Solid Edge ST9 for Designers

(14th Revised and Updated Edition)

Sham Tickoo
Professor
Purdue University Northwest
Hammond, Indiana, USA

Contributing Authors
Tickoo Institute of Emerging Technologies (TIET)
Gurgaon, India

CADCIM Technologies
Indiana, USA

BPB PUBLICATIONS

ISBN: 978-93-86551-20-7
14th Revised and Updated Edition
(For distribution in SAARC countries only)

Limits of Liability and Disclaimer of Warranty

The information contained in this book is the best of Author's & Publisher's knowledge. We are committed to serve students with best of our knowledge and resources. We have taken utmost care and attention while editing and printing of this book but Author and Publisher should not be held responsible for errors, omissions and any other unintentional mistake that might have crept in. However, errors brought to our notice shall be gratefully acknowledged and attended to.

Distributors

COMPUTER BOOK CENTRE
12, Shrungar Shopping Centre
M.G. Road
BENGALURU–560001
Ph: 25587923/25584641

BPB BOOK CENTRE
376 Old Lajpat Rai Market
DELHI-110006
Ph: 23861747

DECCAN AGENCIES
4-3-329, Bank Street
HYDERABAD-500195
Ph: 24756967/24756400

INFOTECH
G-2, Sidhartha Building, 96 Nehru Place
NEW DELHI-110019
Ph: 26438245

MICRO MEDIA
Shop No. 5, Mahendra Chambers
150 DN Rd. Next to Capital Cinema
V.T (C.S.T.) Station
MUMBAI-400001

BPB PUBLICATIONS
20, Ansari Road, Darya Ganj
New Delhi-110002
Ph: 23254990/23254991

Published by Manish Jain for BPB Publications, 20 Ansari Road, Darya Ganj New Delhi-110002 and Printed Repro India Pvt. Ltd, Mumbai

DEDICATION

To teachers, who make it possible to disseminate knowledge to enlighten the young and curious minds of our future generations

To students, who are dedicated to learning new technologies and making the world a better place to live in

THANKS

To employees of CADCIM Technologies and Tickoo Institute of Emerging Technologies (TIET) for their valuable help

Note

If you are a faculty member, you can register by clicking on the following link to access the teaching resources: ***http://www.cadcim.com/Registration.aspx***. The student resources are available at ***http://www.cadcim.com***. We also provide **Live Virtual Online Training** on various software packages. For more information, write us at ***sales@cadcim.com***.

Table of Contents

Chapter 3: Adding Relationships and Dimensions to Sketches

Chapter 5: Working with Additional Reference Geometries

Chapter 7: Editing Features

Chapter 12: Generating, Editing, and Dimensioning the Drawing Views

Chapter 13: Surface Modeling

Preface

Solid Edge ST9

Solid Edge, a product of Siemens, is one of the world's fastest growing solid modeling software. Solid Edge with Synchronous Technology combines the speed and flexibility of direct modeling with precise control of dimension-driven design through precision sketching, region selection, face selection, and handle selection. Solid Edge ST9 integrates the synchronous modeling with the traditional modeling into a single environment. It is an integrated solid modeling tool, which not only unites the synchronous modeling with traditional modeling but also addresses every design-through-manufacturing process. Solid Edge ST9 allows the users to convert any selected ordered feature in existing models into a synchronous feature. This solid modeling package allows the manufacturing companies to get an insight into the design intent, thereby promoting collaboration and allowing the companies have an edge over their competitors. This package is remarkably user-friendly and helps the users to be productive from day one.

In Solid Edge, the 2D drawing views can be easily generated in the drafting environment after creating solid models and assemblies. The drawing views that can be generated include orthographic views, isometric views, auxiliary views, section views, detail views, and so on. You can use any predefined drawing standard file for generating the drawing views. You can display model dimensions in the drawing views or add reference dimensions whenever you want.

The **Solid Edge ST9 for Designers** textbook has been written to help the readers use Solid Edge ST9 effectively. This textbook covers both Synchronous and Ordered environments of Solid Edge ST9 such as Part, Assembly, Sheet Metal, and Drafting. A number of mechanical engineering industry examples are used as tutorials in this textbook so that the users can relate the knowledge gained with the actual mechanical industry designs. Some of the other salient features of this textbook are as follows:

- **Tutorial Approach**

  The author has adopted the tutorial point-of-view and the learn-by-doing approach throughout the textbook. This approach guides the users through the process of creating the models in the tutorials.

- **Heavily Illustrated Text**
  The text in this book is heavily illustrated with about 1100 line diagrams and screen capture images.

- **Real-World Projects as Tutorials**
  The author has used about 50 real world mechanical engineering projects as tutorials in this textbook. This enables the readers to relate the tutorials to the real-world models in the mechanical engineering industry. In addition, there are about 44 exercises that are also based on the real-world mechanical engineering projects.

- **Tips and Notes**
  Additional information related to various topics is provided to the users in the form of tips and notes.

- **Learning Objectives**
  The first page of every chapter summarizes the topics that are covered in the chapter.

- **Self-Evaluation Test, Review Questions, and Exercises**
  Every chapter ends with Self-Evaluation Test so that the users can assess their knowledge of the chapter. The answers to Self-Evaluation Test are given at the end of the chapter. Also, Review Questions and Exercises are given at the end of each chapter and they can be used by the instructors as test questions and exercises.

Symbols Used in the Textbook

Note
The author has provided additional information in the form of notes.

Tip
The author has provided useful information to the users about the topic being discussed in the form of tips.

New
This icon indicates that the command or tool being discussed is new.

Enhanced
This icon indicates that the command or tool being discussed is enhanced.

Formatting Conventions Used in the Textbook

Please refer to the following list for the formatting conventions used in this textbook.

- Names of tools, buttons, options, panels, tabs, and ribbon are written in boldface.

  Example: The **Extrude** tool, the **Finish Sketch** button, the **Modify** panel, the **Sketch** tab, and so on.

- Names of dialog boxes, drop-downs, drop-down lists, list boxes, areas, edit boxes, check boxes, and radio buttons are written in boldface.

  Example: The **Revolve** dialog box, the **Create 2D Sketch** drop-down in the **Sketch** panel of the **Model** tab, the **Placement** drop-down of **Hole** dialog box, the **Distance** edit box in the **Extrude** dialog box, the **Extended Profile** check box in the **Rib** dialog box, the **Drilled** radio button in the **Hole** dialog box, and so on.

- Values entered in edit boxes are written in boldface.

  Example: Enter **5** in the **Radius** edit box.

- Names and paths of the files are written in italics.

  Example: *C:\Solid Edge\c03*, *c03tut03.prt*, and so on

The methods of invoking a tool/option from the **Ribbon**, **Quick Access** toolbar, and **Application Menu** are given in a shaded box.

Ribbon: Get Started > Launch > New
Quick Access Toolbar: New
Application Menu: New

Naming Conventions Used in the Textbook

Tool

If you click on an item in a toolbar or a panel of the **Ribbon** and a command is invoked to create/edit an object or perform some action, then that item is termed as **tool**.

For example:
To Create: **Line** tool, **Dimension** tool, **Extrude** tool
To Edit: **Fillet** tool, **Draft** tool, **Trim Surface** tool
Action: **Zoom All** tool, **Pan** tool, **Copy Object** tool

If you click on an item in a toolbar or a panel of the **Ribbon** and a dialog box is invoked wherein you can set the properties to create/edit an object, then that item is also termed as **tool**, refer to Figure 1.

For example:
To Create: **Create iPart** tool, **Parameters** tool, **Create** tool
To Edit: **Styles Editor** tool, **Document Settings** tool

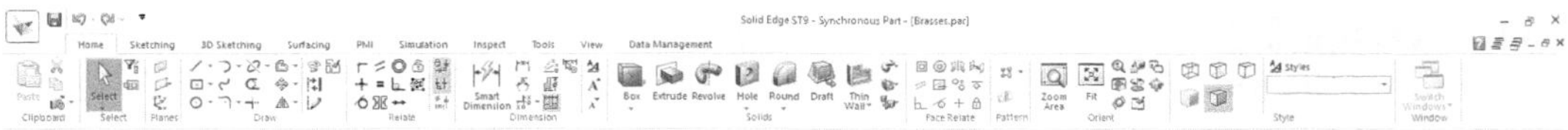

*Figure 1 The **Home** tab in the **Part** environment*

Button

The item in a dialog box that has a 3d shape like a button is termed as **Button**. For example, **OK** button, **Cancel** button, **Apply** button, and so on.

Dialog Box

In this textbook, different terms are used for referring to the components of a dialog box. Refer to Figure 2 for the terminology used.

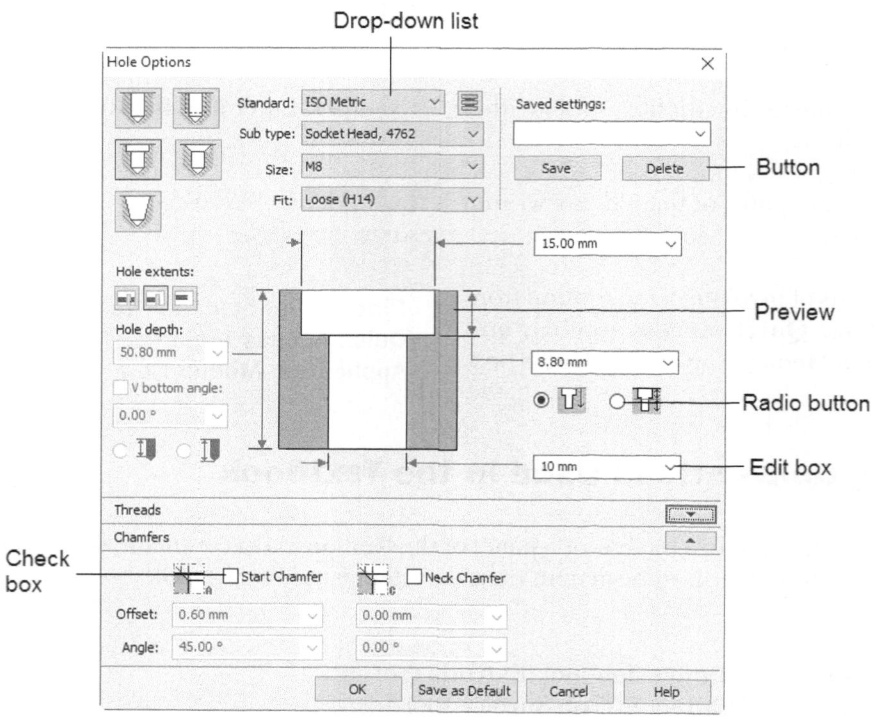

Figure 2 The components in a dialog box

Drop-down

A drop-down is one in which a set of common tools are grouped together. You can identify a drop-down with a down arrow on it. These drop-downs are given a name based on the tools grouped in them. For example, **Rectangle** drop-down, **Line** drop-down, **More planes** drop-down, and so on; refer to Figure 3.

*Figure 3 The **Rectangle**, **Line**, and **More planes** drop-downs*

Drop-down List

A drop-down list is the one in which a set of options are grouped together. You can set parameters by using these options. You can identify a drop-down list with a down arrow on it. For example, the **Selection Type** drop-down list, the **Select from** drop-down list, and so on, refer to Figure 4.

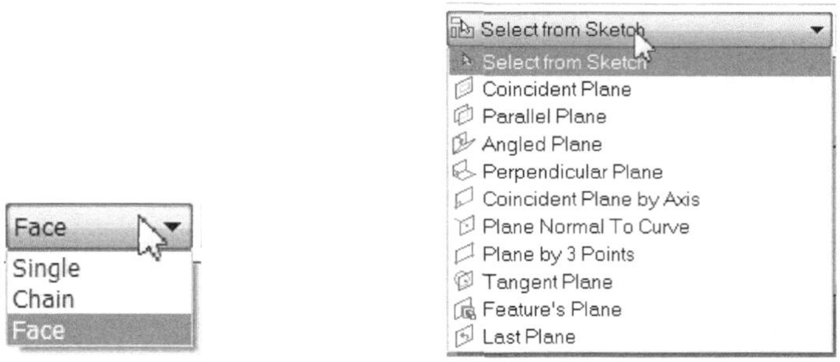

*Figure 4 The **Selection Type** and **Select from** drop-down lists*

Free Companion Website

It has been our constant endeavor to provide you the best textbooks and services at affordable price. In this endeavor, we have come out with a Free Companion website that will facilitate the process of teaching and learning of Solid Edge ST9. If you purchase this textbook, you will get access to the files on the Companion website.

The following resources are available for the faculty and students in this website:

Faculty Resources

- **Technical Support**
  You can get online technical support by contacting ***info@tiet.in***

- **Instructor Guide**
  Solutions to all review questions and exercises in the textbook are provided in this guide to help the faculty members test the skills of the students.

- **PowerPoint Presentations**
  The contents of the book are arranged in PowerPoint slides that can be used by the faculty for their lectures.

- **Part Files**
  The part files used in illustrations, tutorials, and exercises are available for free download.

Student Resources

- **Technical Support**
  You can get online technical support by contacting ***info@tiet.in***

- **Part Files**
  The part files used in illustrations and tutorials are available for free download.

- **Additional Students Projects**
  Various projects are provided for the students to practice.

If you face any problem in accessing these files, please contact the publisher at ***info@tiet.in***or the author at ***stickoo@pnw.edu*** or ***tickoo525@gmail.com***.

Stay Connected

You can now stay connected with us through Facebook and Twitter to get the latest information about our textbooks, videos, and teaching/learning resources. To stay informed of such updates, follow us on Facebook (***www.facebook.com/cadcim***) and Twitter (***@cadcimtech***). You can also subscribe to our YouTube channel (***www.youtube.com/cadcimtech***) to get the information about our latest video tutorials.

Chapter 1

Introduction to Solid Edge ST9

Learning Objectives

After completing this chapter, you will be able to:

- *Understand the basic properties and different environments of Solid Edge*
- *Know the system requirements for installing Solid Edge ST9*
- *Get familiar with important terms and definitions*
- *Understand the user interface*
- *Save the Solid Edge designs automatically after regular intervals*
- *Modify the color scheme*

INTRODUCTION TO Solid Edge ST9

Welcome to the world of Solid Edge ST9, a product of SIEMENS. If you are a new user of this software, you will join hands with thousands of users of this high-end CAD tool worldwide. This software helps the users to improve their design skills. Also, in this software, the user interaction has been taken to a new level, thus making Solid Edge one of the easiest and popular mechanical CAD products.

Solid Edge is a powerful software that is used to create complex designs with great ease. The design intent of any three-dimensional (3D) model or an assembly is defined by its specification and use. You can use the powerful tools of Solid Edge to capture the design intent of any complex model by incorporating intelligence into the design. With Synchronous Technology, Solid Edge redefines the rules of 3D modeling. It combines the speed and flexibility of modeling with precise control of dimension-driven design, thereby generating tremendous productivity gains over traditional methods.

In Solid Edge, the synchronous and traditional (now called Ordered) modeling environments are combined into a single modeling environment. This means, you do not need two separate environments to work with synchronous and traditional modeling technologies. The most interesting feature is that you can switch between the **Synchronous** and **Ordered** environments and can convert a particular Ordered feature into a Synchronous feature.

To make the design process simple and efficient, this software package divides the steps of designing into different environments. This means each step of the design process is completed in a different environment. Generally, a design process involves the following steps:

- Sketching by using the basic sketch entities and converting them into features or parts.
- These parts can be sheet metal parts, surface parts, or solid parts.
- Assembling different parts and analyzing them.
- Generating drawing views of the parts and the assembly.

All these steps are performed in different environments of Solid Edge, namely **Synchronous Part/Ordered Part**, **Assembly**, **Synchronous Sheet Metal/Ordered Sheet Metal**, **Weldment**, and **Draft**.

Solid Edge provides Software Development Kit (SDK) that helps you customize Solid Edge according to your requirement. Solid Edge also provides assistance, tutorials, and technical support to the users. The tutorials can be browsed from the welcome screen. You can view as well as work on the models simultaneously. Solid Edge helps you find commands quickly by using the Command Finder. The enhanced tooltip in Solid Edge provides you complete information of a tool such as its name and description as well as the shortcut keys to invoke the tool.

Solid Edge supports data migration from various CAD packages such as AutoCAD, Mechanical Desktop, Pro/E, Inventor, CATIA, and NX. As a result, you can convert all the files and documents created in these software into a Solid Edge document. You can also view or change the settings of a file while importing it. Solid Edge allows you to evolve a 3D model from a 2D drawing created in the Draft environment of Solid Edge or imported from any other software.

Solid Edge ST9 is a synchronous, parametric, and feature-based solid modeling software. The bidirectional associative nature of this solid modeling software makes the design process very simple and less time-consuming. The synchronous, parametric, feature-based, and bidirectional properties of this software are explained next.

Synchronous Technology

The Synchronous Technology and the new commands and workflow concepts of Solid Edge has made modeling in this software much easier, faster, and accurate than in any other parametric modeling software package. This is because the synchronous technology enables you to create sketches as well as to develop features in the same environment. Note that the features created in the **Synchronous** environment do not depend on the order of their creation. Therefore, the editing of the model becomes a lot easier. This state-of-the-art technology makes Solid Edge ST9 a completely feature-based 2D/3D CAD software package.

Parametric Nature

Parametric nature of a solid modeling package means that the sketch is driven by dimensions, or in other words, the geometry of a model is controlled by its dimensions. For example, to model a rectangular plate of 100X80 units, you can draw a rectangle of any dimension and then modify its dimensions to the required dimensions of the plate. You will notice that the dimensions drive the geometry of the sketch.

Therefore, using this parametric property, any modification in the design of a product can be accomplished at any stage of the product development. This makes the design flexible.

Feature-based Modeling

A feature is defined as the smallest building block of a model. Any solid model created in Solid Edge is an integration of a number of features. Each feature can be edited individually to make any change in the solid model. As a result, the feature-based property provides greater flexibility to the created parts.

The advantage of dividing a model into a number of features is that it becomes easy to modify the model by modifying the features individually. For example, Figure 1-1 shows a model with four simple holes near the corners of the plate.

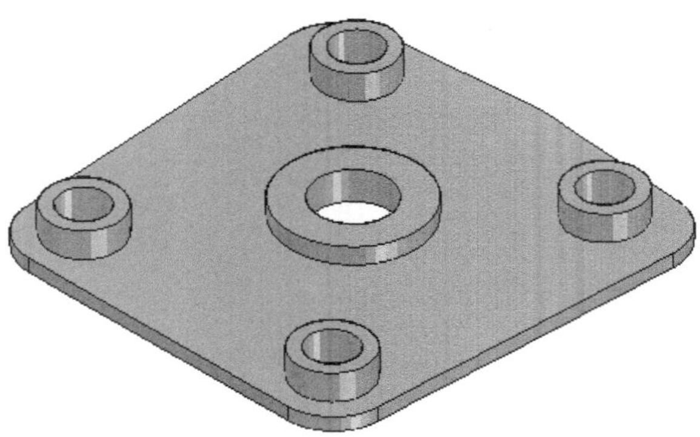

Figure 1-1 *Model with simple holes*

Now, consider a case where you need to change all outer holes to counterbore holes. In a non-feature based modeling package, you need to delete all the holes and then create the counterbore holes. However, in Solid Edge, you can modify some parameters of the holes in the same part and convert the simple holes into counterbore holes, see Figure 1-2.

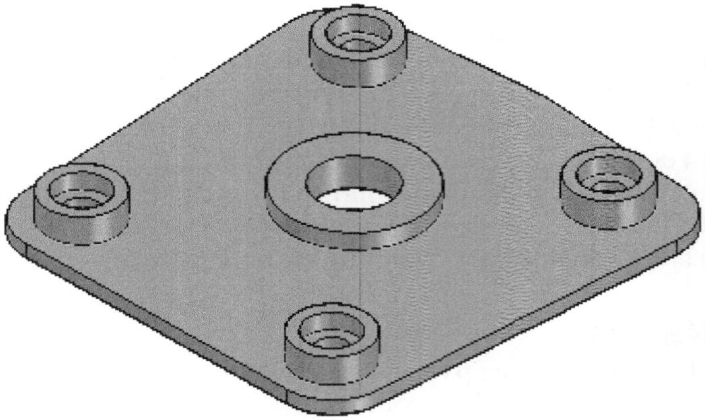

Figure 1-2 *Model with counterbore holes*

Bidirectional Associativity

The bidirectional associativity of a software package is defined as its ability to ensure that any modification made in a particular model in one environment is also reflected in the same model in the other environments. For example, if you make any changes in a model in the **Part** environment, the changes will reflect in the same model in the **Assembly** environment and vice-versa.

Consider the assembly shown in Figure 1-3. The piston is connected to the connecting rod through a pin. It is clear from the assembly that the diameter of the hole is more than what is required. In an ideal case, the diameter of the hole on the piston should be equal to the diameter of the pin.

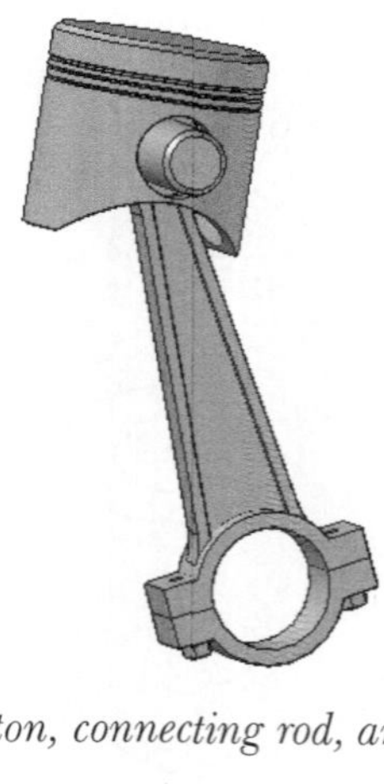

Figure 1-3 *Piston, connecting rod, and pin assembly*

Now, when you open the piston in the **Part** environment and modify the diameter of the hole on it, the same modification is also reflected in the **Assembly** environment, as shown in Figure 1-4.

This is due to the bidirectional associative nature of Solid Edge.

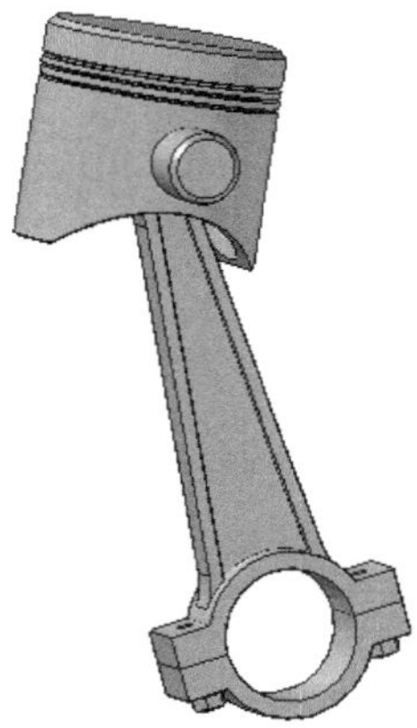

Figure 1-4 *Assembly after modifying the diameter of the hole on the piston*

Similarly, if the modification is made in the **Assembly** environment, the piston, when opened in the **Part** environment, is also modified automatically. This shows that the **Part** and **Assembly** environments of Solid Edge are associative by nature.

Now consider a model, refer to Figure 1-1. Its top view and the sectioned front view are shown in Figure 1-5. Now, when you open the model in the **Part** environment and modify the simple holes near the corners of the plate, refer to Figure 1-1, into the counterbore holes, refer to Figure 1-2. The same modification will not reflect automatically in the drawing views of the model in the **Draft** environment. To reflect the modifications in the **Draft** environment, you need to update them manually using the **Drawing View Tracker** or **Update Views** tool. These tools will be discussed in Chapter 12. After updating the views using the **Drawing View Tracker** or **Update Views** tool, the drawing will be displayed as shown in Figure 1-6.

Note

The modifications done in the views in the ***Draft*** *environment do not reflect in other environments.*

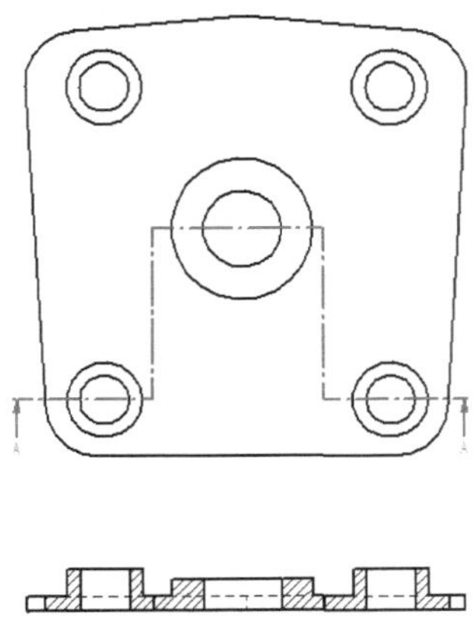

Figure 1-5 *Drawing views of the model before modification*

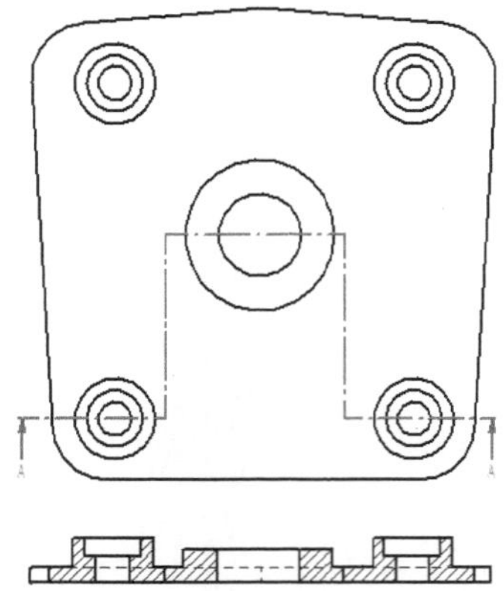

Figure 1-6 Drawing views of the model after modification

Solid Edge ENVIRONMENTS

To reduce the complexity of a design, this software package provides you with various design environments. You can capture the design intent easily by individually incorporating the intelligence of each design environment into the design. The design environments available in Solid Edge are discussed next.

Part Environment

This environment of Solid Edge ST9 is used to create solid as well as surface models. The **Part** environment consists of two environments namely **Synchronous Part** and **Ordered Part**. You can switch between these environments and create a model which consists of both synchronous and ordered features. To invoke this environment, start Solid Edge ST9 by double-clicking on the shortcut icon of Solid Edge ST9 on the desktop of your computer. After Solid Edge ST9 starts, the theme selection window will be displayed. In the theme selection window, select the required user interface theme and then choose the **OK** button; the Solid Edge ST9 window along with the welcome screen will be displayed. From this screen, choose the **ISO Metric Part** option from the **Create** area; the part environment gets started with the ISO units. By default, the **Synchronous Part** environment is invoked. However, you can switch to the **Ordered Part** environment by choosing the **Ordered** radio button from the **Model** group of the **Tools** tab.

Note

1. The theme selection window will only be displayed when you start Solid Edge for the first time after installation.

*2. In this textbook, the **Balanced (Solid Edge Default)** theme is used as the user interface theme.*

Synchronous Part

Solid Edge ST9 with the Synchronous Technology makes it a complete feature-based 2D/3D CAD system. This technology combines the speed and flexibility of direct modeling with precise control of dimension-driven design. In this environment, there is no separate environment to draw sketches; rather the sketching tools are available in the **Synchronous Part** environment itself. It includes direct model creation and modification through precision sketching, region selection, face selection, and handle selection.

Ordered Part

The **Ordered Part** environment of Solid Edge ST9 is used to create parametric and feature-based solids as well as surface models. You can draw sketches of models or features by invoking the sketching environment. Once the sketch is drawn, you can convert it into a solid model using simple but highly effective modeling tools. One of the major advantages of using Solid Edge is the availability of Command bar. The Command bar is displayed in the drawing window. In this environment, you can create a feature step by step by using the Command bar. You can also use the Command bar to easily go one or more steps backward to modify a parameter. You can also convert the features created in this environment to the synchronous features for editing them directly. The models created in the part environment can also be used in other environments of Solid Edge to complete the model's life cycle, also known as the Product Life Cycle.

Assembly Environment

This environment of Solid Edge is used to create an assembly by assembling the components that were created in the **Synchronous/Ordered Part** environment. Both the synchronous and ordered tools are combined in this environment. This environment supports animation, rendering, piping, and wiring. Other visualization and presentation tools are also available in this environment. In addition to that, you can apply a relation between the faces of two different synchronous components in an assembly. For example, you can make the selected face of a component tangent with the target face of another component.

Draft Environment

This environment is used for the documentation of the parts or the assemblies in the form of drawing views. The drawing views can be generated or created. All the dimensions added to the component in the part environment during its creation can be displayed in the drawing views in this environment.

Sheet Metal Environment

This environment is used to create sheet metal components. If you are familiar with the part environment, then modeling in this environment becomes easy. This is because in addition to the sheet metal modeling tools, this environment works in a way similar to the part environment. To invoke this environment, start Solid Edge ST9; a welcome screen will be displayed. Choose the **ISO Metric Sheet Metal** option from the **Create** area in the welcome screen; the Sheet Metal environment gets started with the ISO units. By default, the **Synchronous Sheet Metal** environment is invoked. However, you can switch to the **Ordered Sheet Metal** environment by choosing the **Ordered** radio button from the **Tools** tab.

Synchronous Sheet Metal

The **Synchronous Sheet Metal** environment is used to create and edit sheet metal components in a history-free approach. The procedure of selection of faces introduced in this environment allows you to model sheet metals directly. You can create a dimension-driven design of the sheet metal components in Solid Edge.

Ordered Sheet Metal

The **Ordered Sheet Metal** environment is used to create parametric and feature-based sheet metal components.

Weldment Environment

This environment enables you to insert components from the **Part** or the **Assembly** environment and apply weld beads to the parts or the assembly. This environment is associative with the **Part** and **Assembly** environments.

SYSTEM REQUIREMENTS FOR INSTALLING Solid Edge ST9

The system requirements for Solid Edge ST9 are as follows:

1. Windows 7 Enterprise, Ultimate, or Professional (64-bit only) with Service Pack 1, Windows 8 or 8.1 Pro or Enterprise (64-bit only), Windows 10 (64-bit only)
2. Internet Explorer 10 or 11 (IE 8 meets minimum requirements)
3. 4GB RAM minimum
4. Disk space for installation = 4 GB
5. Screen Resolution: 1280 x 1024 or higher
6. 65K colors

IMPORTANT TERMS AND DEFINITIONS

Some important terms that are used in this textbook are discussed next.

Relationships

Relationships are the logical operations that are performed on a selected geometry to make it more accurate by defining its position and size with respect to the other geometry. There are two types of relationships available in Solid Edge and they are discussed next.

Geometry Relationships

These logical operations are performed on the basic sketched entities to relate them to the standard properties such as collinearity, concentricity, perpendicularity, and so on. Although Solid Edge automatically applies these relationships to the sketched entities at the time of drawing, you can also apply them manually. You can apply different types of geometry relationships, which are discussed next.

Connect

This relationship connects a point to another point or entity.

Concentric

This relationship forces two selected curves to share the same center point. The curves that can be made concentric are circles, arcs, and ellipses.

Horizontal/Vertical

This relationship forces the selected line segment or two points to become horizontal or vertical.

Collinear

This relationship forces two line segments to lie on the same line.

Parallel
This relationship is used to make two line segments parallel.

Perpendicular
This relationship makes a line segment perpendicular to another line segment or series of line segments.

Lock
This relationship is used to fix an element or a dimension such that it cannot be modified.

Tangent
This relationship is used to make the selected line segment or curve tangent to the selected line or curve.

Equal
This relationship forces the selected line segments to be of equal length. It also forces two curves to be of equal radius.

Symmetric
This relationship is used to force the selected sketched entities to become symmetrical about a sketched line segment, which may or may not be a center line.

Rigid Set
This relationship is used to group the selected sketched entities into a rigid set so that they behave as a single unit.

Feature Relationships (Only in Synchronous Part Environment)

The feature relationships are the relationships that are applied on a selected face to make it geometrically related to the target face. These relationships are used to modify the parts created in the **Synchronous Part** environment. These relationships are available in the **Face Relate** group of the **Home** tab in the ribbon in the **Synchronous Part** environment. The following types of feature relationships can be applied between faces:

Concentric
This relationship makes the selected faces concentric with the target face.

Coplanar
This relationship makes the selected faces coplanar with the target face.

Parallel
This relationship enables you to make the selected faces parallel to the target face.

Perpendicular
This relationship helps you to make the selected faces perpendicular to the target face.

Tangent
This relationship makes the selected faces tangent with the target face.

Rigid
This relationship is used to make all the faces in the selection set rigid with respect to each other. This means, if either of the face is moved or rotated, then all the related faces will also move or rotate, thereby maintaining the distance and orientation between them.

Ground
This relationship grounds or constrains the selected face in the model space. As a result, the grounded faces can be neither moved nor rotated.

Symmetry
This relationship makes a selected face symmetric to a target face about a symmetry plane.

Equal
This relationship makes the radius of a selected cylindrical face equal to the radius of a target cylindrical face.

Aligned Holes
This relationship is used to make the axes of multiple cylindrical faces coplanar.

Offset
This relationship is used to offset a face with respect to another face.

Horizontal/Vertical
This relationship forces a horizontal/vertical face or keypoint to align with another horizontal/vertical face or keypoint.

Assembly Relationships
The assembly relationships are the logical operations that are performed on the components to assemble them at their respective working positions in an assembly. These relationships are applied to reduce the degrees of freedom of the components.

Flash Fit
This relationship minimizes the efforts of applying various relationships like: Mate, Planar Align, and so on by automatically positioning the component wherever required.

Mate
This relationship is used to make the selected faces of different components coplanar. You can also specify some offset distance between the selected faces.

Planar Align
This relationship enables you to align a planar face with the other planar face.

Axial Align
This relationship enables you to make a cylindrical surface coaxial with the other cylindrical surface.

Insert
This relationship is used to mate the faces of two components that are axially symmetric and also to make their axes coaxial.

Connect
This relationship enables you to connect two keypoints, line, or a face on two different parts.

Angle
This relationship is used to place the selected faces of different components at some angle with respect to each other.

Tangent
This relationship is used to make the selected face of a component tangent to the cylindrical, circular, or conical faces of the other component.

Cam
This relationship applies the cam-follower relationship between a closed loop of tangent face and the follower face.

Parallel
The **Parallel** relationship is used to force two edges, axes, or an edge and an axis parallel to each other.

Gear
The **Gear** relationship allows you to apply rotation-rotation, rotation-linear, or a linear-linear relationship between two components.

Center-Plane
This relationship is used to align a component at an equal distance between the two faces of other component, planes, or key points.

Path
This relationship is used to apply a mate such that the part moves along a path.

Match Coordinate Systems
This relationship is used to match the coordinate system of one component/part with the coordinate system of another component/part.

Rigid Set
This relationship is used between two or more components to fix them such that they become rigid with respect to each other.

Ground
This relationship is used to fix a component at a specified location and orientation. Solid Edge automatically applies a ground relationship to the first part placed in an assembly.

Entity
An element of a geometry is called an entity. An entity can be an arc, line, circle, point, and so on.

Concept of a Profile and a Sketch
In Solid Edge, there are two methods of drawing a sketch. The first method is to draw a sketch in the sketching environment by invoking the **Sketch** tool from the **Home** tab. The second method is to invoke a feature creation tool such as **Extrude**, **Revolve**, and so on and then draw the sketch for the feature. The sketch drawn using the first method is called a Sketch and the sketch drawn using the second method is called a Profile. You will learn more about this in the later chapters of this book.

Note

1. If you are working in the ***Synchronous Part*** *environment, you can not invoke a feature creation tool such as* ***Extrude, Revolve****, and so on if you do not have a sketch.*

2. In the ***Synchronous Part*** *environment, you can select the sketching tools without switching to another environment.*

Intent Zone
The intent zone is defined by a circular area that is divided into four quadrants. It is used while drawing an arc or a circle from a line, or vice-versa. The quadrants define whether the element is perpendicular, tangent or at some other orientation from the other element. This zone enables you to draw or modify various elements of a geometry within the same tool. For example, while drawing a line tangent to an arc, you can draw a tangent arc or a perpendicular arc by moving the cursor in the intent zone. The movement of the cursor in the intent zone determines the creation of a tangent or a perpendicular arc. The intent zone while drawing a tangent arc and a three point arc is shown in Figure 1-7 and 1-8, respectively.

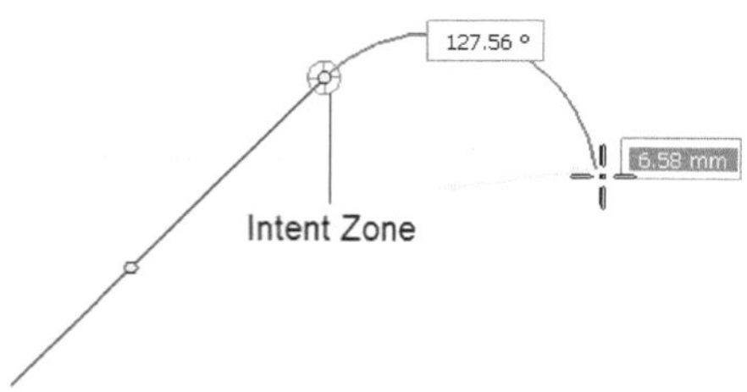

Figure 1-7 *Intent zone displayed while drawing a tangent arc*

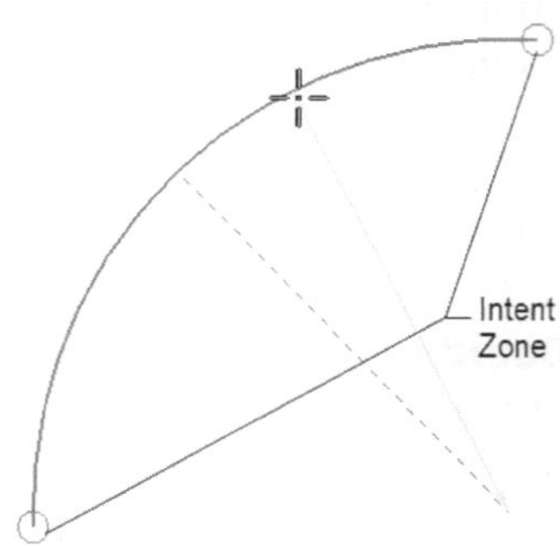

Figure 1-8 *Intent zone displayed while drawing a three point arc*

GETTING STARTED WITH Solid Edge ST9
After you have installed Solid Edge on your computer, double-click on the shortcut icon of Solid Edge ST9 on the desktop of your computer; the welcome screen will be displayed. In this screen, links for various environments will be displayed in the **Create** area. You can start a new document in the desired environment by clicking on the corresponding link in this area. As discussed earlier, the designing steps in Solid Edge are performed in different environment.

You can open the existing documents by choosing the **Open an existing document** button from the **Open** area. The links for the recently used documents are displayed in the **Recent Documents** area. You can click on the link of the required document in this area to open that document. The welcome screen also displays the link for step-by-step tutorials in the **Learn Solid Edge** area. The **Links** area contains the links for the home page and the components catalog page of Solid Edge. However, you can add or remove links by using the **Edit Links** option available below the **Links** area. Choose the **ISO Metric Part** from the **Create** area of the welcome screen; a new Solid Edge document in the **Synchronous Part** environment will be displayed, as shown in Figure 1-9.

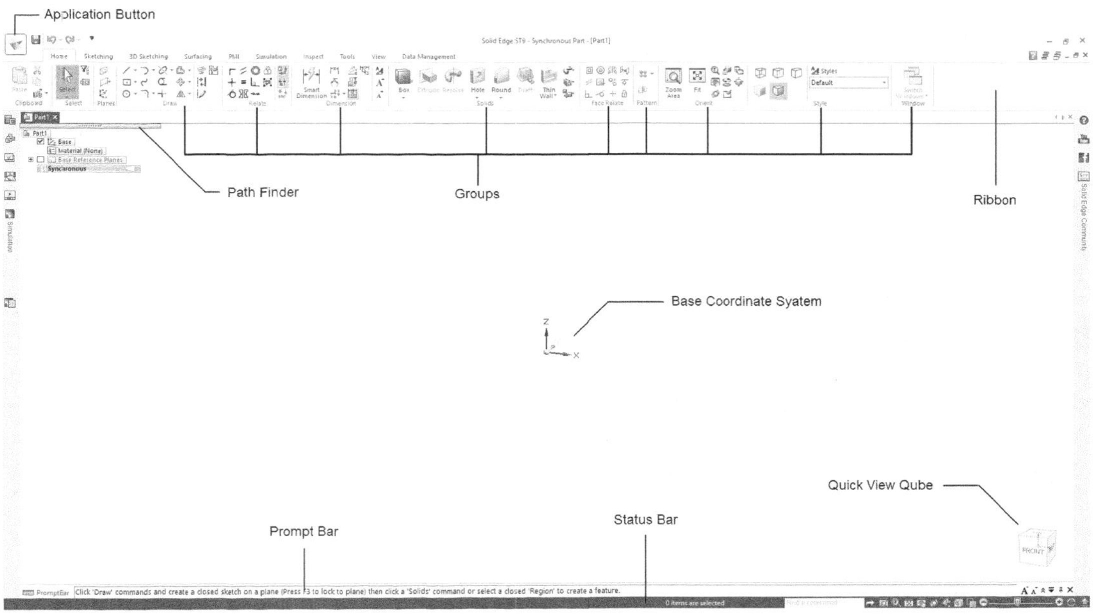

*Figure 1-9 New document in the **Synchronous Part** environment*

USER INTERFACE OF Solid Edge

Solid Edge provides you a **Ribbon** with different tabs and groups. These tabs and groups available while working in the **Synchronous Part/Ordered Part**, **Assembly**, **Draft** and **Synchronous Sheet Metal/Ordered Sheet Metal** environments will be different. Every environment has the **PathFinder** and the prompt line that assist you in creating the design. Various components of the interface are discussed next.

Prompt Line

If you invoke a tool, the prompt line is displayed in the prompt bar. This line is very useful for creating a model because it provides you with the prompt sequences to use a tool.

PathFinder

The **PathFinder**, as shown in Figure 1-10, is on the left in the drawing area. It lists all the occurrences of features and sketches of a model in a chronicle sequence.

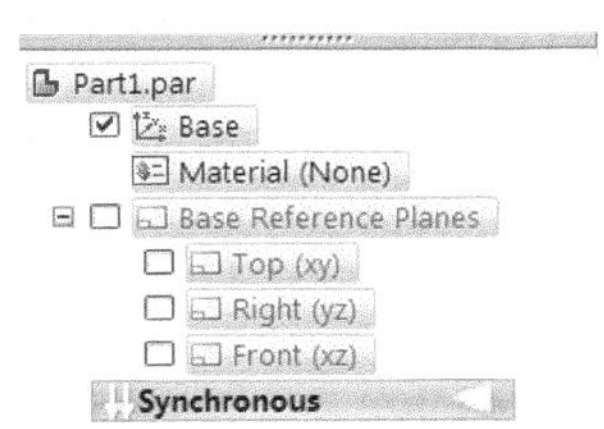

*Figure 1-10 The **PathFinder***

Docking Window

The docking window is available on the left and right of the screen and it remains collapsed by default. It has different tabs on the top. These tabs can be used to activate the feature library, family of parts, and so on. The docking window expands when you move the cursor over the left or right pane of the screen. In case, any tab is missing in it, choose the **Panes** button from the **Show** group in the **View** tab; a flyout will be displayed with various options. Choose the required option; the tab corresponding to that option will be added to the docking window. The options available in the docking window are discussed later in this textbook.

Note

Remember that though the profiles of the features are not displayed in the PathFinder but the sketches are displayed. You will learn about the difference between sketches and profiles later in this textbook.

Application Button

The **Application Button** is available on the top left corner of the Solid Edge window. It is present in all environments. On choosing this button, the Application menu containing the options for creating, opening, saving, and managing documents will be displayed.

Quick Access Toolbar

The **Quick Access** toolbar is available on the top-left of the title bar of the Solid Edge window, refer to Figure 1-11. It provides you an access to the frequently used commands such as **New**, **Open**, **Undo**, **Redo**, **Save**, and **Print**. However, by default, only the **Save**, **Undo**, and **Redo** options are displayed in the **Quick Access** toolbar. To add commands such as **New**, **Open**, and so on, choose the black arrow on the right of the **Quick Access** toolbar; the **Customize** flyout will be displayed. Choose the required command from the flyout; the **Save theme as** dialog box will be displayed if you have chosen the command to add for the first time. Enter the theme name in the **New theme** edit box and the selected command will be added to the **Quick Access** toolbar. You can also deselect a command name from flyout to removed it from the **Quick Access** toolbar.

*Figure 1-11 The **Quick Access** toolbar*

You can also customize the **Quick Access** toolbar to add more commands to it. To do so, invoke the **Customize** flyout again and then choose **Customize** from it; the **Customize** dialog box will be displayed. Choose the **Quick Access** tab, if not chosen. In this dialog box, select the required option from the **Choose commands from** drop-down list; the corresponding menus will be available in a list box displayed below it. Select the required tool from the list box and then choose the **Add** button to add the tool to the **Quick Access** toolbar. Similarly, you can also remove commands by using the **Customize** dialog box. To do so, select the required command from the list box at the right in this dialog box; the **Remove** button will be activated. Choose the **Remove** button; the selected command will be removed from the **Quick Access** toolbar. Choose the **Close** button from the **Customize** dialog box; the **Customize** message box will be displayed. Choose the **Yes** button from the message box; the **Save Theme As** dialog box will be displayed. Enter the name of the theme in the **New Theme** text box in the **Save Theme As** dialog box and choose **OK**.

To remove any tool directly from the **Quick Access** toolbar, right-click on the required tool; a shortcut menu will be displayed. Choose **Remove from Quick Access Toolbar** from the shortcut menu; the corresponding tool will be removed from the toolbar.

Ribbon

The **Ribbon** is available at the top of the Solid Edge window and contains all application tools. It is a collection of tabs. Each tab has different groups and each group is a collection of similar tools. You can increase the drawing area by minimizing the **Ribbon**. To do so, right-click on a tab in the **Ribbon** and choose **Minimize the Ribbon** from the shortcut menu displayed.

You can also add commands in a group of the tab in the **Ribbon**. To do so, invoke the **Customize** dialog box and choose the **Ribbon** tab from it. Select the **All Commands** option from the **Choose commands from** drop-down list, the corresponding tools will be displayed in the left list box below it. Select the required tool from the list box and then click on the required group of the tab (where you want to add the command) in the list box at the right side in the **Customize** dialog box. After selecting the required group in the tab, the **Add** button will be activated. Choose the **Add** button; the selected command will be added to the selected group in the tab of the **Ribbon**. Choose the **Close** button from the **Customize** dialog box; the **Customize** message box will be displayed. Choose the **Yes** button from the message box; the **Save Theme As** dialog box will be displayed. Enter the name of the theme in the **New Theme** text box of the **Save Theme As** dialog box and Choose **OK**.

Status Bar

The status bar is available at the bottom of the Solid Edge window. It enables you to quickly access all the view controls like **Zoom Area**, **Zoom**, **Fit**, **Pan**, **Rotate**, **Sketch View**, **View Orientation**, and **View Styles**. A slider on the right of the status bar controls the amount of zooming. Most importantly, it consists of the Command Finder that helps you to locate the required command.

Record

In SolidEdge, you can use the **Record** button (located at the bottom right corner) to record a video while creating models, assemblies, drawings, and so on. On choosing this button, the **Record Video** dialog box will be displayed, as shown in Figure 1-12. The options in this dialog box can be used to specify various settings such as area to record, audio settings, video compression settings, and so on. After specifying the required settings, choose the **Record** button or press SHIFT+F9 to record a video. To stop recording the video, choose the **Stop** button or press SHIFT+F10; the recorded video will be played in the default video player. To save the video, switch back to the Solid Edge window and choose the **Save** button from the **Record Video** dialog box; the **Save Video** dialog box will be displayed. Specify the name and location of the file and choose the **Save** button in the **Save Video** dialog box. To play the recorded video, choose the **Play** button from the **Record Video** dialog box. Alternatively, you can play the video from the location where it is saved.

*Figure 1-12 The **Record Video** dialog box*

Upload to YouTube

This button is available at the bottom right corner of the drawing window and is used to upload a recorded video to YouTube. On choosing this button, the **Upload to YouTube** dialog box will be displayed, as shown in Figure 1-13. In the dialog box, you can sign in a Youtube account using the **Sign in** button. You can select the video to be uploaded by using the **Browse** button. The other options in the **Video Information** area of this dialog box are the same as that available in the Youtube upload page. After entering all the details, choose the **Upload** button to upload the video.

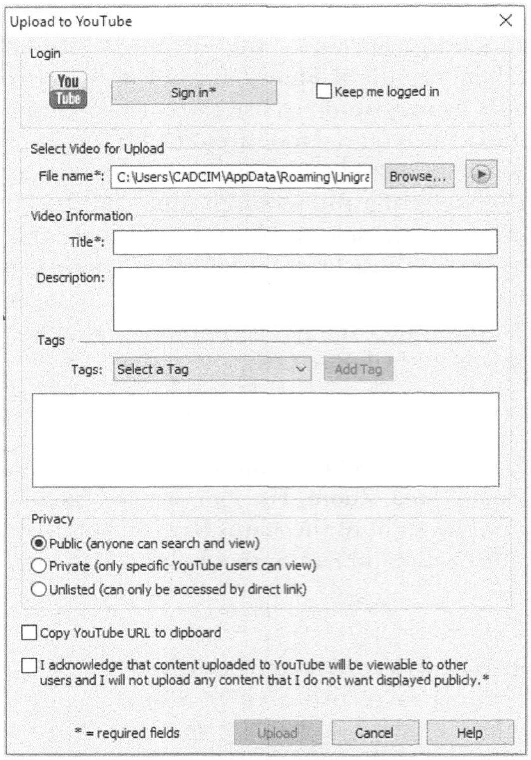

*Figure 1-13 The **Upload to YouTube** dialog box*

Command bar

The Command bar provides the command options for the active tool. It enables you to switch back and forth while creating a model, an assembly, or a drawing. It is available in all the environments of Solid Edge and contains different buttons/steps. The Command bar that is available for the **Extrude** tool is shown in Figure 1-14. However, the buttons displayed in the Command bar depend upon the tool invoked from the **Part** environment. For example, on invoking the **Extrude** tool, the buttons/steps displayed will have different options.

Figure 1-14 The Command bar

QuickPick

This tool enables you to select elements from the drawing window. This tool is used when the elements or the components are overlapping and you need to make a selection. The following steps explain the procedure of using this tool:

1. Bring the cursor near the element or the component that you need to select. Now, pause the cursor, and when three dots appear close to it, right-click on the screen. On doing so, the **QuickPick** dialog box will appear with an entry of each possible selection, as shown in Figure 1-15.

2. In the **QuickPick** dialog box, each entry represents an element. As you move the cursor over the elements in this list, the corresponding components will get highlighted in the drawing window.

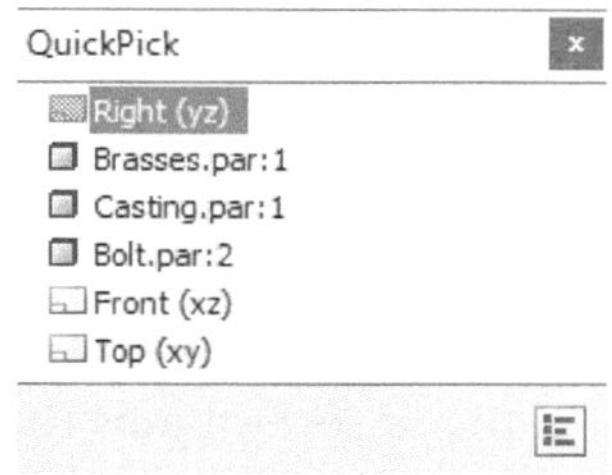

***Figure 1-15** The **QuickPick** dialog box*

3. To exit the **QuickPick** dialog box, simply click on the screen.

Tip
*You can use the **Options** button available at the bottom right corner in the **QuickPick** dialog box to invoke the **QuickPick Options** dialog box. You can use the options in this dialog box to modify the **QuickPick** options.*

Part Environment Tabs

There are several tabs in the **Ribbon** that can be invoked in the **Part** environment. The tabs that are extensively used during the designing process in this environment are discussed next.

The View Tab

This tab is available in all the environments of Solid Edge. The **View** tab of the **Ribbon** is shown in Figure 1-16.

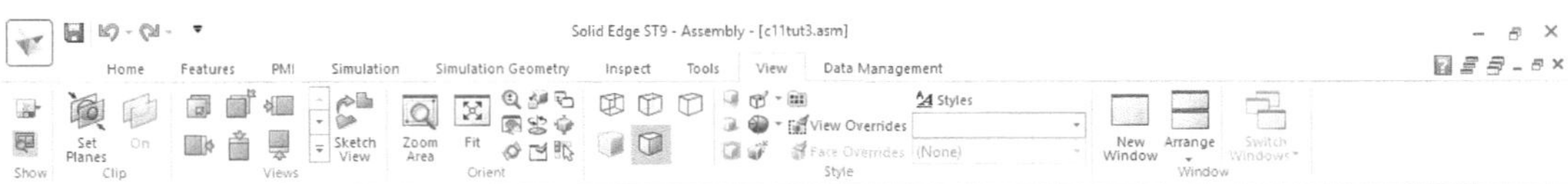

***Figure 1-16** The **View** tab in the **Part** environment*

The Home Tab

This tab consists of the modeling tools that are used to convert a sketch into a solid model. The **Home** tab along with all its tools is shown in Figure 1-17.

***Figure 1-17** The **Home** tab in the **Part** environment*

The Surfacing Tab

This tab contains the modeling tools that are used to create surface models. This tab is available only when you are in the **Part** environment. The **Surfacing** tab, along with all its tools, is shown in Figure 1-18.

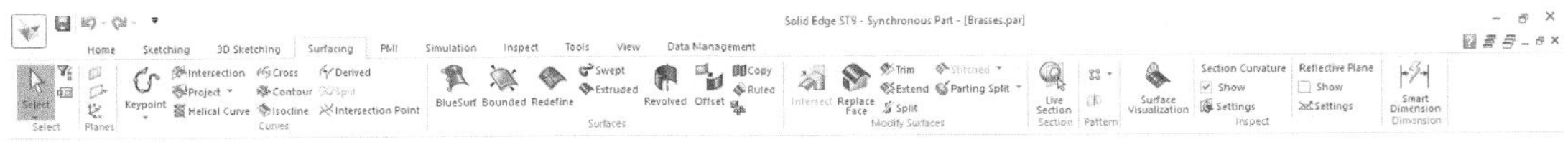

*Figure 1-18 The **Surfacing** tab in the **Part** environment*

Assembly Environment Tabs

There are several tabs that can be invoked to create and manage assemblies in the **Assembly** environment of Solid Edge.

The Assemble Group

The **Assemble** group is available in the **Home** tab of the **Ribbon**. The tools in this tab are used to create and manage assemblies. The **Home** tab in the **Assembly** environment is shown in Figure 1-19.

*Figure 1-19 The **Home** tab in the **Assembly** environment*

Draft Environment Tabs

The **Ribbon** in the **Draft** environment provides you with various tools to generate and create drawing views. Various drafting tools available in the **Home** tab are shown in Figure 1-20.

*Figure 1-20 The **Home** tab of the **Draft** environment*

Radial Menu

The **Radial Menu** is a set of tools arranged radially, as shown in Figure 1-21. To invoke a tool from the radial menu, press the right mouse button and drag the cursor; the radial menu will be displayed. Keeping the right mouse button pressed, move the cursor over the tool to be invoked and then release the mouse button; the tool will be invoked. You can add or remove the tools from the radial menu. To do so, right-click on the **Ribbon** and choose the **Customize the Ribbon** option from the shortcut menu displayed; the **Customize** dialog box will be displayed. Choose the **Radial Menu** tab. Next, select the category that contains the tool that you want to add to the radial menu from the **Choose commands from** drop-down list. On doing so, the categories and the commands are displayed in the list box. Next, drag and place the tool onto the radial menu image in the dialog box; the tool will be displayed in the radial menu. To remove a tool from the radial menu, click on the tool in the radial menu image and drag it into the white space. Next, choose the **Close** button; the **Customize** message box will be displayed. Choose the **Yes** button from it to exit the **Customize** dialog box.

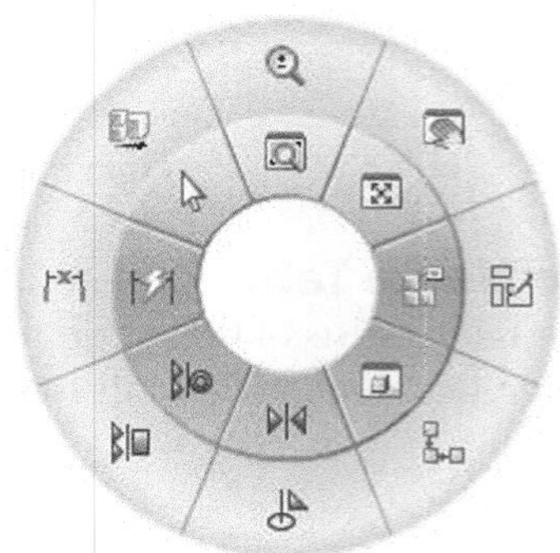

*Figure 1-21 The **Radial Menu** in the **Part** environment*

SIMULATION EXPRESS

Solid Edge provides you an analysis tool called **Simulation Express**. This tool is used to execute the linear static analysis and to calculate the displacement, strain, and stresses applied on a component with respect to the material, loading, and restraint conditions applied to a model. A component fails when the stress applied to it reaches a certain permissible limit. The Static Nodal displacement plot of the Master rod of the engine, designed and analyzed by using the **Simulation Express** tool is shown in the Figure 1-22. Both the Femap and industry standard NX Nastran solvers are used in Solid Edge's **Simulation Express**.

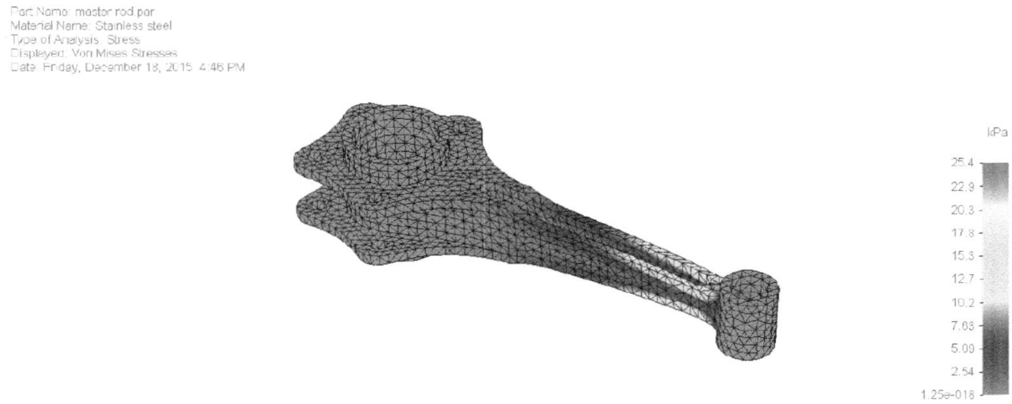

Figure 1-22 The Master Rod analyzed using ***Simulation Express***

USING INTELLISKETCH

The **IntelliSketch** is a dynamic drawing tool that allows you to draw a sketch with accuracy by specifying various relations like endpoint, midpoint, perpendicular, parallel, tangent, horizontal, vertical, and so on. The **IntelliSketch** shows the dynamic display of the relation while drawing a sketch. Moreover, while sketching a relationship indicator will be displayed at the cursor. Click when the indicator is displayed to apply the respective relation to the drawing. You can also apply a relation after drawing the sketch. Additionally, these relationships are maintained even when you modify the sketch. In the **Sketch** environment of the Ordered environment, the relations will be available in the **IntelliSketch** of the **Home** tab whereas in the Synchronous environment, the relations will be available in the in the **IntelliSketch** of the **Sketching** tab.

UNITS FOR DIMENSIONS

The units for dimensioning a sketch or feature can be the Metric and English templates. The Metric templates are prefixed as **ANSI**, **DIN**, **ISO**, **JIS**, **Metric**, **UNI**, **GB**, and **ESKD** and the English templates are prefixed as **ANSI**.

AUTOMATIC SAVING OPTION

In Solid Edge, you can set the option for saving the files automatically after a regular interval of time. While working on a design project, if the system crashes, you may lose the unsaved design data. If the option of automatic saving is on, your data is saved automatically after regular intervals. To set this option, choose **Application Button > Settings > Options**; the **Solid Edge Options** dialog box will be displayed. Choose the **Save** tab and select the **Automatically preserve documents by** check box. You can also select the **Prompt me to save all documents every** radio button and set the minutes in the spinner. You can also select to save uniquely named copies of the documents at a specified location. By default, the files will be saved in the default folder. You can change the default backup folder location by selecting the **File Locations** tab from the dialog box.

COLOR SCHEME IN Solid Edge

In Solid Edge, you can use various color schemes as the background color of the drawing window and for displaying the entities in it. Note that this book uses white as the background color. To change the background color, choose **Application Button > Settings > Options**; the **Solid Edge Options** dialog box will be displayed. Choose the **Colors** tab from this dialog box to display various colors, as shown in Figure 1-23. You can set the different color scheme from there.

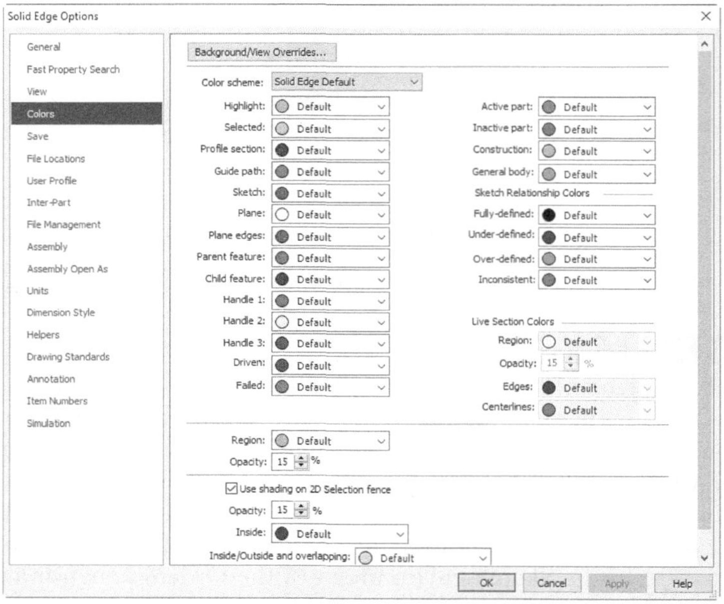

*Figure 1-23 The **Colors** tab of the **Solid Edge Options** dialog box*

To change the background color, choose the **Background/View Overrides** button from the dialog box; the **View Overrides** dialog box will be displayed with the **Background** tab chosen, as shown in Figure 1-24. Select the **White** color from the **Color1** drop-down list; the background color will change to white. Next, choose **OK** from the **View Overrides** dialog box and then from the **Solid Edge Options** dialog box.

To set background color to default, invoke the **View Overrides** dialog box from the **Solid Edge Options** dialog box or you can also invoke the **View Override** dialog box by choosing the **View Overrides** tool from the **Style** group of the **View** tab; the **View Overrides** dialog box will be displayed. Choose the **Background** tab and select **Default** from the **Color1** drop-down list. Choose **OK** to exit this dialog box; the background color will change to default color.

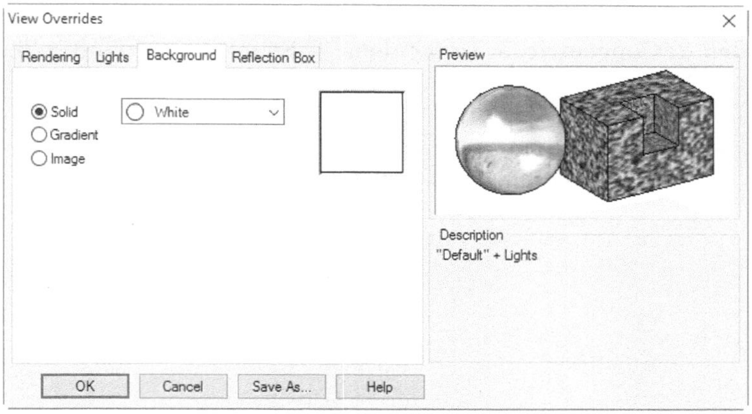

Figure 1-24 *The* ***View Overrides*** *dialog box*

Self-Evaluation Test

Answer the following questions and then compare them to those given at the end of this chapter:

1. The _________ dialog box is used to change the background color of the drawing window in Solid Edge.

2. The _________ relation forces two selected arcs, circles, a point and an arc, a point and a circle, or an arc and a circle to share the same center point.

3. The _________ relation is used to make two points, a point and a line, or a point and an arc coincident.

4. The _________ relation forces two selected lines to become equal in length.

5. The _________ lists all occurrences of features and sketches of a model in a chronological sequence.

6. The _________ relationship is used between two or more components to fix them such that they become rigid with respect to each other.

7. The **Ordered Part** environment of Solid Edge is a feature-based parametric environment in which you can create solid models. (T/F)

8. Any solid model created in Solid Edge is an integration of a number of features. (T/F)

9. The welcome screen of Solid Edge displays the link for step-by-step tutorials in the **Learn Solid Edge** area. (T/F)

10. In Solid Edge, the solid models that are not created by integrating a number of building blocks are called features. (T/F)

Answers to Self-Evaluation Test

1. View Overrides, **2.** Concentric, **3.** Coincident, **4.** Equal, **5.** PathFinder, **6.** Rigid Set, **7.** T, **8.** T, **9.** T, **10.** F

Chapter 2

Drawing Sketches

Learning Objectives

After completing this chapter, you will be able to:

- *Understand various sketching tools*
- *Understand various drawing display tools*
- *Use various selection methods*
- *Delete sketched entities*

SKETCHING IN THE PART ENVIRONMENT

Most solid models consist of closed sketches, placed features, and reference features. A closed sketch is a combination of two-dimensional (2D) entities such as lines, arcs, circles, and so on. The features based on a closed sketch are created by using these entities. Generally, a closed sketch-based feature is the base feature or the first feature. For example, the solid model shown in Figure 2-1 is created by using the sketch shown in Figure 2-2.

Figure 2-1 *Solid model*

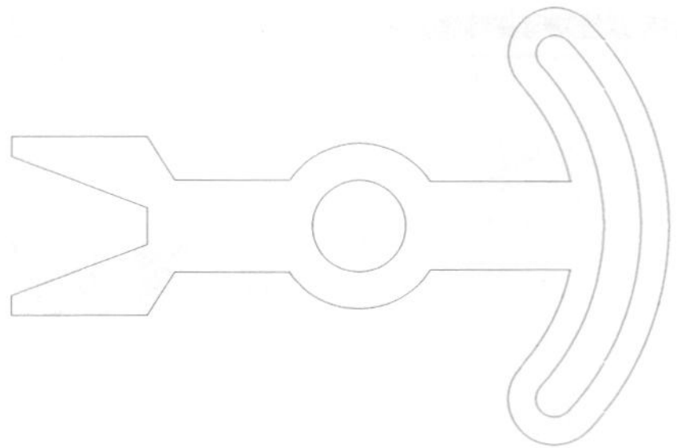

Figure 2-2 *Profile of the solid model*

In most designs, you first need to draw a sketch, add relationships and dimensions to it, and then convert it into a base feature. After doing so, you can create advanced features like cuts, holes, ribs, shells, rounds, chamfers, and so on, on the base feature.

There are two methods to start a new part document. The first one is start a new part document is using the **Application Button** in the home screen and the second one is using the **New** button from the **Quick Access** toolbar. These methods are discussed next.

Starting a New Part File by using the Application Button

To start the **Part** environment, first you need to start Solid Edge. To do so, double-click on the shortcut icon of Solid Edge on the desktop of your computer.

If you are starting the Solid Edge ST9 for the first time, the system will prepare to start the Solid Edge ST9. Once all files have been loaded, the Solid Edge ST9 home screen along with the theme selection window will be displayed. In the theme selection window, refer to Figure 2-3, select the required user interface theme and then choose the **OK** button; the **Solid Edge** home screen will be displayed, as shown in Figure 2-4. Next, click on the **Application Button** and choose **New** > **ISO Metric Part** from the Application menu to start a new part document in the part modeling environment. The **ISO Metric** templates in the **New** area of the Application menu will be displayed only when you have selected **ISO Metric** in the **Modeling Standard** drop-down during the installation.

Note

1. The theme selection window will be displayed, when you start the Solid Edge for the first time after installation.

2. In this textbook, the ***Balanced (Solid Edge Default)*** *theme is used as the user interface theme.*

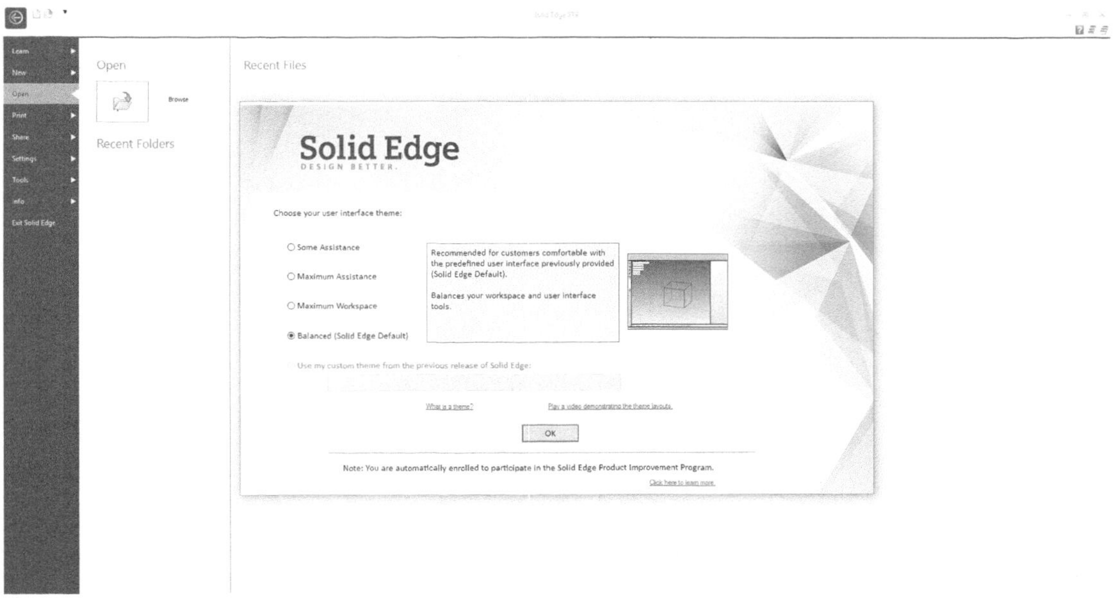

Figure 2-3 Theme selection window of Solid Edge ST9

Figure 2-4 Home screen of Solid Edge ST9

Starting a New Part File by Using the New Dialog Box

You can start a new part file by using the **New** dialog box. To invoke this dialog box. Choose the **New** tool from the **Quick Access** toolbar of the home screen; the **New** dialog box will be displayed, as shown in Figure 2-5. Alternatively, you can choose **Application Button > New** to invoke the **New** dialog box.

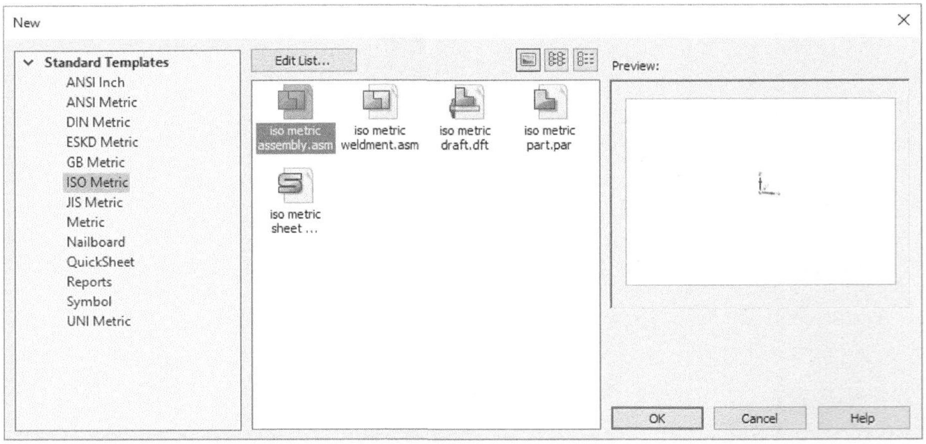

Figure 2-5 *The **New** dialog box*

The left pane of the **New** dialog box contains the **Standard Templates** drop-down list such as **ANSI Metric**, **GB Metric**, **ISO Metric**, and so on. In this list, the **ISO Metric** standard template is selected by default. In the **ISO Metric** standard template, the default templates for starting various environments are displayed in the area adjacent to the **Standard Templates** drop-down list in the **New** dialog box.

To open a new document in the **Synchronous Part** environment of Solid Edge ST9, select the **iso metric part.par** template and then choose the **OK** button from the **New** dialog box. Alternatively, double-click on **iso metric part.par**; the new document will open in the **Synchronous Part** environment as it is the default environment.

The options in the **New** dialog box are discussed next.

Edit List Button

The **Edit List** button is available adjacent to the **Standard Templates** drop-down list. When you choose this button, the **Template List Creation** dialog box will be displayed, as shown in Figure 2-6.

In this dialog box, you can change the position of the templates displayed in the **Templates** area. To do so, choose the **Move Up** or **Move Down** button to move the selected template up or down. You can also create a new customized standard template and also rename and delete it by choosing the corresponding button available at the left corner of the **Template List Creation** dialog box. The newly created standard template name will be displayed under the **Custom Templates** drop-down list available on the left pane of the dialog box. The newly created custom standard templates will also be displayed in the **Custom Templates** drop-down list in the **New** dialog box.

Note

*You can also create a customized standard template in the dialog box by creating a folder with the name Custom Template at the location Program File > Solid Edge ST9 > Template and then saving a customized template in it. This template will automatically be added to the **Standard Templates** drop-down list.*

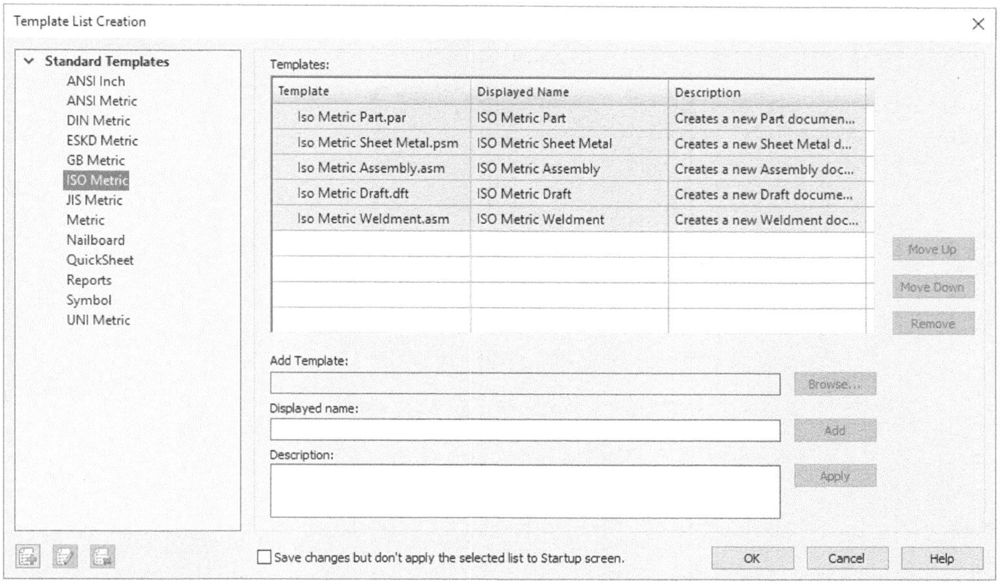

*Figure 2-6 The **Template List Creation** dialog box*

Large Icon

The **Large Icon** button is used to display the templates of the **New** dialog box in the form of large icons.

List

The **List** button is used to display the templates of the **New** dialog box in the form of a list.

Detail

The **Detail** button is used to list the details of the templates in various tabs of the **New** dialog box. When you choose this button, the area on the left will be divided into four columns. The first column lists the names of the templates, the second column lists the sizes, the third column lists the type of the template files, and the last column lists the dates when the templates were last modified.

Preview Area

The **Preview** area shows a preview of the selected template.

Figure 2-7 shows a new Solid Edge document in the **Synchronous Part** environment. This figure also shows various components in the part document of Solid Edge. On invoking this environment, two triads are displayed. Also, the **Sketching** tab is added to the **Ribbon**. This tab is used to create sketches.

Note

*In the **Synchronous Part** environment, the basic drawing tools are available in the **Home** tab as well as in the **Sketching** tab.*

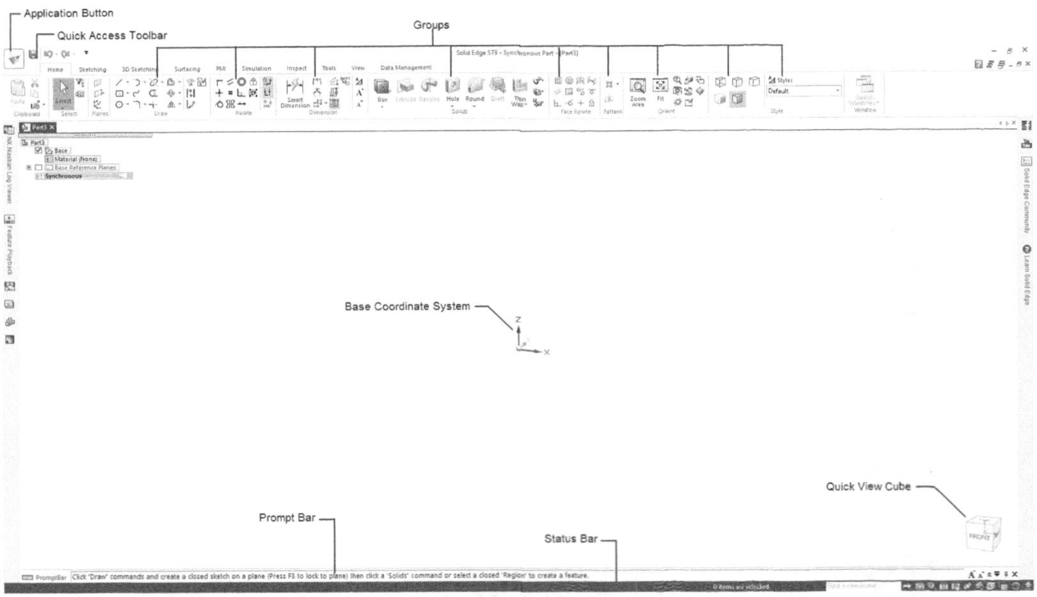

Figure 2-7 *New document in the* ***Synchronous Part*** *environment*

TRANSITION BETWEEN PART ENVIRONMENTS

In Solid Edge, there are two modeling environments coexisting in the same file, the **Synchronous Part** environment and **Ordered Part** environment. The **Synchronous Part** environment is used to create synchronous features whereas the **Ordered Part** environment is used to create ordered features. In Solid Edge, you can work in both the environments in the same file. You can switch between the Synchronous and Ordered environments at any time during the modeling process. To do so, right-click in the graphics window; a shortcut menu will be displayed. Choose the **Transition to Ordered** or **Transition to Synchronous** option from the shortcut menu to switch from **Synchronous Part** environment to **Ordered Part** or vice-versa. You can also switch between environments by choosing the required modeling environment from the **Model** group of the **Tools** tab.

STARTING A SKETCH IN THE PART ENVIRONMENT

In the **Synchronous Part** environment, a triad representing the base coordinate system is displayed at the center of the graphics area. You can draw sketches on any of the principal planes of the base coordinate system. To draw a sketch, invoke a sketching tool from the **Draw** group; two green lines of infinite length get attached to the cursor. Move the cursor toward the axis of the base coordinate system; you will notice that the respective plane gets highlighted and a Lock symbol is displayed on it.

You can also select the required plane by using the **QuickPick** listbox. To do so, move the cursor toward the base coordinate system and wait for a while; a mouse symbol will be displayed near the cursor. Next, right-click; the **QuickPick** list box will be displayed with a list of alternate planes that can be selected for drawing the sketches, as shown in Figure 2-8. Now, you can select the required plane for sketching.

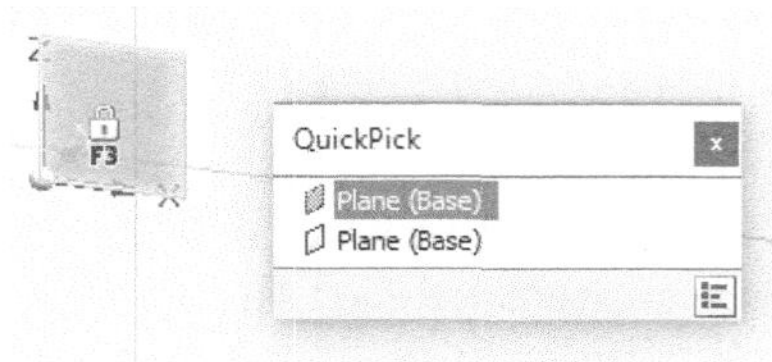

***Figure 2-8** The **QuickPick** list box with the list of planes*

Note

*In Solid Edge, the base reference planes are hidden by default. You can display the base reference planes individually or in group by selecting the **Base Reference Planes** check box in the **PathFinder**.*

Locking and Unlocking Sketching Plane

If you want all input commands to be in the same plane, you can lock that sketch plane. It implies that all the sketches and their dimensions are drawn on the same plane. To lock the plane, click on the Lock symbol that will be displayed on selecting any principal plane or face of the solid. On doing so, the sketch plane will get locked and the Lock symbol will be displayed at the upper right corner of the drawing window. Now, you can draw sketches, add dimensions to them, and so on. In this case, you will notice that the sketches along with their relationships and dimensions are on the same plane, and will be added as a single sketched entity under the **Sketches** node of the **PathFinder**. The plane will remain locked until you unlock it by clicking on the Lock symbol again. If you want to draw a sketch in some other plane, first you need to unlock the plane and then invoke a sketching tool again. Next, select the required plane.

However, to draw a sketch in the **Ordered Part** environment, switch to the **Ordered Part** environment and choose the **Sketch** tool from the **Sketch** group of the **Home** tab; you will be prompted to click on a planar face or a reference plane. Select a reference plane, the selected plane will be oriented parallel to the screen and the sketching environment will be invoked. Now, you can draw the sketch using various sketching tools that are discussed next.

SKETCHING TOOLS

In the **Synchronous Part** environment, the sketching tools are available in the ribbon of the synchronous part environment. But in the **Ordered Part** environment, you first need to invoke the sketch environment to use a sketching tool. All the tools required to create a profile or a sketch in Solid Edge are available in the **Draw** group and are discussed next.

Line Tool

Ribbon: Home > Draw > Line

In any design, lines are the most widely used sketched entities. In Solid Edge, the **Line** tool is used to draw straight lines, symmetric lines as well as to draw the tangent or normal arcs originating from the endpoint of a selected line. The properties of the line are displayed in the Command bar.

Drawing Straight Lines

To draw a straight line, choose the **Line** tool; the **Line** Command bar will be displayed, refer to Figure 2-9. Also you will be prompted to select the first point for the line. Specify the point (click) in the drawing window by pressing the left mouse button; a rubber-band line will be attached to the cursor. Also, you will be prompted to select the second point for the line. Note that on moving the cursor in the drawing window, the length and angle of the line also gets modified accordingly in the **Line** Command bar. Next, specify the endpoint of the line in the drawing window by pressing the left mouse button. Alternatively, you can draw a line by specifying its length and angle in the **Line** Command bar.

***Figure 2-9** The **Line** Command bar*

While drawing a line, you will notice that some symbols are displayed on the right of the cursor. For example, after specifying the start point of the line, if you move the cursor in the horizontal direction, a symbol similar to a horizontal line will be displayed. This symbol is called the relationship handle and it indicates the relationship that will be applied to the entity being drawn. In the above-mentioned case, the horizontal relationship handle is displayed on the right of the cursor. This relationship will ensure that the line you draw is horizontal. These relationships are automatically applied to the profile while drawing a line.

Note

Relationships are also applied between the sketched entities and the reference planes. You will learn more about relationships in the later chapters.

The process of drawing lines does not end after defining the first line. You will notice that as soon as you define the endpoint of the first line, another rubber-band line starts. The start point of this line becomes the endpoint of the first line and the endpoint of the new line is attached to the cursor.

The process of drawing consecutive lines continues until you right-click to terminate it. However, even after right-clicking, the **Line** tool will remain active and you will be prompted to specify the first point of the line. You can terminate the **Line** tool by choosing the **Select** tool from the **Select** group or by pressing the ESC key. Figures 2-10 and 2-11 show the continuous lines being drawn.

While drawing lines, you will notice that if the cursor is horizontally or vertically aligned with the endpoint or midpoint of a line or reference plane, then the dashed lines are displayed. These dashed lines are called alignment indicators and are used to indicate the horizontal or vertical alignment of the current location of the cursor with a point. Figure 2-12 shows the alignment indicators originating from the endpoints of the existing lines.

Tip

If the alignment indicator is not displayed, move the cursor over the entity from which you want the alignment indicator to originate; the entity will turn orange in color and the alignment indicator will be displayed.

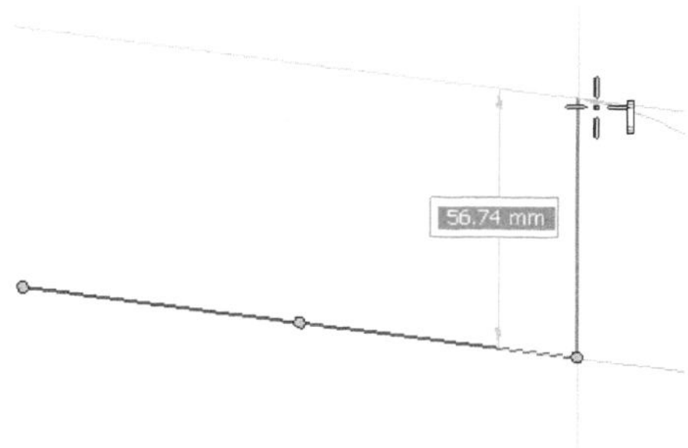

Figure 2-10 *Vertical relationship handle displayed while drawing the vertical line*

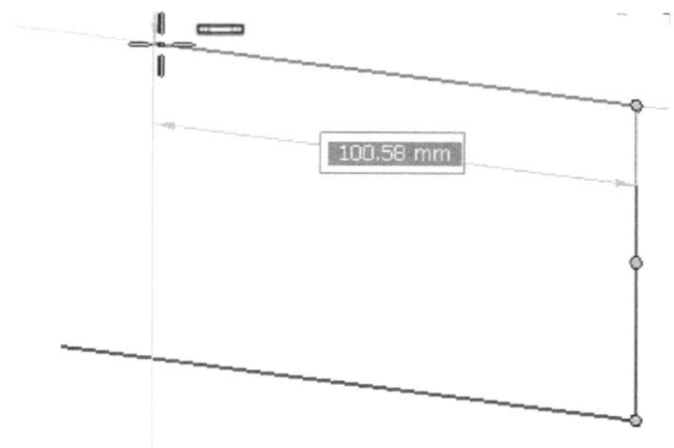

Figure 2-11 *Horizontal relationship handle displayed while drawing the horizontal line*

Drawing Symmetric Lines

To draw a symmetric line, when the **Line** tool is active, press the S key; you will be prompted to select the first point for the line. Specify the point (click) in the drawing window by pressing the left mouse button; a symmetric rubber-band line extendible equally to both sides will be displayed attached to the cursor. Also, you will be prompted to select the second point for the line. Click to specify the endpoint of the symmetric line. After drawing the required symmetric line, the system will automatically switch back to the line mode. You can activate the line mode or the symmetric line mode by pressing the L or S key, respectively.

Drawing Tangent and Normal Arcs

As mentioned earlier, you can draw a tangent or a normal arc by using the **Line** tool. To draw an arc when the **Line** tool is activated, press the A key or choose the **Arc** button from the Command bar. On doing so, you will notice that the **Length** and **Angle** edit boxes in the Command bar are replaced by the **Radius** and **Sweep** edit boxes, respectively. These edit boxes can be used to define the radius and the included angle of the resulting arc.

Also, a small circle will be displayed at the start point of the arc. This circle is divided into four regions. These regions are called intent zones and are used to define the type of the arc to be created. To create an arc tangent to a line, move the cursor through a small distance in the zone that is tangent to the line; the tangent arc will be displayed. Next, click to specify the endpoint of the arc. Similarly, if you move the cursor in the zone that is normal to the line, the normal arc will be displayed. Next, click to specify the endpoint of the arc. After drawing the required arc, the system will automatically switch back to the line mode. You can activate the line mode or the arc mode by pressing the L or the A key, respectively. Figure 2-13 shows a tangent arc being drawn using the **Line** tool.

Tip

If you have selected an incorrect point as the start point of a line, right-click to cancel it; you will again be prompted to specify the first point of the line.

The buttons in the **Line** Command bar are used to specify the color, type, and width of lines. You can also draw a projection line of infinite length by choosing the **Projection Line** button from the **Line** Command bar. Projection lines are generally used in the **Draft** environment.

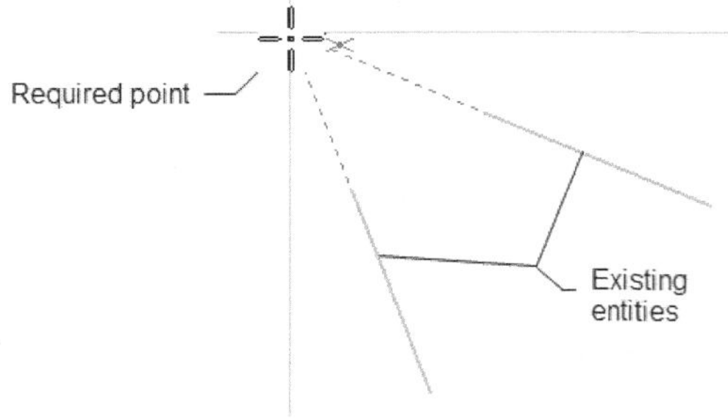

Figure 2-12 The alignment indicators originating from the endpoints of the existing lines

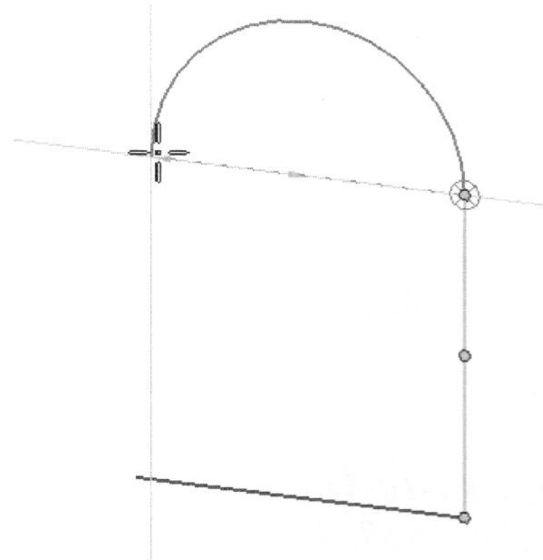

*Figure 2-13 A tangent arc drawn using the **Line** tool*

Point Tool

Ribbon: Home > Draw > Line drop-down > Point

Points are generally used as references for drawing other sketched entities. To place a point, choose the **Point** tool from the **Line** drop-down in the **Draw** group, as shown in Figure 2-14; you will be prompted to click for the point. Place the point by defining its location in the drawing window or by entering its coordinates in the **Point** Command bar.

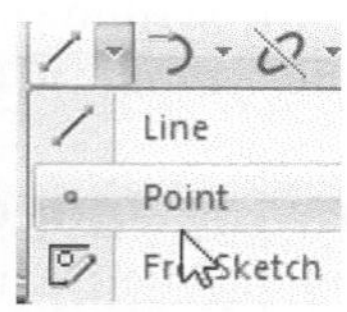

*Figure 2-14 The **Line** drop-down*

FreeSketch Tool

Ribbon: Home > Draw > Line drop-down > FreeSketch

The **FreeSketch** tool enables you to draw lines, arcs, rectangles, and circles by converting a rough sketch into a precision drawing. When you choose the **FreeSketch** tool from the **Line** drop-down, the **FreeSketch** Command bar will be displayed, as shown in Figure 2-15. The commonly used buttons in the **FreeSketch** Command bar are discussed next.

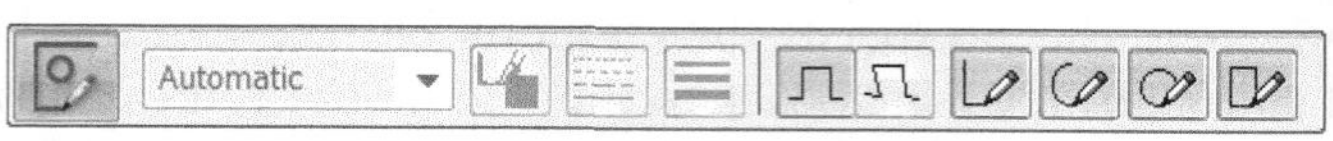

*Figure 2-15 The **FreeSketch** Command bar*

Adjust On

This button is chosen by default. As a result, when you draw a rough line sketch, the software recognizes the sketch and adjusts its orientation as horizontal or vertical. When you draw a rough curve, the sketch is automatically recognized as an arc.

Adjust Off

When you choose this button, the software does not recognize the rough sketch and the sketch will remain the same as drawn.

Drawing Circles

In Solid Edge, circles can be drawn by using three tools. These tools and the tools to draw ellipses are grouped together in the **Circle** drop-down of the **Draw** group, as shown in Figure 2-16. The tools used to draw circles are discussed next.

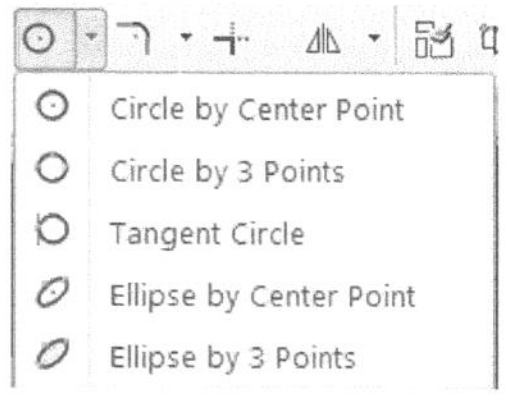

***Figure 2-16** The **Circle** drop-down*

Circle by Center Point Tool

Ribbon:	Home > Draw > Circle drop-down > Circle by Center Point

This is the most widely used tool for drawing circles. In this method, you need to specify the center point for the circle and a point on it. The point on the circle defines the radius of the circle. To draw a circle using this method, choose the **Circle by Center Point** tool from the **Draw** group; the **Circle by Center Point** Command bar will be displayed and you will be prompted to specify the center point of the circle. Specify the center point of the circle in the drawing window; you will be prompted to specify a point on the circle. Specify a point on the circle to define the radius. Alternatively, you can enter the value of the diameter or radius in the Command bar. Figure 2-17 shows a circle drawn using this method.

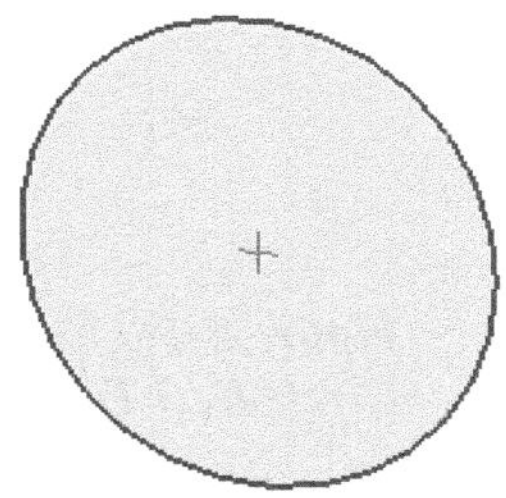

***Figure 2-17** Circle drawn using the **Circle by Center Point** tool*

Circle by 3 Point Tool

Ribbon:	Home > Draw > Circle drop-down > Circle by 3 Points

This tool is used to draw a circle by specifying three points lying on it. To draw a circle using this method, choose the **Circle by 3 Points** tool in the **Draw** group; you will be prompted to specify the first point and then the second point for the circle. Specify these two points; small reference circles will be displayed on these two points, as shown in Figure 2-18. Also, you will be prompted to specify the third point. Specify the third point for the circle to create it.

Tangent Circle Tool

Ribbon:	Home > Draw > Circle drop-down > Tangent Circle

This tool is used to draw a circle tangent to one or two existing entities. To draw a circle using this method, choose the **Tangent Circle** tool from the **Circle** drop-down in the **Draw** group; you will be prompted to specify the first point on the circle. The circle will be drawn using two or three points, depending upon how you specify the first point of the circle. If you specify the first point on an existing entity, then you will be prompted to specify the second point and the circle will be drawn using these two points. However, if you do not specify the first point on any existing entity, then you need to define the circle using three points.

When you move the cursor close to an existing entity to specify the second or third point, the tangent relationship handle will be displayed. Now, if you specify the point, the resulting circle will be tangent to the selected entities. Also, small reference circles will be displayed at the points where the circle is tangent to the selected entities. Figure 2-19 shows a circle tangent to two lines.

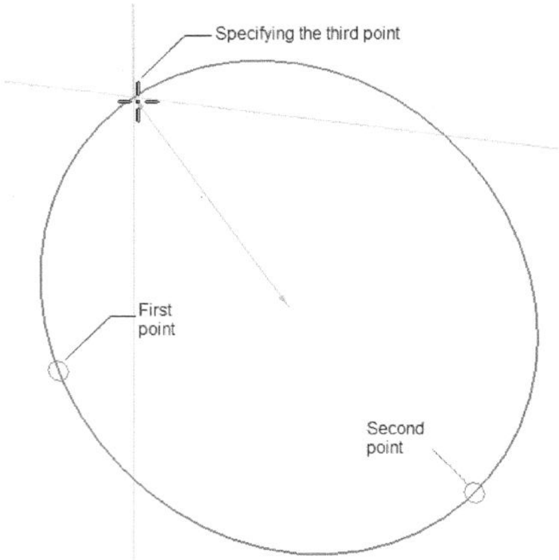

Figure 2-18 *Circle drawn using the* ***Circle by 3 Points*** *tool*

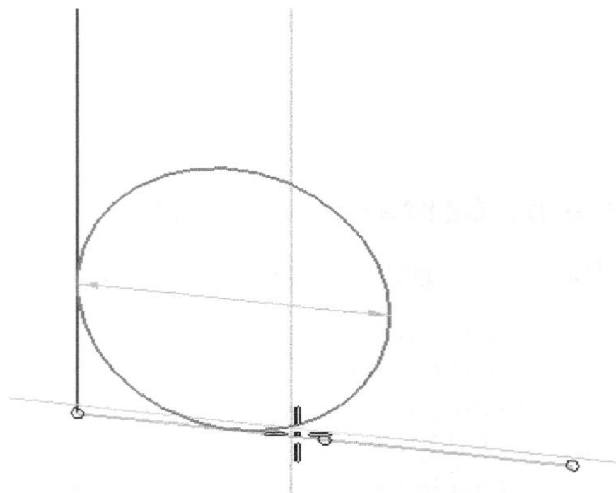

Figure 2-19 *Circle drawn using the* ***Tangent Circle*** *tool*

Drawing Ellipses

In Solid Edge, you can draw ellipses using two methods that are discussed next.

Ellipse by Center Point Tool

Ribbon: Home > Draw > Circle drop-down > Ellipse by Center Point

This tool is used to draw a center point ellipse. In this method, first you need to define the center point of an ellipse. On doing so, you will be prompted to specify the endpoint of the primary axis. Specify the endpoint of the primary axis; you will be prompted to specify the endpoint of the secondary axis. Specify the endpoint of the secondary axis; the ellipse will be created. You can also draw an ellipse by entering the required dimensions in the Command bar and then specifying its center point.

Ellipse by 3 Point Tool

Ribbon: Home > Draw > Circle drop-down > Ellipse by 3 Points

This tool is used to draw an ellipse by specifying three points. The first two points are the first and second endpoints of the primary axis of the ellipse and the third point is a point on the ellipse. To draw an ellipse by using this method, choose the **Ellipse by 3 Points** tool from the **Draw** group; you will be prompted to specify the first endpoint. Specify the first endpoint, you will be prompted to specify the second endpoint of the primary axis of an ellipse. Specify the second point; a reference ellipse will be displayed and you will be prompted to specify a point on the ellipse. The primary axis will act as the major axis or the minor axis, depending upon the location of point specification. Figure 2-20 shows a profile in which the cursor is moved to define the third point on the ellipse to create it. Note that you can also draw an ellipse by specifying values in the Ellipse by 3 Points Command bar, which is displayed on invoking this tool.

Drawing Arcs

In Solid Edge, tools to draw an arc are grouped together in the **Arc** drop-down, as shown in Figure 2-21. You can draw arcs using three methods. These methods are discussed next.

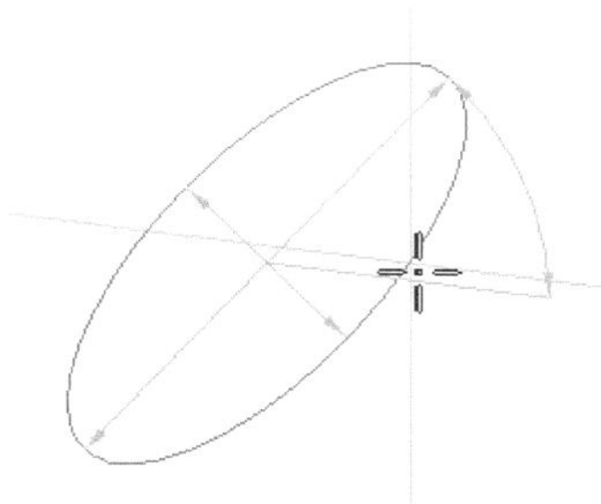

Figure 2-20 An ellipse drawn by specifying three points

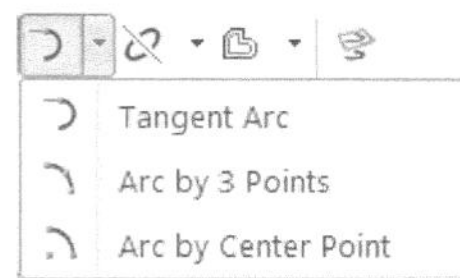

*Figure 2-21 The **Arc** drop-down*

Tangent Arc Tool

Ribbon:	Home > Draw > Arc drop-down > Tangent Arc

The tool of drawing an arc using the **Tangent Arc** tool is similar to drawing the tangent and normal arcs using the **Line** tool. To draw a tangent arc, choose the **Tangent Arc** tool from the **Arc** drop-down, refer to Figure 2-21. On doing so, you will be prompted to specify the start point of the arc. Move the cursor close to the endpoint of the entity where you want to start the tangent arc. You will notice that the endpoint relationship handle is displayed to the right of the cursor. This handle has a small inclined line with a point at the upper end, which suggests that if you select the point now, the endpoint of the entity will be snapped. Select the endpoint and then move the cursor; the intent zones will be displayed. Move the cursor through a small distance in the required intent zone and then specify the endpoint of the arc. Alternatively, you can enter the radius and the included angle of the arc in the **Tangent Arc** Command bar, which is displayed when you invoke this tool.

Arc by 3 Points Tool

Ribbon:	Home > Draw > Arc drop-down > Arc by 3 Points

This tool is used to draw an arc by specifying its start point, endpoint, and the third point on its periphery. The third point is used to specify the direction in which the arc will be drawn. You can specify the radius of this arc in the Command bar. Figure 2-22 shows a three-points arc drawn by this method.

Arc by Center Point Tool

Ribbon:	Home > Draw > Arc drop-down > Arc by Center Point

This tool is used to draw an arc by specifying its center point, start point, and endpoint. Invoke the **Arc by Center Point** tool; you will be prompted to specify the center point of the arc. Specify the center point of the arc; you will be prompted to specify its start point and then the endpoint. Note that when you specify the start point of the arc, the radius will be automatically defined. And on specifying the endpoint of the arc, the length of the arc will be defined. Figure 2-23 shows an arc drawn by using this method.

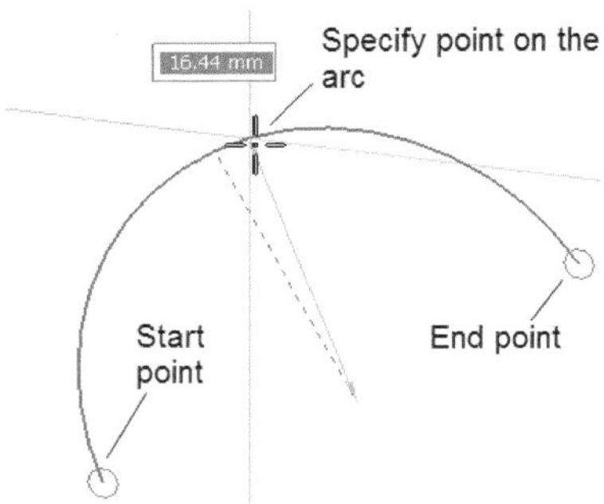

Figure 2-22 *An arc drawn by specifying 3 points*

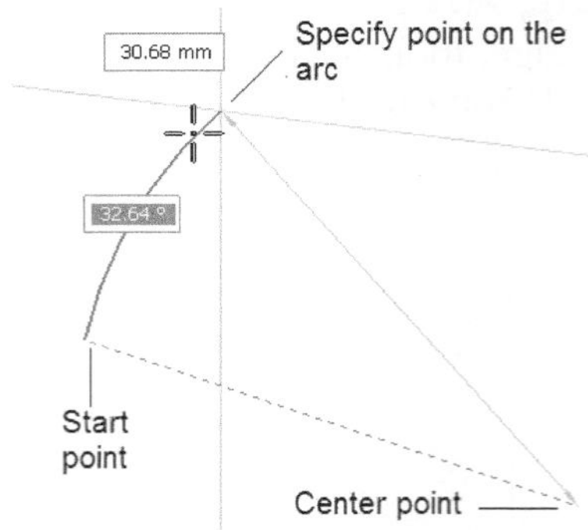

Figure 2-23 *An arc drawn by specifying center point*

Drawing Rectangles

In Solid Edge, you can draw rectangles using three methods that are discussed next.

Rectangle by Center Tool

Ribbon:	Home > Draw > Rectangle drop-down > Rectangle by Center

In Solid Edge, you can draw a rectangle by specifying its center point and any of its vertices. To draw a rectangle by using this tool, choose the **Rectangle by Center** tool from the **Rectangle** drop-down, refer to Figure 2-24; you will be prompted to specify the center point of the rectangle.

Click in the drawing window to specify the center point of the rectangle and move the cursor; the dynamic preview of the rectangle will be displayed in the graphics window, as shown in Figure 2-25 and you will be prompted to specify a point to create a rectangle. Specify a point; the point specified will define the height and width of the rectangle. Alternatively, you can specify the width, height, and angle of the rectangle in the Command bar.

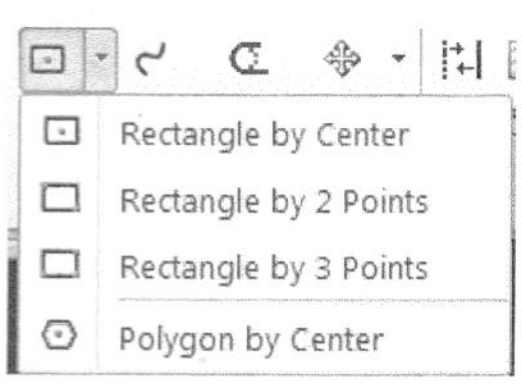

Figure 2-24 *The **Rectangle** drop-down*

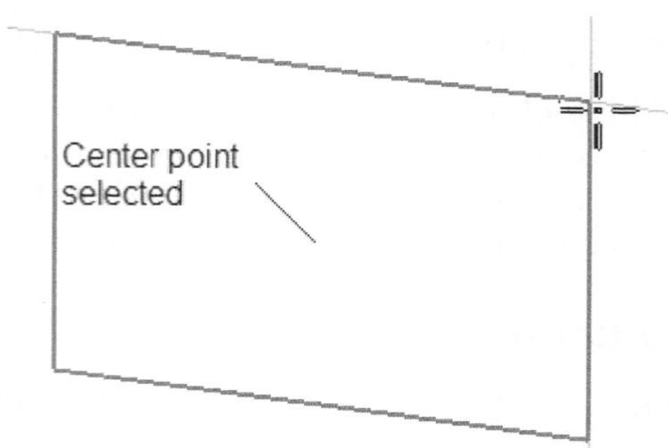

Figure 2-25 *Dynamic preview of the rectangle displayed on specifying its center*

Tip

You can also draw a rectangle by pressing and holding the left mouse button at a point and dragging the cursor across to define the opposite corner of the rectangle. When you release the left mouse button, the rectangle will be drawn.

Rectangle by 2 Points Tool

Ribbon: Home > Draw > Rectangle drop-down > Rectangle by 2 Points

You can also draw a rectangle by specifying two diagonally opposite corners. To draw a rectangle by using this method, choose the **Rectangle by 2 Points** tool; you will be prompted to specify the first corner of the rectangle. Click in the drawing window to specify the first corner of the rectangle; the dynamic preview of the rectangle will be displayed in the graphics window, as shown in Figure 2-26, and you will be prompted to click in the drawing window to specify the second corner. Click in the drawing window or specify the values width and height values in the **Rectangle by 2 Points** Command bar to specify the diagonally opposite corner; a rectangle will be created.

Rectangle by 3 Points Tool

Ribbon: Home > Draw > Rectangle drop-down > Rectangle by 3 Points

You can also draw rectangles by specifying three points. The first two points define the width and orientation of the rectangle and the third point defines its height. To draw a rectangle by specifying three points, invoke the **Rectangle by 3 Points** tool; you will be prompted to specify the first corner. Specify a point in the drawing window to define the start point of the rectangle; you will be prompted to specify the second point. This point will define the width of the rectangle. You can also define this point at an angle. On doing so, the rectangle will be drawn at an angle. After specifying the width of the rectangle, you will be prompted to specify a point that will define the height of the rectangle. Specify the point; the rectangle will be created. Alternatively, you can specify the width, height, and angle of the rectangle in the **Rectangle by 3 points** Command bar. Figure 2-27 shows a rectangle drawn at an angle.

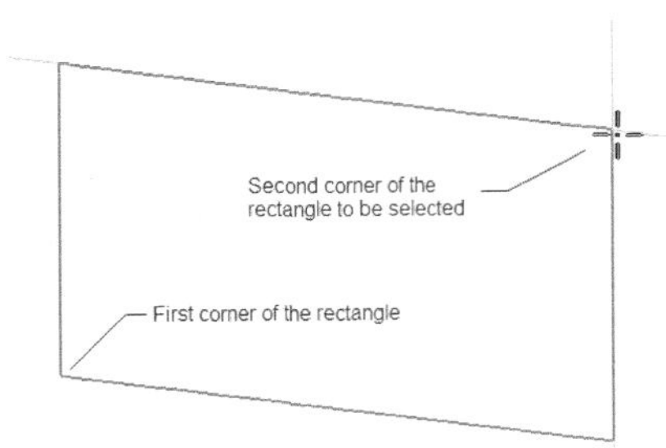

Figure 2-26 *Drawing a rectangle by specifying two diagonally opposite corners*

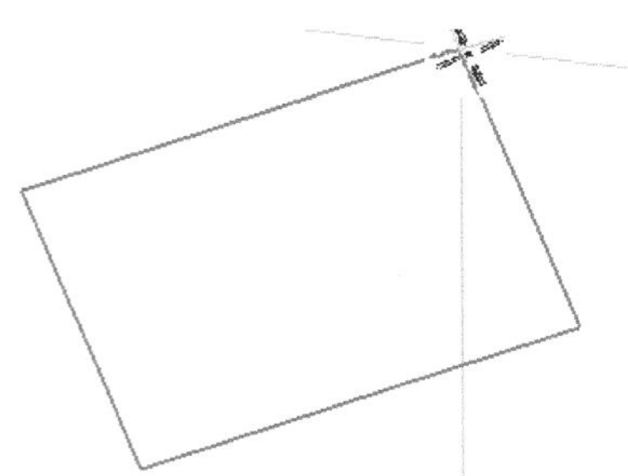

Figure 2-27 *Rectangle drawn at an angle by using the* ***Rectangle by 3 points***

Drawing Polygons

Ribbon: Home > Draw > Rectangle drop-down > Polygon by Center

The polygons drawn in Solid Edge are regular polygons. A regular polygon is a geometric figure with many sides, and in it the length of all sides and the angle between them are the same. In Solid Edge, you can draw a polygon with the number of sides ranging from 3 to 200. To create a polygon, choose the **Polygon by Center** tool from the **Rectangle** drop-down of the **Draw** group; you will be prompted to specify the center point of the polygon. Click in the graphics window to specify the center point of the polygon; you will be prompted to specify the point to create the polygon. Click in the graphics window to specify the point of the polygon; the polygon will be created. You will notice that an imaginary circle is drawn such that all its vertices touch the circle. This imaginary circle will be used as the construction geometry for creating the polygon.

Note that if the **By Midpoint** button is chosen in the **Polygon by Center** Command bar, you can specify the midpoint of an edge of the polygon, as shown in Figure 2-28. If you choose the **By Vertex** button from the **Polygon by Center** Command bar, you can specify the vertex of the polygon, as shown in Figure 2-29.

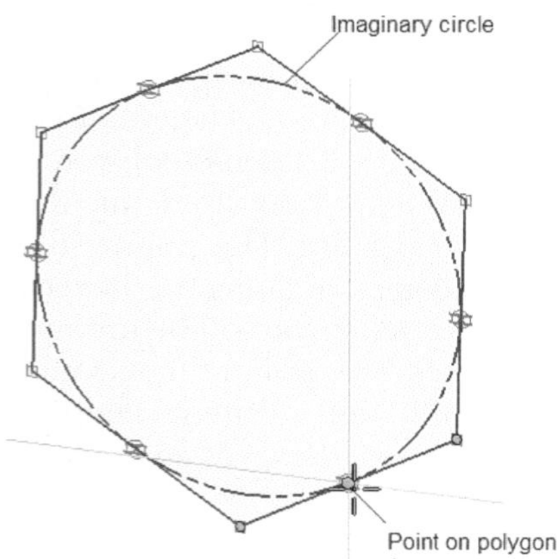

*Figure 2-28 Drawing a polygon by using the **By Midpoint** button*

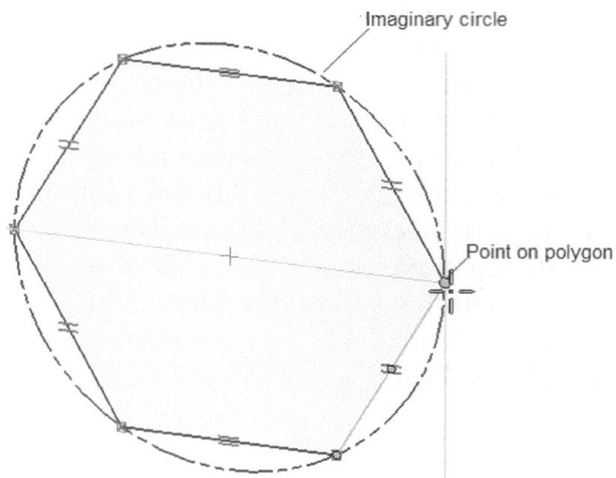

*Figure 2-29 Drawing a polygon by using the **By Vertex** button*

Next, in the **Polygon by Center** Command bar, specify the number of sides of the polygon in the **Sides** spinner. In the **Distance** edit box, specify the distance between the two specified points of the polygon. In the **Angle** edit box, specify the orientation of the polygon with respect to the horizontal axis.

Drawing Curves

Ribbon: Home > Draw > Curve

To draw the curve, choose the **Curve** tool from the **Draw** group of the **Home** tab; the **Curve** Command bar will be displayed. The **Curve** tool allows you to draw curves by using two methods: by specifying points in the drawing window, and by dragging the cursor in the drawing window. These methods are discussed next.

Drawing a Curve by Specifying Points in the Drawing Window

In this method, you need to continuously specify points in the drawing area to draw a curve passing through them. After specifying the first point, move the cursor and specify the second point. Continue specifying points until you have specified all the points required for drawing the curve. Figure 2-30 shows a curve drawn by using this method.

Drawing a Curve by Dragging the Cursor

In this method, you need to press and hold the left mouse button and drag the cursor to create a curve. A reference curve will be displayed in the drawing window as you drag the cursor. Once you release the left mouse button, a curve will be drawn that has approximately the same shape as that of the reference curve. Figure 2-31 shows a curve drawn by using this method.

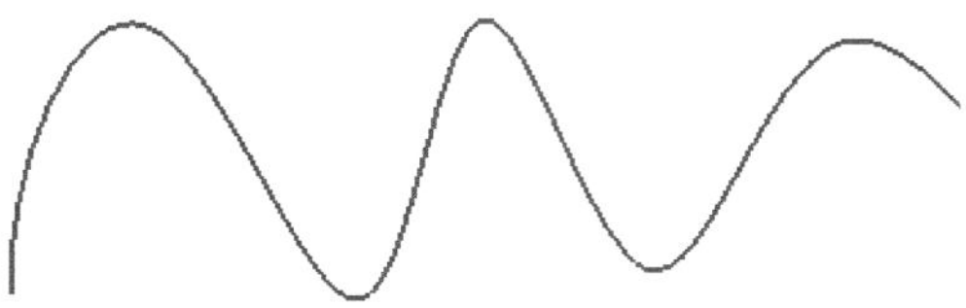

Figure 2-30 *Curve drawn by specifying points in the drawing window*

Figure 2-31 *Curve drawn by dragging the cursor in the drawing window*

You can also create a closed curve by using the **Curve** tool. To do so, invoke the **Curve** tool from the **Draw** group and then choose the **Close Curve** button from the **Curve** Command bar. Next, specify the first point to start the curve; a rubber line will get attached to the cursor. Specify the end point and move the cursor in the drawing area and click for the third point to create the closed curve.

Clean Sketch Tool

Ribbon: Home > Draw > Clean Sketch

The **Clean Sketch** tool is used to remove unnecessary or overlapping elements from the imported sketch. To remove the overlapping entities, choose the **Clean Sketch** tool from the **Draw** group in the **Home** tab; the **Clean Sketch** Command bar will be displayed, refer to Figure 2-32. Now, choose the **Clean Sketch - Clean Sketch Options** button from this Command bar; the **Clean Sketch Options** dialog box will be displayed, refer to Figure 2-33. The options in this dialog box are discussed next.

Figure 2-32 *The **Clean Sketch** Command bar*

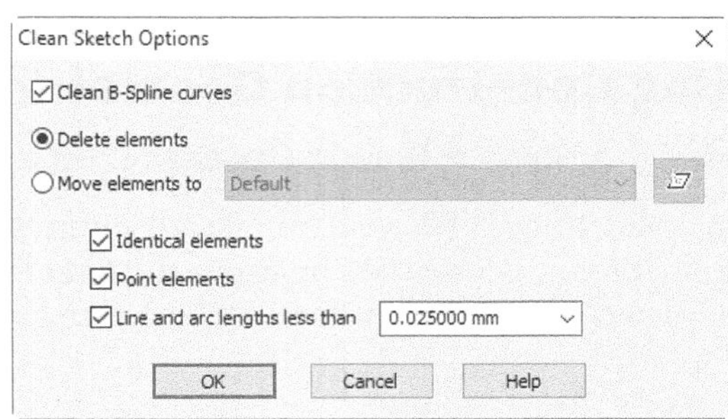

Figure 2-33 *The **Clean Sketch Options** dialog box*

Clean B-Spline curves

The **Clean B-Spline curves** check box in the **Clean Sketch Options** dialog box is selected to delete the B-spline curves from the sketch, refer to Figure 2-33.

Delete elements

The **Delete elements** radio button in the dialog box is selected to delete the duplicate entities.

Move elements to

The **Move elements to** radio button is selected to move the duplicate entities to a separate layer. To move the duplicate entities, select this radio button from the **Clean Sketch Options** dialog box; the **Move elements to** drop-down list and the **New Layer** button on its right will be activated, refer to Figure 2-33. Next, choose the **New Layer** button to create a new layer; the **New Layer** dialog box will be displayed, refer to Figure 2-34. Enter the required layer name in the **New Layer name** edit box and choose the **OK** button, a new layer will be created and displayed in the **Layer** drop-down list. Now, you can select the required layer from this drop-down list.

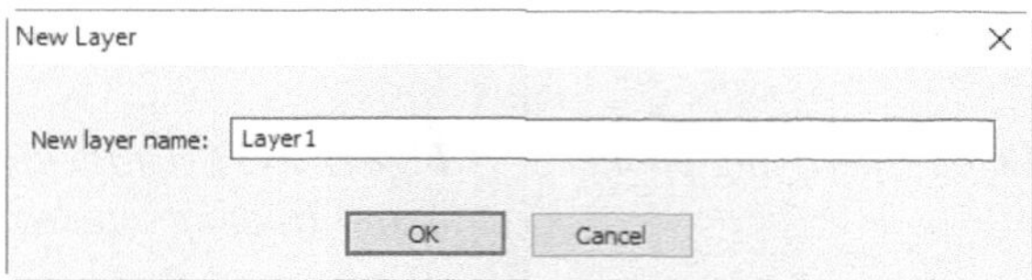

*Figure 2-34 The **New Layer** dialog box*

Identical elements

The **Identical elements** check box is selected to remove the identical entities in the sketch.

Point elements

The **Point elements** check box is selected to remove the point entities in the sketch.

Line and arc lengths less than

The **Line and arc lengths less than** check box is selected to remove the line and arc entities of a value lesser than the user defined value from the sketch.

Note

You cannot move or delete the sketched entities using this command on which any relationship is applied.

Creating Construction Geometries

Ribbon: Home > Draw > Create as Construction

In Solid Edge ST9, you can sketch entities such as lines, arcs, circles, and ellipses as construction geometries by using the **Create as Construction** button. When this button is turned on, all the entities will be created as construction geometry.

Converting Sketched Entities into Construction Geometries

Ribbon: Home > Draw > Construction

This button is used to toggle between sketched entities and construction geometries. Choose the **Construction** button from the **Draw** group of the **Home** tab; the **Construction** Command bar will be displayed and you will be prompted to select or fence the elements to toggle between sketch or construction. Next, select the sketched elements to convert them into construction geometry.

Converting Sketched Entities into Curves

Ribbon: Home > Draw > Convert to Curve

In Solid Edge, you can convert the sketched entities such as lines, arcs, circles, and ellipses into bezier spline curves by using the **Convert to Curve** tool. On invoking this tool, you will be prompted to select an element to be converted into a curve. As soon as you select the element, it will be converted into a bezier spline curve. Note that you may not be able to view the changes in the sketched entity unless you select it. When you select the sketched entity, you will notice that the number of handles in it has increased and the control polygon is displayed on that entity. If you drag the converted entity using any of its handles, it will become a curve.

Filleting Sketched Entities

Ribbon: Home > Draw > Fillet drop-down > Fillet

Filleting is a process of rounding sharp corners of a profile. You can create a fillet by removing sharp corners and then replacing them with round corners. In Solid Edge, you can create a fillet between any two sketched entities. To create a fillet, choose the **Fillet** tool from the **Fillet** drop-down in the **Draw** group, refer to Figure 2-35; the **Fillet** Command bar will be displayed. Enter the radius of the fillet in the **Radius** edit box of the Command bar and press ENTER. Next, select the two entities that you want to fillet; the fillet will be created. You can also directly select the sharp corners to be filleted. The two entities comprising the corner will be highlighted in orange when you move the cursor over the corner. Select the corners at this stage to create the fillet. Figure 2-36 shows a profile before and after filleting the corner.

***Figure 2-35** The **Fillet** drop-down*

You can retain the sharp corner even after creating the fillet. To do so, choose the **No Trim** button from the **Fillet** Command bar and then select the corner to be filleted; the fillet will be created and the sharp corner will be retained. Figure 2-37 shows a profile in which the fillet is created with the sharp corner retained.

Note

Ideally, the profiles that have the fillet created with the sharp corners retained may not give the desired result when used for creating features. Therefore, they should be avoided.

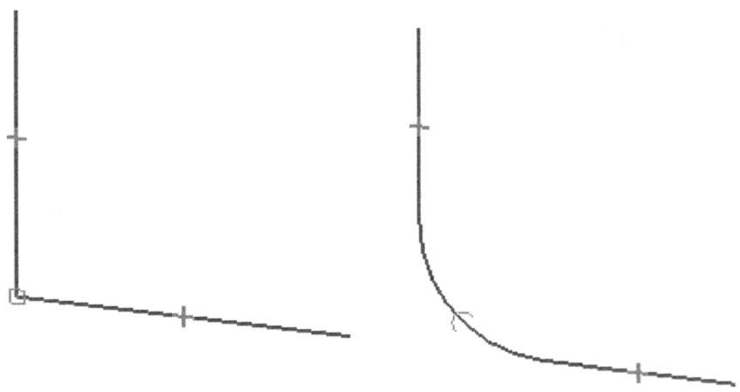

Figure 2-36 Sketch before and after creating the fillet

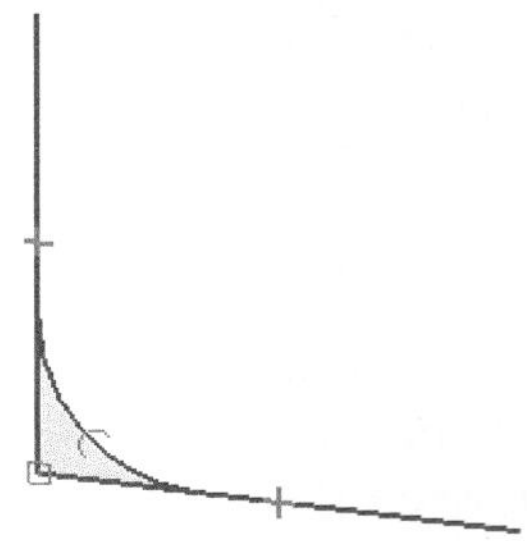

Figure 2-37 Sharp corner retained after creating the fillet

Chamfering Sketched Entities

Ribbon: Home > Draw > Fillet drop-down > Chamfer

Chamfering is a process of beveling the sharp corners of a profile to reduce the stress concentration. You can create a chamfer only between two linear entities. A chamfer can be created by defining the distance of the corner being chamfered from the two edges of the profile, or by defining the angle of the chamfer and the distance along one of the edges. To create a chamfer, invoke the **Chamfer** tool; the **Chamfer** Command bar will be displayed. In this Command bar, the **Angle**, **Setback A**, and **Setback B** edit boxes are available. The **Setback A** and **Setback B** values define the chamfer distance along the first and second edges, respectively. The **Angle** edit box defines the inclination angle of the chamfer. Note that you can specify any two of the three values. The third value is automatically updated on the basis of the two values that you defined.

After setting any two values in the **Chamfer** Command bar, select the first line and the second line to be chamfered; the preview of the resulting chamfer will be displayed. Next, click to create the chamfer. Note that the first line is taken as the setback A element and the second line is taken as the setback B element, by default. If you want to reverse the order, move the cursor over the first line. You will notice that now the second line is taken as the setback A element, and the first line is taken as the setback B element. Consequently, the preview will also change. By default, the setbacks A and B are displayed in orange. Figure 2-38 shows the preview of the chamfer.

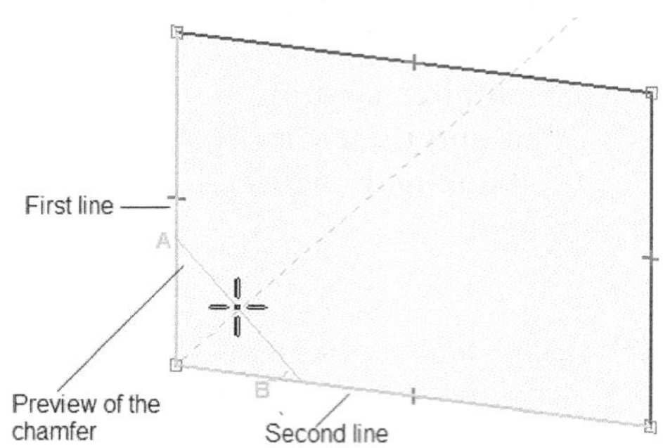

Figure 2-38 Preview of the chamfer

THE DRAWING DISPLAY TOOLS

The drawing display tools are an integral part of any solid modeling tool. They enable you to zoom, fit, and pan the drawing so that you can view it clearly. The drawing display tools available in Solid Edge are discussed next.

Zoom Area Tool

Ribbon:	View > Orient > Zoom Area
Status Bar:	Zoom Area

The **Zoom Area** tool allows you to zoom into a particular area by defining a box around it. You can invoke this tool from the **Orient** group in the **View** tab or directly from the Status bar. On invoking this tool, a plus sign (+) of infinite length will be attached to the tip of the cursor and you will be prompted to click to define the first corner or drag to specify the box. Specify a point on the screen to define the first corner of the zoom area. Next, move the cursor and specify another point to define the opposite corner of the zoom area. The area defined inside the box will be zoomed and displayed on the screen.

Zoom Tool

Ribbon:	View > Orient > Zoom
Status Bar:	Zoom

The **Zoom** tool enables you to dynamically zoom in or out the drawing. You can also use this tool to increase the display area to double the current size. To zoom into the drawing, press and hold the left mouse button in the center of the screen and then drag the cursor down. To zoom out the drawing, press and hold the left mouse button in the center of the screen and drag the cursor up.

To increase the drawing display area upto double of the current size, invoke this tool and click anywhere in the drawing window. On doing so, the drawing display area will increase such that the point at which you clicked will be moved to the center of the screen. Alternatively, you can zoom in and zoom out of the drawing area by scrolling the mouse, when no other tool is active.

Fit Tool

Ribbon:	View > Orient > Fit
Status Bar:	Fit

The **Fit** tool enables you to modify the drawing display area such that all entities in the drawing fit in the current display.

Pan Tool

Ribbon:	View > Orient > Pan
Status Bar:	Pan

The **Pan** tool allows you to dynamically pan the drawing in the drawing window. When you invoke this tool, the arrow cursor will be replaced by a hand cursor and you will be prompted to click to select the origin or drag the cursor for the dynamic pan. Press and hold the left mouse button in the drawing window, and then drag the cursor to pan the drawing. You can also pan the drawing by specifying two points in the drawing window. First, specify a point anywhere in the drawing window and then move the cursor. You will notice that a rubber-band line is displayed. One end of this line will be fixed at the point you specified and the other end will be attached to the hand cursor. Move the cursor and specify another point in the drawing window to pan the drawing. Alternatively, you can press the SHIFT key and drag the mouse by pressing the middle mouse button for panning.

Sketch View Tool

Ribbon:	View > Views > Sketch View
Status Bar:	Sketch View

Sometimes while using the drawing display tools, the orientation of the sketching plane may change. The **Sketch View** tool enables you to restore the original orientation that was active when you invoked the sketching environment. Note that this tool is available only in the sketching environment.

Tip

You can also use the keyboard to modify the drawing display area. To do so, the following combination of keys can be used:

CTRL+ Bottom arrow key = Zoom out
CTRL + SHIFT+ Bottom arrow key = Pan downward
SHIFT+ Top/Right arrow key = Rotate clockwise
SHIFT+ Bottom/Left arrow key = Rotate counter clockwise

SELECTING SKETCHED ENTITIES

You can select the sketched entities available in the drawing window by invoking the **Select** mode. To do so, choose the **Select** tool from the **Select** group; the **Select** mode will be invoked. Next, click on the required entity to select it. Note that you can exit from any active tool by activating the **Select** mode or by pressing the ESC key. The other tools available in the **Select** group are discussed next.

Overlapping

This selection option ensures that all the entities that either lie partially inside the boundary or even touch the boundary are selected.

Selection Filter

This option is used to control whether the element type can be selected or not. A check mark is displayed adjacent to the element types that can be selected.

DELETING SKETCHED ENTITIES

To delete sketched entities, select them using any one of the object selection methods discussed above; the selected entities will turn green in color. Next, press the DELETE key; all the selected entities will be deleted.

GRID

In Solid Edge, you can display the grid while creating a sketch. Also, you can configure the grid settings using the grid tools available in the **Draw** group of the **Sketching** tab. These tools are discussed next.

Show Grid

This button is used to toggle the grid display on/off in the Solid Edge drawing area. To turn the grid display on, choose the **Show Grid** button from the **Draw** group in the **Sketching** tab. Figure 2-39 shows the rectangle drawn after turning the grid display on. Choose the **Show Grid** button again; the grid display turns off.

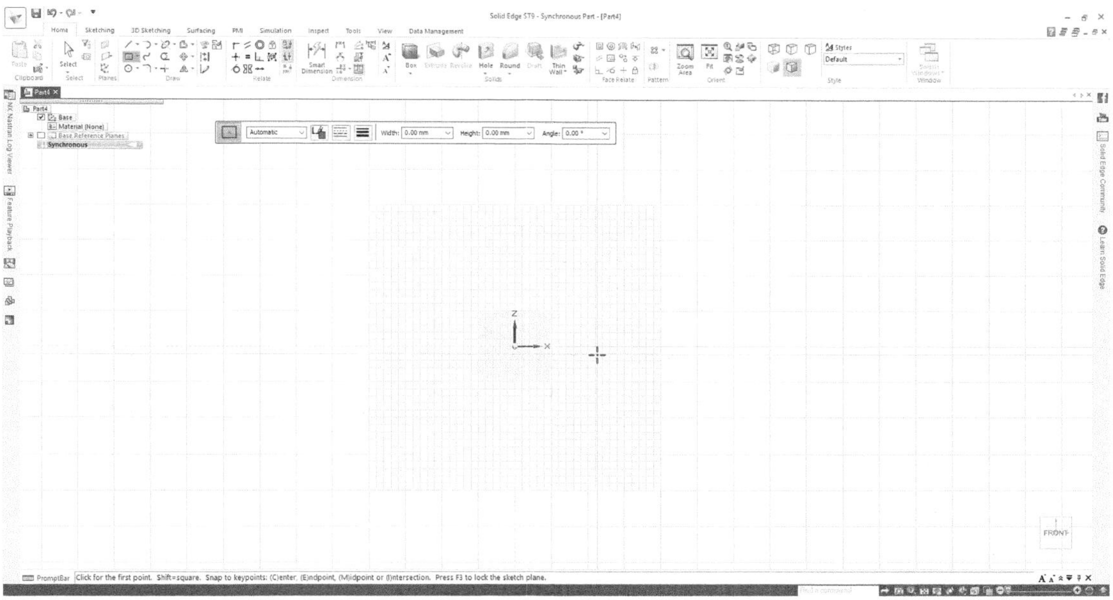

*Figure 2-39 Sketch created on choosing the **Show Grid** button*

Snap to Grid

When this button is chosen, the cursor will snap to grid points.

XY Key-in

This button is used to move the drawn entity up to the required length by specifying the values in the **X** and **Y** edit boxes. To specify the value, choose the **XY key-in** button from the **Sketching** tab; the **X** and **Y** edit boxes will be displayed, as shown in Figure 2-40.

Figure 2-40 X and Y edit boxes displayed

Grid Options

You can also configure the grid settings by using the **Grid Options** dialog box. To invoke this dialog box, choose **Sketching > Draw > Grid Options** from the **Ribbon**. Figure 2-41 shows the **Grid Options** dialog box. The options in this dialog box are used to control the grid settings.

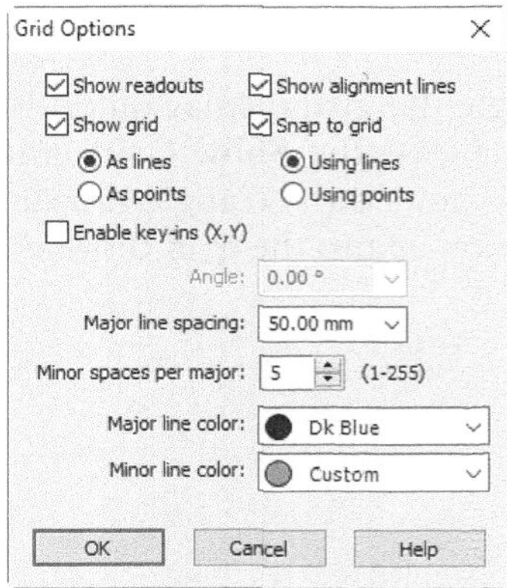

*Figure 2-41 The **Grid Options** dialog box*

REPOSITION ORIGIN

Using this tool you can change the position of the origin point. Note that this tool will be available only when the sketching plane is locked. On choosing this tool, the steering wheel will be displayed, as shown in Figure 2-42. You can use the steering wheel to change the location of the origin point. To change the location of the origin point, select the origin knob of the steering wheel and move the cursor to the required location, refer to Figure 2-43. You can select a part edge, a keypoint, a grid point, or another type of point to define the new location of the origin.

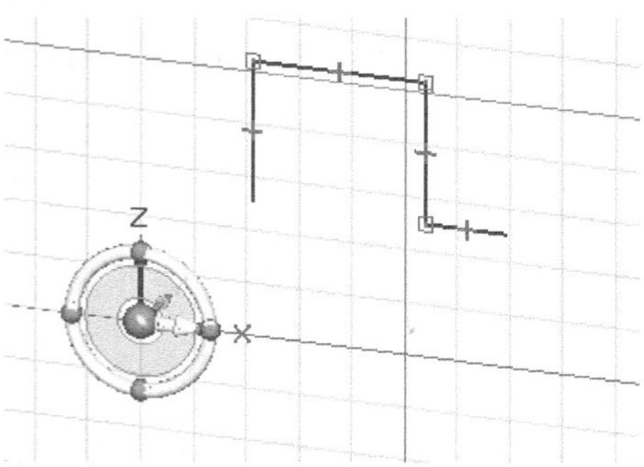

Figure 2-42 Steering wheel displayed in the drawing area

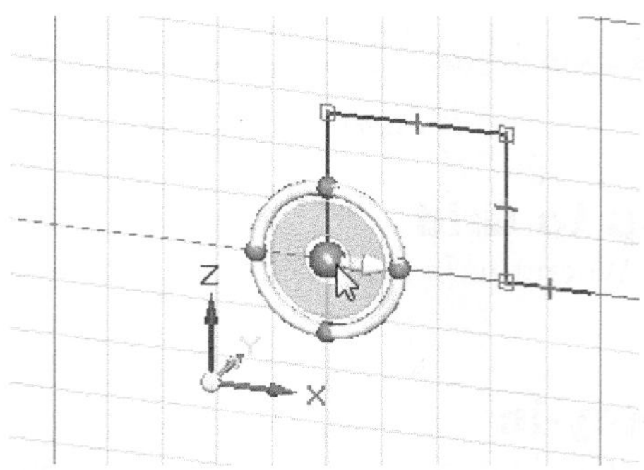

Figure 2-43 Specifying the new location of the origin

ZERO ORIGIN

On choosing this tool, the origin point is reset to the default location.

TUTORIALS

Tutorial 1 Synchronous

In this tutorial, you will draw the profile of the model shown in Figure 2-44. The profile to be drawn is shown in Figure 2-45. Do not dimension the profile as dimensions are given for reference only. **(Expected time: 30 min)**

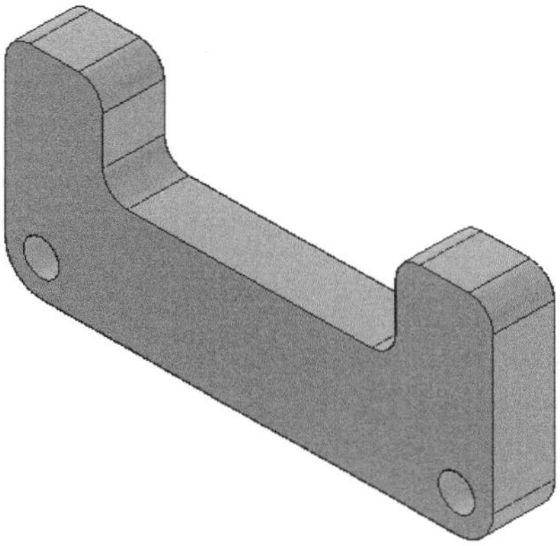

Figure 2-44 *Model for Tutorial 1*

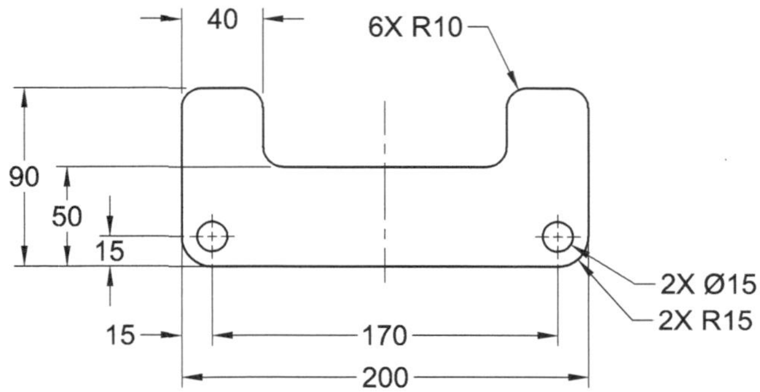

Figure 2-45 *Profile for Tutorial 1*

The following steps are required to complete this tutorial:

a. Start Solid Edge ST9 and then start a new file in the **Synchronous Part** environment.
b. Draw the outer loop of the profile using the **Line** tool.
c. Fillet the sharp corners of the outer loop by using the **Fillet** tool.
d. Draw circles using the centers of fillets to complete the profile.
e. Save the file and close it.

Starting a Solid Edge Document

You will create the profile of the model using the tools in the **Sketching** tab of the **Synchronous Part** environment of Solid Edge. To create this profile, first you need to start a new part file.

1. Double-click on the shortcut icon of Solid Edge ST9 on the desktop of your computer.

   Now, you need to start a new part file to draw the sketch of the given model.

2. Choose the **New** tool from the **Quick Access** toolbar of the home screen; the **New** dialog box will be displayed. Next, select **iso metric part.par** and click **OK** to start a new Solid Edge part file.

Creating the Outer Loop of the Profile

You need to draw the outer loop of the profile by using the **Line** tool. The sharp corners of the outer loop will be rounded by using the **Fillet** tool. In this tutorial, you will use the dynamic edit box displayed in the drawing area to enter the exact dimension of the sketched entities.

1. Choose the **Line** tool from the **Draw** group of the **Home** tab; the **Line** Command bar is displayed and the alignment lines are attached to the cursor. 

2. Next, you need to define the plane on which you want to draw the profile of the base feature. Hover the cursor on the base coordinate system until a mouse symbol is displayed, and then right-click; the **QuickPick** list box is displayed with the possible nearest selection. Next, choose the XZ plane for sketching.

3. By default, the view orientation of the part document is set to Diametric. Choose **Sketch View** from the **Views** group of the **View** tab; the sketching plane orients parallel to the screen. 

4. Move the cursor toward the origin and click when an endpoint snap is displayed at the origin; the start point of the line is specified.

   The point specified by you is selected as the start point of the line and an endpoint of the line is attached to the cursor. As you move the cursor on the screen, the line stretches and its length and angle values get dynamically modified in the Command bar.

   Next, you need to specify the end point to define the first line and the other remaining lines by using the **Length** and **Angle** dynamic edit boxes.

5. Enter **200** in the **Length** dynamic edit box and press ENTER. Next, enter **0** in the **Angle** dynamic edit box and press ENTER.

   On specifying the length and angle values, you will notice that the line is drawn but it is not completely displayed. To include it into the current display, you need to modify the drawing display area by using the **Fit** tool.

6. Choose the **Fit** tool from the Status bar; the current drawing display area is modified and the complete line is displayed in the current view. Also, the **Line** tool still remains active, and you are prompted to specify the second point of the line. 

7. Enter **90** in the **Length** dynamic edit box and press ENTER. Next, enter **-90** in the **Angle** dynamic edit box and press ENTER; a vertical line of length 90 mm is drawn. You can use the **Fit** tool to modify the current drawing display area as discussed earlier.

8. Enter **40** in the **Length** dynamic edit box and press ENTER. Enter **180** in the **Angle** dynamic edit box and press ENTER; a horizontal line of 40 mm is drawn toward the left of the last line.

9. Enter **40** in the **Length** dynamic edit box and press ENTER. Enter **90** in the **Angle** dynamic edit box and press ENTER; a vertical line of 40 mm is drawn downward.

10. Enter **120** in the **Length** dynamic edit box and press ENTER. Enter **180** in the **Angle** dynamic edit box and press ENTER; a horizontal line of 120 mm length is drawn.

11. Move the cursor vertically upward; a rubber-band line is displayed with its start point at the endpoint of the previous line and the endpoint attached to the cursor. When the line becomes vertical, the vertical relationship handle is displayed.

12. Move the cursor vertically upward until the horizontal alignment indicator (dotted line) is displayed at the top endpoint of the vertical line of 40 mm length. If the horizontal alignment indicator is not displayed, move the cursor once to the top end-point of the vertical line and then move it back to its original position. Note that at this point, the value in the **Length** dynamic edit box is **40** and the value in the **Angle** dynamic edit box is **-90**. Next, click on the dotted line to specify the endpoint of this line.

13. Move the cursor horizontally toward the left above the vertical plane and then make sure that the horizontal relationship handle is displayed. Next, move the cursor once on the vertical plane and then vertically upward. Click when the intersection relationship handle is displayed.

14. Move the cursor vertically downward toward the origin. If the first line is not highlighted in orange, move the cursor once over it and then move it back to the origin. The endpoint relationship handle is displayed. This relationship ensures that this line ends at the start point of the first line.

15. Click to specify the endpoint of the line when the endpoint relationship handle is displayed. Choose the **Fit** button to fit the sketch into the drawing window.

16. Choose the **Select** tool from the **Select** group of the **Home** tab to exit the **Line** tool. On doing so, the profile gets shaded, indicating that it is a closed region. The sketch after drawing the lines is shown in Figure 2-46.

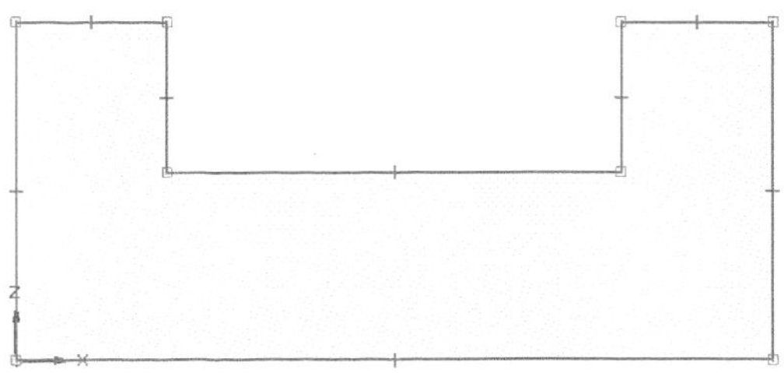

***Figure 2-46** Sketch after drawing the lines*

Filleting Sharp Corners

Next, you need to fillet sharp corners so that the sharp edges are not there in the final model. You can fillet corners by using the **Fillet** tool.

1. Invoke the **Fillet** tool from the **Draw** group; the **Fillet** Command bar is displayed.

To fillet a sharp corner, you first need to specify the fillet radius. You can fillet the lower left and lower right corners first and then the remaining corners. This is because the fillet radii of both the bottom left and the bottom right corners are equal. Also, the fillet radii of the remaining corners are equal.

2. Enter **15** in the **Radius** edit box in the **Fillet** Command bar and press ENTER. Next, move the cursor over the lower left corner of the sketch; the two lines forming a corner are highlighted in orange.

3. Click to select this corner; a fillet is created at the lower left corner of the sketch.

4. Similarly, move the cursor over the lower right corner and click to select it when the two lines forming this corner are highlighted in orange.

   Next, you need to modify the fillet radius value and fillet the remaining corners.

5. Enter **10** in the **Radius** edit box in the Command bar and press ENTER.

6. Select the remaining corners of the sketch one by one and then fillet them with a radius of 10. The sketch after creating fillets is shown in Figure 2-47. Next, exit the tool by choosing the **Select** tool from the **Select** group of the **Home** tab.

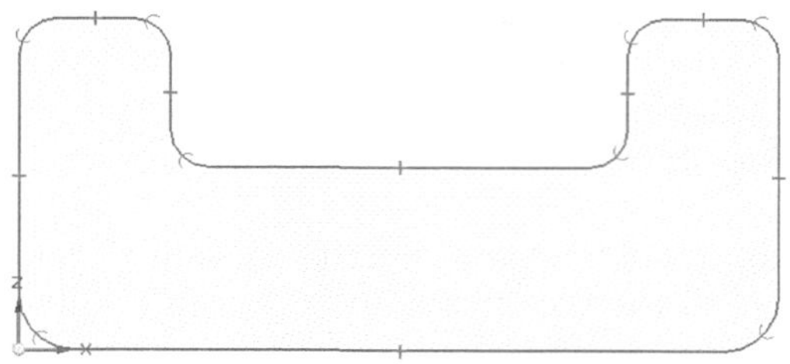

Figure 2-47 *Sketch after creating fillets*

Drawing Circles

Finally, you need to draw circles by using the **Circle by Center Point** tool to complete the profile. You will use the center points of fillets as the center points of the circles.

1. Choose the **Circle by Center Point** tool from the **Draw** group of the **Home** tab; the **Circle by Center Point** Command bar is displayed and you are prompted to select the center point of the circle.

2. Enter **15** in the **Diameter** edit box of the **Circle by Center Point** Command bar and press ENTER.

3. Move the cursor over the fillet at the lower left corner; the fillet is highlighted in orange and the center point of the Fillet arc is displayed. The center point is represented by a plus sign (+).

4. Move the cursor over the center point of the fillet represented by a plus sign (+); the fillet is highlighted in orange color and the concentric relationship handle is displayed on the right of the cursor.

5. Click to specify this point as the center point of the circle; a circle is drawn at this point and you are prompted again to specify the center point of the circle. Also, a circle of the specified diameter is attached to the cursor.

6. Move the cursor over the lower right fillet arc so that its center point is also displayed.

7. Move the cursor over the center point of the lower right fillet and click when the concentric relationship handle is displayed. The final profile for Tutorial 1 is shown in Figure 2-48.

8. Press the ESC key to exit the tool.

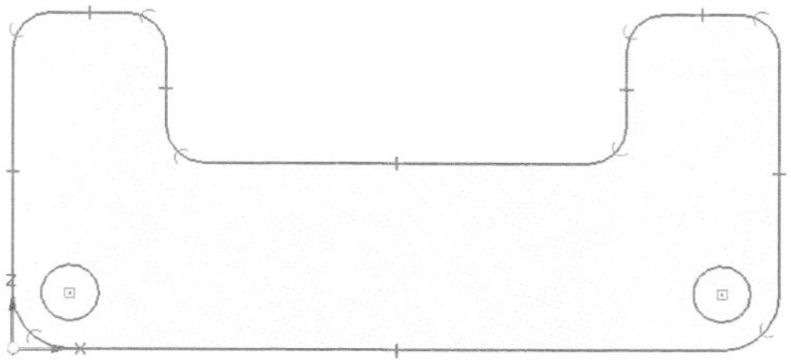

Figure 2-48 *Final profile for Tutorial 1*

Saving the File

1. Choose the **Save** tool from the **Quick Access** toolbar; the **Save As** dialog box is displayed.

   It is recommended that you create a separate folder for every chapter in the textbook.

2. Browse to the *C* drive and then create a folder with the name *Solid Edge* in it. In the *Solid Edge* folder, create a folder with the name *c02*.

3. Make the *c02* folder and save the file with the name *c02tut1.par*.

4. Choose the **Close** button from the file tab bar to close the file.

Tutorial 2 — Synchronous

In this tutorial, you will draw the profile of the model shown in Figure 2-49. The profile to be drawn is shown in Figure 2-50. Do not dimension the profile as dimensions are for reference only. **(Expected Time: 30 min)**

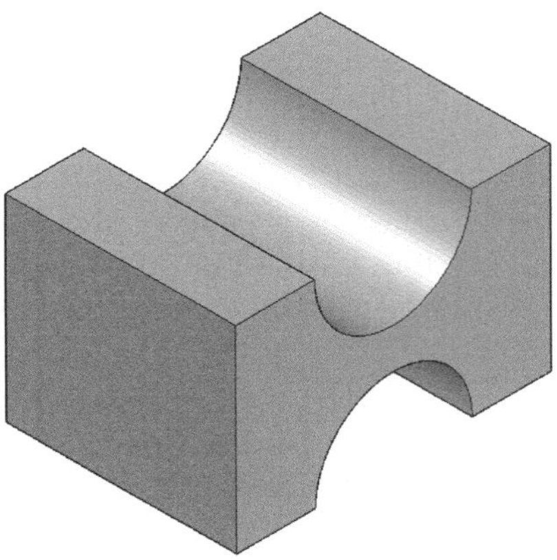

Figure 2-49 *Model for Tutorial 2*

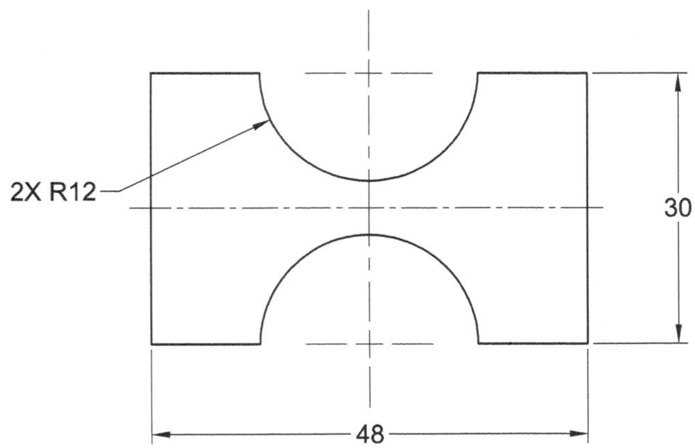

Figure 2-50 *Profile for Tutorial 2*

The following steps are required to complete this tutorial:

a. Start a new part file.
b. Draw the profile of the model by using the **Line** tool.
c. Save the file and close it.

Starting a New Part File and Selecting the Sketching Plane

You can start a new part file by choosing the **New** tool from the **Quick Access** toolbar, which will be available on the screen after you close all the files.

1. Choose the **New** tool from the **Quick Access** toolbar; the **New** dialog box is displayed, as shown in Figure 2-51. 

2. In this dialog box, select the **iso metric part.par** template, refer Figure 2-51. Next, choose **OK** to start a new part file.

Drawing the Profile

You need to draw the profile by using the **Line** and **Arc** tools.

1. Choose the **Line** tool from the **Draw** group of the **Home** tab; the **Line** Command bar is displayed and the alignment lines are attached to the cursor.

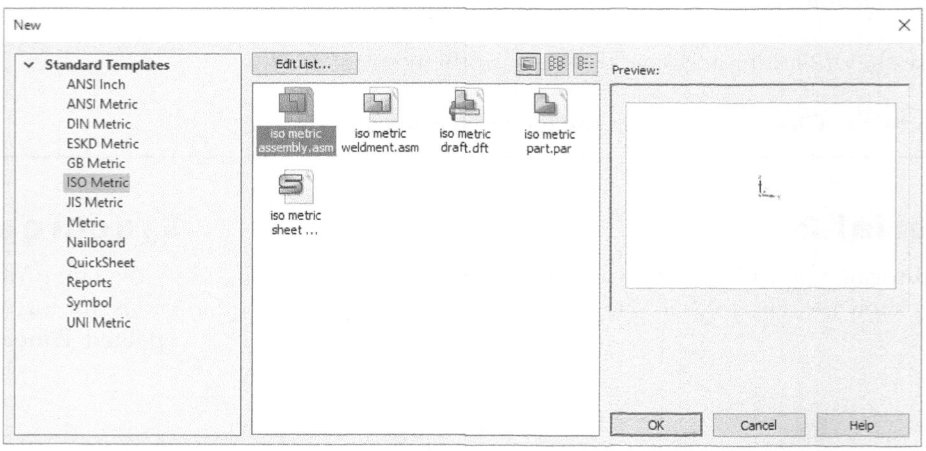

*Figure 2-51 The **New** dialog box to start a new file in ST9*

2. Next, you need to define the plane on which you want to draw the profile of the base feature. To do so, hover the cursor on the base coordinate system until a mouse symbol is displayed and then right-click; the **Quick Pick** list box is displayed with the possible nearest selections. Next, choose the YZ plane for sketching.

   Alternatively, you can select the YZ plane from the **PathFinder**. To do so, click on the plus sign (+) located on the left of the **Base Reference Planes** in the **PathFinder** to expand it. Next, select the YZ plane from it.

Note

The base reference planes are hidden by default. You can display them in the graphics window by selecting the check box located on the left of the ***Base Reference Planes*** *in the* ***PathFinder****.*

3. By default, the view orientation of the part document is set to Dimetric. Choose **Sketch View** from the status bar; the sketching plane is oriented parallel to the screen.

4. Click when an endpoint snap is displayed at the origin to specify the start point of the line.

   The point specified is selected as the start point of the line and the endpoint is attached to the cursor. When you move the cursor on the screen, the line stretches and its length and angle values vary dynamically in the Command bar.

5. Enter **12** in the **Length** dynamic edit box and press ENTER. Next, enter **0** in the **Angle** dynamic edit box and press ENTER.

   The first line is drawn and another rubber-band line with the start point at the endpoint of the previous line and the endpoint attached to the cursor is displayed. But as the next entity is an arc, you need to invoke the arc mode.

6. Press the A key to invoke the arc mode and click on the end point of the line. On doing so, a rubber-band arc with the start point fixed at the endpoint of the last line and the endpoint attached to the cursor is displayed. Also, the intent zones are displayed at the start point of the arc.

7. Move the cursor to the start point of the arc and then move it vertically upward through a small distance. Next, move the cursor toward the right. You will notice that a normal arc starts from the endpoint of the last line.

8. Enter **12** and **180** in the **Radius** and **Sweep** dynamic edit boxes respectively; the preview of the resulting arc is displayed. To draw the arc, you need to specify a point on the screen for defining the direction of the arc.

9. Move the cursor horizontally toward the right and then click; the arc is drawn and the line mode is invoked again. Now, click on the end point of the arc. Zoom out the drawing area.

10. Enter **12** and **0** in the **Length** and **Angle** dynamic edit boxes, respectively, and then press ENTER.

11. Enter **30** and **90** in the **Length** and **Angle** dynamic edit boxes, respectively, and then press ENTER.

12. Move the cursor horizontally toward the left. Make sure the horizontal relationship handle is displayed. Click to specify the endpoint of the line when the vertical alignment indicator is displayed at the endpoint of the arc. If the alignment indicator is not displayed, move the cursor once on the endpoint of the arc and then move it back.

    Next, you need to draw an arc. To do so, you need to invoke the arc mode.

13. Press the A key to invoke the arc mode; a rubber-band arc is displayed with its start point fixed at the endpoint of the last line.

14. Move the cursor to the start point of the arc and then move it vertically downward through a small distance. When the normal arc appears, move the cursor toward the left.

15. Move the cursor once over the lower arc and then move it toward the left, in line with the upper right horizontal line from where this arc starts. On doing so, a horizontal dotted line originating from the upper right horizontal line is displayed. At the point where the cursor is vertically in line with the start point of the lower arc, a vertical dotted line appears from the start point of the lower arc, as shown in Figure 2-52.

16. Click to define the endpoint of the arc at the intersection of the horizontal and vertical alignment dotted lines displayed; the arc is drawn and the line mode is invoked again.

17. Move the cursor horizontally toward the left and click to define the endpoint of the line when the vertical reference plane is highlighted in orange.

18. Move the cursor to the start point of the first line; the endpoint relationship handle is displayed and the first line is highlighted in orange.

19. Click to define the endpoint of this line when the endpoint relationship handle is displayed. The final profile of the model is shown in Figure 2-53.

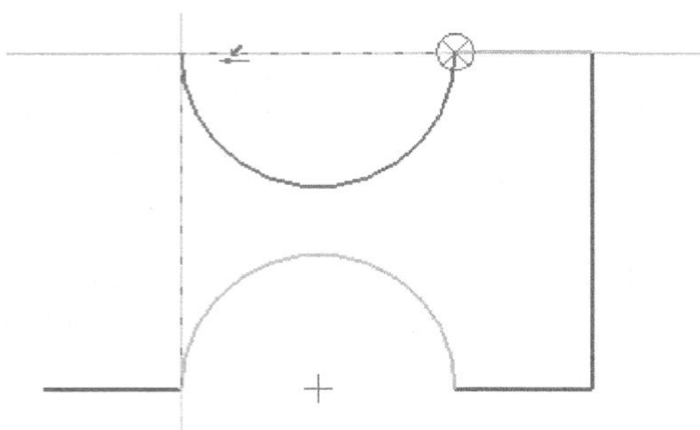

Figure 2-52 *Horizontal and vertical dotted lines displayed to define the endpoint of the arc*

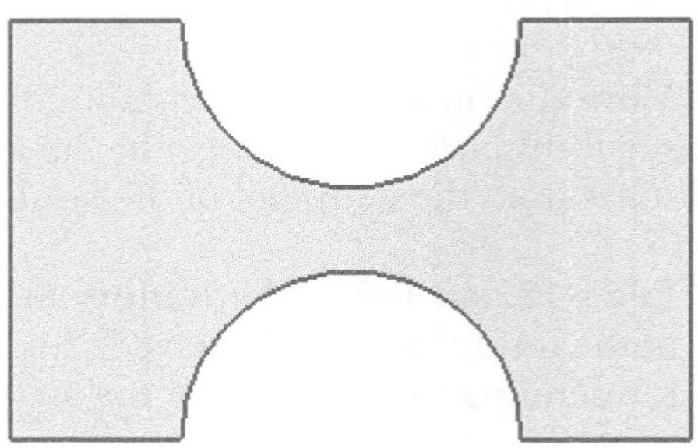

Figure 2-53 *Final profile for Tutorial 2*

20. Press the ESC key to exit the current tool.

Saving the File

1. Choose the **Save** button from the **Quick Access** toolbar and save the file with name *c02tut2* at following location:
   C:\Solid Edge\c02

2. Choose the **Close** button from the file tab bar to close the file.

Tutorial 3 Ordered

In this tutorial, you will draw the profile of the base feature of the model shown in Figure 2-54. The profile to be drawn is shown in Figure 2-55. Do not dimensions the profile as they are for reference only. **(Expected time: 30 min)**

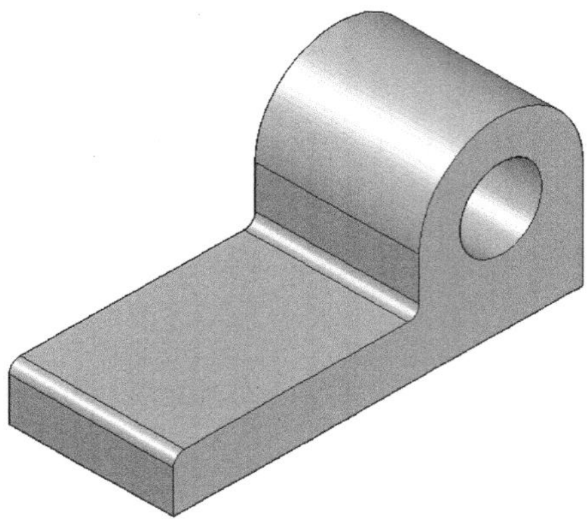

Figure 2-54 Model for Tutorial 3

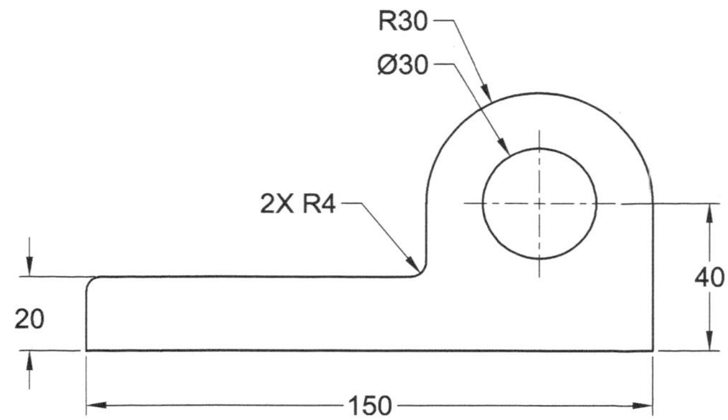

Figure 2-55 Profile for Tutorial 3

The following steps are required to complete this tutorial:

a. Start a new part file.
b. Switch to the ordered environment.
c. Invoke the sketching environment.
d. Draw the profile of the model by using the **Line** tool.
e. Fillet the two corners of the outer loop and then draw the inner circle.
f. Save the file and close it.

Starting a New Part File and Selecting the Sketching Plane

As mentioned earlier, you need to start a new part file by choosing the **New** button from the **Quick Access** toolbar.

1. Choose the **New** button from the **Quick Access** toolbar; the **New** dialog box is displayed.

2. In this dialog box, select the **iso metric part.par** template and then choose **OK** to start a new part file.

3. Select the **Ordered** radio button from the **Model** group of the **Tools** tab; the **Ordered Part** environment is invoked. Next, select the **Base Reference Planes** check box from the **PathFinder** to view the reference planes.

4. Choose the **Sketch** tool from the **Sketch** group of the **Home** tab; the **Sketch** command bar is displayed and you are prompted to select a planar face or a reference plane.

5. Next, move the cursor toward the YZ plane and select it when it is highlighted in orange color; the plane gets oriented parallel to the screen. Also, the **Line** tool is invoked automatically.

Drawing the Profile

As the **Line** tool is active, its Command bar is displayed in the graphics window and you are prompted to specify the start point of the line. You can start drawing the line from the origin.

1. Move the cursor close to the origin; one of the two axes is highlighted and the endpoint relationship handle is displayed.

2. Click when the endpoint relationship handle is displayed to specify the start point of the line.

   The point you specify is selected as the start point of the line and the endpoint is attached to the cursor.

3. Enter **150** in the **Length** dynamic edit box and press ENTER. Enter **0** in the **Angle** dynamic edit box and press ENTER; a line of 150 mm length is drawn.

   If this line is not completely visible on the screen, then to display the complete line, you need to modify the drawing display area by using the **Fit** tool.

4. Choose the **Fit** tool from the status bar; the line is completely visible in the current view.

5. Enter **40** and **90** in the **Length** and **Angle** dynamic edit boxes of the Command bar, respectively. Next press ENTER; a vertical line of 40 mm is drawn.

   Next, you need to draw a tangent arc from the end point of this line.

6. Press the A key to invoke the arc mode. Move the cursor back to the start point of the arc and then move it vertically upward through a small distance.

7. Move the cursor toward the left when the tangent arc is displayed. Enter **30** and **180** in the **Radius** and **Sweep** dynamic edit boxes, respectively. Next, press ENTER.

8. Specify a point in the drawing window to place the arc; the arc is drawn and the line mode is invoked again.

9. Enter **20** and **-90** in the **Length** and **Angle** dynamic edit boxes, respectively, and then press ENTER.

10. Move the cursor horizontally toward the left and make sure that the horizontal relationship handle is displayed. Click to define the endpoint of the line when the vertical plane is highlighted in orange color.

11. Move the cursor to the first line to highlight it and then move it to the start point of the first line; the first line is highlighted in orange color and the endpoint relationship handle is displayed.

12. Click to specify the endpoint of the line. The profile after drawing the outer loop is displayed in Figure 2-56. Next, press ESC to exit the tool.

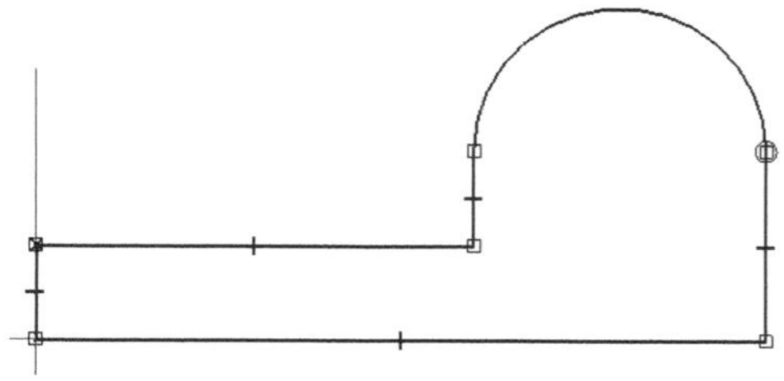

***Figure 2-56** Outer loop of the profile for Tutorial 3*

Filleting Sharp Corners

Next, you need to fillet sharp corners so that sharp edges are not there in the final model. You can fillet corners by using the **Fillet** tool.

1. Choose the **Fillet** tool from the **Draw** group of the **Home** tab; the **Fillet** Command bar is displayed.

2. Enter **4** in the **Radius** edit box of the **Fillet** Command bar and press ENTER. Now, move the cursor over the corner where the outer left vertical line and the upper horizontal line intersects; the two lines forming this corner are highlighted in orange.

3. Next, click to select this corner; a fillet is created at this corner.

4. Similarly, move the cursor over the corner where the upper horizontal line intersects the vertical line originating from the left endpoint of the arc. Now, click to select this corner; a fillet is created at this corner. Figure 2-57 shows the fillets created in the model.

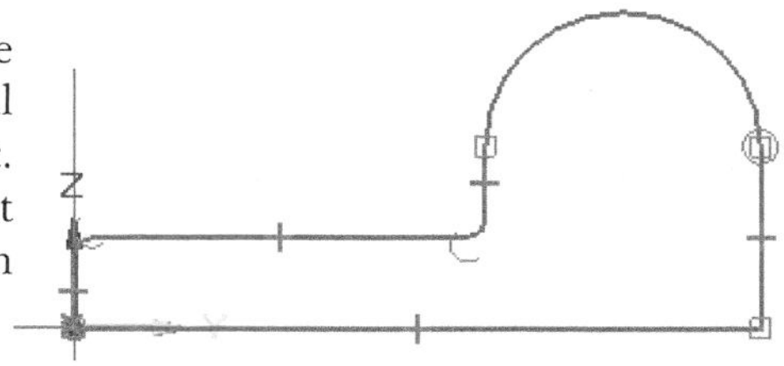

***Figure 2-57** Fillets created in the model*

Drawing the Circle

Next, you need to draw a circle to complete the profile. The circle will be drawn by using the **Circle by Center Point** tool.

1. Choose the **Circle by Center Point** tool from the **Draw** group of the **Home** tab; the **Circle by Center Point** Command bar is displayed.

2. Enter **30** in the **Diameter** edit box of the Command bar and press ENTER; a circle of **30** mm is attached to the cursor.

3. Move the cursor over the arc of radius 30 units; the arc is highlighted in orange color and its center point is displayed, which is represented by a plus sign (+).

4. Move the cursor over the center point of the arc and click to define this point as the center point of the circle when the concentric relationship handle is displayed. This completes the profile. The final profile for Tutorial 3 is shown in Figure 2-58.

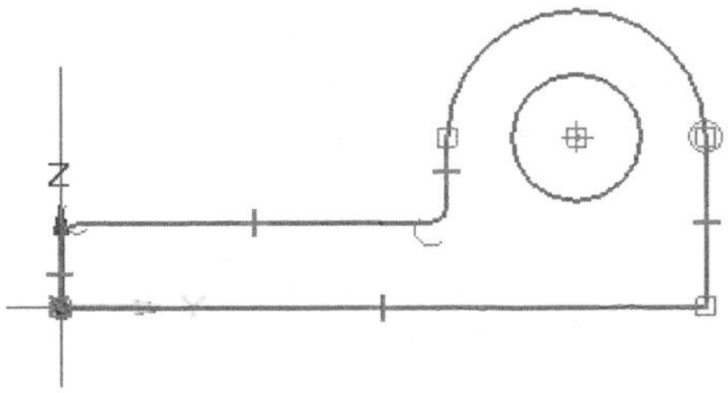

Figure 2-58 Final profile for Tutorial 3

5. Press the ESC key to exit the current tool.

6. Choose the **Close Sketch** tool from the **Close** group; the sketching environment is closed and the **Sketch** Command bar is displayed. Also, the current view is automatically changed to the dimetric view.

Saving the File

1. Choose the **Save** button from the **Quick Access** toolbar and save the file with name *c02tut3* at the following location:
   C:\Solid Edge\c02

2. Choose the **Close** button from the file tab bar to close the file.

Self-Evaluation Test

Answer the following questions and then compare them to those given at the end of this chapter:

1. You can restore the original orientation of the sketching plane by using the __________ tool in the status bar.

2. You can invoke the arc mode while the **Line** tool is already active by pressing the __________ key.

3. You can bevel corners in a sketch by using the __________ tool.

4. You can retain sharp corners even after filleting them by choosing the __________ button from the **Fillet** Command bar.

5. In Solid Edge, you can draw a polygon of sides ranging from 3 to __________.

6. The __________ tool is used to draw an arc by specifying its start point, endpoint, and the third point in the drawing area.

7. In the **Synchronous Part** environment, the reference planes are not displayed by default. (T/F)

8. When you open a new **ISO Metric Part** document, two triads are displayed in the graphics window. (T/F)

9. In the Synchronous modeling, you can create sketches as well as develop features in the same environment. (T/F)

10. You can use the Command bar to specify the exact values of the sketched entities. (T/F)

Review Questions

Answer the following questions:

1. Which of the following options is need to be selected from the **New** dialog box to start a new part file?

   (a) **iso metric assembly.asm** (b) **iso metric draft.dft**
   (c) **iso metric part.par** (d) **iso metric sheet metal.psm**

2. Which of the following tools is used to round sharp corners in a sketch?

   (a) **Fillet** (b) **Chamfer**
   (c) **Round** (d) None of these

3. Which of the following edit boxes in the arc mode replaces the **Angle** edit box in the **Line** Command bar?

   (a) **Arc** (b) **Sweep**
   (c) **Value** (d) None of these

4. Which of the following tools is used to convert an existing sketched entity into a bezier spline curve?

   (a) **Convert to Sketch** (b) **Convert to Arc**
   (c) **Convert** (d) **Convert to Curve**

5. You can use the __________ key to lock or unlock a plane.

6. To invoke the sketching environment, invoke a sketching tool from the **Draw** group in the **Home** tab and then select a reference plane. (T/F)

7. The part file in Solid Edge is saved with a *.prt* extension. (T/F)

8. You can select entities by dragging a box around them. (T/F)

9. If Overlapping is the current selection mode, all entities that lie inside the box or even intersect the box will be selected. (T/F)

10. In Solid Edge, you can create fillets or chamfers by simply dragging the cursor across the entities that you want to fillet or chamfer. (T/F)

EXERCISE

Exercise 1

Draw the profile of the base feature of the model shown in Figure 2-59. The profile to be drawn is shown in Figure 2-60. Do not dimension the profile as dimensions are given for reference only. **(Expected time: 30 min)**

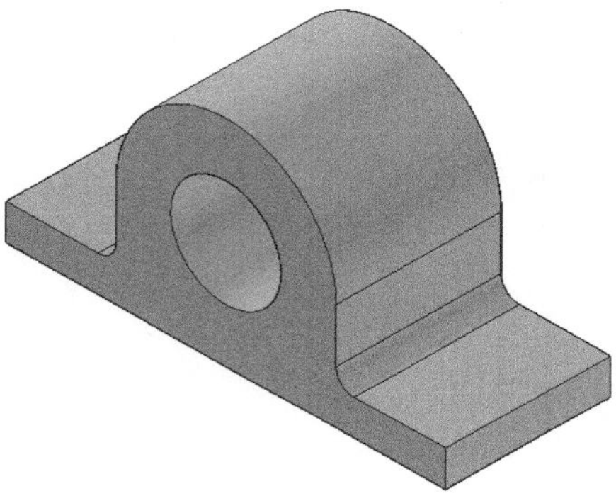

Figure 2-59 *Model for Exercise 1*

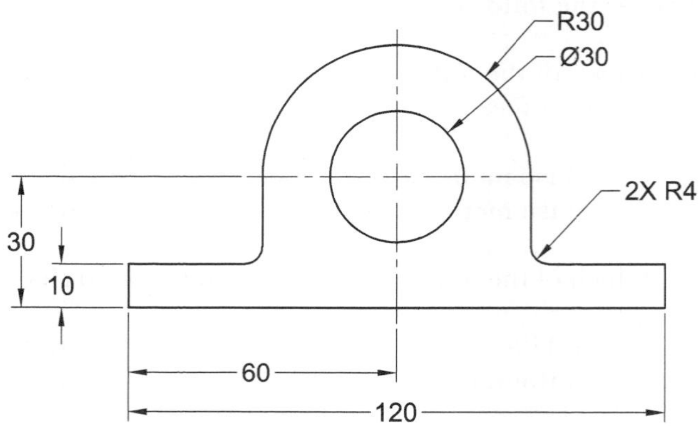

Figure 2-60 *Profile for Exercise 1*

Exercise 2

Draw the profile of the base feature of the model shown in Figure 2-61. The profile to be drawn is shown in Figure 2-62. Do not dimension the profile as dimensions are given for reference only. **(Expected time: 30 min)**

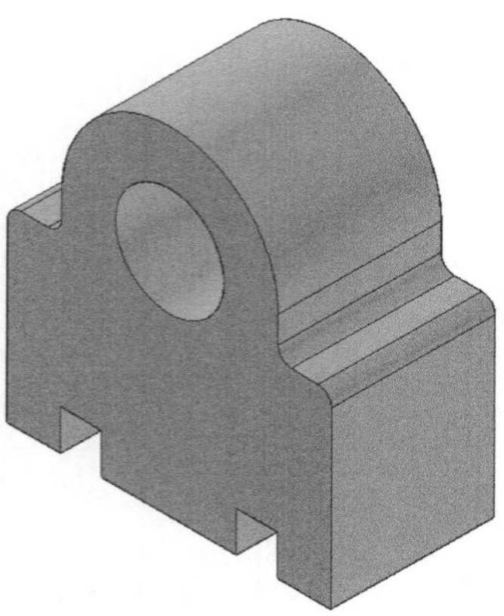

Figure 2-61 *Model for Exercise 2*

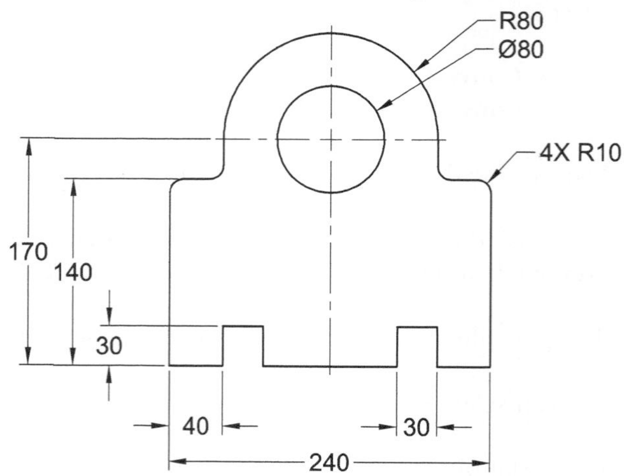

Figure 2-62 *Profile for Exercise 2*

Exercise 3

Draw the profile of the base feature of the model shown in Figure 2-63. The profile to be drawn is shown in Figure 2-64. Do not dimension the profile as dimensions are given for reference only.
(Expected time: 30 min)

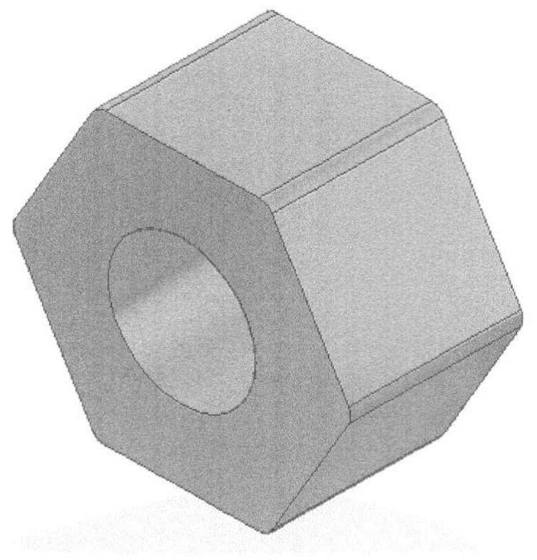

Figure 2-63 *Model for Exercise 3*

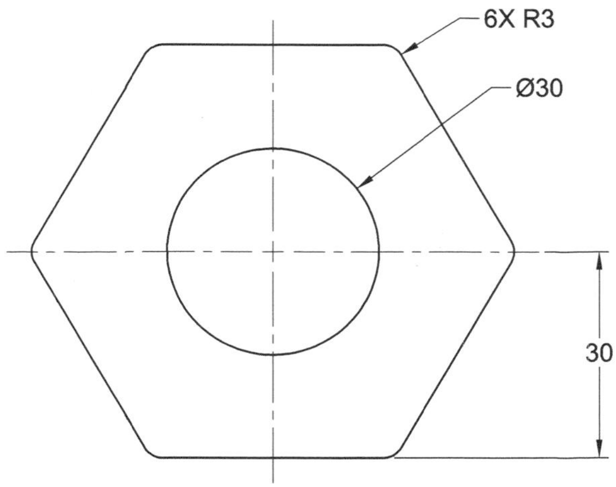

Figure 2-64 *Profile for Exercise 3*

Answers to Self-Evaluation Test

1. Sketch View, **2.** A, **3.** Chamfer, **4.** No Trim, **5.** 200, **6.** Arc by 3 points, **7.** T, **8.** T, **9.** T, **10.** T

Chapter 3

Adding Relationships and Dimensions to Sketches

Learning Objectives

After completing this chapter, you will be able to:

- *Understand different types of geometric relationships*
- *Force additional geometric relationships to sketches*
- *View and delete geometric relationships from sketches*
- *Understand the methods of dimensioning*
- *Modify the values of dimensions*
- *Add automatic dimensions to sketches while drawing them*

GEOMETRIC RELATIONSHIPS

Geometric relationships are the logical operations performed on the sketched entities to relate it to the other sketched entities using the standard properties such as collinearity, concentricity, tangency, and so on. These relationships constrain the degrees of freedom of the sketched entities and stabilize a sketch so that it does not change its shape and location unpredictably at any stage of the design. Most of the relationships are automatically applied to the sketched entities while drawing.

All geometric relationships have separate relationship handles associated with them. These handles can be seen on the sketched entities when relationships are applied to them. In the sketching environment of Solid Edge, you can add eleven types of relationships. These relationships are discussed next.

Connect Relationship

Ribbon:	Home > Relate > Connect

The **Connect** relationship is used to connect the keypoints such as endpoint, midpoint, or center point of a sketched entity to another sketched entity or to its keypoints. When the keypoint of the first entity is connected to the keypoint of the second entity, it is called a two-point connect. It is represented by a square with a dot inside it on the geometry. However, when the keypoint of the first entity is directly connected to the second entity, it is called a one-point connect and is represented by a cross on the geometry.

To add this relationship between the two keypoints of two different sketched entities, choose the **Connect** tool from the **Relate** group of the **Home** tab. Next, move the cursor over the keypoint of the first sketched entity and then click to select the entity when the handle of the keypoint is displayed. After selecting the keypoint of the first entity, move the cursor over the other sketched entity. Depending on whether you connect the keypoint of the first entity to the keypoint of the second entity or to the second entity itself, the relationship will be a one-point connect or a two-point connect. Figure 3-1 shows the entities selected for one-point connect. Figure 3-2 shows the relationship handle displayed after adding the relationship.

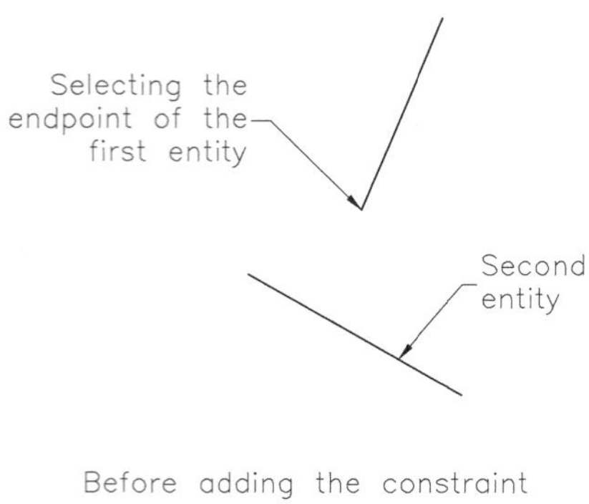

Figure 3-1 Selecting entities for one-point connect relationship

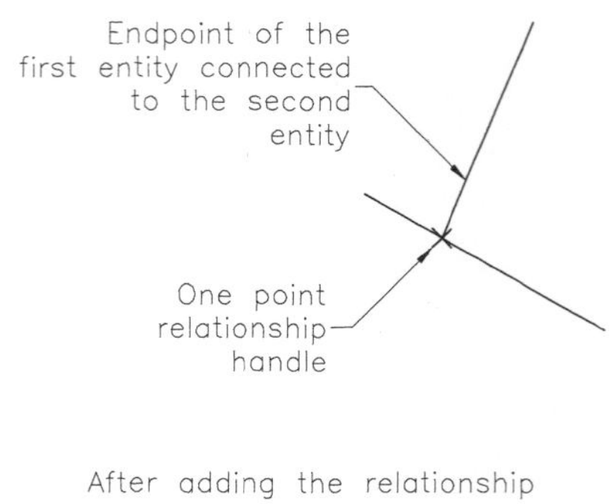

Figure 3-2 Entities after adding the one-point connect relationship

Note

If the handles that represent the relationship are not displayed in the drawing area by default, you need to choose the ***Relationship Handles*** *button from the* ***Relate*** *group of the* ***Home*** *tab to display them.*

Figure 3-3 shows the endpoint of the first entity being connected to the endpoint of the second entity. This is a two-point connect. Therefore, the relationship handle shows a dot inside the square, as shown in Figure 3-4.

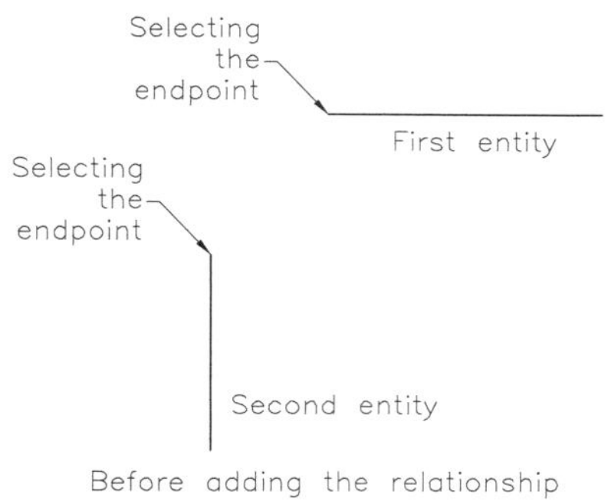

Figure 3-3 *Entities selected for two-point connect relationship*

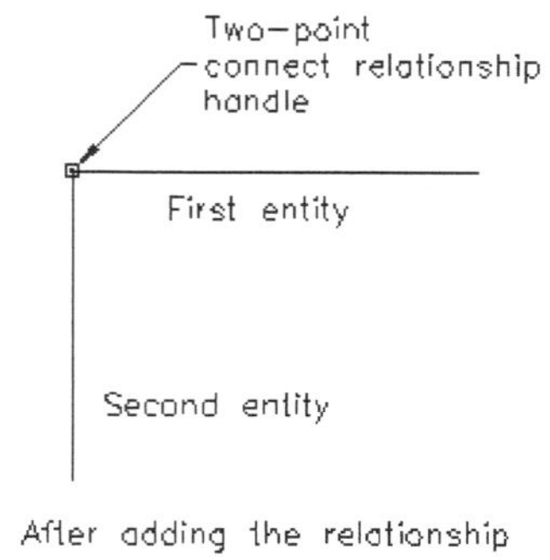

Figure 3-4 *Entities after adding the two-point connect relationship*

Concentric Relationship

Ribbon: Home > Relate > Concentric

The **Concentric** relationship forces two arcs and two circles or an arc and a circle to share the same center point. If there are two arcs and two circles or an arc and a circle with center points at different locations, this relationship will force the first selected arc or circle to move such that its center point is placed over the center point of the second arc or circle. The handle of this relationship is represented by two concentric circles. Figure 3-5 shows two circles before and after applying this relationship.

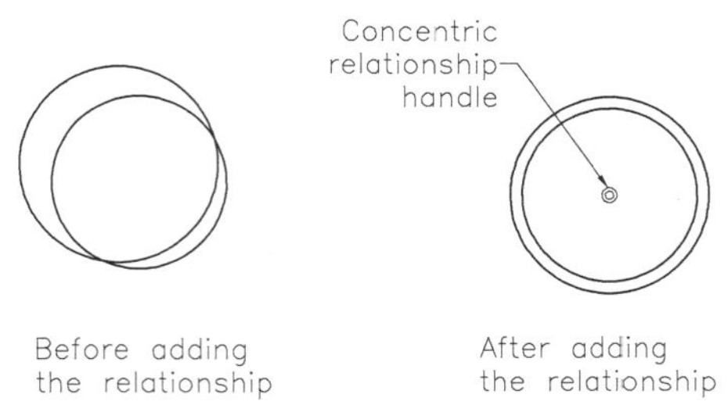

Figure 3-5 *Sketch before and after applying the concentric relationship*

Horizontal/Vertical Relationship

Ribbon: Home > Relate > Horizontal/Vertical

The **Horizontal/Vertical** relationship forces an inclined line to become horizontal or vertical. If the angle of the inclined line is less than 45 degrees, it will become horizontal. But if the angle is equal to or greater than 45 degrees, it will become vertical. You can also select two points and force them to be placed horizontally or vertically. The handle of this relationship is a plus sign (+).

Collinear Relationship

Ribbon: Home > Relate > Collinear

The **Collinear** relationship forces the selected line segment(s) to be placed in a straight line. To add the collinear relationship, invoke the **Collinear** tool; you will be prompted to click on the first line. After making the first selection, you will be prompted to click on the next line. The first line segment is automatically forced to be placed in line with the second line segment. The handle of this relationship is represented by circles, which appear on the collinear lines.

Parallel Relationship

Ribbon: Home > Relate > Parallel

The **Parallel** relationship forces a selected line segment to become parallel to another line segment. On invoking the **Parallel** tool, you will be prompted to click on a line. Click on a line; you will be prompted to click on the next line. After you click on the second line, the first line will become parallel to the second line. The handle of this relationship is represented by two parallel lines.

Perpendicular Relationship

Ribbon: Home > Relate > Perpendicular

The **Perpendicular** relationship forces a selected line to become perpendicular to another line, arc, circle, or ellipse. When you invoke the **Perpendicular** tool, you will be prompted to click on the first line to make it perpendicular. On clicking the first line, you will be prompted to click on the second line, arc, circle, or ellipse to make it perpendicular. On clicking the second entity, the first line will become perpendicular to the second entity. The handle of this relationship is a perpendicular symbol.

Lock Relationship

Ribbon: Home > Relate > Lock

The **Lock** constraint is used to fix the orientation or the location of the selected sketched entity or the keypoint of the sketched entity. If you apply this constraint to the keypoint of a sketched entity, the entity will be fixed at that keypoint and you will not be able to modify the entity using that keypoint. However, you can modify the entity from other keypoints.

Note

*A keypoint that has a lock on it cannot be modified during recomputation by changing the value of dimension manually or by dragging, but it can be modified by manipulation commands such as **Move**, **Rotate**, **Mirror**, and so on, and will be fixed at the new location after manipulations.*

Rigid Set Relationship

Ribbon: Home > Relate > Rigid Set

The **Rigid Set** relationship is used to group the selected sketched entities into a rigid set. When the entities are grouped in a rigid set, they behave as a single entity. Therefore, if you drag one of the entities, all entities in the rigid set are automatically dragged. Note that you cannot include dimensions or a text entity in a rigid set.

Note
*The **Rigid Set** and **Lock** tools will only be enabled when the **Maintain Relationships** button in the **Relate** group of the **Home** tab is chosen.*

Tangent Relationship

Ribbon: Home > Relate > Tangent

The **Tangent** relationship forces a selected sketched entity to become tangent to another sketched entity, refer to Figure 3-6. Note that one of the two entities selected should be an arc, circle, curve, or an ellipse. The handle of this relationship is a circle that appears at the point of tangency.

To add the tangent relationship, invoke the **Tangent** tool and click on the elements; the tangent relationship is applied between the selected elements, as shown in Figure 3-7.

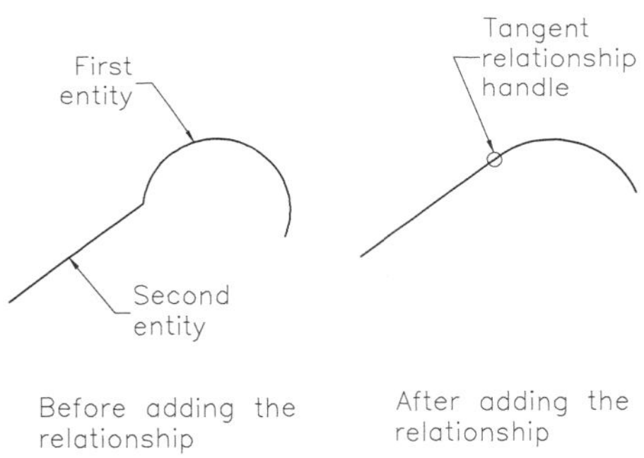

*Figure 3-6 Adding the **Tangent** relationship*

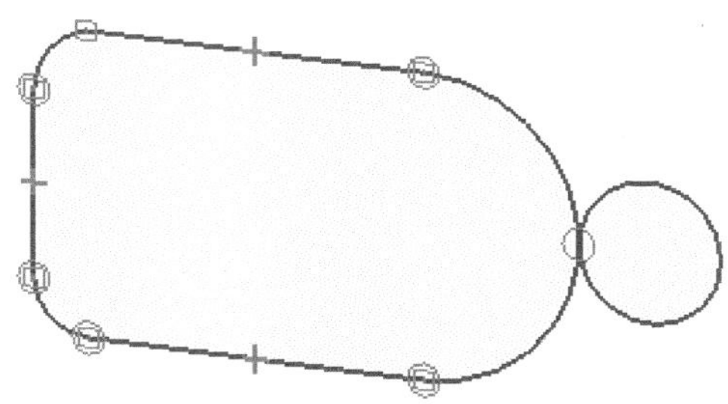

***Figure 3-7** Making a curve tangent to a chain of tangentially connected entities*

Equal Relationship

Ribbon: Home > Relate > Equal

The **Equal** relationship can be used for line segments, ellipses, arcs, or circles. If you select two line segments, this relationship will force the length of the first selected line segment to become equal to the length of the second selected line segment. In case of arcs or circles, this relationship will force the radius of the first selected entity to become equal to the radius of the second selected entity. Similarly, you can force two ellipses to become equal in size using this relationship. The handle of this relationship is an equal sign (=).

Symmetric Relationship

Ribbon: Home > Relate > Symmetric

The **Symmetric** relationship is used to force the selected sketched entities to become symmetrical about a symmetry axis, which can be a sketched line or a reference plane.

This relationship is used in the sketches of the models that are symmetrical about a line. When you invoke the **Symmetric** tool, you will be prompted to click on the symmetry axis. Click on the symmetry axis; you will be prompted to click on an entity. Note that you can select only one entity at a time to apply this relationship. Once you have selected the first sketched entity, you will be prompted to click on the entity. Remember that the second entity should be the same as the first element. This means that if the first entity is a line, the second entity should also be a line. As soon as you select the second entity, the first selected entity will be modified such that its distance and orientation from the axis of symmetry becomes equal to the distance and orientation of the second selected entity. After you have applied this constraint to one set of entities, you will be prompted to click on the next set of first and second entities. However, this time you will not be prompted to select the axis of symmetry. The last axis of symmetry will be automatically selected to add this relationship.

Figure 3-8 shows the sketched entities and the symmetry axis before applying the symmetric relationship and Figure 3-9 shows the sketch after applying the relationship.

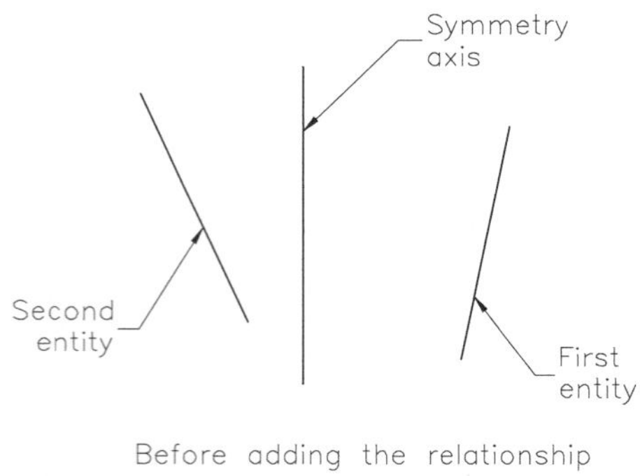

Figure 3-8 Selecting the entities to apply the symmetric relationship

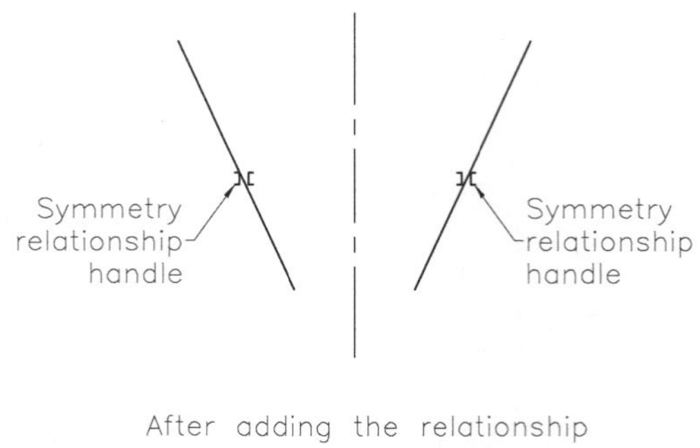

Figure 3-9 Entities after applying the symmetric relationship

Setting the Symmetry Axis (Ordered Environment)

Ribbon: Home > Relate > Symmetry Axis

In Solid Edge, you can set the symmetry axis before invoking the **Symmetric** relationship. After doing that, when you invoke the **Symmetric** tool, you will not be prompted to select the axis of symmetry. The symmetry axis set earlier will be automatically selected as the axis of symmetry. To set the axis of symmetry, choose the **Symmetry Axis** tool from the **Relate** group, you will be prompted to click on the symmetry axis. The line that you select will be automatically changed to the symmetry axis along with its line type.

Note

You may need to apply a number of relationships to constrain all degrees of freedom of a sketch. Generally, while applying relationships to the sketched entities, the first selected entity is modified with respect to the second one. However, if all degrees of freedom of the first entity are restricted, then the second entity is modified.

Controlling the Display of Relationship Handles

Ribbon:	Home > Relate > Relationship Handles

The **Relationship Handles** button is used to turn on or off the display of relationship handles in the sketch. If the **Relationship Handles** button is chosen in the **Relate** group, the handles of all relationships will be displayed in the sketch. You can turn off the display of the relationship handles for better visualization by choosing this button again.

CONFLICTS IN RELATIONSHIPS

Sometimes when you try to apply multiple relationships to an entity and the entity is not able to accommodate all those changes, then the **Solid Edge ST9** information box is displayed, as shown in Figure 3-10.

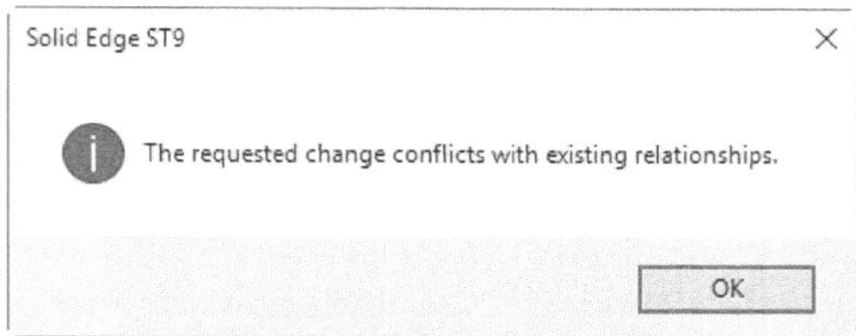

Figure 3-10 *The* ***Solid Edge ST9*** *information box*

This box informs you that applying this relationship will create conflicts in the existing relationships. Therefore, you may need to delete the existing relationships before applying the new ones, depending upon the requirement of the design. For example, if you want to apply the vertical relationship to a horizontal line, you need to delete the horizontal relationship before applying the vertical relationship.

DELETING RELATIONSHIPS

As mentioned earlier, whenever a relationship is applied to a sketched entity, the relationship handle is displayed on the entity. You can delete the applied relationship by selecting that handle and pressing the DELETE key.

DIMENSIONING THE SKETCHED ENTITIES

In Solid Edge, you can use different types of dimensions to dimension the sketched entities. You can create these dimensions using their individual tools or by using the **Smart Dimension** tool. You can also use the options available in the respective Command bars that are displayed for these dimensions. As mentioned earlier, Solid Edge is parametric by nature. Therefore, irrespective of the original size of the entity, you can enter a new value in the **Dimension Value** edit box to modify the size of the entity to the required value. The methods of dimensioning the entities using these dimensions are discussed next.

Adding Linear Dimensions

Ribbon:	Home > Dimension > Smart Dimension / Distance Between

Linear dimensions measure the linear distance of a line segment or the distance between two points. To add this dimension, you can use the **Smart Dimension** tool or the **Distance Between** tool. The points that you can select to add dimension include all the keypoints

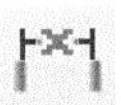

such as endpoints, midpoints, and so on of lines, curves, arcs, circles, or ellipses. You can add linear dimensions to a vertical or a horizontal line by choosing the **Smart Dimension** tool and then directly selecting the line. Once you have selected the line, the linear dimension will be attached to the cursor. Now, you can place the dimension at any desired location.

To place the dimension between two points, invoke the **Smart Dimension** tool or the Distance **Between** tool and select the points one by one. Now, move the cursor vertically to place the horizontal linear dimension or move the cursor horizontally to place the vertical linear dimension.

To add linear dimensions between arcs and circles by using the **Smart Dimension** tool, you can directly select the arc and the circle. However, to create these dimensions by using the **Distance Between** tool, first you need to move the cursor over the entities to highlight their center points and then select the center points to create the dimensions. Figure 3-11 shows the linear dimensioning between the center points of an arc and a circle.

Note

In order to highlight the center points of the entities, you must select the ***Center*** *check box in the* ***IntelliSketch*** *group of the* ***Sketching*** *tab in the* ***Synchronous Part*** *environment. The* ***IntelliSketch*** *group is available in the* ***Home*** *tab of the sketching environment in the* ***Ordered Part*** *environment.*

You can also add the horizontal or vertical dimension to the inclined lines, see Figure 3-12. If you select an inclined line after invoking the **Smart Dimension** tool to add a linear dimension, the aligned dimension will be attached to the cursor by default. You need to press and hold the SHIFT key to add the horizontal or vertical dimension. But if you are using the **Distance Between** tool, you can select the endpoints of the inclined line and move the cursor in the horizontal or vertical direction to place the dimension.

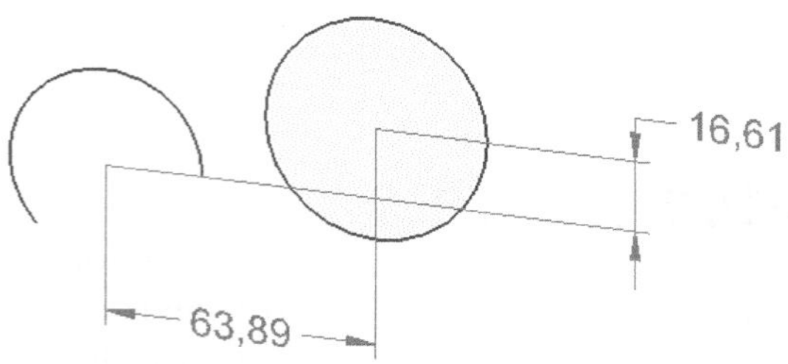

Figure 3-11 *Linear dimensioning of points*

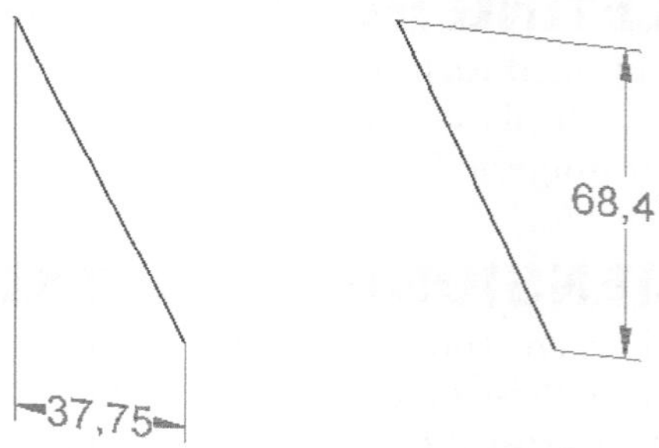

Figure 3-12 *Linear dimensioning of inclined lines*

Command bar Options

While dimensioning the sketched entities, the corresponding Command bars are displayed. Figure 3-13 shows the Command bar displayed on invoking the **Smart Dimension** tool. This Command bar has some additional options and buttons, which should be set before creating dimensions. These options are discussed next.

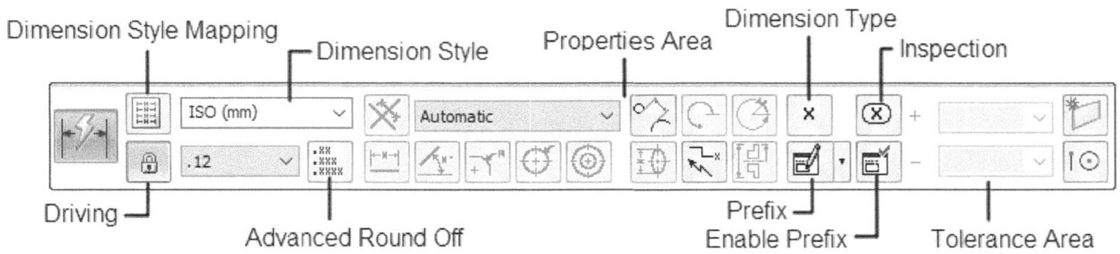

Figure 3-13 The Command bar options

Dimension Style
This drop-down list shows the dimension styles, namely **ANSI(ft)**, **ANSI(in)**, **ISO(cm)**, **ISO(m)**, and **ISO(mm)**. By default, **ISO(mm)** is selected in the drop-down list. You can select the required dimension style from it. If this drop-down list is not activated in the Command bar, then you need to choose the **Dimension Style Mapping** button in the Command bar to activate it.

Driving
The **Driving** button is chosen by default. This means the applied dimension is a driving dimension. A driving dimension is the dimension that drives the size of an entity and is displayed in red color. Therefore, if this button is chosen and you modify the value of an applied dimension in the edit box that is displayed on selecting the entity to be dimensioned, then the size of the entity will change accordingly. If you deactivate the **Driving** button while placing the dimension, the dimension will be called as driven dimension and will be displayed in blue color. If you modify its value, the size of the entity will not change and the value of dimension will be displayed underlined. The **Dimension Round-off** drop-down list adjacent to the **Driving** button is also used to set the round off precision for dimensions. The default round off precision is two decimal places. You can select any other round off precision from this drop-down list.

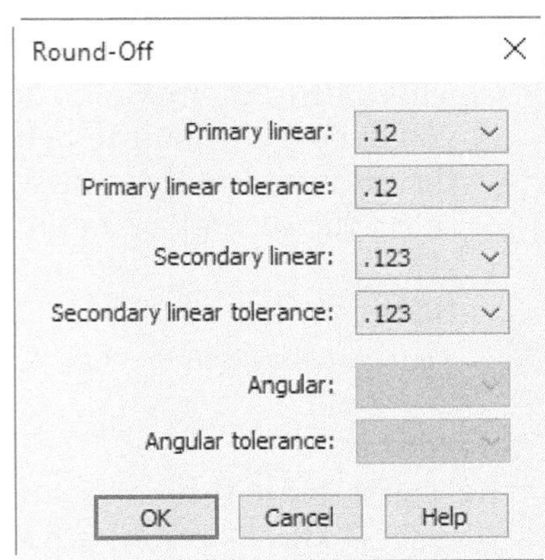

*Figure 3-14 The **Round-Off** dialog box*

Advanced Round-Off
The **Advanced Round-Off** button is used to specify the round off options. When you choose this button, the **Round-Off** dialog box will be displayed, as shown in Figure 3-14. The options in this dialog box are discussed next.

Primary linear
The **Primary linear** drop-down list is used to define the round-off value for the primary linear dimension.

Primary linear tolerance
This drop-down list is used to define the round-off value for the primary linear tolerance.

Secondary linear
This drop-down list is used to define the round-off value for the secondary linear dimension.

Secondary linear tolerance
This drop-down list is used to define the round-off value for the secondary linear tolerance.

Angular
This drop-down list is used to define the round-off value for the angular dimension.

Angular tolerance
This drop-down list is used to define the round-off value for the angular tolerance.

Properties

The options in the **Properties** area are used to specify the orientation of the dimension and also the other properties. Specify the orientation by selecting an appropriate option from the **Orientation** drop-down list. Select the **Horizontal/Vertical** option if you need to dimension the horizontal or vertical distance. Select the **By 2 Points** option, if you need to measure the aligned dimension. Select the **Use Dimension Axis** option, if you need to measure the entity from a baseline.

The other buttons in this area have to be chosen based on the specific segment. The **Tangent** button is discussed next. The remaining buttons will be discussed later.

Tangent
This button allows you to add a dimension between the tangent points of two entities. If you choose this button before selecting entities, the dimension will be tangent to both the entities. But if you first select an arc or a circle, then choose this button and finally select the second arc or circle, the dimension will be tangent to only the second entity.

Note
The remaining options of the Command bar will be available for the other dimensioning techniques.

Tolerance

The options in this area are used to specify the dimension type and the related tolerances. These options are discussed next.

Dimension Type
This button is chosen to specify the type of dimension to be applied. When you choose this button from the **Tolerance** area of the Command bar, a flyout with options such as **Nominal**, **Unit Tolerance**, **Alpha Tolerance**, **Class**, **Limit**, **Basic**, and so on is displayed. These options are used to specify the type of dimensions. For example, to add a tolerance dimension to a sketch, you can choose the **Unit Tolerance** or **Alpha Tolerance** option from this flyout.

You can specify the parameters related to the type of dimensions to be applied in the edit boxes displayed in the **Tolerance** area. Similarly, you can specify the limit dimensions of the selected entity by choosing the **Limit** option. On doing so, the **Upper Tolerance** and **Lower Tolerance** edit boxes will be displayed. You can enter the upper and lower tolerance values in these edit boxes. Figure 3-15 shows a sketch dimensioned by using the limit and tolerance dimensions.

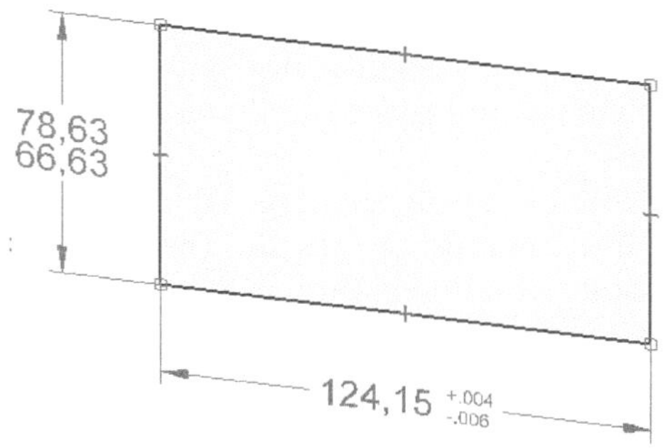

***Figure 3-15** Sketch dimensioned by using the limit and unit tolerance dimension types*

Inspection

This button is chosen from the **Tolerance** area of the Command bar to add an oblong around the dimension for inspection.

Prefix

This button is chosen to add a prefix, suffix, superfix, or subfix to a dimension. If you choose this button from the **Tolerance** area of the Command bar, the **Dimension Prefix** dialog box will be displayed, as shown in Figure 3-16. You can use this dialog box to add a special symbol or add your own text to the dimension. You can toggle between enabling and disabling the data defined in this dialog box by using the **Enable Prefix** button which is also available in the **Tolerance** area of the Command bar.

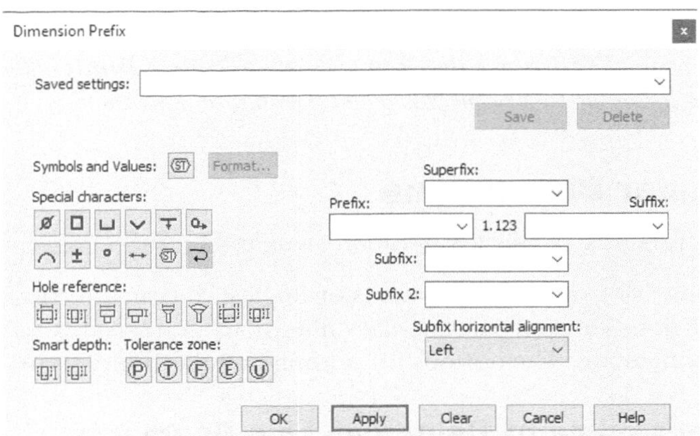

***Figure 3-16** The **Dimension Prefix** dialog box*

Adding Aligned Dimensions

Ribbon: Home > Dimension > Smart Dimension

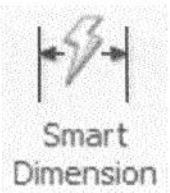

Aligned dimensions are used to dimension the lines that are not parallel to the X-axis or the Y-axis. This type of dimensioning measures the actual distance of the aligned lines. You can invoke the **Smart Dimension** tool and directly select the inclined line to apply this dimension. When you select the line, an aligned dimension will be attached to the cursor. Move the cursor and place the dimension at the required location.

You can also select two points to apply the aligned dimensions. The points that can be used include the endpoints of lines, curves, or arcs and the center points of arcs, circles, or ellipses. If you select these two points, the linear dimensions will be displayed by default. To add the aligned dimensions, press and hold the SHIFT key; the aligned dimension will be displayed. Move the cursor and place the dimension at the desired location. Figures 3-17 and 3-18 show the aligned dimensions applied to various objects.

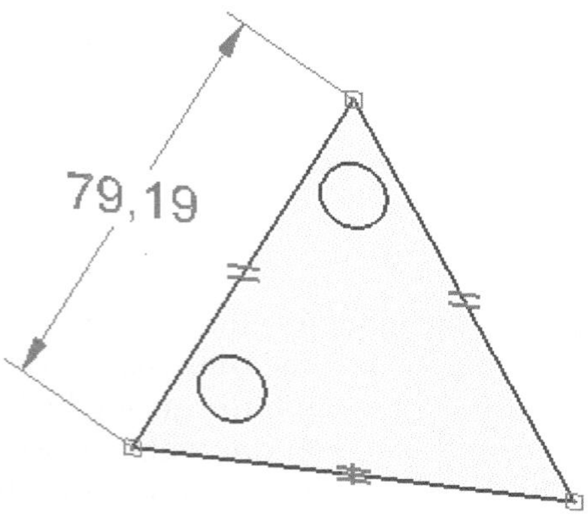

Figure 3-17 *Aligned dimensioning of lines*

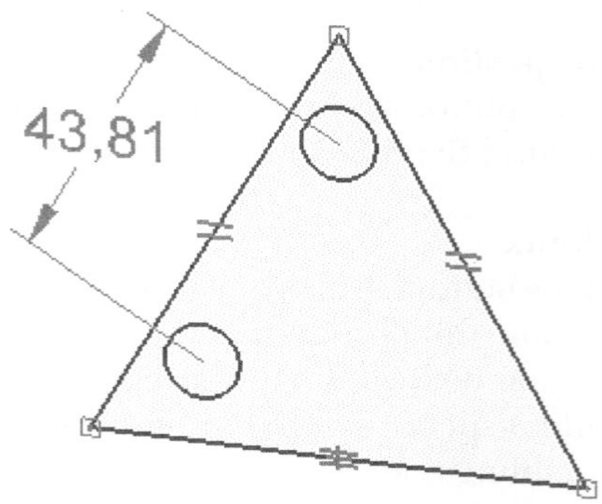

Figure 3-18 *Aligned dimensioning of points*

Note

*If you are using the **Distance Between** tool, select the **By 2 Points** option from the **Orientation** drop-down list in the Command bar to add the aligned dimension.*

Adding Angular Dimensions

Ribbon: Home > Dimension > Smart Dimension / Angle Between

Angular dimensions are used to dimension angles. You can directly select two line segments or use three points to apply the angular dimensions. You can also use angular dimensioning to dimension an arc. The options for adding angular dimensions are discussed next.

Angular Dimensioning by Using Two Line Segments

You can directly select two line segments to apply angular dimensions between them. Invoke the **Smart Dimension** tool and then select a line segment; a linear or an aligned dimension will be attached to the cursor, choose the **Angle** button from the Command bar and then select the second line. Next, place the dimension to measure the angle between the two lines. While placing the dimension, you need to be careful about its point of placement of the dimension because depending on this point of the placement, the interior or the exterior angle will be displayed. Figure 3-19 shows the angular dimensioning between two lines and Figure 3-20 shows the exterior angle between same two lines.

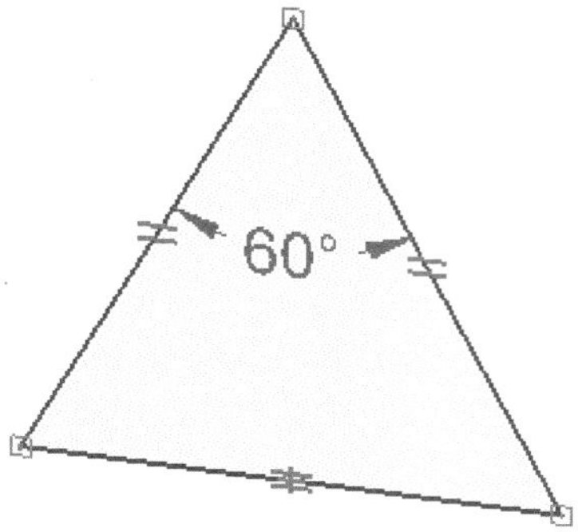

Figure 3-19 *Angular dimensioning between two lines*

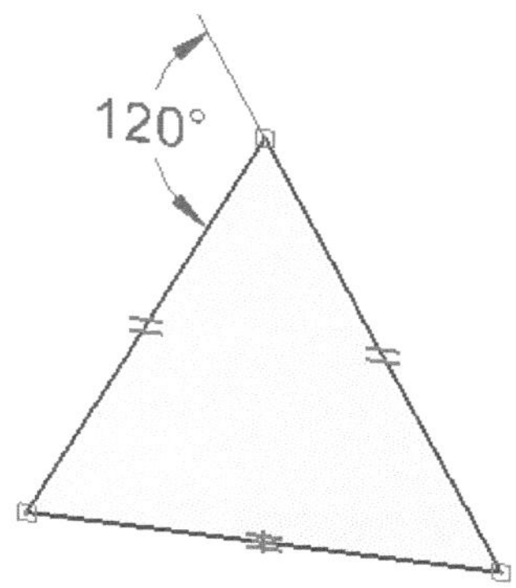

Figure 3-20 *Exterior angle between two lines*

Before placing the angular dimension, if you choose the **Major-Minor** button from the Command bar, you can specify the angle between the lines or its complimentary angle. Figure 3-21 shows the major angle dimension between two lines.

Tip

After placing the dimension, you can drag it to a new location. To do so, exit the dimensioning tool and then select the dimension lines or the dimension text. The dimension lines are the ones between which the dimension text is placed. After selecting the dimension lines or the dimension text, press and hold the left mouse button and drag the cursor to a new location. The dimension will be placed at the new location. Also, note that you cannot change the dimension type by dragging. For example, you cannot drag a major angle dimension to a new location to make it a minor angle dimension.

Angular Dimensioning by Using Three Points

You can also add angular dimensions by using three keypoints using the **Angle Between** tool. The keypoints should be selected in the clockwise or counterclockwise direction.

Note that while selecting the points, the vertex of the angle should be selected last. Also, make sure that the **By 2 Points** option is selected in the **Orientation** drop-down list of the Command bar. Figure 3-22 shows the angular dimensioning by using three points.

Angular Dimensioning of the Sweep Angle of an Arc

You can use angular dimensions to dimension the sweep angle of an arc. To do so, invoke the **Smart Dimension** tool and select an arc. Next, choose the **Angle** button from the Command bar; the angular dimension of the sweep angle of the arc will be displayed, as shown in Figure 3-23.

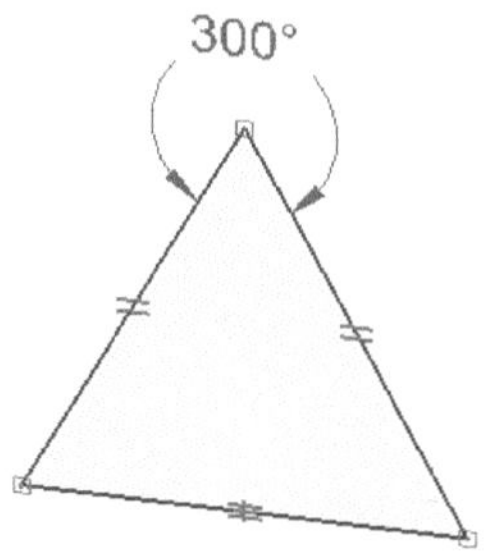

Figure 3-21 *Major angle between two lines*

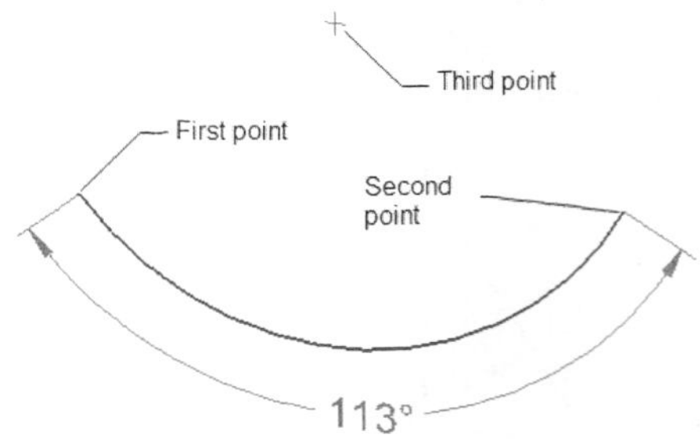

Figure 3-22 *Angular dimensioning by using three points*

Adding Diameter Dimensions

Ribbon: Home > Dimension > Smart Dimension

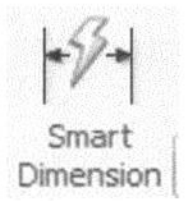

Diameter dimensions are applied to dimension a circle or an arc in terms of its diameter. In Solid Edge, when you select a circle to dimension, the diameter dimension is applied to it by default. However, if you select an arc to dimension, the radius dimension will be applied to it. You can also apply the diameter dimension to an arc. To do so, invoke the **Smart Dimension** tool and then select the arc. Now, choose the **Diameter** button from the Command bar to apply the diameter dimension. Figure 3-24 shows an arc and a circle with the diameter dimensions.

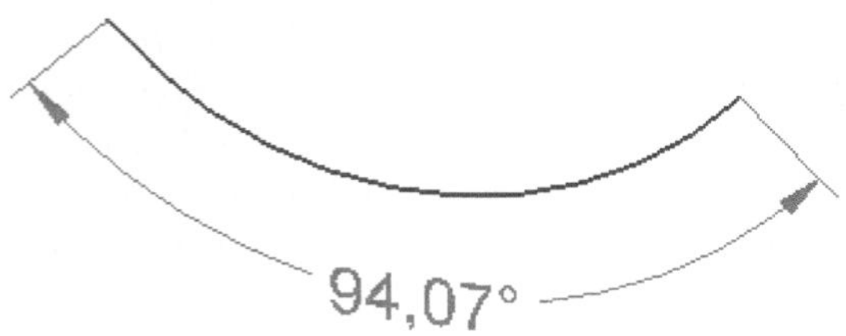

Figure 3-23 *Dimensioning the sweep angle of an arc*

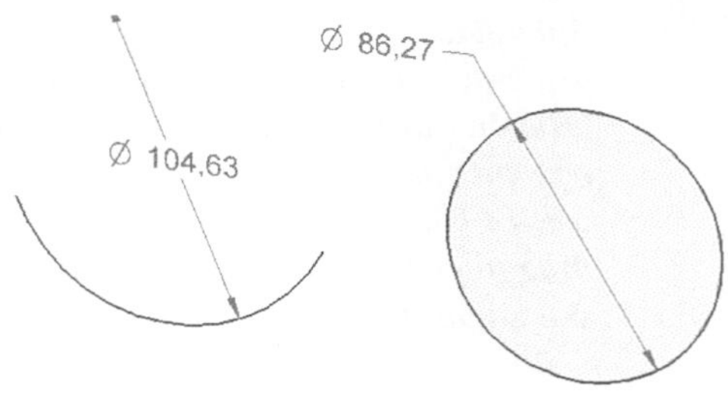

Figure 3-24 *Diameter dimensioning of an arc and a circle*

Adding Radial Dimensions

Ribbon: Home > Dimension > Smart Dimension

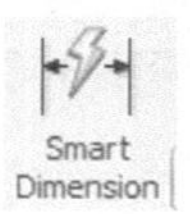

Radial dimensions are applied to dimension an arc, a circle, a curve, or an ellipse in terms of its radius. As mentioned earlier, by default, the circles will be assigned the diameter dimensions and the arcs will be applied the radius dimensions. However, you can also apply the radius dimensions to a circle. To do so, invoke the **Smart Dimension** tool and then select the circle. Now, choose the **Radius** button from the Command bar to apply the radius dimension. Figure 3-25 shows an arc and a circle with the radius dimensions.

Adding Symmetric Diameter Dimensions

Ribbon: Home > Dimension > Symmetric Diameter

Symmetric diameter dimensioning is used to dimension the sketches of the revolved components. The sketch for a revolved component is drawn using the simple sketching entities. For example, if you draw a rectangle and revolve it, it will result in a cylinder. Now, if you dimension the rectangle using the linear dimension, the same dimensions will be displayed when you generate the drawing views of the cylinder. Also, the same dimensions will be used while manufacturing the component. But these linear dimensions will result in a confusion while manufacturing the component. This is because while manufacturing a revolved component, the dimensions have to be in terms of the diameter of the revolved component. The linear dimensions will not be acceptable during the manufacturing of a revolved component.

To overcome this confusion, the sketches of the revolved features are dimensioned using the symmetric diameter dimensions. These dimensions display the distance between the two selected line segments in terms of diameter, which is double of the original length. Also, the **Ø** symbol is placed as a prefix to the dimension. For example, if the original dimension between two entities is 10, the symmetric diameter dimension will display it as **Ø**20. This is because when you revolve a rectangle with a 10 mm width, the diameter of the resultant cylinder will be 20 mm.

To add these dimensions, choose the **Symmetric Diameter** tool from the **Dimension** group of the **Home** tab; you will be prompted to click on the dimension origin element. Note that the dimension origin element should be the line or the axis in the sketch about which the sketch will be revolved. After selecting the axis or the line, you will be prompted to select the dimension measurement element. Select the line or the keypoint in the sketch to which you want to add the linear diameter dimensions. Now, choose the **Half/Full** button from the Command bar. You will notice that a dimension, which is twice the measured distance, is attached to the cursor. Place the dimension at the desired location. Figure 3-26 shows the dimension value preceded by the **Ø** symbol which indicates the symmetric diameter dimension.

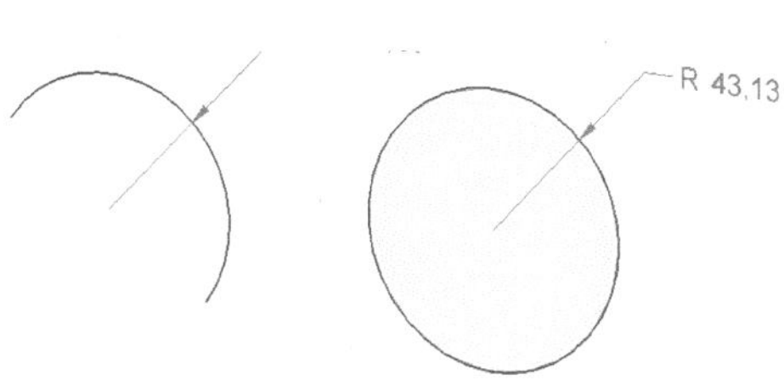

Figure 3-25 *Radial dimensioning of an arc and a circle*

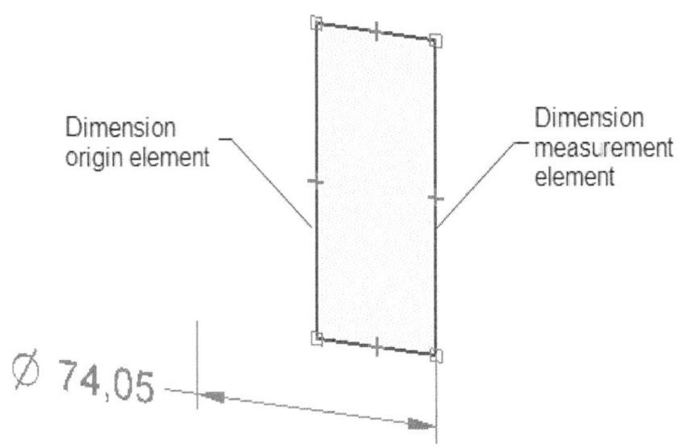

Figure 3-26 *Symmetric diameter dimensioning of a sketch*

Adding Coordinate Dimensions

Ribbon:	Home > Dimension > Coordinate Dimension drop-down > Coordinate Dimension

Coordinate dimensions are used to dimension a sketch with respect to a common origin point, which can be one of the vertices in the sketch. Figure 3-27 shows the coordinate dimensions of a sketch. In this case, the lower left corner of the sketch is taken as the common origin. The remaining entities are dimensioned with respect to this point.

To add this dimension, choose the **Coordinate Dimension** tool from the **Coordinate Dimension** drop-down in the **Dimension** group of the **Home** tab; you will be prompted to click on the common origin element. Select a vertex, keypoint, or a line segment that you want to use as the common origin. Note that if you select a vertex or a keypoint, you can take it as a common origin for the horizontal or the vertical coordinate dimension. But in case of line segments, the vertical line will be taken as the origin for the horizontal dimensions and the horizontal line will be taken as the origin for the vertical dimensions.

After selecting the common origin, move the cursor horizontally or vertically to place the common origin dimension, which is 0, refer to Figure 3-27. If you have placed zero for the X direction, which is represented by a vertical dimension line, move the cursor in the horizontal direction and select a point or a line segment. Next, move the cursor in the direction of the zero dimension and place it. Follow this procedure to place the remaining dimensions along that direction.

Next, right-click to place the coordinate dimensions along the second direction; you will be prompted again to click on the common origin element. Select the origin element and place the dimension along the second direction and then select the points to place the coordinate dimensions along that direction.

Change Coordinate Origin

Ribbon:	Home > Dimension > Coordinate Dimension drop-down > Change Coordinate Origin

After dimensioning the sketch by using the **Coordinate Dimension** tool, you can also change the common origin element. To change the common origin element, choose the **Change Coordinate Origin** tool from the **Coordinate Dimension** drop-down in the **Dimension** group of the **Home** tab; you will be prompted to click on the dimension. Now, choose the dimension where you want to place the new common origin element by moving the cursor horizontally or vertically.

Adding Angular Coordinate Dimensions

Ribbon:	Home > Dimension > Angular Coordinate Dimension

As the name suggests, this tool is used to add angular coordinate dimensions with respect to a common origin point, as shown in Figure 3-28. On invoking this tool, you will be prompted to click on the group center element. This point will be taken as the center point and the angular coordinate dimensions will be created around this point. After selecting this point, you will be prompted to select the common origin element. This is the element that will be taken as the origin for the angular coordinate dimensions. Select the origin point and move the cursor to place the zero dimension; you will be prompted to click on the dimension measurement element. Select the point to which you want to add the angular coordinate dimension. After selecting the element, the preview of the angular coordinate dimension will be displayed. If the dimension is placed clockwise, you can display the counterclockwise dimension by choosing the **Counterclockwise** button from the Command bar. Move the cursor and place the dimension. Continue this process to add all angular coordinate dimensions.

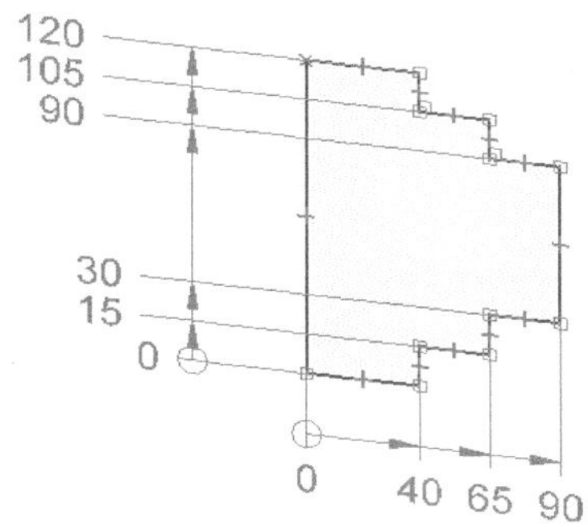

Figure 3-27 Coordinate dimensioning of a sketch

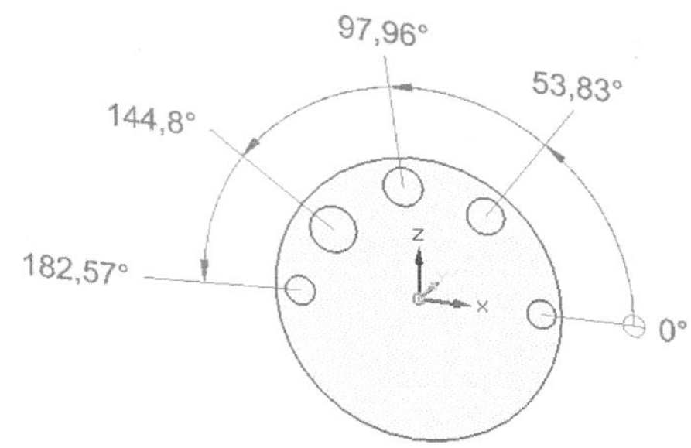

Figure 3-28 Angular coordinate dimensioning of a sketch

ADDING AUTOMATIC DIMENSIONS (ORDERED ENVIRONMENT)

Ribbon: Home > Dimension > Auto-Dimension

The **Auto-Dimension** tool is used to add dimensions to the sketched entities automatically when you draw them. You can set options for the automatic display of dimensions while drawing an entity by choosing the **IntelliSketch Options** button from the **Intellisketch** group of the **Home** tab. When you choose this button, the **IntelliSketch** dialog box will be displayed with the **Auto-Dimension** tab chosen by default, refer to Figure 3-29. The options in this tab are discussed next.

Automatic Dimensioning Options Area

The options in this area are used to specify the automatic dimensions. These options are discussed next.

Automatically create dimensions for new geometry

If this check box is selected then the dimensions will be created automatically in the newly created geometry. The other options in this dialog box will be activated only if this check box is selected. These options are discussed next.

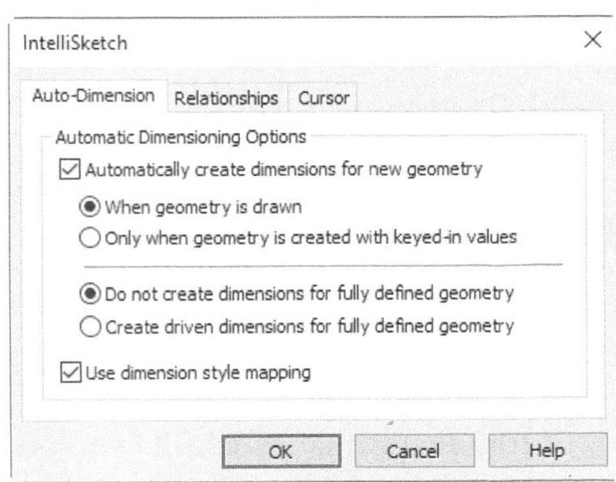

*Figure 3-29 The **IntelliSketch** dialog box*

When geometry is drawn

This radio button is selected by default. As a result, the automatic dimensions are applied as you draw the sketched entities.

Only when geometry is created with keyed-in values

If this radio button is selected, the automatic dimensions will be applied only to the entities that are created by entering the values in the Command bar.

Do not create dimensions for fully defined geometry

This radio button is selected by default. As a result, the automatic dimensions are not added if the sketch is already fully defined.

Create driven dimensions for fully defined geometry

If this radio button is selected, the automatic driven dimensions will be added for the fully defined sketches.

Use dimension style mapping

If this check box is selected, the placed dimensions automatically inherit the dimension style specified in the **Dimension Style** tab of the **Solid Edge Options** dialog box.

UNDERSTANDING THE CONCEPT OF FULLY CONSTRAINED SKETCHES

A fully constrained sketch is the one in which all the entities are completely constrained to their surroundings using constraints and dimensions. It has a definite shape, size, orientation, and location. Whenever you draw a sketched entity, it becomes blue in color. If you add dimensions and constraints to fully constrain it, the entity will turn black. If it does not turn black, choose the **Relationship Colors** button from the **Evaluate** group of the **Inspect** tab. Note that while creating the base sketch in Solid Edge, you need to relate or dimension it with respect to the reference planes in order to fully constrain it.

MEASURING SKETCHED ENTITIES

In Solid Edge, you can measure the distance between the sketched entities, the total length of a closed loop or an open entity, and the area of a loop. To do so, choose the **Smart Measure** tool from the **2D Measure** group of the **Inspect tab**. This tool works similar to the **Smart Dimension** tool. You can also calculate the area properties of the sketched entities. The techniques to measure the area properties are discussed next.

Measuring Distances

Ribbon: Inspect > 2D Measure > Distance

The **Distance** tool is used to measure the linear distance between any two selected points. To measure the linear distance, choose the **Distance** tool from the **2D Measure** group of the **Inspect** tab; you will be prompted to click on the first point. Select the first point to measure the linear distance; you will be prompted to click on the next point. If you move the cursor over a keypoint to select it as the second point, the linear distance, the ΔX distance, and the ΔY distance between the two points will be displayed on the right of the cursor without even selecting the point, as shown in Figure 3-30. If the second point is not a keypoint, the values will not be displayed on the side of the cursor. You need to click on the left mouse button to display the distance value. In this case, the delta values will not be displayed. You can continue to select multiple points to measure the distance between any two points.

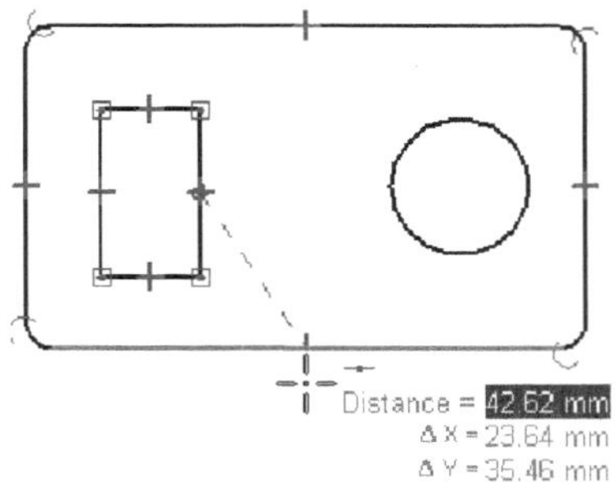

Figure 3-30 *Measuring the distance between the two keypoints*

Measuring the Total Length of a Closed Loop or an Open Sketch

Ribbon:	Inspect > 2D Measure > Total Length

The **Total Length** tool is used to measure the total length of a closed loop or an open sketch. When you invoke this tool, the Command bar will be displayed and you will be prompted to click on the element(s) to be measured. By default, the **Chain** option is selected from the drop-down list in the Command bar. As a result, the complete chain of entities will be selected and the total length of the chain will be displayed. You can also select the **Single** option from this drop-down list to measure the total length of a single entity.

The total length is displayed in the **Length** edit box of the Command bar. If you want to measure the total length of a new set of entities, then choose the **Deselect** button from the Command bar. This will clear the currently selected set and allows you to select a new set of entities.

Measuring an Area

Ribbon:	Inspect > 2D Measure > Area

The **Area** tool is used to measure the area inside a closed loop. To do so, invoke the **Area** tool; you will be prompted to click on the area. Click inside the closed loop; the area will be highlighted in the drawing window and will be displayed on the right of the cursor. You will notice that all the closed loops inside the selected area get removed automatically and are not highlighted, as shown in Figure 3-31.

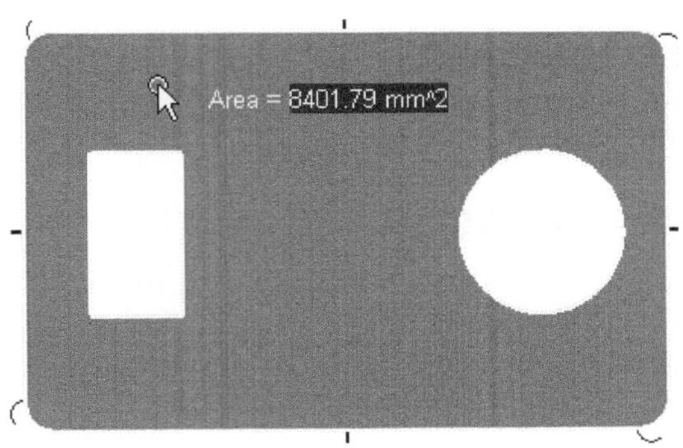

Figure 3-31 *Measuring the area of a closed loop*

If you also want to include the inner closed loops for measuring, then press and hold the CTRL key and click inside the inner closed loop. The area inside the inner closed loop will also get highlighted and two values will be displayed on the right of the cursor. The first value will be the area of the second loop and the other value will be the second or combined area of the two loops. You can continue to add or remove the closed loops by pressing and holding the CTRL key and then clicking inside them.

Calculating the Area Properties

Ribbon: Inspect > Evaluate > Area

The **Area** tool is used to calculate the properties of a selected area. On invoking this tool, you will be prompted to click on an area. Click inside a closed loop; the area of that loop will be highlighted. Accept the inputs in the Command bar and right-click in the area; a shortcut menu will be displayed. Choose the **Properties** option from it to display the **Info** dialog box. This dialog box lists all the properties of the selected area, as shown in Figure 3-32.

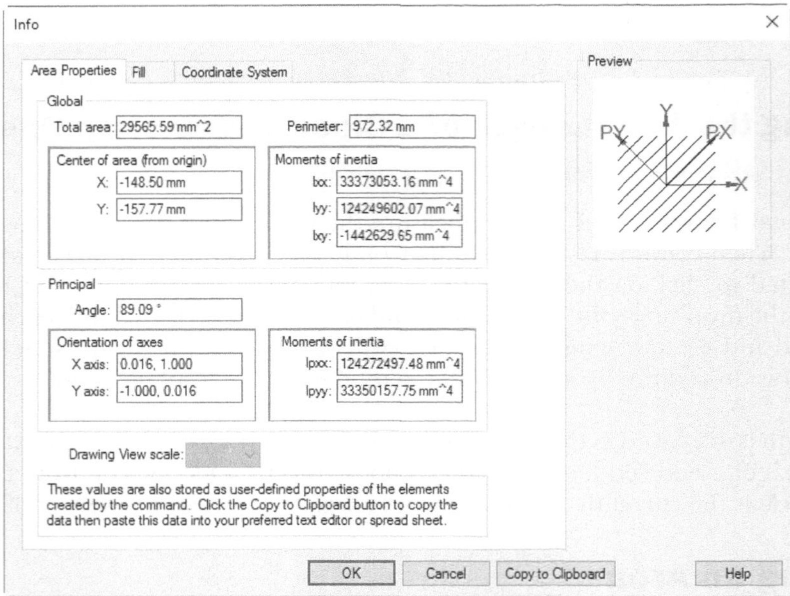

*Figure 3-32 The **Info** dialog box*

TUTORIALS

You will use relationships and parametric dimensions to complete the models in the following tutorials.

Tutorial 1 Synchronous

In this tutorial, you will draw the profile of the model shown in Figure 3-33. The profile shown in Figure 3-34 should be symmetric about the origin. You need not use the edit boxes available in the Command bar to enter the values of the entities. Instead, you can use the parametric dimensions to complete the sketch. **(Expected time: 30 min)**

The following steps are required to complete this tutorial:

Figure 3-33 Model for Tutorial 1

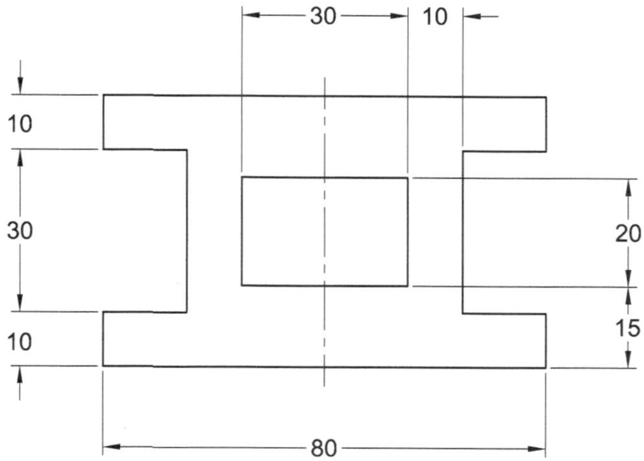

Figure 3-34 Profile to be drawn for Tutorial 1

a. Start Solid Edge and then start a new part file.
b. Draw the outer loop of the profile by using the **Line** tool, refer to Figure 3-35.
c. Add relationships and dimensions to the outer loop, refer to Figures 3-36 and 3-37.
d. Draw a rectangle inside the outer loop by using the **Rectangle** tool and add dimensions and relations to it, refer to Figures 3-38 and 3-39.
e. Save the sketch and close the file.

Starting a Solid Edge Document

The profile of the model will be created using the tools in the **Home** tab of the Solid Edge's **Synchronous Part** environment. Therefore, you need to start a new part file first.

1. Double-click on the Solid Edge ST9 shortcut icon on the desktop of your computer.

   Next, you need to start a new part file to draw the sketch of the given model.

2. Choose the **New** tool from the **Quick Access** toolbar of the home screen; the **New** dialog box is displayed. Next, select the **iso metric part.par** and click **OK** to start a new Solid Edge part file.

Drawing the Outer Loop and Adding Relationships

If the sketch consists of more than one closed loop, it is recommended to draw the outer loop first and then add the required relationships and dimensions to it. This makes it easier to draw and dimension the inner loop.

1. Choose the **Line** tool from the **Draw** group of the **Home** tab; the **Line** Command bar is displayed and the alignment lines are attached to the cursor.

2. Next, you need to define the plane on which you want to draw the profile of the base feature. To do so, select the **Base Reference Planes** check box in the **PathFinder** and move the cursor toward the XZ plane, and then select it for sketching.

3. The view orientation of the part document is set to **Dimetric** by default. Choose **Sketch View** from the status bar to view the horizontal and vertical settings properly.

4. Draw the sketch of the outer loop, as shown in Figure 3-35. It is evident from this figure that the sketch is drawn around the origin and it is not symmetric at this stage. It will become symmetric after adding all relationships and dimensions to it. You can use the alignment indicators to draw the sketch. For your reference, the lines in the sketch are indicated by numbers.

   Next, you need to add relationships to the sketch. First, you need to apply the **Equal** relationship and then the **Symmetric** relationship to the sketch.

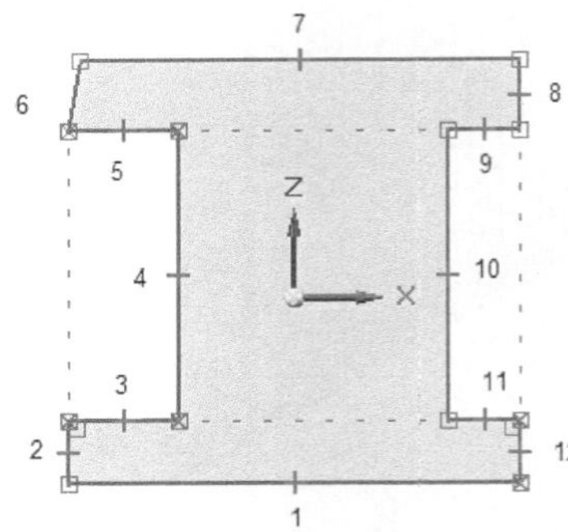

Figure 3-35 *Outer loop of the profile*

5. Choose the **Equal** tool from the **Relate** group; you are prompted to click on an element.

Note

*1. If the relationship handles are not visible by default, choose the **Relationship Handles** button from the **Relate** group of the **Home** tab; the relationship handles will be displayed. As the **Relationship Handles** button is a toggle button, you can hide the relationship handle by choosing the button again.*

*2. Make sure that in the **Relationships** tab of the **IntelliSketch** dialog box, the **Extension (point-on and tangent)** check box is selected. Also, ensure that the **Maintain Relationships** button is chosen in the **Relate** group of the **Home** tab.*

6. Select line 2; the color of this line is changed and you are prompted to select the next line. Select line 6; the **Equal** relationship is applied to lines 2 and 6, and you are again prompted to click on an element. Select line 6 as the first line and then line 8 as the second line.

   If the **Solid Edge ST9** information box is displayed while applying any of these constraints, choose **OK** to exit the information box.

7. Similarly, select lines 8 and 12, 1 and 7, 3 and 5, 5 and 9, 9 and 11, and then lines 4 and 10. The **Equal** relationship is applied to all these pairs of lines.

   Next, you need to make this sketch symmetric about the two reference planes that appear as the vertical and horizontal lines in this view.

8. Choose the **Symmetric** tool from the **Relate** group; you are prompted to click on the symmetry axis.

9. Select the Z axis as the symmetry axis; a symmetry axis is created over the reference plane and you are prompted to click on an element.

10. Select lines 2 and 12.

    Similarly, select lines 3 and 11, 4 and 10, 5 and 9, and 6 and 8. Next, you need to make lines 1 and 7 symmetric about the horizontal reference axis. Note that you need to set the symmetry axis again because the vertical reference axis has already been set as the symmetry axis.

11. Choose the **Symmetric** tool from the **Relate** group; you are prompted to click on an element. Specify the X axis as the symmetry axis; you are prompted to click on an element.

12. Select lines 1 and 7 to add the **Symmetric** relationship between them.

13. Press the ESC key to exit the current tool. The sketch after adding all relationships is shown in Figure 3-36. Notice that all the relationships handles are displayed on the sketch.

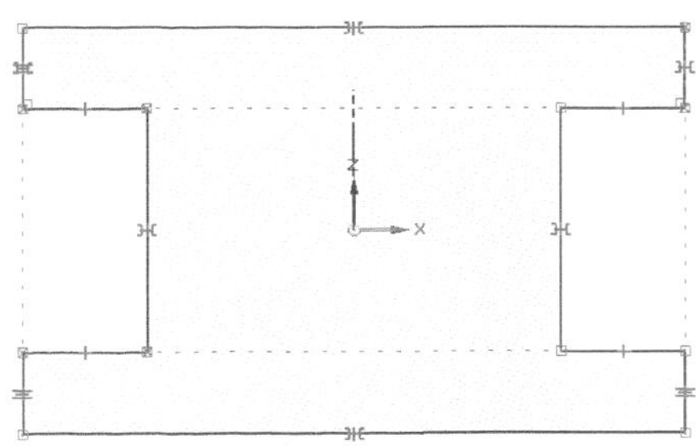

Figure 3-36 Profile after adding relationships

Dimensioning the Sketch

Once all the required relationships have been added to the profile, you can dimension it. As mentioned earlier, when you add dimensions to a sketch and modify the value of the dimension, the entity is also modified accordingly.

Before dimensioning the sketch, it is recommended that you turn on the option to display the text in black color once it is fully constrained.

1. Choose the **Relationship Colors** button from the **Evaluate** group of the **Inspect** tab, if not chosen earlier; the relationship option turns on.

2. Choose the **Smart Dimension** tool from the **Dimension** group of the **Sketching** tab; you are prompted to click on the element(s) to dimension. Next, select line 1.

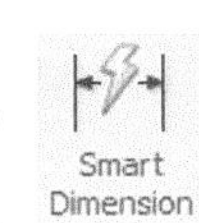

   As soon as you select line 1, a linear dimension to measure the length of line 1 is attached to the cursor.

3. Place the dimension below line 1; the **Dimension Value** edit box is displayed below the dimension. Enter **80** in this edit box and press ENTER.

The length of the line is forced to 80 units and as the sketch is symmetric the line is modified symmetrically.

4. As the **Smart Dimension** tool is still active, you are again prompted to click on the element(s) to dimension. Select line 2 and place the dimension on the left of this line. Enter **10** in the **Dimension Value** edit box and press ENTER.

   You will notice that the length of lines 6, 8, and 12 is also forced to 10 units each because the **Equal** relationship has been applied to all these lines.

5. Select line 3 and place the dimension below this line. Next, enter **15** in the **Dimension Value** edit box and press ENTER.

6. Select line 4 and place it along the previous dimension and relationships; the color of the sketch turns black, indicating that it is fully constrained. Modify the dimension value to **30** in the **Dimension Value** edit box and press ENTER. Notice that the length of line 10 is also modified.

   This completes the dimensioning of the outer profile. The profile after adding these dimensions is shown in Figure 3-37.

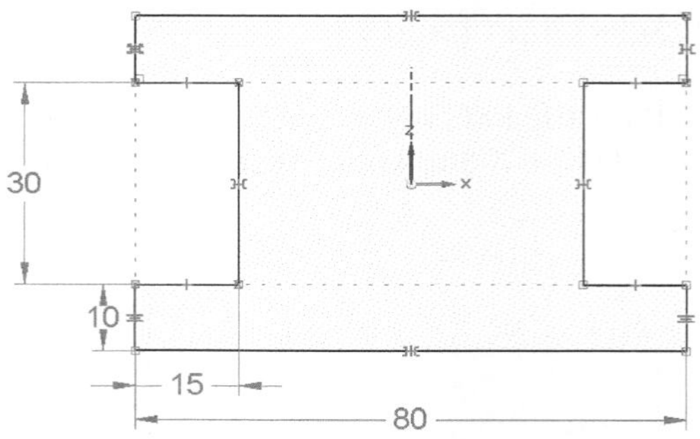

Figure 3-37 *Profile after adding the relationships and dimensions*

Drawing the Inner Loop and Adding Relationships

Next, you need to draw the inner loop, which is a rectangle, and add relationships to the base feature.

1. Choose the **Rectangle by Center** tool from **Home > Draw > Rectangle** drop-down; you are prompted to click for the first point.

2. Click on the origin to specify it as the center point of the rectangle; a dynamic preview of the rectangle is displayed and you are prompted to click to create a rectangle.

3. Click on the graphics window to create a rectangle. Refer to Figure 3-34 for the location of the rectangle.

4. Choose the **Symmetric** tool from the **Relate** group of the **Home** tab and set X axis as the symmetry axis. 

5. Select the upper and lower horizontal lines of the rectangle to add symmetric relationship between them.

   Next, you need to change the symmetry axis to make the vertical lines symmetrical.

6. Choose the **Symmetric** tool from the **Relate** group; you are prompted to click on an element. Select the Z axis as the symmetry axis.

7. Select the two vertical lines of rectangle to make them symmetrical about the Z axis.

   This completes the process of adding relationships to the inner loop. The sketch at this stage will look similar to the model shown in Figure 3-38.

Dimensioning the Inner Loop

1. Choose the **Smart Dimension** tool from the **Dimension** group of the **Home** tab and select the upper horizontal line of the inner loop.

2. Place the dimension above the sketch. Enter **30** in the **Dimension Value** edit box and press ENTER.

3. Next, select the right vertical line of the inner loop and place the dimension on the right of the sketch. Enter **20** in the **Dimension Value** edit box and then press ENTER; the inner loop turns black, indicating that it is fully constrained. This completes the dimensioning of the profile. The final profile, after adding all dimensions, is shown in Figure 3-39.

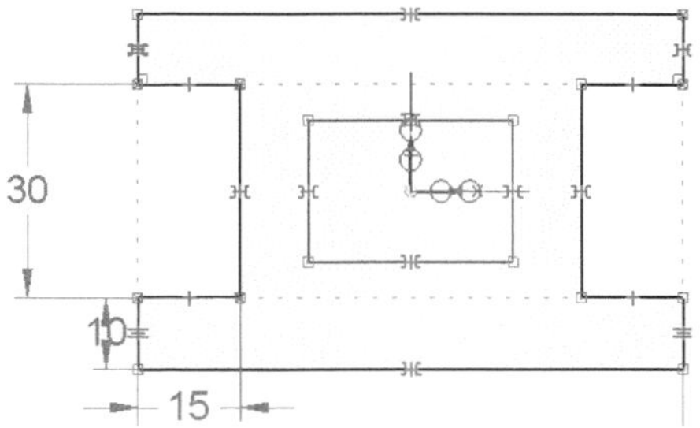

Figure 3-38 *Profile after adding relationships to the inner loop*

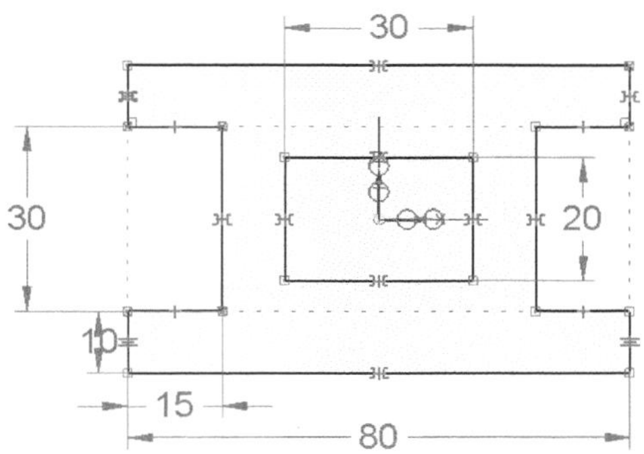

Figure 3-39 *Final profile after adding all dimensions*

As mentioned in the previous chapter, it is recommended that you exit the sketching environment before saving or closing the file because you cannot close a file in the sketching environment.

4. Press the ESC key to exit the current tool.

Saving the File

1. Choose the **Save** button from the **Quick Access** toolbar; the **Save As** dialog box is displayed.

   As mentioned in the previous chapter, you need to create a separate folder for every chapter in the textbook.

2. Browse to the *C:|Solid Edge* folder and then create a folder with the name *c03*.

3. Double-click on the *c03* folder to open it and save the file with the name *c03tut1*.

4. Choose the **Close** button from the file tab bar to close the file.

Tutorial 2 — Ordered

In this tutorial, you will create the profile for the model shown in Figure 3-40. The profile to be drawn is shown in Figure 3-41. You will use relationships and parametric dimensions to complete the sketch. **(Expected time: 30 min)**

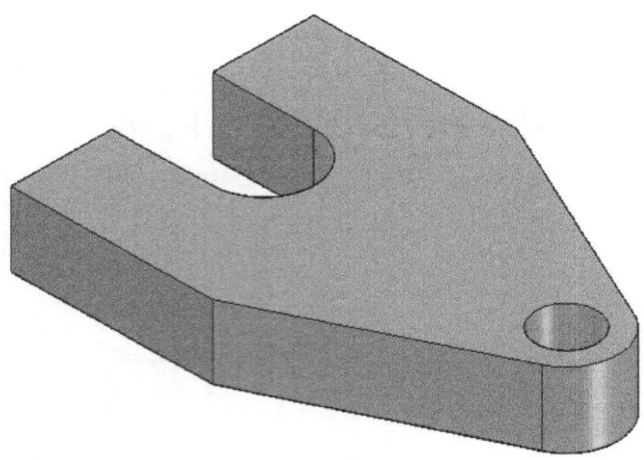

Figure 3-40 Model for Tutorial 2

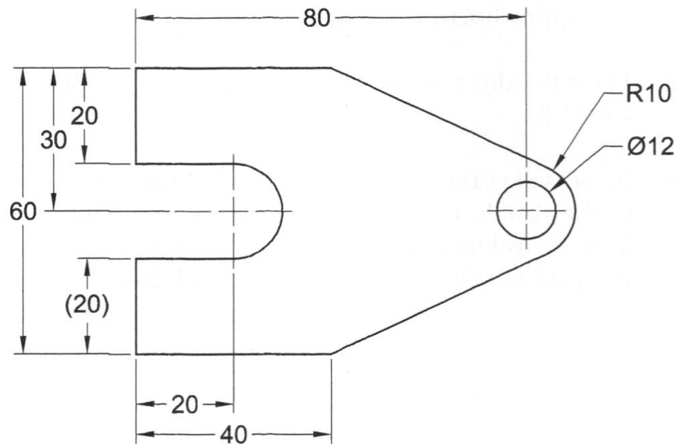

Figure 3-41 Profile to be drawn for Tutorial 2

The following steps are required to complete this tutorial:

a. Start a new part file.
b. Switch to the **Ordered Part** environment.
c. Invoke the sketching environment.
d. Draw the required profile by using the **Line** and **Circle by Center Point** tools, refer to Figure 3-42.
e. Add the required relationships and dimensions to the sketch, refer to Figure 3-44.
f. Save the file and close it.

Starting a New Part File and Selecting the Sketching Plane

1. Choose the **New** tool from the **Quick Access** toolbar; the **New** dialog box is displayed.

2. In this dialog box, select **iso metric part.par** and choose **OK** to start a new part file.

3. Select the **Ordered** radio button from the **Model** group of the **Tools** tab; the **Ordered Part** environment is invoked.

4. Select the check box adjacent to the **Base Reference Planes** node under **PathFinder**; the visibility of the reference plane is turned on.

5. Choose the **Sketch** tool from the **Sketch** group of the **Home** tab; the **Sketch** Command bar is displayed and you are prompted to select a planar face or a reference plane.

6. Select the top plane to draw the profile; the selected plane gets oriented to the normal view.

Drawing the Profile

It is recommended that you draw the first entity in the sketch by entering its exact values in the Command bar. This allows you to modify the drawing display area to fit the first entity. You can draw the other entities taking the reference of the first entity. This also helps you dimension the entities at a later stage.

1. Using the **Line** tool and options in the Command bar, draw a line of length 40 units with its start point at the origin.

2. Taking the reference of the first line, draw the remaining entities in the profile to complete it. Use the arc mode of the **Line** tool to draw the tangent arcs in the profile.

Now, draw the circle by using the **Circle by Center Point** tool while drawing the circle, if the center point of the arc is not displayed, then move the cursor over the arc to display its center point. Use this center point to define the center point of the circle. The profile after drawing all entities is shown in Figure 3-42. For your reference, the entities in the sketch are indicated by numbers.

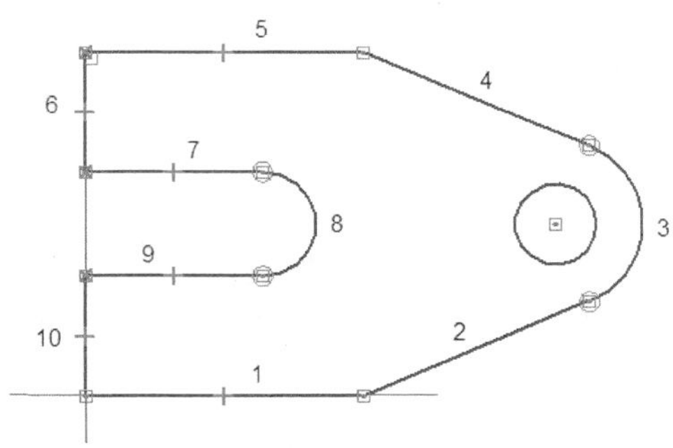

Figure 3-42 *Profile after drawing all entities*

Adding Relationships to the Profile

Next, you need to add relationships to the profile.

1. Choose the **Equal** tool from the **Relate** group of the **Home** tab and add this relationship between lines 1 and 5, 2 and 4, 6 and 10, and 7 and 9.

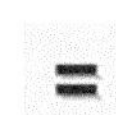

Next, you need to make the two arcs in the sketch tangent to the lines to which they are connected. The tangent relationship could have been applied to the sketch while drawing it. To check this relationship, see whether a small circle is displayed at all points where the arcs and the lines meet. The small circle is the relationship handle of the tangent relationship. Ideally, this handle must be displayed at four locations: the points where arc 3 meets lines 2 and 4 and the points where arc 8 meets lines 7 and 9.

2. Choose the **Tangent** tool from the **Relate** group of the **Home** tab and add the tangent relationship between the entities where it is missing.

Note

If you add a relationship that has already been added, the ***Solid Edge ST9*** *message box is displayed informing that the requested change conflicts with the existing relationships.*

Next, you need to horizontally align the center point of arc 8 with the center point of the circle by using the **Horizontal/Vertical** relationship.

3. Choose the **Horizontal/Vertical** tool from the **Relate** group of the **Home** tab. Move the cursor over arc 8 to display its center point. Select the center point when it is displayed. Similarly, select the center point of the circle; a horizontal dashed line is displayed between the two centers indicating that they are horizontally aligned.

   This completes the process of adding relationships to the profile. The profile after adding all relationships is shown in Figure 3-43.

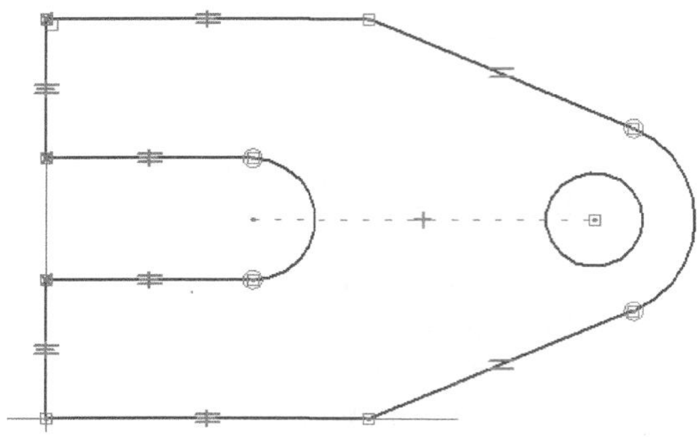

Figure 3-43 *Profile after adding all relationships*

Dimensioning the Profile

After adding relationships, you need to dimension the profile.

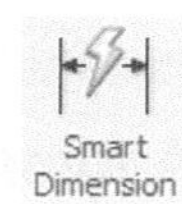

1. Choose the **Smart Dimension** tool from the **Dimension** group of the **Home** tab; you are prompted to click on the elements to dimension.

2. Select line 9 and place the dimension below the profile. Modify the value of the dimension to **20** in the **Dimension Value** edit box displayed with the dimension and then press ENTER.

3. Select line 1 and place the dimension below the previous dimension. Enter **40** in the **Dimension Value** edit box.

4. Select line 6 and the circle. Next, place the dimension above the profile and modify the value of the dimension to **80** in the **Dimension Value** edit box.

5. Select line 10 and place the dimension on the left of the profile. Enter **20** in the **Dimension Value** edit box.

6. Select lines 5 and 1, and place the dimension on the left of the previous dimension. Enter **60** in the **Dimension Value** edit box.

7. Select arc 3 and place the dimension on the right of the sketch. Enter **10** in the **Dimension Value** edit box.

8. Select the circle and place the dimension on the right of the sketch. Enter **12** in the **Dimension Value** edit box.

This completes the dimensioning of the profile. The profile after adding all required dimensions is shown in Figure 3-44.

9. Choose the **Select** tool from the **Select** group of the **Home** tab to exit the active sketching tool.

10. Choose the **Close Sketch** tool from the **Ribbon**; the sketching environment is closed and the **Sketch** Command bar is displayed. Also, the current view is automatically changed to the Dimetric view.

11. Enter **Base Sketch** as the name of the sketch in the **Name** edit box of the Command bar. Choose the **Finish** button and then the **Cancel** button to exit the sketching environment; the sketch is displayed by the specified name in the **PathFinder**.

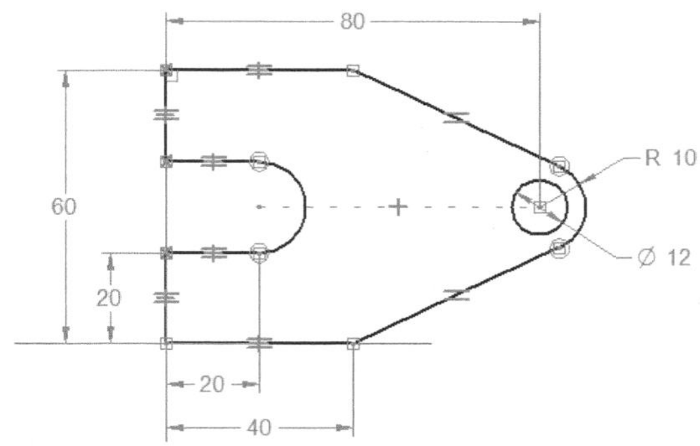

Figure 3-44 *Profile after adding all dimensions*

Saving the File

1. Choose the **Save** button from the **Quick Access** toolbar and save the file with the name *c03tut2* at the location given below.

   C:\Solid Edge\c03

2. Choose the **Close** button from the file tab bar to close the file.

Tutorial 3 — Ordered

In this tutorial, you will create the profile for the revolved model shown in Figure 3-45. The profile is shown in Figure 3-46. You will use the parametric dimensions to complete the sketch.

(Expected time: 30 min)

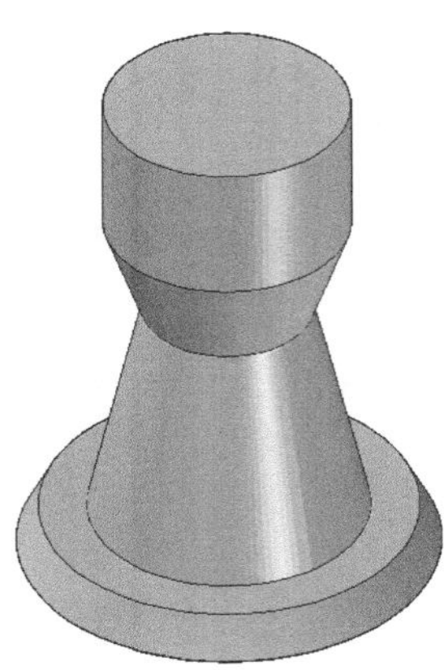

Figure 3-45 *Model for Tutorial 3*

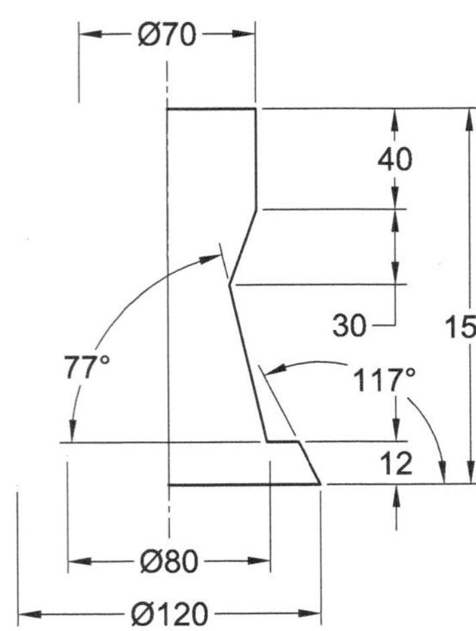

Figure 3-46 *Profile to be drawn for Tutorial 3*

The following steps are required to complete this tutorial:

a. Start a new part file.
b. Switch to the **Ordered Part** environment.
c. Invoke the sketching environment.
d. Draw the required profile by using the **Line** tool, refer to Figure 3-47.
e. Add the required dimensions to the sketch.
f. Save the file and close it.

Starting a New Part File and Selecting the Sketching Plane

You can start a new part file by choosing the **New** tool from the **Quick Access** toolbar, which remains on the screen after you close all the files.

1. Choose the **New** tool from the **Quick Access** toolbar to display the **New** dialog box.

2. Select **iso metric part.par** and choose **OK** to start a new part file.

3. Select the **Ordered** radio button from the **Model** group of the **Tools** tab; the **Ordered Part** environment is invoked.

4. Select the check box adjacent to the **Base Reference Planes** node in the **PathFinder**; the visibility of the reference plane is turned on.

5. Choose the **Sketch** tool from the **Sketch** group of the **Home** tab; the **Sketch** Command bar is displayed and you are prompted to select a planar face or a reference plane.

6. Select the front plane to draw the profile; the selected plane is oriented normal to the viewing direction. Also, the **Line** tool will be invoked by default.

Drawing the Profile Using the Line Tool

To draw the profile, you need to draw the sketch from the lower left corner. The bottom horizontal line will be the first entity to be drawn.

1. Move the cursor to the origin and specify it as the start point of the first line.

2. Enter **60** as the value of length and **0** as the value of angle for the first line in the dynamic edit box. Then, press ENTER to draw the first line segment.

3. Pan the drawing by using the **Pan** tool available in the status bar such that the origin is moved close to the middle of the bottom edge of the drawing window.

4. Complete the sketch of the revolved model by drawing the remaining lines by taking the reference of the first line, refer to Figure 3-47. The lines in this sketch have been numbered for your reference.

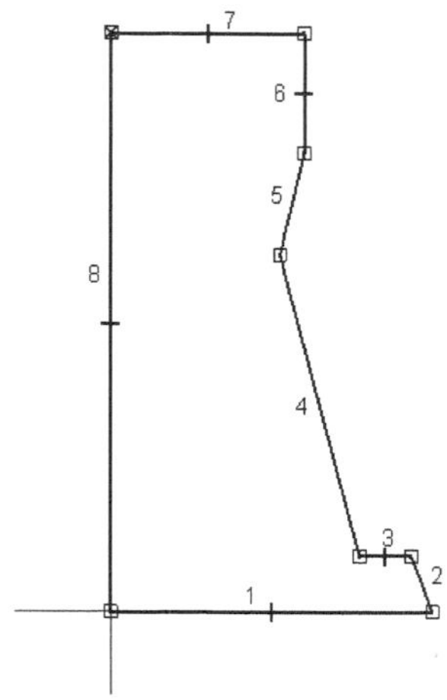

Figure 3-47 Profile for the revolved model

Adding Dimensions to the Profile

Next, you need to add dimensions to the profile. Since it is a profile for the revolved model, you need to add symmetric diameter dimensions to define the diameter of the revolved feature, refer to Figure 3-46.

1. Make sure that the **Relationship Colors** button is chosen in the **Evaluate** group of the **Inspect** tab.

2. Choose the **Symmetric Diameter** button from the **Dimension** group of the **Home** tab ; you are prompted to select the dimension origin element, which acts as the axis of revolution. In this profile, line 8 is the dimension origin element. 

3. Select line 8 and then select the right endpoint of line 1. Choose the **Half/Full** button from the Command bar, if it has not been chosen.

4. Place the dimension below the sketch. You may need to change the drawing display area by choosing the **Zoom** button.

5. Enter **120** as the value of the dimension in the **Dimension Value** edit box.

   Line 8, which was selected as the dimension origin element, is not required to be selected again. You can directly select other dimension measurement elements to add symmetric diameter dimensions.

6. Select the lower endpoint of line 4 and place the dimension below the sketch. Modify the value of dimension to **80** in the **Dimension Value** edit box.

   You will notice that as you place this dimension, the previous symmetric dimension also moves. Now, if you add the symmetric dimension to line 7 in the same sequence, the first two dimensions will also move while placing the third dimension. Therefore, you first need to exit the current sequence of dimensioning.

7. Right-click to exit the current sequence of dimensioning; you are again prompted to select the dimension origin element.

8. Select line 8 and then the right endpoint of line 7; the symmetric diameter dimension is attached to the cursor.

9. Place the dimension above the sketch and modify its value to **70.** Then, press ENTER. Next, you need to add the linear and angular dimensions to the remaining entities by using the **Smart Dimension** tool.

10. Choose the **Smart Dimension** tool from the **Dimension** group of the **Home** tab; you are prompted to click on the element(s) to dimension.

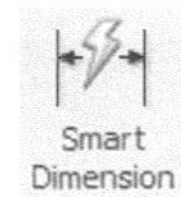

11. Select line 2; an aligned dimension is attached to the cursor. Press and hold the SHIFT key and move the cursor to the right of the sketch. The vertical dimension of line 2 is displayed.

12. Place the dimension on the right of the sketch and modify its value to **12** in the **Dimension Value** edit box. Next, press ENTER.

13. Select lines 1 and 2, and then choose the **Angle** button from the Command bar. Move the cursor to the right of the sketch to display the major angle dimension. Place the dimension on the right of the sketch and enter **117** in the **Dimension Value** edit box.

14. Select line 3 and choose the **Angle** button from the Command bar, and then select line 4. Next, move the cursor to the left of line 4 to display the angular dimension. Place the dimension on the left of line 4 and enter **77** in the **Dimension Value** edit box.

15. Select line 5 and press and hold the SHIFT key to display the vertical dimension of line 5. Place the dimension on the right of the sketch and enter **30** in the **Dimension Value** edit box.

16. Select line 6 and place the dimension on the right of the sketch in line with the previous dimension. Modify the value of dimension to **40**.

17. Select line 8 and place the dimension on the left of the sketch. Modify the dimension value to **150**.

    This completes the dimensioning of the sketch. The sketch after adding all dimensions is shown in Figure 3-48. Notice that as the option for displaying the fully constrained sketch in a different color was chosen from the **Evaluate** group of the **Inspect** tab, the sketch will turn black after placing the last dimension.

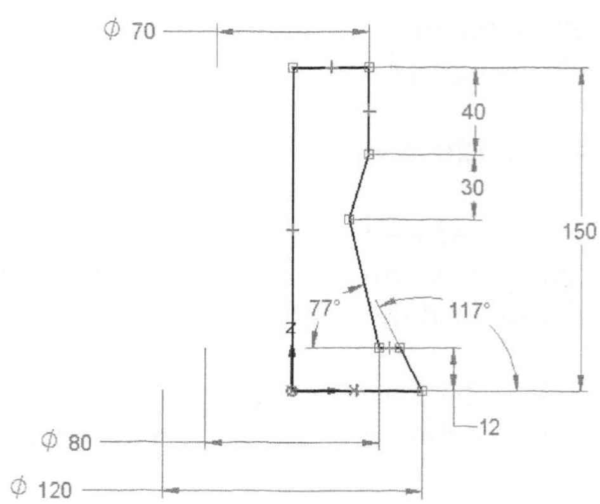

Figure 3-48 *The final model with all dimensions*

Saving the File

1. Choose the **Select** tool from the **Select** group of the **Home** tab.

2. Choose the **Close Sketch** tool from the **Close** group of the **Home** tab; the sketching environment is closed and the **Sketch** Command bar is displayed. Also, the current view is automatically changed to the isometric view.

3. Choose the **Save** button from the **Quick Access** toolbar and save the file with the name *c03tut3* at the location given below:

   C:\Solid Edge\c03

4. Choose the **Close** button from the file tab bar to close the file.

Self-Evaluation Test

Answer the following questions and then compare them to those given at the end of this chapter:

1. The __________ relation forces two arcs, two circles, or an arc and a circle to share the same center point.

2. The __________ dimensions are applied to dimension a circle or an arc in terms of its diameter.

3. The tools available in the __________ drop-down are used to specify the orientation of dimensions.

4. The __________ dimensions measure the actual distance of the inclined lines.

5. The __________ constraint is used to fix the orientation or the location of the selected sketched entity or the keypoint of the sketched entity.

6. By default, circles are assigned to the __________ dimensions.

7. All geometric relationships have the same relationship handles associated with them. (T/F)

8. You can set the symmetry axis before invoking the **Symmetric** tool in the **Ordered Part** environment. (T/F)

9. The **Coordinate Dimensions** tool is used to dimension a sketch with respect to a common origin point. (T/F)

10. The symmetric diameter dimensions are used to dimension the sketches of the revolved components. (T/F)

Review Questions

Answer the following questions:

1. Which of the following dimensions is applied to the arcs by default?

   (a) Radial (b) Diameter
   (c) Angular (d) Linear

2. Which of the following dimensions is used to create angular coordinate dimensions with respect to a common origin point?

   (a) Angular (b) Angular Coordinate
   (c) Linear (d) Coordinate

3. Which of the following relationships is used to fix the orientation or location of a selected sketched entity or a keypoint of the sketched entity?

   (a) **Fix** (b) **Lock**
   (c) **Hide** (d) None of these

4. Which of the following relationships is used to force the selected sketched entities to become symmetrical about a symmetry axis?

   (a) **Symmetric** (b) **Collinear**
   (c) **Coincident** (d) **Horizontal**

5. Which of the following relationships forces a selected line to become normal to another line, arc, circle, or ellipse?

   (a) **Symmetrical** (b) **Collinear**
   (c) **Coincident** (d) **Perpendicular**

6. You cannot modify a dimension after placing it. (T/F)

7. While placing the angular dimensions, you can select the option to display the major or minor angular value. (T/F)

8. You can add a prefix or a suffix to the dimension values. (T/F)

9. In Solid Edge, you can also add tolerance to dimensions in the sketching environment. (T/F)

10. The aligned dimensions cannot be used to dimension the lines that are not parallel to the X axis or the Y axis. (T/F)

EXERCISES

Exercise 1

Draw a profile for the base feature of the model shown in Figure 3-49. The profile to be drawn is shown in Figure 3-50. Use the relationships and parametric dimensions to complete the profile. **(Expected time: 30 min)**

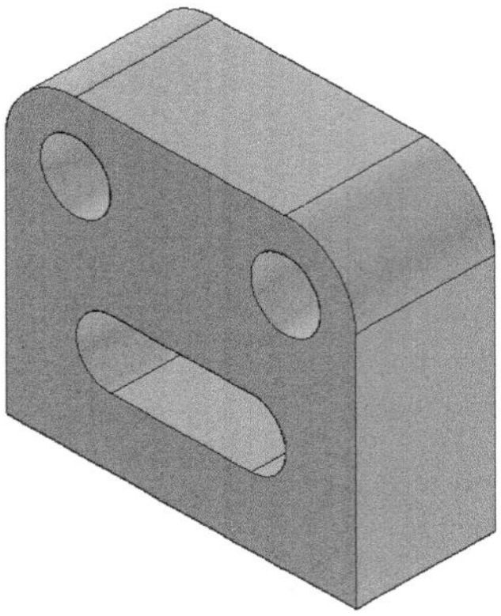

Figure 3-49 Model for Exercise 1

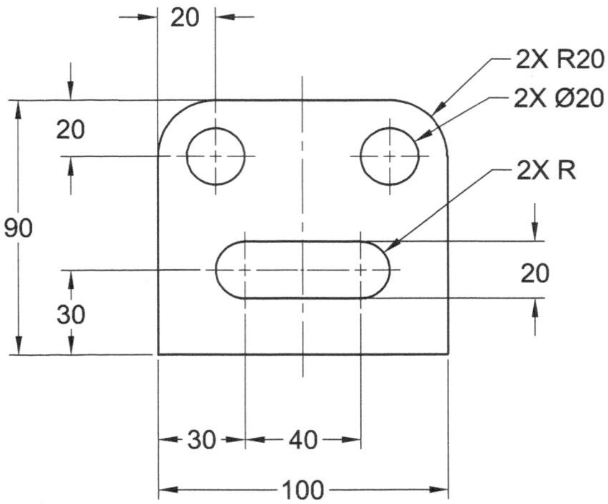

Figure 3-50 Profile for Exercise 1

Exercise 2

Draw the sketch of the model shown in Figure 3-51. The sketch is shown in Figure 3-52. After drawing the sketch, add the required relations and dimensions to it.

(Expected time: 30 min)

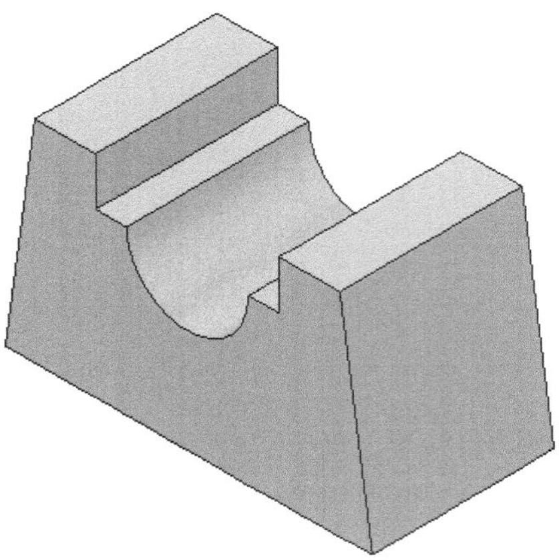

Figure 3-51 Model for Exercise 2

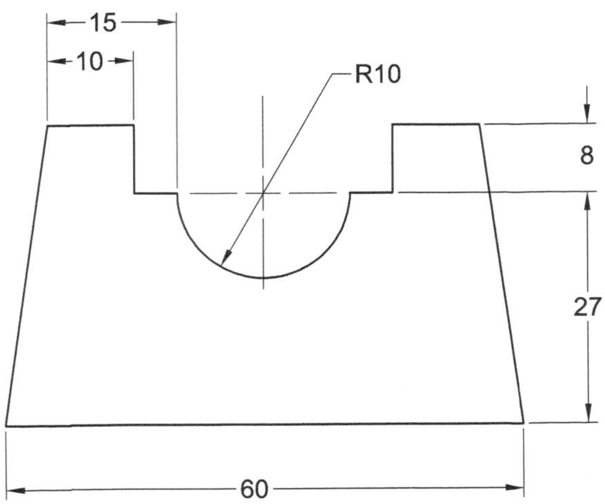

Figure 3-52 Sketch for Exercise 2

Exercise 3

Draw the profile for the base feature of the model shown in Figure 3-53. The profile to be drawn is shown in Figure 3-54. Use the relationships and parametric dimensions to complete the profile. **(Expected time: 30 min)**

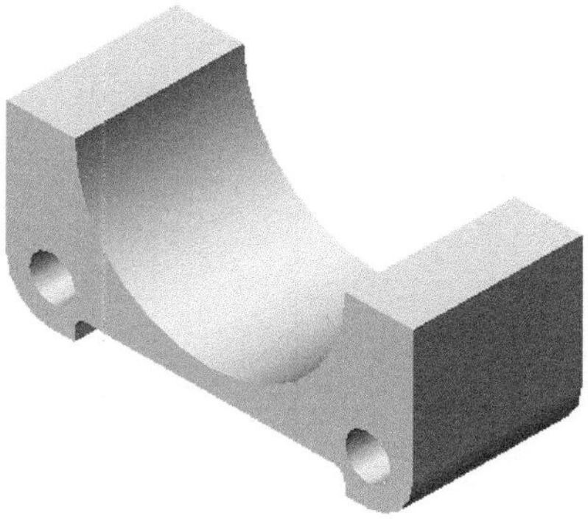

Figure 3-53 Solid model for Exercise 3

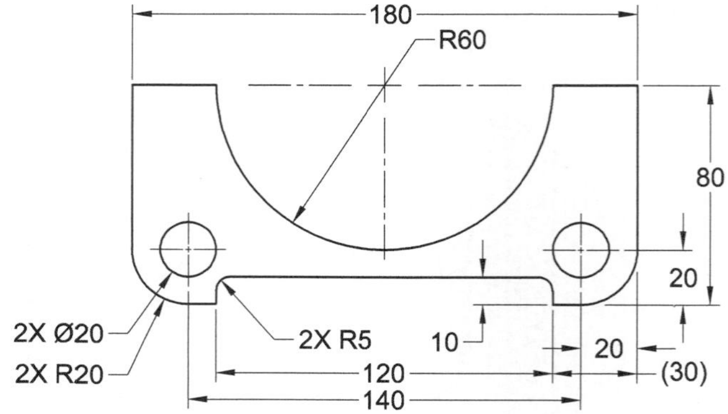

Figure 3-54 Sketch for Exercise 3

Exercise 4

Draw the profile for the revolve feature of the model shown in Figure 3-55. The profile to be drawn is shown in Figure 3-56. Use the relationships and parametric dimensions to complete the profile. **(Expected time: 30 min)**

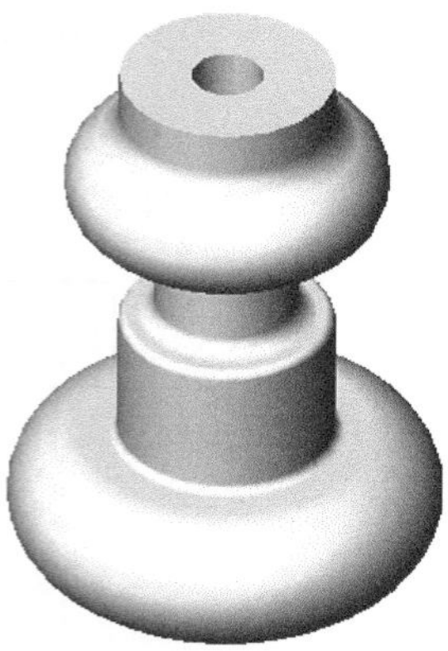

Figure 3-55 Solid model for Exercise 4

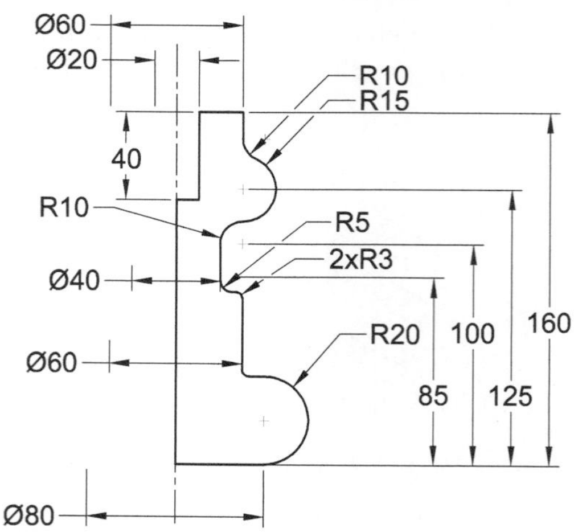

Figure 3-56 Sketch for Exercise 4

Exercise 5

Draw the profile for the base feature of the model shown in Figure 3-57. The profile to be drawn is shown in Figure 3-58. Use the relationships and parametric dimensions to complete the profile. **(Expected time: 30 min)**

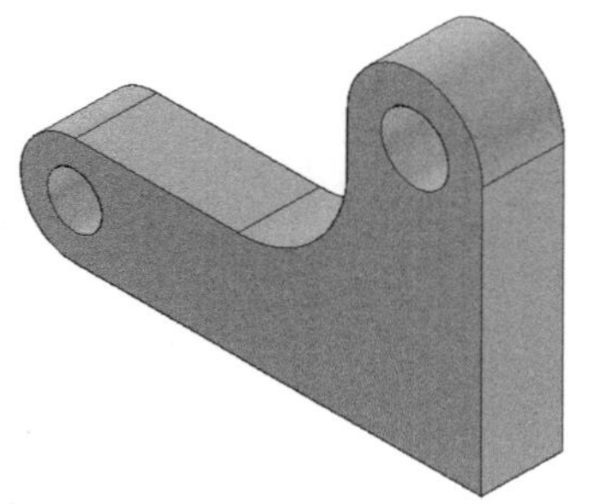

Figure 3-57 *Model for Exercise 5*

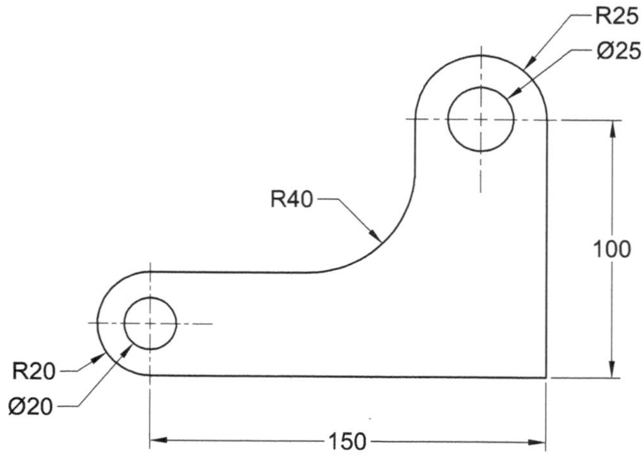

Figure 3-58 *Profile for Exercise 5*

Answers to Self-Evaluation Test

1. Concentric, **2.** Diameter, **3. Orientation**, **4.** Aligned, **5. Lock**, **6.** Diameter, **7.** F, **8.** T, **9.** T, **10.** T

Chapter 4

Editing, Extruding, and Revolving the Sketches

Learning Objectives

After completing this chapter, you will be able to:

- *Edit sketches using the editing tools*
- *Write text and insert images*
- *Edit sketched entities by using the Command bar or by dragging them*
- *Convert sketches into base features by extruding and revolving them*
- *Create primitive features*
- *Rotate the view of a model dynamically in 3D space*
- *Change the view and the display type of models*

EDITING THE SKETCHES

Editing is a very important part of the sketching process in any modeling software. Solid Edge provides a number of tools that can be used to edit the sketched entities. When you design a model, you need to edit the sketch at various stages by using different editing tools. These tools are discussed next.

Trimming the Sketched Entities

Ribbon: Home > Draw > Trim

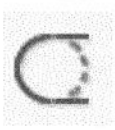

You can remove a portion of a sketched entity by using the **Trim** tool. Figure 4-1 shows the sketched entities before trimming the entities and Figure 4-2 shows the sketch after trimming the entities. Note that when this tool is used on an isolated entity, it deletes the entity.

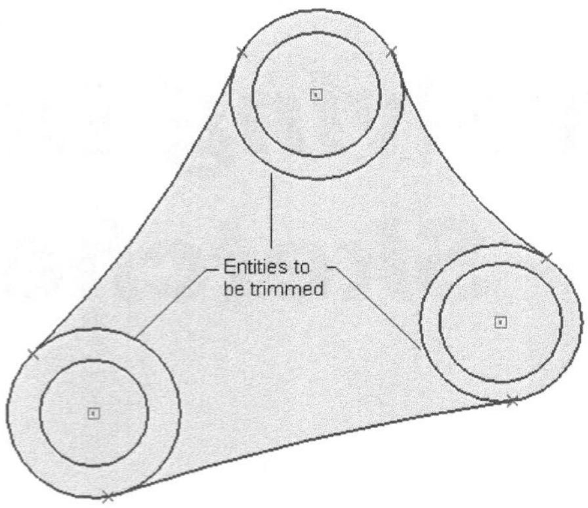

Figure 4-1 *Sketch before trimming the entities*

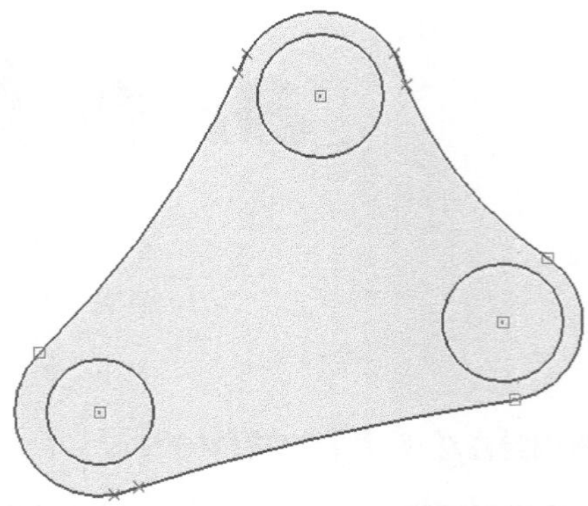

Figure 4-2 *Sketch after trimming the entities*

To trim entities, invoke the **Trim** tool and move the cursor over the portion to be trimmed; it will be highlighted in orange. Click to trim the highlighted portion; you will be prompted again to click on the entity to trim. After trimming all the entities, press ESC to exit this tool.

Creating Splits in the Sketched Entities

Ribbon: Home > Draw > Split drop-down >Split

The **Split** tool is used to split a selected sketched entity at a specified point. To split an entity, invoke the **Split** tool from the **Split** drop-down of the **Draw** group in the **Ribbon**; you will be prompted to select an element. After selecting the element, specify a point from where the element has to be split; the element will break into two parts. The first point of the split element is the nearest endpoint of the element and the second point is the one that you have specified.

Extending the Sketched Entities

Ribbon: Home > Draw > Split drop-down > Extend to Next

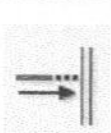

You can extend or lengthen an open sketched entity up to the next entity by using the **Extend to Next** tool. Figure 4-3 shows the entities to be extended and Figure 4-4 shows the sketch after extending the entities. This tool will not work on an entity that does not intersect with any existing sketched entity.

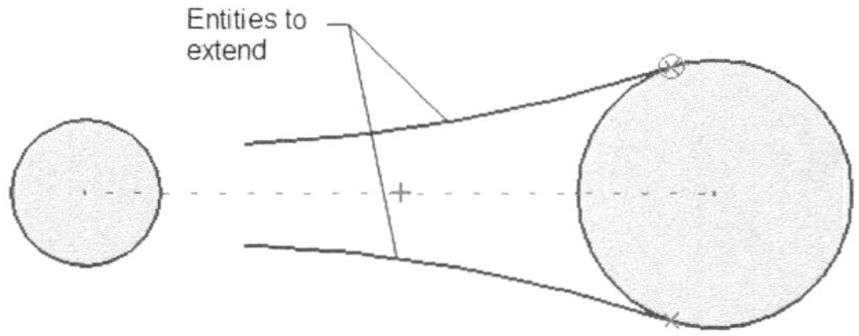

Figure 4-3 Entities to be extended

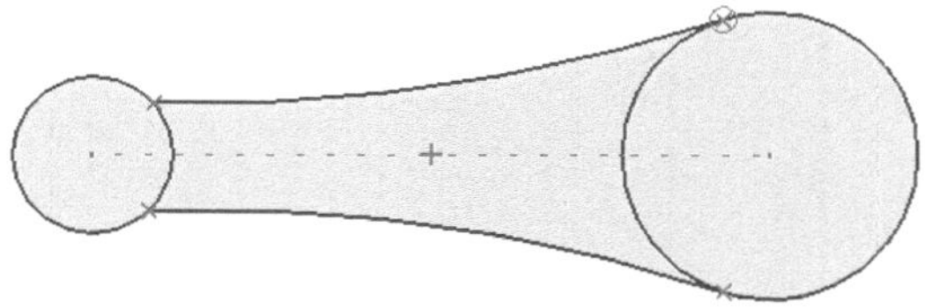

Figure 4-4 Sketch after extending the entities

Trimming/Extending Entities to a Corner

Ribbon:	Home > Draw > Trim Corner

The **Trim Corner** tool is used to trim or extend any two open sketched entities such that they result in a corner. Note that you can select only open entities to create a corner trim. To create a corner trim, invoke this tool and then select two open entities; the selected open entities will be extended or trimmed to create a corner, as shown in Figures 4-5 and 4-6.

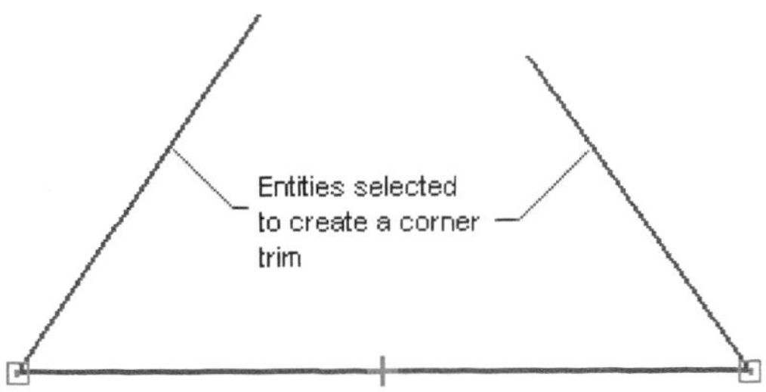

Figure 4-5 Entities selected to create a corner trim

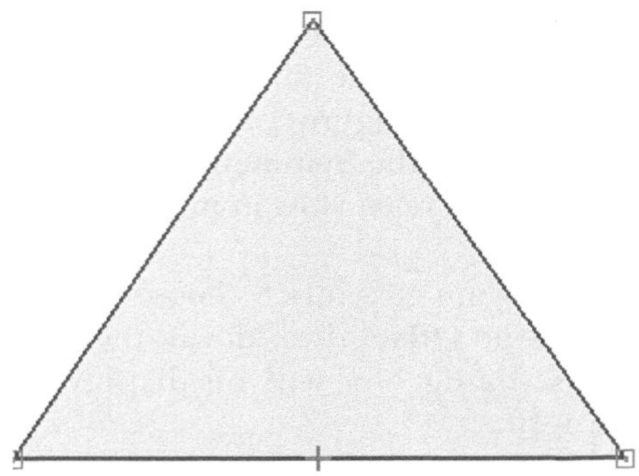

Figure 4-6 Sketch after creating the corner trim

Creating Offset Copies

Ribbon:	Home > Draw > Offset drop-down > Offset

You can create the offset copies of a selected sketched entity or a chain of entities using the **Offset** tool. To create the offset copy of an entity, invoke the **Offset** tool from the **Offset** drop-down, refer to Figure 4-7; the **Offset** Command bar will be displayed with the **Select Step** button chosen by default. Also, you will be prompted to click on the element whose offset copies you want to create. Depending on whether you want to offset a single entity or a chain of entities, select the option from the **Select** drop-down list in the Command bar. Specify the offset distance by entering a value in the **Distance** edit box. After selecting the entity or the chain of entities, choose the **Accept** button or the **Side Step** button; you will be prompted to click to place the offset element(s). Click outside or inside the original entity; the offset entity will be placed accordingly. After placing the offset entity, you will again be prompted to click to place the offset entity. Continue clicking until the required numbers of offsets have been created and then press the ESC key to exit the command. Figure 4-8 shows multiple offset triangles created by offsetting the outer triangle.

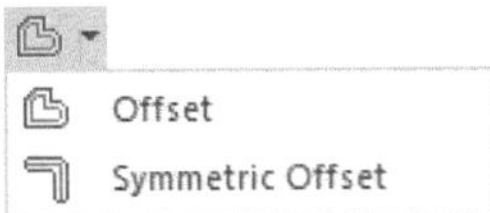

Figure 4-7 *The **Offset** drop-down*

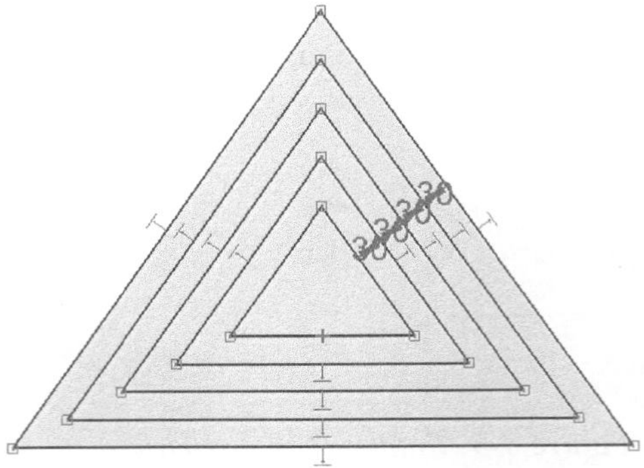

Figure 4-8 *Multiple offset triangles created by offsetting the outer triangle*

Creating Symmetric Offset Copies

Ribbon: Home > Draw > Offset drop-down > Symmetric Offset

You can create a symmetric offset on both sides of the open sketched entities or closed loops by using the **Symmetric Offset** tool. An open sketched entity can be a center line about which you can create a symmetric offset. Figure 4-9 shows a slot created from a centerline using the **Symmetric Offset** tool. This tool is widely used to create slots in models.

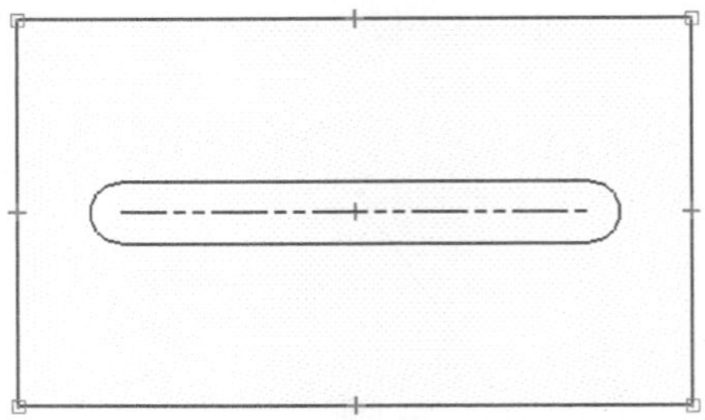

Figure 4-9 *A slot created using the **Symmetric Offset** tool*

To create a symmetric offset, choose the **Symmetric Offset** tool from the **Offset** drop-down; the **Symmetric Offset Options** dialog box will be displayed, as shown in Figure 4-10.

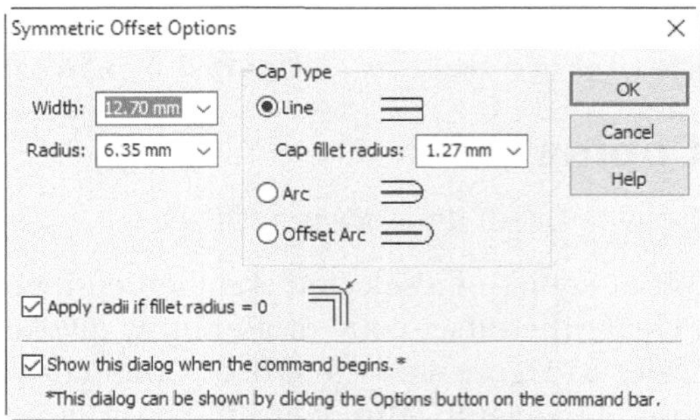

Figure 4-10 *The **Symmetric Offset Options** dialog box*

The options in this dialog box are discussed next.

Width

The **Width** edit box is used to set the width of the slot that will be created by the **Symmetric Offset** tool. You can enter a new value in this edit box or select a preset value from the drop-down list.

Radius

If the selected entities have bends, which result in sharp corners, then this edit box will define the radius of the arc inside the resulting slot. Figure 4-11 shows the slots with different radius values. If you do not want to apply arcs at bends, enter **0** in this edit box.

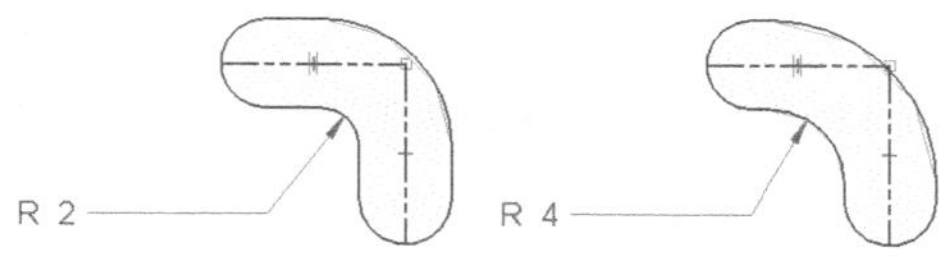

Figure 4-11 *Slots with different fillet radii*

Cap Type Area

This area provides the options to specify the cap type at the end of the slots. These options are discussed next.

Line

This radio button is selected to place a line at the end of the slot. You can define a fillet at the sharp corners of the resulting slot by entering its radius in the **Cap fillet radius** edit box provided below this radio button. Figure 4-12 shows a line cap without a fillet and Figure 4-13 shows a line cap with a fillet.

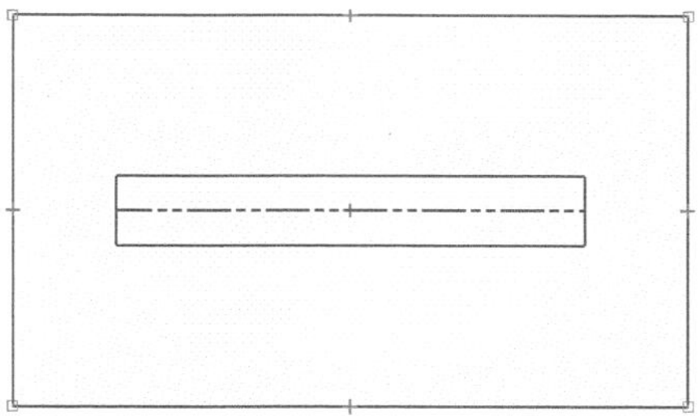

Figure 4-12 *Line cap without fillet*

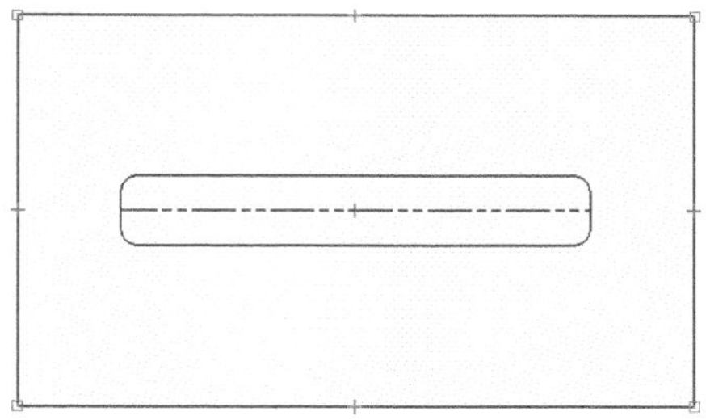

Figure 4-13 *Line cap with a fillet*

Arc

This radio button is used to place an arc at the end of the slot. The endpoint of the entity, that is used to create a symmetric offset, will lie on one of the quadrants of the cap created. The radius of the arc will be half the width of the arc.

Offset Arc

This radio button is selected to place an offset arc at the end of the slot. Remember that the two ends of the arc will be in line with the endpoint of the entity that is used to create the symmetric offset. The radius of the arc will be equal to half of the width value.

Apply radii if fillet radius = 0

This check box is selected to create an arc at the outer corner of the resulting slot if the **0** value is entered in the **Radius** edit box. The radius of the arc will be equal to the value of the width specified in the **Width** edit box.

Show this dialog when the command begins

This check box is selected to display the **Symmetric Offset Options** dialog box whenever you invoke the **Symmetric Offset** tool. After setting the parameters in the **Symmetric Offset Options** dialog box, choose **OK**; you will be prompted to click on the elements to offset. You can select a single entity or a chain of entities by selecting the required option from the **Select** drop-down list. Choose the **Accept** button after selecting the entities; the symmetric offset based on the defined parameters will be created.

Moving/Copying the Sketched Entities

Ribbon: Draw > Move drop-down > Move

The **Move** tool is used to move the selected sketched entities in the drawing window. To move an entity, choose the **Move** tool from the **Move** drop-down in the **Draw** group of the **Home** tab, as shown in Figure 4-14; the **Move** Command bar will be displayed and you will be prompted to click on the element(s) to be modified. You can select single or multiple elements. Select the entities to be moved; you will be prompted to click for the point to move from. This is the base point where you will hold the entities to be moved. This point can be any keypoint in the sketch or any arbitrary point in the drawing window.

Specify the base point; you will be prompted to click for specifying the point to move the elements to. This is the point where the base point will be moved. Specify this point by entering its X and Y coordinates in the Command bar or by specifying a point in the drawing window. If you are specifying the point in the drawing window, you can enter the step value in the **Step** edit box of the Command bar. The step value defines the distance by which the cursor jumps while moving on the screen. Figure 4-15 shows a sketch being moved from its original location.

Figure 4-14 *The **Move** drop-down*

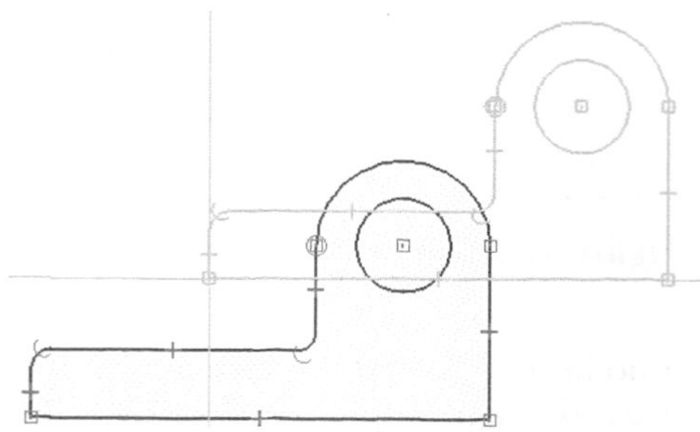

Figure 4-15 *Moving a sketch from its original location*

By default, the **Copy** button is not chosen in the Command bar and therefore the entities are only moved and not copied. If you want a copy of the selected entities to be created while moving them, choose the **Copy** button; the original entities will remain at their original location and a copy of the selected entities will move to the new location.

Rotating the Sketched Entities

Ribbon: Draw > Move drop-down > Rotate

You can rotate the selected sketched entities around a specified center point by using the **Rotate** tool. On invoking this tool, the **Rotate** Command bar will be displayed and you will be prompted to click on the element(s) to modify. Select the entities to be rotated by dragging a box around them; you will be prompted to click at the center of rotation. Select a point in the sketch or in the drawing window around which the selected entities will be rotated; you will be prompted to click on the point to rotate from. This point will define the position angle that will be taken as the base angle to rotate the selected entities. You can specify a point in the drawing window to define the position angle or enter the value of this angle directly in the **Position Angle** edit box of the Command bar.

After defining the position angle, you will be prompted to click on the point to be rotated. Move the cursor in the drawing window; you will notice that the preview of the rotated entities is attached to the cursor. Specify a point in the drawing window to define the rotation angle or enter the value of this angle directly in the **Angle** edit box. If you enter the value in the Command bar, you will be prompted to click on the side of the reference line to place the rotated object(s). You can place the rotated entities in a clockwise or a counterclockwise direction by specifying the point. Figure 4-16 shows a sketch being rotated.

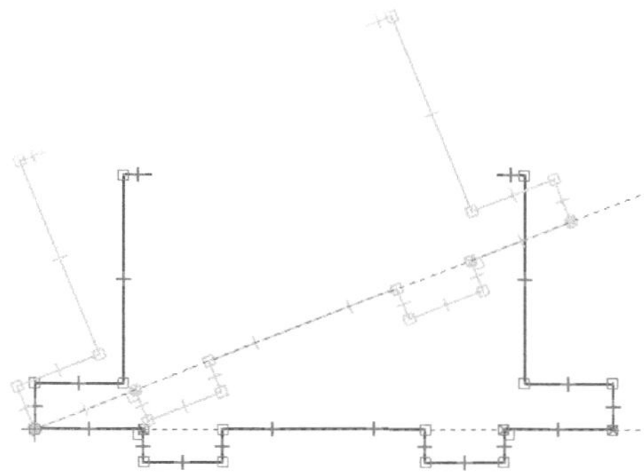

Figure 4-16 *Preview of the sketch being rotated*

> **Tip**
> *You can also create a copy of the selected sketched entities dynamically in the drawing window. To do so, select the entities and then press and hold the CTRL key. Next, drag the cursor; a copy of the selected entities will be placed at the point where you release the left mouse button.*

By default, when you rotate the selected entities, their copy is created. This is because the **Copy** button is chosen by default in the Command bar. You can deactivate this button, if you do not want to create a copy of the rotated entities. You can specify the step value by which the cursor will jump to rotate the sketch using the **Step** edit box in the Command bar.

Mirroring the Sketched Entities

Ribbon:	Draw > Mirror drop-down > Mirror

The **Mirror** tool is used to create a mirrored copy of the selected sketched entities. To mirror the sketched entities, invoke the **Mirror** tool from the **Mirror** drop-down, as shown in Figure 4-17; the **Mirror** Command bar will be displayed and you will be prompted to click on the element(s) to modify. You can select multiple entities to be mirrored by dragging a box around them. On selecting the entities, you will be prompted to click for the first point of the mirror line. You can select an existing line segment to be used as the mirror line or specify a point in the drawing window to define the first point of the mirror line. Next, you will be prompted to click for the second point of the mirror line. Move the cursor to draw a reference line. Place the cursor at the required location and specify the endpoint of

Figure 4-17 *The* ***Mirror*** *drop-down*

the mirror line. You can also specify the angle of the mirror line by entering its value in the **Angle** edit box in the Command bar.

Once you define the mirror line, the mirrored entities will be created and highlighted. Also, you will again be prompted to specify the first point of the mirror line. This allows you to create another mirrored copy of the highlighted entities. This process continues until you terminate the current sequence by right-clicking or exit the tool by pressing the ESC key. Figure 4-18 shows the entities selected for mirroring and Figure 4-19 shows the sketch after mirroring the entities. Note that the entities are mirrored by defining a vertical line passing through the endpoint of the extreme left horizontal line.

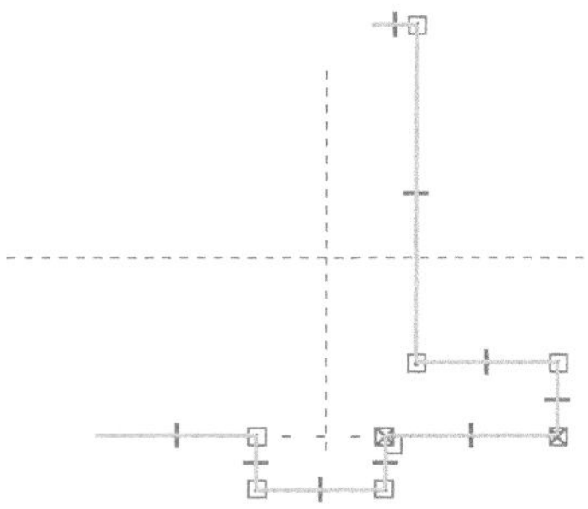

Figure 4-18 *Entities selected for mirroring*

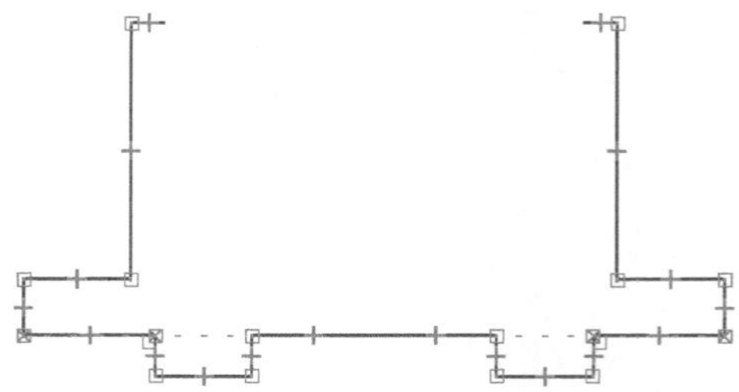

Figure 4-19 *Resultant mirrored sketch*

When you mirror the entities, a mirrored copy of the selected entities is created and the original entities are also retained. This is because the **Copy** button is chosen by default in the Command bar. If this button is not chosen, the original entities are deleted after the mirrored copy is created.

Scaling the Sketched Entities

Ribbon: Draw > Mirror drop-down > Scale

The **Scale** tool is used to modify the size of a sketch maintaining its aspect ratio. You can also create a copy of the scaled sketch using this tool. To scale the sketched entities, invoke this tool; you will be prompted to click on the element(s) to modify. Select the entities that you want to scale by dragging a box around them; you will be prompted to click for the scale center point. Click to specify the scale center; you will be prompted to click for the new scale. The scale center point is the base point that will be used for scaling entities. You can move the cursor on the screen to scale the entities or enter the scale factor in the **Scale Factor** edit box in the Command bar.

The **Reference Length** edit box in the Command bar is used to set the relationship between the distance moved by the cursor and the scale factor. For example, if the value in the **Reference Length** edit box is entered as **50**, the scale factor will be 1 on moving the cursor 50 units away from the scale center point. Similarly, when the cursor is moved 75 units away from the scale center point, the scale factor will become 1.5. To create a copy of the selected entities while scaling, choose the **Copy** button from the Command bar. Figure 4-20 shows a sketch being scaled.

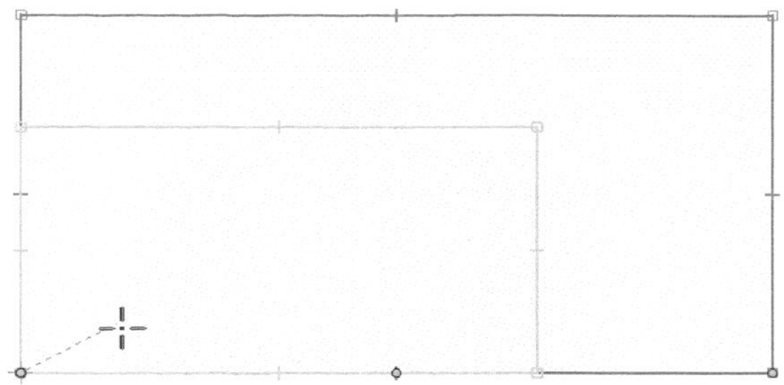

Figure 4-20 Preview of the sketch being scaled

Stretching the Sketched Entities

Ribbon: Draw > Mirror drop-down > Stretch

The **Stretch** tool is used to stretch objects thereby modifying the selected portions of the objects. This command can be used to lengthen or shorten the objects and alter their shapes. On invoking this tool, the **Stretch** Command bar will be displayed and you will be prompted to specify the first point of the fence. In Solid Edge, the entities that you need to stretch are selected by defining a box around them. This box is termed as fence. Specify the first corner of the fence. Next, move the cursor and specify the diagonally opposite corners of the fence. By defining the fence, you are selecting objects and specifying the portions of those selected objects to be stretched. After defining the fence, you will be prompted to click for the point to move from. Specify the base point from where you will hold the entities to be stretched; you will be prompted to click for the point to move to. Move the cursor to specify the point in the drawing window; the entities will be stretched. Figure 4-21 shows a fence defined to select the entities to be stretched. This figure also shows the entities being stretched.

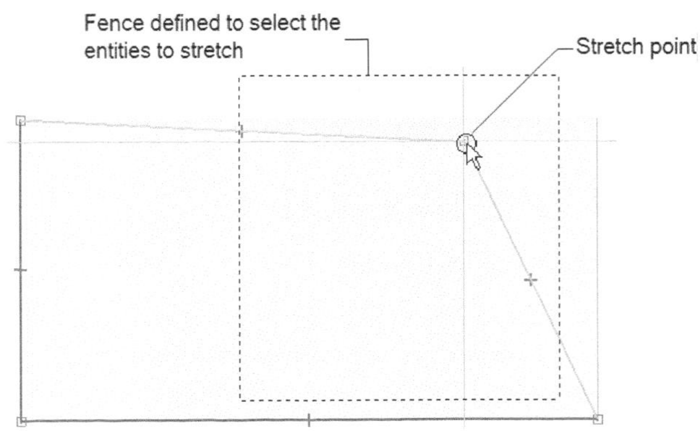

Figure 4-21 Preview of the sketch being stretched

Editing the Sketched Entities by Dragging

You can also edit the sketched entities by dragging them. The object will be moved or stretched depending on the type of entity selected, and the point of selection. For example, if you select a line at any point other than the endpoints, it will be moved. If you select it at an endpoint, it will be stretched. Similarly, if you select an arc at its circumference, it will be moved. But if you select the arc at a keypoint, it will be stretched. Therefore, editing the sketched entities by dragging is entirely based on their selection points. Note that while editing the sketched entities using the keypoints, all related entities will also be moved or stretched. The following table gives you the details of the operation that will be performed when you drag various objects:

Object	Selection point	Operation
Circle	On circumference/center point	Move
	Keypoint on circumference	Stretch+Move
Arc	On circumference	Move
	Keypoints	Stretch
Line	Anywhere other than the Endpoints	Move
	Endpoints	Stretch
Curve	Any point other than the keypoints	Move
	Keypoints	Stretch
Rectangle	Any one line or any endpoint	Stretch
Ellipse	Center point or anywhere other than the keypoints	Move
	Keypoints other than the center point	Stretch

WRITING TEXT IN THE SKETCH

Ribbon: Sketching > Insert > Text Profile

In Solid Edge, you can write text in the Sketching environment and use it to create features at a later stage. Based on the option selected to place the text, you can write a straight line text or a text along a curve. To write a text, choose the **Text Profile** tool from the **Insert** group of the **Sketching** tab; the **Text** dialog box will be displayed, as shown in Figure 4-22. The **Text Profile** tool works in two steps: the **Text** step and the **Location** step. When you invoke this tool, the **Text** step is activated.

You can set the font, size, alignment, spacing, and other formatting options of the text using the options available in this dialog box. You can also set the smoothing of the text by using the vertical slider given on the right of this dialog box. To write text in the second line, press ENTER; the cursor will move to the second line. After entering the required text in this line, choose OK; the **Location Step** will be invoked and the text will be attached to the cursor. If a curve exists in the drawing, move the cursor close to it; the preview of the text placed along the curve will be displayed, depending upon the option chosen in the **Anchor** flyout. This flyout is displayed on choosing the **Anchor** button from the Command bar. You can use this option to position the text properly. Alternatively, you can press the T key on the keyboard to toggle the orientation of the text. Figure 4-23 shows a text written along a circle.

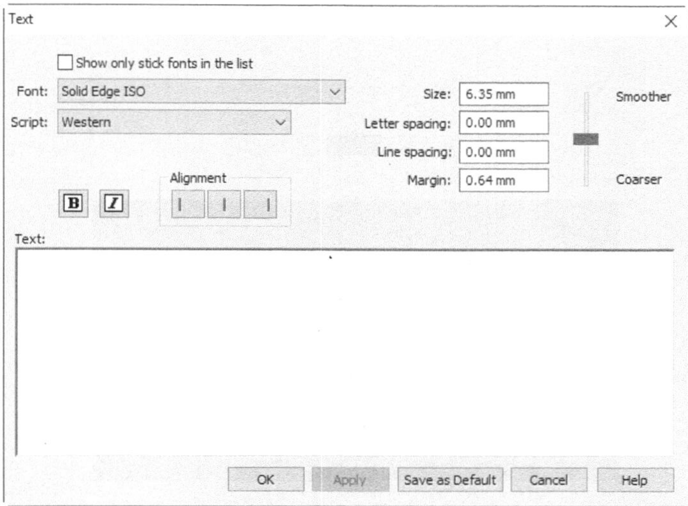

Figure 4-22 *The* ***Text*** *dialog box*

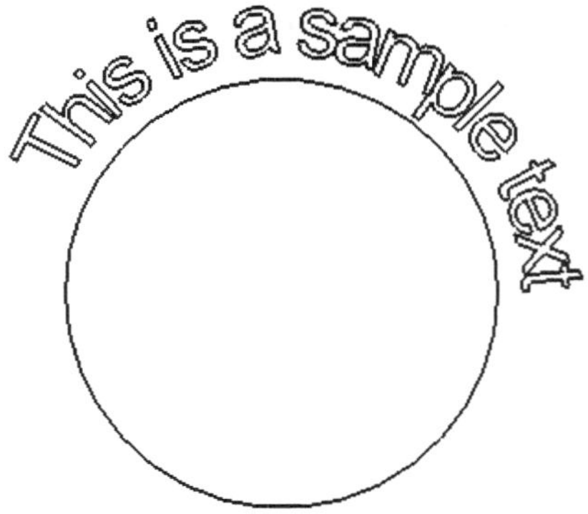

Figure 4-23 *Text written along a circle*

Note

It may be possible that the text displayed in the drawing area is not oriented properly. To get the correct orientation of the text, you need to reorient the plane as required.

INSERTING IMAGES INTO SKETCHES

Ribbon: Sketching > Insert > Image

In Solid Edge, you can insert external images into a sketch and then use them as a label on the model. The images that can be inserted are bitmap image (*.bmp*), png image (*.png*), jpeg image (*.jpg*), or tiff image (*.tif*). To insert an image, invoke the **Image** tool from the

Insert group of the **Sketching** tab; the **Insert Image** dialog box will be displayed, as shown in Figure 4-24. The options in this dialog box are discussed next.

*Figure 4-24 The **Insert Image** dialog box*

General Tab

The options in the **General** tab are discussed next.

Browse

To select an image, choose the **Browse** button; the **Open a File** dialog box will be displayed. Browse to the image file that you want to insert using this dialog box. After selecting the file, choose **Open** from the dialog box. You will return to the **Insert Image** dialog box and the image will be displayed in the preview window.

Link to file

Select the **Link to file** check box to create a link between the selected file and the image inserted in Solid Edge. As a result, if the original image file is changed, the image in Solid Edge can be updated to view the changes.

Use transparent color

This check box will be available only when you select the image to be inserted. When you select this check box, the **Pick Color** button will be enabled and you can choose it to set the transparency color for the image.

Opacity

You can set the opacity of the image using the **Opacity** slider bar.

Border Tab

The options in the **Border** tab of the **Insert Image** dialog box are used to specify the color, width, and linetype of the border for a selected image. After selecting the image and setting the parameters, choose **OK**; the dialog box will be closed and the cursor with aligned lines will be displayed in the drawing window. Now, click anywhere in the drawing window to place the selected image. You can relocate the image by selecting its edges. Also, the **Modify** Command bar is displayed along with the options to modify the properties and position of the image. To resize the image, you can use the handles at the four corners. Figure 4-25 shows an image placed in the graphics window of Solid Edge.

Figure 4-25 *Image inserted in the Sketching environment*

CONVERTING SKETCHES INTO BASE FEATURES

As mentioned in the earlier chapters, most of the designs are a combination of sketched, placed, and reference features. So far, you have learned how to draw sketches and add relationships and dimensions to them. After drawing and dimensioning a sketch, you need to convert it into the base feature.

You can create features dynamically in the **Synchronous Part** environment by selecting a sketch. In addition, Solid Edge provides you with a number of tools such as **Extrude**, **Revolve**, and so on to convert sketches into base features. In this chapter, you will learn how to use the **Select** tool and create the extruded and revolved features. The remaining tools will be discussed in the later chapters. The methods of converting a sketch into the base feature are discussed next.

Creating Base Features in the Synchronous Part Environment

When you select area of the closed sketch, a handle is displayed on the sketch and also the **QuickBar** is displayed in the graphics area. The **QuickBar** has all possible tools and their options to convert a sketch into a feature. Note that the options available in the **QuickBar** depend upon the tool chosen. Figure 4-26 shows the **QuickBar** which is displayed after selecting the base sketch. You can choose the **Extrude** or **Revolve** tool from the **QuickBar**. On doing so, you will notice that all the options related to the tool are available in the **QuickBar**.

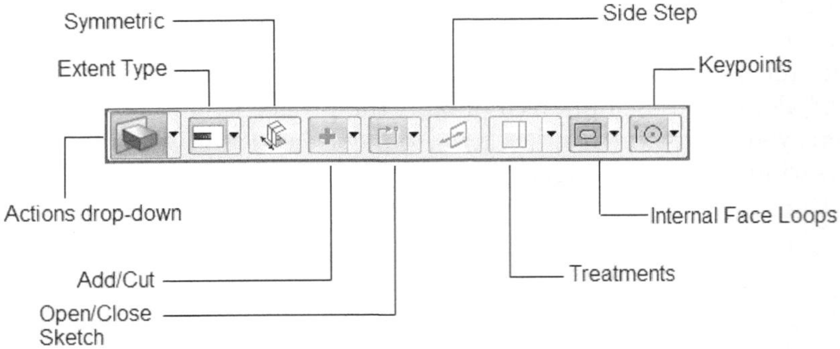

Figure 4-26 The options available in the QuickBar

The tools available in the **QuickBar** are discussed next.

Extrude

The **Extrude** tool is chosen by default in the **QuickBar** and is used to add the material normal to the area defined by a sketch region.

Revolve

This tool is used to create circular features by revolving a sketch about an axis. You can create a revolved feature by choosing this tool from the **Actions** drop-down in the **QuickBar**.

The options related to the **Extrude** and **Revolve** tools are discussed next.

Add/Cut

This drop-down is used to add or cut material. If you are creating the base feature, only the **Add** option will be available because there will be no existing feature from which you can remove material.

Extent Type

The options in this drop-down are used to specify the depth of the resulting extruded feature and are discussed next.

Finite

This option is selected by default and is used to specify the depth of an extruded feature by entering a value in the dynamic edit box displayed on the preview of an extruded feature.

From-To

This option is used to create a protrusion feature by extruding a sketch from a selected plane to another selected plane. When you select this option, the **"From"** surface is automatically set to the sketch plane. The **"From"** surface can be redefined by dragging the origin of the extrude handle to another face or plane. After selecting the **"From"** surface, you will be prompted to specify the "**To**" surface. Select a planar face up to which you want the feature to be extruded.

Symmetric

The **Symmetric** button is used to extrude a profile symmetrically on both the sides of the plane on which the profile is created.

Treatments

This drop-down list is used to apply the draft or the crown treatment to the extrusion feature. The options in this drop-down will be discussed in later chapters.

Internal Face Loops

This drop-down list is used while extruding a sketch which has internal loops in it. There are three options in this drop-down list: **Include Internal Loops**, **Exclude Internal Loops**, and **Use Only Internal Loops**. By default, the **Include Internal Loops** option is selected. Figure 4-27 through 4-29 show the application of these options.

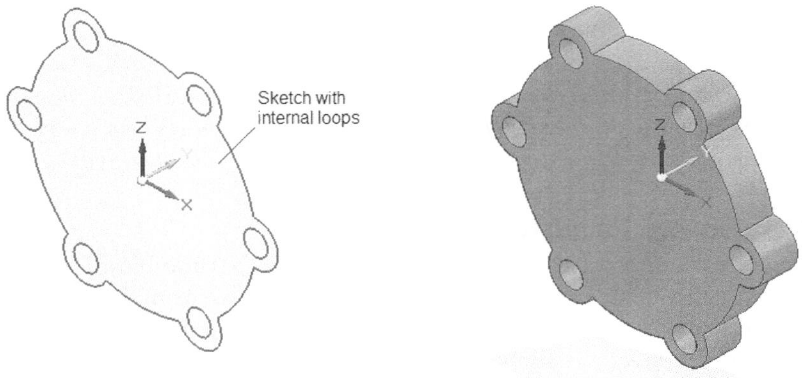

*Figure 4-27 Sketch extruded with the **Include Internal Loops** option selected*

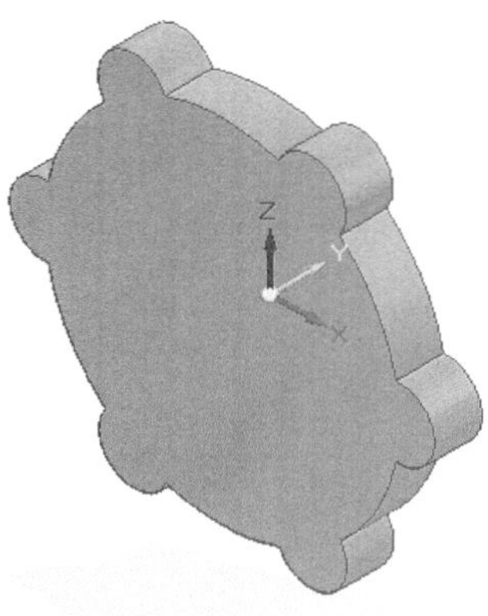

*Figure 4-28 Sketch extruded with the **Exclude Internal Loops** option selected*

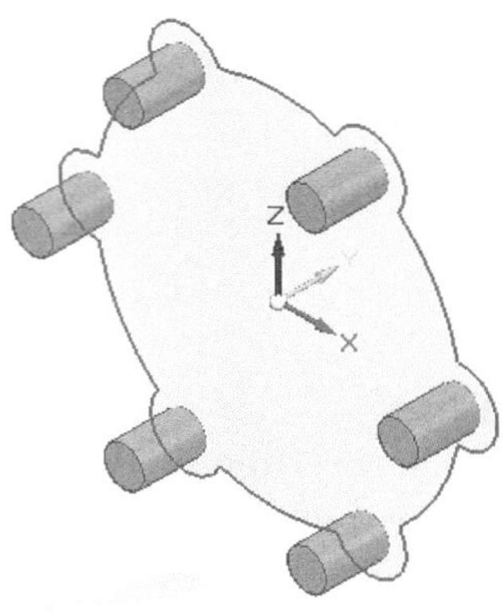

*Figure 4-29 Sketch extruded with the **Use Only Internal Loops** option selected*

Keypoints

This option is used to set the type of keypoint snap for defining extrusion. You can define the depth of the extrusion by specifying a keypoint on the other existing entity.

Creating Extruded Features

When you select a closed sketch, an Extrude handle and a **QuickBar** are displayed, refer to Figure 4-30. To create the extruded features, click on the Extrude handle and move the cursor in the direction in which you want to add the material, the preview of the feature will be displayed in the drawing window. You can set the value of extrusion either dynamically by dragging the cursor or by entering a value in the edit box that will be displayed when you click on the handle. You can also set the symmetry, draft, and crown parameters in the **QuickBar.**

Alternatively, you can create an extruded feature by using the **Extrude** tool from the **Solids** group of the **Home** tab.

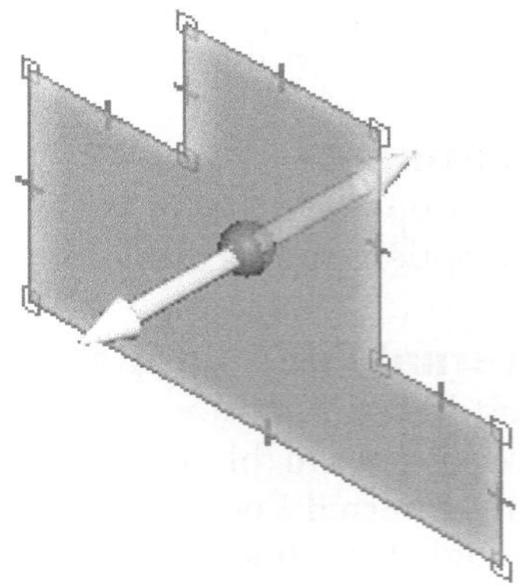

Figure 4-30 *The Extrude handle*

Note

When a sketch is converted into a feature, you will notice that the sketch is moved to the ***Used Sketches*** *node of the* ***PathFinder****. If you want to reuse the sketch, click on the + sign adjacent to the* ***Used Sketches*** *node; the* ***sketch*** *node will displayed. Right-click on it and then choose the* ***Restore*** *option from the shortcut menu displayed; the sketch will become available on the screen.*

Creating Revolved Features

As mentioned earlier, on selecting a closed sketch, an Extrude handle and a **QuickBar** will be displayed. To create revolved features, choose **Revolve** from the **Actions** drop-down in the **QuickBar**; the options in the **QuickBar** will change, refer to Figure 4-31. Also, the revolve handle will be displayed, as shown in Figure 4-32. Drag the origin knob of this handle and align it with the revolution axis. Next, you can set the angle of revolution dynamically by clicking and dragging the torus of the handle, or by entering the required value in the edit box that will be displayed at the handle. In order to revolve the sketch symmetrically, choose the **Symmetric** button from the **QuickBar**. The options in this **QuickBar** are discussed next.

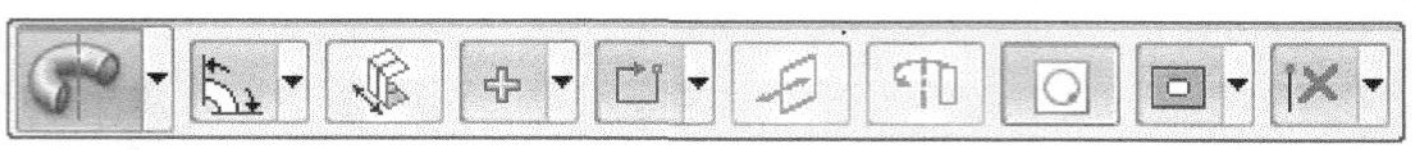

Figure 4-31 *The* ***Revolve QuickBar***

Extent Type

The options in this drop-down are used to specify the depth of the resulting revolved feature and are discussed next.

Finite

The **Finite** option is used to revolve the profile to a specified angle. To do so, enter the angle in the dynamic edit box displayed on the graphics window. This option is chosen by default.

360°

This button is used to revolve the profile to 360 degrees, refer to Figure 4-33.

Note that while creating the revolve feature, the **Create Live Section** button is activated by default in the **Revolve QuickBar**. Therefore, the live sections are automatically created and collected in the **Live Sections** collector of the **PathFinder**. You will learn more about **Live Sections** in the later chapters.

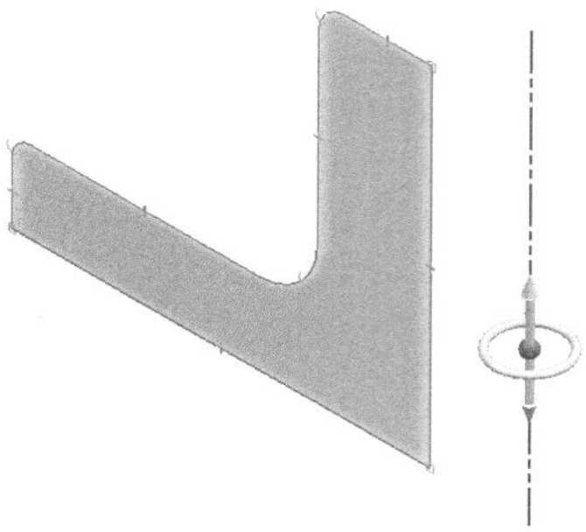

Figure 4-32 The Revolve handle

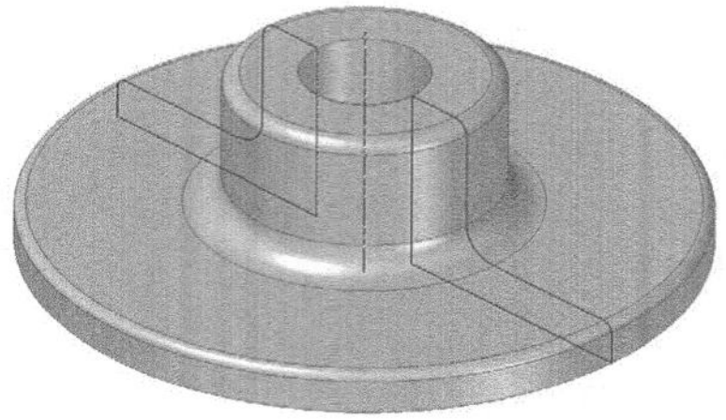

Figure 4-33 Profile revolved to 360 degrees

Note

*Since the axis element gets separated from the sketch elements, the axis element does not move to the **Used Sketches** list in the **PathFinder**.*

CREATING PRIMITIVE FEATURES (SYNCHRONOUS ENVIRONMENT)

In the **Synchronous Part** environment, you can create 3D primitive features without creating the sketches. To do so, choose the desired tool from the **Box** drop-down in the **Solids** group of the **Home** tab. The tools in the **Box** drop-down are discussed next.

Creating a Box Feature

Ribbon: Home > Solids > Box drop-down > Box

The **Box** tool is used to create a box feature in the **Synchronous Part** environment. When you invoke the **Box** tool, the **Box** Command bar will be displayed and you will be prompted to specify the first point. Specify the first point by clicking on the desired plane; you will notice that a rubber line gets attached to the cursor and you are prompted to specify the second point. Specify the second point; you will be prompted to specify the third point to create the rectangle. Click to specify the third point. After specifying the third point, you need to specify the depth of the rectangle. You can specify the depth by moving the cursor dynamically or entering the value in the dynamic edit box. After specifying the depth, the box will be created. Note that the above procedure is followed when the **by 3 point** option is selected in the **Selection Type** drop-down list in the **Box** Command bar for creating the rectangle. You can also select the **by center** or **by 2 point** option from this drop-down list. The method of creating a rectangle for box is same as discussed in Chapter 2.

Creating a Cylinder Feature

Ribbon: Home > Solids > Box drop-down > Cylinder

The **Cylinder** tool is used to create a cylinder feature in the **Synchronous Part** environment. When you invoke the **Cylinder** tool, the **Cylinder** Command bar will be displayed and you will be prompted to specify the center point of the circle. Specify the center point by clicking on the desired plane; you will be prompted to specify a point to define the radius or the diameter of the circle. You can also specify the radius or diameter in their respective dynamic edit boxes available in the drawing area. After specifying the radius or diameter, you need to define the depth of the circle to make the cylinder. You can specify the depth by moving the cursor dynamically or entering the value in the dynamic edit box. After specifying the depth, the cylinder will be created.

Creating a Sphere Feature

Ribbon: Home > Solids > Box drop-down > Sphere

The **Sphere** tool is used to create a sphere without creating the sketch. When you invoke the **Sphere** tool, the **Sphere** Command bar will be displayed and you will be prompted to specify the center point of the sphere. Specify the center point by clicking on the desired plane; you will be prompted to specify a point to define the radius of the sphere. After specifying the radius by clicking or entering the value in the dynamic edit box, the sphere will be created.

CREATING ORDERED FEATURES

In the **Ordered Part** environment, you can create profile-based features by following a step by step procedure. First, you need to switch to the **Ordered Part** environment. To do so, select the **Ordered** radio button in the **Model** group of the **Tools** tab in the **Ribbon.**

Creating Extruded Features

To create an extrude feature, choose the **Extrude** tool from the **Solids** group in the **Home** tab; the **Extrude** Command bar will be displayed, as shown in Figure 4-34. You need to specify the parameters in different steps in this Command bar to create an extrude feature.

***Figure 4-34** The **Extrude** Command bar*

The steps to create an extruded feature are given next.

Sketch Step

This step becomes active whenever you invoke the **Extrude** tool. In this step, you select the plane to draw a profile. You can also select an existing sketch by selecting the **Select from Sketch** option from the **Create-From Options** drop-down list, which is available in the Command bar in this step.

Draw Profile Step
This step allows you to draw the profile of the base feature. This step is automatically invoked when you select a plane to draw the profile.

Extent Step
This step allows you to define the extents of the resulting extrusion feature by specifying its depth.

Side Step
This step will get activated when you try to extrude an open sketch. You will learn more about this step in the next chapter.

Treatment Step
This step allows you to define the draft angle or the crown treatment for the extrude feature.

Creating Revolved Features
To create a revolved feature, choose the **Revolve** tool from the **Solids** group in the **Home** tab; the **Revolve** Command bar will be displayed. The **Revolve** Command bar has four steps: **Sketch Step**, **Draw Profile Step**, **Side Step**, and **Extent Step**, refer to Figure 4-35. These steps are discussed next.

*Figure 4-35 The **Revolve** Command bar*

Sketch Step
In this step, you need to select the plane to draw a profile. You can also select an existing sketch by selecting the **Select from Sketch** option from the **Create-From Options** drop-down list which will be available in the Command bar in this step.

Draw Profile Step
This step allows you to draw the profile of the revolved feature. Remember that while drawing the profile of the revolved feature, you also need to specify the axis about which the profile will be revolved. To specify the axis of revolution, choose the **Axis of Revolution** tool from the **Draw** group in the **Home** tab of the **Ribbon** and select an entity from the drawing area.

Extent Step
The **Extent Step** is automatically invoked when you exit the Sketching environment. This step is used to specify parameters such as angle of revolution and extent type (symmetric and non-symmetric).

ROTATING THE VIEW OF A MODEL IN 3D SPACE

Ribbon:	View > Orient > Rotate
Status Bar:	Rotate

Solid Edge provides you with an option to rotate the view of a solid model freely in three-dimensional (3D) space. This makes it possible for you to visually maneuver around the solid model and view it from any direction. To rotate the view of a model, choose the **Rotate** tool from the status bar; a 3D indicator with three axes and the origin will be displayed at the center of the current view. Also, the **Rotate** Command bar will be displayed. The three axes of the 3D indicator represent the positive X, Y, and Z axes. This indicator allows you to rotate the view freely in 3D space or around any of these three axes.

To rotate the view freely around the center of the current view, left-click once on the center of the 3D indicator and then press and hold the left mouse button and drag the cursor; the view of the model will be rotated and you can visually maneuver around it. You can also freely rotate the view around a vertex in the model by simply selecting the vertex. The 3D indicator will be relocated such that its origin will then lie at the selected vertex.

You can rotate the view around one of the axes of the 3D indicator or around an edge in the model. To do so, invoke the **Rotate** tool and select the edge or the axis. Press and hold the left mouse button and drag the cursor; the view will rotate around the selected edge or axis. After rotating the view, right-click to exit the **Rotate** tool.

RESTORING STANDARD VIEWS

Once you have rotated the views of a model using the **Rotate** tool, you can restore the standard views to view the model from the standard orientations. To restore the standard views, choose the **View Orientation** tool from the status bar; a flyout will be displayed with the standard views, as shown in Figure 4-36. You can select any standard view from this flyout.

You can also save a view other than the standard views. To do so, keep the model in a view other than the standard views and choose the **Save Current View** option from the **View Orientation** flyout; the **New Named View** dialog box will be displayed, as shown in Figure 4-37. Enter the name of the view in the **New view name** edit box. Enter the description of the view in the **Description** edit box. The name that you will enter in the **New view name** edit box will be displayed in the **View Orientation** flyout.

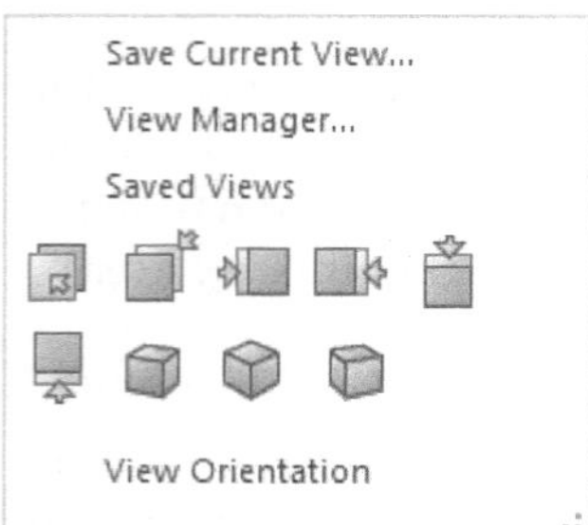

*Figure 4-36 The **View Orientation** flyout*

*Figure 4-37 The **New Named View** dialog box*

You can manage the number of views that are default and additionally saved. To do so, choose the **View Manager** option from the **View Orientation** flyout in the **Status Bar**; the **Named Views** dialog box will be displayed, as shown in Figure 4-38. By using the options in this dialog box, you can apply new views, redefine the views and delete the views.

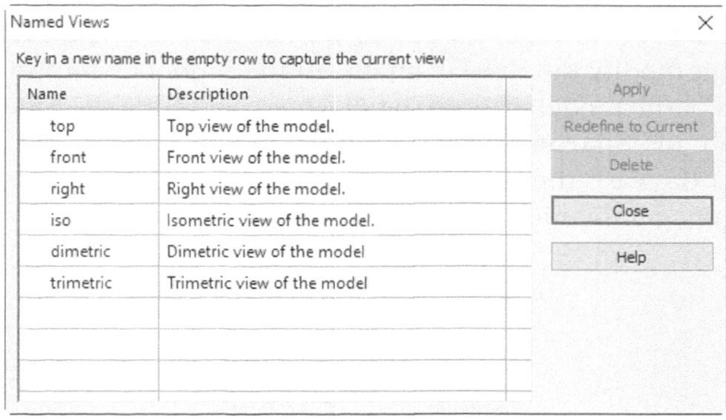

*Figure 4-38 The **Named Views** dialog box*

SETTING THE DISPLAY MODES

You can set the display modes for the solid models using the tools provided in the **Style** group of the **View** tab. Alternatively, you can choose the **View Styles** tool from the status bar to set the display modes. The display modes that can be set for the solid models are discussed next.

Shaded with Visible Edges

In this mode, the models are displayed shaded along with all visible edges in them. As the display is set to shaded, the model will be assigned a material and will behave as a solid model with an opaque material assigned to it.

Shaded

In the **Shaded** display mode, the models are displayed shaded without highlighting any edge of the model.

Visible and Hidden Edges

In this display mode, all visible and hidden edges are displayed in the model. The visible edges are displayed in black and the hidden edges are displayed in gray. You can view the entities placed behind the model in this display mode.

Visible Edges

In this display mode, only the visible edges are displayed in the model. You cannot view the hidden edges.

Wire Frame

In this display mode, all the edges are displayed as continuous lines in the model.

Floor Shadow

This tool is chosen to display the shadow of the solid model. The shadow will be displayed below the model.

IMPROVING THE DISPLAY QUALITY OF A MODEL

In Solid Edge, you can modify the display quality of the model by improving its sharpness. To modify the sharpness of the model, choose the down arrow beside the **Sharpen** tool in the **Style** group of the **View** tab; the **Sharpness Set** cascading menu will be displayed. Next, choose the required option from the cascading menu to improve the display quality of the model. Note that the sharper the image, the more time it will take to regenerate.

TUTORIALS

Tutorial 1 Synchronous

In this tutorial, you will create the model shown in Figure 4-39. Its dimensions are given in the drawing views shown in Figure 4-40. **(Expected time: 30 min)**

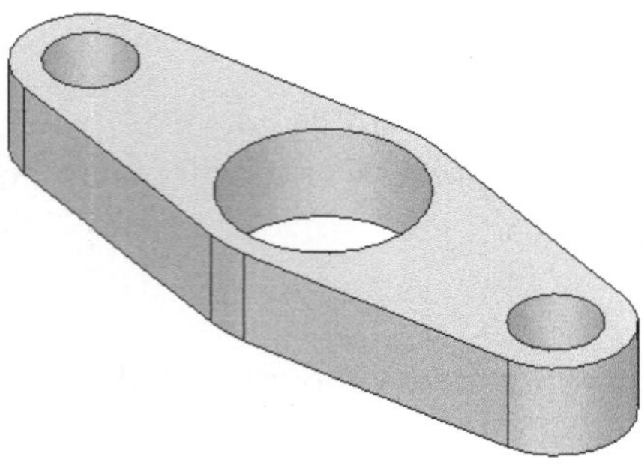

Figure 4-39 *Model for Tutorial 1*

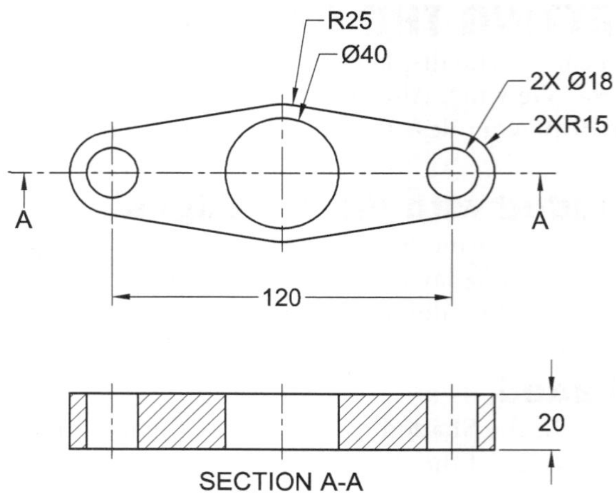

Figure 4-40 *Top and sectioned front views displaying the dimensions of the model*

The following steps are required to complete this tutorial:

a. Start a new part file and then draw the profile of the outer loop, refer to Figures 4-41 and 4-42.
b. Add the required dimensions and relationships to the profile, refer to Figure 4-43.
c. Draw the inner circles and add the required dimensions to them, refer to Figure 4-44.
d. Select the sketch and create the extruded feature, refer to Figure 4-45.
e. Increase the sharpness of the model and rotate the view in 3D space.
f. Save the file and close it.

Drawing the Sketch with Dimensions and Relationships

The sketch of this model can be created by invoking a sketching tool and then selecting a plane. The inner circles will be automatically subtracted from the outer profile when you extrude the sketch.

1. Start a new part file and choose the **Circle by Center Point** tool from the **Draw** group in the **Home** tab; the **Circle** Command bar is displayed and the alignment lines get attached to the cursor.

2. Next, you need to define the plane on which you want to draw the profile of the base feature. To do so, invoke the base reference planes by selecting the **Base Reference Planes** check box in the **PathFinder**. On doing so, the base reference planes are displayed in the graphics window. Next, choose the XY plane for sketching and click on the lock symbol.

3. Make the XY plane normal to the drawing view and draw the sketch, as shown in Figure 4-41, by using the **Circle by Center Point** and **Line** tools. Make sure that the tangent and connect relationships are applied between the lines and the circles whenever a line intersects a circle. The tangent relationship is represented by a small circle and the connect relationship is represented by a cross, refer to Figure 4-41. Also, note that the centers of the circles are collinear.

   Next, you need to trim the unwanted portion of the circles to retain the outer profile of the model. This can be done by using the **Trim** tool.

4. Choose the **Trim** tool from the **Draw** group of the **Ribbon**; you are prompted to select the element to trim. 

5. Move the cursor on the right portion of the left circle; the portion to be trimmed is highlighted in orange.

6. Click on the highlighted portion of the circle; the highlighted portion is removed.

Note

If the entire circle is highlighted, it means that the connect relationship was not applied between the lines and the circle. In such a case, you need to add this relationship manually to the circle and the lines.

7. Similarly, trim the unwanted portion of other circles to get the sketch shown in Figure 4-42.

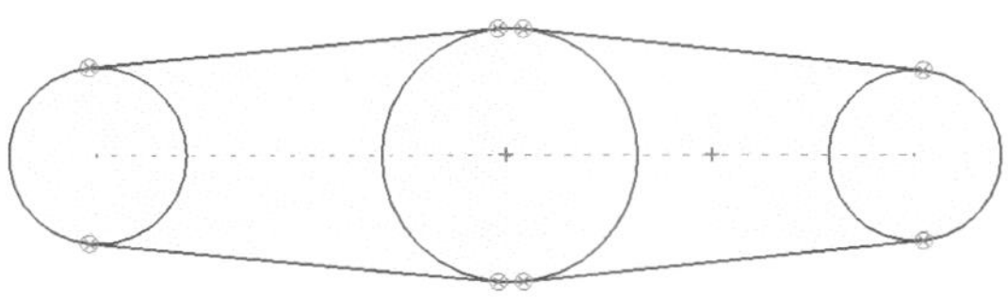

Figure 4-41 *Initial sketch for the base feature*

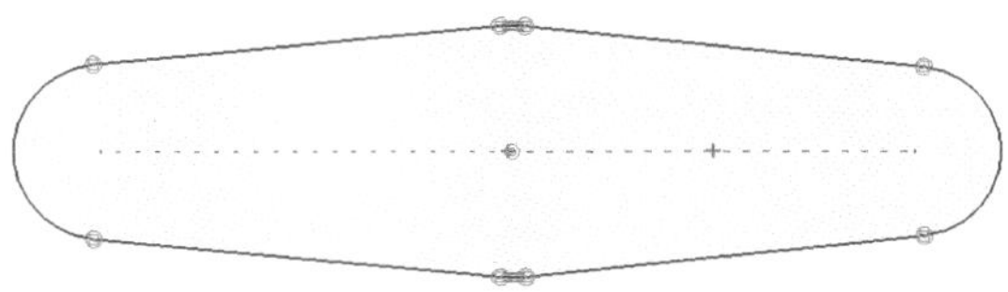

Figure 4-42 *Sketch after trimming the unwanted portion of circles*

   Next, you need to add relationships to the sketch.

8. Choose the **Equal** tool from the **Relate** group of the **Home** tab and make the left and right arcs equal. Similarly, make all lines equal by using the same relationship.

9. Now, if you drag the left arc, the position of the arc will change indicating that the center point of the arc is not constrained with the vertical direction. To constrain it, invoke the **Horizontal/Vertical** tool and select the center points of the left and right arcs. Similarly, align the center point of the left arc with the origin horizontally.

10. Add dimensions to the sketch by using the **Smart Dimension** tool, as shown in Figure 4-43.

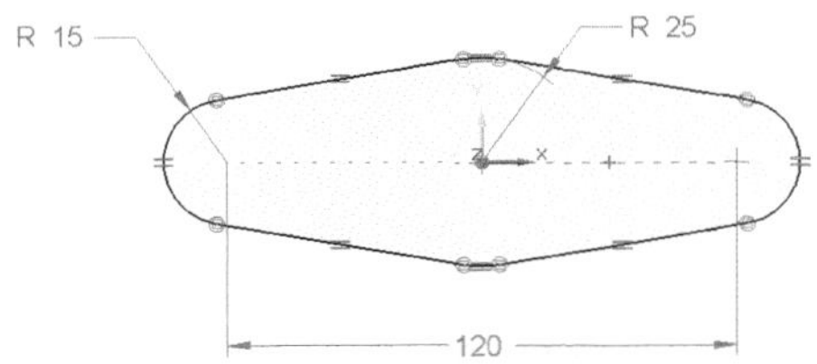

Figure 4-43 *Sketch after adding relationships and dimensions*

Next, you need to draw the inner circles. You can use the center points of the arcs to draw them.

11. Draw three circles using the center points of the existing arcs, refer to Figure 4-44. Before creating the circles, make sure that the **Center** check box is selected in the **IntelliSketch** group of the **Sketching** tab so that you can use the center points of the arcs as the center points of the circles to be created.

12. Add the **Equal** relationship to the left and right circles. Next, add the required dimensions to the circles to complete the sketch. The final sketch of the model is shown in Figure 4-44.

Converting the Sketch into an Extruded Feature

Next, you will create the extrude feature dynamically by using the profile created in the previous step.

1. Click inside the sketch region; an extrude handle is displayed. Also, the **Extrude** quick bar is displayed.

2. Select the **Include Internal Loops** option from the **Internal Face Loops** drop-down list in the **Extrude** Command bar.

3. Click on the extrude handle and drag the cursor in the drawing window; a preview of extrusion and an edit box are displayed in the drawing window.

4. Enter **20** in the edit box and press ENTER; the extruded feature is created, as shown in Figure 4-45.

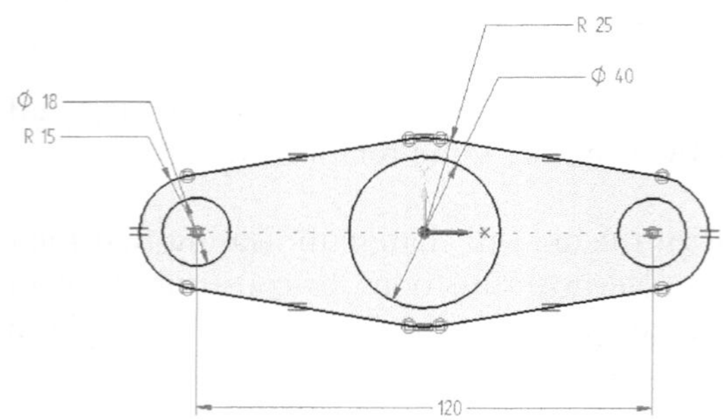

Figure 4-44 *Final sketch of the model*

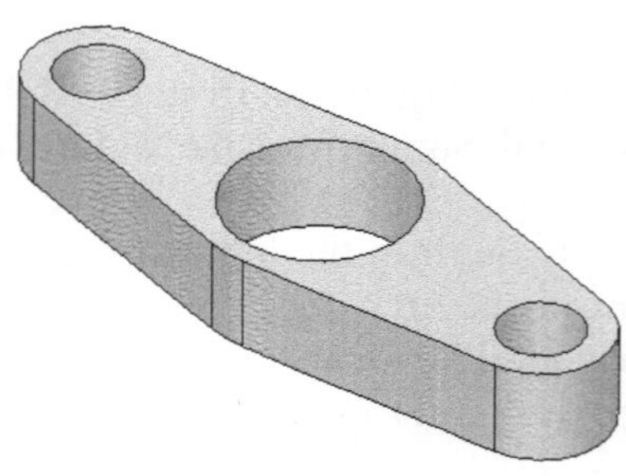

Figure 4-45 *The final extruded model*

Note

You can hide the dimensions of the features in the ***Synchronous Part*** *environment by clearing the* ***PMI*** *check box in the* ***PathFinder****.*

Rotating the View of the Model

Next, you need to rotate the view of the model and view it from different directions.

1. Choose the **Rotate** tool from the **Orient** group of the **View** tab; the 3D indicator along with three axes is displayed at the center of the current view.

2. Press and hold the left mouse button and drag the cursor in the drawing window to rotate the model. Alternatively, you can use the middle mouse button for rotating the model.

   Note that, when you rotate the view, the display quality of the model decreases as the sharpness of the model is set to minimum. You need to increase the sharpness of the model so that the display quality remains the same while rotating the view.

3. Click on the down arrow adjacent to the **Sharpen** tool in the **Style** group of the **View** tab to display the **Sharpness Set** cascading menu, as shown in Figure 4-46.

4. Choose the **5 Finer display** option from the cascading menu; the **Sharpen** message box will be displayed. Choose **Yes** from the message box; the sharpness of the model increases to the maximum value.

5. Next, rotate the view of the model. You will notice that the model remains sharp and the curved features in the model are displayed curved while rotating the view.

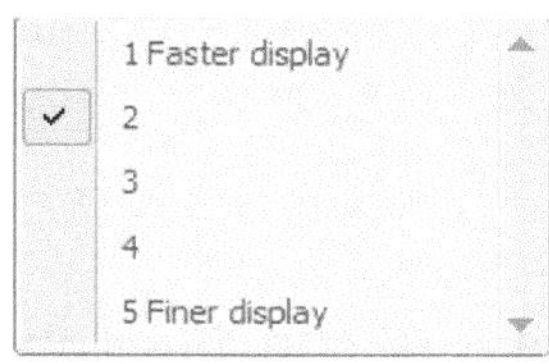

Figure 4-46 *The* ***Sharpness Set*** *cascading menu*

6. Right-click to exit the **Rotate** tool.

   Since the view of the model gets changed while rotating it, you need to restore the view to the isometric view. The isometric view can be restored by using the **View Orientation** flyout.

7. Choose the **View Orientation** button from the status bar; a flyout is displayed.

8. Select **ISO View** from the views displayed in the flyout to change the current view to the isometric view.

9. Right-click in the drawing window and then choose **Fit** from the shortcut menu displayed; the model fits in the drawing window.

Saving and Closing the File

1. Choose the **Save** tool from the **Quick Access** toolbar to display the **Save As** dialog box.

2. Browse to the location *C:\Solid Edge* and then create a folder with the name *c04* at this location.

3. Make the *c04* folder as the current folder and then save the file with the name *c04tut1.par* in it.

4. Choose the **Close** button from the file tab bar to close the file.

Tutorial 2 Synchronous

In this tutorial, you will open the sketch created in Exercise 1 of Chapter 3. Then, you will convert the sketch into an extrusion feature by using the **Extrude** tool. The depth of extrusion is 30 units. **(Expected time: 15 min)**

The following steps are required to complete this tutorial:

a. Open the *c03exe1.par* sketch from the *c03* folder and save it with the name *c04tut2.par* in the *c04* folder.
b. Extrude the sketch to a distance of 30 units using the **Extrude** tool, refer to Figure 4-48.
c. Rotate the view of the model in 3D space using the **Rotate** tool.
d. Save and close the file.

Opening the Sketch

1. Choose the **Open** tool from the **Quick Access** toolbar to display the **Open File** dialog box. If the **Open** tool is not available, then click on the down arrow available in the **Quick Access** toolbar; a drop-down is displayed. Choose **Open** from this drop-down.

2. Browse to *C:\Solid Edge\c03* and then open the *c03exr1.par* file.

Saving the Sketch with a Different Name

After opening the sketch, refer to Figure 4-47, you need to first save it with a new name so that the original sketch is not modified.

1. Choose **Application Button** and then the **Save As** option to display the **Save As** dialog box.

2. Browse to the *C:\Solid Edge\c04* folder and save the sketch with the name *c04tut2.par*; the file is saved with the new name and is opened in the drawing window. To cross-check, refer to the name of the file on top of the screen. The name shows *c04tut2.par*.

***Figure 4-47** Sketch for Tutorial 2*

Extruding the Sketch

Next, you need to convert this sketch into an extruded feature using the **Extrude** tool. The depth of extrusion is 30.

1. Choose the **Select** tool and then select the middle portion of the sketch; the extrude handle and the **Extrude** Command bar are displayed.

2. Select the **Include Internal Loops** option from the **Internal Face Loops** drop-down list in the **Extrude** quick bar.

3. Click on the extrude handle and drag the cursor in the drawing window; a preview of the extrusion and an edit box are displayed in the drawing window.

4. Enter **30** in the edit box and press ENTER; the extruded feature is created. The final extruded model is shown in Figure 4-48.

Figure 4-48 *The extruded model*

Rotating the View of the Model

Next, you need to rotate the view of the model so that you can maneuver around it and view it from different directions.

1. Choose the **Rotate** tool from the status bar to invoke this tool. On doing so, the 3D indicator along with the three axes is displayed at the center of the current view. 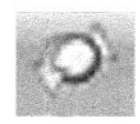

2. Press and hold the left mouse button and drag the cursor in the drawing window. The view of the model rotates in the 3D space and you can view it from different directions.

> **Tip**
> *While rotating the view of the model, if you select an edge or an axis in the 3D indicator, the view will rotate around that edge or axis. To freely rotate the view again, select the origin of the 3D indicator.*

When you rotate the view, the quality of the view will be changed because the sharpness of the model is set to minimum. You need to increase the sharpness of the model to make sure the display quality remains the same while rotating the view.

3. Choose the down arrow adjacent to the **Sharpen** tool in the **Style** group of the **View** tab to display the **Sharpness Set** cascading menu.

4. Choose **5 Finer display** from the cascading menu; the **Sharpen** message box is displayed. Choose **Yes** from the message box to sharpen the display of the model to the maximum.

5. Choose the **Rotate** tool from the status bar and rotate the view of the model.

   You will notice that the model remains sharp and the curved features in the model are displayed as curved.

6. Right-click to exit the **Rotate** tool.

   Next, you need to restore the isometric view of the model which got changed while rotating it.

7. Choose the **View Orientation** button from the status bar; a flyout is displayed.

8. Choose **ISO View** from the views displayed in the flyout in order to change the current view to the isometric view.

9. Right-click in the drawing window, and then choose **Fit** from the shortcut menu displayed. The model fits in the drawing window.

Saving and Closing the File

1. Choose the **Save** tool from the **Quick Access** toolbar. The file is saved with the name *c04tut2*.

2. Choose the **Close** button from the file tab bar to close the file.

Tutorial 3 Ordered

In this tutorial, you will open the sketch created in Tutorial 3 of Chapter 3, refer to Figure 4-49. You will then convert the sketch into a revolved feature by using the **Revolve** tool.

(Expected time: 15 min)

The following steps are required to complete this tutorial:

a. Open the *c03tut3.par* sketch from the *c03* folder and save it as *c04tut3.par* in the *c04* folder.
b. Revolve the sketch using the **Revolve** tool.
c. Rotate the model in 3D space using the **Rotate** tool.
d. Save and close the file.

Opening the Sketch

1. Choose the **Open** tool from the **Quick Access** toolbar to display the **Open File** dialog box.

2. Browse to *C:\Solid Edge\c03* and open the *c03tut3.par* file.

Saving the Sketch with a Different Name

After opening the sketch, you need to first save it with a different name so that the original sketch is not modified.

1. Choose **Application Button > Save As** to display the **Save As** dialog box.

2. Browse to *C:\Solid Edge\c04* and save the sketch with the name *c04tut3.par*; the file is saved with the new name and is opened in the drawing window. Figure 4-49 shows the sketch for the revolved model.

***Figure 4-49** Sketch for the revolved model*

Revolving the Sketch

Next, you need to convert this sketch into a revolved feature using the **Revolve** tool. As there is no revolution axis in this sketch, you need to use the left vertical line as the axis of revolution.

1. Choose the **Revolve** tool from the **Solids** group in the **Home** tab; the **Revolve** Command bar is displayed.

2. Select the **Select from Sketch** option from the **Create-From Options** drop-down list in the Command bar and then select the sketch for the revolved feature.

3. Right-click to accept the selection; you are prompted to click on a line in the sketch to be used as the axis of revolution.

4. Select the left vertical line of the sketch as the revolution axis; the **Extent Step** option is activated. Next, you need to revolve the sketch through an angle of 360-degree to create the revolved feature.

5. Choose the **Revolve 360°** button from the Command bar; the fully revolved feature is displayed in the drawing window.

6. Choose the **Finish** button and then the **Cancel** button from the Command bar to exit the **Revolve** tool.

7. Clear the check box on the left of **Sketch1** and the **Base Reference Planes** check box in the **PathFinder**, if it is selected. The final revolved model is shown in Figure 4-50.

Rotating the View of the Model

1. Press the middle mouse button and drag the cursor to rotate the view of the model.

2. Right-click in the drawing window, and then choose **Fit** from the shortcut menu displayed; the model fits in the drawing window.

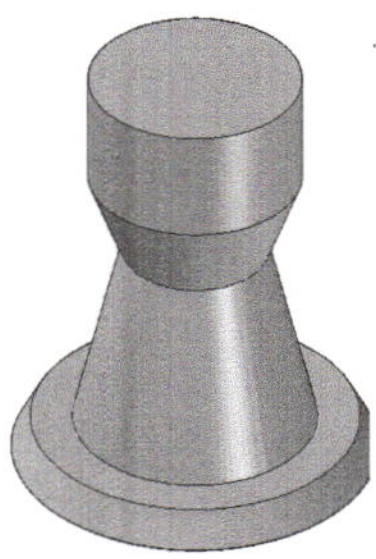

Figure 4-50 The final revolved model

Saving and Closing the File

1. Choose the **Save** tool from the **Quick Access** toolbar. The file is saved with the name *c04tut3*.

2. Choose the **Close** button from the file tab bar to close the file.

Self-Evaluation Test

Answer the following questions and then compare them to those given at the end of this chapter:

1. When you select an entity or invoke a command, the __________ is displayed that helps you to use the options easily.

2. In Solid Edge, you can modify the display quality of a model by improving the __________ of the model.

3. You need to choose the __________ button to extrude a profile symmetrically on both sides of the plane on which the profile is created.

4. The __________ tool allows you to create a mirrored copy of the selected sketched entities.

5. You can create a copy of the selected sketched entities by pressing and holding the __________ key and dragging the cursor.

6. The __________ tool is used to create a feature by revolving a sketch around an axis to add material.

7. You can restore the standard views by invoking the __________ tool from the status bar.

8. In Solid Edge, you can insert external images into a sketch and then use them as labels on the model. (T/F)

9. You need to manually invoke the **Extent Type** in the **QuickBar** when you select the sketch region. (T/F)

10. You can set the display modes for solid models by using the buttons in the status bar. (T/F)

Review Questions

Answer the following questions:

1. Which of the following image types cannot be inserted into the Sketching environment of Solid Edge?

   (a) JPG (b) BMP
   (c) PCX (d) PNG

2. Which one of the following tools is used to create a symmetric offset on both sides of the open sketched entity?

   (a) **Offset** (b) **Symmetric**
   (c) **Symmetric Offset** (d) **Symmetric Extent**

3. Which of the following buttons needs to be chosen from the **Revolve** Command bar to revolve a profile through an angle of 270 degrees?

   (a) **Revolve 360°** (b) **Finite Extent**
   (c) Both (a) and (b) (d) **Through Next**

4. Which of the following buttons needs to be chosen from the **Mirror** Command bar to make sure that the original entities are retained after creating their mirrored copies?

   (a) **Copy** (b) **Mirror**
   (c) **Double** (d) **Scale**

5. Which of the following display modes displays only the visible edges in the model?

   (a) **Shaded** (b) **Visible Edges**
   (c) **Visible and Hidden Edges** (d) **Wire Frame**

6. When you mirror an entity, a mirrored copy of the selected entity is created by default and the original entity is deleted. (T/F)

7. In the **Shaded** display mode, models appear shaded and their edges are displayed. (T/F)

8. You can use the **Rotate** tool to rotate the selected sketched entities around a specified center point. (T/F)

9. The **Offset** tool is used to create a symmetric offset on both sides of the selected entities. (T/F)

10. You can use the **Move** tool to modify the size of a sketch while maintaining its aspect ratio. (T/F)

EXERCISES

Exercise 1

Open the part file created in Exercise 5 of Chapter 3, as shown in Figure 4-51 and convert it into an extrusion feature. The depth of extrusion is 40 units. After creating the model, use the **Rotate** tool to rotate the view of the model. Before saving and closing the file, restore the diametric view of the model. **(Expected time: 15 min)**

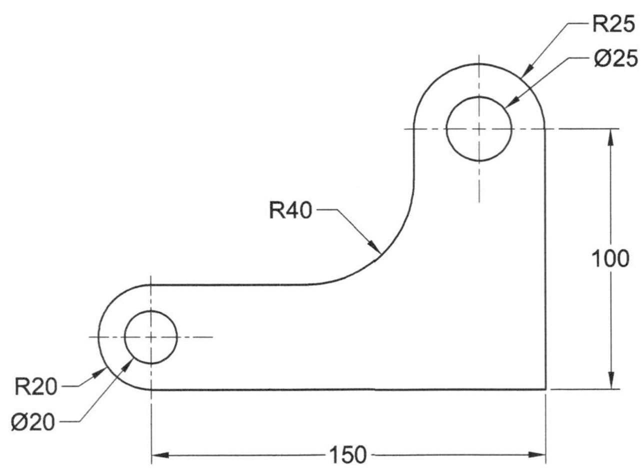

Figure 4-51 *Sketch for Exercise 1*

Exercise 2

Open the part file created in Tutorial 1 of Chapter 3, as shown in Figure 4-52 and convert it into an extrude feature. The depth of extrusion is 40 units. After creating the model, use the **Rotate** tool to rotate the view of the model. Before saving and closing the file, restore the diametric view of the model. **(Expected time: 15 min)**

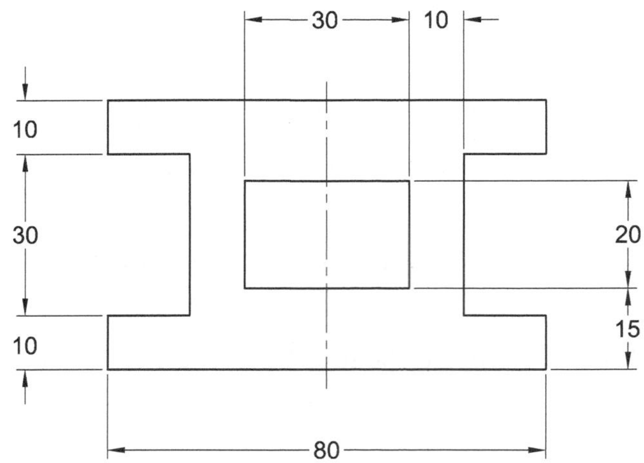

Figure 4-52 Sketch for Exercise 2

Exercise 3

In this exercise, you will create the model shown in Figure 4-53. Its dimensions are given in the drawing views shown in Figure 4-54. The depth of extrusion is 60 units.

(Expected time: 30 min)

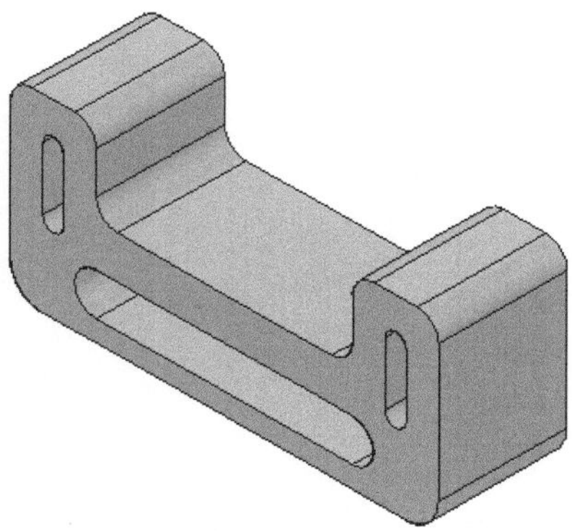

Figure 4-53 The model for Exercise 3

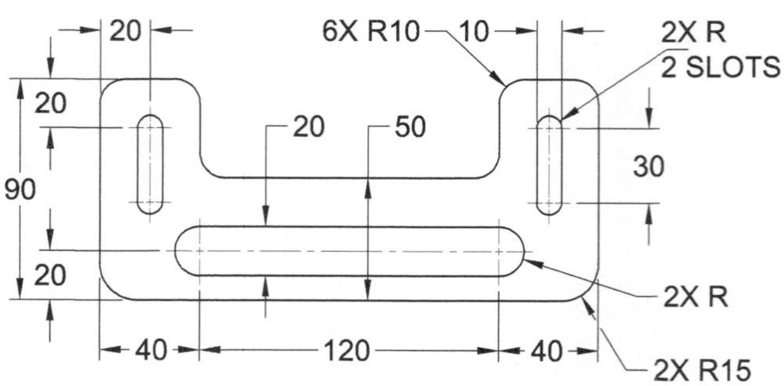

Figure 4-54 Dimensions of the model

Exercise 4

In this exercise, you will create the model shown in Figure 4-55. Its dimensions are given in the drawing views shown in Figure 4-56. Convert the sketch into a 270 degree revolve feature by using the **Revolve** tool.

(Expected time: 30 min)

Figure 4-55 *The model for Exercise 4*

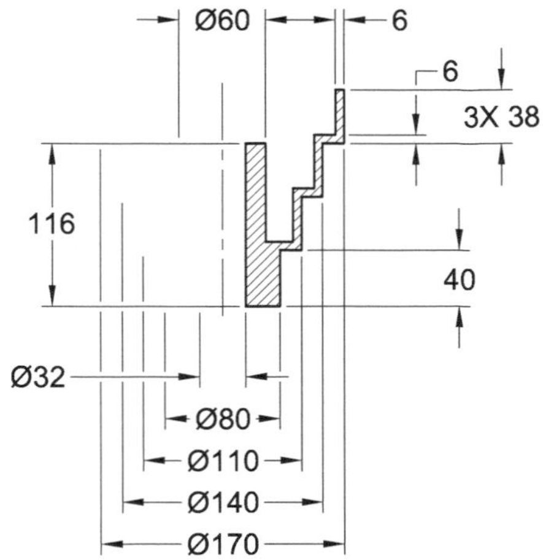

Figure 4-56 *Dimensions of the model*

Answers to Self-Evaluation Test

1. **QuickBar**, **2.** sharpness, **3.** **Symmetric**, **4.** **Mirror**, **5.** CTRL, **6.** **Revolve**, **7.** **View Orientation**, **8.** T, **9.** T, **10.** T

Chapter 5

Working with Additional Reference Geometries

Learning Objectives

After completing this chapter, you will be able to:

- *Understand the use of reference planes*
- *Create reference planes*
- *Control the display of reference axes*
- *Create new coordinate systems*
- *Use additional termination options of the extruded features*
- *Create the extruded and revolved cutouts*
- *Include the edges of existing features as sketched entities in the current sketch*
- *Work with advanced drawing display tools*

ADDITIONAL SKETCHING AND REFERENCE PLANES

As mentioned earlier, most of the mechanical designs consist of a number of sketched, references, and placed features that are integrated together. In the previous chapter, you learned to create the base feature which is the first feature in a model. After creating the base feature, you need to add other features to create the complete model. Generally, the additional features are not created on the default plane on which the base feature is created and therefore you require additional sketching or reference planes to draw sketches and create other features. Consider a model shown in Figure 5-1 that has extruded features, rib features, and a cut feature. In this model, only the base feature will be created on the default plane and rest of the features will require you to specify reference planes to draw sketches and then create the required features.

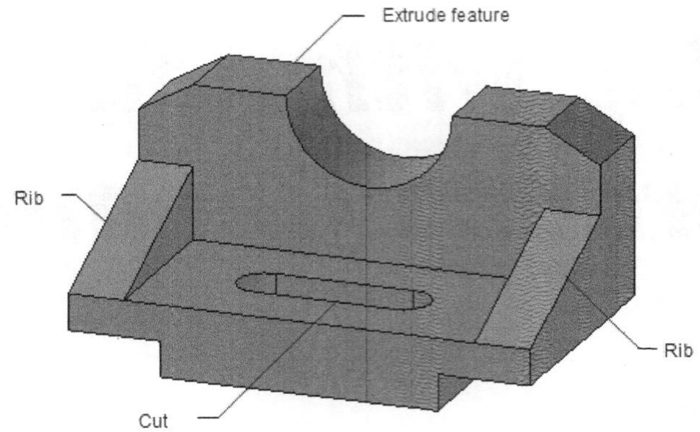

Figure 5-1 *Various features in the model*

The base feature for the model given in Figure 5-1 is shown in Figure 5-2. It is an extruded feature created on a default plane. Figure 5-3 shows the other extruded feature of the model created on a reference plane on the base feature. Similarly, other features of the model such as rib and cut will be created. By default, the top, right, and front planes are available in the part file. These default planes are called the base reference planes. You can use any of these reference planes or the planar faces of the base feature to draw the sketches of the additional features.

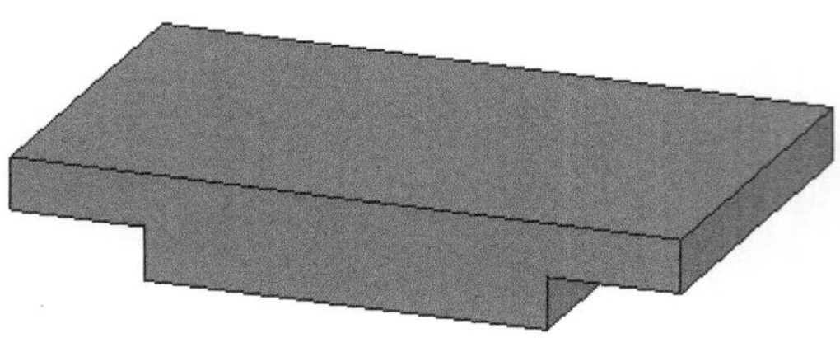

Figure 5-2 *Base feature of the model*

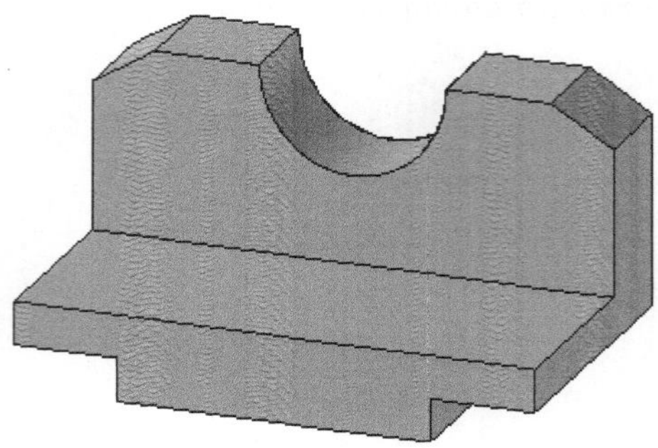

Figure 5-3 *Model with multiple features*

However, you cannot use the existing planes for drawing the sketch of a feature that is at a certain offset or angle from an existing reference plane or planar face of a feature. In this case, you need to create additional reference planes. In addition to the base reference planes, you can create two more types of reference planes which are discussed next.

Local Reference Planes

Local reference planes are those that are created while defining a feature in the Part environment. For example, whenever you invoke a tool to create a sketch-based feature in the **Ordered** environment, the Command bar provides tools to create reference planes. The reference plane created at this stage will be used to create only this particular feature. Therefore, these types of reference planes are called local reference planes. These planes are not displayed in the drawing window or in the **PathFinder**.

Global Reference Planes

The planes that are created separately as features with the help of the tools in the **Planes** group of the **Ribbon** are called global reference planes. These planes are displayed in the drawing window as well as in the path finder and can be used to create additional features.

CREATING REFERENCE PLANES (SYNCHRONOUS)

In Solid Edge, you can create various types of global reference planes. The procedures to create various types of reference planes are discussed next.

Creating a Coincident Plane

Ribbon: Home > Planes > Coincident Plane

Using the **Coincident Plane** tool, you can create a reference plane coincident to the base reference plane or any other reference plane, or the planar face of the model.

To create a coincident plane, invoke the **Coincident Plane** tool; you will be prompted to click on a planar face or a reference plane. Move the cursor on the reference plane or planar face on which you want to create the coincident plane; the plane will be highlighted in orange. Also, the preview of the reference plane being created will be displayed in the drawing window. You can select the other edges of the planar face or the reference plane to define the X-axis of the new plane by pressing the N or the B key. Pressing the N key highlights the next edge to define the X axis of the new plane and pressing the B key highlights the previous edge to define the X-axis. Click at this point; the plane coincident to the selected entity will be created.

Figures 5-4 and 5-5 show the coincident planes being created on the same plane but with different edges defining the X-axis of the plane. You can also toggle the X-axis direction of a new plane to a positive or negative X-axis by pressing the T key. For example, if a reference plane is created, as shown in Figure 5-5, the positive X-axis direction of this plane will be from the top endpoint to the bottom endpoint of the inclined edge. This is indicated by a triad displayed at the center of the plane. To reverse the direction of the positive X axis, press the T key; the direction of the positive X-axis, which was pointing toward the right (Figure 5-5) will be reversed and will point toward the left, refer to Figure 5-6. The triad at the origin of the plane indicates the direction of the positive X-axis.

After you have selected all the options for creating a reference plane, its preview will be displayed in the drawing window. At this stage, click in the drawing area to create the plane.

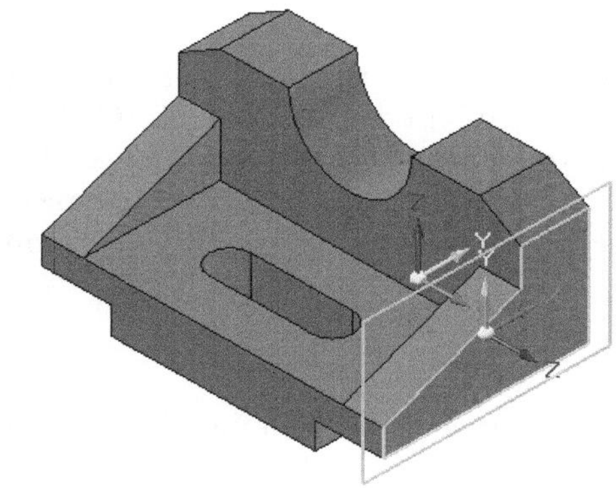

Figure 5-4 Creating a coincident plane with the bottom edge defining the orientation of the X-axis

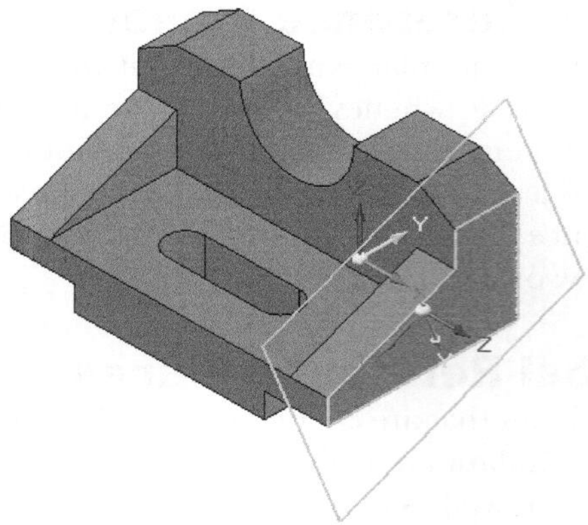

Figure 5-5 Creating a coincident plane with the inclined edge defining the orientation of the X-axis

Modifying Planes Using the Steering Wheel

After creating a reference plane, the steering wheel and the **Move** Command bar will be displayed. Also, the **Design Intent** panel will be displayed. You will learn about this panel in Chapter 7. By using the steering wheel, you can modify the position of a reference face. The various components of the steering wheel are shown in Figure 5-7. If you press and drag the origin knob, the steering wheel will move to a new location. Press the X, Y, or Z axis and drag to move the selected entity along the respective axis. In order to set the direction of the axes, press and drag the knob that is attached to the corresponding axis. You can specify the offset distance in the edit box displayed on moving the plane. The tool plane of the steering wheel allows the selected entities to move along the tool plane. The torus of the steering wheel is used for modifying the inclination of the selected entities. Click on the torus of the steering wheel; the dynamic angle edit box will be displayed. You can enter the value for the inclination angle in this edit box.

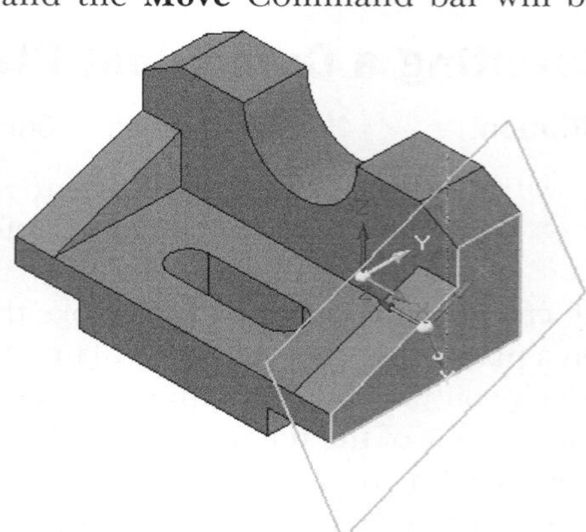

Figure 5-6 Preview of the reference plane after reversing the positive X-axis direction

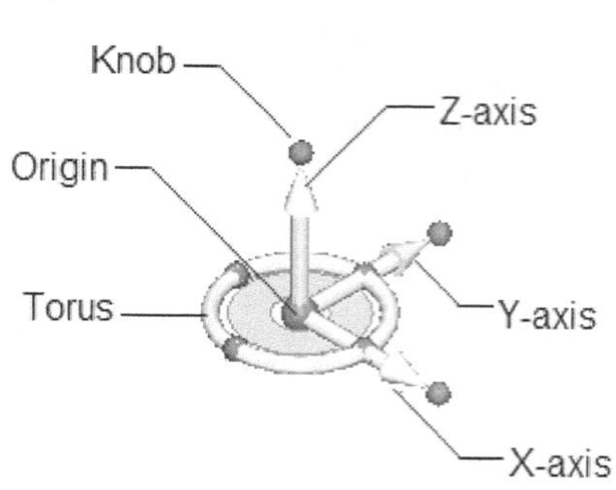

Figure 5-7 The components of the steering wheel

Creating a Plane Normal to an Edge or a Sketched Curve

Ribbon: Home > Planes > More Planes drop-down > Normal to Curve

You can create a plane that is normal to a selected sketched curve or an edge of the model using the **Normal to Curve** tool. You can define a point along the curve where the normal plane needs to be placed. To create a plane normal to a curve or an edge of the model, invoke this tool; you will be prompted to click on the curve or the edge for the normal plane. Once you move the cursor close to the sketched curve or the edge of the model, the nearest endpoint of the curve or the edge will be highlighted. At this point, select the curve; the preview of the normal plane will be displayed and you will be prompted to click on a keypoint or key in a distance or position. Also, the **Position** and **Distance** edit boxes will be displayed in the drawing window. These edit boxes are used to specify the location of the plane along the curve. The **Position** edit box defines the position in terms of percentage. The total length of the edge or the curve is taken as 1 and you are allowed to enter any value between 0 and 1. Similarly, the **Distance** edit box defines the distance of the normal plane from the endpoint that is highlighted while selecting the edge or the curve.

You can also define the location of the normal plane by specifying a point along the edge or the curve in the drawing window. Figure 5-8 shows a plane being created normal to a sketched curve.

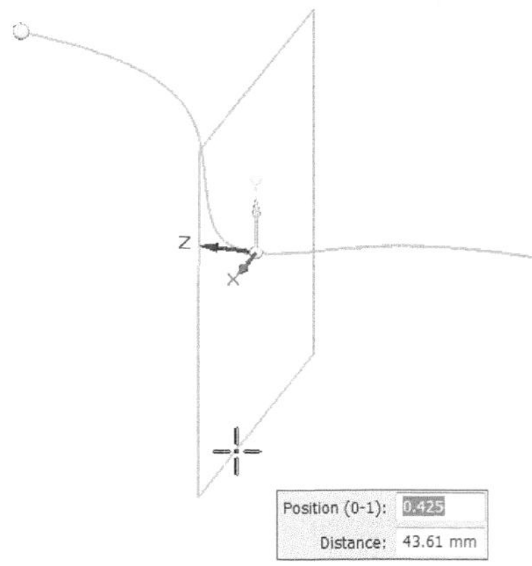

Figure 5-8 *Creating a plane normal to a sketched curve*

Creating a Plane Using 3 Points

Ribbon: Home > Planes > More Planes drop-down > By 3 Points

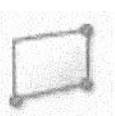

You can create a reference plane on any three specified points of the model by using the **By 3 Points** tool. The three points define the origin of the plane, the direction of the positive X axis, and the direction of the positive Y axis. The length and width of the plane are determined by the distance of the second and third points from the origin.

To define a reference plane using three points, invoke the **By 3 Points** tool; you will be prompted to click on a point to define the origin of the plane. Select a point in the model that you want to use as the origin of the new plane. You can use the **Keypoints** drop-down from the Command bar to select the point. On specifying the origin, you will be prompted to click on a point to define the base of the plane. Select a point that will define the direction of the positive X axis.

Also, note that this point will define the length of the plane. On selecting the point, you will be prompted to click on a point to complete the plane. Select a point that will define the direction of the positive Y axis and the width of the plane.

Figure 5-9 shows a plane being created using three points.

Creating a Tangent Plane

Ribbon: Home > Planes > More Planes drop-down > Tangent

You can create a reference plane tangent to a selected curved surface using the **Tangent** tool. To create a tangent plane, invoke this tool; you will be prompted to click on a curved surface. Select the curved surface from the drawing area; the 3D indicator with three axes and an origin will be displayed in the preview of the plane. The indicator allows you to rotate the view freely in 3D space or around any of these three axes. Next, you need to click on the curved surface at the required angle or you can enter the value of angle in the angle edit box. Figure 5-10 shows the tangent plane being created on the curved surface. A tangent plane can be created on a cylinder, sphere, cone, torus, or b-line surface.

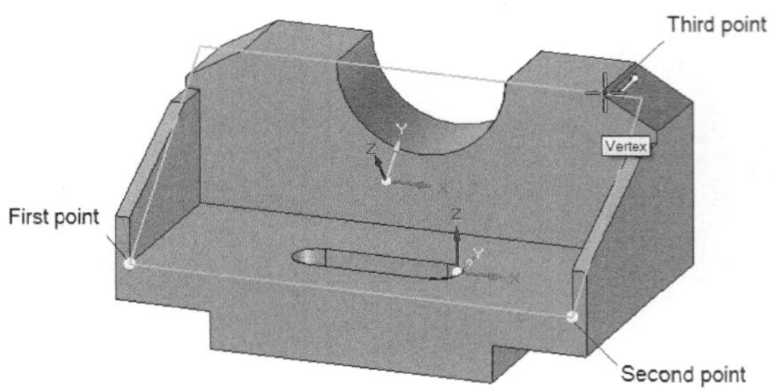

Figure 5-9 Creating a plane using three points

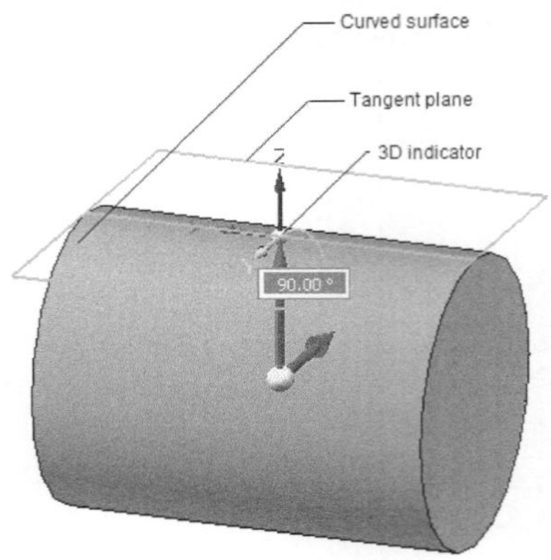

Figure 5-10 Creating a tangent plane on a curved surface

In addition to the tools mentioned earlier, there are some other tools that can be used for creating reference planes. But these tools are available only in the **Ordered Part** environment. In order to use these tools, you need to switch over to the **Ordered Part** environment. However, you can create these types of reference planes in the **Synchronous Part** environment by using the steering wheel. The procedures to create reference planes in the **Ordered Part** environment are discussed next.

CREATING REFERENCE PLANES (ORDERED)

You can create various types of local or global reference planes in the **Ordered** environment. The procedures to create various types of reference planes are discussed next.

Creating a Parallel Plane

Ribbon:	Home > Planes > More Planes drop-down> Parallel

In the **Ordered Part** environment, you can create a reference plane parallel to a selected base reference plane, another reference plane, or a planar face using the **Parallel** tool. To create a parallel plane, invoke the **Parallel** tool from the **More Planes** drop-down, as shown in Figure 5-11; you will be prompted to click on a planar face or a reference plane. Define the orientation of the new plane by selecting the required planar face. As you select the planar face, the Command bar will be displayed with the options to define the location of the plane and you will be prompted to set the offset distance.

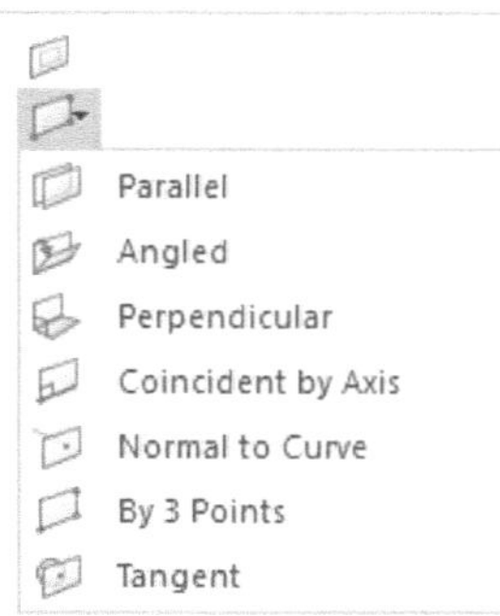

***Figure 5-11** The **More Planes** drop-down*

You can enter the offset value directly in the **Distance** edit box or use the keypoints in the model to define the location of the parallel plane. To use the keypoints in the model, choose the **Keypoints** button in the Command bar to display the flyout that has the keypoint options such as **End Point**, **Midpoint**, **Center Point**, **Edit Point**, and so on. Choose the required option from this flyout and then select the corresponding keypoint in the model; the new parallel plane will be placed at the selected keypoint. Figure 5-12 shows a parallel plane being created by using the center keypoint in the model and Figure 5-13 shows a parallel plane created by using the tangent keypoint in the model.

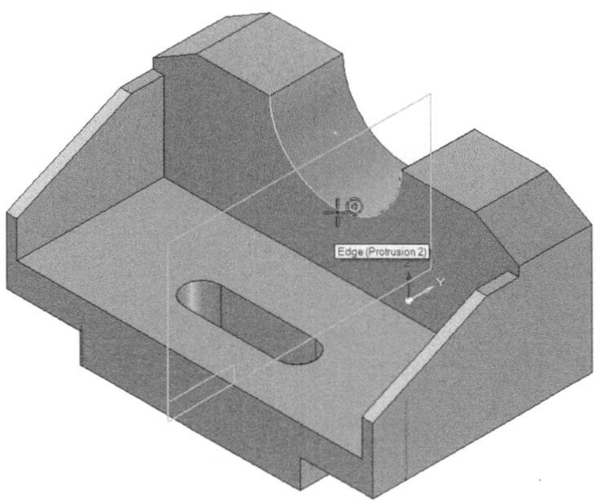

***Figure 5-12** Creating a parallel plane by defining the center keypoint*

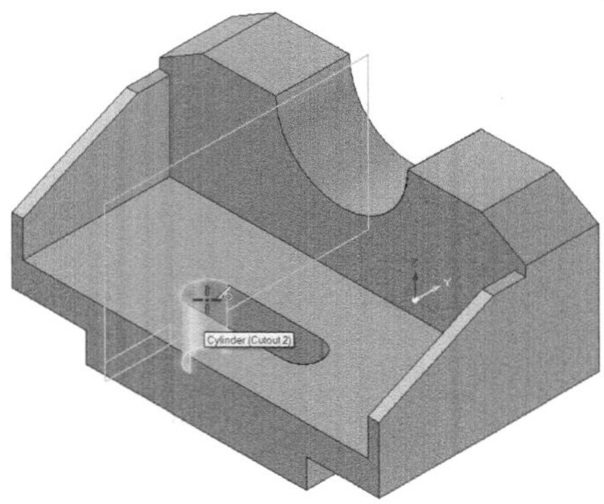

***Figure 5-13** Creating a parallel plane by defining the tangent keypoint*

You can also create a plane parallel to a planar face in the **Synchronous Part** environment. To do so, create a coincident plane on the selected planar face; a steering wheel will be displayed. Click on the primary axis and drag it; an edit box will be displayed. Enter a value in it to define the location of the plane and press ENTER; a parallel plane will be created at the specified distance.

Creating an Angled Plane

Ribbon:	Home > Planes > More Planes drop-down > Angled

In the **Ordered Part** environment, using the **Angled** tool, you can create a reference plane that is at an angle to the selected plane and passes through a specified edge, axis, or plane. On invoking this tool, you will be prompted to click on a planar face or a reference plane. The new reference plane will be defined at an angle to the selected plane. After selecting the plane, you will be prompted to click on the face, edge, or plane to form the base of the profile plane. This will define the edge or the plane through which the new plane will pass. You may need to use the **QuickPick** tool to select the required edge or plane. To invoke this tool, place the cursor over the entity for a while; a mouse symbol will be displayed. Right-click; the **QuickPick** list box will be displayed with all the entities that can be selected at that location. Select the required entity from this list box.

Next, you need to define the direction of the positive X axis for the orientation of the new plane. You will be prompted to click near the end of the axis for the reference plane orientation. As you move the cursor in the drawing window, the direction of the X axis will toggle. Click to define the positive or negative X axis direction of the new plane.

Finally, you will be prompted to click to set the angle or key-in a value. You can enter the angle value directly in the **Angle** edit box of the Command bar or use the keypoints to define the angle of the plane. Note that in this case, you can use only the endpoint, midpoint, or center point to define the plane. Figure 5-14 shows various selections to create an angled plane and also the preview of the resulting plane.

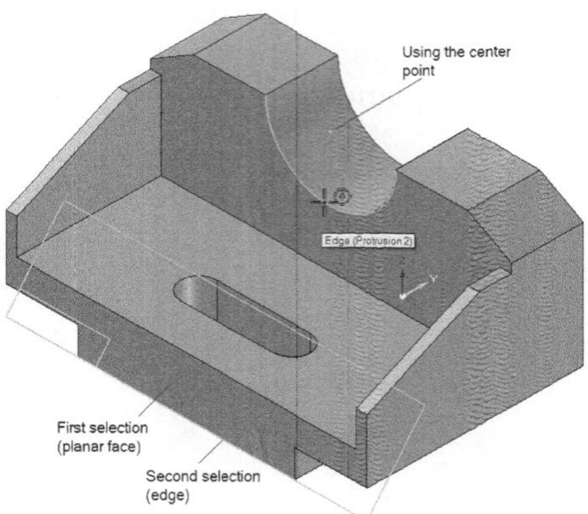

Figure 5-14 *Various selections made to create an angled reference plane*

You can also create a plane at an angle to a planar face in the **Synchronous Part** environment using the steering wheel. To do so, invoke the **Coincident Plane** tool from the **Planes** group; you will be prompted to select a planar face. Move the cursor toward the model and select the required face; the steering wheel will be displayed on the selected face. Click and drag the origin knob of the steering wheel and place it on the edge through which the new plane will pass. On doing so, the primary or secondary axis of the steering wheel will coincide with the edge. Next, click on the torus of the steering wheel; an angle edit box will be displayed. Specify a value in it and press ENTER; a plane will be created at an angle specified in the edit box. When you enter 90 in the edit box, a perpendicular plane will be created.

Creating a Perpendicular Plane

Ribbon: Home > Planes > More Planes drop-down > Perpendicular

The **Perpendicular** tool is used to create a reference plane that is normal to a selected plane and passes through a specified edge or axis. To create a perpendicular plane, invoke this tool; you will be prompted to click on a planar face or a reference plane. The new reference plane will be defined normal to the plane that you select. After selecting the plane, you will be prompted to click on a face, edge, or a plane to form the base of the profile plane. This will define the edge or the plane through which the new plane will pass. You may need to use the **QuickPick** tool to select the required edge or the plane.

Next, you need to define the direction of the positive X of the new plane. You will be prompted to click near the end of the axis for the reference plane orientation. As you move the cursor in the drawing window, the direction of the X axis will toggle. Click to define the positive X axis direction of the new plane.

Finally, you will be prompted to click to set the angle or key-in the value. You can move the cursor in the drawing window to define the side of the plane. Figure 5-15 shows various selections to create a perpendicular plane and the preview of the resulting plane.

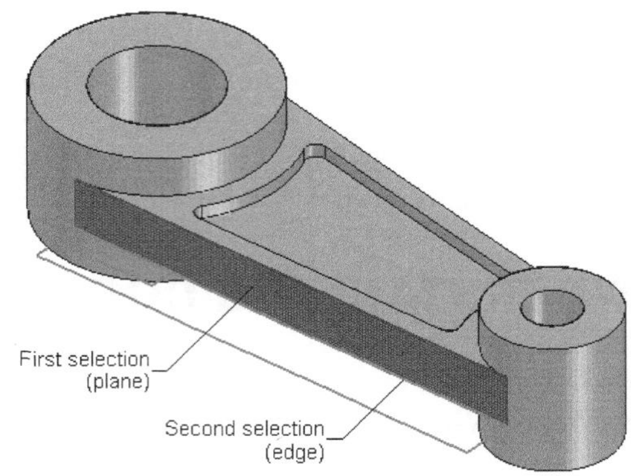

Figure 5-15 *Various selections made to create a perpendicular reference plane*

Creating a Plane Using Coincident by Axis

Ribbon: Home > Planes > More Planes drop-down > Coincident by Axis

The **Coincident by Axis** tool works the same way as the **Coincident Plane** tool. The only difference is that in this tool, after selecting the plane, you will also be prompted to select the edge to define the direction of the positive X axis and the orientation of the plane. Unlike the **Coincident Plane** tool where you use the keyboard shortcuts to define these parameters, in this tool you need to select these parameters in the drawing window.

Note

*If you select the option from the **Create-From Options** drop-down list in the Command bar, for creating local reference planes on the existing feature in the **Ordered Part** environment, the **Feature's Plane** and **Last Plane** options will also be available. The **Feature's Plane** option uses the plane on which the profile of the selected feature was created whereas the **Last Plane** option uses the previous plane selected to create the feature.*

Displaying the Reference Axes (Ordered)

Solid Edge automatically creates reference axes when you create a revolved feature, hole feature, or any other circular or semicircular feature. However, the display of these reference axes is turned off by default. To turn the display of the axes on, right-click in the drawing window; a shortcut menu will be displayed. Choose **Show All > Reference Axes** from the shortcut menu;

the reference axes of all the revolved features will be displayed in the drawing window. But the reference axes of the circular, semicircular, or hole features will not be displayed. To display the axes of these features, choose **Show All > Toggle Axes** from the shortcut menu that will be displayed on right-clicking in the drawing window; you will be prompted to click on the feature or the surface containing reference axis. Select the features whose reference axes you want to display; the reference axes of the selected features will be displayed.

Similarly, you can turn the display of the reference axes off by choosing **Hide All > Reference Axes** from the shortcut menu that is displayed on right-clicking in the drawing window.

Note

*1. Once you have toggled the display of reference axes using the **Toggle Axes** option, you can turn the display of reference axes on or off. To do so, choose **Hide All > Reference Axes** or **Show All > Reference Axes** from the shortcut menu that is displayed on right-clicking in the drawing window.*

*2. You can use the options in the **Show All** or **Hide All** cascading menu to modify the display of other entities such as reference planes.*

UNDERSTANDING COORDINATE SYSTEMS

Each part file that you start in Solid Edge has a coordinate system defined in it. This default coordinate system is called the base coordinate system. In Solid Edge, you can create additional coordinate systems according to your design requirements. These coordinate systems can be used as references to create reference planes, measure distances, copy parts, and so on.

Creating a Coordinate System

Ribbon:	Home > Planes > Coordinate System

In the **Ordered Part** environment, you can create coordinate systems in two ways: by defining the orientations of any of the two axes using the edit boxes or by defining the orientation of any of the two axes by selecting the edges in the model. The options required to create a coordinate system are available in the **Coordinate System Options** dialog box, refer to Figure 5-16. To invoke this dialog box, choose **Coordinate System** from the **Planes** group of the **Home** tab.

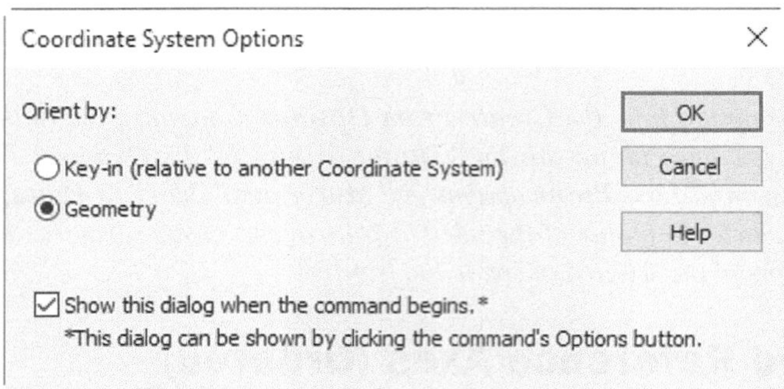

*Figure 5-16 The **Coordinate System Options** dialog box*

Select the **Key-in (relative to another Coordinate System)** radio button if you want to create a coordinate system with respect to an existing coordinate system. Select the **Geometry** radio button, if you want to create a coordinate system by specifying the axis with respect to an existing geometry. When you select the **Key-in (relative to another Coordinate System)** and choose **OK**, the **Coordinate System** Command bar will be displayed. The following steps will be available in the Command bar.

Origin Step

This step is common to both the options for creating a coordinate system and is active by default when the **Coordinate System** Command bar is displayed. In this step, you need to define the point where the origin of the coordinate system will be placed. To define the origin, you can select a keypoint in the model or enter the coordinates of the point in the **X**, **Y**, and **Z** edit boxes in the Command bar. By default, the points will be defined with respect to the default coordinate system. This is because the **Model Space** option is selected from the **Relative to** drop-down list in the Command bar. However, if there are other coordinate systems in the current drawing, they will be listed in this drop-down list and you can define the coordinates of the points with respect to them. After entering the values in the **X**, **Y**, and **Z** coordinates edit boxes, click on the **Next** button in the Command bar; the Command bar will be changed and **Orientation Step** will be activated.

Orientation Step

In this step, you need to define the orientation of the X, Y, and Z axes of the new coordinate system with respect to those of the default coordinate system (model space) or any other coordinate system selected from the **Relative to** drop-down list. The coordinate system will be rotated around the axis by the angle that you define in the **X°, Y°,** and **Z°** edit boxes. For example, if you enter **20** as the value in the **X°** edit box, then the new coordinate system will be rotated by 20-degree around the X axis.

Note

Solid Edge uses the right-hand thumb rule to determine the direction of the rotation of the axes. The right-hand thumb rule states that if the thumb points in the direction of the axis, then the direction of the curled fingers points toward the direction of rotation.

Enter the rotation angles in the **X°**, **Y°**, and **Z°** edit boxes and choose the **Preview** button; the preview of the resulting coordinate system will be displayed. Choose the **Finish** button to create the coordinate system.

On selecting the **Geometry** radio button from the **Coordinate System Options** dialog box, the following steps will be displayed in the Command bar:

Origin Step

This step is similar to the **Origin Step** described previously for creating coordinate systems.

First Axis Step

This step will be activated automatically as soon as you define the origin of the coordinate system. In this step, you need to define the orientation of the first axis of the coordinate system. By default, the **X-Axis** button is chosen from the Command bar. Therefore, the axis that you define will be taken as the X axis of the coordinate system. However, if you want to define any other axis as the first axis, you can choose the button corresponding to that axis from the Command bar.

You can select a point, linear element, or an edge to define the axis after selecting the corresponding option from the **Select** drop-down list. After selecting the element to define the first axis, choose the **Accept** button from the Command bar. You can also press ENTER or right-click to accept the selection. Next, you need to define the direction of the positive side. It is represented by an arrow along the entity that you selected to define the first axis. You can move the cursor to either side of the origin to define the direction of the positive side. Click on the desired side to accept the selection.

Second Axis Step

This step will be activated automatically as soon as you define the first axis of the coordinate system. In this step, you need to define the orientation of the second axis of the coordinate system. If you have defined the X axis of the coordinate system in the previous step, then you need to define the Y or Z axis in this step. You can choose the button corresponding to the axis that you want to define from the Command bar. Note that the button of the axis, which is already defined, is not enabled in the Command bar. The method of defining the axis is the same as that of defining the first axis.

As soon as you define the second axis, the coordinate system will be created and displayed in the model. Choose **Finish** from the Command bar to confirm the creation of the coordinate system. You can also choose the button of any of the steps to modify the selection made in that particular step.

Note

1. *Solid Edge uses the right-hand rule to determine the direction of the third axis. This rule states that if the thumb of the right hand points in the direction of the positive X axis and the first finger points in the direction of the positive Y axis, then the middle finger will point in the direction of the positive Z axis.*

2. *The coordinate system is displayed as a feature in the docking window.*

In the **Synchronous Part** environment, you can create a new coordinate system by specifying its position on a plane. To do so, choose the **Coordinate System** tool from the **Planes** group; a coordinate system will be attached to the cursor and you will be prompted to specify the origin of the new coordinate system. Move the cursor to any plane and specify the orientation by using the N, B, F, P, or G keys in the keyboard. Next, click in the graphics area; the new coordinate system will be placed on the plane. You can also snap to the keypoints in the model space to place a coordinate system.

USING THE OTHER OPTIONS OF THE EXTRUDE TOOL

In the previous chapter, you have learned about some options of the **Extrude** tool. In this chapter, you will learn about the remaining options of this tool.

Side Step

The **Side Step** is required while creating additional features on the base feature using open sketches. In this step, you will be prompted to specify the side of the open sketch on which the material will be added. Figure 5-17 shows an open sketch and the side on which the material will be added and Figure 5-18 shows the model after creating the protrusion feature using the open sketch.

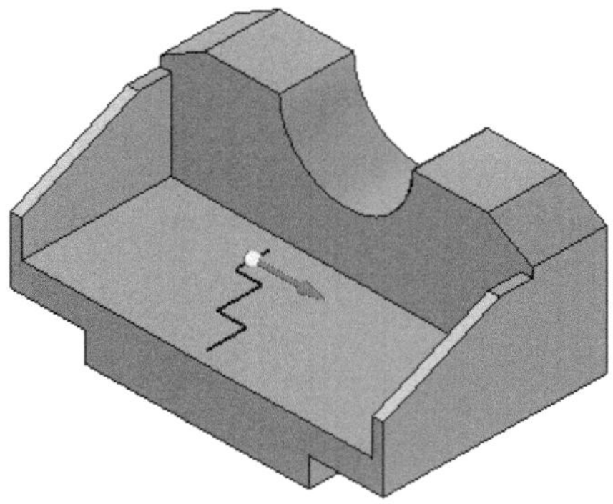

Figure 5-17 *Open sketch and the side on which the material will be added*

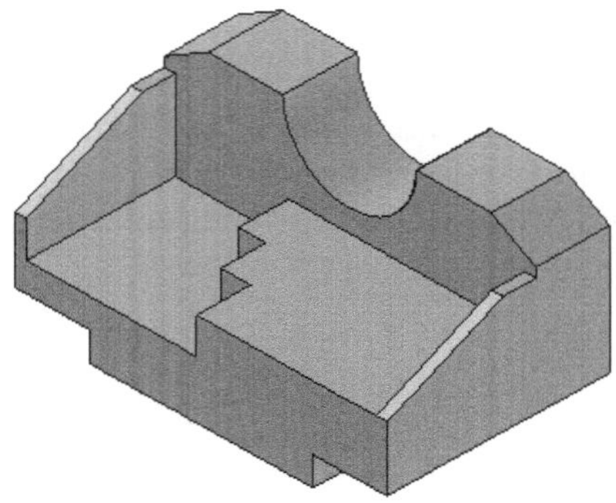

Figure 5-18 *The resultant feature*

Extent Step

In the previous chapter, you learned about the use of the **Finite** and **From-To** options of the **Extent Type** flyout while creating an extruded feature. There are some more options available in the Command bar that enables you to define the depth of the extrusion. These options become available while creating the second feature. These options are discussed next.

Through All

This option is used to create a feature by extruding the sketch through all the features available in the model. The feature will be terminated at the last face of the model. On selecting this option, an Extrude handle will be displayed on the sketch and you will be prompted to click to select the side. Click on the Extrude Handle and move the cursor on either side of the sketching plane to define the direction of extrusion. Note that if you select the side in which the sketch does not intersect with any face of the model, an error message will be displayed informing you that the operation was unsuccessful. Figure 5-19 shows a sketch extruded in the downward direction using the **Through All** option.

Through Next

This option is used to create a feature by extruding the sketch up to the next surface of the model. On selecting this option, you will be prompted to define the side of extrusion of the sketch. Figure 5-20 shows a sketch extruded up to the next surface in the downward direction.

From/To Extent

While using the **From/To Extent** option in the **Ordered Part** environment, you can also define the offset values from the **From** surface and the **To** surface by entering the value in the **Offset** edit box before selecting the respective surface. For example, if you want to use this option with an offset, choose the **From/To Extent** button from the Command bar; you will be prompted to select the '**From**' surface. In the **Offset** edit box, enter the offset distance for the surface from which the feature should start and then select the surface; an arrow will be displayed and you will be prompted to select the side for the offset. After selecting this side, you will be prompted to select the surface up to which the feature will be created. Again, enter the offset distance and select the surface; an arrow will be displayed and you will be prompted to select a side for the offset. Move the cursor to define the direction of the offset. Figure 5-21 shows an extruded feature created by defining the offset values for the '**From**' and '**To**' surfaces.

Note that you can also use the **Through All**, **Through Next**, and **From /To Extent** options to extrude the sketch on both sides. Figure 5-22 shows a sketch extruded on both sides of the sketching plane using the **Through All** option in combination with the **Non-symmetric Extent** option.

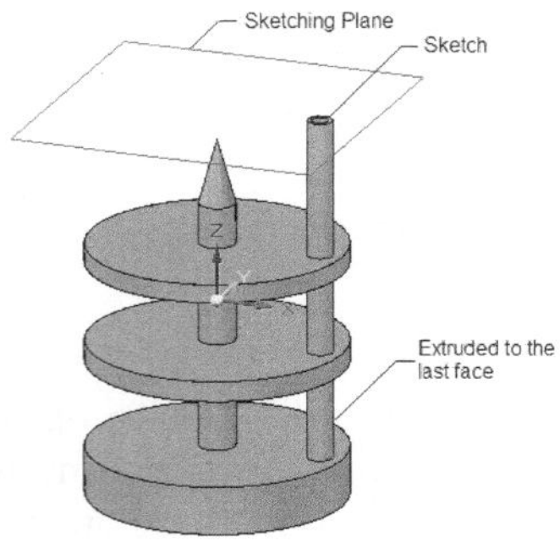

*Figure 5-19 Extruding the sketch downward using the **Through All** option*

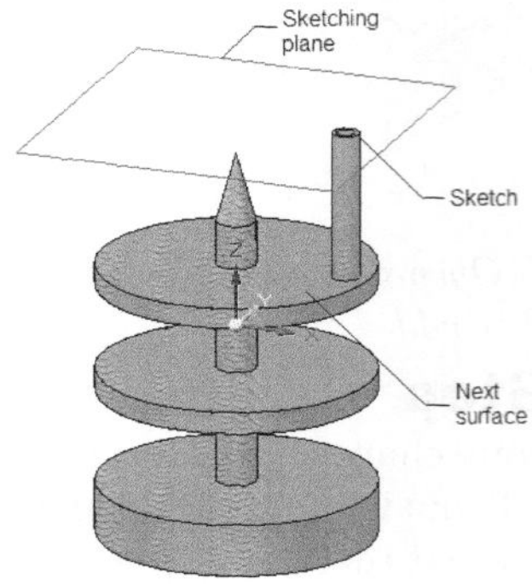

*Figure 5-20 Extruding the sketch using the **Through Next** option*

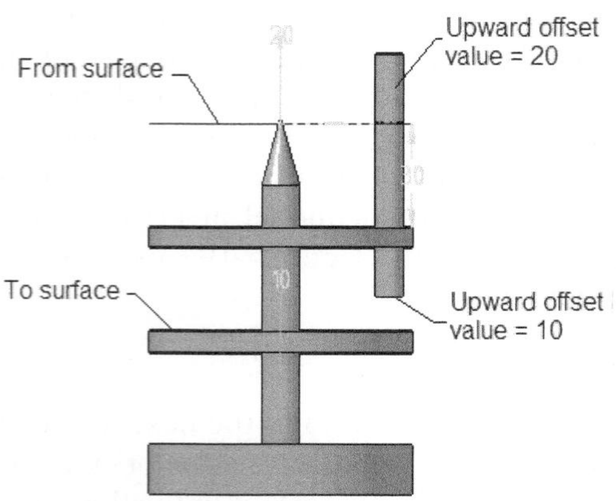

*Figure 5-21 Creating a protrusion feature by defining offset values for the **From** and **To** surfaces*

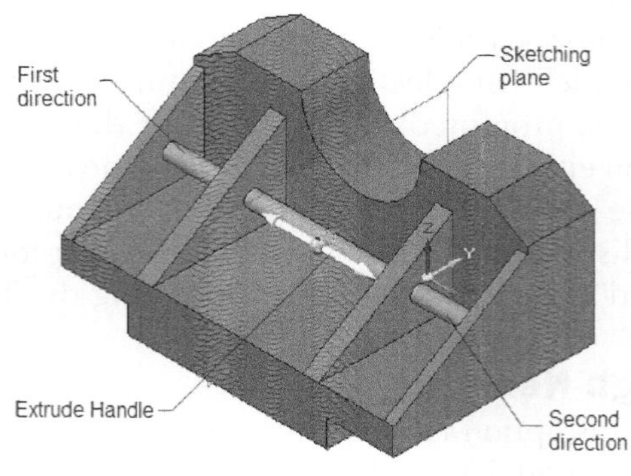

*Figure 5-22 Sketch extruded using the **Through All** option on both sides of the sketching plane in combination with the **Non-symmetric Extent** option*

Treatments Step Flyout

You can add a draft or a crown to a protrusion feature by choosing the required button from the

Treatments Step flyout in the **Extrude** Command bar. The draft or crown features are added to improve the design aesthetically and to remove the model from its mold easily. By adding a draft, you can add a linear taper to the model, as shown in Figure 5-23. This figure shows different drafts applied to both sides of a non-symmetric feature. By adding a crown, you can add a curved taper to the model, as shown in Figure 5-24. This figure shows different crowns applied to both sides of a non-symmetric feature. Note that in both cases, the basic sketch is a circle.

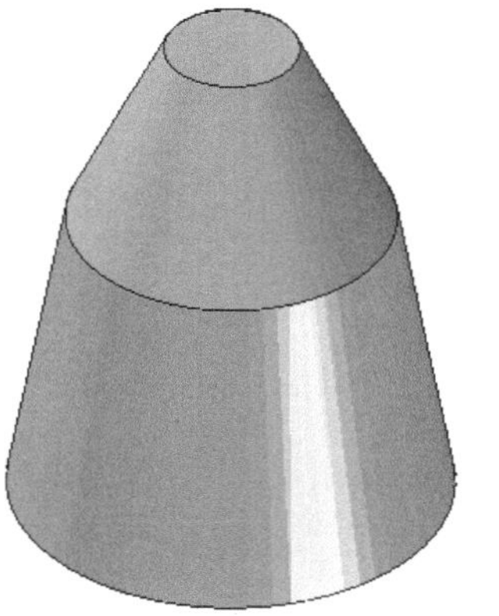

***Figure 5-23** Different drafts added to both sides of the protrusion feature*

***Figure 5-24** Different crowns added to both sides of the protrusion feature*

The options in the **Treatments Step** flyout are discussed next.

No Treatment

This button is chosen by default in the **Treatments Step** flyout. As a result, no treatment is applied to the model.

Draft

The **Draft** button is chosen to add a draft to the extruded feature. When you choose this button, the **Angle** edit box and the **Flip 1** button will be displayed in the Command bar. You can enter the draft angle in the **Angle** edit box. The default direction in which the draft will be created is displayed in the preview of the model. If you want to reverse the direction of the draft, choose the **Flip 1** button. If the draft was initially inward, the preview will now show the draft outward, indicating that the draft will be applied in the reverse direction now. In case of symmetric extend extrude features, the **Angle 1**, **Angle 2**, **Flip 1**, and **Flip 2** edit boxes are displayed in the Command bar.

Crown

The **Crown** button is chosen to add a crown to the extruded feature. When you choose this button, the **Crown Parameters** dialog box will be displayed. If you extrude the sketch symmetrically or non-symmetrically on both sides of the sketching plane, the dialog box will be displayed with the **Direction 1** and **Direction 2** areas, as shown in Figure 5-25. However, if you extrude the sketch only in one direction, the **Direction 1** area of this dialog box will be active. The options available in both areas of the **Crown Parameters** dialog box are the same and are discussed next.

Crown Type

The **Crown Type** drop-down list is used to select the technique of applying a crown to the feature. The options available in this drop-down list are discussed next.

No Crown: This option is used when you do not want to apply the crown in any direction.

Radius: This option is used to apply the crown by defining its radius. The radius value is specified in the **Radius** edit box, which is available below the **Crown Type** drop-down list.

Radius and take-off: This option is used to apply the crown by defining its radius and the take off angle. These values are specified in the edit boxes that are available below the **Crown Type** drop-down list.

Offset: This option is used to apply the crown by defining the offset value between the sections at the start and end of the crown. The offset value is specified in the **Offset** edit box available below the **Crown Type** drop-down list.

Offset and take-off: This option is used to apply the crown by defining the take off angle and offset value between the sections at the start and end of the crown. These values are specified in the edit boxes available below the **Crown Type** drop-down list.

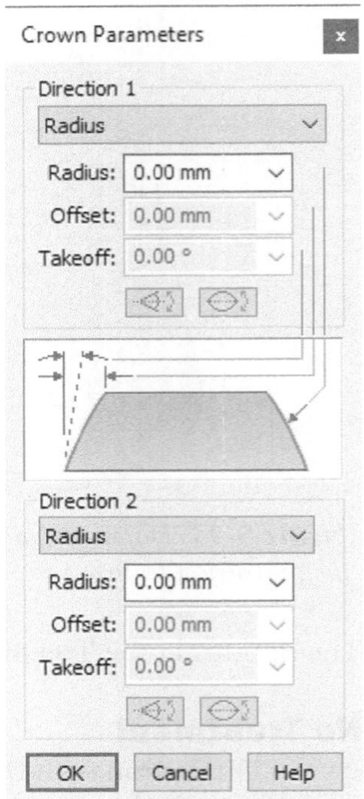

*Figure 5-25 The **Crown Parameters** dialog box*

Radius

The **Radius** edit box is used to specify the radius value of the crown and will be available only when you select the **Radius** or the **Radius and take-off** crown option.

Offset

The **Offset** edit box is used to specify the offset value of the crown and will be available only when you select the **Offset** or the **Offset and take-off** crown option.

Takeoff

The **Takeoff** edit box is used to specify the angle value of the crown and will be available only when you select the **Radius and take-off** or the **Offset and take-off** crown type.

Flip Side

This button is used to reverse the side on which the crown is applied. If the crown is applied inside the feature, choosing this button will apply the crown outside the feature.

Flip Curvature

The **Flip Curvature** button is used to reverse the curvature of the crown.

CREATING CUTOUT FEATURES

Cutouts are created by removing the material, defined by a profile, from one or more existing features. In Solid Edge, you can create various types of cutouts such as extruded cutouts, revolved cutouts, swept cutouts, and so on. In this chapter, you will learn about the extruded or revolved cutouts. The remaining types of cutouts will be discussed in the later chapters.

Creating Extruded Cutouts (Ordered Environment)

Ribbon: Home > Solids > Cut

Extruded cutouts are created by extruding a profile to remove material from one or more features. Figure 5-26 shows the base feature and the sketch that will be used to create a cutout and Figure 5-27 shows the model after creating the cutout.

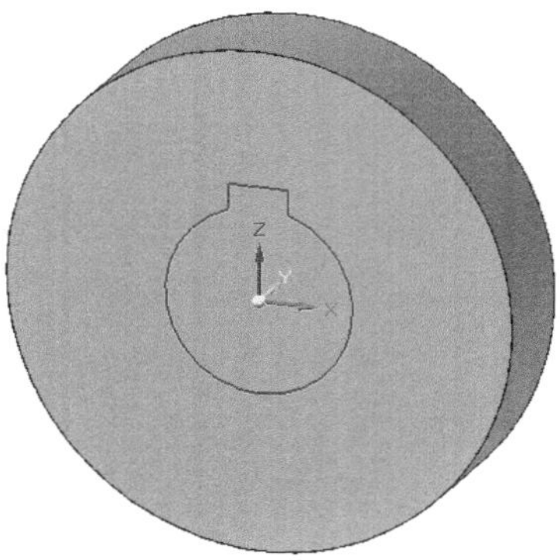

Figure 5-26 *Base feature and the sketch for the cutout*

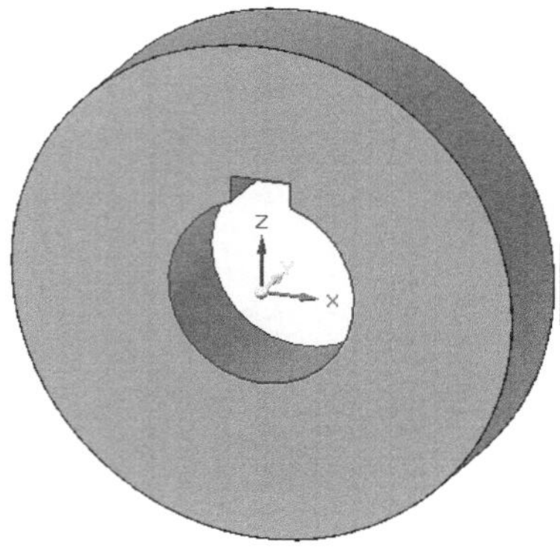

Figure 5-27 *Model after creating the cutout*

In Solid Edge, the cutouts are created using the **Cut** tool. This tool works in the same manner as the **Extrude** tool. Note that while creating the cutouts, you can create close and open profiles and use the **Side Step** extensively to define the direction of the material removal. Figures 5-28 through 5-31 show the side of the material removal and the resulting features.

You can also use open profiles to create the cutouts. However, you need to carefully define the side of the material removal for the cutout, see Figures 5-32 through 5-35.

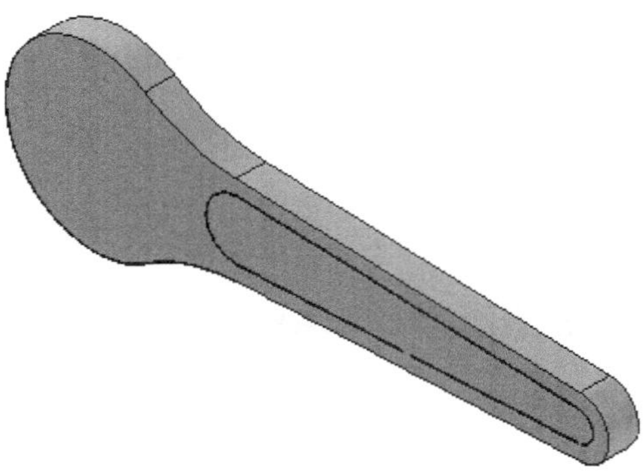

Figure 5-28 *Sketch for the cutout and the direction for the cutout pointing inside the sketch*

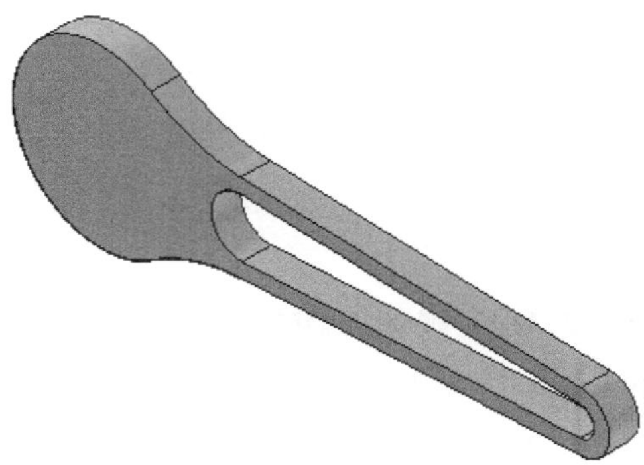

Figure 5-29 *Cutout created by removing the material from inside the sketch*

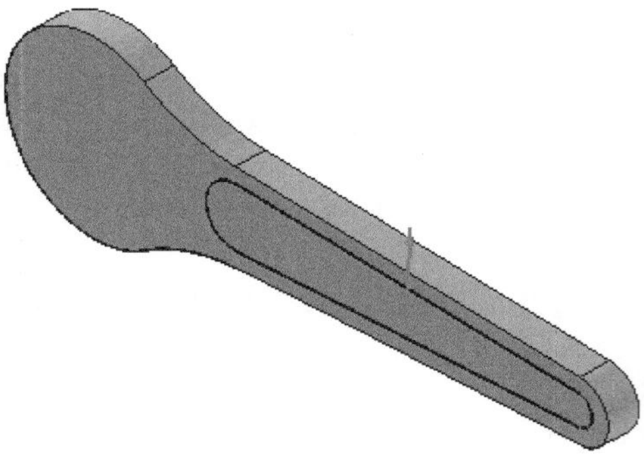

Figure 5-30 Sketch for the cutout and the direction for the cutout pointing outside the sketch

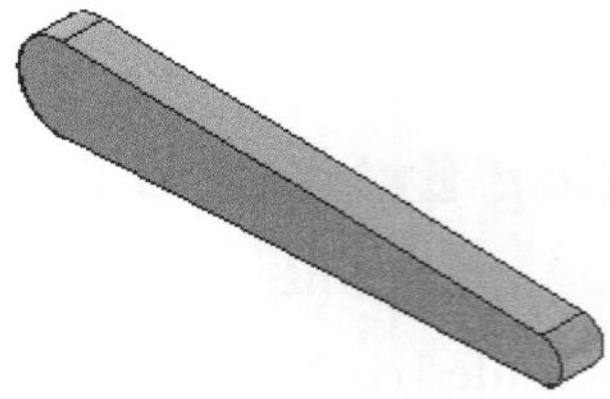

Figure 5-31 Cutout created by removing the material from outside the sketch

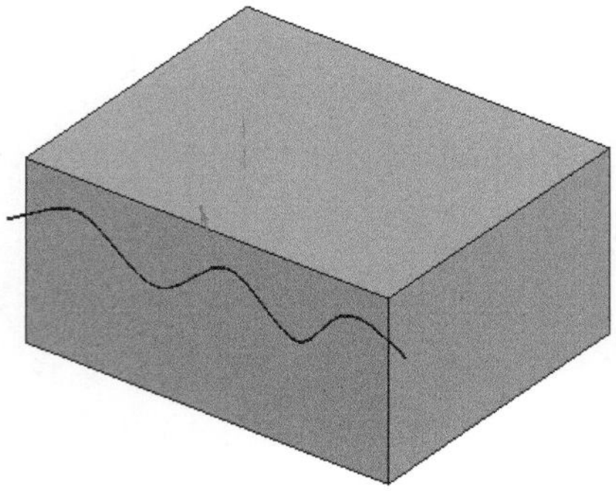

Figure 5-32 Open profile and the side of material removal

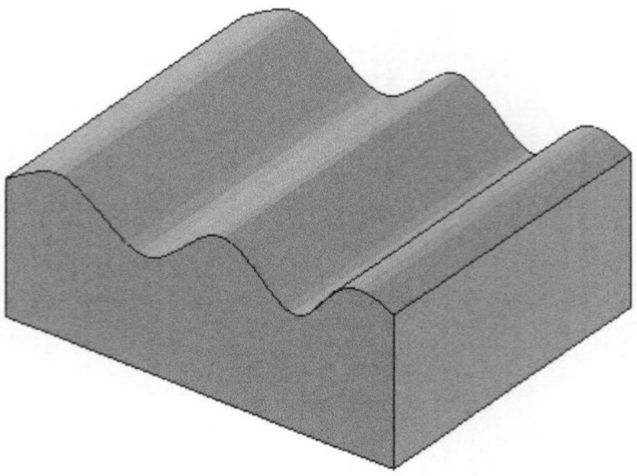

Figure 5-33 Resultant cutout created by removing the material above the open profile

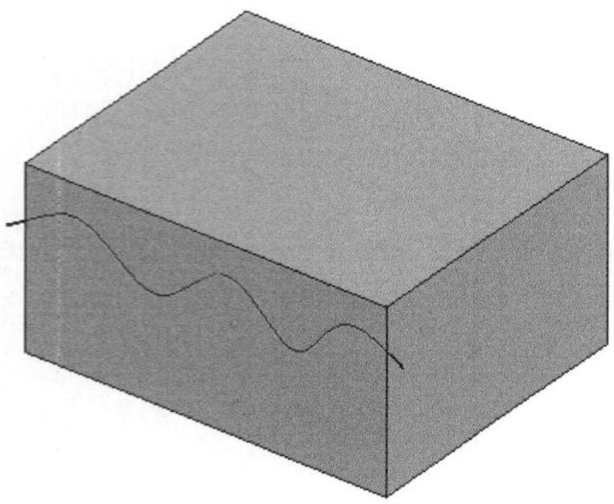

Figure 5-34 Open profile and the side of material removal

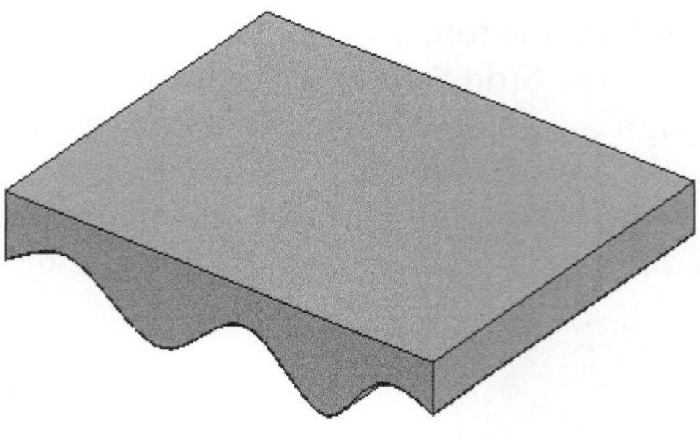

Figure 5-35 Resultant cutout created by removing the material below the open profile

Creating Revolved Cutouts (Ordered Environment)

Ribbon: Home > Solids > Revolved Cut

The **Revolved Cut** tool is used to create a revolved cutout by removing the material defined by the sketch. This tool will be active only when a feature exits in the modeling window. This tool works in the same manner as the **Revolve** tool with the only difference being that the **Revolved Cut** tool removes the material only from an existing feature. Similar to the extruded cutouts, you can also use the **Side Step** extensively in the revolved cutouts to specify the side of material removal. Figures 5-36 through 5-39 show the side of material removal and the resulting models after creating a symmetric semicircular revolved cutout.

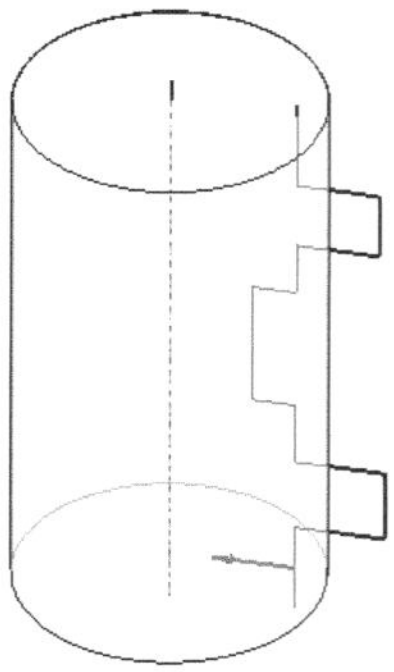

Figure 5-36 *Open profile and the side of the material removal*

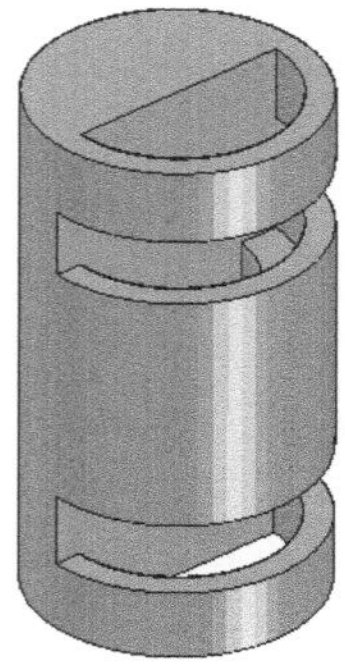

Figure 5-37 *Resultant revolved cutout created by removing the material on the left of the profile*

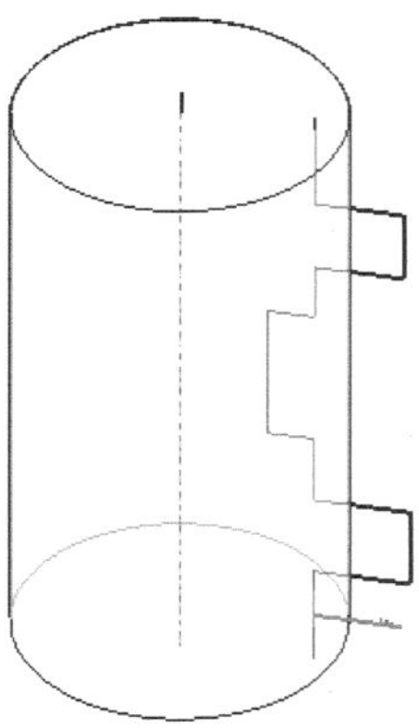

Figure 5-38 *Open profile and the side of the material removal*

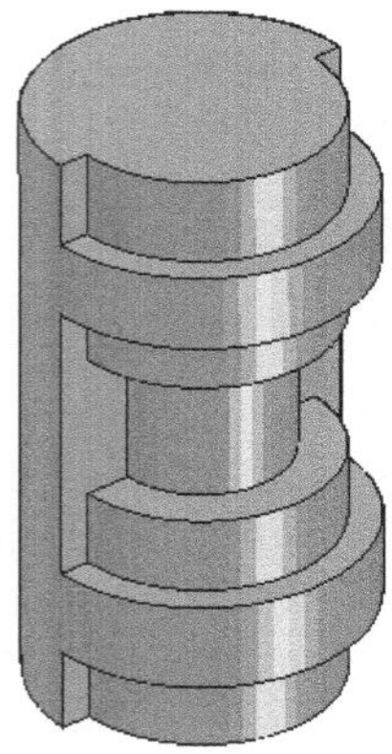

Figure 5-39 *Resultant revolved cutout created by removing the material on the right of the profile*

Creating Cutouts (Synchronous Environment)

Just as adding material to a solid by using the Extrude and Revolve handles, you can also remove material from a solid. To do so, first draw a profile at the required position and then select the profile; an Extrude handle and a Command bar will be displayed. Click on the handle; the preview of extrusion will be displayed by default. But to create a cut, you need to choose **Cut** from the **Add/Cut** drop-down list in the Command bar. Next, you can specify the extent type, symmetry, draft, and crown parameters for the cut in the same way as you did while extruding the profile. Similarly, you can create revolved cutouts using the revolve handle.

Open/Closed sketch

This option in the Command bar is used to specify whether the edges of an adjacent model are considered as a part of the sketch region.

Open

When you choose this option, the edges of the adjacent model are ignored. Figure 5-40 shows the cutout created by using the **Open** sketch option.

Closed

When you choose this option, the edges of the adjacent model are considered as a part of the profile. Figure 5-41 shows the cutout created by using the **Closed** sketch option.

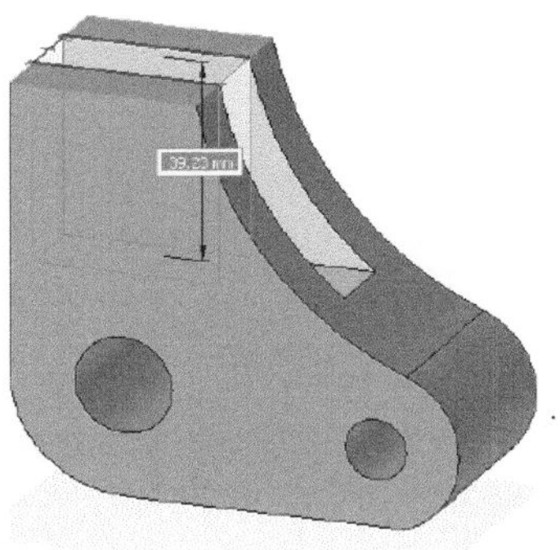

*Figure 5-40 Cutout created by using the **Open** sketch option*

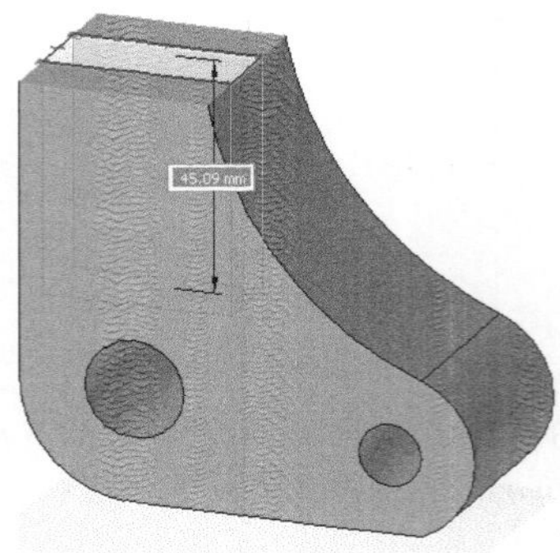

*Figure 5-41 Cutout created by using the **Closed** sketch option*

USING THE EDGES OF EXISTING FEATURES

Ribbon:	Home > Draw > Project to Sketch

Sometimes, while drawing the profiles of some features, you may need to use the edges of the existing features as the sketched entities in the current profile. In Solid Edge, you can do this using the **Project to Sketch** tool after selecting a sketching plane. You can copy the edges of the existing features by projecting them exactly as they are on the current sketching plane or by copying them with some offset. Note that because you are projecting the entities that are already used in the model, you do not need to add dimensions to the projected entities. They will automatically take the dimensions from the original entities.

To project entities in the model, invoke the **Project to Sketch** tool from the **Draw** group; the **Project to Sketch Options** dialog box will be displayed, as shown in the Figure 5-42. The options in the dialog box are discussed next.

Project with offset

This check box is used to project the geometries with some offset value. If this check box is selected, the options to offset the projected geometry will be displayed in the Command bar.

Project internal face loops

If this check box is selected, the geometries of all the internal loops on a face will also be projected when you select a face to project the edges. After setting the options in this dialog box, choose the **OK** button to display the **Project to Sketch** Command bar. If you have selected the **Project with offset** check box, this tool works in one or two steps, which are discussed next.

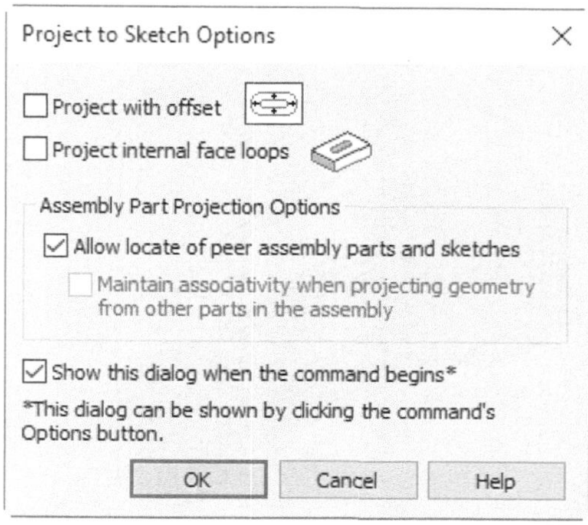

*Figure 5-42 The **Project to Sketch Options** dialog box*

Select

By default, this button is chosen in the **Project to Sketch** Command bar. As a result, you can select the geometries that you want to include in the profile. Also, you can select an option from the **Select** drop-down list based on which the geometries will be included in the profile. Select the required option to select the corresponding entities. You need to choose the **Accept** button after selecting the entities if you have selected the option to project the geometries with an offset. Else, the **Accept** button does not get activated and the selecting entities get included. As mentioned earlier, you do not need to dimension the projected entities. The dimensions are adopted from the original geometries that are projected.

Offset

This button will be available only if you select the option that allows you to project the geometries with an offset. In this case, select the geometries using the **Select** tool and then choose the **Accept** button from the Command bar; the **Offset** step will be invoked and the **Distance** edit box will be displayed in the Command bar. Enter the offset distance in this edit box and then move the cursor in the drawing window to specify the side for the offset. After selecting the side, click to project and offset the selected geometry.

Figure 5-43 shows a model after projecting some of the geometries from the existing features on a reference plane from the top face of the model.

Assembly Part Projection Options Area

The options available in this area are used in the assembly modeling environment. These options are discussed next.

Allow locate of peer assembly parts and sketches

If this check box is selected, you will be allowed to select the geometries from the other parts in the assembly.

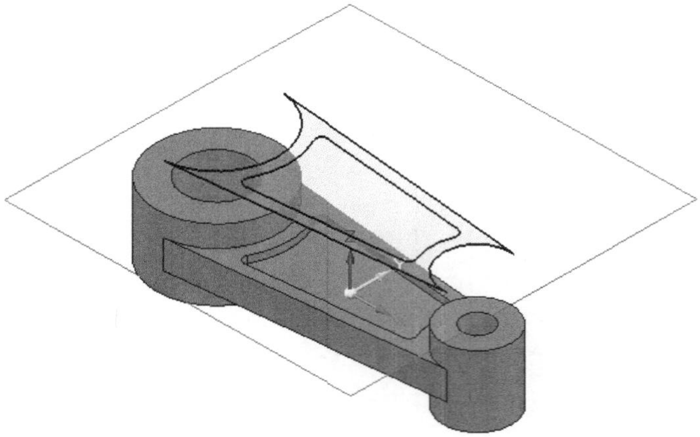

Figure 5-43 Geometries projected on a reference plane

Maintain associativity when projecting geometry from other parts in the assembly

If this check box is selected, the geometries that you project from the other parts in the assembly will be associative.

ADVANCED DRAWING DISPLAY TOOLS

In the earlier chapters, you learned about some of the basic drawing display tools. In this chapter, you will learn about the advanced drawing display tools which are discussed next.

Creating User-defined Named Views

As mentioned earlier, the **View Orientation** palette in the status bar is used to invoke the standard named views. In Solid Edge, you can also create user-defined standard views. These views are automatically added to the **View Orientation** palette, and therefore, can be invoked whenever required.

To create the user-defined named views, set the current view to the view to be saved using the **Rotate** tool or any other drawing display tool. After setting the view, choose **View Orientation > View Manager** from the status bar; the **Named Views** dialog box will be displayed with six standard named views, as shown in Figure 5-44. Enter the name of the new user-defined view in the **Name** column of the seventh row of the **Named Views** dialog box. You can also enter a brief description about the view in the **Description** column. After entering the required information, close the dialog box; the newly created view will be displayed in the **View Orientation** palette and can be selected from this palette.

Using Common Views

Solid Edge provides you with the **Common Views** tool, which is a very user-friendly tool and is used to set the current view to some standard common views. You can invoke this tool by right-clicking in the drawing window when the **Select** tool is active. Then, choose **Common Views** from the shortcut menu displayed; the **Common Views** dialog box will be displayed with a cube in it. You can use this cube to rotate the view of the model by clicking on the corners or faces of the cube. As you move the cursor over any vertex or face of the cube in the **Common Views** dialog box, a message will be displayed in this dialog box that will inform you about the direction of rotation of the view. While working with the **Common Views** tool, you can press the HOME key at any point of time to invoke the standard isometric view.

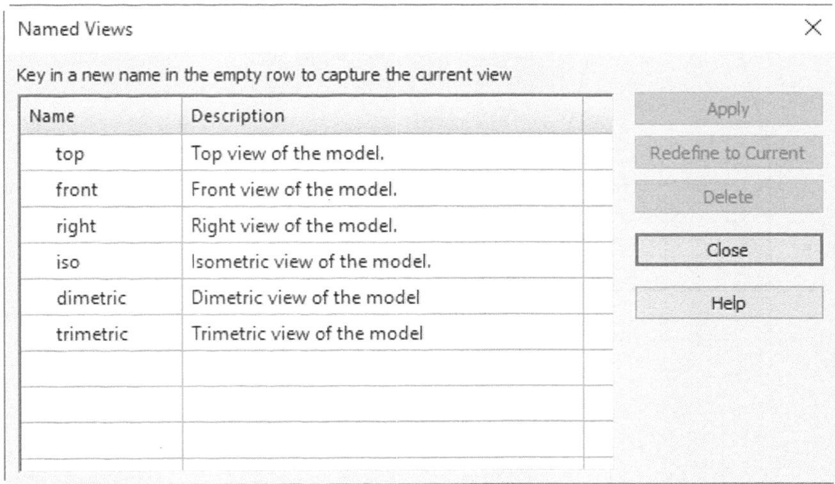

*Figure 5-44 The **Named Views** dialog box*

TUTORIALS

Tutorial 1 — Synchronous

In this tutorial, you will create the model shown in Figure 5-45. The dimensions of the model are given in Figure 5-46. After creating the model, save it with the name *c05tut1.par* at the location given next.

C:\Solid Edge\c05 **(Expected time: 45 min)**

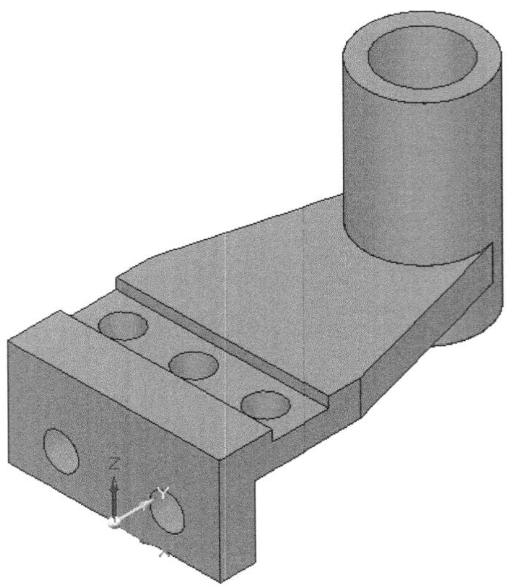

Figure 5-45 Model for Tutorial 1

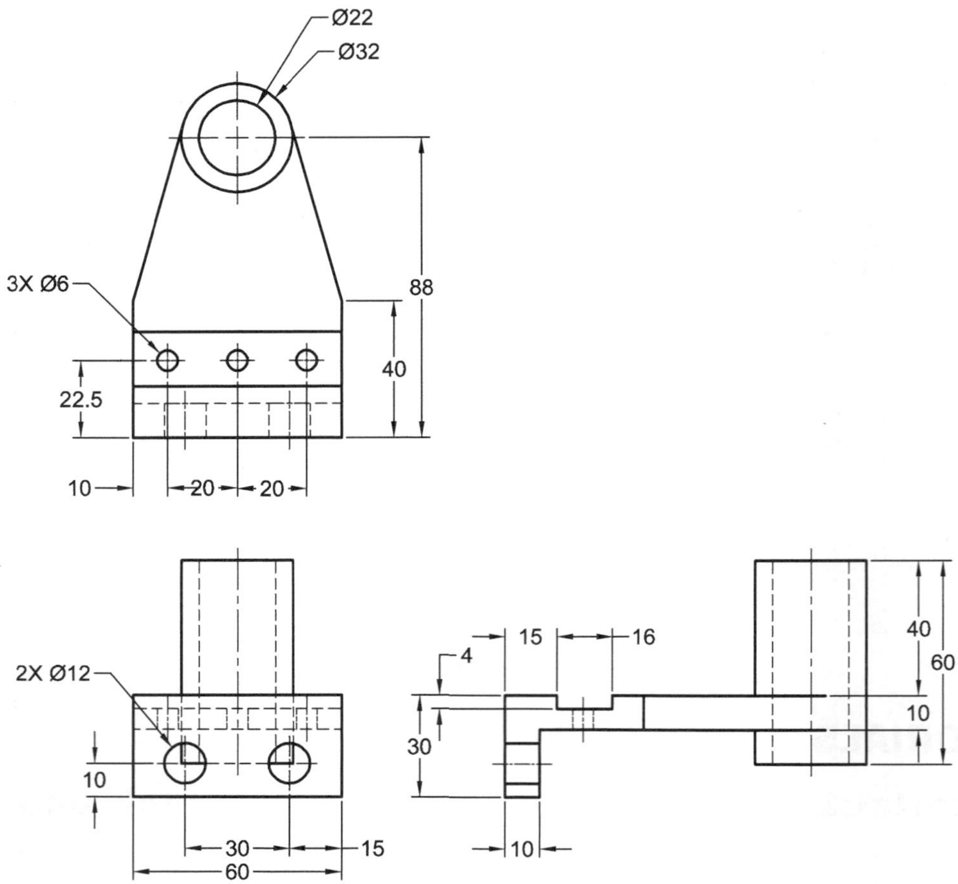

Figure 5-46 *Dimensions of the model*

Before you create the model, first you need to determine the number of features in it and then the sequence in which they will be created. The model for Tutorial 1 is the combination of three extruded features and three cutouts (holes). The base feature will be created on the YZ plane. The second feature will be created on the top face of the base feature. The third extruded feature will be created on the reference plane created at an offset of 10 units from the bottom face of the second feature. The cutouts will be created on the planar face of the protrusion features.

The following steps are required to complete this tutorial:

a. Create the base feature by selecting the YZ plane as a reference plane, refer to Figures 5-47 and 5-48.
b. Create the second feature by selecting the top planar face of the base feature as the sketching plane, refer to Figures 5-49 through 5-52.
c. Create the third feature by defining a reference plane at an offset of 10 units from the bottom face of the second feature, refer to Figure 5-53.
d. Create two hole cut outs on the left face of the base feature using the **Cut** tool, refer to Figure 5-54 and 5-55.

e. Create the remaining cutouts to complete the model, refer to Figure 5-56.
f. Save the model.

Creating the Base Feature

As mentioned earlier, the base feature is an extruded feature and the profile of this feature will be created on the right plane.

1. Start a new part file and then choose the **Line** tool from the **Draw** group of the **Home** tab; the **Line** Command bar is displayed and the alignment lines are attached to the cursor.

   Next, you need to define the YZ plane to draw the profile of the base feature.

2. As you move the cursor toward the base coordinate system, the nearest principal plane gets highlighted. Wait for a while and then right-click; the **QuickPick** list box is displayed with the nearest possible selection. Next, select the YZ plane to sketch.

3. Orient the view normal to the sketching plane by using the **Sketch View** tool from the **Status Bar**.

4. Draw the profile for the base feature and then add the required relations and dimensions by using the tools from the **Sketching** tab, as shown in Figure 5-47. Change the orientation of the view to isometric.

5. Choose the **Select** tool from the **Home** tab and select the middle portion of the sketch; an extrude handle and a Command bar are displayed.

6. Choose the **Symmetric** button from the Command bar and drag the arrow in the drawing window; the preview of extrusion and an edit box are displayed in the drawing window.

7. Enter **60** in the edit box and press ENTER; an extruded feature is created. Figure 5-48 shows the base feature of the model after hiding the dimensions.

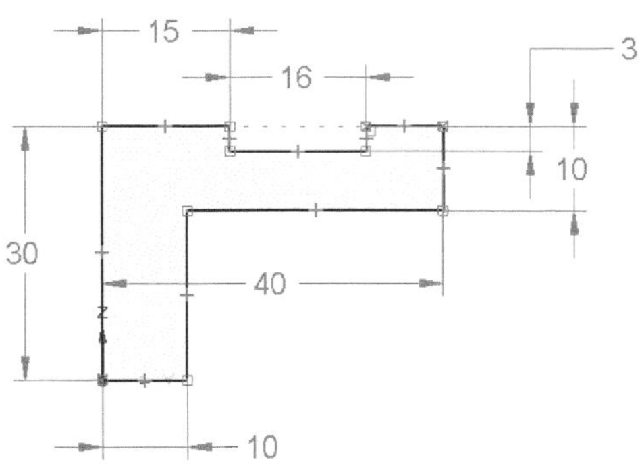

Figure 5-47 *Dimensioned profile for the base feature*

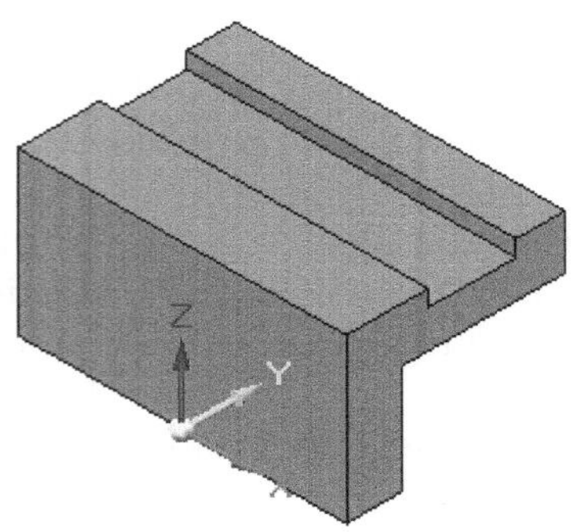

Figure 5-48 *Base feature of the model*

Creating the Second Feature

As mentioned earlier, the second feature is also an extruded feature and its profile is created on the top face of the base feature.

1. Choose the **Line** tool from the **Draw** group; you are prompted to select a planar face or the principal plane for sketching the profile.

2. Move the cursor on the top face of the base feature and click on the lock symbol, refer to Figure 5-49.

3. Orient the view normal to the sketching plane. Draw the profile for the second feature by using the sketching tools and then add the required dimensions and relationships to the profile, as shown in Figure 5-50. Note that you need not draw the horizontal line to close the sketch.

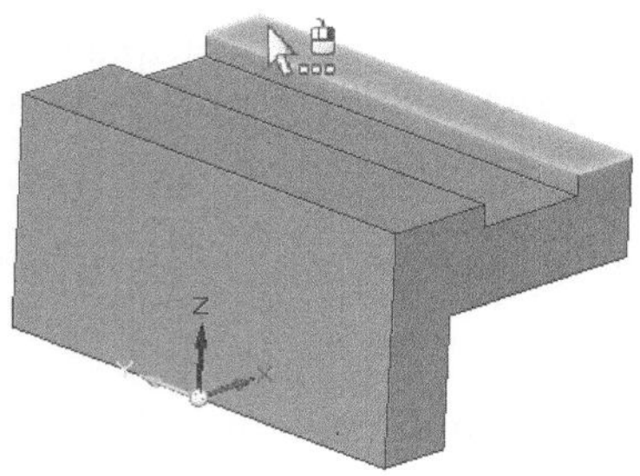

Figure 5-49 Specifying the sketching plane for the second feature

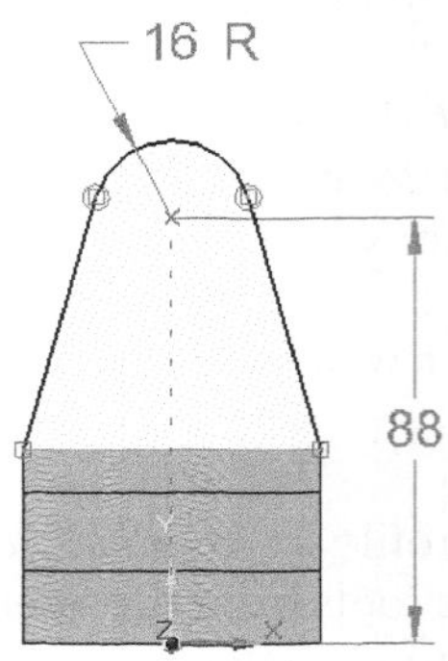

Figure 5-50 Open profile for the second feature

4. Click on the lock symbol on the right in the graphics window; the sketching plane is unlocked. Next, orient the view to isometric.

5. Invoke the **Select** tool and then click inside the closed region; an extrude handle is displayed.

   You need to add material inside the sketch region.

6. Click on the down arrow of the extrude handle and then choose the **From-To** option from the **Extent Type** drop-down list in the Command bar; you are prompted to select the **To** surface because the profile plane is automatically selected as the **From** surface.

7. Place the mouse on the right face for few seconds; the mouse symbol is attached to the cursor. Next, right-click to invoke the **QuickPick** list box. In this list box, select the bottom face of the base feature, as shown in Figure 5-51.

   The model after creating the second feature is shown in Figure 5-52.

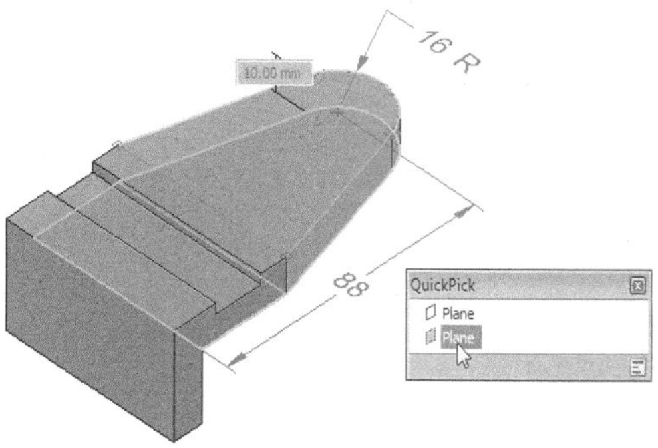

Figure 5-51 *Selecting the bottom face*

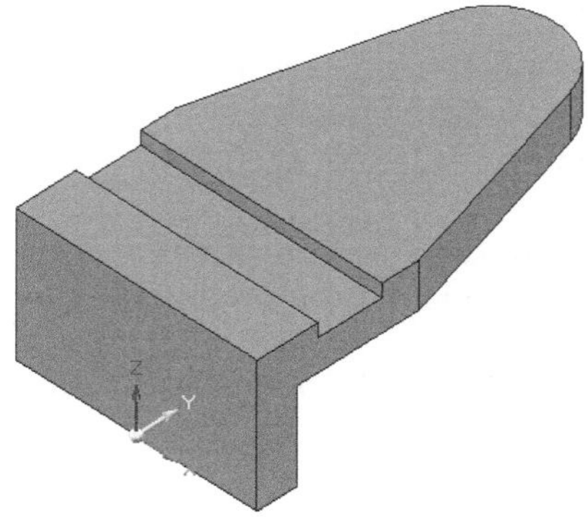

Figure 5-52 *Model after creating the second feature*

Creating the Third Feature

The third feature is also an extruded feature. Its profile can be created on the top face of the second feature and then extruded along both sides of the top face. However, in this tutorial, you will create a profile on a reference plane at an offset of 40 units from the top face of the second feature.

1. Choose the **Coincident Plane** tool from the **Planes** group; you are prompted to click on the planar face. Select the top face of the second feature; a coincident plane is created on the top face of the second feature. Also, a steering wheel is displayed on the newly created plane.

2. Select the primary axis of the steering wheel. Next, move the cursor in upward direction and then enter **40** in the edit box; a parallel plane is created at an offset from the bottom face of the second feature.

3. Draw a circle of diameter 32 units on the new reference plane. The circle should be concentric with the arc in the second feature.

4. Choose the **Select** tool from the **Home** tab and then select the middle portion of the sketch; a steering wheel and an **Extrude** Command bar are displayed.

5. Make sure the **Finite** option is selected in the **Extent Type** drop-down list, and then drag the extrude handle downward; the preview of extrusion and an edit box are displayed in the drawing window.

6. Enter **60** in the edit box and press ENTER. The model after creating the third protrusion feature is shown in Figure 5-53.

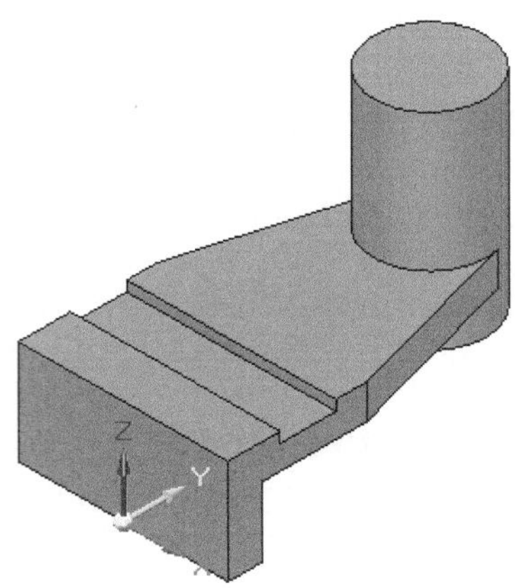

Figure 5-53 *Model after creating the third feature*

Creating the Two Holes on the Left Face of the Base Feature

The fourth feature is a cutout feature that is required to define a hole on the left face of the base feature. The profile of this cutout needs to be created on the left face of the base feature.

1. Choose the **Circle by Center Point** tool from the **Draw** group; you are prompted to click on the planar face.

2. Select the left face of the base feature to define a sketching plane.

3. Orient the view normal to the sketching plane. Draw the profile for the cutout. The profile consists of two circles, each with a diameter of 10 mm, refer to Figure 5-54.

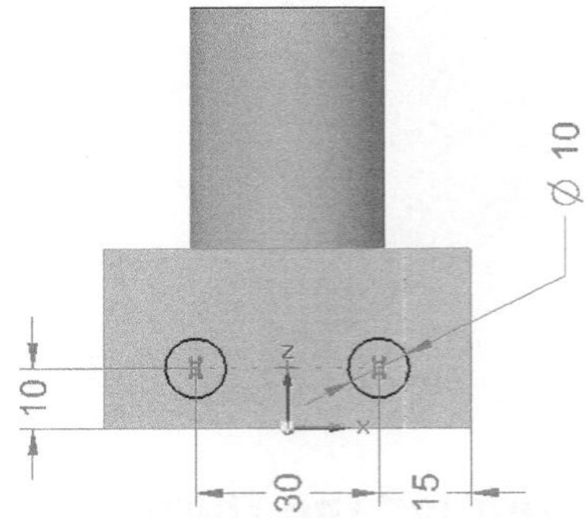

Figure 5-54 *Profile for the cutout feature*

4. Choose the **Extrude** tool from the **Solids** group; the **Extrude** Command bar is displayed. Next, select the **Chain** option from the **Selection Type** drop-down list in the Command bar and select the circles.

5. Select the **Through Next** option from the **Extent Type** drop-down list in the Command bar; the **Add/Cut** drop-down list is activated.

6. Select the **Cut** option from the **Add/Cut** drop-down list.

7. Move the cursor to the right of the model and right-click to specify the direction of the cutout feature creation. The model after creating the cutout feature is shown in Figure 5-55.

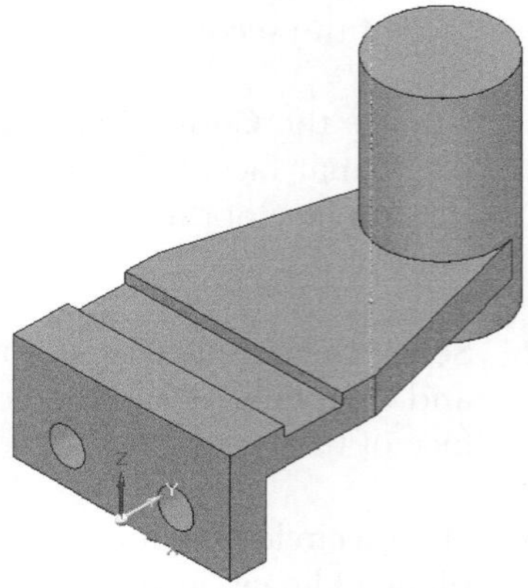

Figure 5-55 *Model after creating the cutout feature*

Creating the Remaining Features

In this step, you will create the remaining cutout features to complete the model.

1. Create the remaining two cutouts. The model after creating all the features is shown in Figure 5-56.

Saving the Model

1. Save the model with the name *c05tut1.par* at the location given next and then close the file.
   C:\Solid Edge\c05

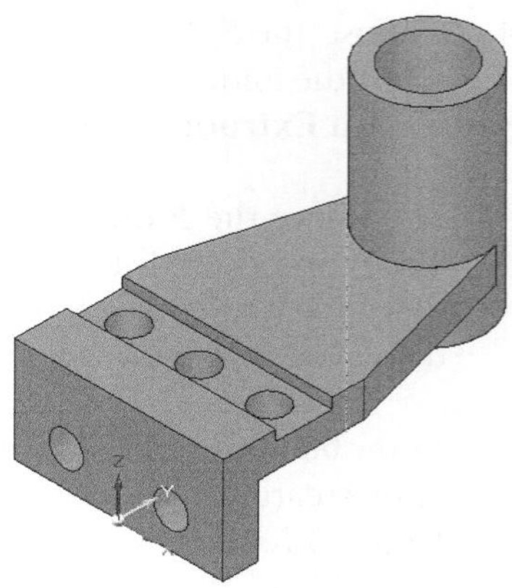

Figure 5-56 *Final model for Tutorial 1*

Tutorial 2 Ordered

In this tutorial, you will create the model shown in Figure 5-57 in the **Ordered Part** environment. The dimensions of the model are given in Figure 5-58. After creating the model, save it with the name *c05tut2.par* at the location given next.

C:\Solid Edge\c05 **(Expected time: 45 min)**

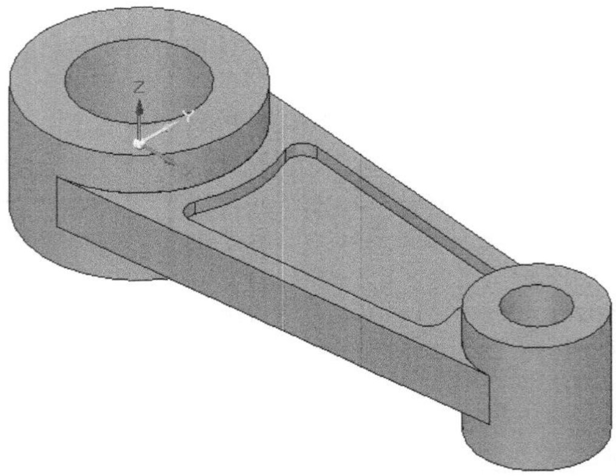

Figure 5-57 *Model for Tutorial 2*

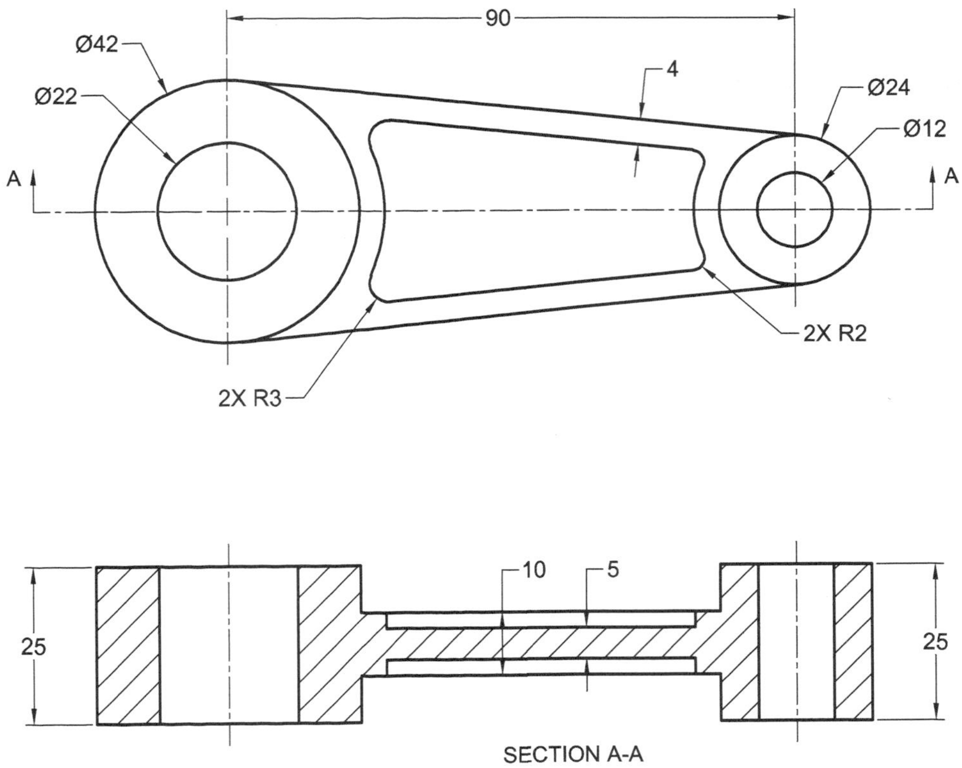

Figure 5-58 *Dimensions of the model for Tutorial 2*

The model for Tutorial 2 can be created by using various combinations of features. However, in this tutorial, the model will be created by using the combination of three extruded features and one cutout feature. The base feature will be created on the top plane and extruded symmetrically. The second feature will also be created on the top plane and then extruded symmetrically. Next, you will create a sketch on the top plane to create a cutout and then an extruded feature.

The following steps are required to complete this tutorial:

a. Start a new part file and switch to the **Ordered Part** environment.
b. Create the base feature on the top plane, refer to Figures 5-59 and 5-60.
c. Create the second feature on the top plane, refer to Figures 5-61 and 5-62.
d. Create the sketch by projecting the edges of the base feature for third and fourth features, refer to Figure 5-63.
e. Create a cutout in the second feature by using the sketch, refer to Figure 5-64.
f. Create an extruded feature by using the same sketch to complete the model, refer to Figure 5-65.

Creating the Base Feature

As mentioned earlier, the base feature is an extruded feature and the profile of this feature will be created on the top plane.

1. Start a new part file and then select the **Ordered** radio button from the **Model** group of the **Tools** tab; the **Ordered Part** environment is invoked.

2. Choose the **Sketch** tool from the **Home** tab; you are prompted to click on the planar face or the reference plane.

3. Turn on the visibility of the **Base Reference Planes** by selecting the check box adjacent to it in the **PathFinder** and then select the top plane as the sketching plane for creating the extrude feature.

4. Draw the profile for the base feature by using the sketching tools and then add the required relationships and dimensions to the profile, as shown in Figure 5-59.

5. Exit the sketching environment and then extrude the sketch symmetrically to a distance of 10 units. The base feature of the model is shown in Figure 5-60.

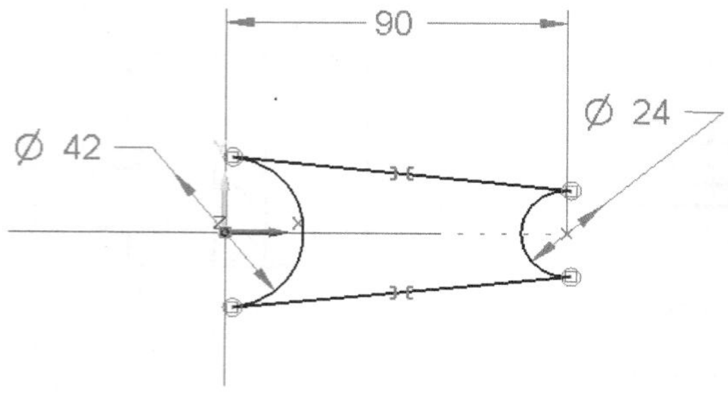

Figure 5-59 *Profile for the base feature*

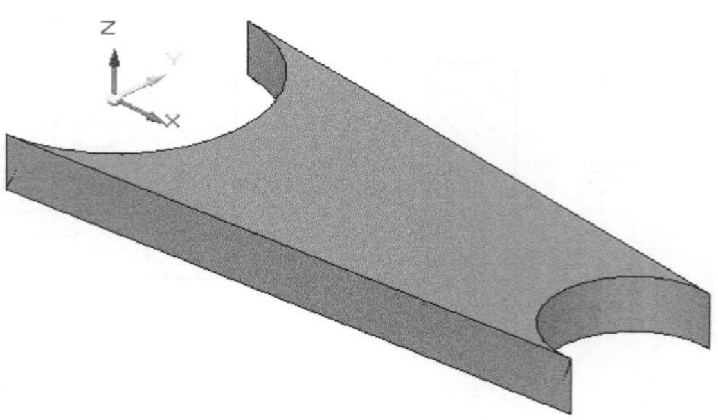

Figure 5-60 *Base feature of the model*

Creating the Second Feature

As mentioned earlier, the second feature is also an extruded feature and the profile of this feature will be created on the top plane.

1. Invoke the **Sketch** tool and select the top plane as the sketching plane. Draw the profile for the second feature by using the sketching tools and then add the required relationships and dimensions to the sketch, as shown in Figure 5-61.

2. Exit the sketching environment and then extrude the sketch symmetrically to a distance of 25 units. The model after creating this feature is shown in Figure 5-62.

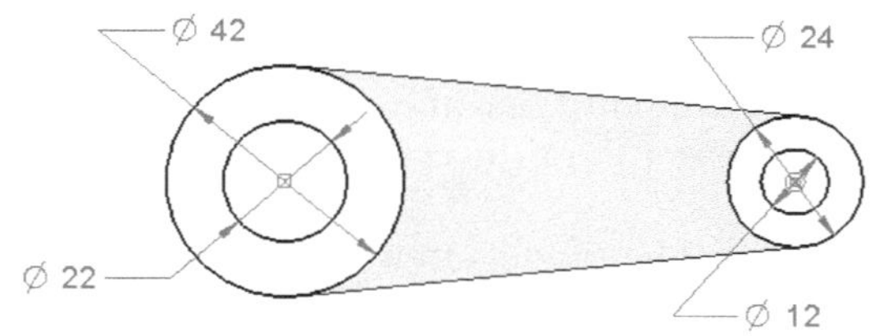

Figure 5-61 *Profile for the second feature*

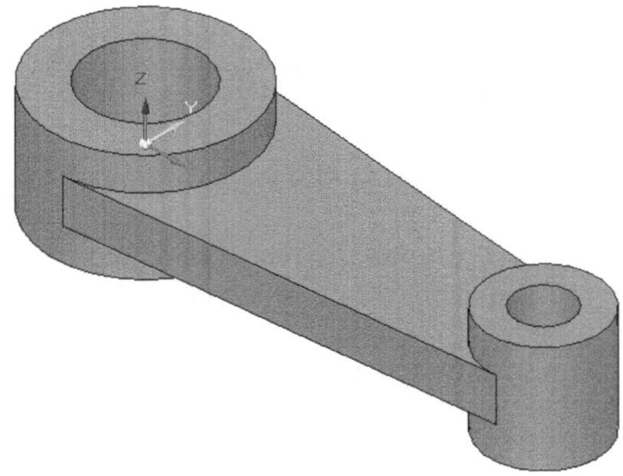

Figure 5-62 *Model after creating the second feature*

Creating the Sketch for the Third and Fourth Features

Next, you need to create a sketch that will be used as a profile for the third and fourth features. This sketch needs to be created on the top plane. To create this sketch, you need to project the edges of the second feature to an offset of 4 units.

1. Invoke the **Sketch** tool and select the top plane as the sketching plane.

2. Choose the **Project to Sketch** tool from the **Draw** group; the **Project to Sketch Options** dialog box is displayed.

3. Select the **Project with offset** check box and make sure that the **Project internal face loops** check box is clear.

4. Choose **OK** to exit the dialog box and then select **Loop** from the **Select** drop-down list in the **Project to Sketch** Command bar.

5. Move the cursor close to the first feature and click when the complete loop defined to create the first feature is highlighted; the complete loop is projected.

6. Right-click to proceed to the **Offset** step. Enter **4** in the **Distance** edit box and press ENTER. Next, move the cursor to the center of the model. Click when the offset arrow points inward in the model; the outer loop is projected at an offset of 4 units.

7. Add a fillet of radius 3 units to all the vertices of the projected loop.

8. Apply dimensions and constraints to the sketch to fully define it, as shown in Figure 5-63.

9. Exit the sketching environment and then the **Sketch** Command bar. This sketch is termed as **Sketch 3** in the **PathFinder**.

Creating the Cutout

Next, you need to create a cutout using the sketch created in the previous step.

1. Choose the **Cut** tool from the **Solids** group; the **Cut** Command bar is displayed.

2. Select the **Select from Sketch** option from the **Create-From Options** drop-down list in the Command bar.

3. Select the sketch and then right-click to proceed to the **Extent Step**.

4. Choose the **Symmetric Extent** button from the Command bar and then enter **10** in the **Distance** edit box. Next, press ENTER to apply the depth of the cutout.

5. Choose **Finish** and then **Cancel** to exit the **Cut** tool. The model after creating the cutout is shown in Figure 5-64.

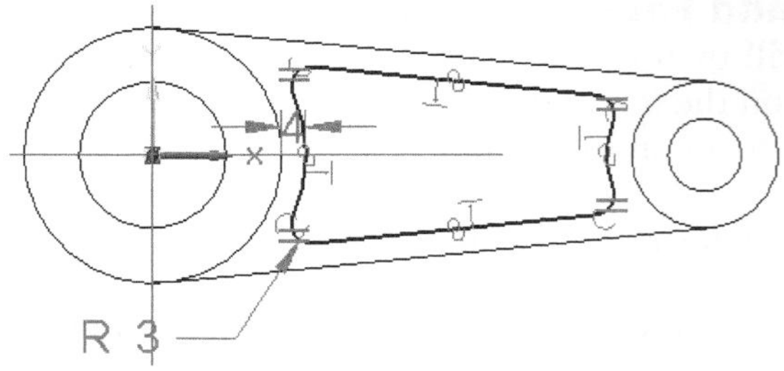

Figure 5-63 Sketch after adding the fillet, dimensions, and constraints

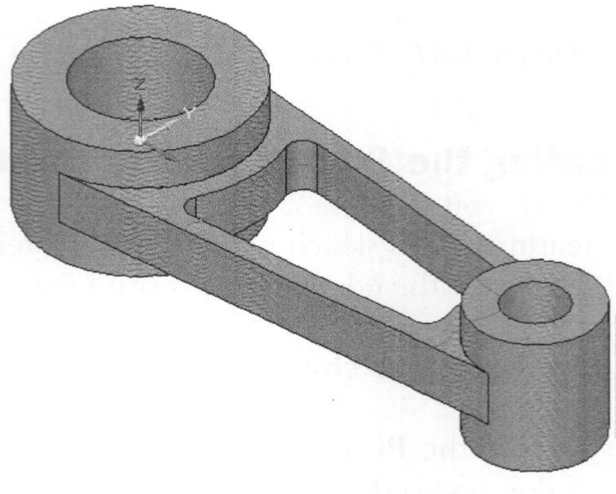

Figure 5-64 Model after creating the cutout

Creating the Extrude Feature

Next you need to create an extrude feature by using the sketch 3.

1. Choose the **Extrude** tool from the **Solids** group and then select the **Select from Sketch** option from the **Create-From Options** drop-down list.

2. Select **Sketch 3** and then right-click to proceed to the **Extent Step**.

3. Choose the **Symmetric Extent** button from the Command bar and then enter **5** in the **Distance** edit box. Next, press ENTER.

4. Choose **Finish** and then **Cancel** from the Command bar to exit the **Extrude** tool.

   Before you save and close the file, it is recommended that you turn off the display of the sketches in the model.

5. Clear the check box beside **Sketch 3** to hide the sketch. Similarly, you can hide planes and other sketches. The final model for Tutorial 2 is shown in Figure 5-65.

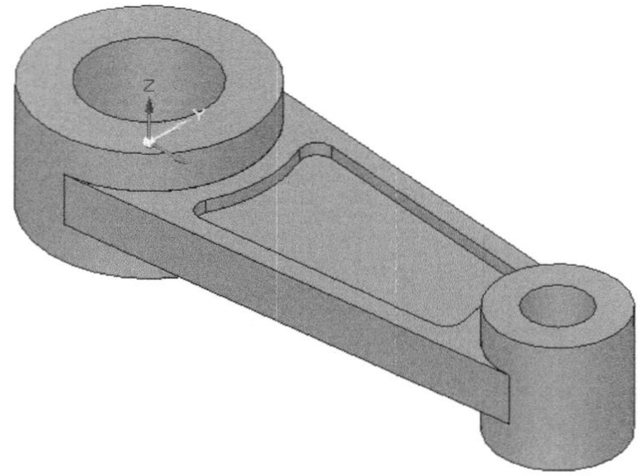

Figure 5-65 *Final model for Tutorial 2*

Saving the Model

1. Save the model with the name *c05tut2.par* at the location given next and then close the file.
   C:\Solid Edge\c05

Tutorial 3 Synchronous

In this tutorial, you will create the model shown in Figure 5-66. Its dimensions are given in Figure 5-67. After creating the model, save it with the name *c05tut3.par* at the location given next.
C:\Solid Edge\c05 **(Expected time: 45 min)**

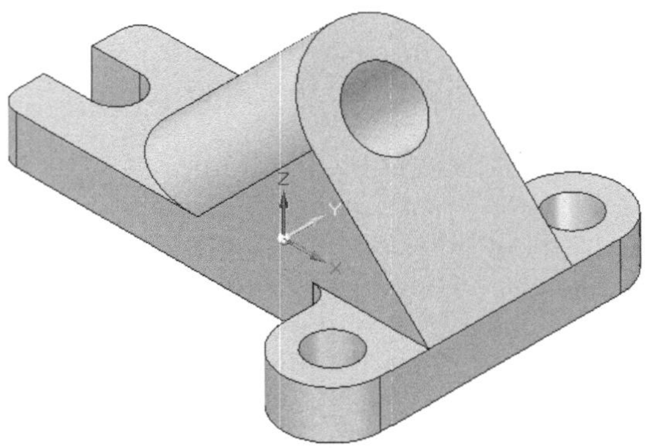

Figure 5-66 *Model for Tutorial 3*

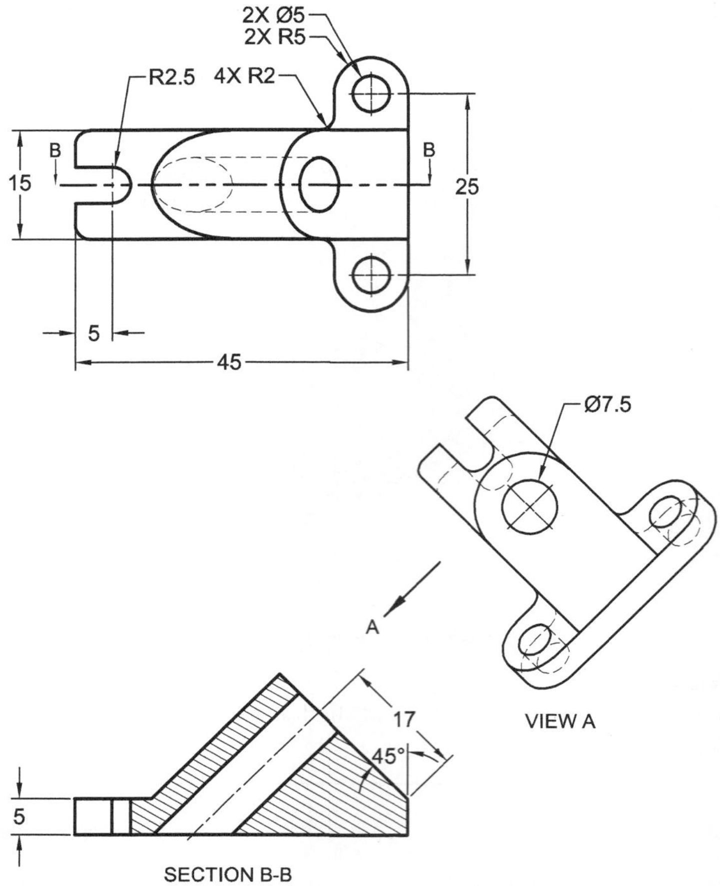

Figure 5-67 *Dimensions of the model for Tutorial 3*

Before you create the model, first you need to determine the number of features in it and then the sequence in which they will be created. The model for Tutorial 3 is a combination of two extruded features. The base feature will be created on the XY plane. The second feature will be created on a plane that is created at 45 degrees to the XY plane.

The following steps are required to complete this tutorial:

a. Create the base feature with two holes on the XY plane, refer to Figure 5-68 and 5-69.
b. Define a new reference plane at an angle of 45 degrees to the right edge of the base feature and use it to draw the profile for the second extruded feature, refer to Figure 5-70 to 5-73.
c. Draw the cutting profile for the third feature using the same reference plane, refer to Figure 5-74.
d. Extrude the cutting profile upto the next surface, refer to Figure 5-74.

Creating the Base Feature

As mentioned earlier, the base feature is a protrusion feature whose profile will be created on the XY plane.

1. Start a new part file and then choose the **Line** tool from the **Draw** group in the **Home** tab; the **Line** Command bar is displayed and alignment lines get attached to the cursor.

2. Select the XY plane as the sketching plane for creating the protrusion feature.

3. Orient the view normal to the sketching plane by using the **Sketch View** tool from the **Status Bar**.

4. Draw the profile for the base feature by using the sketching tools and then add the required relationships and dimensions to the sketch, as shown in Figure 5-68.

5. Choose the **Extrude** tool from the **Solids** group; the **Extrude** Command bar is displayed.

6. Choose the **Face** option in the **Selection Type** drop-down list and the **Include Internal Loops** option in the **Internal Face Loops** drop-down list from the **Extrude** Command bar.

7. Select the sketch and right-click in the graphics window; the preview of the extrude feature is displayed.

8. Choose the **Symmetric** button from the **Extrude** Command bar and enter **5** in the edit box and press ENTER; an extruded feature is created, as shown in Figure 5-69.

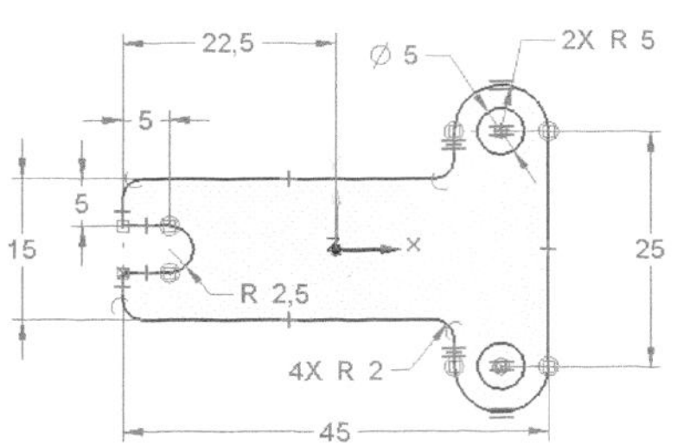

Figure 5-68 *Dimensioned profile of the base feature*

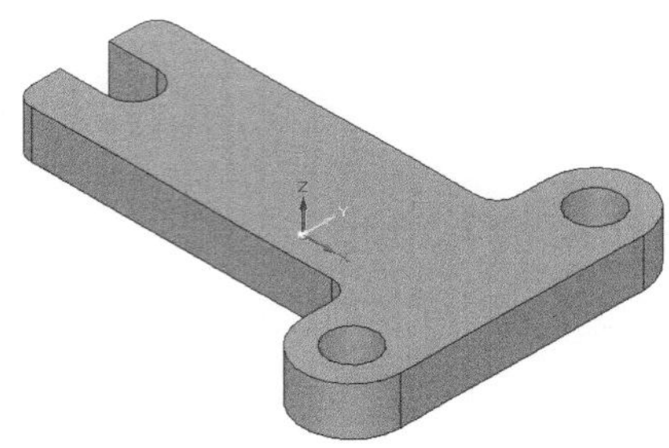

Figure 5-69 *Base feature of the model*

Creating the Second Feature

The second feature needs to be created by using an angled reference plane, which in turn will be created by using the right edge of the top face of the base feature.

1. Choose the **Coincident Plane** tool from the **Planes** group; you are prompted to click on the planar face. Rotate the model and select the top face of the first feature; a coincident plane is created on the top face of the feature. Also, a steering wheel is displayed on the newly created plane.

2. Press and hold the Origin knob of the steering wheel and move the steering wheel toward the right edge of the face and then release it, as shown in Figure 5-70.

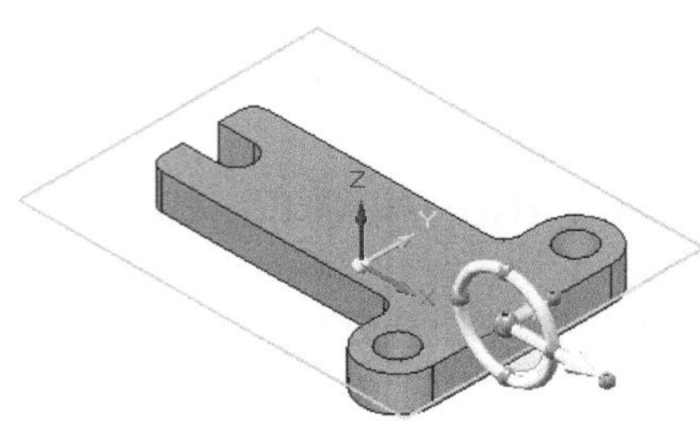

Figure 5-70 *Positioning the steering wheel to create an angled plane*

3. Click on the torus of the steering wheel to rotate the plane. Next, specify the angle by entering **45** in the edit box. After specifying the value, an angled plane is created.

   To create the profile for the second feature, you can project entities from the base feature onto the newly created plane and then modify them to complete the profile.

4. Choose the **Project to Sketch** tool from the **Draw** group and select the angled plane; the **Project to Sketch Options** dialog box is displayed.

   Make sure the **Project with offset** and **Project internal face loops** check boxes are cleared in this dialog box.

5. Next, choose **OK** in this dialog box: the **Project to Sketch** Command bar is displayed. Then select the edges to project, as shown in Figure 5-71.

6. Trim and extend the projected entities by using the **Trim Corner** tool from the **Draw** group in the **Home** tab and then draw a tangent arc to create a closed profile, as shown in Figure 5-72.

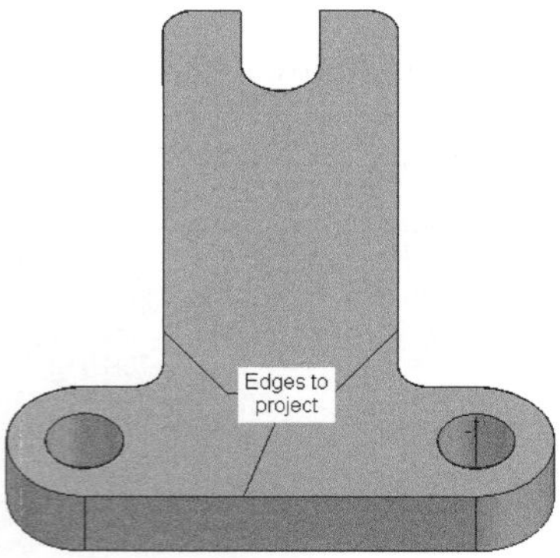

Figure 5-71 *Selecting the entities to project*

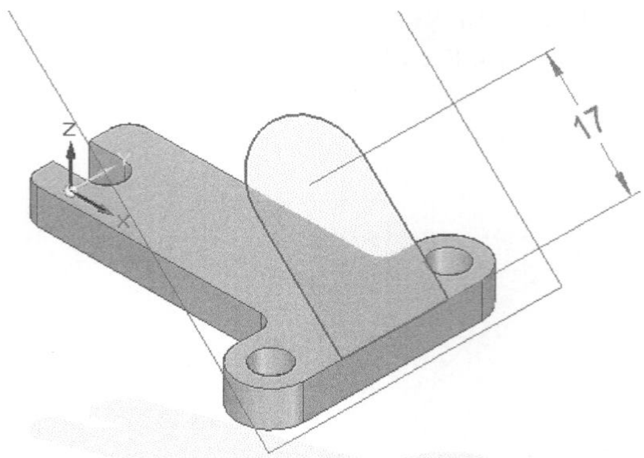

Figure 5-72 *Profile for the second feature*

7. Choose the **Select** tool from the **Home** tab and then select the middle portion of the sketch; an extrude handle and a Command bar are displayed.

8. Select the **Through Next** option from the **Extent type** drop-down list in the Command bar and click on the downward arrow of the extrude handle; the preview of the second feature is displayed merging with the base feature. Click on the downward direction arrow to create the second feature of the model, as shown in Figure 5-73.

Creating the Third Feature

The cut feature is an extrude feature and will be created by using the **Remove** option in the **Extrude** Command bar. You will draw the sketch of this feature on the inclined face of the second feature.

1. Choose the **Circle by Center Point** tool from the **Draw** group of the **Home** tab; you will be prompted to specify the center point of the circle.

2. Select the inclined face of the second feature and draw a circle of diameter **7.5** on it.

3. Choose the **Select** tool from the **Home** tab and select the circle; an extrude handle and the Command bar will be displayed.

4. Choose the **Cut** button from the **Add/Cut** drop-down in the Command bar and also choose the **Through All** button from the **Extent Type** drop-down. Next, select the downward arrow of the extrude handle; the preview of the third feature is displayed.

5. Click on the downward direction arrow to create the third feature of the model. The final model for Tutorial 3 is shown in Figure 5-74.

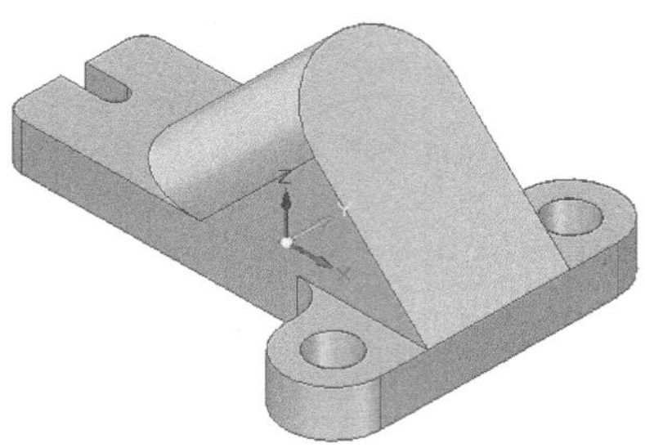

***Figure 5-73** Model for second feature*

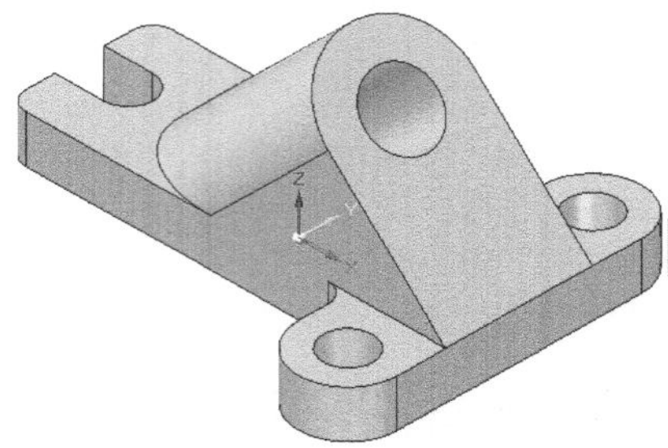

***Figure 5-74** Final model for Tutorial 3*

Saving the Model

1. Save the model with the name *c05tut3.par* at the location given next and then close the file.
   C:\Solid Edge\c05

Note
*The holes shown in the model in Tutorial 3 can also be created by using the **Hole** tool. The use of this tool will be discussed in the later chapters.*

Self-Evaluation Test

Answer the following questions and then compare them to those given at the end of this chapter:

1. While creating cutouts, you can create open profiles and use the __________ extensively to define the direction of material removal.

2. The __________ tool is used to create a plane normal to a selected sketched curve or an edge of a model.

3. In the **Ordered Part** environment of Solid Edge, you can create coordinate systems by using the __________ and __________ options.

4. The _________ tool is used in the **Ordered Part** environment to create a revolved cutout by removing the material defined by a sketch.

5. If a plane selected to define the coincident plane does not have a linear edge, the _________ direction is defined by using the base reference plane.

6. While creating an extruded feature, you can use the _________ to add a draft or a crown to it.

7. In the **Synchronous Part** environment, the steering wheel can be used to create parallel planes as well as angle planes. (T/F)

8. Cutouts are created by removing the material defined by a profile, from one or more existing features. (T/F)

9. A coordinate system is displayed as a feature in the **PathFinder**. (T/F)

10. You can create an extruded feature at an offset distance from the sketching plane while using the **From/To Extent** option. (T/F)

Review Questions

Answer the following questions:

1. Which of the following tools in Solid Edge is used to project the edges of an existing feature on the current sketching plane?

   (a) **Project to Sketch** (b) **Include**
   (c) **Insert** (d) both (a) and (b)

2. Which of the following is not a type of reference plane?

   (a) Base reference planes (b) Global reference planes
   (c) Local reference planes (d) Sample reference planes

3. The _________ of the steering wheel is used to create a parallel plane in the **Synchronous Part** environment.

4. In the **Ordered Part** environment, select the _________ radio button to create a coordinate system with respect to an existing coordinate system.

5. The _________ option is used to apply the crown by defining its radius and take off angle.

6. The _________ check box needs to be selected in the **Project to Sketch Options** dialog box to select geometries from other parts in an assembly.

7. The _________option in the **Create-From Options** drop-down list is used to create sketches on the plane on which the profile of the selected feature was created.

8. The **Coincident Plane** tool is used to create a reference plane that is coincident to a base reference plane, another reference plane, or the planar face of a model. (T/F)

9. You cannot use open profiles to create cutouts. (T/F)

10. The **By 3 Points** tool is used to create reference planes by selecting three points. (T/F)

EXERCISE

Exercise 1

Create the model shown in Figure 5-75. The dimensions of the model are given in the views shown in Figure 5-76. After creating the model, save it with the name *c05exr1.par* at the location given next.

C:\Solid Edge\c05 **(Expected time: 30 min)**

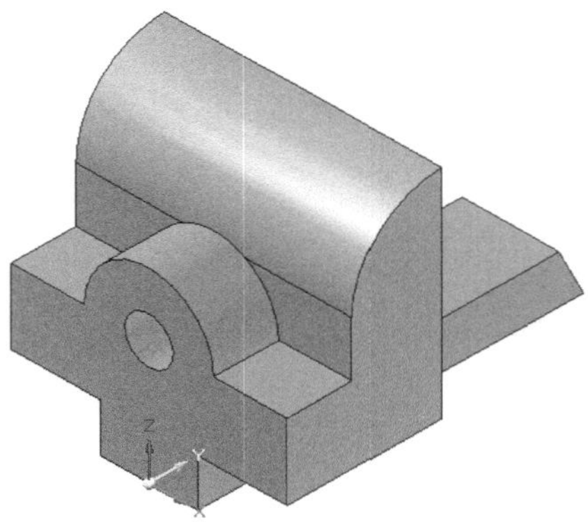

Figure 5-75 *Model for Exercise 1*

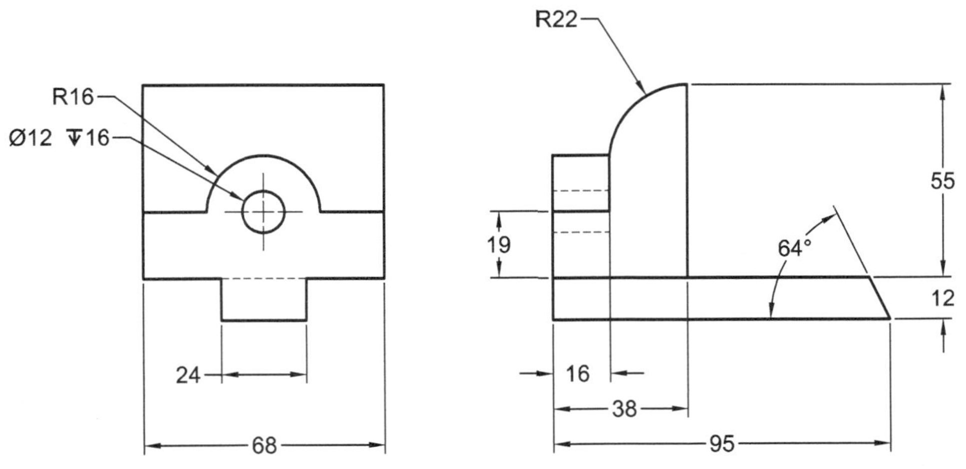

Figure 5-76 *Dimensions of the model for Exercise 1*

Exercise 2

Create the model shown in Figure 5-77. Its dimensions are given in the views shown in Figure 5-78. After creating the model, save it with the name *c05exr2.par* at the location given next.

C:\Solid Edge\c05 **(Expected time: 30 min)**

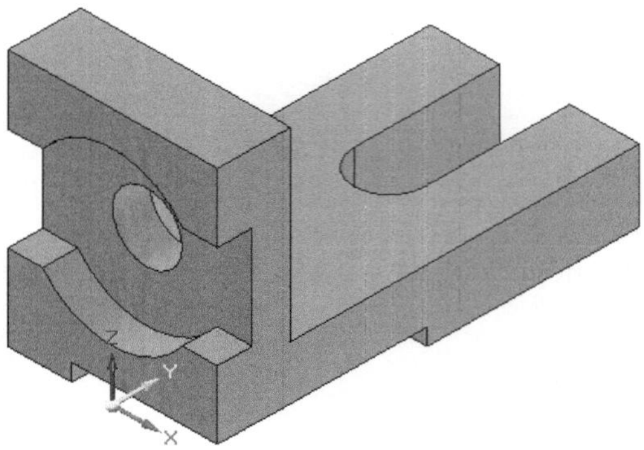

Figure 5-77 *Model for Exercise 2*

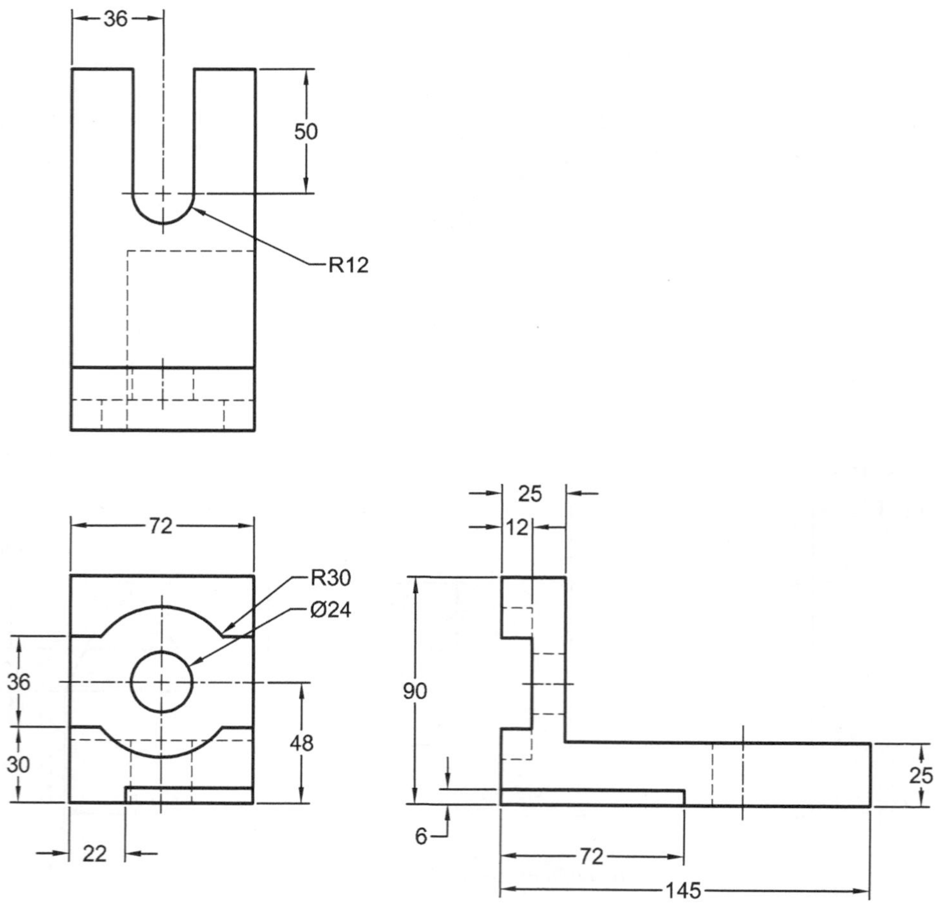

Figure 5-78 *Dimensions of the model for Exercise 2*

Exercise 3

Create the model shown in Figure 5-79. The dimensions are shown in Figure 5-80.

(Expected time: 20 min)

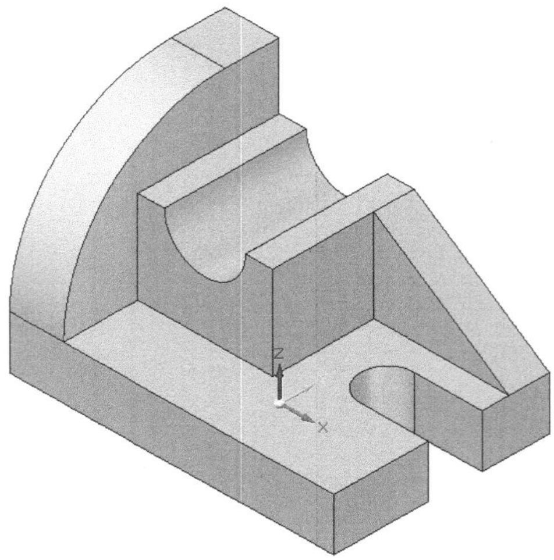

Figure 5-79 Model for Exercise 3

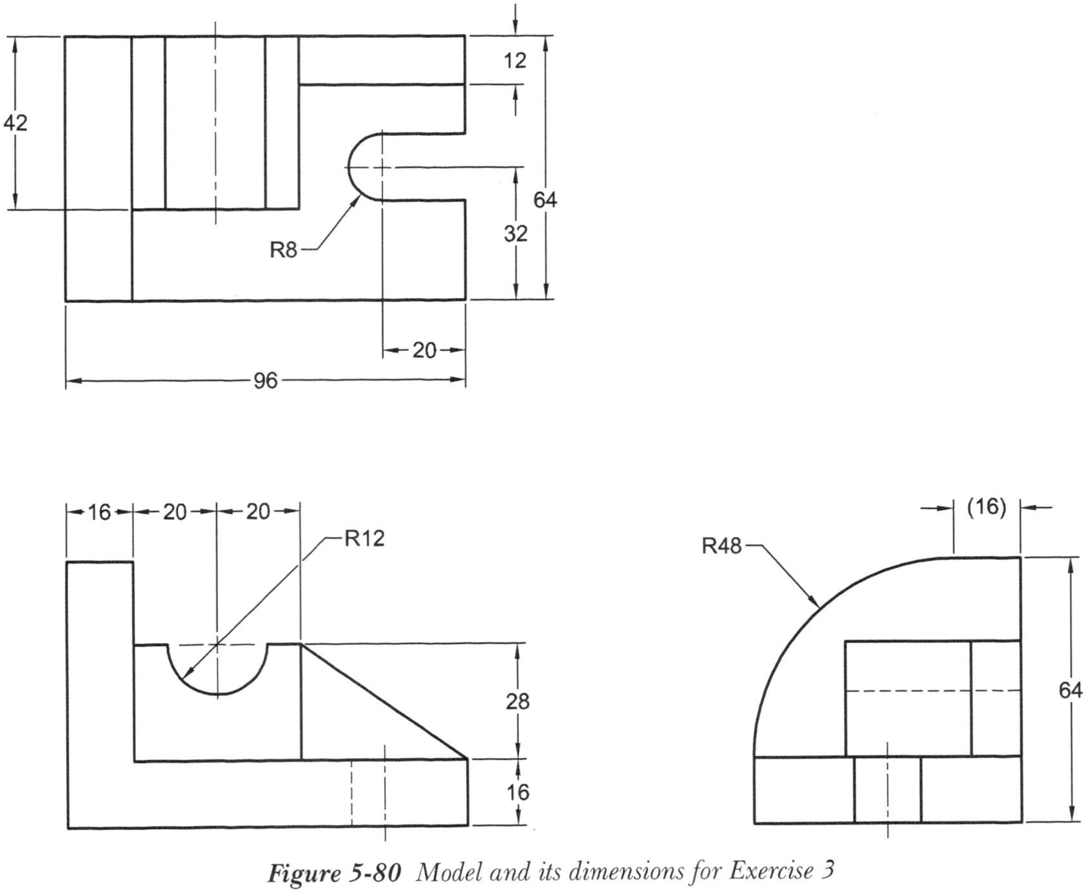

Figure 5-80 Model and its dimensions for Exercise 3

Answers to Self-Evaluation Test

1. Side Step, **2.** Normal To Curve, **3.** Key-in (relative to another coordinate system), Geometry, **4.** Revolved Cut, **5.** X-axis, **6.** Treatment Step, **7.** T, **8.** T, **9.** T, **10.** T

Chapter 6

Advanced Modeling Tools-I

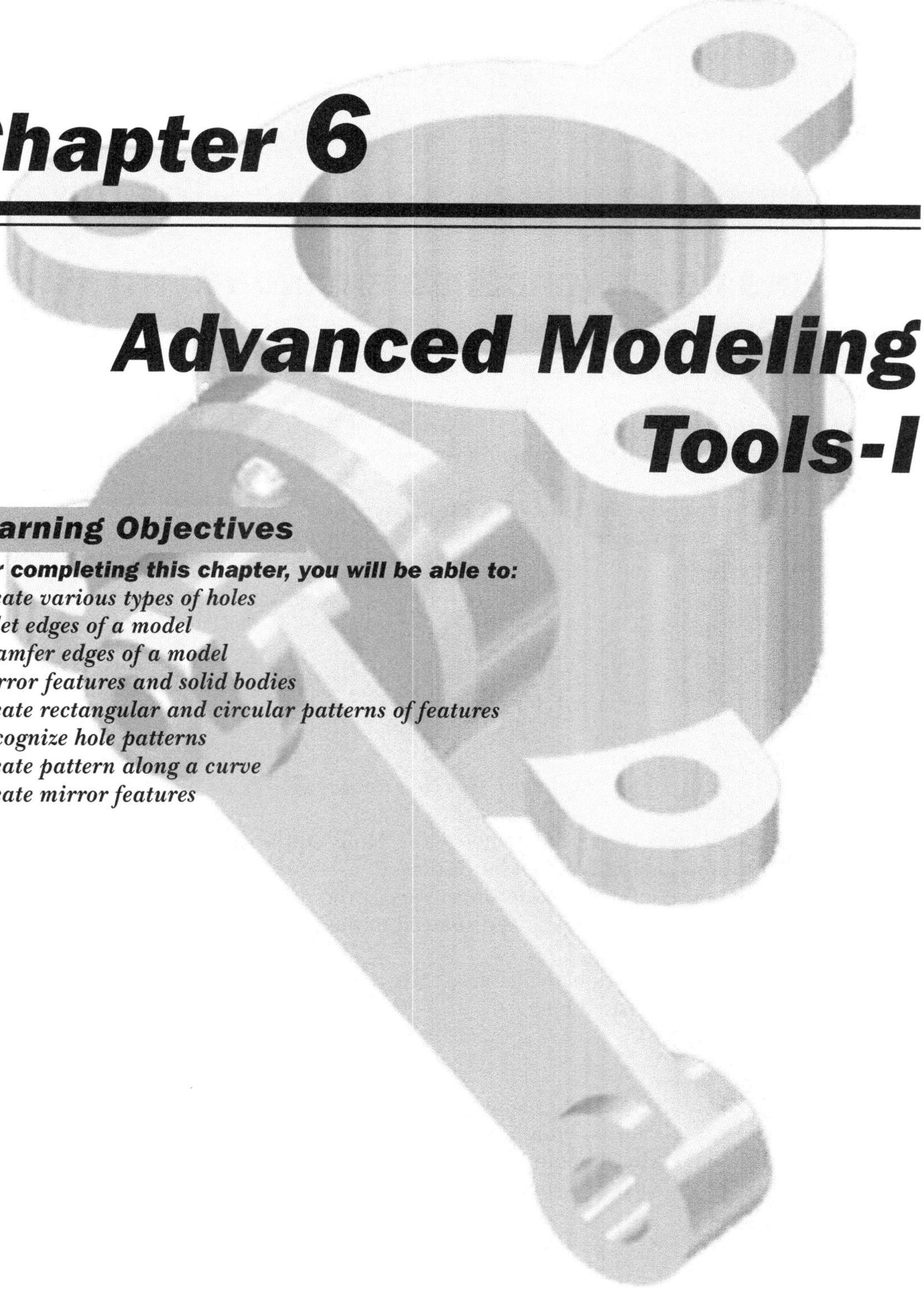

Learning Objectives

After completing this chapter, you will be able to:

- *Create various types of holes*
- *Fillet edges of a model*
- *Chamfer edges of a model*
- *Mirror features and solid bodies*
- *Create rectangular and circular patterns of features*
- *Recognize hole patterns*
- *Create pattern along a curve*
- *Create mirror features*

ADVANCED MODELING TOOLS

Most of the designs consist of advanced features such as counterbore/countersink holes, ribs, webs, shells, and so on. These features can be created by using a number of advanced modeling tools provided in Solid Edge. The advanced features are parametric by nature, and can be modified or edited. The advanced modeling tools appreciably reduce the time taken in creating the features in the models, thereby reducing the designing time.

In this chapter, you will learn about some advanced modeling tools. The remaining advanced modeling tools will be discussed in the later chapters.

CREATING HOLES (ORDERED ENVIRONMENT)

Ribbon: Home > Solids > Hole

Holes are circular cut features that are generally provided for assembling a model. In an assembly, components such as bolts and shafts are inserted into the hole. In the **Ordered Part** environment, a hole is created by first specifying its type and then its location in the model by using the sketching environment.

To create a hole, invoke the **Hole** tool; the **Hole** Command bar will be displayed, as shown in Figure 6-1. As mentioned earlier, first you need to specify the type of hole you want to create and its related settings.

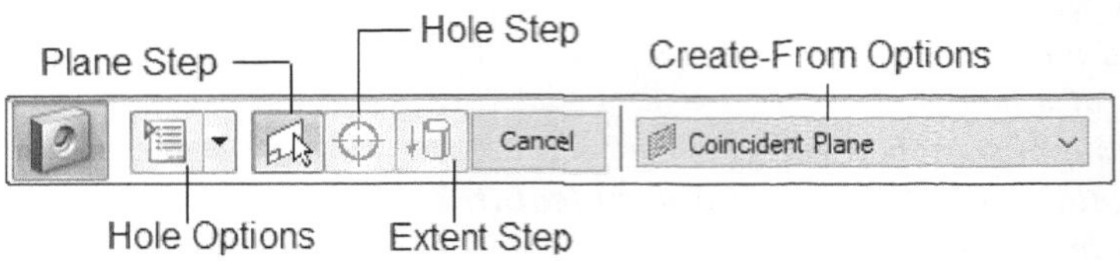

***Figure 6-1** The **Hole** command bar*

To specify the parameters of the hole, choose the **Hole Options** button from the Command bar; the **Hole Options** dialog box will be displayed, as shown in Figure 6-2. By default, this dialog box has some predefined hole settings. Specify the required settings in this dialog box. The preview of the specified hole will be displayed in the preview window in this dialog box.

There are five types of hole buttons available at the upper left corner of the **Hole Options** dialog box. These buttons are discussed next.

Simple

Choose this button to create a simple hole. A simple hole is the one that has a uniform diameter throughout its length. The diameter and the depth of the hole need to be specified in the **Hole Diameter** and **Hole depth** drop-down lists, respectively. Figure 6-3 shows the section view of a simple hole.

Note

*The **Hole depth** drop-down list will be activated only when you choose the **Finite Extent** button from the **Hole extents** area.*

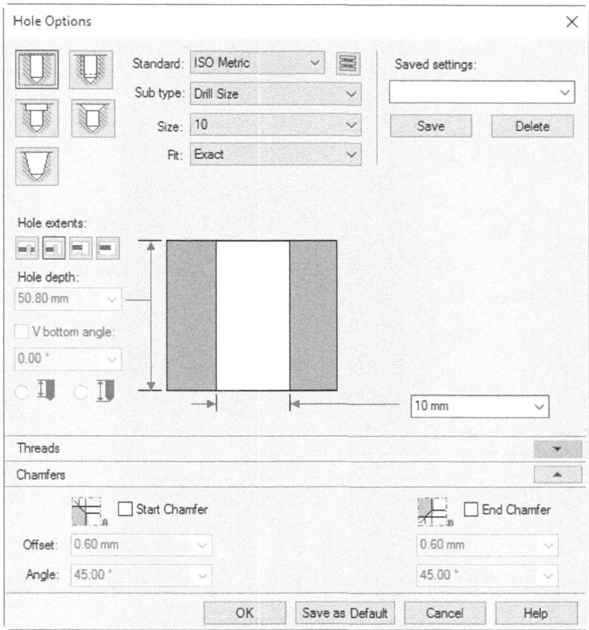

Figure 6-2 *The **Hole Options** dialog box*

Figure 6-3 *Section view of a simple hole*

Threaded

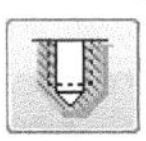
This button is used to create a threaded hole. Note that the threaded surface can be shown with a predefined depiction standard in the drafting environment.

Counterbore

This button is chosen to create a counterbore hole. A counterbore hole is a stepped hole and has two diameters: the counterbore diameter and the hole diameter. In this type of hole, you also need to specify two depths. The first depth is the counterbore depth, which is the depth up to which the bigger diameter will be defined. The second depth is the depth of the hole. Figure 6-4 shows the section view of a counterbore hole.

Countersink

This button is used to create a countersink hole. A countersink hole also has two diameters, but the transition between the bigger diameter and the smaller diameter is in the form

of a tapered cone. In this type of hole, you will need to define the countersink diameter, hole diameter, countersink angle, and depth of the hole. Figure 6-5 shows the section view of a countersink hole.

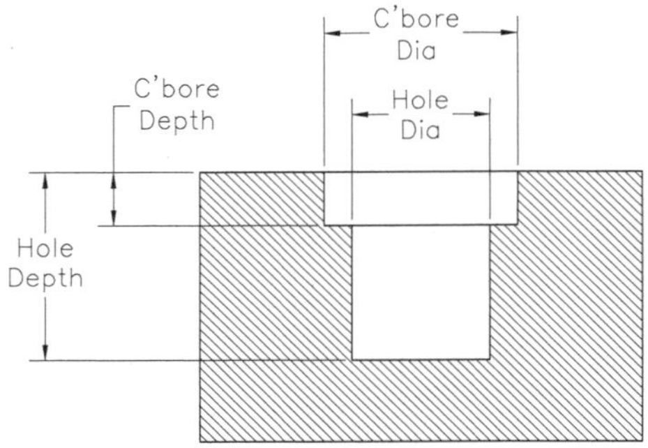

Figure 6-4 Section view of a counterbore hole

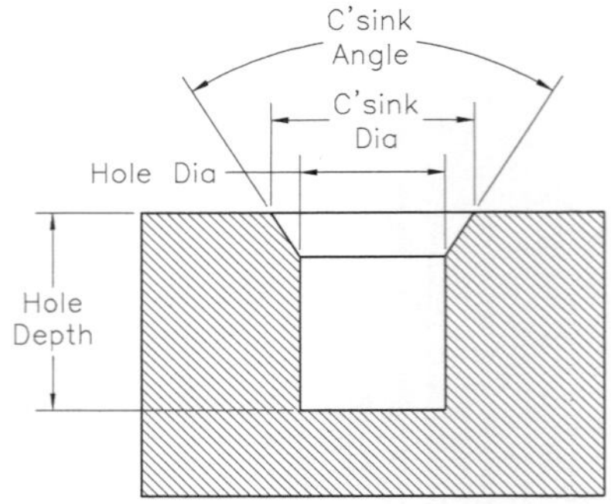

Figure 6-5 Section view of a countersink hole

Tapered

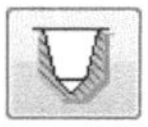

This button is used to create a tapered hole, as shown in Figure 6-6.

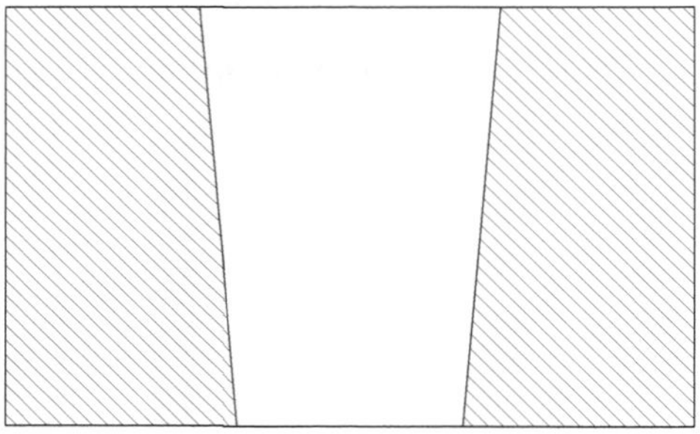

Figure 6-6 Section view of a tapered hole

The other options available in this dialog box are discussed next.

Standard

The **Standard** drop-down list is used to specify the dimensioning and hole standards. By default, the **ISO Metric** standard is selected in this list. Other dimensioning standards available in this drop-down list are: **ANSI Inch**, **ANSI Metric**, **DIN Metric**, **GB Metric**, **GOST Metric**, **JIS Metric**, **UNI Metric**, **Inch**, and **mm**.

Sub type

The **Sub type** drop-down list is used to specify the sub type of the selected hole type.

Size

The **Size** drop-down list is used to define the size of the fastener to be inserted in the hole that is created using the **Hole** tool. The size of the fasteners in the **Size** drop-down list depends on the standard selected from the **Standard** drop-down list.

Fit

The **Fit** drop-down list is used to specify the type of contact between the hole and the fastener. Note that this option is not available for the **Threaded** and **Tapered** hole types.

Note

*The **Sub type**, **Size**, and **Fit** options are not available when you select the **Inch** or **mm** option from the **Standard** drop-down list.*

Saved settings

This drop-down list is used to select the hole settings already saved. But if you want to use some hole settings frequently, you can specify the required settings and save them with a particular name. On doing so, the name will then be displayed in this drop-down list. Whenever you select this name, the settings configured under the name will automatically be set in the **Hole Options** dialog box.

Save

Choose this button to save the hole settings with the specified name. To do so, enter a name in the **Saved settings** edit box and then choose this button; the current hole settings defined in the **Hole Options** dialog box will be saved with the specified name.

Delete

Choose this button to delete the hole setting that is currently saved in the **Saved settings** drop-down list.

Hole extents Area

Most of the options available in the **Hole extents** area are the standard termination options that are discussed in the **Extrude** tool. If you choose the **Finite Extent** button to terminate the hole, the following options will be available in this area.

Hole depth

This drop-down list is used to specifying depth of the hole.

V bottom angle

If the **V bottom angle** check box is selected, the end of the hole will be tapered and it will converge at a point, refer to the preview in the preview window of the dialog box. The angle for the V bottom is specified in the edit box available below this check box. Figure 6-7 shows the section view of a countersink hole with a V bottom. On selecting this check box, the **Dimension to flat** and **Dimension to V** radio buttons will be activated. These radio buttons are discussed next.

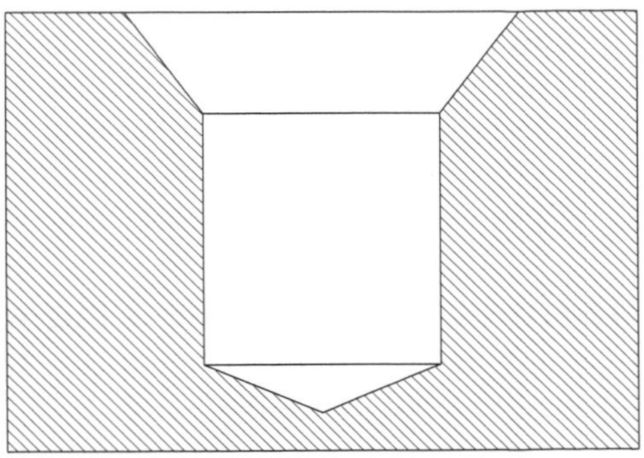

Figure 6-7 *Section view of the countersink hole with V bottom*

Dimension to flat

The **Dimension to flat** radio button is selected to define the depth of the hole up to the flat face of the hole.

Dimension to V

The **Dimension to V** radio button is selected to define the depth of the hole up to the tip of the bottom V of the hole.

The remaining options in the **Hole Options** dialog box depend upon the type of hole selected. These options are discussed next.

Options for Simple Hole

The options available for simple hole type are discussed next.

Hole Diameter

The **Hole Diameter** drop-down list is used to set the diameter of the hole. You can select the diameter from the predefined values available in this drop-down list or enter a value in the edit box available. Note that the units of the diameters in this drop-down list depend on the type of unit selected from the **Standard** drop-down list.

Note

*The default hole diameter values available in the **Hole Diameter** drop-down list are displayed based on the diameters available in the **HOLES.TXT** file. This file is available at the location C:/Program Files/Solid Edge ST8 /Preferences.*

Chamfers Rollout

The **Chamfers** rollout is used to specify the type and location of the chamfer to be applied on the hole. The options available under this rollout are discussed next.

Start Chamfer

The **Start Chamfer** check box is used to apply chamfer at the start face of the hole. When you select this check box, the **Offset** and **Angle** edit boxes will be activated. These edit boxes are used to specify the chamfer parameters.

End Chamfer

The **End Chamfer** check box is used to apply chamfer at the end face of the hole. When you select this check box, the **Offset** and **Angle** edit boxes will be activated. These edit boxes are used to specify the chamfer parameters. Note that this option is not available in the **Hole Options** dialog box of the **Synchronous** environment.

Options for Threaded Hole

In addition to the **Chamfer** rollout, the **Hole Options** dialog box provides the following options for the threaded hole type:

Nominal Diameter

This drop-down list is used to define the nominal diameter of the thread for threaded type hole.

Threads Rollout

The **Threads** rollout list in the **Hole Options** dialog box is used to set the thread type for the selected hole diameter. You can select any predefined thread type from this rollout. The options available in the **Thread Extent** area are discussed next.

To hole extent

The **To hole extent** radio button is selected to create threads throughout the length of the hole. Observe the change in the preview window when you select this radio button.

Finite extent

The **Finite extent** radio button is selected to create threads up to a specified depth. The depth is specified in the edit box available beside this radio button.

Options for Counterbore Hole

In addition to the **Hole Diameter** drop-down list, the **Threads** and **Chamfer** rollouts, the **Hole Options** dialog box provides the following options for the counterbore hole type:

Counterbore Diameter

The **Counterbore Diameter** drop-down list is used to specify the counterbore diameter. You can select the diameter from this drop-down list or enter a value in this edit box.

Counterbore Depth

The **Counterbore Depth** drop-down list is used to specify the depth up to which the counterbore diameter will be defined in the hole. You can select the depth from this drop-down list or enter a value in this edit box.

Profile at top

If this radio button is selected, then the plane you define to place the hole will be taken as the plane from where the counterbore depth starts. This is the top face of the hole feature.

Profile at bottom

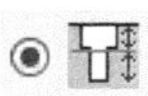

If the **Profile at bottom** radio button is selected, then the plane you define to place the hole will be taken as the plane at which the counterbore depth ends. This is also the plane from where the hole diameter starts. Refer to the preview of the hole shown in the preview window in the dialog box.

Note

*Apart from the **Start Chamfer** and **End Chamfer** options, the **Neck Chamfer** option in the **Chamfers** rollout of the **Hole Options** dialog box will be available in case of the counterbore hole type. This option is used to apply chamfer at the start of the nominal diameter of a counterbore hole.*

Options For Countersink Hole

In addition to the **Hole Diameter** drop-down list, the **Threads**, and **Chamfer** rollouts, the **Hole Options** dialog box provides the following options for the countersink hole type:

Countersink diameter

The **Countersink diameter** drop-down list is used to specify the countersink diameter. You can select the diameter from this drop-down list or enter a value in this edit box.

Countersink angle

The **Countersink angle** drop-down list is used to specify the countersink angle. You can select the angle from this drop-down list or enter a value in this edit box.

Head clearance

The **Head clearance** check box is used to create a cylindrical bore above the face where the countersink depth starts. When you select this check box, the preview of the section view will be displayed in the preview window. The value for the head clearance depth is specified in the edit box available below the **Head clearance** check box. When you select the **Head clearance** check box, the **Profile at top** and **Profile at bottom** radio buttons will also be displayed in the **Hole Options** dialog box. These options are same as discussed in the counterbore hole. Figure 6-8 shows the section view of a countersink hole with the **Head clearance** check box selected.

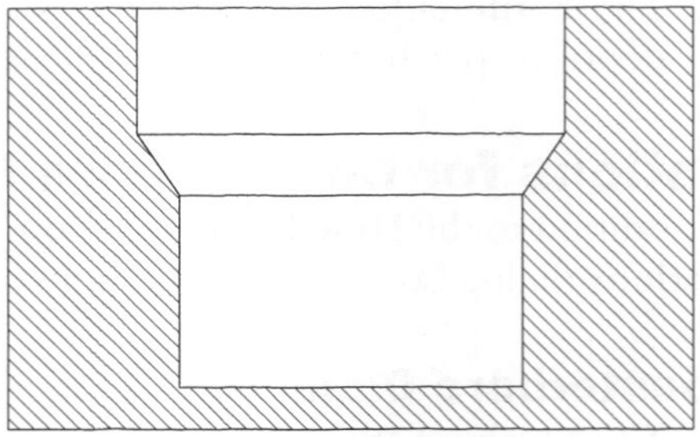

Figure 6-8 *Section view of a countersink hole with the **Head clearance** check box selected*

Options for Tapered Hole

In addition to the **Hole Diameter** drop-down list, the **Chamfer** rollout, the **Hole Options** dialog box provides the following options for the tapered hole type.

Profile at bottom

The **Profile at bottom** radio button is the first button on the bottom of the **Saved Setting** drop-down list. If this radio button is selected, the tapering parameters will be set based on the bottom diameter of the hole.

Profile at top

The **Profile at top** radio button is selected to set the tapering parameters based on the top diameter of the hole.

Angle

This radio button is selected to specify the value of the taper angle for creating a tapered hole.

Decimal (R/L)

This radio button is selected to specify the taper angle value that is calculated by dividing the radius of the hole by its length.

Ratio (R:L)

This radio button is selected to specify the taper angle value that is calculated by the ratio of the radius of the hole to its length.

Note

*The **Sub type**, **Size**, and **Fit** options are not available when the **Tapered** button is chosen in the **Hole Options** dialog box.*

After setting the parameters in the **Hole Options** dialog box, you may need to perform the following three steps to create a hole:

Plane Step

Choose the **OK** button from the **Hole Options** dialog box; the **Plane Step** will be invoked. The **Plane Step** is used to select the plane on which the profile of the hole will be placed. By default, this step is active on invoking this tool. Therefore, you are prompted to click on a planar face or on a reference plane. You can also use the **Create-From Options** drop-down list to create a new reference plane to place the hole profile.

Hole Step

The **Hole Step** will automatically be invoked after you specify the plane to place the hole profile. In this step, you need to define the location of the hole profile, therefore, the sketching environment is invoked. Depending upon the type of hole selected from the **Hole Options** dialog box, one or two concentric circles are attached to the cursor in the sketching environment. You can place single or multiple hole profiles by specifying their locations in the model. You can use relationships and dimensions to specify the exact location of the hole. Figure 6-9 shows the four profiles of counterbore holes placed in the sketching environment in the **Hole Step**. After placing the hole profile, adding dimensions and relationships to hole profiles, you need to choose the **Close Sketch** button to exit the sketching environment.

Extent Step

The **Extent Step** will not be invoked automatically. By default, the extent option that you have specified from the **Hole Options** dialog box will be applied on the hole termination. However, if you want to change the hole termination options, you need to click on the **Extent Step** button from the **Hole** Command bar. On doing so, the **Hole** Command bar will be modified and display the same options as are available in the **Hole Options** dialog box. Also, you will be prompted to select the side for the hole termination. Move the cursor in the direction in which you want to create the hole feature and then click to accept the direction. The preview of the hole feature will be displayed. Choose the **Finish** button and then the **Cancel** button to exit this tool. Figure 6-10 shows a model with four holes created by using the hole profile.

Tip

*To change the hole parameters while defining the location of the hole in the sketching environment, first make sure the **Hole Circle** button is chosen. Next, choose the **Hole Options** button from the command bar to invoke the **Hole Options** dialog box. The changes that you make in this dialog box will reflect in the hole profiles that are already placed and also in the new ones that have to be placed.*

Note

*Even if you create multiple holes by placing more than one hole profile using a single sequence of the **Hole** tool, they will be displayed as a single hole feature in the **PathFinder**.*

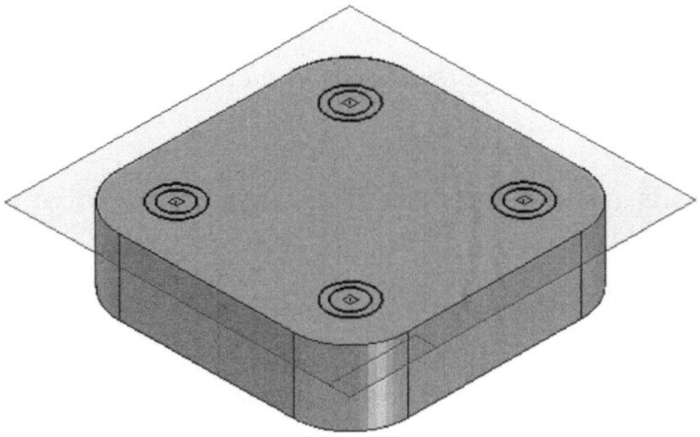

Figure 6-9 *Profiles of four counterbore holes placed in the sketching environment*

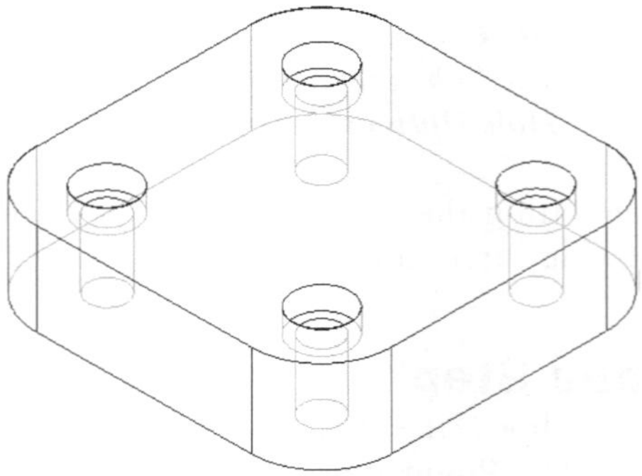

Figure 6-10 *Model after creating four counterbore holes*

CREATING HOLES (SYNCHRONOUS ENVIRONMENT)

In the **Synchronous Part** environment, you can create holes dynamically by placing them on any face of the model. You can place holes on multiple faces in one instance of the command. Holes created in one instance of the command will have the same dimensions.

When you invoke the **Hole** tool in the **Synchronous Part** environment, the preview of the hole with the default dimensions will be attached to the cursor. You can specify the dimensions of the hole based on your requirements by invoking the **Hole Options** dialog box. The **Hole Options** dialog box in the **Synchronous Part** environment has the same options as in the **Ordered Part** environment. After setting the hole parameters and closing the dialog box, move the cursor toward the face where you want to place the hole and click on the lock symbol displayed, or press F3; the plane will be locked and a lock symbol will be displayed at the upper right corner of the graphics window, as shown in Figure 6-11. Now click at any point on the locked face to place the hole. Then position the hole at the desired location by applying dimensions between the center point of the hole and the linear edges of the model.

You can also place a hole with respect to the midpoint of a linear edge. To do so, after locking the placement plane for placing hole feature, move the cursor on an edge and then press the M key; the preview of the hole will snap to the midpoint of that edge. Then move the cursor horizontally or vertically toward the center of the placement face to display a reference line, refer to Figure 6-12. You can now specify the placement point by clicking the left mouse button.

You can also position a hole at the center of any circular edge of the model. To do so, after locking the placement plane to place the hole, move the cursor over the circular edge; the center of the circular edge will be highlighted. Move the cursor over the highlighted center point; the cursor will be snapped to it. Now left click at this point; the hole will be placed at the center of the circular edge.

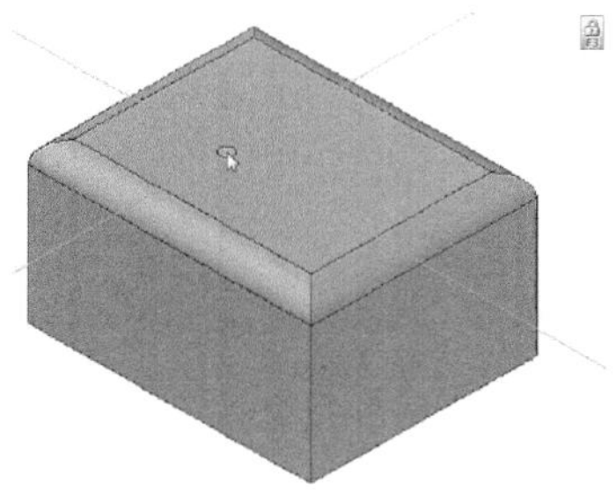

Figure 6-11 *Placing a hole on the locked plane*

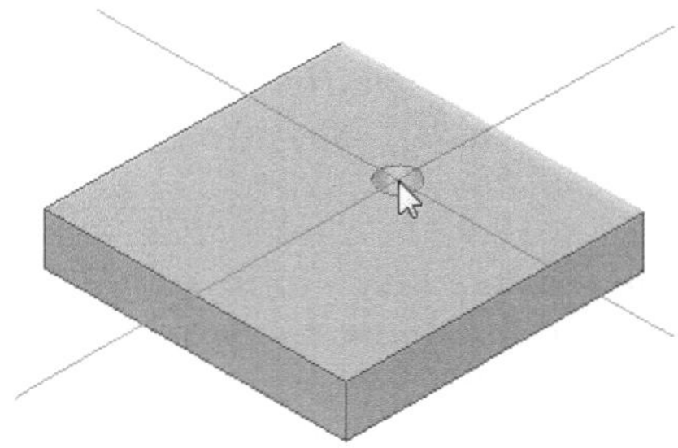

Figure 6-12 *The hole aligned with the midpoint of the edge*

If you place the cursor on an edge and press the E key; the dimension between the center point of the hole and the endpoint of the edge will be displayed, as shown in Figure 6-13. You can toggle the dimensional reference edge by using the **Toggle Dimension Axis** button on the Command bar, refer to Figure 6-14.

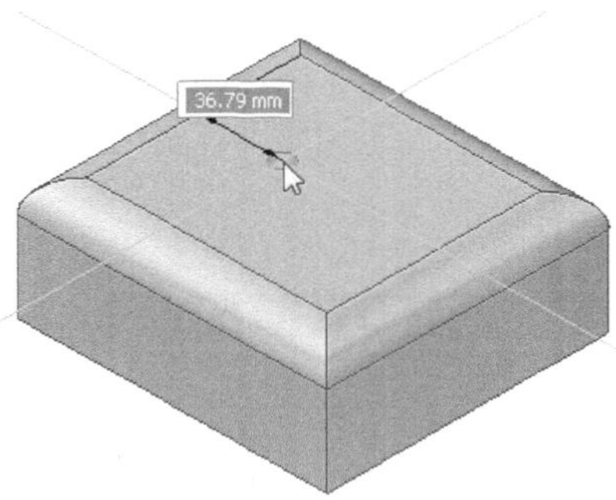

Figure 6-13 *Dimension between the center of the hole and the endpoint of an edge*

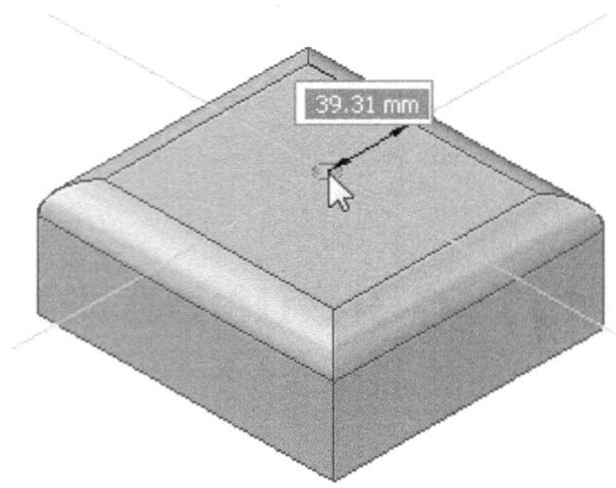

Figure 6-14 *Vertically oriented dimension*

You can also position a hole with reference to a circular edge. If the model has circular edges, place the cursor on a circular edge or a fillet; the center point of the circular edge will be highlighted. Next, press C to display the dimension between the center point of the hole and the center point of the circular edge, as shown in Figure 6-15. You can toggle the dimensional reference by using the **Toggle Dimension Axis** button on the Command bar, refer to Figure 6-16. Enter a value in the dimension edit box to lock the dynamic movement of the hole.

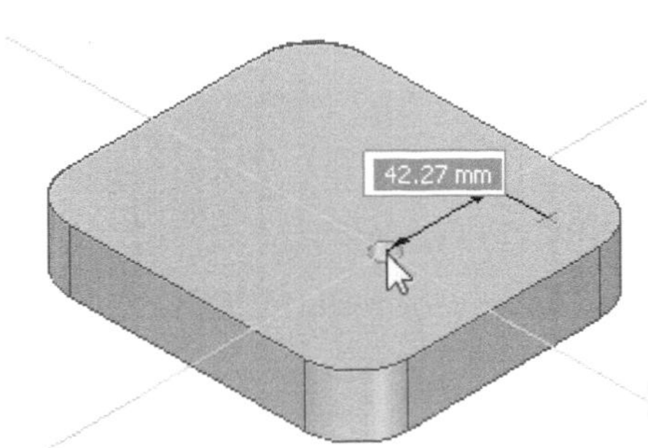

Figure 6-15 *Dimension between the center point of the hole and the center point of the circular edge*

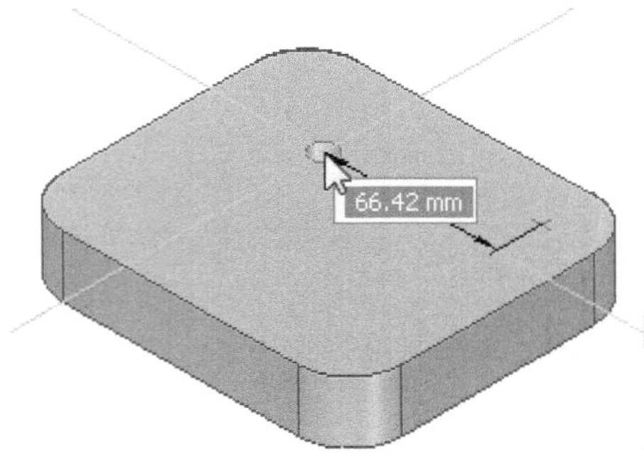

Figure 6-16 *Horizontally oriented dimension*

Note

*After invoking the **Hole** tool, if you continuously place two holes on a single plane then the plane gets locked automatically. To place holes on a different plane, you first need to unlock the current plane.*

You can also create a hole on the cylindrical surface. To do so, invoke the **Hole** tool from the **Solids** group of the **Home** tab; you will be prompted to place the hole on the cylindrical face of the model. Move the cursor on the cylindrical face and press the F3 function key on the keyboard; a plane tangent to the surface of the cylinder will be attached to the cursor and the **Tangent** Command bar will be displayed. On moving the cursor on the surface of the cylinder, the plane will also change its position. Next, enter an angle value in the edit box displayed on the graphics window and press ENTER; a plane tangent to the cylindrical face will be created, refer to Figure 6-17. Also, a tangent line is displayed on the cylinder. Next, place the hole on the newly created plane. You can precisely place the hole on this plane. You can also create dimensions between the lines and the centers of the holes.

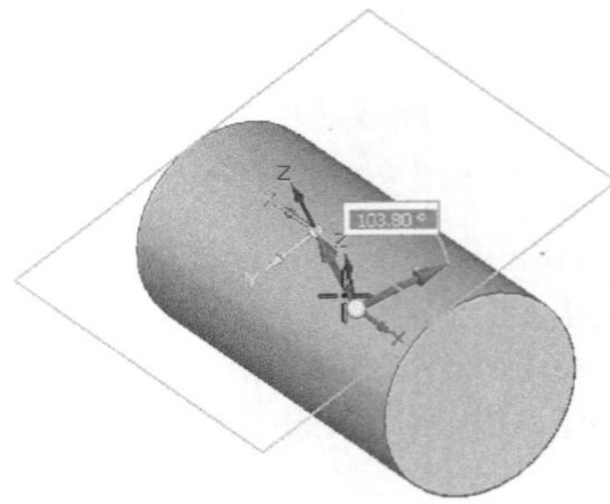

Figure 6-17 *Plane created tangent to the cylinder*

CREATING ROUNDS (ORDERED ENVIRONMENT)

Ribbon: Home > Solids > Round drop-down > Round

In Solid Edge, you can add fillets or rounds to the sharp edges of models by using the **Round** tool. This tool allows you to create four types of rounds. You can select the type of round that you want to create from the **Round Options** dialog box, as shown in Figure 6-18. This dialog box is invoked by choosing the **Round Options** button from the **Round** Command bar.

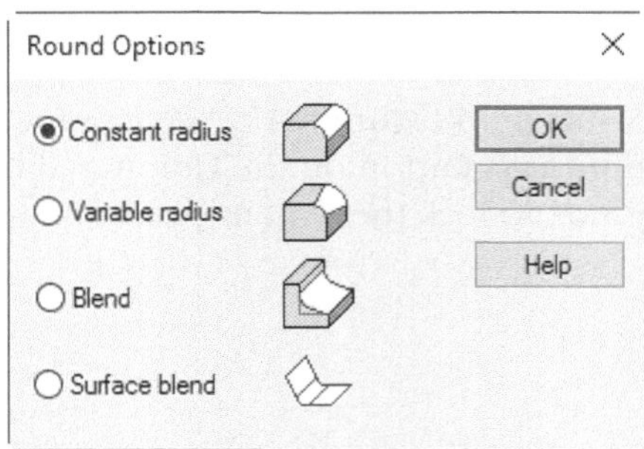

Figure 6-18 *The **Round Options** dialog box*

In this chapter, you will learn how to create the first two types of rounds. The remaining two types of rounds will be discussed in later chapters.

Creating the Constant Radius Round

To create this type of round, select the **Constant radius** radio button from the **Round Options** dialog box.

When you invoke the **Round** tool or exit the **Round Options** dialog box after selecting the **Constant radius** radio button, the **Select Step** will be activated and you will be prompted to click on an edge chain. The options available in the Command bar in this step are discussed next.

Select

The **Select** drop-down list provides various selection types for selecting the entities to fillet. These selection types are discussed next.

Edge/Corner

This option is used to select an individual edge or a corner defined by multiple edges.

Chain

This is the default option and is used to select the chain of tangentially continuous edges.

Face

This option is used to select a face, thus selecting all its edges. As you move the cursor close to a face, all its edges will be highlighted. Click anywhere on the face to select all the edges of that face.

Loop

This option is used to select a specified loop on a selected face. When you select this option, you will be prompted to select a face containing loops.

Feature

This option is used to fillet all the edges of a selected feature. You can select the feature from the drawing window or from the **PathFinder**.

All Fillets

This option is used to fillet all inward facing edges of a model. The fillets are created by adding material to the model and the surface thus created will be concave in shape. When you select this option, you will be prompted to select the part. Select the required part; all the edges to which the fillet is added will be highlighted. Next, choose the **Accept** button and then choose the **Preview** button from the Command bar to create a round feature. Figure 6-19 shows the model with fillets added to all possible edges.

All Rounds

This option is used to add rounds to all the external edges of the model. The rounds result in convex surfaces and are created by removing the material from the model. When you select this option, you will be prompted to click on the part to accept. Select the part; all the edges to which the rounds are added will be highlighted. Figure 6-20 shows a model with rounds added to all possible edges.

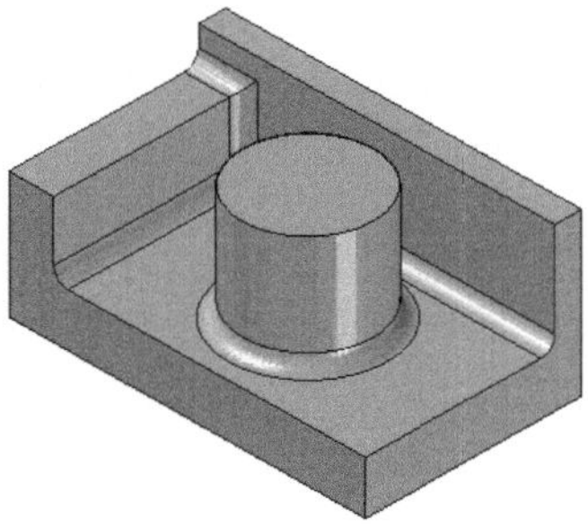

Figure 6-19 Round added to the model by using the ***All Fillets*** *option*

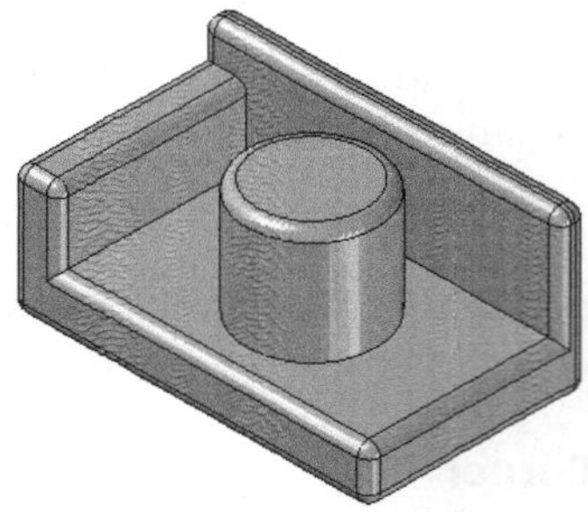

Figure 6-20 Round added to the model by using the ***All Rounds*** *option*

Radius

The **Radius** edit box is used to specify the radius value. To set the radius value, select the edges to round and then specify the radius. Next, choose the **Accept** button from the **Round** Command bar; the preview of the resulting fillet will be displayed.

In Solid Edge, you can modify the parameters of a round by using the **Round Parameters** dialog box shown in Figure 6-21. You can invoke this dialog box by choosing the **Round Parameters** button from the **Round** Command bar.

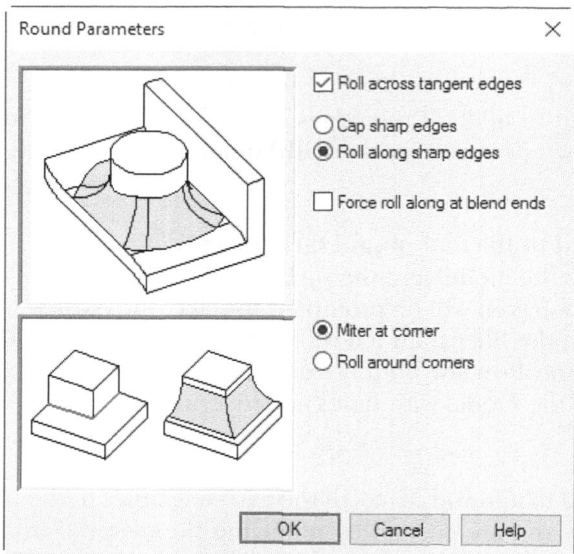

Figure 6-21 *The* ***Round Parameters*** *dialog box*

The options in the **Round Parameters** dialog box are discussed next.

Roll across tangent edges

If the round in a model comes across its tangent edges, then selecting this check box will roll the round across these tangent edges. If you clear this check box, the round will terminate as soon as it comes across a tangent edge. Figure 6-22 shows the model before adding a round. Figure 6-23 shows a model created with the **Roll across tangent edges** check box selected and Figure 6-24 shows a model created with the **Roll across tangent edges** check box cleared.

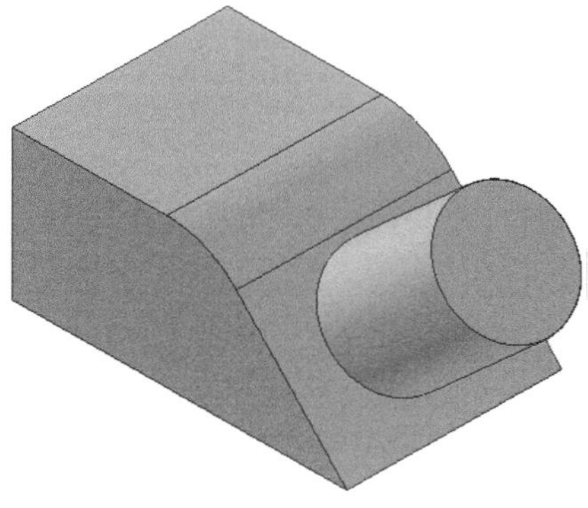

Figure 6-22 *Model before adding the round*

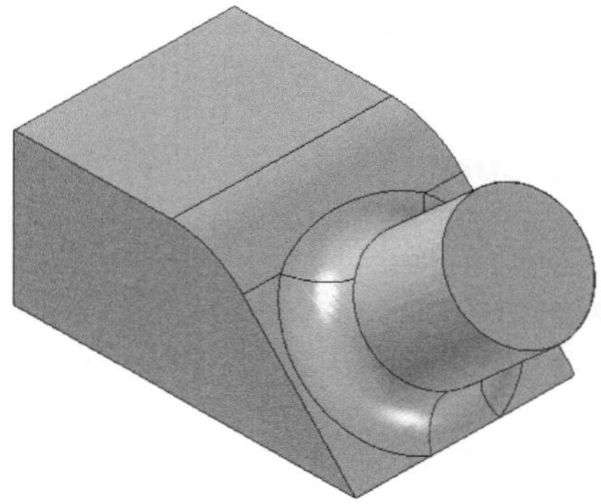

Figure 6-23 *Round created with the* ***Roll across tangent edge*** *check box selected*

Cap sharp edges

If the round in a model comes across its sharp edges, selecting this radio button will extend the face defined by sharp edges to maintain the round, as shown in Figure 6-25.

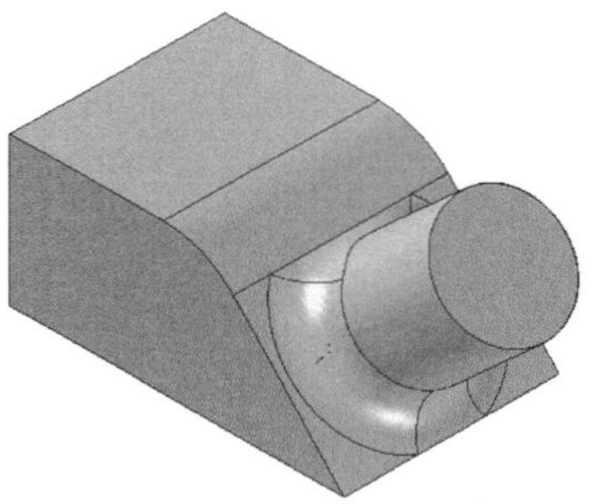

Figure 6-24 *Round created with the* ***Roll across tangent edge*** *check box cleared*

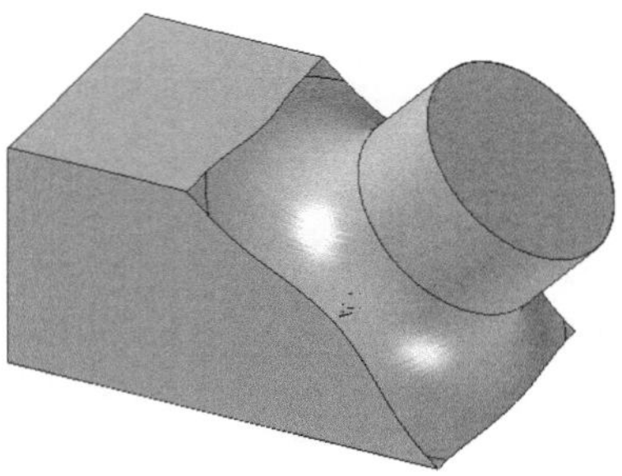

Figure 6-25 *Round created by capping the sharp edges*

Roll along sharp edges

If the round in a model comes across the sharpedges, selecting this radio button will terminate the round such that the sharpness of edges is retained, as shown in Figure 6-26.

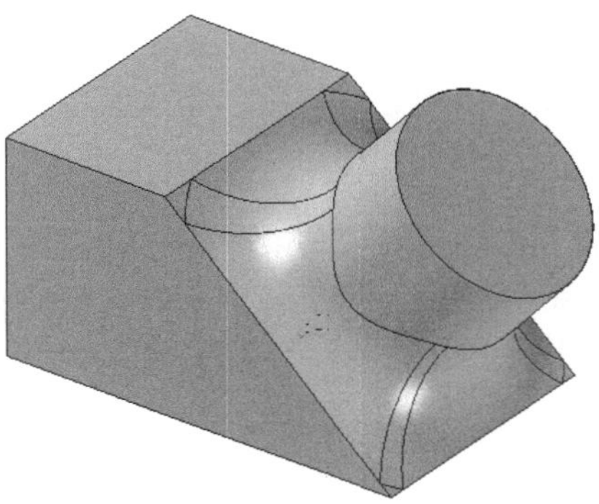

Figure 6-26 *Round created by rolling along sharp edges*

Force roll along at blend ends
This check box is used to force the round such that the shape of the original edge is retained.

Miter at corner
This radio button is selected to create a miter at the sharp corner.

Roll around corner
When this radio button is selected, the round will be rolled around the corners.

After specifying the parameters in the **Round Parameters** dialog box, choose **OK** to close it.

If you select the three edges that form a corner and then right-click, the **Soften Corner Step** button will be available, adjacent to the **Select Step** button in the **Round** Command bar. On choosing this button, the **Soften Corner Step** will be activated. This step allows you to add a setback to the selected corner. Figures 6-27 and 6-28 show the rounds in the model without and with the setback added to the corner, respectively.

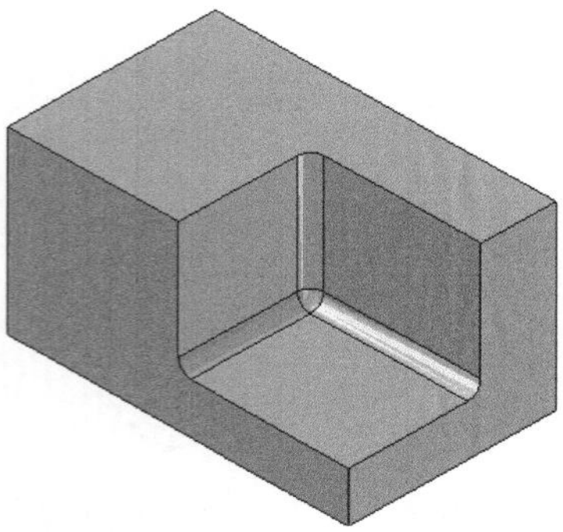

Figure 6-27 *Edges rounded without setback*

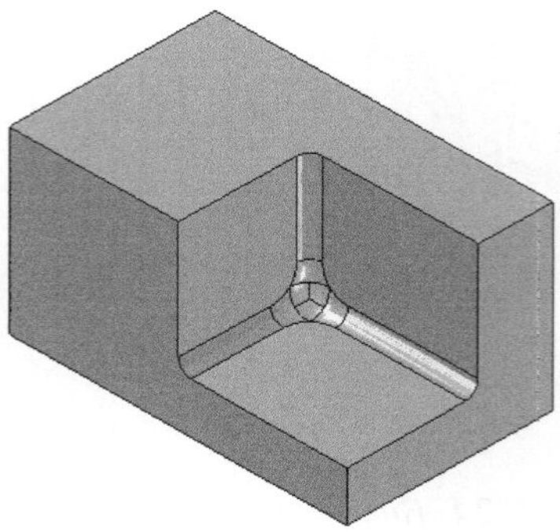

Figure 6-28 *Edges rounded with setback*

The options available in the Command bar of the **Soften Corner Step** are discussed next.

Select
This drop-down list enables you to select the corner to soften. By default, the **Corner** option is selected from this drop-down list. This option allows you to select the individual corner to soften. If you select the **All Corners** option, all corners of the feature will be selected.

Method
This drop-down list is used to specify the method of adding a setback to the corner. You can specify a numeric value for the setback by selecting the **Distance** option. If you select the **Multiple of radius** option, you can specify the setback value in terms of multiples of the fillet radius.

Shape
This drop-down list is used to specify the shape of the round. There are two options available in this drop-down: **Tangent Continuous** and **Curvature Continuous**. If you select the **Tangent Continuous** option, the round will be tangent to the adjacent faces. If the **Curvature Continuous** option is selected, the round created will be smoothly connected to the adjacent faces and also

maintains the same curvature of the adjacent faces. Figure 6-29 shows the difference between these two options.

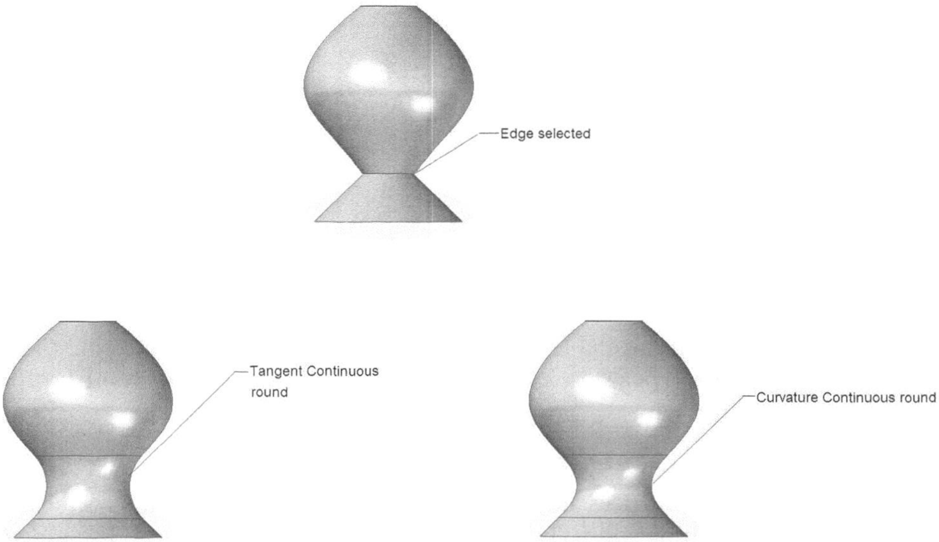

Figure 6-29 The difference between the tangent continuous and curvature continuous rounds

Value

This edit box is used to specify the setback value.

> **Tip**
> *If you return to the **Soften Corner Step** and you had earlier selected the corner to add a setback, then the selected corner will be available in the **Select** drop-down list. The name of that corner will be suffixed by the value of the setback.*

Unique Edge Values

This button is activated only when you choose the **Multiple of radius** option from methods drop-down. This button is chosen when you want to specify different setback values along every edge that forms the corner. When you choose this button, the **Edge Setbacks** dialog box will be displayed. You can enter the setback for each edge in this dialog box. Figure 6-30 shows the round edges setback of different values along each edge.

> **Tip**
> *If you return to the **Soften Corner Step** and you had earlier specified a unique edge value setback, then the edges that comprised the corner will be available as **Edge-Corner** in the **Select** drop-down list. The value suffixed to the corner is the setback value along that edge.*

Creating the Variable Radius Round

In this type of round, you can specify multiple radius values along the length of the edge selected to be filleted, as shown in Figure 6-31.To create this type of round, select the **Variable radius** radio button from the **Round Options** dialog box and choose **OK** to exit the dialog box. When you exit the **Round Options** dialog box, the **Select Step** will be activated and you will be prompted to click on an edge chain.

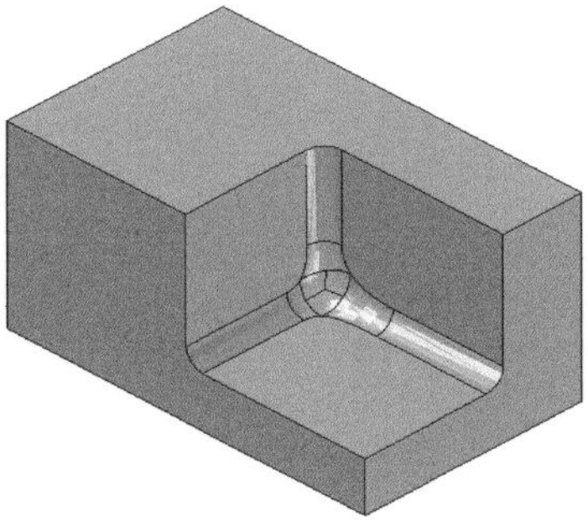

Figure 6-30 *Setback with different values along each edge*

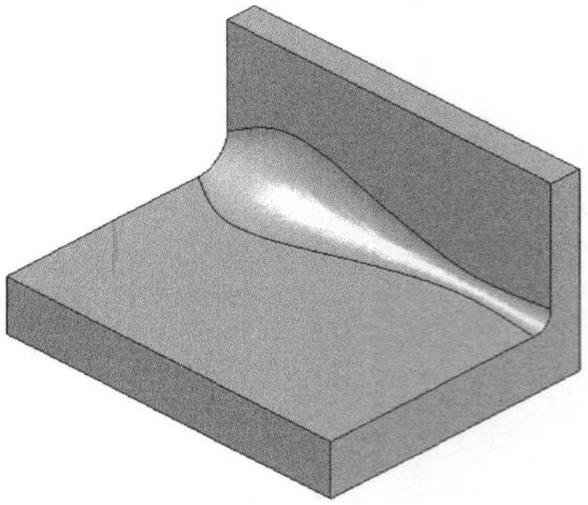

Figure 6-31 *Variable radius round*

You can use the other options available in the **Select** drop-down list for selecting the entities to be filleted. These selection types were discussed in the **Creating the Constant Radius Round** section.

After selecting the edge, choose the **Accept** button to invoke the **Select Vertices** button. This button is used to specify the vertices along the edge to define different radius values. When this button is invoked, the **Point** option will be selected in the **Select** drop-down list and you will be prompted to click on the point to edit. Select the first point on the edge to enable the **Radius** edit box. Enter the radius value at this vertex in the **Radius** edit box. Note that you can select only the keypoints along the edge such as the endpoints and the midpoint. To define some intermediate points, you need to sketch them using the **Sketch** tool.

As you press the ENTER key after specifying the radius value at a selected vertex, the **Radius** edit box will be disabled. Now again select a vertex and then enter the radius of the vertex. Continue this procedure until you select all the vertices and also specify their corresponding radii. Next, choose the **Preview** button to display the preview of the resultant round and then choose the **Finish** button to create it. You can click on the radius value in the preview to modify it.

CREATING ROUNDS (SYNCHRONOUS ENVIRONMENT)

In the **Synchronous Part** environment, you can add rounds or fillets to sharp edges of the model. To do so, invoke the **Round** tool from the **Solids** group of the **Home** tab; the **Round** Command bar will be displayed. Select the edges to be rounded or filleted. Next, enter the radius value in the dynamic edit box displayed in the graphics window and press ENTER.

Creating Variable Radius Rounds (Synchronous Environment)

In the **Synchronous Part** environment, you can create a variable radius round using the **Blend** tool. To do so, choose the **Blend** tool from the **Round** drop-down in the **Solids** group of the **Home** tab; the **Blend** Command bar will be displayed, as shown in Figure 6-32. Select the **Variable radius** radio button from the Command bar; the Command bar will get modified and you will be prompted to select an edge. Select the required edge and choose the **Accept** button. Next, select a point on the selected edge; the **Radius** edit box will be enabled. Enter a value in the **Radius** edit box and choose the **Accept** button; you will be prompted to select another point. Similarly, select another point on the selected edge and specify a different radius value in the **Radius** edit box. Next, choose the **Accept** button; the preview of the variable radius will be displayed. Similarly, you can select more points on the selected edge and specify desired radius values. Next, choose the **Finish** button and then the **Cancel** button to exit the tool.

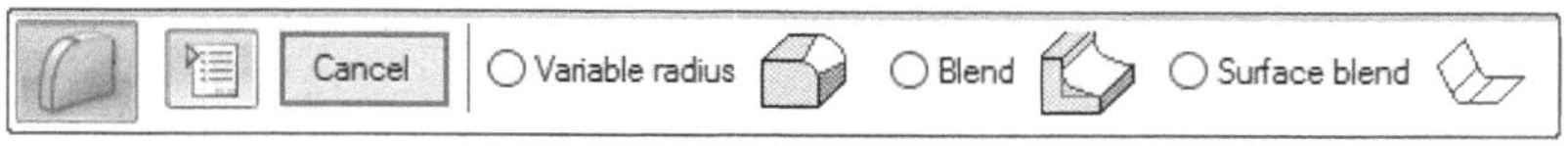

*Figure 6-32 The **Blend** command bar*

Note

While creating the variable radius round, you can select only the intersection points and keypoints along the edge or face.

CREATING CHAMFERS (ORDERED ENVIRONMENT)

Ribbon: Home > Solids > Round drop-down > Chamfer

Chamfering is defined as the process of beveling sharp edges of a model to reduce the area of stress concentration. In Solid Edge, chamfers are created using the **Chamfer** tool. If you invoke this tool, the **Chamfer** Command bar will be displayed. Before creating a chamfer, you need to specify the type of chamfer by choosing the **Chamfer Options** button in the **Chamfer** Command bar. On choosing this button, the **Chamfer Options** dialog box will be displayed, as shown in Figure 6-33. The options in this dialog box are discussed next.

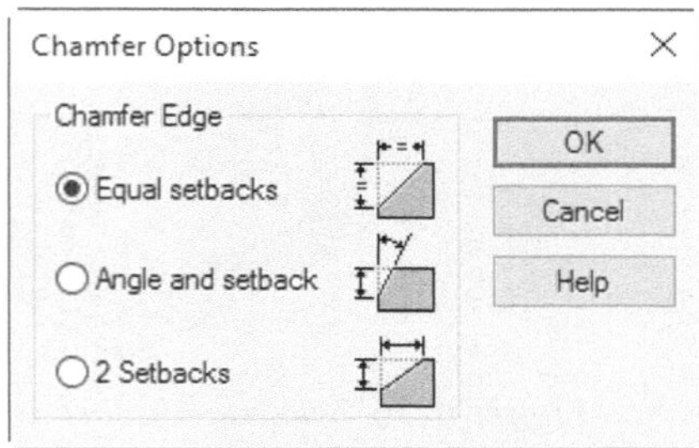

*Figure 6-33 The **Chamfer Options** dialog box*

Equal setbacks

This radio button is selected to create a chamfer with equal setback values of the selected edges from both the faces. The chamfer thus created will be at 45-degree. This is the default option. Therefore, on invoking this tool, you will be prompted to select the edge to be treated. The setback value can be specified in the **Setback** edit box. Figure 6-34 shows a model without adding the setback for chamfer and Figure 6-35 shows a model after adding the equal setback for the chamfer.

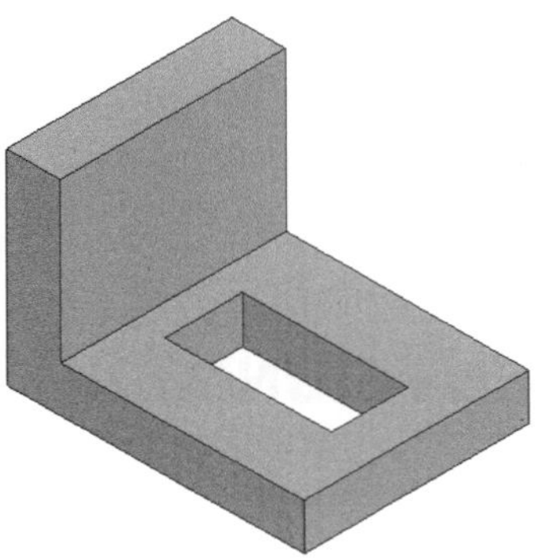

Figure 6-34 Model without chamfer

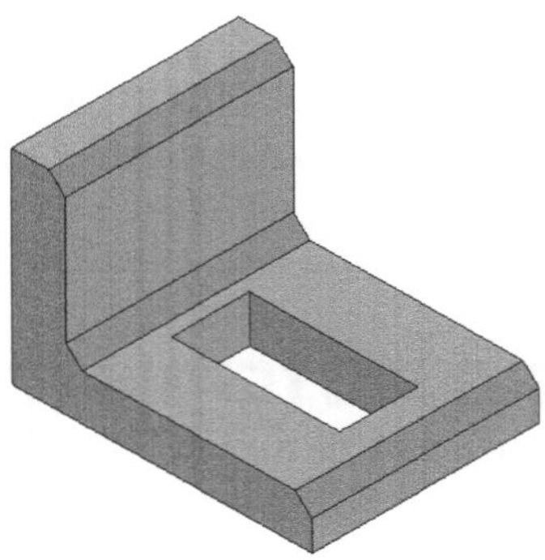

Figure 6-35 Model after creating the chamfer

Angle and setback

This is the second method of creating chamfers. In this method, a chamfer is created by defining one setback distance value and one angle value. When you exit the **Chamfer Options** dialog box after selecting this option, you will be prompted to select the face containing the edges to be chamfered. This is the face against which the angle will be measured. After selecting the face, choose the **Accept** button from the Command bar; you will be prompted to select the edge chain to be chamfered. Note that you can select only the edges that are part of the selected face. The setback distance and the angle value can be specified in their respective edit boxes in the Command bar. Figure 6-36 shows the face to measure the angle and also the edge selected to be chamfered. Figure 6-37 shows the model after chamfering the selected edges with the setback value 10 and the angle value 50 degrees. You can edit these values for a chamfer by clicking them and then entering new values.

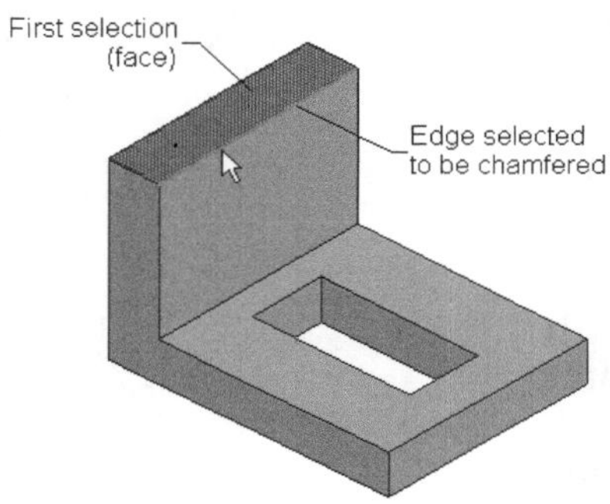

Figure 6-36 Selecting the face and the edge to chamfer

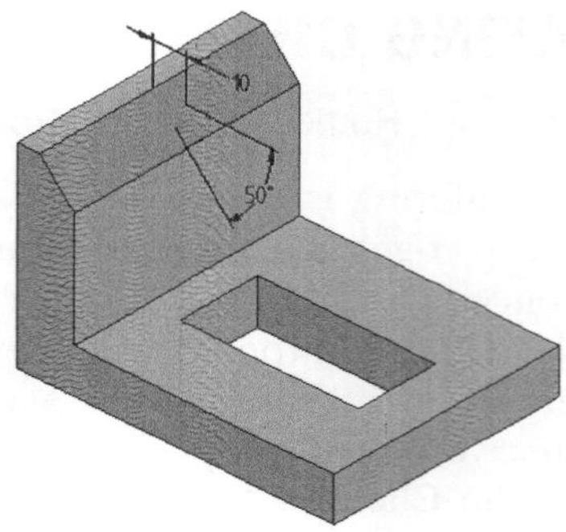

Figure 6-37 Model after creating the chamfer

2 Setbacks

This radio button is selected to create a chamfer by using two different distances. When you exit the **Chamfer Options** dialog box after selecting this option, you will be prompted to select the face containing the edges to be chamfered. This is the face along which the first setback distance will be measured. After selecting the face, choose the **Accept** button; you will be prompted to select the edge chain to be chamfered. Note that you can select only those edges that are part of the selected face. You can specify the two setback distances in the **Setback 1** and **Setback 2** edit boxes in the Command bar. You can edit the setback values by clicking on the setback dimension displayed on the model.

Note

*You can create chamfers in the **Synchronous Part** environment by using the **Chamfer Equal Setbacks** and **Chamfer Unequal Setbacks** tools available in the **Round** drop-down of the **Solid** group in the **Home** tab. The procedures to create chamfers with equal setbacks and unequal setbacks are the same as discussed in the **Ordered Part** environment.*

CREATING PATTERNS (ORDERED ENVIRONMENT)

Most of the mechanical designs consist of multiple copies of some features arranged in a rectangular or circular fashion. For example, the grooves on the base of the pedestal bearing, as shown in Figure 6-38, or the holes on a particular bolt circle diameter on a flange, as shown in Figure 6-39.

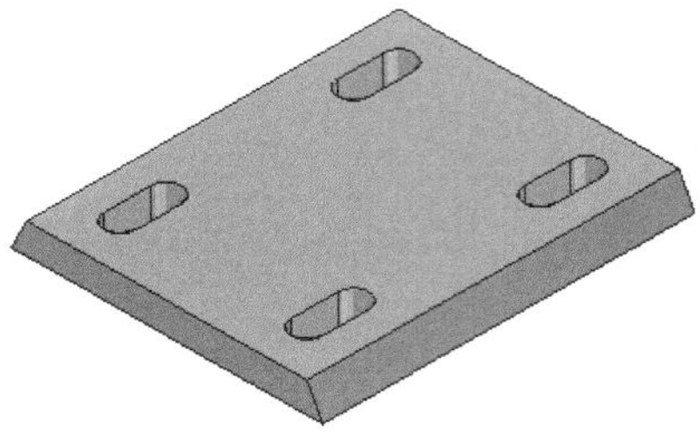

Figure 6-38 *Model with features arranged in rectangular fashion*

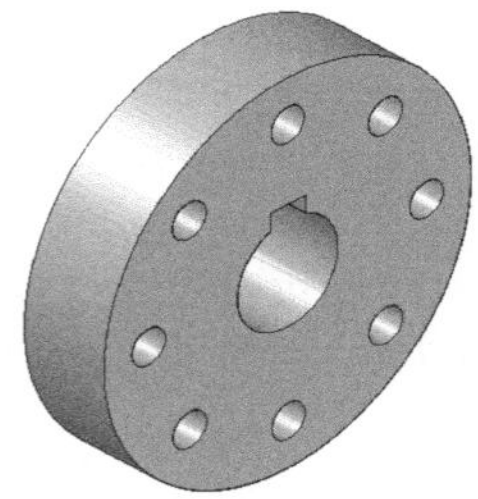

Figure 6-39 *Model with features arranged in circular fashion*

Creating such features individually is very tedious and time consuming. To make the process easier and faster, Solid Edge provides you with the **Pattern** tool. This tool can be used to create rectangular as well as circular patterns.

Creating Rectangular Patterns

Ribbon: Home > Pattern > Pattern drop-down > Pattern

When you invoke the **Pattern** tool, the **Rectangular** tool gets activated by default. The process of creating a pattern is completed in three steps: **Select Step**, **Sketch Step**, and **Draw Profile Step**. The first two steps are the same for creating the rectangular pattern and the circular pattern. In the **Draw Profile Step**, you need to specify whether you want to create a rectangular pattern or a circular pattern by drawing a rectangular or a circular profile. All these steps and their corresponding options are discussed next.

Select Step

When you invoke the **Pattern** tool, the **Select Step** is activated and you are prompted to click on a feature. Select the feature to be patterned and then choose the **Accept** button; the **Sketch Step** will be invoked.

Sketch Step

This step is used to select the plane on which the profile of a rectangular or a circular pattern will be drawn. You can select the option from the **Create-From Options** drop-down list to specify the plane on which the profile will be drawn. As soon as you select the plane, the **Draw Profile Step** will be activated and the sketching environment will be invoked.

Draw Profile Step

On invoking this step, the **Rectangular Pattern** tool in the **Features** group from the **Home** tab of the **Ribbon** will be invoked in the sketching environment. Also, the **Rectangular Pattern** Command bar will be displayed, as shown in Figure 6-40. Using this Command bar, draw a rectangular profile along which you need to create the rectangular pattern. On drawing a rectangle, the pattern instances will be represented by small dots and the **Select** Command bar will be displayed. Choose the **Close Sketch** button and then the **Finish** button on the **Rectangular Pattern** Command bar; a rectangular pattern will be created.

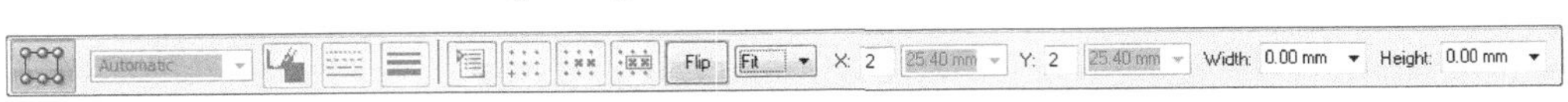

Figure 6-40 *The* ***Rectangular Pattern*** *command bar*

Note

1. The rectangle profile may not necessarily pass through the feature selected to be patterned because the rectangle is used only for reference.

2. The profiles of the patterns are like any other sketched entities. Therefore, it is recommended that you add dimensions and relationships to make them stable.

The options in the Command bar for the rectangular pattern are discussed next.

Pattern Type Drop-down List

This drop-down list is used to specify the method of defining the placement of occurrences in the rectangular pattern. These methods are discussed next.

Fit: If this option is selected, you can specify the number of occurrences along the X and Y directions and these will be fitted inside the specified rectangle. The spacing between the occurrences along the X and Y directions will be automatically calculated.

Fill: If you select this option, you can specify the spacing between the occurrences along the X and Y directions and the length and width of the rectangle. The total number of occurrences along the X and Y directions are automatically determined by the values of the individual spacing and the length and width of the rectangle.

Fixed: You can select this option when you want to specify the total number of occurrences along the X and Y directions as well as the spacing between the occurrences along these directions. The height and width of the rectangular pattern will be automatically calculated.

X/Y Edit Boxes

These edit boxes are used to specify the number of occurrences along the X and Y directions and are available only for the **Fit** and **Fixed** pattern types.

The X spacing and Y spacing Edit Boxes

These edit boxes are available next to the **X** and **Y** edit boxes, respectively and are used to specify the individual spacing between the occurrences along the X and Y directions. These edit boxes are only available for the **Fill** and **Fixed** pattern types.

Width/Height Edit Boxes

These edit boxes are used to specify the width and height of a rectangle profile, and are only available for the **Fit** and **Fill** pattern types.

Tip

*If you exit the **Rectangular Pattern** command bar by mistake, you can invoke it again by choosing the **Rectangular** tool from the **Features** group.*

Stagger Options

In Solid Edge, you can create a rectangular pattern in which every alternate row or column is offset from its original location. To do so, choose the **Stagger Options** button from the **Rectangular Pattern** Command bar; the **Stagger Options** dialog box will be displayed, as shown in Figure 6-41.

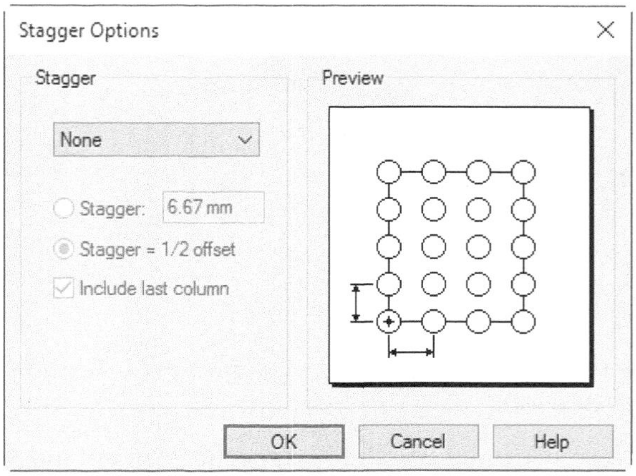

*Figure 6-41 The **Stagger Options** dialog box*

To create a staggered rectangular pattern, you need to select an option from the drop-down list available in the **Stagger** area. You can specify whether you want to stagger a row or the column. By default, the staggering distance is half of the offset value. However, you can also specify any other numeric value by selecting the **Stagger** radio button. The **Include last column** check box is selected to specify that you want to create the last row or column in the staggered pattern. Figure 6-42 shows a rectangular pattern staggered along the row and Figure 6-43 shows the same pattern staggered along the column.

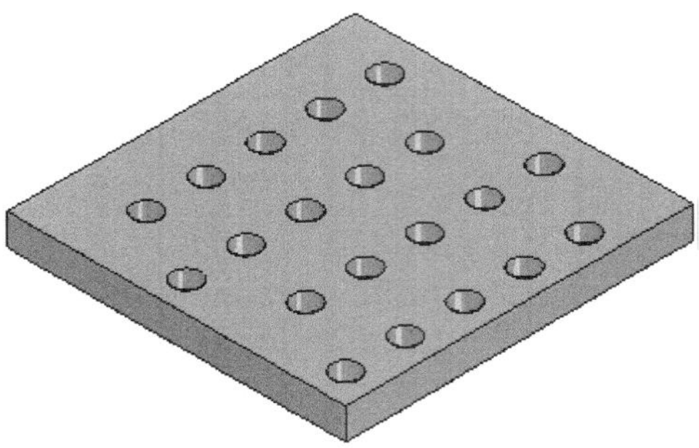

Figure 6-42 Rectangular pattern staggered along the row

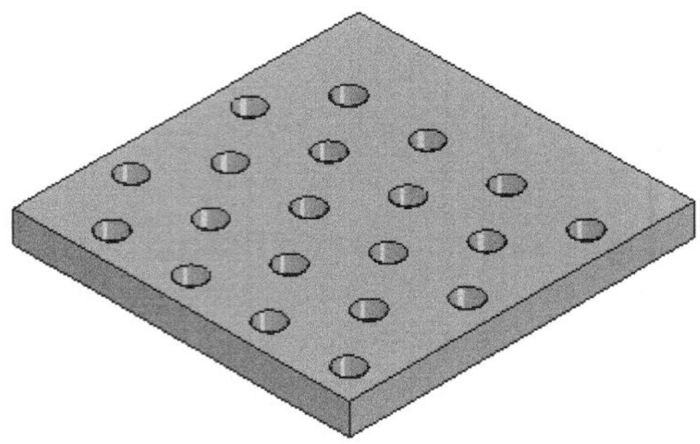

Figure 6-43 Rectangular pattern staggered along the column

Reference Point

While defining a pattern, the reference point plays an important role in determining the direction in which the pattern elements will be placed. By default, the first corner of the rectangle is taken as the reference point and is designated by a bold cross (**x**). The pattern is created from this first point in the direction in which the rectangle is drawn. If you want to change the reference point, choose the **Reference Point** button from the Command bar and then select the point you want to use as the reference point. For example, refer to Figure 6-44. In this figure, the reference point is at the lower left corner of the rectangle that is at the center of the circular cut feature. Figure 6-45 shows the resulting pattern.

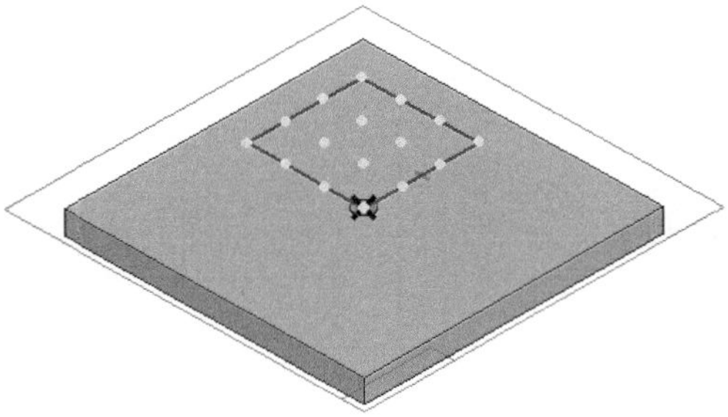

Figure 6-44 *Selecting the lower left corner of the rectangle as the reference point*

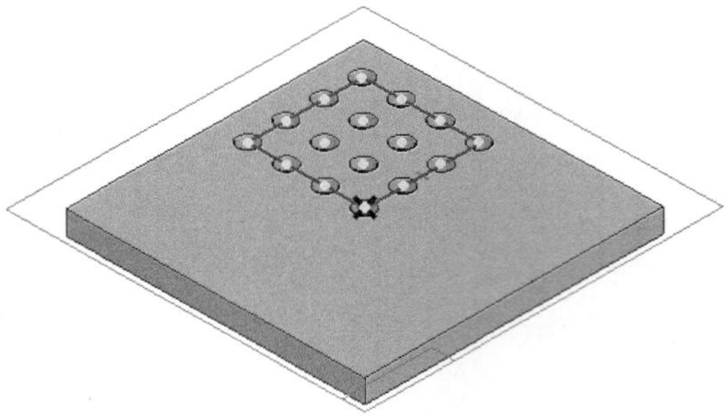

Figure 6-45 *Resulting rectangular pattern*

In Figure 6-46, the reference point is at the lower right corner of the rectangle and Figure 6-47 shows the resulting pattern.

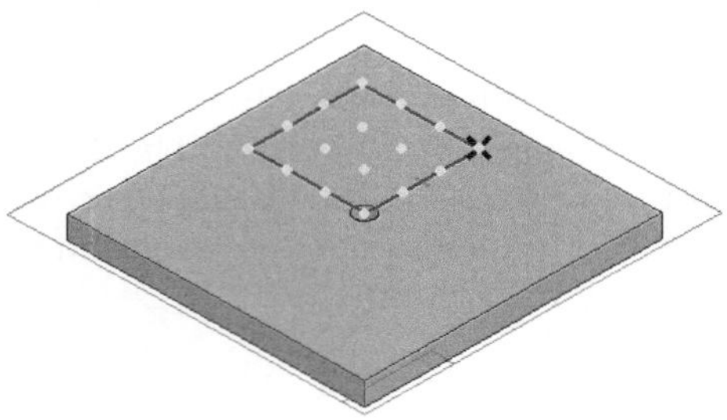

Figure 6-46 *Selecting the lower right corner of the rectangle as the reference point*

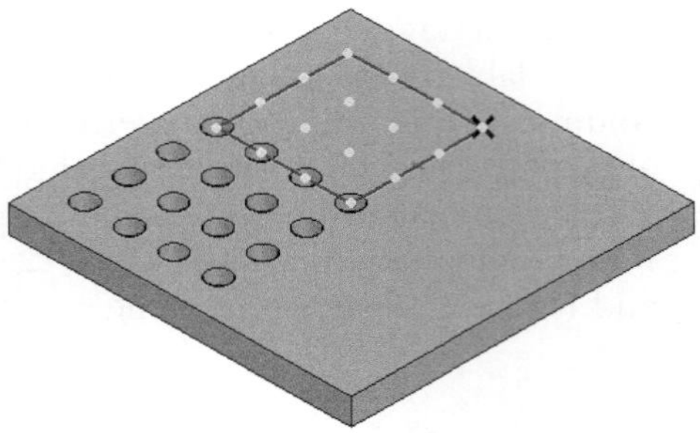

Figure 6-47 *Resulting rectangular pattern*

Suppress Occurrence Button

This button is chosen to suppress some of the occurrences in the rectangular pattern. To suppress occurrences, choose this button and then click the green point on the occurrence to be suppressed in the pattern. You can unsuppress occurrences by again clicking on them. After suppressing the occurrences, right-click to continue. Figure 6-48 shows a pattern without suppressing occurrences and Figure 6-49 shows the same pattern with some occurrences suppressed.

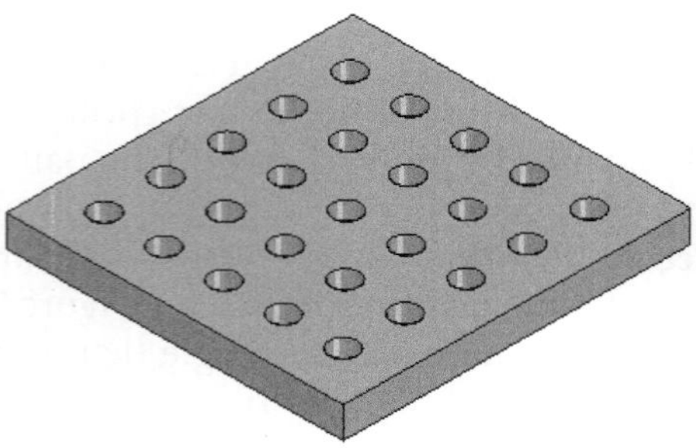

Figure 6-48 *Pattern without suppressing the occurrences*

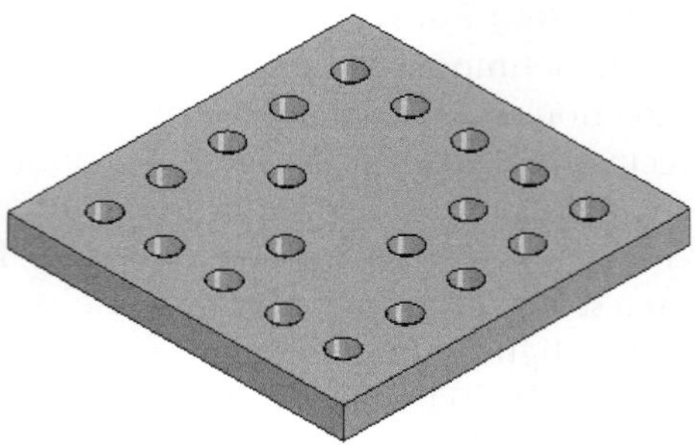

Figure 6-49 *Pattern with some occurrences suppressed*

After specifying the parameters of the pattern in the sketching environment, choose **Close Sketch**; the preview of the resulting pattern will be displayed.

In addition to the buttons of various steps, the Command bar provides two more buttons, **Smart** and **Fast**. The functions of these two buttons are discussed next.

Smart/Fast Button

The **Smart** button is used to create patterns with more complex designs. For example, refer to Figure 6-50. This figure shows a staggered pattern in which the occurrences in the last column do not lie completely inside the model. Such cases cannot be handled by the **Fast** option. Therefore, you must use the **Smart** option to create the pattern. Note that if you try to create this pattern using the **Fast** option, the last column will not be created.

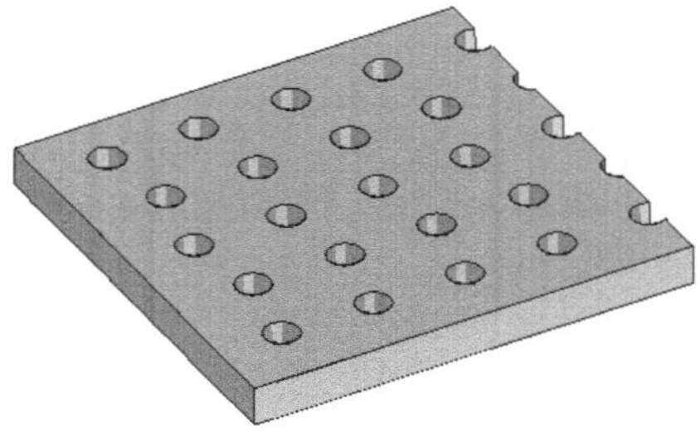

Figure 6-50 *Model with complex pattern designs*

Note

Generally, the coplanar features can be patterned by using the ***Fast*** *pattern option and the features that are not coplanar can be patterned using the* ***Smart*** *pattern option.*

Creating Circular Patterns

Ribbon: Home > Pattern > Pattern drop-down > Pattern

As mentioned earlier, the process of creating circular patterns is the same as that of creating rectangular patterns. The only difference is in the **Draw Profile Step**. To invoke this step, you first need to select the feature to pattern and then select the plane or the planar face on which the profile of the circular pattern will be drawn.

Draw Profile Step

To create a circular pattern, you need to draw its profile, which can be a circle or an arc. This circle or arc acts as a reference to arrange the occurrences in a circular fashion. Invoke this step in the sketching environment and choose the **Circular Pattern** tool from the **Features** group of the **Home** tab in the **Ribbon**; you will be prompted to click for the center point of the arc. Specify the center point of the circular pattern; you will be prompted to specify the start point of the arc and radius for the circle. Specify a point to define the radius of the circle for the circular pattern. Finally, you will be prompted to click for a point on the circle to define the direction of the pattern. On doing so, you will notice that an arrow is displayed at the point you defined as the start point of the circle. You can move the cursor to either side of the start point to define the circular pattern in the clockwise or counterclockwise direction. After selecting the direction, the **Select** Command bar will be displayed. Choose the **Close Sketch** button and then the **Finish** button on the **Pattern** Command bar; a circular pattern will be created.

The options in the Command bar for the circular pattern are discussed next.

Reference Point Button

This button is chosen to change the reference point of the pattern.

Suppress Occurrence Button

This button is chosen to suppress some of the occurrences in the circular pattern. To suppress the occurrences, choose this button and then click on the green points of the occurrence that you do not want in the pattern. After suppressing them, right-click to exit.

Pattern Type Drop-down List

This drop-down list is used to specify the method of defining the placement of occurrences in the circular pattern. The options in this list are discussed next.

Fit: If this option is selected, then the number of occurrences that you specify in the **Count** edit box are fitted inside the profile of the circular pattern.

Fill: This option allows you to specify the spacing between the occurrences along the profile of the circular pattern.

Fixed: This option is available only when you choose the **Partial Circle** button. It is used to specify the total number of occurrences and spacing between them.

Partial Circle Button

Choose this button when you do not want to create a circular pattern through a complete circle. You can specify the angle of sweep for the partial circle in the **Sweep** edit box. Figure 6-51 shows a circular pattern of eight holes arranged around a partial circle of 270-degree angle. In this case, the original feature is the circle at the bottom and the occurrences are placed in the counterclockwise direction. Figure 6-52 shows the same pattern, but the occurrences are placed in the clockwise direction.

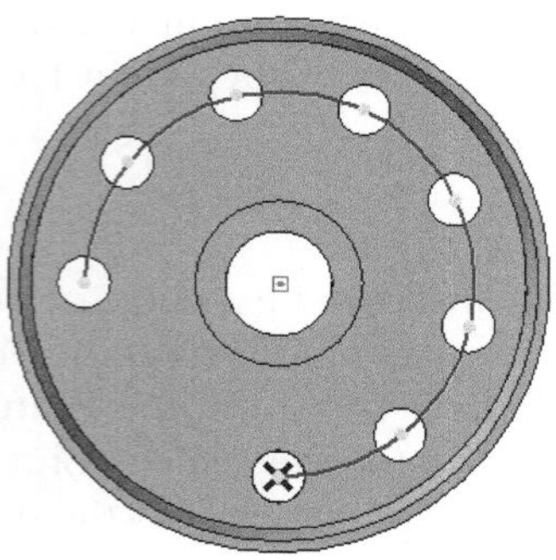

Figure 6-51 *Circular pattern placed along a partial circle in the counterclockwise direction*

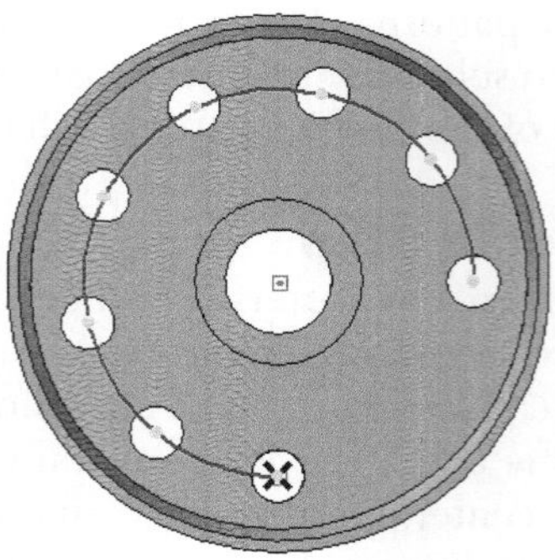

Figure 6-52 *Circular pattern placed along a partial circle in the clockwise direction*

Tip

If you have already created the profile of a pattern by using the ***Rectangular Pattern*** *or* ***Circular Patterns*** *tool in the sketching environment, then you can select that profile by using the* ***Select from Sketch*** *option in the* ***Create-From Options*** *drop-down list.*

Full Circle Button

This button is used to create a circular pattern through a complete circle, as shown in Figure 6-53.

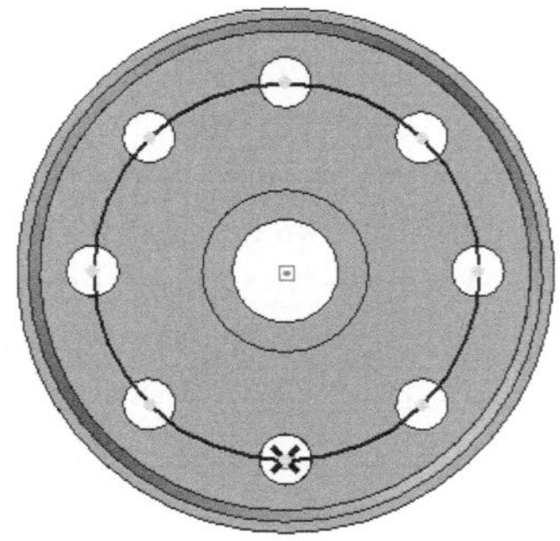

Figure 6-53 Circular pattern through a complete circle

Radius Edit Box

This edit box is used to specify the radius of the profile of the circular pattern.

Sweep Edit Box

This edit box is available only when you choose the **Partial Circle** button and is used to specify the angle of the partial circle. This edit box is available only for the **Fit** and **Fill** pattern types.

Count Edit Box

This edit box is available only for the **Fit** and **Fixed** pattern types and is used to specify the occurrences of patterns in the circular pattern.

Spacing Edit Box

This edit box is available only for the **Fill** and **Fixed** pattern types and is used to specify the spacing between the occurrences of the patterns in the circular pattern.

Creating a Pattern along a Curve

Ribbon: Home > Pattern > Pattern drop-down > Curved

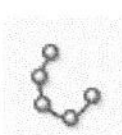

In Solid Edge, you can also pattern the selected features along an existing curve or an edge using the **Curved** tool. You need to perform following steps for creating a pattern along a curve using the **Curved** tool:

Select Step

This step will be activated when you invoke the **Curved** tool. In this step, you are prompted to click on a feature to pattern. You can select one or more features to pattern. After selecting the features, choose the **Accept** button to invoke the **Select Curve Step**.

Select Curve Step

This step is used to select the curve along which the pattern will be created. You will be allowed to specify other options such as the anchor point and the total number of occurrences in the pattern. The options available in the Command bar for this step are discussed next.

Pattern Curve

This button is automatically chosen when the **Select Curve Step** is invoked. This button enables you to select the curve along which the selected feature will be patterned. You can select an existing sketched entity or an edge as the curve for creating the pattern. After selecting the curve, choose the **Accept** button.

Anchor Point

This button will be automatically chosen when you choose **Accept** after selecting the pattern curve. It enables you to select the anchor point in the selected curve to specify the alignment of the pattern occurrences. You can select any of the endpoints of the curve or the joining points of a chain of entities. As soon as you select the anchor point, an arrow will be displayed at that point and you will be prompted to click to accept the displayed side or select the other side in the view. This arrow defines the direction in which the occurrences will be placed along the curve. While defining the anchor point, you can also specify the distance by which the occurrences will be offset from the anchor point in the **Offset** edit box. This edit box is available while defining the anchor point. Figures 6-54 and 6-55 show the preview of a pattern of counterbore holes along the curve with different anchor points.

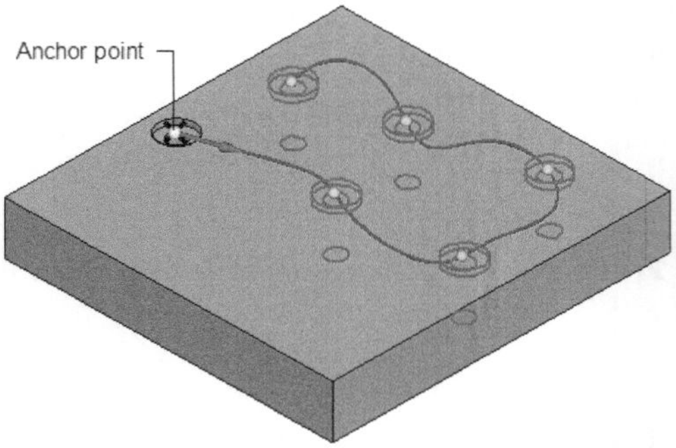

Figure 6-54 *Preview of the pattern along the curve*

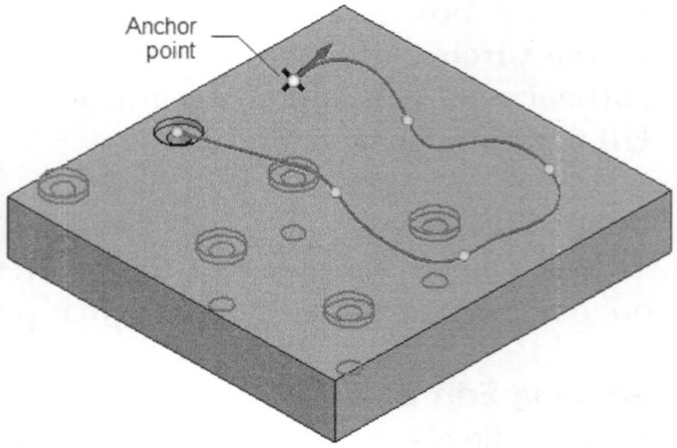

Figure 6-55 *Preview of the pattern with different anchor points*

Note

*The other options in the **Select Curve Step** are similar to those discussed in the rectangular and circular patterns.*

Spacing Step

This step is invoked automatically when you choose the **Accept** button from the **Select Curve Step**. This step is used to specify the placement of occurrences, occurrences of pattern, and spacing between the occurrences in the **Pattern Type**, **Count**, and **Spacing** edit boxes, respectively.

Path Curve Step

The **Path Curve Step** is not invoked automatically. You need to click this button to invoke it. This step is used to select a path curve that defines the second direction along which the occurrences of a pattern will be arranged. The curve that you define in this step will define the direction and the total distance between all occurrences of the pattern along the second direction. After selecting the path curve, specify an anchor point. The options available in this step are the same as those discussed in the **Select Curve Step**. Figure 6-56 shows the preview of a pattern along a curve with the second direction, defined along an edge. Note that the number of occurrences of the pattern in the path curve direction is 3.

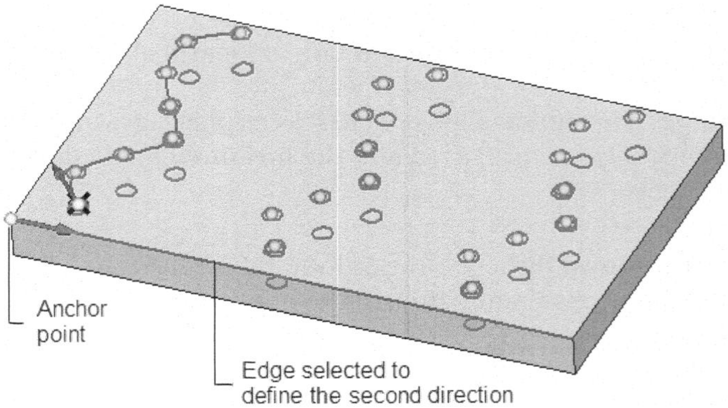

Figure 6-56 Preview of the pattern with the direction and path curves

Alignment Step

This step is used to specify the advanced parameters of the pattern along the curve. The options available in the Command bar for this step are discussed next.

Occurrence Orientation drop-down list

This drop-down list is used to specify the types of occurrences of the pattern in the resulting pattern. The options available in this drop-down list are discussed next.

Simple: If you select this option, the occurrences of the pattern will have the same orientation as that of the original pattern, as shown in the preview of the pattern in Figure 6-57.

Follow Curve: If you select this option, the occurrences of the pattern will be oriented along the direction of the selected curve at a particular point, as shown in the preview of the pattern in Figure 6-58.

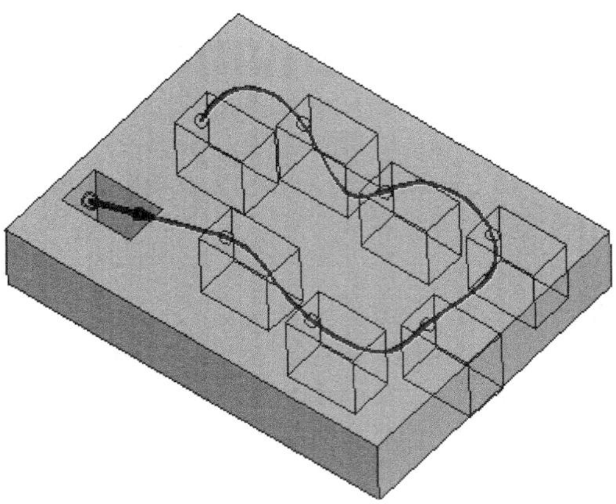

Figure 6-57 Pattern with linear transformation

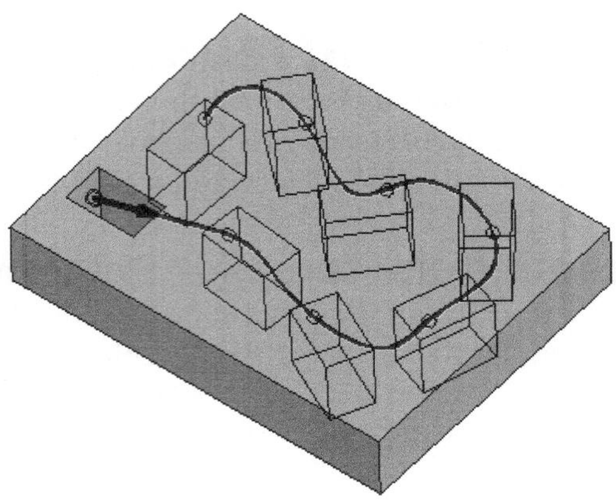

Figure 6-58 Pattern with full transformation

Follow Curve Chord: If you select this option, a line segment is drawn between all the instances and the orientation of the surface is set based on these segments rather than the actual curve.

Follow Using Surface: If you select this option, the occurrences of the pattern will be oriented along the direction of the selected face at a particular point.

Follow Using Plane: This option allows you to select a plane on which the original occurrence and a pattern occurrence are projected and the measured angle defines the orientation of the pattern occurrence.

Rotation Type drop-down list: This drop-down list is used to specify the types of rotation of the occurrences in the resultant pattern. The options available in this drop-down list are discussed next.

Curve Position: If you select this option, the curve position will determine the rotation of the occurrences of the pattern, as shown in the preview of the pattern in Figure 6-59.

Feature Position: If you select this option, the feature position will determine the rotation of occurrences of the pattern, as shown in the preview of the pattern in Figure 6-60.

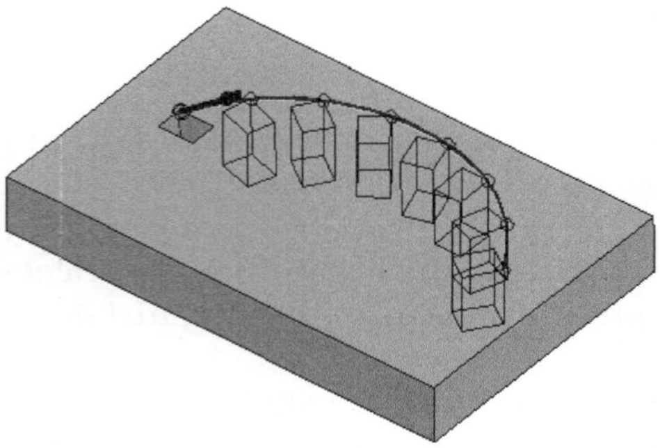

Figure 6-59 Pattern with curve position rotation

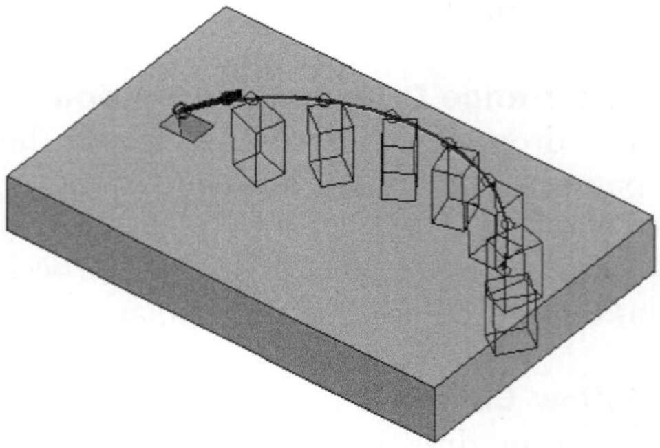

Figure 6-60 Pattern with feature position rotation

CREATING PATTERNS (SYNCHRONOUS ENVIRONMENT)

In the **Synchronous Part** environment, you can create the patterns of a selected feature in less time compared to creating them in the **Ordered Part** environment. This can be done by using the advanced tools in the **Pattern** group. The tools available in the **Pattern** group are discussed next.

Creating Rectangular Patterns

To create a rectangular pattern, first you need to select the feature to pattern and then choose the **Rectangular** tool from the **Rectangular** drop-down in the **Pattern** group of the **Home** tab. You will notice that the first corner of an imaginary rectangle will be attached to the selected feature. Specify the second corner of the rectangle; the preview of the rectangular pattern along with several on-screen tools will be displayed, as shown in Figure 6-61. These tools are Command bar, the occurrence count box, dynamic edit boxes, occurrence handles, and the orient vector handle. You can define and edit the parameters of the pattern using these tools.

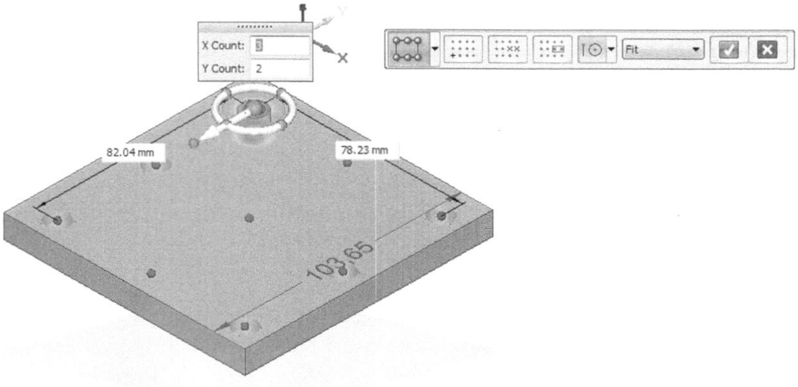

Figure 6-61 Various on-screen tools displayed while creating a pattern

Command bar

The options available in the Command bar are discussed next.

Pattern

This drop-down contains all types of pattern tools that are used to pattern a feature.

Reference Point

This button is used to change the reference point of a pattern.

Suppress Instance

This button is used to select the occurrence to be suppressed in a rectangular pattern.

Suppress Region

This button is used to suppress the occurrences of a pattern by using a sketch region or a planar face. Note that you need to create the sketch region prior to creating the pattern. To suppress the occurrences of a pattern in a region, choose this button and then select the sketch region that encloses the occurrences that you do not want in the pattern. On selecting the sketch, an arrow pointing along the direction of suppression will be displayed in the region. You can use the arrow to specify whether the occurrences lying inside or outside the region have to be suppressed, as shown in Figure 6-62.

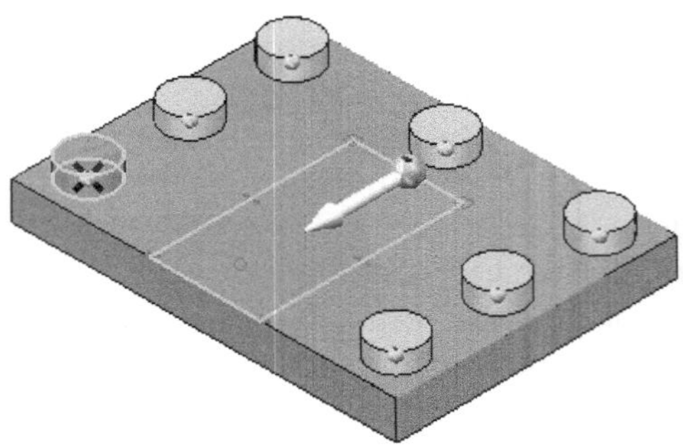

Figure 6-62 Suppressing the occurrences inside the region

Fill Style

This drop-down list is used to specify the option to be used for defining the number of occurrences and spacing between them. The options in this drop-down list have already been discussed.

Occurrence Count Boxes

These count boxes are used to specify the number of occurrences along the X and Y directions.

Dynamic Edit Boxes

These edit boxes are used to specify the exact values for the spacing between occurrences. When the **Fit** option is set, the dynamic edit boxes are used to specify the total height and the width of the pattern, as shown in Figure 6-63. However, if you select the **Fixed** option from the **Fill Style** drop-down list, then the edit boxes are used to specify the spacing between the occurrences along the X and Y directions, as shown in Figure 6-64.

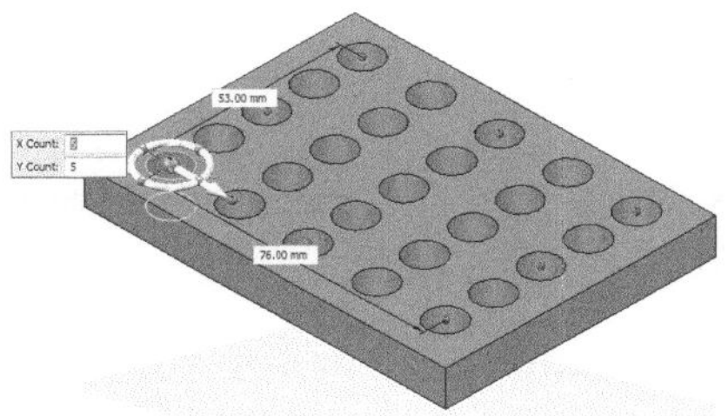

Figure 6-63 *Creating a rectangular pattern using the* ***Fit*** *option*

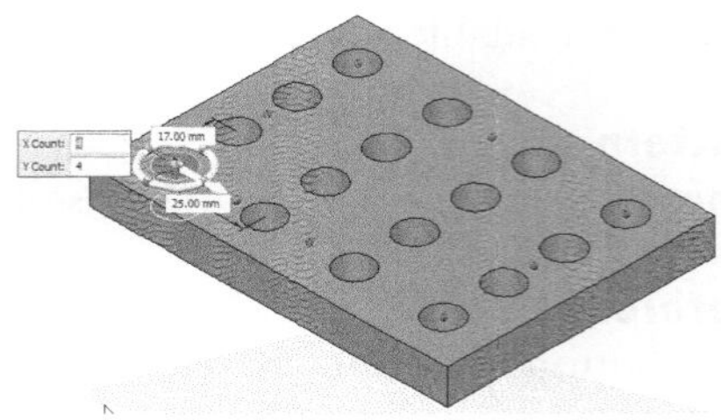

Figure 6-64 *Creating a rectangular pattern using the* ***Fixed*** *option*

Occurrence Handles

Occurrence handles are the red color spheres that appear on the occurrences. These handles are used to change the length and width of a pattern dynamically. To change the height and the width values, position the cursor on an occurrence handle and drag it to a new location; the values in the height and width boxes are updated accordingly.

Orient Vector Handle

This handle works in the same way as a steering wheel. It is used to change the orientation and position of a pattern. To change the angular orientation of a pattern, position the cursor on the torus. Now rotate the torus either dynamically by dragging the cursor or by entering the desired angle in the edit box, as shown in Figure 6-65. You can reorient the pattern in 90-degree increment by using the knobs on the torus. You can redefine the origin of the pattern by selecting the origin of the handle and then repositioning it.

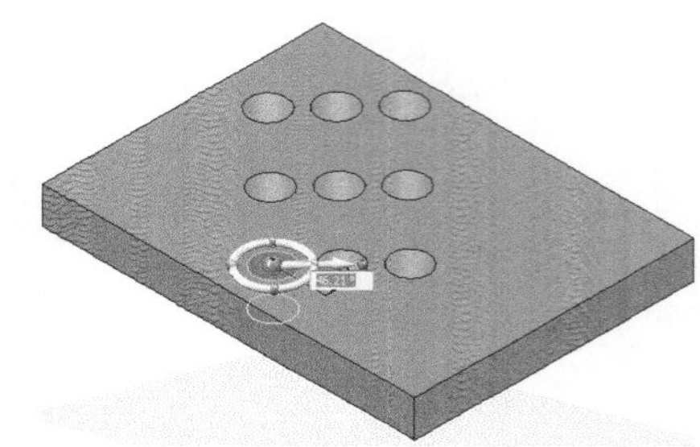

Figure 6-65 *Changing the orientation of the pattern by using the torus of the orient vector handle*

After specifying the parameters of the pattern, choose the **Accept** button in the Command bar; a new pattern will be displayed.

Creating Circular Patterns

To create a circular pattern, first you need to select the feature to be patterned. Next, choose the **Circular** tool from the **Rectangular** drop-down; an imaginary circle along with the pattern axis will be displayed, as shown in Figure 6-66. Move the cursor and select the center point of the circular pattern. You can also select a keypoint such as a center point of a circular edge. On doing so, the preview of the circular pattern is displayed. You can use the Command bar to specify the parameters of the circular pattern.

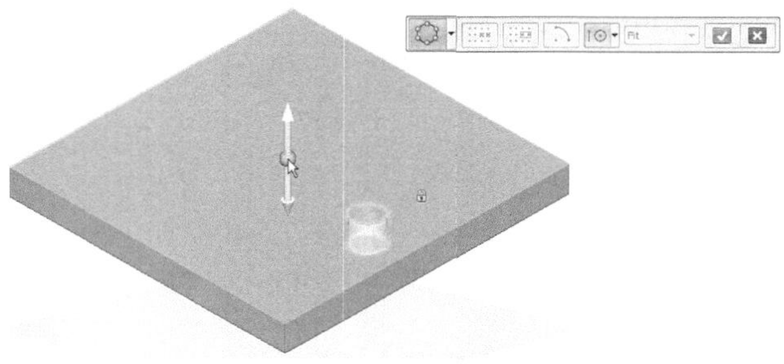

Figure 6-66 *Imaginary circle displayed along with the pattern axis*

Command bar

The options in the Command bar are discussed next.

Circle/Arc Pattern

You need to choose this button if you do not want to create a circular pattern through a complete circle. You can specify the sweep angle for arc in the **Sweep** edit box displayed on the pattern. Figure 6-67 shows a circular pattern of eight holes arranged around an arc of 270 degrees.

Suppress Region

This button is chosen to suppress the occurrences of a pattern by using a sketch region or a planar face. Figure 6-68 shows the suppressing of occurrences inside the region.

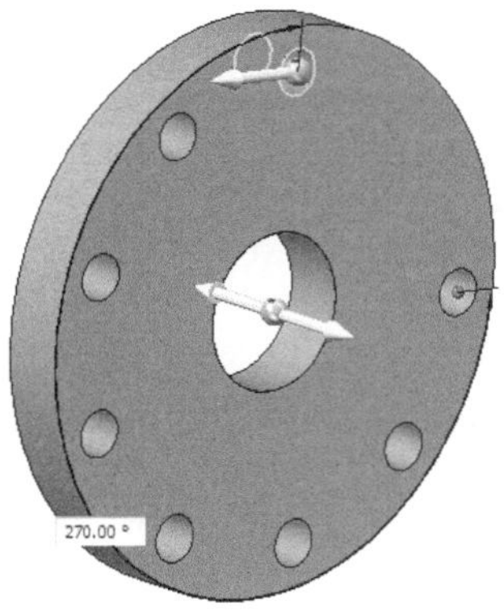

Figure 6-67 *Circular pattern created by specifying the sweep angle*

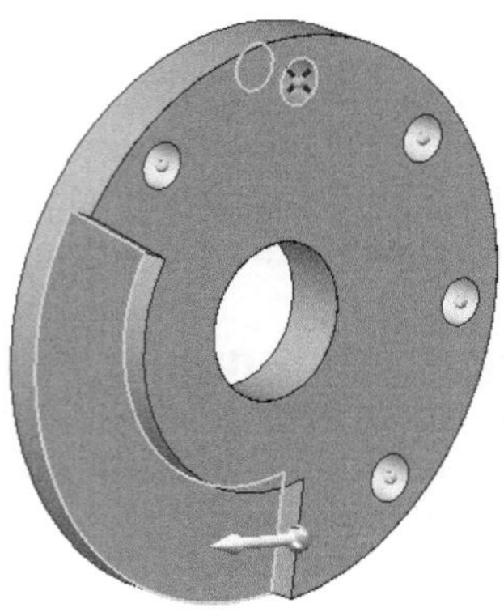

Figure 6-68 *Suppressing individual occurrences inside the region*

Creating a Pattern along a Curve

You can create a pattern of selected features such as a face, feature, surface, or design body along a curve using the **Along Curve** tool. To invoke this tool, first you need to select the feature to be patterned and then choose the **Along curve** tool from the **Rectangular** drop-down. The Command bar will be displayed and you will be prompted to select the curve along which the feature is to patterned. Select a 2D or 3D sketch, a curve, or an edge to create a pattern.

After selecting the curve, choose the **Accept** button. Now, you need to select the anchor point on the curve. The anchor point is the starting point of the pattern. On selecting the anchor point, a dynamic arrow will be displayed on the anchor point to specify the direction of the pattern creation.

Advanced Button

This button is used to specify the advanced parameters of the pattern along a curve. On choosing this button, the **Occurrence Orientation** and **Rotation Type** drop-down list will be displayed.

Occurrence Orientation Drop-down List

This drop-down list is used to specify the types of the occurrences of the pattern in the resulting pattern. The options available in this drop-down list have already been discussed.

Rotation Type Drop-down List

This drop-down list is used to specify the types of rotation of the occurrences in the resultant pattern. The options available in this drop-down list have already been discussed.

Creating Fill Pattern

Ribbon: Home > Pattern > Rectangular drop-down > Fill Pattern

The **Fill Pattern** tool is used to fill a defined region with the pattern of features, faces, bodies, or holes. There are three fill styles available in the **Fill Pattern** tool: **Rectangular**, **Stagger**, and **Radial**. Each fill style has a set of options that are used to define the pattern. To create a fill pattern, select the feature to be patterned from the graphics window or from the **PathFinder**. Next, choose the **Fill Pattern** tool in the **Rectangular** drop-down from **Pattern** group; the **Fill Pattern** Command bar will be displayed. You need to select a face or region on which the fill pattern is to be created. Next, choose the **Accept** button in the Command bar; the preview of the fill pattern will be placed on the region. You can define the fill style by selecting it from the **Fill style** drop-down. The procedures to create various fill styles are discussed next.

Creating a Rectangular Fill Pattern

The rectangular fill style is used to fill the region with the rows and columns of occurrences. By default, this fill style is selected in the Command bar. As a result, you will be prompted to select the region for the pattern to fill. Select the face on which you want to create the fill pattern. Next, choose the **Accept** button; two edit boxes defining the spacing between rows and columns are displayed along with the steering wheel. You need to enter values in the edit boxes to define the row and column spacing. The TAB key can be used to jump between the two edit boxes. You can use the steering wheel to change the orientation of rows. The columns are always aligned perpendicular to the rows.

Creating a Stagger Fill Pattern

The Stagger fill style is used to create a pattern with staggered rows of occurrences. When you select this option, the **Fill spacing method** drop-down gets activated. This drop-down has three options that can be used to control the spacing in the staggered fill pattern. These options are discussed next.

Polar

On choosing this option, the spacing of occurrences can be defined by specifying values in the linear and angle edit boxes. The linear value defines the spacing between individual occurrences, whereas the angular value determines the spacing between rows, refer to Figure 6-69.

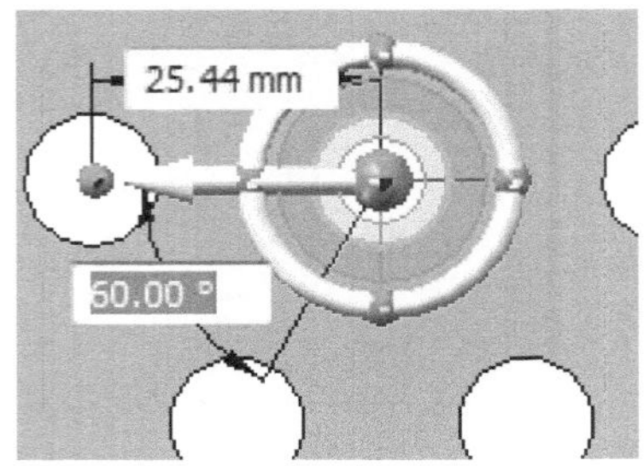

*Figure 6-69 Creating the stagger fill style using the **Polar** option*

Linear Offset

The **Linear Offset** option is used to create a stagger fill pattern by defining the offset spacing of occurrences and the spacing between rows, as shown in Figure 6-70.

Complex Linear Offset

On choosing the **Complex Linear Offset** option, you can create a stagger fill pattern by defining the occurrence spacing, offset spacing, and the row spacing, as shown in Figure 6-71.

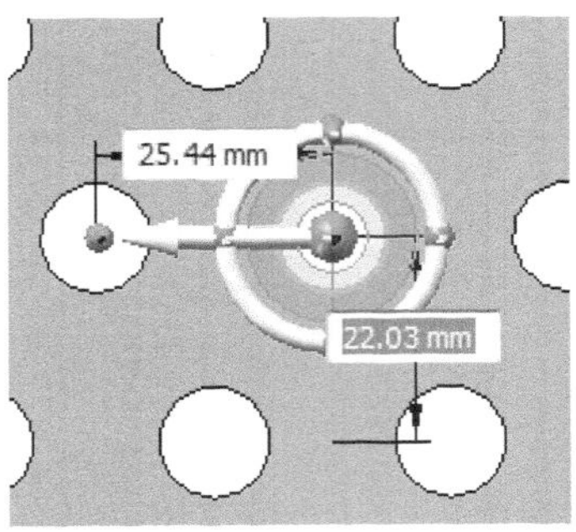

*Figure 6-70 Creating a staggered fill style using the **Linear Offset** option*

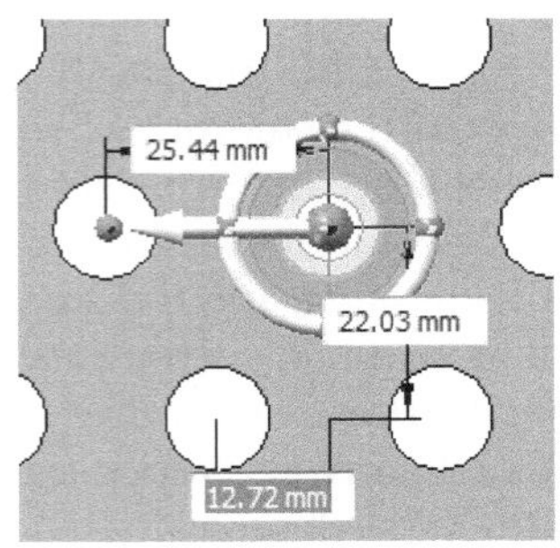

*Figure 6-71 Creating a staggered fill style using the **Complex Linear Offset** option*

Creating a Radial Fill Pattern

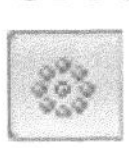

To create the radial fill pattern, select the **Radial** option from the **Fill Style** drop-down; the **Fill Spacing method** drop-down list gets activated. This drop-down has two options: **Occurrence count** and **Target spacing**. These options are used to control the spacing between the occurrences.

Occurrence Count

The **Occurrence Count** option is chosen by default while creating the radial fill pattern. As a result, you need to specify the number of instances per ring and the radial spacing between them. Figure 6-72 shows a pattern with the **Occurrence Count** option selected.

Target Spacing

On choosing this option, you need to define the radial spacing of occurrences and the spacing between individual occurrences on each ring. The total number of occurrences in each ring is automatically determined by the values that you enter for the individual spacing of occurrences, refer to Figure 6-73.

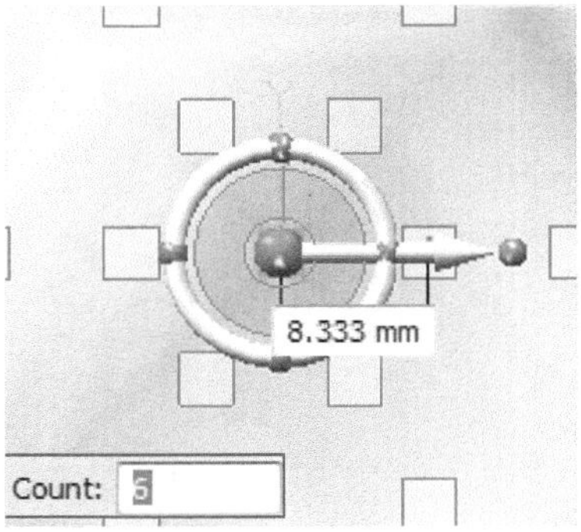

*Figure 6-72 Creating a radial fill pattern using the **Occurrence Count** option*

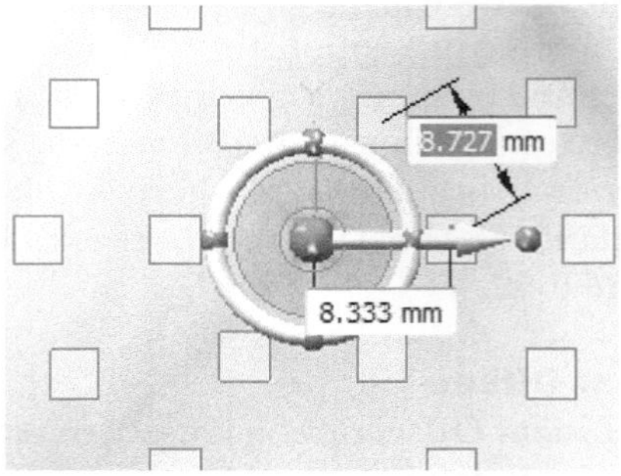

*Figure 6-73 Creating a radial fill pattern using the **Target Spacing** option*

Center Orient

The **Center Orient** button is available only when you create a radial fill pattern. On choosing this button, an arrow is displayed inside the torus of the steering wheel indicating the orientation of the occurrence, refer to Figure 6-74. To change the orientation of the occurrence, you need to click on the arrow inside the steering wheel and then rotate it to an angle keeping the arrow pressed. You can specify the exact value in the edit box displayed near the arrow. Notice the change in the orientation after specifying values.

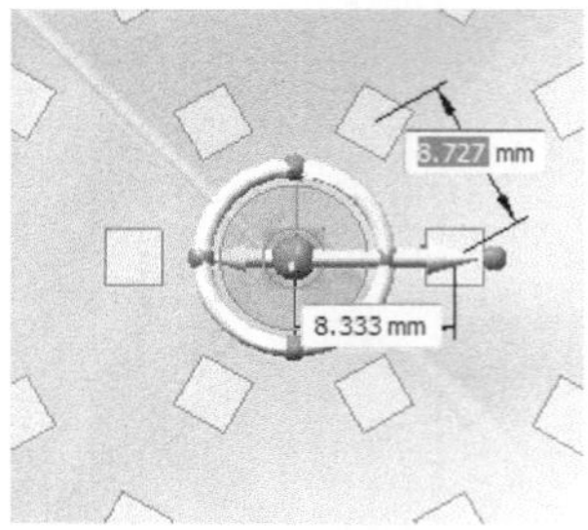

*Figure 6-74 Creating the radial fill pattern using the **Center Orient** button*

Suppress Instance

You can suppress the occurrences in the fill pattern by choosing the **Suppress Instance** button. On choosing this button, the Command bar will be modified. There are two options to set the visibility of the occurrences to be suppressed. These two options available in the Command bar are discussed next.

Use Occurrence Footprint

This button is chosen by default. As a result, occurrences that lie completely inside the fill region are displayed, refer to Figure 6-75. It means that you cannot see the occurrences that lie on the boundary of the fill region.

Allow Boundary Touching

If you choose this button, the occurrences touching the boundary will be visible. Figure 6-76 shows occurrences overlapping the boundary.

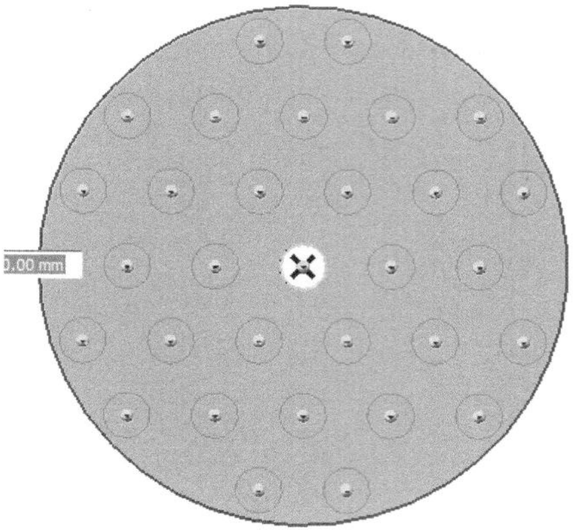

Figure 6-75 *Suppressing occurrences using the **Use Occurrence Footprint** button*

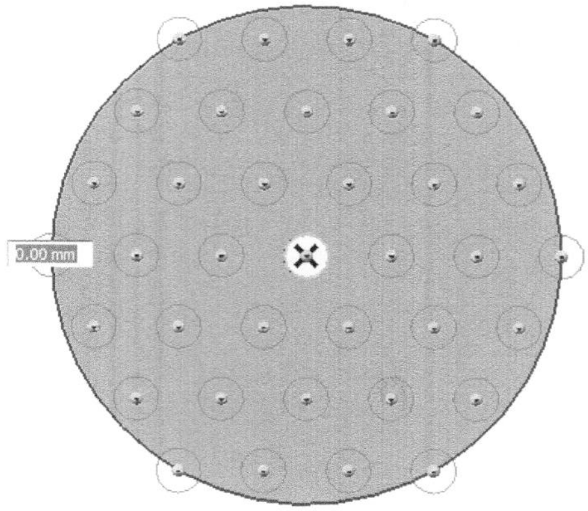

Figure 6-76 *Suppressing occurrences using the **Allow Boundary Touching** button*

On setting any one of the visibility options, the occurrences will be displayed with green dot. Click on the green dots displayed on the occurrences to suppress them; the suppressed occurrences will be displayed with red circles. You can use the **Reset** button in the Command bar to make all occurrences unsuppressed. To suppress the occurrences that overlap the boundary, you need to decrease the boundary of the fill region. You can decrease or increase the boundary size of the fill region by using the value box displayed on the boundary. By entering a negative offset value in the value box, you can suppress the occurrences that lie on the boundary of the fill region. If you enter a positive offset value in value box, the occurrences outside the boundary of the fill region will be displayed.

Editing the Pattern

You can change the pattern by changing its parameters even after it has been created. To do so, double-click the pattern in the **PathFinder**; the **Fill Pattern** Command bar and Pattern action handle with dynamic boxes will be displayed on the pattern. Next, click on the Pattern action handle or in dynamic boxes to edit the parameters of the pattern.

Adding a New Feature to the Pattern

You can add new features to an existing pattern by using the **Add to Pattern** button. This button will be available on the Command bar only when you are editing the pattern. Note that you need to add a new feature to any one of the occurrence on the pattern before editing the pattern. Next, select the feature that is to be added to the pattern and then choose the **Accept** button; you will be prompted to select the reference point. Specify any occurrence position onto which the feature is to be added; the new feature will be added to the existing pattern.

RECOGNIZING HOLE PATTERNS (SYNCHRONOUS ENVIRONMENT)

In Solid Edge, you can recognize holes of an imported model as rectangular or circular patterns. Figure 6-77 shows a rectangular arrangement and a recognized hole pattern. To recognize hole patterns, first you need to recognize holes in the **Synchronous Part** environment. To do so, choose the **Recognize Holes** tool from the **Hole** drop-down of the **Solids** group in the **Home** tab; the **Hole Recognition** dialog box will be displayed. Next, choose the **OK** button from the dialog box; the holes available in the model will be recognized.

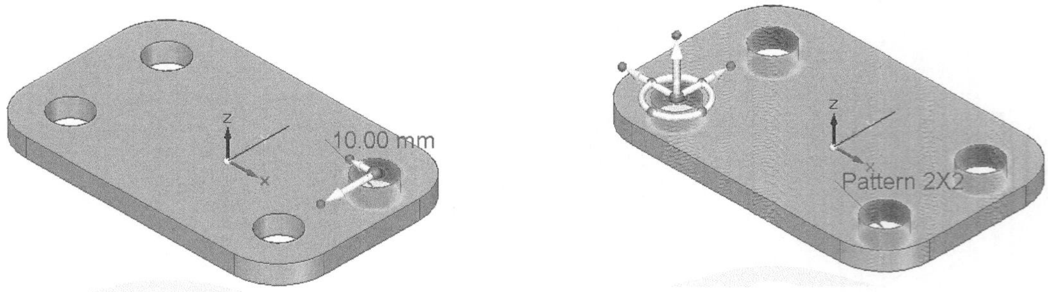

***Figure 6-77** A rectangular arrangement and a recognized hole pattern*

After recognizing the holes, you can recognize hole patterns. To do so, choose the **Recognize Hole Patterns** tool from the **Pattern** drop-down in the **Pattern** group and then select the holes of the model by cross-window selection method and right click; the **Hole Pattern Recognition** dialog box will be displayed, as shown in Figure 6-78. In the dialog box, choose the **Define Master Occurrence** button to define the reference point for the pattern; the **Hole Pattern Recognition** dialog box will disappear. Specify the reference point for the pattern in the model; the **Hole Pattern Recognition** dialog box will reappear. You can also enter the name of the pattern in the **Feature Name** field in the dialog box. After specifying the required settings, choose the **OK** button; the hole arrangements will be recognized as rectangular and circular patterns. Also, new entries of patterns will be added in the **PathFinder**.

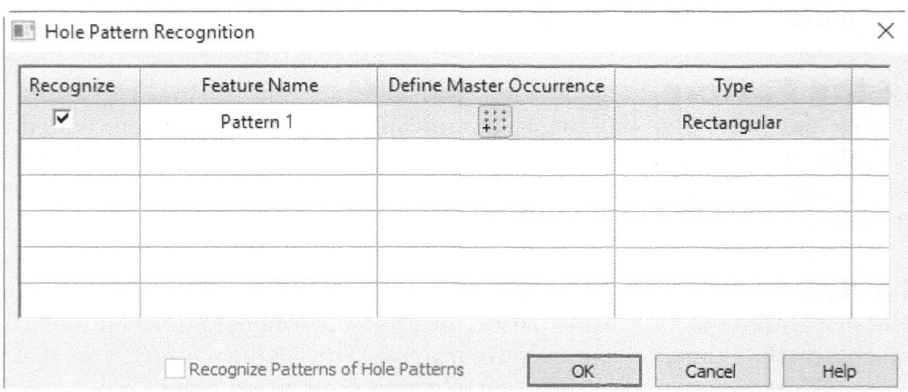

***Figure 6-78** The **Hole Pattern Recognition** dialog box*

RECOGNIZING PATTERNS (SYNCHRONOUS ENVIRONMENT)

In Solid Edge ST8, you can recognize the pattern of a model that is imported into it if the pattern is rectangular or circular. To recognize a pattern, select all the faces of the feature whose pattern needs to be recognized, as shown in Figure 6-79.

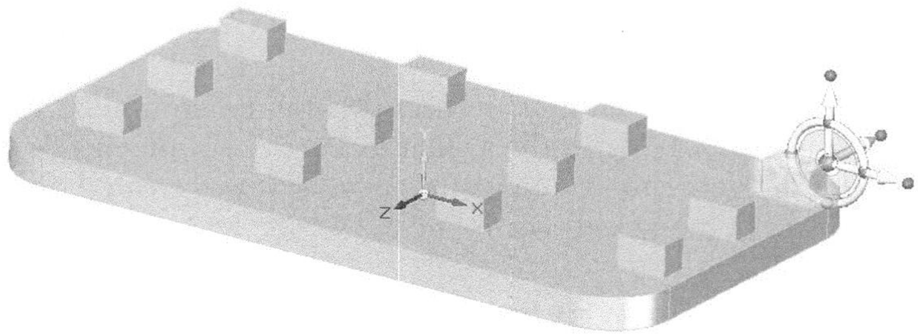

Figure 6-79 Selected faces of feature

After selecting the faces, choose the **Recognize Patterns** tool from the **Rectangular** drop-down in the **Pattern** group; the **Pattern Recognition** dialog box will be displayed, as shown in Figure 6-80. In the dialog box, choose the **Define Master Occurrence** button to define the reference point for the pattern; the **Pattern Recognition** dialog box will disappear. Specify the reference point for the pattern in the model; the **Pattern Recognition** dialog box will reappear. You can specify the name of the pattern in the **Feature Name** field in the dialog box. After specifying the required settings, choose the **OK** button; the arrangements will be recognized as rectangular or circular pattern as shown in Figure 6-81. Also, new entries of patterns will be added in the **PathFinder**.

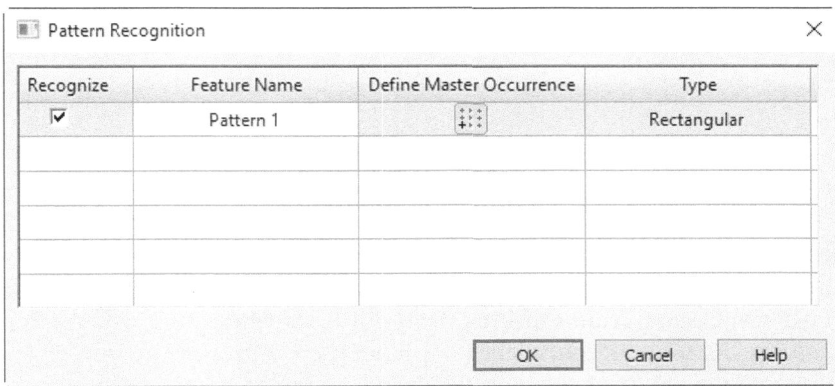

*Figure 6-80 The **Pattern Recognition** dialog box*

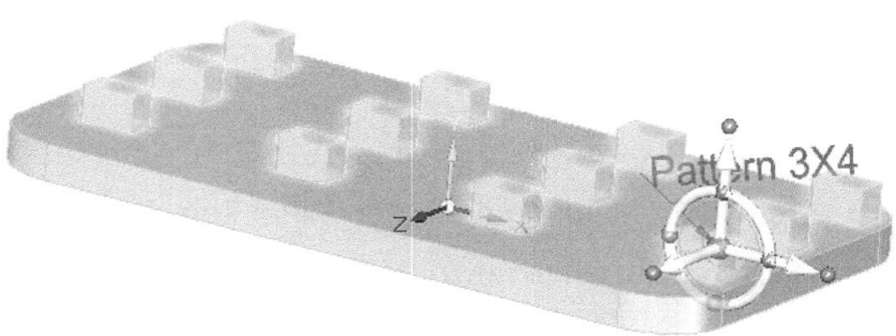

Figure 6-81 A rectangular pattern recognized

MIRRORING FEATURES AND BODIES (ORDERED ENVIRONMENT)

Similar to mirroring the sketched entities in the sketching environment, you can also mirror selected features or the entire body in the **Ordered Part** environment. As mentioned in the introduction, a body is the entire model consisting of all features created till now. The methods of mirroring features and bodies are discussed next.

Mirroring Selected Features

Ribbon:	Home > Pattern > Mirror Copy Feature drop-down > Mirror Copy Feature

The **Mirror Copy Feature** tool enables you to mirror the selected features about a selected reference plane or a planar face. This helps in saving a lot of time in modeling a symmetric feature. Invoke the **Mirror Copy Feature** tool; the **Mirror Copy Feature** Command bar will be displayed. The **Mirror Copy Feature** tool works in two steps which are discussed next.

Select Features Step

This step enables you to select the features that you want to mirror. You can select the features from the drawing window or from the **PathFinder**. After selecting the features, you can choose the **Accept** button or right-click to accept the selected features. On doing so, the **Plane Step** will be invoked.

Note

By pressing and holding the CTRL key, select the features to be mirrored and then invoke the ***Mirror Copy Feature*** *tool. In this case, the* ***Select Features Step*** *will not be invoked.*

Plane Step

This step enables you to select a reference plane or a planar face to mirror the selected feature. You can also use the **Create-From Options** drop-down list to create a new reference plane to mirror the features. As soon as you select the plane, the preview of the mirror feature will be displayed. Note that if an error message is displayed, you need to change the fast mirror to the smart mirror by choosing the **Smart** button from the Command bar.

Figure 6-82 shows the model before mirroring the features and Figure 6-83 shows the same model after mirroring the features about the reference plane passing through the center of the model.

Mirroring Bodies

Ribbon:	Home > Pattern > Mirror drop-down > Mirror Copy Part

The **Mirror Copy Part** tool is used to mirror the selected body about a selected reference plane or a planar face. This tool also works in two steps which are discussed next.

Select Step

This step allows you to select the body that you want to mirror. You need to select the body in the drawing window. As soon as you move the cursor over the body, it will be highlighted. Click to select the body; the **Plane Step** will be invoked.

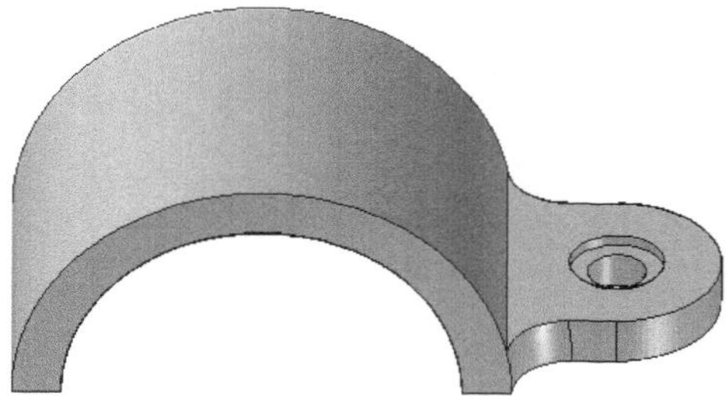

Figure 6-82 Model before mirroring the features

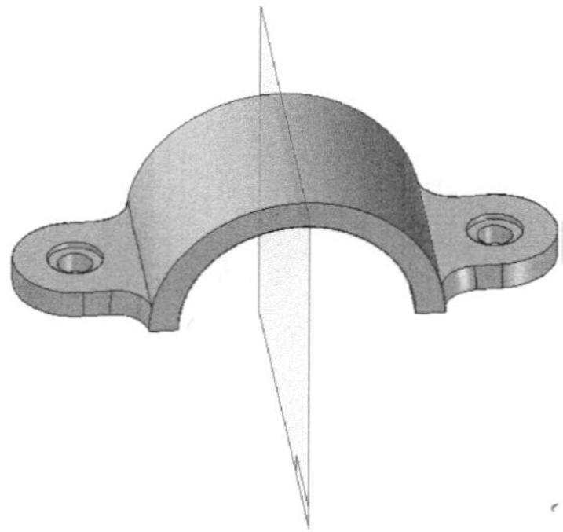

Figure 6-83 Model after mirroring the features about the reference plane that passes through the center of the model

Plane Step

This step allows you to select a reference plane or a planar face to mirror the selected feature. As soon as you select the plane, the preview of the mirror body will be displayed.

Figure 6-84 shows the body selected to be mirrored and the planar face being selected as the mirror plane. Figure 6-85 shows the same model after mirroring the body.

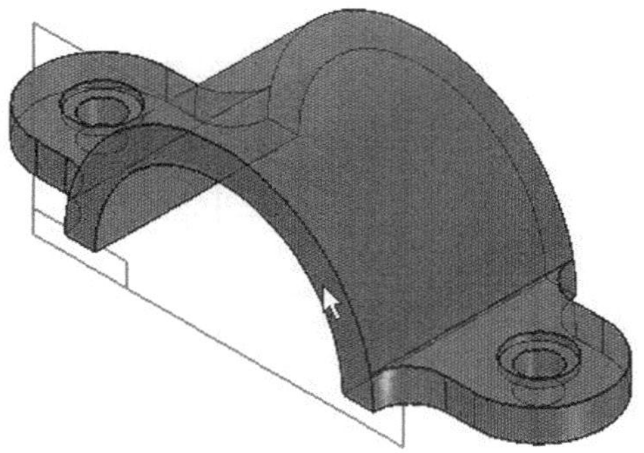

Figure 6-84 Body selected to be mirror and the mirror plane

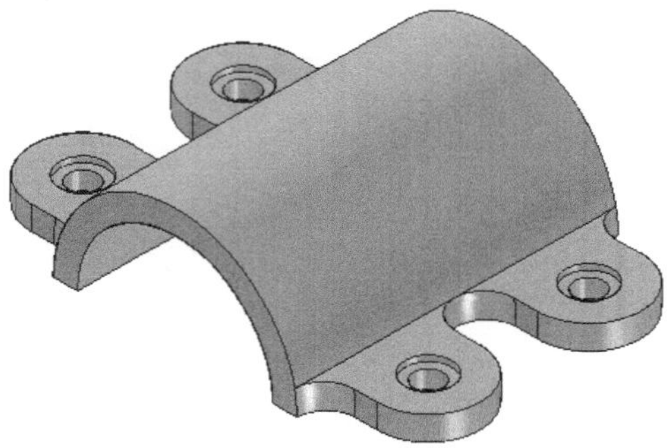

Figure 6-85 Model after mirroring the body

Note

*You can also mirror a selected feature in the **Synchronous Part** environment by invoking the **Mirror** tool and then selecting the plane about which the feature is to be mirrored. Note that the **Detach Faces** button in the Command bar should remain deactivated while mirroring the features.*

TUTORIALS

Tutorial 1 Synchronous

In this tutorial, you will create the model shown in Figure 6-86. The dimensions of this model are shown in Figure 6-87. After creating the model, save it with the name *c06tut1.par* at the following location:

C:\Solid Edge\c06 **(Expected time: 30 min)**

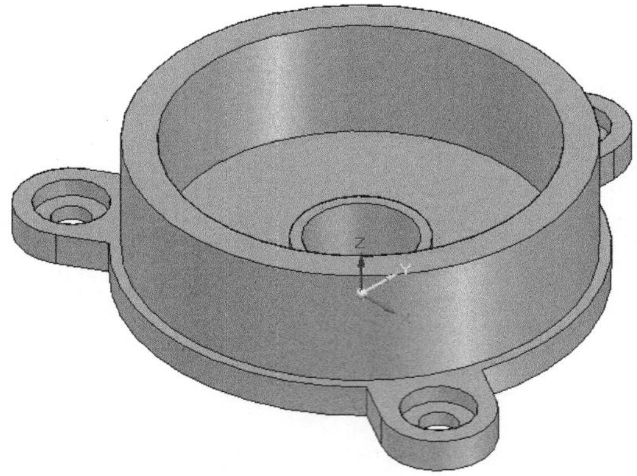

Figure 6-86 *Model for Tutorial 1*

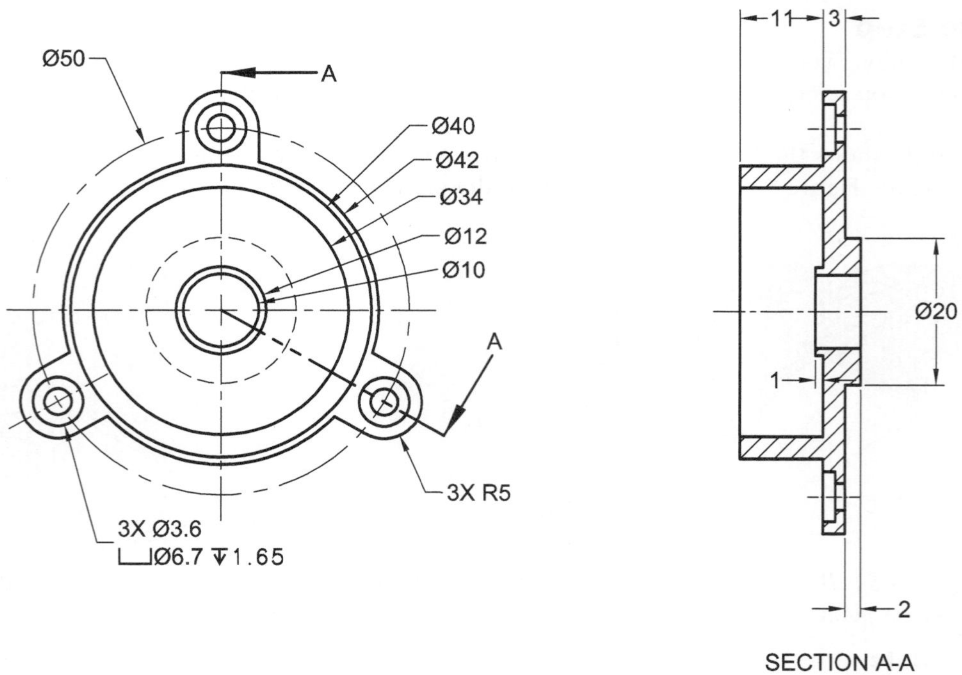

Figure 6-87 *Dimensions of the model for Tutorial 1*

The following steps are required to complete this tutorial:

a. Start Solid Edge in the **Synchronous Part** environment. Create the profile for the revolved base feature on the front plane and revolve it through 360 degrees, refer to Figures 6-88 and 6-89.
b. Create the second feature, refer to Figures 6-91 and 6-92.
c. Create a counterbore hole on the new feature, refer to Figure 6-93.
d. Create a circular pattern of the second feature and a hole, refer to Figures 6-95 and 6-96.
e. Save the model and then close the file.

Creating the Base Feature

As mentioned earlier, the base feature is a revolved protrusion feature. You need to create its profile on the front plane.

1. Start Solid Edge in the **Synchronous Part** environment. Choose the **Line** tool from the **Draw** group and then select the XZ plane as the sketching plane for the revolved feature.
2. Draw the profile of the revolved feature and the axis of revolution using the sketching tools.
3. Add the required relationships and dimensions to the sketch, as shown in Figure 6-88. In this figure, the visibility of the relationship handles is turned off by using the **Relationship Handles** button.

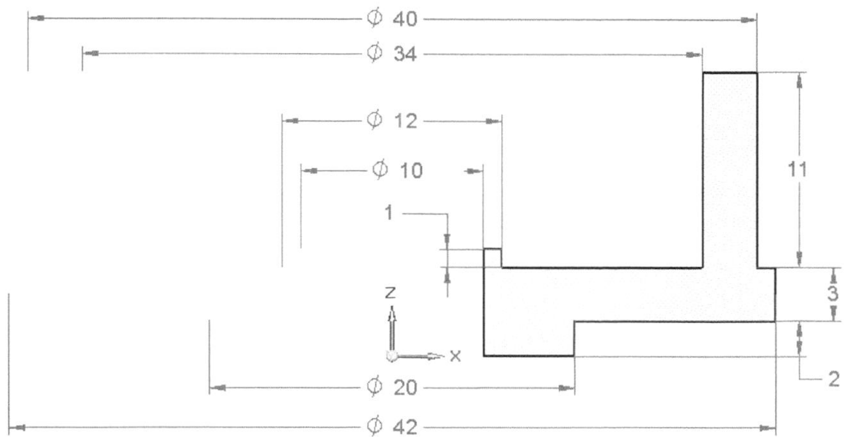

Figure 6-88 Sketch for the revolved feature

4. Select the sketch region; an extrude handle is displayed. Pick the origin of the handle and place it on the z-axis of the base coordinate system, and then revolve the sketch through 360 degrees to create the base feature, as shown in Figure 6-89.

Creating the Second Feature

The second feature is an extruded feature. You need to create this feature at the bottom of the base feature. Note that to get the proper orientation of the model, you need to be careful while defining the sketching plane for this feature.

1. Invoke the **Rotate** tool, and then rotate the model around the vertical edge of the rotate tool such that the bottom face of the model is displayed.
2. Choose the **Line** tool, and then select the bottom face of the base feature as the sketching plane, refer to Figure 6-90.

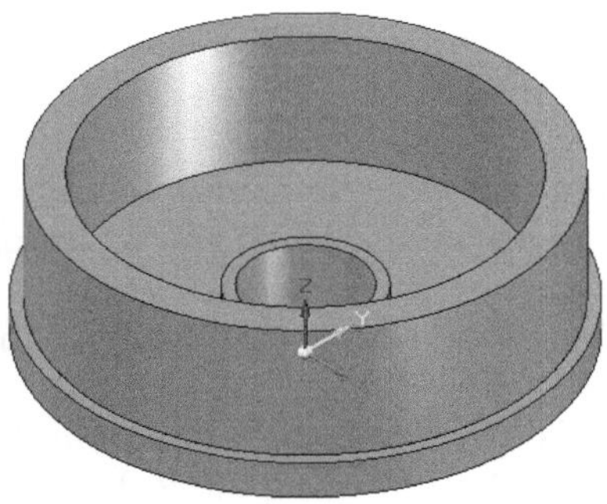

Figure 6-89 Revolved feature

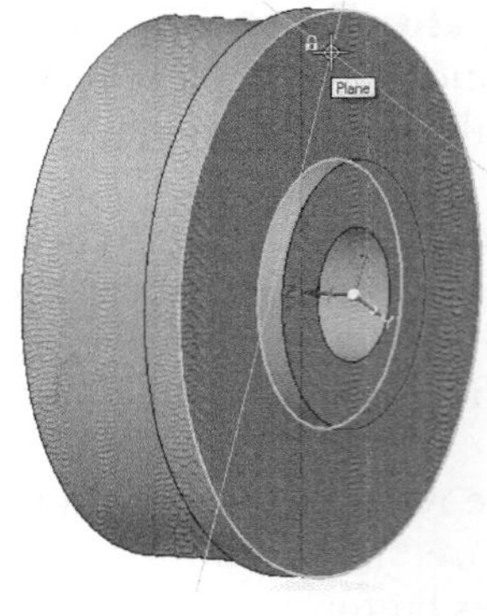

Figure 6-90 Selecting the bottom face of the model as the sketching plane

3. Draw the sketch of the extruded feature and then add the required relations and dimensions to it, as shown in Figure 6-91.

4. Select the sketch region and then extrude it up to the next planar face by using the **From-To** option from the **Extent Type** drop-down. The isometric view of the model after creating the extruded feature is shown in Figure 6-92.

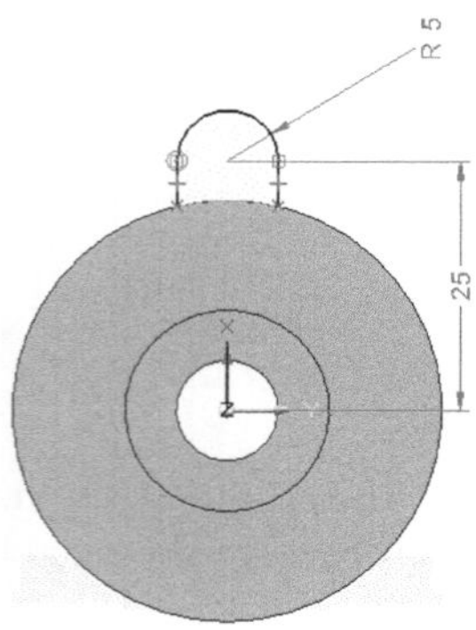

Figure 6-91 Sketch for the extruded feature

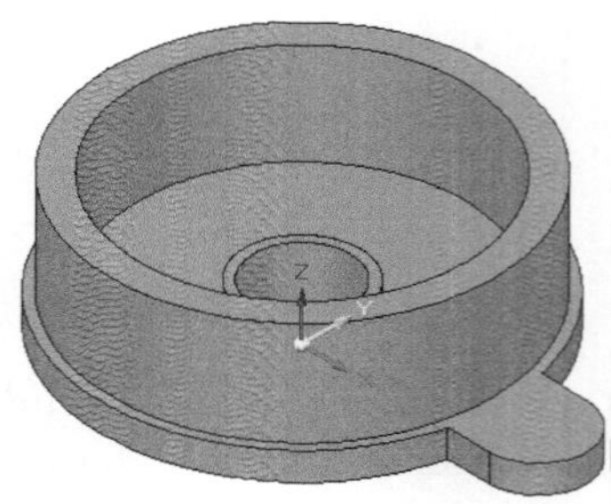

Figure 6-92 Isometric view of the model after creating the extruded feature

Creating the Counterbore Hole

Next, you need to create a counterbore hole on the extruded feature by using the **Hole** tool.

1. Choose the **Hole** tool from the **Solids** group of the **Home** tab; the **Hole** Command bar is displayed.

2. Choose the **Hole Options** button from the Command bar to display the **Hole Options** dialog box.

3. In this dialog box, choose the **Counterbore** button from the upper left corner. Select **mm** from the **Standard** drop-down list. Enter **3.6** in the **Hole Diameter** edit box available on the right side.

4. Enter **6.7** in the **Counterbore diameter** edit box and **1.65** in the **Counterbore depth** edit box.

5. Choose the **Through All** button from the **Hole extents** area and then **OK** from the **Hole Options** dialog box; the preview of the hole is attached to the cursor and you are prompted to click on a planar face or a reference plane.

6. Select the top face of the second feature and lock the plane. Place the hole concentric to the arc of the second feature; the preview of the hole feature is displayed, as shown in Figure 6-93. The model after creating the counterbore hole is shown in Figure 6-94.

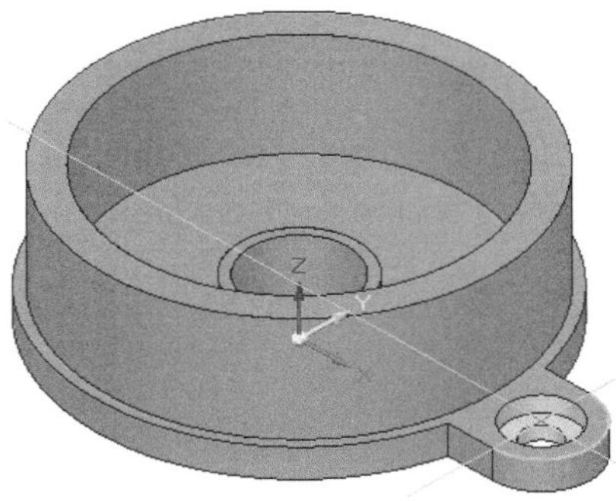

Figure 6-93 Preview of the counterbore hole

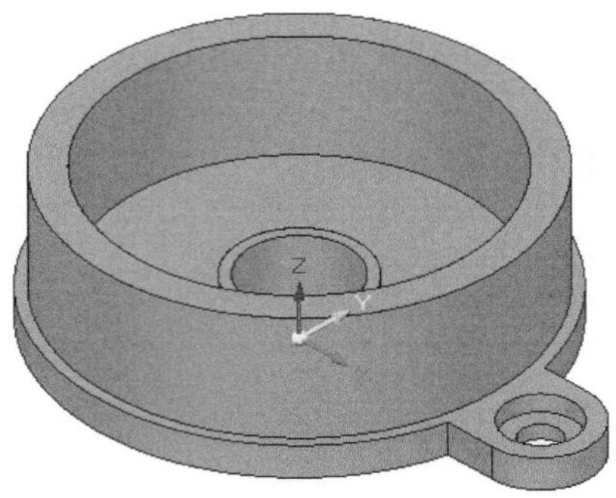

Figure 6-94 Model after creating the counterbore hole

7. Press the ESC key to exit from the **Hole** Command bar.

Creating a Circular Pattern of Features

Next, you need to create a circular pattern of the second feature and the hole. As mentioned earlier, you need to select the features to activate the tools in the **Pattern** group.

1. Select the second extruded feature and the hole feature from the **PathFinder** or the drawing area.

2. Choose the **Circular** tool from the **Rectangular** drop-down of the **Pattern** group to display the **Pattern** Command bar and the Pattern axis handle.

3. Move the handle and place it on the center point of the model to specify it as the axis of rotation. You can also use the **Keypoints** options to easily select the axis of rotation. On selecting the axis of rotation, the preview of the circular pattern along with the **Count** box is displayed, as shown in Figure 6-95.

4. Enter **3** in the **Count** box and click on the **Accept** button in the Command bar; the circular pattern is created.

The final model after creating the pattern is shown in Figure 6-96.

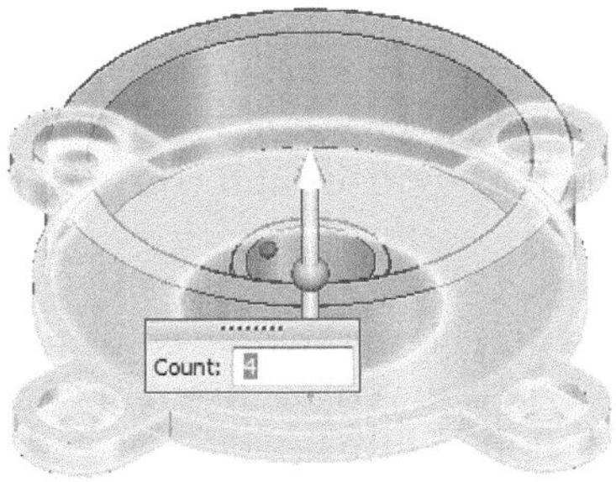

Figure 6-95 Preview of the circular pattern

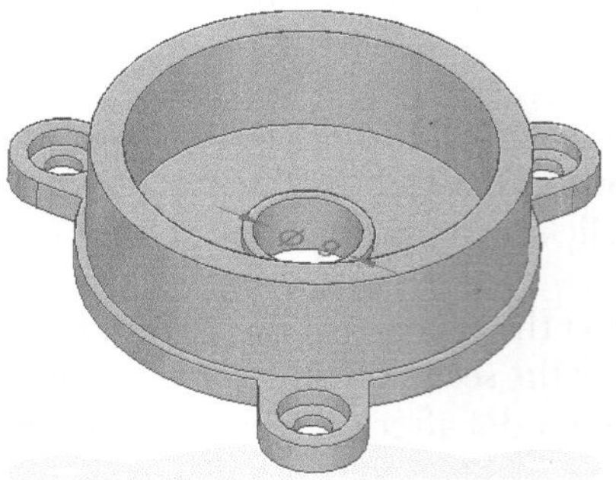

Figure 6-96 Final model for Tutorial 1

Saving the Model

1. Save the model with the name *c06tut1.par* at the following location given next and then close the file.
   C:\Solid Edge\c06

Tutorial 2 Ordered

In this tutorial, you will create the model of the Guide bracket shown in Figure 6-97. The dimensions of the model are given in the drawing shown in Figure 6-98. After creating the model, save it with the name *c06tut2.par* at the location given next.
C:\Solid Edge\c06 **(Expected time: 30 min)**

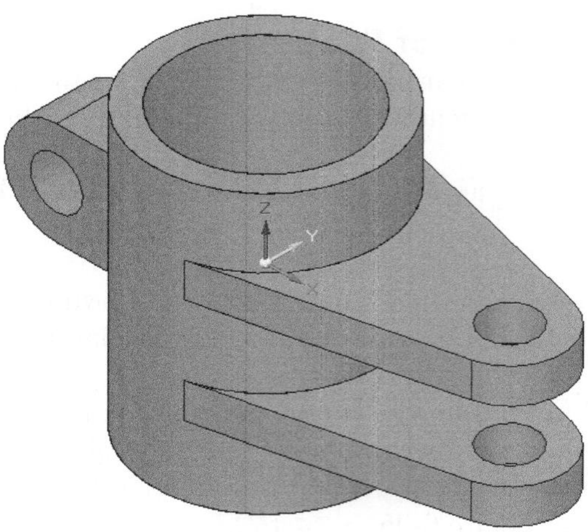

Figure 6-97 Model for Tutorial 2

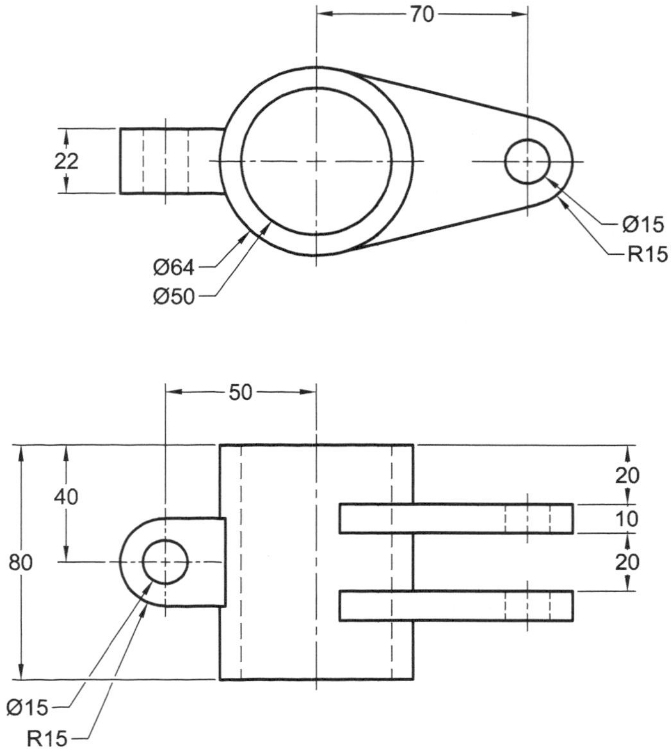

Figure 6-98 Dimensions of the model for Tutorial 2

The following steps are required to complete this tutorial:

a. Create the profile of the base feature on the top plane and then extrude it symmetrically about the sketching plane, refer to Figure 6-99.
b. Create a reference plane at an offset of 15 in the upward direction from the XY plane. Use this reference plane to create the second protrusion feature, refer to Figure 6-100.
c. Mirror the second feature about the top plane, refer to Figure 6-101.
d. Create the fourth feature on the front plane and extrude it symmetrically through a distance of 22, refer to Figure 6-103.
e. Create simple holes on the second and fourth features to complete the model, refer to Figure 6-104.

Creating the Base Feature

First, you need to create the base feature of the model.

1. Start a new part file.

2. Switch to the **Ordered Part** environment and then draw the sketch of the base protrusion feature on the top plane. The sketch consists of two concentric circles of diameters 64 mm and 50 mm.

3. Exit the sketching environment and then extrude the sketch symmetrically through a distance of 80 mm. The isometric view of the base feature of the model is shown in Figure 6-99.

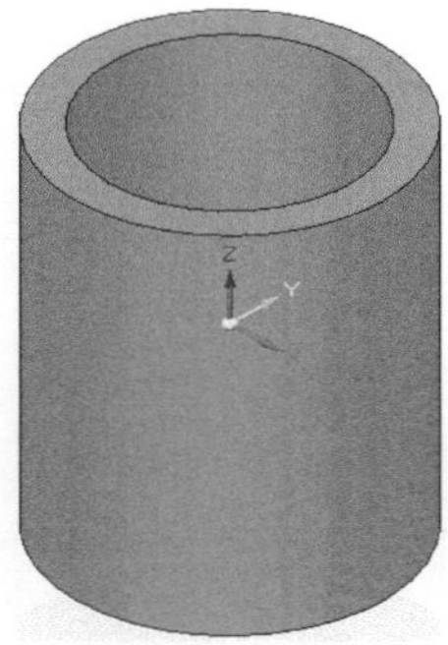

Figure 6-99 Base feature of the model

Creating the Second Feature

The second feature is a protrusion feature and will be created by using an open profile. You need to draw the open profile on a parallel plane 20 mm above the top plane.

1. Invoke the **Extrude** tool, if it is not active, and then select the **Parallel Plane** option from the **Create-From Options** drop-down list of the Command bar.
2. Select the XY plane, enter **15** in the **Distance** edit box of the Command bar, and press ENTER.
3. Move the cursor in the upward direction of the model and click; a new local reference plane is created and the sketching environment is invoked.
4. Create the open profile of the second extruded feature, and then add the required dimensions and relationships to the profile. For the shape and dimension of the open profile, refer to Figure 6-98.
5. Exit the sketching environment and then extrude the profile up to a distance of 10 units symmetrically. The model after creating this feature is shown in Figure 6-100.

Mirroring the Second Feature

Since the base feature was created symmetrically to the top plane, you can create the third feature by mirroring the second feature about the top plane.

1. Choose the **Mirror Copy Feature** tool from the **Mirror Copy Feature** drop-down of the **Pattern** group to invoke the **Mirror Copy Feature** Command bar. On doing so, the **Select Features Step** is activated and you are prompted to select the features to be included in the mirror feature.
2. Select the second feature and then right-click to accept the selection; the **Plane Step** is invoked and you are prompted to click on a planar face or a reference plane.
3. Select the top plane from the drawing window or from the docking window to display the preview of the mirror feature.
4. Choose the **Finish** and **Cancel** buttons to create the feature. The model after mirroring the feature is shown in Figure 6-101.

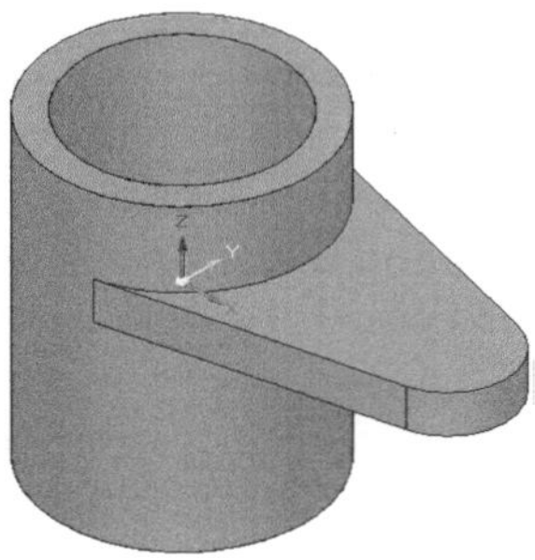

Figure 6-100 Model after creating the second feature

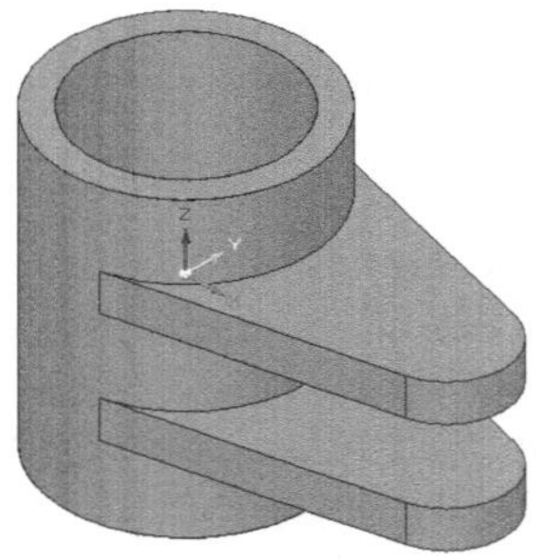

Figure 6-101 Model after mirroring the second feature

Creating the Fourth Feature

1. Create an open profile on the front plane for the fourth feature and then add the required dimensions and relationships to the profile, as shown in Figure 6-102.

2. Exit the sketching environment and then extrude the profile symmetrically up to a distance of 22 mm. The model after creating the fourth feature is shown in Figure 6-103.

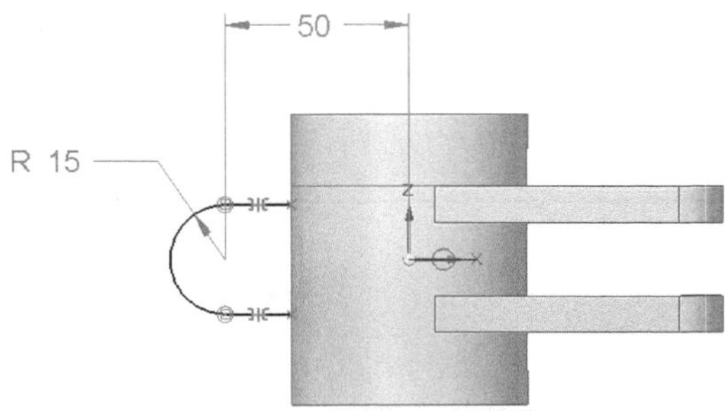

Figure 6-102 Open profile for the fourth feature

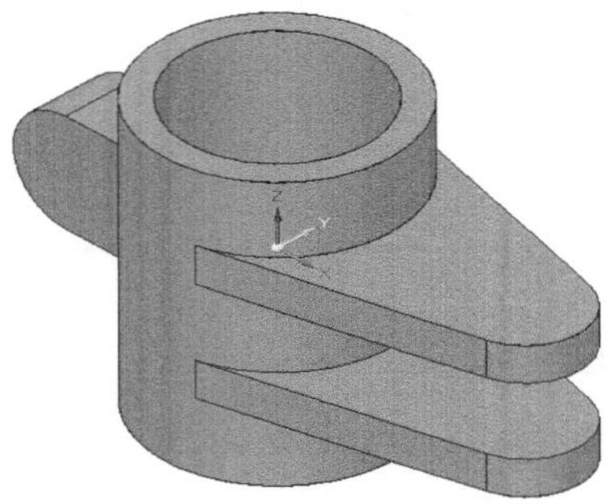

Figure 6-103 Model after creating the fourth feature

Creating Holes

Next, you need to create two through holes: one for the second and third features, and the other for the fourth feature.

1. Invoke the **Hole** tool and then choose the **Hole Options** button from the Command bar; the **Hole Options** dialog box is displayed.

2. Select **mm** from the **Standard** drop-down list of the **Hole Options** dialog box. Enter **15** in the **Hole Diameter** edit box available on right side.

3. Choose the **Through All** button from the **Hole extents** area and then choose **OK** to exit the dialog box.

4. Move the cursor to the top face of the second feature and then select it as the sketching plane.

5. Place the profile of the hole concentric to the arc in the second feature and then exit the sketching environment; the preview of the hole passing through the mirrored feature is also displayed.

6. Choose the **Finish** button from the Command bar to complete the feature creation. The **Hole** tool is still active and you are prompted to click on a planar face or a reference plane.

7. Select the front planar face of the fourth feature as the sketching plane; a circle having dimensions as that of the previous hole is attached to the circle. If required, you can modify the hole settings by invoking the **Hole Options** dialog box.

8. Place the hole concentric to the arc in the fourth feature and then exit the sketching environment.

   The final model of the Guide bracket is shown in Figure 6-104.

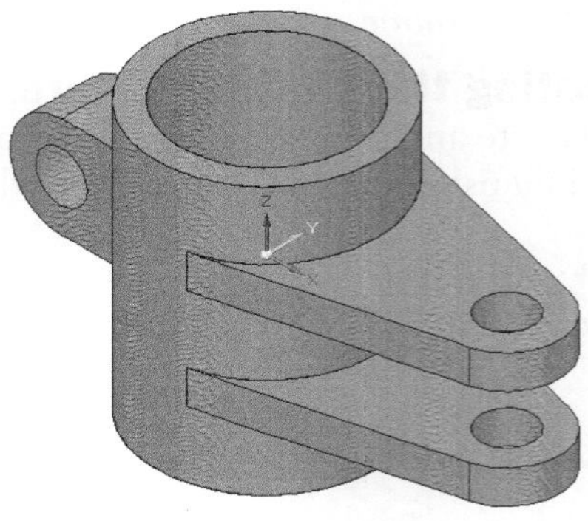

Figure 6-104 *Final model of the Guide bracket*

Saving the Model

1. Save the model with the name *c06tut2.par* at the following location and then close the file.
   C:\Solid Edge\c06

Tutorial 3 Synchronous

In this tutorial, you will create the model shown in Figure 6-105. The dimensions of the model are given in the drawing shown in Figure 6-106. After creating the model, save it with the name *c06tut3.par* at the location given next.
C:\Solid Edge\c06 **(Expected time: 30 min)**

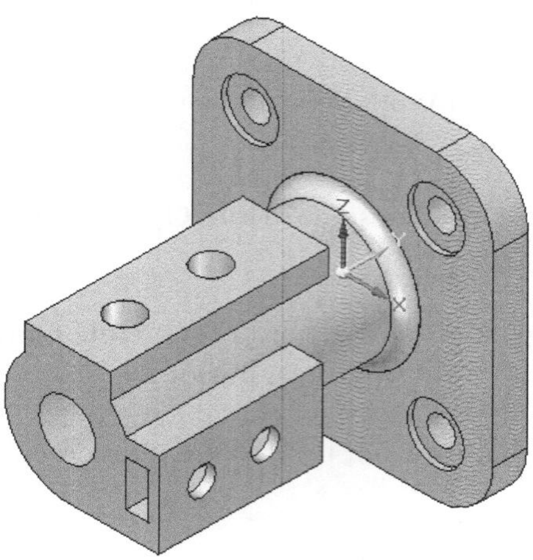

Figure 6-105 *Model for Tutorial 3*

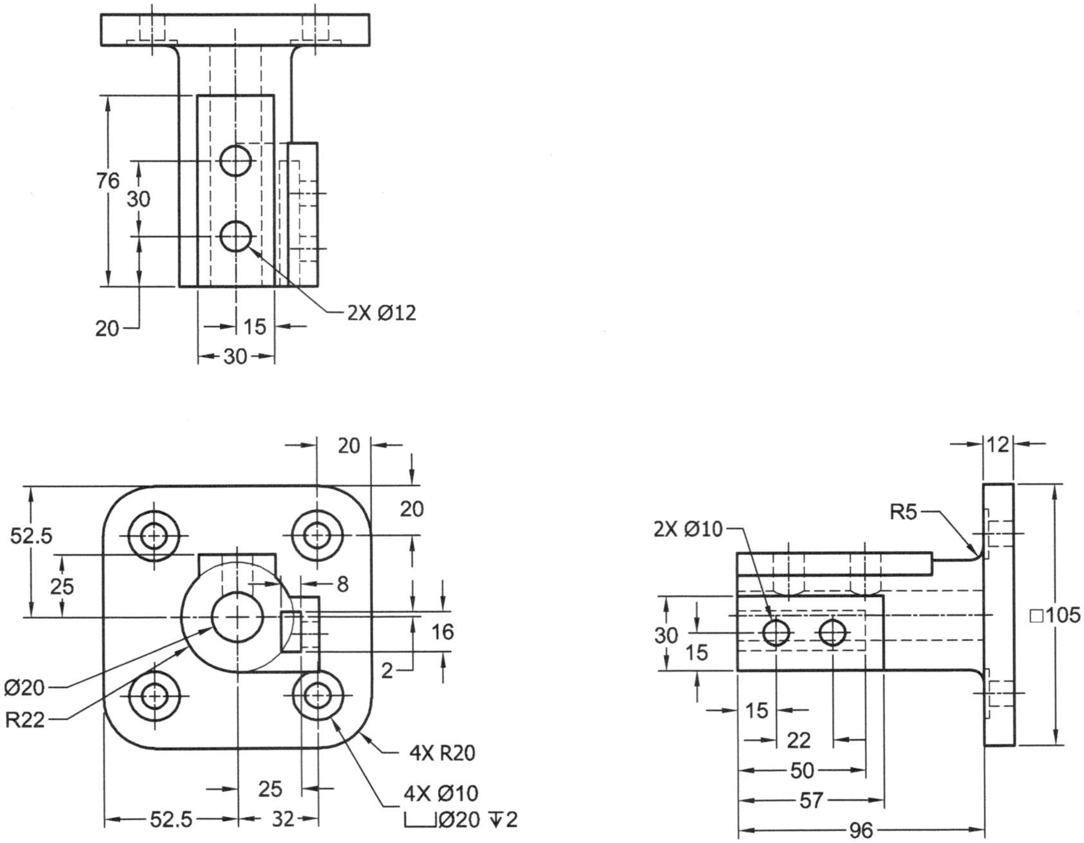

***Figure 6-106** Dimensions of the model for Tutorial 3*

The following steps are required to complete this tutorial:

a. Create the base feature on the front plane, refer to Figure 6-107. The sketch for the base feature consists of a square with a fillet on all the four corners.
b. Create the circular protrusion feature on the front face of the base feature, refer to Figure 6-109.
c. Add two rectangular join features to the cylindrical feature, refer to Figures 6-110 and 6-111.
d. Create the rectangular cut feature on one of the rectangular join features, refer to Figure 6-112.
e. Create simple holes on the rectangular features, refer to Figures 6-112 and 6-113.
f. Create one counterbore hole on the front face of the base feature.
g. Create a rectangular pattern of the counterbore hole, refer to Figure 6-114.
h. Create a fillet on the circular protrusion feature to complete the model, refer to Figure 6-115.

Creating the Base Feature

1. Start a new part file and then draw the sketch for the base protrusion feature on the XZ plane. The sketch for the base feature is a square of side 105 units. It has all four corners filleted

with a fillet of radius 20 mm, as shown in Figure 6-107. As evident from this figure, the sketch is symmetric about the origin of the sketching plane.

2. Select the sketch region and then extrude the sketch to a distance of 12 units. Make sure that the **Finite** option is selected from the **Extent Type** drop-down list in the **Extrude** Command bar. The isometric view of the base feature of the model is shown in Figure 6-108.

Creating the Circular Extrude Feature

1. Choose the **Circle by Center Point** tool and then select the front face of the base feature as the sketching plane.

2. Draw a circle of 44 mm diameter as the profile for the second feature. Remember that the center of the circle is at the origin.

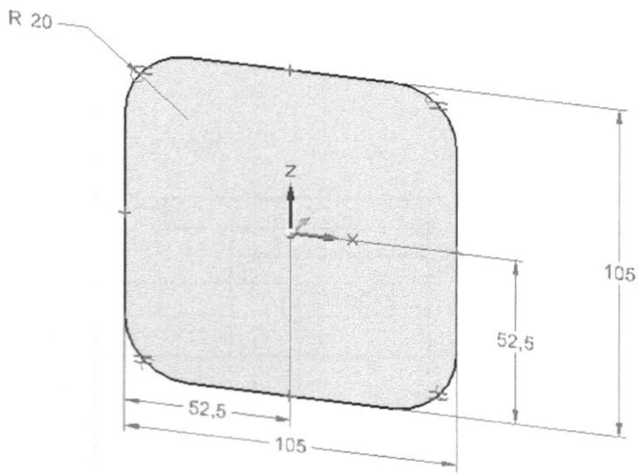

Figure 6-107 *Sketch for the base feature*

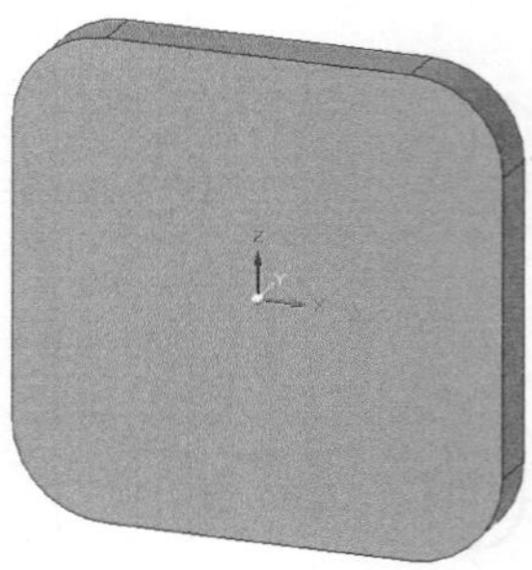

Figure 6-108 *Base feature of the model*

3. Select the circular region and then extrude the sketch up to a distance of 96 mm in forward direction. The model after creating this feature is shown in Figure 6-109.

Creating Rectangular Extruded Features

Next, you need to create two rectangular extruded features on the circular feature. Both these features will be created by defining parallel planes from the base reference planes and then extruding the sketch up to the circular protrusion feature.

1. Select the check box adjacent to the **Base Reference Planes** node in the **PathFinder**; the visibility of the base reference planes is turned on.

2. Create a coincident plane on the top plane of the base reference planes; a new plane is created on the top plane and the steering wheel is displayed on it.

3. Select the Z axis of the steering wheel and drag it upward. Then, enter **25** in the edit box displayed on the plane; the plane is moved to a distance of 25 mm.

4. Draw the profile of the rectangular feature 76X30 on the newly created plane and add the required dimensions and relationships to it.

5. Select the sketch region and extrude the profile up to the circular extruded feature by using the **Through Next** option. The model after creating this feature is shown in Figure 6-110.

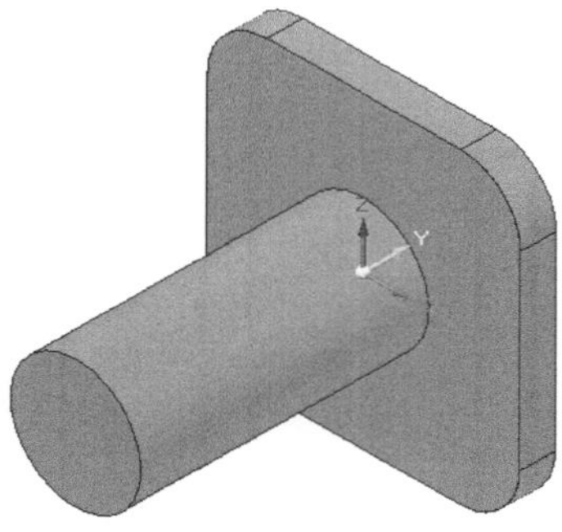

Figure 6-109 *Model after creating the circular protrusion feature*

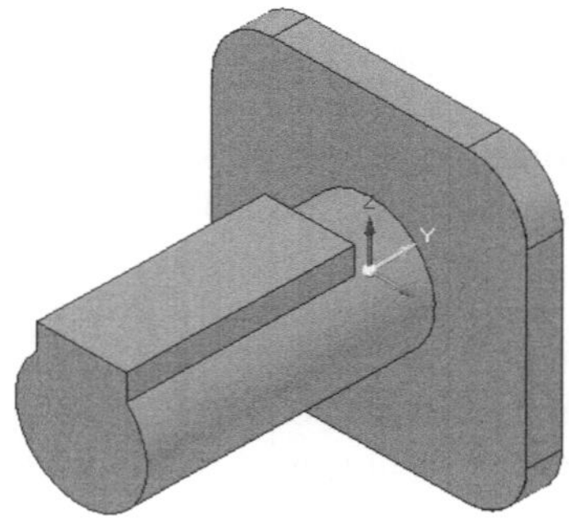

Figure 6-110 *Model after creating the top rectangular join features*

6. Define a parallel plane at a distance of 32 mm from the YZ plane toward the right and use it to draw the sketch for the side rectangular feature, refer to Figure 6-106 for dimensions.

7. Select the sketch region and extrude the profile up to the circular extruded feature by using the **Through Next** option. The model after creating this feature is shown in Figure 6-111.

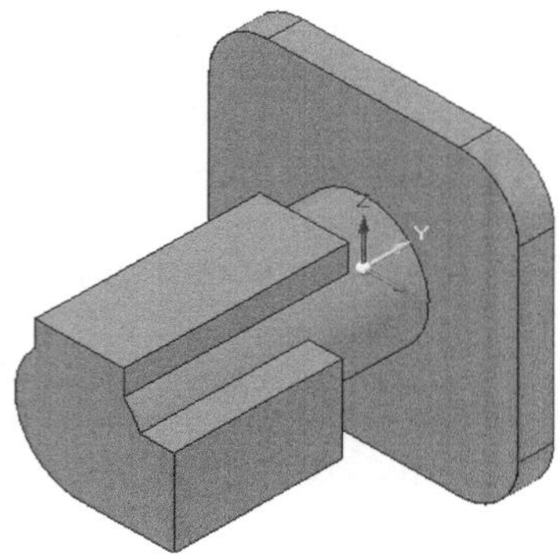

Figure 6-111 *Model after creating the side rectangular join features*

Creating the Rectangular Cut Feature

1. Draw the rectangular profile (16X8 units) on the front face of the second feature and add the required dimensions to it. For dimensions, refer to Figure 6-106.

2. Select the sketch region and then move the cursor inside the body to create a cut. Next, specify the depth of the cut as 50 units.

Creating Simple Holes

Next, you need to create simple holes. You need to use the **Hole** tool three times to create simple holes on the circular extruded feature and the two rectangular extruded features. First, you need to create a simple hole on the circular extruded feature because this hole will be used to terminate the hole on the top rectangular extruded feature.

1. Invoke the **Hole** tool and then choose the **Hole Options** button from the Command bar; the **Hole Options** dialog box is displayed.

2. In this dialog box, select **mm** from the **Standard** drop-down list. Enter **20** in the **Diameter** edit box on right side.

3. Choose the **Finite Extent** button from the **Hole extents** area and enter **96** in the **Hole depth** edit box. Then, choose **OK** to exit the dialog box.

4. Move the cursor to the front face of the circular protrusion feature and then lock the plane.

5. Place a hole concentric to the circular feature; a hole is created on the second feature of the model. You can use the **Keypoints** options for easy placement of the hole.

6. Click on the lock plane symbol displayed on the top right corner of the graphics window; the front face of the second feature is unlocked.

   Next, you need to create a hole on the top planar face of the top rectangular feature. The **Hole** tool is still active and you are prompted to click on a planar face or a reference plane. For the next hole sequence, you need to change the dimensions of the hole. You can also change the dimensions of the hole after placing it.

7. Choose the **Hole Options** button from the Command bar; the **Hole Options** dialog box is invoked. Enter **12** as the value of the hole diameter in the **Hole Diameter** edit box.

8. Choose the **Through Next** button from the **Hole extents** area, and then choose **OK** to exit the dialog box.

9. Lock the top planar face of the top rectangular extruded feature.

   Next, you need to position the holes with reference to the adjacent edges.

10. Place the cursor on the right edge of the rectangular feature and press E; the dimension is displayed between the center point of the hole and the endpoint of the edge. Enter **15** in the edit box. Similarly, create dimension between the center point of the hole and the front edge of the rectangular feature, and then enter **20** in the edit box.

11. Similarly, create another hole on the top face of the rectangular feature. For dimensions, refer to Figure 6-106.

    Now you need to place holes on the right planar face of the side rectangular extruded feature, refer to Figure 6-112. For the dimensions of the hole location, refer to Figure 6-106.

12. Modify the hole diameter to 10 units before placing the two instances of the hole. For dimensions, refer to Figure 6-106.

    The isometric view of the model after creating simple holes is shown in Figure 6-113.

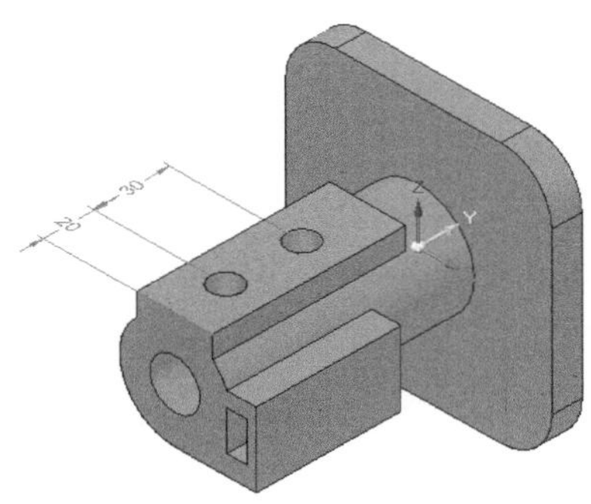

Figure 6-112 *Dimensioned holes*

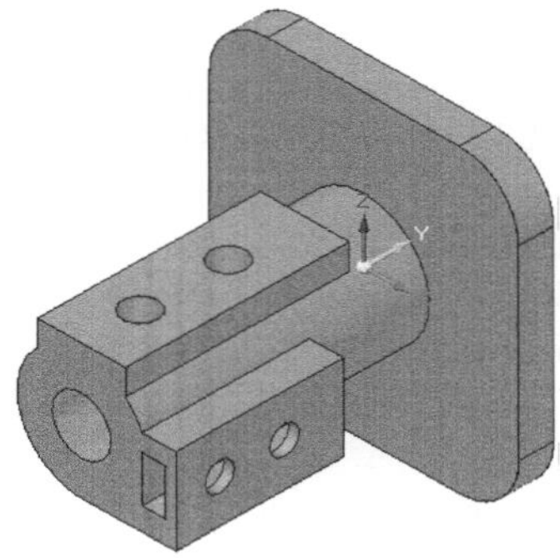

Figure 6-113 *Model after creating simple holes*

Creating the Counterbore Hole

The next feature is a counterbore hole. This hole will be created on the front planar face of the base feature and it will be concentric to the fillet on the top left corner of the base feature.

1. Invoke the **Hole** tool, if it is not active and then choose the **Hole Options** button from the Command bar; the **Hole Options** dialog box is invoked.

2. Choose the **Counterbore** button from the upper left corner of the **Hole Options** dialog box. Make sure that units are in mm. Next, enter **10** as the value of the diameter of the hole in the **Hole Diameter** edit box.

3. Enter **20** in the **Counterbore Diameter** edit box and **2** in the **Counterbore Depth** edit box.

4. Choose the **Through All** button from the **Hole extents** area and then choose **OK** to exit the dialog box; you are prompted to click on a planar face or a reference plane.

5. Lock the front planar face of the base feature and place the hole concentric to the center of the fillet on the top left corner.

6. Press the ESC key to exit the tool.

Creating the Rectangular Pattern of the Counterbore Hole

Next, you need to create the rectangular pattern of the counterbore hole. The rectangular pattern will have two rows and two columns and the pattern will be created on the front face of the base feature.

1. Select the counterbore hole on the base feature; the tools in the **Pattern** group get activated.

2. Choose the **Rectangular** tool from the **Pattern** group; the first corner of an imaginary rectangle is attached to the center point of the counterbore hole.

3. Specify the second corner of the rectangle on the center point of the fillet on the lower right corner; the preview of the rectangular pattern is displayed, as shown in Figure 6-114.

4. Enter **2** in the X count box as well as in the Y count box.

5. Right-click to create the rectangular pattern of the counterbore hole.

Creating the Round

To complete this model, you need to create a round on the edge where the circular protrusion feature connects with the base feature. You will create the fillet by using the constant radius fillet.

1. Choose the **Round** tool from the **Solids** group and then select the circular edge of the circular protrusion feature where it connects to the base feature.

2. Enter **5** in the **Radius** edit box and then press ENTER; a round is created on the edge.

3. Press the ESC key to exit the tool. The final model for Tutorial 3 is shown in Figure 6-115.

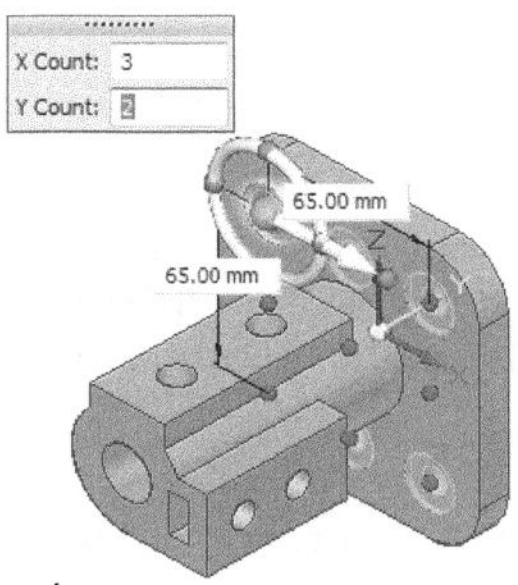

Figure 6-114 *Preview of the rectangular pattern of the counterbore hole*

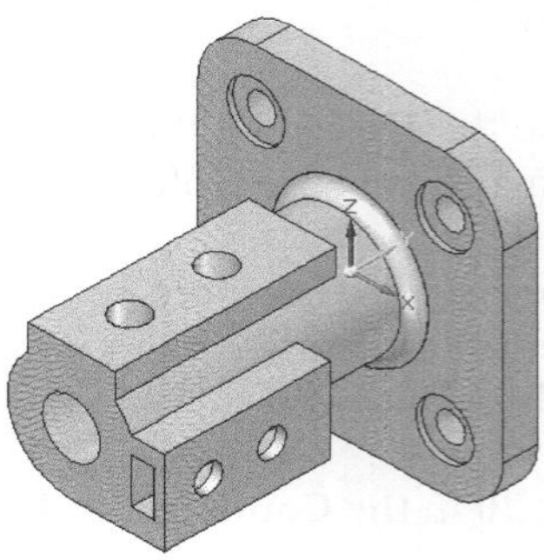

Figure 6-115 *Final model for Tutorial 3*

Saving the Model

1. Save the model with the name *c06tut3.par* at the location given below and then close the file.

   C:\Solid Edge\c06

Self-Evaluation Test

Answer the following questions and then compare them to those given at the end of this chapter:

1. In Solid Edge, you can also pattern the selected features along with an existing curve or an edge by using the __________ tool.

2. Choose the __________ button from the **Pattern** Command bar to create the patterns that involve more complex situations.

3. __________ is defined as the process of beveling the sharp edges of a model to reduce the area of stress concentration.

4. In the **Ordered Part** environment, you can select the round type from the __________ dialog box.

5. In the **Ordered Part** environment, the __________ radio button needs to be selected from the **Chamfer Options** dialog box to create a chamfer with equal setback.

6. Using the **Round** tool, you can create __________ types of rounds.

7. In the **Synchronous Part** environment, the ____________ handle is used to change the orientation of the rectangular pattern.

8. You can suppress the occurrences that overlap the boundaries by choosing the ________ option.

9. You can specify a hole type in the **Hole Options** dialog box. (T/F)

10. The advanced modeling tools considerably reduce the time taken for creating features in models and thus reduce the designing time. (T/F)

Review Questions

Answer the following questions:

1. Which one of the following is not a type of hole in Solid Edge?

   (a) **Counterbore** (b) **Countersink**
   (c) **Simple** (d) **Sectional**

2. Which of the following pattern tools is used to create a staggered pattern in the **Ordered Part** environment?

   (a) **Rectangular** (b) **Along the curve**
   (c) **Circular** (d) **Fill**

3. Which one of the following is not a type of round in Solid Edge?

   (a) **Constant radius** (b) **Variable radius**
   (c) **Smooth** (d) **Blend**

4. Which one of the following tools is used to mirror bodies in Solid Edge?

   (a) **Mirror Copy Part** (b) **Mirror Copy Feature**
   (c) Both (d) None of these

5. Which of the following options is used to create a chamfer by defining one setback distance value and one angle value?

   (a) **Equal setbacks** (b) **2 Setbacks**
   (c) **Angle and setback** (d) None of these

6. In the **Ordered Part** environment, which of the following types of round can be used to specify multiple radius values along the length of the edge selected to fillet?

   (a) **Constant radius** (b) **Variable radius**
   (c) **Point** (d) **Blend**

7. Which of the following options is used to define the radial spacing and the spacing between individual occurrences when you create a radial fill pattern?

   (a) **Target spacing** (b) **Occurrences count**
   (c) **Polar** (d) **Complex Linear offset**

8. You cannot specify multiple radius values along the length of the edge while creating a variable radius round. (T/F)

9. A counterbore hole is the one that has a uniform diameter throughout the length of the hole. (T/F)

10. If the **V bottom angle** check box is selected while creating a hole, the end of the hole will be tapered and it will convert into a point. (T/F)

EXERCISES

Exercise 1

Create the model shown in Figure 6-116. The dimensions of the model are given in the views shown in Figure 6-117. After creating the model, save it with the name *c06exr1.par* at the following location given next:

C:\Solid Edge\c06 **(Expected time: 30 min)**

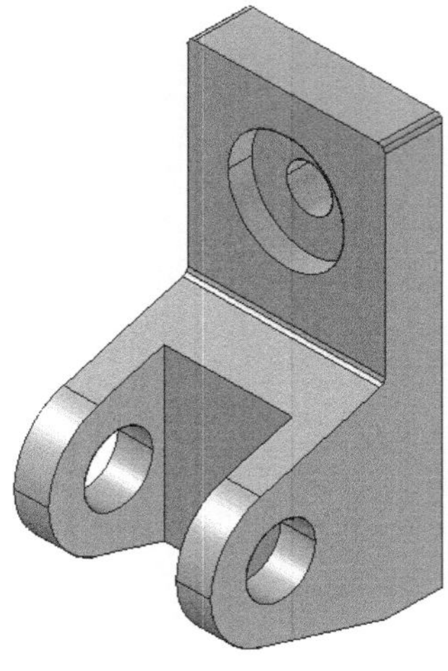

Figure 6-116 Model for Exercise 1

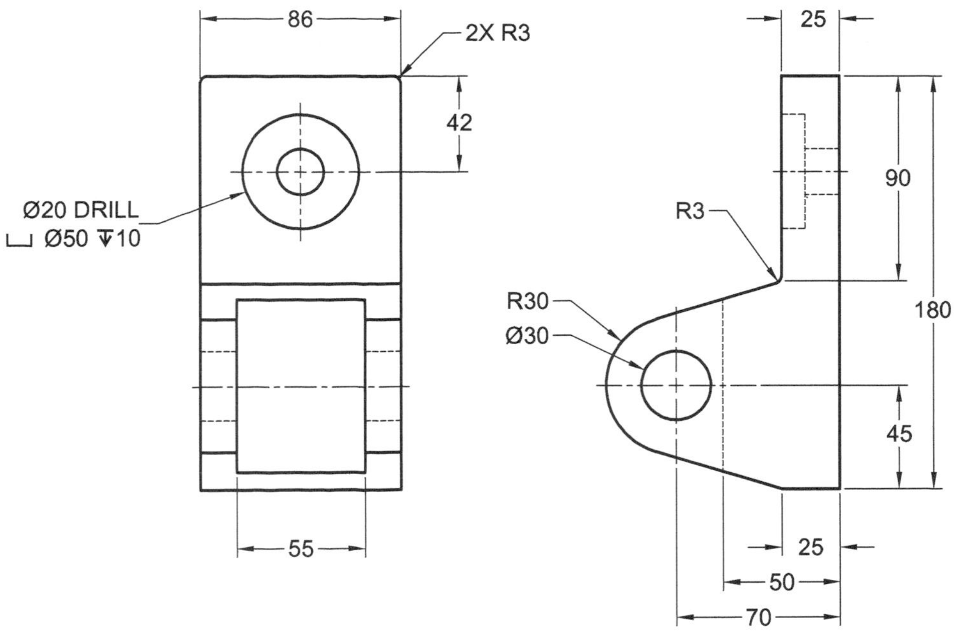

Figure 6-117 Dimensions of the model for Exercise 1

Exercise 2

Create the model shown in Figure 6-118. The dimensions of the model are given in the views shown in Figure 6-119. After creating the model, save it with the name *c06exr2.par* at the following location:

C:\Solid Edge\c06 **(Expected time: 30 min)**

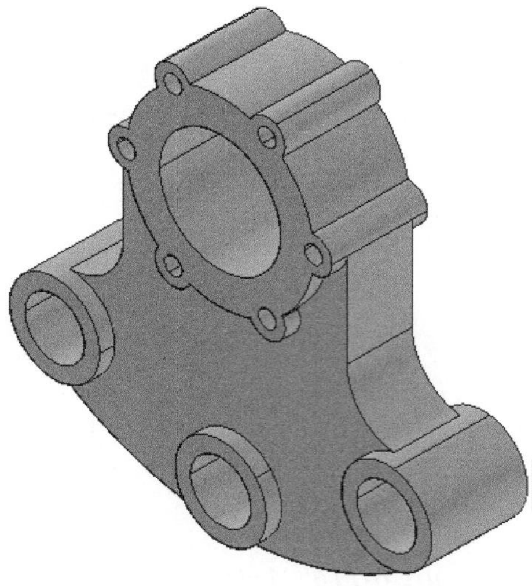

Figure 6-118 Model for Exercise 2

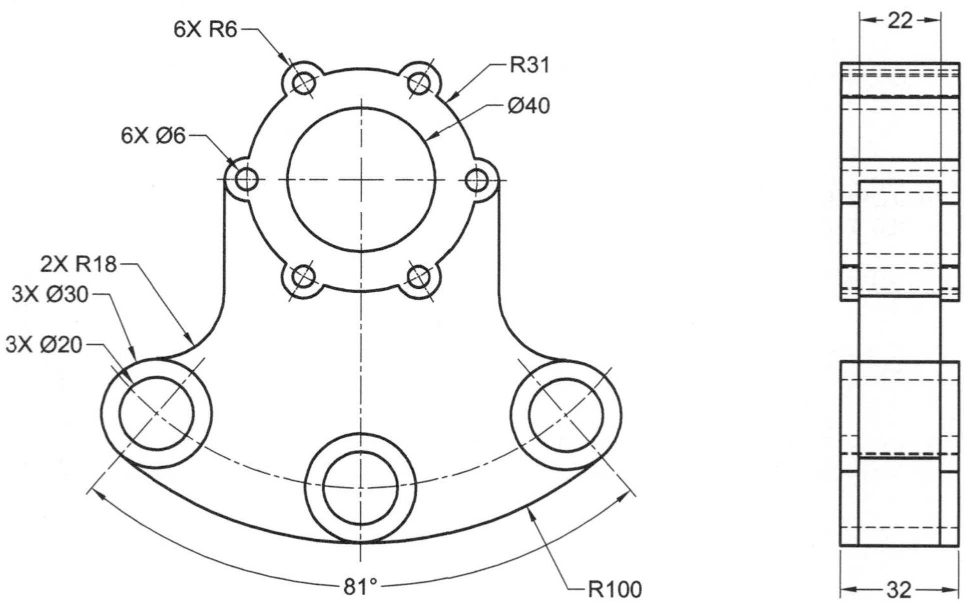

Figure 6-119 Dimensions of the model for Exercise 2

Exercise 3

Create the model shown in Figure 6-120. The dimensions of the model are given in the views shown in Figure 6-121. After creating the model, save it with the name *c06exr3.par* at the following location:

C:\Solid Edge\c06 **(Expected time: 30 min)**

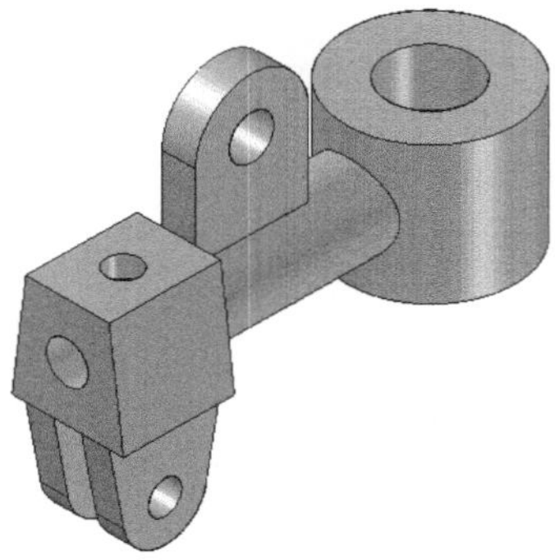

***Figure 6-120** Model for Exercise 3*

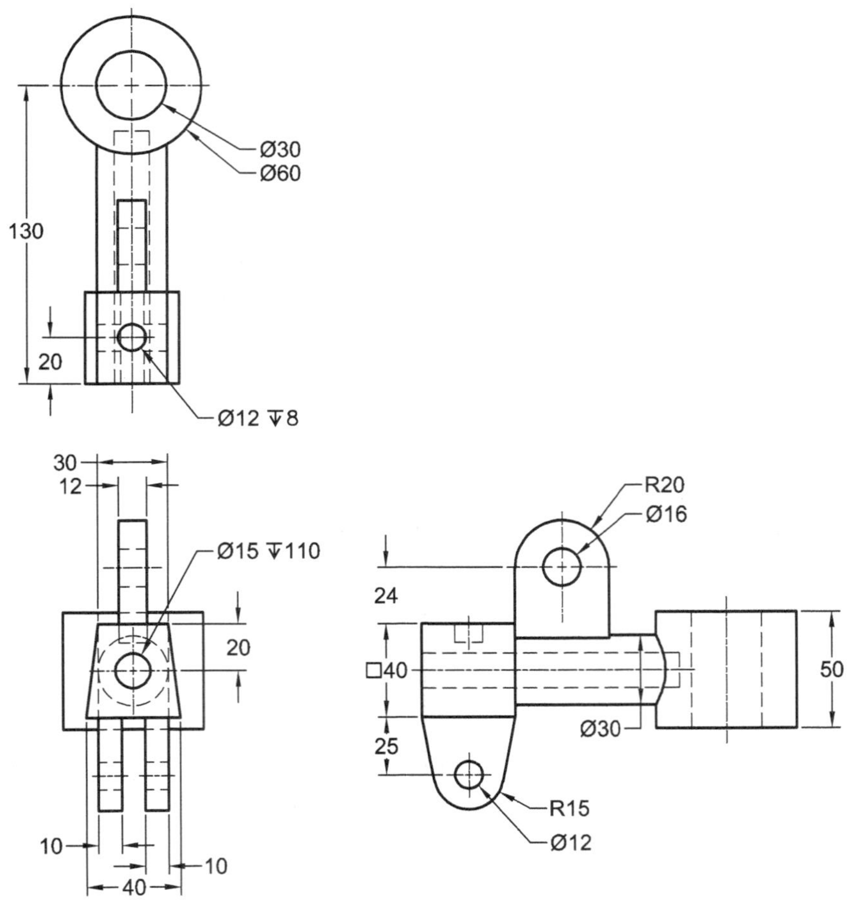

***Figure 6-121** Dimensions of the model for Exercise 3*

Exercise 4

Create the model shown in Figure 6-122. The dimensions of the model are given in the views shown in Figure 6-123. After creating the model, save it with the name *c06exr4.par* at the following location:

C:\Solid Edge\c06 **(Expected time: 30 min)**

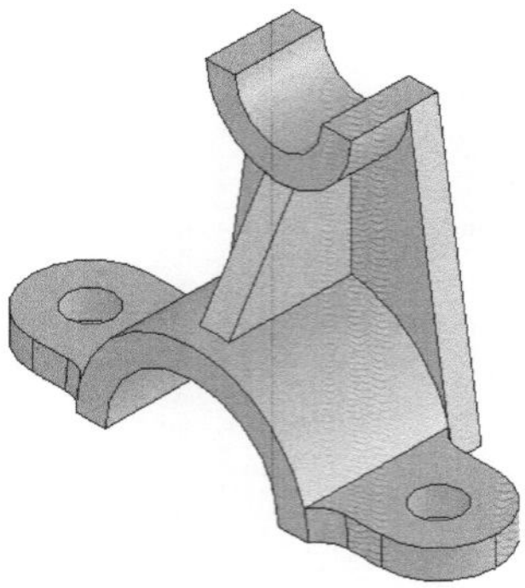

Figure 6-122 *Model for Exercise 4*

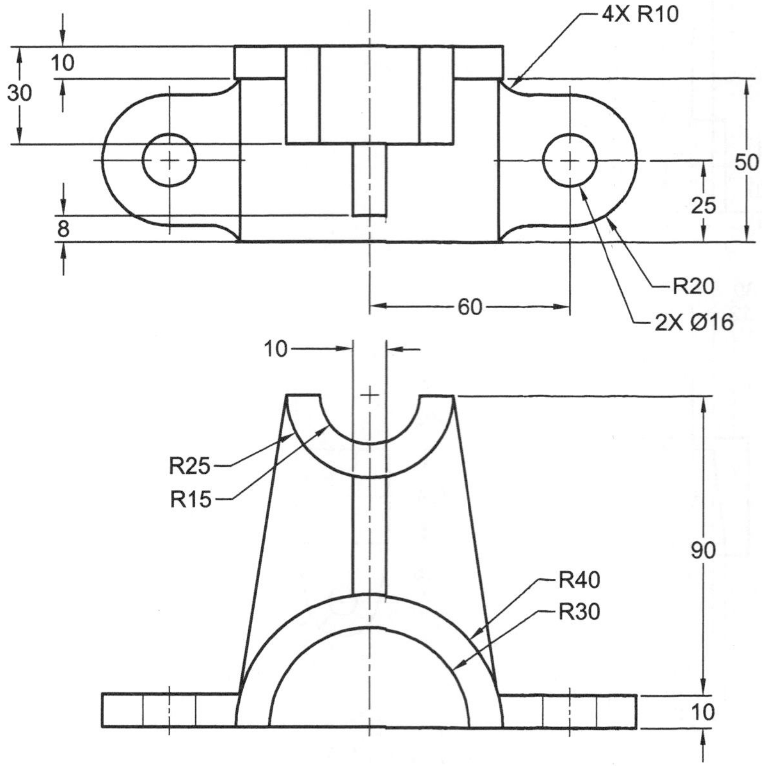

Figure 6-123 *Dimensions of the model for Exercise 4*

Answers to Self-Evaluation Test

1. Curved, **2. Smart**, **3.** Chamfering, **4. Round Options**, **5. Equal setbacks**, **6.** Four, **7. Orient vector**, **8. Allow Boundary Touching**, **9.** T, **10.** T

Chapter 7

Editing Features

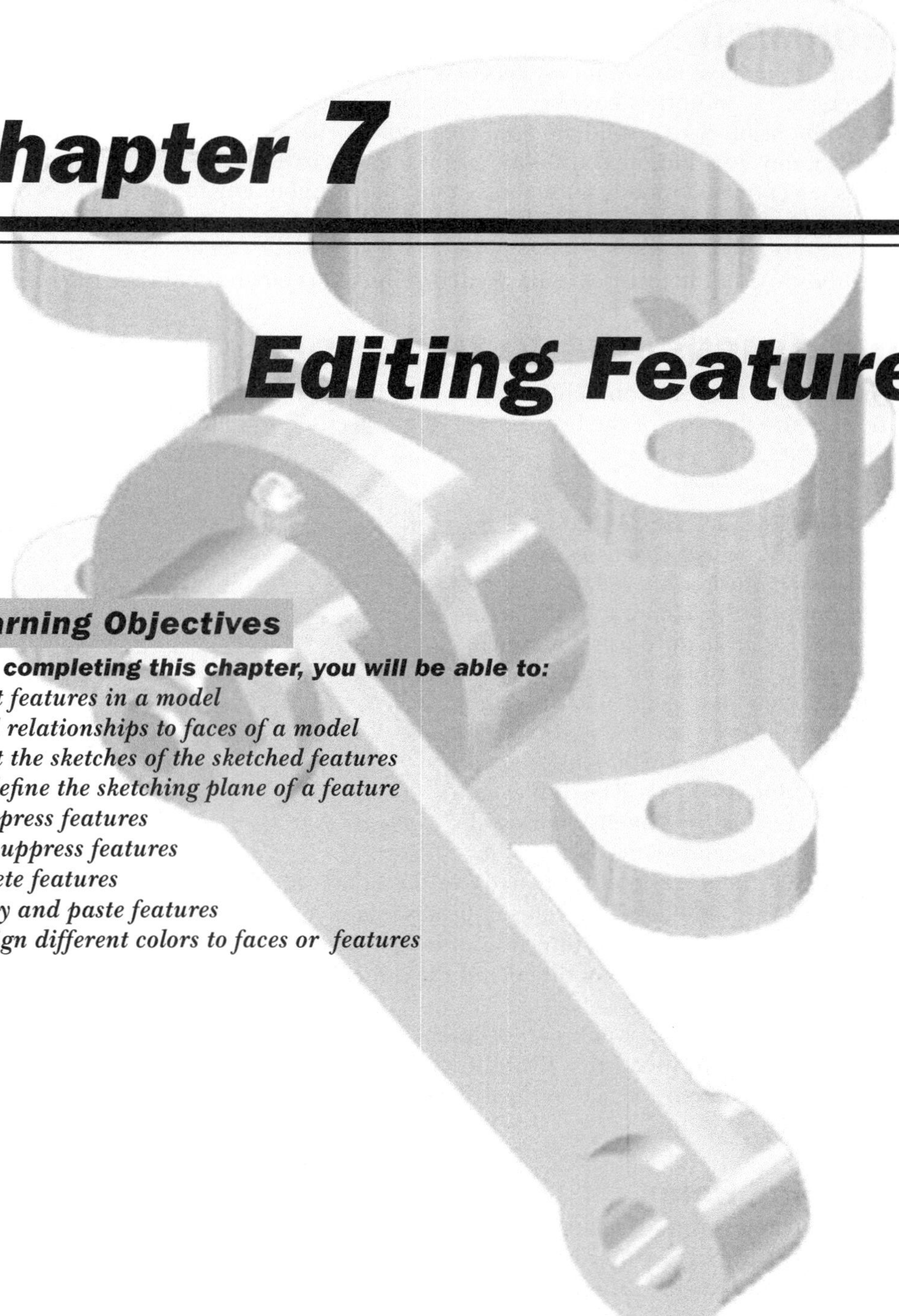

Learning Objectives

After completing this chapter, you will be able to:

- *Edit features in a model*
- *Add relationships to faces of a model*
- *Edit the sketches of the sketched features*
- *Redefine the sketching plane of a feature*
- *Suppress features*
- *Unsuppress features*
- *Delete features*
- *Copy and paste features*
- *Assign different colors to faces or features*

EDITING MODELS IN THE SYNCHRONOUS ENVIRONMENT

Editing is one of the most important aspects of a design process. Most designs require editing while being created or after they have been created. In Solid Edge, Synchronous technology is a history-free, dimension-driven solid modeling technology that makes you work on models with speed and flexibility. In addition, the ability to edit features irrespective of their 2D geometries using various selection and modification tools in the Synchronous environment allows the users to apply unpredictable changes to a model.

Various methods to edit the features in the **Synchronous Part** environment are discussed next.

ADDING DIMENSIONS TO THE MODEL

In the **Synchronous Part** environment, you can add dimensions to a feature and edit them to change the size and location of the feature. The methods used to dimension and edit features are discussed next.

Dimensioning a Feature

You can add dimensions to the sketches as well as the features using the tools available in the **Dimension** group of the **Home** tab. But note that once you create a feature using a sketch, you cannot edit the dimensions of the sketch. In such a case, you first need to apply the dimensions to the feature and then edit them. To edit a dimension, select the dimension text; the **Dimension value** edit box will be displayed, refer to Figure 7-1. Also, the dimension text will have a dot on one side and arrow on the other.

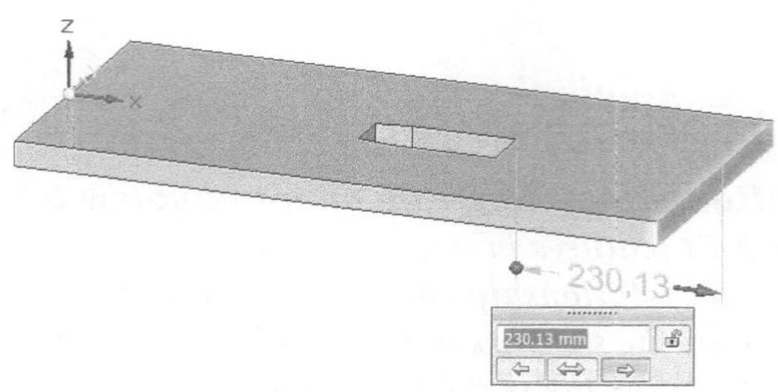

*Figure 7-1 The **Dimension value** edit box*

You will notice that the direction of the arrow in the dimension callout and in the dimension text, point toward the same direction. This indicates that if you change the value in the callout, the feature will be modified in the direction of arrow. After specifying the dimension, if you press ENTER, the feature will be modified and the dimension will be displayed in blue color.

However, if you need to modify a value in the**Dimension value** edit box, choose the lock button in the dimension callout and then press ENTER; the dimension will be locked and displayed in red color. This locked dimension acts as the driving dimension and the blue colored dimension acts as the driven dimension.

Dimensioning Holes

When you select holes, rounds, patterns, or thin wall features, the steering wheel and the dimensions of the feature are displayed on the screen. When you click on a dimension value, the **Edit Definition** callout will be displayed with the parameters of the feature selected, as shown in Figure 7-2. The parameters that will be displayed in the callout depend upon the feature selected. For example, if you select a counterbore hole, the parameters displayed in the callout will be the diameters and depths of counterbore hole. In order to modify the parameters of the feature, you need to enter the required data in the respective edit boxes available in the callout and then press the ENTER key to accept the new values.

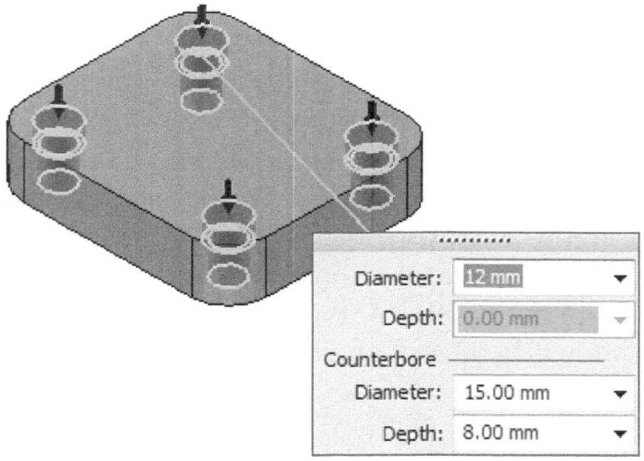

*Figure 7-2 The **Edit Definition** callout*

Note

*If you press the TAB key after entering the new value in the edit box in the **Edit Definition** callout, the dimension will be modified and the next edit box will be activated. However, if you press ENTER after modifying a dimension, the corresponding dimension will get modified and the **Edit Definition** callout will be closed.*

EDITING THE ROUND FEATURE (SYNCHRONOUS)

In the **Synchronous Part** environment, you can edit a round feature. To do so, select it from the model and then click on the dimension value displayed; the **Edit Definition** callout will be displayed, as shown in Figure 7-3. The options available in the callout are discussed next.

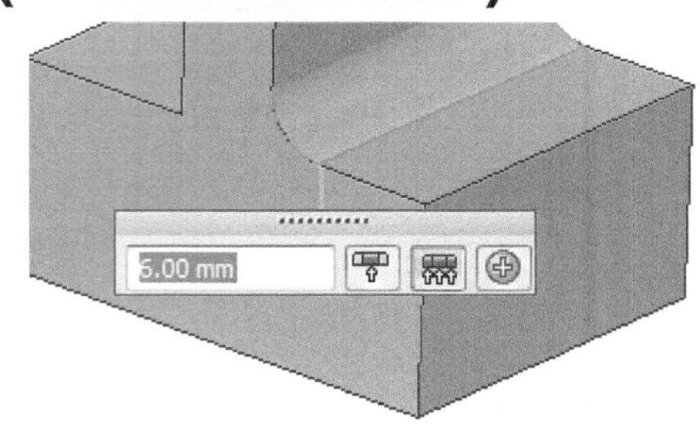

*Figure 7-3 The **Edit Definition** callout*

Selected Faces Only

 This button is used to modify the selected faces only.

All Feature Faces

 This button is used to modify all round or fillet features on the model.

Selection Manager

 This button is used to modify all round or fillet features that have the same radius value.

ADDING RELATIONS

Besides adding dimensions to features, you can also add relations between different faces of a feature to modify the part created in Synchronous environment. You can also control the behavior of a feature/face with respect to a selected entity while applying a relation. In Solid Edge, these relations are placed separately in the **Face Relate** group of the **Home** tab.

Aligning Faces

To align the faces of a feature, you need to define a relationship between one or more faces with respect to the selected face. The tools to define relationships between faces are available in the **Face Relate** group of the **Home** tab. To apply the **Coplanar** relationship, choose the **Coplanar** tool from the **Face Relate** group in the **Home** tab; the **Coplanar** Command bar will be displayed, as shown in Figure 7-4. Also, you will be prompted to click on the planes of the model. Select a face from the model and choose the **Accept** button from the Command bar. Next, select another face from the model; the first face will get aligned with the selected face. Figure 7-5 and Figure 7-6 shows the faces before and after applying the **Coplanar** face relation.

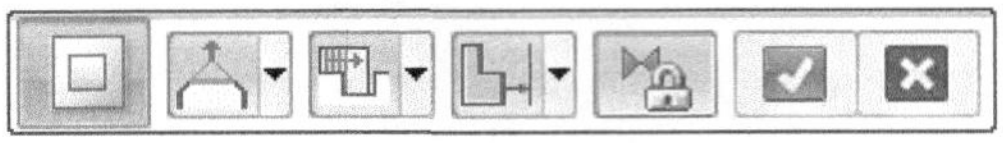

Figure 7-4 *The* ***Coplanar*** *Command bar*

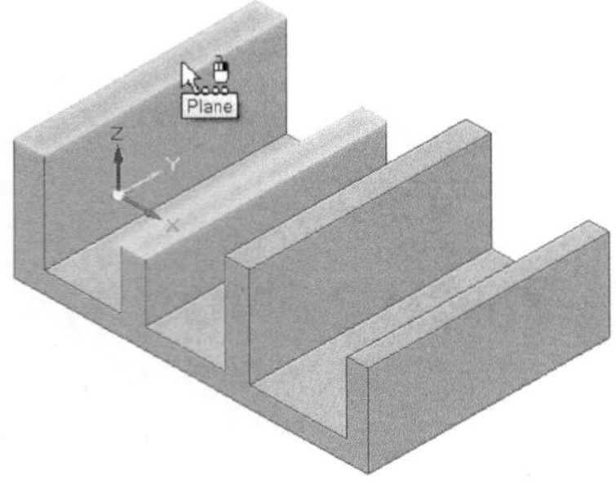

Figure 7-5 *Model before applying the relation*

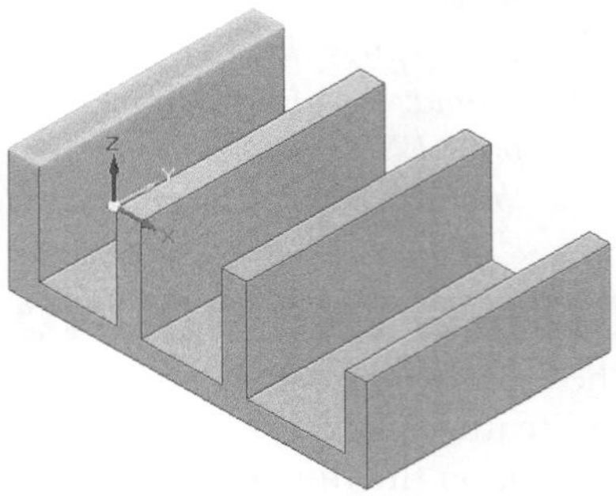

Figure 7-6 *Model after applying the* ***Coplanar*** *relation*

The options available in the **Coplanar** Command bar are discussed next.

Precedence

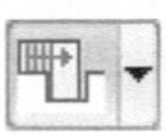

This drop-down is used to specify the priority of the selected and non-selected faces while adding relations to the model. The options in this drop-down are discussed next.

Select Set Priority

This option is used to set the priority of the selected face. The selected face can be moved to any extent without affecting the remaining faces. Figure 7-7 shows the model in which the face is being moved when the **Select Set Priority** option is chosen.

Model Priority

This option is used to set the priority of the unselected faces of the model. The selected face cannot move beyond the model geometry. Figure 7-8 shows the model in which the selected face is being moved when the **Model Priority** option is chosen.

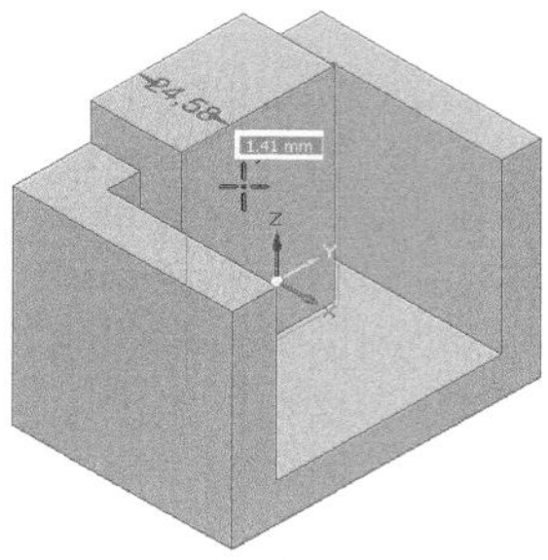

*Figure 7-7 Model generated by using the **Select Set Priority** option*

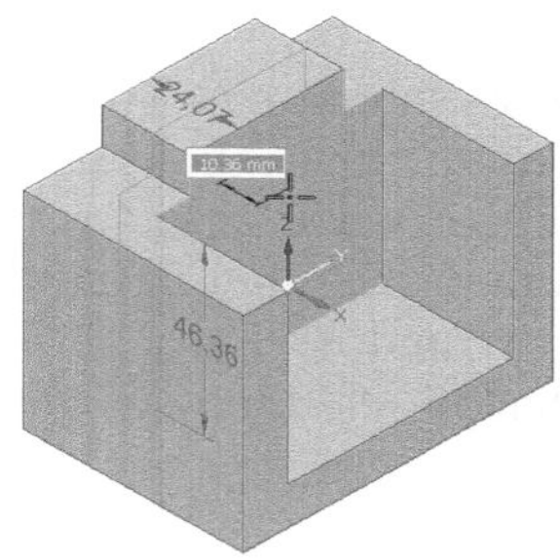

*Figure 7-8 Model generated by using the **Model Priority** option*

Single/All

The options in the **Single/All** drop-down are used to specify whether you want to apply the selected relation to a single element or to all selected elements. There are two options in this drop-down: **Single Align** and **Multiple Align**. You can choose the required option from this drop-down. These options are discussed next.

Single Align

When you choose the **Single Align** option from the drop-down, the relationship is applied to the first selected element only and the rest of the elements in the selection set maintain the original spatial relationship with the first selected element. Figure 7-9 shows multiple faces selected to be coincident with the top left face. Figure 7-10 shows the resultant model on choosing the **Single Align** option from the **Single/All** drop-down in the Command bar. Notice that only the first selected face is aligned with the target face in the figure.

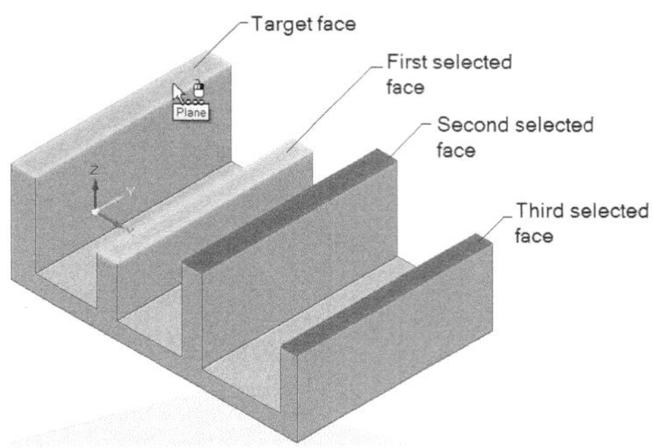

Figure 7-9 Multiple faces selected to be made coincident

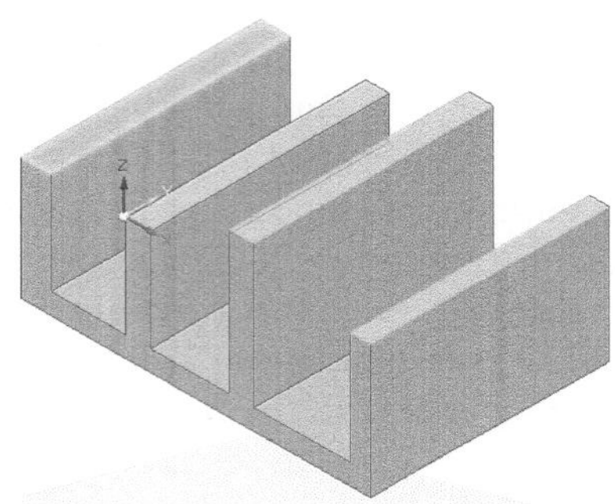

*Figure 7-10 Resultant model after choosing the **Single Align** option*

Multiple Align

If you want all elements in the selection set to follow the relationship with the target element, and then choose the **Multiple Align** option from the **Single/All** drop-down. Figure 7-11 shows the resultant model with the **Multiple Align** option chosen. Notice that in the figure, all selected faces are aligned with the target face.

Persist

The **Persist** button is chosen by default in the **Coplanar** Command bar. As a result, the applied relations will persist even if an entity is modified. For example, if you apply the **Coincident** relation to any two faces and then modify the length of any one of these faces, the length of the other face will automatically be modified, which means the **Coincident** relation has persisted. Figure 7-12 shows the resultant model with the **Persist** button chosen. Also, notice that all selected faces get modified on modifying a single face.

Note

The other options available in this Command bar are discussed later in this chapter.

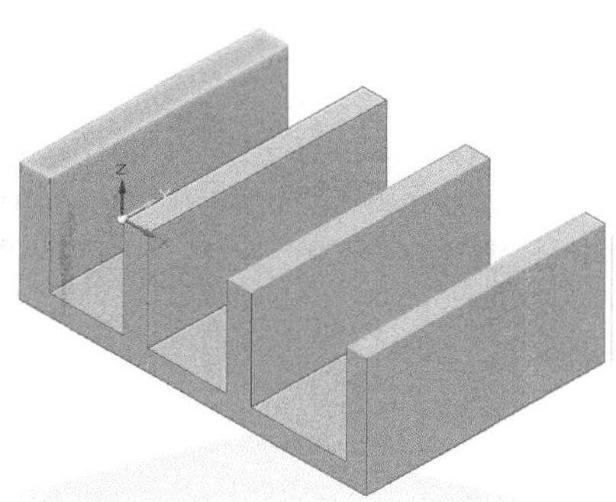

Figure 7-11 *Resultant model after choosing the* ***Multiple Align*** *option*

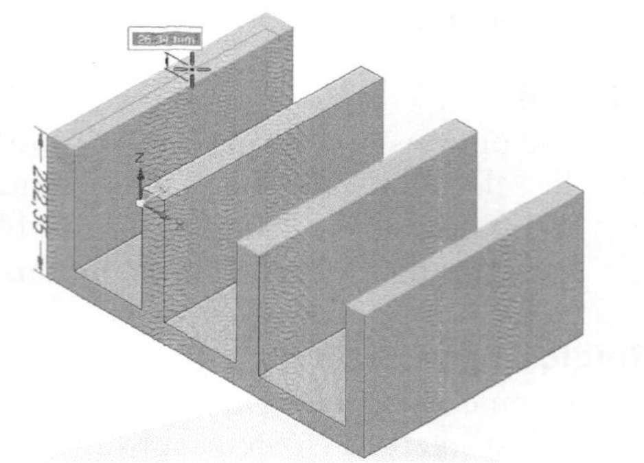

Figure 7-12 *Modifying a face with the* ***Persist*** *button chosen*

Design Intent

The **Design Intent** panel is displayed, refer to Figure 7-13 automatically displayed when you move/rotate faces, align faces, or edit dimensions of a model, refer to Figure 7-13. The check boxes available in this panel are used to control the behavior of a model with respect to a selected entity while modifying it. If you want more control over the behavior of the model then click on the **Advanced** option from the **Design Intent** panel; the **Advanced Design Intent** panel will be displayed, as shown in Figure 7-14. Now, you can activate or deactivate the buttons available in the **Advanced Design Intent** panel to define the relations between the selected elements and the rest of elements of the model. For example, when you move a single planar face with the steering wheel, you can use **Advanced Design Intent** panel to specify whether other coplanar faces that are not selected should stay coplanar during the move operation or not. You can also use the **Advanced Design Intent** panel to specify how the model will behave after a relation is applied to it. For example, if you are applying the **Coincident** relationship between the faces, you need to deactivate the **maintains coplanar faces** button from the **Advanced Design Intent** panel so that only the selected faces are aligned to the target face.

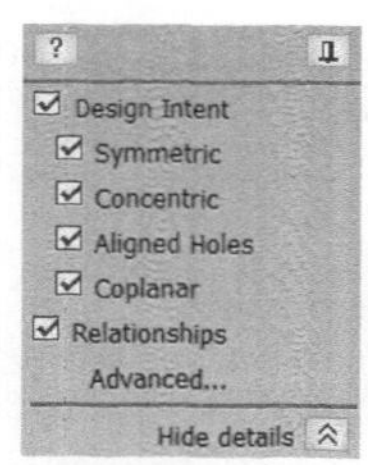

Figure 7-13 *The* ***Design Intent***

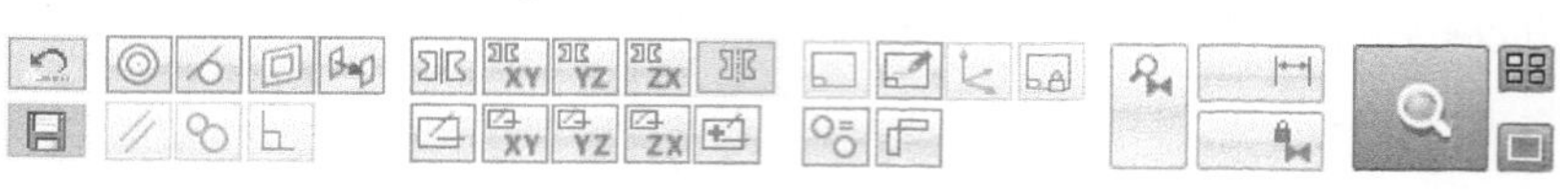

Figure 7-14 *The* ***Advanced Design Intent*** *panel*

The **Maintain Relationships** button of the **Advanced Design Intent** panel contains all geometric relations that can be maintained between the selected element and the rest of the elements while modifying it. For example, if the **Maintain Coplanar Faces** button is activated, and you move a planar face, all unselected elements that are coplanar to the selected face will also move. You can maintain the following relationships between a selected face and rest of the faces in the model:

Maintain Concentric Faces

Maintain Tangent Faces

Maintain Coplanar Faces

Maintain Parallel Faces

Tangent Touching

Maintain Perpendicular Faces

Maintain Symmetry About Base Planes (XY, YZ, ZX Planes)

Local Symmetry

Maintain Aligned Holes (X, Y, Z axes)

Lock to Base Reference

Same radius if Possible

Keep Orthogonal to base if possible

If you choose the **Suspend Design Intent Settings** button, all design intent settings will get suspended. Choose the **Relax Dimensions** button to suspend the locked dimensions while modifying the faces. The **Relax Persistent Relationships** button is used to suspend the applied relationships while editing the model. The **Restore** button is used to restore the default settings. In addition to applying the relationships, the buttons used to filter the reference elements are **Consider Reference Planes**, **Consider Sketch Planes**, and **Consider Coordinate Systems**. The options selected from the **Advanced Design Intent** panel will be applied to the selected **filter** buttons.

The **Solution Manager** button is used to solve the model in over-constrained condition. This also helps you in controlling all the relationships of the model. Also, if you select the **Auto Solution Manager** check box, you do not need to manually invoke the solution manager. The **Options** button is used to displays the **Solution Manager Colors** dialog box. You can set the colors of various solutions while modifying faces.

The procedures to apply different face relations in the **Synchronous** environment are discussed next.

Applying Concentric Relationship

Ribbon: Home > Face Relate > Concentric

You can make two different cylindrical faces of a component concentric using the **Concentric** tool. To do so, choose the **Concentric** tool from the **Face Relate** group in the **Synchronous** environment; the **Concentric** Command bar will be displayed and you will be prompted to select model elements to relate. Select a cylindrical face and right-click to accept the selection; you will be prompted to select an element to position the previous selection. Select another cylindrical face and right-click; the two faces will become concentric. Figure 7-15 shows the faces selected to be made concentric and Figure 7-16 shows the preview of the resultant model.

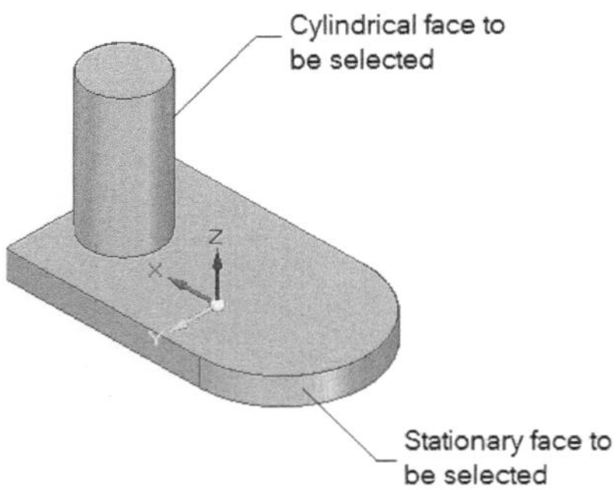

Figure 7-15 *Faces selected to be made concentric*

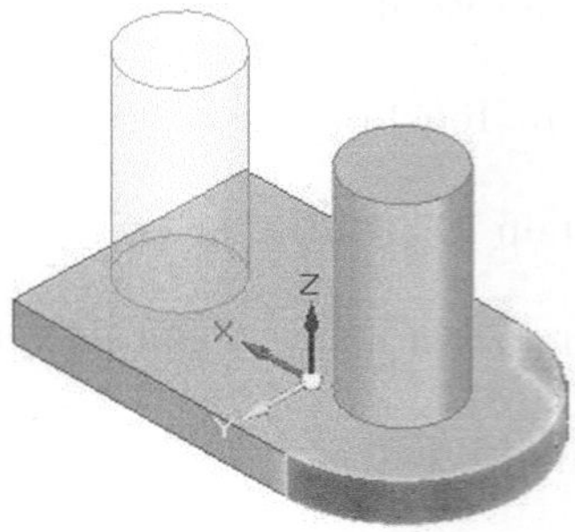

Figure 7-16 *Preview of the resultant model*

Applying Tangent Relationship

Ribbon: Home > Face Relate > Tangent

You can make a face of a component tangent to another face using the **Tangent** tool. To do so, choose the **Tangent** tool from the **Face Relate** group in the **Synchronous** environment; the **Tangent** Command bar will be displayed and you will be prompted to select model elements to relate. Select a face to be made tangent and right-click to accept; you will be prompted to select a face to position the previous selection. Select a face to remain stationary and then choose the **Accept** button. Figure 7-17 shows the selected faces to be made tangent and Figure 7-18 shows the preview of the resultant model.

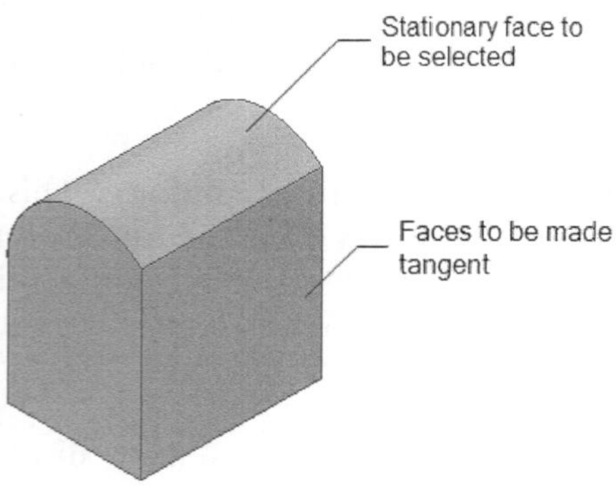

Figure 7-17 *Face selected to be made tangent*

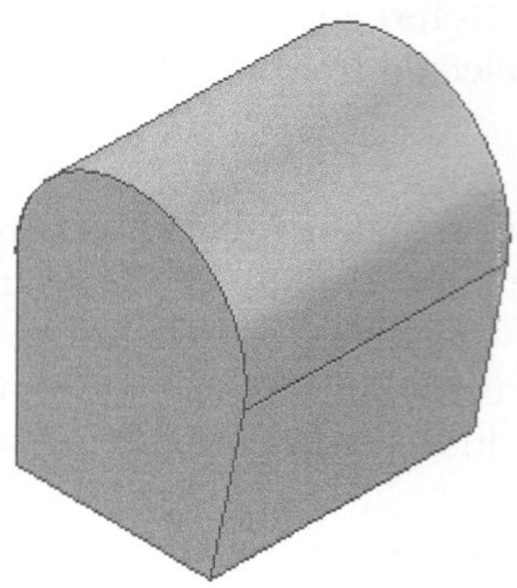

Figure 7-18 *Preview of the resultant model*

Applying Symmetric Relationship

Ribbon: Home > Face Relate > Symmetry

You can make a face of a component symmetric to another face about any specified plane using the **Symmetry** tool. To do so, choose the **Symmetry** tool from the **Face Relate** group in the **Synchronous** toolbar; the **Symmetry** Command bar will be displayed and you will be prompted to select elements to be aligned. Select a face from the model and right-click to accept the selection; you will be prompted to select face to be made symmetric to the previous selection. Select another face and right-click. Next, select a plane or a face to define the symmetry and choose the **Accept** button; the symmetric relation is applied between the selected faces. Figure 7-19 shows the faces selected to apply symmetry and Figure 7-20 shows the preview of the resultant model.

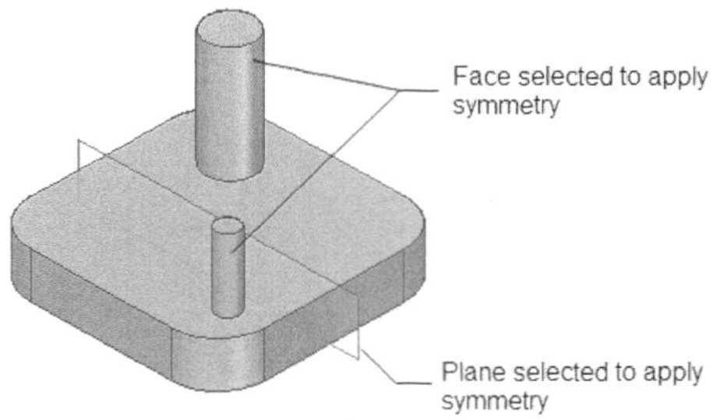

Figure 7-19 *Faces selected to apply symmetry*

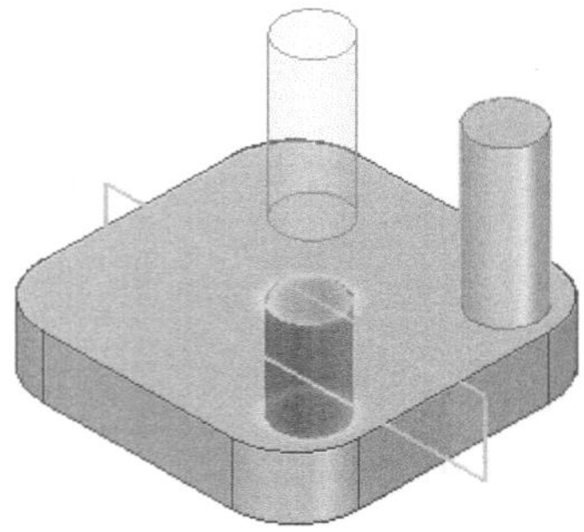

Figure 7-20 *Preview of the resultant model*

Applying Parallel Relationship

Ribbon: Home > Face Relate > Parallel

You can make a planar face of a component parallel to another planar face using the **Parallel** tool. To do so, choose the **Parallel** tool from the **Face Relate** group in the **Synchronous** environment; the **Parallel** Command bar will be displayed and you will be prompted to select the planar faces to be made parallel. Select the planar face that you want to modify, refer to Figure 7-21 and right-click; the selection will be accepted and you will be prompted to select the planar face or plane that has to remain stationary. Select the required planar face or plane; the preview of the resultant component will be displayed, refer to Figure 7-22.

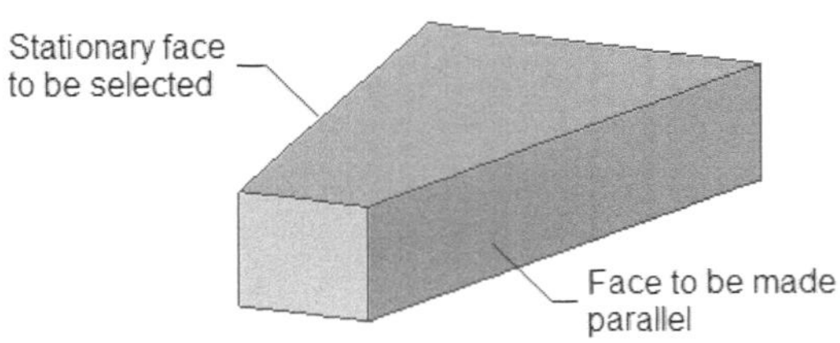

Figure 7-21 *Faces selected to be made parallel*

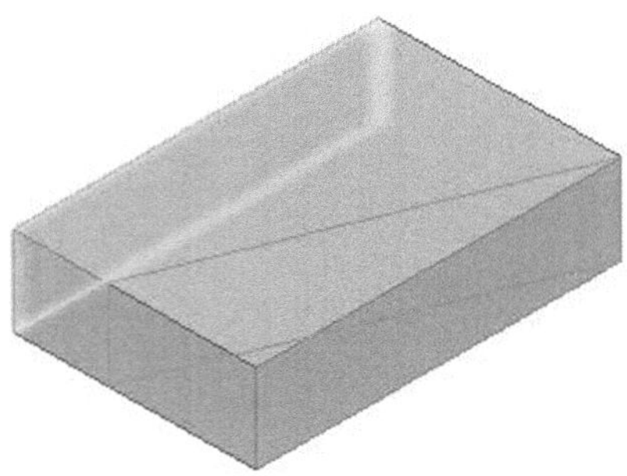

Figure 7-22 *Preview of the resultant model*

Applying Perpendicular Relationship

Ribbon: Home > Face Relate > Perpendicular

You can make a planar face of a component perpendicular to another planar face using the **Perpendicular** tool. Choose the **Perpendicular** tool from the **Face Relate** group in the **Synchronous** environment; the **Perpendicular** Command bar will be displayed and you will be prompted to select the planar faces to be made perpendicular. Select the required planar face to be modified, refer to Figure 7-23, and right-click to accept the selection. Now, you will be prompted to select the planar face or plane that has to remain stationary. Select the required planar face or plane; the preview of the resultant component will be displayed, refer to Figure 7-24.

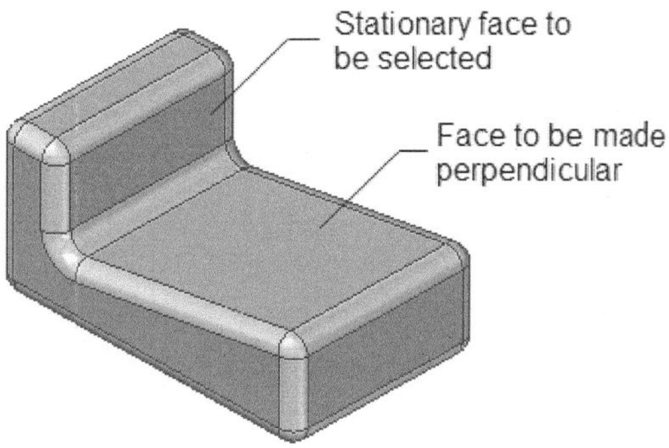

Figure 7-23 *Faces selected to apply the* ***Perpendicular*** *tool*

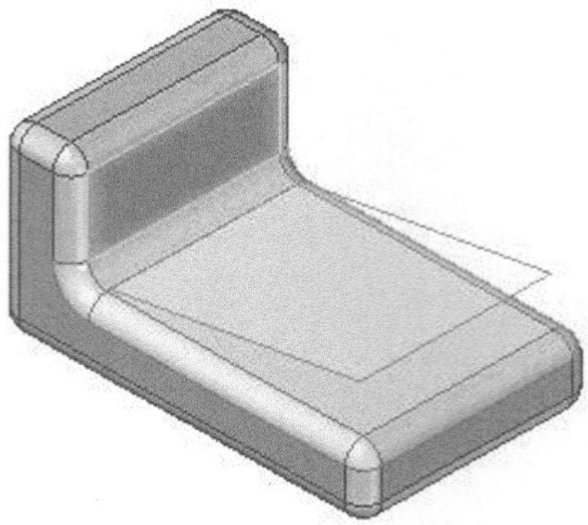

Figure 7-24 *Preview of the resultant model*

Applying Offset Relationship

Ribbon: Home > Face Relate > Offset

You can offset a face from a stationary face using the **Offset** tool. To do so, choose the **Offset** tool from the **Face Relate** group; the **Offset** Command bar will be displayed and you will be prompted to select the face to offset. Select a face from the model and right-click to accept the selection; you will be prompted to select a face to remain stationary. Select the stationary face from the model; a dynamic edit box will be displayed. Enter the offset distance in this edit box and press ENTER; the face will be offset from the stationary face. Figure 7-25 shows the offset face and stationary face selected. Figure 7-26 shows the resultant model.

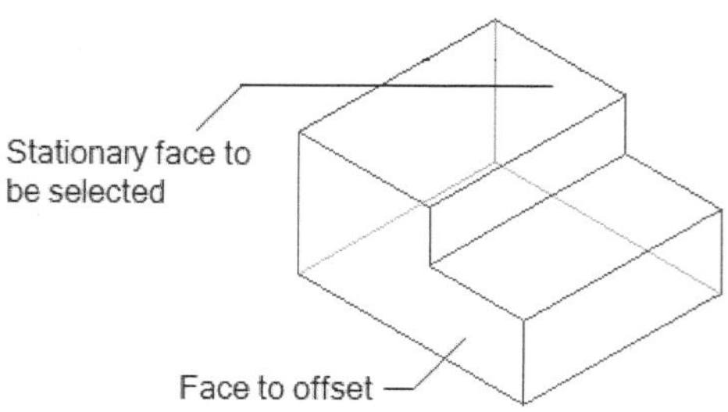

Figure 7-25 *Faces selected to be made offset*

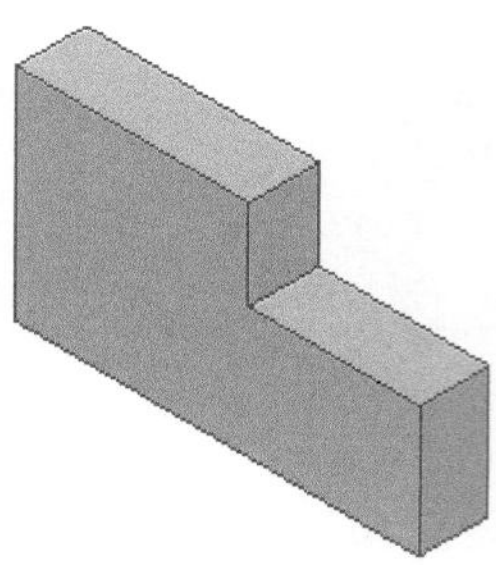

Figure 7-26 *Preview of the resultant model*

Applying Equal Radius Relationship

Ribbon: Home > Face Relate > Equal

You can make radius of cylindrical face equal to the radius of the second stationary cylindrical face using the **Equal** tool. Choose the **Equal** tool from the **Face Relate** group in the **Synchronous** environment; the **Equal** Command bar will be displayed and you will be prompted to select the cylindrical face to be modified. Select the required cylindrical face, refer to Figure 7-27 and right-click to accept the selected feature. On doing so, you will be prompted to select a cylindrical face to set the diameter of the selected faces. Select a cylindrical face from the model and right-click; the preview of the resultant model will be displayed, as shown in Figure 7-28.

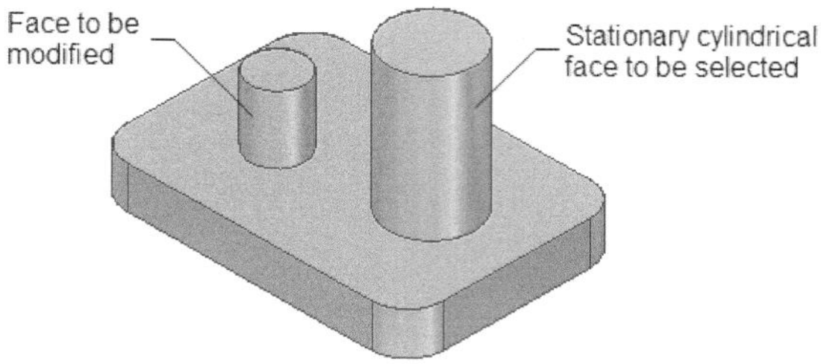

Figure 7-27 *Faces selected to be made equal radius*

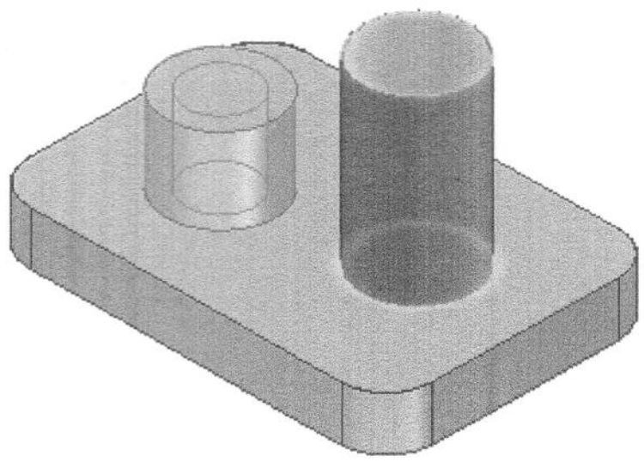

Figure 7-28 *Preview of the resultant model*

Applying Horizontal/Vertical Relationship

Ribbon: Home > Face Relate > Horizontal/Vertical

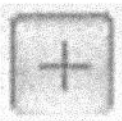

You can align a horizontal or vertical face or keypoint to the another horizontal or vertical face or keypoint using the **Horizontal/Vertical** tool. Choose the **Horizontal/Vertical** tool from the **Face Relate** group in the **Synchronous** environment; the **Horizontal/Vertical** Command bar will be displayed and you will be prompted to select a face or keypoint to place the horizontal or vertical relationship. Select the required faces or edges or keypoints from the model and choose the **Accept** button; the selected entities will be aligned horizontally or vertically. Figure 7-29 shows two keypoints selected and Figure 7-30 shows the preview of the resultant model.

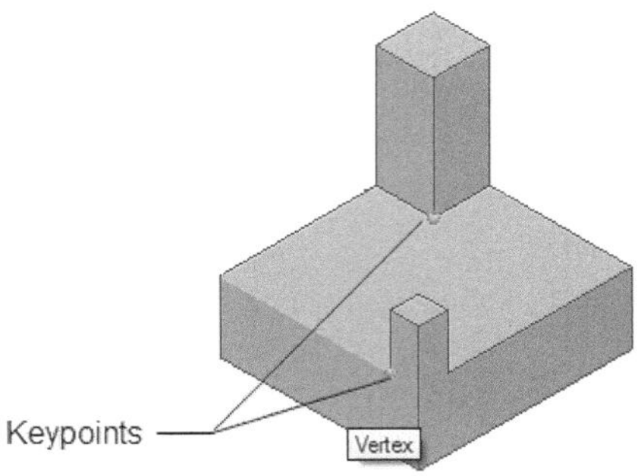

Figure 7-29 *Keypoints selected to apply horizontal/vertical relationship*

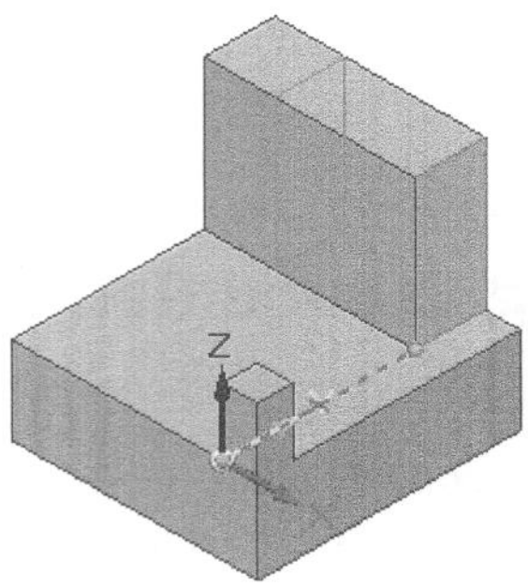

Figure 7-30 *Preview of the resultant model*

Applying Aligned Holes Relationship

Ribbon: Home > Face Relate > Aligned Holes

You can make the axes of multi cylindrical, conical or round faces align/coplanar using the **Aligned Holes** tool. To do so, choose the **Aligned Holes** tool from the **Face Relate** group in the **Synchronous** environment; the **Aligned Holes** Command bar will be displayed and you will be prompted to select cylinders, rounds, or cones to align to a common plane. Select the required faces to modify, refer to Figure 7-31, and right-click to accept the selection. Now, you will be prompted to select the planar face or datum plane or a point to which the axis of the selected faces will be aligned. Select the required planar face or plane; the preview of the resultant component will be displayed, refer to Figure 7-32. Note that, the first selected axis/face remains stationary and the remaining axes move according to the selected axis.

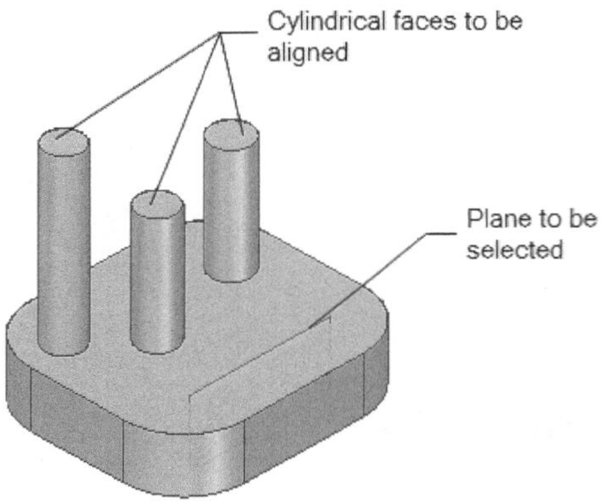

Figure 7-31 Cylindrical faces and plane selected to be made coplanar

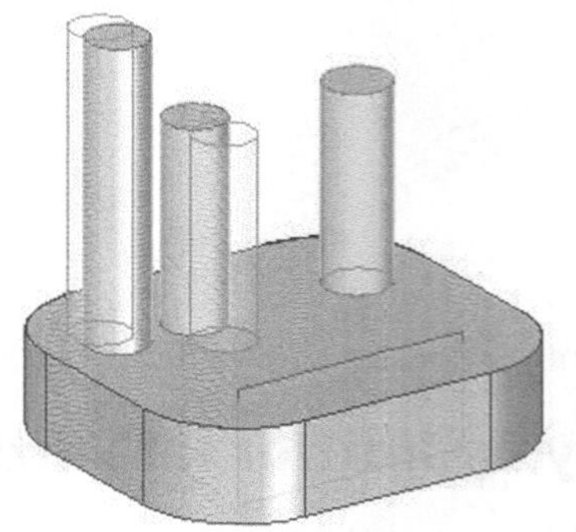

Figure 7-32 Preview of the resultant model

Applying Rigid Relationship

Ribbon: Home > Face Relate > Rigid

You can make a selected set of faces rigid with respect to each other using the **Rigid** tool. To do so, choose the **Rigid** tool from the **Face Relate** group in the **Synchronous** environment; the **Rigid** Command bar will be displayed and you will be prompted to select elements to be included in the set. Select the required face to apply rigid relationship and then right-click to accept the selected relationship; the selected set of faces will be fixed together. As a result, if you move one of the faces, the other faces fixed to that face will also move.

Applying Ground Relationship

Ribbon: Home > Face Relate > Ground

The **Ground** tool is used to make a face grounded by adding the ground constraint to it. You can use this tool to prevent any change in the selected face. To ground a face, choose the **Ground** tool from the **Face Relate** group in the **Synchronous** environment; the **Ground** Command bar will be displayed and you will be prompted to select the faces to be grounded. Select the required faces and choose the **OK** button; the selected faces will become grounded.

OTHER SELECTION HANDLES

Different selection handles are displayed on selecting different entities of a model. The entities can be individual or group of elements, sketched profiles, dimensions, relationships, features, holes, cuts, and so on. Depending on the entity selected, the selection handle can be an Extrude handle, a steering wheel, Revolved Protrusion handle, Selection Manager, Edit Definition handle, Dimension value edit handle, Reference Plane handle, or Align Face. Most of the handle types have been discussed earlier and the remaining ones are discussed next.

Reference Plane Handle

In the **Synchronous Part** environment, you can resize and relocate the construction reference plane. Note that you cannot resize or relocate the default plane. To resize or relocate a plane, select the global reference plane; the steering wheel and a Command bar will be displayed. Next, choose **Resize** from the **Move** drop-down of the Command bar; the reference plane handles will be displayed, as shown in Figure 7-33. You can click and drag any of the yellow points on this handle to resize the reference plane. In order to move the reference plane, you need to click and drag the straight lines in between the yellow points. You can also choose the **Resize** button from the Command bar to resize the selected reference plane.

Selection Manager

The **Selection Manager** tool is used to create a selection set in relation to the selected element. To do so, choose the **Selection Manager Mode** option from the **Select** drop-down in the **Select** group of the **Home** tab; the cursor with a green circle and a plus mark in it will be displayed. This indicates that the **Selection Manager** tool is activated. Now, select the face to be modified; the **Selection Manager** menu will be displayed. By default, the **Use Box Selection** option is chosen in this menu, as shown in Figure 7-34. Choose the required selection criteria from the menu; all elements matching the selection criteria will be selected.

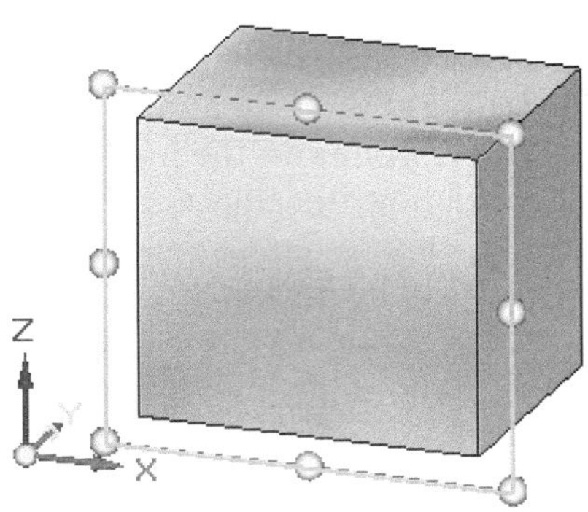

Figure 7-33 The reference plane handle

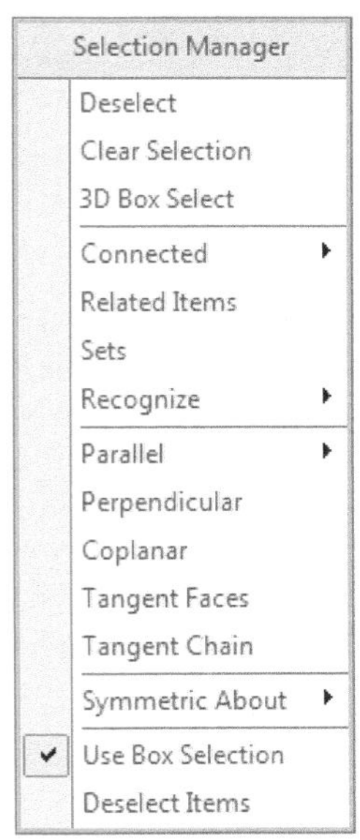

*Figure 7-34 The **Selection Manager** menu*

Additional options in the **Selection Manager** will help you to deselect the selected items, clear the entire selection, or to create a 3D box to select the elements. Using the 3D box, all elements within the box will be selected, irrespective of the selection criteria.

You can also choose the **Selection Filter** option from the **Select** group of the **Home** tab in the **Ribbon** to control the selected items. The **Selection Filter** option from the **Select** drop-down list allows you to filter the selection and the **Clear Selection** button allows you to clear the entire selection.

MODIFYING FACES USING THE STEERING WHEEL

The steering wheel is used to move or rotate an entity. The entities can be faces, features, reference planes (other than the base reference plane), coordinate system (other than the base coordinate system), sketches, or sketched entities.

Moving or Rotating the Selected Entities

Moving or rotating the selected entities using the steering wheel is similar to the common move or rotate operation. You can perform these operations using various components of the steering wheel. For example, the selected entity can be moved along the primary axis, the secondary axis, or along the tool plane of the steering wheel by using the Torus of the steering wheel. Figure 7-35 shows a placed feature being moved and Figure 7-36 shows a placed feature being rotated.

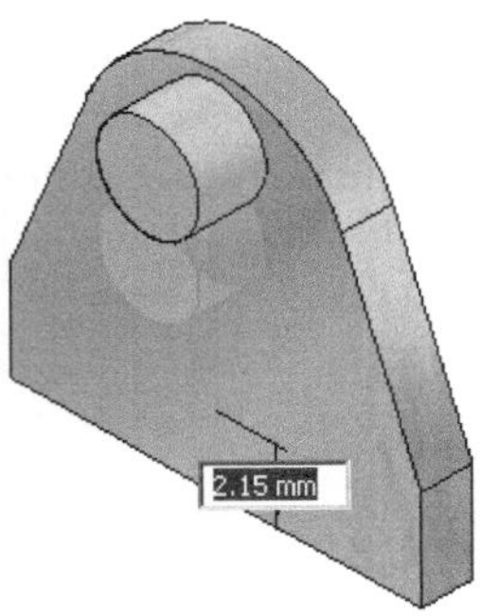

***Figure 7-35** A placed feature being moved*

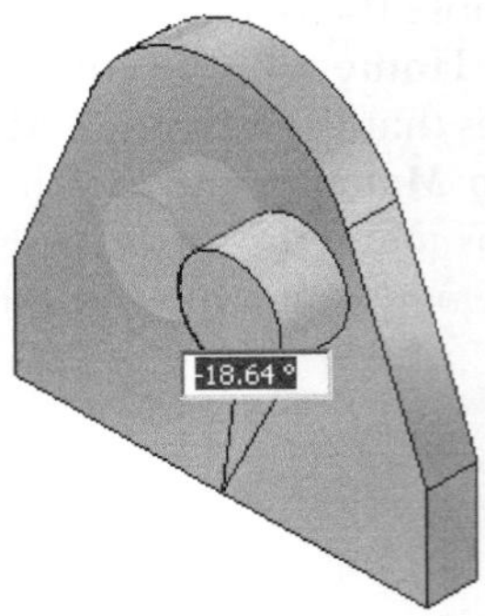

***Figure 7-36** A placed feature being rotated*

Other than moving or rotating the placed features, the steering wheel can also be used to move or rotate the faces of the base feature. To move a face, select it; a steering wheel and a Command bar will be displayed. Now, specify the direction of movement and the distance to be moved in the edit box. You can also specify the snapping points on the model to define the extent of movement. While moving a face, you can control how the adjacent faces will behave with respect to the operation being performed. To do so, choose the **Connected faces** button from the Command bar. On choosing this button, a flyout will be displayed with three options: **Extend/Trim**, **Tip**, and **Lift** connected faces.

Extend/Trim

When you choose the **Extend/Trim** option and move the selected face, the adjacent faces extend or trim without changing the angular orientation of the selected face, as shown in Figure 7-37.

Tip

When you choose the **Tip** option, the adjacent faces change their angular orientation to maintain the original dimension of the selected face, as shown in Figure 7-38.

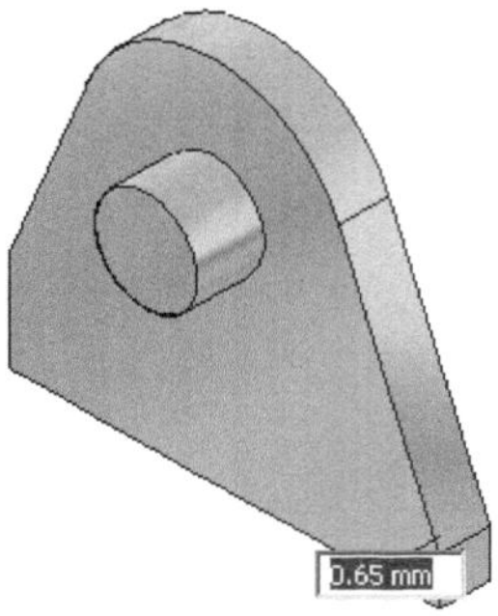

*Figure 7-37 The face being moved with the **Extend/Trim** option chosen*

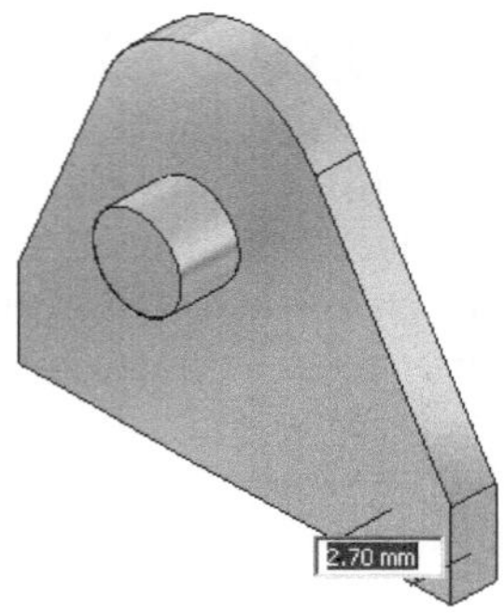

*Figure 7-38 The face being moved with the **Tip** option chosen*

Lift

When you choose the **Lift** option, the adjacent faces will remain unchanged and some new faces may be generated to accommodate the changes, as shown in Figure 7-39.

Using the steering wheel, you can also rotate the faces in order to create angular ends like tapers. To do so, select the required face; the steering wheel will be displayed. Move the steering wheel to the axis of rotation, which means the primary axis of steering wheel should coincide with the axis of rotation. Next, click on the Torus and specify the angle of rotation. Figure 7-40 shows the selected face being rotated. Using the Command bar, you can create copies of the selected entities while moving or rotating them. You can also detach the selected entities and then reattach them either at the same location or at a new location. You will learn more about it later in this chapter.

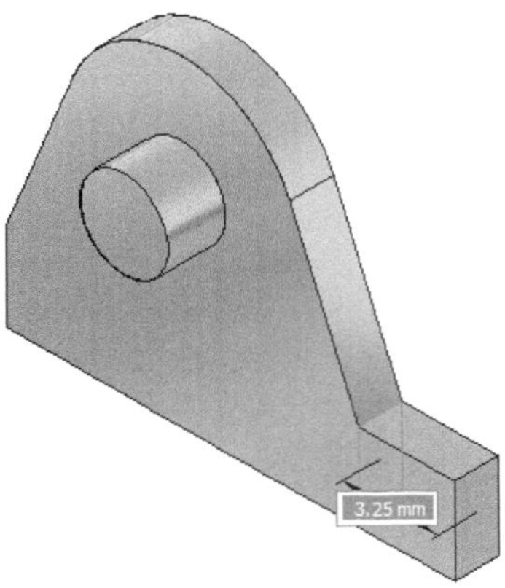

*Figure 7-39 The selected face being moved with the **Lift** option chosen*

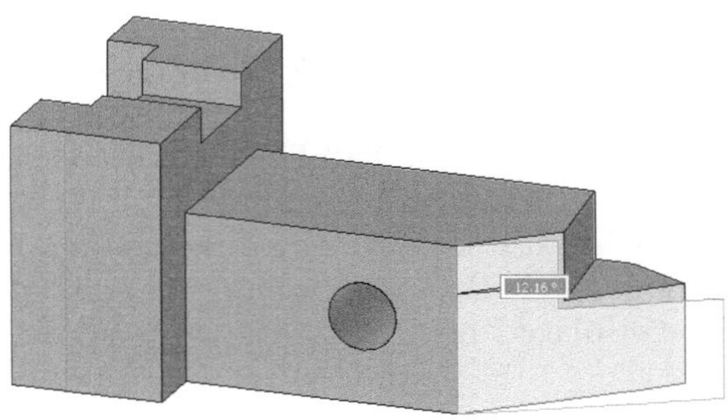

Figure 7-40 The selected face being rotated using the steering wheel

MODIFYING THE MODEL BY EDITING DIMENSIONS

You can modify the shape and size of a model by editing its dimensions directly on the model. When you click on a dimension text, the **Dimension value** edit box, Command bar, and **Design Intent** panel will be displayed. You can define the dimensions and also specify the side in which you want to make changes in the model by using the **Dimension value** edit handle. Using the lock button, you can lock a dimension to ensure that it does not change when other dimensions are getting changed. All this has already been discussed earlier in this chapter.

CREATING LIVE SECTIONS

In earlier chapters, you have learned that a live section is created while creating a revolved feature. With the help of a live section, you can view the cross-section of a model and create its section on a selected plane. The live section can be used to view and modify the cross-section of the 3D model easily. You can also create a live section on the non-revolved features. To do so, choose the **Live Section** tool from the **Section** group of the **Surfacing** tab; you will be prompted to select a plane. Click on a planar face or a reference plane; the steering wheel will be displayed on the plane, as shown in Figure 7-41. Use the primary axis of the steering wheel and move the plane to the cross-section at which you want to create a live section.

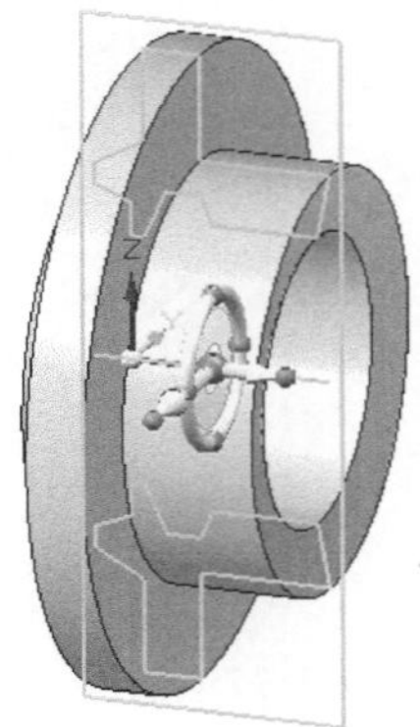

***Figure 7-41** Steering Wheel displayed on the reference plane*

You can edit the cross-section of the model by dimensioning the live section or by using the 2D steering wheel. While editing the live section, the current settings in the **Design Intent** panel are used to control the behavior of the model.

MODIFYING THE MODEL BY DETACHING AND ATTACHING FACES OR FEATURES

You can modify the Synchronous models by detaching the selected faces or features from the model and then reattaching the detached faces or features to the model.

Detaching Faces or Features

The **Detach** tool is used to remove the selected faces or features from the model, without actually deleting them. Figure 7-42 shows a feature selected to be detached. To detach a feature, select it from the **PathFinder** and right-click; a shortcut menu will be displayed. Choose **Detach** from the shortcut menu; the selected feature will be hidden in the graphics window. Also, the feature will get blurred in the **PathFinder** and a cleared check box will be displayed in front of the node of the corresponding feature. After the selected feature is detached, the adjacent faces of the detached feature will be modified in the solid model, as shown in Figure 7-43. However, on selecting the check box in front of the node of the feature, the detached profile of the feature will be displayed again at its original location.

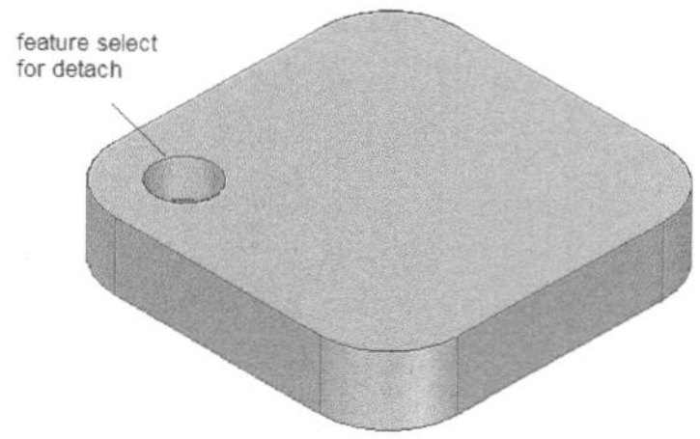

Figure 7-42 *Model before detaching the round*

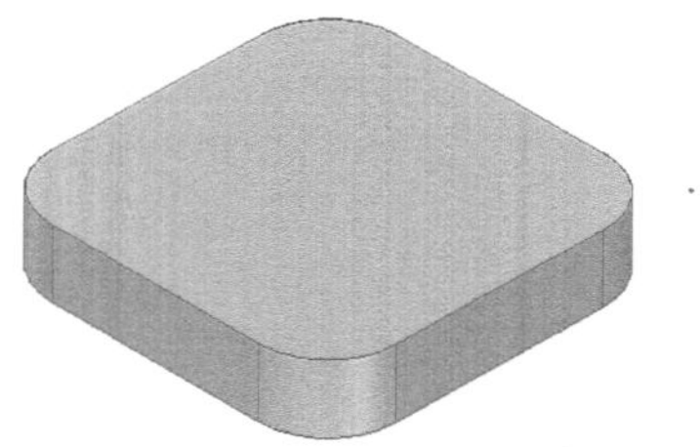

Figure 7-43 *Model after detaching the round*

Attaching Faces or Features

The **Attach** tool is used to attach the detached faces or features to the model. To do so, right-click on the detached feature in the **PathFinder**; a shortcut menu will be displayed. Choose **Attach** from the shortcut menu; the feature will get reattached to the model at the same location.

You can also reposition the detached feature using the steering wheel and then attach it at a new location. To do so, select a feature; a steering wheel and a Command bar will be displayed. Choose the **Detach faces** button from the Command bar to detach the selected feature from the model. You can choose the **Copy** button from the Command bar, if you want to create a copy of the detached feature. Next, move the detached feature to a new location, as shown in Figure 7-44, using the steering wheel. On doing so, a profile of the detached feature will be created at the new location and a selected check box will be displayed in front of the detached feature in the **PathFinder**. On clearing the check box, the profile will be hidden. In order to reattach the feature at a new location, select the feature from the **PathFinder** and right-click; a shortcut menu will be displayed. Choose **Attach** from the shortcut menu; the feature will be attached at a new location. Figure 7-44 shows the detached hole being moved to a new location. Notice that the detached feature is copied to the new location and its profile is created at the new location.

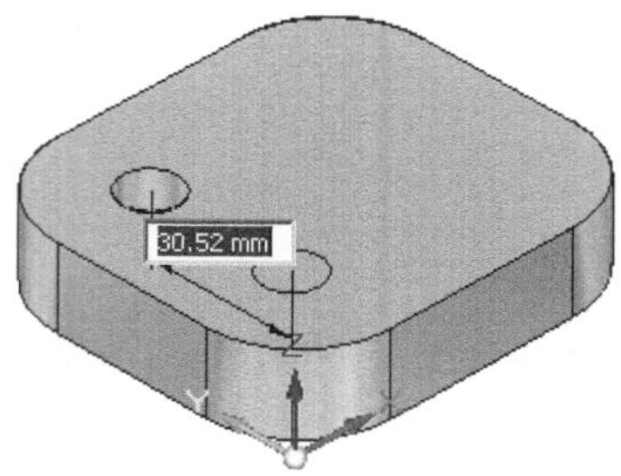

Figure 7-44 *The detached feature being moved to a new location*

MODIFYING THE MODEL BY ISOLATING FEATURES

You can isolate a selected feature from the model, so that you can edit it individually. You can do so by using the **Break** or **Separate** option. This option becomes available in the shortcut menu when you select a set of features like Hole, Rectangular or circular pattern, or Pattern along curve and then right-click.

When you create a pattern of a feature, all features in thepattern are displayed as a set in a node in the **PathFinder**. Now if you modify a single feature, all features will be modified simultaneously. But to edit them individually, you need to separate or break the features from the set.

Separating Features from the Set

If you create multiple holes using the **Hole** tool and then edit the diameter of a single hole, the diameter of all holes will be modified. To edit the diameter of an individual hole, you need to separate that hole from the set of multiple holes. You can use the **Separate** Command to separate a feature (hole) from the feature set and edit it separately. To do so, select the required hole and right-click; a shortcut menu will be displayed. Choose the **Separate** option from the shortcut menu, as shown in Figure 7-45; the selected hole will be placed in a separate node. Now, you can edit the parameters of this hole individually.

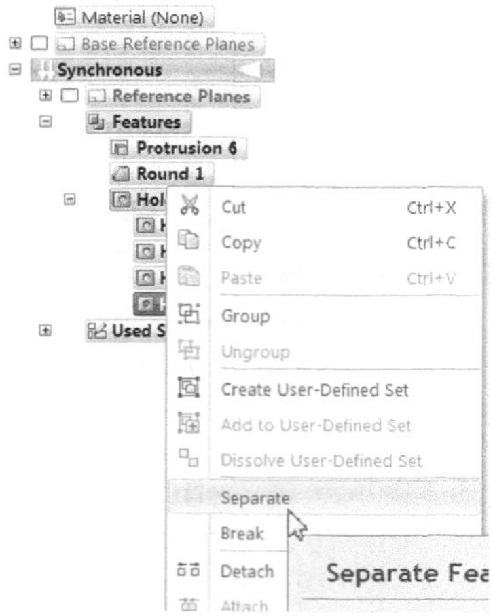

*Figure 7-45 The **Separate** option chosen from the shortcut menu*

Breaking Features from the Set

Sometimes, you need to edit features that are part of a rectangular or a circular pattern individually. To do so, select the required instances and right-click. Then, choose the **Break** option from the shortcut menu displayed; a new **Face Set** node will be created in the **PathFinder**. In this way, you can break as many instances as you want and create various face sets. Next, separate the parent feature. Now, if you modify the individual instance of a face set, the modifications will occur in all instances of the related face set.

EDITING FEATURES IN THE ORDERED ENVIRONMENT

To edit features in the ordered environment of Solid Edge, select a feature from the **PathFinder** or from the drawing window; the **Select** Command bar will be displayed with three options: **Edit Definition**, **Edit Profile**, and **Dynamic Edit**. Alternatively, you can choose these options from the shortcut menu that is displayed when you right-click on a feature. These options are used to edit the features and are discussed next.

Edit Definition

To edit the parameters of a feature, select the feature from the **PathFinder** or from the graphics area and then choose the **Edit Definition** tool from the **Select** Command bar. On selecting the feature and invoking this editing tool, the Command bar of the tool that was used to create that feature will be displayed with all the steps. For example, if you select an protrusion feature and choose the **Edit Definition** button, the **Extrude** Command bar will be displayed with the steps required for creating the extrusion feature. Also, the basic profile of the extrusion feature will be displayed in the model.

Now, you can choose the required step from the Command bar and modify the parameters of the feature as per your requirement. For example, if you want to change the plane on which the profile is drawn, choose the **Sketch Step** button from the Command bar and then select a reference plane or a planar face to place the profile. On doing so, the **Solid Edge** message box will be displayed; informing that the profile is placed on new plane and some of the relationship may be lost. Choose **OK** from this message box to continue to change the plane of the profile.

Edit Profile

The **Edit Profile** tool is used to directly invoke the sketching environment to edit the profile of a profile-based feature. You can choose this option from the shortcut menu that is displayed when you right-click on the feature. Note that this button will not be available for a non profile-based feature such as a fillet or a chamfer. After editing the profile, exit the sketching environment; the Command bar of the tool that was used to create the profile-based feature will be displayed. Note that the changes made in the profile are reflected in the model. Exit this Command bar.

Dynamic Edit

When you choose the **Dynamic Edit** tool, all dimensions of the selected feature will be displayed. You can select any dimension and modify its value using the Command bar options. In case, there are entities that have not been dimensioned, press and hold the left mouse button on such entities and then drag the cursor to dynamically edit the feature. Figure 7-46 shows a model being dynamically edited by dragging the entities and Figure 7-47 shows the same model after dynamically editing the sketch of the model.

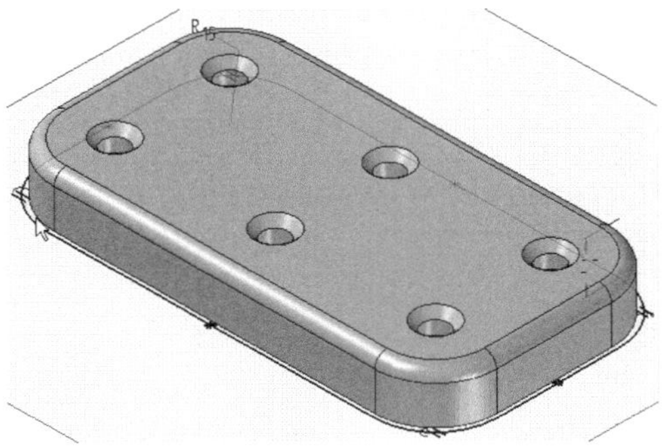

Figure 7-46 *Dynamically editing the model by dragging the sketch*

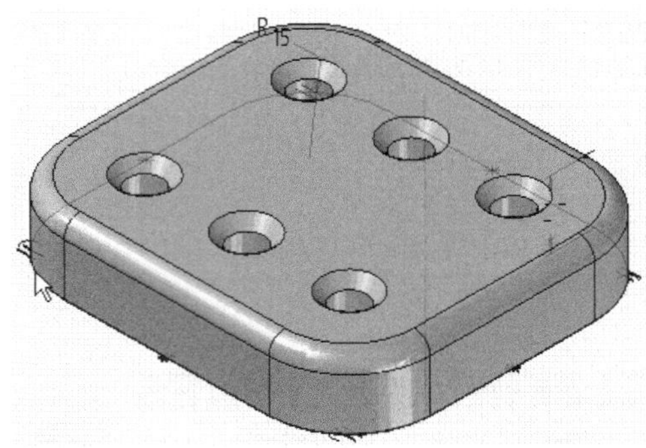

Figure 7-47 *The model after dynamically editing its profile*

Tip

1. You can edit the profile of a profile-based feature dynamically by dragging it. If you want to turn off the option of dynamic editing of profiles by dragging, choose the ***Application Button*** *from the top left corner of the screen; a flyout will be displayed. Choose* ***Options*** *from the* ***Settings*** *tab to invoke the* ***Solid Edge Options*** *dialog box. Next, choose the* ***General*** *tab, and then clear the* ***Enable Dynamic Edit of profiles/sketches*** *check box in this tab.*

2. If you select the ***Recompute after edit*** *radio button in this tab, the model will be regenerated after the dragging is completed. By default, the model is recomputed as you drag the cursor to edit the profile.*

Note

Sometimes, if a feature of a model is not updated after editing the selected feature, an arrow or an exclamation mark is displayed on the left of the dependent features in the ***PathFinder****. You may also need to edit this feature to make sure that the model is error free.*

SUPPRESSING FEATURES

Sometimes, there may be a situation when you do not want some of the features to be displayed in the drawing views or in the printout of the model. In the **Ordered Part** environment, you can simply suppress the feature that you do not want at a particular stage. Once the feature is suppressed, it will not be displayed in the drawing window, drawing views of that model, or in the printout of the model. Remember that in such cases, the features are not deleted, they are only temporarily turned off.

In this process, all features that are dependent on the feature that you select to suppress are also suppressed. To suppress a feature, right-click on it in the **PathFinder**. Alternatively, select the feature that you need to suppress from the drawing area and right-click on it; a shortcut menu will be displayed. Choose **Suppress** from the shortcut menu. All the features that are suppressed will have a red circle icon with an inclined line on their left in the **PathFinder**. The features dependent on the suppressed feature will have a red exclamatory mark in the **PathFinder**.

UNSUPPRESSING THE SUPPRESSED FEATURES

To unsuppress a feature, right-click on the suppressed feature in the **PathFinder** and then choose **Unsuppress** from the shortcut menu; the selected feature will be displayed in the model again.

Tip

If you generate the drawing views of the model that has some suppressed features, the suppressed features will not be displayed in the views. However, as soon as you unsuppress the features, they will be displayed in the drawing views.

DELETING FEATURES

Select the feature to be deleted from the **PathFinder** or from the model in the drawing window and press the DELETE key; the selected feature will be deleted. You can also right-click on a feature and choose **Delete** from the shortcut menu to delete it.

COPYING AND PASTING FEATURES

In Solid Edge, you can copy and paste a feature from the current file to any other file or at some other location in the same file. Note that if you select a non profile-based feature to copy, you must select the parent feature also. For example, you cannot select a fillet feature alone to copy. You also need to select the parent feature to which the fillet will be applied.

To copy a feature, right-click on the feature in the **PathFinder** or in the drawing window and then choose **Copy** from the shortcut menu. You can also press the CTRL+C keys to copy the selected features. When copying a synchronous feature, make sure that the position of the steering wheel is at a point that coincides with the face to be attached. Also, the secondary axis should point upward. To paste the feature in another file, you need to open the file. Right-click in the drawing window to display the shortcut menu and then choose **Paste** from it; you will be prompted to select a planar face or a reference plane. Select the reference plane or the planar face on which you want to paste the feature; the preview of the profile of the selected feature will be attached to the cursor. Also, you will be prompted to click on a point where the feature will be pasted. You can paste multiple copies of the feature by specifying the points.

Figure 7-48 shows the plane selected for pasting the hole feature on a different planar face and Figure 7-49 shows the model after placing three copies of the selected hole feature.

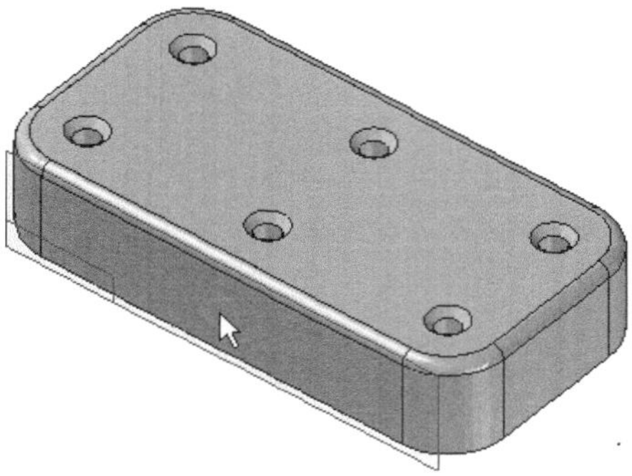

Figure 7-48 *Plane selected for pasting the hole feature*

Figure 7-49 *Three copies of the hole feature placed on the selected plane*

Note
*You cannot paste the cut feature in the **Synchronous Part** environment.*

ROLLING BACK A MODEL TO A FEATURE

Solid Edge enables you to roll back a model to a particular feature in such a way that all features created after the selected features are suppressed. Also, if you create a new feature in the rolled back state, it will be placed after the feature up to which the model is rolled back and before all the suppressed features. To roll back the model to a particular feature, select the feature in the **PathFinder** and right-click to display a shortcut menu. Choose **Go To** from the shortcut menu; the model will be rolled back to the selected feature. To retain the original state of the model, you need to select the last feature and choose **Go To** from the shortcut menu. On doing so, all features of the model will be unsuppressed and the model will regain its original state.

CONVERTING ORDERED FEATURES TO SYNCHRONOUS

In Solid Edge, you can convert the ordered features to synchronous features. In order to do so, right-click on an ordered feature in the **PathFinder**; a shortcut menu will be displayed. Choose the **Move to Synchronous** option from the shortcut menu, refer to Figure 7-50. Note that the ordered features can be converted to synchronous features only when you are working in the **Ordered Part** environment. The conversion will start from the top-level of the model. For example, if you are converting a feature created on the base feature of the model, first the base feature will be converted and then the selected feature.

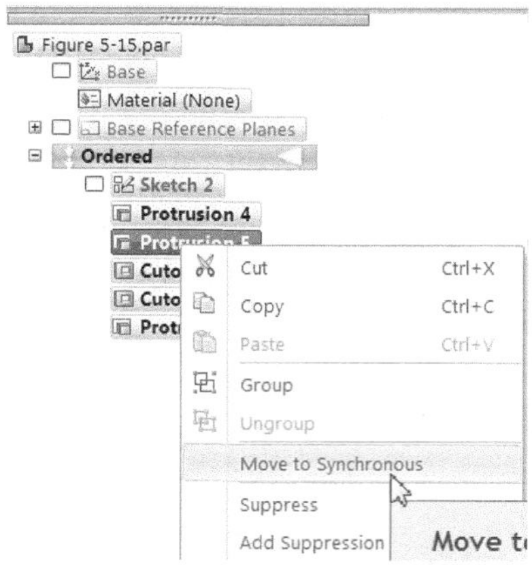

*Figure 7-50 The **Move to Synchronous** option chosen from the shortcut menu*

Note

Ordered features can be converted into synchronous features. But, the synchronous features cannot be converted into ordered features.

ASSIGNING COLOR TO A PART, FEATURE, OR FACE

Ribbon: View > Style > Part Painter

Sometimes, you may need to represent a face or a feature of a model differently from others for presentation. In Solid Edge, you can do so by assigning a different color to the selected face or feature. The remaining features will have the color of the model, but the selected face or feature can be assigned a different color.

To assign a different color to a face, choose the **Part Painter** tool from the **Style** group of the **View** tab; the **Part Painter** Command bar will be displayed. From the **Select** drop-down list in the Command bar, select the required option for the selection of the item from the model. Now, from the **Style** drop-down list, select the color that you want to assign to the selected item. Next, select the item in the model; the selected item will be assigned the specified color.

Note

*The **Part Painter** tool will be available only when the **Use individual part styles** radio button is selected in the **Color Manager** dialog box. The **Color Manager** dialog box will be displayed when you choose the **Color Manager** button from the **Style** group of the **View** tab.*

PLAYING BACK THE CONSTRUCTION OF FEATURES

In Solid Edge, you can view the animation of the sequence of the feature construction by using the **Feature Playback** tab of the docking window. If this tab is not displayed in the docking window, choose the **Feature Playback** option from the **Panes** drop-down list of the **Show** group from the **View** Tab; the features and animation features will be displayed in the docking window. To view the animation of the feature construction of the model, you can choose the **Play** button available at the bottom of the docking window. All features in the model will be replayed in the sequence in which they were created. You can use other control buttons to control the playback of features. You can also modify the time gap between the playback of the features by entering the required value in the **seconds between features** edit box available in this tab. After playing back the features of the model, you can directly close the docking window.

Note

*The **Feature Playback** tool is only available in the **Ordered** environment.*

MODIFYING FACES IN THE ORDERED ENVIRONMENT

SolidEdge provides a set of tools to modify the faces of a 3D geometry in the **Ordered** environment. These tools are available in the **Modify faces** drop-down of the **Modify** group. You can move, rotate, or offset faces using these tools.

Moving Faces

Ribbon:	Home > Modify > Move Faces drop-down > Move Faces

To move faces of a 3D geometry in the ordered environment, choose the **Move Faces** tool from the **Modify** panel; the **Move Faces** Command bar will be displayed. Select a face and right-click to accept the selection. Next, move the cursor in the direction normal to the selected face and specify the distance in the **Distance** edit box of the Command bar and left-click; the face will be moved upto the specified distance.

Rotating Faces

Ribbon:	Home > Modify > Move Faces drop-down > Rotate Faces

To rotate faces of a 3D geometry in the ordered environment, choose the **Rotate Faces** tool from the **Modify** panel; the **Rotate Faces** Command bar will be displayed. Select the face to be rotated and right-click. Next, you need to define the axis of rotation. You can use the **Movement Type** drop-down list to define the rotation axis. If you select the **By Geometry** option from this drop-down list, you need to select an edge to define the rotation axis, as shown in Figure 7-51. If you select the **By Points** option, the rotation axis can be defined by selecting two points, as shown in Figure 7-51. After defining the rotation axis, specify the angle of rotation in the **Angle** edit box.

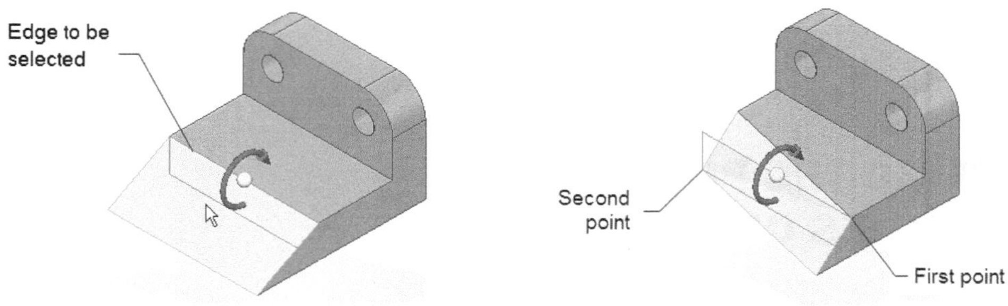

Figure 7-51 *Rotation axes defined using the **By Geometry** and **By Points** options*

Offsetting Faces

Ribbon: Home > Modify > Move Faces drop-down > Offset Faces

To offset faces of a 3D geometry in the ordered environment, choose the **Offset Faces** tool from the **Modify** panel; the **Offset Faces** Command bar will be displayed. Select the faces to be offset and right-click to accept the selection; the direction arrow will be displayed on the selected faces. Click to specify the offset direction. Next, specify the offset distance in the **Distance** edit box; the selected faces will be offset, as shown in Figure 7-52. Choose the **Finish** button on the Command bar to exit.

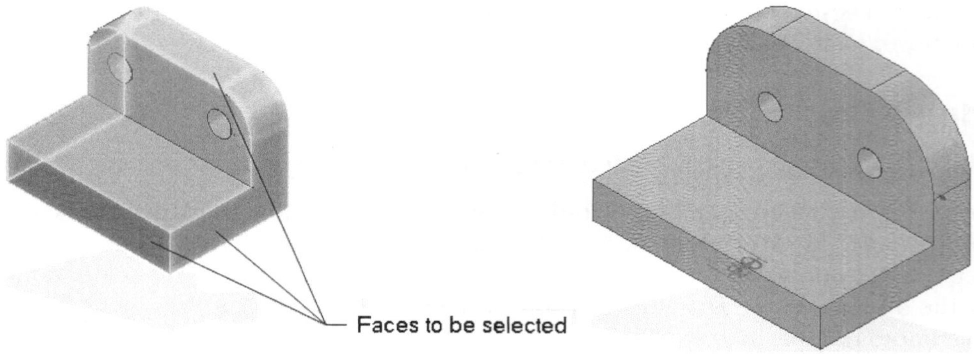

Figure 7-52 Offsetting Faces using the ***Offset Faces*** *tool*

COPYING SKETCH OBJECTS TO ANOTHER SKETCH

Ribbon: Home > Sketch > Tear Off

In Ordered environment, you can copy sketch entities from an already existing sketch to a new sketching plane using the **Tear Off** tool. On invoking this tool, the **Tear Off** Command bar will be displayed. Next, define the sketching plane of a new sketch; you will be prompted to select the sketch entities to be copied. Select the entities and right-click; the selected entities will be copied to the new sketching plane, as shown in Figure 7-53. Choose the **Finish** and **Cancel** buttons to close the Command bar.

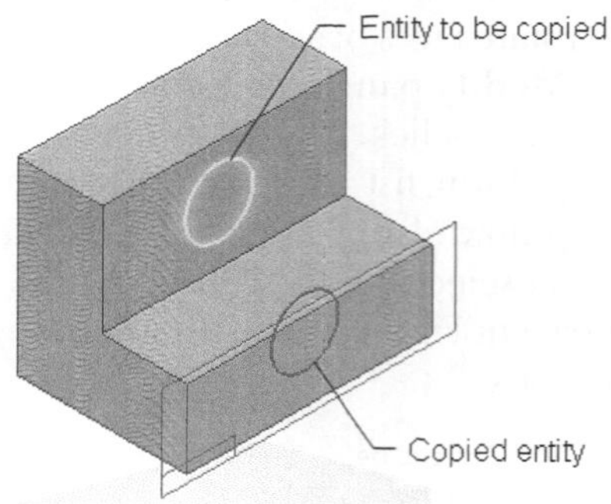

Figure 7-53 Sketch entity copied using the ***Tear Off*** *tool*

CHECKING THE PHYSICAL PROPERTIES OF A MODEL

Ribbon: Inspect > Physical Properties > Properties

Checking the physical properties of a model and storing them for further use is an integral part of any designing process. To check the physical properties of a model in Solid Edge, choose the **Properties** button from the **Physical Properties** group of the **Inspect** tab; the **Physical Properties** dialog box will be displayed, as shown in Figure 7-54.

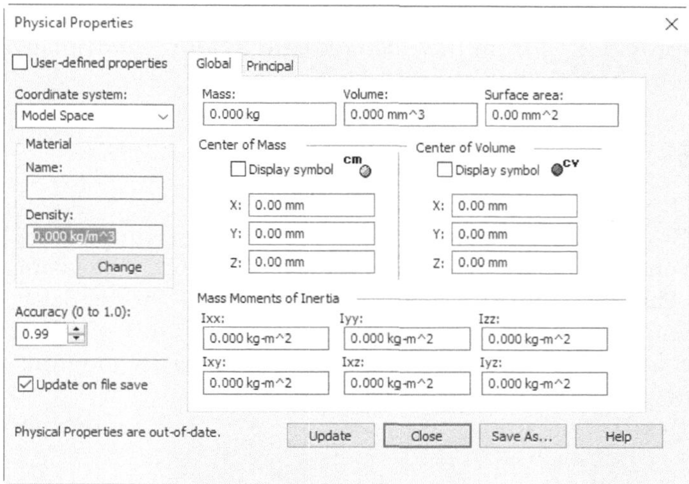

Figure 7-54 *The* ***Physical Properties*** *dialog box*

As is evident from this dialog box, the default density of the material is taken as 0.000 kg/m ^ 3. To specify the density of the required material, choose the **Change** button; the **Solid Edge Material Table** dialog box will be displayed. You can choose the required material and also you can change the value of the required parameters in this dialog box. Next, choose the **Apply to Model** button and then the **Update** button; the physical properties of the model will be modified. The modified properties will be displayed in the **Global** and **Principal** tabs. You can also save the physical properties as text files by choosing the **Save As** button in Solid Edge.

MODIFYING THE DISPLAY OF CONSTRUCTION ENTITIES

Ribbon: View > Show > Construction Display

Solid Edge allows you to show or hide all construction entities together through the **Show All/Hide All** dialog box, as shown in Figure 7-55. To invoke this dialog box, choose the **Construction Display** option from the **Show** group of the **View** tab.

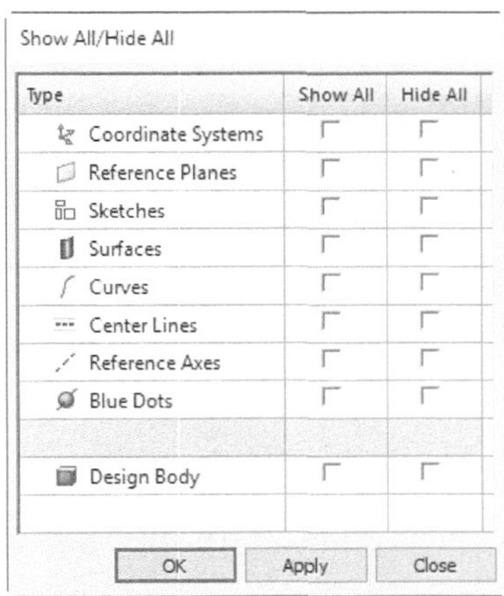

Figure 7-55 *The* ***Show All/Hide All*** *dialog box*

You can choose the required check box in the **Show All** column or in the **Hide All** column, and then choose the **Apply** button from the dialog box to modify the display of the construction entities based on your requirement.

TUTORIALS

Tutorial 1 Synchronous

In this tutorial, you will create the model shown in Figure 7-56 using various tools of the **Synchronous Part** environment. The extrude depth of the model is 50mm and other dimensions of the model are given for your reference in Figure 7-57. Then, you will create a taper of 60 degrees at the base, as shown in Figure 7-58. After creating the model, save it with the name *c07tut1.par* at the location given next:

C:\Solid Edge\c07 **(Expected time: 45 min)**

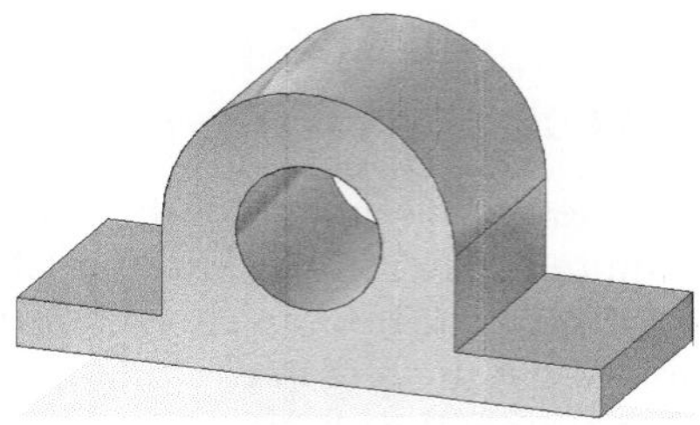

Figure 7-56 *The model for Tutorial 1*

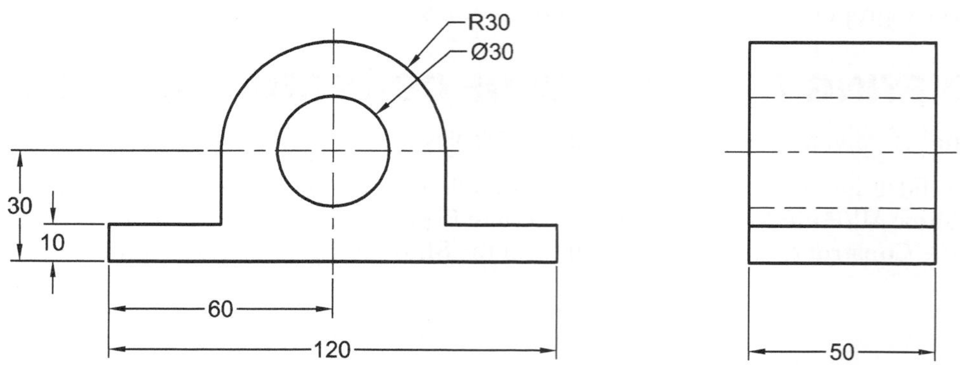

Figure 7-57 *Dimensions of the model*

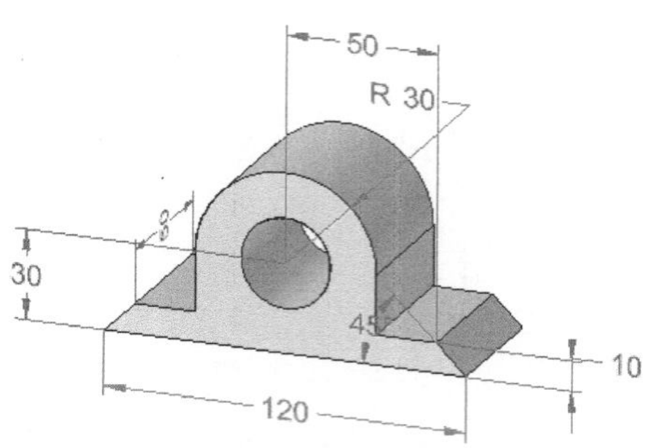

Figure 7-58 *The final model*

The following steps are required to complete this tutorial:

a. Create the base sketch on the front plane, refer to Figure 7-59.
b. Create the base feature, refer to Figure 7-60.
c. Create the sketch for second feature, refer to Figure 7-61.
d. Align the front face of the second feature with the front face of the base feature, refer to Figure 7-62.
e Center align the second feature, refer to Figures 7-63 and 7-64.
f. Create the hole feature, refer to Figure 7-65.
g. Create the taper feature, refer to Figures 7-67 through 7-68.
h. Save the model.

Creating the Base Profile

1. Start a new Solid Edge part file.

2. Choose the **Rectangle by Center** tool from the **Draw** group of the **Sketching** tab; the **Rectangle by Center** Command bar is displayed and the alignment lines are attached to the cursor.

3. Next, you need to define the plane on which you want to draw the profile of the base feature. To do so, select the **Base Reference Planes** check box in the **PathFinder** to display the base reference planes. Next, move the cursor on the XZ plane for sketching and then click on the lock symbol.

   The view orientation of the part document is set to **Dimetric** by default. Choose **Sketch View** from the status bar to view the horizontal and vertical settings properly.

4. Draw a rectangle on the XZ plane; the rectangle gets shaded. This indicates that it is a closed region.

5. Press the ESC key to exit the **Rectangle by Center** tool.

   Note that you can first create a fully-defined sketch and then convert it into a model. However, for this tutorial, you will not dimension the sketch but the feature only. So, you need to proceed without dimensioning the sketch.

Creating the Base Feature

Next, you will create the extruded feature dynamically using the rectangle created in the previous step.

1. Choose the **Select** tool and click inside the rectangle; the Extrude handle is displayed, as shown in Figure 7-59.

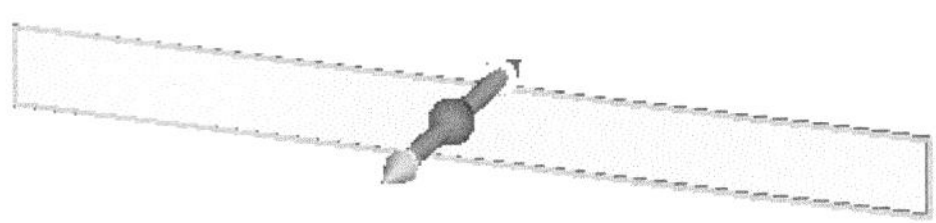

Figure 7-59 *Extrude handle displayed on selecting the rectangle*

2. Click on the Extrude handle and drag the cursor in the drawing window; the preview of extrusion and an edit box are displayed in the drawing window.

3. Make sure that the **Symmetric** button from the **Extrude** Command bar is not activated. Next, click in the drawing window after extruding to a considerable distance; the extruded feature is created.

4. Dimension the length, width, and height of the extruded feature by using the **Smart Dimension** tool from the **Dimension** group and exit the **Smart Dimension** tool.

5. Click on the dimension value of length; the **Dimension value** edit box is displayed. Enter **120** in it.

6. Similarly, modify the height and width of the extruded feature to **10** and **50**, respectively, as shown in Figure 7-60.

Creating the Second Feature

1. Create the profile for the second feature, as shown in Figure 7-61. It is displayed in blue color.

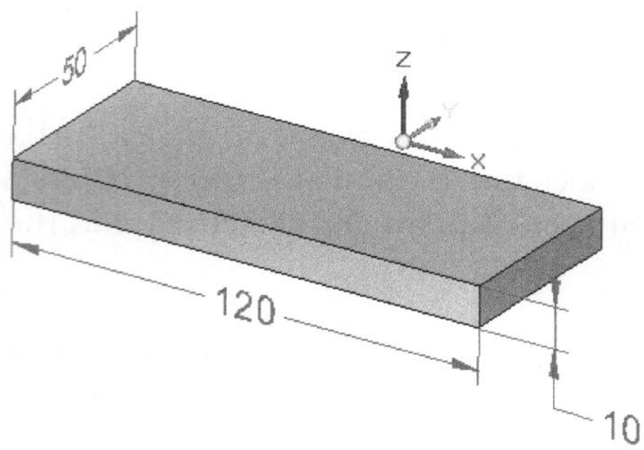

Figure 7-60 *Model after modifying the dimensions*

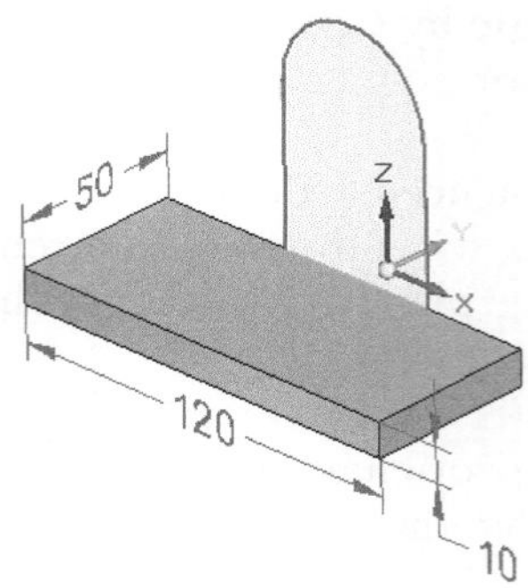

Figure 7-61 *Model after creating the profile for the second feature*

2. Invoke the **Select** tool and then click inside the closed region; an Extrude handle is displayed.

3. Click on the Extrude handle; the **Extrude** Command bar is displayed. Deactivate the **Symmetric** button on the Command bar and drag the handle toward the front to a suitable distance. The feature does not need to be aligned to the front face because later on you will need to apply the relationship between the faces.

4. Click at a point in the graphics area; the second feature is created.

   Next, you need to tangentially connect the curved face and the planar face of the second feature.

5. Invoke the **Tangent** tool from the **Face Relate** group; the **Tangent** Command bar is displayed and you are prompted to select an element from the model. Select the planar face on the right-side of the second feature and choose the **Accept** button; you are prompted to click on the element to position the selection.

6. Select the top curved face of the second feature and choose the **Accept** button from the Command bar; the tangent relation is applied between the selected faces.

7. Similarly, apply the tangent relationship between the curved face and the planar face on the left side of the second feature.

Aligning the Face of the Second Feature with the Face of the Base Feature

In this section, you need to align the front face of the base feature with the front face of the second feature.

1. Invoke the **Coplanar** tool from the **Face Relate** group; a Command bar is displayed and you are prompted to select the face on which you want to apply the relation.

2. Select the front face of the second feature and choose the **Accept** button in the Command bar.

3. Next, select the front face of the base feature, refer to Figure 7-62; the selected face of the second feature coincides with the selected face of the base feature.

4. Choose the **Accept** button from the Command bar.

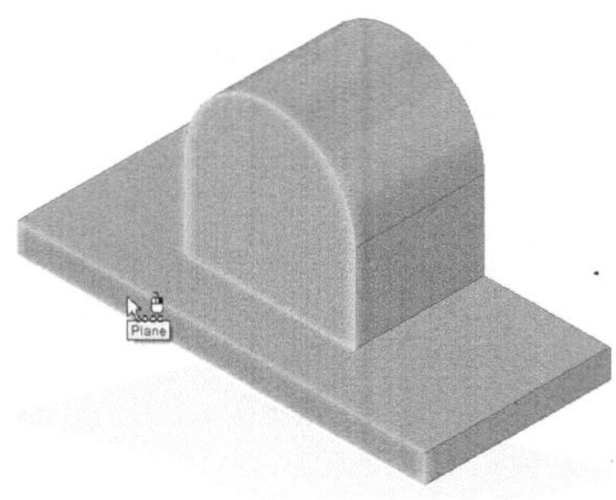

Figure 7-62 *Aligning the faces*

Aligning the Second Feature to the Center

Next, you need to align the second feature to the center.

1. Choose the **Smart Dimension** tool from the **Dimension** group. Next, dimension the distance between the center point of the second feature and the right edge of the first feature. Next, exit the active tool.

2. Click on the dimension text; the **Dimension Value** edit handle is displayed, as shown in Figure 7-63. Enter **60** in the **Value** edit box.

3. Choose the **Left** direction control button from the **Dimension Value** edit handle to move the second feature in the left direction and then right-click to update the dimension.

4. Similarly, dimension the radius of the second feature and modify it to **30**. Also, modify the height between the center of the arc of the second feature and the base to **30**. The final model after adding dimensions is shown in Figure 7-64.

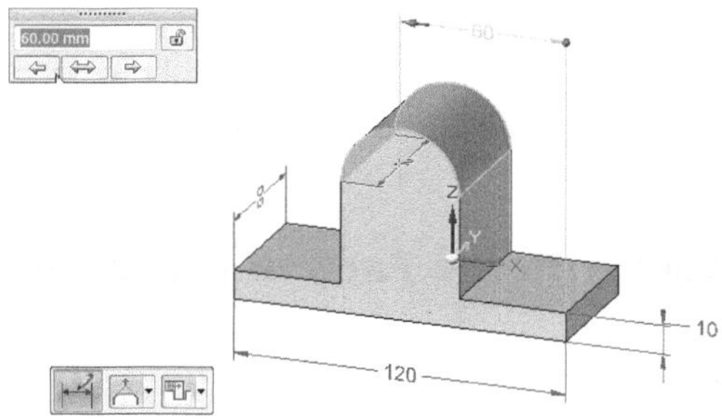

*Figure 7-63 The **Dimension value** edit handle*

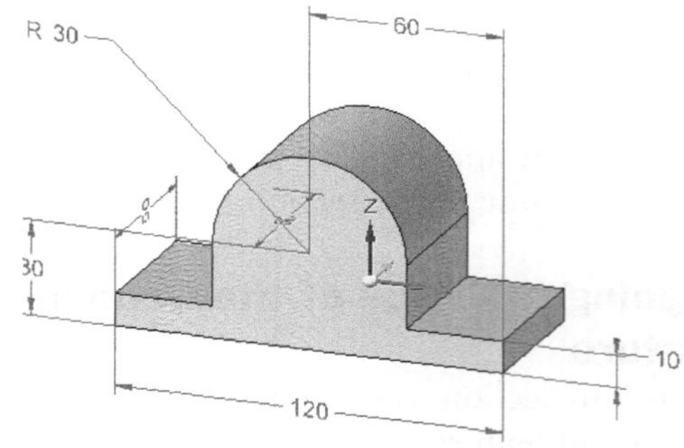

Figure 7-64 Model after adding dimensions

Creating the Hole Feature

1. Choose the **Hole** tool from the **Solids** group of the **Home** tab; a transparent hole with default settings is attached to the cursor.

2. Place the hole on the front face of the second feature and press the ESC key; the hole is created and an Edit Definition handle along with the hole diameter is displayed.

   Now, you need to edit its dimensions and then make it concentric to the arc of the second feature.

3. Click on the hole diameter text; the **Edit Definition** box is displayed with the default dimension of the hole, as shown in Figure 7-65. Enter **30** in the **Diameter** edit box of the **Edit Definition** box and press the ESC key.

4. Choose the **Concentric** tool from the **Face Relate** group of the **Home** tab and then select the hole. Choose the **Accept** button from the Command bar; you are prompted to select another face that you need to align with the hole.

5. Select the top circular face of the second feature, as shown in Figure 7-66. Next, choose the **Accept** button from the Command bar to accept the selection. On doing so, the hole feature is created based on the dimension specified and it is concentric to the second feature.

Creating the Taper Face

1. Select the vertical face on the right of the base feature; the move handle and a Command bar are displayed.

2. Click on the origin knob of the move handle to activate the steering wheel, and move the steering wheel towards the bottom edge of the face, and then release the origin knob, refer to Figure 7-67.

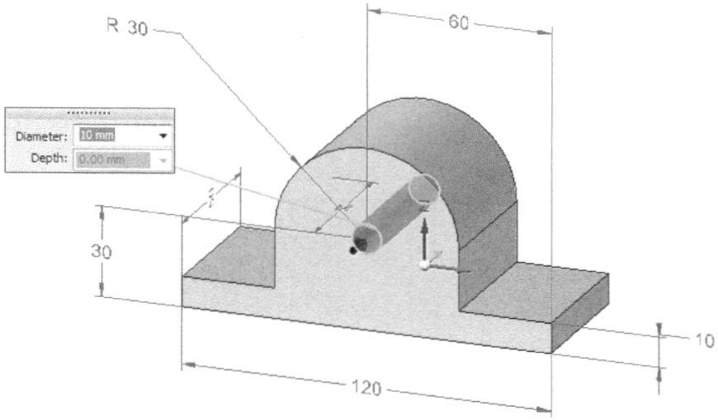

*Figure 7-65 The **Edit Definition** box displayed after clicking on the hole*

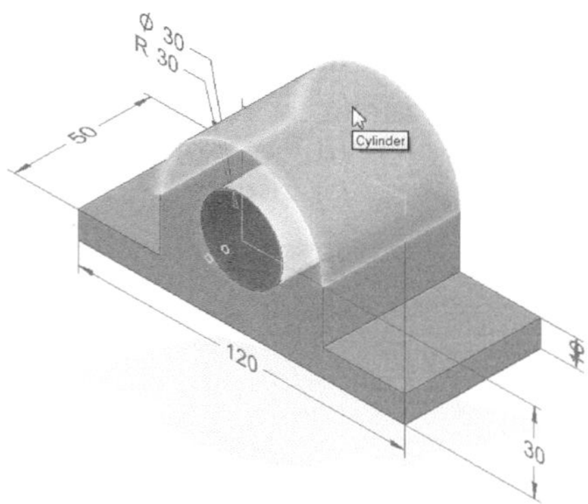

Figure 7-66 Applying the concentric relationship

3. Click on the Torus of the steering wheel; the preview of the taper with an edit box is displayed in the drawing window. Specify **45** as the taper angle by entering this value in the edit box; the taper is created. Note that the same modification will occur at the opposite side of the base feature. This is because the sketch of the base feature is created by using the **Rectangle by Center** tool at the origin.

4. Final model after providing the taper angle is shown in Figure 7-68.

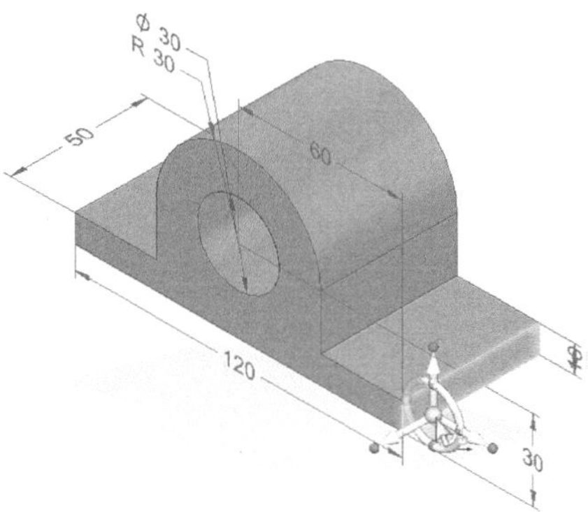

Figure 7-67 Rotating the face

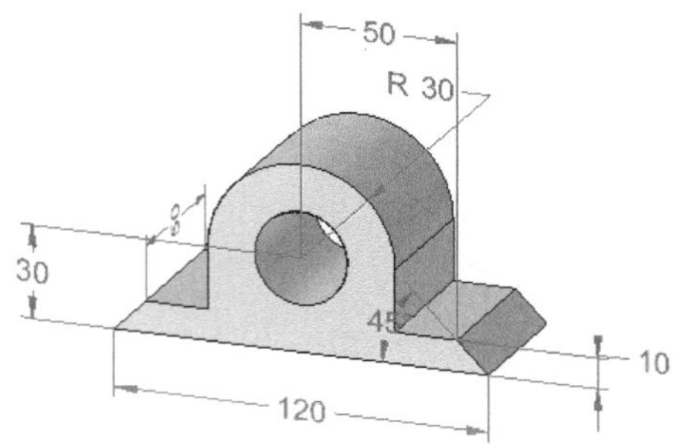

Figure 7-68 The final model

Saving the Model

1. Save the model with the name *c07tut1.par* at the location given next and close the file.
   C:\Solid Edge\c07

Tutorial 2 Ordered

In this tutorial, you will create the model shown in Figure 7-69. Its dimensions are given in the drawing views shown in Figure 7-70. After creating the model, you will modify the central hole in the cylindrical feature into a counterbore hole. The counterbore diameter should be 36 units and the hole diameter should be 24 units. The counterbore depth should be 10 units.

Also, you will change the holes on the top planar face of the model to countersink holes with the countersink diameter as 14 units and the hole diameter as 8 units. The countersink angle should be 82-degree. You will increase the number of occurrences along the shorter side to 3 units. Next, you will save the model with the name *c07tut2.par* at the location given next:

C:\Solid Edge\c07 **(Expected time: 30 min)**

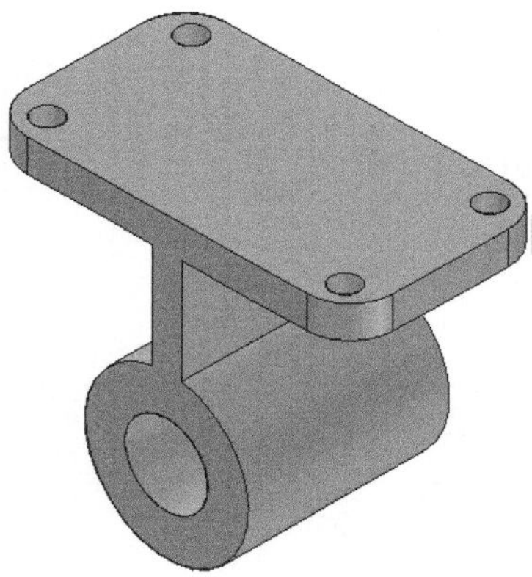

Figure 7-69 *Model for Tutorial 2*

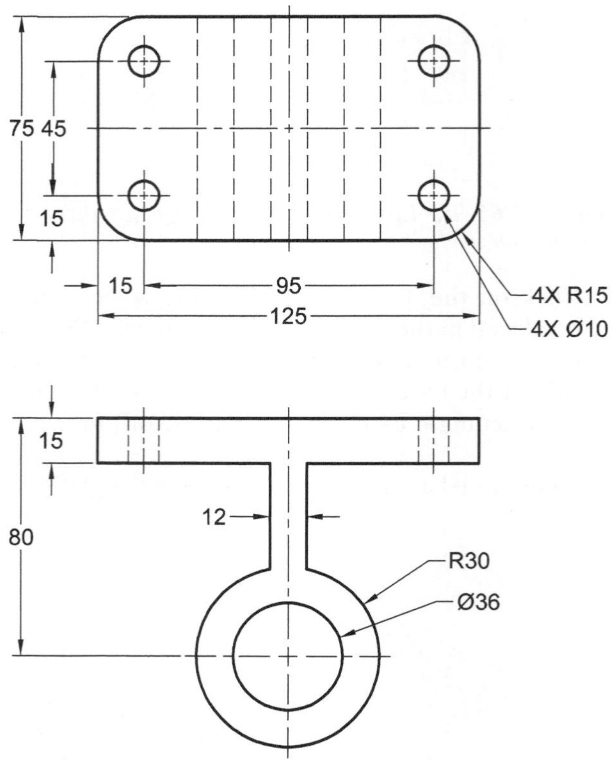

Figure 7-70 *Dimensions of the model for Tutorial 2*

The following steps are required to complete this tutorial:

a. Start Solid Edge in the **Ordered Part** environment and create the base feature on the front plane, refer to Figures 7-71 and 7-72.
b. Create a simple hole in the cylindrical feature of the model, refer to Figure 7-73.
c. Create the round features on the vertical edges of the top of the base feature, refer to Figure 7-74.
d. Create a simple hole on the top face of the base feature, refer to Figure 7-75.
e. Create a rectangular pattern of the holes on the top face of the base feature, refer to Figure 7-76.
f. Modify the central hole and the hole on the top face of the base feature.
g. Modify the number of items in the rectangular pattern of holes.
h. Save the model and close the file.

Creating the Base Feature

As mentioned earlier, the base feature is an extrusion feature and you need to create the profile of the base feature on the front plane. The profile thus created will be extruded symmetrically.

1. Start a new ISO part document and then switch to the **Ordered Part** environment.

2. Select the front plane as the sketching plane for the extrusion feature.

3. Draw the profile of the extrusion feature, as shown in Figure 7-71, and then add the required relationships and dimensions to the profile.

4. Exit the sketching environment and extrude the profile **75** mm symmetrically to create the base feature, as shown in Figure 7-72.

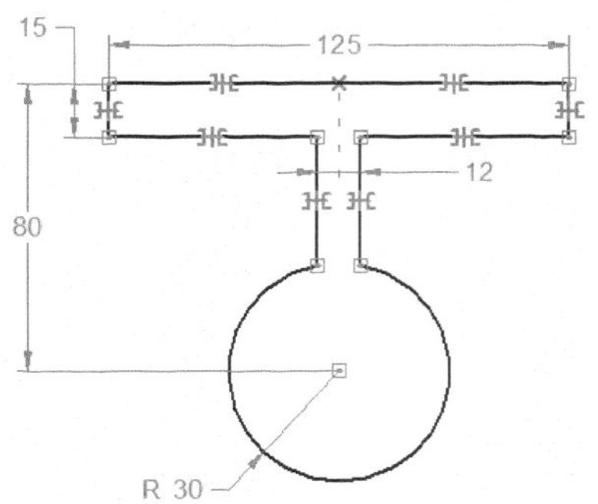

Figure 7-71 *Sketch of the base feature*

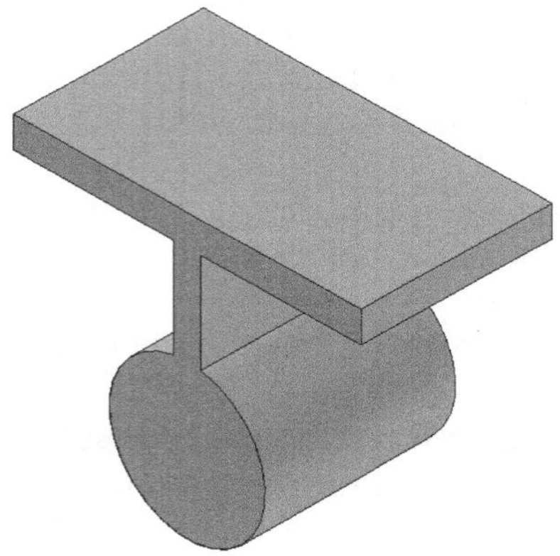

Figure 7-72 *Base feature of the model*

Creating a Simple Hole in the Cylindrical Feature

1. Invoke the **Hole** tool and then modify the diameter of the simple hole to **36** in the **Hole Options** dialog box. Make sure that **mm** is selected in the **Standard** drop-down list.

2. Select the front planar face of the base feature as the sketching plane and place the profile of the hole concentric to the cylindrical feature.

3. Exit the sketching environment and create the hole, as shown in Figure 7-73.

Creating the Round Feature

1. Invoke the **Round** tool and select the vertical edges on the top planar face of the base of the feature.

2. Specify the radius of the round as **15** mm in the **Round** Command bar and then exit the tool after completing the operation. The model after creating the round is shown in Figure 7-74.

Figure 7-73 Model after creating the central hole

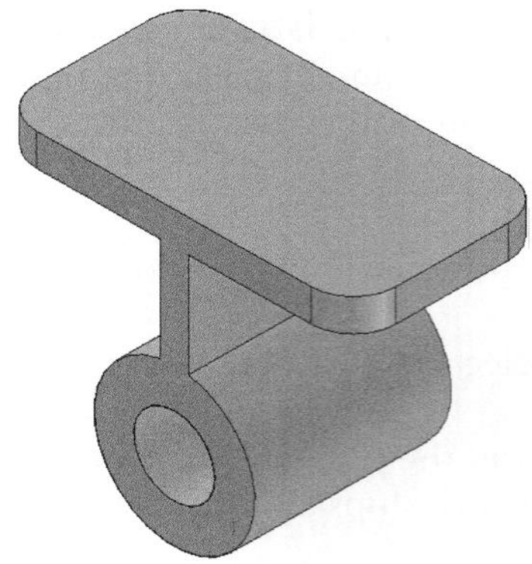

Figure 7-74 Model after creating the round

Creating a Simple Hole on the Top Face

1. Invoke the **Hole** tool from the **Solids** group and then modify the diameter of the simple hole to **10** in the **Hole Options** dialog box. Make sure that **mm** is selected in the **Standard** drop-down list.

2. Select the top planar face of the base feature as the sketching plane and then place the profile of the hole, concentric to the fillet on the upper left vertex.

3. Exit the sketching environment and create the hole, as shown in Figure 7-75.

Creating a Rectangular Pattern of the Hole

1. Invoke the **Pattern** tool from the **Pattern** group; the **Pattern** Command bar is invoked. Next, select the hole on the top planar face as the feature to pattern and choose the **Accept** button; the **Sketch Step** is activated.

2. Choose the **Coincident Plane** option from the **Create-From Options** drop-down list in the Command bar and then select the top planar face of the model; the sketching environment is invoked.

3. Choose the **Rectangular Pattern** button from the **Features** group, if it is not chosen by default; you are prompted to click for the first point. Specify a point by clicking on the center point of the hole; you are prompted to click for the second point.

4. Next, move the cursor toward the center point of the lower right fillet to specify the diagonal point of the rectangular profile. Specify **2** in the **X** and **Y** edit boxes in the Command bar. and exit the sketching environment; the pattern is created. Next, choose **Finish** to create a hole and exit the tool. The model after creating the pattern is shown in Figure 7-76.

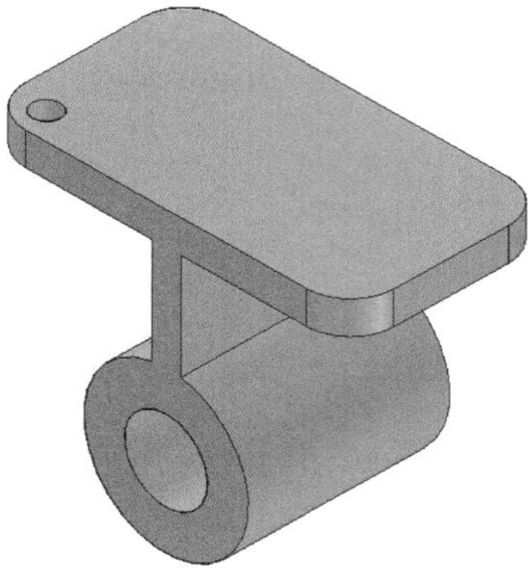

Figure 7-75 Model after creating a simple hole on the top plane

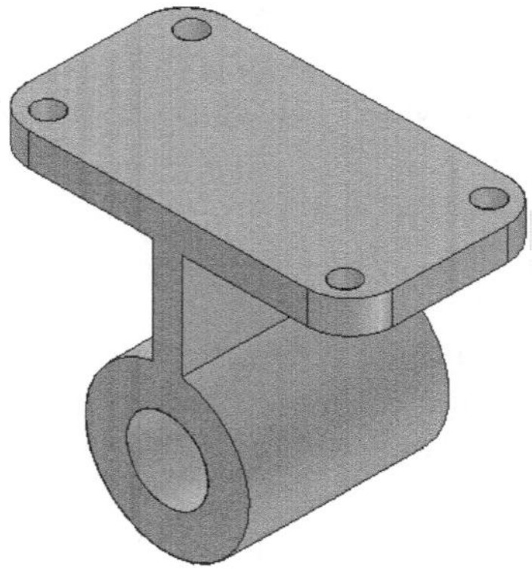

Figure 7-76 Model after patterning the hole

Modifying the Holes

As mentioned in the beginning of this tutorial, you need to modify the simple hole on the cylindrical feature to a counterbore hole and the simple hole on the top face to a countersink hole. Therefore, you need to edit both these holes. As the first hole was the central hole on the cylindrical feature, it will be displayed as **Hole 1** in the **PathFinder**.

1. Select **Hole 1** from the **PathFinder** and then choose the **Edit Definition** button from the **Select** Command bar to display the **Hole** Command bar. 

2. Choose the **Hole Options** button from the Command bar; the **Hole Options** dialog box is displayed. Choose the **Counterbore** button from the upper left corner of this dialog box.

3. Enter **24** in the **Hole Diameter** edit box, **36** in the **Counterbore diameter** edit box, and **10** in the **Counterbore depth** edit box and then choose **OK**; the preview of the counterbore hole along with its profile is displayed on the model.

4. Choose the **Finish** button to complete the modification in the hole.

5. Now, select **Hole 2** from the **PathFinder** and then choose the **Edit Definition** button from the Command bar to display the **Hole** Command bar.

6. Choose the **Hole Options** button from the Command bar and then choose **Countersink** button from the upper left corner of the **Hole Options** dialog box.

7. Enter **8** in the **Hole Diameter** edit box, **14** in the **Countersink diameter** edit box, **82** in the **Countersink angle** edit box and then choose **OK**; the preview of countersink hole along with its profile is displayed on the model.

8. Again, choose the **Finish** button to complete the modification in the hole.

   Note that the remaining three holes are also countersink holes and an arrow is displayed on the left of **Pattern 1** in the **PathFinder**. This arrow shows that the pattern feature is not recomputed properly and it needs to be edited. The model after making the changes in both the holes is shown in Figure 7-77.

Modifying the Pattern

Next, you need to edit the pattern of the holes by increasing the number of occurrences along the short side of the top face to **3**.

1. Click on **Pattern 1** in the **PathFinder** and then choose the **Edit Profile** button from the Command bar to invoke the sketching environment.

   It is recommended that you delete the original profile and create the profile of the rectangular pattern again. This is because, if you try to edit the existing profile, the arrow on the left of the pattern may still be displayed after editing the pattern.

2. Delete the existing profile of the rectangular pattern and then draw the profile again.

3. Specify **2** and **3** as the number of occurrences of the pattern along the X and Y directions respectively.

4. Exit the sketching environment and then choose **Finish** from the Command bar. The model after editing the required features is shown in Figure 7-78.

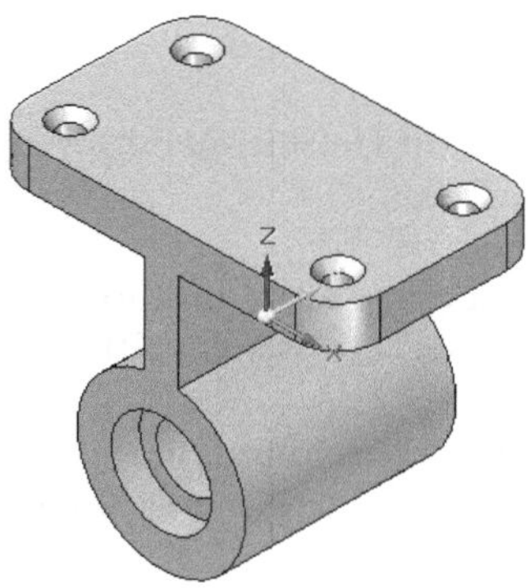

Figure 7-77 Model after editing the holes

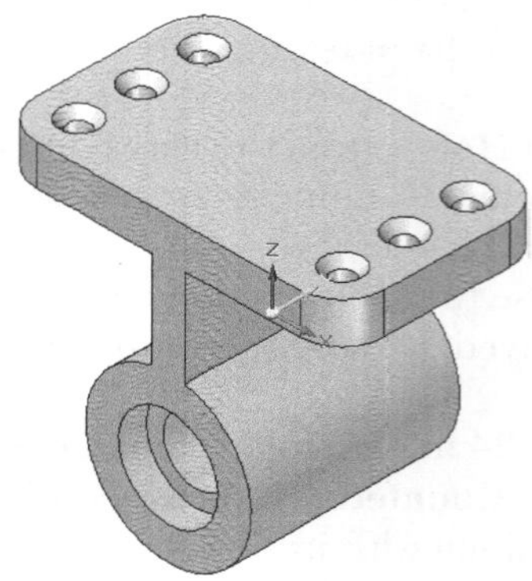

Figure 7-78 Final model after editing the pattern of holes

Saving the Model

1. Save the model with the name *c07tut2.par* at the location given next and then close it.
   C:\Solid Edge\c07

Tutorial 3 Ordered

In this tutorial, you will create the model shown in Figure 7-79. The dimensions of the model are given in the drawing views shown in Figure 7-80. In this model, you will create one of the holes by using the **Hole** tool and the remaining holes by copying and pasting the first hole. Next, you will save the model with the name *c07tut3.par* at the location given next:
C:\Solid Edge\c07 **(Expected time: 30 min)**

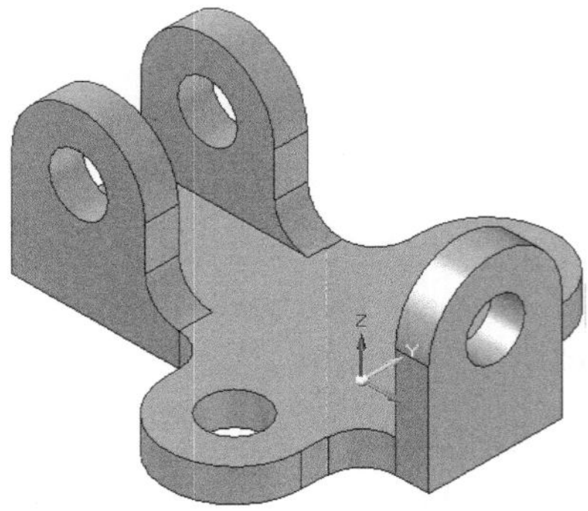

Figure 7-79 *Model for Tutorial 3*

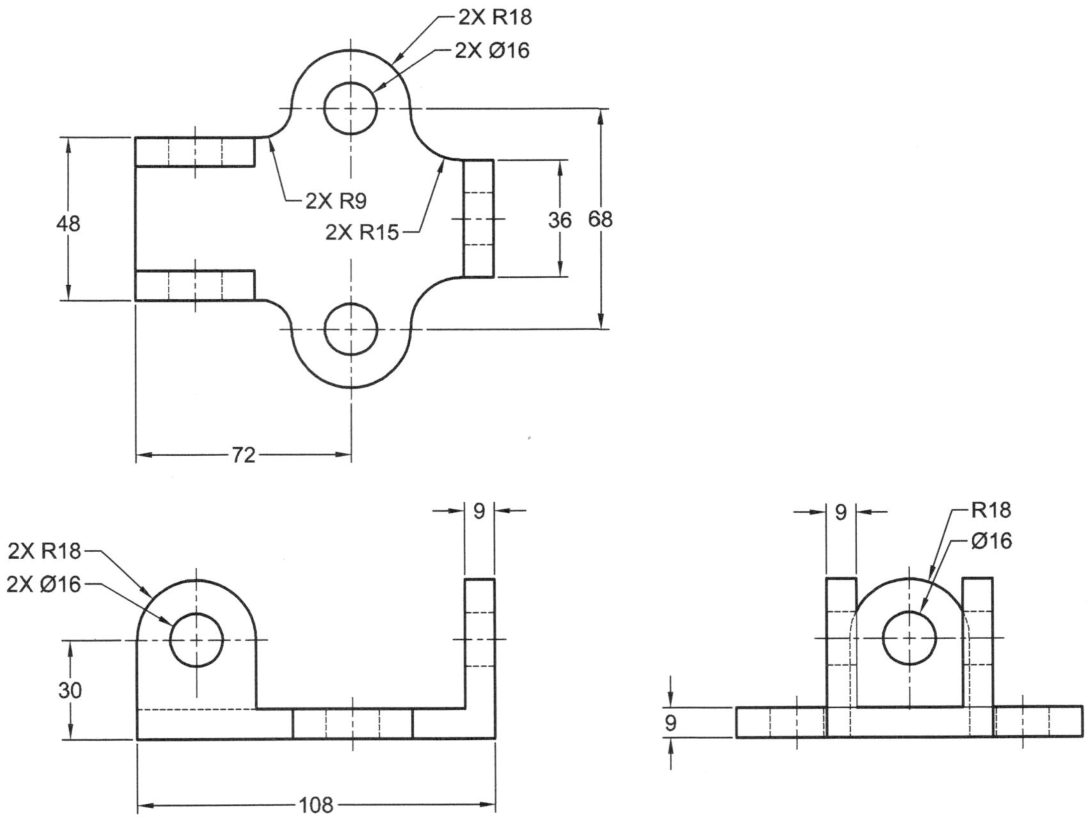

Figure 7-80 *Dimensions of the model for Tutorial 3*

The following steps are required to complete this tutorial:

a. Create the base feature on the top plane, refer to Figures 7-81 and 7-82.
b. Add extruded features and round features to the model, refer to Figures 7-83 and 7-84.
c. Create a simple hole on one of the faces of the model, refer to Figure 7-85.
d. Copy and paste hole on the other faces, refer to Figures 7-86 and 7-87.
e. Edit the profiles of the copied holes and make them concentric to the arc on the faces of the model, refer to Figure 7-88.

f. Save the model and close the file.

Creating the Base Feature

As mentioned earlier, the base feature is an extrusion feature. You need to create its profile on the top plane.

1. Start a new part file in the **Ordered Part** environment and then select the top plane as the sketching plane for the extrusion feature.

2. Create the profile of the base feature, as shown in Figure 7-81, and then extrude the profile to 9 units. The base feature of the model is created, as shown in Figure 7-82.

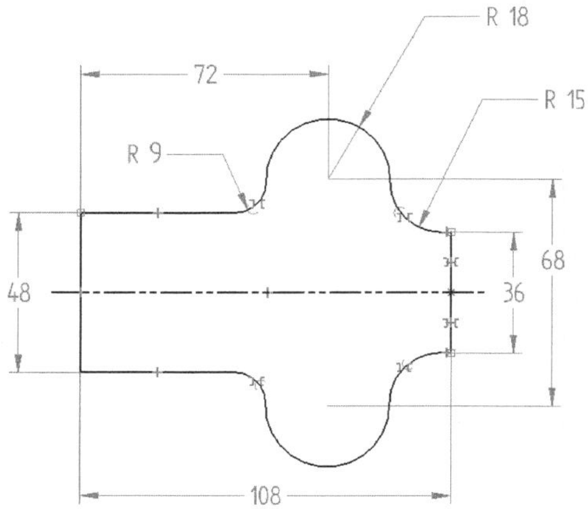

Figure 7-81 The profile of the base feature

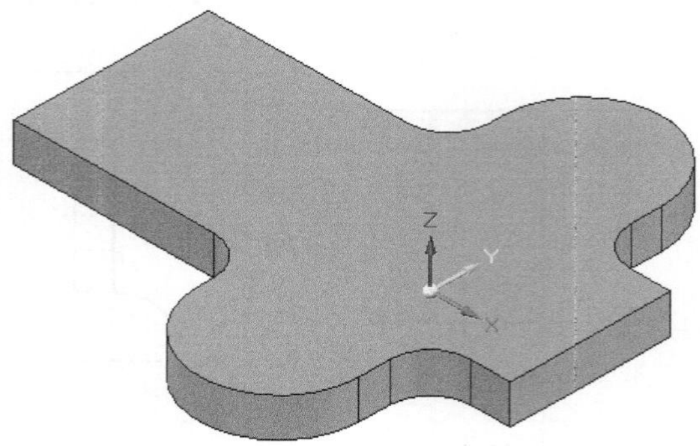

Figure 7-82 Base feature of the model

Adding the Extruded Features and Round Feature

1. Invoke the **Extrude** tool and then add two extruded features to the model, as shown in Figure 7-83.

2. Mirror one of the extruded features about the front plane by using the **Mirror Copy Feature** tool and then add the required rounds to the model, as shown in Figure 7-84.

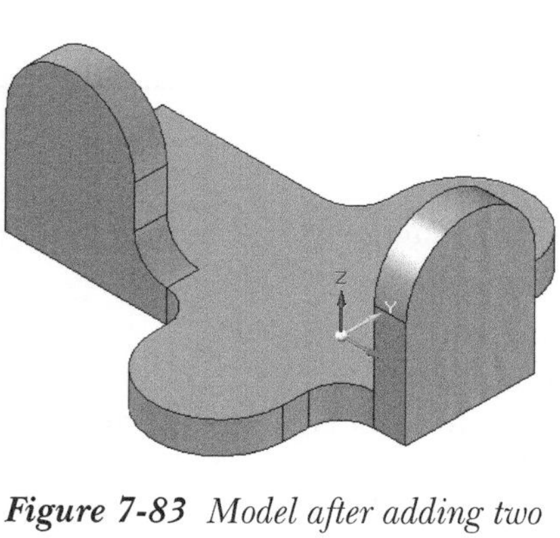

Figure 7-83 Model after adding two more extruded features

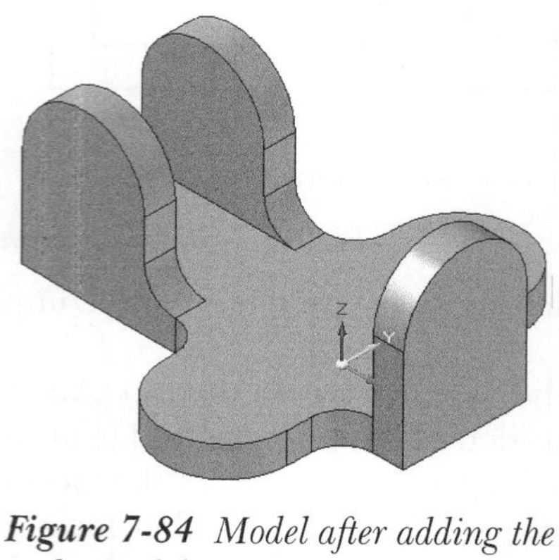

Figure 7-84 Model after adding the extruded and round features

Creating a Simple Hole on a Face

1. Invoke the **Hole** tool and then create a simple hole of 16 mm diameter on one of the faces of the model, as shown in Figure 7-85. Make sure the hole is created by choosing the **Through All** button from the **Hole Extent**.

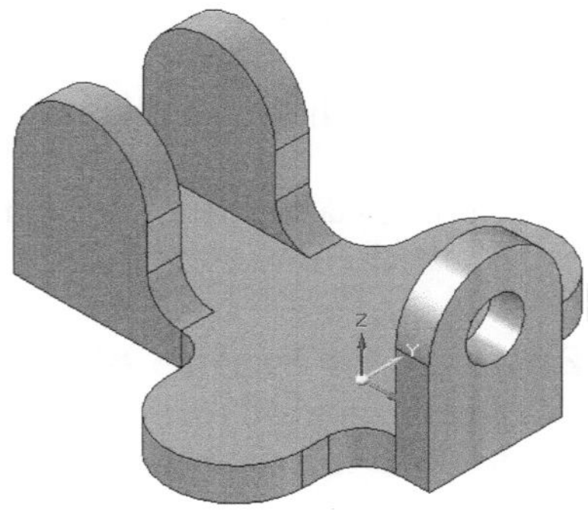

Figure 7-85 *Model after creating the simple hole*

Copying and Pasting Holes on the other Faces

Next, you need to copy and paste holes on other faces. Note that you need to edit the profiles of the holes after placing them so as to make sure that the holes are concentric to the arc features on the faces on which they are placed.

1. Select the hole in the drawing window or in the **PathFinder**, and then right-click to display the shortcut menu. Choose **Copy** from the shortcut menu.

2. Click anywhere in the drawing window to make sure that the hole is no more selected.

3. Right-click in the drawing window, and then choose **Paste** from the shortcut menu displayed; the **Paste** Command bar is displayed with the **Plane Step** activated in it. Also, the profile of the hole is attached to the cursor and you are prompted to click on a planar face or on a reference plane.

4. Select the front planar face of the vertical feature, refer to Figure 7-86; the hole is created. You will notice that the hole feature is also created on the other extruded feature which is on the opposite side, as shown in Figure 7-87. This is because the original hole was created by using the **Through All** button.

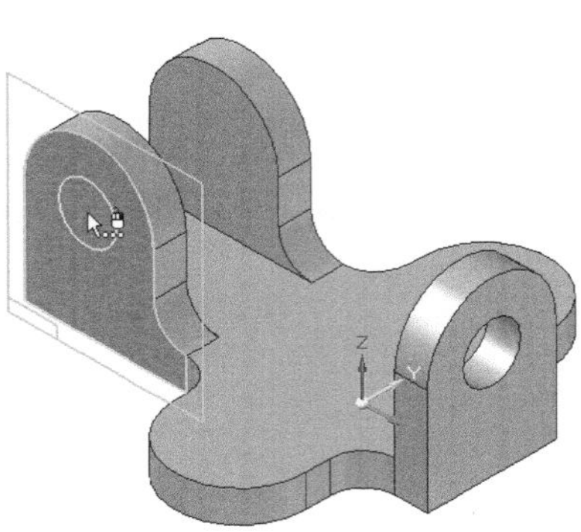

Figure 7-86 *Selecting the face to paste the hole feature*

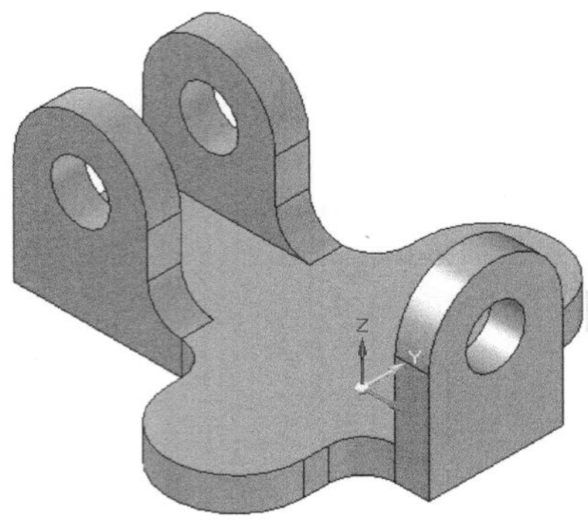

Figure 7-87 *Model after pasting the hole on the selected face*

Next, you need to paste the hole on the top face of the base feature. Therefore, you need to select the top planar face of the base feature as the sketching plane.

5. Move the cursor toward the feature over the top planar face of the base feature.

6. Place two holes on the top planar face, close to the two arcs on the base feature.

7. Choose **Cancel** from the Command bar; all holes are displayed as separate hole features in the **PathFinder**.

Editing the Profile of the Holes and Applying Relationships

Next, you need to edit the profiles of these placed holes and apply concentric relationships to them to properly position the holes.

1. Right-click on **Hole 2** in the **PathFinder**, and then choose **Edit Profile** from the shortcut menu displayed; the sketching environment is invoked and the profile of the hole feature is displayed.

2. Add the concentric relationship to the hole profile and the arc in the feature. Exit the sketching environment and then choose **Finish** to exit the tool.

3. Similarly, edit the profiles of the remaining two holes. The final model after editing the profiles of all holes is shown in Figure 7-88.

Figure 7-88 *Final model for Tutorial 3*

Saving the Model

1. Save the model with the name *c07tut3.par* at the location given next and then close the file.
   C:\Solid Edge\c07

Tutorial 4 — Ordered & Synchronous

In this tutorial, you will create the model shown in Figure 7-89. The dimensions of the model are given in Figure 7-90. After completing the model creation, you will convert all ordered features of the model to synchronous features and modify the features. Save the model with the name *c07tut4.par* at the location given next.
C:\Solid Edge\c07 **(Expected time: 30 min)**

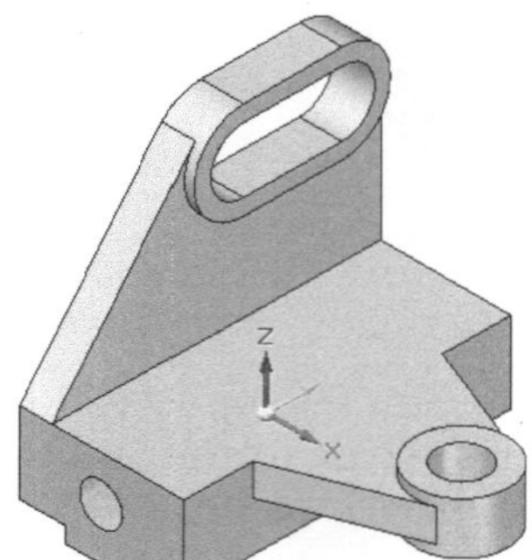

Figure 7-89 *Model for Tutorial 4*

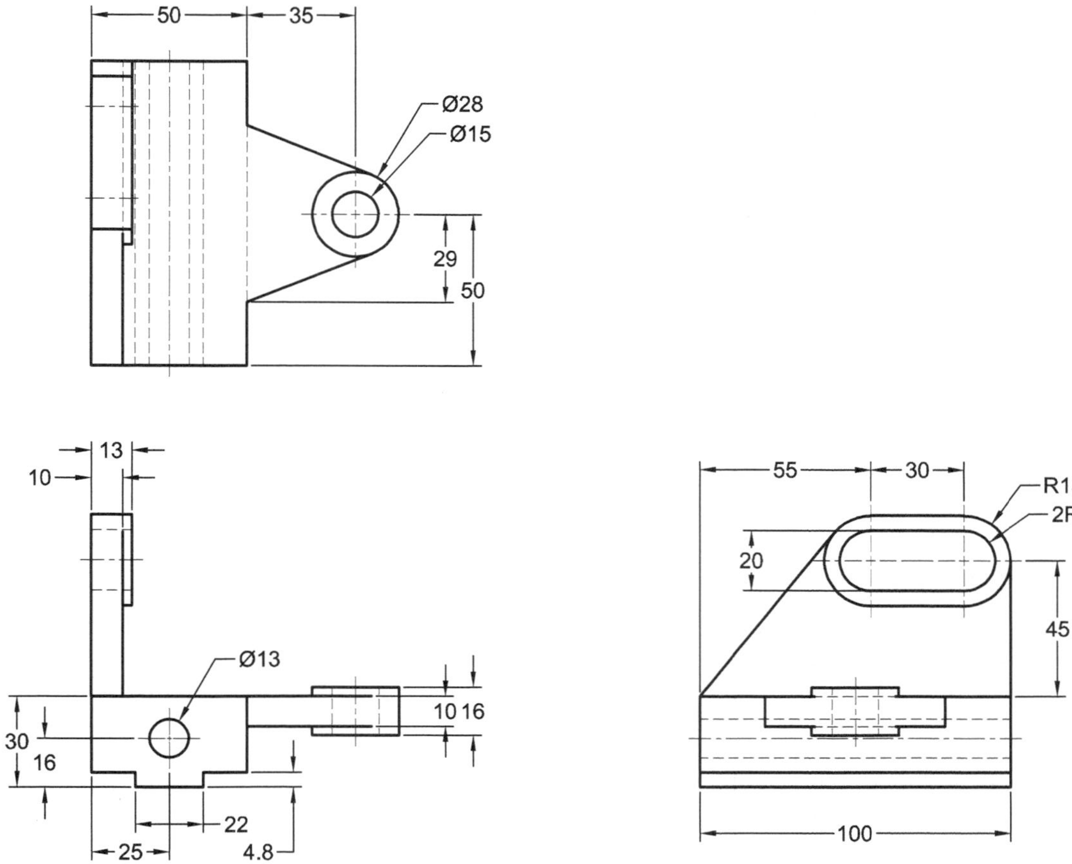

Figure 7-90 Dimensions of the model for Tutorial 4

The following steps are required to complete this tutorial:

a. Start a new part file and switch to the **Ordered Part** environment.
b. Create the base feature on the front plane, refer to Figure 7-91.
c. Create the other extruded features on the top face of the model, refer to Figure 7-92.
d. Create the extrude features on the back face of the model, refer to Figure 7-93.
e. Create two hole features, refer to Figure 7-94.
f. Convert all the features into synchronous features.
g. Edit the features of the model using the synchronous editing tools, refer to Figure 7-95.
h. Change the color of the model to copper.
i. Save the model and close the file.

Creating the Base Feature

1. Start a new part file and switch to the **Ordered Part** environment.

2. Create the base feature of the model on the front plane, as shown in Figure 7-91. Make sure you create the feature by extruding the profile symmetrically. For dimension refer to Figure 7-92.

Creating Extruded Features on the Top Face of the Base Feature

1. Create two extruded features on the top face of the base feature, as shown in Figure 7-92. It is recommended that you add the **Horizontal/Vertical** relationship to the center of the arc in the second feature and the vertical plane. This ensures that even if the depth of extrusion of the base feature is modified, the second and third features will remain at the center of the base feature.

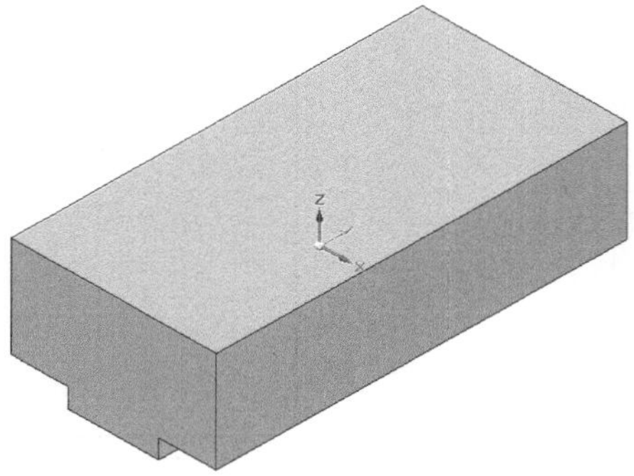

Figure 7-91 *Base feature of the model*

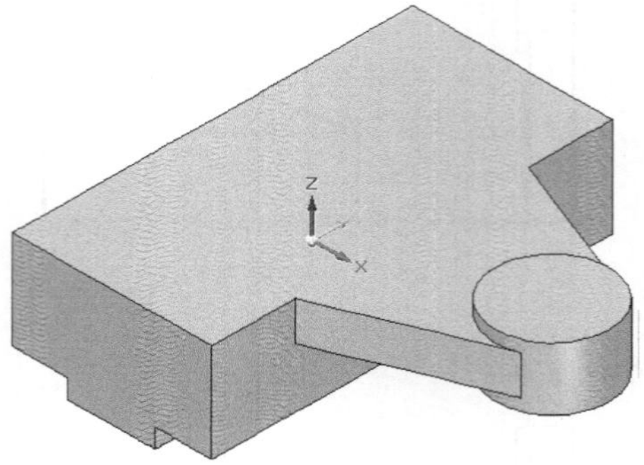

Figure 7-92 *Model after adding features on the top face of the base feature*

Creating Features on the Back Face of the Base Feature

1. Create two extruded features and the cutout on the back face of the base feature, as shown in Figure 7-90. It is recommended that you include the horizontal edge of the base feature to create the protrusion feature. This is because when you edit the depth of the base feature, the protrusion feature is modified accordingly. Also, do not add the dimension 55 that defines the cutout on the back face, refer to Figure 7-93. Instead, apply the **Vertical** relationship to the right edge. This helps in editing the base feature.

Creating Simple Holes

1. Create two simple holes in the model to complete it, as shown in Figure 7-94.

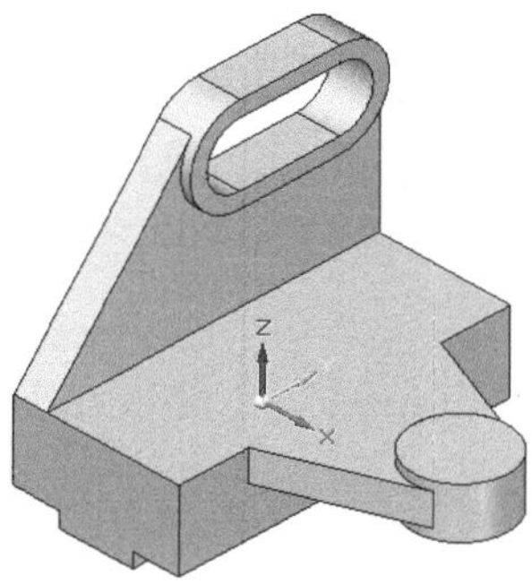

Figure 7-93 *Model after creating features on the back face*

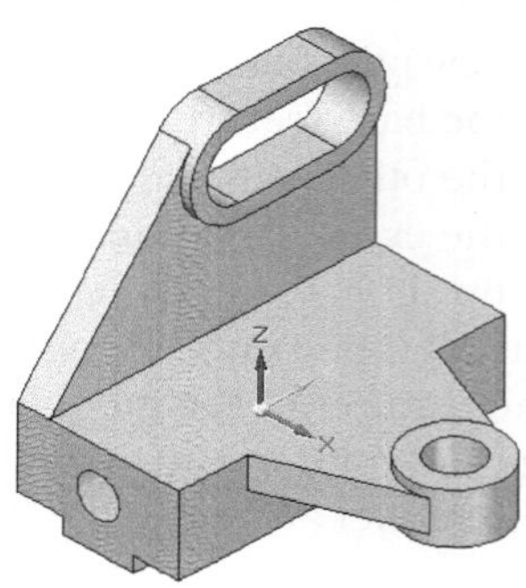

Figure 7-94 *Model after creating holes*

Converting Ordered Features to Synchronous Features

1. Right-click on the last feature of the model in the **PathFinder** tree; a shortcut menu will be displayed. Choose the **Move to Synchronous** option from the shortcut menu; all the ordered features will be converted into synchronous features.

Editing the Features using the Synchronous Editing Tools

1. Select the inclined face of the model; a move handle is displayed on it. Click on the origin knob of the move handle; the steering wheel gets activated. Position the steering wheel, as shown in Figure 7-95. Next, select the torus and rotate and then enter **-5** in the edit box.

Changing the Color of the Model

Next, you need to change the color of the model to copper by using the **Part Painter** tool.

1. Choose the **Part Painter** tool from the **Style** group of the **View** tab to display the **Part Painter** Command bar.

2. Select **Copper** from the **Style** drop-down list and **Body** from the **Select** drop-down list.

3. Select the model in the drawing window; the color of the model is automatically changed to copper. Choose **Close** to exit the Command bar. The final model is shown in Figure 7-96.

Saving the Model

1. Save the model with the name *c07tut4.par* at the location given next and then close the file.
   C:\Solid Edge\c07

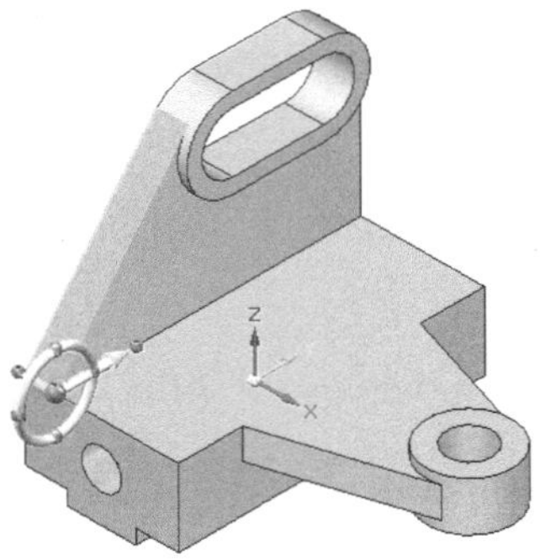

Figure 7-95 *Positioning the steering wheel to rotate the inclined face*

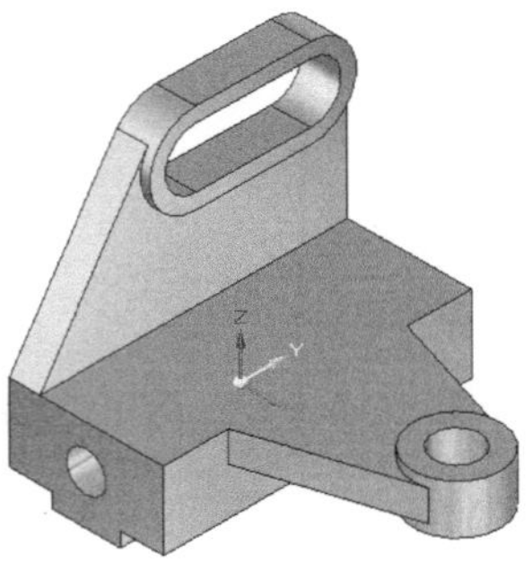

Figure 7-96 *Final model after editing the base feature*

Self-Evaluation Test

Answer the following questions and then compare them to those given at the end of this chapter:

1. The _________ is used to move or rotate faces or features.

2. The **Use Box Selection** option is used for selecting the entities for using the_________ tool.

3. When you select the text of the dimension, the _________ edit box is displayed.

4. The _________ controls the behavior of a model, while it is being edited.

5. The __________ tool is used to remove the selected faces or features from a model without actually deleting them.

6. To check the physical properties of a model, choose __________ from the **Physical Properties** group of the **Inspect** tab.

7. To delete features, select them from the **PathFinder** or from the drawing window and then press the __________ key.

8. To suppress a feature, right-click on it, and then choose __________ from the shortcut menu displayed.

9. While calculating the physical properties of a model, the default density of the material is taken as __________.

10. In the **Ordered** environment of Solid Edge, you can view the animation of the sequence of the feature construction. (T/F)

Review Questions

Answer the following questions:

1. Which of the following components of the steering wheel is used to rotate the selected entities?

   (a) Primary axis (b) Secondary axis
   (c) Torus (d) Tool plane

2. Which of the following features needs to be selected to display the **Edit Definition** handle?

   (a) Holes (b) Thin Wall
   (c) Pattern (d) All

3. Which of the following relationships cannot be applied to align faces?

   (a) **Concentric** (b) **Coincident**
   (c) **Parallel** (d) **Equal**

4. Which of the following options is displayed automatically when you move/rotate faces, align faces, or edit dimensions?

   (a) **Rules** (b) **Design Intent**
   (c) **Advanced Design Intent** (d) All of these

5. Which of the following nodes is added in the **PathFinder** tab after using the **Break** Command?

   (a) **Face Set** (b) **Break**
   (c) **Relationship** (d) **Hole**

6. The _________ tool is used to separate a feature (hole) from the set of features for editing it separately.

7. If the **Feature Playback** tab is not added in the docking window, you need to select the **Feature Playback** option from the _________ drop-down of the **Show** group in the **View** tab.

8. To copy a feature, right-click on it, and then choose _________ from the shortcut menu displayed.

9. You can modify the dimension of a feature in the desired direction. (T/F)

10. You can change the dimension value in the **Dimension Value** edit box by scrolling the wheel of the mouse. (T/F)

EXERCISES

Exercise 1

Open the model created in Exercise 1 of Chapter 6 and modify its dimensions, as shown in Figures 7-97 and 7-98. After modifying the dimensions, save the model with the name *c07exr1.par* at the location given next so that the original file is not modified.

C:\Solid Edge\c07 **(Expected time: 15 min)**

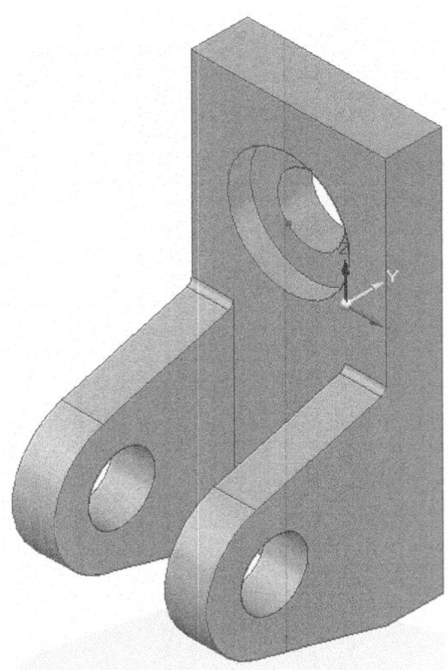

Figure 7-97 *Model for Exercise 1*

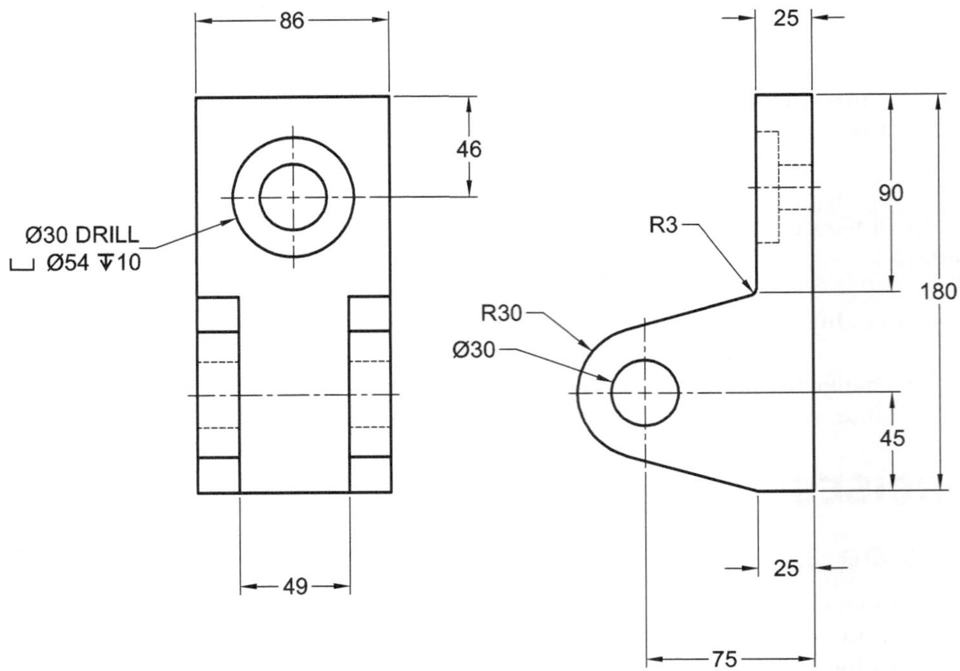

Figure 7-98 Dimensions of the model for Exercise 1

Exercise 2

Create the model shown in Figure 7-99. The dimensions of the model are given in the views shown in Figure 7-100. After creating the model, edit some of its dimensions and then save it with the name *c07exr2.par* at the location given next.

C:\Solid Edge\c07 **(Expected time: 30 min)**

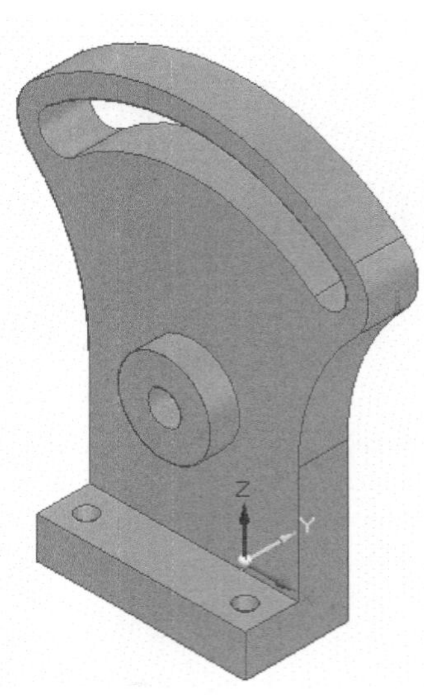

Figure 7-99 Model for Exercise 2

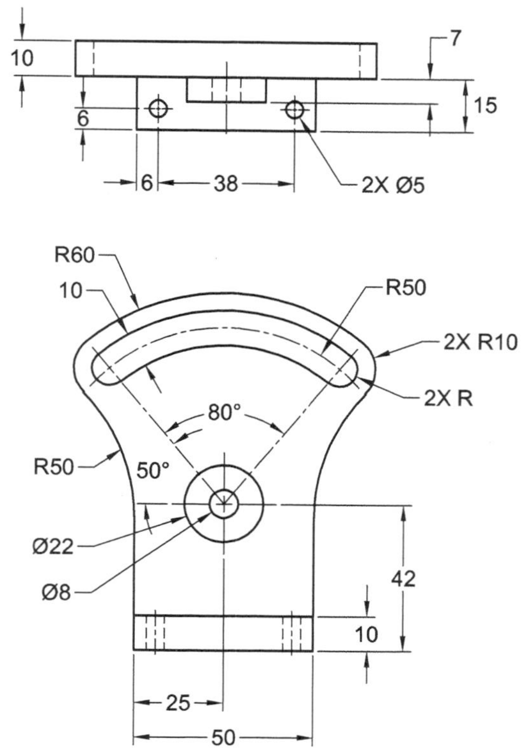

Figure 7-100 Dimensions of the model for Exercise 2

Exercise 3

Create the model shown in Figure 7-101. The dimensions of the model are given in the views shown in Figure 7-102. After creating the model, edit some of its dimensions and then save it with the name *c07exr3.par* at the location given next.

C:\Solid Edge\c07 **(Expected time: 30 min)**

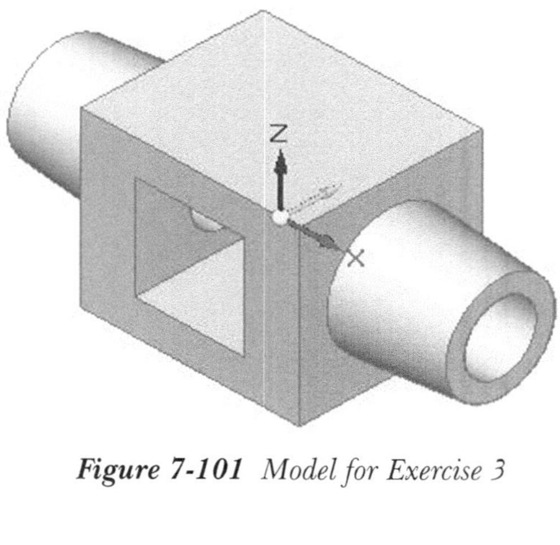

Figure 7-101 Model for Exercise 3

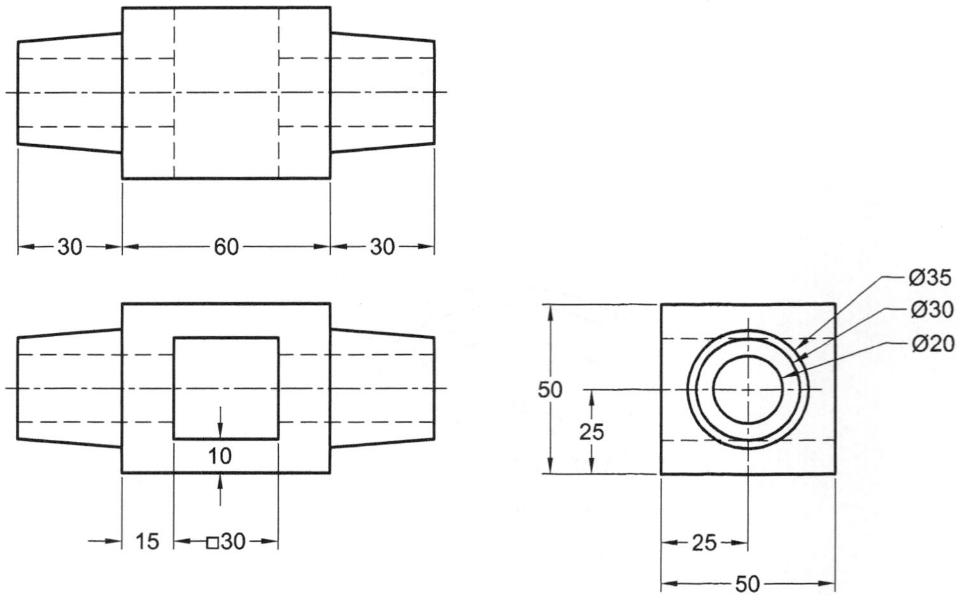

Figure 7-102 Dimensions of the model for Exercise 3

Answers to Self-Evaluation Test

1. Steering wheel, **2. Selection Manager**, **3. Dimension value**, **4. Design Intent**, **5. Detach**, **6. Properties**, **7.** DELETE, **8. Suppress**, **9.** 0 **10.** T

Chapter 8

Advanced Modeling Tools-II

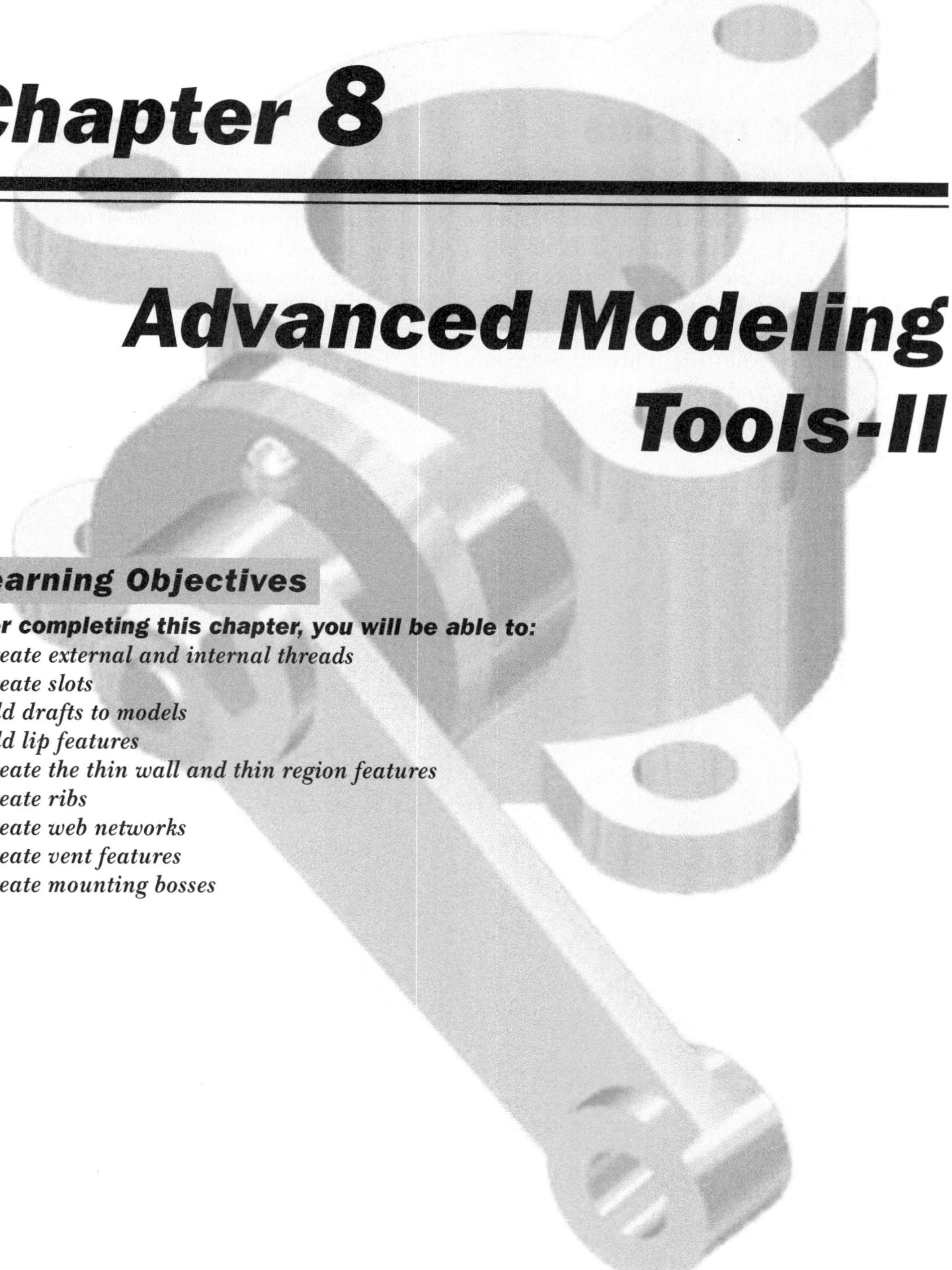

Learning Objectives

After completing this chapter, you will be able to:

- *Create external and internal threads*
- *Create slots*
- *Add drafts to models*
- *Add lip features*
- *Create the thin wall and thin region features*
- *Create ribs*
- *Create web networks*
- *Create vent features*
- *Create mounting bosses*

ADVANCED MODELING TOOLS

In previous chapters, you learned to create and edit features. In this chapter, you will learn about some of the advanced modeling tools that are used to create some complicated models. The remaining advanced modeling tools will be discussed in the later chapters.

CREATING THREADS

Ribbon: Home > Solids > Hole drop-down > Thread

In Solid Edge, you can create internal or external threads using the **Thread** tool. Internal threads are created in a hole or in circular cut features whereas external threads are created on the external surface of a cylindrical feature. Figure 8-1 shows the external thread. These standard sizes are available in the **Hole Diameter** edit box of the **Hole Options** dialog box that was discussed earlier. To create threads, invoke the **Thread** tool and choose the **Options** button from the **Thread** Command bar; the **Thread Options** dialog box will be displayed, as shown in Figure 8-2. The options in this dialog box are discussed next.

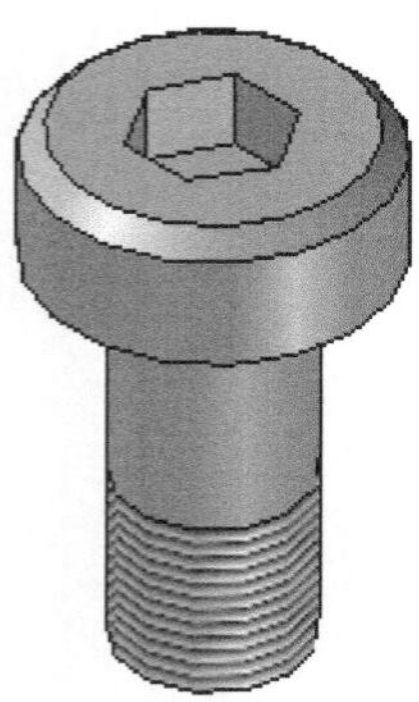

Figure 8-1 External threads

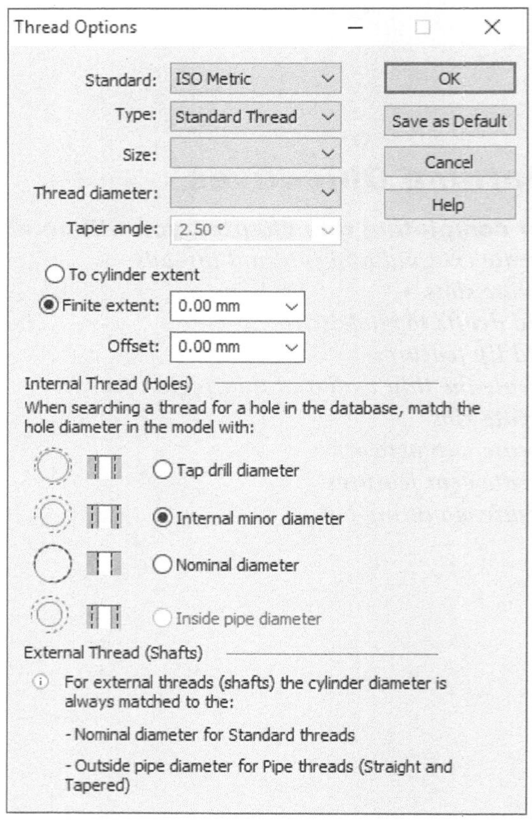

*Figure 8-2 The **Thread Options** dialog box*

Standard

The options in this drop-down list are used to specify the dimensions for the thread standards. By default, the **ISO Metric** standard is selected in this drop-down list. Other thread standards available in this drop down list are **ANSI Inch**, **ANSI Metric**, **DIN Metric**, **GB Metric**, **GOST Metric**, **JIS Metric**, and **UNI Metric**.

Type

This drop-down list is used to specify the type of thread that you want to create. The options in this drop-down list are available depending upon the size of the selected cylinder. You can select any of the following option from this drop-down list to create threads.

Standard Thread

This option allows you to create threads on standard feature.

Straight Pipe Thread

This option allows you to create threads on a straight feature.

Tapered Pipe Thread

This option allows you to create threads on a tapered feature.

Thread Diameter

The **Thread Diameter** drop-down list is used to set the diameter of the hole using the predefined values available in this drop-down list. Note that the units of the thread diameters in this drop-down list depend on the type of standard selected from the **Standard** drop-down list.

Size

This drop-down list displays the standard size of the threads. The standard size of the threads in this drop-down list depends on the diameter selected from the **Thread Diameter** drop-down list.

Taper angle

This edit box is available when you select the **Tapered** thread type. You can enter the taper angle in this edit box or select the predefined taper angles from the **Taper angle** drop-down list.

To cylinder extent

This radio button is available only when you are creating the straight and standard threads. It is used to create threads through the entire length of the cylinder.

Finite extent

This option enables you to create threads upto a specified depth. If you select the **Finite extent** radio button, the **Finite extent** edit box adjacent to the **Finite extent** radio button will be activated. You can use this edit box to specify the depth value.

Offset

This edit box is used to specify the distance between the start of the thread and end face of the cylinder. This edit box is activated only when you select the **Straight Pipe Threads** or **Standard Threads** option in the **Type** drop-down list.

After you specify the parameters in the **Thread Options** dialog box, select the cylindrical face on which the thread is to be created; a warning box will be displayed, informing that the diameter of the cylinder will be changed to match the diameter of the thread. Choose the **OK** button to create a thread.

Note

1. While applying the thread feature, the diameter of the part should not be constrained. This is because in Solid Edge the diameter of the part automatically changes to match the diameter of the thread feature.

*2. If the threaded portion is not visible, you need to change the color of the threads by using the **Color Manager** dialog box. To do so, choose the **Color Manager** tool from the **Style** group in the **View** tab; the **Color Manager** dialog box will be displayed. Select the **Use individual part styles** radio button and then select the **Thread** option from the **Threaded Cylinder** drop-down list.*

CREATING SLOTS

Ribbon: Home > Solids > Hole drop-down > Slot

In Solid Edge, you can create a slot feature on to the model by using the **Slot** tool. To do so, you need to create the sketch for the required slot feature. Note that you can only create slot feature along a tangent continuous sketch. In **Synchronous** environment, you need to create sketch before invoking the **Slot** Command bar but in **Ordered** environment, you can create the sketch after invoking the **Slot** Command bar. The methods for creating the slot features are discussed next.

Creating a Slot in Synchronous Environment

To create a slot feature in the **Synchronous** environment, first draw the sketch for the slot on a planar surface of the model. Note that all the entities of the sketch created for creating a slot should be tangent to each other. Figure 8-3 shows the sketch created on the model surface. Next, choose the **Slot** tool; the **Slot** Command bar will be displayed, refer to Figure 8-4. Next, choose the **Slot Options** button from the Command bar; the **Slot Options** dialog box will be displayed, as shown in Figure 8-5. By default, the **Flat end** radio button is selected and the value 10 mm is displayed in the **Slot width** edit box. Select the **Arc end** radio button and choose **OK**. Now select the recently drawn sketch and move the cursor toward right and click; the slot feature will be created, refer to Figure 8-6. The options in the **Slot Options** dialog box are discussed next.

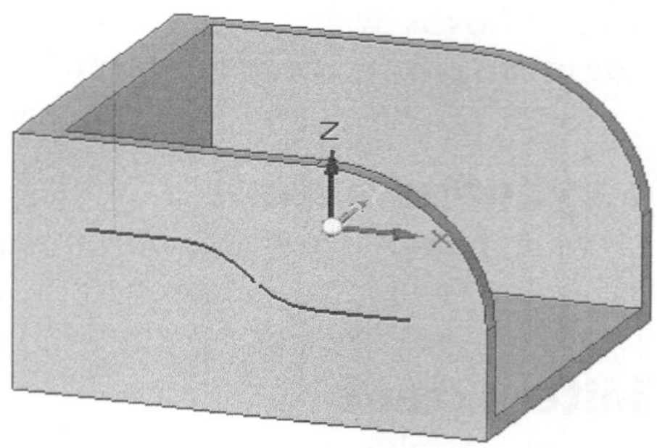

Figure 8-3 *Sketch drawn for the slot feature*

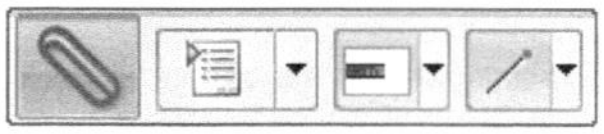

*Figure 8-4 The **Slot** Command bar*

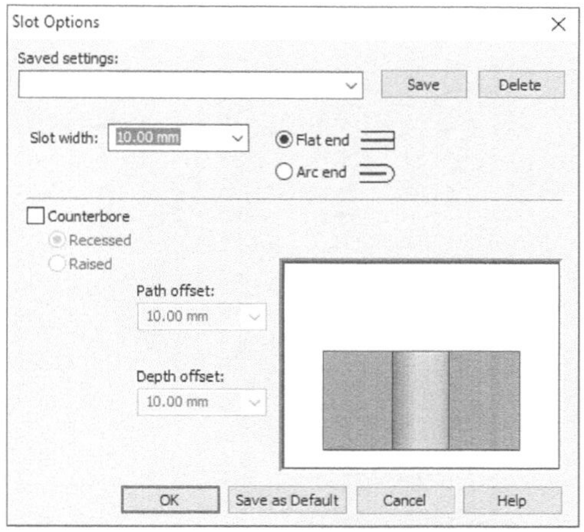

*Figure 8-5 The **Slot Options** dialog box*

Saved settings
This drop-down list is used to display the list of all the previously saved slot settings. You can select the required slot setting from this drop-down.

Slot width
The **Slot width** edit box is used for specifying the width for the applied slot feature.

Flat end
This radio button is selected to create a slot feature with flat ends.

Arc end
This radio button is selected to create a slot feature with arc ends.

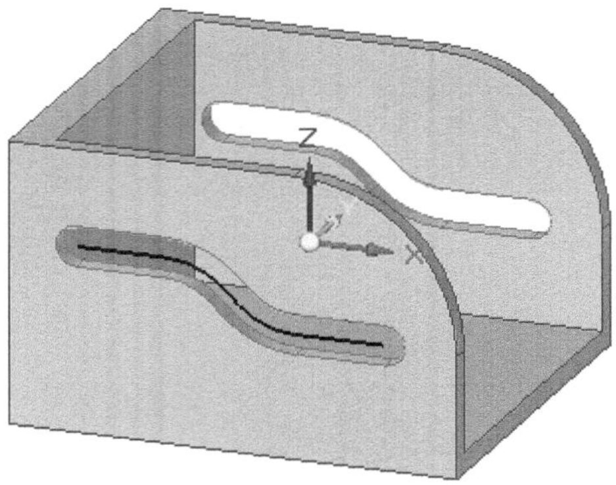

Figure 8-6 Slot feature created over the model

Counterbore
This check box is selected for creating counterbore shaped slots. On selecting this check box, the **Recessed** and **Raised** radio buttons are activated and these options are discussed next.

Recessed
This radio button is selected for creating a slot of a fully recessed counterbore shape. To create a slot of recessed counterbore shape, select this radio button and enter the values in the **Path Offset** and **Depth Offset** edit boxes. The **Path Offset** edit box is used to specify the width of the counterbore recess. The **Depth Offset** edit box is used to specify the counterbore depth. Figure 8-7 shows the sketch of the slot and Figure 8-8 shows a recessed counterbore slot.

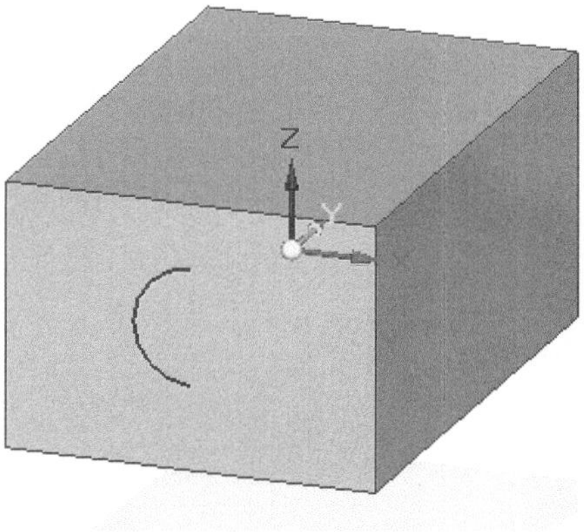

Figure 8-7 Sketch for the counterbore slot

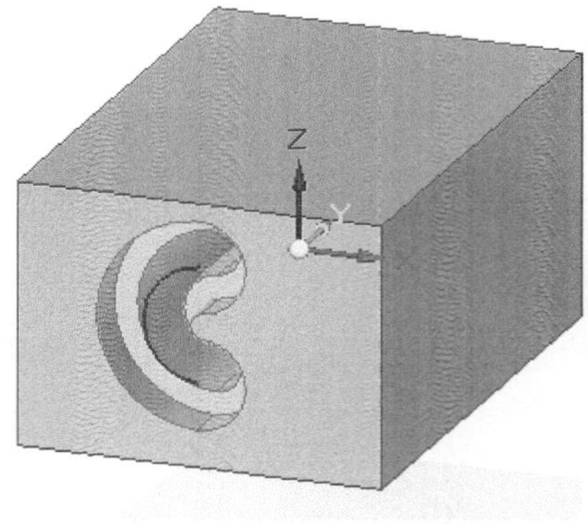

Figure 8-8 Counterbore slot created on the model surface

Raised

This radio button is selected to create a slot of a raised counterbore shape. To create a raised counterbore slot, select this radio button and enter the values in the **Path Offset** and **Depth Offset** edit boxes. The preview area in the dialog box shows the slots created using these edit boxes. Figures 8-9 and 8-10 show the counterbore slot raised outside and inside, respectively.

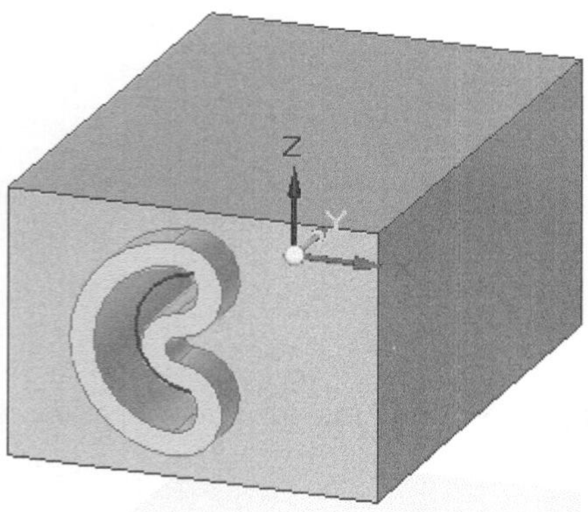

Figure 8-9 Counterbore slot raised outside

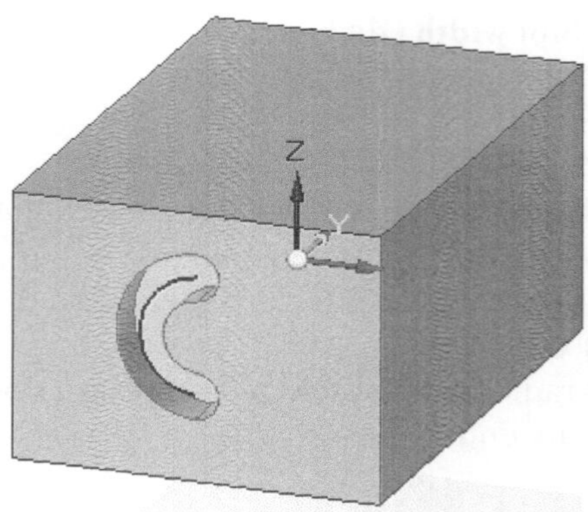

Figure 8-10 Counterbore slot raised inside

Creating a Slot in Ordered Environment

The method of creating slots in the **Ordered** environment is same as that of creating a slot in the **Synchronous** environment. To do so, invoke the **Slot** tool; the **Slot** Command bar will be displayed with the **Sketch Step** button chosen by default. And, you will be prompted to select the sketch drawn for creating the slot feature. Select or draw the required sketch and choose the **Accept** button from the Command bar; a slot feature is created. Click anywhere in the drawing area and choose the **Finish** and **Cancel** buttons to close the Command bar.

Note

*The options in the **Slot** Command bar in the **Ordered** environment are same as those discussed earlier.*

ADDING DRAFTS TO THE MODEL

Ribbon: Home > Solids > Draft

This tool is used for tapering the faces of a model. Tapering the faces enables you to easily remove the component from the mold during the casting. You can add a draft to a model using the **Draft** tool. To do so, invoke the **Draft** tool from the **Solids** group; the **Draft** Command bar will be displayed. Choose the **Draft Options** button from it; the **Draft Options** dialog box will be displayed, as shown in Figure 8-11. This dialog box consists of four radio buttons (options) to create a draft. In this chapter, you will learn to create a draft using the first two options of the dialog box. The remaining options will be discussed in the later chapters.

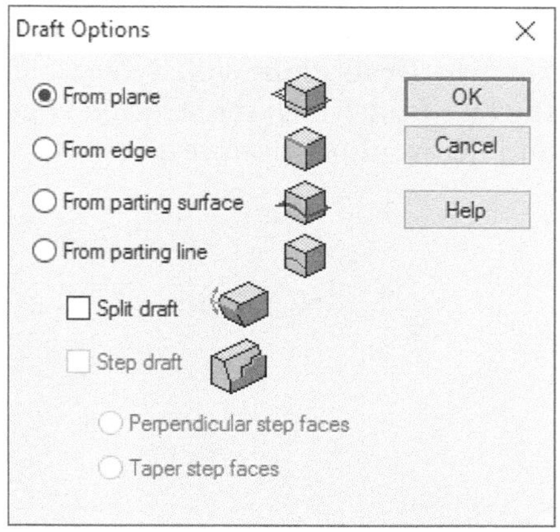

Figure 8-11 *The **Draft Options** dialog box*

Creating a Draft Using the From Plane Method

By default, the **From Plane** radio button is selected in the **Draft Options** dialog box. Choose **OK** to exit the dialog box; you will be prompted to click on a planar face or on a reference plane. The draft plane is a plane whose normal is used to define the draft angle. After defining the draft plane, you are prompted to select one or more faces on which the draft will be added. You can select the required option from the **Selection Type** drop-down list available in the **Draft** Command bar to select the faces to draft. After selecting the draft faces, a draft direction handle along with the **Draft Angle** edit box will be displayed. Next, enter the draft angle in the **Draft Angle** edit box; a preview of the draft will be displayed. Note that you cannot enter a negative draft angle value because you need to define the direction of the draft using the draft direction handle. Figures 8-12 and 8-13 show the draft directions and the resulting drafts, respectively.

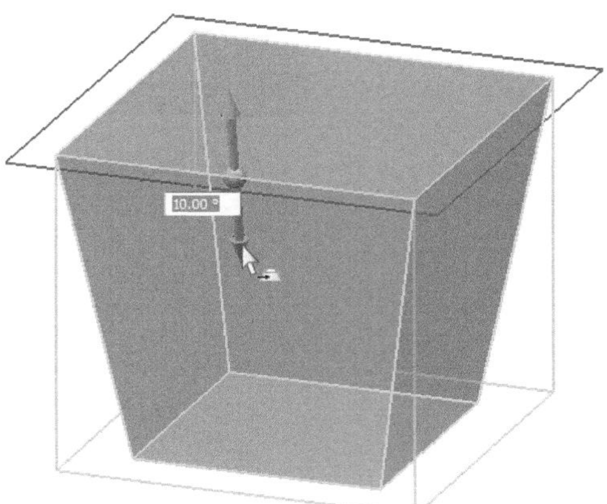

Figure 8-12 *Defining the draft direction using the draft direction handle*

Figure 8-13 *Resulting draft*

Creating a Draft Using the From Edge Method

The method of creating a draft from an edge is similar to that of creating a draft from a plane. The only difference is that in the edge draft, you are allowed to select an edge from where the draft angle will be measured. This is done in the **Select Parting Geometry Step** that is invoked after the **Draft Plane** step. Note that out of all the selected faces, the draft will be added only to the face from which the selected edge will pass. Figures 8-14 and 8-15 show the draft directions and the resulting draft respectively.

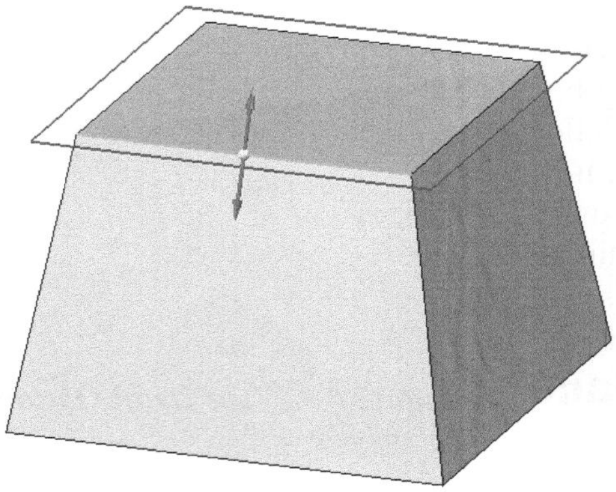

Figure 8-14 *Defining the direction of draft creation*

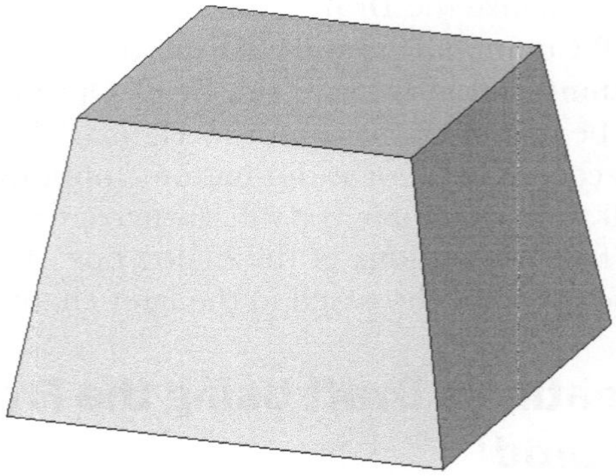

Figure 8-15 *Resultant draft*

The remaining methods used for creating drafts are discussed in the Chapter 13, 'Surface Modeling'.

ADDING RIBS TO THE MODEL (ORDERED)

Ribbon:	Solids > Thin Wall drop-down > Rib

Ribs are defined as the thin wall-like structures used to bind joints together so that they do not fail under an increased load. In Solid Edge, ribs are created using an open profile, refer to Figures 8-16 and 8-17.

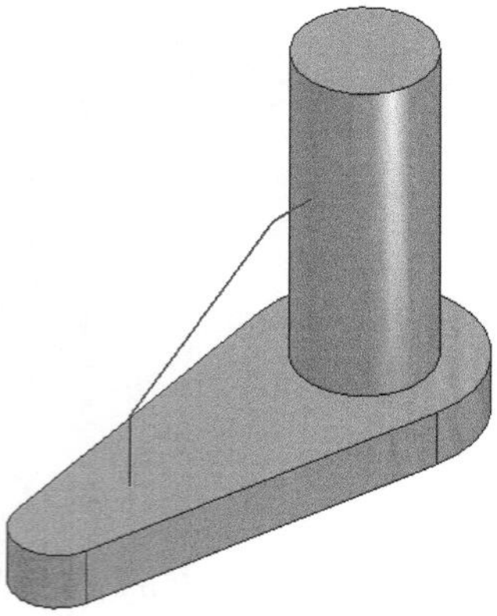

Figure 8-16 *Open profile to create a rib*

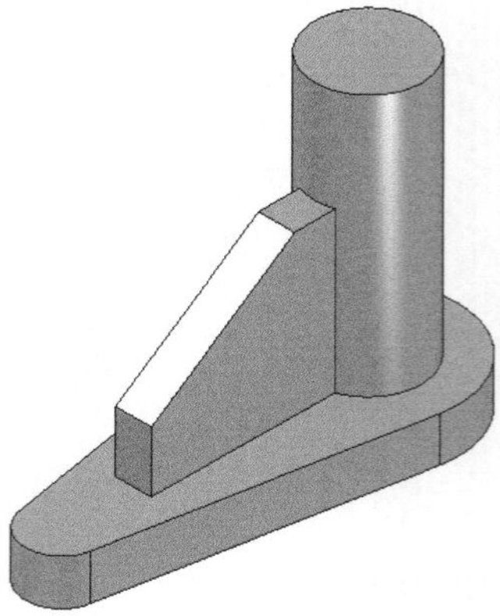

Figure 8-17 *Resulting rib feature*

The process of creating ribs is completed in four steps which are discussed next.

Sketch Step

This step enables you to select a sketching plane for drawing the profile of the rib feature. You can also select an existing profile using the **Select from Sketch** option from the **Create-From Options** drop-down list. It is recommended that the profile of the rib feature should be extruded symmetrically. Therefore, you need to select the sketching plane for drawing the profile accordingly.

Draw Profile Step

This step will be automatically invoked when you select the sketching plane for drawing the profile of the rib feature.

Direction Step

This step is invoked automatically when you select the profile and accept it or draw the profile and exit the sketching environment. This step enables you to define the direction of the rib creation, and therefore, you are prompted to click to accept the displayed side or select the other side in the view. The feature can be created in a direction normal or parallel to the profile. If you move the cursor in the drawing window, a dynamic preview of the rib feature will be displayed in various directions. If the feature cannot be created, an error symbol will be displayed in the preview of the rib, as shown in Figure 8-18. The rib feature will be successfully created if the direction defined for the feature creation is toward the faces of the existing feature, as shown in Figure 8-19. Next, click to specify the side of the feature creation.

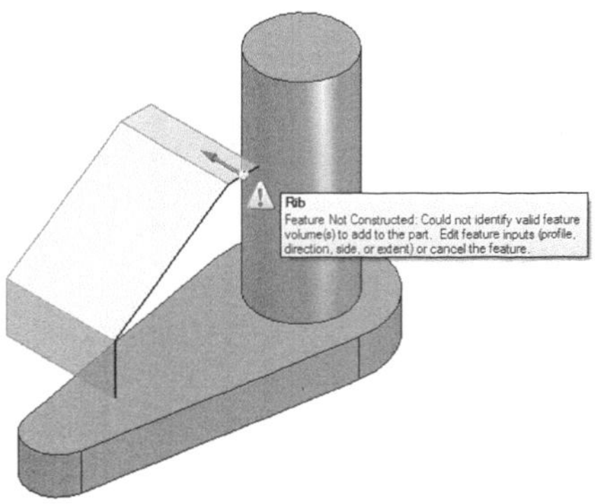

Figure 8-18 *Error symbol displayed in the preview of the rib*

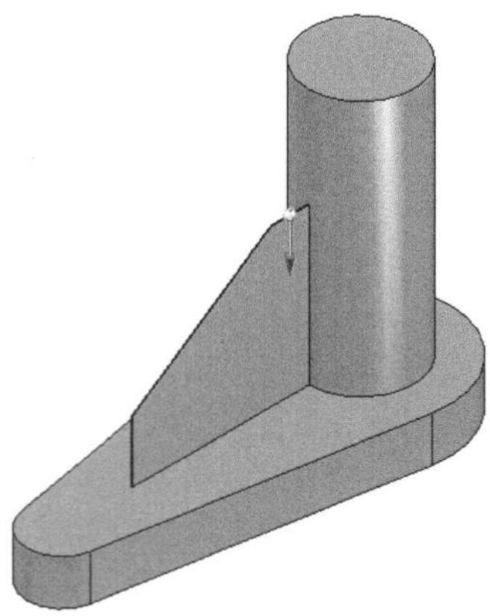

Figure 8-19 *Preview of the direction in which the rib feature will be created*

Side Step

Choose the **Side Step** button in the Command bar to define the direction of the rib creation. In the **Side Step**, you are allowed to specify the side of the sketching plane on which the rib will be created. You can move the cursor on either side of the profile to define it. As mentioned earlier, it is recommended to create the rib symmetrically on both sides of the sketching plane. To create a symmetric rib, move the cursor close to the profile; the preview of the symmetric rib will be displayed, as shown in Figure 8-20. Next, click to create the symmetric rib.

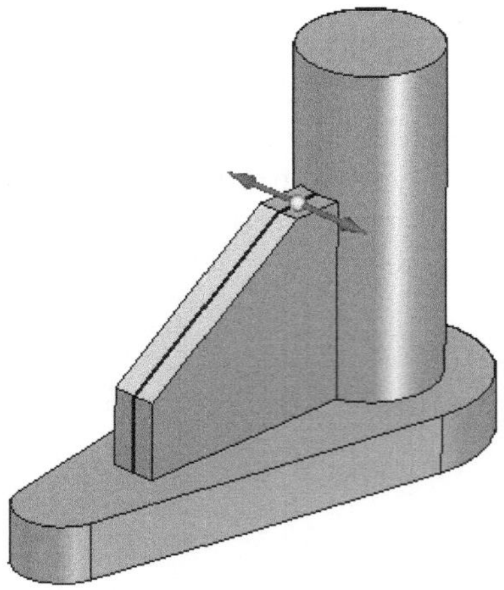

Figure 8-20 Preview of the symmetric rib

In the **Direction Step** and **Side Step**, some additional options are available in the Command bar and are discussed next.

Extend Profile

This button is chosen by default and is used to extend the rib feature to the adjacent features, even if the profile does not extend to them. Figure 8-21 shows an open profile for creating the rib. As is evident in this figure, the open profile does not extend to the adjacent features. Figure 8-22 shows the rib feature created using the same profile with the **Extend Profile** button chosen. As is evident from this figure, the rib feature has been extended to the adjacent features.

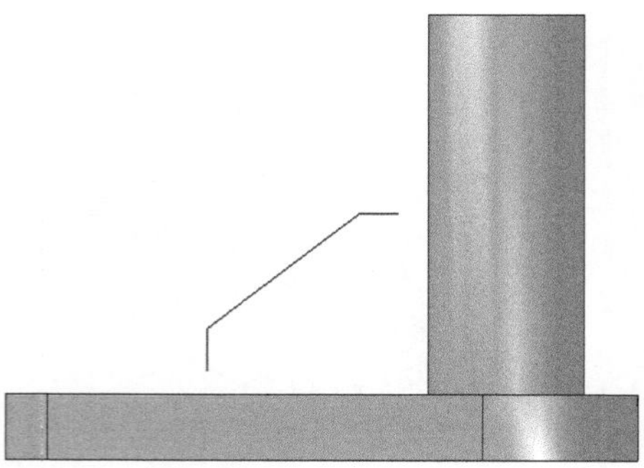

Figure 8-21 Open profile for creating the rib

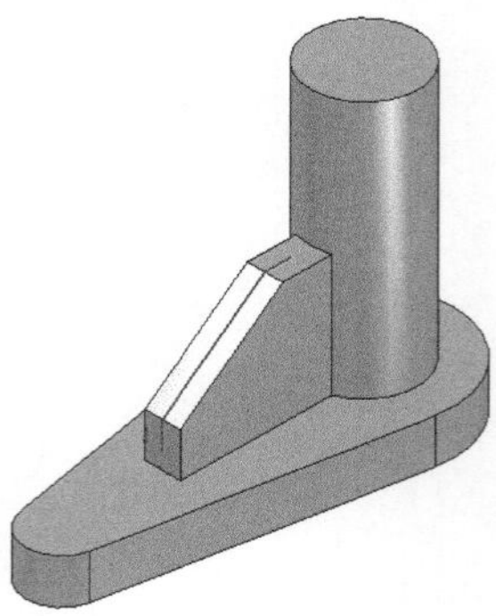

*Figure 8-22 Rib feature created with the **Extend Profile** button chosen*

No Extend

This button should be chosen when you do not want the rib to extend to the adjacent faces. Figure 8-23 shows the profile and the resulting rib created by choosing the **Extend Profile** button and Figure 8-24 shows the rib feature created by choosing the **No Extend** button.

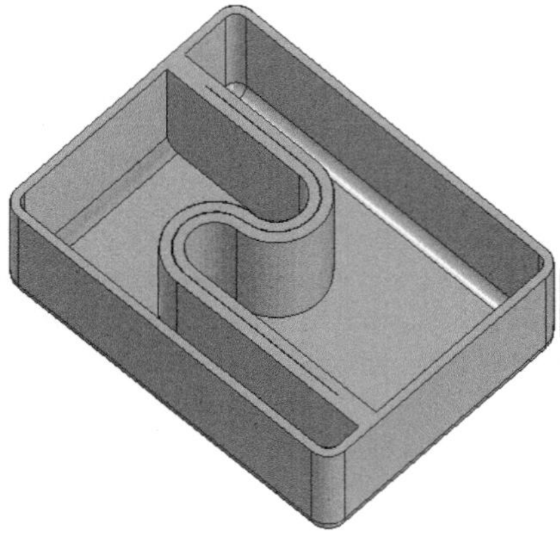

Figure 8-23 *Rib feature created with the* ***Extend Profile*** *button chosen*

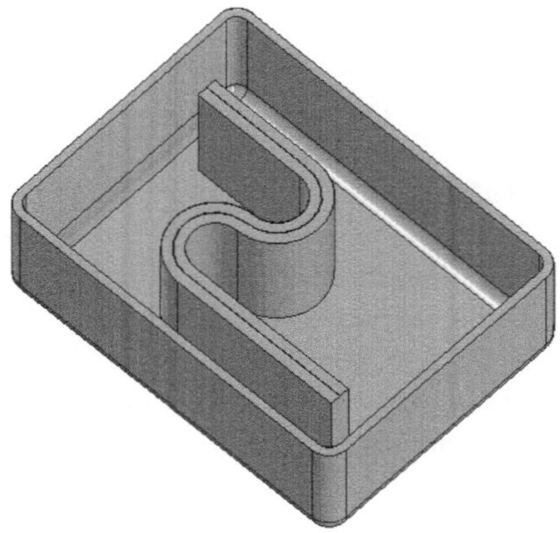

Figure 8-24 *Rib feature created with the* ***No Extend*** *button chosen*

Extend to Next

This button is chosen to extend the rib to the next features in the direction specified in the **Direction Step**. Figure 8-25 shows the rib feature created using this option.

Finite Depth

This button is chosen when you want to extend the rib to a finite depth in the direction that you have specified in the **Direction Step**. You can specify the depth of the rib in the **Depth** edit box that is displayed next to the **Thickness** edit box when you choose the **Finite Depth** button. Figure 8-26 shows the rib feature created using this option.

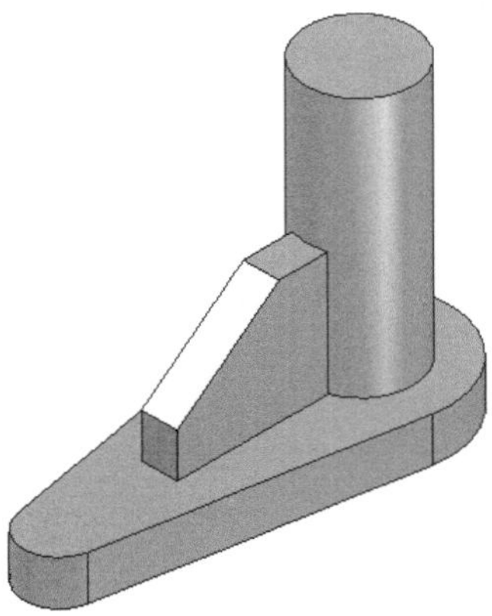

Figure 8-25 *Rib feature created with the* ***Extend to Next*** *button chosen*

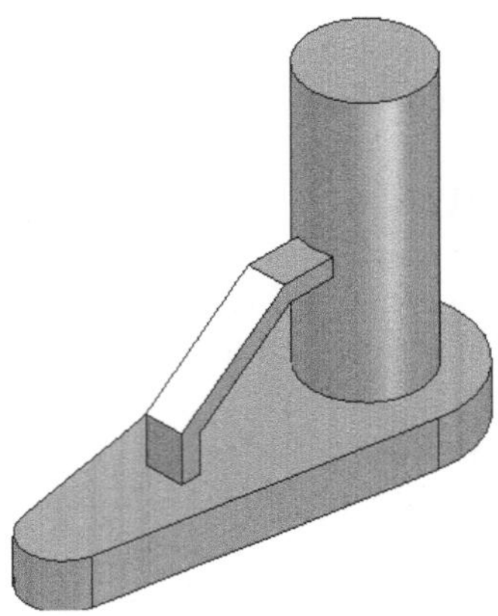

Figure 8-26 *Rib feature created up to a finite depth*

Thickness

This edit box is used to specify the thickness of the rib feature. You can enter any desired thickness value for the rib in this edit box. You can also select the predefined thickness values using the **Thickness** edit box.

Depth

This edit box will be available when you choose the **Finite Depth** button. It is used to specify the depth of the rib when you want to extend it to a finite depth.

Note

You can also create a rib feature in the ***Synchronous Part*** *environment. To do so, invoke the* ***Rib*** *tool from the* ***Thin Wall*** *drop-down of the* ***Solids*** *group in the* ***Home*** *tab; the* ***Rib*** *Command bar will be displayed and you will be prompted to select the sketched entities. Select the chain of entities or a single sketched entity and then choose the* ***Accept*** *button from the Command bar; a preview of the rib feature will be displayed. Specify the direction and enter the thickness of the rib in the* ***Dimension*** *edit box displayed. Choose the* ***Accept*** *button to create the rib feature.*

ADDING THIN WALL FEATURES (ORDERED)

Ribbon: Home > Solids > Thin Wall drop-down > Thin Wall

By adding a thin wall feature, you can scoop out the material from a model and make it hollow from inside. The resulting model becomes the structure of walls with a cavity inside. You can also remove some of the faces of the model or apply different wall thicknesses to some of them. Figure 8-27 shows the model with the thin wall feature added and the front face removed.

The **Thin Wall** tool works in the following three steps:

Common Thickness

This step enables you to specify the common thickness for the thin wall feature. You can also specify the side of the solid toward which the thin wall will be created. The options in the Command bar under this step are discussed next.

Offset Outside

The **Offset Outside** button is chosen to define the wall thickness outside the model with respect to its outer faces. In this case, the outer faces of the model will be considered as the inner walls of the resulting thin wall feature.

Offset Inside

The **Offset Inside** button is chosen by default and is used to define the wall thickness inside the model with respect to its outer faces. In this case, the outer faces of the model will be considered as the outer walls of the resulting thin wall feature.

Symmetrical

The **Symmetrical** button is chosen to calculate the wall thickness equally in both the directions of the outer faces of the model.

Common thickness

This edit box is used to specify the common thickness for the thin wall feature.

Open Faces

This step will be automatically invoked when you specify the common thickness and press ENTER. In this step, you can specify the face that you want to remove from the thin wall feature. You can use the **Selection Type** list to define the selection method. After specifying the faces to be removed, choose the **Accept** button and then choose the **Preview** button to preview the thin wall feature. Figure 8-28 shows a thin wall model with the front and left side faces removed.

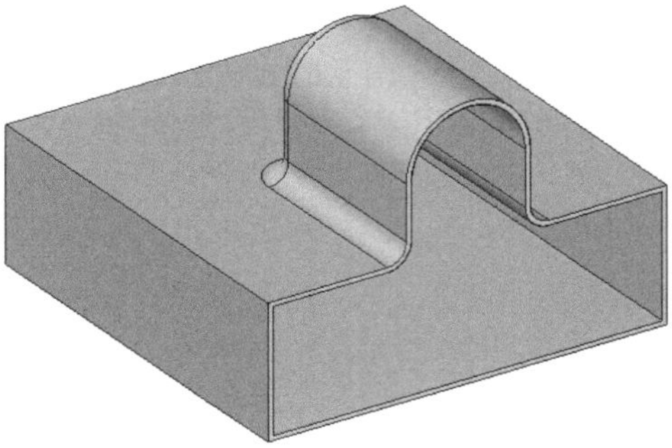

Figure 8-27 *Model with the thin wall feature added and front face removed*

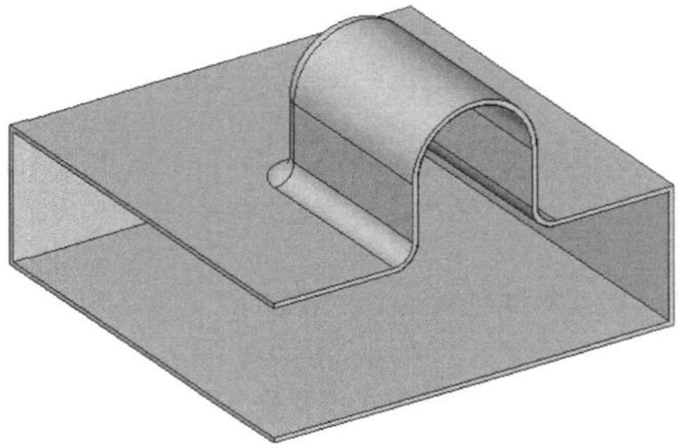

Figure 8-28 *Thin wall model with the front and left faces removed*

Unique Thickness

This step is used to specify different wall thicknesses. After selecting the face or faces, specify the unique thickness value in the **Unique Thickness** edit box in the Command bar and press ENTER. Again, select another face or faces to which you want to add different wall thicknesses and specify the wall thickness in the edit box. Continue this process till you have selected all the faces to which you want to add different wall thicknesses. Figure 8-29 shows a thin wall model with an open face and a unique thickness added to the left and bottom faces.

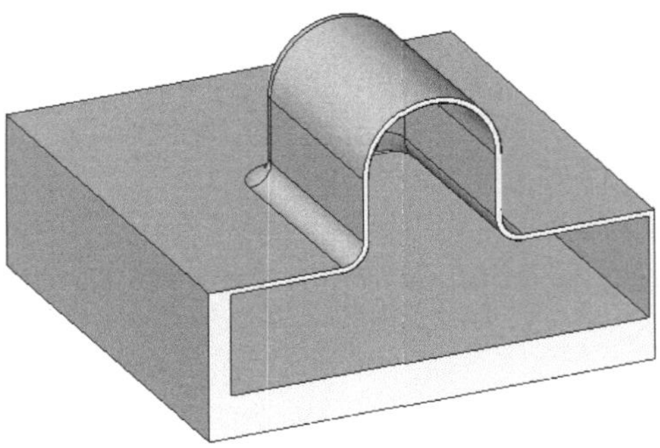

Figure 8-29 *Model with multiple wall thicknesses*

To create thin walls in the **Synchronous Part** environment, invoke the **Thin Wall** tool from the **Solids** group. Next, click on the face that you want to leave open and then enter the common thickness value in the edit box; a preview of the thin wall will be displayed dynamically. Use the handle to specify whether the thickness should be added with reference to inner faces or outer faces. Right-click to accept the thin feature.

Note

Make sure that when you are applying a unique thickness to a thin wall feature, the model is not in symmetric condition. To turn off the symmetric condition, check the advanced design intent of the selected faces and deactivate the symmetric rules.

ADDING THIN REGION FEATURES (ORDERED)

Ribbon: Home > Solids > Thin Wall drop-down > Thin Region

Sometimes, instead of the complete model, you may need to add the thin wall feature to a particular region. For example, refer to the model shown in Figure 8-30. You can add thin wall to a particular region using the **Thin Region** tool. This tool is available only in the **Ordered Part** environment.

The **Thin Region** tool works in the following four steps:

Faces To Thin Step

This is the first step and it is activated automatically when you invoke the **Thin Region** tool. In this step, you need to select a particular feature or the faces of a region to add the thin wall feature. Next, specify the common thickness in the **Common Thickness** edit box. Note that while selecting the faces, you need to make sure that they result in a closed volume. For example, to create a thin wall region shown in Figure 8-30, you need to select the top curved face, side tangent faces, the back face, and the front face of the region, as shown in Figure 8-31.

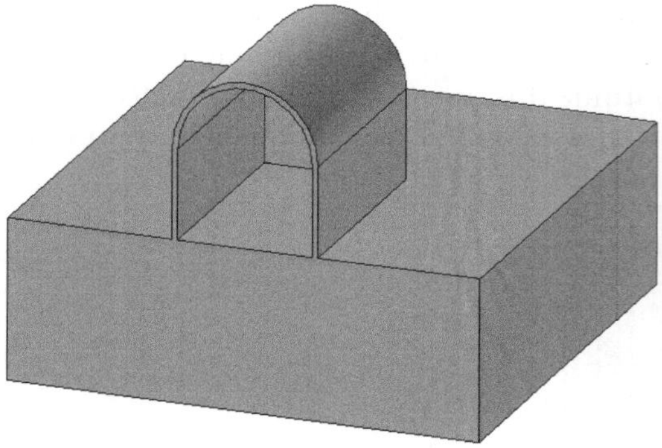

Figure 8-30 Model with a thin wall feature added to a particular region

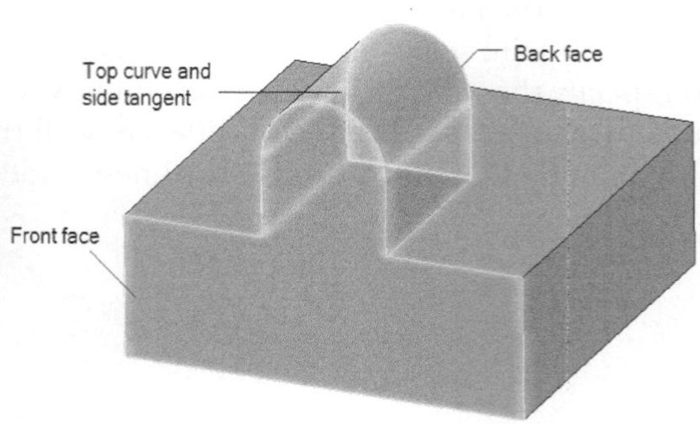

Figure 8-31 Selecting faces to create a thin wall region

Open Faces Step

This step will be automatically invoked when you exit the previous step. In this step, you can select the faces that you want to remove from the thin wall region. For example, to create the model shown in Figure 8-30, you need to remove the front face.

Note

While creating the thin region feature, if the face that you selected to remove is still displayed, then you need to edit the feature and again select the face to be removed in the ***Open Faces*** *step.*

Capping Faces Step

Capping face can be considered as the face that defines the termination of the thin region. You can select any face of the model or an existing surface to define the capping faces. You can also define an offset value from the capping face using the **Offset** edit box that is displayed in the Command bar. Figure 8-32 shows a face used as the capping face. After selecting the capping face, choose the **Accept** button from the Command bar and press ENTER; the model will be created, refer to Figure 8-30. Figure 8-33 shows an extruded surface used as the capping face. Figure 8-34 shows the same surface used as the capping face but with an offset of 2 unit. You will learn more about surfaces in the later chapters.

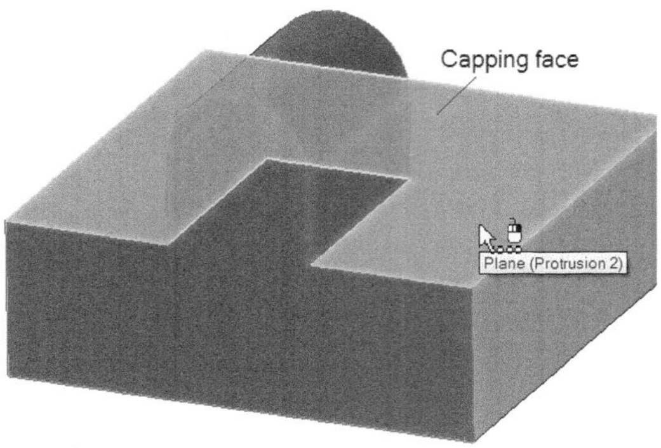

Figure 8-32 Face used as capping face

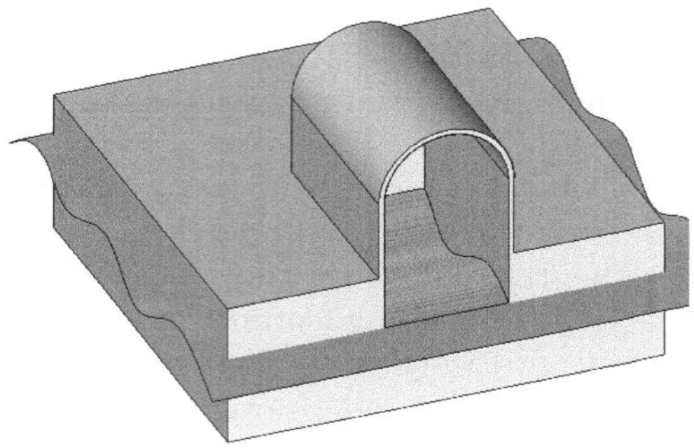

Figure 8-33 Surface used as the capping face

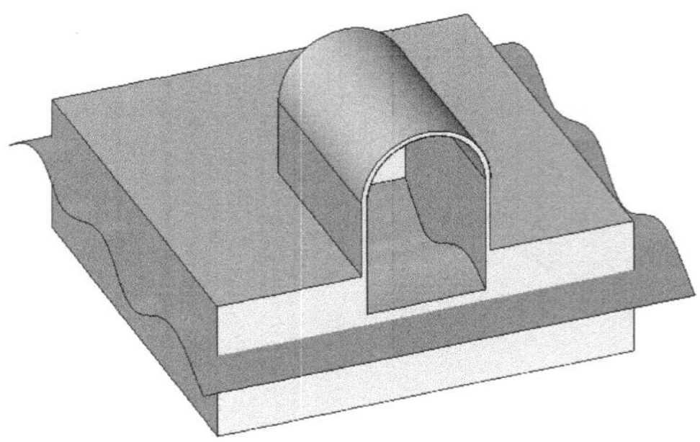

Figure 8-34 Surface used as the capping face with an offset of 2 unit

Unique Thickness Step

This step is used to define different thicknesses to the selected faces and works similar to the **Unique Thickness** step in the **Thin Wall** tool.

ADDING A LIP TO THE MODEL

Ribbon: Home > Solids > Thin Wall drop-down > Lip

The **Lip** tool is used to add a lip to the model by adding material along the selected edges, or by adding a groove to the model by removing the material along the selected edges. The amount of material to be added or removed is defined by a rectangle whose width and height can be specified on invoking this tool.

The **Lip** tool works in the following two steps:

Select Edge Step

This step allows you to select the edge along which you want to add a lip or groove. You can use the options in the **Select** drop-down list to select an individual edge or a chain of edges.

Direction Step

This step enables you to specify the direction and size of the lip feature. When this step is invoked, the **Width** and **Height** edit boxes will be displayed. Specify the width and height of the rectangle in these edit boxes to define the profile of the lip.

After specifying the width and height of the lip, move the cursor in the drawing window. You will notice that an orange colored rectangle is displayed at the start of the edge. Move the cursor around the start of the edge and specify the location of the lip. Note that if the rectangle is inside the feature, the resulting feature will be a groove and if the rectangle is outside the feature, the resulting feature will be a lip. Figures 8-35 through 8-38 show different positions of the rectangle and the resulting lip and groove features.

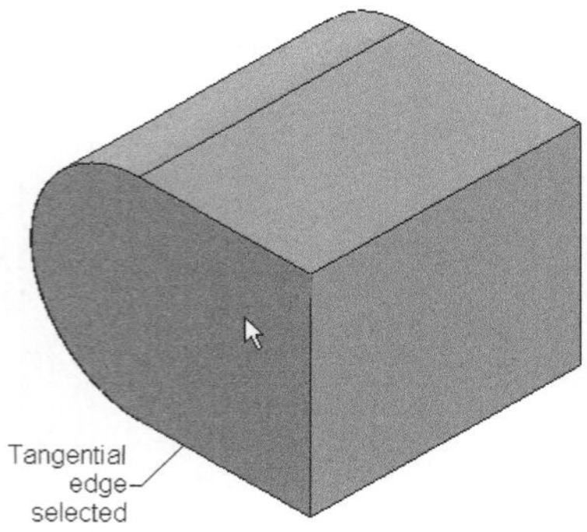

Figure 8-35 *Location of the rectangle*

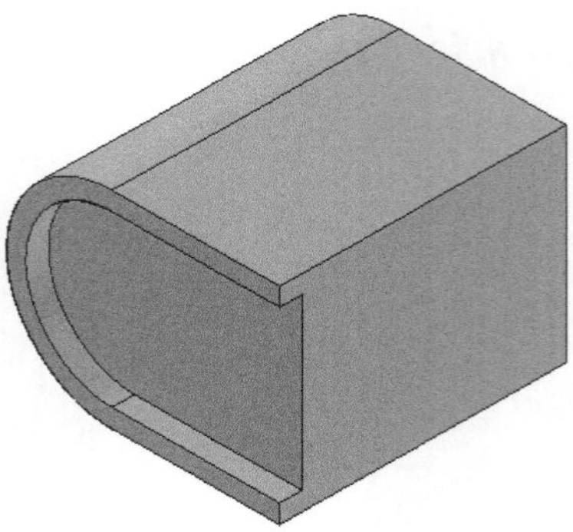

Figure 8-36 *Resulting lip feature*

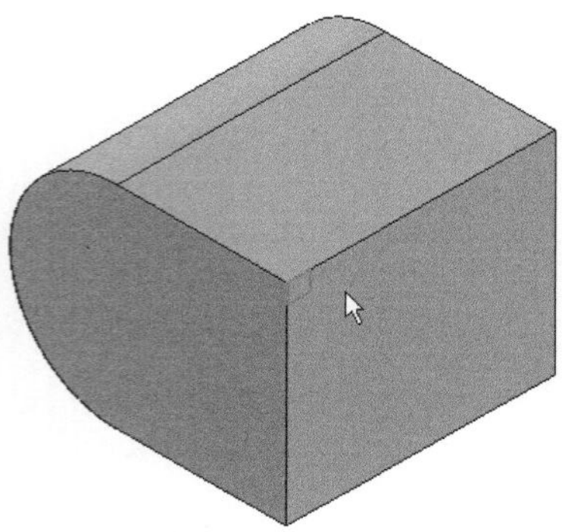

Figure 8-37 *Location of the rectangle*

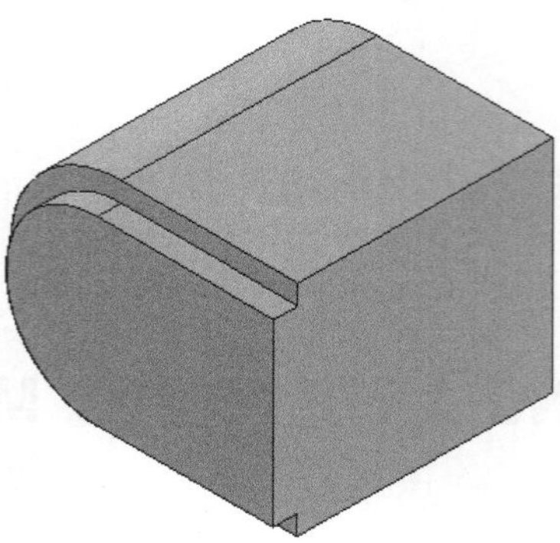

Figure 8-38 *Resulting groove feature*

CREATING WEB NETWORKS (ORDERED)

Ribbon:	Home > Solids > Thin Wall drop-down > Web Network

The **Web Network** tool enables you to create a web network using open entities. Figures 8-39 shows the open sketch entities and Figure 8-40 shows the resulting web network. You can also create a web network as a base feature.

Figure 8-39 *Thin wall model and a network of lines*

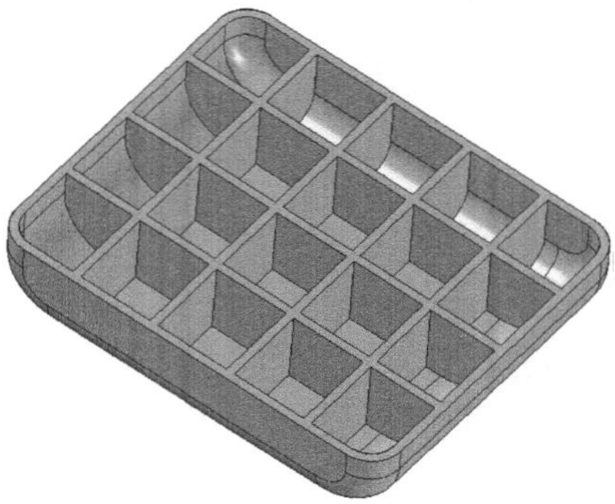

Figure 8-40 *Resulting web network*

This tool works similar to the **Rib** tool and the web network is created in the following four steps:

Sketch Step

This step enables you to select a sketching plane for drawing the profile of the web network. You can also select an existing profile using the **Select from Sketch** option from the **Create-From Options** drop-down list.

Draw Profile Step

This step will be automatically invoked when you select the sketching plane for drawing the profile of the web network.

Direction Step

This step will be automatically invoked when you select the profile and accept it or draw the profile and exit the sketching environment. This step enables you to define the direction in which the web network will be created. It is recommended to define the direction of the web network toward the bottom of the part.

You can specify the thickness of the webs in the web network in the **Thickness** edit box. The functions of the other buttons in the Command bar of this step are the same as those in the **Rib** tool. Figure 8-41 shows a web network in which webs are not extended. Figure 8-42 shows a web network in which webs are extended, but defined up to a finite depth.

Treatment Step

This step is used to add a draft to webs in a web network. It works similar to the **Treatment Step** in the **Protrusion** tool.

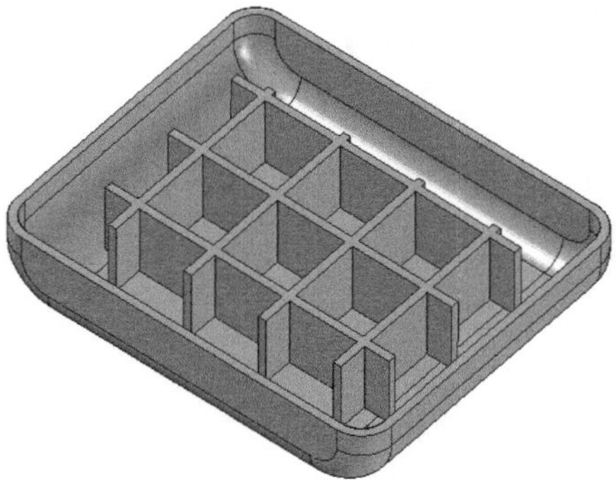

Figure 8-41 *Web network with webs not extended*

Figure 8-42 *Webs defined up to a finite depth*

Tip

To select multiple entities, refer to Figure 8-39, select the ***Single*** *option from the* ***Select*** *drop-down list, and then drag a box around the entities to select them.*

Note

You can also create a web network feature in the ***Synchronous Part*** *environment. To do so, draw a sketch to create the web network and then invoke the* ***Web Network*** *tool from the* ***Thin Wall*** *drop-down of the* ***Solids*** *group in the* ***Home*** *tab; the* ***Web Network*** *Command bar will be displayed and you will be prompted to select a chain of entities or a single entity. Select the sketch and then choose the* ***Accept*** *button; a preview of the web network will be displayed and you will be prompted to modify the network. Specify the direction of the web network and enter the thickness value in the* ***Dynamic*** *edit box. Next, choose the* ***Accept*** *button from the Command bar; the web network will be created.*

CREATING VENTS

Ribbon: Home > Solids > Thin Wall drop-down > Vent

The **Vent** tool enables you to create a vent in an existing model by defining the boundary of the vent, ribs, and spars in the vent. This tool is available only after you have drawn the sketch for the vent. Figure 8-43 shows a model and a profile that defines the boundary. Note that in the vent, all the vertical lines are selected as spars and all the horizontal lines are selected as ribs. Figure 8-44 shows the resulting model with the vent.

To create a vent, invoke the **Vent** tool; the **Vent Options** dialog box will be displayed, as shown in Figure 8-45.

Vent Options dialog box

The options in this dialog box are discussed next.

Saved settings

This drop-down list displays the list of settings that you have saved. By default, this drop-down list is blank. To save the settings, set the required parameters in this dialog box, enter a name for the parameters set in the **Saved settings** edit box, and then choose the **Save** button; the settings will be saved. Now, if you want to view the parameters set under any set, select the required name from the **Saved settings** drop-down list. You can delete the unwanted settings by selecting them from this drop-down list and choosing the **Delete** button.

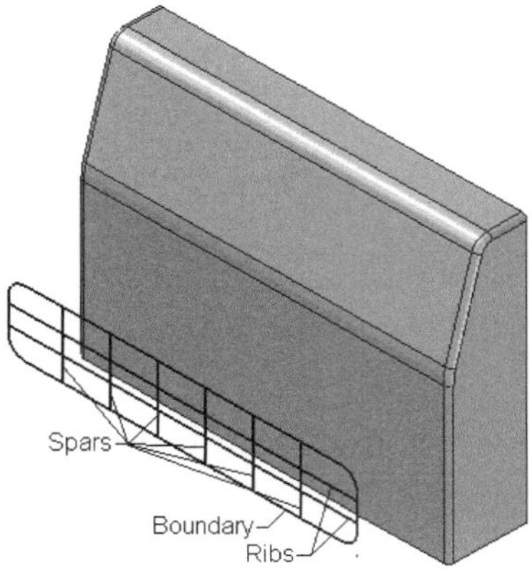

***Figure 8-43** Parameters of the vent*

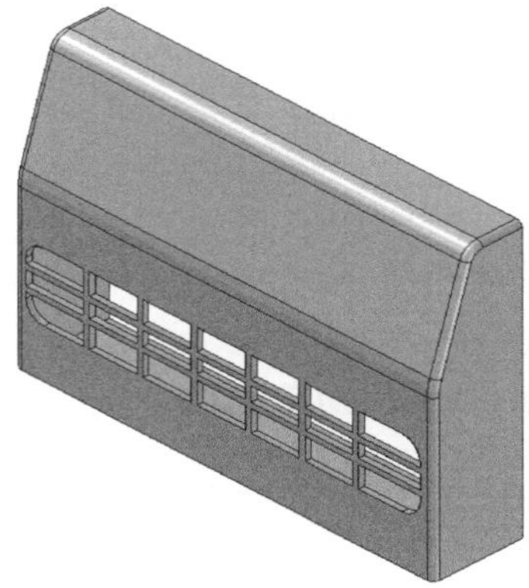

***Figure 8-44** Resulting model with the vent*

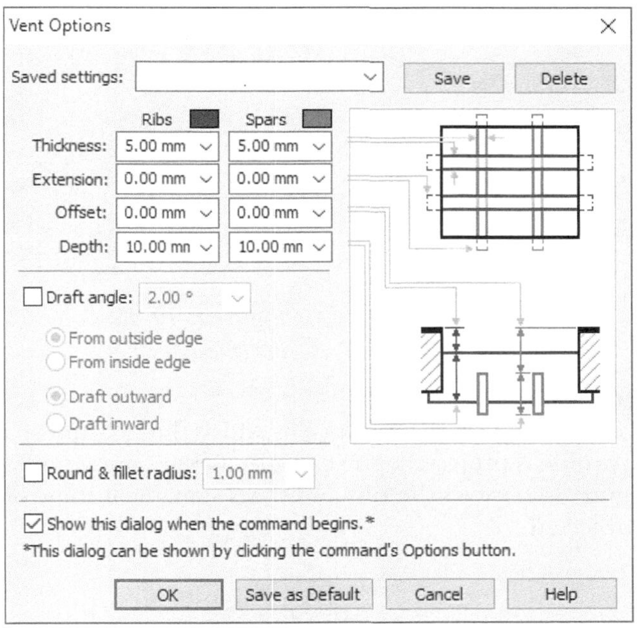

***Figure 8-45** The **Vent Options** dialog box*

Thickness Ribs/Spars

These edit boxes are used to specify the thickness of ribs and spars. Figure 8-46 shows a vent with the thickness of ribs and spars as 2. Figure 8-47 shows a vent with the thickness of ribs and spars as 5. You can have the same or different thickness values for the ribs and spars.

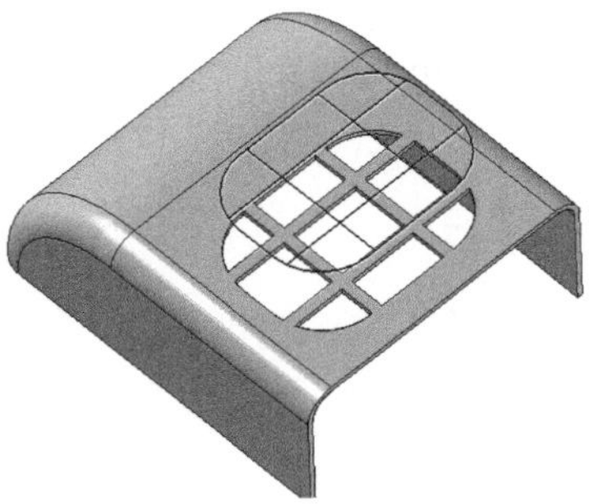

Figure 8-46 Vent with ribs and spars thickness as 2

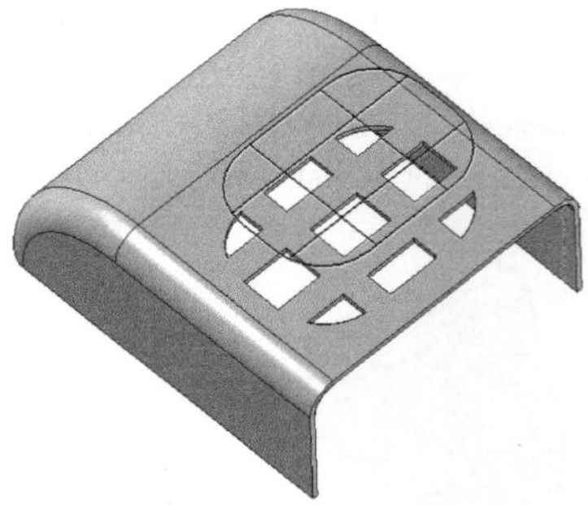

Figure 8-47 Vent with ribs and spars thickness as 5

Extension Ribs/Spars

These edit boxes are used to specify the distance by which the ribs and spars will extend beyond the boundary of the vent. You can have the same or different extension values for the ribs and spars. Figure 8-48 shows the ribs and spars without extension and Figure 8-49 shows the ribs and spars extended beyond the boundary.

Figure 8-48 Ribs and spars not extended

Figure 8-49 Ribs and spars extended beyond the boundary

Offset Ribs/Spars

These edit boxes are used to specify the distance by which the ribs and spars will be offset from the face on which the profile is projected. You can specify the same or different offset values for the ribs and spars. Figure 8-50 shows the ribs and spars starting at some offset from the face on which the profile is projected.

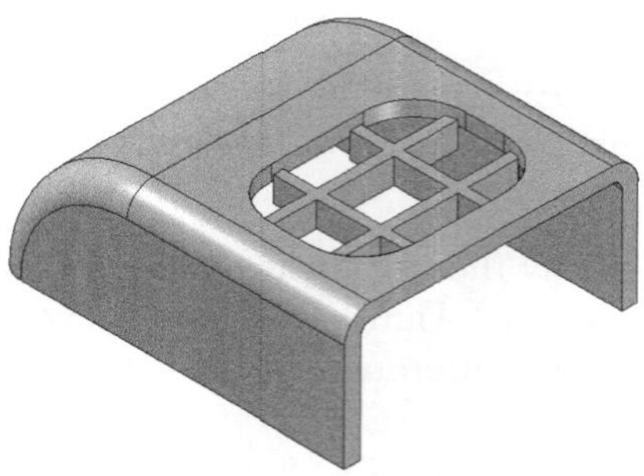

Figure 8-50 Ribs and spars starting at an offset from the top face

Note

If the offset value of the ribs and spars is more than the thickness of the face on which the profile of the vent is created, then the feature may not be created.

Depth Ribs/Spars

These edit boxes are used to specify the depth of ribs and spars. You can have the same or different depth values for each one of them. Figures 8-51 and 8-52 show vent features with different depth values for ribs and spars.

Figure 8-51 *Ribs and spars depth = 2*

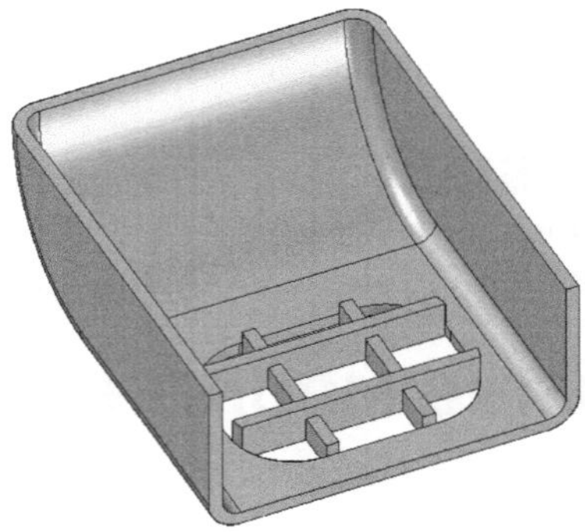

Figure 8-52 *Ribs depth = 4, spars depth = 6*

Draft angle

The **Draft angle** check box is selected to add a draft to the ribs and spars in the vent. The draft angle can be specified in the edit box available on the right of this check box. You can also specify whether the draft should be specified from the outside or the inside edge, and whether the draft should be outward or inward. You can do so by selecting the required radio button below the **Draft angle** edit box.

Round & fillet radius

The **Round & fillet radius** check box is selected to add rounds and fillets to the vent. The radius of the round and fillet can be specified in the edit box available on the right of this check box. Figure 8-53 shows a vent with fillets and rounds.

Figure 8-53 *Vent with fillets and rounds*

After specifying the required parameters in the **Vent Options** dialog box, choose **OK**. The **Vent** tool works in the following four steps:

Select Boundary Step

This step will be activated automatically in the Command bar when you exit the **Vent Options** dialog box. In this step, you can select a chain of entities that will act as the boundary of the vent. You can also select the options in the **Selection Type** list to select a chain of entities or an individual entity.

Select Ribs Step

This step will be automatically invoked when you accept the boundary in the **Select Boundary Step**. In this step, you can select closed or open entities to define the ribs in the vent. After selecting the entities, right-click to accept the selection.

Select Spars Step

This step will be automatically invoked when you accept the entities to define the ribs in the **Select Ribs Step**. In this step, you can select the entities that you want to use as spars in the vent. You can select closed or open entities to define the spars. After selecting the entities, right-click to accept the selection.

Extent Step

This step is used to specify the side and the extent of the vent. You can use the buttons in the Command bar of this step to define the extent.

CREATING MOUNTING BOSSES (ORDERED)

Ribbon: Home > Solids > Thin Wall drop-down > Mounting Boss

The **Mounting Boss** tool enables you to create mounting boss features, which are used in plastic components to accommodate fasteners. Figure 8-54 shows a model with four mounting boss features.

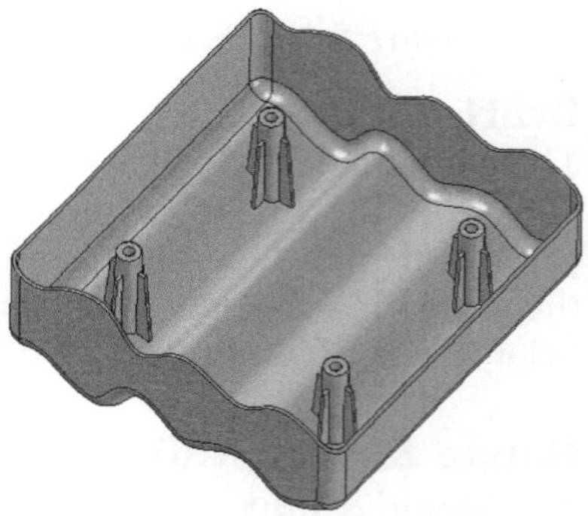

Figure 8-54 *Model with four mounting bosses*

To create mounting boss features, invoke the **Mounting Boss** tool; the **Mounting Boss** Command bar will be displayed. It is recommended that before proceeding further, you set the parameters of the mounting boss features in the **Mounting Boss Options** dialog box, as shown in Figure 8-55. This dialog box is invoked on choosing the **Mounting Boss Options** button from the **Mounting Boss** Command bar.

Mounting Boss Options Dialog Box

The options in this dialog box are discussed next.

Saved settings

This drop-down list displays the list of settings that you have saved. By default, this drop-down list is blank. To save the settings, set the required parameters in this dialog box, enter a name for the parameters set in the **Saved settings** edit box, and then choose the **Save** button; the settings will be saved. Now, if you want to view the parameters set, select the required name from the **Saved settings** drop-down list. You can delete the unwanted settings by selecting them from this drop-down list and choosing the **Delete** button.

Settings

The options available in this area are used to set the parameters of the mounting boss feature. All these options have a grey arrow on the right that leads to a parameter in the preview window.

The preview window explains the use of the options available in the **Settings** area. These options are discussed next.

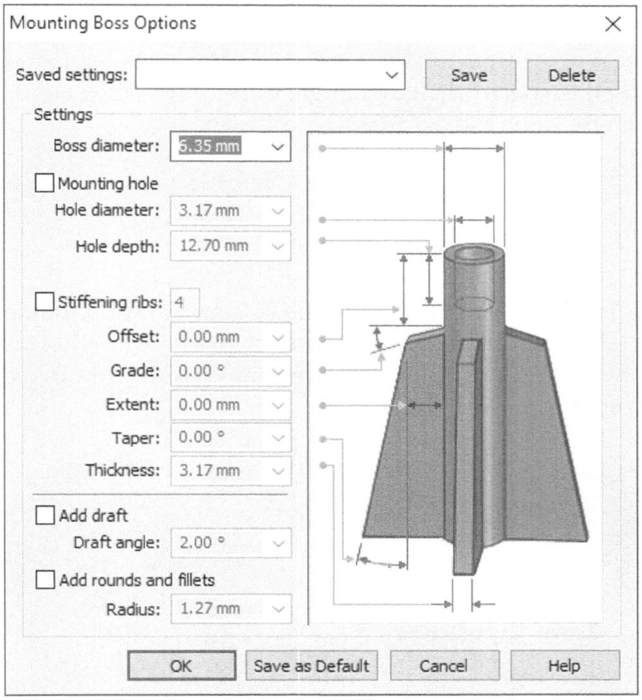

*Figure 8-55 The **Mounting Boss Options** dialog box*

Boss diameter

This edit box is used to specify the diameter of the mounting boss.

Mounting hole

This check box is selected to create a hole on the top face of the mounting boss. On selecting this check box, the **Hole diameter** and **Hole depth** edit boxes will become available and you can specify the diameter and the depth of the hole in these edit boxes, respectively.

Stiffening ribs

This check box is used to create a mounting box with ribs. If this check box is not selected, only a cylindrical feature will be created as the mounting boss. You can specify the number of stiffening ribs in the edit box available on the right of this check box.

Offset

This edit box will be available only when you select the **Stiffening ribs** check box and is used to specify the distance between the start of the rib and the top face of the mounting boss.

Grade

This edit box is used to specify the angle of the top face of the ribs with respect to the top face of the mounting boss.

Extent
This edit box is used to specify the extrusion depth of the top face of the ribs from the cylindrical surface of the mounting boss.

Taper
This edit box is used to specify the taper angle value of the rib. Note that you can enter only a positive taper angle value for the rib.

Thickness
This edit box is used to specify the thickness of the rib.

Add draft
This check box is selected to add a draft to the mounting boss. On selecting this check box, the **Draft angle** edit box will be activated and then you can enter the draft angle in this edit box. Figure 8-56 shows a model with mounting bosses without a draft and Figure 8-57 shows the mounting bosses with draft.

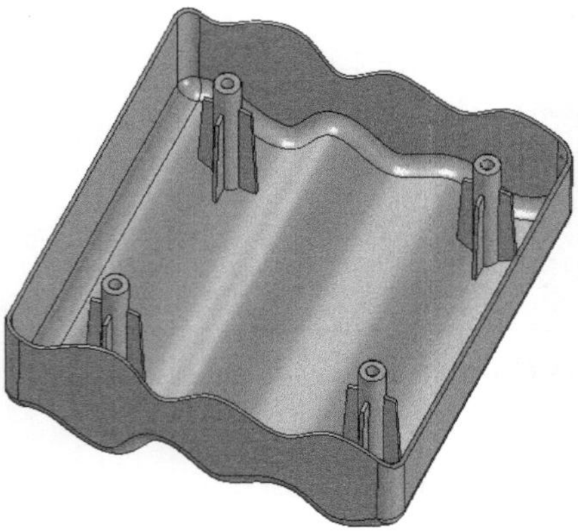

Figure 8-56 *Mounting bosses without draft*

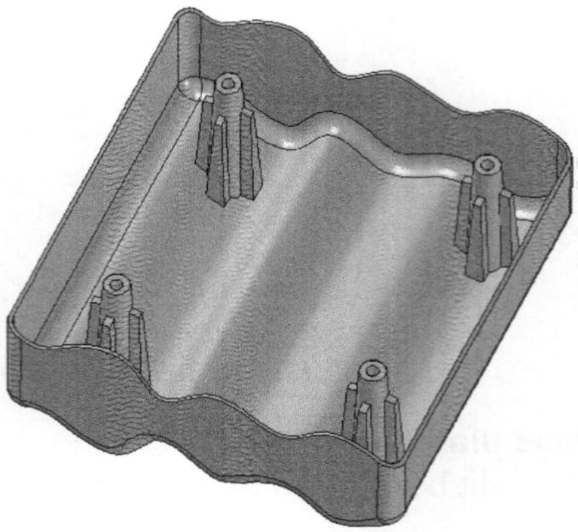

Figure 8-57 *Mounting bosses with draft*

Add rounds and fillets
This check box is selected to add rounds and fillets to the mounting boss. On selecting this check box, the **Radius** edit box will be activated and now you can enter the radius value in this edit box.

After setting the options in the **Mounting Boss Options** dialog box, you need to use the following three steps to create the mounting bosses:

Plane Step

This step enables you to select a plane for placing the profiles of the mounting bosses. Note that the profiles of the mounting bosses are placed at a planar face or a reference plane parallel to the face on which you want to project them. The distance between the parallel plane and the face on which the mounting bosses are projected defines their depth. It is similar to extruding the profile from the parallel plane up to the face.

By default, the **Parallel Plane** option is selected in the **Create-From Options** drop-down list. If the face on which you want to project the profiles is curved, you can select the base reference plane that is parallel to the face.

Mounting Boss Step

This step will automatically be invoked when you select the parallel plane. On doing so, the sketching environment is invoked and the **Mounting Boss Location** button will be chosen in the **Features** group of the **Home** tab. In addition, the profile of the mounting boss will be attached to the cursor. Now, you can place the profiles of the mounting boss on the selected plane to place the mounting boss.

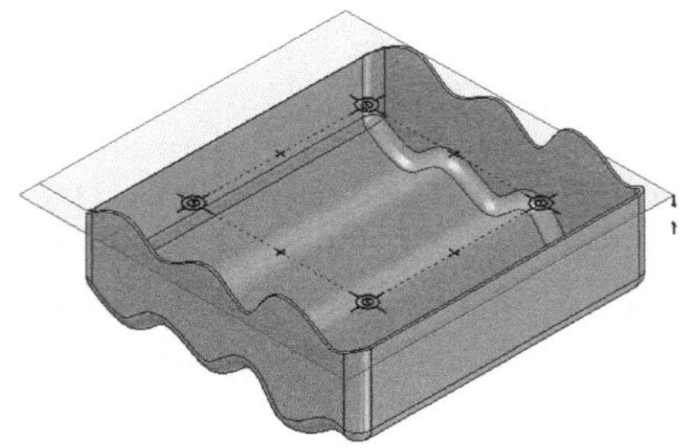

Figure 8-58 Profile of four Mounting bosses

You can also modify the mounting boss options by choosing the **Mounting Boss Options** button. This button will be available in the Command bar when you choose the **Mounting Boss Location** button from the **Features** group of the **Home** tab. Figure 8-58 shows the profile of the four mounting bosses placed on a parallel plane.

Extent Step

This step will automatically be invoked when you choose the **Close Sketch** button from the sketching environment of the **Mounting Boss Step**. In this step, you can specify the side for creating mounting boss. You can move the cursor on the side of the face where you want to project the profiles and click to accept the side. As soon as you specify the side, a preview of the mounting boss will be displayed. If the feature is correct, you can choose the **Finish** button to accept the feature; else, choose the **Mounting Box Options** button or the button of any other step to modify the options.

REORDERING FEATURES

While working on designs, you may sometime need to reorder the features. By reordering features, you can change the sequence in which the features were created in the model. For example, in the model shown in Figure 8-59, cavities were created first, followed by the thin wall feature. As a result, a thin wall is also created around the cavities, resulting in a protrusion feature. The original model required is the one shown in Figure 8-60.

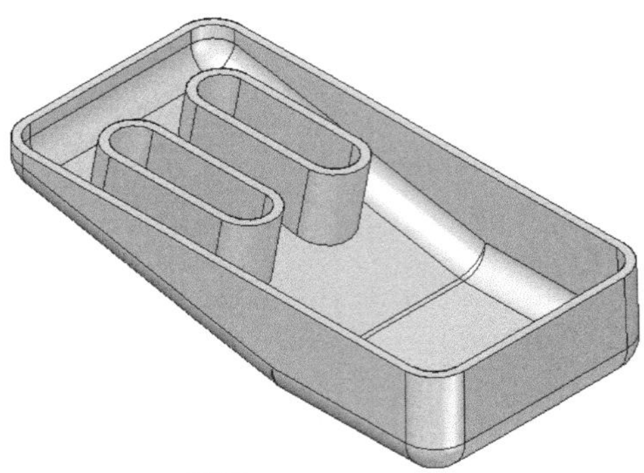

Figure 8-59 Thin wall created around cavities

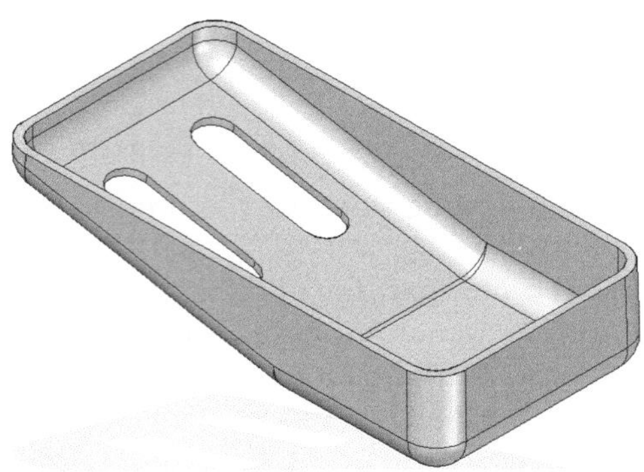

Figure 8-60 Original model

To resolve this problem, Solid Edge allows you to change the order of the feature creation in the model. You can move a feature before or after another feature. However, note that the reordering is possible only between the features that are independent of each other. For example, if a part of any feature is dependent on another feature, then you cannot reorder the dependent feature above the parent feature.

In Solid Edge, the features are reordered using the **PathFinder**. Select the feature in the **PathFinder** and drag it above or below the other features. If a feature cannot be dragged above a feature in the **PathFinder**, then you cannot reorder the feature before it because the selected feature is dependent on the feature above which you want to drag it. However, if the feature is not dependent, a green arrow will be displayed on the left of the feature in the **PathFinder** while you reorder it. Figure 8-61 shows the thin wall feature being dragged above the cutout feature to reorder it before the cutout feature. If you reorder the thin wall feature before the cutout, you will get the model shown in Figure 8-60.

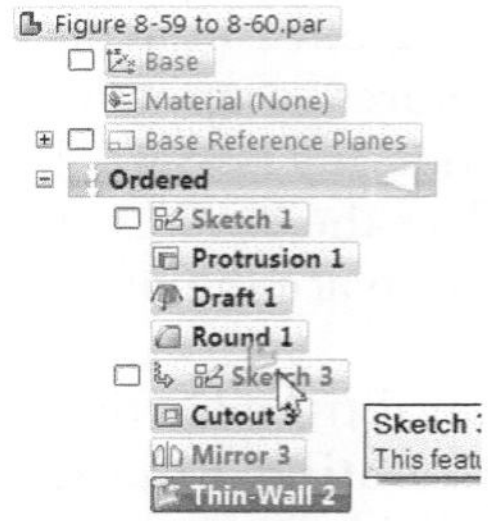

Figure 8-61 *Reordering features in the* ***PathFinder***

TUTORIALS

Tutorial 1 Synchronous and Ordered

In this tutorial, you will create the model shown in Figure 8-62. Its dimensions are given in the drawing views shown in Figure 8-63. Save the model with the name *c08tut1.par* at the location given next:

C:\Solid Edge\c08 **(Expected time: 30 min)**

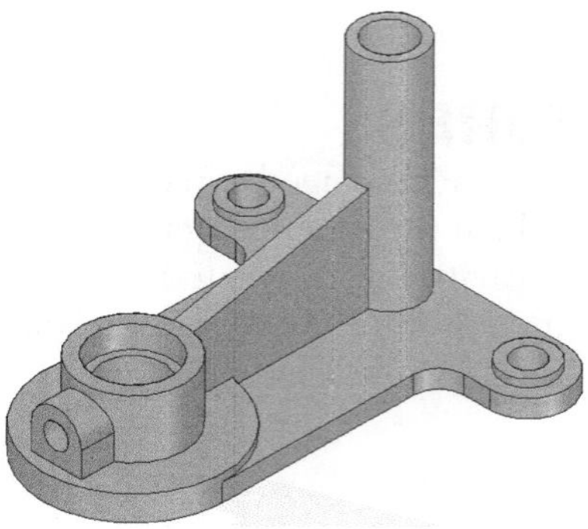

Figure 8-62 *Model for Tutorial 1*

The following steps are required to complete this tutorial:

a. Start a new part file and create the base feature on the top plane, refer to Figure 8-64.
b. Add the remaining protrusion features to the base feature, refer to Figure 8-65.
c. Add holes to the model, refer to Figure 8-66.
d. Switch to the **Ordered Part** environment and create the rib feature, refer to Figure 8-67 and Figure 8-68.
e. Save the model and close the file.

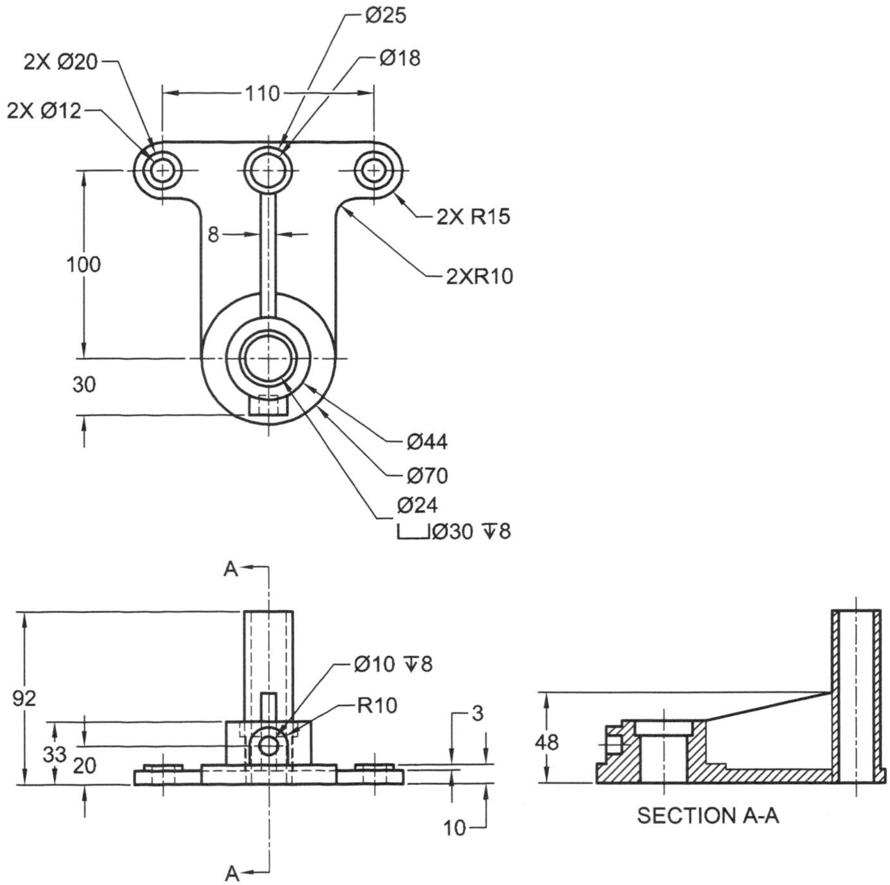

Figure 8-63 Dimensions of the model for Tutorial 1

Creating the Base Feature

1. Start a new part document in Solid Edge. Create the sketch of the base feature on the top (xy) plane and then extrude it. The extruded base feature is shown in Figure 8-64.

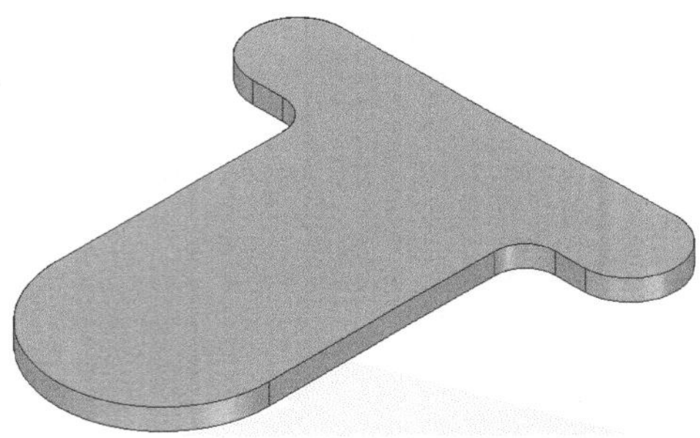

Figure 8-64 Base feature of the model

Adding the Remaining Extruded Features and Holes

1. Add the remaining protrusion features to the model, as shown in Figure 8-65.

2. Create holes in the model, as shown in Figure 8-66.

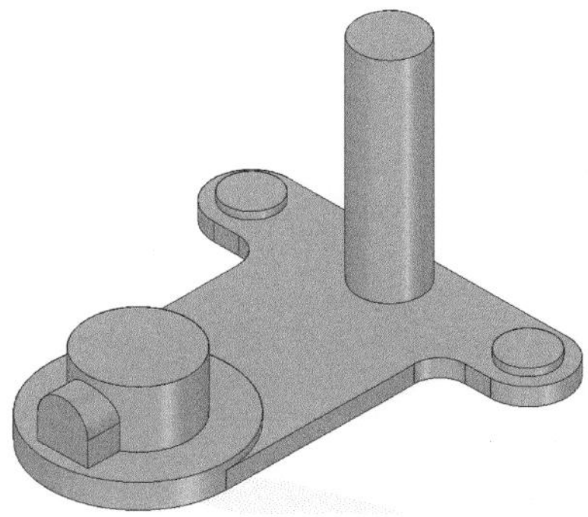

Figure 8-65 Model after adding the remaining protrusion features

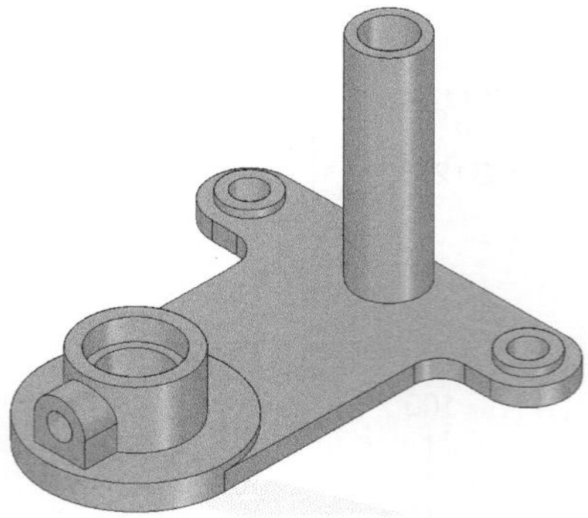

Figure 8-66 Model after adding holes

Creating the Rib Feature

Next, you need to switch to the **Ordered Part** environment and create the rib feature. The profile for this rib is a single line and needs to be extruded symmetrically on both sides of the sketching plane.

1. Choose the **Rib** tool from the **Thin Wall** drop-down in the **Solids** group of the **Home** tab; the **Sketch Step** is activated in the Command bar.

2. Select the **Coincident Plane** option from the **Create-From Options** drop-down list, if it is not already selected; you are prompted to click on a planar face or on a reference plane.

3. Select or create a reference plane passing through the center of the circular features in the middle of the model.

4. Draw a single line as the profile of the rib feature and add the required relationships and dimensions to it, as shown in Figure 8-67.

5. Exit the sketching environment; the **Direction Step** is activated and you are prompted to click to accept the displayed side or select the other side in the view.

6. Enter **8** in the **Thickness** edit box and specify the direction of the rib, as shown in Figure 8-68.

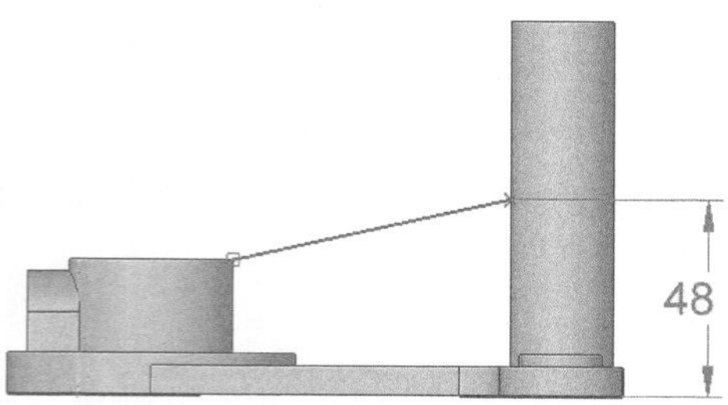

Figure 8-67 Profile for the rib feature

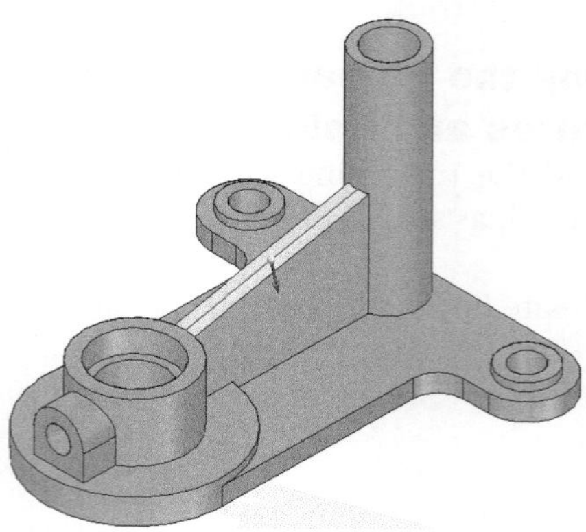

Figure 8-68 Specifying the direction of the rib

7. Choose **Finish** and then **Cancel** from the Command bar to create the rib feature. The final model after creating the rib feature is shown in Figure 8-69.

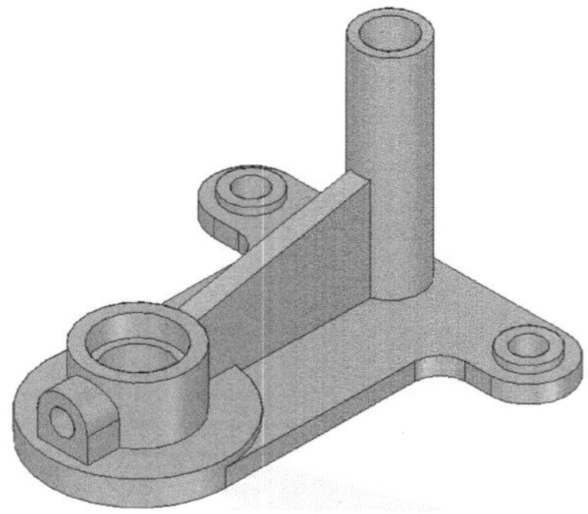

Figure 8-69 *Model after creating the rib feature*

Saving the Model

1. Save the model with the name *c08tut1.par* at the location given below and then close the file.

   C:\Solid Edge\c08

Tutorial 2 — Synchronous and Ordered

In this tutorial, you will create the model of the ice tray shown in Figure 8-70. Its dimensions are given in the drawing views shown in Figure 8-71. Save the model with the name *c08tut2.par* at the location given next:

C:\Solid Edge\c08 **(Expected time: 30 min)**

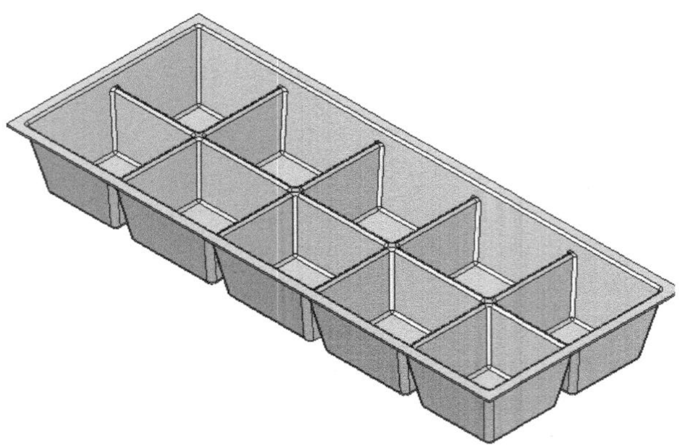

Figure 8-70 *Model for Tutorial 2*

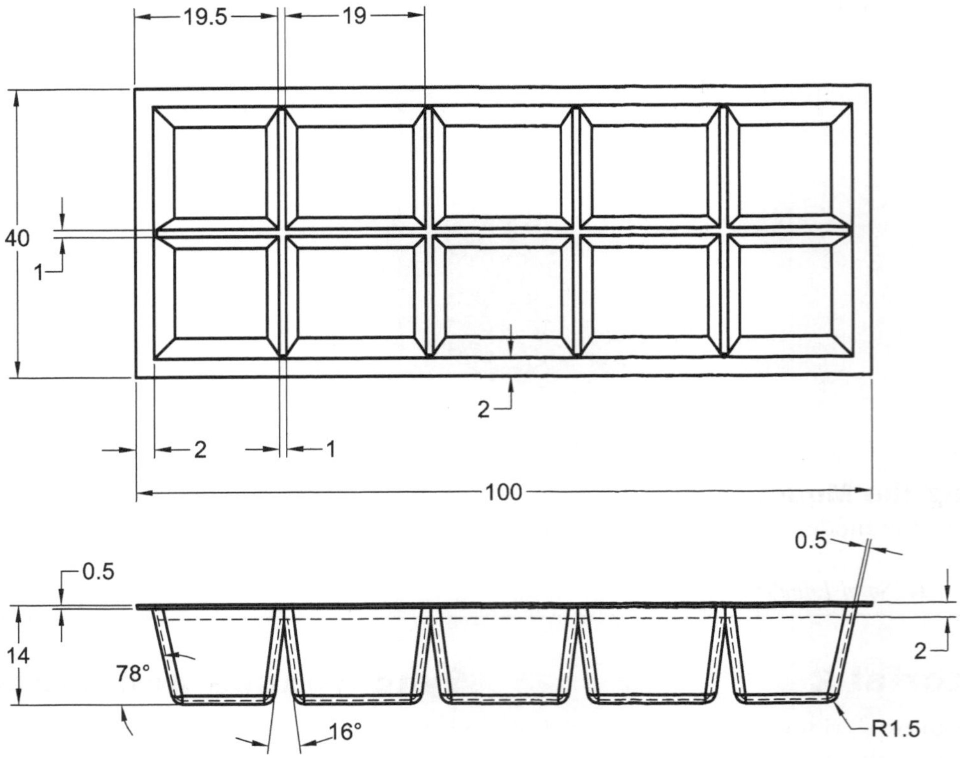

Figure 8-71 Dimensions of the model for Tutorial 2

The following steps are required to complete this tutorial:

a. Start a new part file and create the base feature on the top plane, refer to Figure 8-72.
b. Add a draft to the base feature, refer to Figure 8-73.
c. Switch to the **Ordered Part** environment.
d. Add a thin wall feature to the model, refer to Figure 8-74.
e. Create a web network in the model, refer to Figures 8-75 and 8-76.
f. Add rounds to the sharp edges of the model, refer to Figure 8-77.
g. Add another thin wall feature, refer to Figure 8-78.
h. Save the model and close the file.

Creating the Base Feature

1. Start a new part file and then create the base feature of the model on the xy plane. The base feature is a box of 100x40x14 size and is shown in Figure 8-72.

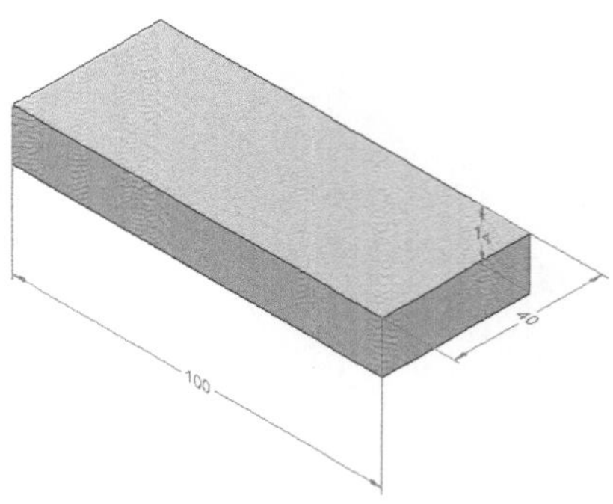

Figure 8-72 Base feature of the model

Adding the Draft to the Base Feature

Next, you need to add a draft to the outer faces of the base feature using the top planar face of the base feature as the draft plane.

1. Choose the **Draft** tool from the **Solids** group of the **Home** tab; the **Draft** Command bar is displayed.

   On invoking the **Draft** tool, you are prompted to click on a planar face or on a reference plane as you need to define the draft plane.

2. Select the top planar face of the base feature as the draft plane.

   Next, you need to select the faces to be tapered.

3. Select all the four side-faces of the model to add the draft. Specify the direction of draft creation as inward by using the Draft direction handle and then enter **12** in the dynamic **Draft angle** edit box.

4. Right-click in the drawing area to create the draft. The model after adding the draft is shown in Figure 8-73.

Adding the Thin Wall Feature (Ordered Part)

Next, you need to scoop out the material from inside the model to create a thin wall model. This is done by using the **Thin Wall** tool. Also, you need to remove the top face of the model while creating the thin wall.

1. Switch to the **Ordered Part** environment and choose the **Thin Wall** tool from the **Solids** group of the **Home** tab; the **Thin Wall** Command bar is displayed with the **Common Thickness** step activated. Also, you are prompted to key in a common thickness value.

2. Enter **2** in the **Common thickness** edit box and press ENTER; the **Open Faces** step is invoked and you are prompted to click on a face chain.

3. Select the top planar face of the model as the face to be removed and then right-click to accept the selection.

4. Choose the **Preview** button and then choose **Finish** to create the thin wall feature. The model after creating the thin wall feature is shown in Figure 8-74.

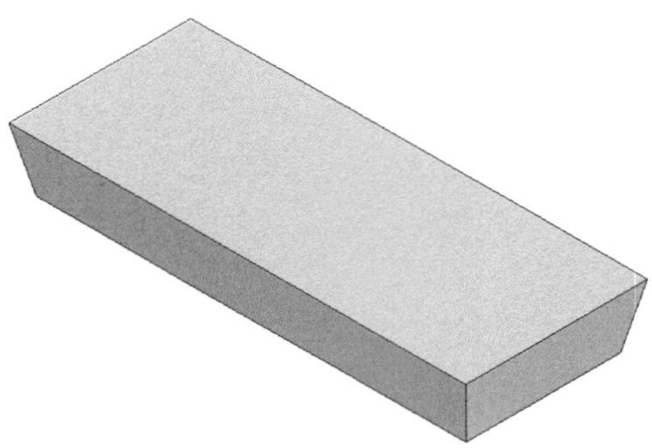

Figure 8-73 *Model after adding the draft*

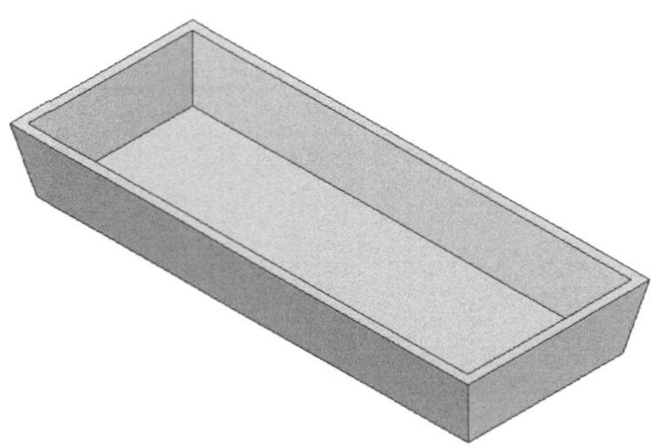

Figure 8-74 *The model after adding the thin wall feature*

Creating the Web Network

Next, you need to create the web network to accommodate the ice cubes. To create the web network, you need to use an open profile consisting of mutually perpendicular lines. Note that this profile needs to be created on a reference plane located at an offset distance of **2** from the top planar face of the thin wall model.

1. Choose the **Web Network** tool from the **Thin Wall** drop-down in the **Solids** group; the **Web Network** Command bar is displayed with the **Sketch Step** activated. Also, you are prompted to click on a planar face or on a reference plane.

2. Define a plane parallel to the top planar face of the thin wall feature. The plane should be at offset distance of **2** units in the downward direction. Make sure that the **Parallel Plane** option is selected in the **Create-From Options** drop-down list.

3. Draw the profile of the web network, as shown in Figure 8-75.

4. Exit the sketching environment; the **Direction Step** is invoked and you are prompted to click to accept the displayed side or select the other side in the view.

   You will notice that only one line is selected in the preview. But, it is just for the display. While creating the web network, all lines will be used.

5. Enter **1** in the **Thickness** edit box and move the cursor to the lower side of the model and click to create the web network in the downward direction.

   To add a draft of **8** degrees to the web network, you need to invoke the **Treatment Step** manually.

6. Choose the **Treatment Step** beside the **Direction Step** in the **Web Network** Command bar. Next, choose the **Draft** button from the **Treatment Step**.

7. Enter **8** in the **Angle** edit box. Choose the **Flip 1** button from the Command bar to make sure that the draft is applied in the outward direction.

8. Choose the **Preview** button and then choose the **Finish** button from the Command bar to complete the web network, see Figure 8-76.

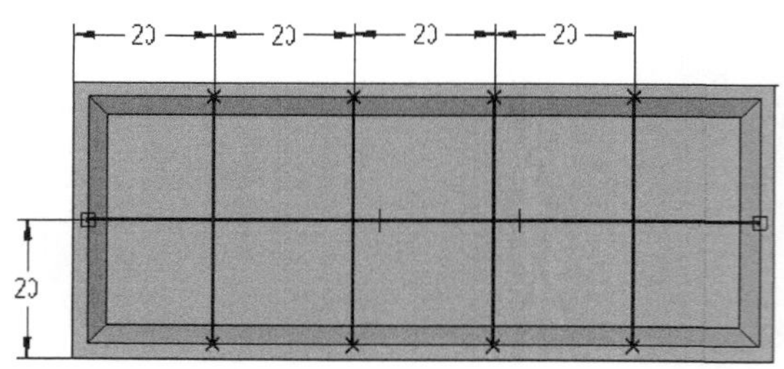

Figure 8-75 *Sketch for the web network*

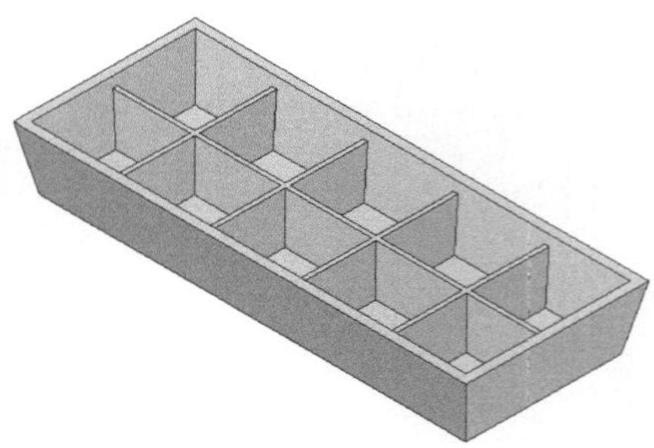

Figure 8-76 *Model after creating the web network*

Creating Rounds

1. Add a round of radius 1 mm to the inner edges of the cavities created by the web network.

2. Next, add a round of radius 0.5 mm to the top face of the web network. The model after adding rounds is shown in Figure 8-77.

Adding the Thin Wall Feature

Next, you need to add a thin wall feature such that all the side faces and the bottom face of the model are removed.

1. Choose the **Thin Wall** button from the **Solids** group; the **Thin Wall** Command bar is displayed and the **Common Thickness** step is activated. Hence, you are prompted to key in a common thickness value.

2. Enter **0.5** in the **Common thickness** edit box and press ENTER; the **Open Faces** step is invoked and you are prompted to click on a face chain.

3. Select the four side-faces and the bottom face of the model as the faces to be removed and then right-click to accept the selection.

4. Choose **Preview** and then the **Finish** button to create the thin wall feature. The final model of the ice tray after creating the thin wall feature is shown in Figure 8-78.

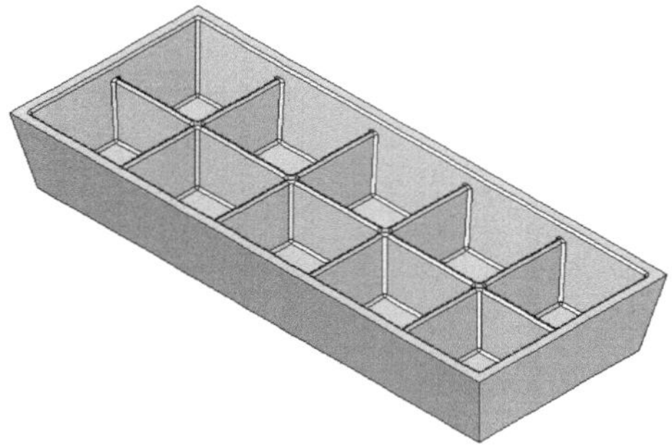

Figure 8-77 *Model after adding rounds*

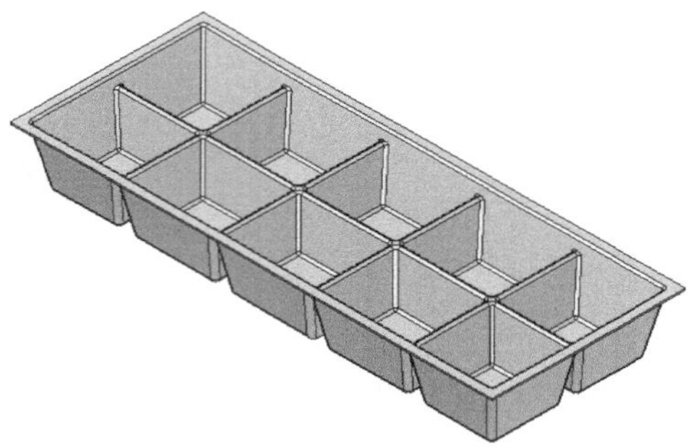

Figure 8-78 *Final model of the ice tray*

Saving the Model

1. Save the model with the name *c08tut2.par* at the location given below and then close the file:

   C:\Solid Edge\c08

Tutorial 3 Synchronous and Ordered

In this tutorial, you will create the model of the cover shown in Figure 8-79. Its dimensions are given in Figure 8-80. The outer fillet in Figure 8-80 is removed for the purpose of dimensioning. The radius of this fillet is 8. A draft of 1 degree needs to be added to the base feature of the model. The parameters of the mounting bosses are as follows:

Boss diameter = 4, hole diameter = 2, hole depth = 5, stiffening rib = 4, rib offset = 3, rib grade = 10 degrees, rib extent = 1, rib taper = 10-degrees, rib thickness = 1.
Save the model with the name *c08tut3.par* at the location given below:
C:\Solid Edge\c08 **(Expected time: 45 min)**

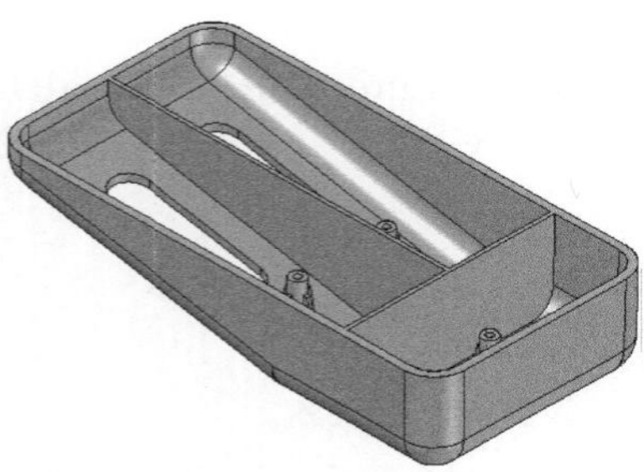

Figure 8-79 *Model for Tutorial 3*

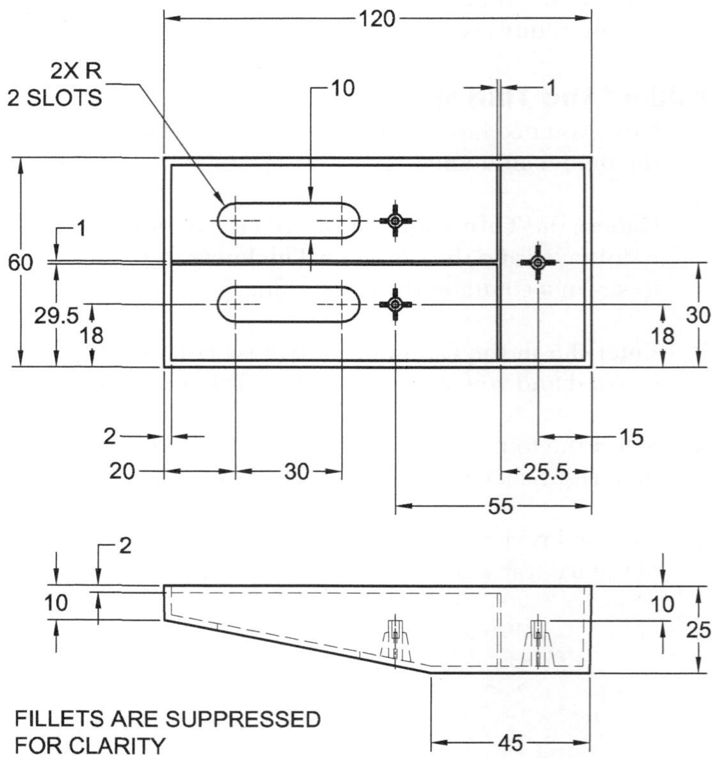

Figure 8-80 *Dimensions of the model for Tutorial 3 with the fillets removed for clarity*

The following steps are required to complete this tutorial:

a. Start Solid Edge in the **ISO Metric Part** environment. Create the base feature on the front (xz) plane, refer to Figure 8-81.
b. Add a draft to the base feature.
c. Add rounds to the sharp edges of the model, refer to Figure 8-82.
d. Add a thin wall feature to the model, refer to Figure 8-83.
e. Create two cutouts in the model, refer to Figure 8-84.
f. Create a web network in the model, refer to Figures 8-85 and 8-86.
g. Switch to the **Ordered Part** environment and add mounting bosses to the model, refer to Figures 8-87 and 8-88.
h. Save the model and close the file.

Creating the Base Feature

1. Start Solid Edge in the **ISO Metric Part** environment and then select the front (xz) plane as the sketching plane for the protrusion feature.

2. Create the profile of the base feature and extrude it symmetrically. The base feature of the model is shown in Figure 8-81.

Figure 8-81 Base feature of the model

Adding the Draft to the Base Feature

As mentioned earlier, drafts are added for the easy removal of component from casting. Therefore, you need to add draft to the side walls of this model before you proceed further. To do so, you need to use the top face as the draft plane.

1. Choose the **Draft** tool from the **Solids** group of the **Home** tab; the **Draft** Command bar is displayed.

   You need to add draft with the top face of the base feature as the draft plane. By default, the **From plane** radio button is selected in the **Draft Options** dialog box. Therefore, you do not need to invoke the **Draft Options** dialog box to select this option.

   When you invoke the **Draft** tool, the **Draft Plane** button is activated and you are prompted to click on a planar face or on a reference plane.

2. Select the top planar face of the base feature as the draft plane; the **Draft Faces** button is activated.

3. Select all the four side-faces of the model to add the draft. Click on the Draft direction handle and make sure that the lower half of the handle lies inside the model.

4. Enter **1** in the dynamic **Draft Angle** edit box. Next, press ENTER.

5. Add a round of radius **8** to the sharp edges of the model, as shown in Figure 8-82.

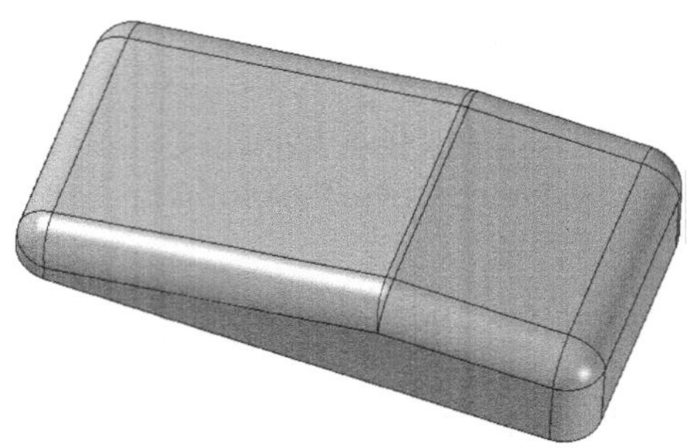

Figure 8-82 Model after adding the rounds

Adding the Thin Wall Feature

Next, you need to scoop out the material from inside the model to create a thin wall model. This is done using the **Thin Wall** tool. Also, you need to remove the top face of the model while creating a thin wall.

1. Choose the **Thin Wall** tool from the **Solids** group; the **Thin Wall** Command bar is displayed and the **Open Faces** button is activated. In addition, the handle and the edit box are displayed on the model.

2. Enter **2** in the edit box; you are prompted to click on a face chain.

3. Select the top planar face of the model as the face to be removed and then right-click to accept the selection. The model after creating the thin wall feature is shown in Figure 8-83.

Creating Cutouts

1. Create two cutouts in the model, as shown in Figure 8-84.

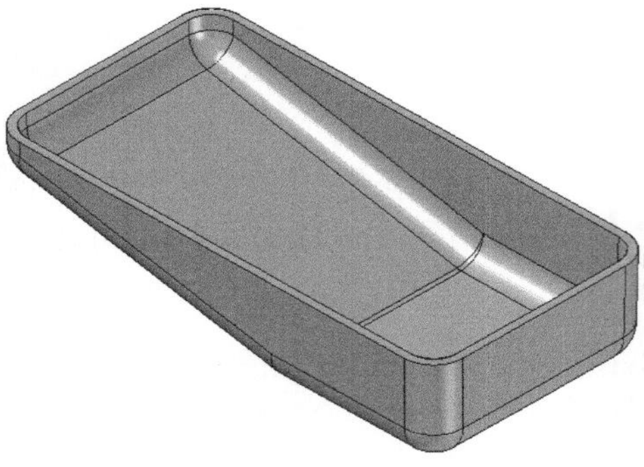

Figure 8-83 Model after creating the thin wall feature

Figure 8-84 Model after creating the cutouts

Creating the Web Network

Next, you need to create a web network by using an open profile that consists of two mutually perpendicular lines. Note that this profile needs to be created on a reference plane located at an offset distance of 2 units below the top planar face of the thin wall model.

1. Define a plane parallel to the top planar face of the thin wall feature. The plane should be offset 2 units inside the model.

2. Draw the profile for the web network, as shown in Figure 8-85.

3. Choose the **Web Network** tool from the **Thin Wall** drop-down in the **Solids** group; the **Web Network** Command bar is displayed. Also, you are prompted to select the sketch. 

4. Select the **Single** option from the **Select** drop-down list and select the sketched entities.

5. Right-click to accept the sketch; the **Direction Step** is invoked and you are prompted to click to accept the displayed side or select the other side in the view.

6. Enter **1** in the dynamic **Thickness** edit box and move the cursor to the bottom of the model to create the web network in the downward direction.

7. Choose the **Accept** button from the Command bar to complete the web network, refer to Figure 8-86.

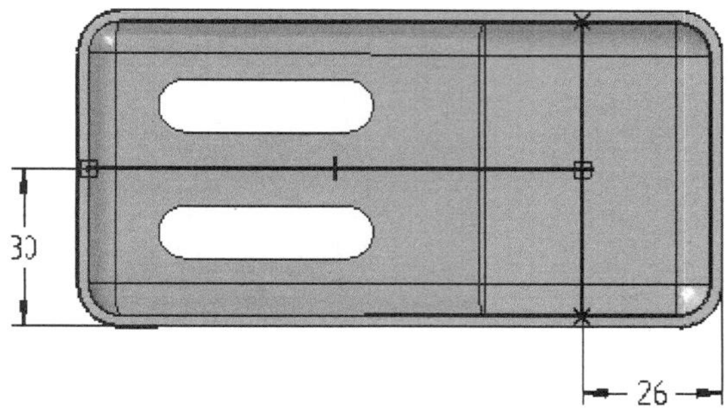

Figure 8-85 *Profile for the web network*

Figure 8-86 *Model after creating the web network*

Creating Mounting Bosses (Ordered Part Environment)

Next, you need to create mounting bosses. To do so, you need to switch to the **Ordered Part** environment because the **Mounting Boss** tool is available only in the **Ordered Part** environment. The profiles of the mounting bosses need to be placed on a reference plane located at an offset distance of 10 from the top planar face of the thin wall model.

1. Choose the **Mounting Boss** tool from the **Thin Wall** drop-down in the **Solids** group of the **Ribbon**. 

   The **Mounting Boss** Command bar is displayed and the **Plane Step** is activated. Also, you are prompted to click on a planar face or on a reference plane. Note that you need to define a reference plane parallel to the top planar face of the thin wall feature.

2. Define a plane parallel to the top planar face of the thin wall feature. The plane should be offset 10 units inside the model.

   As you define the parallel plane, the **Mounting Boss Location** step is activated and the sketching environment is invoked. Now, before placing the mounting boss profile, you need to modify the parameters of the mounting boss. To do so, follow the steps given below.

3. Make sure the **Mounting Boss Location** button is chosen in the **Features** group of the **Ribbon**. Next, choose the **Mounting Boss Options** button from the Command bar.

4. Set the parameters in the **Mounting Boss Options** dialog box, based on the values given in the tutorial statement.

5. Place three instances of the mounting boss profiles and then add the required dimensions, as shown in Figure 8-87. It is recommended that you select the edge of the model as the first entity and the mounting boss profile as the second entity while dimensioning.

6. Exit the sketching environment and specify downward as the direction of the feature creation. Choose the **Finish** button and then the **Cancel** button to exit the tool. The final model of the cover after creating the mounting bosses is shown in Figure 8-88.

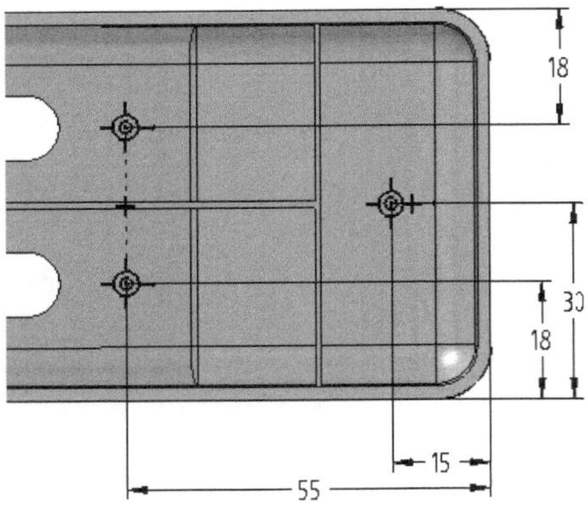

Figure 8-87 *Partial view of the model with profiles for mounting bosses*

Figure 8-88 *Final model after creating the mounting bosses*

Saving the Model

1. Save the model with the name *c08tut3.par* at the location given below and then close the file.

   C:\Solid Edge\c08

Tutorial 4 Synchronous

In this tutorial, you will create the model as shown in Figure 8-89. Its dimensions are given in Figure 8-90. Save the model with the name *c08tut4.par* at the location given next.

C:\Solid Edge\c08 **(Expected time : 30 min)**

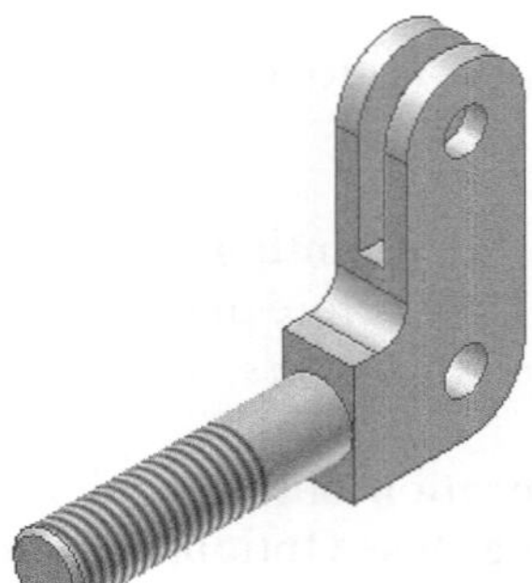

Figure 8-89 *Solid model for Tutorial 4*

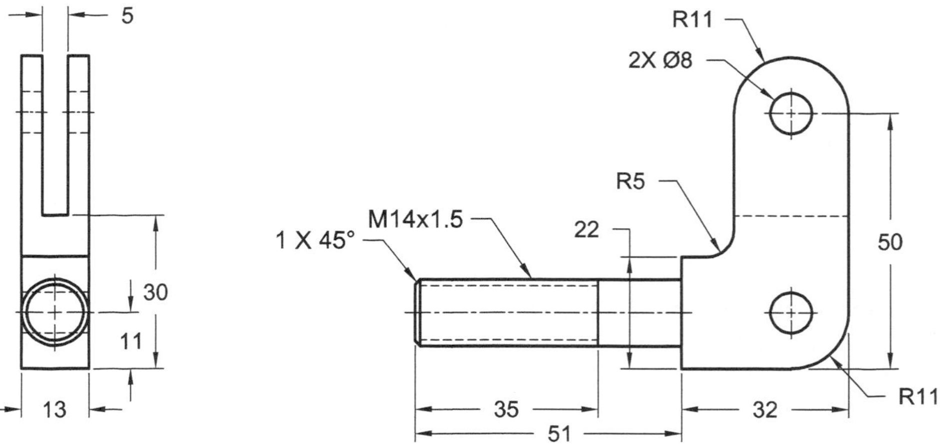

Figure 8-90 *Left and front side views of the model*

The following steps are required to complete this tutorial:

a. Start Solid Edge in the **ISO Metric Part** environment and then create the base feature on the right (yz) plane, refer to Figure 8-91.
b. Create the cutout feature, refer to Figure 8-92.
c. Create the cylindrical feature on the left face of the base feature and then create the hole features, refer to Figure 8-93.
d. Create threads on the cylindrical feature and then chamfer its front end, refer to Figure 8-94.
e. Save the model and close the file.

Creating the Base Feature

1. Start Solid Edge in the **ISO Metric Part** environment and then select the right (yz) plane as the sketching plane for the protrusion feature.

2. Create the profile of the base feature and extrude it symmetrically, as shown in Figure 8-91. For dimensions, refer to Figures 8-90 and 8-91.

Creating Cut Feature

1. Create the cut feature on the model, as shown in Figure 8-92. For dimensions of the cut feature, refer to Figure 8-90.

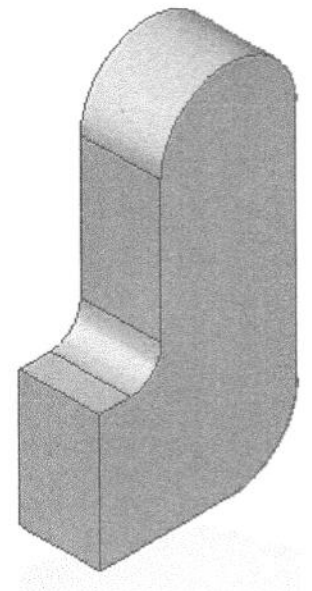

Figure 8-91 *Base feature for the model*

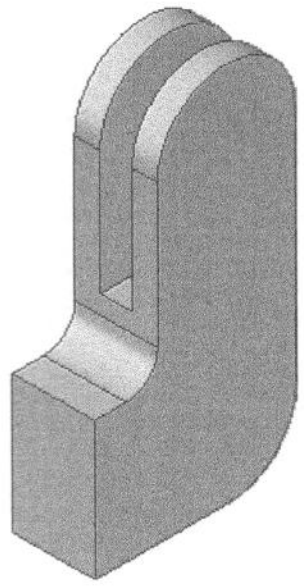

Figure 8-92 *Model after creating the cut feature*

Creating the Cylindrical Feature and Holes

1. Create the cylindrical feature, as shown in Figure 8-93. For dimensions, refer to Figure 8-90.

Note

In Solid Edge, while creating the thread feature, the diameter of the shaft should not be constrained as the diameter of the shaft will automatically change to match with the diameter of the thread feature.

2. Create two holes on the base feature, refer to Figure 8-93. For dimensions, refer to Figure 8-91.

Creating the Thread Feature

1. Choose the **Thread** tool from the **Hole** drop-down in the **Solid** group of the **Home** tab; the **Thread** Command bar is displayed and you are prompted to select a cylinder to apply thread.

2. Choose the **Thread Options** button from the Command bar; the **Thread Options** dialog box is displayed. In this dialog box, select the **Standard Thread** option from the **Type** drop-down list.

3. Select **ISO Metric** from the **Standard** drop-down list and select **14 mm** from the **Thread Diameter** drop-down list. Next, set the thread type and the thread length.

4. Select **M14x1.5** from the **Size** drop-down list and then select the **Finite extent** radio button, if not already selected and then choose the **OK** button.

5. Select the cylindrical surface; the **Changes Diameter** message box is displayed stating that the diameter of the selected cylinder will change to match the specification of thread **M14x1.5**. Choose the **OK** button from the message box to apply the thread on the cylindrical feature. Next, enter **34** in the **Finite extent** dynamic edit box.

Creating the Chamfer

1. Choose the **Chamfer Equal Setbacks** tool from the **Round** drop-down list in the **Solids** group of the **Home** tab; you are prompted to select the edge to be chamfered. Select the front edge of the cylindrical feature. Next, enter **1** in the **Dimension** edit box. The final model after chamfering is shown in Figure 8-94.

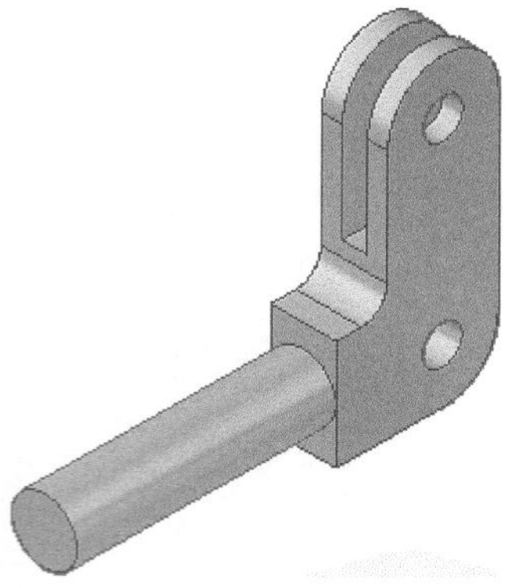

Figure 8-93 *Model after creating the join feature*

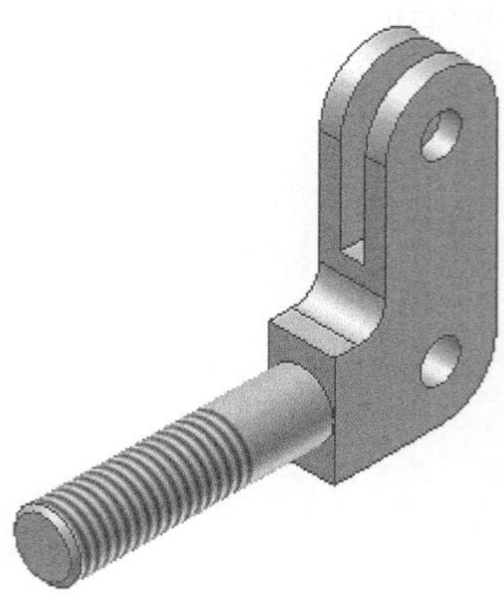

Figure 8-94 *Model after chamfering*

Saving the Model

1. Save the model with the name *c08tut4.par* at the location given below and then close the file.
   C:\Solid Edge\c08

Self-Evaluation Test

Answer the following questions and then compare them to those given at the end of this chapter:

1. The __________ features are used to accommodate fasteners in plastic components.
2. In Solid Edge, features are reordered using the __________.
3. The __________ tool is used to taper the selected faces of a model.
4. After setting the options in the **Mounting Boss Options** dialog box, the **Mounting Boss** tool works in __________ steps.
5. You can add a thin wall feature to a particular region of a model by using the __________ tool.
6. In the **Lip** tool, the amount of material to be added or removed is defined by a __________ whose width and height can be specified on the basis of the requirement.
7. The **Thin Wall** tool scoops out the material from a model and makes it hollow. (T/F)
8. The **Taper** radio button needs to be selected to create threads on a tapered feature. (T/F)
9. Internal threads are created in holes or circular cut features and external threads are created on the external surface of a cylindrical feature. (T/F)
10. Ribs are defined as thin wall-like structures used to bind joints together so that they do not fail under an increased load. (T/F)

Review Questions

Answer the following questions:

1. Which of the following tools enables you to create a network of webs using open entities?

   (a) **Lip** (b) **Rib**
   (c) **Web Network** (d) **Thin Wall**

2. Which of the following tools enables you to add a taper to the selected faces of a model?

   (a) **Draft** (b) **Taper**
   (c) **Rib** (d) None of these

3. Which of the following tools enables you to create a vent in an existing model by defining its boundary, ribs, and spars?

   (a) **Draft** (b) **Taper**
   (c) **Rib** (d) **Vent**

4. Which of the following tools is used to add a thin wall to the entire model?

   (a) **Draft** (b) **Thin Region**
   (c) **Rib** (d) **Thin Wall**

5. Which of the following steps is used to place the profiles of the mounting boss on the plane?

   (a) **Mounting Boss Location** (b) **Sketch Step**
   (c) **Profile Step** (d) None of these

6. Which of the following buttons is chosen to extend the rib feature to the adjacent features, even if the profile does not extend to them?

   (a) **Extend Profile** (b) **Extend**
   (c) Both of these (d) None of these

7. The **Lip** tool enables you to add a lip to a model by adding the material or by adding a groove to the model by removing the material. (T/F)

8. In Solid Edge, you can create internal or external threads by using the **Thread** tool. (T/F)

9. In Solid Edge, you can add drafts in five ways. (T/F)

10. Using the **Thin Wall** tool, you can also remove some of the faces of a model or apply different wall thicknesses to some of them. (T/F)

EXERCISES

Exercise 1

Create the model shown in Figure 8-95. The dimensions of the model are shown in the Figure 8-96. After creating the model, save it with the name *c08exr1.par* at the location given next:

C:\Solid Edge\c08 **(Expected time: 30 min)**

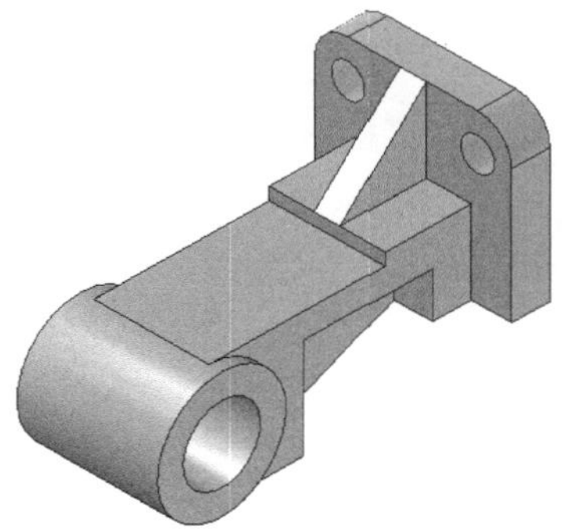

Figure 8-95 Model for Exercise 1

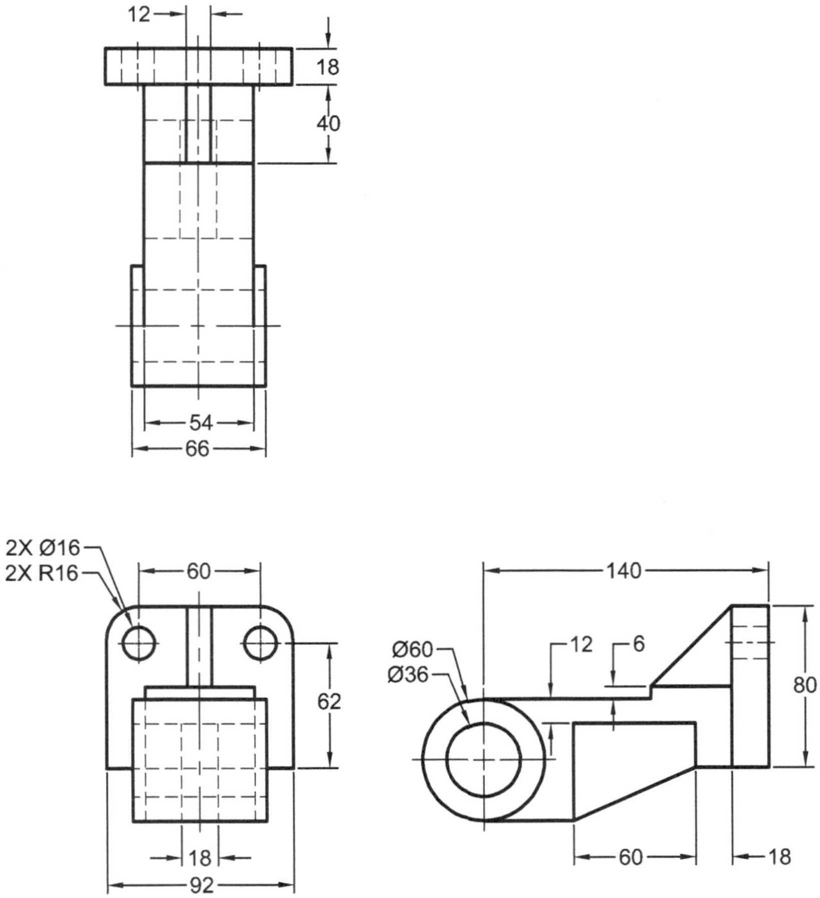

Figure 8-96 The model and dimensions for Exercise 1

Exercise 2

Create the model shown in Figure 8-97. Its dimensions are given in Figure 8-98. Save it with the name *c08exr2.par* at the location given next:

C:\Solid Edge\c08 **(Expected time: 30 min)**

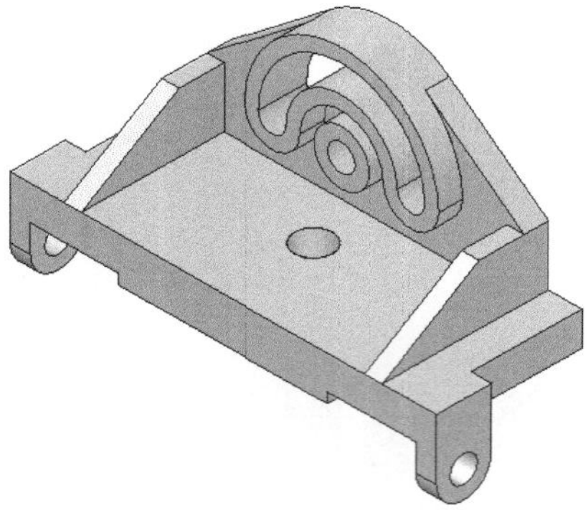

Figure 8-97 Model for Exercise 2

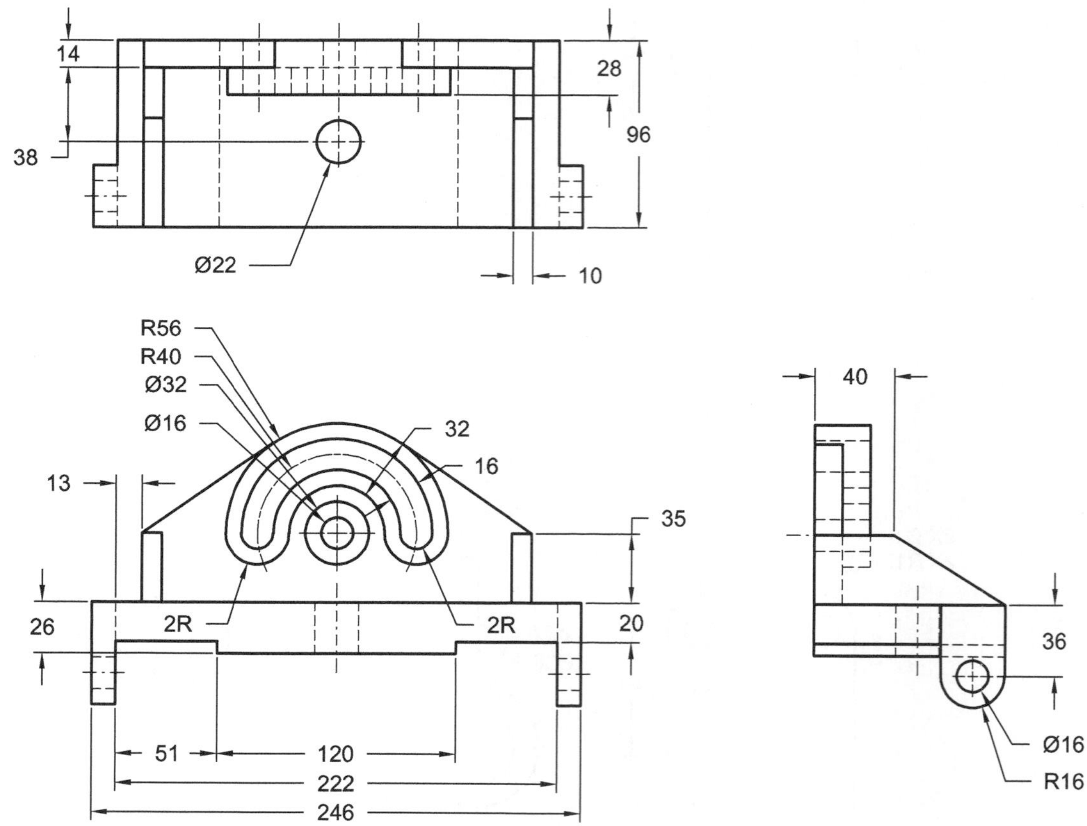

Figure 8-98 Dimensions of the model

Exercise 3

Create the model shown in Figure 8-99. Its dimensions are given in Figure 8-100. Save it with the name *c08exr3.par* at the location given next:

C:\Solid Edge\c08 **(Expected time: 30 min)**

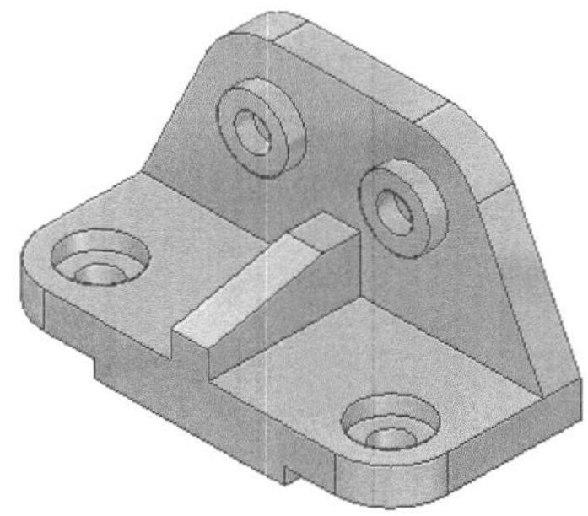

Figure 8-99 Model for Exercise 3

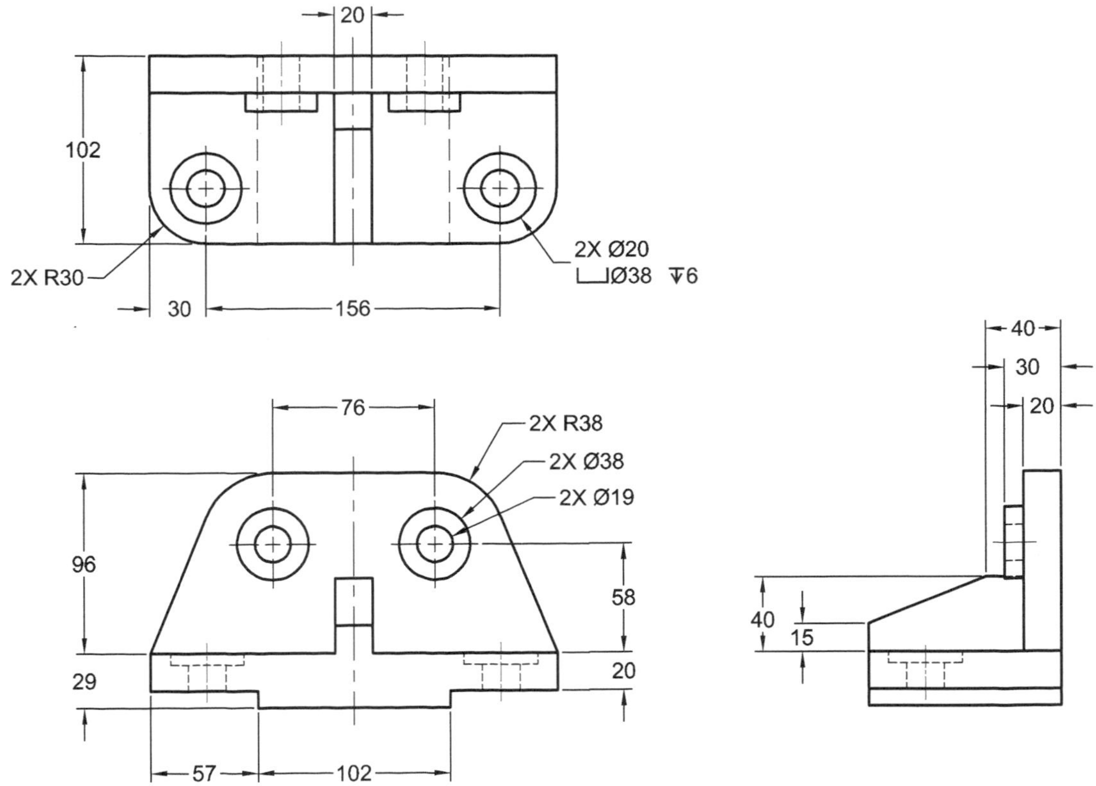

Figure 8-100 Dimensions of the model

Answers to Self-Evaluation Test

1. Mounting boss, **2. PathFinder**, **3. Draft**, **4.** three, **5. Thin Region**, **6.** rectangle, **7.** T, **8.** F, **9.** T, **10.** T

Chapter 9

Advanced Modeling Tools-III

Learning Objectives

After completing this chapter, you will be able to:

- *Create swept protrusions and cutouts*
- *Create lofted protrusions and lofted cutouts*
- *Create 3D sketches*
- *Create helical protrusions*
- *Create normal protrusions and cutouts*
- *Work with additional bodies*

ADVANCED MODELING TOOLS

In the earlier chapters, you learned about some of the advanced modeling tools. In this chapter, you will learn about the remaining advanced modeling tools.

Advanced Tools to Create Protrusions

In the earlier chapters, you learned about the basic protrusion tools such as **Extrude** and **Revolve** that are used to create base features. As mentioned earlier, these tools add material to the sketch. In this chapter, you will learn about some advanced tools that apart from adding material also have the capability of creating base features. You will also learn how to remove the material using these advanced tools. This chapter will cover the tools that are used for creating the following features:

- Swept Protrusion and Cutout
- Lofted Protrusion and Cutout
- Helical Protrusion and Cutout
- Normal Protrusion and Cutout

CREATING SWEPT PROTRUSIONS

Ribbon: Home > Solids > Add drop-down > Sweep

You can create swept protrusions along an open or a closed path using the **Sweep** tool. To create a swept protrusion, sketch the path and the cross-section normal to the path. Next, invoke the **Sweep** tool and select a path and then a section. Using the **Sweep** tool, you can sweep a single section along a single path or multiple sections along multiple paths. This tool is similar to the **Extrude** tool with the only difference that on using the **Sweep** tool, the section is swept along a specified path.

Sketching the Path and the Cross-section

You first need to create path on a plane by invoking the sketching tool. Next, you need to create a plane normal to the path or curve by invoking the **Normal to Curve** tool from the **Planes** group. On doing so, you will be prompted to click on a point on the curve. Move the cursor close to one of the endpoints on the path to draw a section for the swept protrusion. Click when the desired endpoint is highlighted in orange. You can move the cursor along the path; the plane also moves with it. Click to specify the location of the plane where the cross-section needs to be drawn. It is not necessary that a cross section drawn for the profile of a sweep feature intersects the path. However, a plane on which the profile is drawn should lie at one of the endpoints of the path. Next, draw the sketch of the cross-section on the plane.

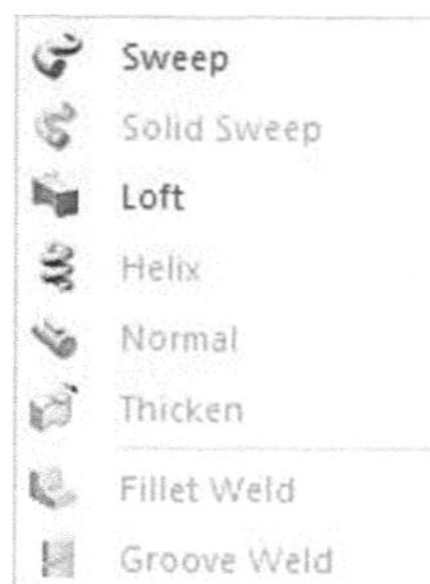

Figure 9-1 The Add drop-down

After creating the path and the cross-section, choose the **Sweep** tool from the **Add** drop-down in the **Solids** group, as shown in Figure 9-1; the **Sweep Options** dialog box will be displayed, as shown in Figure 9-2. You can create a sweep feature by two methods, which are discussed next.

Single path and cross section Method

The **Single path and cross section** radio button is selected by default and is used to sweep a section along an open or a closed path, as shown in Figures 9-3 and 9-4.

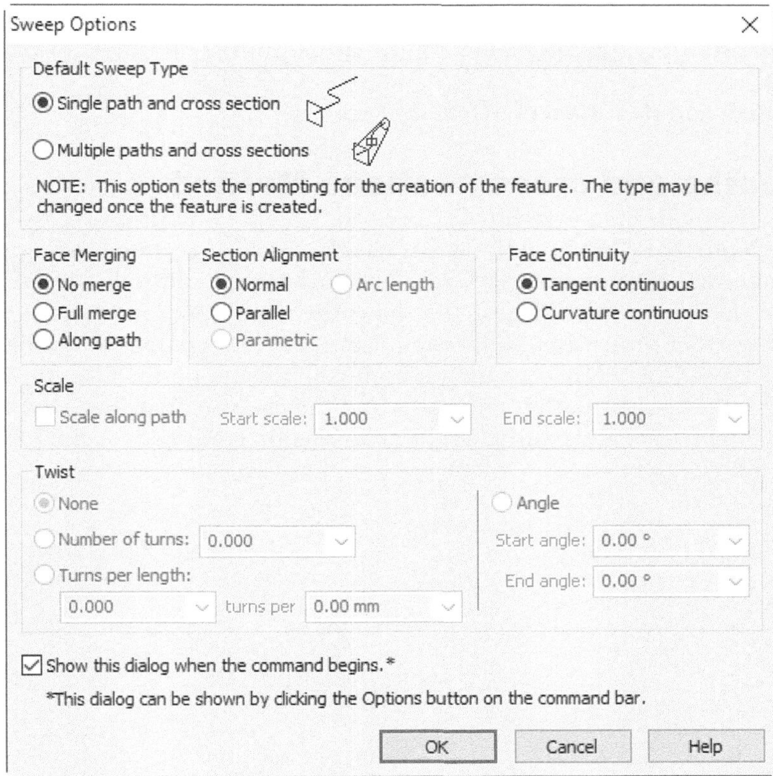

*Figure 9-2 The **Sweep Options** dialog box*

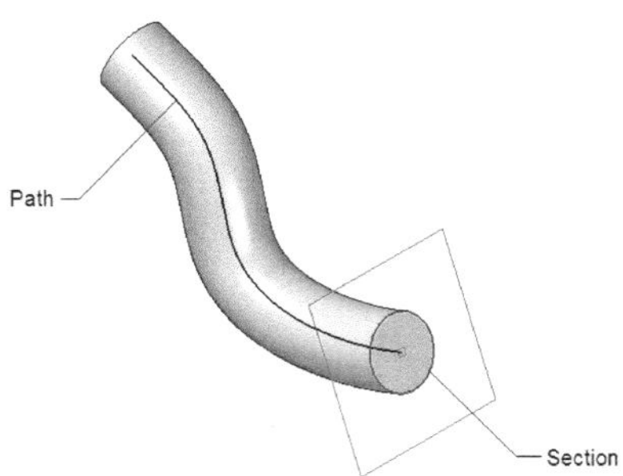

Figure 9-3 Path and cross-section selected to create the swept protrusion

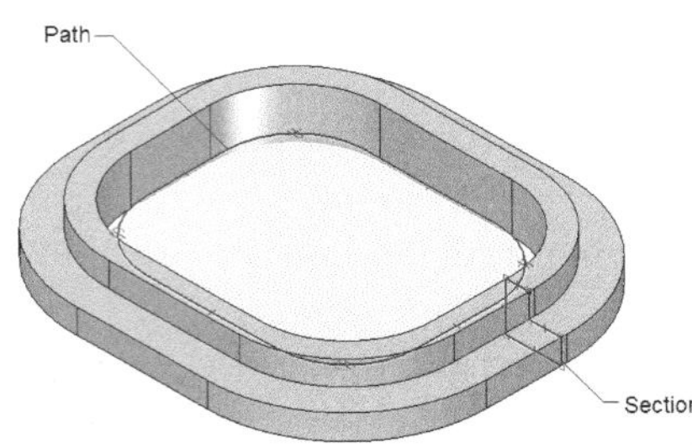

Figure 9-4 Closed path and closed cross-section selected to create the swept protrusion

The following steps explain the procedure for creating a swept protrusion using this method:

1. Select the **Single path and cross section** radio button from the **Sweep Options** dialog box and choose **OK** to exit the dialog box; the **Swept Protrusion** command bar will be displayed with the **Path Step** option chosen. Also, by default, the **Select Sketch Step** option is chosen. As a result, you can select any existing sketch or edge as a path.

2. Select an existing sketch as a path, refer to Figure 9-3. Next, choose the **Accept** button from the command bar or right-click in the drawing area; the **Cross Section Step** will be invoked in the command bar.

3. Select the profile of the cross section and move the cursor to the point that you want to specify as the starting point; a preview of the swept protrusion will be displayed.

4. Choose **Finish** and then **Cancel** to exit the tool.

Multiple paths and cross sections Method

In Solid Edge, you can create sweep features by sweeping multiple cross-sections along multiple paths. Note that you can at the most select three cross-sections. Generally, this option is used when you want to vary cross-sections. The variation is controlled by paths and not by the geometry of the cross-section. Figure 9-5 shows the three paths and a cross-section that are used to create the swept protrusion, as shown in Figure 9-6. Remember that while sketching the cross-section, it should be aligned to the endpoints of all the paths. Else, the feature will be created without following the paths. The paths and the cross-sections have to be created prior to invoking the **Sweep** tool. Make sure that the cross-section is aligned to all the three endpoints of the three paths.

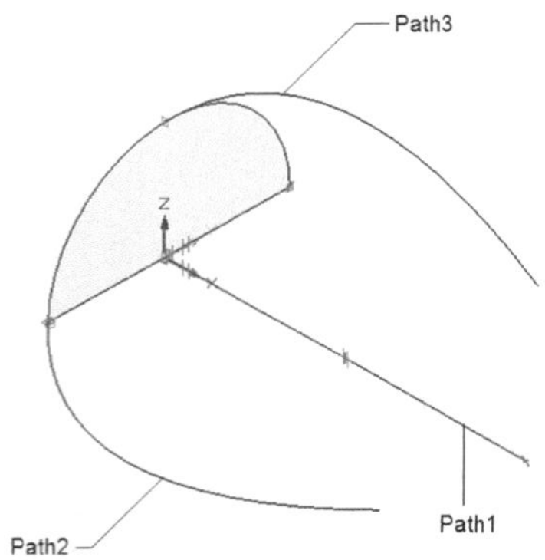

Figure 9-5 *Three paths and a cross-section*

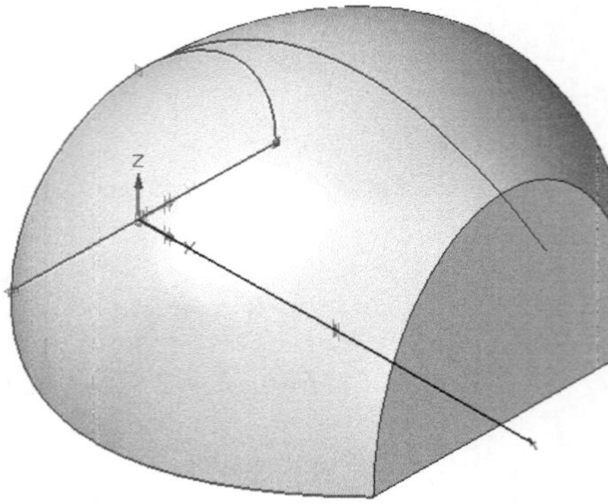

Figure 9-6 *Swept protrusion*

The following steps explain the procedure for creating the swept protrusion shown in Figure 9-6:

1. Draw the sketch of the first, second, and third path on three different planes. Next, you need to create the cross-section.
2. Invoke the **Normal to Curve** tool from the **Planes** group and move the cursor to the point on the path where you will draw the section for the swept protrusion. Click on the point. The reference plane will be displayed at the selected point.
3. Draw the sketch for the cross-section and make sure that the cross-section is aligned to all the three endpoints of the three paths.
4. Choose the **Sweep** tool; the **Sweep Options** dialog box will be displayed. Select the **Multiple paths and cross sections** radio button and then choose **OK** to exit this dialog box; the **Swept Protrusion** command bar will be displayed with the **Path Step** activated.

5. Select the first path from the drawing area and choose the **Accept** button.
6. Similarly, select the second and third paths and then choose the **Accept** button; the **Cross Section Step** will be activated automatically. If it is not activated, first terminate the **Path Step** and then activate the **Cross Section Step** by choosing the **Next** button after selecting the first or second path.
7. Select the cross-section; you will be prompted to select the second and third cross-sections.
8. You can terminate the **Cross Section Step** after the selecting the first cross-section by choosing the **Preview** button. On doing so, a preview of the swept protrusion will be displayed.
9. Next, choose the **Finish** and then **Cancel** button from the command bar to exit the tool.

You can also create a sweep feature by specifying a single path and multiple cross-sections. Figure 9-7 shows a single path and two cross-sections that are used to create the swept protrusion feature shown in Figure 9-8. To create a sweep feature by using a single path and multiple cross-sections, first you need to sketch a path and cross-sections. Next, invoke the **Sweep** tool and select the **Multiple paths and cross sections** radio button from the **Sweep Options** dialog box. Select the path and then choose the **Accept** button from the command bar. Choose the **Next** button to invoke the **Cross Section Step**. Select the first and second cross-sections. Choose the **Preview** button from the command bar; a preview of the swept protrusion will be displayed. Then, choose the **Finish** and **Cancel** button from the command bar to exit the tool.

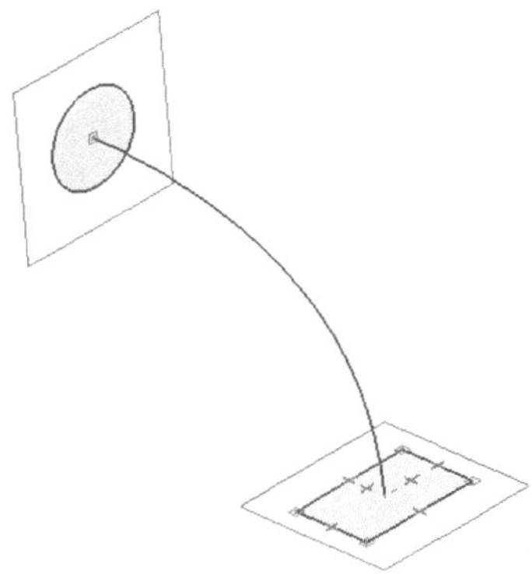

Figure 9-7 *Two cross-sections and a path to create a multiple section swept protrusion*

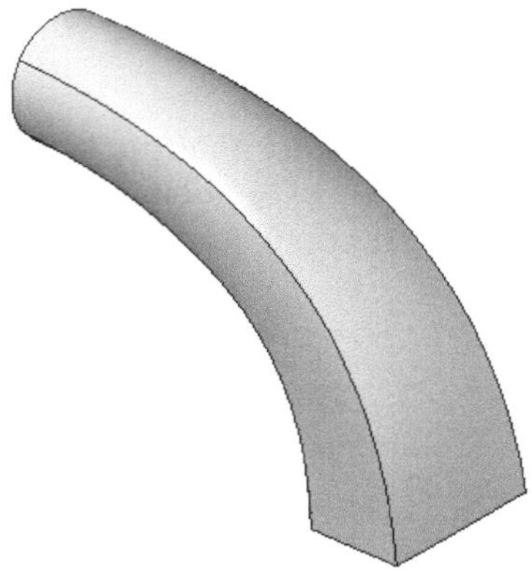

Figure 9-8 *Swept protrusion*

Axis step

This option is available after selecting the path and cross-section of the swept protrusion. You can choose this option to specify the axis of the swept protrusion. The axis is selected in order to lock the cross-section to the axis. It ensures that the cross-section will be oriented normal to the plane. This option will be useful when you create a path that is non-planar or when you use more than one cross-section to create a swept protrusion.

Sweep Options Dialog Box

The options available in the **Sweep Options** dialog box are discussed next.

Face Merging Area

The options available in this area are used to specify the methods for merging the faces of the sweep feature. These options are discussed next.

No merge

This option ensures that the faces of the sweep feature are not merged, as shown in Figure 9-9. The black lines in the model show different faces of the model.

Full merge

This option ensures that the faces of the sweep feature are fully merged, as shown in Figure 9-10.

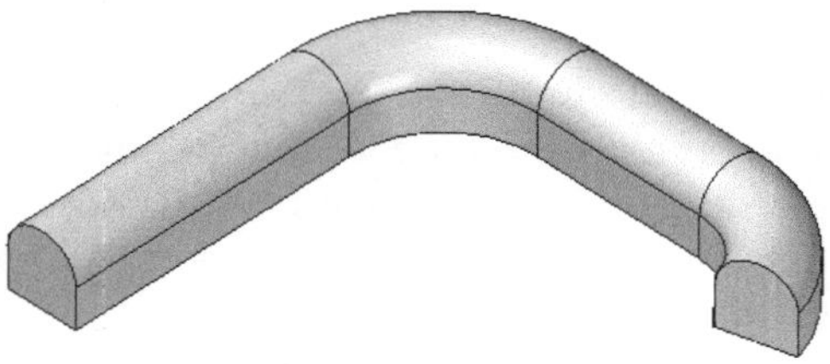

Figure 9-9 Swept protrusion with the faces not merged

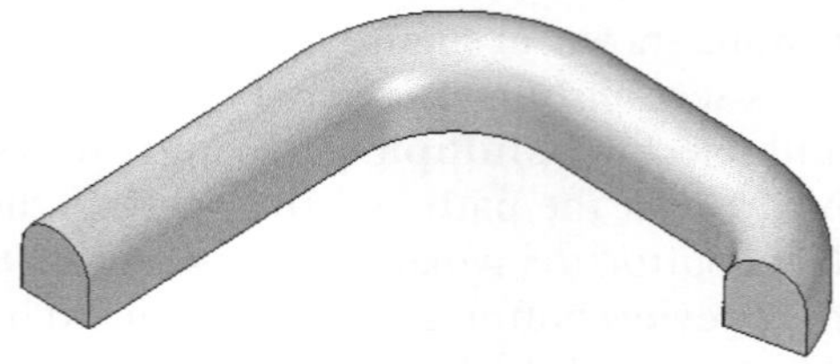

Figure 9-10 Swept protrusion with the faces fully merged

Along path

This option ensures that the faces along the direction of the path of the sweep feature are merged. Figure 9-11 shows the swept protrusion with the faces that are merged along the path of the sweep feature. The black lines in the model show different faces of the model.

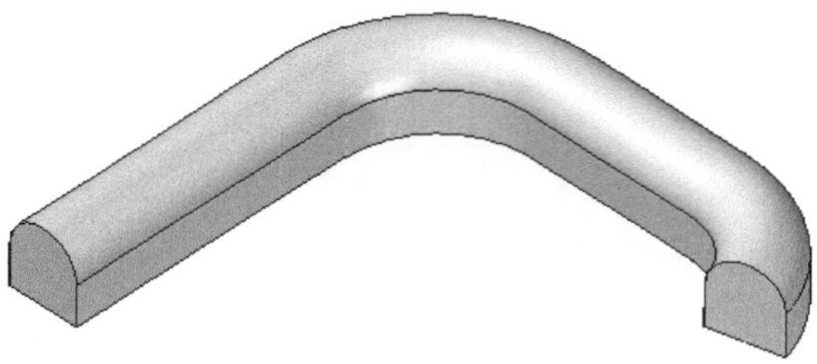

Figure 9-11 Swept protrusion with faces along the path curve merged

Section Alignment Area

The options available in this area are used to specify the alignment of the sections along the path curve. These options are discussed next.

Normal

This option ensures that the cross-section remains oriented relative to the path used for creating a sweep. Figure 9-12 shows the swept protrusion created using this option.

Parallel

This option is used when you want the cross-section to remain oriented parallel to the sketch plane while sweeping. Figure 9-13 shows the swept protrusion created using this option.

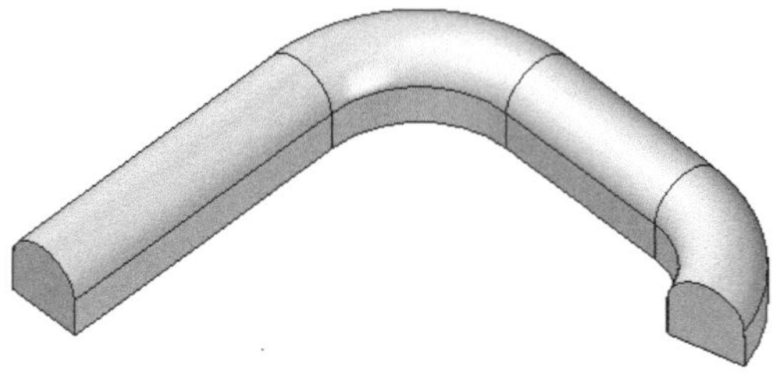

Figure 9-12 *Swept protrusion created using the normal section alignment*

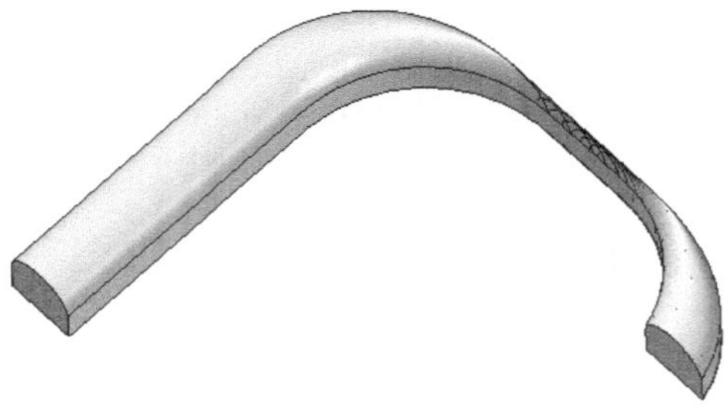

Figure 9-13 *Swept protrusion created using the parallel section alignment*

Parametric

This option is available only when you use multiple paths. It ensures that the orientation of the cross-section varies on the basis of the parameter distance of the path curve. Note that the paths that you select in this option should be created from a single entity. Figure 9-14 shows the multiple paths swept protrusion created using the **Normal** option and Figure 9-15 shows the multiple paths swept protrusion created using the **Parametric** option. These figures also show the cross-section and the paths used to create them.

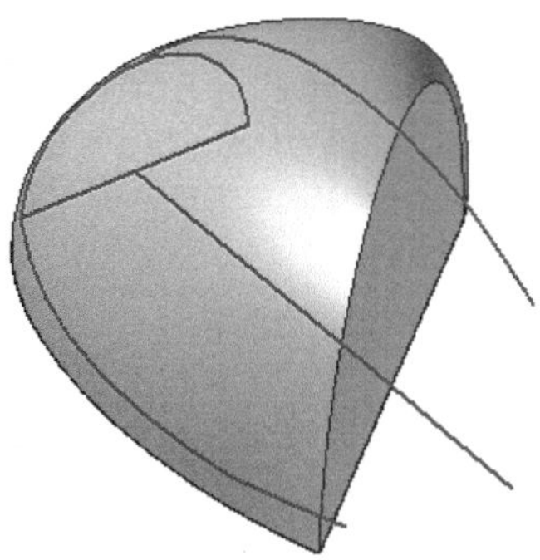

Figure 9-14 *Swept protrusion created using the normal section alignment*

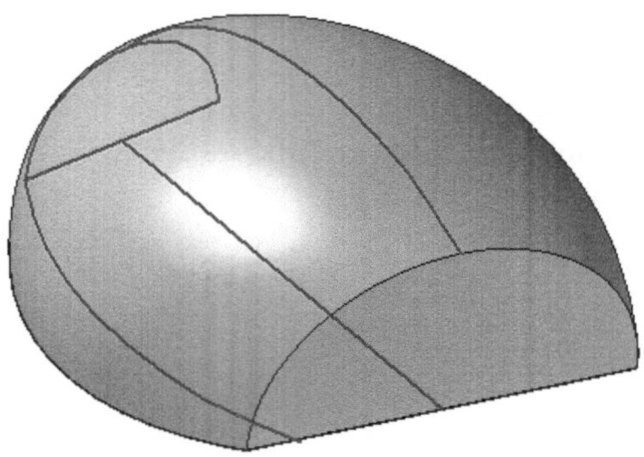

Figure 9-15 *Swept protrusion created using the parametric section alignment*

Arc Length

This option is also available only when you use multiple paths. It is similar to the **Parametric** option, but in this case the cross-section varies on the basis of the arc length distance of the path curve. Also, the paths that you select for this option may consist of multiple entities.

Face Continuity Area

The options available in this area are used to specify the methods of face continuity. You can select the option of tangent continuity and curvature continuity.

Scale Area

The options in this area are used to create a sweep feature by scaling the cross-section along a path. This area is available for both the sweep types only after you have selected the path and the cross-section. To create the sweep feature by scaling the cross-section along the path, select the **Scale along path** check box; the **Start scale** and **End scale** drop-down lists will be activated.

Specify the scale factors in these drop-down lists to scale the profile at the start and end of the sweep. Next, choose **OK**; the sweep feature with the scaled profile will be created, as shown in Figure 9-16. Note that if the scale factor is more than 1, the cross-section at that end will increase in size. Similarly, if the scale factor is less than 1, the cross-section will decrease in size.

Twist Area

The options in this area are used to create a sweep feature by twisting the cross-section along the path curve. The options in this area are discussed next.

None

On selecting this radio button, no twist will be applied to the sweep feature.

Number of turns

On selecting this radio button, you need to specify the number of turns the cross-section will be twisted along the path.

Turns per length

On selecting this radio button, you need to specify the number of turns per length the cross-section will be twisted along the path.

Angle

Select this radio button to apply the twist to the cross-section along the path. You can define the value of the twist in degrees at the start and end of the sweep in the **Start angle** and **End angle** drop-down lists, respectively. Figure 9-17 shows the swept feature with both scale and twist applied.

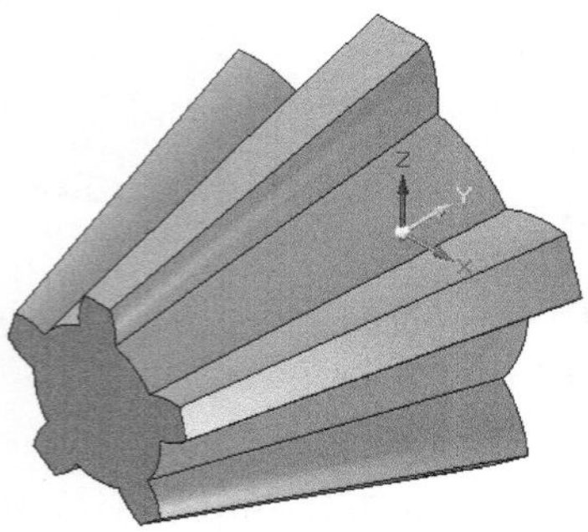

Figure 9-16 *Sweep feature with different scale factors at start point and endpoint*

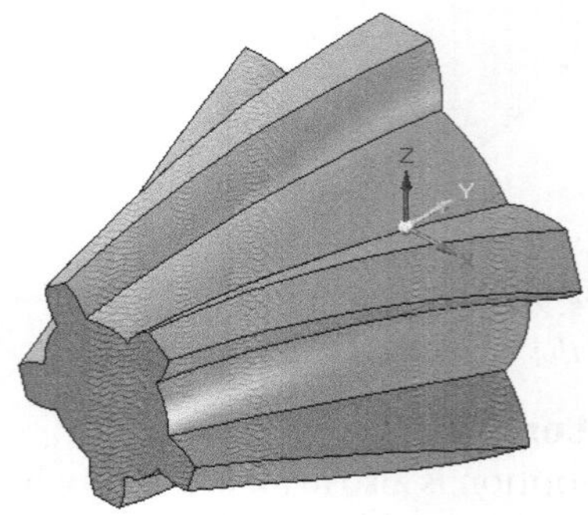

Figure 9-17 *Sweep feature with both scale and twist applied*

CREATING SWEPT CUTOUTS

Ribbon: Home > Solids > Cut drop-down > Sweep

You can create swept cutouts using the **Sweep** tool available in the **Cut** drop-down of the **Solids** group. Note that the tool will be available only when a base feature has already been created in the drawing window. The procedure to create the swept cutout is the same as the one used to create a swept protrusion. Figure 9-18 shows the swept cutout created on a base feature.

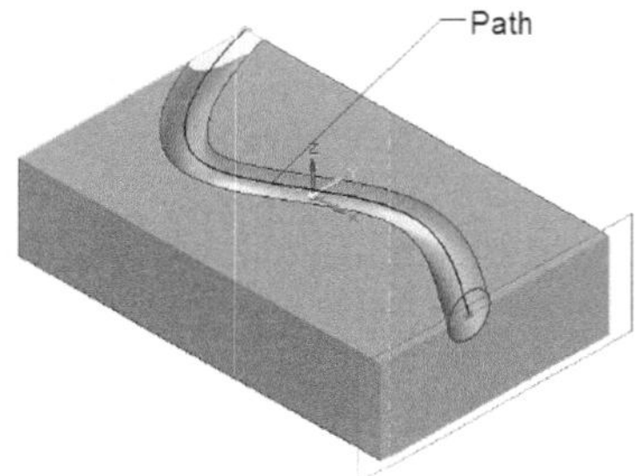

Figure 9-18 Swept cutout created using the cross-section and the path

CREATING LOFTED PROTRUSIONS

Ribbon: Home > Solids > Add drop-down > Loft

You can create a lofted protrusion feature by blending more than one similar or dissimilar cross-section together using the **Loft** tool. These cross-sections may or may not be parallel to each other. However, all cross-sections must be closed profiles. You can choose the **Loft** tool from the **Add** drop-down of the **Solids** group.

You can create a lofted protrusion by selecting the existing sketches or edges. When you choose the **Loft** tool, you will be prompted to select an edge, a sketch, or a curve chain. Select the existing sketches shown in Figure 9-19 and choose the **Preview** button; the lofted protrusion will be created, as shown in Figure 9-20. On the other hand, to draw the sketches of the cross-sections, you need to select a reference plane to draw them one by one.

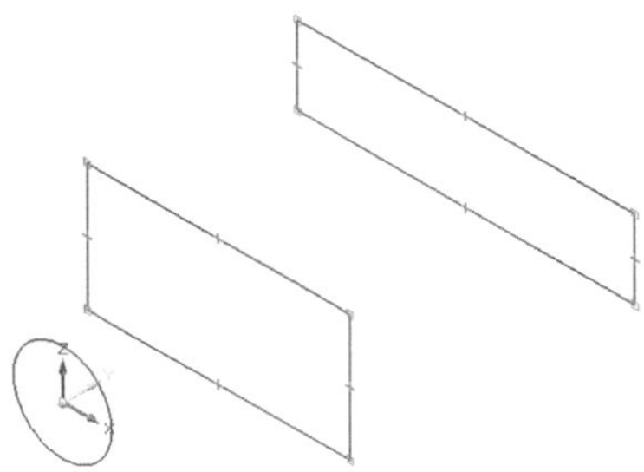

Figure 9-19 Three cross-sections to create a lofted protrusion

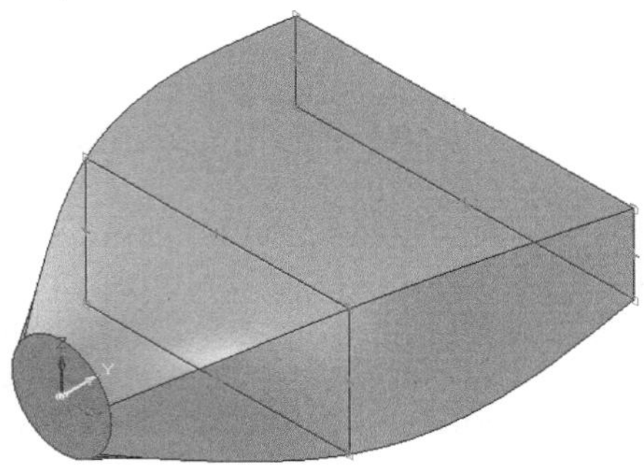

Figure 9-20 Resulting lofted protrusion

The following steps explain the procedure for creating a lofted protrusion:

1. Draw the first cross-section on any of the **Base Reference Planes**.
2. Create a plane parallel to the previous plane and draw the second profile on this plane.
3. Similarly, create the third plane and draw the third cross-section on it. You can also select the second plane and move it to the location of the third plane by using the Steering Wheel.
4. Invoke the **Loft** tool from the **Add** drop-down of the **Solids** group; the **Cross Section Step** will be activated in the command bar. Next, you need to select the first cross-section. Move the cursor closer to the point that you want to specify as the start point. You do not need to specify the start point if you are selecting a circle as the first cross-section.

5. Next, specify the endpoint while selecting the second and third cross-sections and then choose the **Preview** button; a preview of the lofted protrusion will be displayed.
6. Choose the **Finish** button and then the **Cancel** button to exit the tool.

After understanding the procedure of creating a lofted protrusion, you will learn about the options available under various steps required for creating a lofted protrusion.

Cross Section Order

The **Cross Section Order** button is used to reorder the sequence of sections that blend with each other. This button will be available only when you choose the **Edit** button on the command bar after selecting the sections. This means that the sections can be reordered only while editing.

When you choose the **Cross Section Order** button, the **Cross Section Order** dialog box will be displayed, as shown in Figure 9-21. This dialog box is used to reorder the sections. As it is evident from Figure 9-22, Section 1 blends with Section 2 and then Section 2 blends with Section 3. You can use the **Up** and **Down** buttons available in the dialog box to reorder the sections. Note that the section you select in this dialog box will be highlighted in green on the screen.

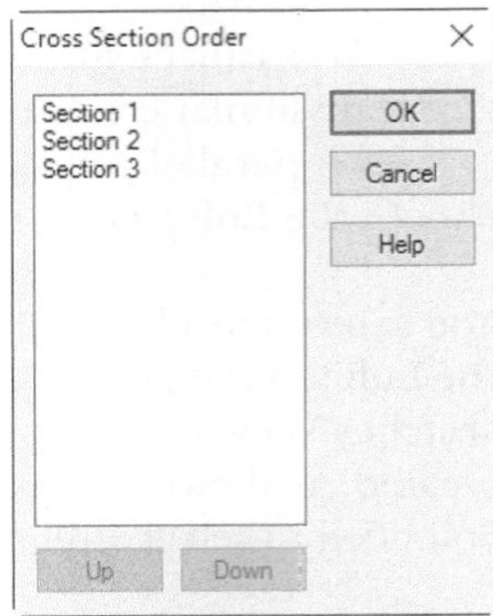

Figure 9-21 *The **Cross Section Order** dialog box*

Define Start Point

The **Define Start Point** button is used to define the start points of the new sections or to redefine the start points of existing sections of the lofted feature. For new sections, this button will be available after creating them. In case of existing sections, this button will be available after choosing the **Edit** button.

When you select the section to blend, a point will be highlighted. This point will be selected as the start point of the section. After selecting the sections, choose the **Edit** button. Now using the **Define Start Point** button, you can redefine the start points on the sections. Figure 9-22 shows the start points of the sections and Figure 9-23 shows the resulting lofted protrusion. Depending on the start points specified, the lofted feature changes its profile.

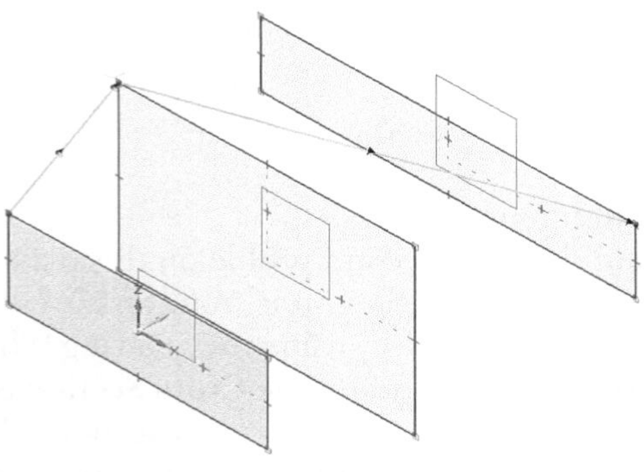

Figure 9-22 *Three sections and their start points joined by a dotted line*

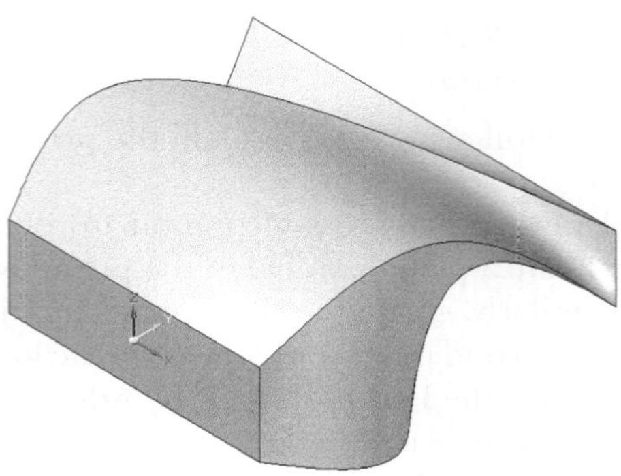

Figure 9-23 *Lofted protrusion*

Vertex Mapping

On selecting atleast two sections for the lofted protrusion, you will notice that the **Guide Curve Step** and **Extent Step** buttons are available in the command bar. When you choose the **Extent Step** button, the **Vertex Mapping** button will be available in the command bar along with the other buttons.

This button is used when you want to control the blending of the sections using their vertices. By default, the start points of the sections are used as mapping points to create the loft. If you want to modify the mapping of the points, choose the **Vertex Mapping** button; the **Vertex Mapping** dialog box will be displayed, as shown in Figure 9-24.

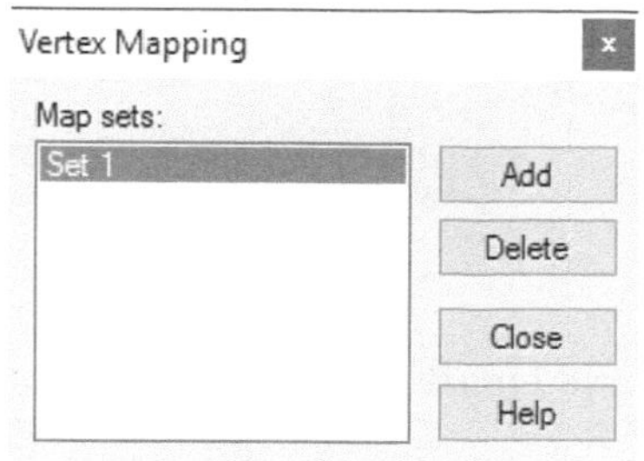

Figure 9-24 The ***Vertex Mapping*** *dialog box*

The sets of mapping points are displayed in the **Vertex Mapping** dialog box and the default mapping is shown by the green lines in the preview, refer to Figures 9-24 and 9-25. To modify the default mapping, select any other point on the sections. The new mapping is shown by continuous lines, refer to Figure 9-25. Figure 9-26 shows the resulting lofted protrusion.

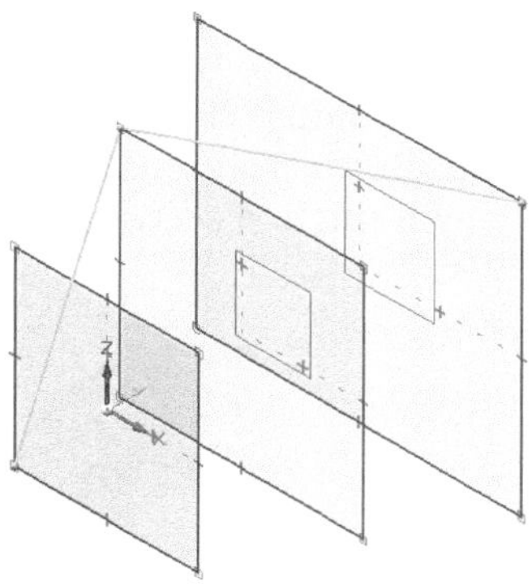

Figure 9-25 *Sections selected to create a loft*

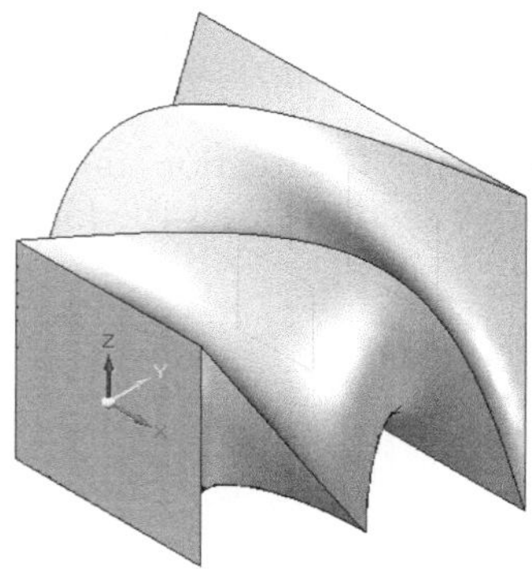

Figure 9-26 *Resulting lofted protrusion*

You can add additional mapping sets by choosing the **Add** button. On doing so, a new set with the name **Set 2** will be added. You can select the vertices of the cross-sections one by one to add the additional vertex mapping. To control the blending points on a circle, sketch the points on the circle while drawing it, refer to Figure 9-27. This means that the points and the circle are in one sketch feature. Next, select a circle and then a pentagon. Choose the **Preview** button; the lofted protrusion will be created, as shown in Figure 9-28. While creating the lofted protrusion, choose the **Extent Step** button from the command bar. Choose the **Vertex Mapping** button from the command bar to display the **Vertex Mapping** dialog box.

Tip

In order to create a smooth loft between a circle and a polygon, it is a good practice to place the required number of points on the circle. The number of points should be equal to the number of sides of the polygon. While creating the loft feature, you can use vertex mapping to add the sets of points to both the sections. This results in a smoother loft protrusion.

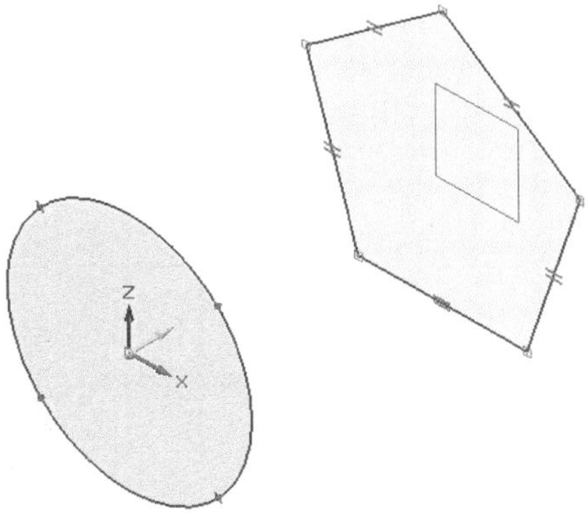

Figure 9-27 *Points added on the circle*

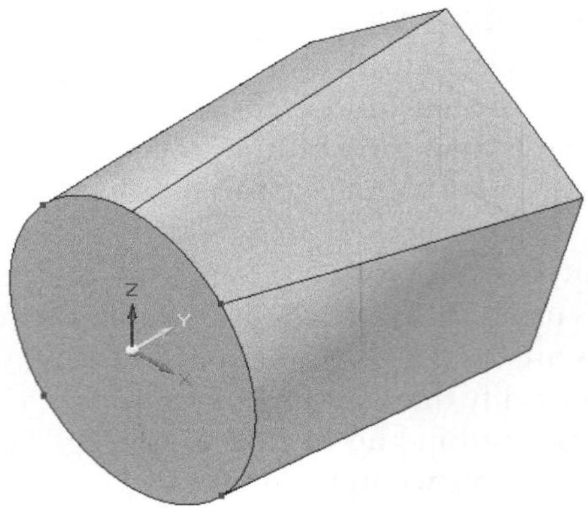

Figure 9-28 *Lofted protrusion created between a circle and a pentagon*

Finite Extent

The **Finite Extent** button is chosen by default. It enables you to blend the first section with the last section.

Closed Extent

The **Closed Extent** button is used to blend the last section with the first section and to close the lofted protrusion. Figure 9-29 shows the four sections to be lofted. Figure 9-30 shows the resulting closed extent loft. If the **Finite Extent** button is chosen, then the blend will start from the first section and end at the fourth section. But in Figure 9-30, it is evident that the fourth section closes the loft feature by blending it with the first section.

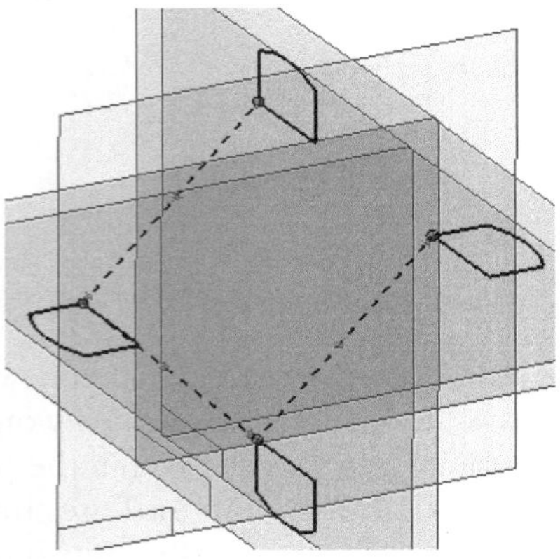

Figure 9-29 *Four sections to be lofted with their start points*

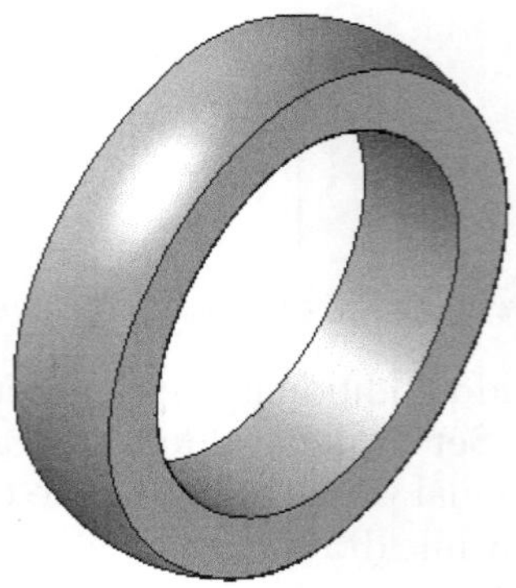

Figure 9-30 *Loft created using the* ***Closed Extent*** *button*

Show/Hide Tangency Control Handles

This button is chosen by default. As a result, the tangency control handles are displayed in the preview of the loft feature. You can control the tangency between the two cross-sections using the control handles or the **Start** and **End** drop-down lists.

Start and End

The **Start** and **End** drop-down lists are available when you hide the tangency control handles. These drop-down lists are available under the **Extent Step** and provide the **Natural** and **Normal to Section** options. These options determine the start and end of the blending from the cross-sections. The **Natural** option, which is selected by default, does not constrain the blending at the start and end cross-sections. Figure 9-31 shows three sections and their start points. Figure 9-32 shows the lofted protrusion whose end conditions are set by using the **Natural** option.

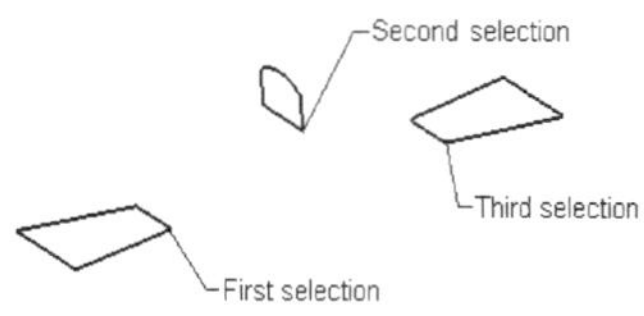

Figure 9-31 Sections, selection points, and sequence of selection

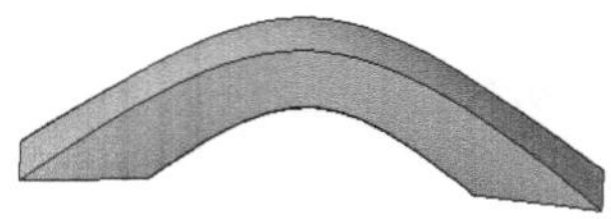

Figure 9-32 Loft feature created using the ***Natural*** *option*

The **Normal to Section** option is used to constrain the end conditions of the loft to be normal to the sections. Figure 9-33 shows the loft feature created using the **Normal to Section** option. Figure 9-34 shows a model created using two different end conditions. In this figure, the left section is set to the **Normal to Section** option, while the right section is set to the **Natural** option.

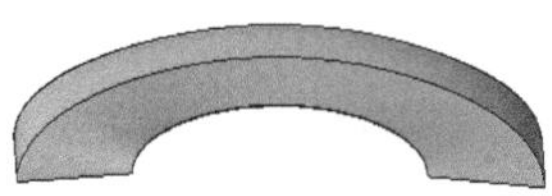

Figure 9-33 Loft feature created using the ***Normal to Section*** *option*

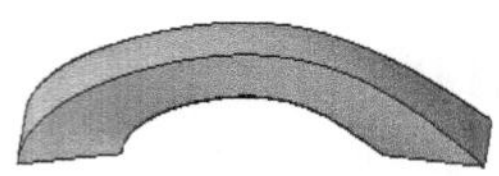

Figure 9-34 Model with two different end conditions

Adding Guide Curves to a Loft

Guide curves are used to control the material flow between the sections of the loft feature. The sketches drawn for the guide curve must have a **Connect** relationship with the sketches that define the loft section.

The **Guide Curve Step** button on the command bar is used to select or create a sketch as a guide curve. To draw the sketch of the guide curve, you need to select or create a reference plane on which the guide curve will be drawn. Figure 9-35 shows the sections and the guide curve used to create the lofted protrusion shown in Figure 9-36. Notice the variation in the section caused by the guide curve.

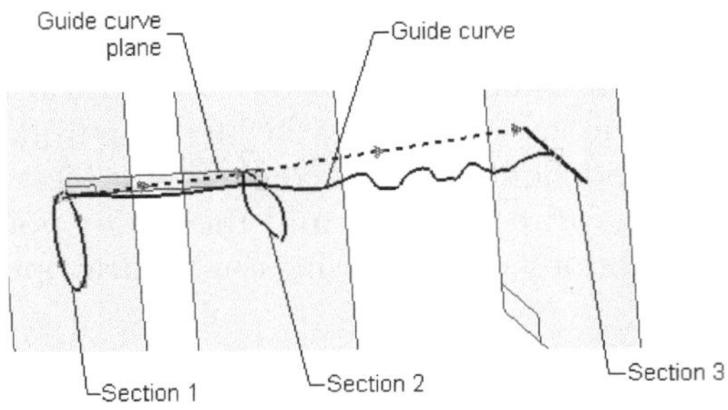

Figure 9-35 Sections and guide curve

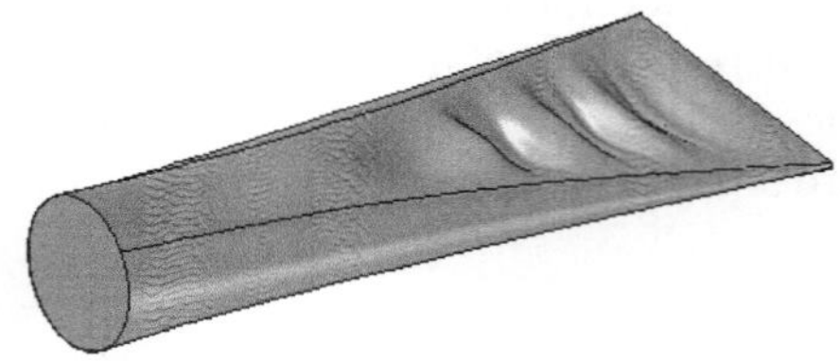

Figure 9-36 Lofted protrusion created using the guide curve

CREATING LOFTED CUTOUTS

Ribbon: Home > Solids > Cut drop-down > Loft

You can create lofted cutouts by using the **Loft** tool available in the **Cut** drop-down of the **Solids** group. This tool is used to remove material and it functions in the same way as the **Loft** tool in the **Add** drop-down. Figure 9-37 shows a lofted cut.

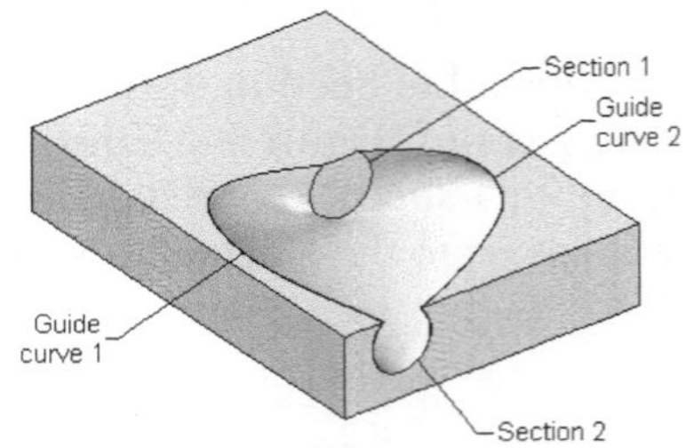

Figure 9-37 Lofted cut

CREATING 3D SKETCHES (SYNCHRONOUS ENVIRONMENT)

Ribbon: 3D Sketching > New 3D Sketch

In the earlier chapters, you have learned to draw 2D sketches in the sketching environment. In this chapter, you will learn to draw 3D sketches. 3D sketches are mostly used to create 3D paths for the sweep features, 3D curves, and so on. Figure 9-38 shows a chair frame created by sweeping a profile along a 3D path.

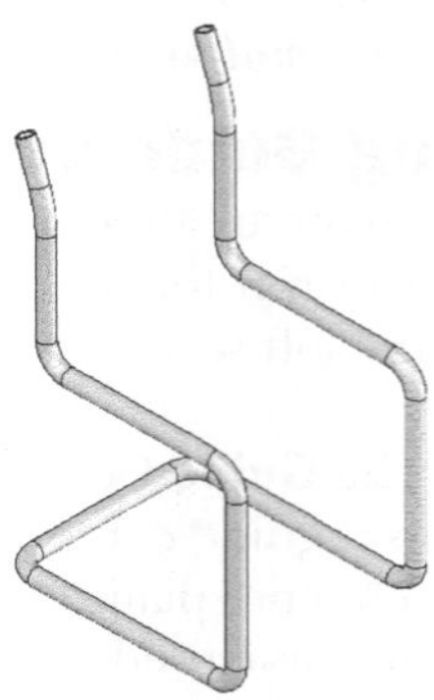

Figure 9-38 A chair frame created by sweeping a profile along a 3D path

To draw a 3D sketch, choose the **New 3D Sketch** tool from the **New Sketch** group of the **3D Sketching** tab; the **3D sketches** node will be added to the **PathFinder**. You do not need to select a sketching plane to draw a 3D sketch. It is better to orient the view to isometric for drawing line. To do so, choose the 3D sketching tool from the **3D Draw** group; 3D aligned lines of infinite length will be attached to the cursor and also a new coordinate system is displayed in the drawing area. The red infinite line represents the X direction, the green infinite line represents the Y direction, and the blue infinite line represents the Z direction. Also, the same colors are reflected in the new coordinate system for the respective axes. The tools available in the **3D Draw** group of the **3D Sketching** tab are used in the 3D sketching environment and are discussed next.

Note

When you invoke a sketching tool, if the 3D aligned lines of infinite length are not attached with the cursor, then you need to activate the ***Show 3D Alignment Lines*** *button available in the* ***3D 3D Intellisketch*** *group of the* ***3D Sketching*** *tab.*

3D Point

Ribbon:	3D Sketching > 3D Draw > 3D Point

The **3D Point** tool is used to create points in the modeling space by defining the X, Y, and Z coordinates. You can also create a 3D point on a locked plane by defining the horizontal and vertical coordinates. To create a 3D point choose the **3D Point** tool; you will be prompted to click for a point. Click in the drawing area; a point will be created. You can also use the **3D Point** command bar to define the X, Y and Z coordinates of the point. To create a point on a locked plane, choose the **Lock Sketch Plane** button from the command bar and you will be prompted to click on a plane to lock. Select a plane and define the X and Y coordinates for the point to create points on the locked plane.

3D Line

Ribbon:	3D Sketching > 3D Draw > 3D Line

The **3D Line** tool is used to draw straight lines as well as to draw the tangent or normal arcs originating from the endpoint of the selected line. To draw a straight line, choose the **3D Line** tool; you will be prompted to select the first point of the line and you will also notice that three alignment lines are attached to the cursor. Specify the point by clicking in the drawing area by using the left mouse button; a rubber band line will be attached to the cursor. Also, you will be prompted to select the second point of the line. Move the cursor to the right. Next, position the cursor where it touches the red alignment line (X direction), and click in the drawing area when the parallel icon is displayed; the line will be drawn in the X direction, as shown in Figure 9-39. Now, move the cursor in the Y direction and when it touches the green line, a parallel icon will be displayed. Now, click in the drawing area; a line will be drawn in the Y direction, as shown in Figure 9-40. Similarly, move the cursor in the Z direction and when it touches the blue line, a parallel icon will be displayed. Now, click in the drawing area; a line will be drawn in the Z direction, as shown in Figure 9-41.

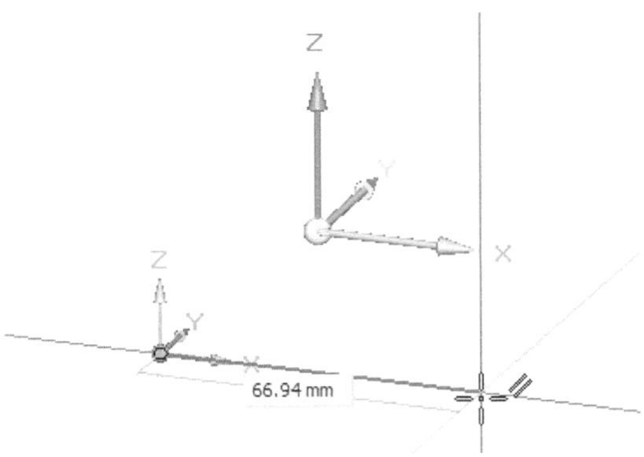

Figure 9-39 Sketching in the X direction

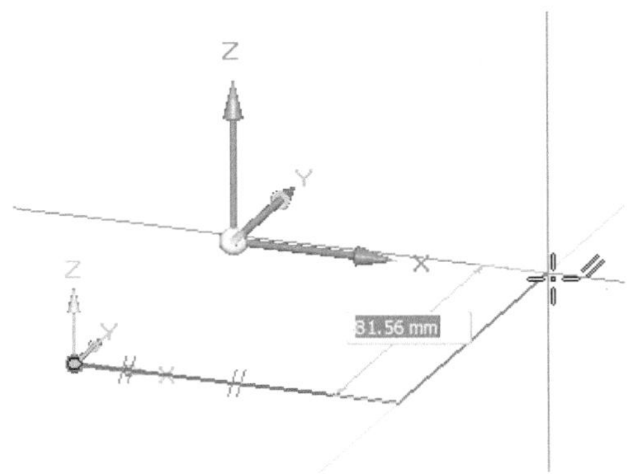

Figure 9-40 Sketching in the X and Y directions

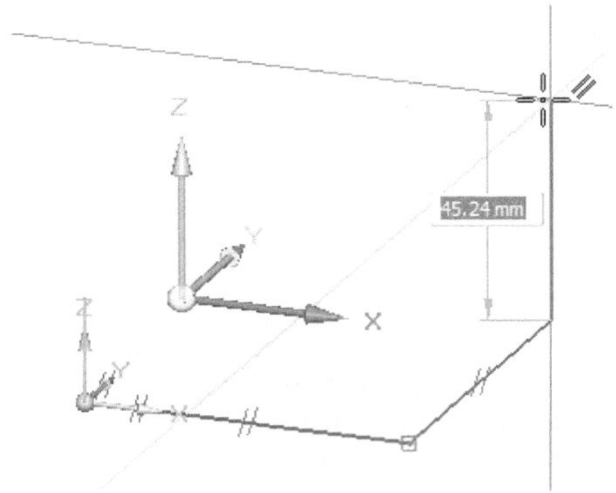

Figure 9-41 *Sketching in the X,Y and Z directions*

You can also draw inclined lines. To do so, click to specify the first point; a rubber line gets attached to the cursor. Now, click to specify the second point when no parallel icon is displayed. You can also draw a tangent or a normal arc by using the **3D Line** tool in the same way as you did by using the **Line** tool in the 2d sketching discussed in Chapter 2.

3D Rectangle by Center

Ribbon: 3D Sketching > 3D Draw > 3D Rectangle by Center

The **3D Rectangle by Center** tool is used to create a rectangle by defining its center point, width, height, and angle. You can use the **3D Rectangle by Center** command bar or dynamic edit boxes to define the rectangle width, height, and angle. You can also create a square by using this tool. To do so, press and hold the SHIFT key while creating the rectangle.

3D Circle by Center Point

Ribbon: 3D Sketching > 3D Draw > 3D Circle by Center Point

The **3D Circle by Center Point** tool is used to create a circle in the 3D sketching environment. You can enter a diameter or radius value in the **3D Circle by Center Point** command bar or in the dynamic edit boxes. When you enter a value in the command bar, a circle will be attached to the cursor and you will be prompted to select the plane to be locked. Now, choose the **Lock Sketch Plane** button from the **3D Circle by Center Point** command bar and select the plane. Click in the drawing area to placed the circle. Note that all subsequent clicks place the circle of same size in the drawing. To create circles of different sizes/radii, you need to right-click to enter a new value in the command bar or dynamically define a circle.

3D Fillet

Ribbon: 3D Sketching > 3D Draw > 3D Fillet

The **3D Fillet** tool is used to create a fillet between lines and arcs or a combination of both and these elements should be coplanar. You can retain the sharp corners even after creating the fillet. To do so, choose the **No Trim** button from the **3D Fillet** command bar and then select the corners to be filleted; a fillet will be created and the sharp corners will be retained.

3D Include

Ribbon: 3D Sketching > 3D Draw > 3D Include

The **3D Include** tool is used to project 2D sketch elements, 3D sketch elements, and part edges into the active 3D sketch. The included elements are associative to the parent elements and maintain their 3D position. On invoking the **3D Include** tool; you will be prompted to select on the edge to project on the active 3D sketch. Click on the edge to project on the active 3D sketch. Figure 9-42 shows the edges projected in 3D sketch using the **3D Include** tool.

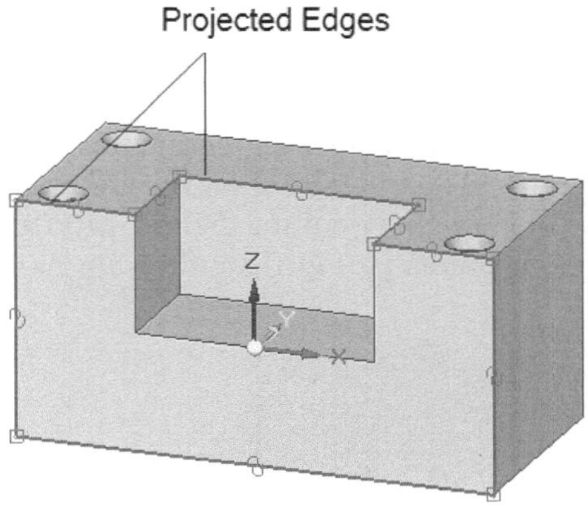

***Figure 9-42** Edges projected in 3D sketch using the **3D Include** tool*

In the 3D sketching environment of Solid Edge, you can add ten types of relationships by using the tools available in the **3D Relate** group of **3D Sketching** tab. The **Connect**, **Horizontal/Vertical**, **Concentric**, **Tangent**, **Perpendicular**, **Equal**, and **Parallel** relationships work in the same way as they did in the sketching environment discussed in Chapter 3. The remaining relationship are discussed next.

Coaxial Relationship

Ribbon: 3D Sketching > 3D Relate > Coaxial

The **Coaxial** relationship forces the selected arc or circle of 3D sketch to share the same axis with a linear segment. You can also make a line in a 3D sketch coaxial with a circular edge or cylindrical face. To add the coaxial relationship, invoke the **Coaxial** tool; you will be prompted to select a line, arc, or circle. Next, click on the line; you will be prompted to select a circular element or feature. The first line segment is automatically forced to place coaxially with the circular element. If you select on the circular element after the first prompt, then in the second prompt, you will be prompted to select a linear element.

On Plane Relationship

Ribbon: 3D Sketching > 3D Relate > On Plane

The **On Plane** relationship forces the selected 3D sketch to become coplanar with the selected plane. When you invoke the **On Plane** tool, you will be prompted to click on the 3D Sketch element. After making the first selection, you will be prompted to click on a planar face or reference plane. Click on the planar face or reference plane; the selected 3D sketch will become coplanar to the selected plane.

Note

*You can create a 3D sketch in the **Ordered** part environment by invoking the 3D sketching environment. To invoke the 3D sketching environment, choose the **3D Sketch** button in the **Sketch** group of the **Home** tab. The tools for creating a 3D sketch are same in this environment as in the **Synchronous** part environment.*

CREATING HELICAL PROTRUSIONS

Ribbon: Home > Solids > Add drop-down > Helix

You can create helical protrusions such as springs, threads, and so on by using the **Helix** tool. To create a helical protrusion, you need to draw an axis and a cross-section. A cross-section can be drawn on the same plane or a plane perpendicular to the axis. The helical protrusion is created depending on the orientation of the cross-section with respect to the axis. Figures 9-43 and 9-45 show the sketches of the cross-section and the axis, and Figures 9-44 and 9-46 show the resulting helical protrusions. The steps to create a helical protrusion in the **Synchronous** part environment are discussed next.

Figure 9-43 *Cross-section and axis*

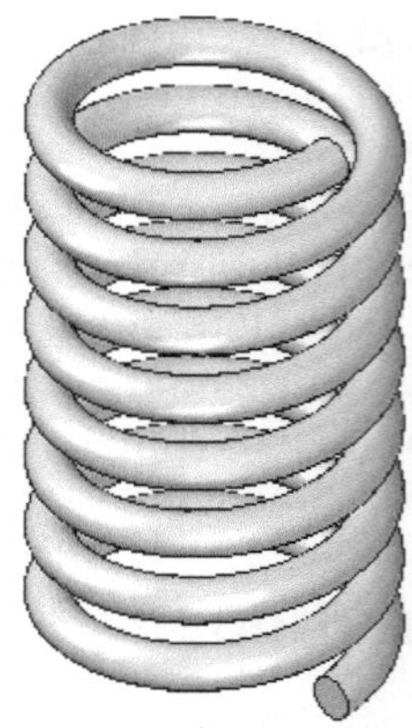

Figure 9-44 *Parallel helical protrusion*

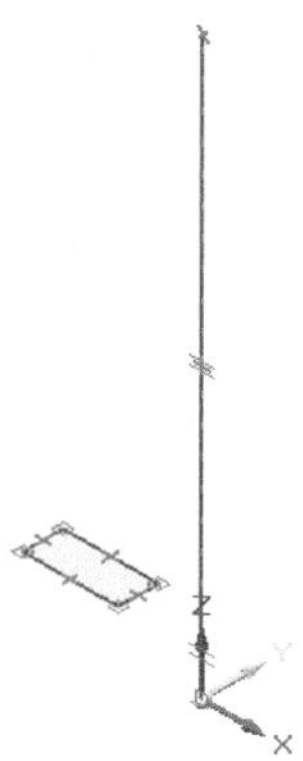

Figure 9-45 *Cross-section and axis*

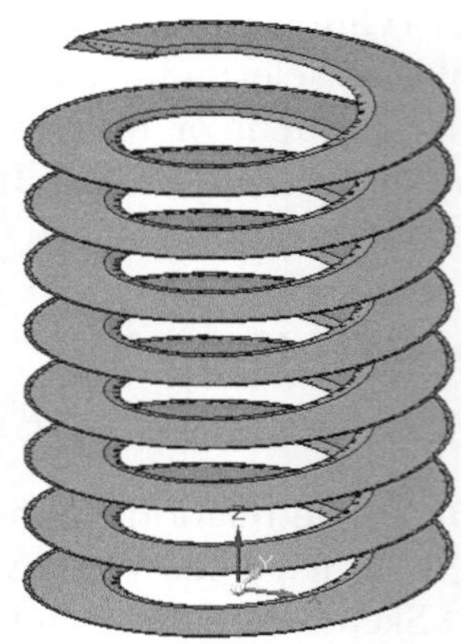

Figure 9-46 *Perpendicular helical protrusion*

Cross section and axis definition

To create a helix feature, first you need to define a cross section and an axis. After that, invoke the **Helix** tool; the **Helix** command bar will be displayed with the **Cross section and axis definition** button chosen by default in it. Also, you will be prompted to select the cross-section and the axis. Select the cross-section and the axis from the existing sketch and choose the **Accept** button; a preview of the helix along with a handle and a dynamic edit box will be displayed. You can specify the number of turns and the pitch of the helix in these edit boxes. The handle can be used to define the direction of the helix creation. Apart from using the edit boxes, you can also use the **Helix Options** button in the command bar to define the helix parameters.

Note
*You can convert an existing line into a construction line by choosing the **Construction** button in the **Draw** group of the **Ribbon** and then selecting the existing line.*

Helix Options

When you choose the **Helix Options** button from the command bar, the **Helix Options** dialog box will be displayed, as shown in Figure 9-47.

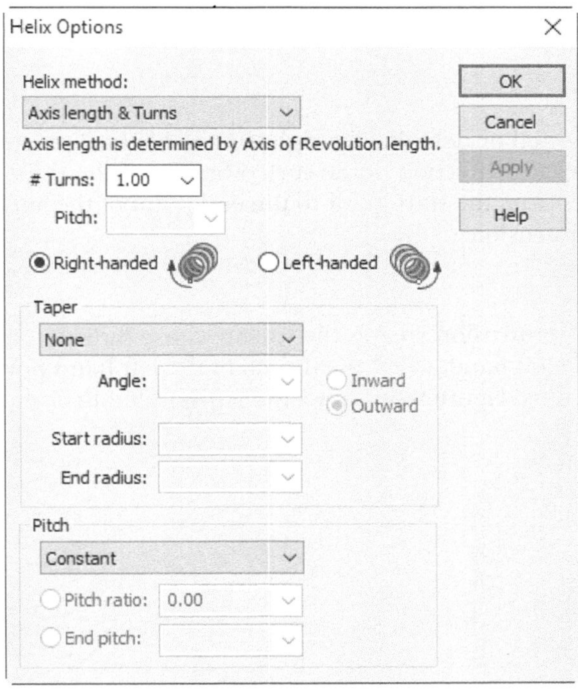

*Figure 9-47 The **Helix Options** dialog box*

Helix Method

There are three options available in this drop-down list which are discussed next.

Note
These options are also available in the command bar.

Axis length & Pitch

The pitch of a helix is the distance measured parallel to the axis and between the corresponding points on the adjacent turns. This option allows you to specify the pitch of the helix and it assumes the length of the axis as the height of the helical protrusion.

Axis length & Turns
This option enables you to specify the number of turns in the helix and assumes the length of the axis as the height of the helical protrusion.

Pitch & Turns
This option enables you to specify the pitch of the helix and the number of turns. The number of turns and the value of the pitch determine the height of the helical protrusion.

Turns
This edit box is used to specify the number of turns of the helical protrusion.

Pitch
This edit box is used to specify the pitch of the helix.

Right-handed
This radio button is selected by default. The right-handed helical protrusion creates the spring whose direction matches the direction of the curled fingers of the right hand, when the thumb of the right hand points from the start point to the end point of the axis. Figure 9-48 shows the right-handed helical protrusion.

Left-handed
The left-handed helical protrusion creates the spring whose direction matches the direction of the curled fingers of the left hand, when the thumb of the left hand points from the start point to the end point of the axis. Figure 9-49 shows the left-handed helical protrusion.

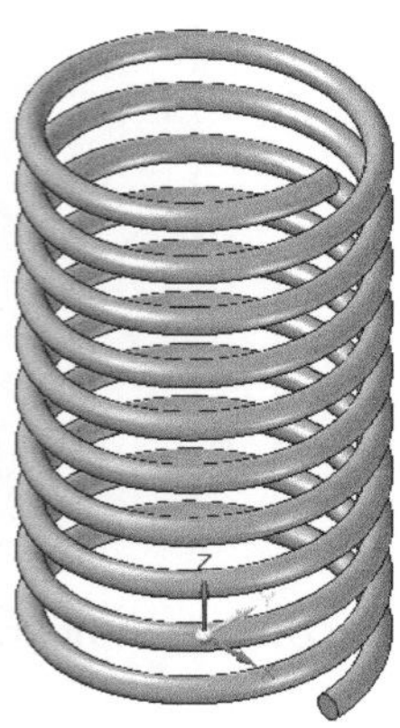

Figure 9-48 *Right-handed helical protrusion*

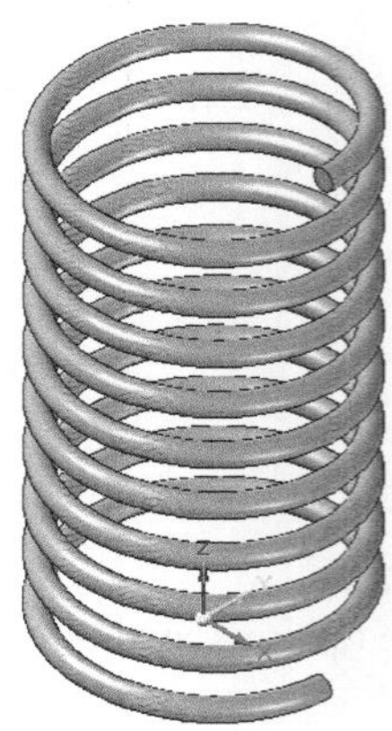

Figure 9-49 *Left-handed helical protrusion*

Taper Area
The options in this area of the dialog box are used to specify the parameters related to the taper of the helix. The options in this area are discussed next.

Taper Drop-down List
This drop-down list is used to specify the taper methods. There are three methods available in this drop-down list: **None**, **By Angle**, and **By Radius**. The **None** option enables you to

create a helix without any taper. The **By Angle** option enables you to specify the taper angle. This taper angle can be inward or outward. When you select the **By Angle** option from the drop-down list, the **Inward** and **Outward** radio buttons will be activated. The **Inward** radio button enables you to create a helical protrusion that tapers inside, that is, toward the axis, see Figure 9-50. The **Outward** radio button is used to create a helical protrusion that tapers outside, that is, away from the axis, see Figure 9-51.

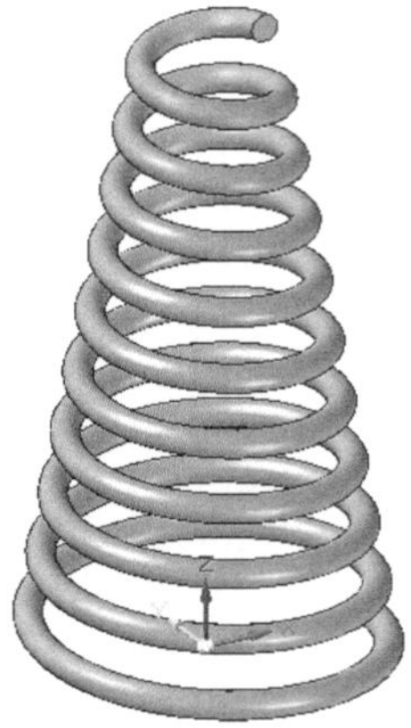

Figure 9-50 *Inward tapered spring*

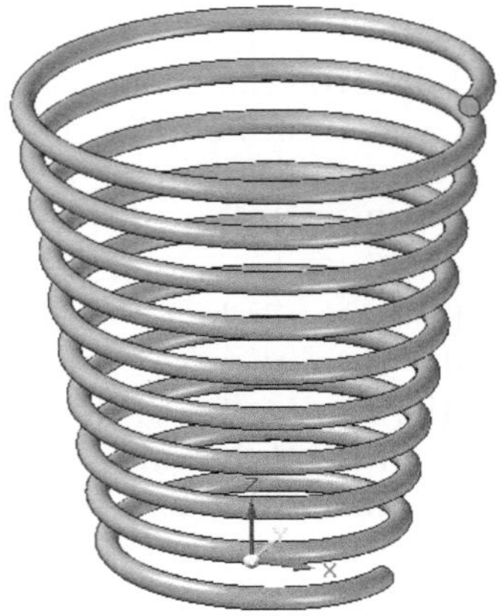

Figure 9-51 *Outward tapered spring*

The **By Radius** option enables you to specify the end and start radii of the helical protrusion. This radius is from the axis of the helical protrusion. When you select the **By Radius** option from the drop-down list, the **Start** and **End radius** edit boxes will be activated. The start radius value is applied at the start end of the helical protrusion and the end radius value is applied at the end of it. Figure 9-52 shows a spring created with the taper specified in terms of the start and end radii.

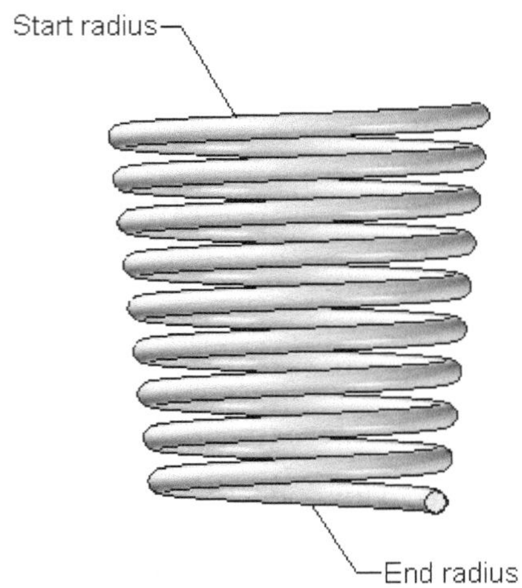

Figure 9-52 *Taper specified by using the start and end radii*

Pitch Area

The options in this area of the dialog box are used to specify the parameters related to the pitch of the helix. These options are discussed next.

Pitch Drop-down List

The drop-down list is used to specify the pitch methods. There are two options available in this drop-down list, **Constant** and **Variable**.

The **Constant** option enables you to maintain a constant pitch throughout the helical protrusion.

When you select the **Variable** option from the drop-down list, the **Pitch ratio** and **End pitch** radio buttons are activated. The **Pitch ratio** specifies the variable pitch ratio for a variable pitch helix. The **End pitch** specifies the ending pitch length for the helix.

Note that if you use the **End pitch** option to create a variable spring, then the actual start pitch and end pitch values will not be equal to the values specified in the **End pitch** and **Pitch** edit boxes of the **Helix Options** dialog box.

In Solid Edge, you can create a variable pitch helical protrusion by specifying the start and end pitch values of the helix. The variable pitch values are defined based on the formula that states that increase in the pitch value (I) is equal to the ratio of difference between the end pitch (EP) and start pitch (SP) values and the number of turns (T). In mathematical notations, this can be written as I=(EP-SP)/T, where I is the increase in pitch, SP is the pitch at start, EP is the pitch at end, and T is the number of turns. For example, if SP is 20, EP is 44, and T is 12, then I=2. Half of this value will be added to the start value specified to calculate the distance for the first turn and the distance for the rest of the turns will be equal to the sum of I and the value of the previous turn, refer to Figure 9-53. In this figure, the actual start pitch (SP) is 20+1 and the value of remaining pitches is calculated by adding 2 to the previous turn's value.

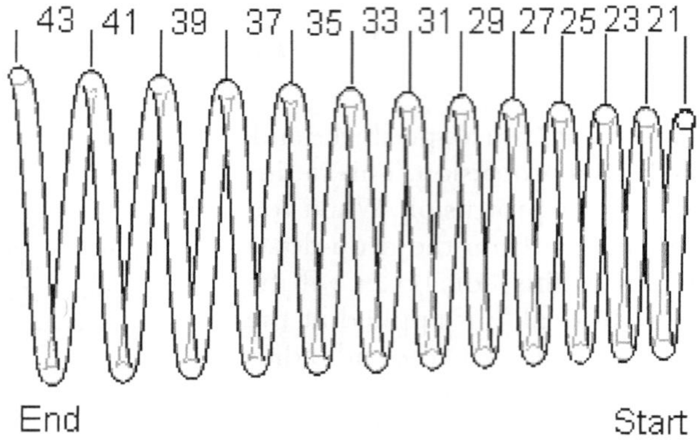

Figure 9-53 *Taper specified by using the start and end pitch values*

After specifying the parameters, choose the **OK** button from the **Helix Options** dialog box. Now, you need to define the extent type for the extrusion. Click on the **Extent Type** drop-down list; the **Finite** option will be selected as default. So, the helix will be created upto specify parameter in the **Helix** dialog box. But if you need to specify the height upto a surface, select the **From-To** button and specify the parameters accordingly.

To create the helical protrusion in the **Ordered** part environment, choose the **Helix** tool from the **Add** drop-down in the **Solids** group of the **Home** tab; the **Helical Protrusion** command bar will be displayed and you will be prompted to click on a planar face or reference plane to create a profile for the helix. By default, the cross-section is created in parallel direction of the revolution axis. However, to create a cross-section in perpendicular direction, you can choose the **Helix Options** button from the command bar to invoke the **Helix Options** dialog box. Now, you can select the **Perpendicular** radio button from the dialog box to create a cross section in the perpendicular direction of the revolution axis. Next, choose the **OK** button to close the dialog box. After selecting the orientation for the helix profile, select a planar face or reference plane and draw a closed sketch for the helix profile and specify an axis of revolution from the **Draw** group of the **Home** tab. Next, choose the **Close Sketch** button; you will be prompted to click on the axis to identify start end of the helix. Select the axis; the **Parameter Step** will be activated and you will be prompted to enter the helix parameters. Now, choose the **More** button from the command bar; the **Helix Parameters** dialog box will be displayed. Note that the options in this dialog box are similar to the options in the **Helix Options** dialog box discussed in the **Synchronous** part environment. After defining the parameters in the dialog box, choose the **OK** button from the dialog box. Next, choose the **Next** button from the command bar; the **Extent Step** will be activated. By default, the **Finite Extent** button will be chosen and the helix will be created upto the length of the axis. Choose the **Preview** and **Finish** buttons from command bar to create the helix.

CREATING HELICAL CUTOUTS

Ribbon: Home > Solids > Cut drop-down > Helix

You can create helical cutouts on any feature by using the **Helix** tool from the **Cut** drop-down in the **Solids** group of the **Home** tab. This tool works in the same way as the **Helix** tool available in the **Add** drop-down of the same group in both the environments. The only difference is that the **Helix** tool in the **Cut** drop-down is used to remove the material from the part.

CREATING NORMAL PROTRUSIONS

Ribbon: Home > Solids > Add drop-down > Normal

In Solid Edge, you can create a normal protrusion by selecting a closed curve. You can do so by using the **Normal** tool. The selected curve can be created or projected on a planar or a non planar face of a model. Note that it is not possible to draw a sketch on a non-planar surface. Therefore, you need to project the curve on it. Projecting a curve on a non planar surface will be discussed in the **Surface Modeling** chapter. Using the **Normal** tool, you can create an embossed feature on a cylindrical or a planar face. To emboss a text, create the text by using the **Text Profile** tool. The **Text Profile** tool is available in the **Tools** tab of the **Ribbon** in the sketching environment of the **Ordered** part environment, and in the **Insert** group of the **Sketching** tab of the **Ribbon** in the **Synchronous** part environment. To understand the use of the **Normal** tool, create a profile on a planar face, as shown in Figure 9-54. Next, invoke this tool by choosing **Normal** from the **Add** drop-down in the **Solids** group. Select the sketch to be extruded normal to the surface. After selecting the sketch, right-click to accept the selection. On doing so, a red arrow will be displayed and you will be prompted to specify the projection direction. You can specify its direction by clicking on the screen. If you specify inward direction, the material will be added inside the profile. If you specify the outward direction, the material will be added on a face outside the profile. You can specify the height of material to be added in the **Height** edit box of the command bar in the **Side Step** before specifying the direction.

Figure 9-54 shows the profile created on a planar face. Figure 9-55 shows the resulting model after adding material of 10 mm height. The direction is specified inward to the profile by using the **Normal** tool.

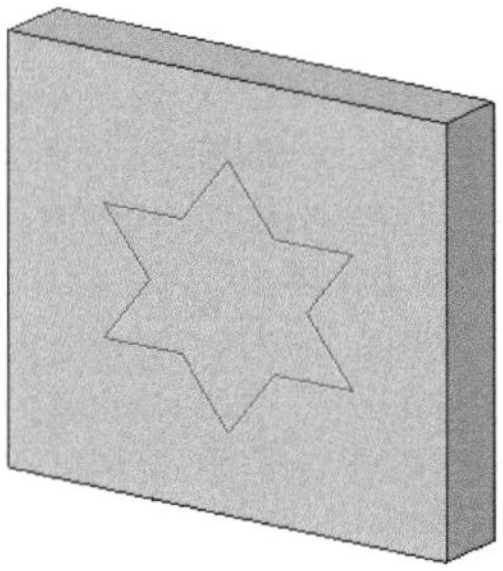

Figure 9-54 Profile created

Figure 9-55 Model after adding material

CREATING NORMAL CUTOUTS

Ribbon:	Home > Solids > Cut drop-down > Normal

You can create a normal cutout by choosing the **Normal** tool from the **Cut** drop-down in the **Solids** group. This tool works in the same way as the **Normal** tool in the **Add** drop-down with the only difference that this tool is used to remove the material.

WORKING WITH ADDITIONAL BODIES

Solid Edge provides you with the tool to insert new bodies in a part or sheet metal file. You can create features in the newly created body and then perform the boolean operations on two or more than two part bodies. You will learn more about boolean operations later in the chapter.

Note

*The options available in the **Add Body** drop-down can be only used over the bodies created using the **Add Body** option.*

Inserting a New Body

Ribbon:	Home > Solids > Add Body > Add Body

In Solid Edge, you can create a new solid body in the existing model by using the **Add Body** tool. To do so, you need to follow the steps discussed next.

1. Create a new body or open a previously created file. The file can be a part or sheet metal file.

2. Invoke the **Add Body** tool from the **Solids** group in the **Home** tab; the **Add Body** dialog box will be displayed, refer to Figure 9-56. The options in the dialog box are discussed later in this chapter.

3. Select the **Add Part body** or **Add Sheet Metal body** radio button from the dialog box.

4. Enter the body name in the **New body name** edit box or use the default name.

5. Choose the **OK** button and then construct a new body by using different sketching and modeling tools, refer to Figure 9-57.

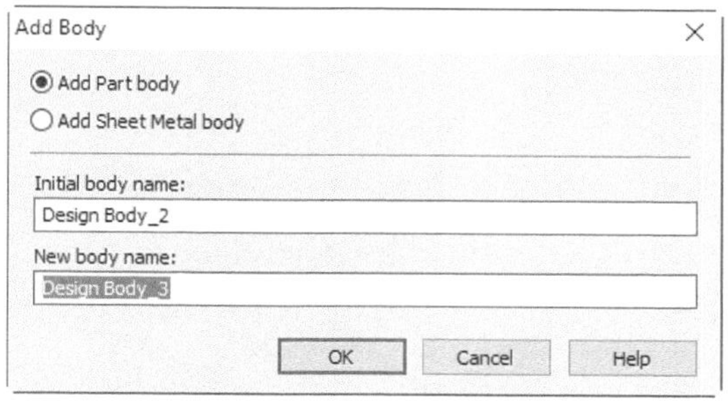

Figure 9-56 The ***Add Body*** *dialog box*

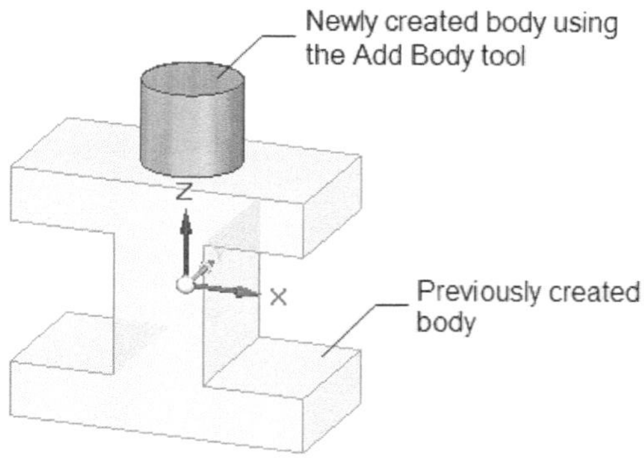

Figure 9-57 New body added

The options available in the **Add Body** dialog box are discussed next.

Add Part body

This radio button is selected to add a part body.

Add Sheet Metal body

This radio button is selected to add a sheet metal body.

Initial body name

This edit box is used to specify the name of the active body. By default, the name of the active body is Design Body_1 and you can change it by entering the desired name.

New body name

This edit box is used to specify the name of the body to be created. By default, the name of the newly created part is Design Body_2 but you can change it by entering the desired name.

Note that after a new body is created, the names of both the bodies get displayed under the **Design Bodies** in the **Path Finder**.

Applying Boolean Operations to Bodies

After inserting the bodies, you can apply boolean operations such as union of two bodies, subtraction of one body from the other, retaining the intersected portion of two bodies, and so on. The operations which are used to manipulate the bodies are discussed next.

Combining Bodies

Ribbon:	Home > Solids > Add Body > Union

In Solid Edge, you can combine different bodies together by using the **Union** tool. To do so, open a multi body file or create multiple bodies in a file. Next, choose the **Union** tool from the **Add Body** drop-down in the **Solids** group; the **Union** command bar will be displayed and you will be prompted to select the bodies to be combined. Select the bodies to be combined and right-click to accept the changes in it; the selected bodies will be combined and thus form a single body. Figure 9-58 shows the bodies to be combined and Figure 9-59 shows a preview of the newly combined bodies. Note that you can use the **Union** tool only on the bodies created using the **Add Body** tool.

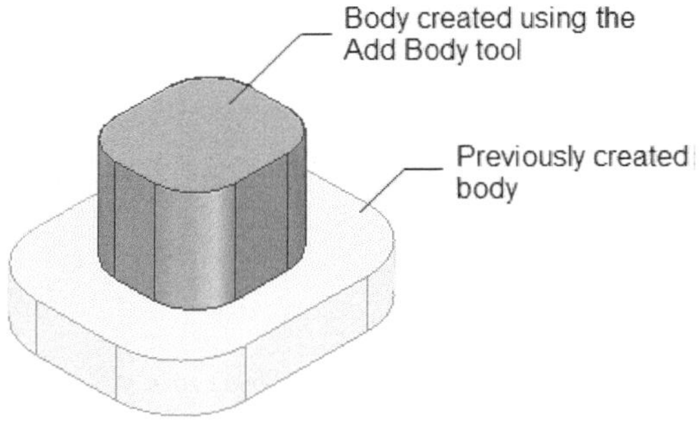

Figure 9-58 Bodies to be combined

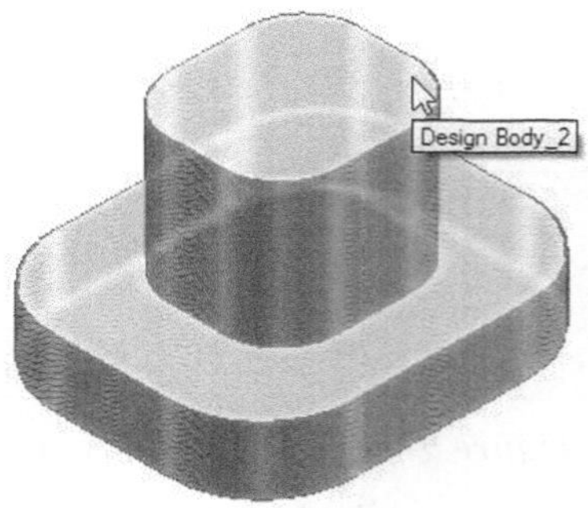

Figure 9-59 Preview of the combined bodies

Subtracting Bodies

Ribbon: Home > Solids > Add Body > Subtract

In Solid Edge, you can subtract a body from another body. To do so, open a multi body file or create multiple bodies in a file, refer to Figure 9-60. Now, invoke the **Subtract** tool from the **Add Body** drop-down; the **Subtract** command bar will be displayed and the **Select Target Step** button is chosen by default in it. You will be prompted to select the target body. Select the target body and then right-click to accept the selection. Now, you will be prompted to select the body to be subtracted from the target body. Select the newly created body; it will be subtracted from the target body, refer to Figure 9-61. Note that by activating the target body, you can view the subtracted part of the body. To view the subtracted part, press the ESC key and then right-click on the target body. Next, choose **Activate Body** from the shortcut menu displayed; the target body will be activated and you can view the subtracted body, refer to Figure 9-62.

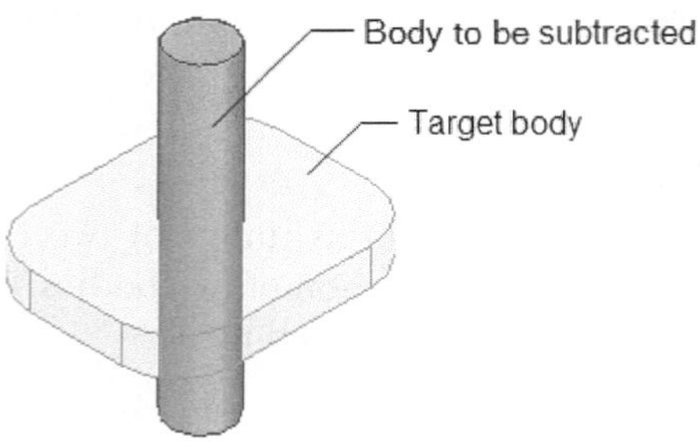

Figure 9-60 Bodies to be selected

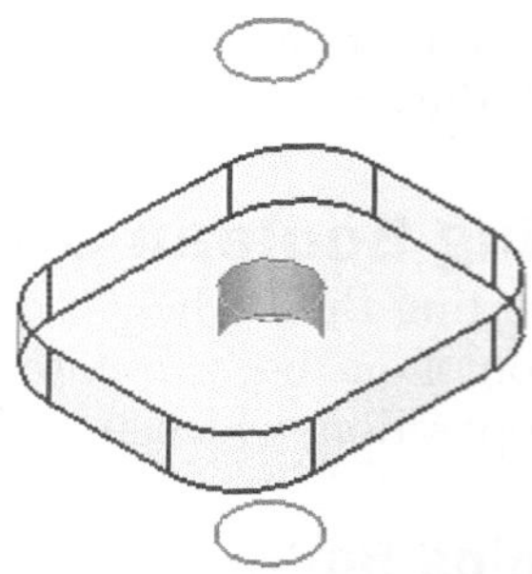

Figure 9-61 Preview of the subtracted body

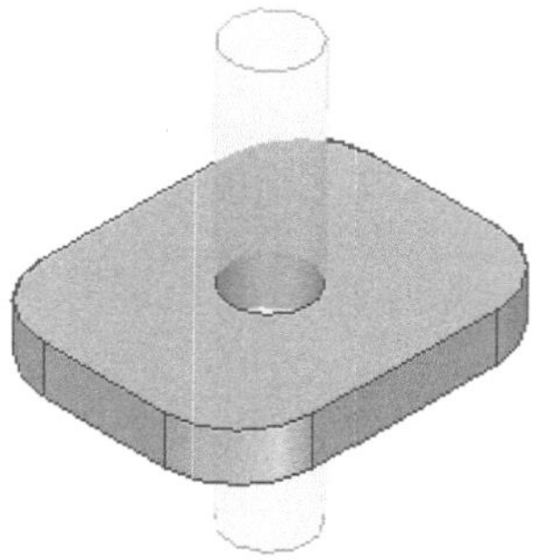

Figure 9-62 Subtracted part of body

Intersecting Bodies

Ribbon:	Home > Solids > Add Body > Intersect

You can retain the intersecting material of two intersecting bodies and remove the rest of the portion of the selected bodies using the **Intersect** tool. You can also create complex geometries very easily using this tool. When you invoke this tool, the **Intersect** command bar will be displayed. Select the intersecting bodies and choose the **Accept** button from the **Intersect** command bar. Figure 9-63 shows bodies to be selected and Figure 9-64 shows a preview of the bodies after selecting them. Figure 9-65 shows the intersecting part between the bodies.

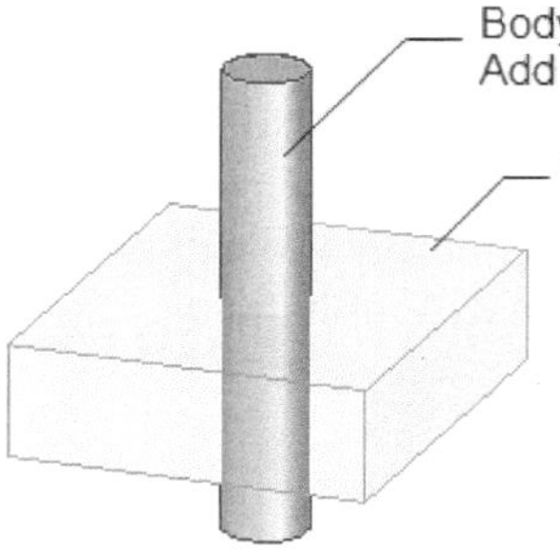

Figure 9-63 Bodies to be selected

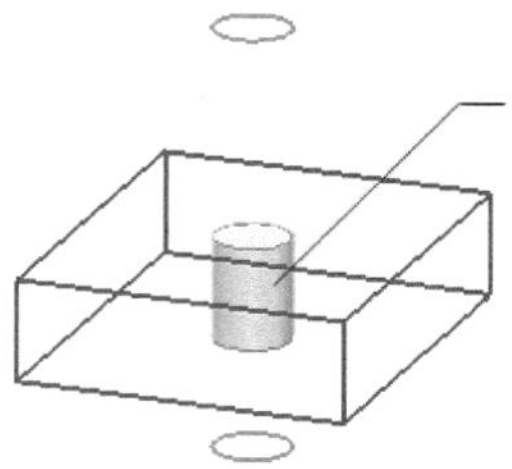

Figure 9-64 Preview of the intersecting part of bodies

Figure 9-65 Intersecting part between the selected bodies

Splitting a Body

Ribbon:	Home > Solids > Add Body > Split

You can split a body into two or multiple bodies using the **Split** tool. When you invoke this tool, the **Split** command bar will be displayed and you will be prompted to select the tool and the target body. Select the tool body (body created using the **Add Body** tool) and then the target body, refer to Figure 9-66. Next, choose the **Accept** button from the command bar; the tool body will split into multiple bodies, as shown in Figure 9-67.

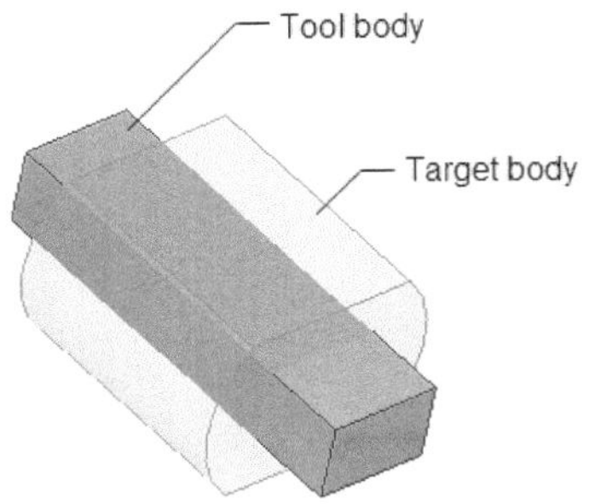

Figure 9-66 Bodies to be selected

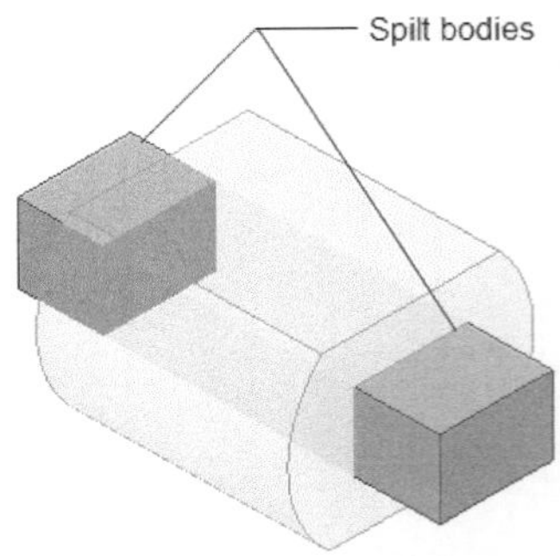

Figure 9-67 Bodies after splitting

Multi-body Publish

Ribbon: Home > Solids > Add Body > Multi-body Publish

You can create an individual file for each body present in a file containing multiple bodies by using the **Multi-body Publish** tool. You can also create an assembly file by using the published bodies as the components. Note that this tool is only available, if you are working over a file that contains multiple bodies. To create an individual file for each body present in a file, invoke the **Multi-body Publish** tool from the **Add Body** drop-down; the **Solid Edge ST9** dialog box will be displayed, refer to Figure 9-68. Choose the **OK** button; the **Save As** dialog box will be displayed. In this dialog box, enter the required file name in the **File name** edit box and select the location when you need to save the file. Next, choose the **Save** button; the **Multi-body Publish** dialog box will be displayed, refer to Figure 9-69. Now, you need to choose the **Save Files** button from this dialog box to save the design bodies present in a multi-body file. The **Create Assembly** check box in this dialog box is selected by default. As a result, an assembly file will be created. You need to uncheck this check box, if you do not want to create an assembly file.

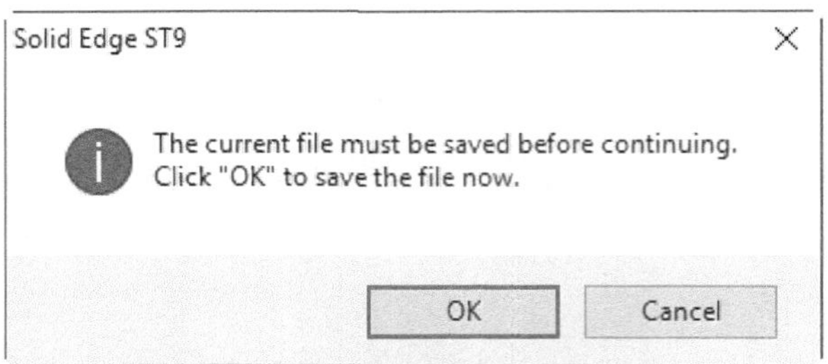

*Figure 9-68 The **Solid Edge ST9** dialog box*

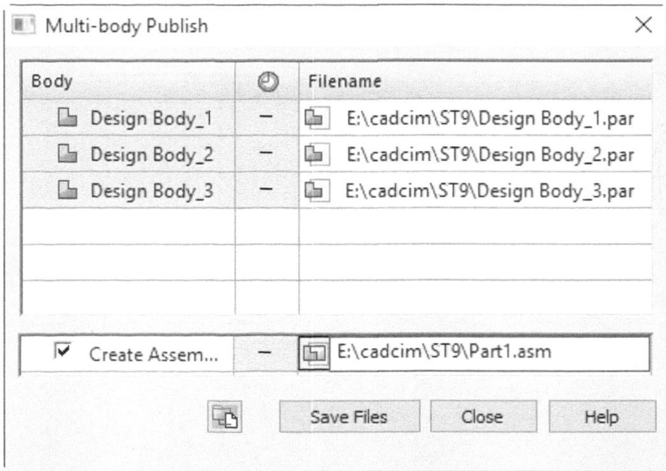

*Figure 9-69 The **Multi-body Publish** dialog box*

TUTORIALS

Tutorial 1 Synchronous and Ordered

In this tutorial, you will create the model of the Upper Housing of a Motor Blower assembly. The model is shown in Figure 9-70. Figure 9-71 shows the left view, top view, front view, and the sectioned left-side view of the model. All dimensions are in inches. After creating the model, save it with the name *c09tut1.par* at the location given next:

C:\Solid Edge\c09 **(Expected time: 45 min)**

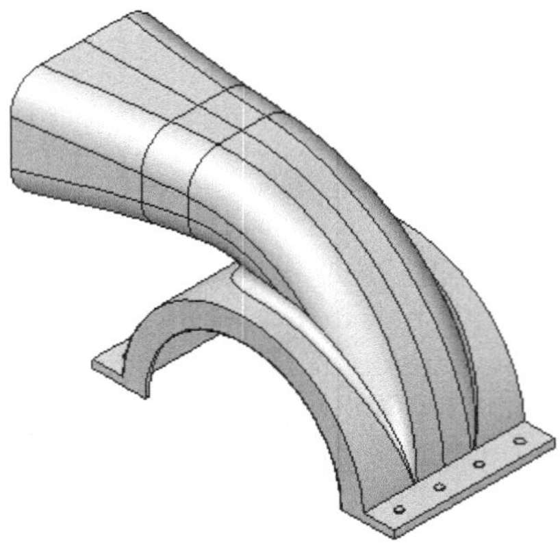

Figure 9-70 Isometric view of the Upper Housing

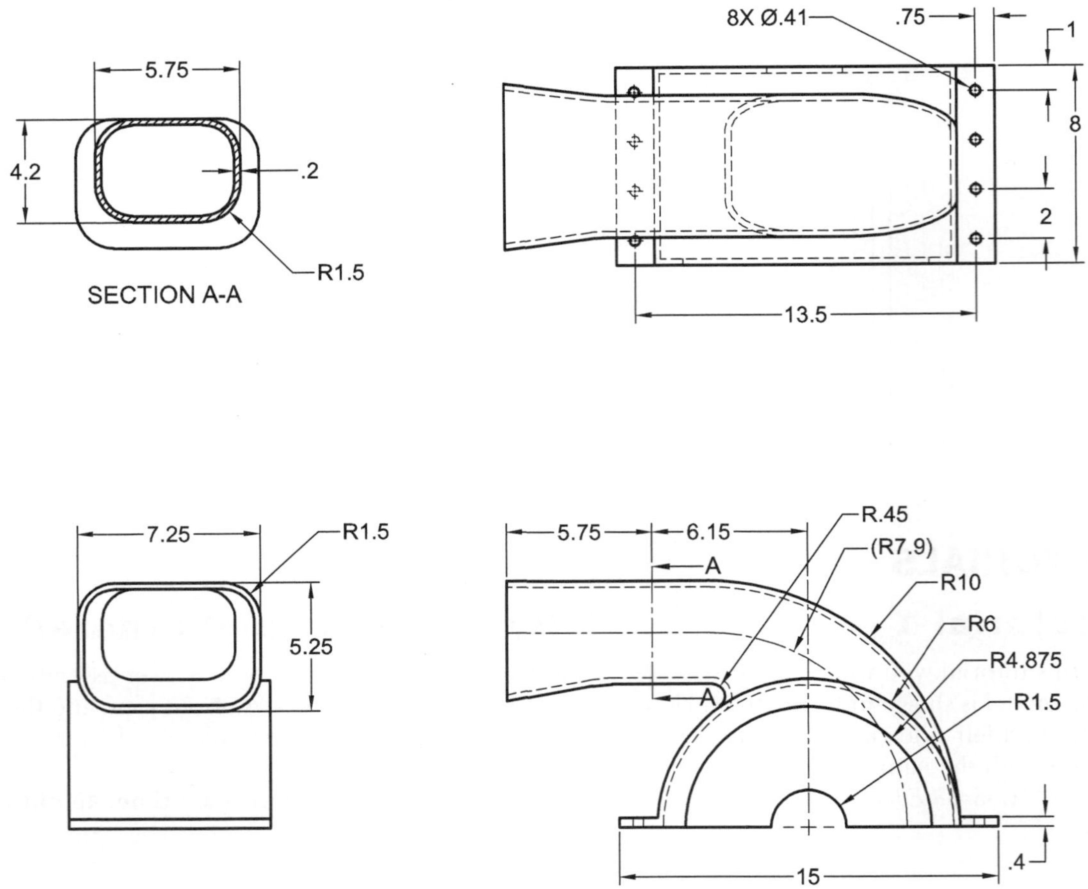

Figure 9-71 *Views and dimensions of the Upper Housing*

The following steps are required to complete this tutorial:

a. Start a new file and create the base feature on the front plane, refer to Figure 9-73. This feature is extruded symmetrically on both sides of the front plane.
b. Create the swept protrusion feature on the front plane, refer to Figures 9-74 through 9-83.
c. Create a round of radius .45 inches on the swept protrusion feature, refer to Figure 9-85.
d. Create the thin wall feature on the model, refer to Figure 9-86.
e. Create cut features on the base feature, refer to Figures 9-87 through 9-90.
f. Create a protrusion feature on the base feature, refer to Figure 9-92.
g. Mirror the previous protrusion feature to the left side of the model, refer to Figure 9-93.
h. Create a hole feature on the previous feature, refer to Figure 9-94.
i. Create a pattern of the hole feature, refer to Figure 9-95.

Starting a New File

The dimensions of this model are in inches. Therefore, you need to select a template that has units in inches.

1. Choose the **New** button from the **Quick Access** toolbar to display the **New** dialog box.

2. Select **ANSI Inch** from **Standard Templates** in the dialog box and double-click on the **ansi inch part.par** option to open a new part file with inch as the unit of length.

Creating the Base Feature

The file that you have opened has units set to inches. Therefore, the model that you will create will have dimensions in inches.

1. Draw the profile of the base feature on the XZ plane and dimension it, as shown in Figure 9-72.

2. Select the sketch and extrude it symmetrically on both sides of the profile plane to the depth of 8 units. The isometric view of the base feature is shown in Figure 9-73.

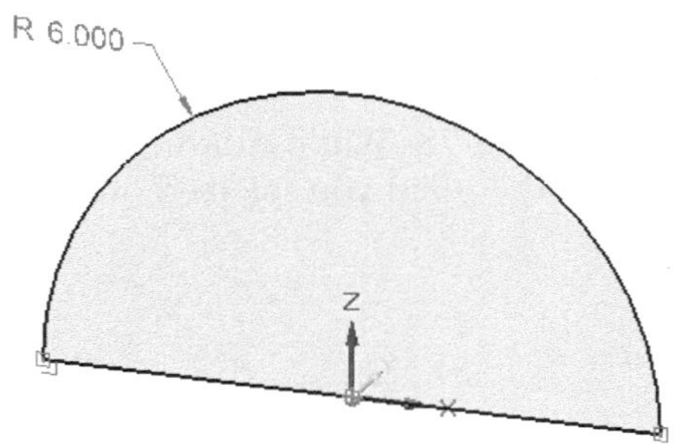

Figure 9-72 *Sketch of the base feature*

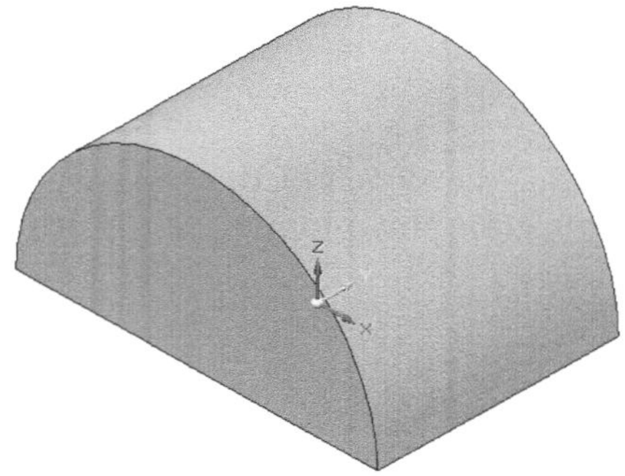

Figure 9-73 *Base feature*

Creating the Swept Protrusion

The second feature is the swept protrusion. You need to draw sketches for the path and the cross-sections to be used for creating the swept protrusion.

1. Draw the sketch of the path on the XZ plane, as shown in Figure 9-74.

2. Choose the **Normal to Curve** tool from the **More Planes** drop-down of the **Planes** group; you are prompted to select the curve.

3. Select the arc close to its lower endpoint; the profile plane is displayed, as shown in Figure 9-75.

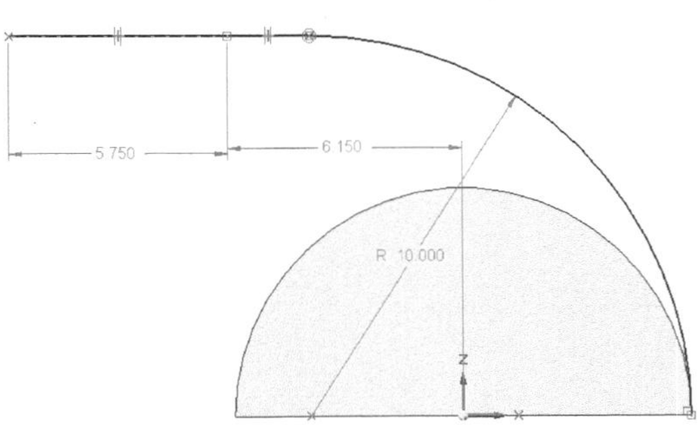

Figure 9-74 *Sketch of the path*

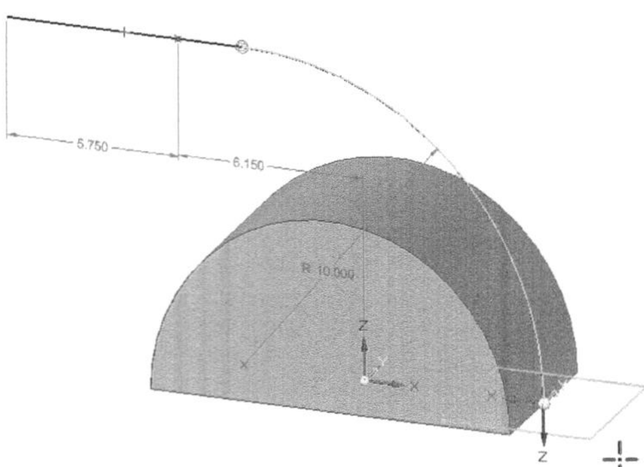

Figure 9-75 *Profile plane at the end of the path*

You will notice that on moving the cursor along the path curve, the profile plane also moves.

4. Click when the plane is at the lower end point of the path; the plane is created normal to the curve.

5. Draw the sketch of the cross-section on the newly created plane, as shown in Figure 9-76.

   Next, you need to draw the second cross-section. It is evident from the drawing views of the model that the second cross-section is to be drawn on the path where the section A-A is drawn, refer to Figure 9-71.

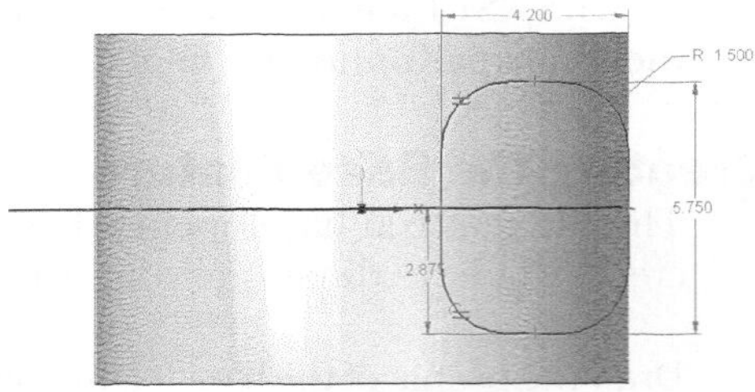

Figure 9-76 *The first cross-section of the swept protrusion*

6. Invoke the **Normal to Curve** tool and click on the point from where a line of length 5.75 units starts, as shown in Figure 9-77, to place the profile plane.

7. Draw the sketch of the cross-section, as shown in Figure 9-78. While drawing the sketch, constrain the midpoint of the upper horizontal line to the point you selected on the curve path.

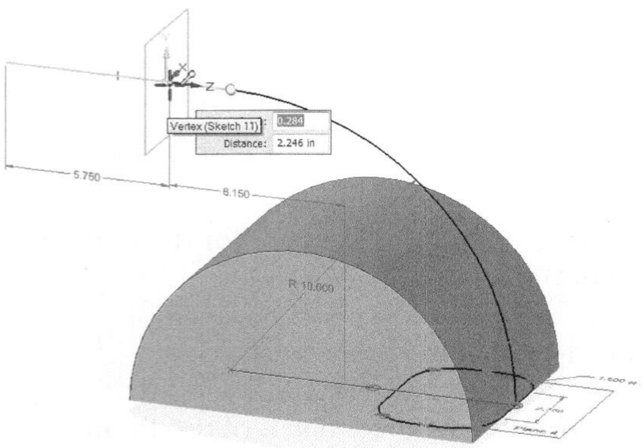

Figure 9-77 *Location for the profile plane*

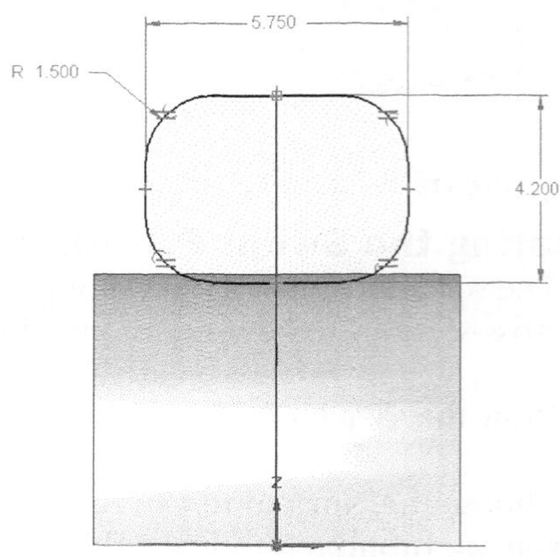

Figure 9-78 *The second cross-section of the swept protrusion*

8. Next, create a profile plane at the extreme left point, as shown in Figure 9-79.

9. Draw the sketch of the cross-section, as shown in Figure 9-80.

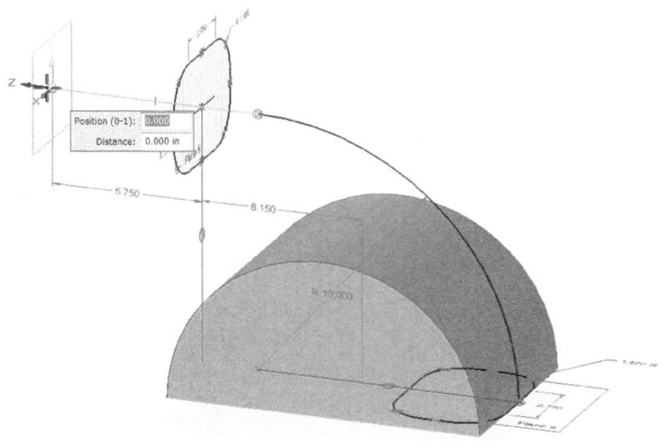

Figure 9-79 Location for the last profile plane

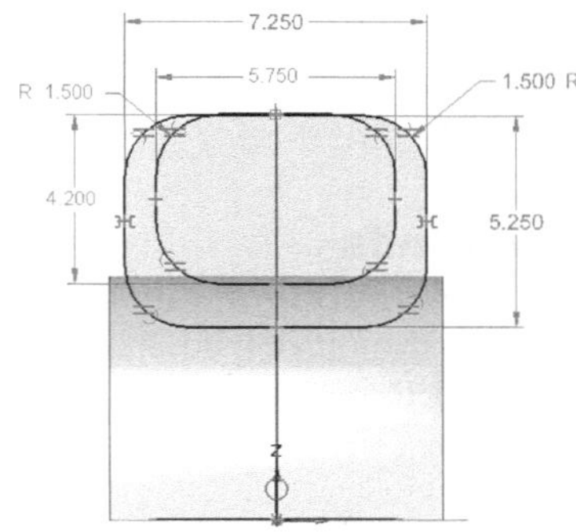

Figure 9-80 The third cross-section of the swept protrusion

Next, you need to create the swept protrusion by using the sketches.

10. Choose the **Sweep** tool from the **Add** drop-down of the **Solids** group; the **Sweep Options** dialog box is displayed.

11. Select the **Multiple paths and cross sections** radio button and make sure that the **No merge** radio button is selected in the **Face Merging** area. Next, choose **OK** to close the dialog box; the **Sweep** command bar is displayed with the **Path Step** invoked.

12. Select the path from the drawing area and choose the **Accept** button; you are prompted to select one more path. Choose the **Next** button to end the **Path Step**; the **Cross section Step** is invoked automatically.

13. Select the first cross-section and specify the start point on it, as shown in Figure 9-81.

14. Similarly, select the second and third cross-sections and then specify the vertex points on them, as shown in Figure 9-82.

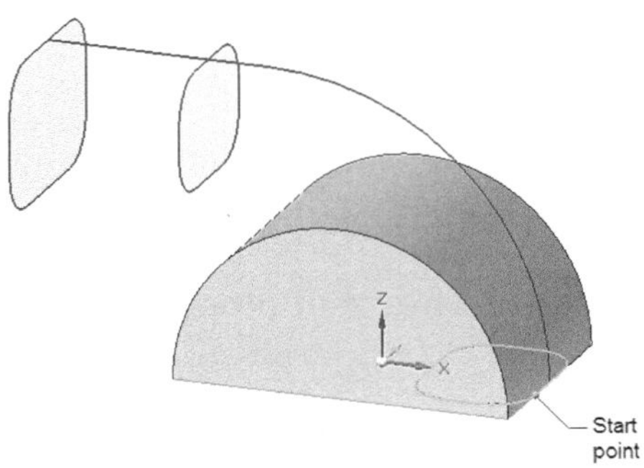

Figure 9-81 Arrow showing the start point on the first cross-section

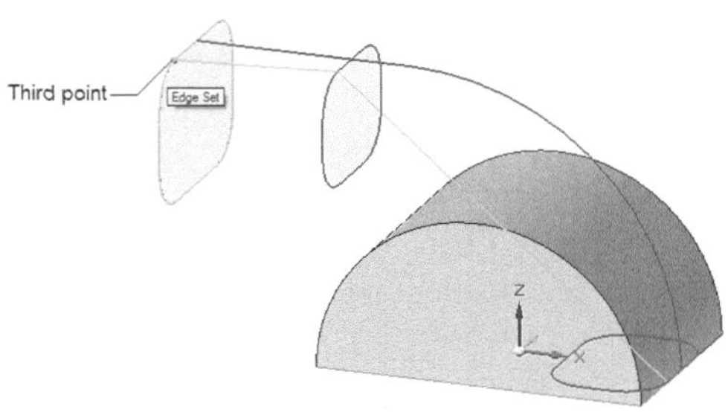

Figure 9-82 Arrow showing the start point on the third cross-section

15. Choose the **Preview** button from the command bar.

16. Choose the **Finish** button and then the **Cancel** button from the command bar to exit the **Sweep** tool. The swept protrusion feature is created, as shown in Figure 9-83.

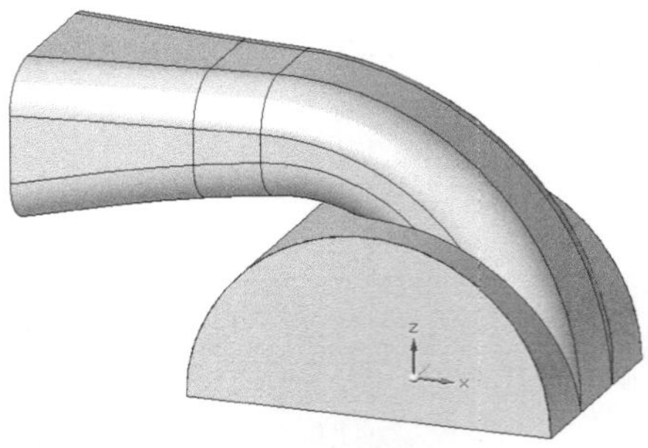

Figure 9-83 *Swept protrusion feature*

Adding Rounds

Before creating a thin wall feature, you need to add a round to the model. This is because while creating a thin wall feature, a round is also included along with the other faces of the model.

1. Choose the **Round** tool from the **Solids** group of the **Home** tab; the **Round** command bar is displayed.
2. Select the edge where the base feature and the swept feature join, as shown in Figure 9-84.
3. Enter **.45** in the **Radius** edit box and then press ENTER to accept.
4. Press the ESC key to exit the **Round** tool; the round is created, as shown in Figure 9-85.

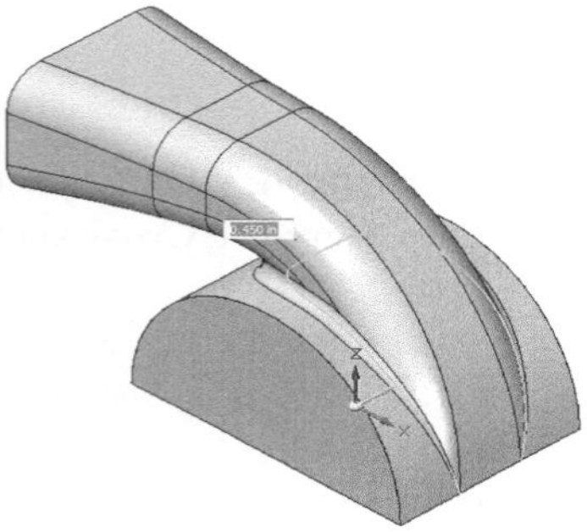

Figure 9-84 *Edge to be selected for round*

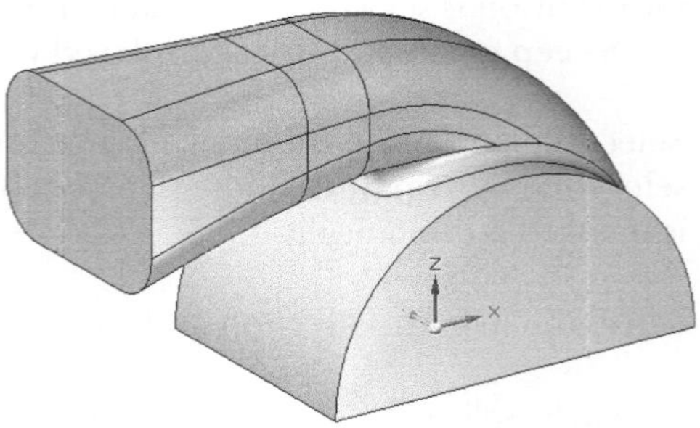

Figure 9-85 *Edge after creating the round*

Creating the Thin Wall Feature

You need to create a thin wall feature of thickness 0.2 units on the model so that it has uniform wall thickness.

1. Choose the **Thin Wall** tool from the **Home > Solids > Thin Wall** drop-down; you are prompted to select the faces to open.
2. Select the front face of the swept protrusion feature and the bottom face of the base feature.
3 Specify the offset direction; a preview of the thin wall feature is displayed.

Next, you need to specify the thickness value.

4. Enter **.2** in the edit box displayed on the model and press ENTER; the thin wall feature is created, as shown in Figure 9-86.

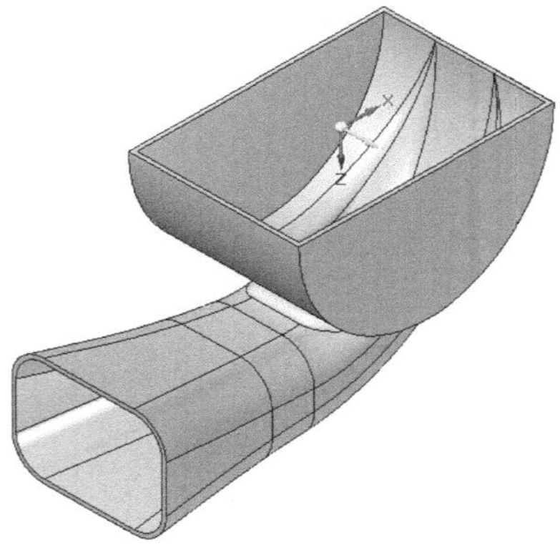

Figure 9-86 *Thin wall feature created*

Creating Cutout Features

1. Create an extrude cutout feature on the front face of the base feature. The sketch of the cutout feature is shown in Figure 9-87.

2. To specify the depth of extrusion, choose the **Through Next** button from the command bar; the cutout is created, as shown in Figure 9-88.

3. Create the next cutout feature whose sketch is shown in Figure 9-89.

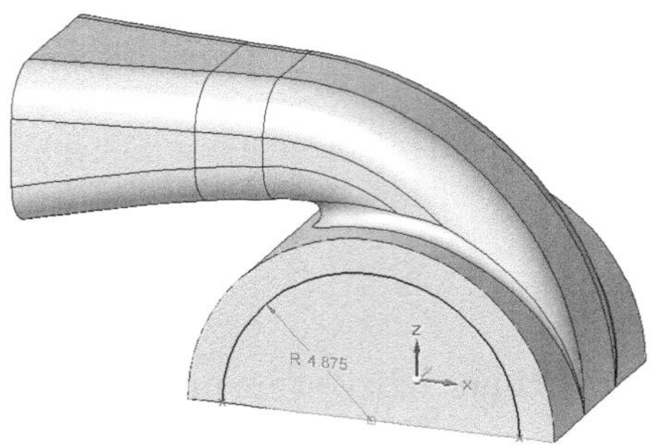

Figure 9-87 *Sketch of the cutout feature*

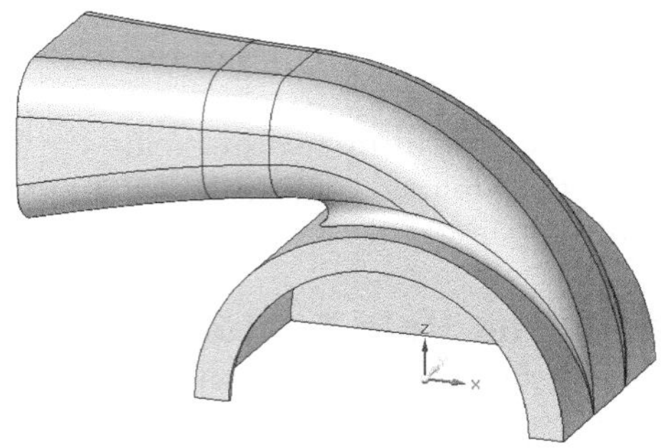

Figure 9-88 *Model after creating the cutout feature*

4. Specify the depth of the cutout feature by using the **Through Next** option. The model after creating this cutout feature is shown in Figure 9-90.

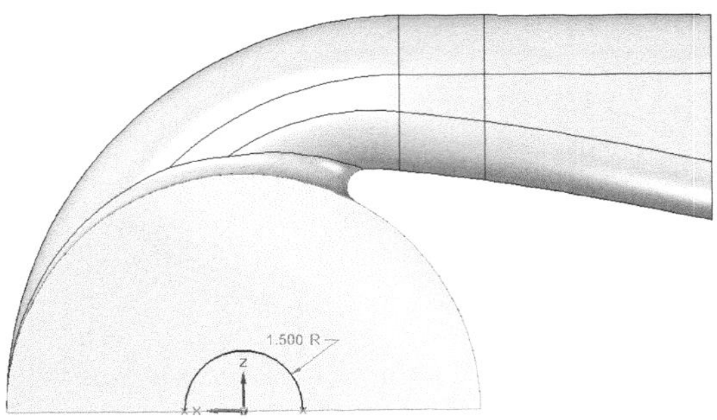

Figure 9-89 *Sketch of the cut feature*

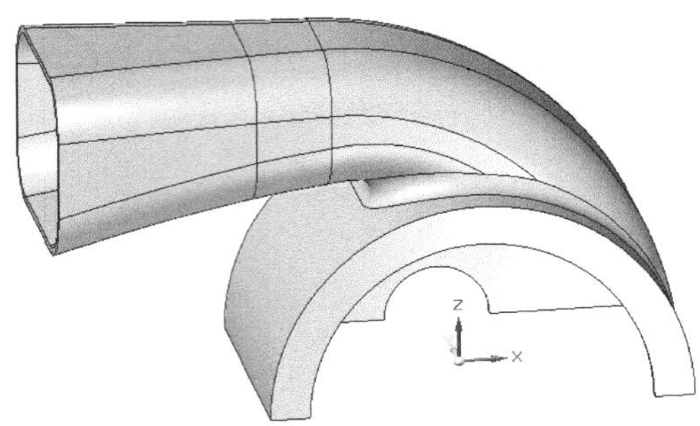

Figure 9-90 *Model after creating the cut feature*

Creating the Protrusion Feature (Ordered)

1. Switch to the **Ordered** part environment and create a protrusion feature on the front face of the base feature. Its sketch is shown in Figure 9-91.

The model after creating the protrusion feature is shown in Figure 9-92.

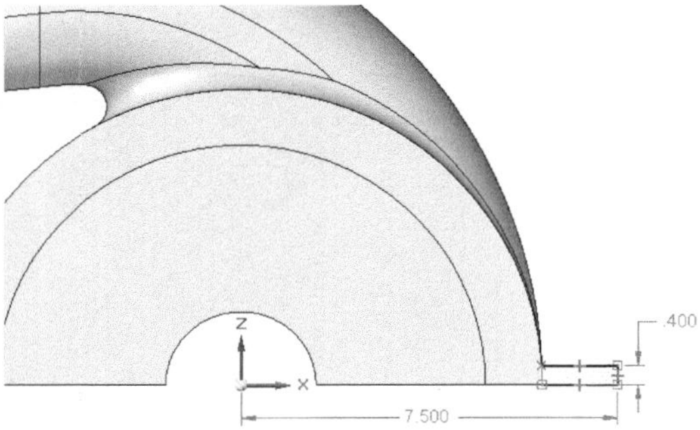

Figure 9-91 *Sketch of the protrusion feature*

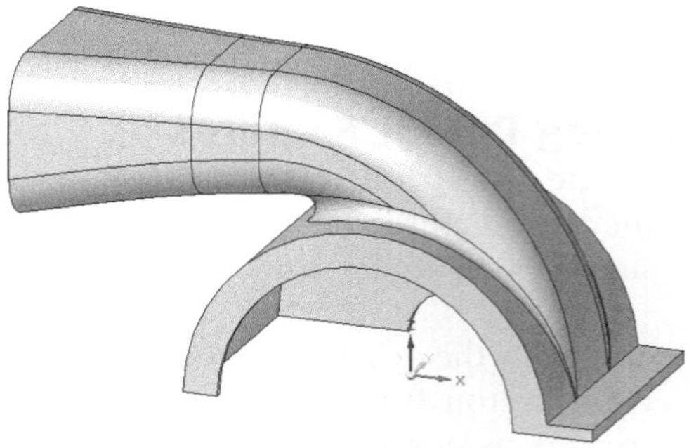

Figure 9-92 *Model after creating the protrusion feature*

Creating the Mirror Copy

1. Choose the **Mirror Copy Feature** tool from the **Mirror** drop-down in the **Pattern** group of the **Home** tab; you are prompted to select the features to be included in the mirror feature.

2. Select the protrusion feature created in the previous step and mirror it about the right plane. Select the **Smart** option to create the mirror of the feature. The model after mirroring the feature is shown in Figure 9-93.

Creating the Hole Feature

1. Choose the **Hole** button from the **Solid** group in the **Home** tab; you are prompted to select a face on which the hole will be created.

2. Select the top face of the protrusion feature on the right. Refer to Figure 9-71 for specifying the hole parameters. Now create the hole, as shown in Figure 9-94.

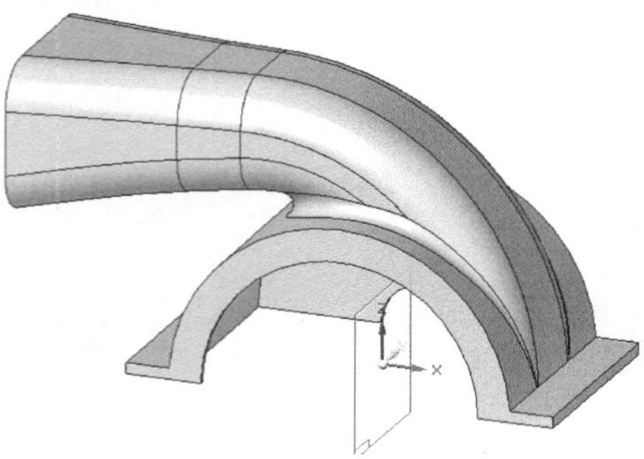

Figure 9-93 *Model after mirroring the protrusion feature*

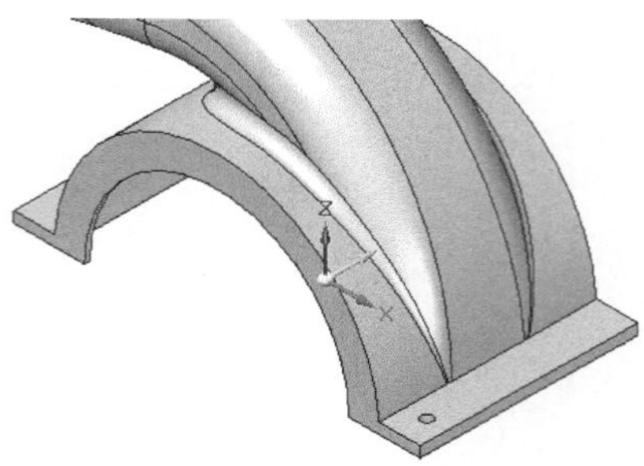

Figure 9-94 *Hole on the protrusion feature*

Creating the Pattern of the Hole Feature

1. Choose the **Pattern** tool from the **Pattern** group of the **Home** tab; you are prompted to select the feature to be patterned.

2. Select the hole feature from the **PathFinder**.

3. Create the pattern of the hole, as shown in Figure 9-95. You may need to use the **Smart** option to create the pattern.

Saving the File

1. Save the model with the name *c09tut1.par* at the location given below and then close the file.

   C:\Solid Edge\c09

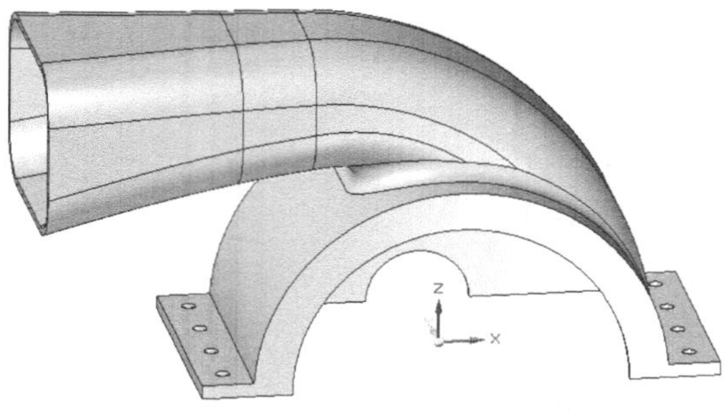

Figure 9-95 *Final model for Tutorial 1*

Tutorial 2 Synchronous

In this tutorial, you will create the model shown in Figure 9-96. Figure 9-97 shows the views and dimensions of the model. Use these sections to create the loft feature. After creating the model, save it with the name *c09tut2.par* at the location given next:

C:\Solid Edge\c09 **(Expected time: 45 min)**

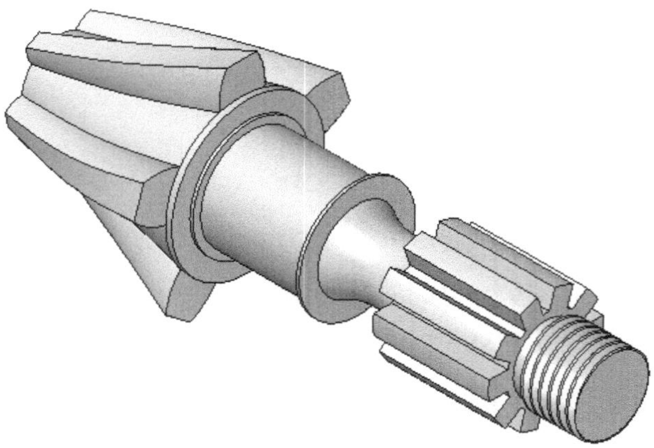

Figure 9-96 *Isometric view of the model for Tutorial 2*

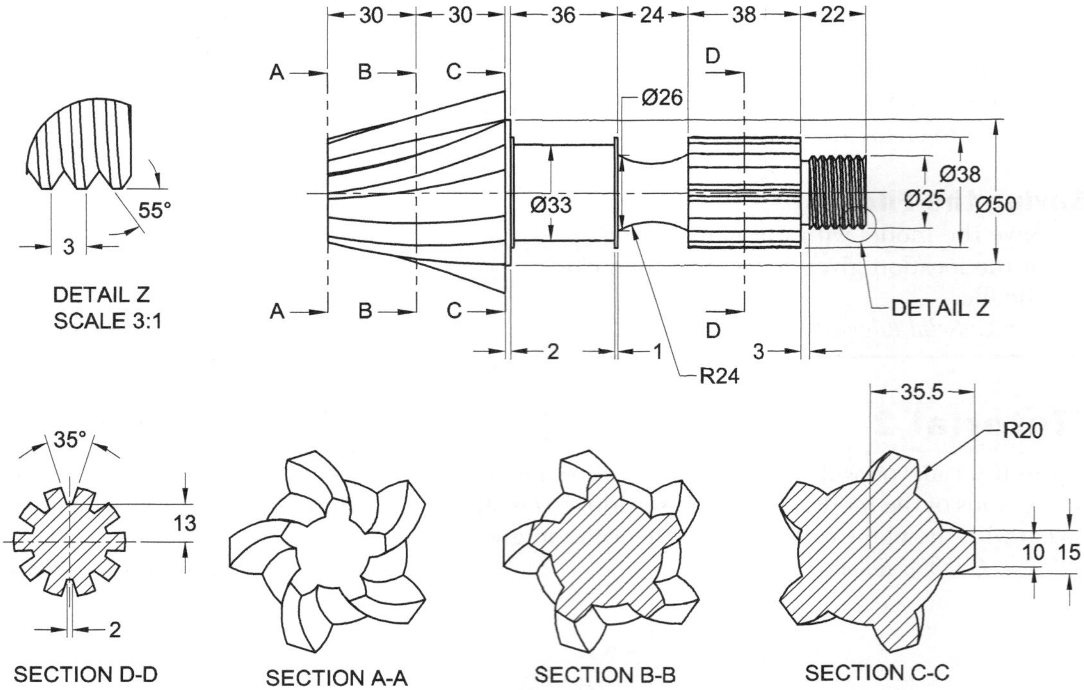

NOTE:
CREATE A LOFT WITH SECTION C-C, B-B AND A-A
THE SIZE OF SECTION B-B AND A-A IS 75% AND 50% OF SECTION C-C
EACH SECTION IS ROTATED AT 15° COUNTERCLOCKWISE

Figure 9-97 *Front and section views of the model*

The following steps are required to complete this tutorial:

a. Start Solid Edge in the **ISO Metric Part** environment. Create the base feature on the right plane, refer to Figure 9-98.
b. Create the undercut revolved feature, refer to Figures 9-99 and 9-100.
c. Create a helical cutout on the base feature, refer to Figures 9-101 and 9-102.
d. Create protrusion feature on the end face of the base feature, refer to Figure 9-103.
e. Create cutout to create a slot on the cylindrical feature and then create a pattern of the slot, see Figures 9-104 through 9-106.
f. Create a revolved protrusion, refer to Figure 9-108.
g. Create a protrusion feature on the end face of the previous feature, refer to Figure 9-110.
h. Create the last feature of the model which is a loft protrusion. Three sections will be used to create this feature, refer to Figures 9-118 through 9-122.

Creating the Base Feature

1. Start Solid Edge in the **ISO Metric Part** environment and then select the right plane as the sketching plane for the base feature.

2. Create a cylindrical feature of diameter 25 mm and length 22 mm on the right plane, as shown in Figure 9-98.

Creating an Undercut

1. Create a revolved cutout on the base feature. The dimensions of the undercut are shown in Figure 9-99.

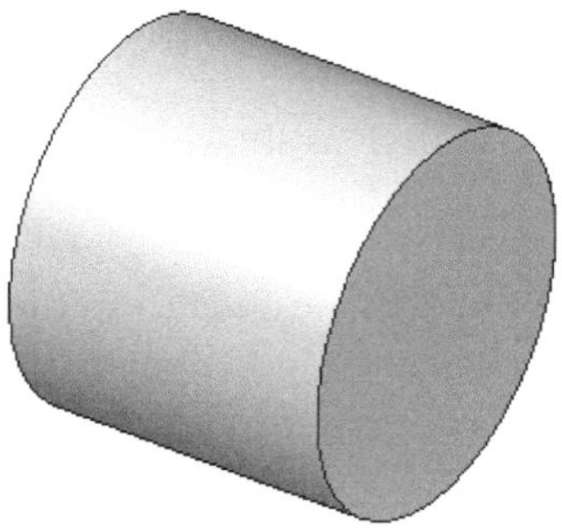

Figure 9-98 Base feature

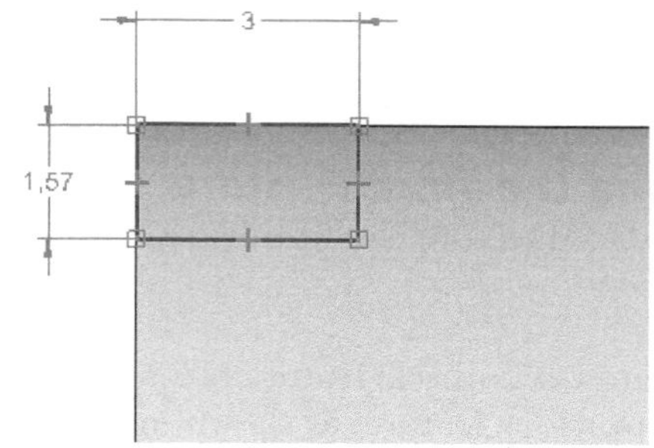

Figure 9-99 Sketch for the undercut

Creating the Helical Cutout

Next, you need to create a helical cutout on the cylindrical feature. The cross-section of the helical cutout will be triangular.

1. Choose the XZ plane and then draw center line and the profile of the section, as shown in Figure 9-100. The dimensions of the profile are shown in Figure 9-101.

2. Choose the **Helix** tool from the **Cut** drop-down in the **Solids** group; the **Helix Cutout** command bar is displayed. The **Cross section and axis definition** button is chosen by default in this command bar. Also, you are prompted to select the axis and the cross-section.

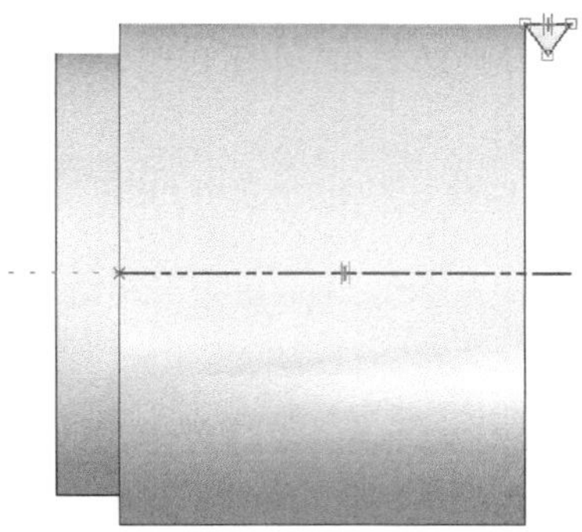

Figure 9-100 Sketch and center line

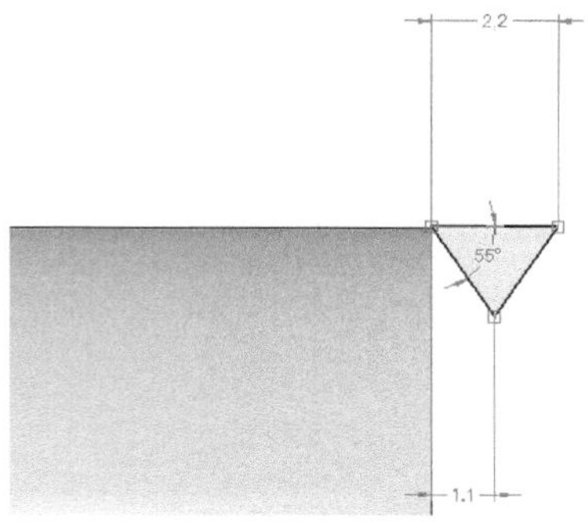

Figure 9-101 Sketch of the section with dimensions

3. Select the axis and the cross-section and then right-click to accept.

Next, you need to specify the helix parameters.

4. Choose the **Helix Options** button in the command bar; the **Helix Options** dialog box is displayed.

5. Select the **Axis length & Pitch** option from the **Helix method** drop-down list; the **Pitch** edit box is activated.

6. Enter **3** as the value of the pitch in the **Pitch** edit box and choose the **OK** button; a preview of the helical cutout is displayed.

7. Right-click to accept the selection; the helical cutout is created, as shown in Figure 9-102.

Creating the Third Feature

The third feature is a cylindrical feature which will be created on the end face of the previous feature.

1. Create a cylindrical feature of 38 mm in diameter and 38 mm in length on the right face of the previous feature, as shown in Figure 9-103.

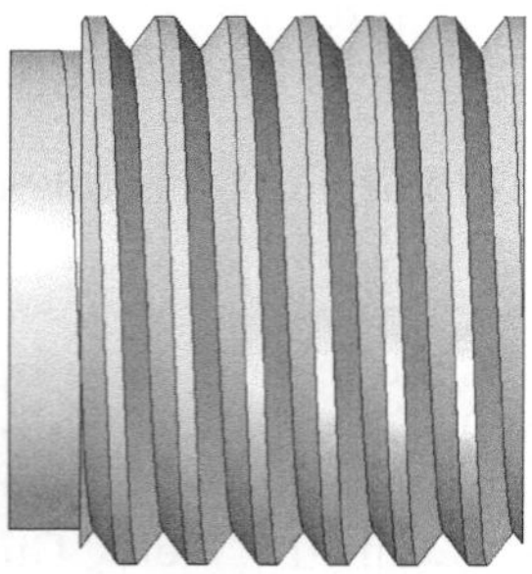

Figure 9-102 *Helical cutout*

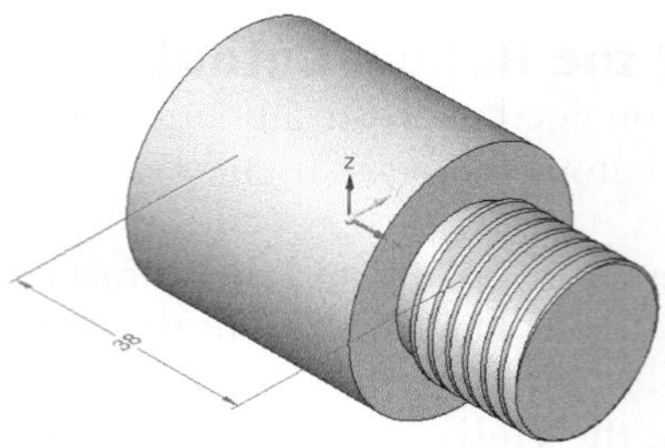

Figure 9-103 *The model after creating the third feature*

Creating the Fourth Feature

The fourth feature is a cutout which will be created on the previous feature. After creating the cutout, you will create its pattern.

1. Create a cutout on the cylindrical feature by drawing the sketch shown in Figure 9-104. The cutout feature is shown in Figure 9-105.

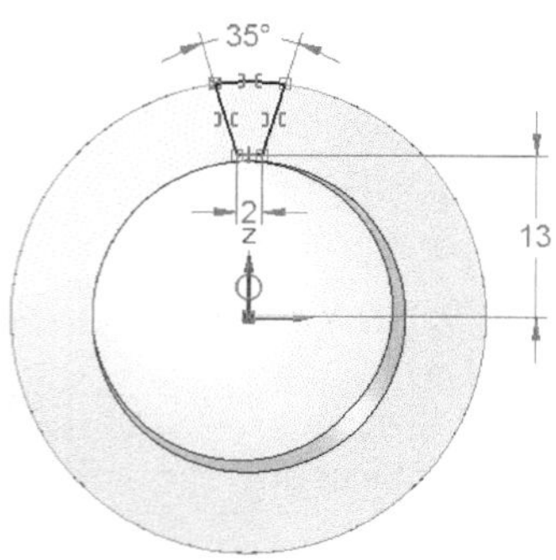

Figure 9-104 *Sketch of the section with dimensions*

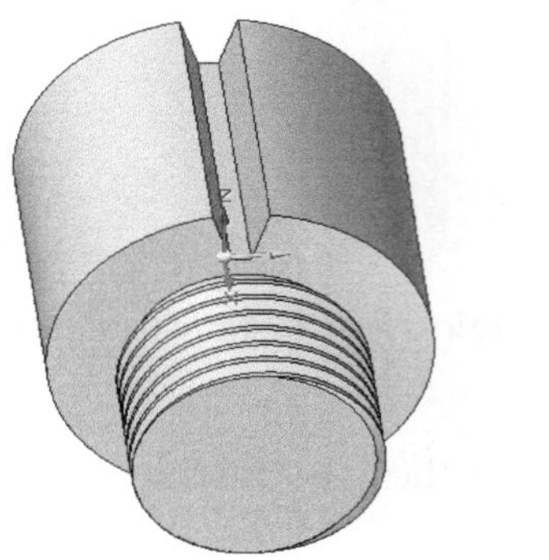

Figure 9-105 *Feature after creating the cutout*

2. Select the cutout from the **PathFinder**. Next, choose the **Circular** tool from the **Pattern** drop-down of the **Pattern** group and create the circular pattern of the cutout feature. The total number of instances in the pattern is 10.

   The pattern is created, as shown in Figure 9-106.

Creating Revolved Protrusions

The next two features are the revolved protrusions.

1. Draw the sketch shown in Figure 9-107 to create a revolved protrusion.

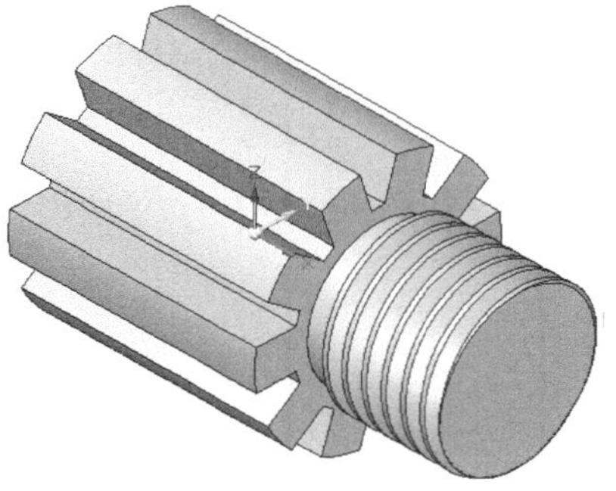

Figure 9-106 *Model after creating the pattern*

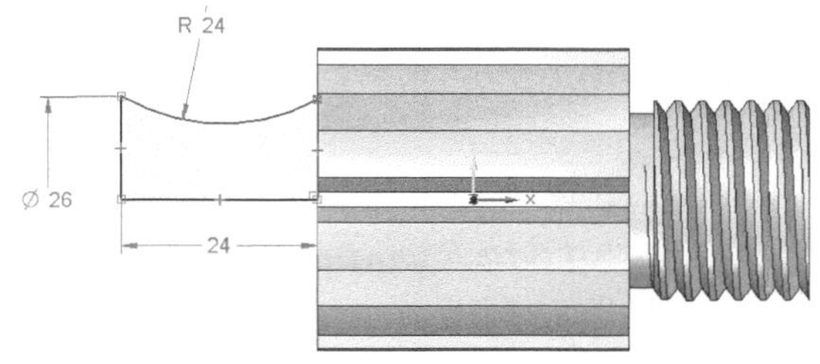

Figure 9-107 *Sketch to revolve*

2. Select the sketch region; the **Extrude** command bar will be displayed.

3. Choose the **Revolve** tool from the **Action** drop-down in the command bar; the revolve handle is displayed on the sketch. Specify the axis of revolution using the revolve handle.

   The revolved feature is created, as shown in Figure 9-108.

4. Create another revolved protrusion on the XZ plane by drawing the sketch, as shown in Figure 9-109.

   The revolved feature is created, as shown in Figure 9-110.

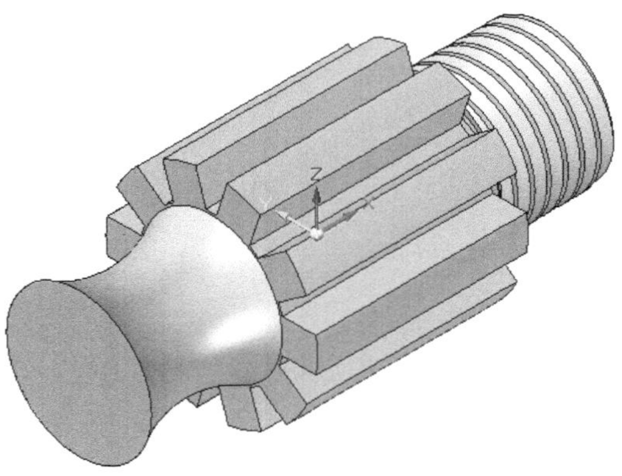

Figure 9-108 *Model after creating the revolved protrusion*

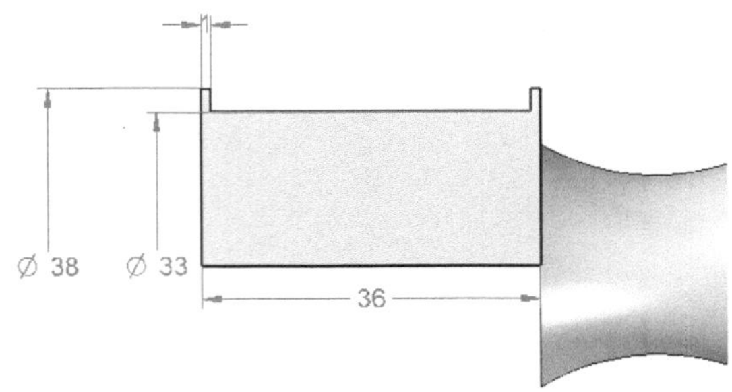

Figure 9-109 *Sketch to revolve*

Creating the Protrusion Feature

1. Create the protrusion feature by using the profile shown in Figure 9-111. The diameter of this protrusion is 50 units and the depth of extrusion is 2 units.

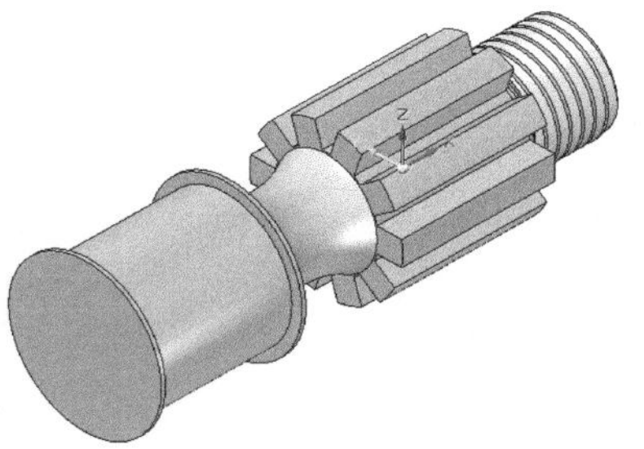

Figure 9-110 *Model after creating the revolved protrusion*

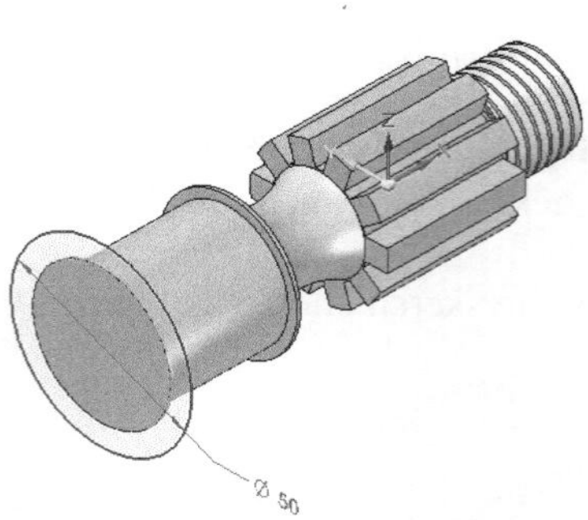

Figure 9-111 *Profile for the protrusion feature*

Note

The last three features could have been created as a single revolved feature. But in that case, it would be difficult to modify the dimensions of the sketch that include all the three features.

Creating the Cross-sections of the Lofted Protrusion Feature

The lofted protrusion that you are going to create uses three cross-sections. The size of the second and third cross-sections of the first cross-section will be 75% and 50%, respectively.

1. Choose a sketching tool and select the end face of the previous feature as the drawing plane. The first cross-section is drawn on this face.

2. Draw the sketch, as shown in Figure 9-112. After drawing the sketch, you need to create four more instances of the same sketch.

3. Choose the **Rotate** tool from the **Move** drop-down in the **Draw** group. Create four instances of the sketch by using the **Copy** button from the **Rotate** command bar, refer to Figure 9-113. The construction lines in this figure are given for your reference only.

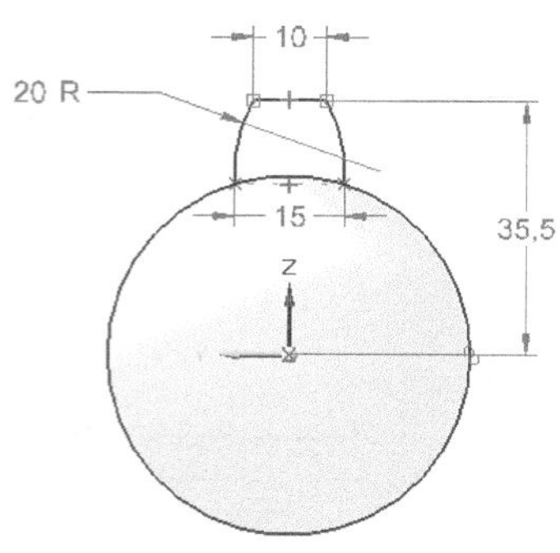

Figure 9-112 *Sketch with dimensions*

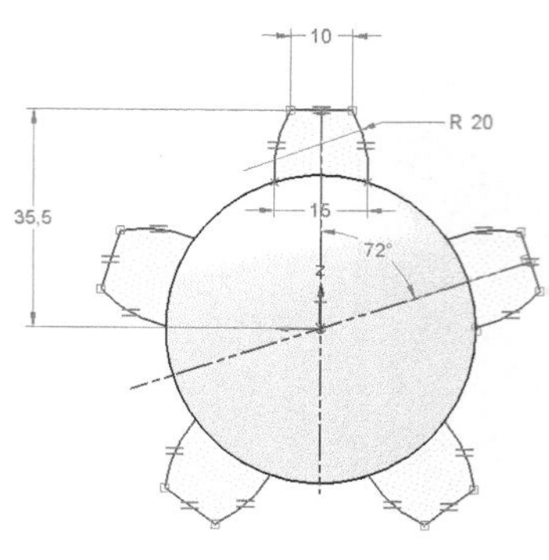

Figure 9-113 *Creating copies of the sketch*

4. Trim the unwanted arcs and add required dimensions to the sketch. Remember that the sketch should be a closed loop and should be fully constrained. Figure 9-114 shows the final sketch of the first cross-section.

5. After drawing the first cross-section, create a reference plane parallel to the previous plane at an offset distance of 30 mm. This plane will be used to draw the sketch of the second cross-section.

   The second cross-section will be the same sketch profile as created earlier but with a difference in the scale factor.

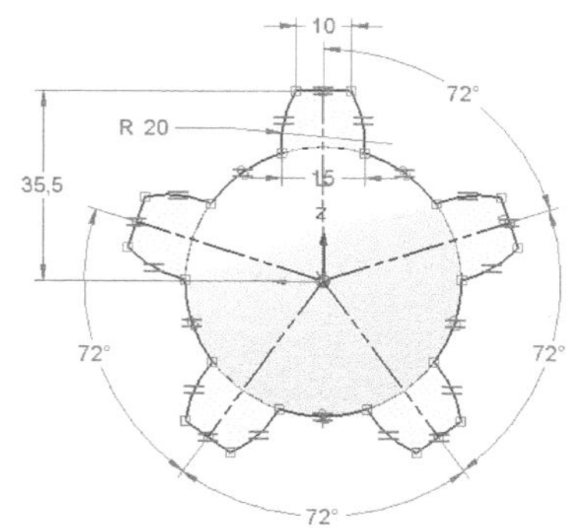

Figure 9-114 *Final sketch of the first section*

6. Choose the **Project To Sketch** tool from the **Draw** group; you are prompted to click on a planar face. Click on the newly created plane; the **Project to Sketch** command bar and the **Project to Sketch Options** dialog box is displayed. Select the **Project internal face loops** check box in the dialog box and then choose the **OK** button to exit the dialog box.

7. Select the **Wireframe Chain** option from the **Selection Type** drop-down list in the command bar and then select the sketch profile.

8. Choose the **Accept** button from the command bar and then press the ESC key.

   Next, you need to scale this profile with some scale factor.

9. Choose the **Scale** tool from the **Mirror** drop-down and enter **0.75** in the **Scale** edit box in the command bar. Make sure that the **Copy** option available on the command bar is not active.

10. Scale the existing sketch, as shown in Figure 9-115.

11. Rotate the sketch by 15 degrees in the clockwise direction by using the **Rotate** tool. Make sure that the **Copy** option available on the command bar is not active. The sketch after rotating it is shown in Figure 9-116.

12. Create another reference plane parallel to the previous plane at a distance of 30 units. This plane will be used to draw the sketch of the third cross-section.

13. Follow steps 6 through 11 to draw the third cross-section. Select the sketch profile and then enter **0.5** as the scale factor in the **Scale** edit box and rotate the sketch by 30 degrees in the clockwise direction. Figure 9-117 shows the sketch of the third cross-section after scaling and rotating the profile.

    Figure 9-118 shows three different cross-sections created on three different planes for creating the lofted protrusion feature.

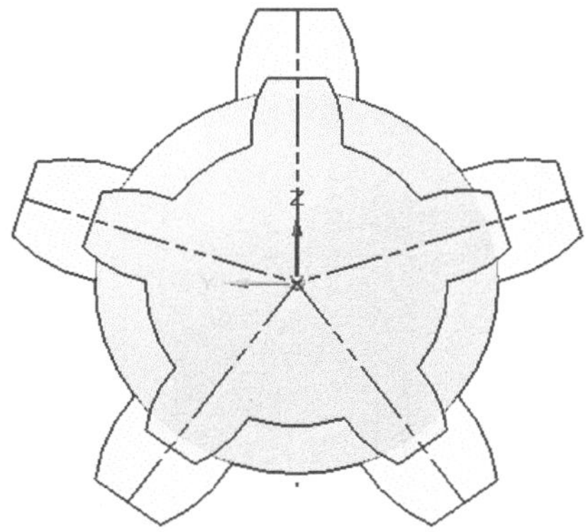

Figure 9-115 Sketch after scaling

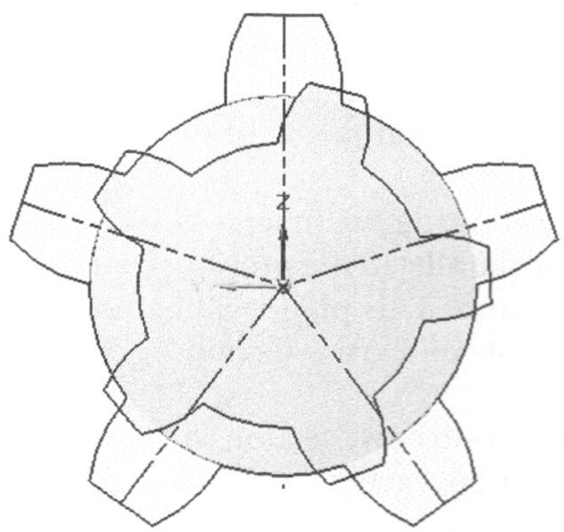

Figure 9-116 Sketch after rotating

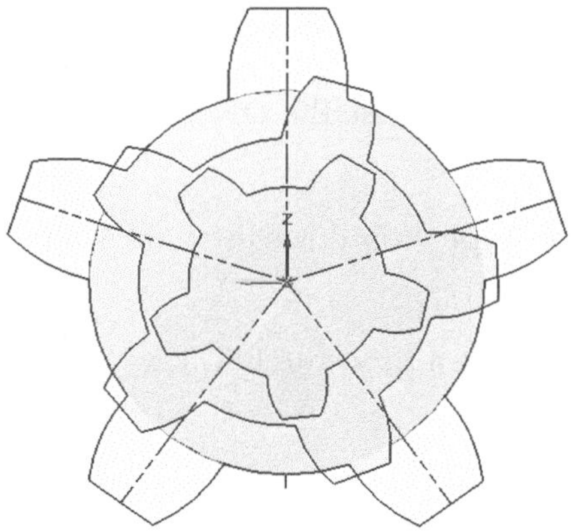

Figure 9-117 Sketch after scaling and rotating the profile

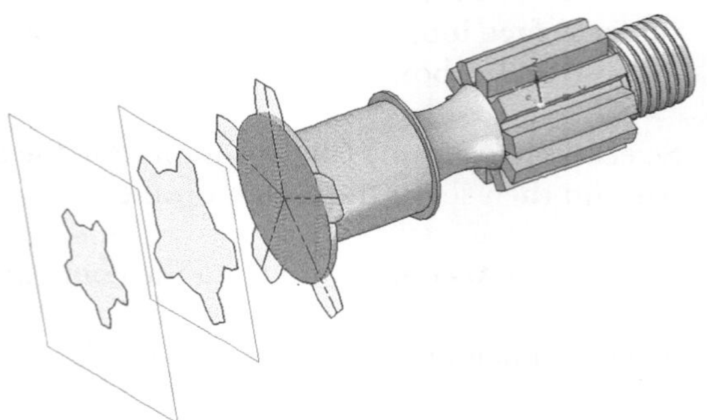

Figure 9-118 Three different cross-sections created on three different planes

Creating the Lofted Protrusion Feature

1. Choose the **Loft** tool from the **Add** drop-down in the **Solids** group; the **Loft** command bar is displayed.

   By default, the **Cross Section Step** is activated. As a result, you are prompted to select a sketch.

2. Select the first cross-section of the loft feature; a vertex nearest to the cursor is highlighted, as shown in Figure 9-119. Select this vertex. The vertex will be used as the start point of the first cross-section.

3. Similarly, select the second cross-section, as shown in Figure 9-120. Note that on selecting the second cross-section, its start point is highlighted. Also, a green temporary line is displayed, indicating the flow of material through the cross-section.

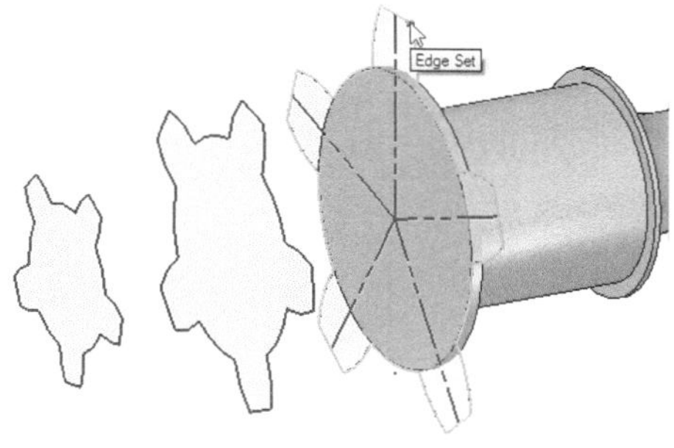

Figure 9-119 Start point on the first section

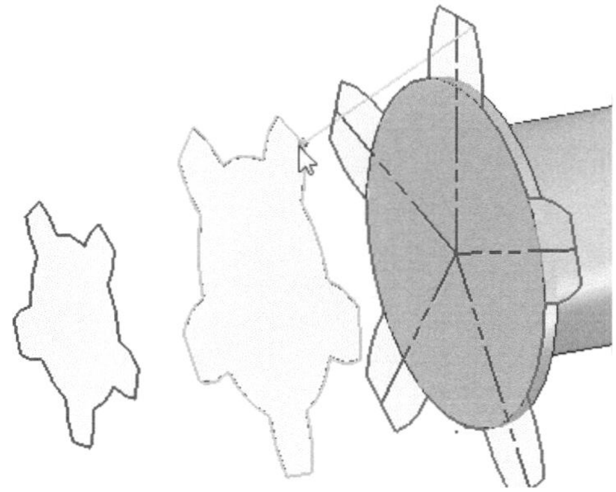

Figure 9-120 Second connecting point of the second section

4. Similarly, select the third cross-section, as shown in Figure 9-121.

5. Choose the **Preview** button and then the **Finish** button from the command bar to create a lofted protrusion feature, as shown in Figure 9-122.

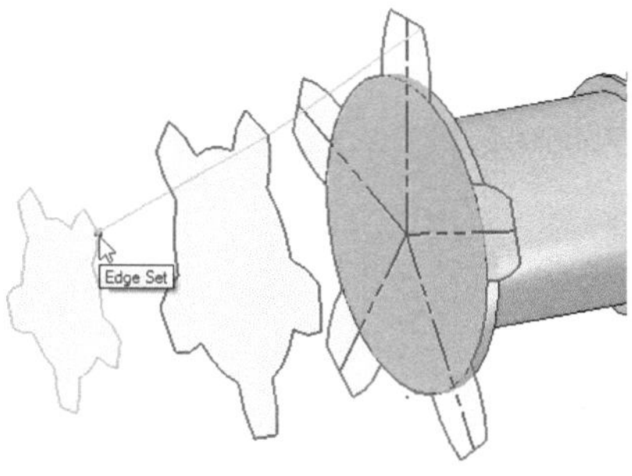

Figure 9-121 Start point on the third section

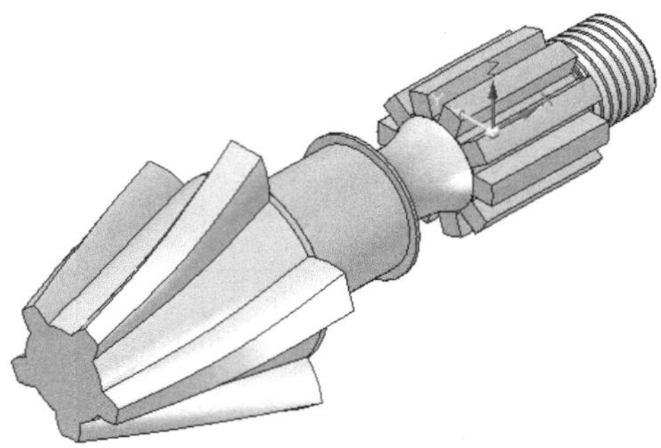

Figure 9-122 Model after creating all features

Tip
Another method of creating this sweep is to draw a single profile and assign a scale factor of 0.5 and twist of 30-degree to it from the ***Sweep Options*** *dialog box.*

Saving the File

1. Save the model with the name *c09tut2.par* at the location given next and then close the file.
   C:\Solid Edge\c09

Tutorial 3 Synchronous and Ordered

In this tutorial, you will create the model shown in Figure 9-123 and Figure 9-124. Its orthographic views and dimensions are shown in Figure 9-125. After creating the model, save it with the name *c09tut3.par* at the location given next:
C:\Solid Edge\c09 **(Expected time: 1hr 15 min)**

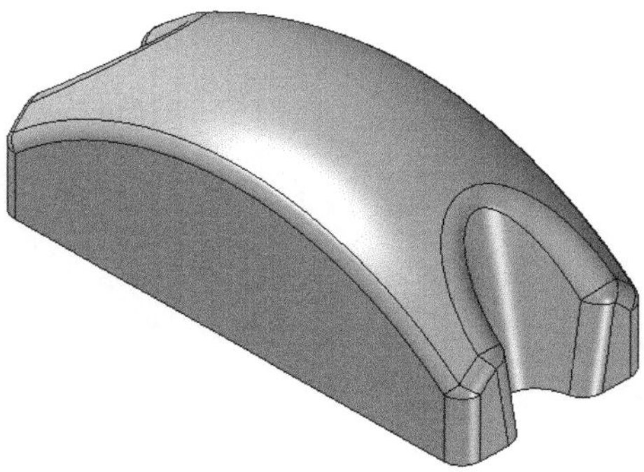

Figure 9-123 Isometric view of the carburetor cover

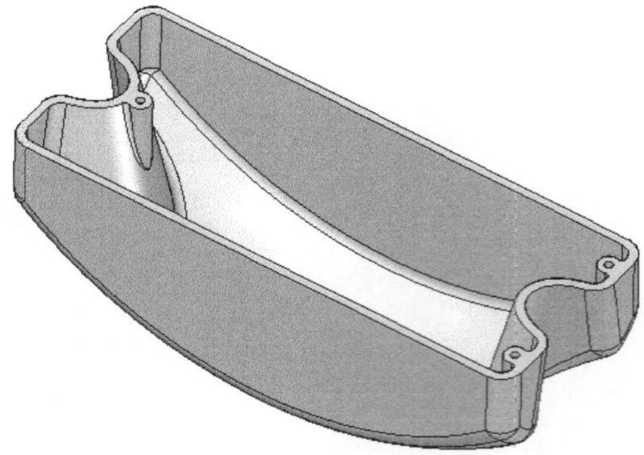

Figure 9-124 Rotated view of the model

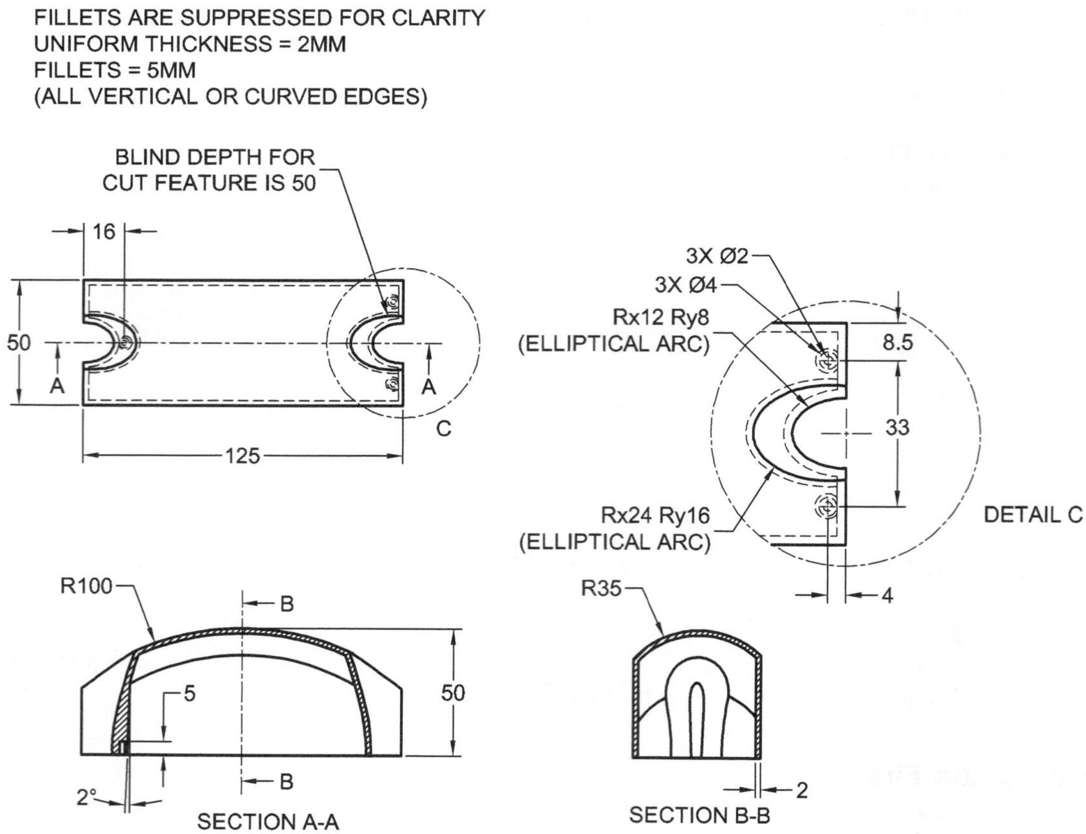

Figure 9-125 Views and dimensions of the Carburetor Cover

The following steps are required to complete this tutorial:

a. Start Solid Edge in the **ISO Metric Part** environment. Create the base feature on the top plane, refer to Figure 9-126.
b. Create a swept cutout on the base feature, refer to Figures 9-127 through 9-130
c. Create a lofted cutout on the bottom face of the base feature, refer to Figures 9-131 through 9-133.

d. Create a mirror copy of the lofted cutout, refer to Figure 9-134.
e. Create rounds, refer to Figure 9-135.
f. Create a thin wall feature, refer to Figure 9-136.
g. Create the mounting boss on the bottom face of the base feature, refer to Figure 9-137.
h. Create rounds on the vertical edges of mounting bosses, refer to Figure 9-138.

Creating the Base Feature

1. Start Solid Edge in the **ISO Metric Part** environment and then select the top plane as the sketching plane for the base feature.

2. Create the base feature, which is a rectangular block, on the top plane, as shown in Figure 9-126. The dimensions of this block are 125X50X50.

Creating the Sweep Cutout

1. Draw the sketch of the path on the XZ plane, as shown in Figure 9-127.

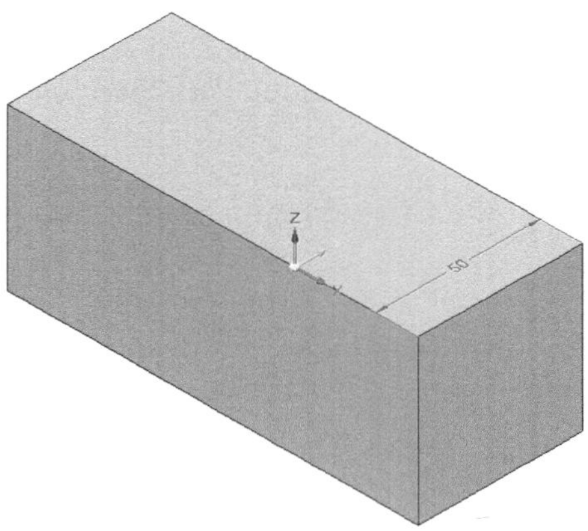

Figure 9-126 Rectangular block

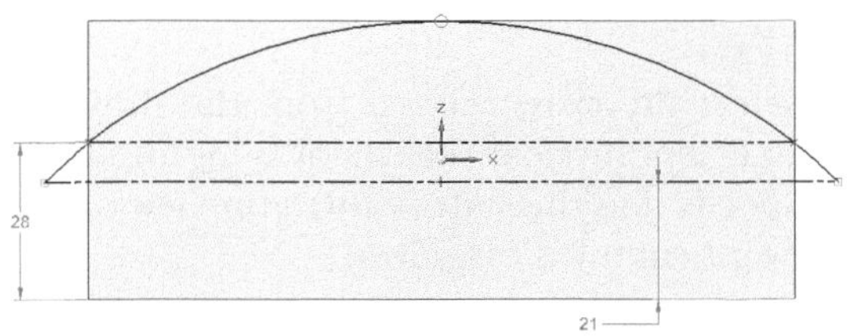

Figure 9-127 Sketch of the path

Next, you need to draw a cross-section on the plane normal to the path.

2. Choose the **Normal To Curve** tool from the **Planes** drop-down in the **Planes** group; you are prompted to select a curve.

3. Click on an arc to select it; the profile plane is displayed, as shown in Figure 9-128. On moving the cursor along the path curve, you will notice that the profile plane also moves along with the cursor.

4. Click when the plane is at the endpoint of the path; a plane normal to the path is created. Next, you can draw the cross-section of the swept protrusion.

5. Draw the sketch of the cross-section on the newly created plane, as shown in Figure 9-129.

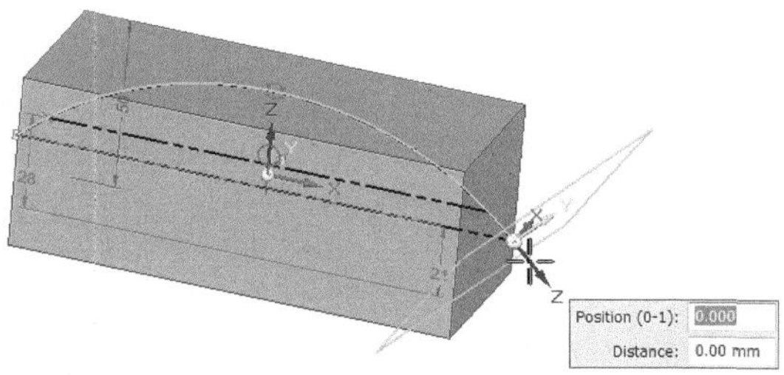

Figure 9-128 Profile plane for the cross-section

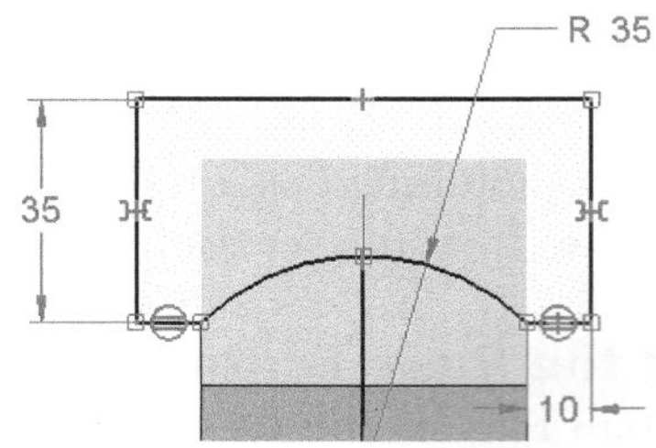

Figure 9-129 Partial view of the sketch with constraints and dimensions

Next you need to create a swept cutout by using the path and the cross-section.

6. Choose the **Sweep** tool from the **Cut** drop-down in the **Solids** group of the **Home** tab; the **Sweep Options** dialog box is displayed.

7. Select the **Single path and cross section** radio button, if it is not selected. Choose **OK** to exit the dialog box; the **Swept Cutout** command bar is displayed with the **Path Step** selected by default.

8. Select the path and right-click to accept the selection; the **Cross Section Step** button gets activated in the command bar.

9. Select the cross section from the drawing area; a point near the cursor is highlighted. Specify it as the start point; a preview of the swept cutout is displayed.

10. Choose **Finish** and then the **Cancel** button in the command bar; the cutout is created, as shown in Figure 9-130.

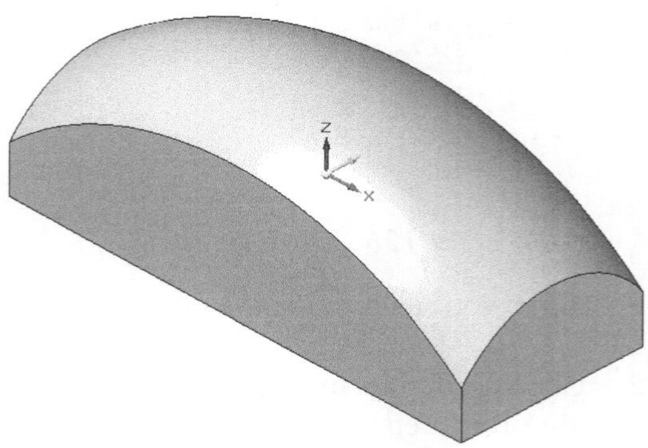

Figure 9-130 Swept cutout

Creating the Loft Cutout

The next feature that you need to create is a lofted cutout. To do so, you need to draw two ellipses on two different planes.

1. Draw the sketch of the first cross-section of the cut feature on the bottom face of the base feature. The orthographic drawing view of this model shows an elliptical lofted cutout. Therefore, you need to draw an ellipse and dimension it, as shown in Figure 9-131.

2. After drawing the first cross-section, create a reference plane parallel to the bottom face of the base feature at a distance of 50 units above the bottom face.

3. Draw the sketch of the second cross-section of the cut feature and dimension it, as shown in Figure 9-132.

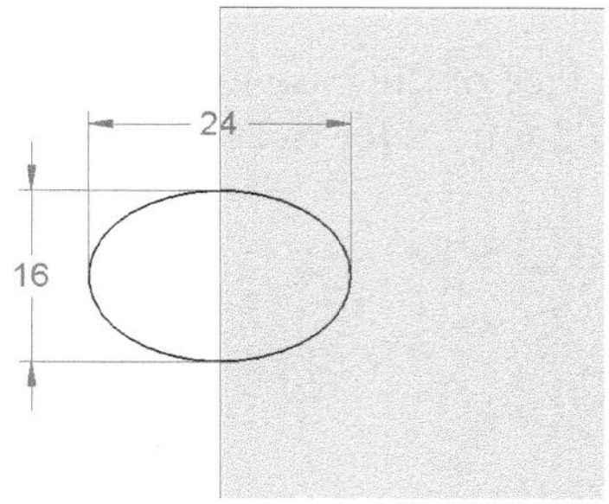

Figure 9-131 Sketch of the first cross-section

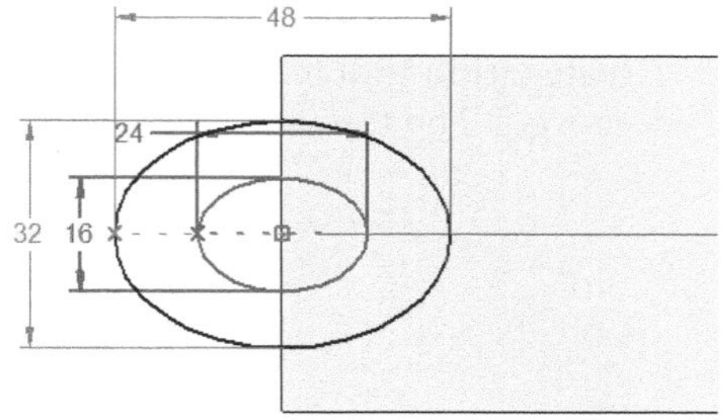

Figure 9-132 Sketch of the second cross-section

Next, create the loft cutout feature using the **Loft** tool.

4. Choose the **Loft** tool from the **Cut** drop-down in the **Solids** group; the **Lofted Cutout** command bar is displayed. Also, the **Cross section Step** is activated by default and you are prompted to select the sketch.

5. Select the first and second cross-sections.

6. Choose the **Preview** button; the preview of the lofted cutout is displayed, as shown in Figure 9-133.

7. Choose the **Finish** button and then the **Cancel** button to exit the **Loft** tool.

Creating the Mirror Copy of the Lofted Cutout

1. Select the loft cutout from the **PathFinder**.

2. Choose the **Mirror** tool from the **Pattern** group and mirror the lofted cutout on the right side of the model, as shown in Figure 9-134. You can use the right reference plane for creating the mirror copy.

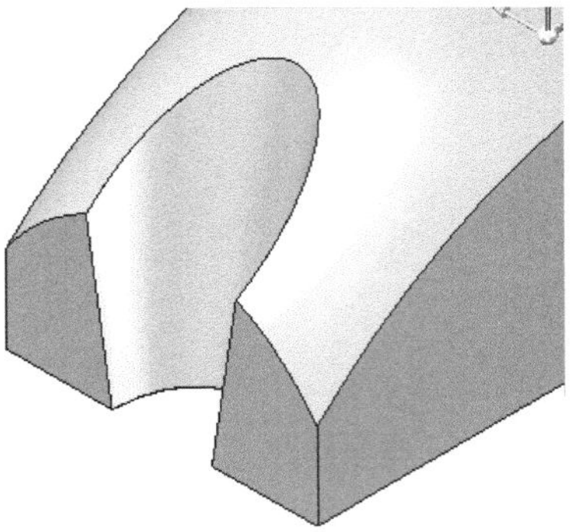

Figure 9-133 Lofted cutout

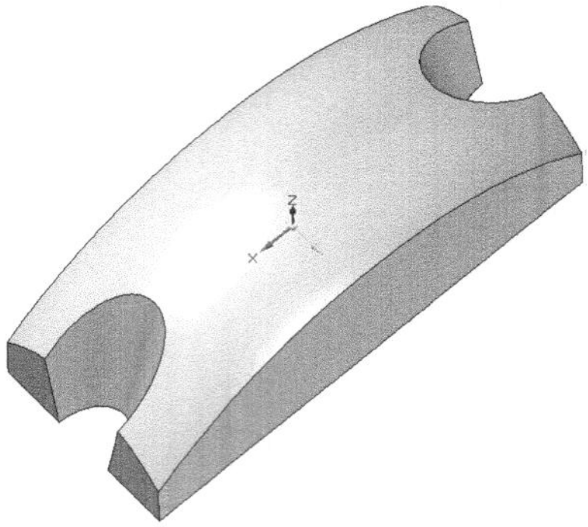

Figure 9-134 Model after mirroring the feature

Creating the Round

1. Choose the **Round** tool from the **Solids** group and create rounds of radius 5 mm. The model after creating rounds is shown in Figure 9-135.

Creating the Thin Wall Feature

1. Create a thin wall feature by selecting the bottom face of the base feature as the face to be removed. The thickness of this thin wall feature is 2 mm, refer to Figure 9-136.

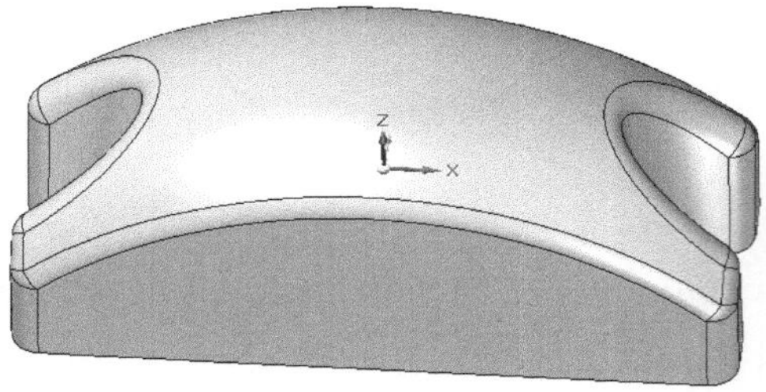

Figure 9-135 *Model after creating the rounds*

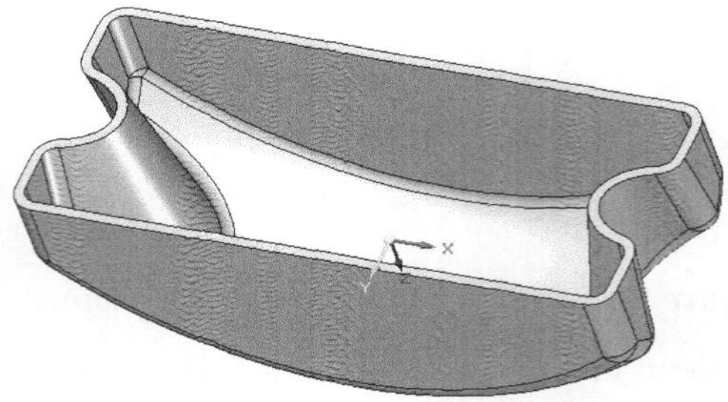

Figure 9-136 *Model after creating the thin wall feature*

Creating the Mounting Boss

Next, you need to create two mounting bosses on the bottom face of the base feature. As you cannot create bosses in the **Synchronous** part environment, you need to switch to the **Ordered** part environment.

1. Switch to the **Ordered** part environment.
2. Choose the **Mounting Boss** tool from the **Thin Wall** drop-down in the **Solids** group. 
3. Set the parameters of the mounting bosses, refer to Figure 9-125. Place the three profiles of the mounting boss on the bottom face of the base feature, as shown in Figure 9-137.
4. Exit the sketching environment and specify upward direction as the direction of creation of this feature.
5. Choose **Finish** and then the **Cancel** button to exit the tool; the mounting boss is created, as shown in Figure 9-138.

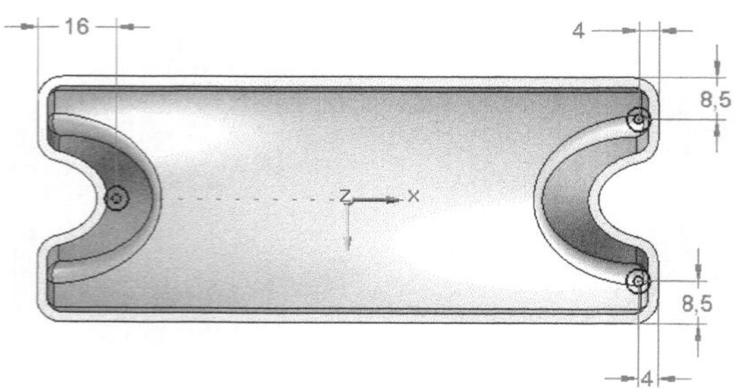

Figure 9-137 *Profile with dimensions*

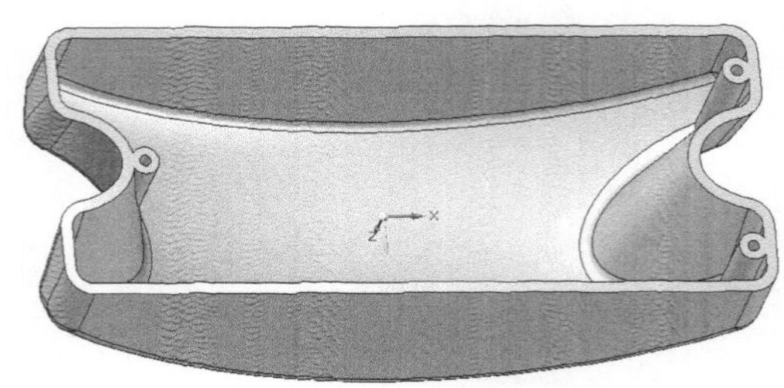

Figure 9-138 *Mounting boss*

Creating Rounds

1. Choose the **Round** tool from the **Solids** group of the **Home** tab; the **Round** command bar will be displayed.

2. Enter **1** in the **Radius** edit box and select the vertical edges of the newly created mounting boss; a preview of the round is displayed, as shown in Figure 9-139.

3. Right-click to accept the selection and then choose **Preview** and then **Finish** from the command bar to create the round feature.

   The model is completed, as shown in Figure 9-140.

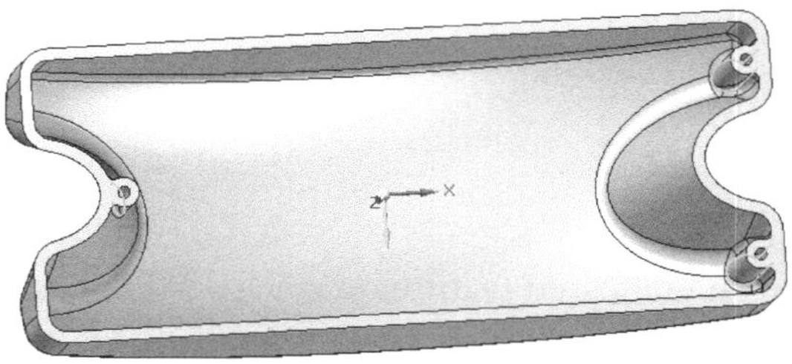

Figure 9-139 *Preview of the resulting round*

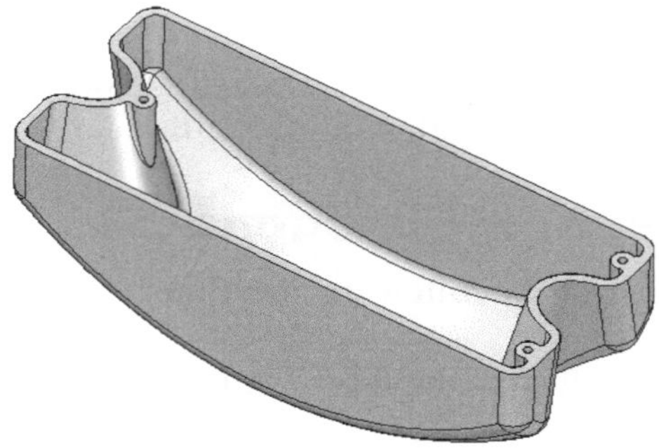

Figure 9-140 *Completed model*

Saving the File

1. Save the model with the name *c09tut3.par* at the location given next and then close the file.
   C:\Solid Edge\c09

Self-Evaluation Test

Answer the following questions and then compare them to those given at the end of this chapter:

1. To create a lofted protrusion, you need to choose the__________ tool from the **Solids** group of the **Ribbon**.

2. While creating a loft feature, the __________ button on the command bar is used to select or create a sketch as a guide curve.

3. The options in the ___________ area of the **Helix Parameters** dialog box are used to specify the parameters related to the taper of the helix.

4. The **Sweep** tool is used to extrude a section along a specified path. The order of operation is to first create or select a path and then create or select a section. (T/F)

5. The **Sweep** tool is used to create a swept feature only along a single path with a single section. (T/F)

6. In Solid Edge, while using the **Sweep** tool, the maximum number of paths that can be drawn is three. (T/F)

7. You can create a lofted protrusion by selecting the existing sketches or edges or by drawing sketches. (T/F)

8. The **Single path and cross sections** radio button is used to sweep a section along a single curve. (T/F)

9. In Solid Edge, a variable pitch helical protrusion is created by increasing the pitch value from the start to the end using formula. (T/F)

10. The **Sweep** tool is used to sweep a single section along a single path or multiple sections with multiple paths. (T/F)

Review Questions

Answer the following questions:

1. Which of the following tools is used to create an embossed feature on a cylindrical face?

   (a) **Loft** (b) **Normal**
   (c) **Sweep** (d) None of these

2. Which of the following buttons is chosen automatically after sketching or selecting the path for creating a sweep feature?

   (a) **Cross Section Step** (b) **Relative Orientation**
   (c) **Path Step** (d) None of these

3. Which of the following areas in the **Sweep Options** dialog box is used to create a sweep feature by twisting the cross-section along a path curve?

   (a) **Scale** (b) **Twist**
   (c) **Section Alignment** (d) None of these

4. Which of the following buttons in the **Loft Protrusion** command bar is used for vertex mapping?

   (a) **Vertex Mapping** (b) **Closed Extent**
   (c) **Finite Extent** (d) None of these

5. To specify a plane for drawing a cross-section, you can also create a reference plane by selecting the options available in the **Create-From Options** drop-down list. (T/F)

6. Guide curves are used to control the material flow between the sections of a loft feature. (T/F)

7. The **Vertex Mapping** dialog box is used to modify the mapping points. (T/F)

8. The sketches drawn for the guide curve must have the **Connect** relationship with the sketches that define the loft section. (T/F)

9. The **Helix** tool is used to create springs, threads, and so on. (T/F)

10. The **Loft** tool is used to create a feature by blending two or more cross-sections together. (T/F)

EXERCISE

Exercise 1

Create the model shown in Figure 9-141. The dimensions of the model are shown in Figure 9-142. After creating the model, save it with the name *c09exr1.par* at the location given next:

C:\Solid Edge\c09 **(Expected time: 30 min)**

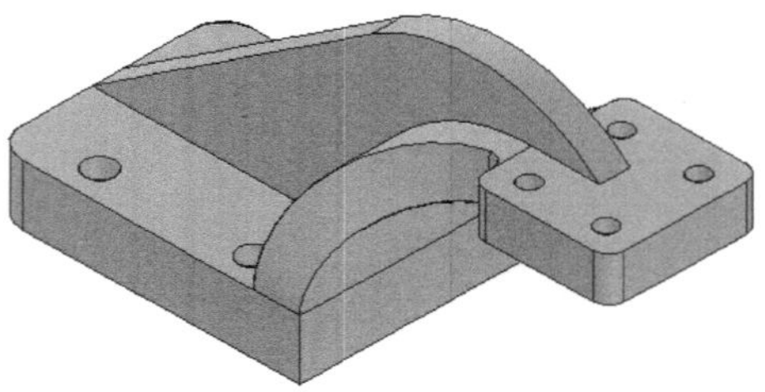

Figure 9-141 *Model for Exercise 1*

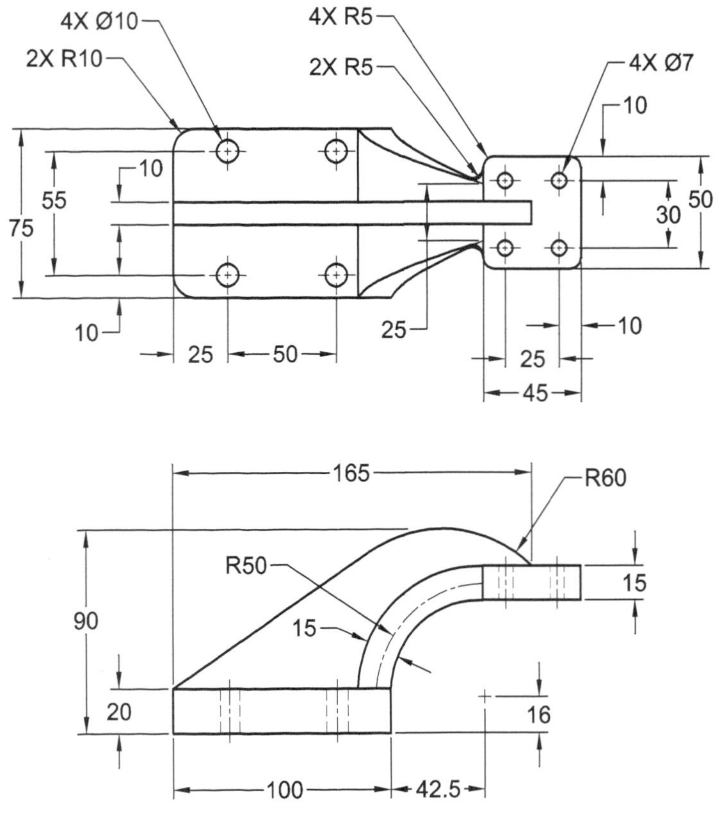

Figure 9-142 *Drawing views of the model*

Exercise 2

Create the model shown in Figures 9-143 and 9-144. Its dimensions are shown in Figure 9-145. After creating the model, save it with the name *c09exr2.par* at the location given next:

C:\Solid Edge\c09 **(Expected time: 30 min)**

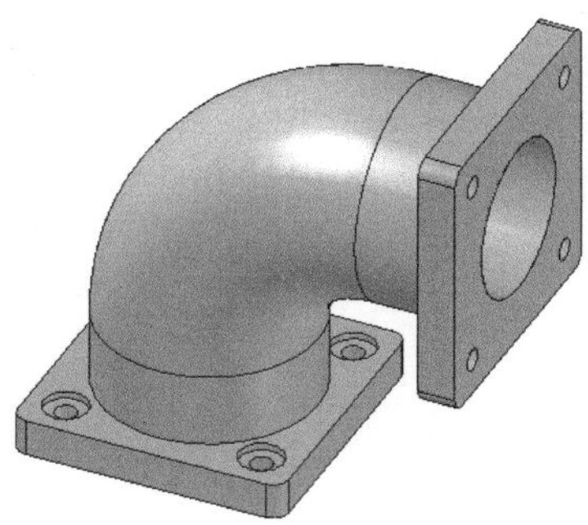

Figure 9-143 *Model for Exercise 2*

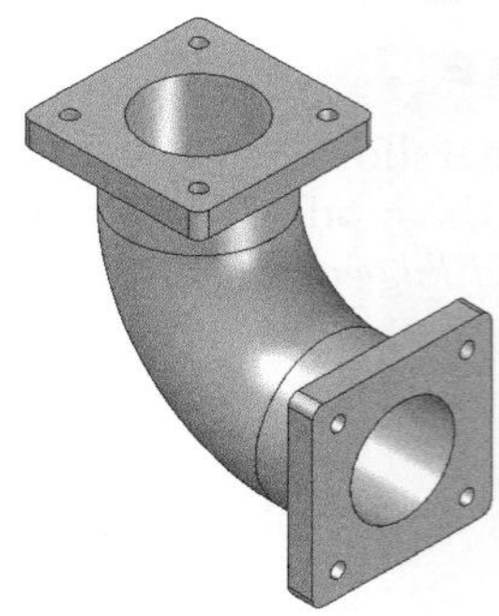

Figure 9-144 *Isometric view of the model for Exercise 2*

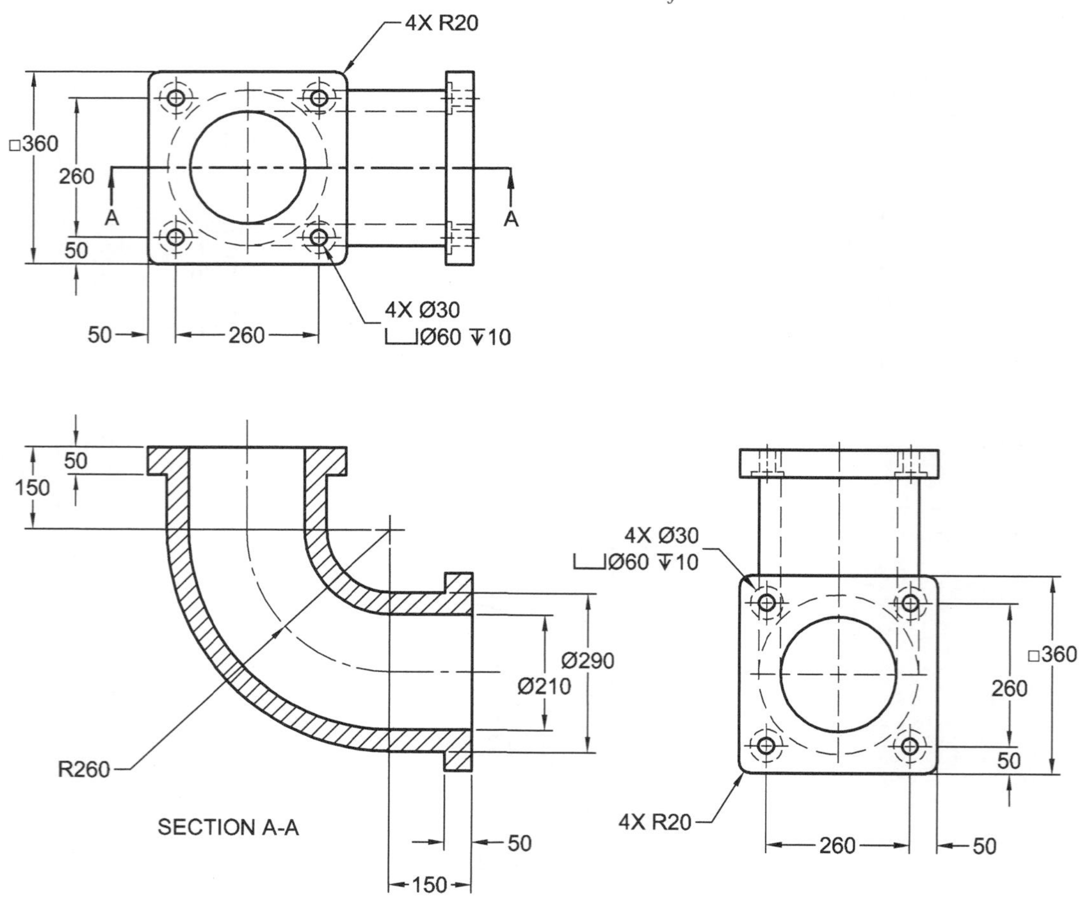

Figure 9-145 *Drawing views of the model*

Exercise 3

Create the model shown in Figure 9-146. Its dimensions are shown in Figure 9-147. After creating the model, save it with the name *c09exr3.par* at the location given next.

C:\Solid Edge\c09 **(Expected time: 30 min)**

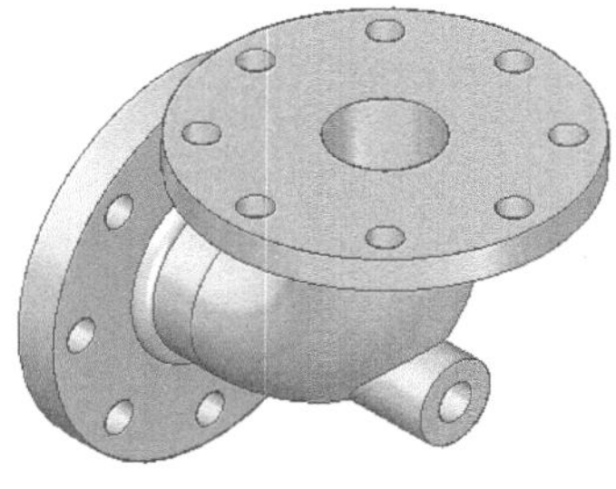

Figure 9-146 *Model for Exercise 3*

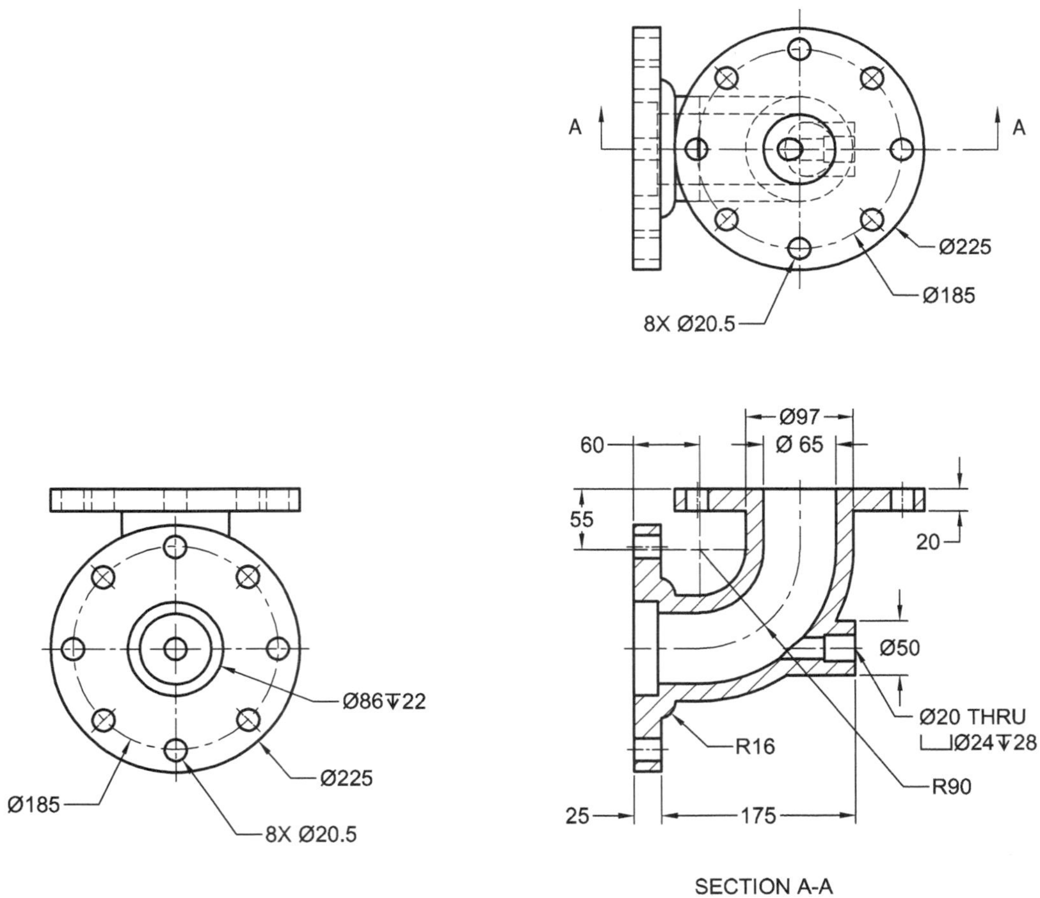

Figure 9-147 *Views and dimensions of the model for Exercise 3*

Answers to Self-Evaluation Test

1. Loft, **2.** Guide Curve Step, **3.** Taper, **4.** T, **5.** F, **6.** T, **7.** T, **8.** T, **9.** T, **10.** T

Chapter 10

Assembly Modeling-I

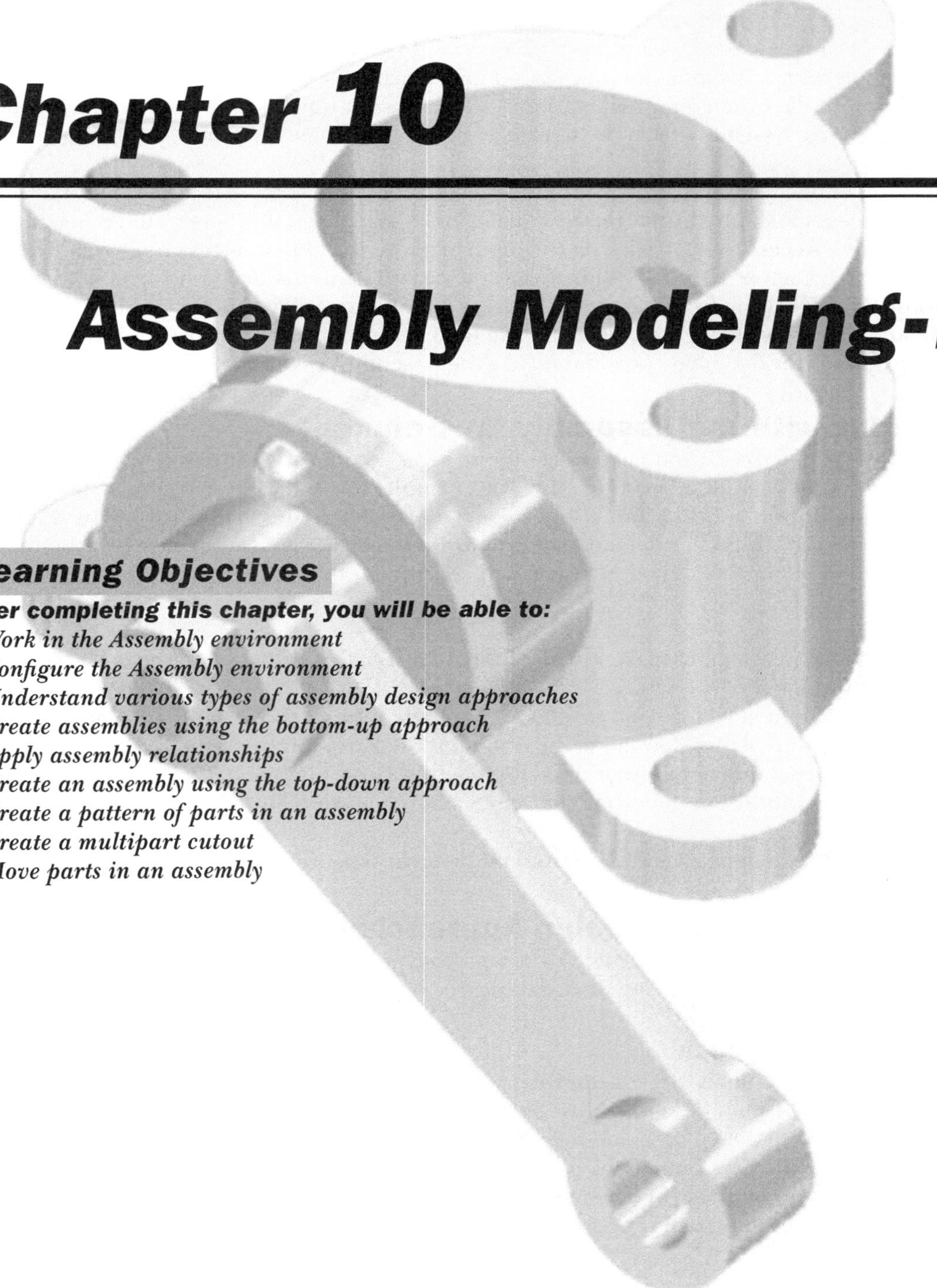

Learning Objectives

After completing this chapter, you will be able to:

- *Work in the Assembly environment*
- *Configure the Assembly environment*
- *Understand various types of assembly design approaches*
- *Create assemblies using the bottom-up approach*
- *Apply assembly relationships*
- *Create an assembly using the top-down approach*
- *Create a pattern of parts in an assembly*
- *Create a multipart cutout*
- *Move parts in an assembly*

THE ASSEMBLY ENVIRONMENT

An assembly consists of two or more components assembled together at their respective work positions using assembly relationships. These relationships help you constrain the degrees of freedom of components at their respective work positions. In Solid Edge software, you can develop an assembly with a combination of ordered and synchronous parts. This assembly document contains both the ordered and synchronous tools. To start the **Assembly** environment, choose the **ISO Metric Assembly** from the **Create** area of the welcome screen.

If the Solid Edge session is already running on your computer, choose the **New** button from the **Quick Access** toolbar to display the **New** dialog box. Note that if the **New** button is not available in the **Quick Access** toolbar, click on the down arrow of the **Quick Access** toolbar; a flyout will be displayed. Choose **New** from this flyout; the **Save Theme As** dialog box will be displayed. Choose the **OK** button from the dialog box; the **New** button will be added to the **Quick Access** toolbar. In the **New** dialog box, select the **iso metric assembly.asm** template. Next, choose the **OK** button to exit the dialog box and invoke the **Assembly** environment.

Working with the Assembly Environment

Before assembling parts, you need to configure some settings to ensure that while working on the assembly, its handling becomes easy. For example, to set the desired unit system, choose **Application Button > Info > File Properties**; the **Asm Properties** dialog box will be displayed. Next, choose the **Units** tab from the **Asm Properties** dialog box to set the units. By using various options available in this dialog box, you can specify the title of the assembly and its related information.

While creating an assembly, make sure the **Parts Library** tab is displayed in the docking window available on the left of the screen. This will be used extensively while assembling parts. If it is not available in the docking window, choose the **Parts Library** tool from the **Panes** drop-down in the **Show** group of the **View** tab in the ribbon. If the **Parts Library** pane is in collapsed state, choose the **Parts Library** tab from the left pane; the **Parts Library** pane will be displayed. To keep the **Parts Library** in the expanded state, choose the **Auto Hide** button of the pane.

The default screen appearance of the **Assembly** environment is shown in Figure 10-1.

Types of Assembly Design Approaches

In Solid Edge, assemblies are created by using two types of design approaches: bottom-up and top-down. These approaches are discussed next.

Bottom-up Approach

The bottom-up assembly design approach is the traditional and the most widely preferred approach of an assembly design. In this approach, all the components are created as separate part documents and are then placed and referenced in the assembly document. The components are created in the part environment as *.par* files. Next, you need to open an assembly document and assemble the components one by one at their respective work positions using the assembly relationships. This approach is preferred while handling large assemblies.

*Figure 10-1 The default **Assembly** environment screen*

Top-down Approach

In the top-down approach of an assembly design, the components are created in the same assembly document. Therefore, this approach is entirely different from the bottom-up approach. In this approach, you start working in the assembly document and then create components one-by-one. The geometry of one part helps you define the geometry of the other part.

Note

Most of the assemblies use a combination of both assembly design approaches.

CREATING THE BOTTOM-UP ASSEMBLY

As mentioned earlier, in the bottom-up assemblies, components are created as separate part files in the **Ordered Part** or **Synchronous Part** environment. After creating the components, they are inserted into the assembly and then assembled using the assembly relationships. To start an assembly design with this approach, you first need to insert components into the assembly. It is recommended to place the first component at the origin of the assembly document. On doing this, the base reference planes of the assembly and the part will coincide and the component will be in the same orientation as it was in the **Ordered Part** or **Synchronous Part** environment. When you place the first component in the assembly, the component will be fixed at its placement position. The technique used to place part files in the assembly file is discussed next.

Assembling the First Component

As stated before, there is an extensive use of the docking window in the **Assembly** environment because parts are inserted into the assembly using the docking window.

The first part that is placed in the assembly is called the base component. Generally, the base component does not have any motion relative to other components in the assembly. This component acts as the foundation of the whole assembly and it is taken as reference for all assembly parts in that assembly. The following steps explain the procedure of inserting the first component into the assembly file:

1. Choose the **Parts Library** tab from the left pane, refer to Figure 10-2.

2. In the drop-down list of the docking window, browse to the folder where the assembly part files are saved.

3. Double-click on the base component in the **Parts Library**; the first component will be placed in the assembly and it will be automatically assigned the **Ground** relationship. You do not need to apply any other assembly relationship to this component.

Assembling the Second Component

After placing the first component, now you will insert the second component into the assembly. But to fully position the second component in the assembly, you need to use the assembly relationships. Following are the steps to insert the second component into the assembly file:

1. Before placing the second component, you need to configure the option for displaying the new component in a separate file. To do so, choose **Application Button > Settings > Options**; the **Solid Edge Options** dialog box will be displayed. In this dialog box, choose the **Assembly** tab and then select the **Do not create new window when placing component** check box, if it is not already selected. Next, choose **OK** to apply the settings to the assembly document and close the dialog box.

2. Double-click or drag the second component from the **Parts Library** and insert it into the assembly window. Next, apply assembly relationships to assemble the component.

3. As you drag and drop the second component into the assembly window, the **Assemble** Command bar will be displayed. Choose the **Options** button from this Command bar; the **Options** dialog box will be displayed. Make sure that the **Use FlashFit as the default placement method** and **Use Reduced Steps when placing parts** check boxes are selected in this dialog box. It will ensure that you do not have to select the target part first to add relationships.

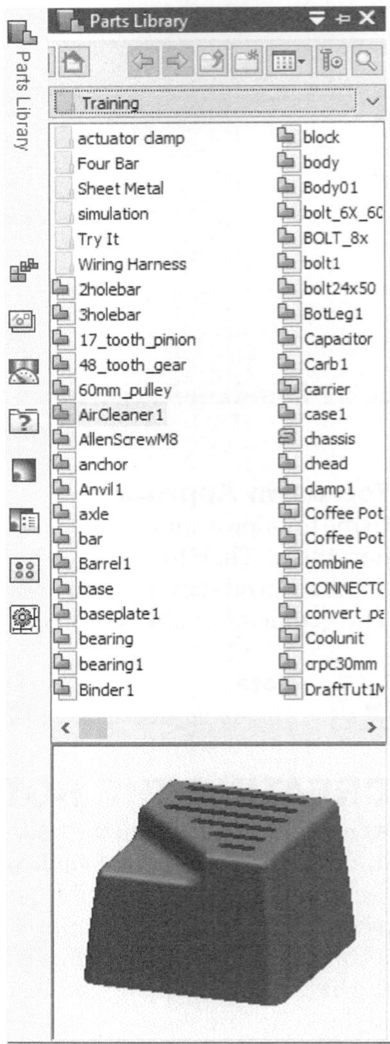

*Figure 10-2 **Parts Library** in the **Assembly** environment*

Note

The part that is to be placed in the assembly is called the placement part, and the part that is in the assembly with respect to which the placement part has to be positioned is called the target part.

Applying Assembly Relationships

After the base component is placed in the assembly, you can insert the second component. To assemble the second component, you need to constrain its degrees of freedom. As mentioned earlier, components are assembled using assembly relationships. These relationships help you place and position a component precisely with respect to other components or surroundings in the assembly. There are two methods of adding relationships to the components in the assembly: using the **FlashFit** button or using any other button from the **Relationship Types** flyout, as shown in Figure 10-3. These two methods are discussed next.

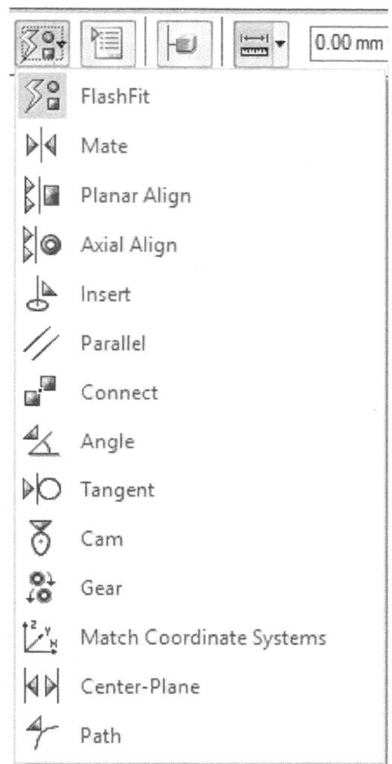

***Figure 10-3** The **Relationship Types** flyout*

Note

To insert parts that have other file formats such as .prt, .sldprt, and so on, you first need to convert them into the .par file format.

Using Assembly Relationships to Assemble Components

There are several types of assembly relationships in the **Relationship Types** flyout. This flyout is displayed on choosing the **Assemble - Relationship Types** button from the **Assemble** Command bar which is displayed on inserting the placement part in the assembly, refer to Figure 10-4.

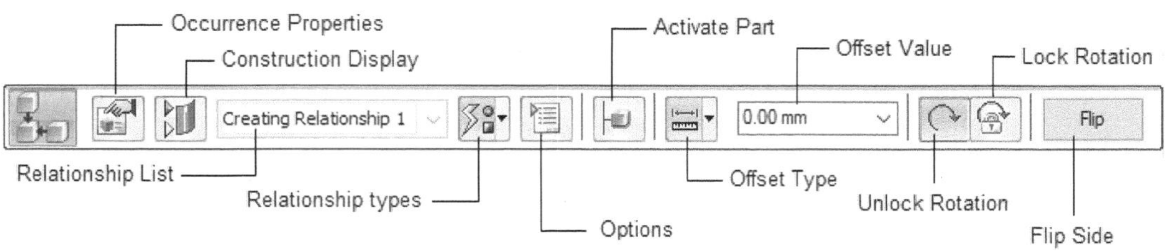

***Figure 10-4** The **Assemble** Command bar*

These relationships are discussed next.

Flash Fit

The **Flash Fit** relationship is used to apply the best possible constraints automatically between the parts. This also speeds up the assembly design process. After choosing this button, select an element on the placement part and move the cursor toward the target part to place the part. Solid Edge infers the potential solution and previews this part in various inferred positions.

Relationships such as **Mate**, **Insert**, **Planar Align**, and **Axial Align** can be easily applied using the **Flash Fit** relationship and are discussed next.

Mate

The **Mate** relationship enables you to make two selected faces or reference planes parallel and reorient them to face each other. To apply the **Mate** constraint, choose the **Mate** button from the **Relationship Types** flyout. Next, select a face from the second component and then select a face from the first component; the second component will be placed in the assembly window with the specified relationship. Figure 10-5 shows the two faces that are selected to apply the **Mate** relationship. After applying this relationship, the two components are placed, as shown in Figure 10-6.

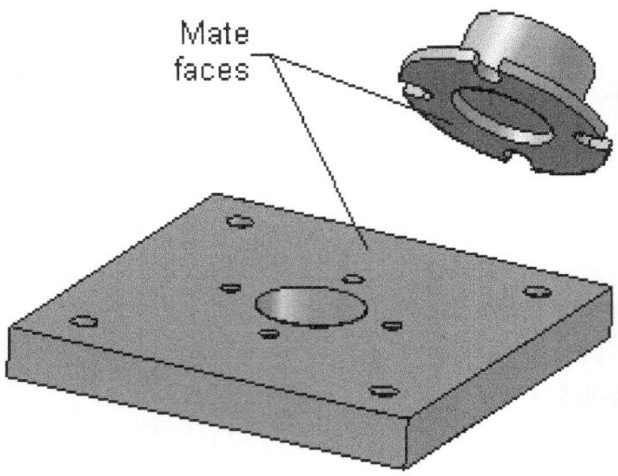

Figure 10-5 *Faces selected to apply the **Mate** relationship*

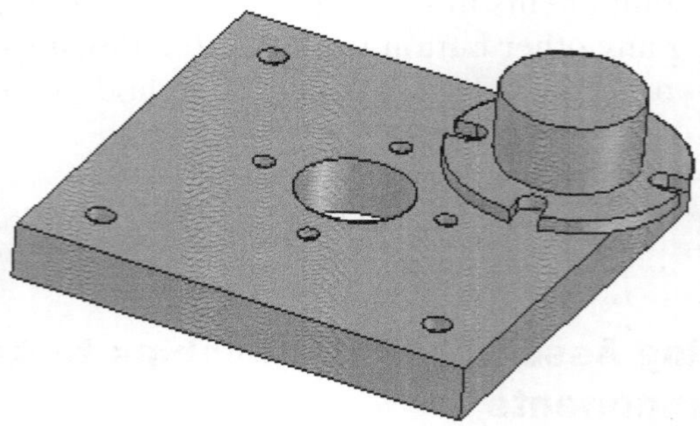

Figure 10-6 *The two components after applying the **Mate** relationship*

While applying the **Mate** relationship, you can choose the **Float**, **Range** or **Fixed** button from the Command bar. These three buttons are used to specify the type of offset that will be applied between the two mating faces. To apply the offset type, click on the **Offset Type** button; a flyout will be displayed. Next, choose the required tool from this flyout.

The **Float** button is chosen when the mating faces have to be made parallel and are not required to be placed at a specified offset distance from each other. In this way, the distance between the two mating faces remains floating, and is not fixed. It will be modified depending on the other relationships that are applied to the placement part.

The **Fixed** button is chosen by default. This button is used when the mating faces are to be placed at a specified offset distance from each other. The offset value can be entered in the **Offset Value** edit box available on the right of this button. By applying the **Mate** relationship with the **Fixed** button chosen, you can restrict the two degrees of freedom of the placement part. These movements are normal to the mating faces and rotatory around the axes normal to the other two faces.

The **Range** button is used when the mating faces are to be kept at a specific distance from each other. The minimum and maximum values of the distance can be specified in the **Range maximum** and **Range minimum** value edit boxes available on the right of this button.

Note

1. Generally, each part of a mechanism has six degrees of freedom (DOFs). Three of these DOFs are rotational DOFs (about the X, Y, and Z axes) and the rest are linear (or translational) DOFs (along the X, Y, and Z axes).

*2. All the fifteen assembly relationships are available in the **Assemble** group of the **Home** tab in the **Ribbon**.*

*3. In Solid Edge, you can modify a relationship. To do so, select the component to which the relationship will be applied from the top pane of the **PathFinder**. Select the symbol of relationship from the bottom pane of the **PathFinder** and double click on it; the **Assemble** Command bar will be displayed. Now you can make modification from the Command bar.*

Planar Align

The **Planar Align** relationship aligns the face or the reference plane of the placement part with the face or the reference plane of the target part. The aligned faces become parallel to each other and face in the same direction. This relationship can also be applied with the fixed or floating offset options. To apply the planar constraint, choose the **Planar Align** button from the **Relationship Types** flyout. Next, select the required face from the second component and then select a face from the first component; the second component will be placed in the assembly window with the specified relationship.

As mentioned earlier, if you use the **Float** button, you can apply an additional relationship to further constrain the placement part to the target part. The **Fixed** button enables you to enter an offset value. Figure 10-7 shows the faces selected on the two parts to apply the **Planar Align** relationship. Figure 10-8 shows the fixed offset after applying the **Planar Align** relationship. In this figure, you will notice that an offset distance is applied to the faces that were selected to be aligned by using the **Fixed** option. You can also maintain a specific distance between the faces by using the **Range** option.

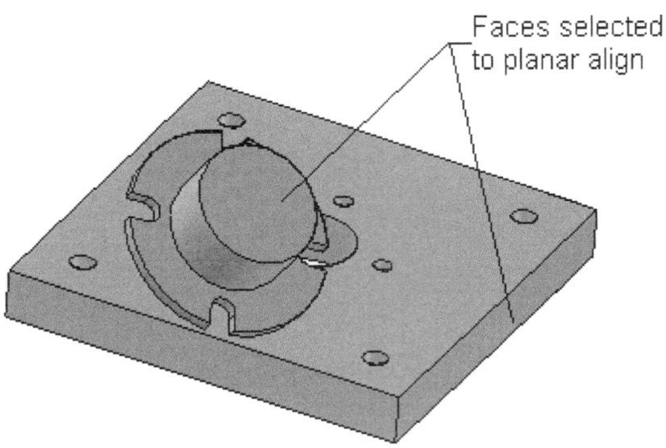

Figure 10-7 *Faces selected*

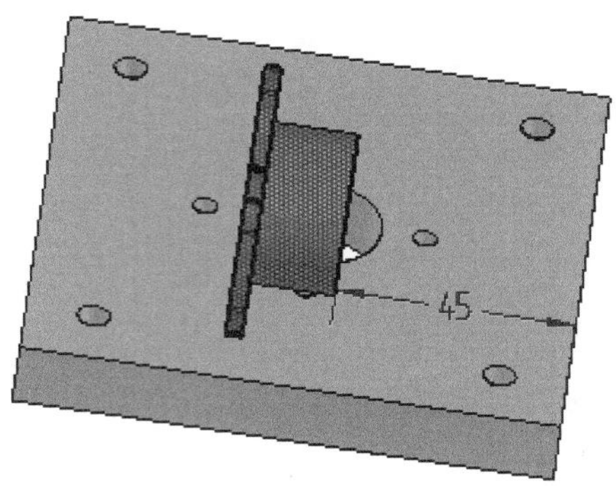

Figure 10-8 *The two parts after applying the **Planar Align** relationship with the fixed offset*

Note

*To change the offset distance value, first select the **Mate** symbol in the graphics screen and then change the value in the edit box displayed.*

Axial Align

The **Axial Align** relationship enables you to align the axis of a cylindrical feature on the placement part with the axis of the cylindrical feature on the target part. To apply this relationship, choose the **Axial Align** button from the **Relationship Types** flyout and then select the cylindrical faces of the two parts, refer to Figure 10-9. The axis of the bolt is aligned with that of the hole. The bolt is assembled with the plate, as shown in Figure 10-10.

You can apply the **Axial Align** relationship with a locked rotation or with an unlocked rotation. If you choose the **Unlock Rotation** button from the **Assemble** Command bar, the rotational degrees of freedom of the part will remain free. You can apply an additional relationship to constrain the rotational movement. If you choose the **Lock Rotation** button, the rotational movement will be locked.

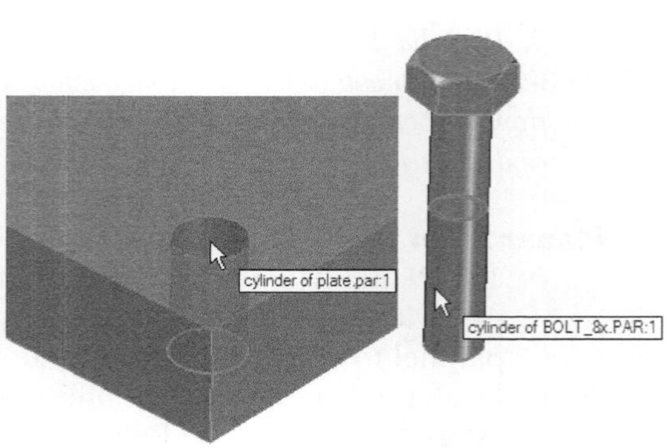

Figure 10-9 Cylindrical surfaces selected to align axes

Figure 10-11 shows the face of the bolt made parallel to the face of the plate. This is made possible by applying three relationships. Firstly, the axes of the bolt and the hole in the plate are aligned using the **Axial Align** relationship with the **Unlock Rotation** button chosen. This option enables you to keep the rotational movement of the bolt free. Then the bottom face of the bolt head and the top face of the plate are mated using the **Mate** relationship. Finally, the **Planar Align** relationship with the floating offset is applied to make the two faces parallel.

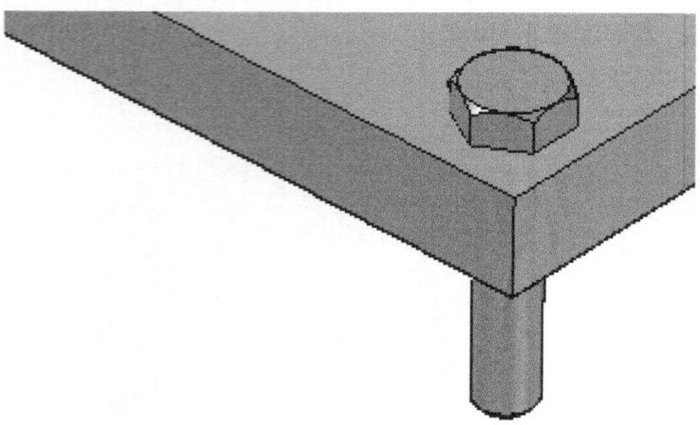

Figure 10-10 Bolt assembled with the plate

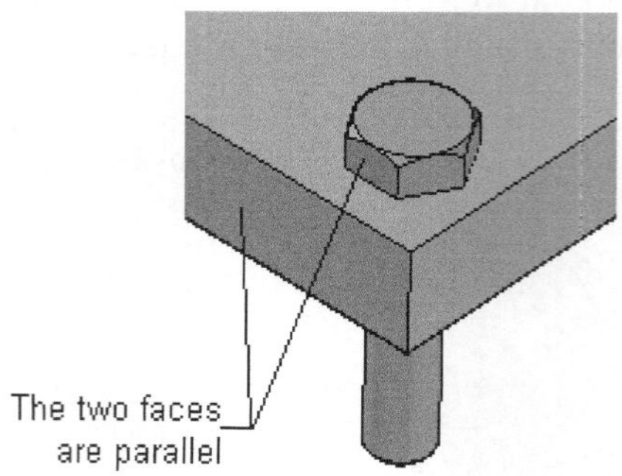

Figure 10-11 The face of the bolt made parallel to the face of the plate

Note

*The dimension edit box in the Command bar will not be available when you apply the **Axial Align** relationship.*

Insert

The **Insert** relationship combines the functions of both the **Mate** and **Axial Align** relationships. This means that you can make the cylindrical faces of the placement and target parts concentric as well as mate their planar faces using a single relationship. For example, the **Insert** relationship can be applied between a bolt and a hole feature. On choosing this button from the **Relationship Types** flyout, you will be prompted to click on the face to mate or on the axis to align. Select the cylindrical surfaces of the bolt and the hole to align their axes. Then, you need to set the two faces to mate. Remember that if you have applied the **Insert** relationship, the rotational degrees of freedom are constrained automatically.

However, you can rotate the placement part to some angle by editing the relationships. You need to modify the **Axial Align** relationship from locked to unlocked. After doing this, you can apply the **Angle** relationship to rotate the placement part.

Parallel

The **Parallel** relationship is used to force two edges, axes, or an edge and an axis parallel to each other. You can apply this relationship with a fixed offset, floating offset, or range offset. Figure 10-12 shows the edges selected to apply the **Parallel** relationship. Figure 10-13 shows the assembly after applying this relationship.

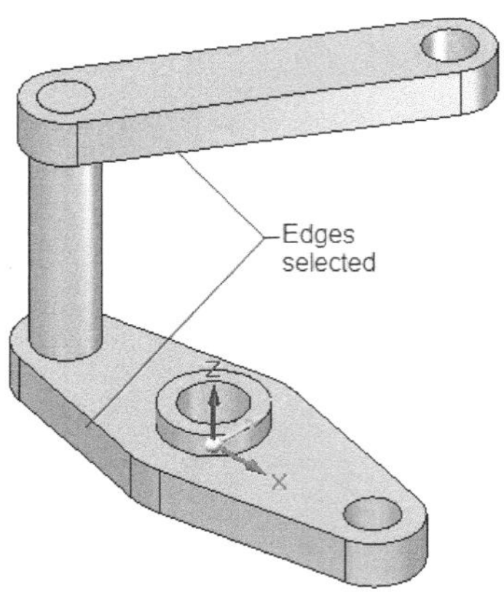

***Figure 10-12** Edges selected to apply the **Parallel** relationship*

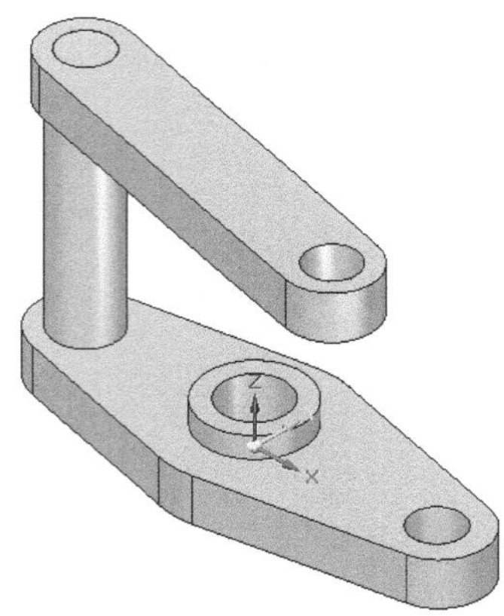

***Figure 10-13** The assembly after applying the **Parallel** relationship*

Connect

The **Connect** relationship is used to connect two parts by positioning a keypoint with another keypoint. A keypoint can also be positioned to a face or an edge. In Figure 10-14, the corner of the block is connected to the center of the hole.

Angle

The **Angle** relationship is applied to specify the angular position between the selected faces, reference planes, or the edges of the two parts. For example in Figure 10-15, the two faces are at an angle. But the two faces need to be at an angle of 60-degree to each other. Here, you can force the two faces to be at a particular angle by applying the **Angle** relationship and specifying the angular value of 60-degree, refer to Figure 10-16.

On choosing the **Angle** button from the **Relationship Types** flyout, you will be prompted to select a planar or linear element to measure to. After selecting the element to measure to, as shown in Figure 10-17, you will be prompted to select the element to measure from.

From the target part, select the plane or element to measure from, refer to Figure 10-17. Now, specify the value for the angle of rotation in the **Angle Value** edit box. Next, select the new angle value to control the measurement from the **Angle Format** drop-down list in the Command bar. On doing so, you will be prompted to select the plane on which the measurement will lie. Select the required plane.

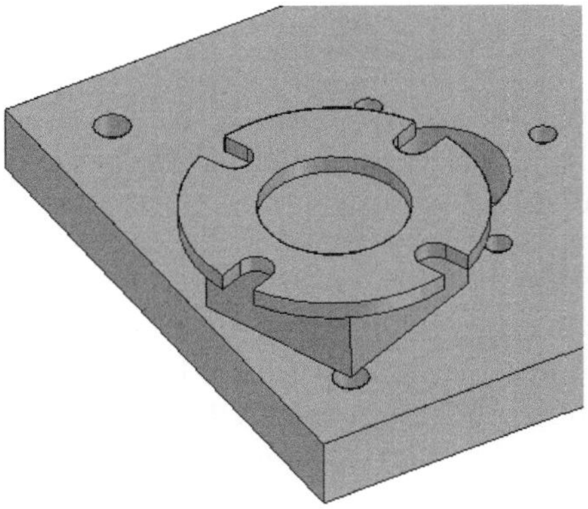

Figure 10-14 *The corner of the block connected to the center of the hole*

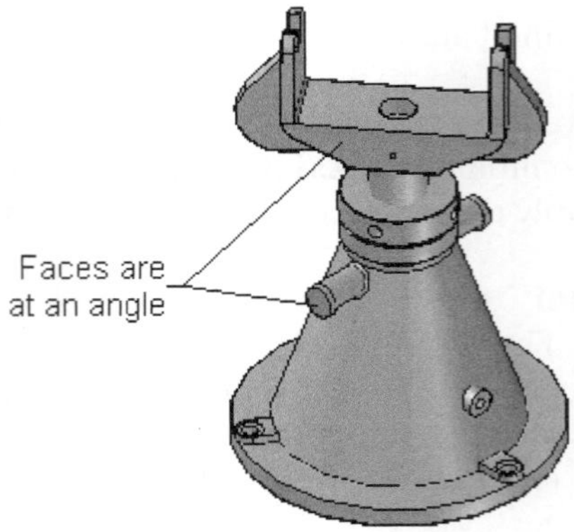

Figure 10-15 *Faces at an angle*

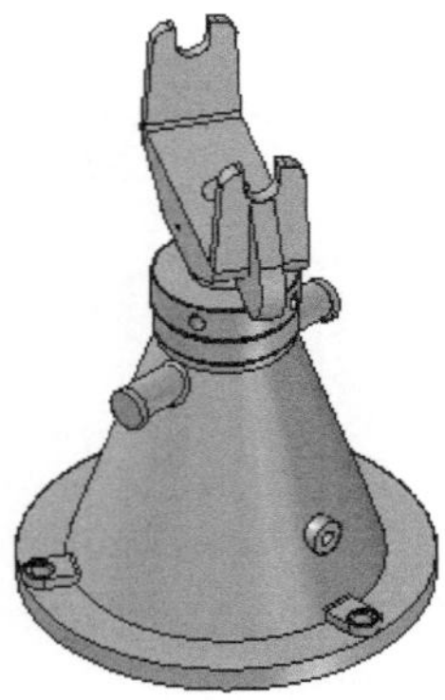

Figure 10-16 *Faces after applying the* ***Angle*** *relationship*

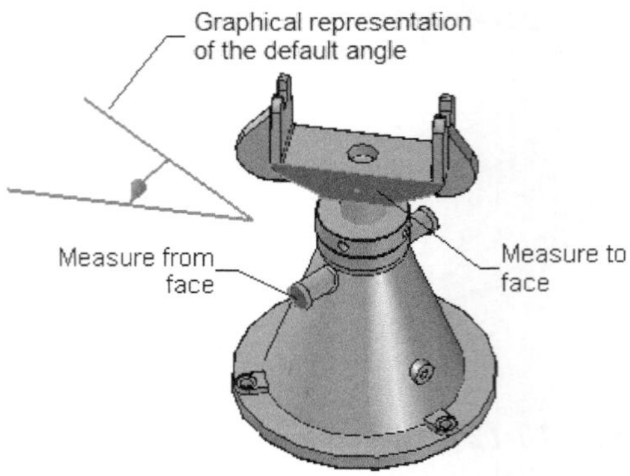

Figure 10-17 *Various parameters to be specified for applying the* ***Angle*** *relationship*

After applying the **Angle** relationship, you can modify the angular value. To do so, invoke the **Select** tool and select the component to which the relationship will be applied from the top pane of the **PathFinder**. Select the symbol of the **Angle** relationship from the bottom pane of the **PathFinder**; the **Angle** Command bar will be displayed at the bottom of the drawing area. By default, **1** is chosen in the **Angle** Command bar. To change the angle format, click on the **1** button; a flyout will be displayed. Before selecting the format, you can move the cursor over the format to preview it in the drawing window. Select the required format and then enter the angular value of the rotation in the **Angle Value** edit box of the **Angle** Command bar.

Tangent

The **Tangent** relationship is used to apply tangency between two surfaces. On choosing the **Tangent** button from the **Relationship Types** flyout, you will be prompted to select the face that you need to make tangent. Also, you will be prompted to select the tangent face of the target part. Select the face that is to be made tangent to the part; the first face will be placed tangent to the second face. Figure 10-18 shows the two faces that are made tangent to each other.

Path

The **Path** relationship is used to apply the path relationship between the two components while assembling them. After applying this relationship, you can define the motion of one component relative to the path chosen. To apply this relationship, choose the **Path** button from the **Path** drop-down in the **Assemble** group; you will be prompted to select a point or an edge to define the follower. After selecting the point or edge, you will be prompted to select the path. Select the path and right click; the path relation will be applied. Figure 10-19 shows the axis (follower) and the path selected and Figure 10-20 shows the resultant assembly after applying the **Path** relationship.

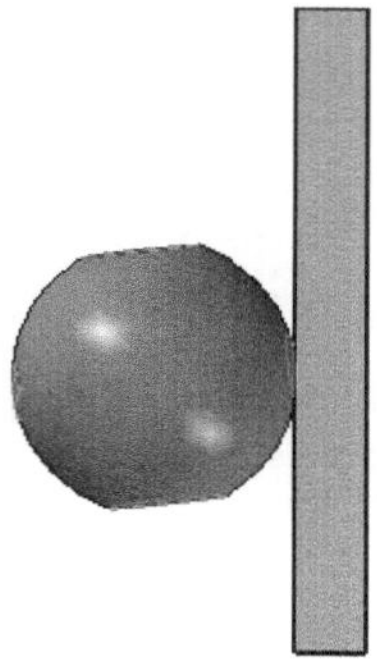

Figure 10-18 *The* ***Tangent*** *relationship applied to two parts*

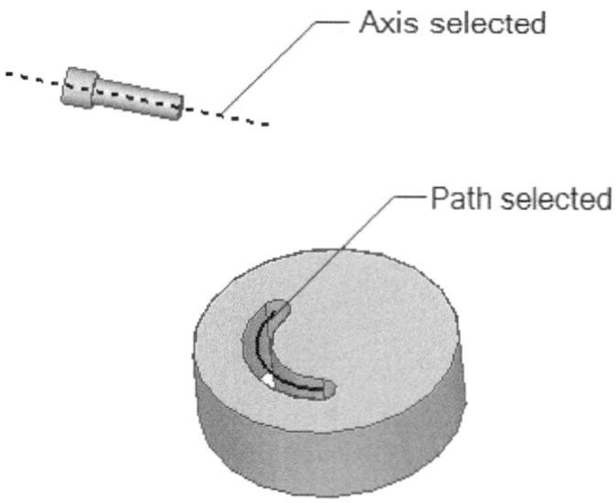

Figure 10-19 *Axis and path selected for applying the* ***Path*** *relationship*

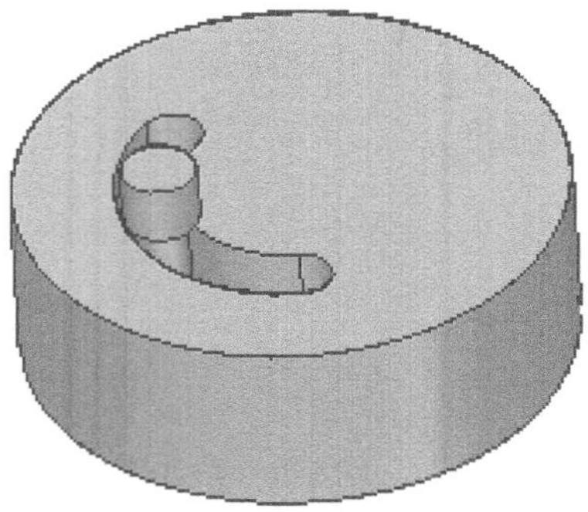

Figure 10-20 *Resultant assembly*

Cam

The **Cam** relationship is applied between the face of the follower and the tangential faces of the cam. The face of the follower that is selected to apply the relationship can be a cylindrical, spherical, or a planar surface. The faces selected on the cam must form a closed loop of tangential surfaces.

Figure 10-21 shows the selected faces and Figure 10-22 shows the cam and the follower assembly.

In Solid Edge, you can also use the **Cam** button available in the **Path** drop-down to model a barrel cam easily. The **Cam** relationship button allows the follower geometry to follow chained curves. Figure 10-23 shows the curved edge and the placement part (follower) to be selected for applying **Cam** relationship. In this arrangement, the placement part will follow through the curved edge. Figure 10-24 shows the resultant barrel cam assembly.

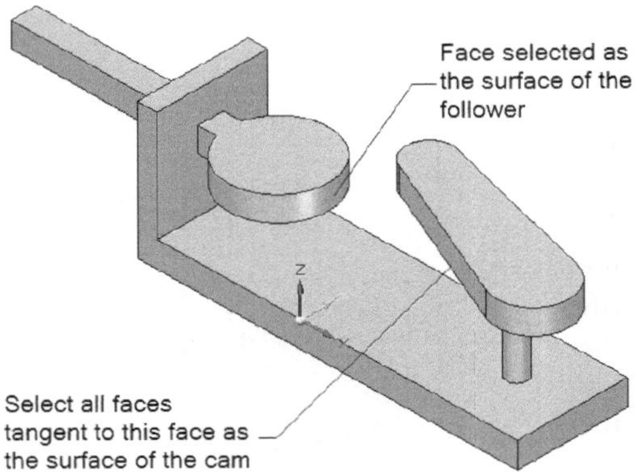

*Figure 10-21 Faces selected to apply the **Cam** relationship*

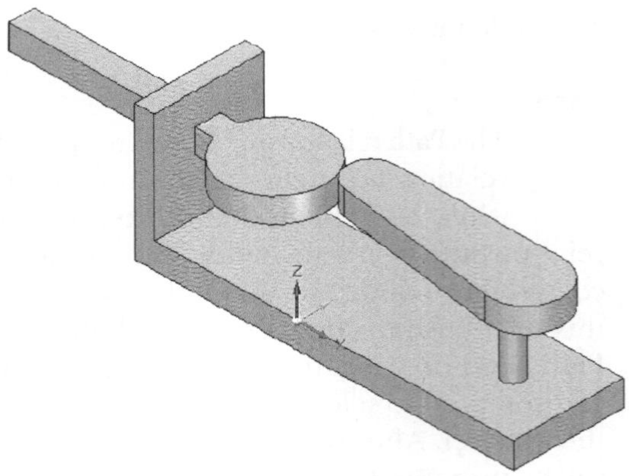

Figure 10-22 Cam and follower assembly

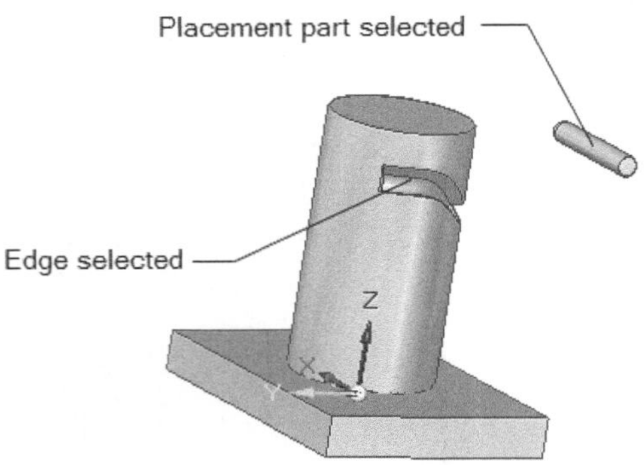

*Figure 10-23 Face and placement part selected to apply **Cam** relationship*

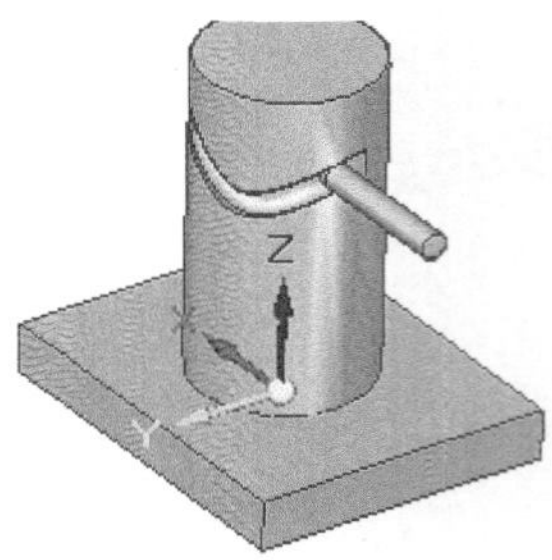

Figure 10-24 Resultant barrel cam assembly

Tip
*It is recommended that you make the front faces of the cam and the follower coplanar so that the **Cam** relationship executes properly.*

Gear

The **Gear** relationship is used to add rotation-rotation, rotation-linear, or linear-linear relation between two components. The components that can be used are gears, pulleys, and pneumatic or hydraulic actuators. On choosing this option from the **Relationship Types** flyout, you will be prompted to select cylindrical faces, linear edges, or axes of rotational components. To select the type of movement between components, choose the **Gear Type** button from the Command bar; a flyout will be displayed. The options in the flyout are **Rotation-Rotation**, **Rotation-Linear**, and **Linear-Linear**. Figure 10-25 shows the selected faces of gear parts with the **Rotation-Rotation** type of movement. The motion of a rack and pinion is an example of the **Rotation-Linear** movement. Rack undergoes a translation motion, whereas pinion undergoes rotational motion. Select the **Ratio** or **Teeth** option from the **Gear Value Type** drop-down list. Next, set the values of the two mating components in the **Value 1** and **Value 2** edit boxes. This option allows you to set the movement of one component relative to the other.

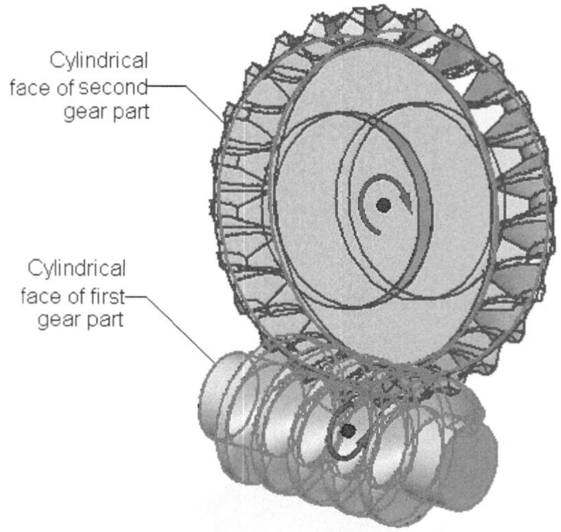

Figure 10-25 *Faces selected for the* ***Gear*** *relationship*

Note

Before applying the ***Gear*** *relationship on components, you need to apply other assembly relationships such as* ***Mate***, ***Axial Align***, *and so on to assemble the components.*

Match Coordinate Systems

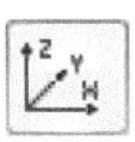

The **Match Coordinate Systems** relationship uses the coordinate systems of both the components to be assembled. To apply this relationship, you need to create the coordinate systems for the placement and target components by using the **Coordinate System** button. This button is available in the **Planes** group of the **Home** tab in the **Part** environment. In the **Assembly** environment, this tool is available in the **Planes** group of the **Features** tab of the **Ribbon**.

Center-Plane

The **Center-Plane** relationship is used to assemble a part at the mid-point of two selected planes, faces, or keypoints. You can select a face or two faces of the target part to be assembled. To do so, choose the **Center-Plane** button from the **Relationship Types** flyout. Next, select the **Double** option from the **Selection Type** drop-down list in the **Assemble** Command bar; you will be prompted to select planar faces, edges, or key points of the placement part. Select the faces, edges, or key points; you will be prompted to select the planar faces, key points, or reference planes. Now, select two planar faces of the target part where you want to place the assembly part. It is not necessary that the target faces are parallel. After applying the **Center-Plane** relationship, you will notice that the selected face of the assembly part is inserted at the midpoint between the two faces of the target part. Figures 10-26 and 10-27 respectively show the models before and after the **Center-Plane** relationship is applied to the faces using the **Double** face option in the **Center-Plane** Command bar.

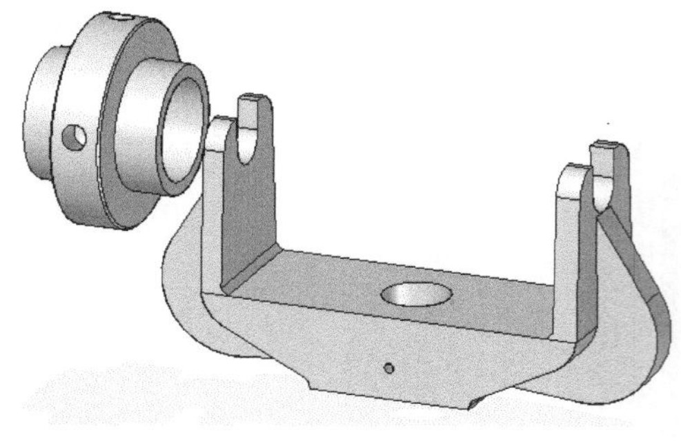

Figure 10-26 Assembly on which the ***Center-Plane*** *relationship is to be applied*

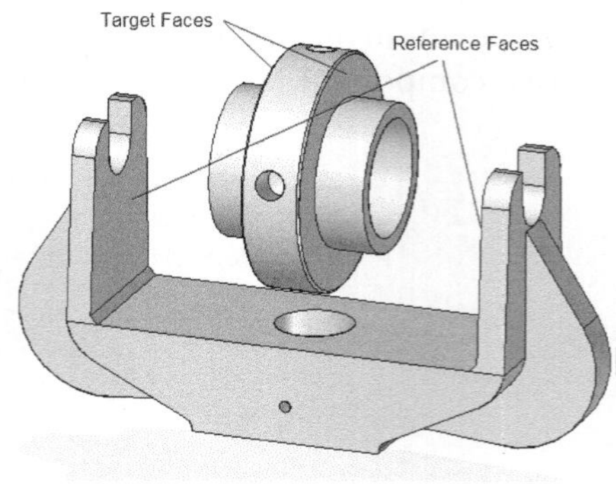

Figure 10-27 Assembly after applying the ***Center-Plane*** *relationship*

Note

You can also select the ***Single*** *option if you want to specify single target face.*

Ground

The **Ground** relationship is used for making a part fixed at some specified position and orientation (relative to the assembly). This relationship is available in the **Assemble** group of the **Home** tab. Note that the grounded part acts as an anchor relative to which other parts will be positioned. Solid Edge automatically applies the ground relationship to the first part placed in the assembly.

Rigid Set

The **Rigid Set** relationship is used to apply the relationship between two or more components and fixes them such that they become rigid with respect to each other. Note that this relationship is created in the active assembly and can contain subassemblies. To apply this relationship, choose the **Rigid Set** button from the **Assemble** group of the **Home** tab; the **Rigid Set** Command bar gets displayed. Next, select the components to add to the rigid set; the components get highlighted. Select the required option from the **Shared Relationships** drop-down list of the Command bar and then choose the **Accept** button; the rigid set will be created.

Points to be Remembered while Assembling Components

The following points should be remembered to work efficiently on the assembly design in Solid Edge:

1. The first assembly relationship you apply to the two parts in the assembly restricts certain degrees of freedom of both the components. As you continue applying additional

relationships, the parts become fully constrained and cannot be moved in the assembly. The process of moving the partially constrained parts in the assembly is discussed later in this chapter.

Figure 10-28 shows the symbols in the **PathFinder** indicating the status of the constraints applied. These symbols help you identify whether a part is fully or partially constrained. It is recommended that all the necessary constraints should be applied on a part as per the design requirement before you proceed to assemble the next part.

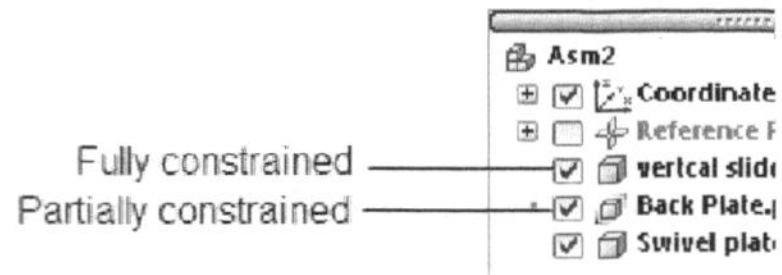

Figure 10-28 *Symbols in the* ***PathFinder***

2. Choose the **Options** button from any of the **Assemble** Command bars to specify the placement options; the **Options** dialog box will be displayed, as shown in Figure 10-29.

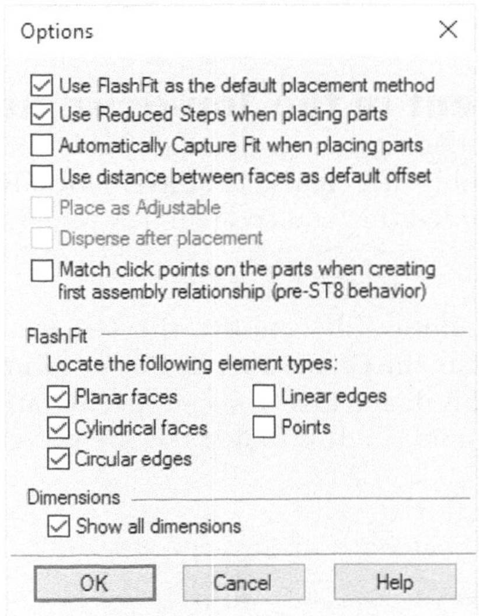

Figure 10-29 *The* ***Options*** *dialog box*

When you select the **Use Flash Fit as the default placement method** check box, the **Flash Fit** option in the **Relationship Types** flyout will be displayed as the default option. If you clear this check box, the **Mate** relationship will be displayed as the default option.

The **Use Reduced Steps when placing parts** check box is used to reduce the number of steps to assemble a part with the assembly. For example, if this check box is cleared, you first need to select the target part and then an element on it. If the check box is selected, you can directly select the element on the target part. This means by selecting this check box, you reduce the steps required to design an assembly by 60 percent.

3. While placing the component at the desired location, you can apply multiple relationships one by one from the **Assemble** Command bar.

4. To apply relationships to a part that is not fully positioned, select the part from the

PathFinder; the bottom pane of the **PathFinder** will display the relationships that are already applied to the selected part. To edit an existing relationship, select it from the bottom pane; a floating toolbar will be displayed. You can edit the relationship using this toolbar. If you want to delete a relationship, select it from the bottom pane and press DELETE. To apply a relationship, choose the **Edit Definition** button from the Command bar and then add relationships to the part selected from the **PathFinder**.

CREATING THE TOP-DOWN ASSEMBLY

As discussed earlier, top-down assemblies are those in which the components are created inside the assembly file. However, to create the components, you require an environment in which you can draw the sketches and then convert them into features. In other words, to create the components in the assembly file, you need the sketcher tools as well as the part environment in the assembly file itself. In Solid Edge, you can invoke the part environment from the Assembly environment. The basic procedure of creating the components in the assembly or the procedure of creating the top-down assembly is discussed next.

Creating a Component in the Top-down Assembly

Before creating the first component in the top-down assembly, first you need to save the assembly file. After starting a new assembly file, choose the **Save** button from the **Quick Access toolbar** to save the file. It is recommended that you create a new folder and save the assembly file and other referenced files in it.

After saving the current assembly file, choose the **Create Part In-Place** tool from the **Assemble** group of the **Home** tab; the **Create Part In-Place Options** dialog box will be displayed, as shown in Figure 10-30. In this dialog box, you can specify various options for creating a part in the assembly. Most of the options in this dialog box are self-explanatory.

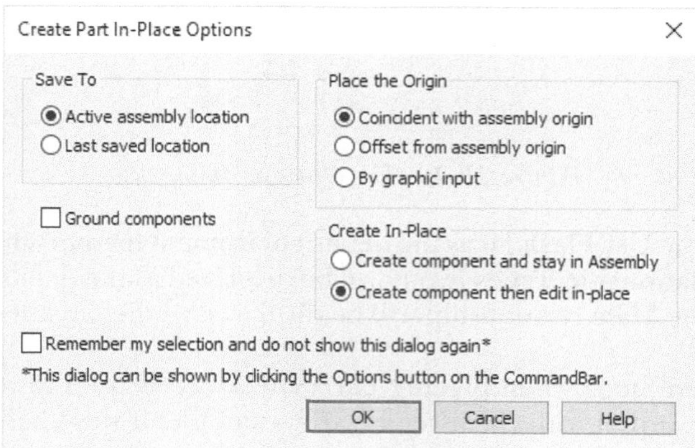

***Figure 10-30** The **Create Part In-Place Options** dialog box in the Assembly environment*

The options in the **Place the Origin** area are used to define the placement of the part. These options are discussed next.

Coincident with assembly origin

On selecting this radio button, the origin of the new part becomes coincident with the assembly origin. Also, the reference planes of the new part become coplanar with the respective reference planes of the assembly. These new reference planes are used to create a new part. You can also create additional reference planes to create new parts.

Offset from assembly origin

This radio button is used to create the reference planes of the part at an offset distance from the assembly origin. The offset distance can be specified by entering the x, y, and z distance values or by specifying a keypoint.

By graphic input

This radio button enables you to select a face or edge, or an existing part to place the reference planes of the new part.

Ground components

On selecting this check box, the newly created part will be assigned the **Ground** relationship.

The options in the **Create In-Place** area are used to specify whether to create and edit the part or not. If you select the **Create component and stay in Assembly** radio button, a new part file will be created within the assembly. If you choose the **Create component and then edit in-place** button, a new part file will be created within the assembly and the Part environment will be invoked. You can build new features to create a new part. After creating the part, save it and then choose the **Close and Return** button from the **Close** group of the **Home** tab to exit the part environment and to enter again in the **Assembly** environment. After specifying the required options, choose the **OK** button; the **Create Part In-Place** Command bar will be displayed. In this Command bar, you can select a template from the **Templates** drop-down list to create a file. You can also use the **Browse for Template** button to open the **New** dialog box. You can use this dialog box to access more templates. Next, choose the **Accept** button from the Command bar; the **Save as** dialog box is displayed. Specify the name and location of the file and choose the **Save** button; the part or the assembly file will be created. Similarly, you can create multiple parts one by one within the assembly. The assembly shown in Figure 10-31 is created by using the top-down assembly approach.

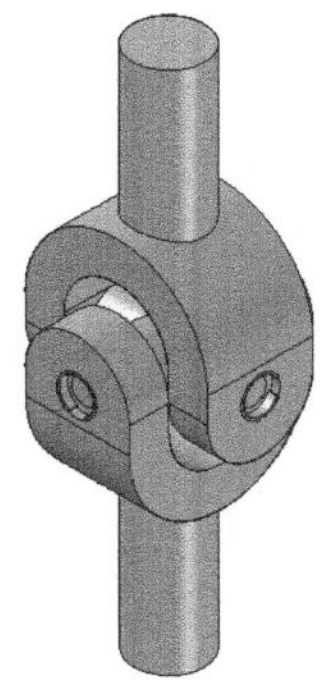

Figure 10-31 *Assembly created using the top-down assembly*

Note

*It is recommended that you save the part file before you exit the part environment. To do so, choose the **Save** button in the part environment.*

CREATING THE PATTERN OF COMPONENTS IN AN ASSEMBLY

Ribbon:	Home > Pattern > Pattern

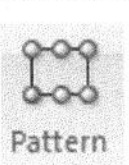

While working in the **Assembly** environment of Solid Edge, you may need to assemble more than one instance of the component about a specified arrangement. Consider the case of a flange coupling where you have to assemble four instances of the bolt to fasten the coupling. You need to assemble all the four bolts manually. Therefore, to reduce the time of the assembly design cycle, Solid Edge has provided a tool to create patterns of the components. This tool is discussed next.

Creating a Reference Pattern

The reference pattern is used to pattern the instances of the components by using an existing pattern feature. This means the pattern on the existing part should be created by using the **Pattern** tool. To create a reference pattern, choose the **Pattern** button from the **Pattern** group of the **Home** tab in the **Ribbon**; you will be prompted to select the parts to be included in the pattern. Select the instance of the part that is already assembled and then right click to accept the selection; you will be prompted to select the part that contains the pattern. After selecting the part, you will be prompted to select the pattern. Select a hole; you will be prompted to select the reference feature in the pattern. Select the instance of the hole, which is the source hole. Choose the **Finish** button from the Command bar; the pattern will be created. Figure 10-32 shows the component to be patterned and the pattern source of the feature. Figure 10-33 shows the resulting pattern.

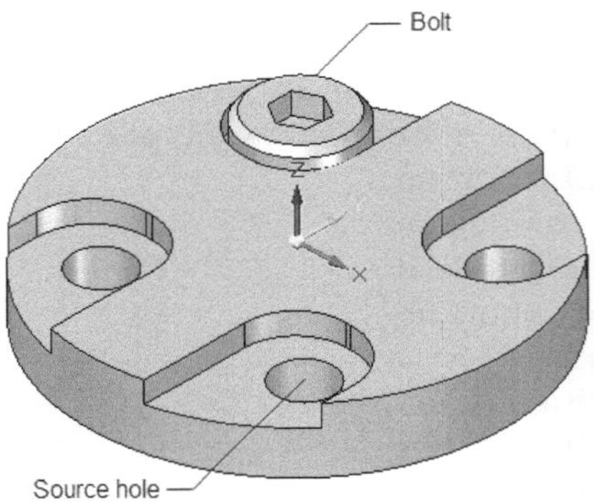

Figure 10-32 Assembly showing the component to be patterned

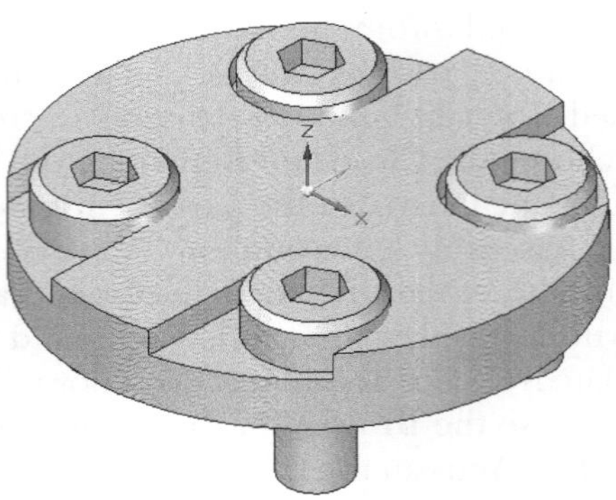

Figure 10-33 Assembly after creating a pattern

If you need to skip some of the instances of the pattern, click on the plus sign (+) on the left of the pattern feature in the **PathFinder**; the list of pattern instances will be displayed. Next, expand the instance and clear the check box in front of the respective part; the instance will be hidden from the drawing window.

Note

1. You do not need to select the reference element if the pattern is created in the ***Synchronous Part*** *environment. The component will show a preview directly after selecting the pattern feature.*

2. All the instances of the pattern are associated with each other. For example, if you give an offset distance to the bottom face of the bolt from the top face of the base plate, all the bolts will be positioned at that offset distance.

MIRRORING A COMPONENT IN AN ASSEMBLY

Ribbon: Home > Pattern > Mirror

In the Assembly environment of Solid Edge, you can mirror the assembly components by using the reference plane as the mirror plane. To do so, choose the **Mirror Components** tool from the **Pattern** group of the **Home** tab in the **Ribbon**; the **Mirror Components** Command bar will be displayed and you will be prompted to select the component to be mirrored. Select the component to be mirrored and choose the **Accept** button from the Command bar; you will be prompted to select the mirror plane about which the component is to be mirrored. Figure 10-34 shows the component to be mirrored and the mirror plane. Select the mirror plane; the preview of the mirrored feature will be displayed. Also, the **Mirror Components** dialog box will be displayed, refer to Figure 10-35. Choose the **OK** button from the dialog box and then choose the **Finish** button from the Command bar; the final mirrored feature will be displayed, refer to Figure 10-36.

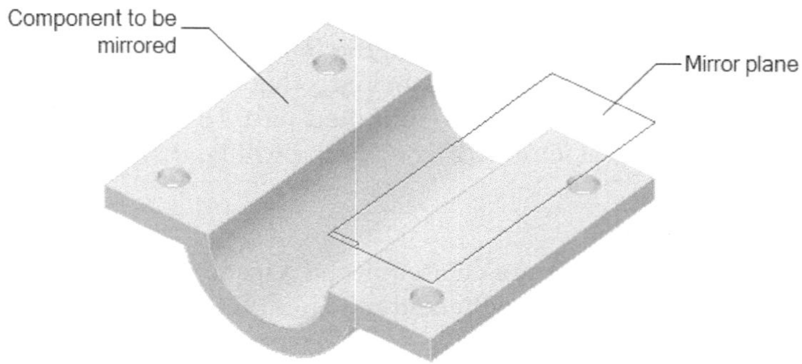

***Figure 10-34** Component and the mirror plane*

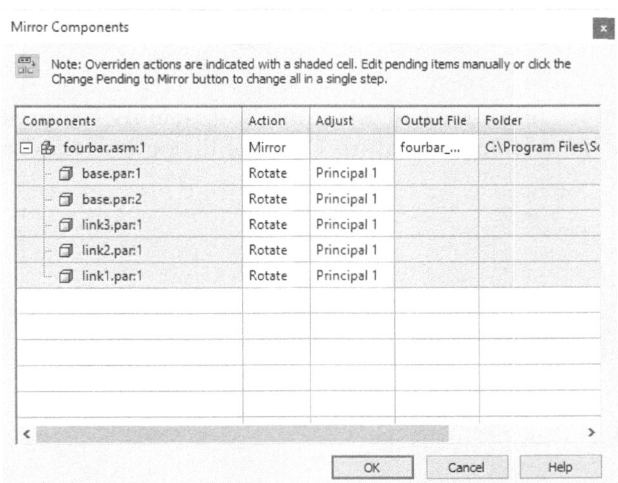
Mirror Components

Note: Overriden actions are indicated with a shaded cell. Edit pending items manually or click the Change Pending to Mirror button to change all in a single step.

Components	Action	Adjust	Output File	Folder
fourbar.asm:1	Mirror		fourbar_...	C:\Program Files\S
base.par:1	Rotate	Principal 1		
base.par:2	Rotate	Principal 1		
link3.par:1	Rotate	Principal 1		
link2.par:1	Rotate	Principal 1		
link1.par:1	Rotate	Principal 1		

OK Cancel Help

***Figure 10-35** The **Mirror Components** dialog box*

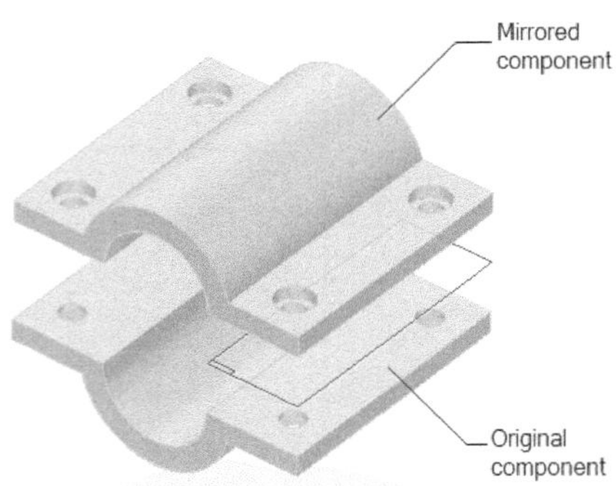

***Figure 10-36** Mirrored component with the original component*

CREATING MATERIAL REMOVAL FEATURES IN AN ASSEMBLY

Sometimes, an assembly design is such that after the components of an assembly are assembled, you need to cut a portion of the assembly. These cuts are generally created for lubrication grooves, keeping the holes concentric, design purposes, and so on. These cutouts can be assembly features or assembly-driven part features. These features are part of the **Assembly** environment only and are discussed next.

Assembly Features

In Solid Edge, the features that are created in the **Assembly** environment are called assembly features. These features are saved in the assembly file only, and not as separate part files. In other words, the assembly features are not associative with the parts on which they are created.

Assembly-driven Part Features

In Solid Edge, assembly-driven part features are the features that are created in the **Assembly** environment and are associatively linked with the parts that are affected by this feature. In other words, they are associatively linked with the modified parts. This means that if you open the part, the assembly cutout or an assembly-driven feature will be displayed.

Create Part Features

In Solid Edge, the part features that are created in the **Assembly** environment are the same as those created using the **Create Part In-Place** tool. These features are not associated with the assembly.

Tools for Material Removal in an Assembly

Solid Edge allows you to create various types of features for material removal using tools such as **Cut**, **Revolved Cut**, **Hole**, and so on.

To create a material removal feature like cutout, choose the **Cut** tool from the **Assembly Features** group of the **Features** tab in the **Ribbon**; the **Assembly Feature Options** dialog box will be displayed, as shown in Figure 10-37.

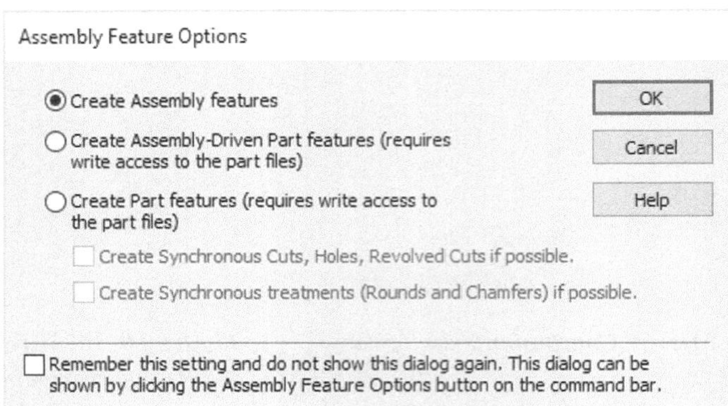

Figure 10-37 *The* ***Assembly Feature Options*** *dialog box*

The options in this dialog box have been discussed earlier. Select any one of the radio buttons and choose **OK** to exit the dialog box; you will be prompted to select a reference plane or a face to draw the sketch. After drawing the sketch, specify the depth of the cut. Next, select the parts to be included in the multipart cutout. Choose **Preview** and then the **Finish** button from the Command bar to create the cut.

The material removal tools are used to create cutouts simultaneously in the assembled components. These tools enable you to select the parts on which the cutout will be created. Figure 10-38 shows the three parts that are to be assembled together with the help of a nut and bolt. To assemble the bolt in the assembly, all the three parts must have a hole cut on them. For the bolt to assemble properly with all the parts, it is necessary that the hole on one part should be concentric to the hole on the other part. For this purpose, a multipart hole is created on the assembly of the three components in the **Assembly** environment. Figure 10-39 shows the assembly after creating the hole.

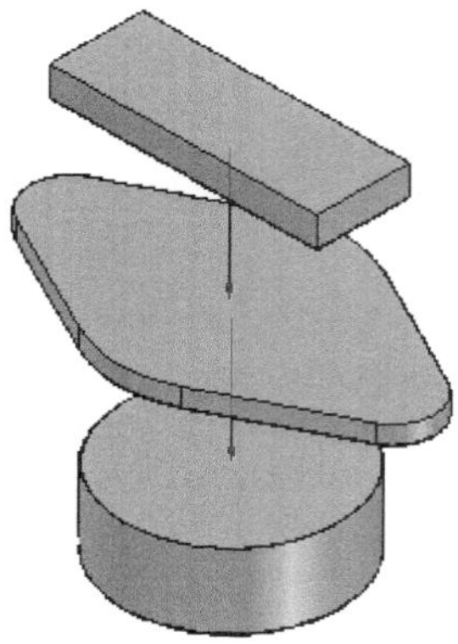

Figure 10-38 *Three parts to be assembled*

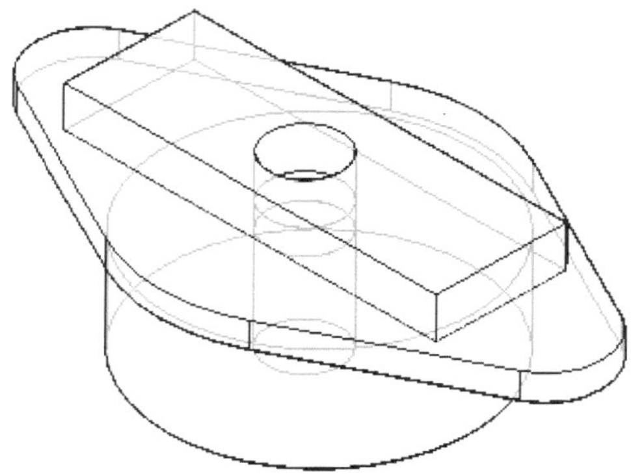

Figure 10-39 *Parts after assembling and creating a multipart cutout*

In the **Assembly** environment, assembly features are listed under the **Assembly Features** node in the **PathFinder**. Remember that because the cutout that you create can be an assembly feature or an assembly-driven part feature, you need to save the existing assembly before creating the cutout.

Subtracting Material from a Part using Another Part

Ribbon: Features > Assembly Features > Subtract

Subtract

In Solid Edge, you can use the **Subtract** tool to subtract material from a part by using another part. On invoking this tool, the **Assembly Subtract Options** dialog box will be displayed, as shown in Figure 10-40. The options in this dialog box are self-explanatory. Select the required options from this dialog box and choose the **OK** button; you will be prompted to select the target bodies for boolean operations. Select the parts from which you need to subtract the material and right-click to accept the selection; you will be prompted to select the tool body. Select the part from the assembly which will act as a tool to remove material and right-click; material will be removed from the target body. Choose **Finish** and **Cancel** to exit the tool.

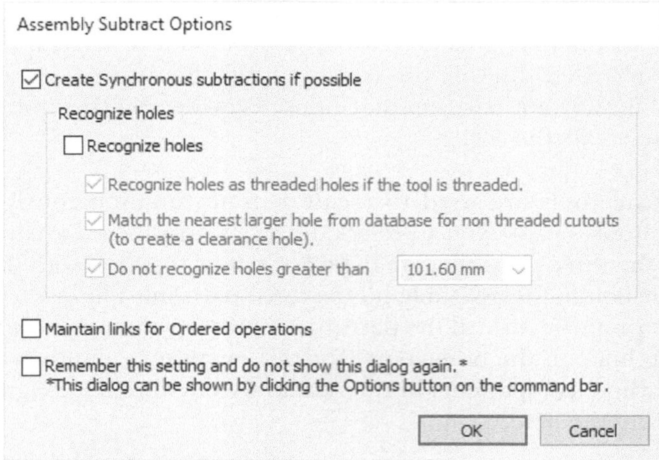

Figure 10-40 The ***Assembly Subtract Options*** *dialog box*

MOVING THE INDIVIDUAL COMPONENTS

Ribbon: Home > Modify > Drag Component

In Solid Edge, you can move unconstrained or partially constrained components in an assembly without affecting the position and location of other components. The partially constrained components are the components of the assembly which have at least one degree of freedom. You can translate or rotate the selected partially positioned components.

Procedure for Moving the Components

To move a component, choose the **Drag Component** tool from the **Modify** group of the **Home** tab; the **Analysis Options** dialog box will be displayed. In this dialog box, specify parameters and choose the **OK** button; the **Drag Component** Command bar will be displayed and you will be prompted to select the component to move. Select the component. Next, choose the **Freeform Move** button from the Command bar and then move the component by dragging it. If you choose the **Move** button in the Command bar, all the three axes will be displayed, as shown in Figure 10-41. You can select any of the three axes and drag the component. Note that if any assembly relationship exists with the selected component such that its movement is restricted in that direction, the component will not move in that direction.

If you want to rotate the component, choose the **Rotate** button from the Command bar and select the axis about which the component's rotatory movement is free.

MOVING MULTIPLE COMPONENTS

Ribbon: Home > Modify > Drag Component > Move Components

Apart from moving or rotating the unconstrained or partially constrained components in an assembly, you can move or rotate multiple components together. To move or rotate multiple components together, choose the **Move Components** tool from the **Modify** group of the **Home** tab in the ribbon; the **Move Components** Command bar and the **Move Options** dialog box will be displayed. Choose the **OK** button from the dialog box; the **Select**

Step will be invoked automatically and you will be prompted to select the components to be moved. Select the required components and right-click to accept the selection. By default, the **Move Components Option** button is chosen in the Command bar. As a result, the **Select From Point Step** will be invoked. Now, you need to specify a reference point from where the entities will be moved. You can use the **Keypoint** flyout to specify the point to snap. You can also specify the coordinates of the point to snap. On selecting the point, the **Select To Point Step** will be invoked and you will be required to specify a point to move the entities.

For rotating the component about an axis, choose the **Rotate Components Option** button from the Command bar; the **Axis Step** will be invoked. Specify the axis of rotation; the **Angle Value** edit box will be displayed, in which you can enter the value of rotation. On choosing the **Repeat** button from the Command bar, the rotation will be repeated. Figure 10-42 shows multiple components to be rotated in the assembly.

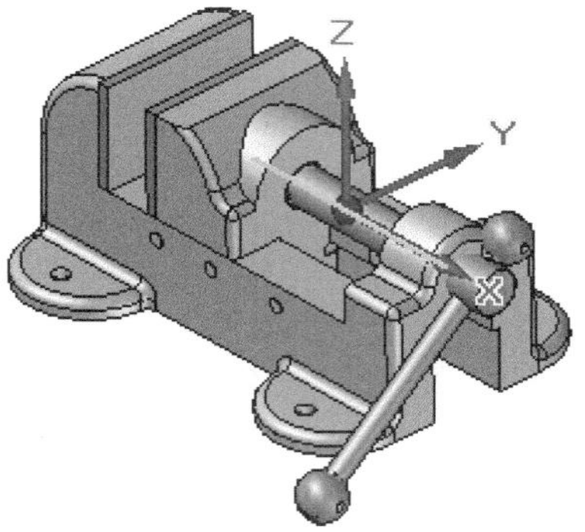

Figure 10-41 *Axes displayed to move the part in the assembly*

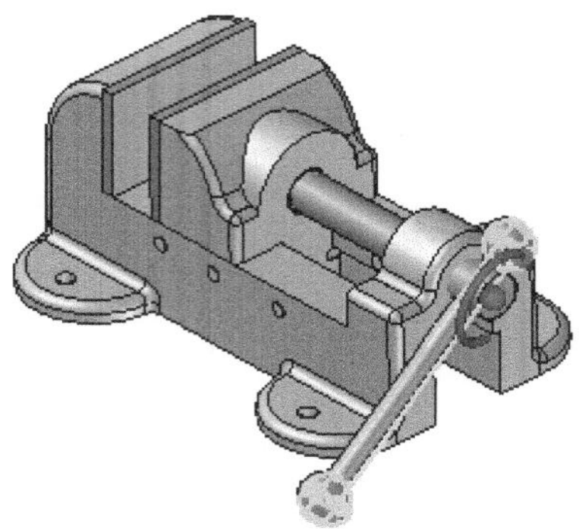

Figure 10-42 *Multiple parts to be rotated in the Assembly*

By choosing the **Copy Components** option from the Command bar, you can create multiple copies of the selected entity while moving or rotating the components.

TUTORIALS

Tutorial 1

In this tutorial, you will create all the components of the Stock Bracket assembly and then assemble them. The Stock Bracket assembly is shown in Figure 10-43. The dimensions of various components are shown in Figures 10-44 through 10-50. Note that all dimensions are in inches. After completing the tutorial, save the file with the name *Stock Bracket.asm* at the location given next:

C:\Solid Edge\c10\Stock Bracket **(Expected time: 3 hr)**

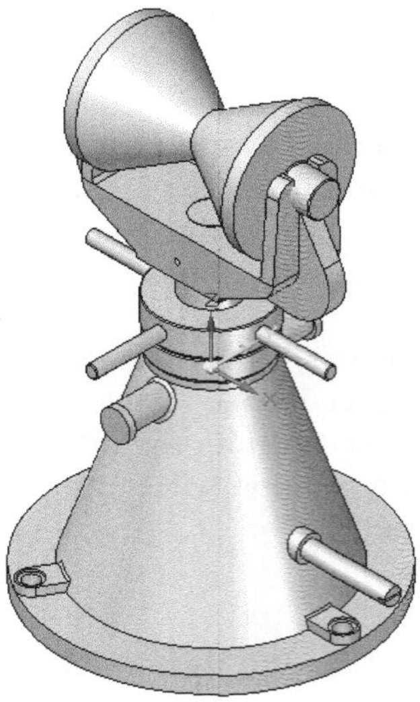

Figure 10-43 Assembly of the Stock Bracket

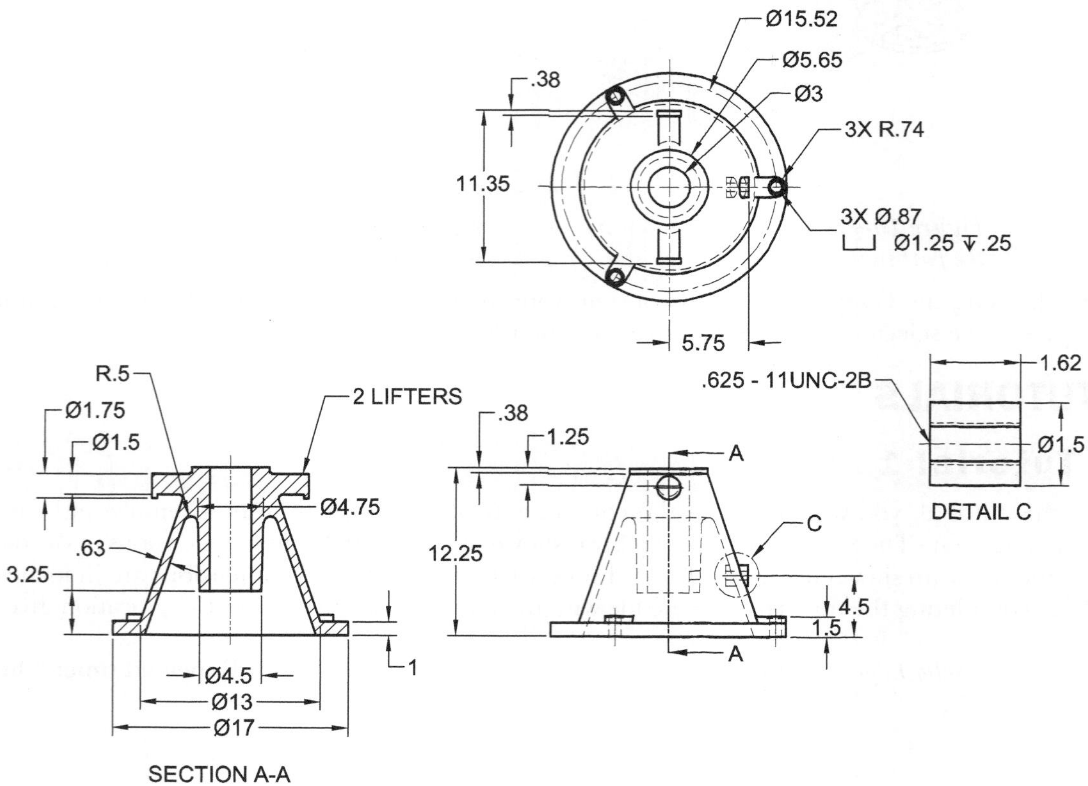

Figure 10-44 Top and front views of the Stock Support Base

The following steps are required to complete this tutorial:

a. Create all the components as individual part files and save them. Note that all the dimensions of the parts are in inches. So you need to use the **ansi inch part.par** template to create part files. Save the files in *C:\Solid Edge\c10\Stock Bracket* folder.
b. Start a new file in the **Assembly** environment.
c. Select the base component, which is the Stock Support Base, and drag it into the assembly window. This component will automatically get assembled with the assembly reference planes, using the **Ground** relationship.
d. Drag the Thrust Bearing into the assembly window. Apply the required relationships, refer to Figure 10-54.
e. Next, assemble the Adjusting Screw Nut with the Thrust Bearing using the assembly relationships, refer to Figure 10-57 through 10-59.
f. Assemble the Support Adjusting Screw with the assembly, refer to Figure 10-61 through 10-62.
g. Assemble the Support Roller Bracket with the assembly, refer to Figure 10-63 to 10-66.
h. Next, assemble the Stock Support Roller with the Support Roller Bracket, refer to Figure 10-67 through 10-70.
i. Assemble one instance of the Adjusting Nut Handle and pattern it to create other instances, refer to Figures 10-72 and 10-73.
j. Assemble the Adjusting Screw Guide with the Stock Support Base, refer to Figure 10-74 through 10-78.
k. Save the assembly file.

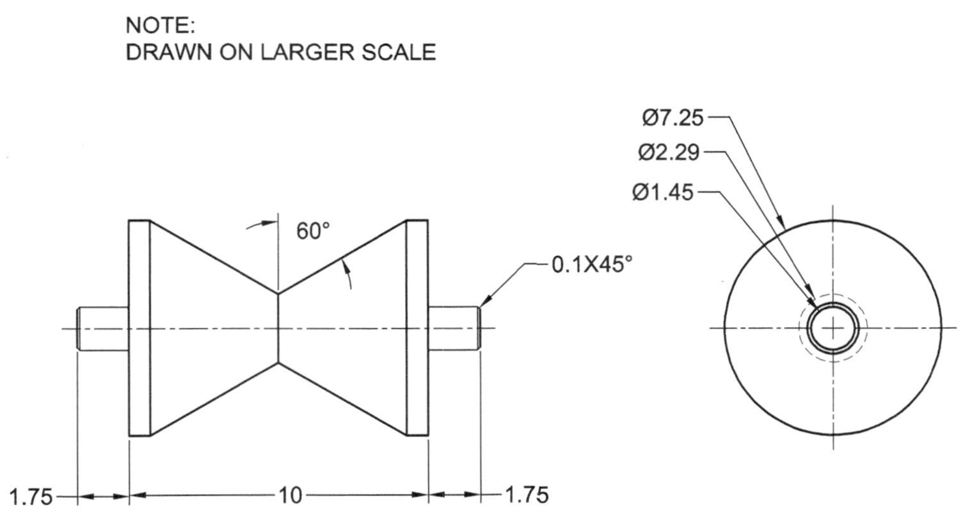

Figure 10-45 *Front and right views of the Stock Support Roller*

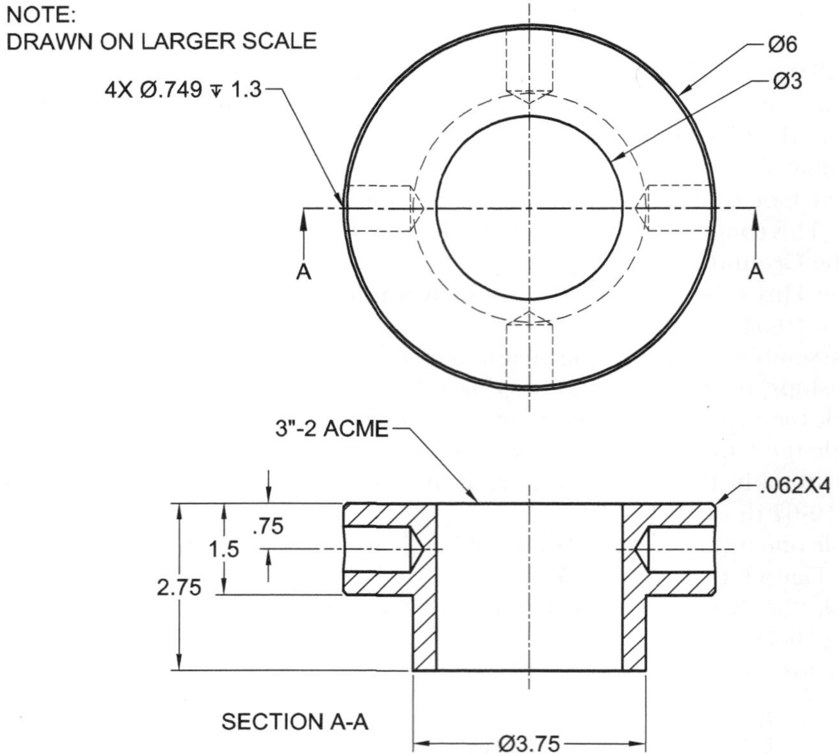

Figure 10-46 *Top and front views of the Adjusting Screw Nut*

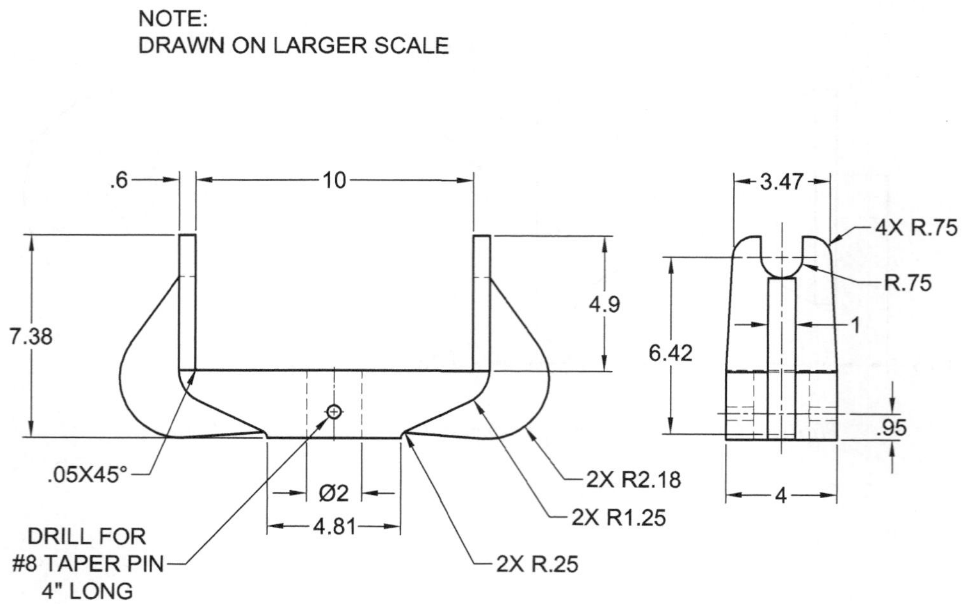

Figure 10-47 *Front and right views of the Support Roller Bracket*

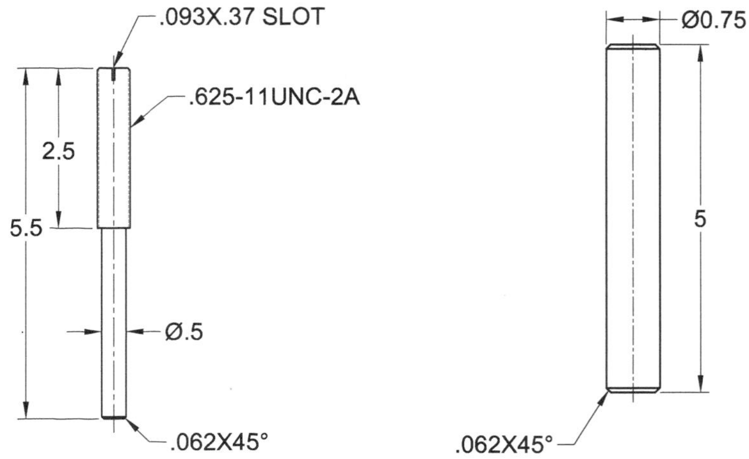

Figure 10-48 *Views of the Adjusting Screw Guide and Adjusting Nut Handle*

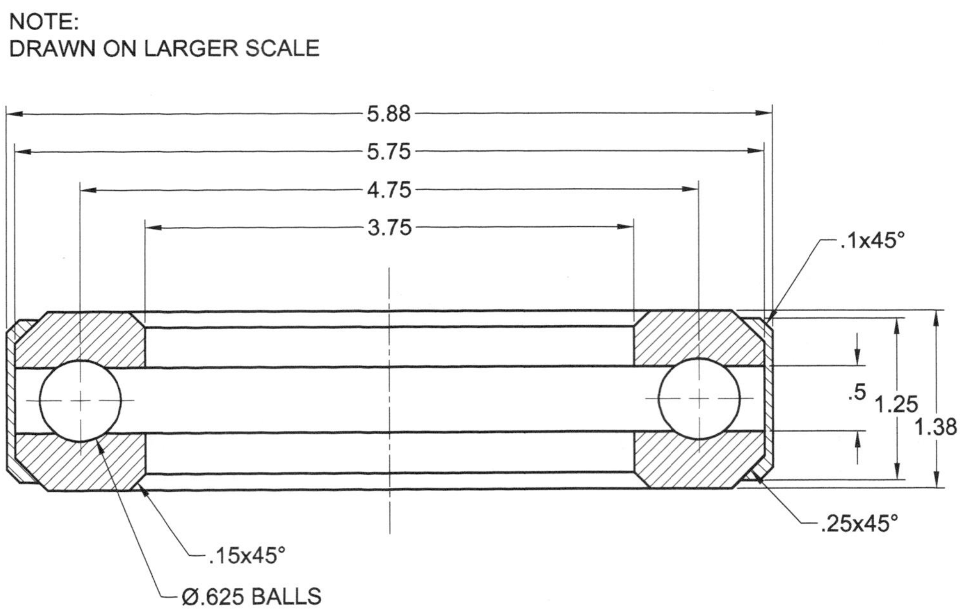

Figure 10-49 *Top and front views of the Thrust Bearing*

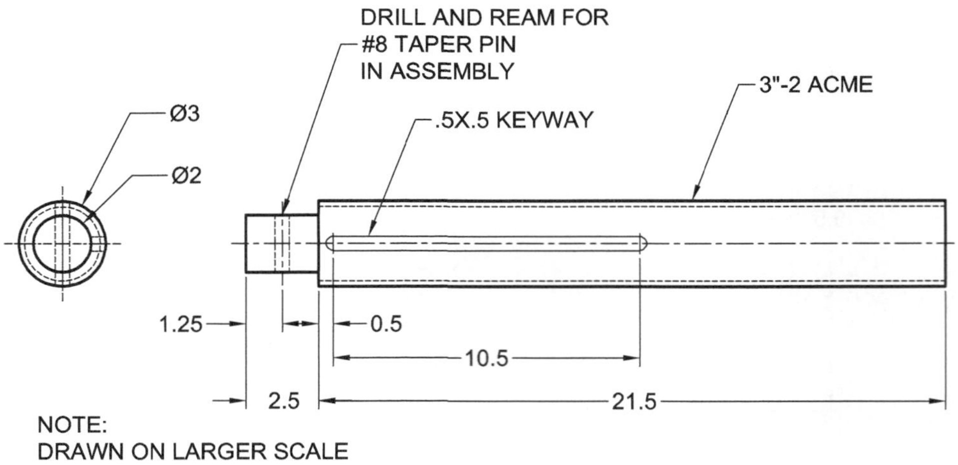

Figure 10-50 *Views of the Support Adjusting Screw*

Creating Assembly Components

1. Create all the components of the Stock Bracket assembly as separate part files. Specify the names of the files, refer to Figures 10-44 through 10-50. The files should be saved in *C:\Solid Edge\c10\Stock Bracket* folder.

   Make sure *Stock Bracket* is your current folder.

Starting a New Document in the Assembly Environment

1. Choose the **New** button from the **Quick Access** toolbar and choose **ANSI Inch** from the **Standard Templates** drop-down list. Then, double-click on the **ansi inch assembly.asm** template in the **New** dialog box to start a new assembly file.

Assembling the Base Component with the Reference Planes

As mentioned earlier, the first part that is placed in the assembly is called the base component. The base component generally does not undergo any motion relative to the other components in the assembly. This is because it is grounded.

1. Choose the **Parts Library** tab from the left pane; a docking window is displayed. 

2. Browse and open the *Stock Bracket* folder.

3. Double-click on the *Stock Support Base* in the docking window; the base component is assembled with the Base coordinate system and the **Ground** relationship is applied.

Assembling the Second Component

After assembling the base component, you need to assemble the second component which is *Thrust Bearing*.

1. Before placing the second component, choose **Setting > Options**; the **Solid Edge Options** dialog box is displayed. Choose the **Assembly** tab and then select the **Do not create** 

new window when placing component check box, if it is not already selected. Finally, choose the **OK** button.

2. Drag the *Thrust Bearing* into the assembly window from the docking window; the **Assemble** Command bar will be displayed.

   You will notice that the placement part is displayed in the same window as the target part, as shown in Figure 10-51.

3. Choose the **Options** button from the **Assemble** Command bar to display the **Options** dialog box.

4. Select the **Use FlashFit as the default placement method** and **Use Reduced Steps when placing parts** check boxes in the dialog box, if they are not already selected, and then exit the dialog box. Make sure that the **FlashFit** button is chosen from the **Relationship Types** flyout.

5. Select the top face of the *Thrust Bearing* and *Stock Support Base*; the two faces will be aligned. Choose the **Flip** button from the **Assemble** Command bar to flip the direction of alignment.

6. Select the cylindrical face of the *Thrust Bearing* and *Stock Support Base*, as shown in Figure 10-52.

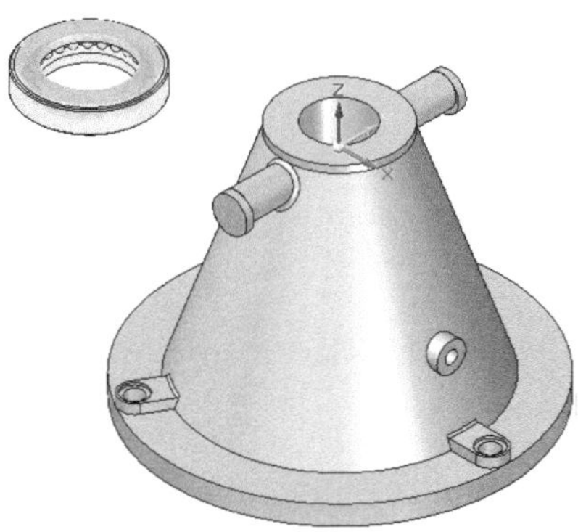

Figure 10-51 *Placement part and target part in the same window*

Figure 10-52 *The selected cylindrical face of the target part*

The placement part is constrained to the target part, as shown in Figure 10-53. You have already applied two relationships to the parts. Next, you need to make sure that the two parts are fully constrained.

7. Choose the **Relationship Types** button from the **Assemble** Command bar; the **Relationship Types** flyout is displayed. Choose the **Planar Align** button from it. 

   The **Planar Align** relationship is used to align the reference plane of the placement part with any of the parallel faces of the target part.

8. Choose the **Construction Display** button from the **Assemble** Command bar to display a flyout.

9. From this flyout, choose the **Show Reference Planes** button to display the reference planes of the placement part and choose the **Float** button from the **Offset Type** flyout of the Command bar.

10. Select the reference plane and the face of the target part, as shown in Figure 10-53.

    Now, the *Thrust Bearing* is fully constrained to the *Stock Support Base*. The assembly at this stage is shown in Figure 10-54.

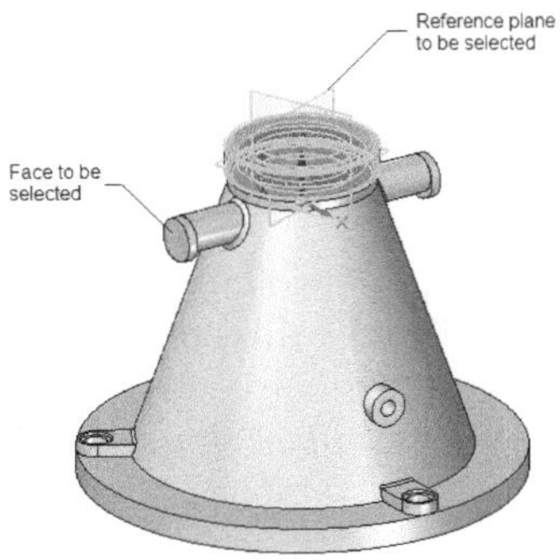

Figure 10-53 *Elements to be selected for aligning the reference plane and the face*

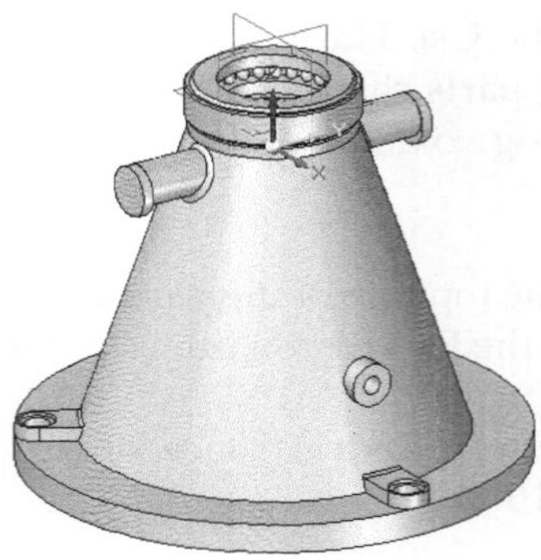

Figure 10-54 *Assembly after aligning the components*

Assembling the Third Component

After assembling the second component, you need to assemble the *Adjusting Screw Nut*, which is the third component.

1. Drag the *Adjusting Screw Nut* into the assembly window; the placement part is displayed in the assembly window.

2. Choose the **Relationship Types** button from the **Assemble** Command bar to display a flyout. Next, choose the **Insert** button from the flyout. Note that the **Insert** relationship uses two constraints, **Axial Align** and **Mate**.

3. Spin the placement part and select the cylindrical face, as shown in Figure 10-55.

   Now, you need to select the corresponding element on the target part.

4. Select the inner cylindrical face of *Thrust Bearing,* as shown in Figure 10-56. On doing so, the **Axial** constraint is applied.

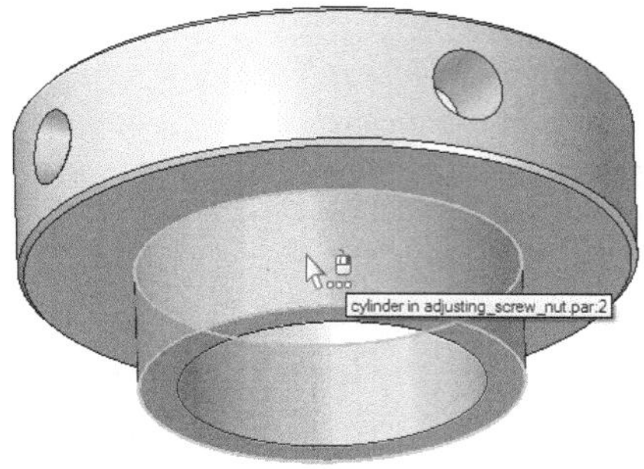

Figure 10-55 *Face to be selected for applying the **Axial** relation*

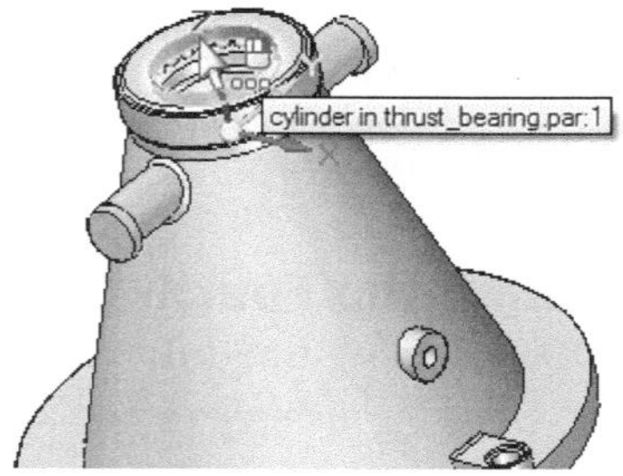

Figure 10-56 *Face to be selected for applying the **Axial** relation*

5. Next, select the face on the placement part, as shown in Figure 10-57.

6. Select the top face of the *Thrust Bearing*, refer to Figure 10-58. On doing so, the **Mate** relationship is applied. The *Adjusting Screw Nut* is assembled with the *Thrust Bearing* in the assembly, as shown in Figure 10-59.

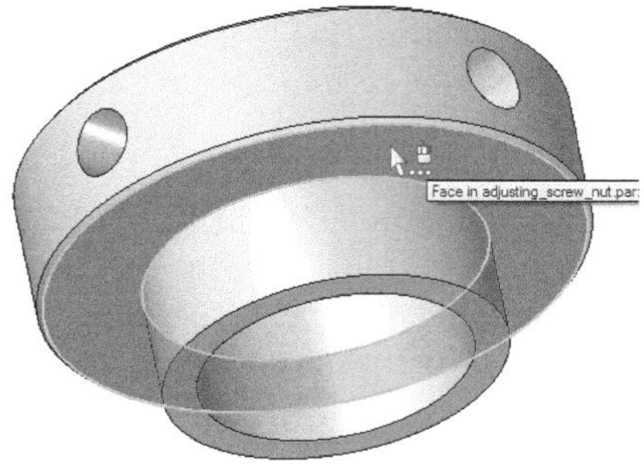

Figure 10-57 *Face to be selected for applying the **Mate** relation*

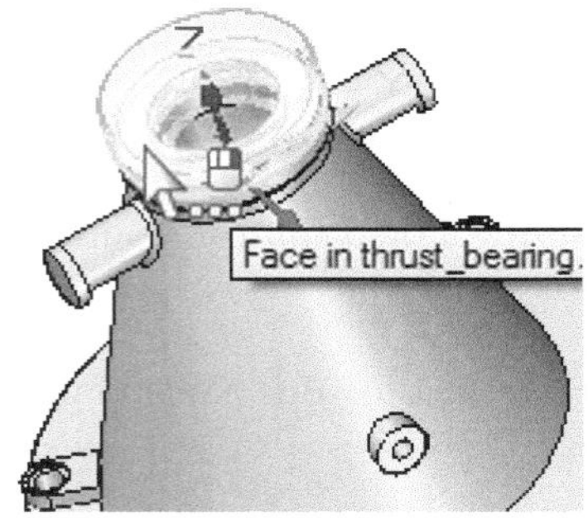

Figure 10-58 *Top face to be selected for applying the **Mate** relation*

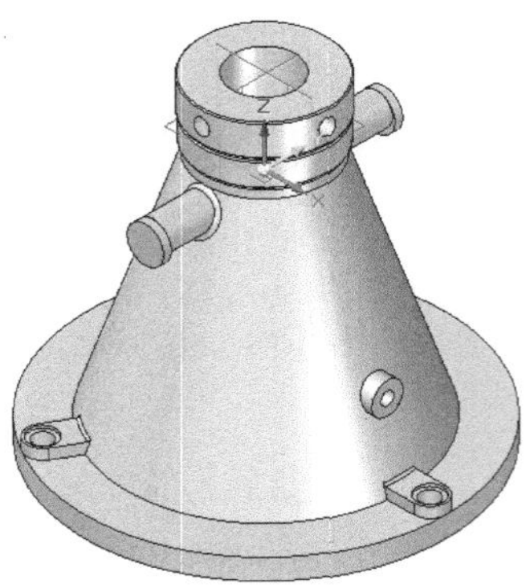

Figure 10-59 *The assembly after assembling three components*

Tip

*Generally, three assembly relationships are needed to fully constrain or fully position a component with respect to the other component. The **Insert** relationship uses two relationships and assumes the third relationship. The third relationship will lock the rotatory movement of the component. This rotatory movement can be unlocked by editing the **Insert** relationship.*

Assembling the Fourth Component

After assembling the third component, you need to assemble the fourth component which is the *Support Adjusting Screw*.

1. From the docking window, drag the *Support Adjusting Screw* into the assembly window; the placement part is displayed in the assembly window.
2. Choose the **Axial Align** button from the **Relationship Types** flyout. 
3. Select any of the cylindrical faces of the placement part that are recently displayed in the assembly window.
4. Now, select the central hole in the *Adjusting Screw Nut*. You will notice that the placement part has moved inside the assembly and is partially displayed.
5. Choose the **Planar Align** button from the **Relationship Types** flyout.
6. Choose the **Fixed** button from the **Offset Type** flyout and enter **-1.5** in the **Offset Value** edit box displayed.
7. Select the face of the placement part and then the face of the target part, as shown in Figure 10-60.
8. Choose the **Construction Display** button from the Command bar to display a flyout. 
9. From this flyout, choose the **Show Reference Planes** button, if it is not already chosen. Notice that the reference planes of the placement part are displayed.
10. Choose the **Float** button from the **Offset Type** flyout in the Command bar. 
11. Select the reference plane and the face of the target part, as shown in Figure 10-61. Make sure that the keyway in the *Support Adjusting Screw* is oriented towards the *Adjusting Screw Guide* hole of the *Stock Support Base*. To do so choose, the **Flip** button in the Command bar.

Note

*If you are unable to select any of the reference planes, open the component in the **Part** environment. Select the check boxes of the respective planes from the **PathFinder**. Now, you can select the **Reference Planes** node from the **Assembly** environment.*

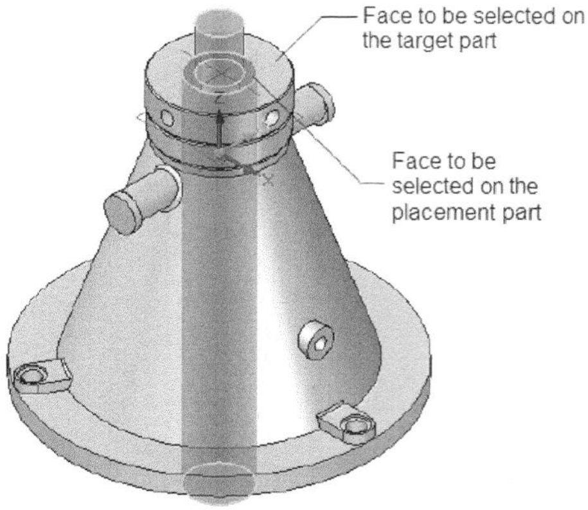

Figure 10-60 Elements to be selected for aligning the two parts

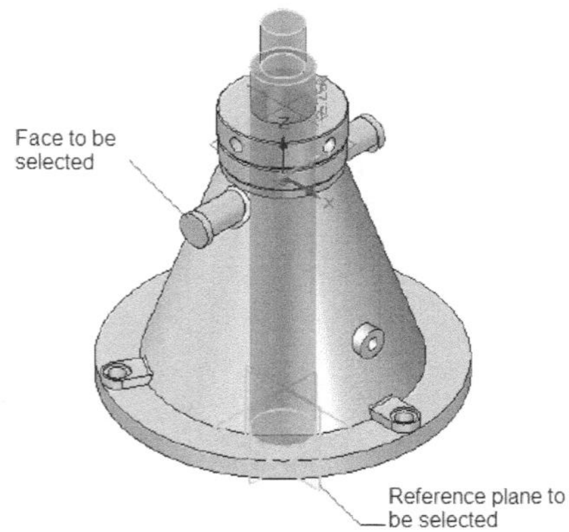

Figure 10-61 Reference plane of the placement part and the face of the target part

The *Support Adjusting Screw* is fully constrained to the assembly. The assembly at this stage looks like the one shown in Figure 10-62.

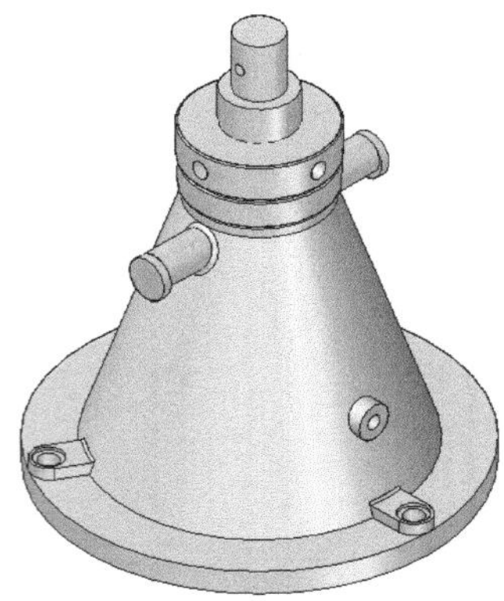

Figure 10-62 Assembly after assembling the four components

Assembling the Fifth Component

The fifth component to be assembled is the *Support Roller Bracket*.

1. Drag the *Support Roller Bracket* from the docking window into the assembly window; the placement part is displayed in the assembly window.
2. Choose the **Axial Align** button from the **Relationship Types** flyout.
3. Select the cylindrical face of the hole in the *Support Roller Bracket* and then select the cylindrical face of the *Support Adjusting Screw,* as shown in Figure 10-63. You will notice that the placement part is moved inside the assembly and is partially placed, as shown in Figure 10-64.
4. Choose the **Mate** button from the **Relationship Types** flyout.

5. Select the cylindrical face of the hole in the *Support Roller Bracket* and then select the cylindrical face of the hole of the target part, as shown in Figure 10-65.

The assembly after assembling the parts is shown in Figure 10-66 and the *Support Roller Bracket* is fully constrained to the assembly.

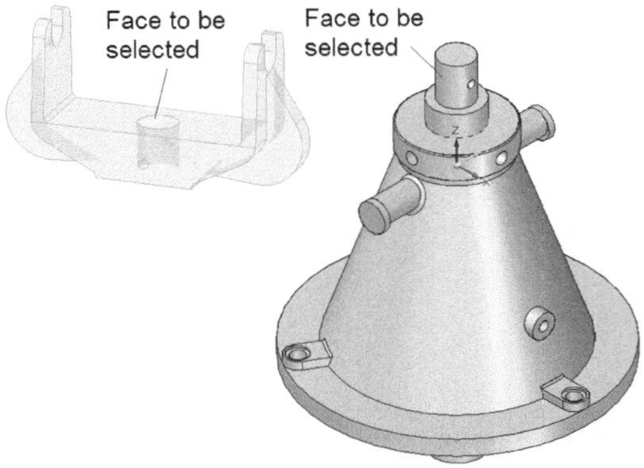

Figure 10-63 Elements to be selected for mating the two faces

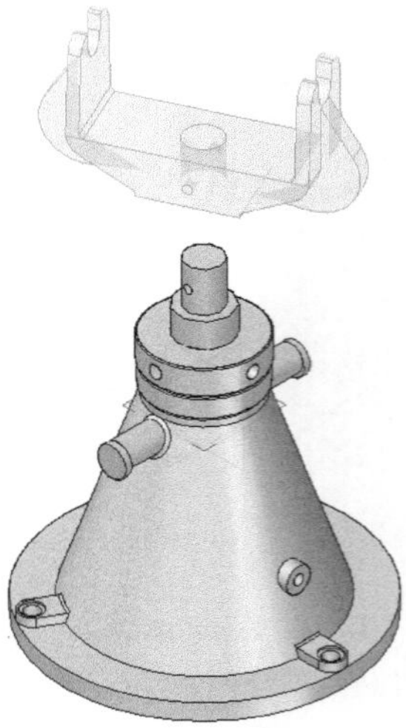

Figure 10-64 Assembly after mating the components

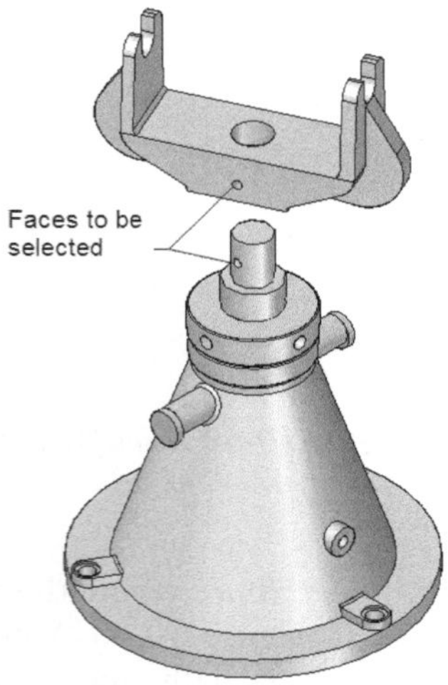

Figure 10-65 Faces to be selected for aligning

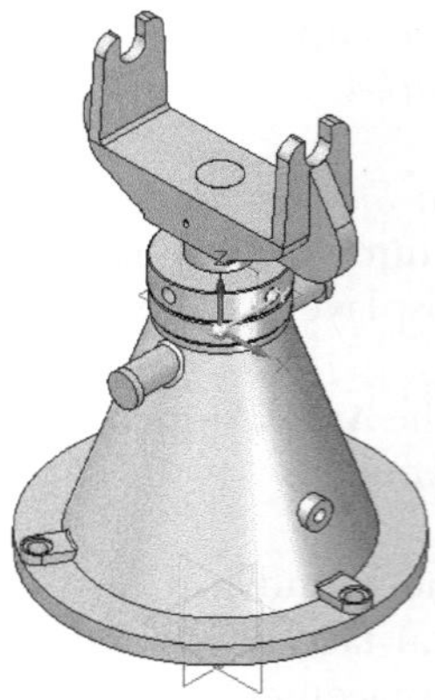

Figure 10-66 Assembly after assembling the Support Roller Bracket

Assembling the Sixth Component

Next, you need to assemble the sixth component, which is the *Stock Support Roller*.

1. Drag the *Stock Support Roller* from the docking window into the assembly window; the placement part is displayed in the assembly window.

2. Choose the **Axial Align** button from the **Relationship Types** flyout.

3. Choose the **Lock Rotation** button from the Command bar.

4. Select the cylindrical face of the placement part, as shown in Figure 10-67. Next, select the cylindrical face of the target part, as shown in Figure 10-68.

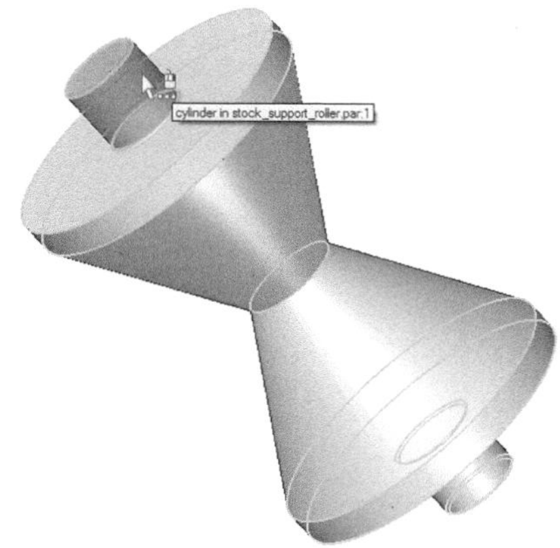

Figure 10-67 *Cylindrical face on the placement part to be selected for aligning the axes*

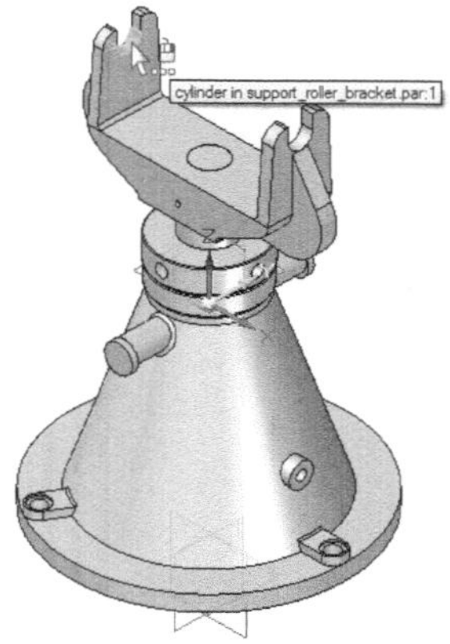

Figure 10-68 *Cylindrical face on the target part to be selected for aligning the axes*

The placement part is partially constrained with the assembly, as shown in Figure 10-69.

5. Choose the **Mate** button from the **Relationship Types** flyout.

6. Select the faces to mate, as shown in Figure 10-70. The *Stock Support Roller* is fully constrained to the assembly, refer to Figure 10-71. You can check the symbol in the **PathFinder** which shows that the *Stock Support Roller* is fully constrained.

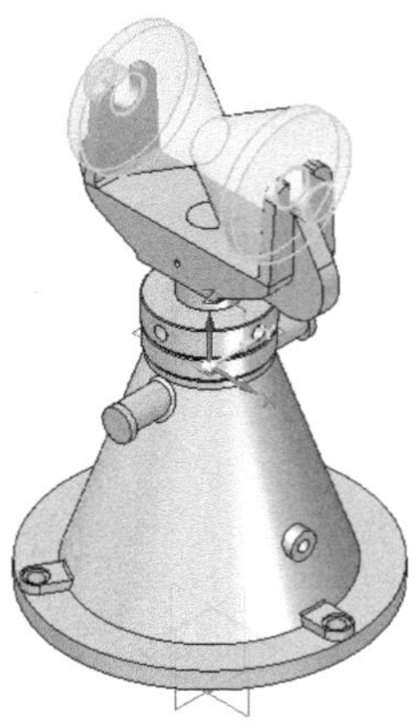

Figure 10-69 *Partially positioned assembly*

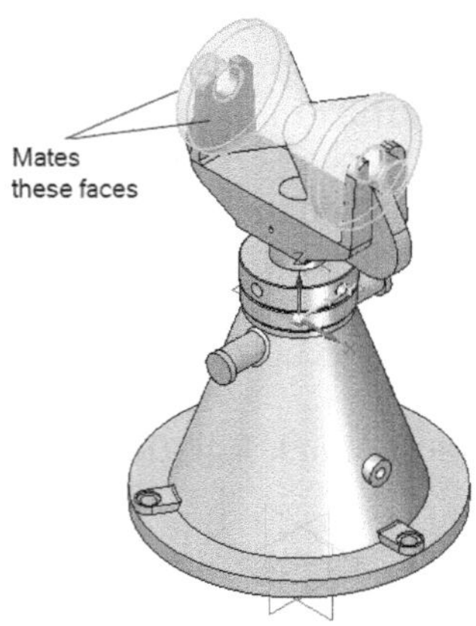

Figure 10-70 *Elements to be selected for mating*

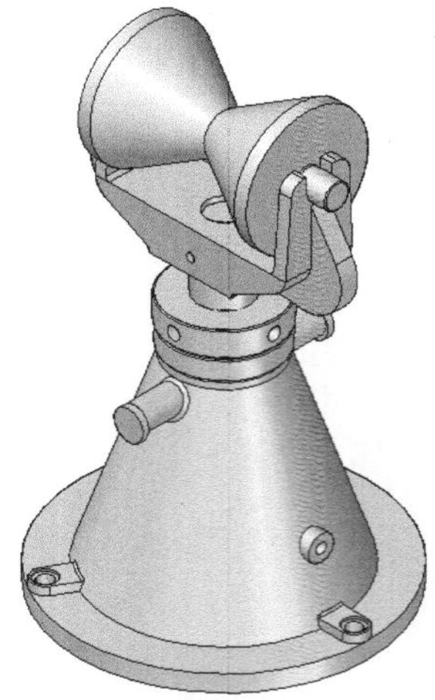

Figure 10-71 *Fully constrained assembly*

Assembling the Seventh Component

Next, you need to assemble the seventh component which is the *Adjusting Nut Handle*. After assembling one instance of the *Adjusting Nut Handle*, you will create its pattern to create the remaining instances. However, before proceeding further, you need to turn on the display of the reference planes of the *Adjusting Screw Nut* in the **PathFinder**. These planes will be used to assemble the *Adjusting Nut Handle*.

1. Right-click on the *Adjusting Screw Nut* in the **PathFinder** and then choose **Show/Hide Component**; the **Show/Hide Component** dialog box is displayed. In this dialog box, select the **On** check box next to the **Reference Planes** and choose **OK** to display the reference planes in the graphics window.

2. Double-click on the *Adjusting Nut Handle* in the **Parts Library**; the placement part is displayed in the assembly window.

3. Choose the **Axial Align** button from the **Relationship Types** flyout.

4. Choose the **Lock Rotation** button from the Command bar.

5. Select the cylindrical face of the *Adjusting Nut Handle*.

6. Select the cylindrical face of any of the holes in the *Adjusting Screw Nut*. Notice that the placement part is partially constrained to the assembly. Next, you will select the faces to mate.

   Remember that the end face of the placement part should be assembled at an offset distance of **2.1** from the center of the assembly.

7. Choose the **Mate** button from the **Relationship Types** flyout.

8. Choose the **Fixed** button from the Command bar and enter **2.1** in the **Offset Value** edit box displayed.

9. Select the right end face of the *Adjusting Nut Handle* and then select the reference plane of the *Adjusting Screw Nut* that is parallel to the selected surface, refer to Figure 10-72.

10. Turn off the display of the reference planes by right-clicking on the component and choosing **Show/Hide Components > Reference Planes** option from the shortcut menu displayed.

    The *Adjusting Nut Handle* is assembled with the assembly, refer to Figure 10-72. Also, one instance of the *Adjusting Screw Nut* is assembled in the assembly.

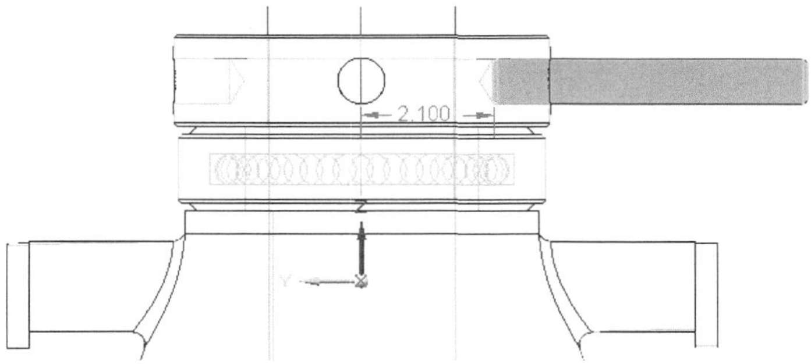

Figure 10-72 *The Adjusting Nut Handle assembled with the assembly*

Creating the Pattern

You need to create the pattern of the *Adjusting Screw Nut* to assemble the remaining instances.

1. Choose the **Pattern** tool from the **Pattern** group; the **Pattern** Command bar is displayed and you are prompted to select the parts to be included in the pattern.

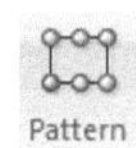

2. Select the *Adjusting Nut Handle* from the assembly and choose the **Accept** button from the Command bar; you are prompted to select the part or the sketch that contains the pattern. This is because Solid Edge will reference the part to be patterned with the existing pattern.

3. Select the *Adjusting Screw Nut* from the assembly; you are prompted to select a pattern.

4. Select the existing pattern by selecting any one of the highlighted holes; you are prompted to click on a reference feature in the pattern. The reference feature is the hole that was the source while the pattern was being created on the part.

5. Select the hole that is highlighted when you move the cursor over it.

Note

*You do not need to select the reference hole if the pattern is created in the **Synchronous Part** environment. The component will show the preview directly after selecting the pattern feature.*

6. Choose the **Finish** button from the Command bar; the pattern is created, as shown in Figure 10-73.

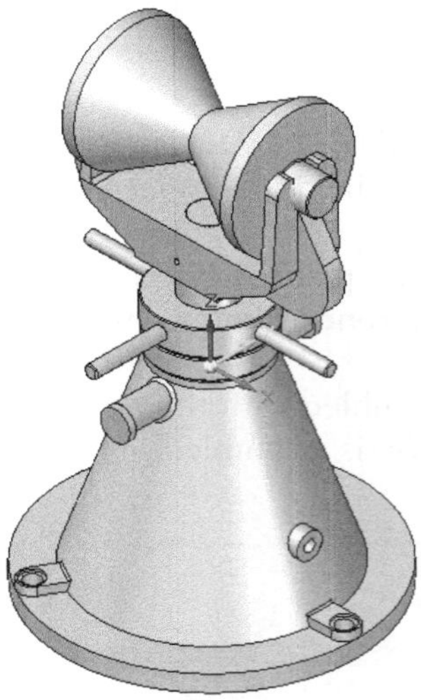

Figure 10-73 *Assembly after creating the pattern*

Assembling the Last Component

Finally, you will assemble the *Adjusting Screw Guide* with the *Stock Support Base*.

1. Drag the *Adjusting Screw Guide* from the docking window into the assembly window.

2. Choose the **Insert** button from the **Relationship Types** flyout.

Remember that the **Insert** relationship uses two constraints, **Mate** and **Axial Align**.

3. Select the cylindrical face of the *Adjusting Screw Guide,* refer to Figure 10-74.

4. Select the cylindrical face of the hole that is on the protruded feature created on the inclined surface of the *Stock Support Base*, as shown in Figure 10-75.

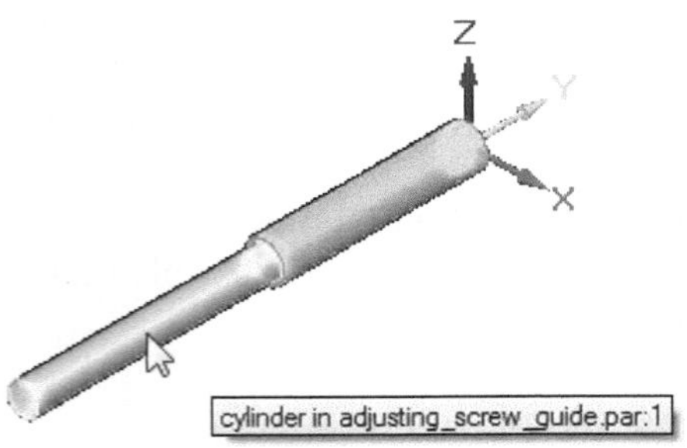

Figure 10-74 *Cylindrical face of the screw to be selected for applying the* ***Mate*** *relationship*

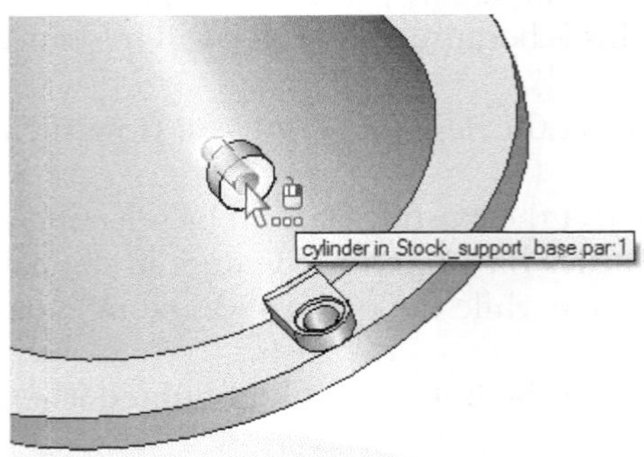

Figure 10-75 *Cylindrical face of the hole to be selected for applying the* ***Mate*** *relationship*

5. Select the faces on the placement part and the bottom face of the keyway in the *Support Adjusting Screw*, as shown in Figures 10-76 and 10-77.

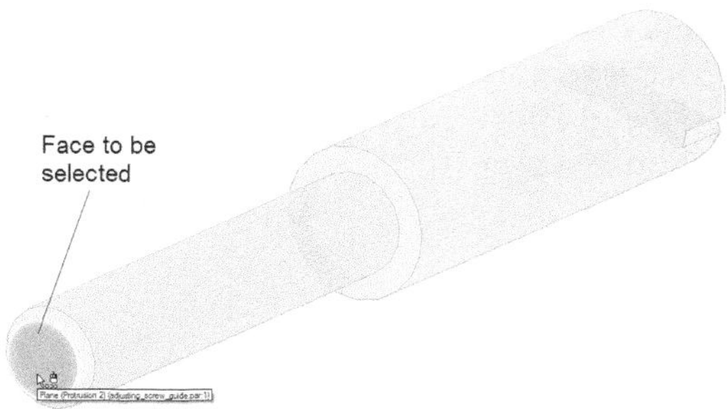

Figure 10-76 *Face to be selected for applying the* ***Mate*** *relationship*

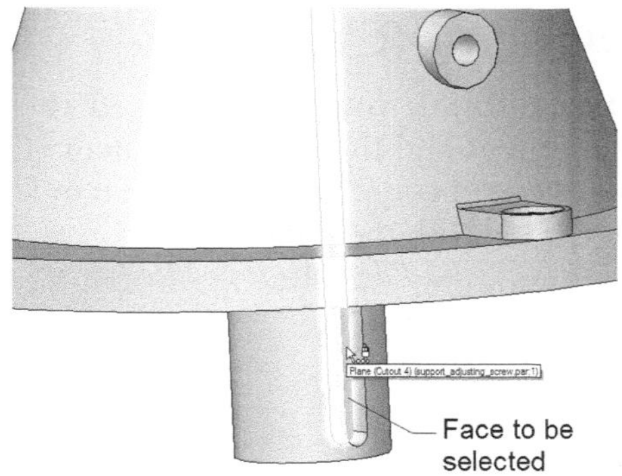

Figure 10-77 *Face to be selected for applying the* ***Mate*** *relationship*

The *Adjusting Screw Nut* is assembled with the assembly, as shown in Figure 10-78.

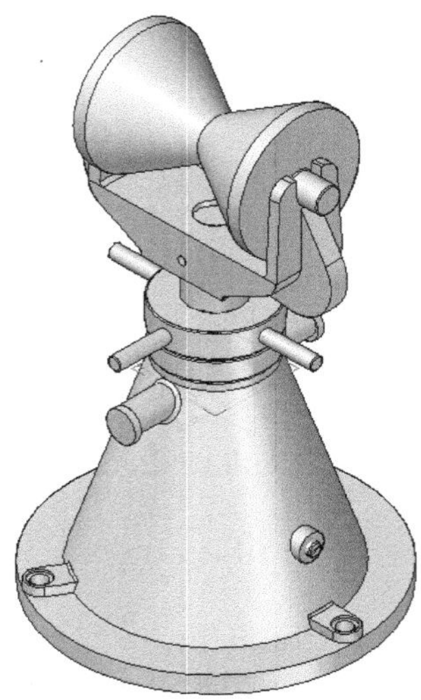

Figure 10-78 *Complete assembly of the Stock Bracket*

Saving the File

1. Choose the **Save** button from the **Quick Access** toolbar to display the **Save As** dialog box.

2. Enter the name of the assembly as **Stock Bracket** and choose the **Save** button to exit the dialog box.

3. Choose **Application Button > Close** to close the file.

Tutorial 2

In this tutorial, you will create all the components of a Pipe Vice assembly in the **Part** environment and then assemble them. The Pipe Vice assembly is shown in Figure 10-79. The dimensions of components are given in Figures 10-80 and 10-81. After completing the tutorial, save the file with the name *Pipe Vice.asm* at the location given next:

C:\Solid Edge\c10\Pipe Vice **(Expected time: 2 hr)**

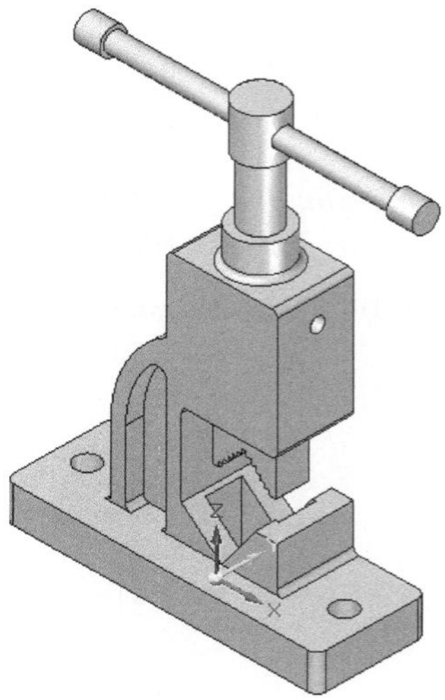

Figure 10-79 *Pipe Vice assembly*

The following steps are required to complete this tutorial:

a. Create all components in individual part files and save them. The part files will be saved at *C:\Solid Edge\c10\Pipe Vice*.
b. Start a new file in the **Assembly** environment.
c. Drag the Base into the assembly window. This component will be automatically assembled with the reference planes using the **Ground** relationship.
d. Drag the Screw into the assembly window and apply the required relationships, refer to Figures 10-82 through 10-87.
e. Drag the Moveable Jaw into the assembly window and apply the required relationships, refer to Figures 10-88 and 10-90.
f. Drag the Handle into the assembly window and apply the required relationships, refer to Figures 10-91 and 10-92.
g. Drag the Handle Screw into the assembly window and apply the required relationships, refer to Figures 10-93 and10-95. Similarly, assemble the other instance of the Handle Screw, refer to Figure 10-96.
h. Save the file.

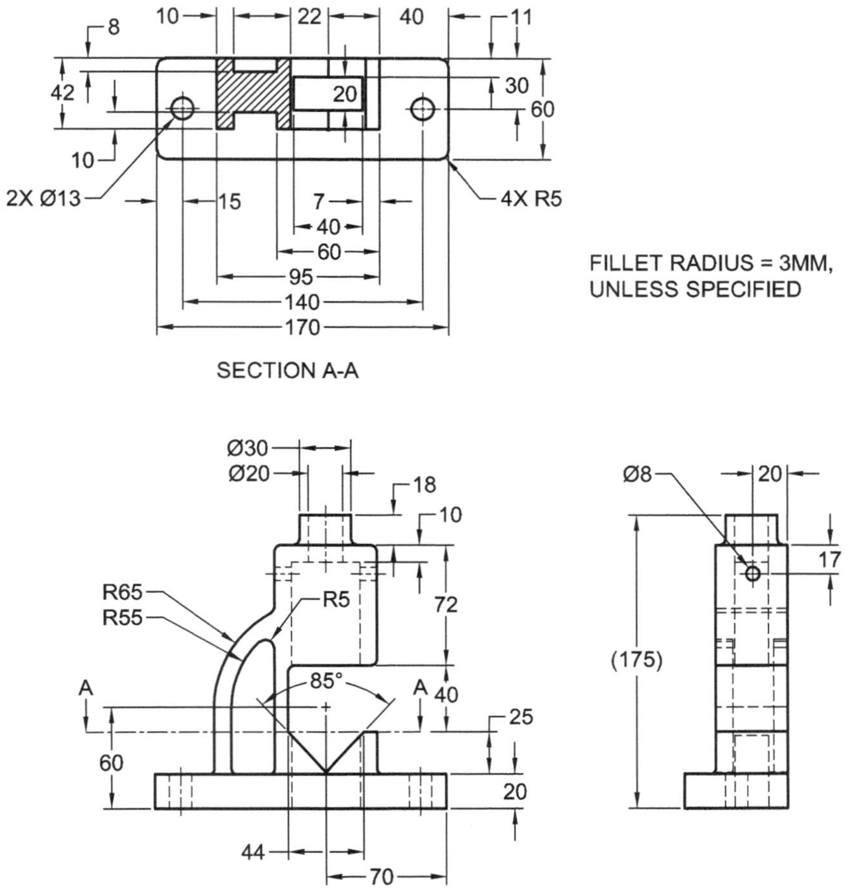

Figure 10-80 Views and dimensions of the Base

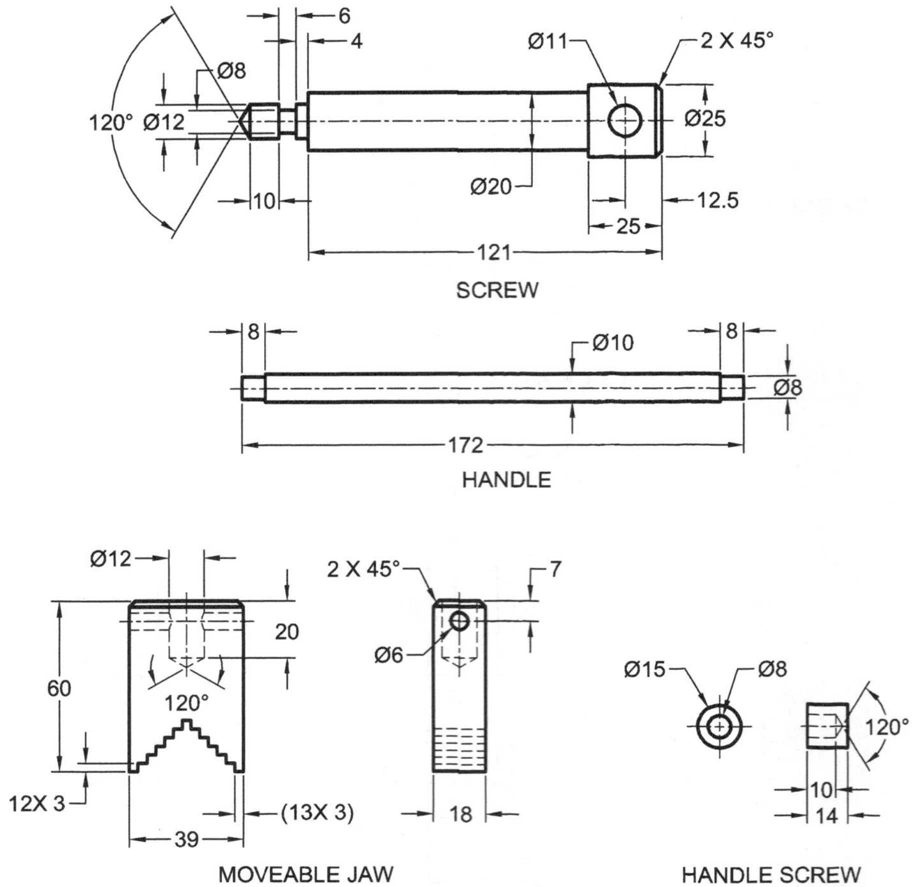

Figure 10-81 Views and dimensions of the Screw, Handle, Moveable Jaw, and Handle Screw

Creating Assembly Components

1. Create all the components of the Pipe Vice assembly as separate part files in the part environment. Specify the names of files, as shown in Figures 10-80 and 10-81. The files should be saved at *C:\Solid Edge\c10\Pipe Vice*. Make sure the *Pipe Vice* is your current folder.

Starting the Solid Edge Session in the Assembly Environment

1. Choose the **New** button from the **Quick Access** toolbar and choose **ISO Metric** from the **Standard templates** drop-down list. Then, double-click on the **iso metric assembly.asm** template to start a new assembly file.

Assembling the Base Component with Reference Planes

As mentioned earlier, the first part that you place in the assembly is called the base component.

1. Choose the **Parts Library** button from the docking window.

2. Browse and open the *Pipe Vice* folder.

3. Double-click on the *Base* in the docking window to assemble the base component with reference planes.

Assembling the Second Component

After assembling the base component, you need to assemble the second component which is a Screw.

1. Before placing the second component, choose **Application Button > Settings > Options**; the **Solid Edge Options** dialog box is displayed. Choose the **Assembly** tab and then select the **Do not create new window when placing component** check box, if it is not already selected. Next, choose the **OK** button.

2. Drag the *Screw* from the docking window into the assembly window.

3. Choose the **Axial Align** button from the **Relationship Types** flyout.

4. Select the cylindrical face on the *Screw*, as shown in Figure 10-82.

5. Select the cylindrical face of the hole that is in the top cylindrical feature of the *Base*, as shown in Figure 10-83.

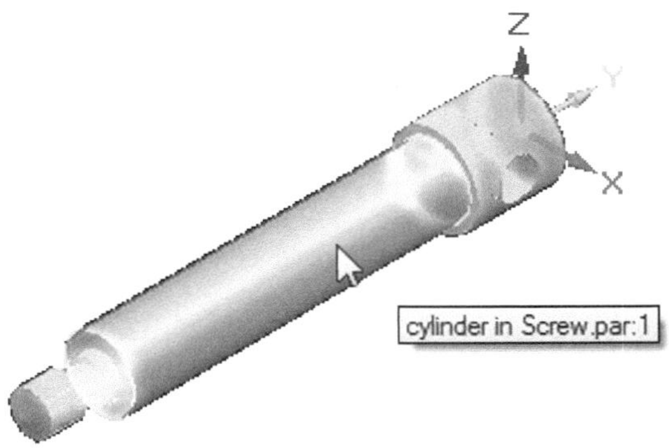

Figure 10-82 *Face of the screw to be selected for applying the* ***Axial*** *relationship*

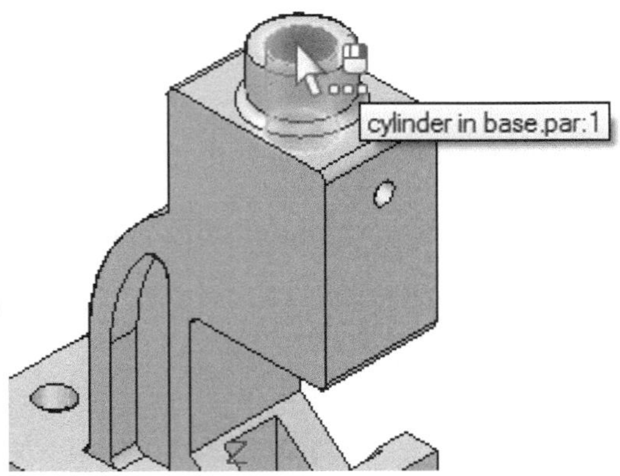

Figure 10-83 *Face of the hole to be selected for applying the* ***Axial*** *relationship*

6. Choose the **Mate** button from the **Relationship Types** flyout. Choose the **Fixed** button from the **Offset Type** flyout and enter **35** in the **Offset Value** edit box.

7. Select the face on the *Screw*, as shown in Figure 10-84.

8. Select the face on the top face of the *Base* corresponding to the face selected on the *Screw*, as shown in Figure 10-85. The *Screw* is assembled with the *Base* in the assembly.

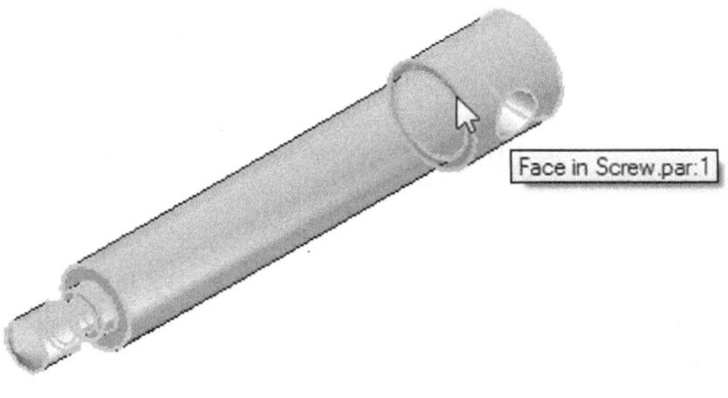

Figure 10-84 Face of the screw to be selected for applying the ***Mate*** *relationship*

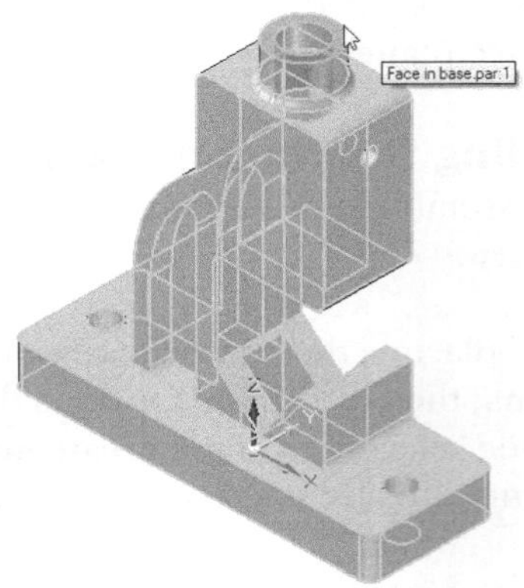

Figure 10-85 Face of the hole to be selected for applying the ***Mate*** *relationship*

9. Choose the **Mate** button from the **Relationship Types** flyout, if it is not already chosen.
10. Choose the **Construction Display** button from the **Assemble** Command bar to display a flyout.
11. Choose the **Show Reference Planes** button from the flyout to display the reference planes of the placement part.

12. Choose the **Float** button from the **Relationship** Command bar.
13. Select the reference plane and the face of the *Base*, as shown in Figure 10-86.

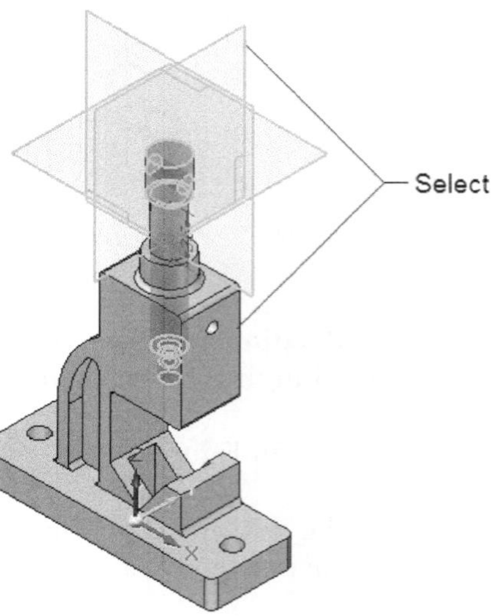

Figure 10-86 Reference plane and the face to be selected

The two components are assembled, as shown in Figure 10-87.

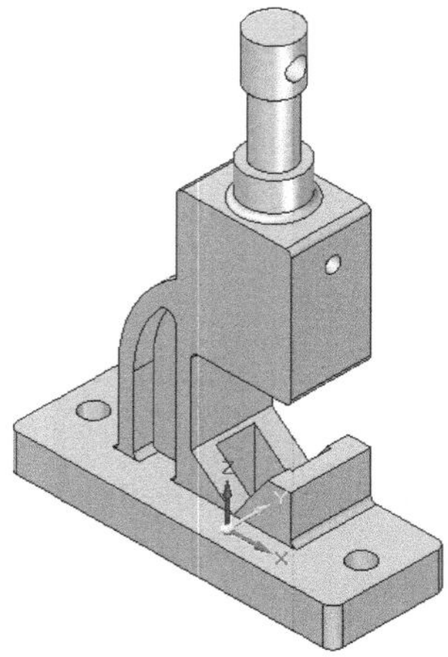

Figure 10-87 *Two components assembled*

Note

*You can also use the **Insert** option instead of the **Mate** and **Axial Align** options for aligning two components.*

Assembling the Third Component

Now, you need to assemble the third component which is the *Moveable Jaw*.

Before placing the component, you need to hide the Base component and show the reference plane of screw.

1. Clear the check box beside the Base component node in the **PathFinder**.

2. Right-click on the *Screw* in the **PathFinder** and then choose **Show/Hide Component**; the **Show/Hide Component** dialog box is displayed. In this dialog box, select the **On** check box next to the **Reference Planes** and choose **OK** to display the reference planes in the graphics window.

3. Drag the *Moveable Jaw* from the **Parts Library** into the assembly window.

4. Choose the **Axial Align** button from the **Relationship Types** flyout.

5. Select the vertical cylindrical face of the hole in the *Moveable Jaw*.

6. Select the cylindrical face of the *Screw*. Next, you need to select the faces to mate.

7. Choose the **Mate** button from the **Relationship Types** flyout. Select the top face of the *Moveable Jaw* and then select the face of the *Screw*, as shown in Figure 10-88.

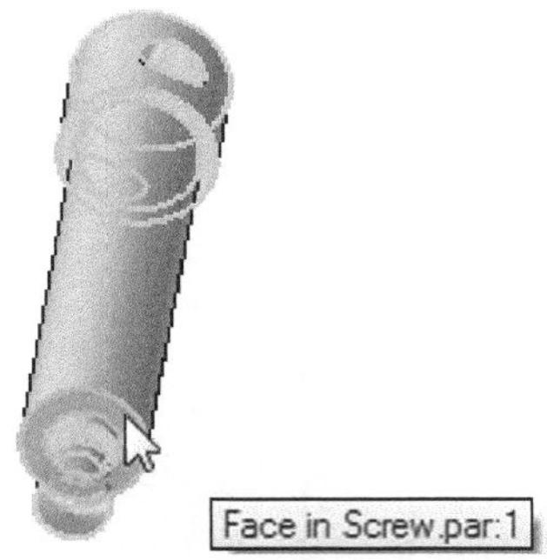

***Figure 10-88** Face to be selected for mating*

8. Choose the **Mate** button from the **Relationship Types**flyout, if it is not already chosen.

9. Choose the **Construction Display** button from the **Assemble** Command bar to display a flyout.

10. Choose the **Show Reference Planes** button from the flyout to display the reference planes of the placement part.

11. Choose the **Float** button from the **Assemble** Command bar.

12. Select the reference planes, as shown in Figure 10-89.

    The two components are assembled, as shown in Figure 10-90.

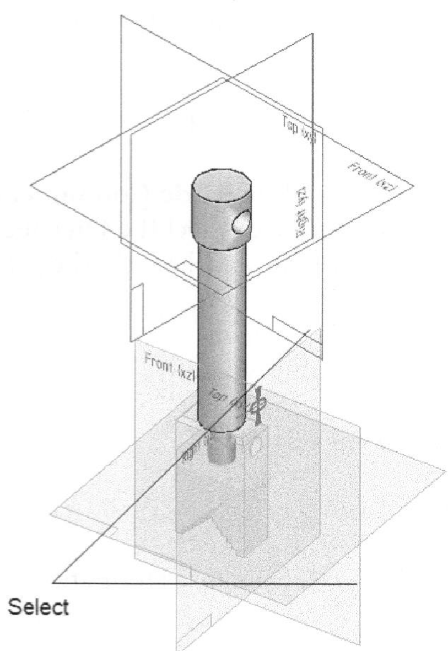

***Figure 10-89** Reference planes to be selected*

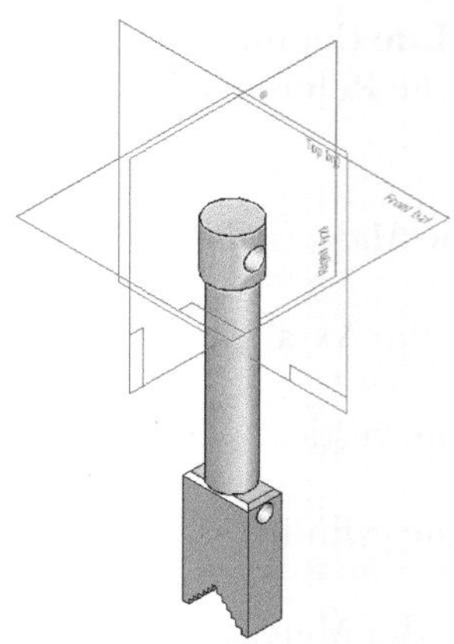

***Figure 10-90** Two components assembled*

13. Select the check box beside the Base component node in the **PathFinder** to display the Base.

Assembling the Handle

Next, you need to assemble the *Handle* with the *Screw*.

1. Drag the *Handle* from the docking window into the assembly window.
2. Choose the **Insert** button from the **Relationship Types** flyout. 
3. Select the cylindrical face of the *Handle*.
4. Next, select the cylindrical face of the hole in the *Screw* which is the second component.
5. Choose the **Construction Display** button from the **Assemble** Command bar to display a flyout.
6. Choose the **Show Reference Planes** button from the flyout. Notice that the reference planes of the placement part are displayed.
7. Select the reference plane, as shown in Figure 10-91.
8. Select the reference plane, as shown in Figure 10-92, to assemble the *Handle* with the *Screw*.

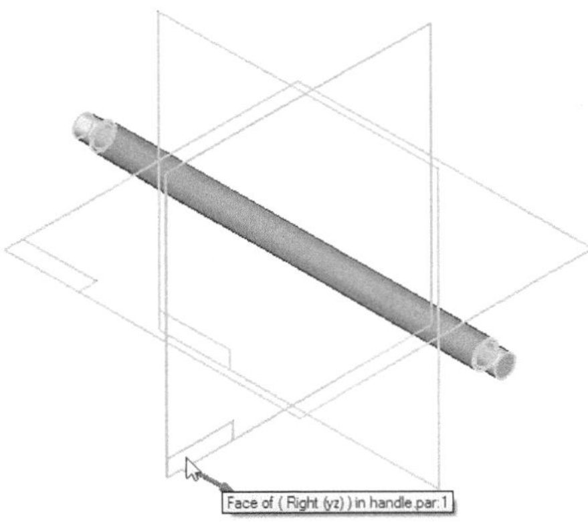

Figure 10-91 *Reference plane to be selected for mating*

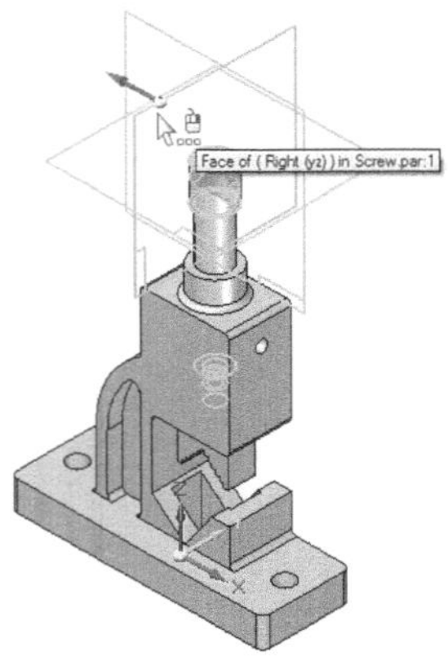

Figure 10-92 *Selecting the reference plane on the target part*

Note

To hide assembly reference planes, right-click on the component in the ***PathFinder*** *and then choose the* ***Show/Hide Component*** *from the shortcut menu displayed; the* ***Show/Hide Component*** *dialog box will be displayed. In this dialog box, select the* ***Off*** *check box corresponding to the* ***Reference Planes*** *and then choose the* ***OK*** *button.*

Assembling the Handle Screw

Next, you need to assemble the *Handle Screw* with the *Handle*.

1. Drag the *Handle Screw* from the docking window into the assembly window. 

2. Choose the **Insert** button from the **Relationship Types** flyout.

3. Select the cylindrical surface of the hole in the placement part and then select the cylindrical surface of the *Handle*.

   Next, you need to select the faces to mate.

4. Select the front face of the placement part, as shown in Figure 10-93. Next, select the face on the target part, as shown in Figure 10-94.

   The *Handle Screw* is assembled with the *Handle*, as shown in Figure 10-95.

5. Similarly, assemble the other instance of the *Handle Screw* at the other end of the *Handle*, refer to Figure 10-96.

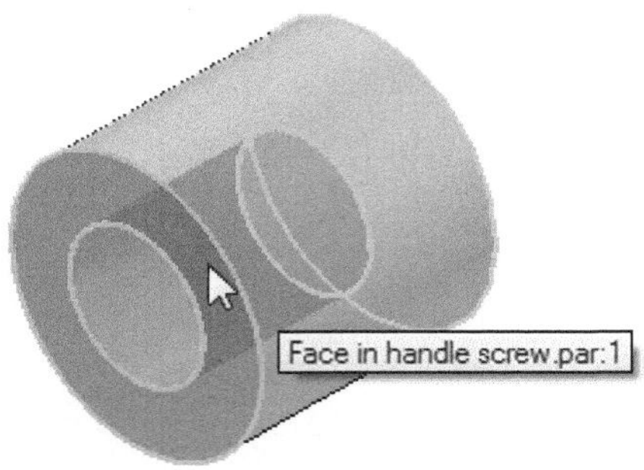

Figure 10-93 *Face to be selected on the placement part*

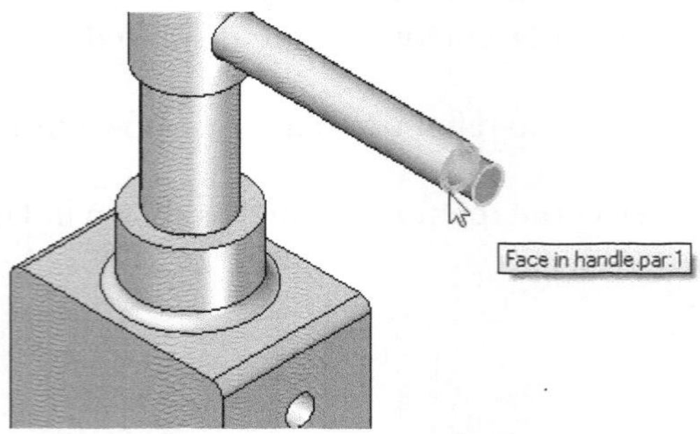

Figure 10-94 *Face to be selected in the target part*

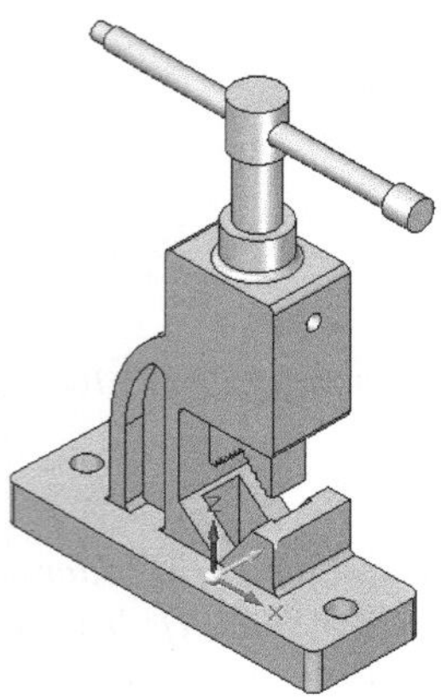

Figure 10-95 *Handle Screw assembled at one end of the Handle*

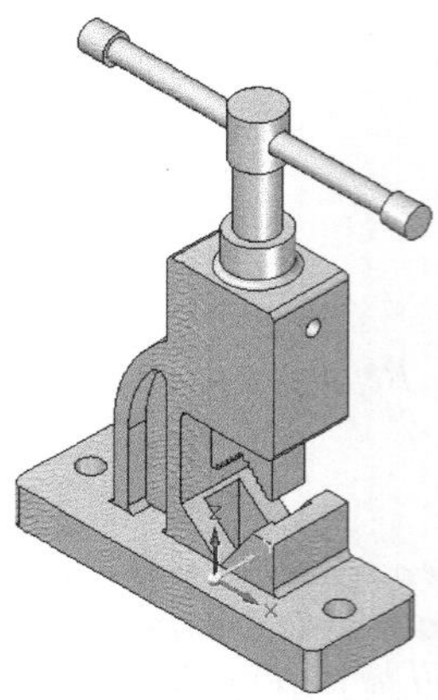

Figure 10-96 *Complete assembly*

Saving the File

1. Choose the **Save** button from the **Quick Access** toolbar to display the **Save As** dialog box.

2. Enter **Pipe Vice** as the name of the assembly and choose the **Save** button to exit the dialog box.

3. Choose **Application Button > Close** to close the file.

Self-Evaluation Test

Answer the following questions and then compare them to those given at the end of this chapter:

1. ___________ is the file extension of the files created in the **Assembly** environment of Solid Edge.
2. To create a reference pattern, choose the ___________ tool from the **Home** tab.
3. The first assembly relationship that you apply to the two parts in an assembly restricts certain ___________ of the two components.
4. The ___________ relationship combines the functions of both the **Mate** and **Axial Align** relationship.
5. In the top-down approach of an assembly design, all the components are created within the same assembly file. (T/F)
6. The **Axial Align** relationship is generally applied to make two faces coplanar. (T/F)
7. In Solid Edge, you can create parts in the **Assembly** environment. (T/F)
8. The base component is the first part that is placed in the assembly. (T/F)
9. The docking window is incorporated many times while assembling components. (T/F)
10. In Solid Edge, you can move an unconstrained or partially constrained component in the assembly without affecting the position and location of other components. (T/F)

Review Questions

Answer the following questions:

1. Which of the following buttons are used to make the Command bar available after applying a relationship?

   (a) **Help** (b) **Edit Definition**
   (c) **Common Views** (d) None of these

2. Which button in the **Relationship Types** flyout is used to constrain two keypoints on two parts?

   (a) **Parallel** (b) **Mate**
   (c) **Connect** (d) None of these

3. Which of the following relationships is used to apply the best possible constraint between the assembly parts automatically?

   (a) **Mate** (b) **Cam**
   (c) **Flash Fit** (d) None of these

4. Which of the following buttons is used to create a new part in the **Assembly** environment?

   (a) **Create In-Place** (b) **PathFinder**
   (c) **Standard Parts** (d) None of these

5. Once the relationships are applied to two parts, they cannot be edited. (T/F)

6. You cannot use the same relationships of a component to place another instance of the same component. (T/F)

7. The **Axial Align** relationship is used to align two axes. (T/F)

8. You cannot select the cylindrical surfaces to align the axes of two cylindrical parts. (T/F)

9. The reference planes of the individual components cannot be displayed while applying assembly relationships. (T/F)

10. You can move a part only in the direction that is not constrained. (T/F)

EXERCISES

Exercise 1

Create the Plummer Block assembly in the Assembly environment, as shown in Figure 10-97. The section view and bill of material of the assembly is shown in Figure 10-98. The dimensions of the components of the assembly are shown in Figures 10-99 through 10-101. You need to create components in the **Synchronous Part** environment. After completing the tutorial, save the file with the name *Plummer Block.asm* at the location given below:

C:\Solid Edge\c10\Plummer Block **(Expected time: 2 hr)**

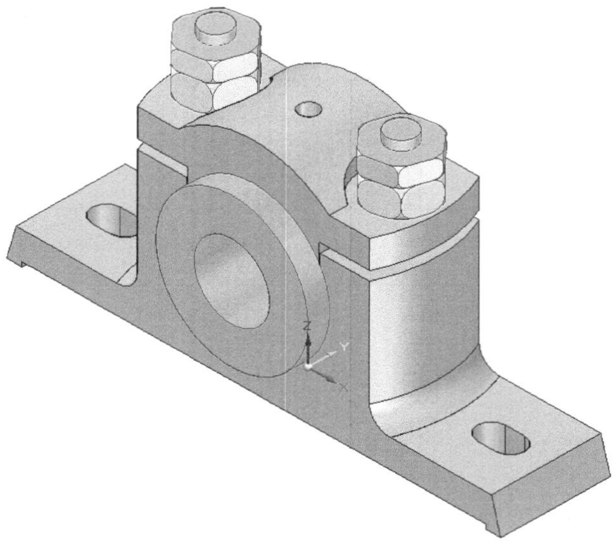

Figure 10-97 Plummer Block assembly

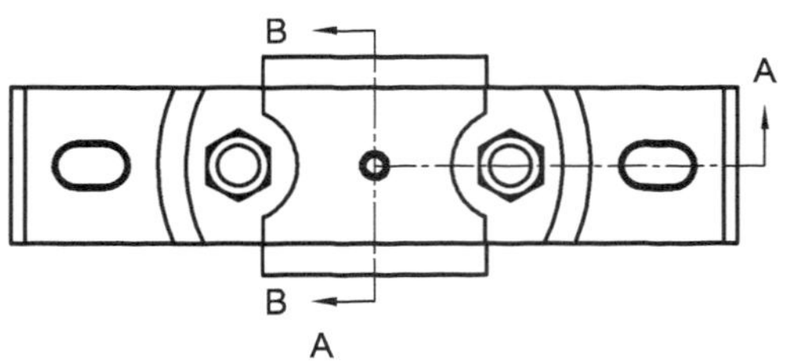

ITEM NO.	PART NO.	DESCRIPTION	QTY.
1	Casting		1
2	Cap		1
3	Bolt		2
4	Nut		2
5	Lock Nut		2
6	Brasses		1

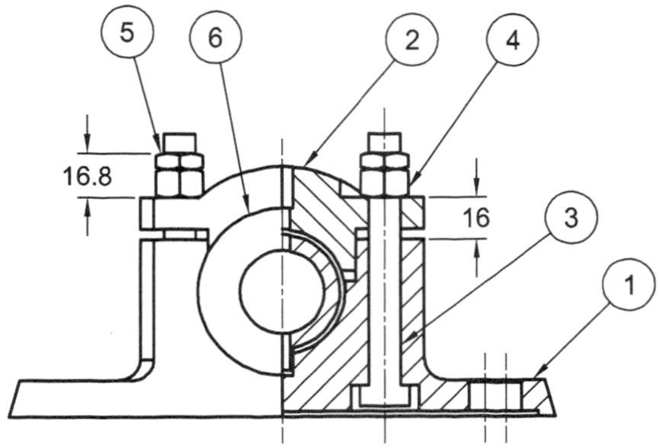

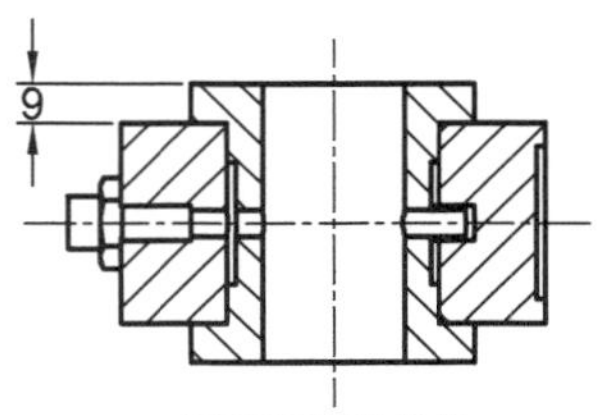

Figure 10-98 *Section view with balloons and Bill of Material of the assembly*

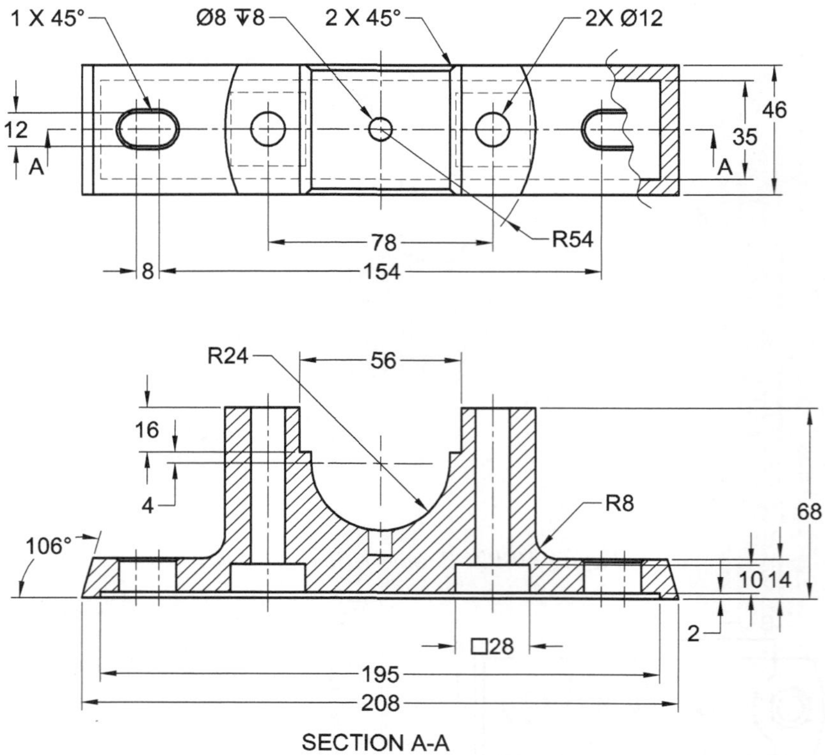

Figure 10-99 Views and dimensions of the Casting

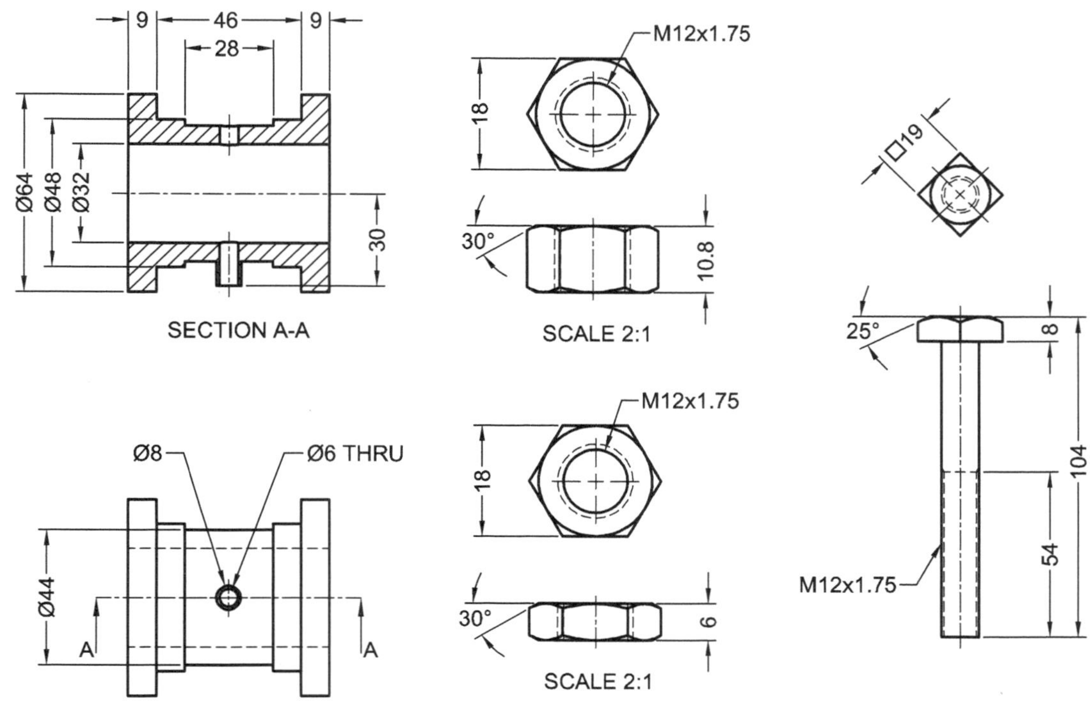

Figure 10-100 *Views and dimensions of the Brasses, Nut, Lock Nut, and Bolt*

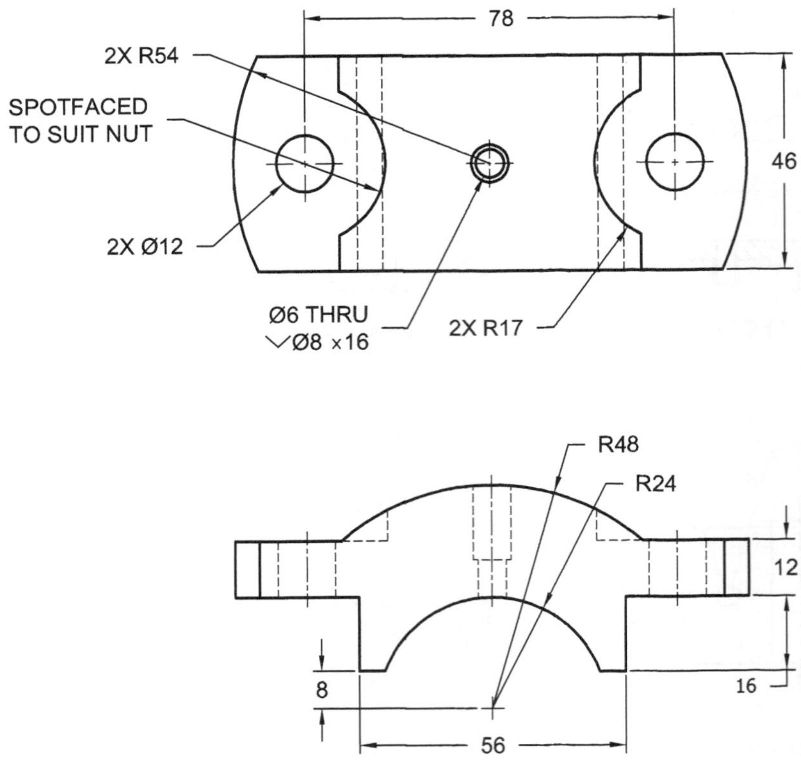

***Figure 10-101** Views and dimensions of the Cap*

Exercise 2

Create the Simple Eccentric assembly in the Assembly environment, as shown in Figure 10-102. The bill of material is shown in Figure 10-103 and the exploded view of the assembly is shown in Figure 10-104. The dimensions of the components of the assembly are shown in Figures 10-105 through 10-109. You need to create components in the **Synchronous Part** environment. After completing the tutorial, save the file with the name *Eccentrics.asm* at the location given next:

C:\Solid Edge\c10\Eccentrics **(Expected time: 2 hr)**

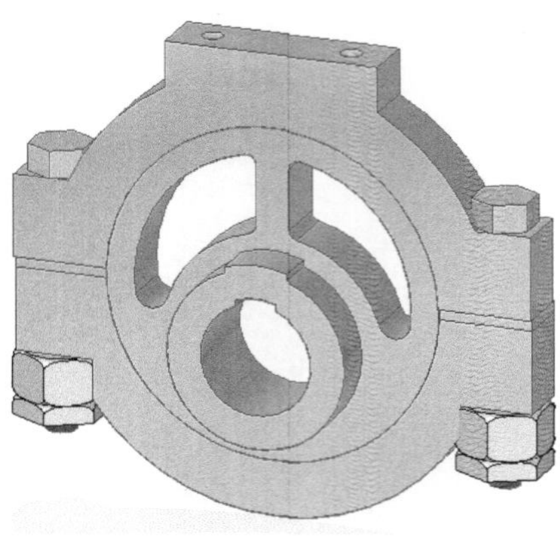

***Figure 10-102** Simple Eccentric assembly*

NUMBER	NAME	QUANTITY
1	BOTTOM STRAP	1
2	PACKING	2
3	SHEAVE	1
4	TOP STRAP	1
5	BOLT	2
6	NUT	2

Figure 10-103 *Bill of Material*

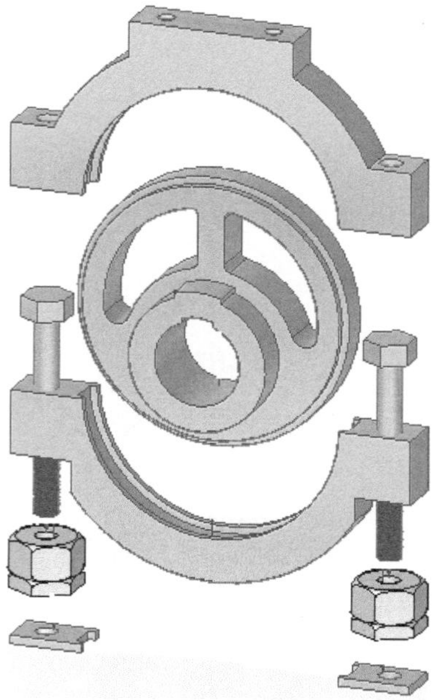

Figure 10-104 *Exploded view of the assembly*

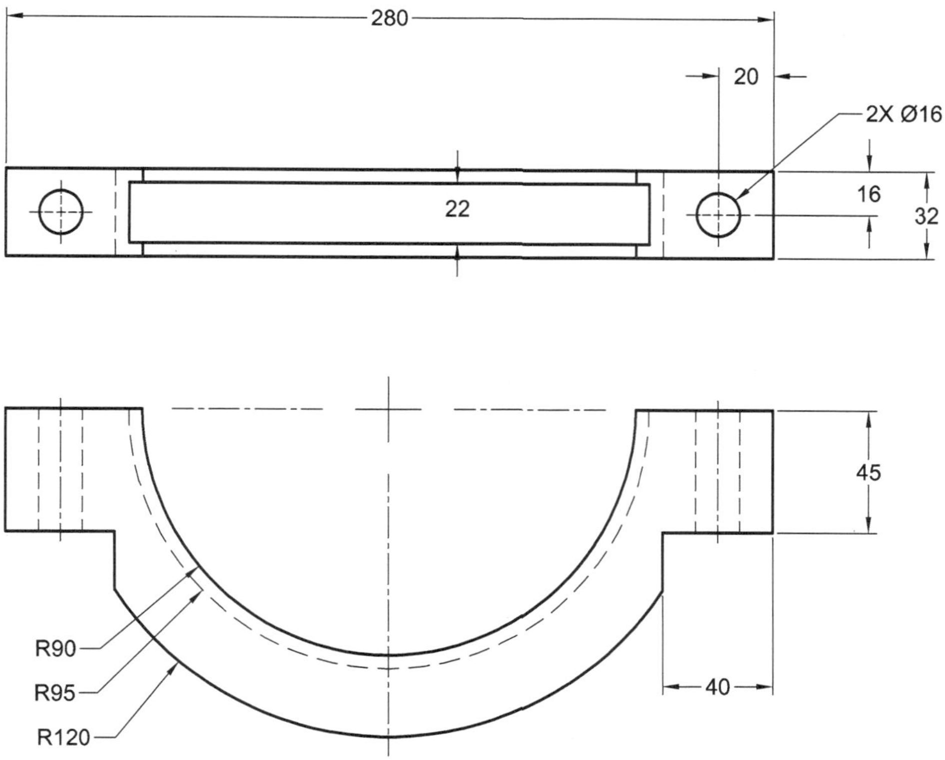

Figure 10-105 *Views and dimensions of the Bottom Strap part*

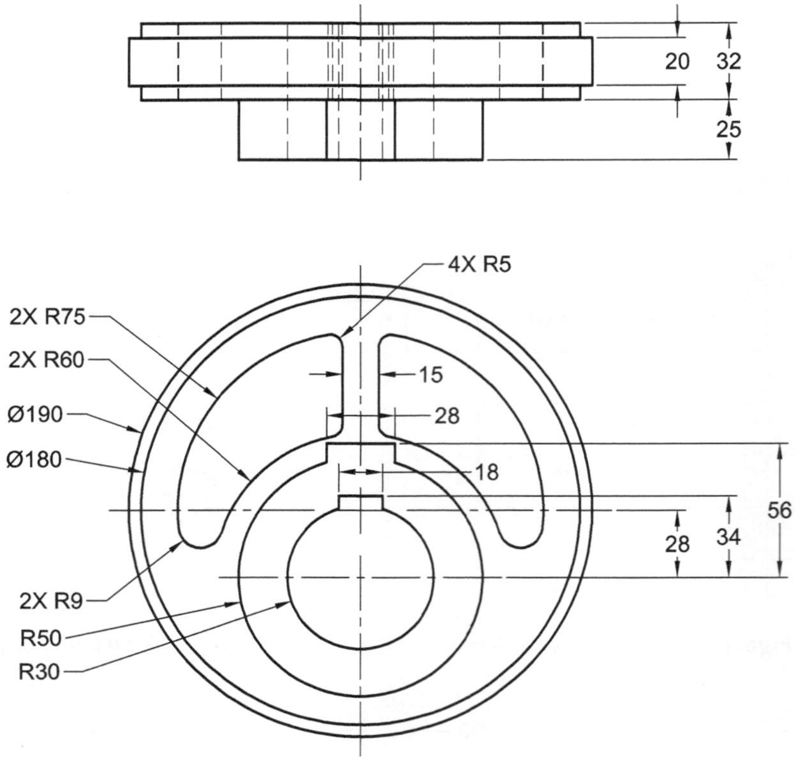

Figure 10-106 *Views and dimensions of the Sheave part*

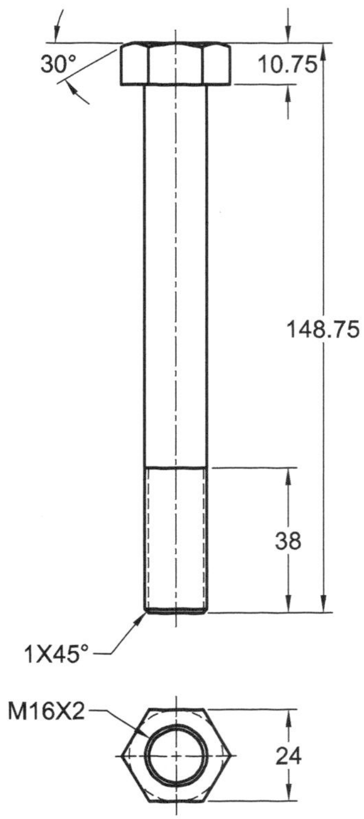

Figure 10-107 *Views and dimensions of Bolt*

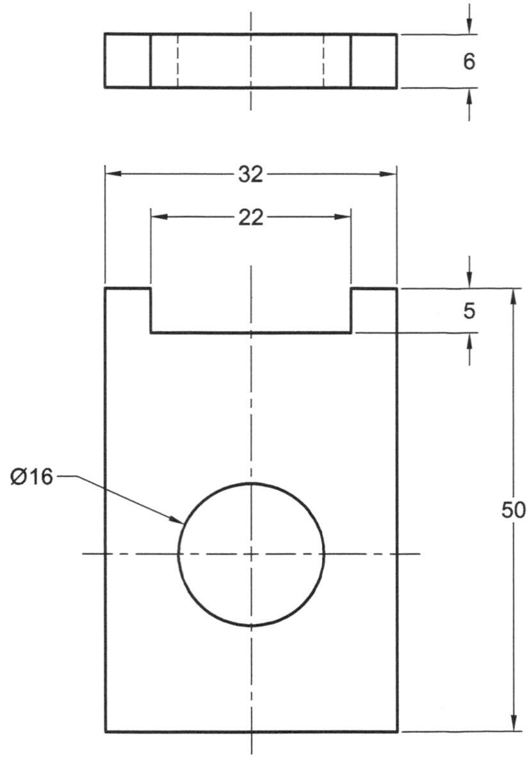

Figure 10-108 *Views and dimensions of Packing*

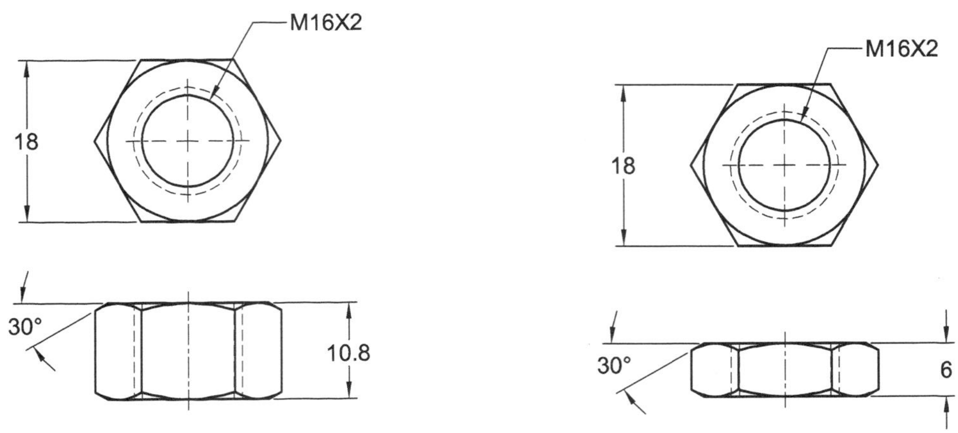

Figure 10-109 *Views and dimensions of Bolt*

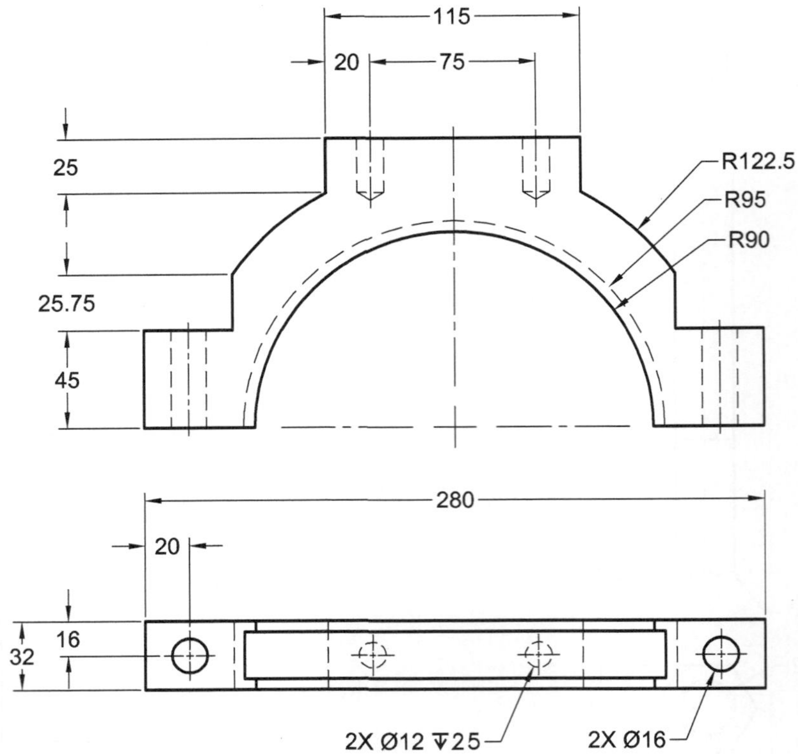

Figure 10-110 *Views and dimensions of the Top Strap*

Answers to Self-Evaluation Test

1. *.asm*, **2. Pattern**, **3.** degrees of freedom, **4. Insert**, **5.** T, **6.** F, **7.** T, **8.** T, **9.** T, **10.** T

Chapter 11

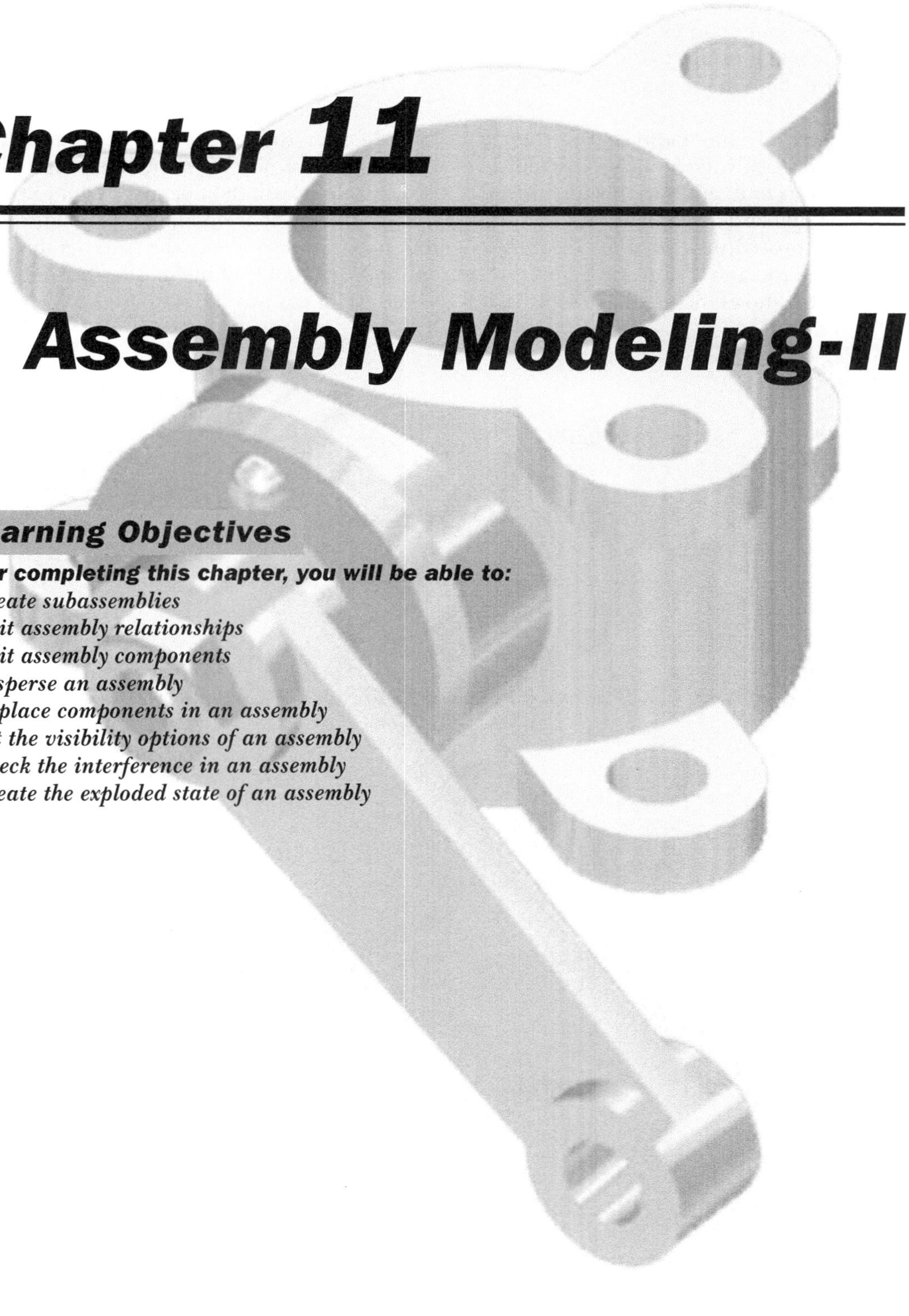

Assembly Modeling-II

Learning Objectives

After completing this chapter, you will be able to:

- *Create subassemblies*
- *Edit assembly relationships*
- *Edit assembly components*
- *Disperse an assembly*
- *Replace components in an assembly*
- *Set the visibility options of an assembly*
- *Check the interference in an assembly*
- *Create the exploded state of an assembly*

CREATING SUBASSEMBLIES

In the previous chapter, you learned to place components in the assembly file and apply the assembly relationships to the components. In this chapter, you will learn to create subassemblies and place them in the main assembly.

If an assembly has many parts, then it becomes easier to design it by segregating into subassemblies. To create a subassembly, you need to start a new assembly file, assemble the components in it, and save it with a name. This subassembly will then be inserted into the new assembly file and assembled with the other parts. To create subassemblies, you need to follow the same procedure as that for creating assemblies. Figure 11-1 shows the subassembly of the articulated rod and piston and Figure 11-2 shows the subassembly of the master rod and piston. Figure 11-3 shows the main assembly that is created using the two subassemblies.

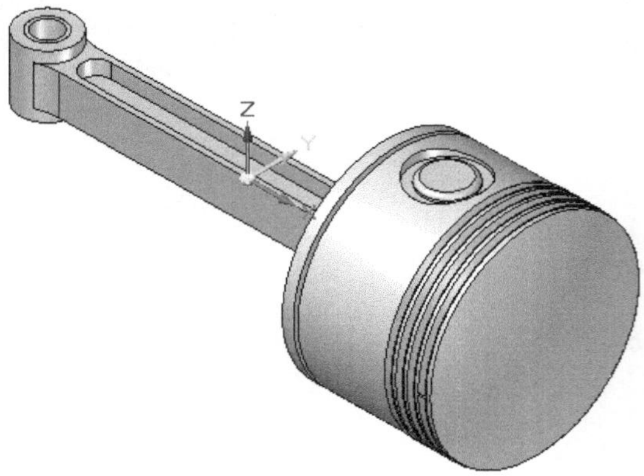

Figure 11-1 *A subassembly of the articulated rod and piston*

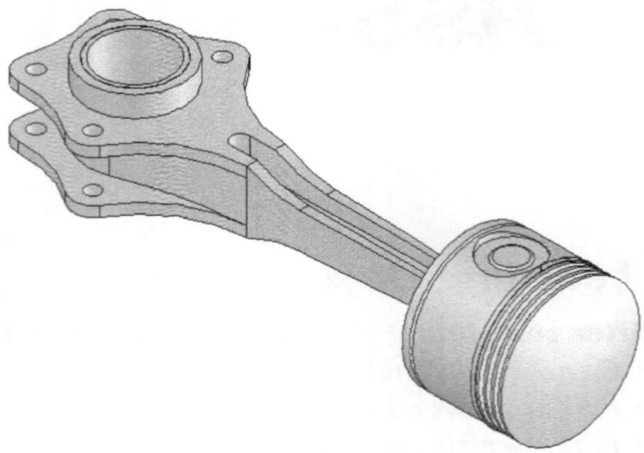

Figure 11-2 *A subassembly of the master rod and piston*

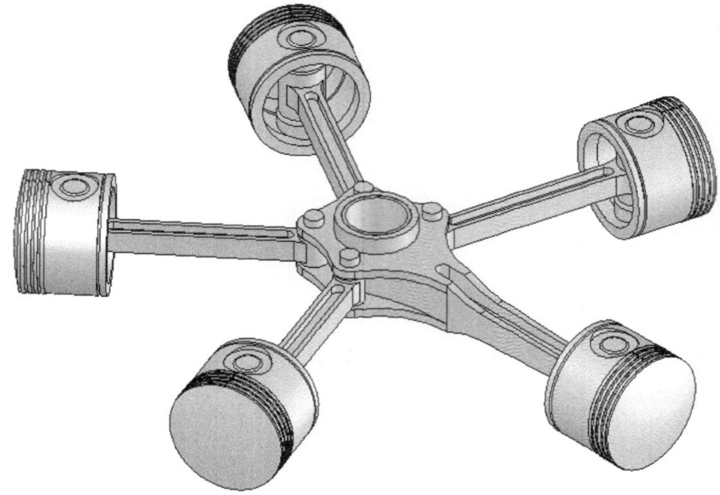

Figure 11-3 *Main assembly created after assembling the two subassemblies*

To create a subassembly, you can follow the top-down approach or the bottom-up approach of the assembly design.

Note

*Right-click on the top pane of the **Parts Library** area and choose the **Assembly-Use Configuration and Open As Settings** option from the shortcut menu displayed. If this option is not chosen, the subassembly you place in the assembly document will not be activated.*

Tip

1. You can also place a subassembly in the main assembly using the drag and drop method discussed in the previous chapter.

*2. If you place a subassembly in the main assembly, an assembly icon will be displayed with the name of the subassembly in the **PathFinder**. If you expand the subassembly in the **PathFinder**, all parts assembled in it will be displayed.*

EDITING THE ASSEMBLY RELATIONSHIPS

Generally, after creating the assembly or during the process of assembling the components, you need to edit the assembly relationships. The editing operations that can be performed on the assembly relationships are discussed next.

Note

*When you select a part from the **PathFinder**, the relationships that are applied to the selected part will be displayed above the dashed line. The remaining relationships of the other parts that are associated with the selected part will be displayed below the dashed line.*

Modifying the Values

The steps required for modifying the angle or distance offset values are as follows:

1. Select a part from the **PathFinder**; the selected part will be highlighted in green color in the drawing area and the relationships will be displayed at the bottom of the **PathFinder** in the assembly window.
2. You can recognize the relationship type by viewing its symbol. Choose the mate relationship from the bottom pane; the faces to which the mate relationship was applied will be highlighted. Also, an edit handle and a floating toolbar will be displayed.
3. Enter a new offset value in the **Offset Value** edit box of the floating toolbar; the distance offset value of the assembly relationship will be modified and the modifications will be updated automatically in the assembly. You can also enter a negative value for the offset distance. The negative value enables you to position the part in the opposite direction.

Similarly, you can also modify the angular value of an assembly relationship.

Applying Additional Relationships

Sometimes, you need to keep a part partially positioned with other parts in an assembly to move the partially positioned parts along the X, Y, or Z axis. As discussed in the previous chapter, the symbol for the partially positioned part is different from that of the fully positioned part. Figure 11-4 shows a list of the symbols and their meanings displayed in the top pane of the **Pathfinder**.

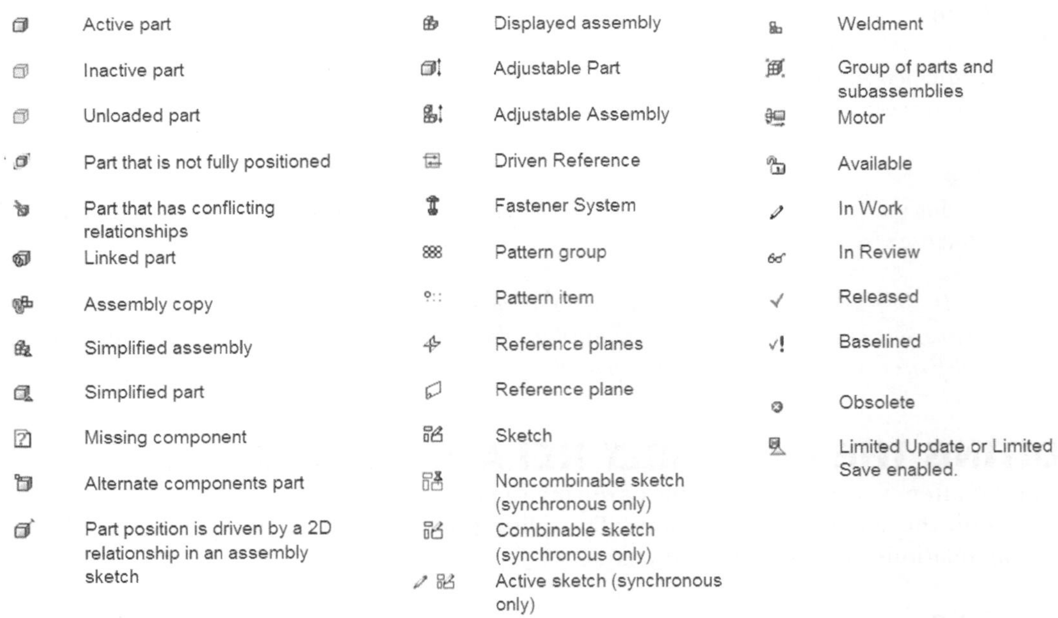

Figure 11-4 *Symbols displayed in the **PathFinder***

The following steps explain the procedure of applying additional relationships to a part:

1. Select the partially positioned part from the **PathFinder**; the selected part will get highlighted in the assembly window and the existing relationships will be displayed at the bottom of the **PathFinder**. Also, the **Select** command bar will be displayed.
2. Choose the **Edit Definition** button from the **Select** command bar; the **Assemble** command bar will be displayed.
3. Choose the assembly relationship from the **Relationship Types** flyout to apply new relationships to the part.

Note

*While editing the parts using the above steps, the **Relationship List** drop-down list is displayed in the **Assemble** command bar consisting a list of existing relationships applied to the selected part.*

Modifying Assembly Relationships

Sometimes, you may need to modify the existing assembly relationships of parts in an assembly. For example, you may need to modify the **Mate** relationship into the **Planar Align** relationship. To do so, select a component in the **PathFinder**. Next, choose the relationship that you want to replace from the bottom of the **PathFinder**. Then, right-click and choose the **Edit Definition** option from the shortcut menu displayed; the **Assemble** command bar will be displayed. Use the **Relationship Types** flyout from the command bar to choose the new relationship. Next, you can select the elements to which the new relationship needs to be applied.

You can also delete the existing relationship by selecting it from the bottom of the **PathFinder**. After selecting the relationship, right-click to invoke the shortcut menu and choose the **Delete**

Relationship option from it. Alternatively, you can also press the DELETE key to delete the selected relationship. After deleting the relationship, you can apply a new relationship to the part.

The bottom of the **PathFinder** is used to view and modify the relationships between the selected part and the other parts in the assembly. Figure 11-5 shows a list of symbols that are displayed at the bottom of the **PathFinder**. The meanings of the symbols are also mentioned in the same figure.

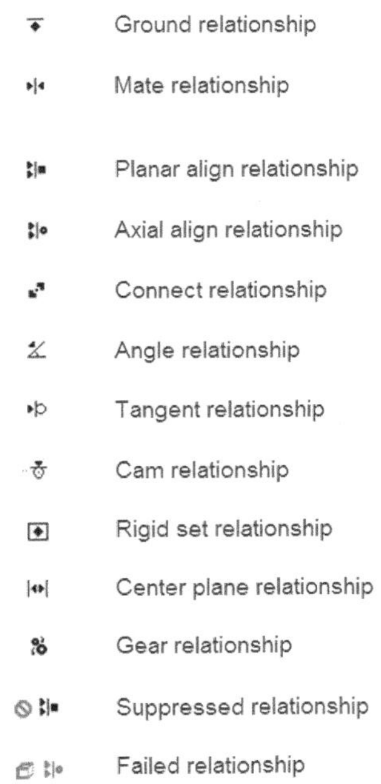

Figure 11-5 *Symbols of relationships*

Reversing the Orientation of a Part

You can reverse the orientation of a part that has been positioned using the **Axial Align**, **Planar Align**, **Mate**, **Parallel**, **Tangent**, or **Cam** relationship. To flip a part, select it and then select the relationship. Right-click to invoke the shortcut menu and choose the **Flip** option from it.

Tip

When you modify a fixed offset type to a floating offset, you may also need to modify other relationships to make the part fully positioned.

Note

*1. You can also use the **Flip** button available in the **Assemble** command bar to reverse the orientation of the part. When you flip a part assembled using the **Mate** relationship, this relationship will be converted into a **Planar Align** relationship.*

*2. The rotatory movement of the part will be locked on applying the **Axial Align** relationship. You can unlock it by editing the relationship from the bottom pane. To do so, select the **Axial Align** relationship; the **Unlock Rotation** and **Lock Rotation** buttons will be displayed in the floating toolbar. Choose the **Unlock Rotation** button to unlock the rotatory movement.*

EDITING THE ASSEMBLY COMPONENTS

After inserting and positioning components in an assembly file, you may need to edit components at some later stage of your assembly design cycle. The editing of components includes editing features, editing sketch profile, and modifying reference planes or faces. The following steps explain the procedure of editing components:

1. Select the component from the top pane of the **PathFinder**. Right-click on the component and choose the **Edit** option from the shortcut menu displayed; the **Part** environment will be invoked in the assembly file.
2. Select the feature to be edited from the **PathFinder**. You can edit or delete an existing feature. Also, you can add a new feature to the assembly component. This type of editing is known as Editing in the Context of Assembly.
3. After editing the part, choose the **Close and Return** tool from the **Close** group to close and return to the **Assembly** environment.

Tip

*To edit a component separately from the **Assembly** environment, select the component and right-click. Next, choose the **Open** option from the shortcut menu; the component will open in the corresponding **Part** environment. Edit the component and then save the changes.*

MODIFYING SYNCHRONOUS COMPONENTS IN THE ASSEMBLY ENVIRONMENT

You can modify the synchronous components assembled in the **Assembly** environment by using the handle. To modify a component, select the faces of the component to be modified; a handle will be displayed. By default, you will not be able to select the faces. To select the required faces, choose the **Face Priority** option from the flyout displayed, on choosing the black arrow below the **Select** tool in the **Select** group. Alternatively, move the cursor toward the required component; the **QuickPick** tool will be displayed. Next, right-click; the **QuickPick** list box with the list of nearest possible selections will be displayed. Select the face to be modified from this list box; a handle will be displayed. Using this handle, you can move or rotate the selected faces of the synchronous components. The working of handle is the same as discussed in Chapter 7.

DISPERSING SUBASSEMBLIES

Ribbon: Home > Modify > Disperse

Dispersing the subassembly means that the components of the subassembly become the components of the next higher level assembly or subassembly. To disperse a subassembly, select it from the **PathFinder** and choose the **Disperse** button from the **Modify** group; the **Disperse Assembly** information box will be displayed, as shown in Figure 11-6. In this information box, choose **Yes** to accept the transfer of components of the subassembly to the next higher level assembly or subassembly.

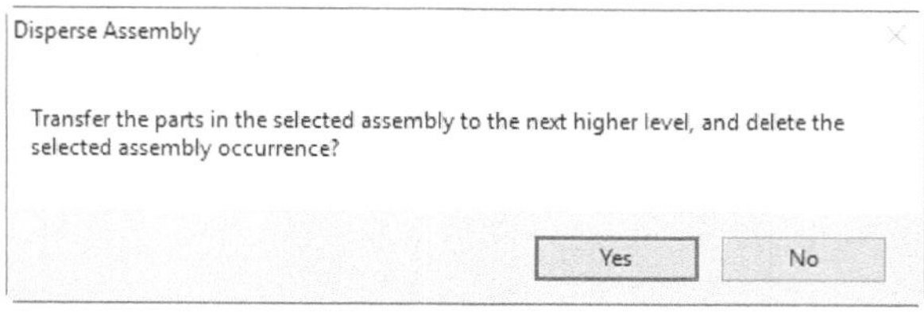

*Figure 11-6 The **Disperse Assembly** information box*

REPLACING COMPONENTS

Sometimes in the assembly design, you may need to replace a component of an assembly with some other components. To replace a component, you can select the required tools from the **Replace Part** drop-down in the **Modify** group. These tools are discussed next.

Replace Part

Ribbon:	Home > Modify > Replace Part

The **Replace Part** tool in the **Modify** group of the **Home** tab is used to replace the required part or component in an assembly. To do so, choose the **Replace Part** tool; the **Replace Part** command bar will be displayed and you will be prompted to select the component to be replaced. Select the component and choose the **Accept** button from the command bar; the **Replacement Part** dialog box will be displayed. Select the replacement component and choose the **Open** button from the **Replacement Part** dialog box; the assembly component will be replaced by a new part. While replacing the components, Solid Edge compares the geometry of the two components, and if their geometry matches properly, the new component will be positioned with the other components in the assembly exactly as that of the replaced part. Solid Edge uses the same relationships that were used to place the original component. However, if there is a change in the geometry of the new component, the assembly relationships may fail and the **Assembly** information box will be displayed, as shown in Figure 11-7.

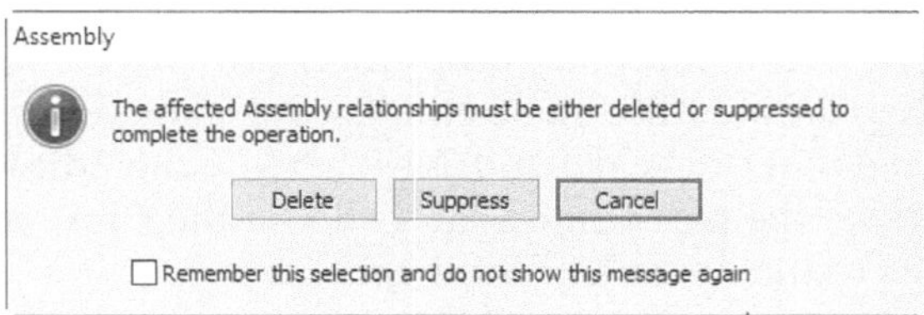

*Figure 11-7 The **Assembly** information box*

If the relationships fail, their symbols will be displayed in red color at the bottom pane of the **PathFinder**. You need to delete these relationships and apply new ones to fully position the replaced component.

Replace Part with Standard Part

The **Replace Part with Standard Part** tool is used to replace an existing part by the standard part in the assembly environment. To replace a part using this tool, choose this tool from the **Replace Part** drop-down; the **Replace Part with Standard Part** command bar will be displayed and you will be prompted to select the part to be replaced. Select the part from the current assembly environment and choose the **Accept** button from the command bar; the **Standard Parts** dialog box will be displayed. Select the required part from this dialog box; the selected part get replaced with the standard part. Figure 11-8 shows a plummer block assembly and Figure 11-9 shows its two parts replaced by the washers. The usage of standard parts are discussed later in this chapter.

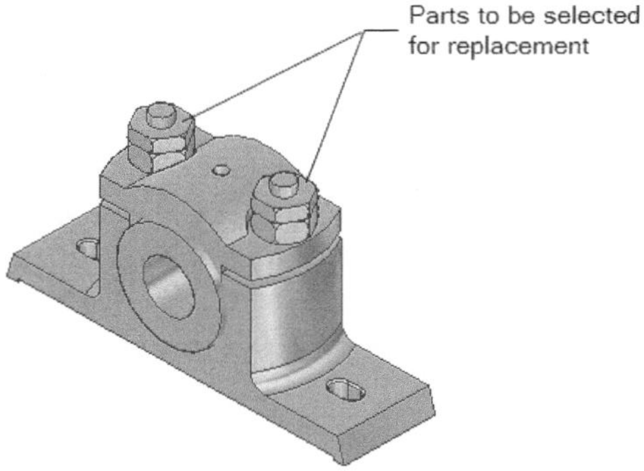

Figure 11-8 Parts of the assembly selected

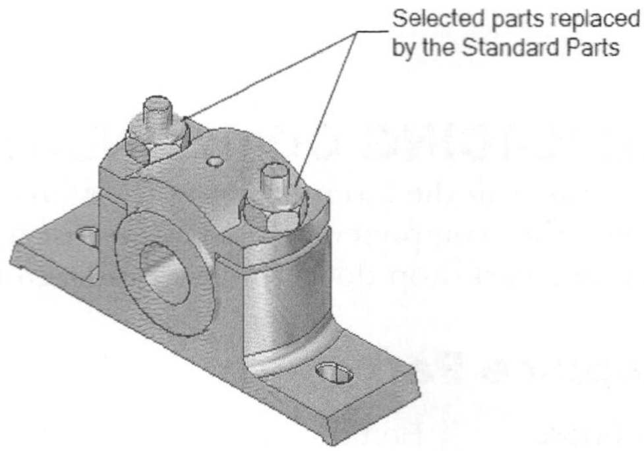

Figure 11-9 Replaced parts

Note

*The **Standard Parts** dialog box will be displayed only if the **Standard Parts Administration** of Solid Edge ST9 is installed in the system.*

Replace Part with New Part

The **Replace Part with New Part** tool in the **Replace Part** drop-down is used to replace an existing part or component in an assembly environment with new part or component. To replace a part using this tool, choose this tool from the **Replace Part** drop-down; the **Replace Part with New Part** command bar will be displayed and you will be prompted to select the component to be replaced. Select the component and choose the **Accept** button from the command bar; the **Replacement Part-New** dialog box will be displayed, as shown in Figure 11-10. Select the **Iso Metric Part.par** option from the **Template** drop-down list. Next, enter the name of the new component to be created in the **New file name** edit box and choose the **Create Part** button from the dialog box; the selected part will be deleted. Next, choose the **Edit In Place** button from the **Select** command bar. Create the part features and choose the **Close and Return** button from the **Close** group to return to the **Assembly** environment.

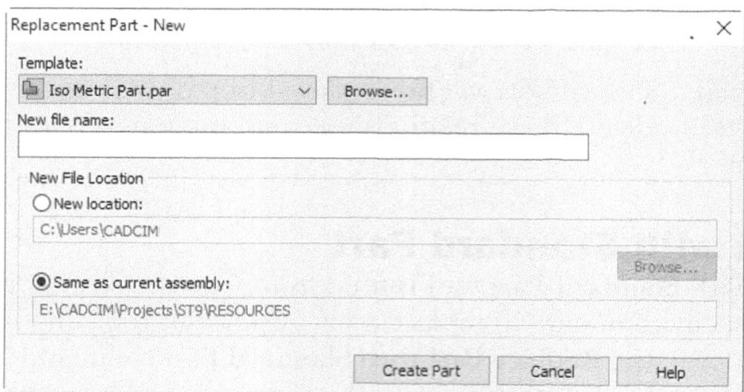

*Figure 11-10 The **Replacement Part - New** dialog box*

Replace Part with Copy

The **Replace Part with Copy** tool is used to replace the original part or component of an assembly with its copy. To do so, invoke the assembly environment and import any assembly file in it. Next, choose the **Replace Part with Copy** tool from the **Replace Part** drop-down; the **Replace Part with Copy** command bar will be displayed and you will be prompted to select the component to be copied. Select the component from the assembly environment or **PathFinder** and choose the **Accept** button from the command bar; the **Replacement Part - Copy** dialog box will be displayed, as shown in Figure 11-11. Note that you need to save the new file in the recently opened assembly folder. Next, browse to the folder location and save it with a different name; a copy of the part will be created and will replace the original part.

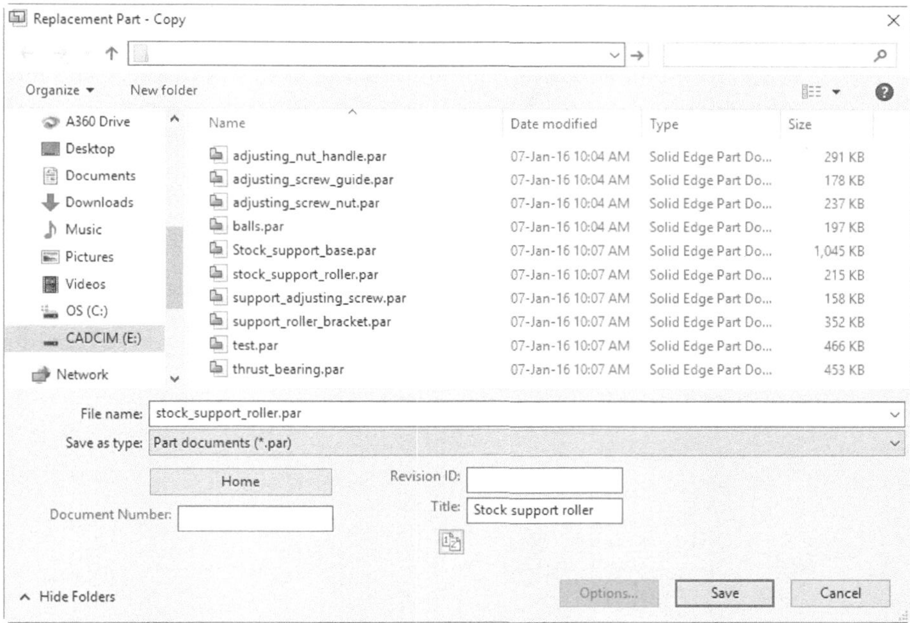

*Figure 11-11 The **Replacement Part - Copy** dialog box*

SIMPLIFYING ASSEMBLIES USING VISIBILITY OPTIONS

When you are assembling components whether it is a large assembly or a small one, you may need to simplify it using the visibility options. By simplifying, you can hide the components at any stage of the design cycle. You can also set the transparency of any component for simplifying the assembly. The methods of simplifying the assembly are discussed next.

Hiding and Displaying Components

To hide a component placed in an assembly, select the component from the assembly or from the **PathFinder** and clear the check box in front of the required component; the display of the component will be turned off. Also, the symbol next to the component in the **PathFinder** will get faded, indicating that the component is hidden. Alternatively, select the component and right-click; a shortcut menu will be displayed. Choose **Hide** from the shortcut menu to hide the component.

To show the hidden component, select the hidden component from the **PathFinder** and then select the check box in front of it; the hidden component will be displayed again in the assembly. Alternatively, select the component and right-click; a shortcut menu will be displayed. Choose **Show** from the shortcut menu to display the component.

Changing Transparency Conditions

In Solid Edge, you can change the transparency of components to simplify the assembly. Select the component to change its transparency. Next, select the required clear or glass color from the **Face Style** drop-down list in the **Style** group of the **View** tab; the color of the selected component will be changed.

INTERFERENCE DETECTION IN ASSEMBLIES

After creating an assembly design, the most essential step is to check the interference between components of an assembly. If there is an interference between components, the components may not assemble properly after they are manufactured. Therefore, before sending components for manufacturing, it is essential to check the assembly for interference. To check interference, choose the **Check Interference** tool from the **Evaluate** group of the **Inspect** tab; the **Check Interference** command bar will be displayed.

Interference Options

The **Interference Options** button is used to set the output options for checking the interference. On choosing this button, the **Interference Options** dialog box will be displayed, as shown in Figure 11-12. The options available in this dialog box are discussed next.

*Figure 11-12 The **Interference Options** dialog box*

Options Tab

This tab is chosen by default. The options available in this tab are discussed next.

Check Select Set 1 Against Area

The options in this area enable you to determine the method of selecting components for checking the interference. These options are discussed next.

Select Set 2: This option is selected by default. When this option is selected, you need to select the second set of components individually from the **PathFinder** or from the assembly window after selecting the first set of components.

All other parts in the assembly: This option considers the remaining parts of the assembly as the second selection set.

Parts currently shown: This option checks the interference between the components you selected as the first set and the remaining components that are correctly displayed in the assembly.

Itself: This option checks the interference among the first set of components.

Output Options Area

The options in this area enable you to determine the format in which you need the output from the interference check. These options are discussed next.

Generate report: This option enables you to save the interference check results into a text file; the configuration of this file can be set in the **Report** tab of the same dialog box.

Interfering volumes: This option enables you to determine the state of the interfering volumes. The **Show** radio button allows you to display the interfering volume in the assembly. Whereas, the **Save as part** option allows you to save the interfering volume as a part file. This volume is saved as a separate part and is automatically grounded.

Hide parts not in Select Sets 1 and 2: This option enables you to hide the parts that are not included in sets 1 and 2.

Highlight interfering parts: As the name suggests, this option highlights the parts that have an interference in the assembly.

Check interference with construction geometry: This option is used to check interference between construction geometries like axes and planes.

Dim parts with no interference: If this option is selected, the parts that do not have interference with any part are displayed as dim.

Hide parts with no interference: This option enables you to hide the parts that are not in any of the selection sets and do not take part in the interference check.

Ignore interferences between matching threads: On selecting this check box, the interference is not detected, if the thread pitch does not match between a bolt and a threaded hole with the same nominal diameters.

Ignore threaded fasteners interfering with non-threaded holes: This option ignores the interference between a threaded cylinder and a non-threaded hole.

Report Tab

When you choose the **Report** tab, the **Interference Options** dialog box will be modified, as shown in Figure 11-13. The options in this tab are discussed next.

*Figure 11-13 The **Report** tab in the **Interference Options** dialog box*

File name

The **File name** edit box is used to specify the name of the report file. You can choose the **Browse** button to locate the folder in which you want to save the file.

Part names

When you choose this option, the names of the parts that are causing the interference will be listed in the report file.

Part centers of gravity

When you choose this option, the centers of gravity of the interfering parts will be listed in the report file.

Interference center of gravity

When you choose this option, the center of gravity of the volume of the interference will be listed in the report file.

Interference volume

When you choose this option, the volume of the interference will be listed in the report file.

Checking for the Interference

After setting the options for the interference check, you need to select the first set of the components. You can select the components from the assembly window or from the **PathFinder**.

After selecting the first set of components, choose the **Accept** button from the **Check Interference** command bar or right-click to accept the selection. Now you need to select the parts for set 2. After selecting the parts, right-click to process the interference check. If there is an interference, then depending on the output options you have set, the interference volume will be displayed. You can use the reference of the interference volume to edit the components for eliminating the interference.

CREATING FASTENER SYSTEM

Ribbon: Home > Assemble > Create Part In-Place drop-down > Fastener System

The **Fastener System** tool is used to add the fasteners like bolts, nuts, and washers into the assembly without modeling the parts. In Solid Edge, you can add a fastener with specified standards that are provided in the software. To add a fastener, choose the **Fastener System** tool from the **Create Part In-Place** drop-down from the **Assemble** group of the **Home** tab in the **Ribbon**; the **Fastener System** command bar will be displayed, as shown in Figure 11-14. The procedure of adding fasteners is discussed next.

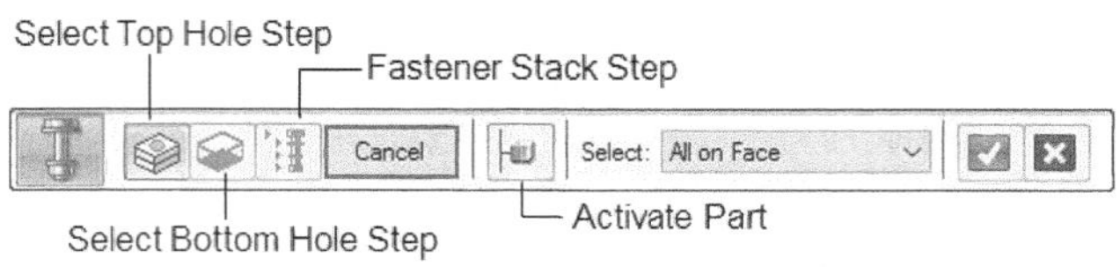

*Figure 11-14 The **Fastener System** command bar*

Note

*The **Fastener System** tool will be available only if the **Standard Parts Administration** of Solid Edge ST9 is installed in the system.*

After invoking the **Fastener System** command bar, you will be prompted to select a top circular edge of a hole to add fastener into the assembly. Note that the hole whose top circular edge you will select must be a through hole. Select the circular edge of the hole, where you need to place the fastener. After selecting the circular edge, choose the **Accept** button from the **Fastener System** command bar. On doing so, you will be prompted to specify the bottom extent of the fastener to be added. Select the cylindrical surface of the hole; the **Fastener System** dialog box will be displayed, refer to Figure 11-15. You can select the required fastener from this dialog box. The options in this dialog box are discussed next.

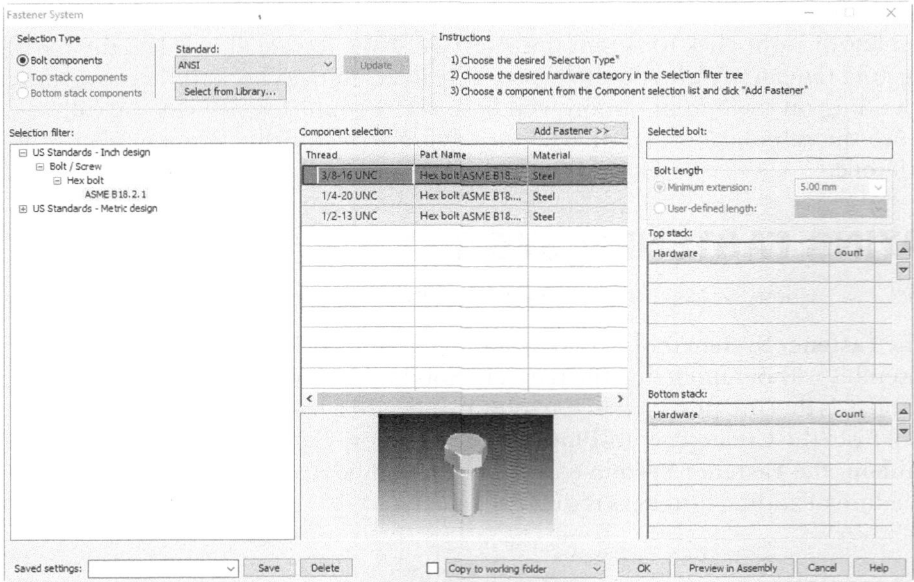

*Figure 11-15 The **Fastener System** dialog box*

Selection Type Area

In this area, you need to specify the type of fasteners that are to be added into the assembly. By default, the **Bolt components** radio button is selected in this area. As a result, the **Selection filter** area displays the information of the bolts and screws that matches the selected hole.

If the **Top stack components** radio button or the **Bottom stack components** radio button is selected, then the **Selection filter** area will display the information about the nut and washer, respectively that match with the bolt or screw that is to be added to the feature in the assembly. Other options in this area are discussed next.

Note

*The **Top stack components** and **Bottom stack components** radio buttons are activated only after you add a fastener by choosing the **Add Fastener** button in the **Fastener System** dialog box.*

Standard

The **Standard** drop-down list contains standards such as **ANSI**, **BS**, **DIN**, **GB**, **GOST**, **ISO**, and so on. You can use these standards for adding the fasteners into the hole. Select the required standard type and choose the **Update** button; the **Selection filter** and **Component selection** areas will display the fasteners available for the selected standard. Next, select the required fastener from the **Component selection** area. You can choose any fastener for adding it to the hole feature. Note that every time you choose a standard type, you have to choose the **Update** button to update the options.

Select From Library

If the required fastener is not displayed in the **Component selection** area, you can select it from the **Standard Parts** dialog box. To invoke this dialog box, choose the **Select From Library** button from **Standard** area; the **Standard Parts** dialog box will be displayed, as shown in

Figure 11-16. In this dialog box, you can select the required fastener from the **Selecting Part** area. On doing so, the preview and the specifications of the selected fastener will be displayed in the **Selected Part** area. After selecting the required fastener from this dialog box, choose the **Select** button to exit the **Standard Parts** dialog box.

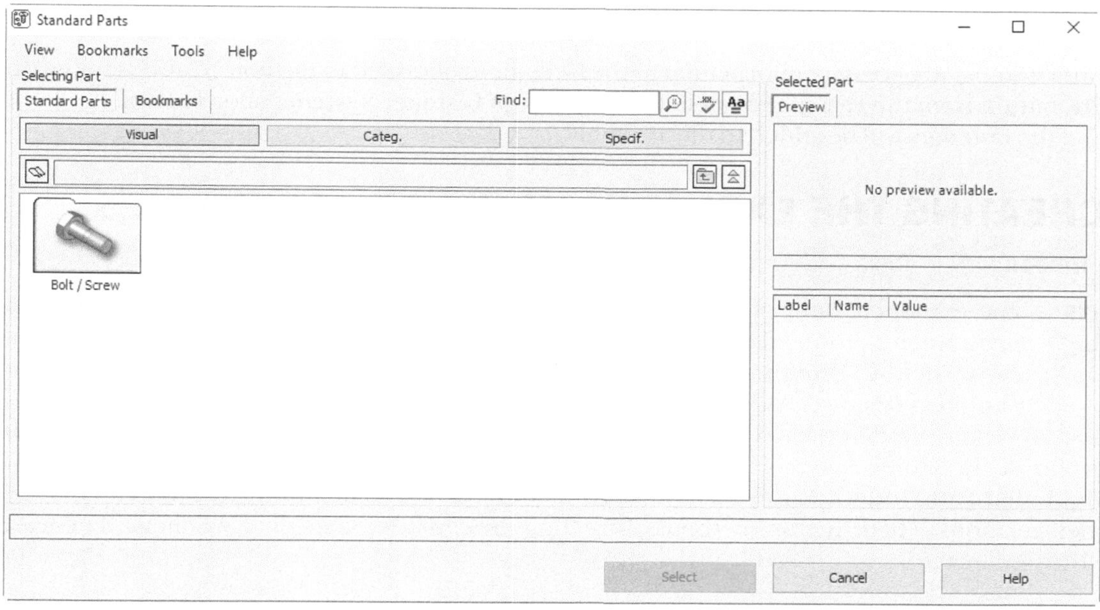

*Figure 11-16 The **Standard Parts** dialog box*

Selection filter Area

This area displays the fastener types that matches the standard selected in the **Standard** drop-down list. You can choose any type of fastener that is to be added based on the standard.

Component selection Area

This area displays different sizes of fasteners that match the selected hole. Select the required fastener from this area and then choose the **Add Fastener** button; the fastener will be selected.

Selected bolt Area

This area displays the name of the selected fastener.

Bolt Length Area

In this area, you can specify the length of the fastener. You can enter the maximum length in the **Maximum Extension** edit box or select a user-defined length from the **User-defined length** drop-down list.

Top Stack

This area displays the list of nuts that are added to the fastener. This area will be activated only after selecting the **Top Stack Component** radio button in the **Selection Type** area. Select the **Top Stack Component** radio button; the **Selection filter** and **Component selection** areas will display the nuts available for the selected bolt size. The procedure to add the nut is same as discussed earlier. After adding the nut, its name will be displayed in the **Top Stack** area.

Bottom Stack
This area displays the list of the washers to be added to the fastener. This area will be activated only after selecting the **Bottom Stack Component** radio button in the **Selection Type** area. The procedure for selecting the washer is same as discussed for selecting the fastener. After adding the washer, the washer name will be displayed in the **Bottom Stack** area.

After adding all necessary information of the fastener to be added to the hole feature, choose the **OK** button from the **Fastener System** dialog box; the **Fastener System** dialog box will be closed and the fasteners will be added to the assembly.

CREATING THE EXPLODED STATE OF ASSEMBLIES

Ribbon: Tools > Environs > ERA

ERA

The exploded state of an assembly is created in the **Explode - Render - Animate** environment. To invoke this environment, choose the **ERA** button from the **Environs** group of the **Tools** tab in the **Assembly** environment. As soon as you enter the **Explode - Render - Animate** environment, the explode, render, and animate tools will be displayed in the **Ribbon** and the **Explode PathFinder** window will be displayed. The **Explode** group of the **Home** tab provides the tools to create the exploded state of an assembly. The **Exploded PathFinder** tab is used to display the exact tree structure of the exploded parts and their relations. There are two methods of creating the exploded state of an assembly. These are discussed next.

Automatic Explode

Ribbon: Home > Explode > Auto Explode

Auto Explode

This option is used to create the exploded view automatically. Whenever you explode an assembly using this method, flowlines are automatically created. To create an automatic exploded state, choose the **Auto Explode** button from the **Explode** group; the **Auto Explode** command bar will be displayed. The options displayed in this command bar on choosing the **Auto Explode** tool are discussed next.

Select Step
The **Select Step** button is chosen by default in the **Auto Explode** command bar. This button enables you to select the assembly that you want to explode.

Select Drop-down List
There are two options in the **Select** drop-down list. These are discussed next.

Top-level assembly
By default, the **Top-level assembly** option is selected in the **Select** drop-down list. As a result, the subassemblies in the assembly are considered as a single component while exploding. Choose the **Accept** button from the command bar to accept the **Top-level assembly** option. Once you accept it, the options in the command bar will change. Next, choose the **Automatic Explode Options** button from the command bar; the **Automatic Explode Options** dialog box will be displayed, as shown in Figure 11-17. Clear the **Bind all subassemblies** check box and select the **By subassembly level** radio button in the

Explode Technique area, if it has not been selected already. Choose the **OK** button from the **Automatic Explode Options** dialog box. Deactivate the **Automatic Spread Distance** button by choosing it in the **Auto Explode** command bar and set the distance value in the **Distance** edit box. Next, choose the **Explode** button from the command bar. Figure 11-18 shows the exploded state created using the **Auto Explode** tool.

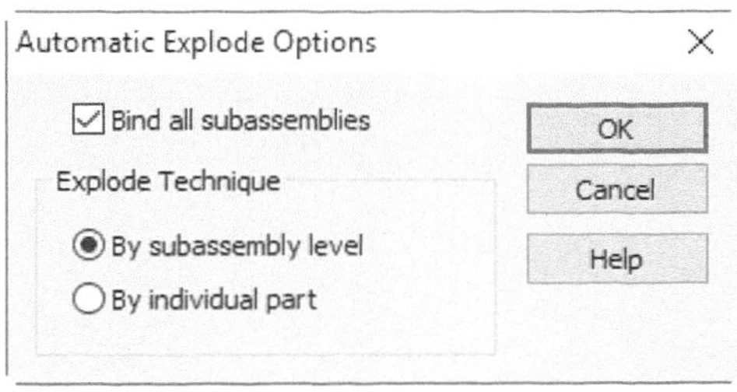

*Figure 11-17 The **Automatic Explode Options** dialog box*

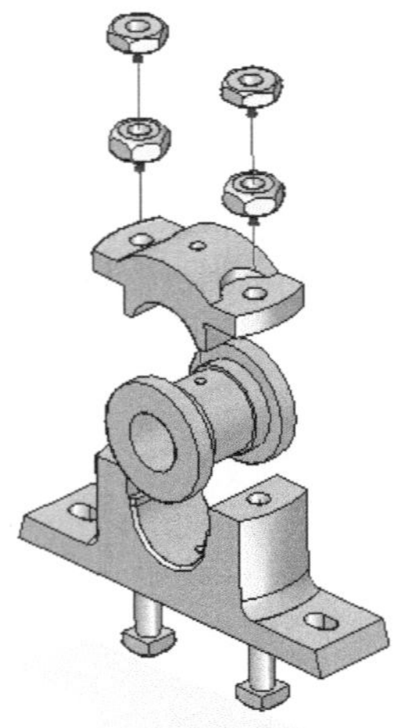

Figure 11-18 Exploded view of the Plummer Block assembly

Subassembly

This option is used to explode the components of the selected subassembly only, as shown in Figure 11-19. The explosion procedure is similar to that discussed earlier for the top-level assemblies.

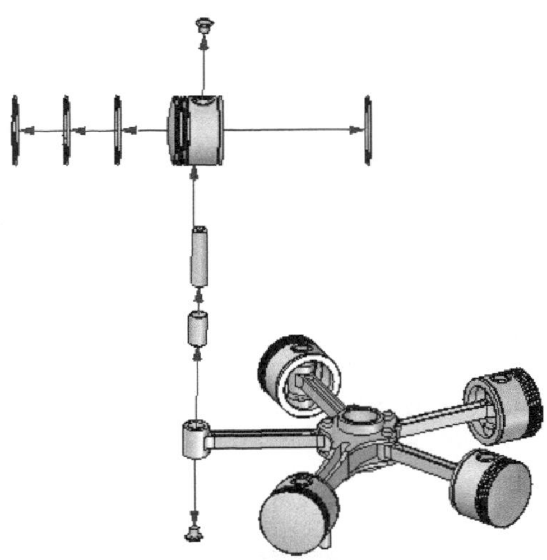

Figure 11-19 The exploded subassembly

> **Tip**
> *The automatic explode method explodes the components of an assembly based on the relationships applied to it.*

Unexploding Assemblies

Ribbon:	Home > Modify > Unexplode

To unexplode an assembly, choose the **Unexplode** button from the **Modify** group; the **Solid Edge** information box will be displayed, as shown in Figure 11-20 informing that the current explosion will be deleted. Choose the **Yes** button from this information box to confirm the deletion of current explosion.

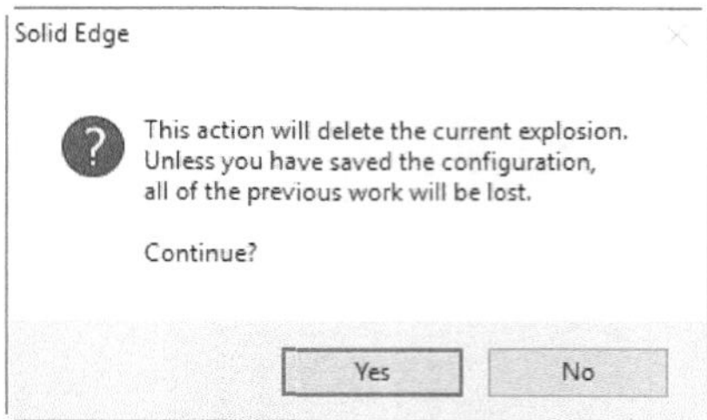

***Figure 11-20** The **Solid Edge** information box*

Exploding Assemblies Manually

Ribbon:	Home > Explode > Explode

The automatic explode method may not give the desired results every time. Therefore, the manual method is used to achieve the required exploded state. To explode the assembly manually, choose the **Explode** button from the **Explode** group of the **Home** tab; the **Explode** command bar will be displayed and you will be prompted to select the parts you need to explode. Note that while selecting the parts, do not select the part that is grounded. Also, select only those components that will be exploded in the same direction. Remember that the order of the selection of the components should be such that the component closest to the stationary part in the exploded state is selected first. For example in Figure 11-21, component A should be selected first and then the component B. The stationary part will remain stationary and the parts that were not selected will also remain at their position. After selecting the parts to be exploded, choose the **Accept** button. Next, select the part that will remain stationary and then select a face or reference plane on the stationary part to specify the direction of explosion. The explosion will take place normal to the selected plane. After you select the explode direction, the **Explode Options** dialog box will be displayed, as shown in Figure 11-22. The options in the **Explode Options** dialog box are discussed next.

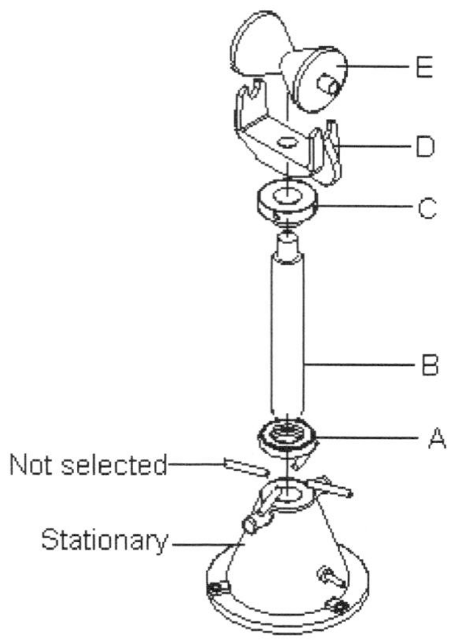

Figure 11-21 Exploded state of an assembly

Figure 11-22 The ***Explode Options*** *dialog box*

Explode Technique Area

There are two options in this area and they are discussed next.

Move components as a unit

This option is used to move the selected components as a single unit from their original position through the distance specified in the **Distance** edit box, refer to Figure 11-23.

Spread components evenly

This option is used to move the selected components individually from their original position through the distance specified in the **Distance** edit box, refer to Figure 11-24. The individual components are listed in the **Explode order** list box.

After specifying the required option, choose the **OK** button from the **Explode Options** dialog box to accept and exit it. Next, choose the **Explode** button from the **Explode** command bar; the component will explode in the graphics area depending upon the option specified. Choose **Finish** and then **Cancel** to exit exploding.

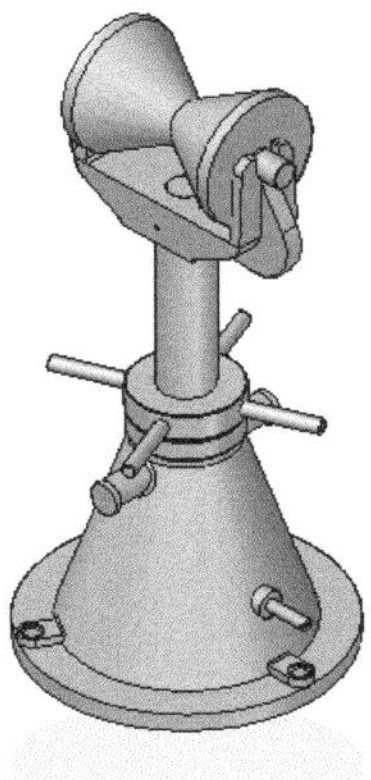

Figure 11-23 Exploding components as a single unit

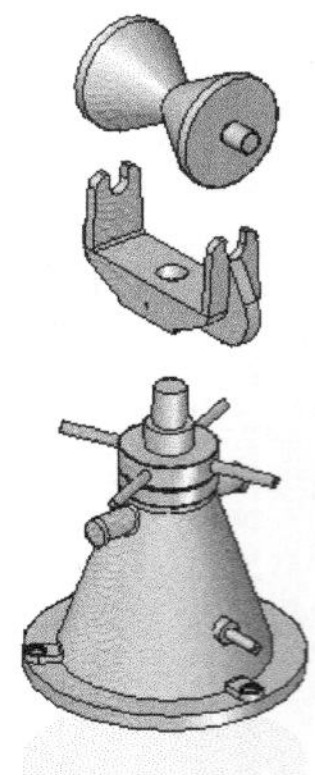

Figure 11-24 Exploding individual parts of components

Changing the Distance between Components

Ribbon: Home > Modify > Drag Component

After exploding an assembly, you may need to modify the distance between the components or the orientation of components. To do so, choose the **Drag Component** button from the **Modify** group; the **Drag Component** command bar will be displayed and you will be prompted to select a component. In the **Drag Component** command bar, choose the **Move Dependent Parts** button, if you want to move the component along with its dependents. To move a single component, choose the **Move Selected Part** button from the command bar. Move the cursor over the component to be moved; the component will be highlighted. Next, select the component and choose the **Accept** button. Now, click and drag the component to be moved. You can also change the orientation of the components by choosing the **Rotate** button from the **Drag Component** command bar. Similarly, on choosing **Move Planar**, you can move the selected component in the same plane.

Repositioning the Parts

Ribbon: Home > Modify > Reposition

When you are not able to move a part beyond its parent part in the exploded state of assembly, you can choose the **Reposition** button from the **Explode - Render - Animate** environment and reposition the selected component with respect to a reference part. To reposition a part, choose the **Reposition** tool from the **Modify** group; the **Reposition** command bar will be displayed and you will be prompted to select the part to reposition. Select the part and you will be prompted to click on another part to place the selected part next to. Next, select the direction in which you want to place the part. You will notice that the repositioned part changes its position in the exploded state of the assembly. Now, if required, you can move the repositioned part to the desired location.

Note

The distance and position of only the exploded parts can be modified.

Removing the Parts

Ribbon: Home > Modify > Remove

The **Remove** button will be enabled in the **Modify** group only after you select an exploded part. When you choose this button, the selected part will be hidden and will move to its original position in the assembly. To redisplay the hidden component, select the check box adjacent to the component in the **PathFinder**. Alternatively, right-click on the hidden component in the **PathFinder**; a shortcut menu will be displayed. Choose the **Show** option from the shortcut menu; the hidden part will be redisplayed.

In Solid Edge, the flow lines of the exploded assembly are generated automatically. The flow lines display the path of the exploded part. Sometimes you may not get the desired flow lines. As a result, you need to modify or create them. The tools to modify the flow lines are available in the **Flow Lines** group of the **Home** tab. These tools are discussed next.

Note

*To generate the flow lines automatically, make sure that the **Flow Lines** button is chosen in the **Flow Lines** group of the **Home** tab.*

Drop

Ribbon: Home > Flow Lines > Drop

On exploding an assembly, the flow lines are generated automatically. If the flow lines are not generated automatically, you can generate them by using the **Drop** tool. To do so, choose the **Drop** tool from the **Flow Lines** group of the **Home** tab; the flow lines will be generated for the assembly, refer to Figures 11-25 and 11-26.

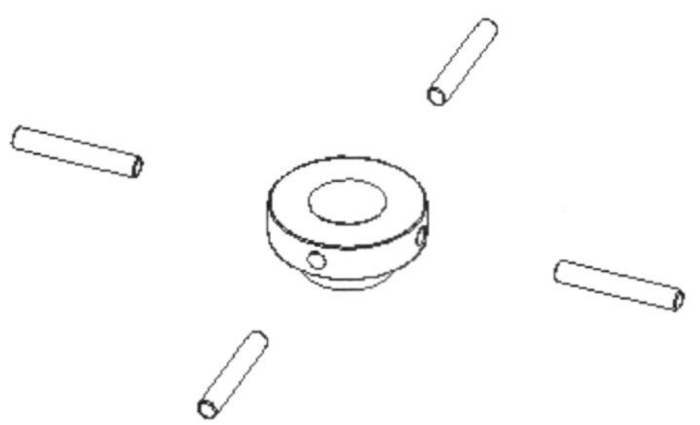

Figure 11-25 *Exploded state without flowlines*

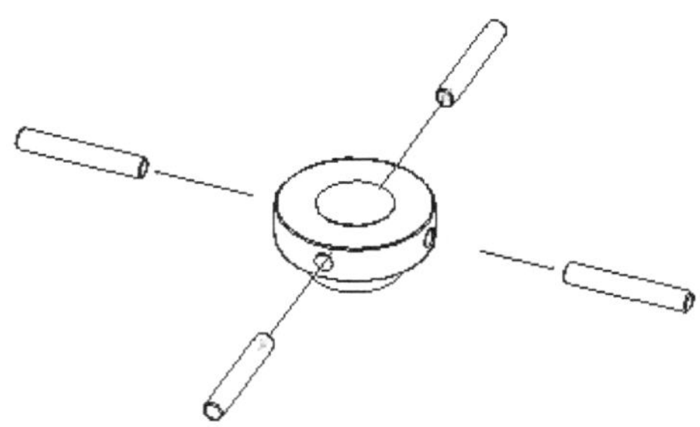

Figure 11-26 *Exploded state with flowlines*

Modify

Ribbon: Home > Flow Lines > Modify

The **Modify** tool is used to modify the flow line by changing the length, location and joggle the position of generated flow lines. Choose the **Modify** tool; the **Modify** command bar will be displayed and you will be prompted to select the flow line segment which is to be modified. Select the required line; arrows with dot will be attached at the ends of flow line. Now, click on the arrow from the side where you want to increase the length; the length of the flow line will be increased as you drag the cursor. After getting the required length of flow line as you drag the cursor and click at a point; the length of the flow line will be changed.

If you want to change the location of the flow line, click on the dot; you will be prompted to select the new location for the flow line. Select the new location; the location of the flow line will be changed.

If you want to joggle the position of the flow line, click on it and two arrows with the line will be attached. Now, click on an arrow in the direction where you want to change or move the flow line and next, drag the mouse to change the position.

Draw

Ribbon: Home > Flow Lines > Draw

On exploding an assembly, the flow lines that are generated automatically may not be in the desired position and therefore, you may need to generate them manually. To do so, invoke the **Draw** tool from the **Flow Lines** group of the **Home** tab; the **Draw** command bar will be displayed and you will be prompted to select the start point of the flow line. Move the cursor to the desired location and select the start point. On selecting the start point, you will be prompted to select the end point of the flow lines. Select any point in the graphics window and choose the **Finish** button and the **Cancel** button from command bar; the flow line will be created.

TUTORIALS

Tutorial 1

In this tutorial, you will create the exploded view of the Stock Bracket assembly created in Tutorial 1 of Chapter 10. The exploded state of the assembly is shown in Figure 11-27. After creating the exploded state, you need to save the configuration with the name *Stock Bracket.cfg* at the location given below:

C:\Solid Edge\c11\Stock Bracket **(Expected time: 30 min)**

The following steps are required to complete this tutorial:

a. Copy all the part and assembly files of the *Stock Bracket* assembly from the *c10* folder to the *c11* folder. The files will be saved at C:*Solid Edge\c11\Stock Bracket*.
b. Create the exploded state of the assembly, refer to Figure 11-28.
c. Collapse the components of the exploded assembly, refer to Figure 11-29.
d. Save the exploded state of the assembly as a configuration file.

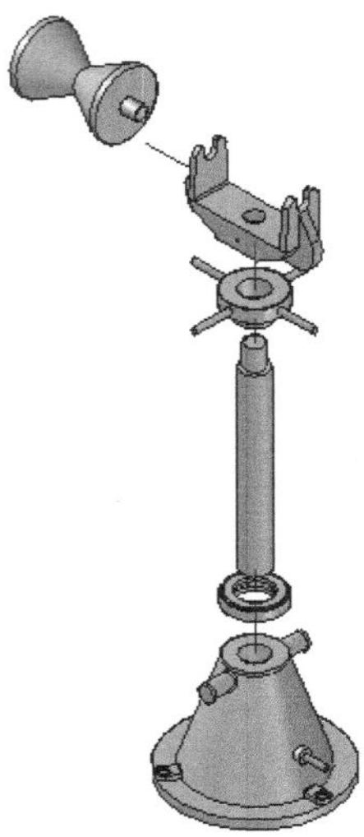

Figure 11-27 Exploded view of the Stock Bracket assembly

Copying the Files to the Current Folder

1. Copy all the part and assembly files of the *Stock Bracket* assembly from the *c10* folder to the *Solid Edge\c11\Stock Bracket* folder. Remember that the extension of the part file is *.par* and that of the assembly file is *.asm*.

Creating the Exploded State of the Assembly

To create the exploded state of the assembly, you need to invoke the **Explode - Render - Animate** environment in the Assembly environment.

1. Open the *stock bracket.asm* file in the **Assembly** environment.

2. Choose the **ERA** tool from the **Environs** group of the **Tools** tab; the **Explode - Render - Animate** environment is invoked.

3. Choose the **Explode** button from the **Explode** group of the **Home** tab; you are prompted to click on the parts to be exploded. Also, the **Explode** command bar is displayed.

   Remember that the part that has to be kept closest to the stationary part must be selected first. In this assembly, the stationary part is the *Stock Support Base*.

4. Select the components in the following order: *Thrust Bearing, Support Adjusting Screw, Adjusting Screw Nut, Support Roller Bracket,* and *Stock Support Roller*.

5. Choose the **Accept** button from the **Explode** command bar; you are prompted to click on the stationary part.

6. Choose the *Stock Support Base* as the stationary part; you are prompted to select a face of the stationary part. Selection of this face is required to determine the direction of explosion.

7. Choose the top face of the *Stock Support Base*; a red arrow pointing upward is displayed. If the arrow does not point upward, move the cursor up to point it upward.

8. Click to specify the direction when the arrow points in the upward direction.

9. When you specify the direction, the **Explode Options** dialog box is displayed. In this dialog box, select the **Spread components evenly** radio button and then choose the **OK** button to close it. Next, enter **20** inches in the **Distance** edit box of the **Explode** command bar.

10. Choose the **Explode** button to explode the assembly.

11. Choose the **Fit** button from the status bar; the exploded view of the assembly is displayed, as shown in Figure 11-28.

12. Now, choose the **Finish** button and then the **Cancel** button from the command bar, to exit the **Explode** tool

    Note that the exploded view obtained is not the desired view. This is because the *Stock Support Roller* is not in the correct direction. Therefore, you need to further apply some operations on it to get the desired view.

Collapsing the Component

Ideally, the *Stock Support Roller* needs to be exploded on the right or left of the *Stock Roller Bracket*. Therefore, you need to unexplode the *Stock Support Roller* first and then explode it again in the horizontal direction.

1. Select the *Stock Support Roller* and choose the **Collapse** button from the **Modify** group of the **Home** tab; the selected component moves to its original position with respect to its parent component, as shown in Figure 11-29.

Figure 11-28 *Exploded view of the assembly*

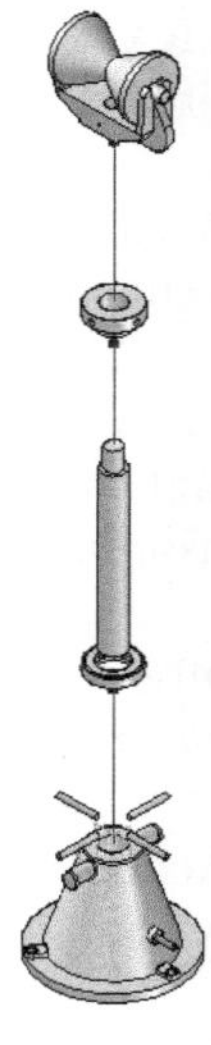

Figure 11-29 *Exploded view after collapsing the Stock Support Roller*

Exploding the Stock Support Roller

Now, you need to explode the *Stock Support Roller* in the horizontal direction.

1. Choose the **Explode** button from the **Explode** group of the **Home** tab; you are prompted to click on the parts to be exploded.
2. Select the *Stock Support Roller* from the assembly window, if it is not selected. Choose the **Accept** button; you are prompted to select the stationary part.
3. Select the *Support Roller Bracket* as the stationary component; you are prompted to select a face on the stationary component to specify the direction of explosion.
4. Select the face of the stationary part to display a red arrow on it, as shown in Figure 11-30.
5. When the arrow points in the direction shown in Figure 11-30, click to specify the direction.
6. Enter **20** in the **Distance** edit box and then choose the **Explode** button from the **Explode** command bar; the selected component is exploded, as shown in Figure 11-31. Choose the **Finish** and then **Cancel** button to exit the tool.

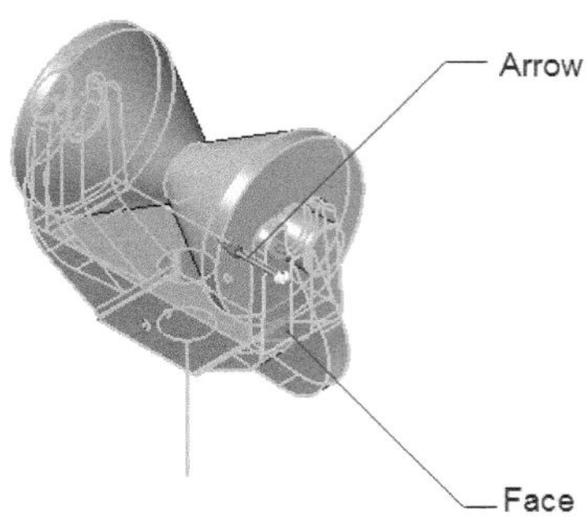

***Figure 11-30** Arrow showing the direction of explosion*

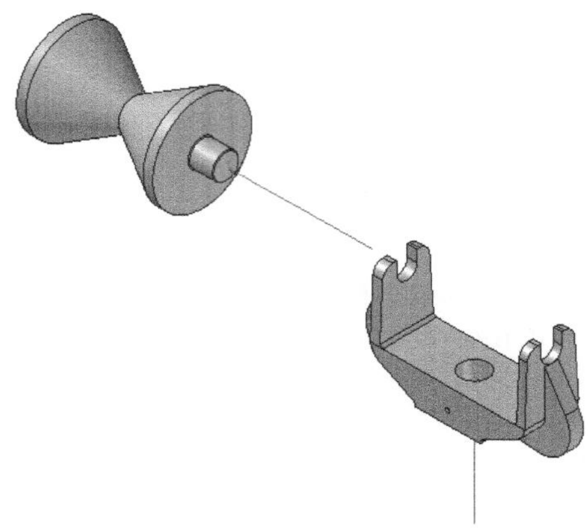

***Figure 11-31** The component exploded*

Reducing the Gap between Components

The distance between the components in the exploded view is large. You need to reduce the gap between the components.

1. Choose the **Drag Component** button from the **Modify** group of the **Home** tab; the **Drag Component** command bar is displayed. 
2. Choose the **Move Selected Part** button, if it is not already chosen. 

3. Select any one of the instances and choose the **Accept** button from the **Drag Component** command bar; a triad is displayed on the selected instance. Select the Z axis of the triad by clicking and dragging it toward the stationary part to reduce the gap between them.

4. After dragging the first component, select the second component and drag it closer to the stationary part, as shown in Figure 11-32.

5. Similarly, drag other components to reduce the gap. The exploded state of the assembly after reducing the gap is shown in Figure 11-33.

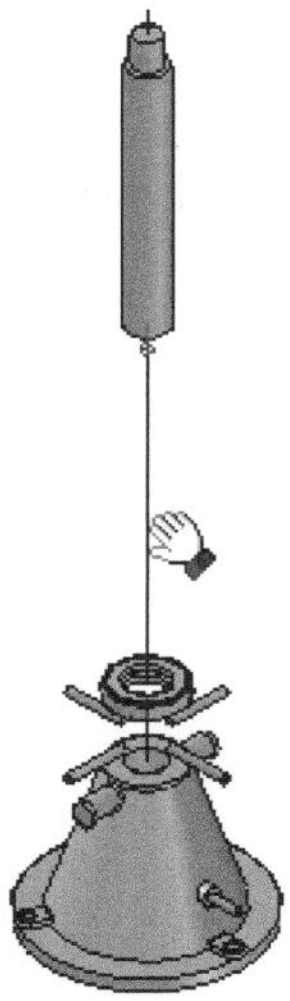

Figure 11-32 *Dragging the components*

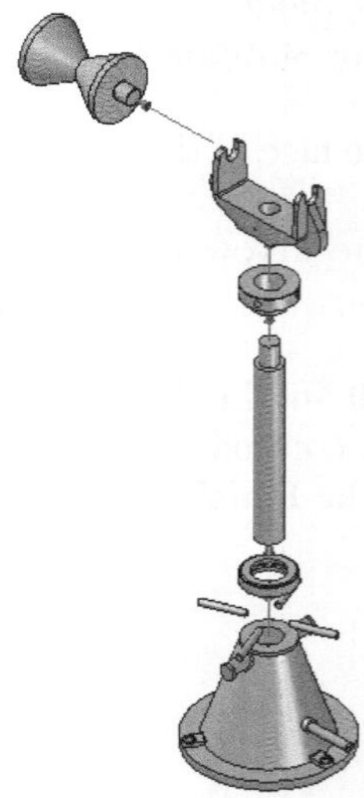

Figure 11-33 *Assembly after reducing the gap*

Moving the Components

The four instances of the *Adjusting Nut Handle* are not at the desired location. Therefore, you need to move them manually one by one.

1. Choose the **Drag Component** button from the **Modify** group; the **Drag Component** command bar is displayed and you are prompted to select the component to move. 

2. Select any one of the instances of the *Adjusting Nut Handle* and choose the **Accept** button from the **Drag Component** command bar; a triad is displayed on the selected instance, as shown in Figure 11-34.

3. Select the Z axis of the triad by clicking on it. Drag the component and place it, as shown in Figure 11-35.

4. Similarly, drag and place other instances of the *Adjusting Nut Handle*. To select the next instance, choose the **Select Part** button from the **Drag Component** command bar.

   The assembly after moving all the instances of the *Adjusting Nut Handle* is shown in Figure 11-36.

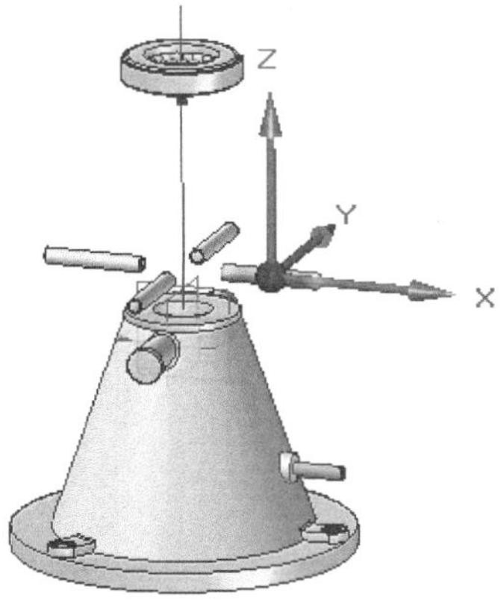

Figure 11-34 *The triad used to move the component*

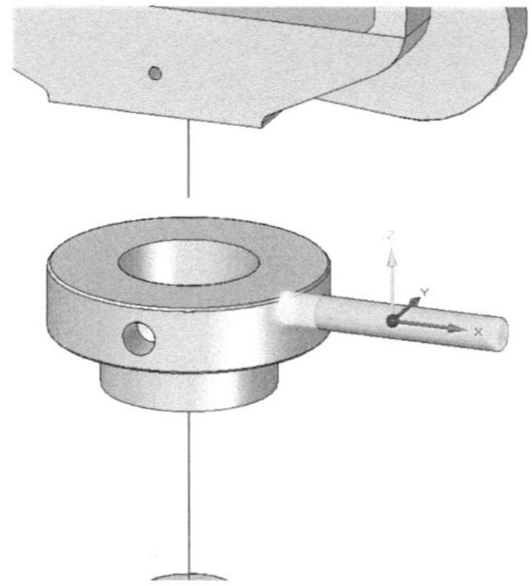

Figure 11-35 *The selected part placed at the required position*

Note

If the triad is not the way you want, choose the ***Rotate Triad*** *button from the command bar to orient the triad.*

Tip

To move the Adjusting Nut Handle more precisely to the desired location in the assembly, zoom in and view the assembly location of this part from the front. While viewing the part from the front view, move it to the desired location. You can also change the display of the assembly by choosing ***View Styles > Visible and Hidden Edges*** *from the status bar.*

After moving the instances, you will notice that the instances are still touching the Adjusting Screw Nut. Therefore, you need to move all the instances of the *Adjusting Nut Handle* away from the *Adjusting Screw Nut* by using the **Drag Component** tool.

5. Choose the **Drag Component** tool from the **Modify** group; the **Drag Component** command bar is displayed.

6. Select any one instance of the *Adjusting Nut Handle* and choose the **Accept** button from the command bar. Drag the instance to the required position. Alternatively, enter the distance value in the **Distance** edit box; the part moves to a new location.

7. Similarly, drag all the instances of the *Adjusting Nut Handle* one by one and place them, as shown in Figure 11-37.

8. Exit the **Drag Component** tool; all the parts are exploded as required.

Exploding the Last Component

The last component is the *Adjusting Screw Guide* and you need to explode it manually.

1. Choose the **Explode** tool from the **Explode** group.

2. Select the *Adjusting Screw Guide* from the assembly and choose the **Accept** button.

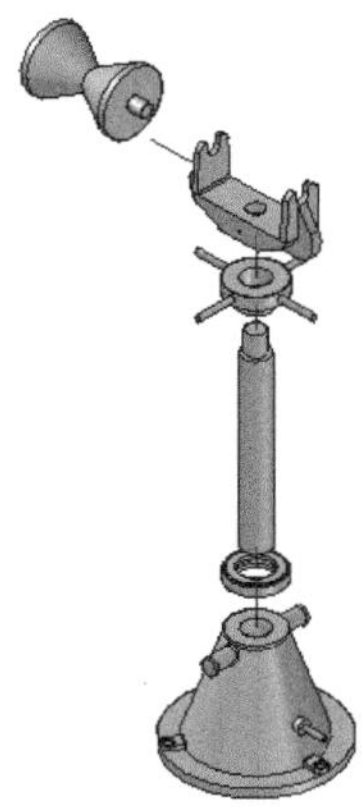

Figure 11-36 *Assembly after moving all instances of the Adjusting Nut Handle*

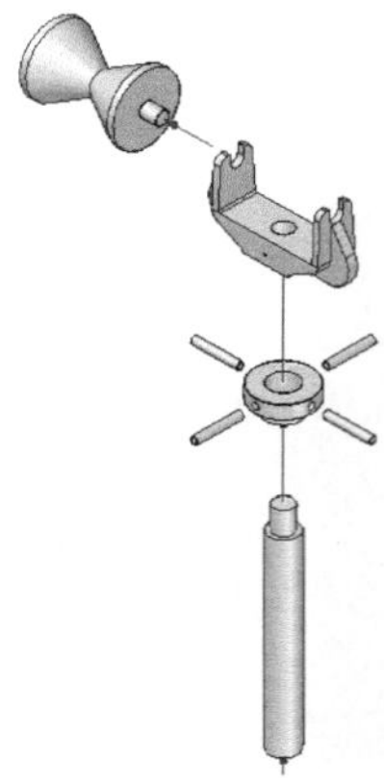

Figure 11-37 *The Adjusting Nut Handle after dragging all instances*

3. Select the *Stock Support Base* as the stationary part.

4. Select the face of the stationary part, as shown in Figure 11-38, to specify the direction of explosion. Click when the red arrow points away from the base.

5. Enter **10** inches in the **Distance** edit box and then choose the **Explode** button from the command bar; the selected part is exploded in the specified direction, as shown in Figure 11-39.

6. Choose **Finish** and then **Cancel** to exit the **Explode** tool.

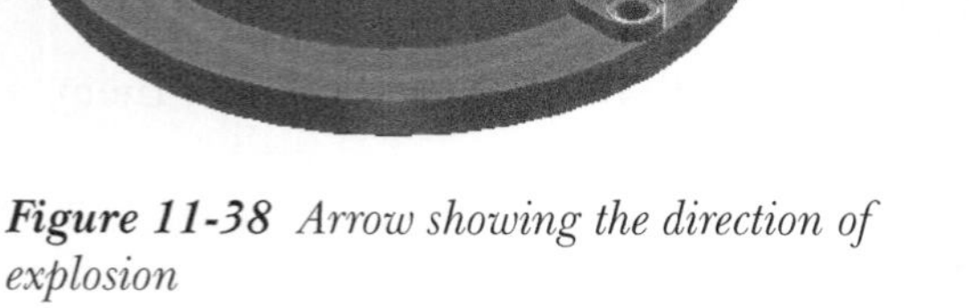

Figure 11-38 *Arrow showing the direction of explosion*

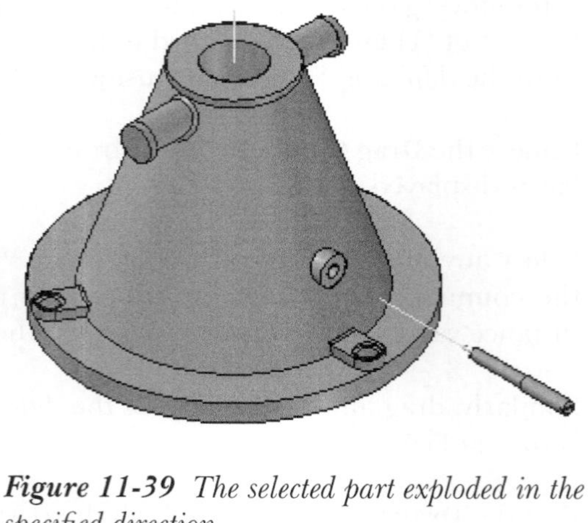

Figure 11-39 *The selected part exploded in the specified direction*

Saving the Configuration

You may need to use this exploded state of the assembly in the later chapters. Therefore, you need to save it in a configuration file. To create the configuration file, follow the steps given next.

1. Choose the **Display Configurations** tool from the **Configurations** group in the **Ribbon**; the **Display Configurations** dialog box is displayed. Make sure that you save the model before choosing the **Display Configurations** tool.

2. Choose the **New** button; the **New Configuration** dialog box is displayed. Next, enter **Stock bracket** as the name of the configuration in the **Configuration name** text box of the **New Configuration** dialog box.

3. Choose the **OK** button from the **New Configuration** dialog box and then choose the **Close** button to exit the dialog box.

4. To return to the assembly window, choose the **Close ERA** button from the **Close** group.

Tutorial 2

In this tutorial, you will create the Radial Engine assembly shown in Figure 11-40. This assembly will be created in two parts, the subassembly and the main assembly. The exploded state of the assembly is shown in Figure 11-41. The views and dimensions of all the components of this assembly are shown in Figures 11-42 through 11-46. After creating the assembly, save it with the name *Radial Engine.asm* at the location given below:

C:\Solid Edge\c11\Radial Engine **(Expected time: 3 hr)**

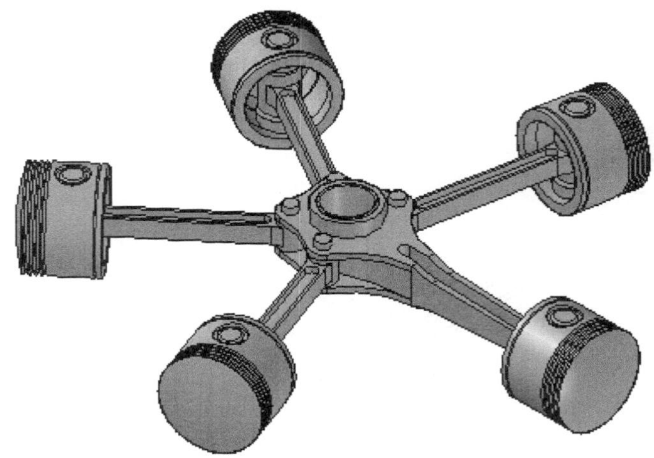

Figure 11-40 *The Radial Engine assembly*

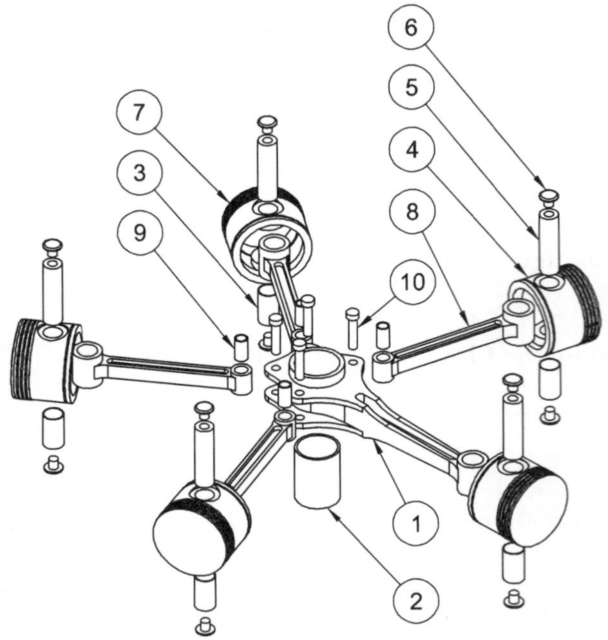

ITEM NO.	PART NO.	QTY.
1	Master Rod	1
2	Master Rod Bearing	1
3	Rod Bush Upper	5
4	Piston	5
5	Piston Pin	5
6	Piston Pin Plug	10
7	Piston Ring	20
8	Articulated Rod	4
9	Rod Bush Lower	4
10	Link Pin	4

Figure 11-41 *Exploded view of the assembly*

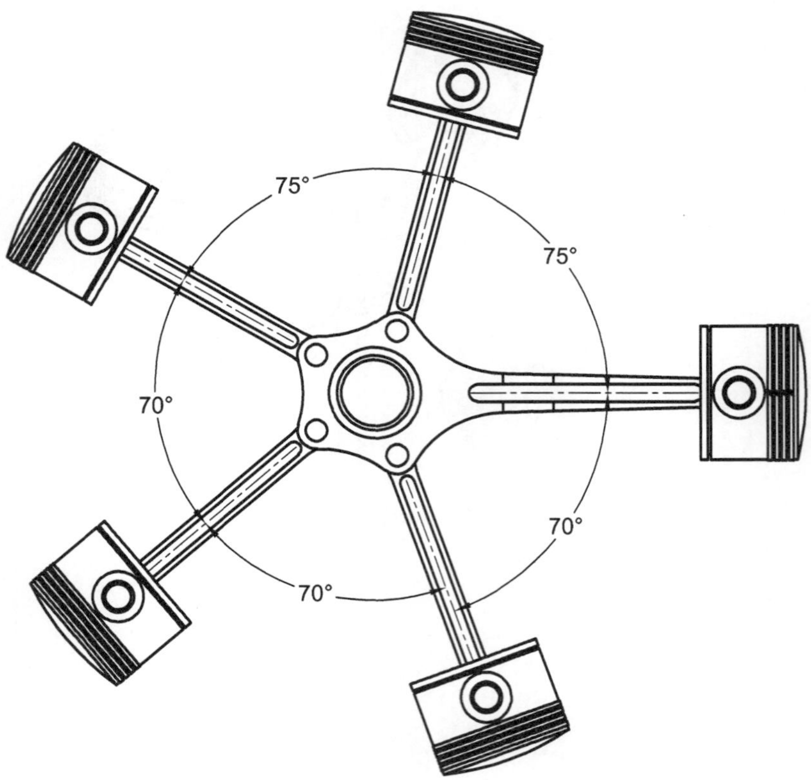

Figure 11-42 *Assembly structure*

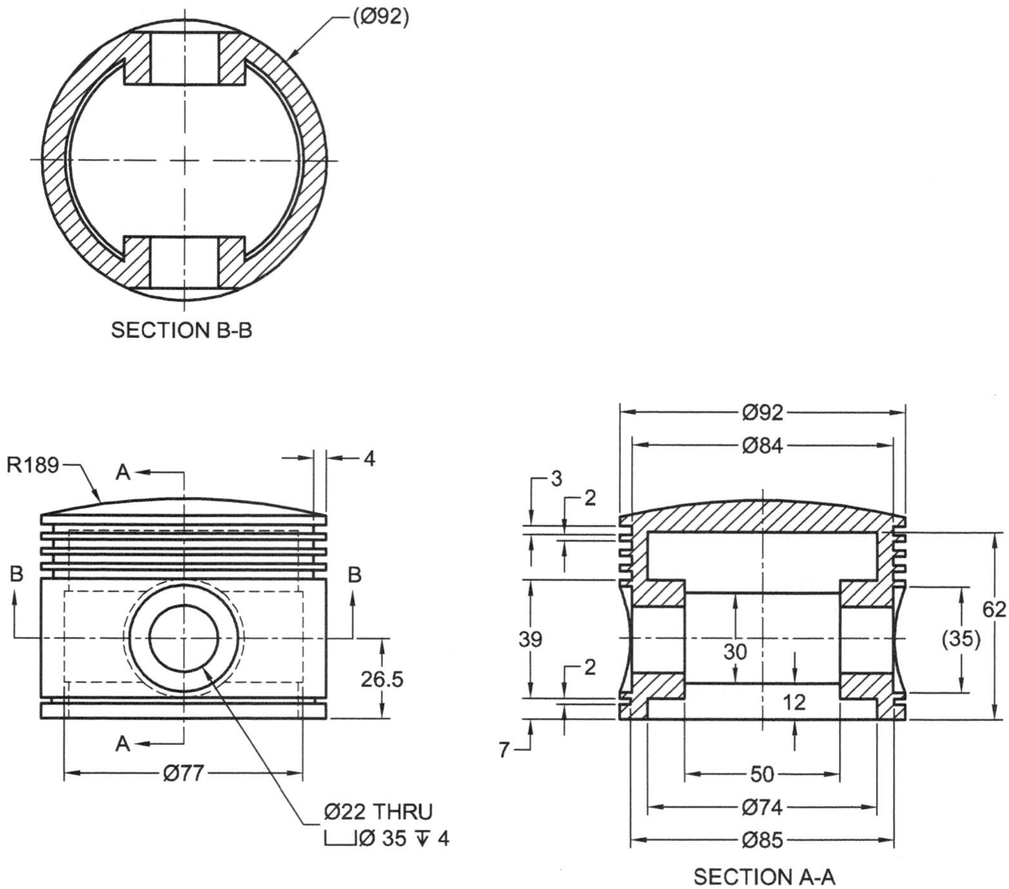

Figure 11-43 *Views and dimensions of the Piston*

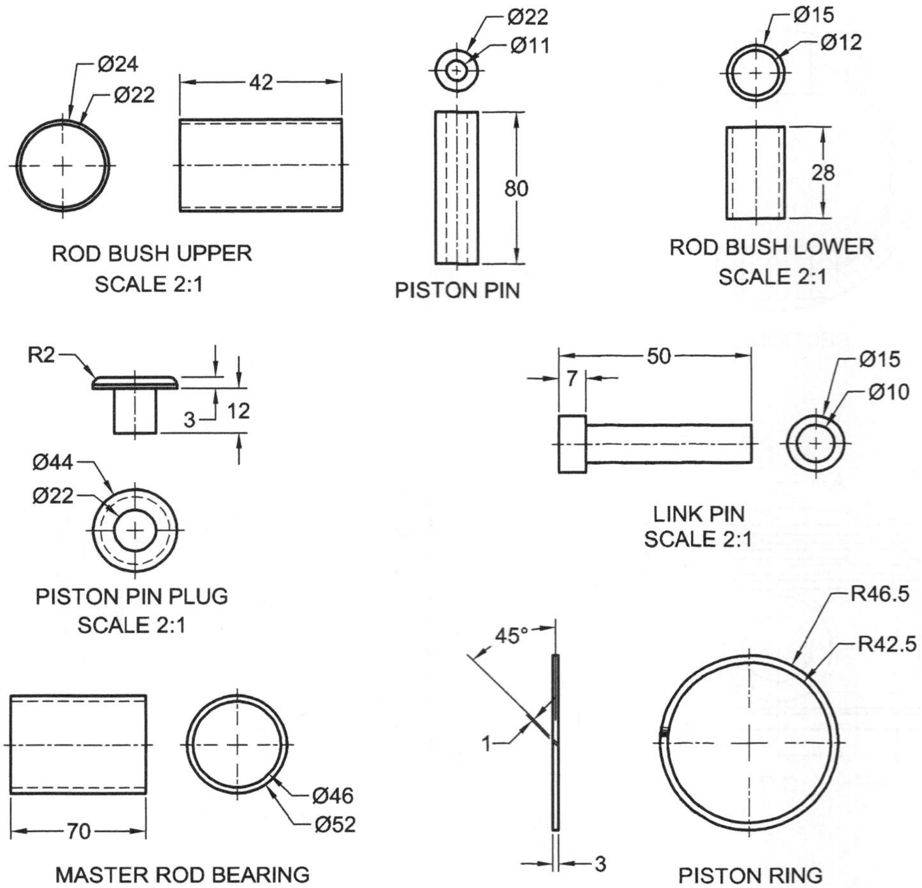

Figure 11-44 *Views and dimensions of other components*

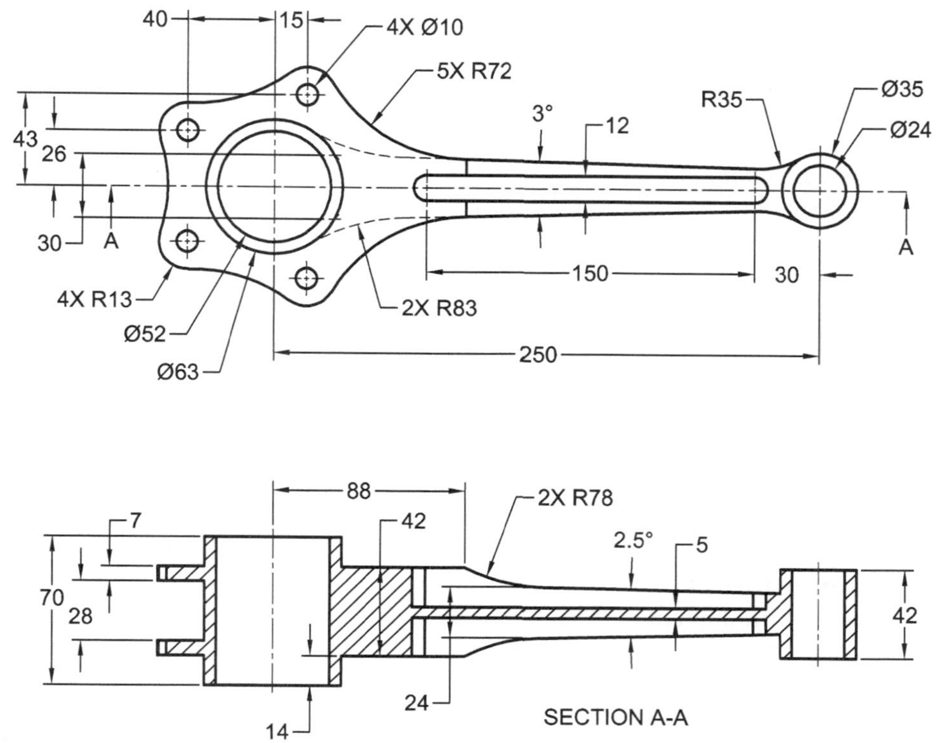

Figure 11-45 Views and dimensions of the Master Rod

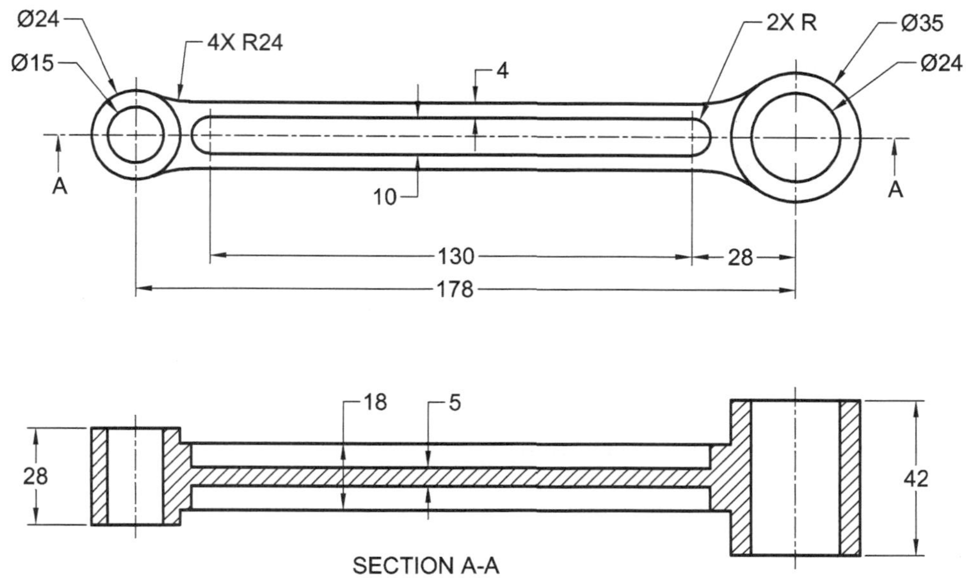

Figure 11-46 Views and dimensions of the Articulated Rod

This assembly has a large number of components, so you need to divide it into two assemblies such that one is the main assembly and the other is the subassembly. First you need to create the subassembly which consists of the *Articulated Rod, Piston, Piston Rings, Piston Pin, Rod Bush Upper, Rod Bush Lower,* and *Piston Pin Plug*. After creating this subassembly, you will create the main assembly in which you will assemble the *Master Rod* with the *Piston, Piston Rings, Piston Pin, Rod Bush Upper,* and *Piston Pin Plug*. After assembling components in the main assembly, you will add the subassembly to the main assembly.

The following steps are required to complete this tutorial:

a. Create all components of the assembly in the **Part** environment and save them in the *Radial Engine* folder.
b. Create the subassembly, refer to Figures 11-47 through 11-49.
c. Create the main assembly, refer to Figure 11-50.
d. Assemble the subassembly to the main assembly, refer to Figures 11-51.
e. Assemble the Link pin to the main assembly and save the assembly, refer to Figures 11-52 and 11-53.

Creating Components

1. Create a folder with the name *Radial Engine* at *Solid Edge\c11*. Create all the components in individual part files and save them in this folder.

Creating the Subassembly

As discussed earlier, first you need to create the subassembly and then assemble it with the main assembly.

1. Start a new file in the **Assembly** environment. Name this file as *Piston Articulated Rod subassem* and save it in the same folder in which the parts were saved.

2. Choose the **Parts Library** tab from the left pane; the **Parts Library** is displayed as a docking window. Browse to the folder where all the files were saved and then drag and drop the Articulated Rod into the assembly window.

3. Assemble the *Rod Bush Upper* with the *Articulated Rod* using the assembly relationships. Figure 11-47 shows the sequence in which you need to assemble the components. The exploded view and the flowlines are shown for your reference only. The assembly after assembling the *Articulated Rod, Rod Bush Upper, Rod Bush Lower, Piston, Piston Pin,* and *Piston Pin Plugs* will look similar to Figure 11-48.

4. Insert the *Piston Ring* in the subassembly and assemble it with the *Piston*, as shown in Figure 11-48. Similarly, assemble other instances of the *Piston Ring* with the *Piston*.

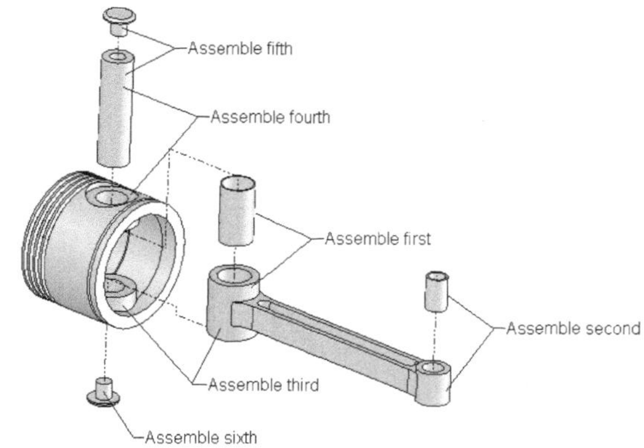

Figure 11-47 *Assembly sequence of the Articulated Rod, Piston, Piston Pin Plug, Piston Pin, Rod Bush Upper, and Rod Bush Lower*

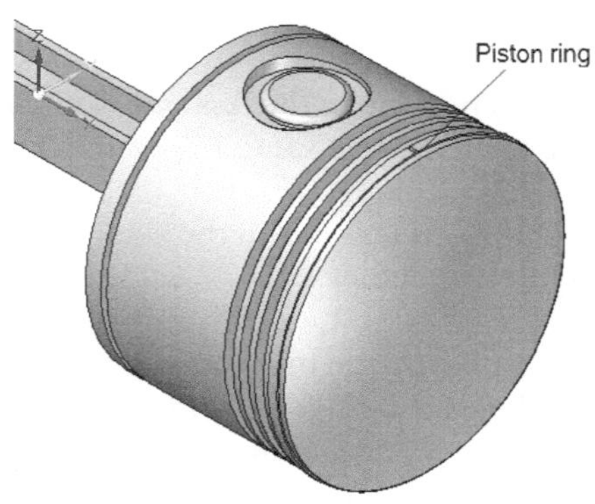

Figure 11-48 *First instance of the Piston Ring assembled with the Piston*

Now, you need to change the color of the *Piston Ring*.

5. Choose the **Color Manager** button from the **Style** group of the **View** tab; the **Color Manager** dialog box is displayed. 

6. Select the **Use individual part styles** radio button, if it is not already selected, and choose **OK** from the dialog box.

7. Now select the *Piston Ring* from the **PathFinder** or from the subassembly.

8. From the **Face Style** drop-down list of the **Style** group, select the color that you want to apply to the selected component. As you select the color; the **Multiple Part Occurrences** message box will be displayed.

9. Choose the **All Occurrences** button from the message box to apply the selected style to all the occurrences of the selected part. The subassembly after assembling the *Piston Rings* and changing their color is shown in Figure 11-49. Next, save and close the subassembly file.

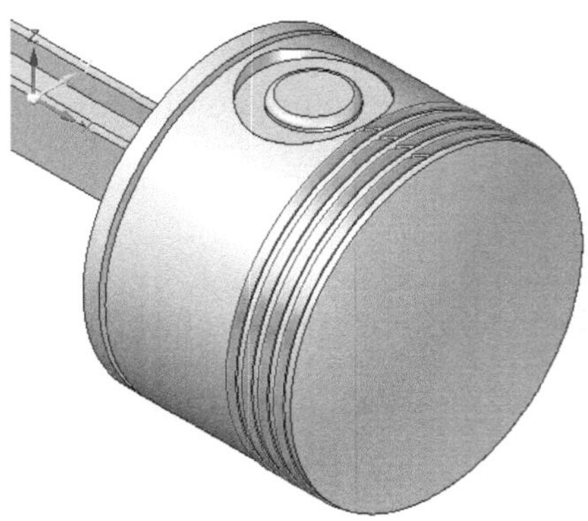

Figure 11-49 *Subassembly after assembling the Piston Rings and changing their color*

Creating the Main Assembly

Next, you need to create the main assembly and then assemble the subassembly with it.

1. Start a new file in the **Assembly** environment and then save it with the name **Radial Engine Assembly** in the same folder in which the parts were saved.

2. Place the *Master Rod* in the assembly so that it automatically gets assembled with the assembly reference planes.

3. After placing the first component, use the assembly relationships to place the *Piston* and then the *Piston Pin, Piston Pin Plugs, Piston Rings, Rod Bush Upper,* and *Master Rod Bearing,* one by one. The components after being assembled with the main assembly will be displayed, as shown in Figure 11-50.

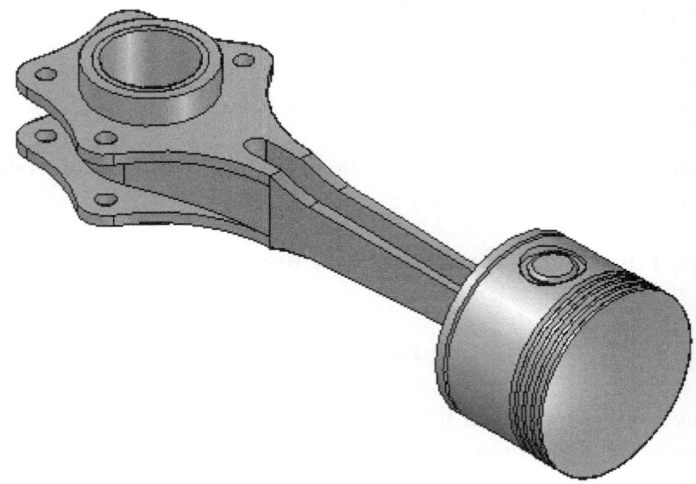

Figure 11-50 *Components assembled with the Main assembly*

Assembling the Subassembly with the Main Assembly

Next, you need to assemble the subassembly with the main assembly using the assembly relationships.

1. Choose the **Parts Library** tab from the left pane to display it.

2. Drag and drop the *Piston Articulation Rod* subassembly into the assembly window;

3. Assemble the subassembly with the main assembly using the **Mate**, **Axial Align**, and **Angle** assembly relationships. The first instance of the subassembly after assembling with the main assembly is shown in Figure 11-51. Note that while applying the **Angle** relationship, you need to choose the **7** button from the **Angle Format** flyout in the **Angle** command bar.

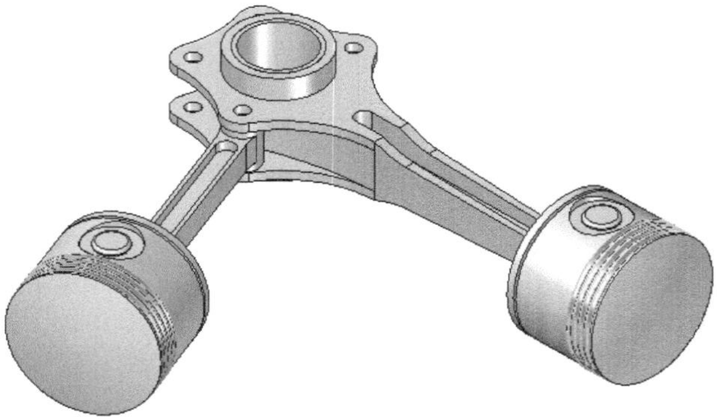

Figure 11-51 *The first instance of the subassembly assembled with the main assembly*

Figure 11-43 shows the assembly structure that will help you in assembling the instances of the subassembly.

Assembling the Link Pin

After assembling the subassembly with the main assembly, you need to assemble the *Link Pin* with the main assembly.

1. Place the *Link Pin* in the current assembly and assemble it with the main assembly by using the assembly relationships. Figure 11-52 shows the first instance of the *Link Pin* assembled with the main assembly.

2. Before placing the other instances of the *Link Pin*, invoke the **Options** dialog box in the command bar and then select the **Automatically Capture Fit when placing parts** check box from it.

Figure 11-53 shows all the instances of the *Link Pin* assembled with the main assembly.

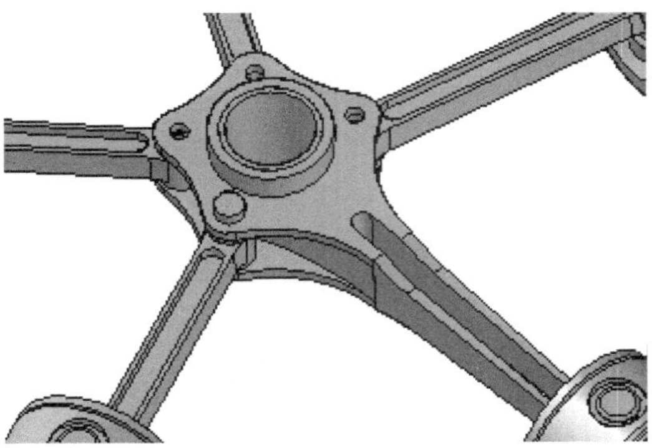

Figure 11-52 *First instance of the Link Pin assembled with the main assembly*

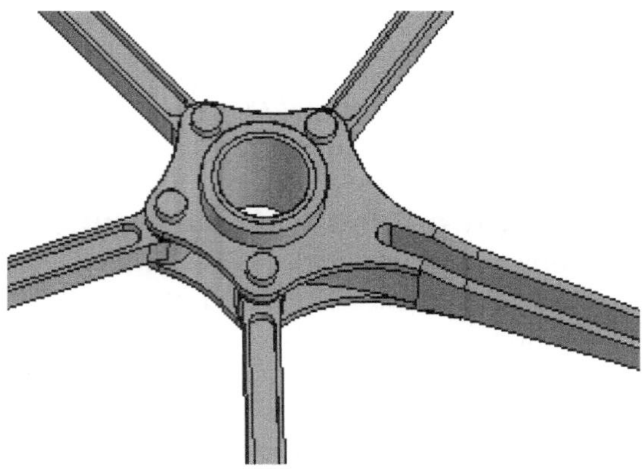

Figure 11-53 *All instances of the Link Pin assembled with the main assembly*

3. Save the assembly with the name *Radial Engine.asm* at the location given next and then close the file.
   C:\Solid Edge\c11\Radial Engine

Tutorial 3

In this tutorial, you will edit the Synchronous parts of the Plummer Block assembly created in Exercise 1 of Chapter 10, as shown in Figure 11-54. Modify the width of the components from **46** to **56** mm. Also, you need to remove the taper of the base element. The resultant model is shown in Figure 11-55. Save the resultant model with the name *Plummer Block* at the location given below:

C:\Solid Edge\c11\Plummer Block **(Expected time: 30 min)**

The following steps are required to complete this tutorial:

a. Copy all the part and assembly files of the Plummer Block assembly from the *c10* folder to the *c11* folder. The files will be saved at *Solid Edge\c11\Plummer Block*.
b. Modify the width of the base component, refer to Figure 11-56.
c. Modify the width of the Brasses, refer to Figures 11-57 and 11-58.
d. Remove the taper of the base component, refer to Figure 11-59.

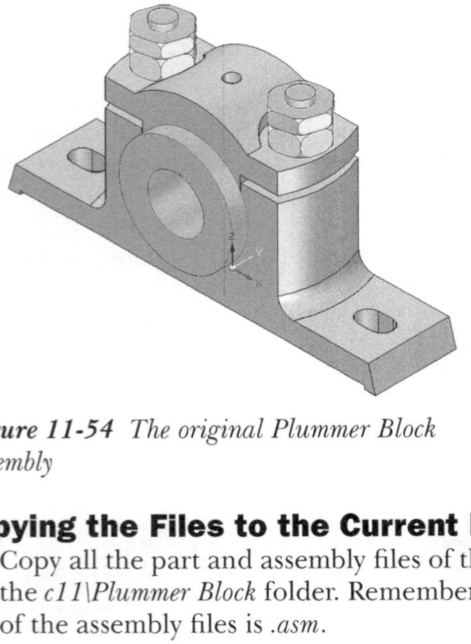

Figure 11-54 *The original Plummer Block assembly*

Figure 11-55 *The Plummer Block assembly after editing*

Copying the Files to the Current Folder

1. Copy all the part and assembly files of the Plummer Block assembly from the *c10* folder to the *c11\Plummer Block* folder. Remember that the extension of the part files is *.par* and that of the assembly files is *.asm*.

2. Choose the **Open** button from the **Quick Access** toolbar; the **Open File** dialog box is displayed. Browse to the location where the plummer block assembly file is saved and then select the *plummer block.asm* file. Next, select the **Small Assembly** option from the **Assembly open as** drop-down list.

3. Choose the **More** button available at the bottom of the **Assembly open as** drop-down list; the **Assembly open as** dialog box is displayed. Select the **Activate all** option from the **Part activation** drop-down list in the dialog box. Next, choose the **OK** and then **Open** button; the file is opened in the **Assembly** environment.

Modifying the Width of the Casting and Cap

To modify the width of the component, you first need to select the front face of the base component and then modify it. Next, you need to make the other components coincident with the base component.

1. Choose the **Select** tool to display a flyout. Choose the **Face Priority** option from the flyout.

2. Move the cursor on the front face of the base component; the face gets highlighted. Select the front face of the base component.

3. On selecting the front face, a handle, **QuickBar**, **Design Intent** panel, and dimensions that were added to the feature are displayed.

4. Unlock the locked dimensions; the locked dimensions turn blue.

5. Click on the primary axis of the handle; an edit box is displayed on the component. Enter **5** in the edit box to specify the distance to move the front face, as shown in Figure 11-56. On doing so, you will notice that both the front face and the back face move to the same distance. But, this will happen only when the base component is extruded symmetrically.

   The base component gets modified. Similarly, modify the Cap component.

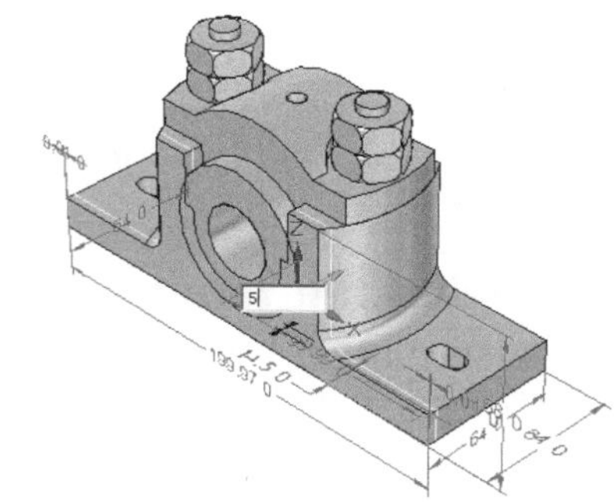

Figure 11-56 Moving the front face of the base component

Modifying the Width of the Brasses

Next, you need to modify the *Brasses*. You cannot modify them in a single modification step because they were not extruded symmetrically. Therefore, you need to modify each face one by one. To do so, first you need to suppress the cap, bolts, nuts, and lock nuts.

1. In the **PathFinder**, clear the check boxes beside the *cap, bolts, nuts,* and *lock nuts*; the respective components are hidden.

2. Invoke the **Select** tool and select the front planar face of the brasses; a handle is displayed.

3. Select the handle is displayed in the drawing area; an edit box is displayed. Enter **7** in the edit box; both the front as well as the back faces of the brasses are modified accordingly.

4. Choose the **Select** tool and select the planar face of the *Brasses*; the handle and the **QuickBar** are displayed, refer to Figure 11-57.

5. Select the handle and move the face toward the back planar face of the base component. Next, select the keypoint of the base component; the selected face of the Brasses is in plane with the base component, as shown in Figure 11-57.

6. Select the planar face of the Brass; a handle is displayed, as shown in Figure 11-58. Click on the handle and move the face outward; an edit box is displayed. Next, enter **3** in the edit box; both the outer cylinders are modified.

   Now, you need to display all hidden components.

7. In the **PathFinder**, select the check boxes beside the hidden components.

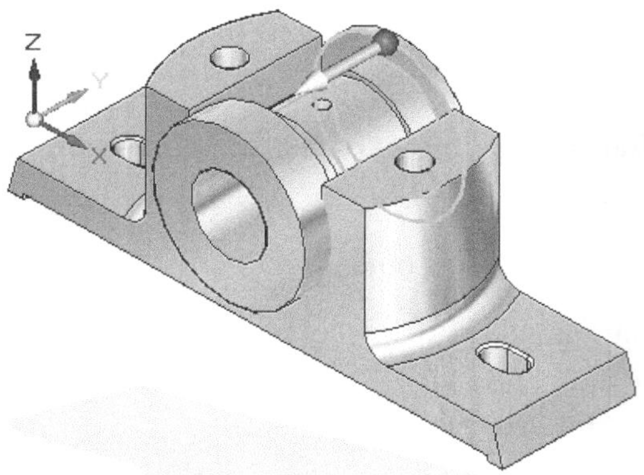

Figure 11-57 *Modifying the outer cylinders of the Brasses*

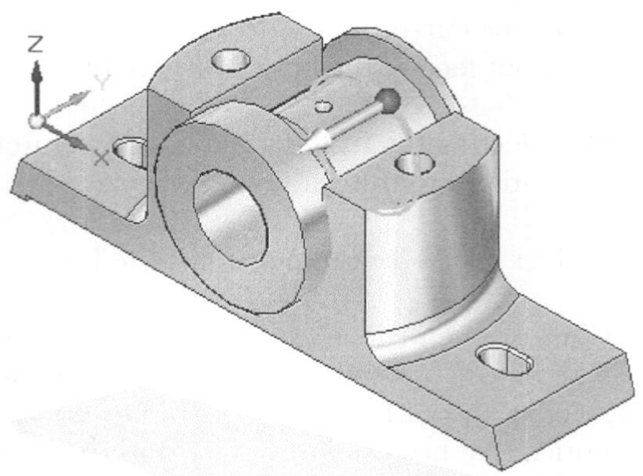

Figure 11-58 *Modifying the next outer cylinders of the Brasses*

Removing the Taper of the Base Component

1. Select the tapered face of the base component, refer to Figure 11-59; a handle, **QuickBar**, and **Design Intent** panel are displayed for the selected face. Make sure that the **Face Priority** option is chosen in the **Select** drop-down of the **Select** group.

2. Move the handle to the edge of the tapered face, as shown in Figure 11-59.

3. Click on the torus of the handle; an edit box along with a preview of rotation is displayed on the screen.

4. Enter **-16** in the **Dimension** edit box to make it perpendicular to the base.

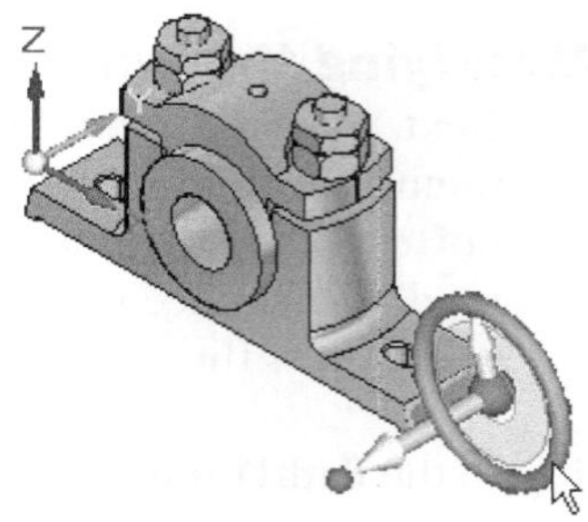

Figure 11-59 *Rotating the face of the base component*

Similarly, rotate the other tapered face if required. The resultant model will be as shown in Figure 11-55.

Note
*If you do not get the desired result on entering **-16** in Step 4, enter **16**.*

Self-Evaluation Test

Answer the following questions and then compare them to those given at the end of this chapter:

1. The ____________ is the file extension of the assembly files created in the **Assembly** environment of Solid Edge.

2. The ____________ environment in the **Assembly** environment is used to create the exploded states of the assembly.

3. You can turn on the display of a hidden component by selecting it and choosing the __________ option from the shortcut menu that is displayed by right-clicking.

4. To explode an assembly manually, choose the _________ button from the **Explode** group of the **Ribbon** in the **Explode-Render-Animate** environment.

5. You can delete an existing assembly relationship by selecting it from the bottom pane of the **PathFinder** and then pressing the DELETE key. (T/F)

6. The bottom pane of the **PathFinder** is used to view and modify the relationships between the selected part and the other parts in the assembly. (T/F)

7. To create subassemblies, you need to follow a different procedure than the one required for creating assemblies. (T/F)

8. By simplifying assemblies, you can hide components at any stage of the design cycle.(T/F)

9. Before sending the **Part** and the **Assembly** files for detailing and drafting, it is essential to check for interference in the assembly. (T/F)

10. You cannot set the output options before starting the interference check. (T/F)

Review Questions

Answer the following questions:

1. Which of the following options is used to open a component separately in a part file?

   (a) **Modify** (b) **Open**
   (c) **Open in Solid Edge Part** (d) **Edit**

2. Which of the following environments within the **Assembly** environment is used to create the exploded state of an assembly?

   (a) **Virtual Studio** (b) **Explode-Render-Animate**
   (c) **Motion** (d) None of these

3. Which of the following tools is used to replace a part with a standard part?

   (a) **Replace Part** (b) **Replace Part with Standard Part**
   (c) **Replace Part with Copy** (d) **Replace Part with New Part**

4. Which of the following options should be chosen from the shortcut menu to hide a component?

   (a) **Show** (b) **Hide**
   (c) **Activate** (d) **Show only**

5. You cannot modify the dimensions of a component in the **Assembly** environment. (T/F)

6. In the exploded state, when you choose the **Remove** button from the **Explode** group in the **Explode-Render-Animate** environment, the selected part gets hidden and moves to its original position in the assembly. (T/F)

7. The exploded state of an assembly is created by changing the environment to the **Explode-Render-Animate** environment in the **Assembly** environment. (T/F)

8. You can set the transparency of any component to simplify the assembly. (T/F)

9. The automatic explode method does not give the desired results every time. Therefore, the manual method is used to achieve the desired exploded state. (T/F)

10. When you place a subassembly in the main assembly, an assembly icon is displayed with the name of the subassembly in the **PathFinder**. (T/F)

EXERCISE

Exercise 1

Create the Shaper Tool Head assembly, as shown in Figure 11-60. After creating the assembly, create its exploded state, as shown in Figure 11-61. The dimensions of the model are given in Figures 11-62 through 11-66. After creating the assembly, save it with the name *Shaper.asm* at the location given below:

C:\Solid Edge\c11\Shaper Tool Head **(Expected time: 4 hr)**

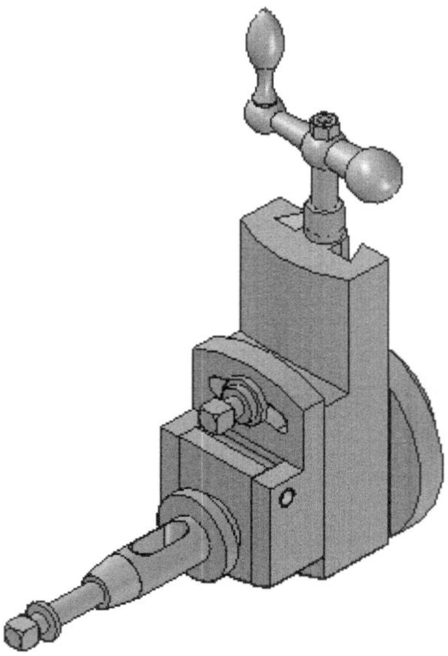

Figure 11-60 *Shaper Tool Head assembly*

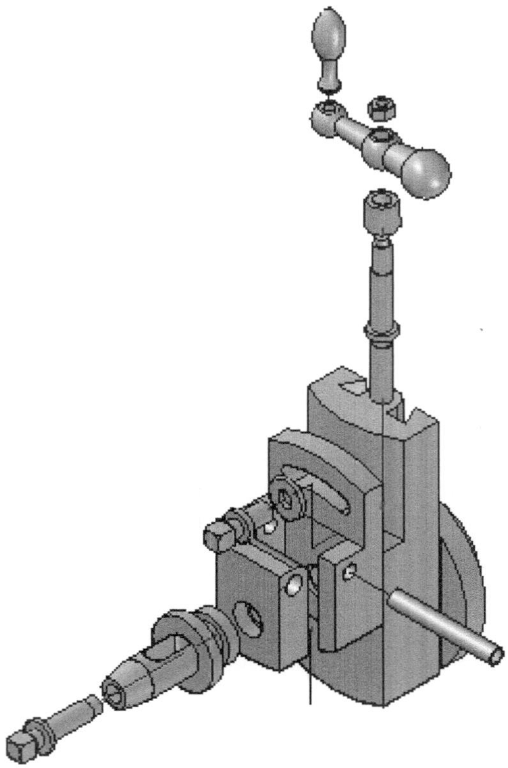

Figure 11-61 *Exploded state of the assembly*

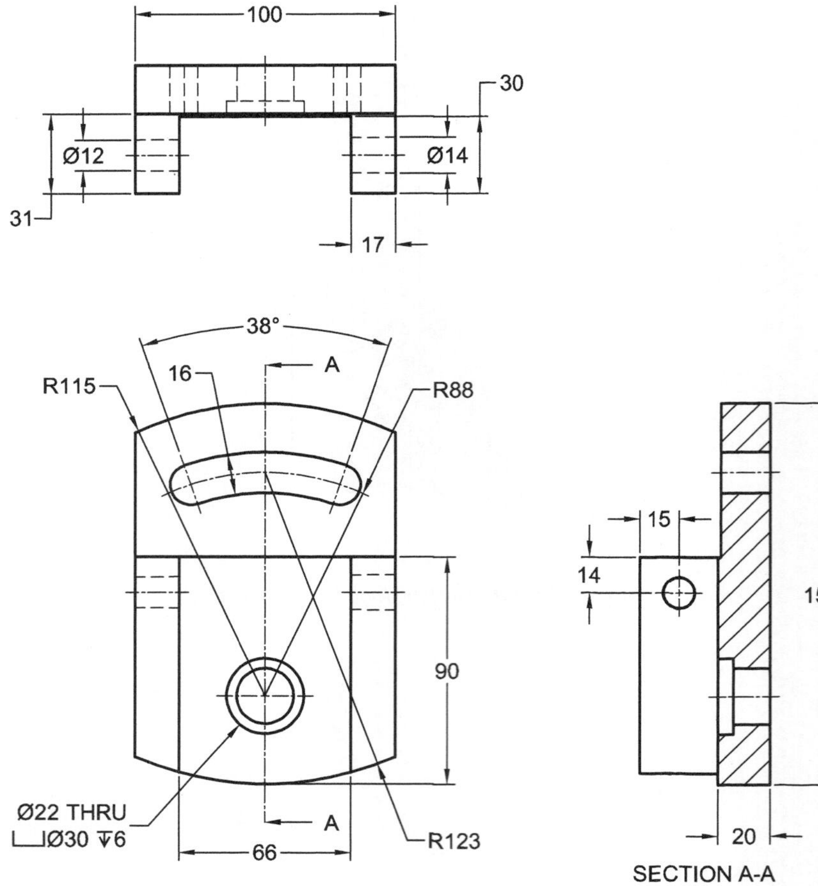

Figure 11-62 *Views and dimensions of the Swivel Plate*

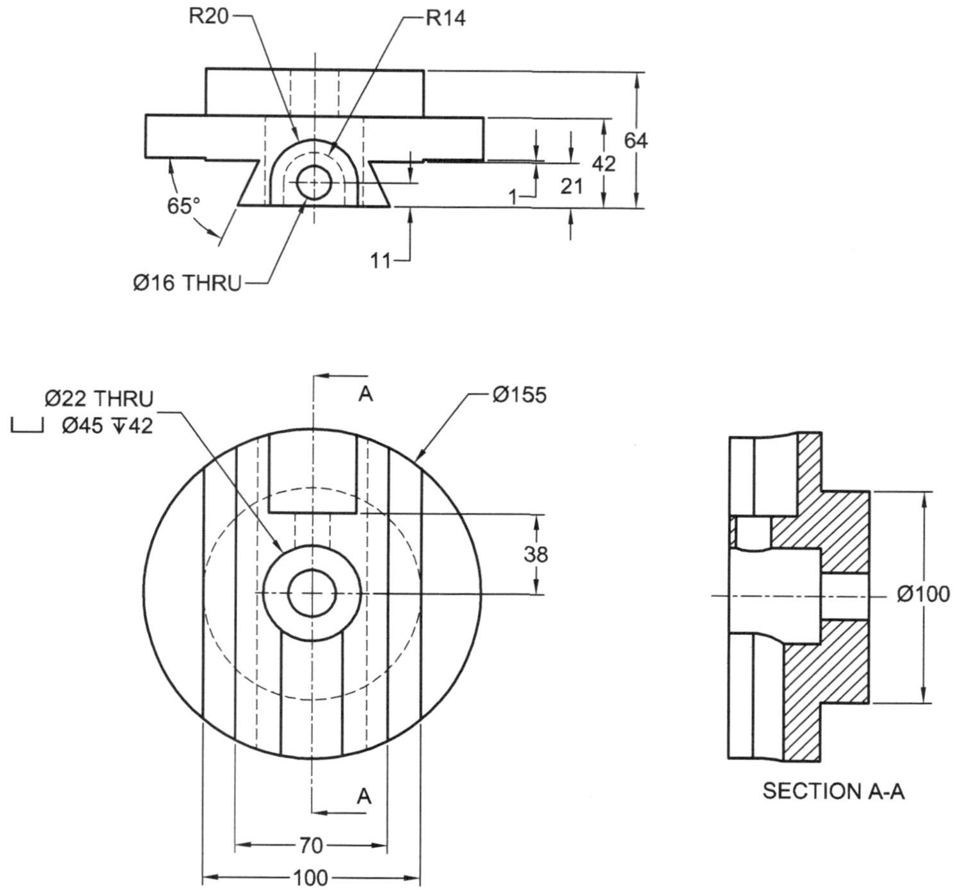

***Figure 11-63** Views and dimensions of the Back Plate*

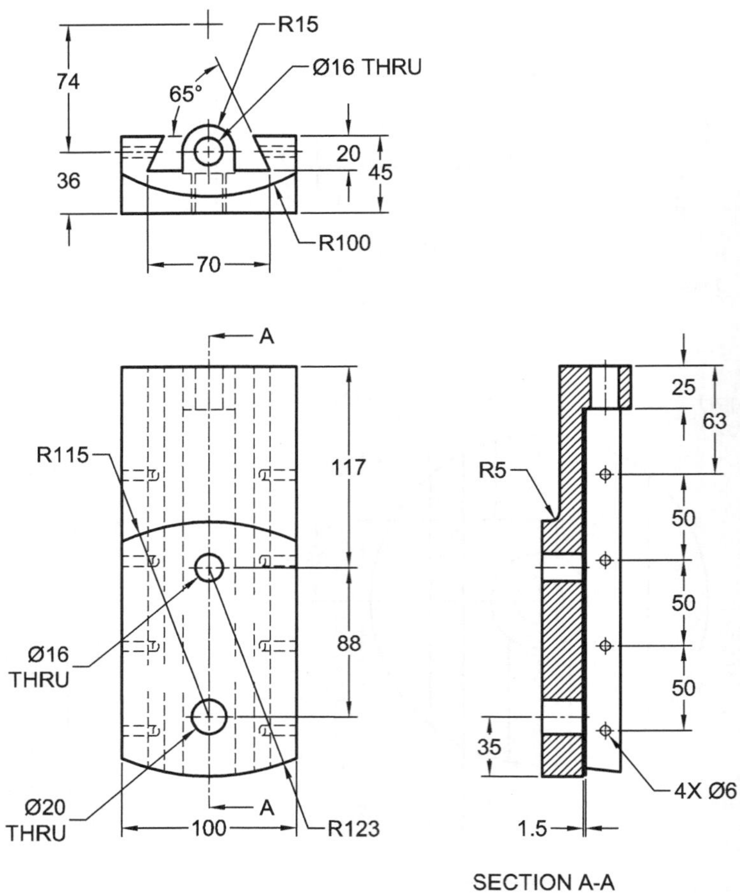

Figure 11-64 *Views and dimensions of the Vertical Slide*

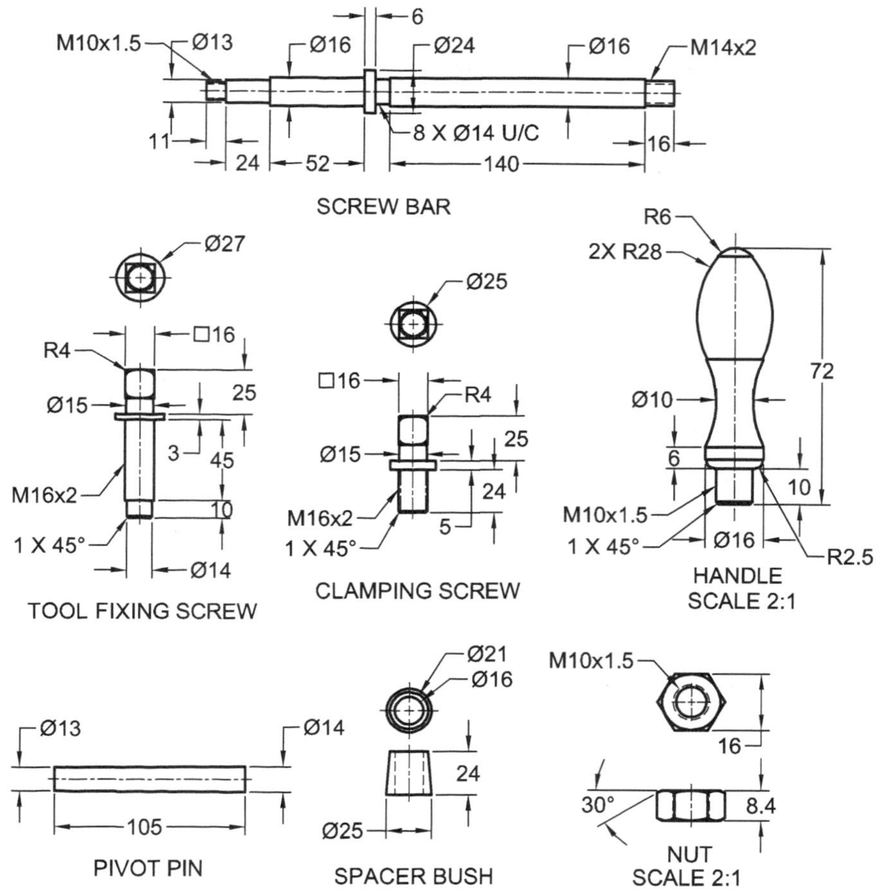

Figure 11-65 Views and dimensions of various components

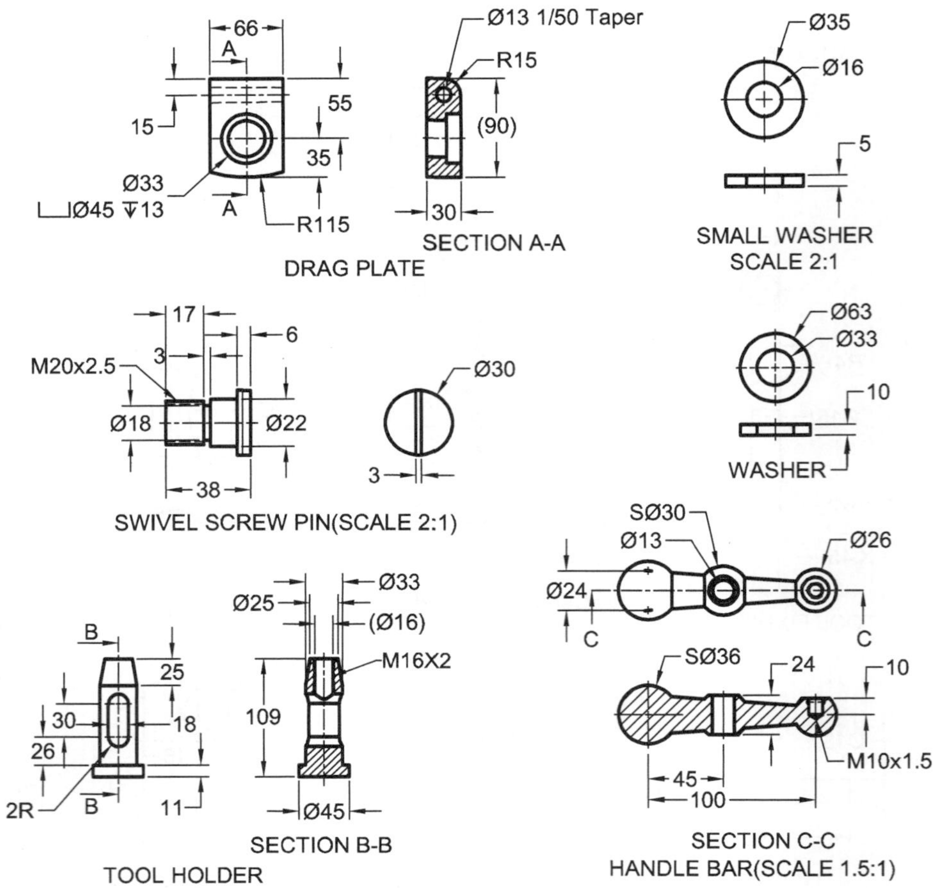

Figure 11-66 *Views and dimensions of various components*

Exercise 2

Create the Bench Vice assembly, as shown in Figure 11-67. The dimensions of the model are given in Figures 11-68 through 11-71. After creating the assembly, save it with the name *Bench Vice.asm* at the location given below:

C:\Solid Edge\c11\Bench Vice **(Expected time: 3 hr)**

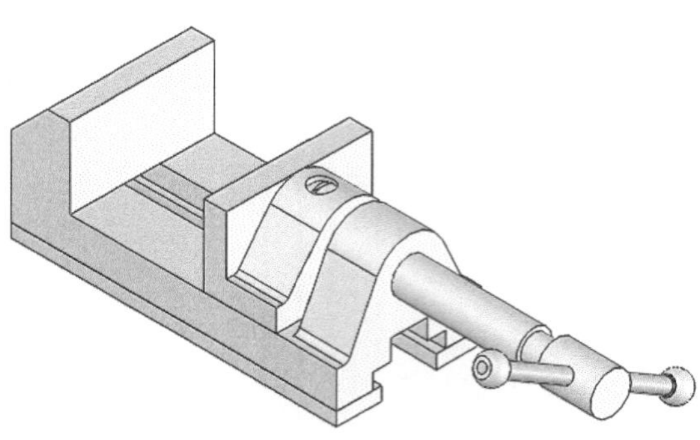

Figure 11-67 *Bench Vice assembly*

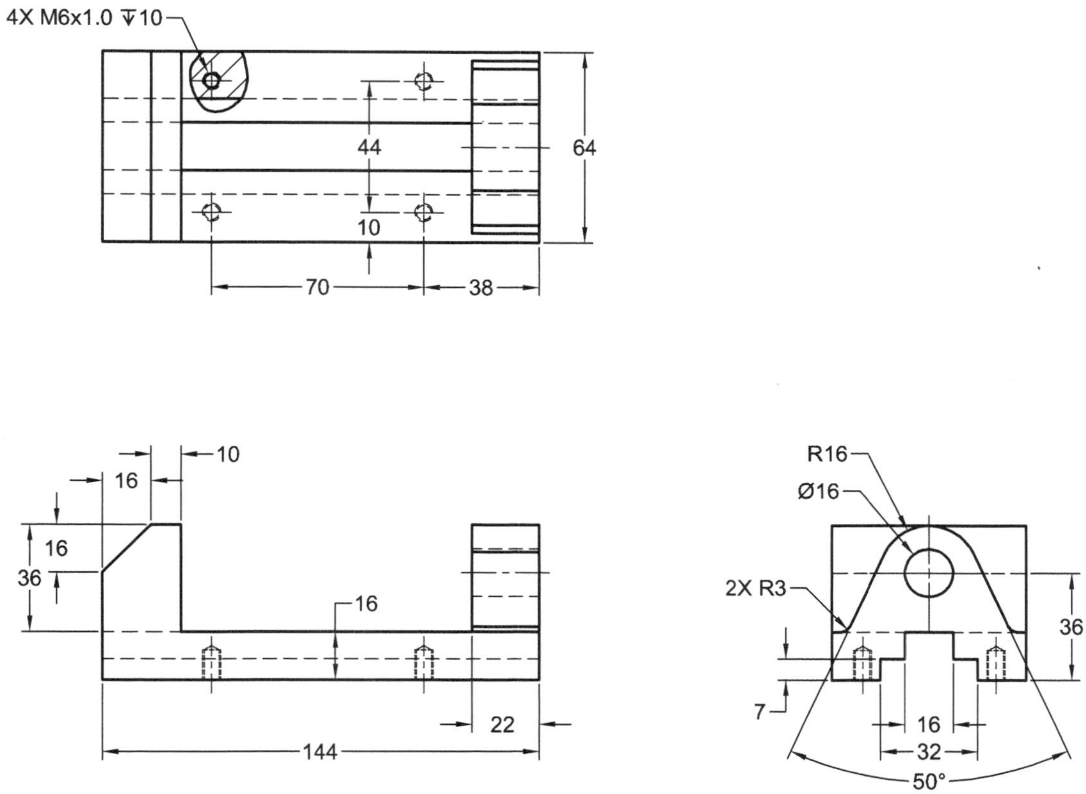

Figure 11-68 *Orthographic views and dimensions of the Vice Body*

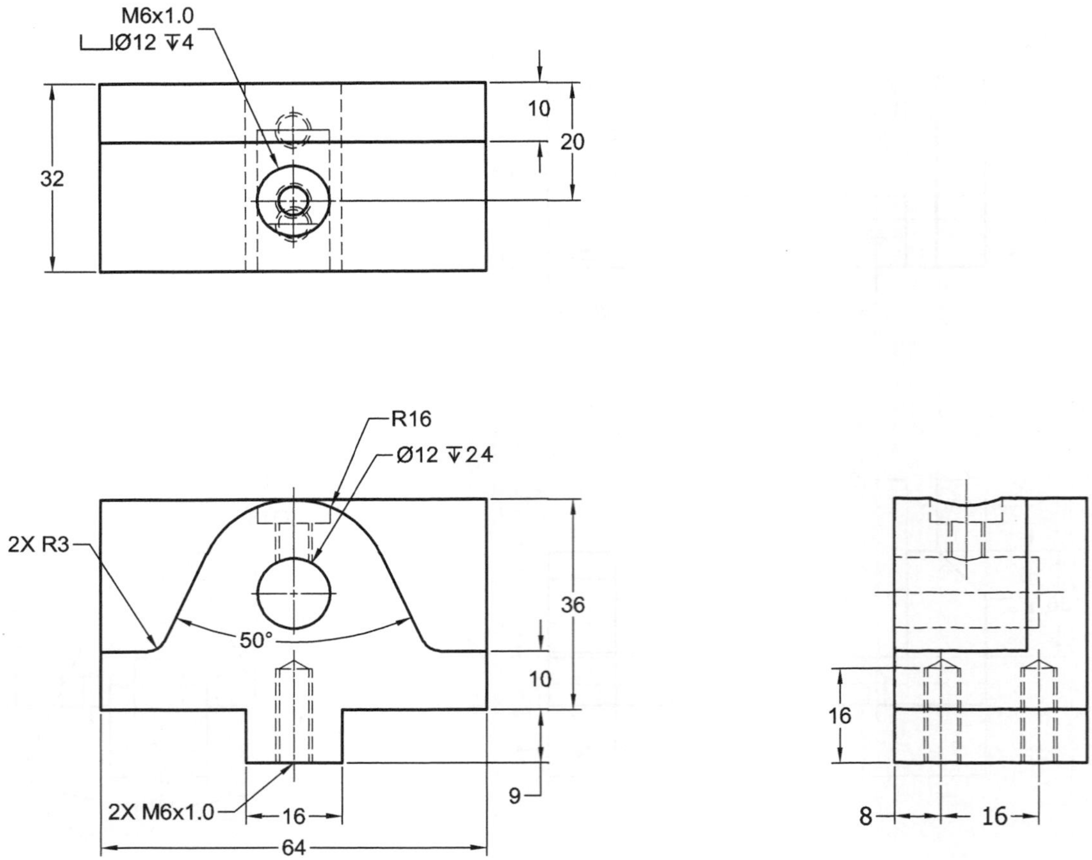

Figure 11-69 Orthographic views and dimensions of the Vice Jaw

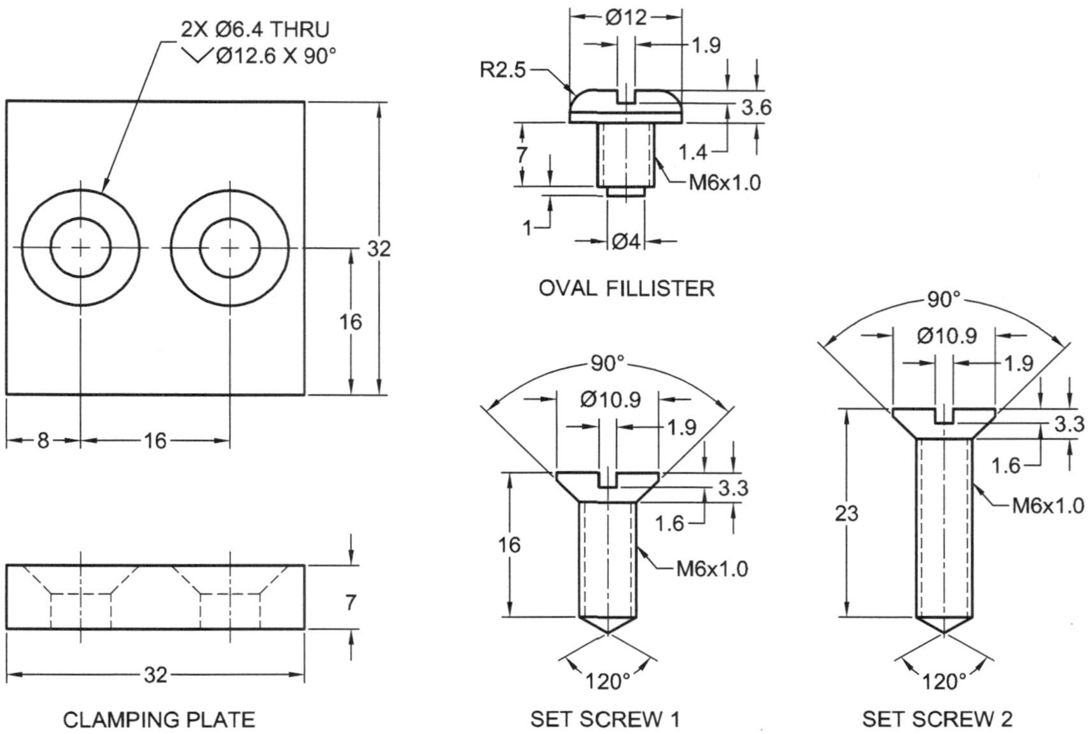

Figure 11-70 *Orthographic views and dimensions of various components of the Bench Vice assembly*

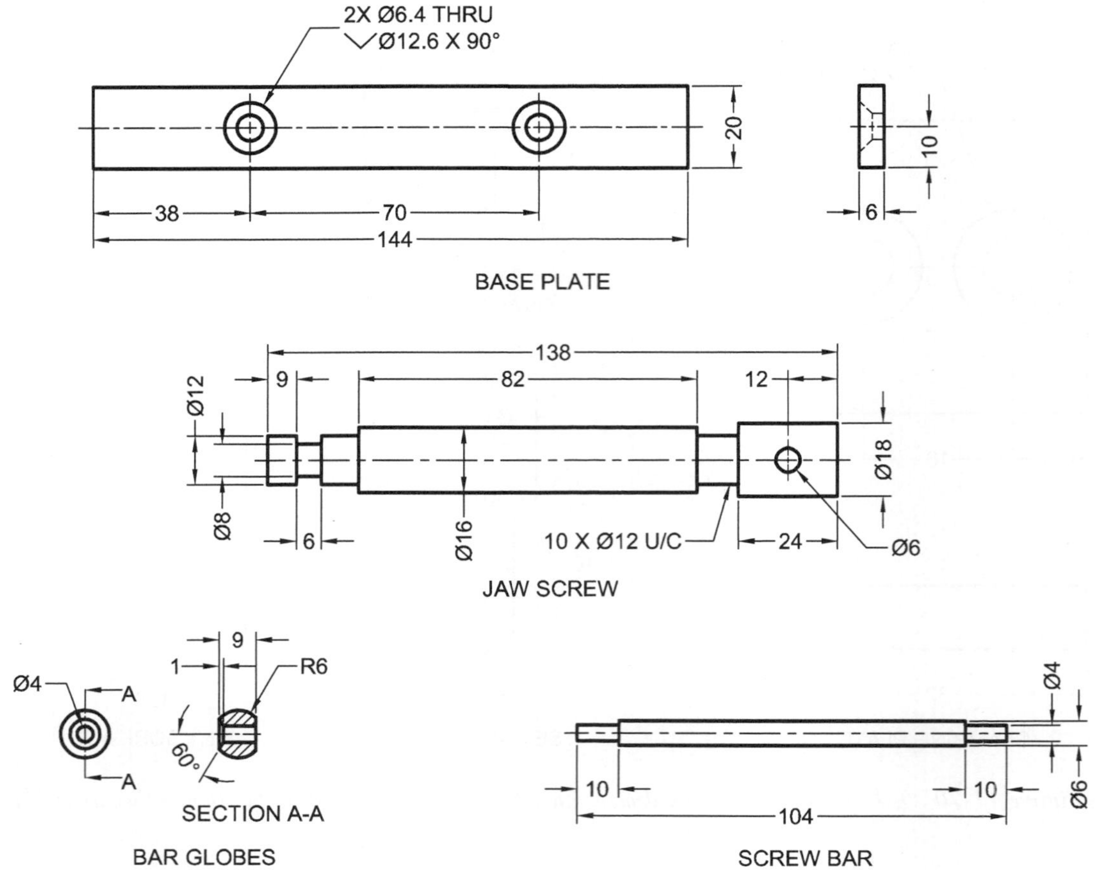

Figure 11-71 Orthographic views and dimensions of various components of the Bench Vice assembly

Answers to Self-Evaluation Test

1. .asm, **2. Explode - Render - Animate**, **3. Show**, **4. Explode**, **5.** T, **6.** T, **7.** F, **8.** T, **9.** T, **10.** F

Chapter 12

Generating, Editing, and Dimensioning the Drawing Views

Learning Objectives

After completing this chapter, you will be able to:

- *Understand the Draft environment*
- *Learn the type of views generated in Solid Edge*
- *Generate drawing views*
- *Manipulate drawing views*
- *Add annotations to drawing views*
- *Evolve 3D Model from 2D drawings*
- *Generate the exploded views of assemblies*
- *Create associative balloons and parts list*

THE DRAFT ENVIRONMENT

After creating a solid model or an assembly, you can generate its two-dimensional (2D) drawing views. Note that you can create a solid model in the part environment and assemble it in the **Assembly** environment. Solid Edge has a separate environment called the **Draft** environment, which is used to generate drawing views. This environment contains tools to generate, edit, and modify the drawing views. To invoke the **Draft** environment, start **Solid Edge ST9** and then choose the **ISO Metric Draft** option from the **New** tab of the welcome screen.

If Solid Edge is already running on your computer and you want to invoke the **Draft** environment, invoke the **New** dialog box and select the **iso metric draft.dft** template from it, refer to Figure 12-1. The *.dft* is the extension of the files created in this environment. After selecting the required template, choose **OK** in the **New** dialog box to enter the **Draft** environment. You can modify the drawing standards of the current file from the **Draft** environment.

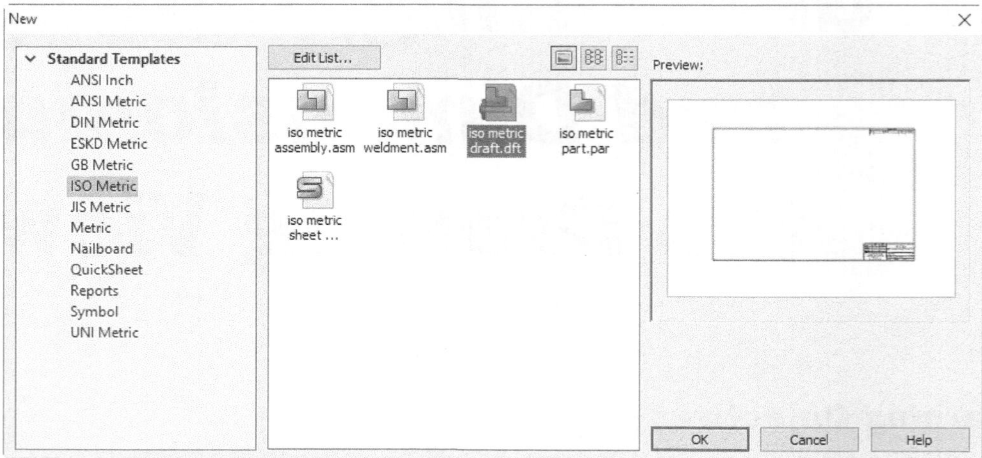

Figure 12-1 *Selecting a draft template from the **New** dialog box*

When you enter the **Draft** environment, the drawing sheet and the background sheet with borders will be displayed, as shown in Figure 12-2. This sheet is the one on which you will generate the drawing views. The background sheet is used to add title blocks. You can set the parameters of the drawing sheet in the **Sheet Setup** dialog box which can be invoked by choosing **Application Button > Settings > Sheet Setup**.

If you have a part file or an assembly file opened and you want to generate its drawing views, choose **Application Button > New > Drawing of Active Model**; the **Create Drawing** dialog box will be displayed. Choose the **Browse** button from this dialog box; the **New** dialog box will be displayed. Select the desired template from the dialog box and choose the **OK** button; the selected template will be displayed in the **Template** box in the **Create Drawing** dialog box. Make sure that the **Run Drawing View Wizard** check box is selected in the **Create Drawing** dialog box and then choose the **OK** button; the **Draft** environment will be invoked and the **View Wizard** tool from the **Drawing Views** group of the **Home** tab is selected as default. You will learn more about this tool later in this chapter.

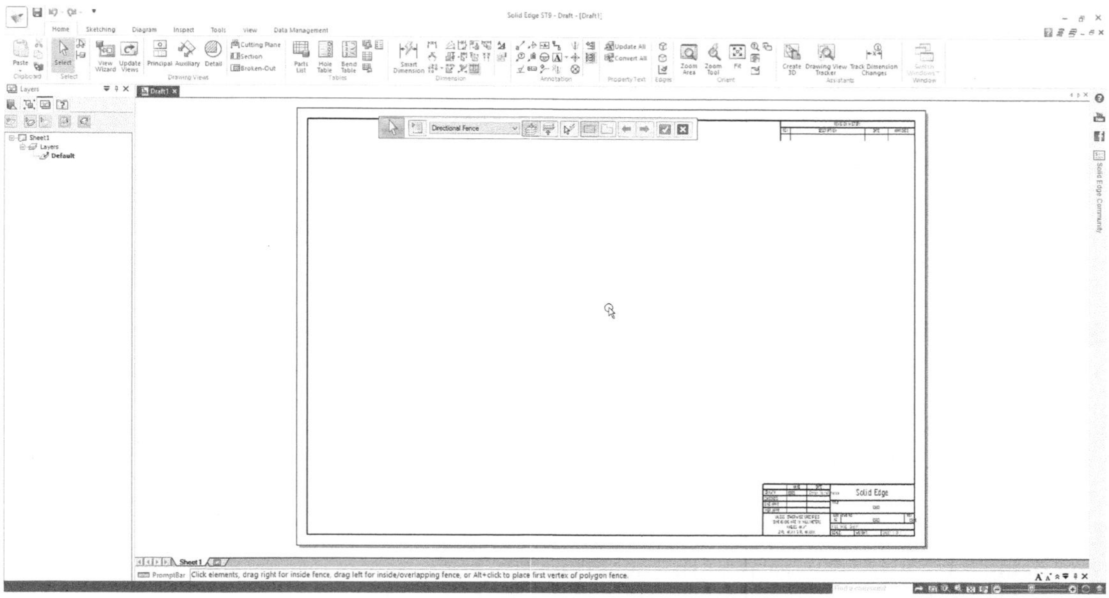

*Figure 12-2 The default screen in the **Draft** environment*

> **Tip**
> *To use an empty sheet without any margin or title block, choose **Application Button > Settings > Sheet Setup**; the **Sheet Setup** dialog box will be displayed. In this dialog box, choose the **Background** tab and select the blank space in the **Background sheet** drop-down list. The preview of an empty sheet will be displayed in the dialog box. Next, choose the **OK** button to exit the dialog box.*

TYPES OF VIEWS GENERATED IN Solid Edge

In Solid Edge, there are two types of drafting techniques: generative drafting and interactive drafting techniques. In the generative drafting, the views are generated from the part or assembly that is already created. In the interactive drafting, the views are sketched using the sketching tools.

> **Note**
> *The reason for generating the drawing views is that these views are associative with their respective solid models or assemblies. Therefore, any change in the model updates the drawing views as well. On the other hand, the sketched view is not associated with any model. Therefore, editing of the views is not automatic.*

In Solid Edge, you can generate six types of views from a model or an assembly. These views are discussed next.

Base View

The base view is the first view and is generated using a parent model or an assembly. This view is an independent view and is not affected by the changes made in any other view in the drawing sheet. Most of the other views are generated taking this view as the parent view.

Principal View

The principal view is an orthographic view that is generated using any other view present in the drawing sheet. This is the most common view generated after the base view.

Auxiliary View

The auxiliary view is a drawing view that is generated by projecting lines normal to a specified edge of an existing view. These views are mainly used when you want to show the true length of an inclined surface.

Section View

The section view is generated by cutting the part of an existing view using a plane or a line and then viewing the parent view from a direction normal to the section plane. These views are generally used for the models that are complicated from inside and it is not possible to display the inner portion of the part using the conventional views.

Detail View

The detail view is used to display the details of a portion of an existing view. This portion is selected from the parent view. The portion that you select will be scaled and placed as a separate view. The scale can be modified, if needed.

Broken-Out View

The broken-out view is used for the parts that have a high length to width ratio. The broken-out area is specified by adding break lines to an existing orthographic view.

GENERATING DRAWING VIEWS

Ribbon:	Home > Drawing Views > View Wizard

In Solid Edge, the first view to be generated is the base view. This view is generated using the **View Wizard** tool. The remaining views are generated by using the base view directly or indirectly. Before you proceed further, you need to set the projection type to the third angle projection. To do so, choose **Application Button > Settings > Options**; the **Solid Edge Options** dialog box will be invoked. Next, choose the **Drawing Standards** tab from this dialog box. In this tab, select the **Third** radio button from the **Projection Angle** area and then choose **OK**.

Generating the Base View

You can generate the base view by using the **View Wizard** tool. When you invoke this tool, the **Select Model** dialog box will be displayed. In this dialog box, select the model whose drawing views need to be generated and then choose the **Open** button; the front view of the model will be attached to the cursor. Also, the **View Wizard** command bar will be displayed, as shown in Figure 12-3. The options in this command bar are used to configure various settings of the drawing view.

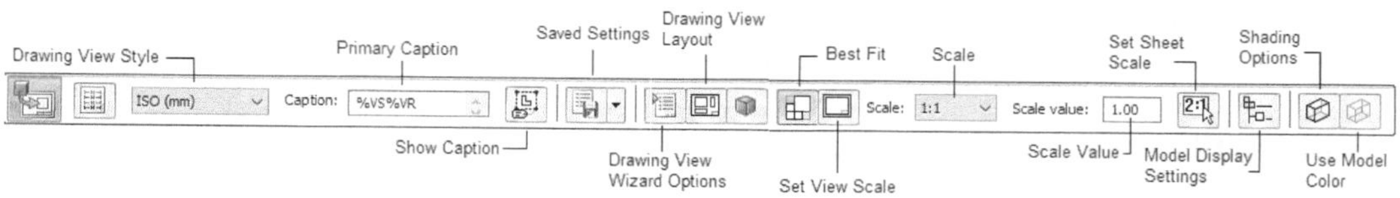

*Figure 12-3 The **View Wizard** command bar*

The **Drawing View Style** drop-down is used to specify the view style of the drawing view. You can enter a caption for the drawing view in the **Primary Caption** edit box and choose the **Show Caption** button to display the caption below the view. The **Drawing View Wizard Options** button is used to display **Drawing View Wizard**, as shown in Figure 12-4. The options in this wizard are discussed next.

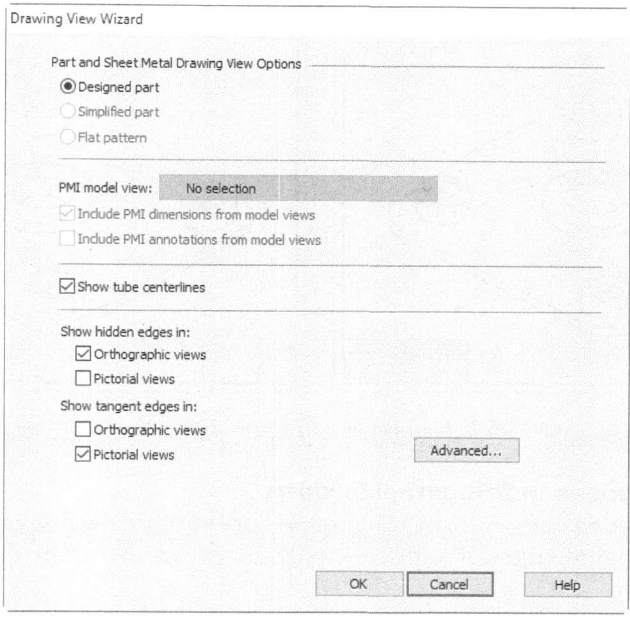

*Figure 12-4 The **Drawing View Wizard***

Part and Sheet Metal Drawing View Options Page

The options in this page enable you to specify the parameters related to the display of the drawing view.

Designed part

This radio button is selected by default and is used to specify whether you need to generate the drawing views of an existing part.

Simplified part

This radio button is used to generate the drawing views of the simplified version of a model. This radio button will be in an inactive state if the simplified version of a model does not exist.

Flat pattern

This radio button is used to generate the drawing views of a flat pattern of the sheet metal part. It is available only for the sheet metal parts having a flat pattern.

Show tube centerlines
This check box is selected to display the centerlines in the tube components.

Show hidden edges in Orthographic views
This check box is selected by default and is used to display the hidden edges, if any, in the orthographic drawing views.

Show hidden edges in Pictorial views
Pictorial views are the drawing views other than orthogonal views. This option is used to display hidden edges, if any, in the pictorial drawing views. Figures 12-5 and 12-6 show the isometric (pictorial) drawing views with visible hidden-edges and suppressed hidden edges, respectively.

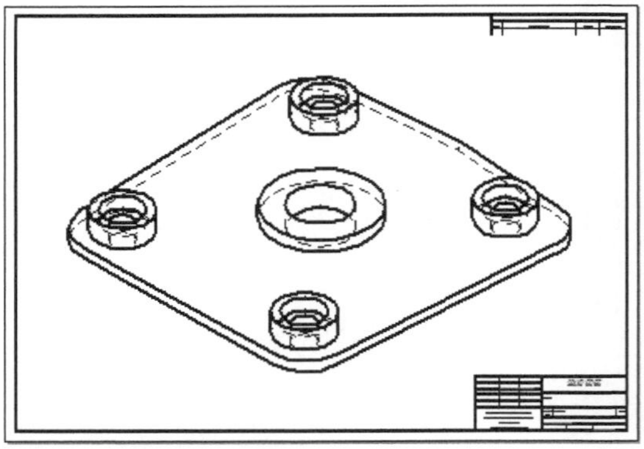

Figure 12-5 *Drawing view with hidden edges*

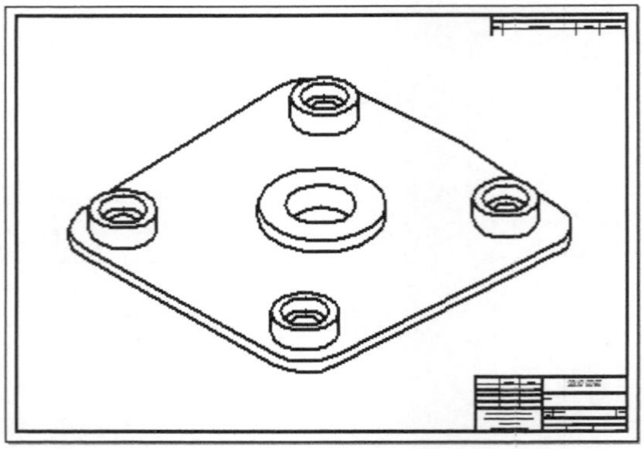

Figure 12-6 *Drawing view without hidden edges*

Show tangent edges in Orthographic views
Tangent edges are the edges formed by rounds or cylindrical features. This option is used to display the tangent edges, if any in the part, in the orthographic drawing views.

Show tangent edges in Pictorial views
This option is used to display the tangent edges, if any, in the pictorial drawing views.

Choose the **OK** button after selecting the required options to close the dialog box.

Drawing View Layout Page

The **Drawing View Layout** button in the **View Wizard** command bar is used to display the **Drawing View Layout** page of the **Drawing View Wizard** dialog box, as shown in Figure 12-7. The options in this page enable you to specify the standard orientation of the drawing view or the pictorial view. These options are discussed next.

Note
*For assembly, the options in the **Drawing View Wizard** will change according to the assembly feature.*

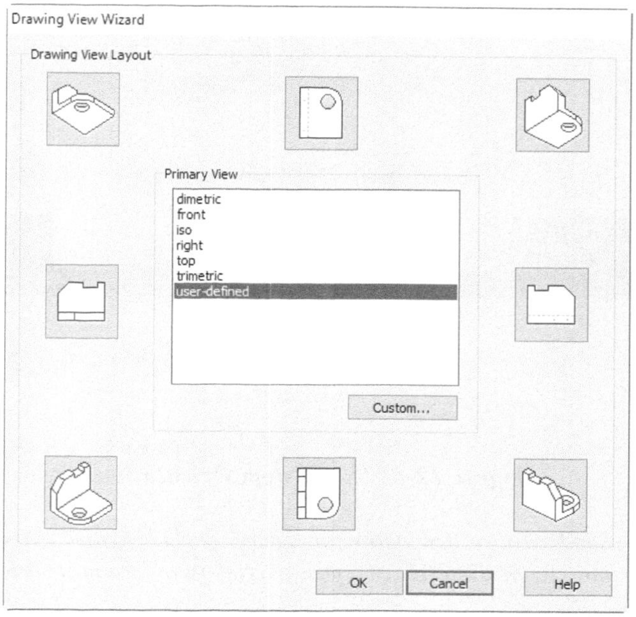

*Figure 12-7 The **Drawing View Layout** page of the **Drawing View Wizard***

Primary View

This display box consists of options for generating views in the standard orientations. You can select any option from the standard orientations. You can also use the **View Orientation** button from the **View Wizard** command bar for a standard orientation.

Custom

When you choose the **Custom** button, the **Custom Orientation** window will be displayed, as shown in Figure 12-8. This window displays the part or the assembly that you had selected earlier from the **Select Model** dialog box. You can use the drawing display tools available in this window to set the orientation of the model. You can also spin the model using the middle mouse button. You can also create the perspective drawing view of a model by choosing the **Perspective** button from the **Custom Orientation** window and specifying the perspective angle in the **Rotation Angle** list after selecting the rotation axis of model. After setting the orientation, choose the **Close** button to exit the window.

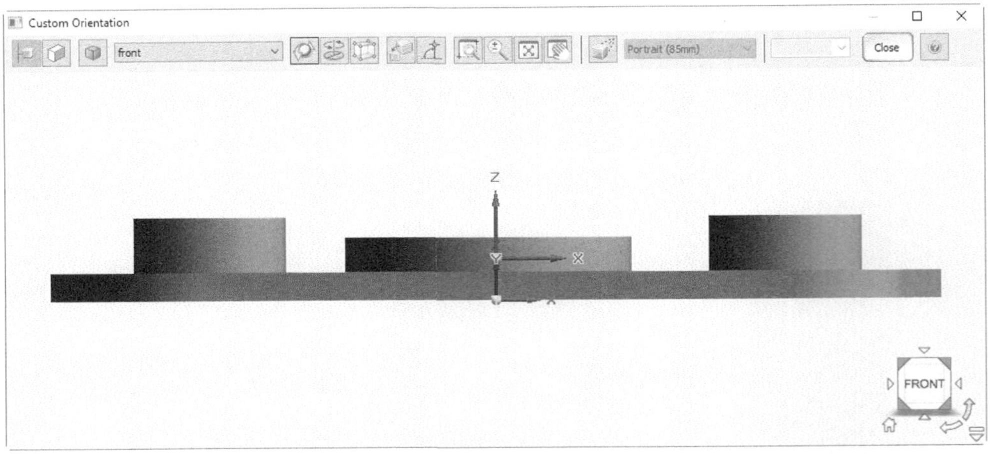

*Figure 12-8 The **Custom Orientation** window*

Note

*1. The buttons indicating different drawing views are not activated in the **Drawing View Wizard**, if the **iso**, **trimetric**, or **dimetric** option is selected in the **Primary Views** area.*

2. If you suppress features of a model whose drawing views are generated, the suppressed features will not be displayed in the drawing views. When unsuppressed, these features will be again displayed in the drawing view.

The other buttons in the **Drawing View Layout** page enable you to generate multiple views at a time with primary view. Choose the **OK** button to close this dialog box.

The other options in the **View Wizard** command bar are self-explanatory. You can examine them and use them as per your requirement. After specifying the required options in the command bar, click in the drawing sheet to place the primary view of the drawing. When you place the primary view of the drawing, the **Principal** tool will be invoked automatically. This tool is discussed in the section followed under the heading "Generating the Principal View".

Tip

When you double-click on a generated drawing view, the part file associated with that view will be opened.

Generating the Principal View

Ribbon: Home > Drawing Views > Principal

To generate the principal view, you need to have an existing view which can be selected to include a base view or another principal view. To generate the principal view, choose the **Principal** tool from the **Drawing Views** group of the **Home** tab; you will be prompted to select a drawing view. Move the cursor to a drawing view or the source view and select it as soon as it is highlighted in red color. On doing so, crossed box will be attached to the cursor. Now, as you move the cursor up, down, left, or right, the box will also move with it. You can place the view at the bottom, top, left, or right of the source view. Note that, if you move the cursor diagonally, you can generate a pictorial view, such as an isometric view, from the source view.

Note

1. A principal view cannot be generated from a detail view, section view, or an auxiliary view.

2. By default, Solid Edge generates drawing views in the first angle projection system. However, the third angle projection system has been used throughout the book. The procedure to change the default projection system to the third angle projection system has already been discussed in this chapter.

Figure 12-9 shows the drawing sheet with the base view and the principal views. The base view is the front view and the top and isometric views are generated from the front view using the **Principal** tool.

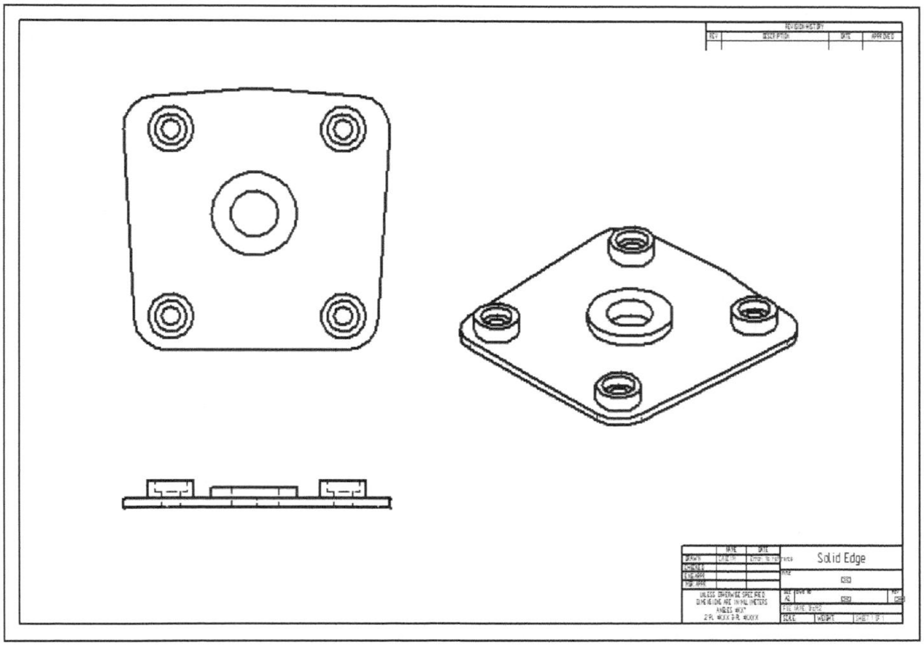

Figure 12-9 *Drawing sheet with the base view and the principal views*

Note

When you generate a drawing view on the drawing sheet, it will be displayed with visible and hidden edges. You can also change the display of the drawing view to shaded view. To change the display, select the drawing view; the ***Principal*** *command bar will be displayed. Choose the* ***Shading options*** *button; a flyout will be displayed. Choose any of the shading options from it.*

Generating the Auxiliary View

Ribbon: Home > Drawing Views > Auxiliary

The auxiliary view is a drawing view that is generated by projecting the lines normal to a specified edge of an existing view. To generate the auxiliary view, choose the **Auxiliary** tool from the **Drawing Views** group of the **Home** tab; the **Auxiliary** command bar will be displayed, as shown in Figure 12-10.

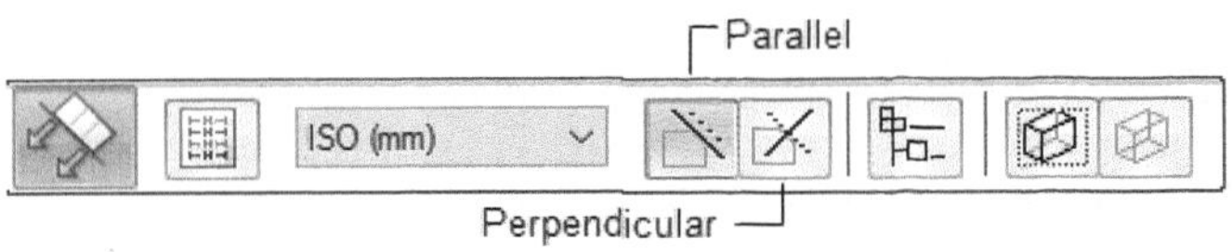

***Figure 12-10** The **Auxiliary** command bar*

Also, you will be prompted to click on a fold line or click on the first point of the fold line. The fold line is an edge of the model or an imaginary line normal to which the view will be projected. Select an edge of the model or a keypoint on the edge and then select another keypoint. An imaginary fold line will be formed. By default, the **Parallel** button is chosen in the command bar. As a result, the auxiliary view will be projected normal to this fold line. Move the cursor and then click to place the view; an arrow pointing in the direction normal to the fold line will be displayed, as shown in Figure 12-11. If you select the **Perpendicular** button, the auxiliary view will be projected parallel to the fold line.

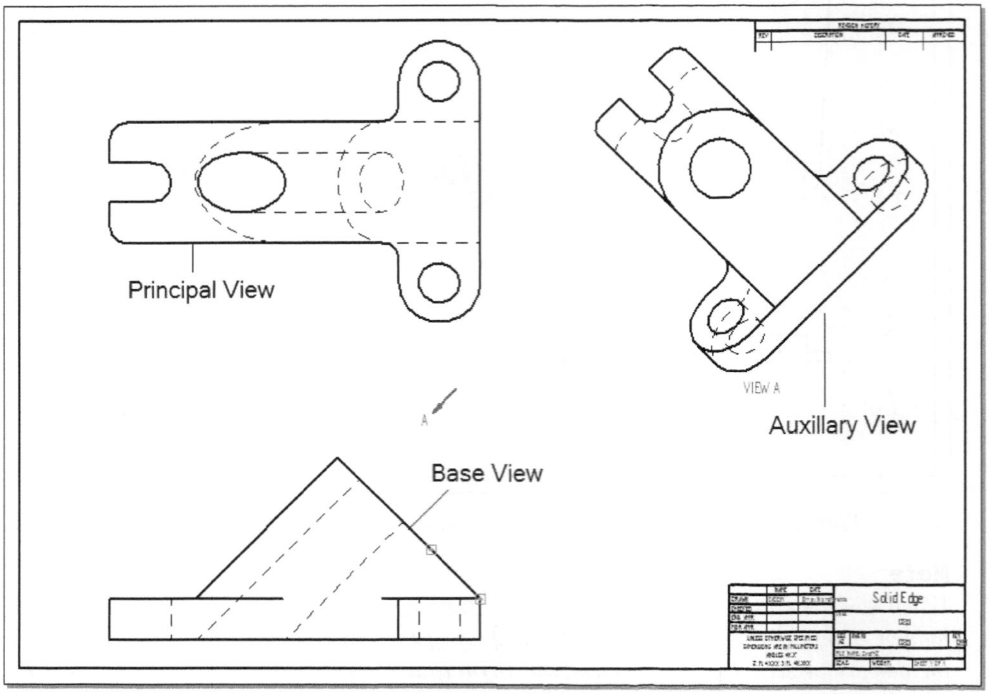

***Figure 12-11** Auxiliary view generated from the principal view*

The display of this arrow can be changed to a line with double arrows. To change the display, select the arrow and right-click to invoke the shortcut menu. Choose the **Properties** option from the shortcut menu; the **Viewing Plane Properties** dialog box will be displayed, as shown in Figure 12-12. Select the **Double** radio button from the **View Direction Lines** area in the dialog box and choose **OK**; the arrow will change into a line with double arrows.

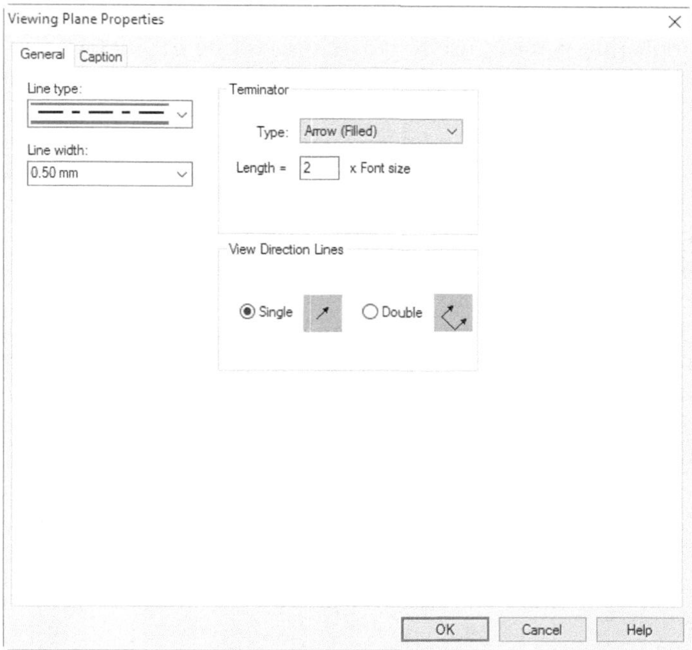

*Figure 12-12 The **Viewing Plane Properties** dialog box*

Need for Auxiliary View

The need for auxiliary view arises when it becomes impossible to dimension the geometry in the orthographic views. For example, in the model refer to Figure 12-11, the profile on the face of the inclined feature cannot be dimensioned until a view is generated normal to the inclination. After the auxiliary view is generated, the profile can easily be dimensioned with true dimensions.

Generating the Section View

Ribbon:	Home > Drawing Views > Section

As mentioned earlier, the section view is generated by cutting a portion of an existing view using a cutting geometry and then viewing the source view from the direction normal to the cutting geometry. In Solid Edge, various types of section views can be generated using the **Section** tool.

To create a section view, you need a geometry that will be used to cut the source view. To create a cutting geometry, the **Cutting Plane** tool is used.

Generating a Simple Section View

The following steps explain the procedure for creating a cutting geometry and generating a simple section view:

1. Choose the **Cutting Plane** tool from the **Drawing Views** group of the **Home** tab; you will be prompted to select a drawing view. This view will be the source view.

2. Select the source view to activate the Sketching environment. This environment contains the sketching tools that you can use to create the cutting geometry.

Note

When you move the cursor over a drawing view to select the source view, it will be highlighted in red color. This indicates that the view can be selected. But, when you move the cursor over the area that does not have any entity, the red color in the drawing view will not appear. And if you click in this area, the view will not be selected. Therefore, note that the red color will appear only when the cursor is on an entity that composes the drawing view.

3. Draw the sketch for the cutting geometry. Remember that the sketch should be a continuous open sketch. You can use the alignment indicators to sketch the cutting geometry.

4. After drawing the sketch for the cutting geometry, choose the **Close Cutting Plane** button from the **Close** group to exit the cutting plane environment.

5. Specify the direction of the viewby clicking in the direction of the arrows.

   Note that when you move the cursor across the cutting geometry, the direction of arrows will also get changed.

6. Choose the **Section** tool from the **Drawing Views** group of the **Home** tab; you will be prompted to select a cutting plane.

7. Select the cutting plane and place the section drawing view parallel to the cutting plane at the desired location on the drawing sheet. A simple section view is shown in Figure 12-13.

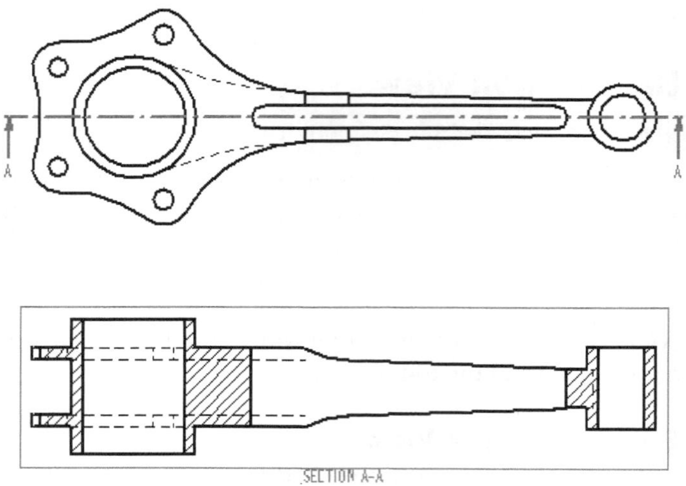

Figure 12-13 *The shaded top view and the front section view*

Points to Remember while Creating Cutting Planes

The following points should be remembered while creating the cutting planes:

1. The sketch drawn can be a combination of arcs and lines, but an arc cannot be the start or the end entity of the sketch.
2. The sketch must be open and all entities should be connected to each other.
3. Relationships and dimensions can be applied between the sketched entities and the drawing view.
4. The cutting plane can be edited by double-clicking on it or by choosing the **Edit** button, which will be displayed in the command bar when you select the cutting plane.

Note

1. When you place the section view, it does not matter on which side of the source view you place it. The section view remains the same on either side of the source view; but it varies with the direction of arrows on the cutting plane.

2. In Solid Edge, the section view hatching is applied automatically and its properties depend on the type of material assigned during the creation of the model. You can change the hatching properties in the ***Style*** *dialog box. To invoke the* ***Style*** *dialog box, choose the* ***Styles*** *button from the* ***Style*** *group of the* ***View*** *tab.*

Generating the Revolved Section Views

The revolved section views are needed when some features in a model are at a certain angle. In a revolved section view, the section portion revolves around an axis normal to the viewing plane such that it is straightened. For example, Figure 12-14 shows the views of a model that has three outer features at angles equal with respect to each other. If you want to show the geometry of at least two outer features, you need to generate a revolved section view.

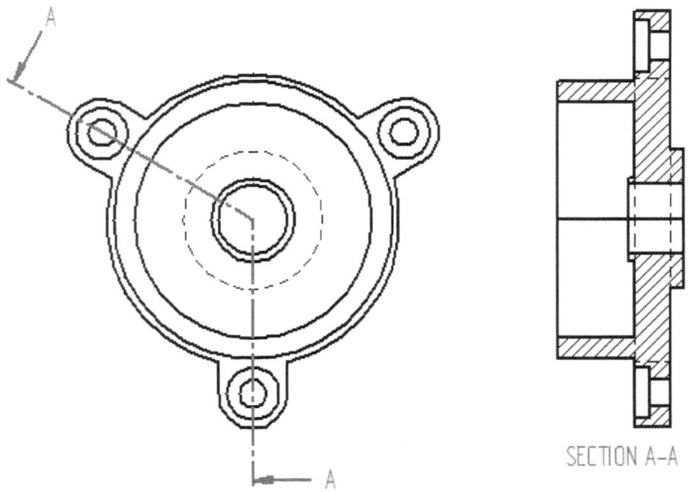

Figure 12-14 *The Front view and the right side revolved section view*

To generate a revolved section view, invoke the **Section** tool and select an existing cutting plane. Since the cutting planes have entities that are at some angle to each other, you need to select the line that will be used as a fold line for generating the section view. For example, in Figure 12-15, the inclined line is used to generate the section view at the top and the vertical line is used to generate the section view on the right. Before placing the view, choose the **Revolved Section View** button from the command bar.

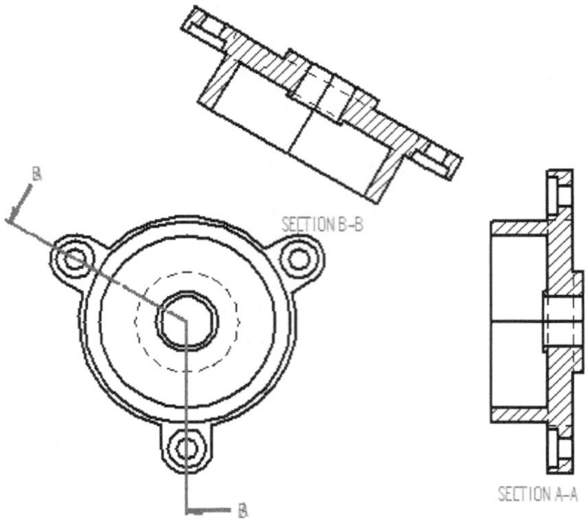

Figure 12-15 *Two different revolved section views generated by selecting two different cutting geometries*

Note

1. The cutting plane of a revolved section view can also have a combination of the curved and linear entities but curved entities must be connected with linear entities from its both ends.

*2. If the cutting plane geometry consists of an arc, the **Revolved Section View** button in the command bar cannot be used.*

3. The cutting plane geometries should be multiline and they should be inclined at an angle to each other.

4. If a multiline cutting geometry exists, you can select only the first entity and the last entity as the cutting plane.

Section View that Displays only the Sectioned Geometry

The **Section Only** button in the command bar is used to generate a section view that displays only that area of the model that is sectioned. Figure 12-16 shows the section view which displays only the section area of the model.

The following steps explain the procedure for creating this type of view:

1. Choose the **Section** tool from the **Drawing Views** group of the **Home** tab; you are prompted to select a cutting plane.
2. Select the cutting plane; a box is attached to the cursor and the options in the **Section** command bar get enabled.

3. Choose the **Section Only** button from the command bar and place the view by clicking on the desired side. The section view is placed, refer to Figure 12-16.

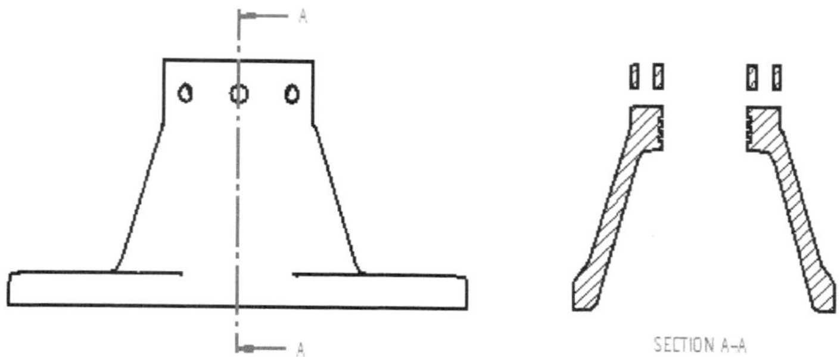

***Figure 12-16** Section view displaying only the section area*

Generating Full Section View of the Existing Section View

The **Section Full Model** button in the command bar is used for generating full section view from the existing created section view of the model. As a result, this button will be activated only if a section view is available in the drawing area. Figure 12-17 shows the full section view generated from the section view of the model using the **Section Full Model** button.

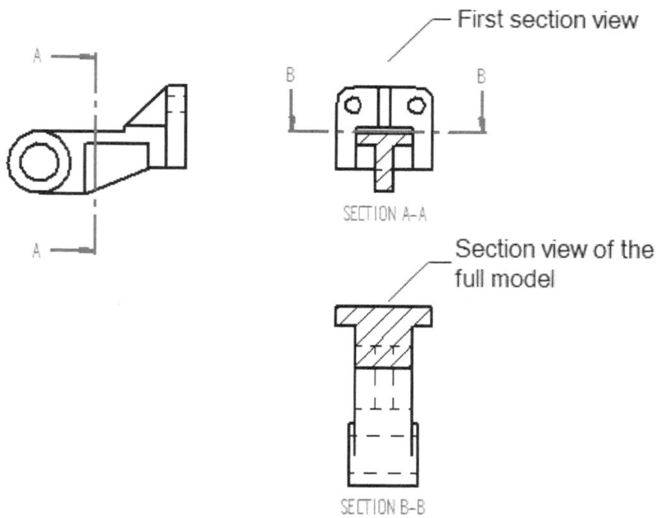

***Figure 12-17** Section view generated using the **Section Full Model** button*

Generating the Broken-Out Section View

Ribbon: Home > Drawing Views > Broken-Out

The broken-out section view is used to display the section of a particular portion of a model without sectioning the model. The **Broken-Out** tool is used to generate the broken section view. This tool is available in the **Drawing Views** group of the **Home** tab. The steps given next explain the procedure for creating this type of view.

1. Choose the **Broken-Out** tool from the **Drawing Views** group of the **Home** tab and select the drawing view where you have to draw the profile for the broken view; you will automatically

enter the sketching environment where all the tools that are used to draw the profile are available.

2. Draw the sketch, refer to Figure 12-18. Next, choose the **Close Broken-Out Section** button from the **Ribbon** to exit the **Broken-Out** environment; you are prompted to specify the distance for the depth of the cut.

3. Specify the distance in the **Depth** edit box available in the command bar or by moving the shaded rectangle line on the other orthographic view, refer to Figure 12-18. After specifying the depth of the cut, you are prompted to select the view that needs to be broken.

4. Select the isometric view (pictorial view) to generate the broken-out section view, as shown in Figure 12-19.

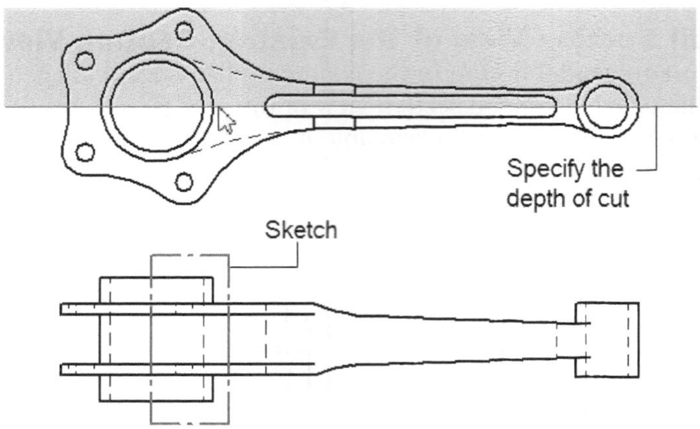

Figure 12-18 *Specifying the profile and the depth of the cut*

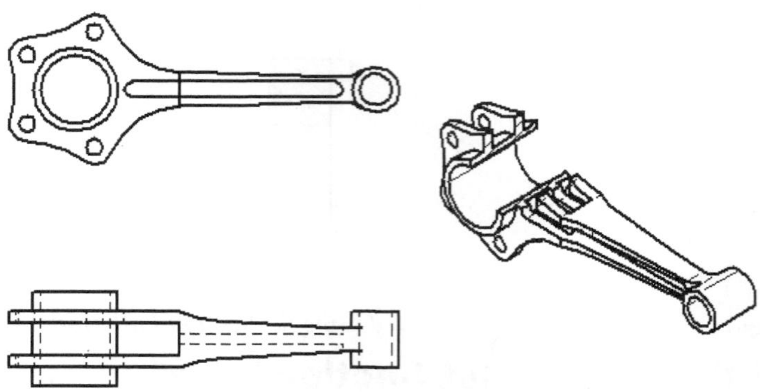

Figure 12-19 *Isometric broken-out section view*

Generating the Detail View

Ribbon: Home > Drawing Views > Detail

Detail

Detailed views are used to provide enlarged view of a particular portion of an existing view. In Solid Edge, the detailed view is generated by drawing a circle or any other user-defined sketch around the portion whose details are needed. When you choose the

Detail button, the **Detail** command bar will be displayed and the **Circular Detail View** button will be chosen by default. Also, you will be prompted to select the center of the circle. After specifying the center of the circle, you will be prompted to specify another point to determine the radius of the circle. As soon as you click, a circle, which is actually the preview of the detail view, will be attached to the cursor. Place the view on the drawing sheet at the desired location, see Figure 12-20.

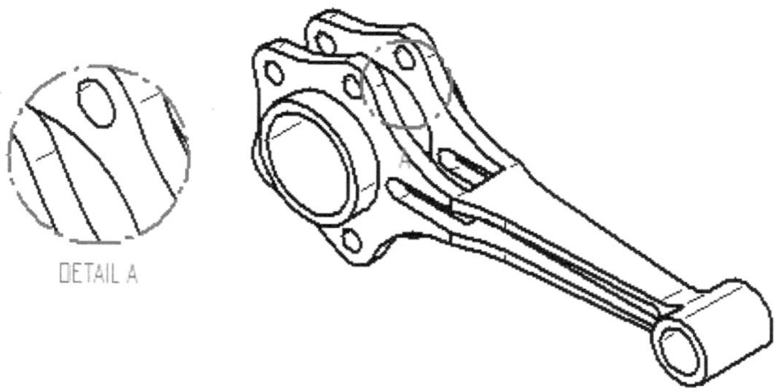

Figure 12-20 Detail view of an isometric view

You can also choose the **Define Profile** button from the command bar to define the boundary of the detail view. Choose this button and then drawing view, the sketching environment will be activated. Draw the required closed profile using the tools available in this environment. Figure 12-21 shows the user-defined closed profile and the detailed view created.

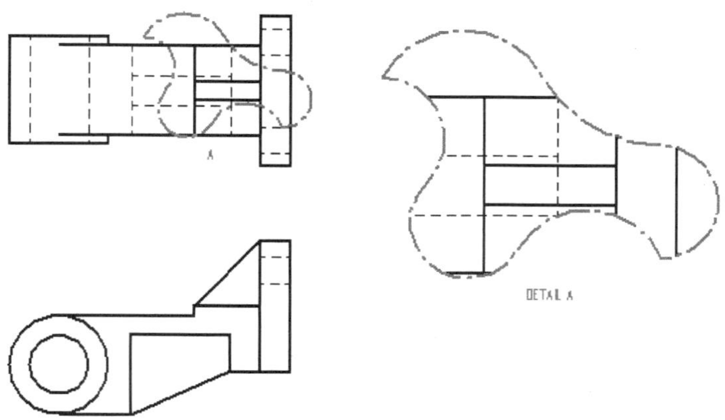

Figure 12-21 User-defined sketch and the resulting detailed view

Tip

1. *If you drag and drop a part file from the docking window on the drawing sheet, then depending on the projection angle system set for the current file, the top, front, and right side views of the part will be generated. If you drag and drop an assembly on the drawing sheet, then an isometric view of the assembly will be generated.*

2. *You can right-click on a detail view and choose* ***Convert to Independent Detail View*** *to convert the view into an independent view.*

Generating the Broken View

This type of view is used for the parts that have a high length to width ratio. This view is generated on an existing orthographic or pictorial view. It is created by breaking the existing view along the horizontal or vertical direction. Various types of broken views are shown in Figure 12-22.

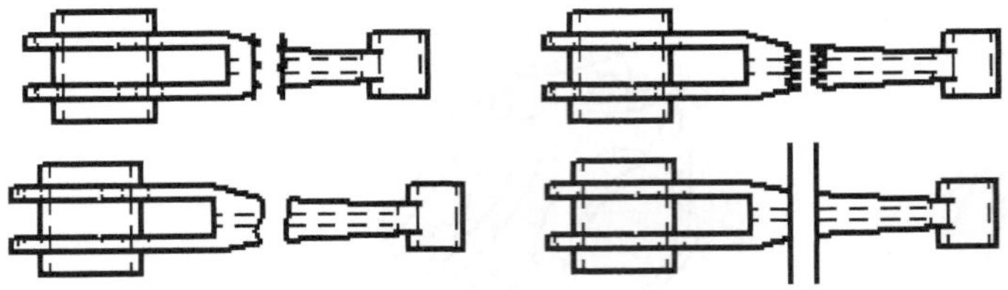

Figure 12-22 *Different types of broken views*

The following steps explain the procedure for creating this type of view:

1. Move the cursor over the drawing view where you have to add the break lines. When the view is highlighted and turns into red color, right-click on it to invoke the shortcut menu.

2. From the shortcut menu, choose the **Add Break Lines** option; you will be prompted to click on the drawing view at the point where you need to place the first break line. Notice that as you move the cursor, the break line also moves with it.

   You can set the style for the break lines from the **Style** drop-down list. By choosing the **Vertical Break** or **Horizontal Break** buttons from the command bar, you can specify whether the drawing view will be broken vertically or horizontally. In the command bar, there are five line types that can be selected for the break line type.

3. Before specifying the first point for the break line, you need to specify the line type for the break lines. To do so, choose the **Break Line Type** button from the command bar; a flyout is displayed with five options. Choose any of the options for selecting a line type. The **Break gap** edit box in the command bar is used to set the distance between the pair of break lines. The **Height** edit box is used to specify the height of the zigzag in the break lines. The **Pitch** edit box is used to specify the pitch of the breaks when you select the zigzag break line type.

Tip

You can add views of different parts and assemblies to a single drawing sheet. This helps you to view the dimensions of different models on a single sheet. To add a new model to the sheet, follow the same procedure that was used to generate the base view.

4. Click on the drawing view to specify the location for the first break line. After placing the first break line, click again on the drawing view to specify the location for the second break line.

5. After specifying the second break line, choose the **Finish** button from the command bar to exit.

Note

*When you select a view with break lines, the **Show Broken View** button will be displayed in the **Select** command bar. This button toggles the display of break lines in the selected drawing view.*

Inheriting Break Lines to a Principle, Section or Auxiliary view

If you create a principal view by using a view with break lines, the break lines will automatically be inherited by it. However, if you have created a principal view prior to adding break lines, then you need to manually inherit them. To do so, right-click on the principal view and choose the **Inherit Break Lines** option from the shortcut menu displayed. Next, select the view with break lines; the break lines will be inherited by the principal view. Similarly, break lines can be inherited by section or auxiliary views.

WORKING WITH INTERACTIVE DRAFTING

As mentioned earlier, you can also sketch the 2D drawing views in the **Draft** environment of Solid Edge. In technical terms, sketching the 2D drawing views is known as interactive drafting. You can draw the 2D drawing views by choosing the **Draft View** button from the **Quick Access** toolbar, after customizing the **Quick Access** toolbar. To customize the toolbar, right-click on the **Ribbon** and choose the **Customize Quick Access toolbar** option from the shortcut menu displayed; the **Customize** dialog box will be displayed. Next, select the **Commands Not in the Ribbon** option from the **Choose commands from** drop-down list and then select **Draft View** from the list box displayed below the drop-down list. Next, choose **Add** to add the **Draft View** as a button to the toolbar and then close the dialog box. Next, choose the **Draft View** button from the **Quick Access** toolbar; you will be prompted to place the view. Select a point on the drawing sheet; the sketching environment will be invoked. The tools in the sketching environment of the **Draft** environment are the same as those in the sketching environment of the **Part** environment. After sketching the drawing view, choose the **Close Draw In View** button from the **Close** group of the **Ribbon** to return to the **Draft** environment.

MANIPULATING DRAWING VIEWS

Once the drawing views are generated, it is very important to learn how they can be modified or edited. The following editing operations can be performed on the existing drawing views:

Aligning Drawing Views

When you generate the principal views from the base views, they are aligned automatically. If you move one of the views, then the other view will also move along with the first one. This shows that the two views are aligned. Also, when you select one of the views, a centerline that connects the two views will be displayed.

To unalign a view, select the view and right-click to invoke a shortcut menu. Choose **Maintain Alignment** from the shortcut menu to deactivate it. The alignment indicator in the view shows a zigzag line suggesting the view is no more aligned. Now, if you move any of the previously aligned views, the other corresponding view will not move. Choose this option again to align the views. Note that a straight line is displayed in the drawing when the views are aligned.

To completely delete the alignment, right-click on the required view; a shortcut menu will be displayed. Choose the **Delete Alignment** option from the shortcut menu and select the alignment line to be deleted.

To create a new alignment of the view right-click in the drawing area and choose the **Create Alignment** option from the shortcut menu; the **Create Alignment** command bar will be displayed. You can select a location for the drawing view alignment using the **Alignment position** drop-down list. The buttons available in the command bar are used to specify whether you want to create a vertical, horizontal, parallel, or a perpendicular alignment. Choose the required options and buttons from the command bar and then select the view with which you want to align the current view.

Modifying the Scale of Drawing Views

In Solid Edge, when you generate a principal or primary view in the drawing sheet, the scale of the view is automatically set, based on to the scale of the drawing sheet. You can modify the scale of a drawing view by selecting it and changing the value in the edit box in the **Select** command bar, refer to Figure 12-23. Alternatively, you can change it by choosing the **Properties** button from the command bar. When you choose the **Properties** button, the **High Quality View Properties** dialog box will be displayed. You can set the scale value in this dialog box. You can also invoke this dialog box by choosing the **Properties** option from the shortcut menu that will be displayed when you select a view and then right-click on it.

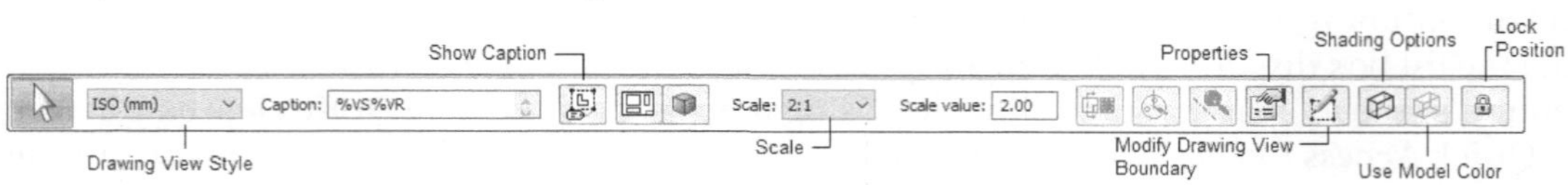

*Figure 12-23 The **Drawing View** command bar*

Note

When you modify the scale of a drawing view that was generated by projecting a view, the scale factors of both the views will be modified.

Cropping Drawing Views

Cropping is a technique that is used to view only a particular portion of the drawing view on the drawing sheet. To crop a drawing view, select the drawing view; a box with dotted outlines will be displayed. The dotted outlines of the box will have snap points in it. Move the cursor on any one of the snap points; a handle will be displayed. Click and drag the handle till the required portion of the drawing is visible. This visible portion will be the cropped view. The portion of the view lying inside the associated box is retained and the remaining portion is hidden.

To bring back the view to its original display, right-click on the view to display the shortcut menu. In the shortcut menu, choose the **Uncrop** option; the cropping in the view is removed.

Note

You cannot crop a detail view and a broken view.

Moving the Drawing Views

To move a drawing view, select and drag it to the drawing sheet. To place the view, release the left mouse button at the desired location on the drawing sheet.

Rotating the Drawing Views

The drawing views can be rotated by invoking the **Sketching** tab in the **Ribbon**. To rotate a drawing view, choose the **Rotate** tool from the **Move** drop-down in the **Draw** group of the **Sketching** tab; you will be prompted to select an element to modify. Select the drawing view you need to rotate; you will be prompted to select the center of rotation. Select a point that acts as the center of rotation. Now, select a point from which you want to start the rotation and then select a point up to which you want to rotate the view. You can also specify the angle of the rotation value in the dimension edit boxes present in the command bar.

Applying the Hatch Pattern

You can also apply a hatch pattern to a closed region by using interactive drafting. To apply the hatch pattern, choose the **Fill** tool from the **Draw** group of the **Sketching** tab; you will be prompted to select the area. As you select a closed region, it will be filled with the hatch pattern. You can modify the hatch pattern by selecting it and right-clicking on it; a shortcut menu will be displayed. Choose the **Properties** option; the **Fill Properties** dialog box will be displayed. Specify the required options and choose the **OK** button to modify the hatch pattern.

Modifying the Properties of Drawing Views

After generating a drawing view, you can modify its properties. To set its properties, right-click on the drawing view to invoke the shortcut menu. Choose the **Properties** option from the shortcut menu to display the **High Quality View Properties** dialog box, refer to Figure 12-24. There are eight tabs in this dialog box and these are discussed next.

The **General** tab contains the options that are used to modify the scale, move the drawing view to another sheet, add caption or description to the drawing view, rotate the drawing view by specifying an angle, and so on. You can also select the options to add 3D dimensions to the pictorial view, retrieve dimensions on the next update of the part, include PMI dimensions as well as annotations from the model views, and so on.

The **Display** tab contains the options that are used to set the display of the drawing view. In this tab, the **Parts list** box displays the components, subassemblies, and construction surfaces. You can select them in this list and choose the display options from this tab. The **Parts List Options** button enables you to select the items that you want to display in the **Parts list** box. From the **Selected Part(s) Display** area, you can set the display style of the entities in the drawing view. The **Restore Default Display Settings** button restores the default settings.

The **Caption** tab contains the options that are used to modify the caption text and the format option for the selected drawing view.

The **Sections** tab lists the 3D sections that can be used to generate the section views.

The **Annotation** tab contains the options that enable you to set the style for the center lines and flowlines.

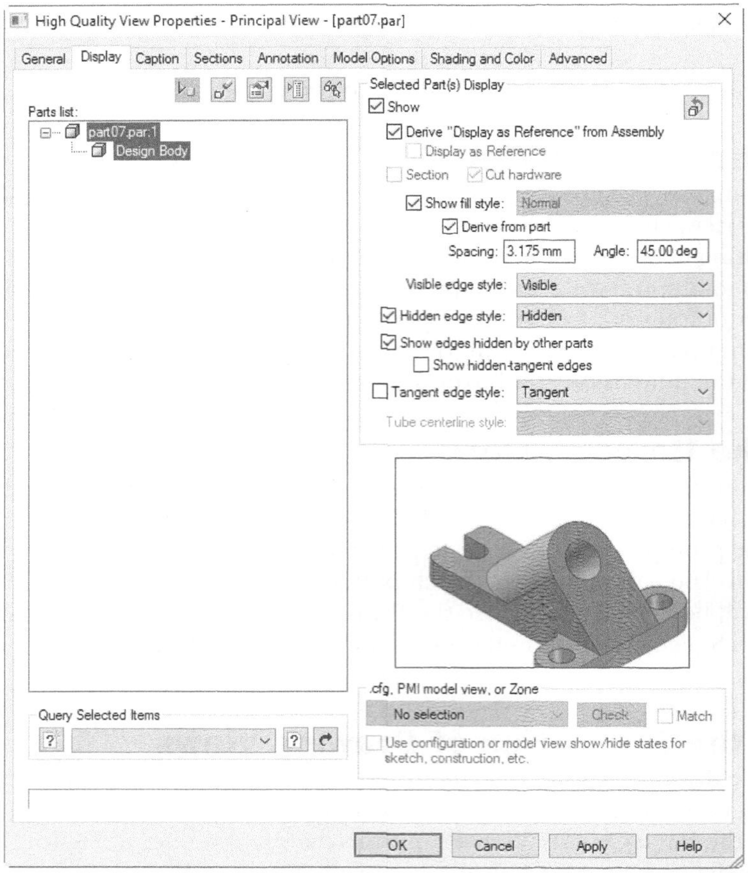

*Figure 12-24 The **High Quality View Properties** dialog box for a principal view*

Tip

*1. To modify the hatch pattern style of a section view, select the view and right-click on it to invoke the shortcut menu. Choose the **Properties** option from the shortcut menu to display the **High Quality View Properties** dialog box. Next, choose the **Display** tab. Now, clear the **Drive from part** check box; the **Changing Drawing View Default Display Properties** will be displayed. Choose the **OK** button from it and then from the **Show fill style** drop-down list in the **Selected Part(s) Display** area, select any one of the hatch pattern styles and then choose **OK** to exit the dialog box.*

*2. If you need to modify the properties of the hatch such as spacing, angle, and so on, right-click on the drawing view and then choose the **Draw in View** option from the shortcut menu displayed when you right-click on the view; the view will open in a separate window. Now, right-click on the hatch and then choose the **Properties** option from the shortcut menu displayed; the **Fill Properties** dialog box will be displayed. Using this dialog box, you can modify the parameters of the hatch. After modifying the parameters of the hatch, choose **OK** and then choose the **Close Draw In View** button from the **Close** group to exit the **Draw View Edit** environment; the changes will be displayed in the drawing view.*

The **Model Options** tab contains the options that are used to specify whether to display the simplified representation of the part in the drawing view.

The **Shading and Color** tab contains the options that are used to set the shading of a drawing view of the part. You can also apply the part base colors using the options under this tab.

The **Advanced** tab contains the advanced drawing options.

ADDING ANNOTATIONS TO DRAWING VIEWS

Once you have generated the drawing views, you need to add annotations such as dimensions, notes, surface finish symbols, geometric tolerances, and so on to them. There are two methods to display these annotations in the drawing views. The first method is to generate the annotations that are defined at the time of creating the model such as dimensions. These dimensions are associative in nature and therefore, can be used to modify or drive the dimensions of a model. The second method of displaying the annotations is to manually add them to the drawing views.

Displaying Center Marks and Center Lines in a Drawing View

Solid Edge allows you to display center marks and center lines in the drawing views. To do so, choose the **Automatic Centerlines** tool from the **Annotation** group of the **Home** tab; the command bar will be displayed with various options. If you choose the **Center Line and Center Mark Options** button from the command bar, the **Center Line and Center Mark Options** dialog box will be displayed. You can select the entities on which you want to display the center marks and center lines using this dialog box. Note that the **Center Line and Center Mark Options** button is available only when the **Add Lines and Marks** button is chosen.

You can set the options for adding or removing the center lines and center marks using the buttons available in the command bar. It is recommended that you choose the **Center Marks** or the **Center Mark Projection Lines** button from the command bar. Choosing both buttons will place the center lines above the center marks.

Figure 12-25 shows a drawing view with center mark projection lines and Figure 12-26 shows a drawing view with center lines.

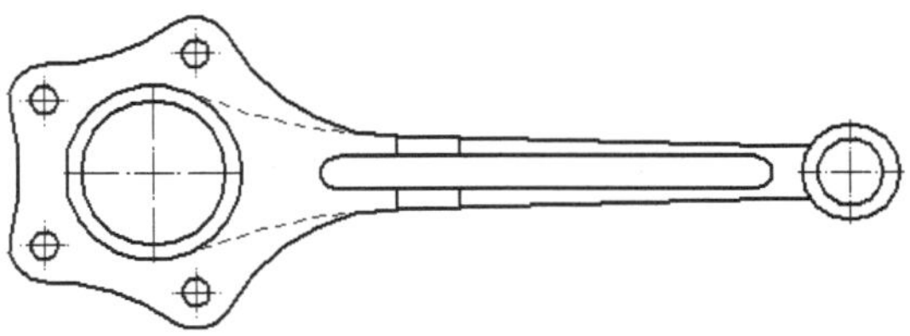

Figure 12-25 *Center marks on the holes in a drawing view*

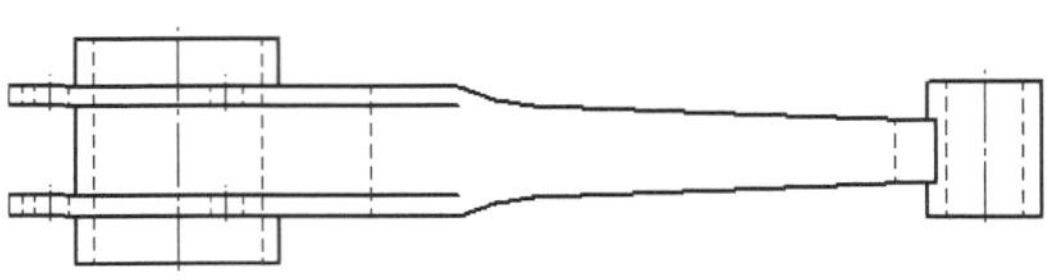

Figure 12-26 *Center lines on the holes in a drawing view*

Note

*You can also create dimensions in the **Draft** environment, but these dimensions cannot drive the dimensions of the part.*

Creating a Bolt Hole circle

A 'bolt hole circle' is a circle on which the center marks of circles are arranged in a circular pattern. In Solid Edge, you can create a bolt hole circle easily by using the **Bolt Hole Circle** tool available in the **Annotation** group of the **Home** tab. To create a bolt hole circle, invoke this tool and specify the center point of the bolt hole circle, refer to Figure 12-27. Next, select the center point of anyone of the circles in the circular pattern; the bolt hole circle will be created.

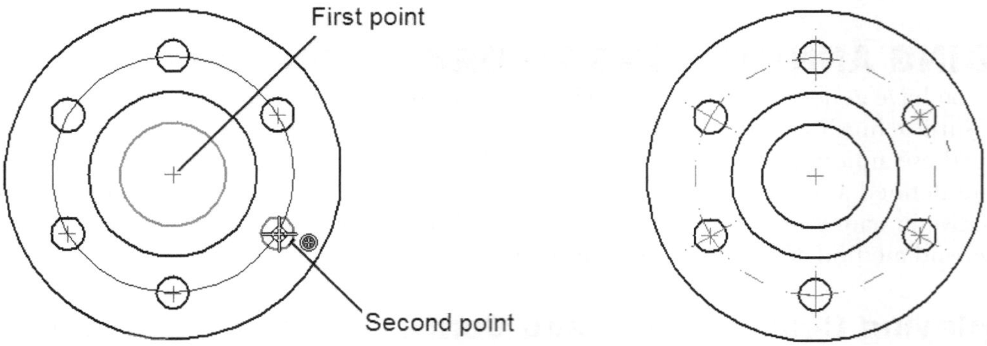

Figure 12-27 *Creating a bolt hole circle*

You can also create a bolt hole circle by selecting the center point of two circles in the circular pattern. You can do so by choosing the **By 2 Points** button from the **Bolt Hole Circle** command bar. The **By 3 Points** button is used to create a bolt circle by selecting three center points of the circles in the circular pattern, refer to Figure 12-28. If you choose the **Trim** button while creating a bolt circle, you will be prompted to select a section of the bolt circle to be trimmed.

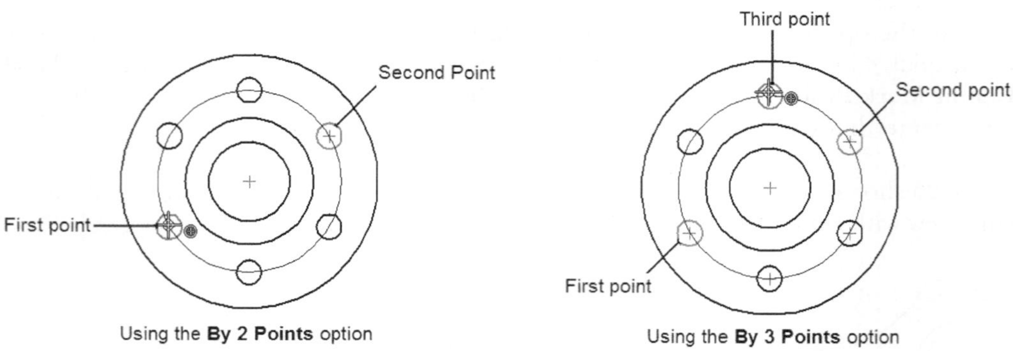

Figure 12-28 *Using the* ***By 2 Points*** *and* ***By 3 Points*** *options*

Generating Annotations

Generating annotations is the process of retrieving dimensions, notes, and so on from the parent model. The annotations that were used to create the model are displayed on the orthographic views of the model.

To retrieve dimensions, choose the **Retrieve Dimensions** tool from the **Dimension** group of the **Home** tab; the command bar will be displayed with various dimensioning options and you will be prompted to select a drawing view. As soon as you select a drawing view, the dimensions will be displayed on it. Various buttons available on the command bar are discussed next.

Dimension Style Mapping

This is a toggle button available in the command bar. It is used to specify whether or not the dimension style mapping set from the **Dimension Style** tab of the **Solid Edge Options** dialog box will be used.

Linear

This button is used to retrieve linear dimensions in the selected drawing view.

Radial

This button is used to retrieve radial dimensions in the selected drawing view.

Angular

This button is used to retrieve angular dimensions in the selected drawing view.

Annotations

This button is used to retrieve annotations that are applied to the model.

Retrieve Duplicate Radial Dimensions

This button is used to retrieve duplicate radial dimensions that have the same value.

Hidden Line Dimensions

This button is used to retrieve dimensions of the hidden lines.

Add Dimensions

If this button is chosen, the dimensions will be added to the drawing view.

Remove Dimensions

If this button is chosen, the dimensions will be removed from the drawing view. Note that the dimensions that are applied using the **Retrieve Dimension** tool can only be removed.

Figure 12-29 shows a drawing view after retrieving dimensions.

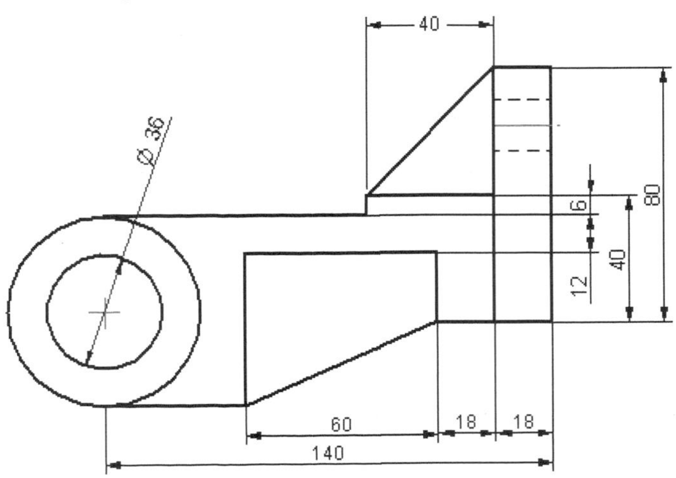

***Figure 12-29** Drawing view with dimensions*

Adding Reference Dimensions to Drawing Views

Although retrieving the dimensions from the parent model is the most effective way of dimensioning, sometimes you may also need to dimension the drawing views manually. The tools for dimensioning a drawing view are available in the **Dimension** group of the **Home** tab in the **Ribbon**. These tools are similar to those discussed in the sketching environment. The dimension tools that were not discussed earlier are: **Line Up Text**, **Attach Dimension**, **Chamfer Dimension**, and **Copy Attributes**. These tools are discussed next.

Line Up Text

This tool is available in the **Dimension** group and is used to align the selected entities in line with the base element. The elements can be dimensions, callouts, or balloons. On choosing this tool, the **Line Up Text** command bar is displayed. To align the selected entities, select the alignment type and specify the alignment offset distance in the command bar. Next, select the base element to which the selected entities will be aligned. Next, select the entities; the selected entities will be aligned with the base element.

In Solid Edge, the **Line Up Text** command bar is provided with two options that are used to align the annotations and the linear dimensions. These options are discussed next.

Vertical Break Point

This option is used to vertically align the leader break points of the selected elements.

Horizontal Break Point

This option is used to horizontally align the leader break points of the selected elements.

Attach Dimension

This tool is available in the **Dimension** group and is used to replace the selected dimension with the new element. However, the new element should be of the same type as the selected entity. For example, you can use this tool to replace the dimension of an arc with a new dimension of another arc, but not to a line. Any prefixes, tolerances, or any other formatting of the old dimension can be applied to the new dimension. To attach or replace a dimension, select the dimension and specify the origin and target elements to attach; the dimension gets replaced.

Chamfer Dimension

This tool is available in the **Dimension** group in the **Home** tab of the **Ribbon**. On choosing this tool, you will be prompted to select the dimension base line. Select a horizontal or vertical line from which you need to measure the chamfer length; you will be prompted to select the dimension measure line. Select the chamfer line; you will notice that the dimension is attached to the cursor. Click to place the dimension.

Copy Attributes

The **Copy Attributes** tool is used to copy or match the dimensions styles, fonts and the data such as prefix, suffix, superfix, subfix strings of the dimension already created in the drawing sheet. You can also use this tool to match the annotations that are placed in the drawing sheet. To do so, choose the **Copy Attributes** tool from the **Dimension** group of the **Home** tab; the **Copy Attributes** command bar will be displayed. Select the required option from the **Copy What?** drop-down list from the command bar. Also, you will be prompted to select the dimension or annotation to copy from. Select a source dimension or annotation; you will be prompted to select the dimension or annotations to copy to. Next, select the dimension that is to be matched with the first one.

Adding Callouts To Drawing View

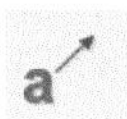

The **Callout** tool is used to generate callouts for the views in the drawing sheet. To generate callouts, choose the **Callout** tool from the **Annotation** group of the **Home** tab; the **Callout Properties** dialog box will be displayed, as shown in the Figure 12-30. There are five tabs in this dialog box and these are discussed next.

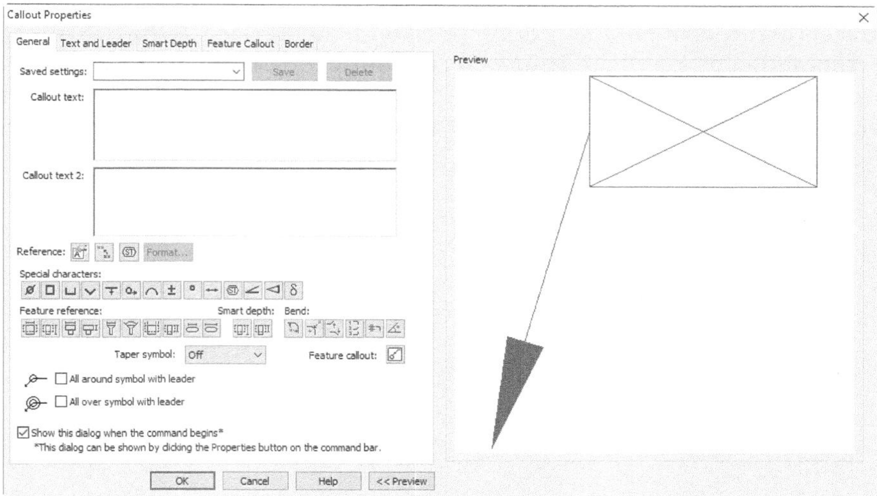

*Figure 12-30 The **Callout Properties** dialog box*

General Tab

The options in this tab are used to specify the text for the callout. You can also specify special characters, hole references, smart depths, bends, and hole cutouts. You can save the callout with a desired name by specifying a name in the **Saved settings** edit box and then choosing the **Save** button.

Text and Leader Tab

The options in this tab are used for specify the annotations such as leaders, balloons, callouts, control frames, and symbols. You can also specify the font, style, size, and color for the callout text.

Smart Depth Tab

The options in this tab are used to create callouts for the holes placed in the views. Using the options in this tab, you can specify the hole depth, thread depth, and so on. You can also insert special characters to annotate holes.

Feature Callout Tab

The options in this tab are used to specify the type of holes and slots that are present in the drawing sheet. You can also use the special characters and symbols available in this tab.

Border Tab

The options in this tab are used to specify the border outline of the callouts. You can also specify the lineweights and the spacing for the text along the horizontal and vertical sides.

After setting the specifications for the callouts in the **Callout Properties** dialog box, choose the **OK** button; you will be prompted to click on an element or free space point. Select the object with which you want to link the callout; the preview of the callout will be attached to the cursor. Specify a point on the drawing sheet to place the callout.

Adding Surface Texture Symbols to a Drawing View

You can add surface texture symbols to edges or faces in the drawing views by using the **Surface Texture Symbol** tool. To do so, choose the **Surface Texture Symbol** tool from the **Annotation** group of the **Home** tab; the **Surface Texture Symbol Properties** dialog box will be displayed, as shown in Figure 12-31, and you will be prompted to click on an element or free space point. Select an edge or a face to apply the surface texture symbol. There are two tabs in the **Surface Texture Symbol Properties** dialog box which are discussed next.

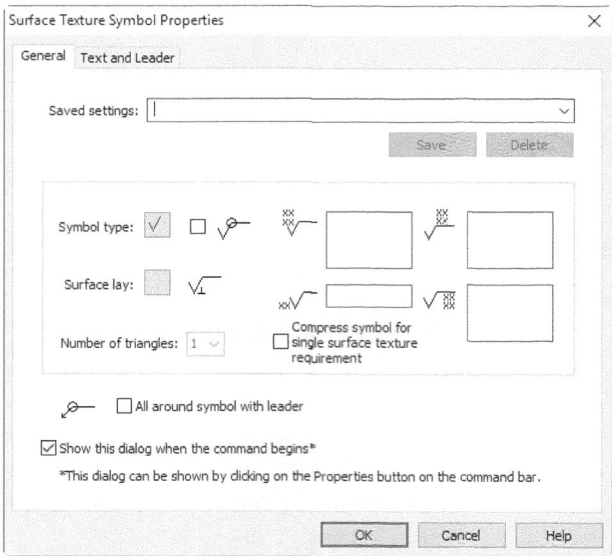

Figure 12-31 *The* ***Surface Texture Symbol Properties*** *dialog box*

General Tab

In this tab, you can select the symbol type for the surface texture. You can also specify the characteristics and applications of the surface finish, roughness, waviness, and lay. To specify the symbol type, select the **Symbol type** button; a flyout will be displayed with surface finish options. Select the desired option from the flyout. To specify the type of surface lay, select the **Surface lay** button; a flyout will be displayed with eight options. Select the desired option from the flyout.

Text and Leader Tab

The options in this tab are used for specify the annotations such as leaders, balloons, callouts, control frames, and symbols. You can also specify the font, style, size and color to the callout text.

After specifying settings in the **Surface Texture Symbol Properties** dialog box, choose the **OK** button; you will be prompted to click on an element or free space point. Select an entity; the surface texture symbol will be attached to the cursor. Notice that this symbol moves along with the cursor. Specify a point in the drawing sheet to place the surface texture symbol.

Specifying the Edge Conditions

Sometimes, you may need to specify the edge conditions for a part or assembly. The edge condition for the part can be specified by using the **Edge Condition** tool. To specify the edge conditions, choose the **Edge Condition** tool from the **Annotation** group of the **Home** tab; the **Edge Condition Properties** dialog box will be displayed, as shown in Figure 12-32 and you will be prompted to click on an element or free space point. Two tabs are available in the **Edge Condition Properties** dialog box.

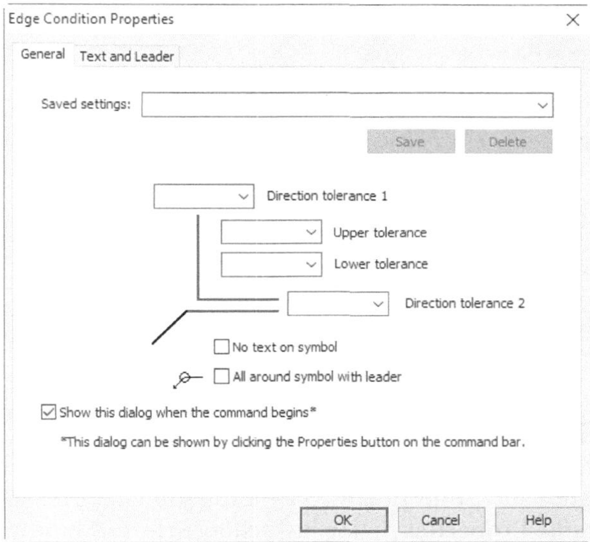

*Figure 12-32 The **Edge Conditions Properties** dialog box*

In the **General** tab, you can set the tolerance. In the **Text and Leader** tab, you can add different fonts, styles, colors, and so on as discussed in the previous topics.

Adding a Feature Control Frame to Drawing View

In shop floor drawing, you need to provide various parameters, along with the dimensions and the dimensional tolerances. The parameters can be geometric conditions, material conditions, tolerance zones, and so on. All these types of parameters are defined by using the **Feature Control Frame** tool. To add feature control frame to the drawing view, choose the **Feature Control Frame** tool from the **Annotation** group of the **Home** tab; the **Feature Control Frame Properties** dialog box will be displayed, as shown in Figure 12-33, along with the command bar. The options in this dialog box are discussed next.

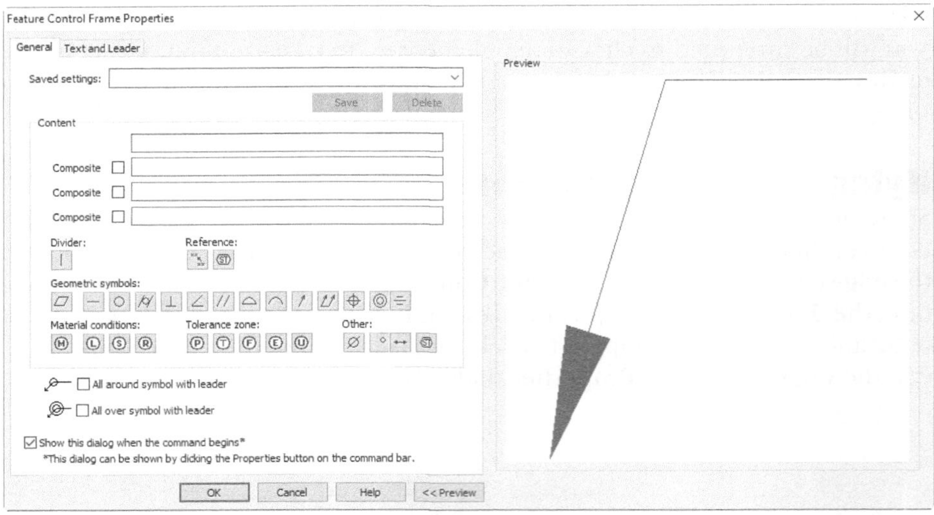

*Figure 12-33 The **Feature Control Frame Properties** dialog box*

General Tab

Using this tab, you can add or edit the feature control frame data. To do so, enter the required data in the **Composite** edit boxes of the **Content** area; a preview of the frame is displayed in the **Preview** area. You can find all types of geometric character symbols, material conditions symbols, tolerance zone symbols, and so on to specify the exact part conditions with preferred values in the **Content** area. The **Divider** button in the **Content** area is used to make divisions in the **Feature Control Frame**.

Text and Leader Tab

Using the options in this tab, you can set the font and the style, size, and color of the font. You can also modify the Leader and projection lines by using this tab. After specifying the settings in the **Feature Control Frame Properties** dialog box, choose the **OK** button; you will be prompted to click on an element or free space point. Select the required element; a preview of the feature control frame will be attached to the cursor. Specify a point in the drawing sheet; the feature control frame will be placed on the required element.

You can also change the orientation of the feature control frames. To do so, choose the **Orientation** option from the **Feature Control Frame** command bar; a flyout will be displayed with options such as **Horizontal**, **Vertical**, **Parallel** and **Perpendicular**. Note that the options in this flyout will be displayed based on the entity on which the feature control frame has to be placed. Choose the required orientation option; the feature control frame will be oriented.

Adding Datum Target to a Drawing View

The **Datum Target** tool is used to add datum targets to the entities in the drawing view. These datum targets are used as reference datum planes in the feature control frames.

To add datum targets, choose the **Datum Target** tool from the **Annotation** group of the **Home** tab; a command bar will be displayed and you will be prompted to select the datum point. Select the **Properties** option from the command bar; the **Datum Target Properties** dialog box will be displayed, as shown in Figure 12-34. There are two tabs in this dialog box and they are discussed next.

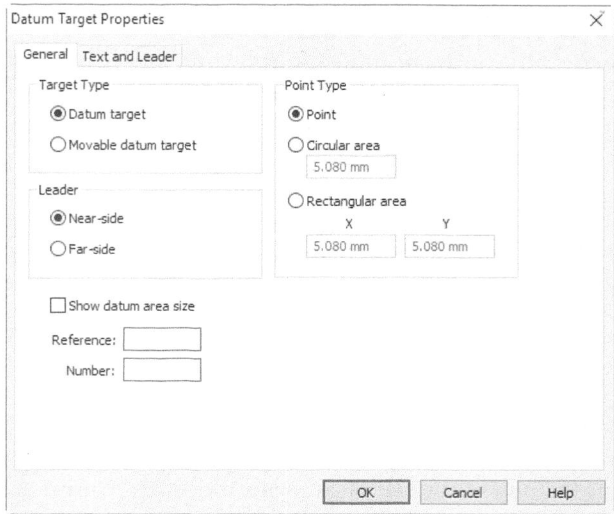

*Figure 12-34 The **Datum Target Properties** dialog box*

General Tab

Using the options in this tab, you can specify the properties of the datum target. The options in the **Target Type** area are used to specify the datum target types. In the **Leader** area, if you select the **Near-side** radio button, a solid leader line will be displayed. To display a dashed leader line, select the **Far-side** radio button from this area.

The options in the **Point Type** area are used to specify the symbol and size of the datum target point. The **Show datum area size** check box, if selected, displays the datum area size in the datum target symbol. The **Reference** edit box is used to enter the reference letter whereas the **Number** edit box is used to enter the datum target number.

Text and Leader Tab

Using the options in this tab, you can set the font and its style, size, and color. You can also modify the Leader and projection lines by using this tab.

Adding a Datum Frame to a Drawing View

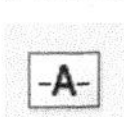

The **Datum Frame** tool is used to add datum frames to drawing view. To add a datum frame to the drawing sheet, choose the **Datum Frame** tool from the **Annotation** group of the **Home** tab; a command bar will be displayed and you will be prompted to click on an element or free space point. In the command bar, enter the datum character in the **Datum Text** edit box and specify the scale value in the **Text Scale** edit box. After entering the values, select an entity in the drawing view; a preview of the datum frame will be attached to the cursor. Specify a point in the drawing sheet to place the datum frame at that point.

Note

*In Solid Edge, you can lock the drawing view to prevent the movements of the view. To do so, select a drawing view; the **Select** command bar will be displayed. Select the **Lock Position** option from the command bar; the selected drawing view will be locked and a lock symbol will be displayed when the cursor is moved on the drawing view.*

ADDING NEW DRAWING SHEETS

In Solid Edge, a drawing file can have multiple drawing sheets. A multisheet drawing file is generally used when you need to generate drawing views of all the parts of an assembly in a single drawing file. You can easily switch between the sheets to refer to the drawing views of different parts within the same file, thus avoiding the step of opening separate drawing files.

To add a new sheet to the drawing file, right-click on **Sheet1** at the bottom of the drawing window and choose the **Insert** option from the shortcut menu; a new sheet named **Sheet2** will be added to the drawing file. Similarly, you can use other options available in the shortcut menu to rename, delete, reorder, and sheet setup. You can also use  button available next to the **Sheet1** to add a new sheet.

EDITING THE DEFAULT SHEET FORMAT

You can edit the default standard sheet format according to your design requirement. To edit the standard sheet format, you need to activate the **Background** sheet and deactivate the **Working** sheet. Choose the **Background** button from the **Sheet Views** group of the **View** tab to activate the **Background** sheet and choose the **Working** button from the **Sheet Views** group of the **View** tab to deactivate the **Working** sheet. You will notice that all entities, annotations, and views are removed from the drawing sheet and four sheet tabs, namely **A4-Sheet**, **A3-Sheet**, **A2-Sheet**, and **A1-Sheet** are displayed at the bottom of the drawing sheet. Right-click on any one of sheet size tab at the bottom of the drawing window and choose the **Sheet Setup** option from the shortcut menu to display the **Sheet Setup** dialog box. You can use the options in this dialog box to modify the size and units of the sheet. You can also edit or delete an existing title block and use the sketching tools to draw a new title block. After editing the sheet, activate the **Working** sheet and deactivate the **Background** sheet.

UPDATING DRAWING VIEWS

As discussed earlier, this software has Bidirectional Associativity due to which when you make any changes in a model in the **Part** environment it automatically reflects in the **Assembly** environment and vice versa. But when you make any changes to the model in the **Part** or **Assembly** environment, it will not reflects changes in its drawing views in the **Draft** environment and its views will be enclosed within a box. This box indicates that the views are out of date and need to be updated. For updating the views you need to select the **Drawing View Tracker** tool from the **Assistants** group of the **Tools** tab; the **Drawing View Tracker** dialog box will be displayed, as shown in Figure 12-35.

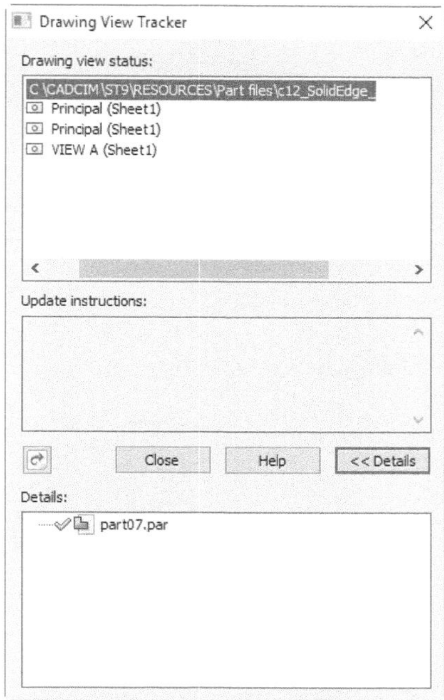

*Figure 12-35 The **Drawing View Tracker** dialog box*

Choose the **Update View** button adjacent to the **Close** button from the dialog box; the drawing views will be updated. Choose the **Close** button from the dialog box; the **Dimension Tracker** dialog box will be displayed. This dialog box displays information about the element that is updated. Choose the **Close** button to exit from the dialog box.

You can also choose the **Update Views** button from the **Drawing Views** group of the **Home** tab; the **Dimension Tracker** dialog box will be displayed. Choose the **Close** button from the dialog box to exit; the drawing views will be updated.

Note

*The modifications done on the views in the **Draft** environment do not reflect in other environments.*

EVOLVING A 3D MODEL FROM A 2D DRAWING

You can evolve a 3D model from a 2D drawing using the **Create 3D** tool. This tool enables the solid edge tools to work with 2D drawing views to quickly create the 3D models. Also, you can use the drafting views or the drawing files created in AutoCAD to generate the 3D model. Figure 12-36 shows a 2D drawing and Figure 12-37 shows a 3D model evolved from the 2D drawing.

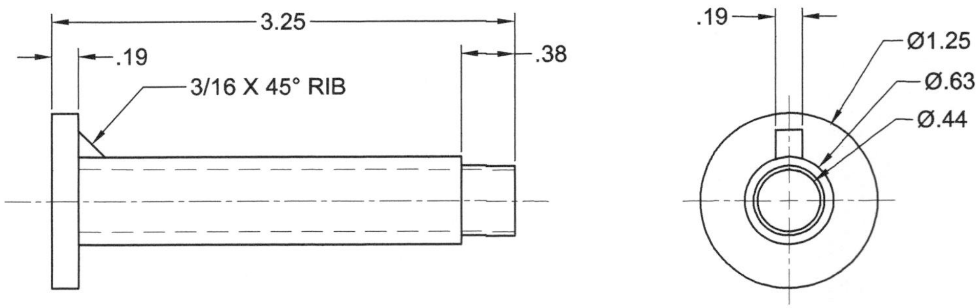

Figure 12-36 *A 2D drawing*

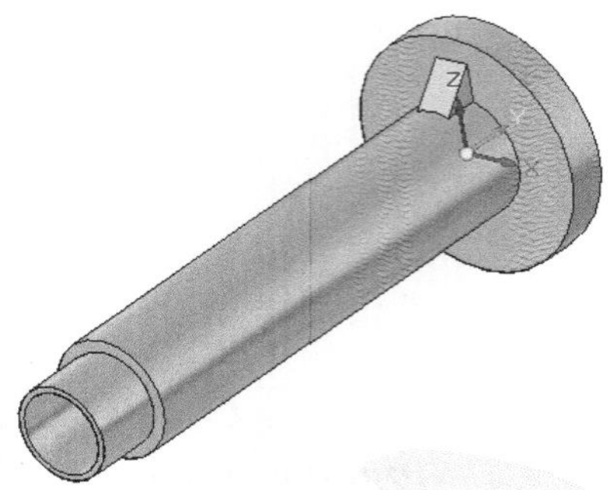

Figure 12-37 *The 3D model evolved from the 2D drawing*

The steps to be followed to evolve a 3d model from a 2d drawing are given below:

1. Open the 2D drawing in Solid Edge.
2. Choose the **Create 3D** tool from the **Assistants** group of the **Tools** tab to invoke the **Create 3D** dialog box.
3. Specify a template file.
4. Choose the **Options** button and select the desired angle of projection (first or third) and choose the **OK** button.
5. Choose the **Next** button and specify the scale for the 3D model, if required.
6. Select the view geometry from the drawing area by drawing a selection window.
7. Choose the **Next** button to select another view geometry, if required.
8. Next, choose the **Set Fold Line** button to draw a fold line. This line defines the position to fold the primary view. This ensures the proper orientation of the sketches.
9. After performing all the steps mentioned above, choose the **Finish** button; the sketches will be oriented as defined.

   Now, you can select the profile from the drawing view and perform the required 3d operation on it. You will be more clear about the usage of the **Create 3D** tool in Tutorial 3.

GENERATING THE EXPLODED VIEW OF ASSEMBLIES

The exploded views are generated by selecting the configuration that was saved at the time of exploding the assembly in the **Assembly** environment. The following steps explain the procedure for generating an exploded view:

1. Choose the **View Wizard** tool from the **Drawing Views** group of the **Home** tab to display the **Select Model** dialog box.
2. Select the assembly from the dialog box and choose the **Open** button; the **View Wizard** command bar will be displayed. Choose the **Drawing View Wizard Options** button from the command bar to display the **Drawing View Wizard** dialog box.
3. From the **.cfg, PMI Model View, or Zone:** drop-down list in the dialog box, select the configuration that represents the exploded state of the assembly.
4. Set the other parameters and then choose the **OK** button from the dialog box.
5. Place the view on the drawing sheet; an exploded view is generated, as shown in Figure 12-38.

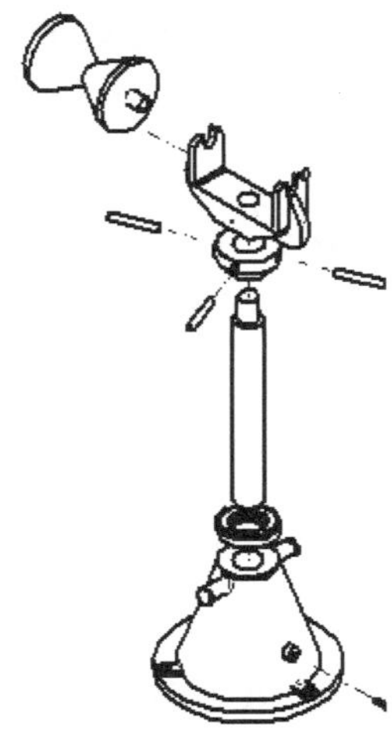

Figure 12-38 Exploded view

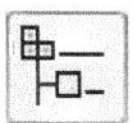

Before placing the view, you can also set the display of the parts in the exploded drawing view by choosing the **Model Display Settings** button from the **View Wizard** command bar. When you choose this button, the **Drawing View Properties** dialog box will be displayed, as shown in Figure 12-39. The options in the **Display** tab of this dialog box are discussed next.

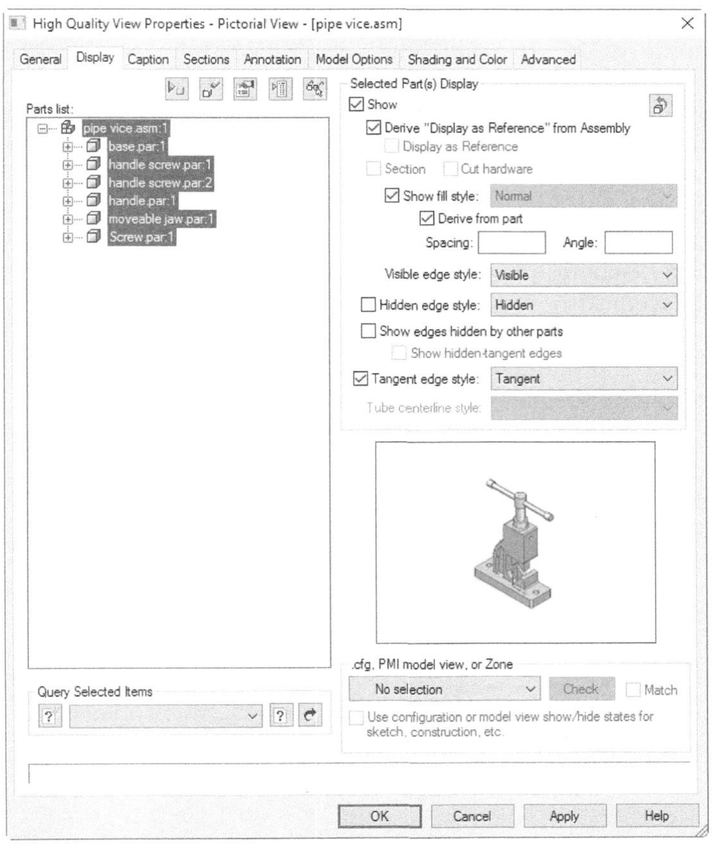

*Figure 12-39 The **Drawing View Properties** dialog box*

Display Tab of the Drawing View Properties Dialog Box

The **Display** tab of this dialog box contains various options for controlling the display of the assembly drawing view. These options are discussed next.

Show

Using the **Show** check box, you can control the display of one or more parts in the assembly. You will also notice that all parts, including the assembly, are selected in the **Parts list** area.

Display as Reference

This check box, when selected, enables you to display the selected part as reference. You can select the part from the **Parts list** area. The selected part is displayed as dotted in the assembly drawing view.

Visible edge style

This drop-down list enables you to select the edge style of the parts in the assembly drawing view. You can also apply different styles to different parts in the assembly drawing view.

CREATING ASSOCIATIVE BALLOONS AND PARTS LIST

Generally, the drawing view of an assembly also contains the list of parts, material of each part, quantity, and other related information in the form of a table, which is called the bill of material (BOM). In Solid Edge, it is called the parts list. The parts list can be generated by choosing the **Parts List** tool from the **Tables** group. The parts list is associative in nature, which means that any modification made in the part files of the assembly will be reflected in the parts list also. The procedure for generating a parts list and balloons is given next.

1. Generate the assembly drawing view.
2. Choose the **Parts List** button from the **Tables** group of the **Home** tab; the **Part List** command bar will be displayed. Also, you will be prompted to select a drawing view.
3. Select the assembly drawing view; the preview of the parts list box will be attached to the cursor and you will be prompted to edit the properties of the parts list or specify a point in the drawing sheet to place the parts list box. Choose the **Properties** button from the command bar; the **Parts List Properties** dialog box will be displayed. Set the display properties of the parts list and balloons in this dialog box and choose **OK**.
4. Choose the **Auto-Balloon** button from the command bar, if it is not already chosen.
5. Click in the drawing area; the parts list and balloons are placed in the drawing sheet automatically, refer to Figure 12-40.

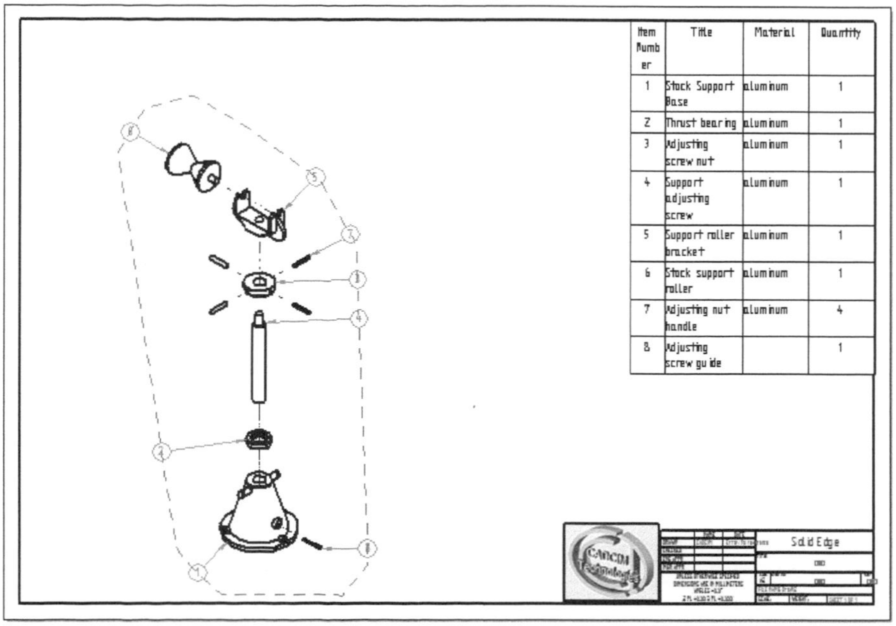

Figure 12-40 The exploded view of the assembly with parts list and balloons

Parts List Properties Dialog Box

While generating a parts list on the drawing sheet, if you choose the **Properties** button from the command bar before placing it, the **Parts List Properties** dialog box will be displayed, as shown in Figure 12-41. This dialog box is used to set the parameters of the parts list and balloons. The options in this dialog box are discussed next.

General Tab

The options in this tab are used to specify the text properties of the text in the parts list and are discussed next.

Saved settings

This drop-down list contains the styles that are saved for the parts list. By default **ANSI**, **ANSI-New Sheet**, **ISO**, **ISO-New Sheet**, and **Exploded** styles are saved. If you need to save a new style, enter a name in this drop-down list and choose the **Save** button. You can also select the required table style from the **Table style** drop-down list available below the **Saved settings** drop-down list.

Height Area

The options in this area are used to specify the location to place the table in the drawing view, set the maximum number of rows, maximum height, and many other parameters of the table.

Margin Area

The options in this area are used to set the spacing between the text and table cell border in the horizontal and vertical directions.

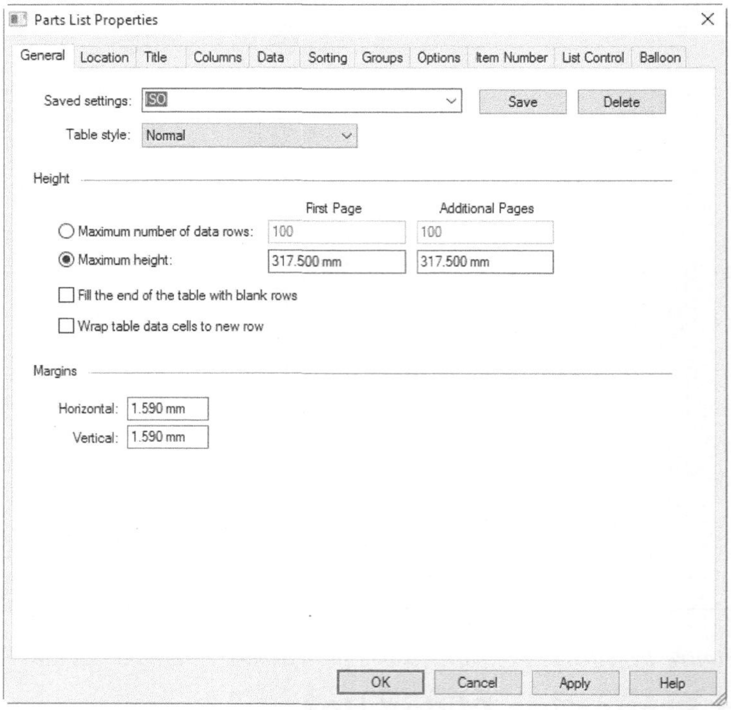

*Figure 12-41 The **Parts List Properties** dialog box*

Location Tab

The options in this tab are used to arrange the sheet placement and size. Some of these options are discussed next.

Anchor corner

The **Anchor corner** drop-down list of the **Location** tab of the dialog box is used to specify the anchor point for the part list.

Location Area

The options in this area are used to specify the location of the part list.

Position Area

The **Page** list in this area displays the pages available in the table. The **Sheet** drop-down list displays the sheets available in the drawing.

Title Tab

You can add titles to the table using the options in this tab. On choosing the **Add Title** button, the **Title text** area will get activated. You can enter the desired title in this area. You can also set the number of titles for the table by using the **Number of Titles** edit box. Additionally, you can specify the sequence of titles by using the **Title** spinner. Using the options in the **Position** drop-down list, you can specify the position of each title in the table. You can delete the selected title by using the **Delete Title** button.

Columns Tab

The options in this tab are used to specify various properties of columns in the parts list. These options are discussed next.

Columns

This display box lists all the columns that will appear in the parts list. It also displays the order in which the columns will be displayed. You can change the order of the columns by using the **Move Up** and **Move Down** buttons. You can add columns to this box by selecting the required column from the **Properties** display box and choosing the **Add Column** button. To remove columns from the table, choose the **Delete Column** button.

Properties

This display box lists all column headings that can be displayed in the parts list. You can also select the **User Defined** property to create a column without any heading.

Column Format Area

The options in this area are used to control the column headings to be displayed in the table. You can specify the required headings by using the **Columns** display box. You can also specify the alignment of the text as well as its position in various cells of the parts list. Moreover, you can set the width of the column in this area.

Data Tab

The options in this tab are used to format the data in the parts list tables. You can insert or delete columns and rows, as well as move the rows up or down by using the options in this tab. You can change the format of any column by choosing the **Format Column** button in this tab. On choosing this button, the **Format Column** dialog box will be displayed. Using this dialog box, you can set the column width, text, position, alignment, and other parameters of the header.

Sorting Tab

The options in this tab are used to specify the criteria to sort the parts in the parts list.

Groups Tab

The options in this tab are used to group the columns by selecting them.

Options Tab

The options in this tab are used to control the numbering of items in the parts list. You can also specify the type of parts to be displayed in the list by using the options in this tab.

Item Number Tab

The options under this tab allow you to edit the item number associated with each item in the parts list.

List Control Tab

The options under this tab are used to control the display of parts in the parts list. From these options, you can select the parts that you want to exclude from the assembly. These options are discussed next.

Top-level list (top-level and expanded components)
When this radio button is selected, only the top-level assembly is searched for the parts to list them in the parts list. If the assembly contains subassemblies, they are listed as a single part and the parts of the subassemblies are not listed in the parts list.

Note
Remember that the title in the parts list will be listed only if you have entered it in the file properties of that part.

Atomic list (all parts)
This radio button, when selected, specifies that all parts will be listed in the parts list. If the assembly contains subassemblies, all parts of the subassemblies will also be listed in the parts list.

Exploded list (all parts and subassemblies)
When this radio button is selected, all parts, subassemblies, and subassembly parts are displayed in the parts list. In this list, a part may be displayed multiple times based on the number of times it has been used in a subassembly. The sub options of exploded list are discussed next.

Use level based item numbers: When this check box is selected, the parts under a subassembly receive the item number based on the hierarchy level of the subassembly. For example, 1.1, 1.2, 1.3 and so on.

Show top assembly in list: When this check box is selected, a row will be inserted in the part list for entering the name of the top level assembly.

Expand weldment subassemblies: When this check box is selected, the weldment assembly will expand and its parts will be displayed in the part list. If this check box is cleared, the weldment assembly will be treated as the single part.

Selected item Area
The options in this area are used to exclude or include the selected part from the parts list. To exclude a part, select it from the adjacent tree and then select the **Exclude** radio button.

Subassemblies Area
The options in this area are used to specify if a subassembly exists and also if you want it to be displayed as a single item or along with its parts in the parts list.

Include all ballooned parts in all drawing views
When this check box is selected, only those parts which were ballooned earlier will be listed in the parts list. This check box is cleared by default.

Exclude parts hidden in all drawing views
When this check box is selected, the hidden parts will be excluded from the parts list. This check box is cleared by default.

Exclude parts marked as reference in all drawing views
If this check box is selected, the reference parts will be excluded from the parts list. This check box is selected by default.

Balloon Tab
The options under this tab enable you to set the display properties of the balloons that appear on the assembly drawing view. The options in the **Auto Balloon** area of this tab are used to specify whether the balloons will be created on all the occurrences of a part in an assembly or only one. You can also select the **Create alignment Shape** check box to arrange the balloons in a systematic pattern. You can select the alignment type from the **Pattern** menu displayed by choosing the **Pattern** button, refer to Figure 12-42. Similarly you can select the rotation type from the **Order** menu displayed on choosing the **Order** button.

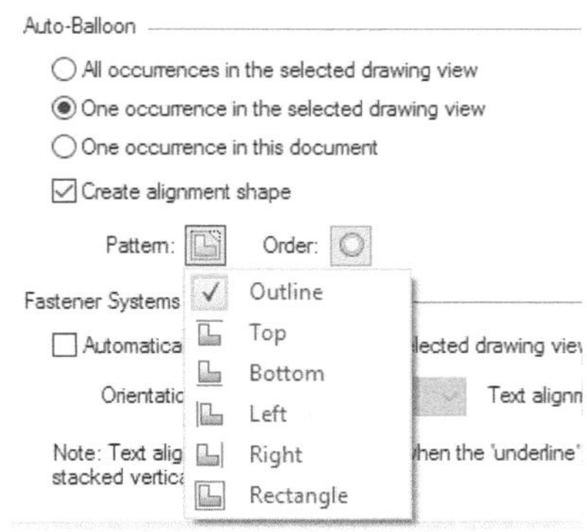

*Figure 12-42 The **Pattern** menu*

Setting the Text Properties
You can set the properties of the text used in the Parts list or BOM. The steps required to modify the text size are as follows:

1. Choose the **Styles** button from the **Styles** group of the **View** tab to display the **Style** window.
2. Select **Table** from the **Style type** area list and then select the current table style from the **Styles** list; the parameters of the current table style are displayed in the **Description** box.
3. To modify the parameters of the table style, choose the **Modify** button from the **Style** dialog box; the **Modify Table Style** dialog box is displayed.
4. Choose the **Text** tab from it and then select **Normal** from the **Text styles** list.
5. Choose the **Modify** button; the **Modify Text Box Style** dialog box gets invoked. Choose the **Paragraph** tab from it; the text settings are displayed in this tab.
6. Specify the required font size in the **Font size** edit box and press ENTER.
7. Choose **OK** from the **Modify Table Style** dialog box and then **Apply** from the **Style** dialog box to accept and exit the settings.

Alternatively, select the parts list; the **Select** command bar will be displayed. Select the **Properties** option from the command bar, the **Parts list Properties** dialog box will be displayed. Select the **Data** tab in the dialog box; the data present in the parts list will be displayed and the options for rearranging the rows and columns, and changing the font styles and sizes will be displayed. By using these options, you can modify the required text in the parts list.

Steps to Generate Parts List and Balloons
In this section, you will learn how to generate the parts list and balloons by setting the options in the **Parts List Properties** dialog box.

The following steps explain the procedure for generating the parts list and balloons:

1. Choose the **Parts List** tool from the **Tables** group; you are prompted to select the drawing view.

2. Select the drawing view that exists on the drawing sheet.
3. Choose the **Properties** button from the command bar to display the **Parts List Properties** dialog box.
4. Choose the **Columns** tab.
5. In the **Columns** display box, select **Author** and choose the **Delete Column** button.
6. Choose the **List Control** tab.
7. From the **Global** area, select the **Atomic List (all parts)** radio button and choose the **OK** button to exit the dialog box.
8. Choose the **Auto-Balloon** button from the command bar, if it is not already chosen.
9. Click in the drawing area to place the BOM and balloons. You will notice that the balloons are displayed showing both the item number and the quantity.
10. To remove the quantity from a balloon, select all the balloons by pressing the CTRL key; the command bar is displayed.
11. Choose the **Item Count** button from the command bar displayed. Now, the balloon will show only the item number.

On performing the above steps, an assembly with parts list and balloons will be generated, as shown in Figure 12-43. This assembly consists of two subassemblies.

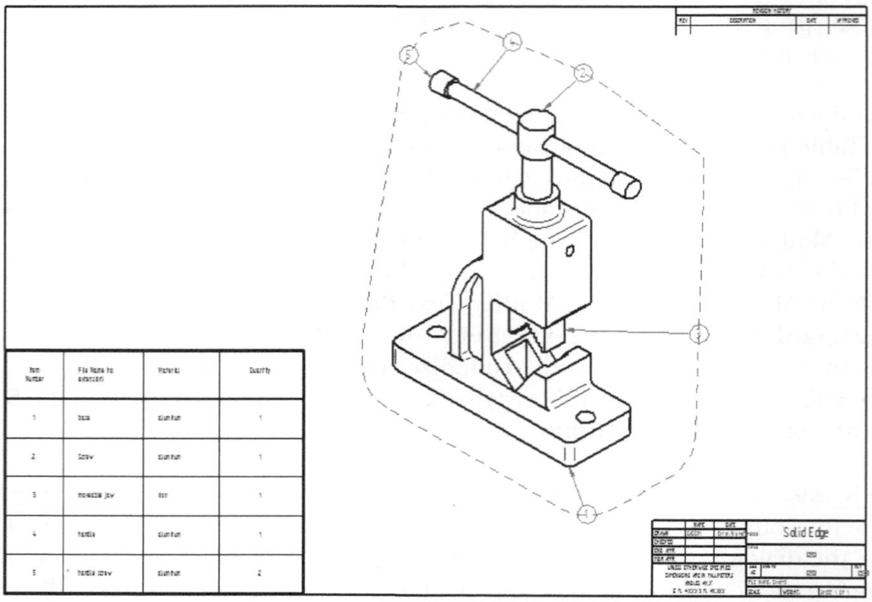

***Figure 12-43** Exploded view of the assembly with BOM and balloons*

TUTORIALS

Tutorial 1

In this tutorial, you will generate the top view, front view, and right view of the part created in Exercise 1 of Chapter 8, as shown in Figure 12-44. You will use the standard A2 sheet format for generating the drawing views. You will also need to insert your company logo in the sheet.

(Expected time: 1 hr)

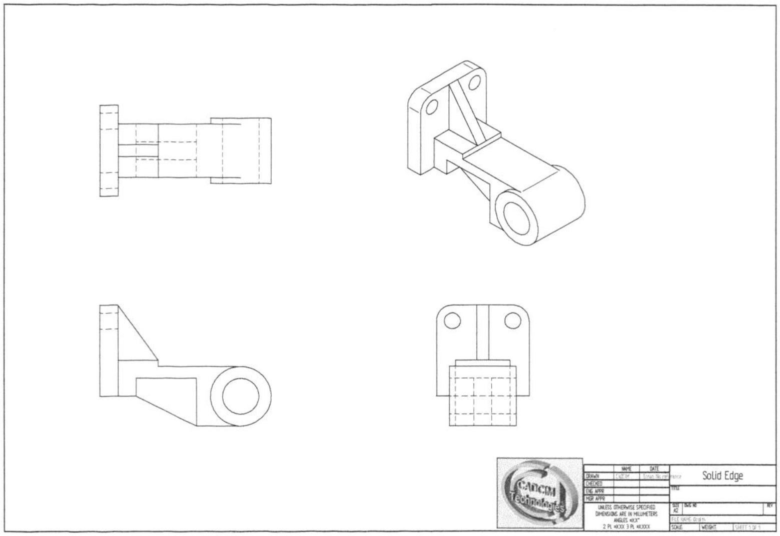

Figure 12-44 *Top, front, right side, and isometric views of the model*

The following steps are required to complete this tutorial:

a. Start a new draft file.
b. Set up the drawing sheet and the background sheet, refer to Figure 12-44.
c. Set the projection angle method and save the draft template file.
d. Generate the drawing views, refer to Figure 12-46.
e. Save the draft file.

Starting a New File in the Draft Environment

Start Solid Edge and then choose the **ISO Metric Draft** option from the **Create** area of the welcome screen.

Setting the Drawing Sheet Options

The drawing sheet in Solid Edge is like a blank sheet of paper on which you can draw views. You can add as many sheets as needed in the same drawing file. When you work in the **Draft** environment, there is only one sheet by default. The sheet on which you place the drawing views is called the worksheet and the sheet on which you create the title blocks is called the background sheet. Based on the size of the worksheet you select, the background sheet automatically adjusts itself to the size of the worksheet. To set the worksheet and the drawing sheet for this tutorial, follow the steps given next.

1. Choose **Application Button > Settings > Sheet Setup**; the **Sheet Setup** dialog box is displayed. In the **Sheet Size** area of the **Size** tab, the **Standard** radio button is selected by default.

2. In the **Standard** drop-down list, select **A2 Wide (594mm x 420mm)**, if it is not already been selected. Note that in the dialog box, the units are set in millimeters.

3. Choose the **Background** tab in the dialog box. Make sure **A2-Sheet** is selected in the **Background sheet** drop-down list. Choose the **OK** button from the dialog box to exit it.

   Next, you need to insert a graphic image as an object in the background sheet. Generally, this method is used to insert a company's logo. As the image has to be inserted in the background sheet, you need to deactivate the working sheet. Also, note that to insert an image, you should have an image editing program installed on your computer.

4. Choose the **Background** button from the **Sheet Views** group of the **View** tab and then choose the **Working** button from the **Sheet Views** group of the **View** tab to deactivate the Working **Sheets** option. Notice that four sheets are displayed in the bar below the drawing window.

5. Choose the **A2-Sheet** tab from the bottom of the drawing window and then zoom to fit it on the screen.

6. Now, you need to delete the table at the top. To do so, select the top table, as shown in Figure 12-45. All entities in the table turn magenta in color which indicates that they are selected.

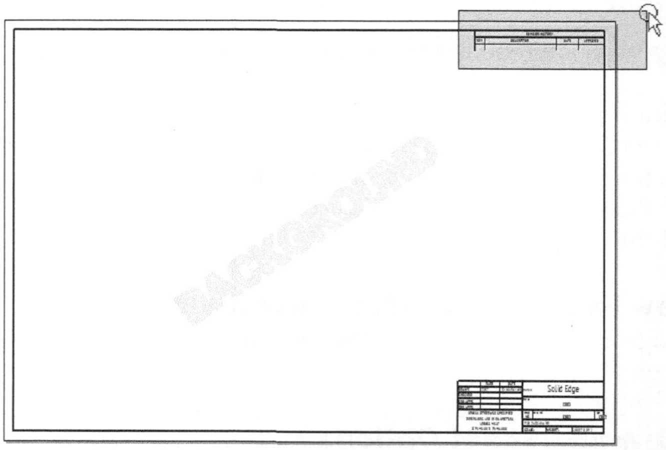

Figure 12-45 *Selecting the table*

7. Press the DELETE key to delete the selected entities.

8. Choose the **Image** button from the **Insert** group of the **Sketching** tab to display the **Insert Image** dialog box.

9. Choose the **Browse** button from this dialog box; the **Open a File** dialog box is displayed.

10. Browse and then select the image file of the logo that you want to use, refer to Figure 12-46.

11. Set the transparency option for the logo, if required.

12. After selecting the file, choose the **OK** button from the **Insert Image** dialog box; the image is placed on the sheet.

13. Drag the handles of the image to resize it and move it to the desired location.

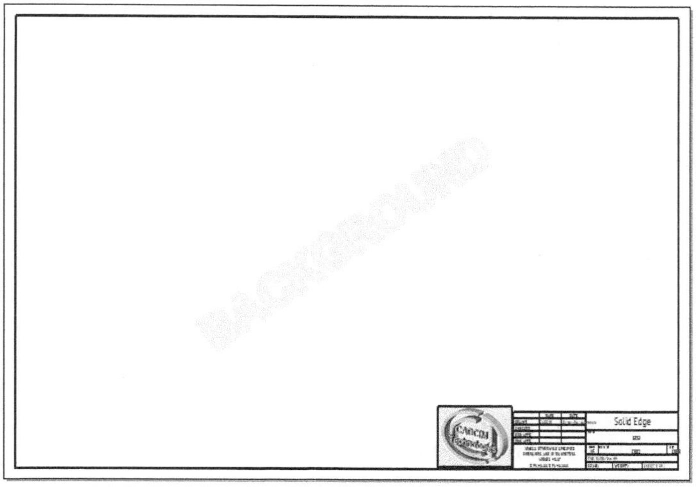

Figure 12-46 *Title block with the image*

14. After placing the image, choose **Application Button > Settings > Options** to display the **Solid Edge Options** dialog box. Then, choose the **Drawing Standards** tab from this dialog box.

15. In the **Projection Angle** area of this dialog box, select the **Third** radio button to set the current projection type to third angle projection. Choose **OK** to exit the dialog box.

16. Choose the **Working** button from the **Sheet Views** group of the **View** tab and then choose the **Background** button from the **Sheet Views** group of the **View** tab to deactivate the **Background** button. Next, the drawing views that you generate will be placed on the worksheet and not on the background sheet. Use the **Fit** button to fit the drawing into the sheet.

17. Save the drawing file with the name *Template.dft* at the following location: *C:\Solid Edge\c12*.

    As the *Template.dft* is to be used in the next tutorial, you need to create a folder with the name **Templates** at the location: *C:\Program Files\Solid Edge ST9\Template*. Then, save the file in it so that it is displayed in the template list of the **New** dialog box.

    You have successfully created a template file. In this textbook, you will further use this drawing file as a template to generate drawing views in the **Draft** environment.

18. Close this file. Next, choose the **New** tool from the **Quick Access** toolbar; the **New** dialog box is displayed.

19. Select the **Template** option from the **Standard Templates** drop-down list and select the **Template.dft** option from the area adjacent to the **Standard Templates** drop-down list. Next, choose **OK** to start the file. The file will open in the **Draft** environment.

Generating Drawing Views

The **Drawing View Wizard** enables you to generate multiple views in a single attempt. All the views required for this tutorial will be generated at the same time using the options on this page or using this wizard.

1. Choose the **View Wizard** tool from the **Drawing Views** group of the **Home** tab to display the **Select Model** dialog box.

2. Select the part created in Exercise 1 of Chapter 8 and then choose the **Open** button to display the **View Wizard** command bar.

3. Choose the **Drawing View Layout** button from the command bar; the **Drawing View Wizard** is displayed.

4. In the **Drawing View Wizard**, select the views from the **Primary View** area, refer to Figure 12-47 and then choose the **OK** button.

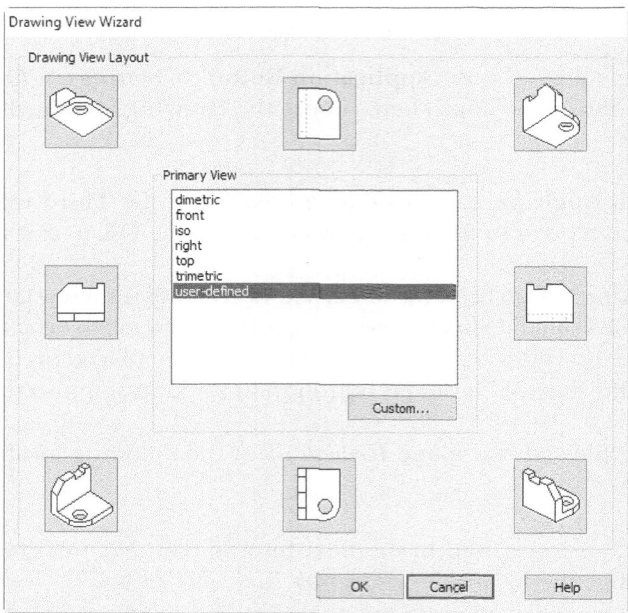

*Figure 12-47 The **Drawing View Wizard***

5. Place the drawing views on the sheet.

   Note that you need to change the scale of the views. When the scale of any one of the orthographic views is modified, it changes the scale of other two orthographic views as well.

6. Select the isometric view to display the command bar.

7. Enter **0.75** in the **Scale value** edit box and press ENTER to modify the scale.

8. Similarly, select any one of the orthographic views to invoke the command bar. Modify the value of the scale to **0.75**.

9. You can move the views on the sheet by dragging them. Arrange all the views as they are shown in Figure 12-48.

Saving the File

1. Choose **Save** from the **Quick Access** toolbar to display the **Save As** dialog box. Next, save the file with the name *c12tut1.dft* at the following location:
   C:\Solid Edge\c12.

2. Choose the **Close** button from the file tab bar to close the file.

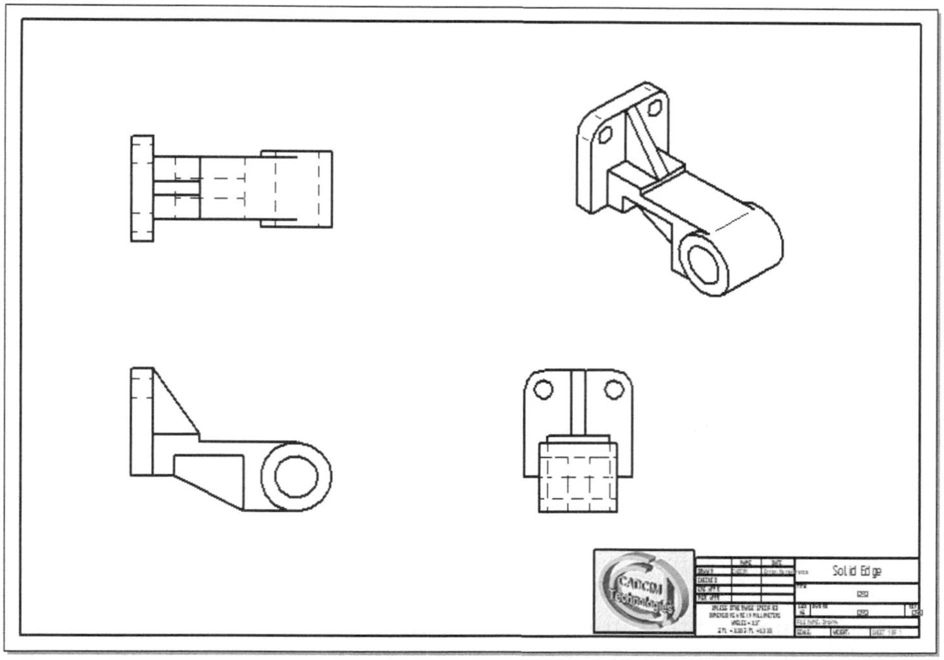

Figure 12-48 *Sheet after generating all drawing views*

Tutorial 2

In this tutorial, you will generate the front view, left-side view, and auxiliary view of the part shown in Figure 12-49. You can download the 3D model from *http://www.cadcim.com*. The path of the file is as follows: *Textbooks>CAD/CAM>Solid Edge>Solid Edge ST9 for Designers>Input Files*. Use the template that was created in Tutorial 1. **(Expected time: 30 min)**

The following steps are required to complete this tutorial:

a. Start a new draft file.
b. Generate drawing views, refer to Figures 12-50 through 12-53.
c. Generate dimensions, refer to Figures 12-54 through 12-56.

d. Create the remaining dimensions that are not generated, refer to Figure 12-57.
e. Save the drawing file and close the window.

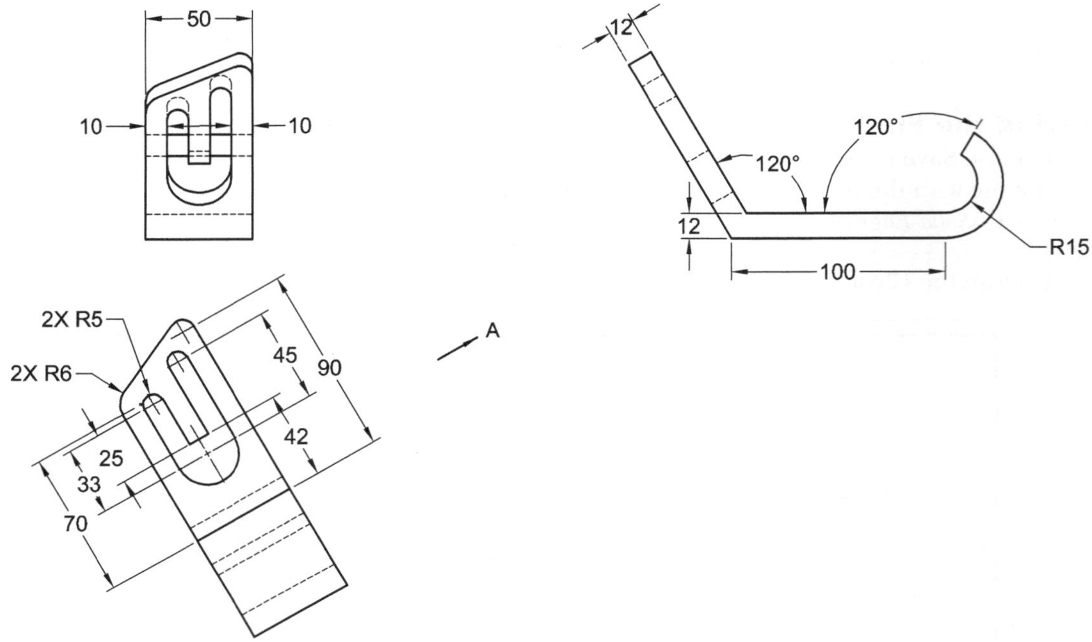

Figure 12-49 Left-side view, auxiliary view, and the front view of the model

Starting a New File in the Draft Environment

You will use the template created in the previous tutorial to generate the drawing views for this tutorial.

1. Choose the **New** button from the **Quick Access** toolbar to display the **New** dialog box.

2. Select the **Template** option from the **Standard Templates** drop-down list. Next, select the **Template.dft** from the area adjacent to the **Standard Templates** drop-down list and choose the **OK** button to exit the dialog box and enter the **Draft** environment.

Generating the Base Drawing Views

As mentioned earlier, the drawing views are generated from their parent part. The following steps are required to generate the drawing views:

1. Choose the **View Wizard** tool from the **Drawing Views** group to display the **Select Model** dialog box.

2. Select the part and choose the **Open** button to display the **View Wizard** command bar.

3. Choose the **Drawing View Layout** button from the command bar; the **Drawing View Wizard** is displayed.

4. Select **front** from the **Primary View** area and then to show the left view of the model, choose the button left to the **Primary View** area.

5. Place the drawing views on the sheet.

   Note that you need to scale the views. When the scale of any one orthographic view is modified, it changes the scale of other two orthographic views as well.

6. Select one of the views to display the command bar.

7. Modify the value of the scale to **1.2** in the **Scale value** edit box in the command bar.

8. You can move the views on the sheet by dragging them. Arrange the views as they are shown in Figure 12-50.

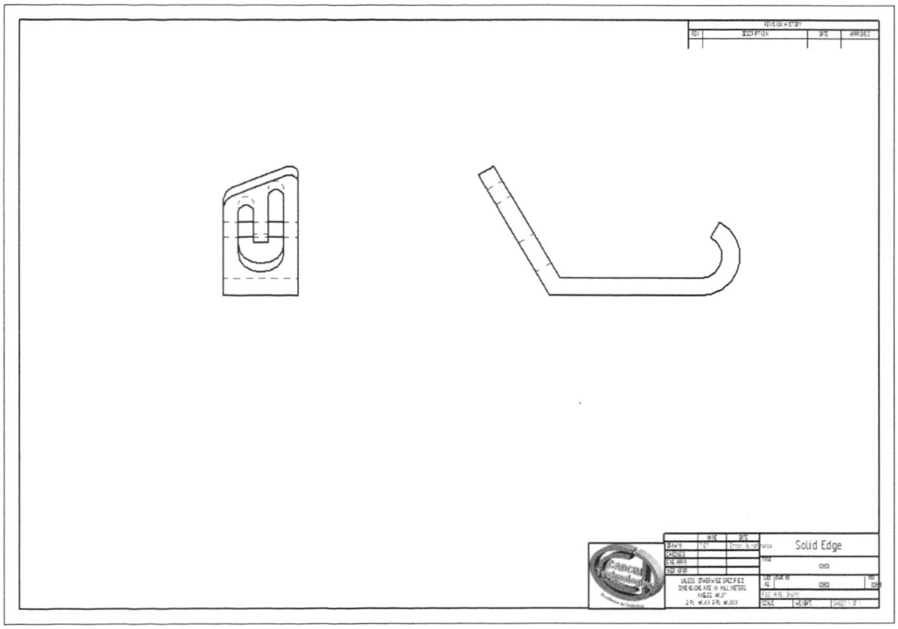

***Figure 12-50** Drawing views after scaling*

Generating the Auxiliary View

You will generate the auxiliary view by selecting the edge perpendicular to which the view will be projected. This view is created because the true shape of the cut profile can be shown in this view. To generate the auxiliary drawing view, follow the steps discussed next.

1. Choose the **Auxiliary** tool from the **Drawing Views** group; you are prompted to click on the first point of the fold line. The fold line is an imaginary line that is created when you select two keypoints. The auxiliary view is projected about this imaginary line.

2. Select the edge, as shown in Figure 12-51; an imaginary fold line is formed and the auxiliary

view is projected normal to this fold line. Move the cursor to the left to place the view, refer to Figure 12-52. After you place the view, an arrow pointing in the direction normal to the fold line is displayed, as shown in Figure 12-53.

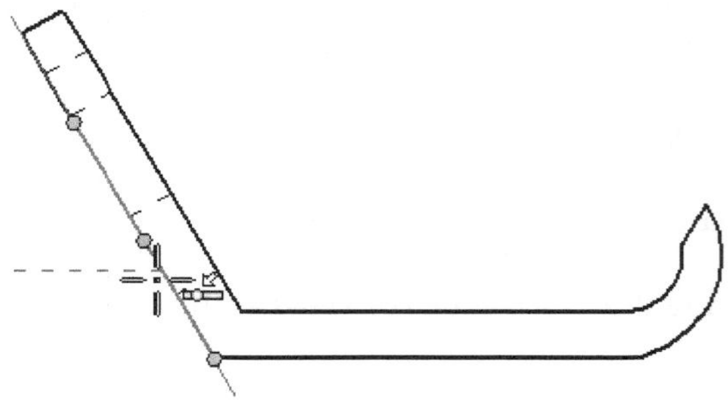

Figure 12-51 *Edge to be selected*

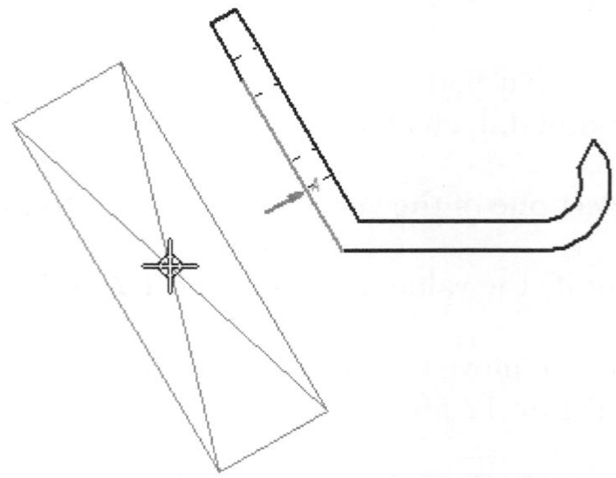

Figure 12-52 *Moving the cursor to place the view*

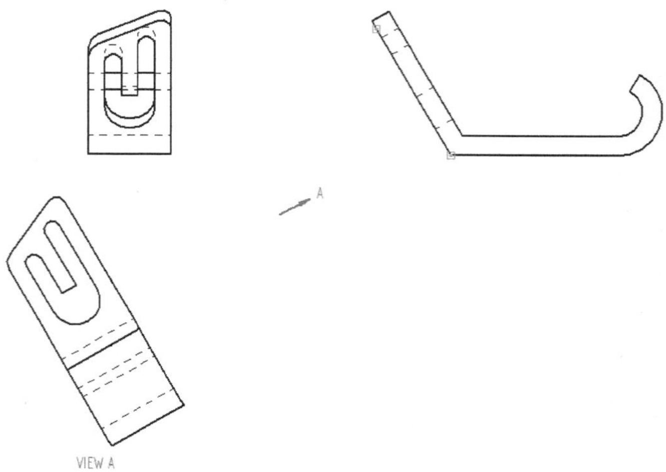

Figure 12-53 *Drawing sheet after generating the auxiliary view*

Generating the Dimensions

In this section, first retrieve the dimensions from the model and then create the remaining dimensions.

1. Choose the **Retrieve Dimensions** tool from the **Dimension** group; you are prompted to select the drawing view. Select the front view and increase the font size of the dimensions.

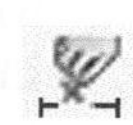

2. Exit the current tool and then select a dimension; the current dimension style is displayed in the **Dimension Style** drop-down list in the command bar. You need to modify the text size for this dimension style.

3. Press the ESC key to remove the dimension from the selection set. Next, choose the **Styles** button from the **Style** group of the **View** tab to display the **Style** dialog box. Select the **Dimension** option from the **Style type** list box and then choose dimension style of the current dimensions from the **Styles** list box and then choose the **Modify** button. The **Modify Dimensions Style** dialog box is displayed.

4. Choose the **Text** tab and modify the value of the font size to **8.5** in the **Font size** edit box. Choose **OK** in the **Modify Dimensions Style** dialog box and then choose **Apply** from the **Style** dialog box.

5. Arrange the dimensions, as shown in Figure 12-54, using the dimensioning tools.

6. Choose the **Distance Between** tool from the **Dimension** group of the **Home** tab and then select the **By 2 Points** option from the **Orientation** drop-down list in the command bar. Dimension the auxiliary view with dimensions 90, 42, and 70, as shown in Figure 12-55.

7. To dimension the auxiliary view with dimensions 45, 25, and 33, draw an axis such that it passes through the center of the arc, refer to Figure 12-56, by using the **Line** tool available in the **Draw** group of the **Sketching** tab.

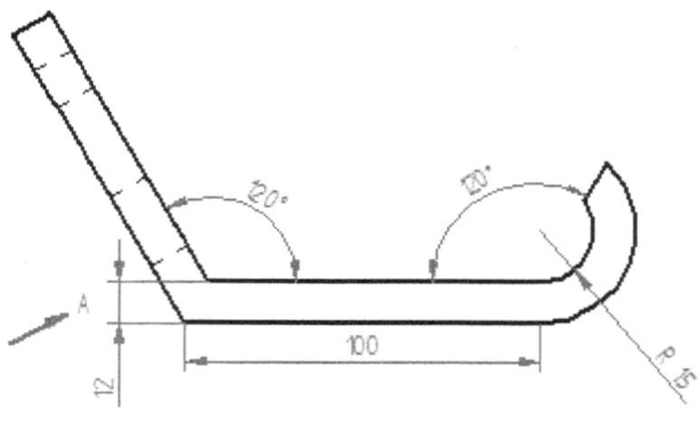

Figure 12-54 *Front view after placing the missing dimensions*

8. Select the center of the arc and then the axis, and place 33 as the dimension, see Figure 12-56.

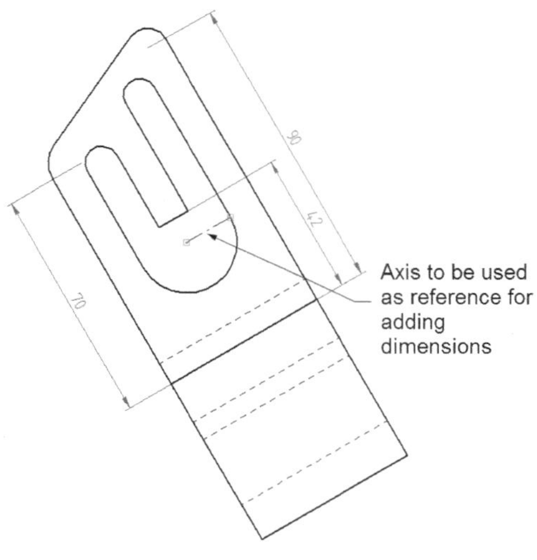

Figure 12-55 *Axis drawn to dimension*

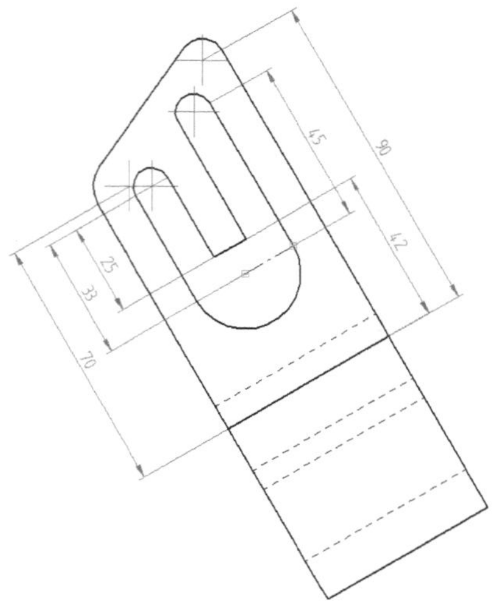

Figure 12-56 *Auxiliary view after dimensioning*

9. Similarly, apply the remaining dimensions to the auxiliary view so that all the dimensions are displayed.

10. After dimensioning the auxiliary view, choose the **Retrieve Dimensions** button and select the left-side view to generate the dimensions. You will notice that only dimension 50 is generated. Create the remaining dimensions manually.

The drawing sheet after dimensioning the drawing views is shown in Figure 12-57.

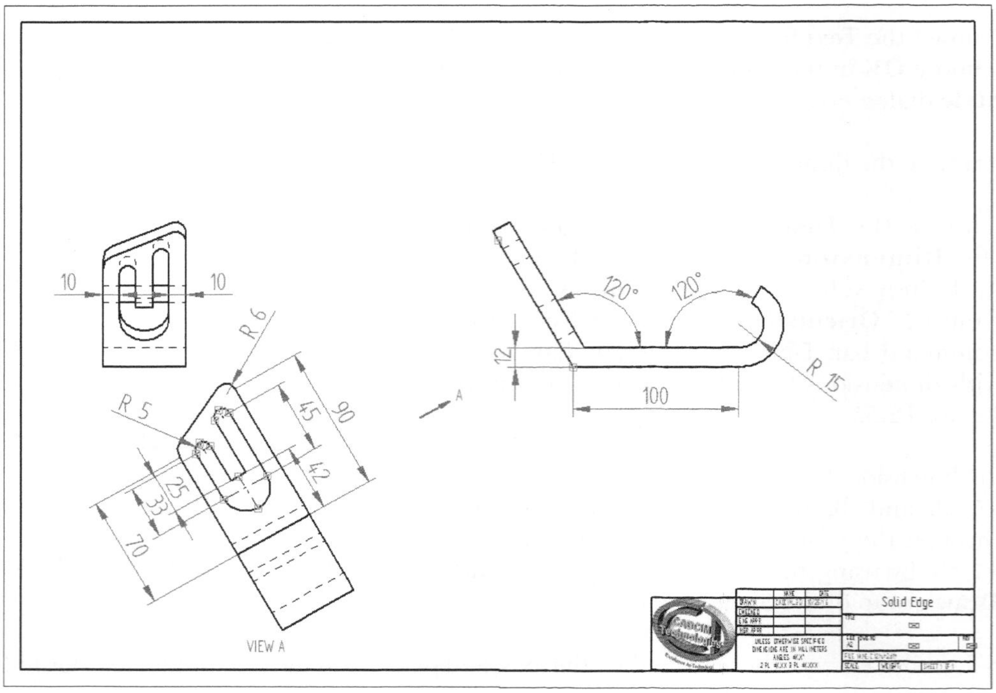

Figure 12-57 Drawing sheet after dimensioning the views

Saving the File

1. Save the file with the name *c12tut2.dft* at the following location: *Solid Edge/c12.*

2. Choose **Application Button > Close** to close the file.

Tutorial 3

In this tutorial, you will create the drawing views shown in Figure 12-58 in AutoCAD. You can also download this drawing file from *http://www.cadcim.com*. The path of the file is as follows: *Textbooks>CAD/CAM>Solid Edge>Solid Edge ST9 for Designers>Input Files*. Next, you will create a 3D model from these drawing views, as shown in Figure 12-59. Finally, you will save the 3D model with the name *c12tut3.par* at the location *C:\Solid Edge\c12*. All dimensions are in inches.

(Expected time: 45 min)

The following steps are required to complete this tutorial:

a. Import the drawing views created in AutoCAD into Solid Edge.
b. Define the settings for placing the views.

c. Create the extrusion features using both the drawing views, refer to Figures 12-60 and 12-61.
d. Create a hole.
e. Create a rib, refer to Figures 12-62 and 12-63.

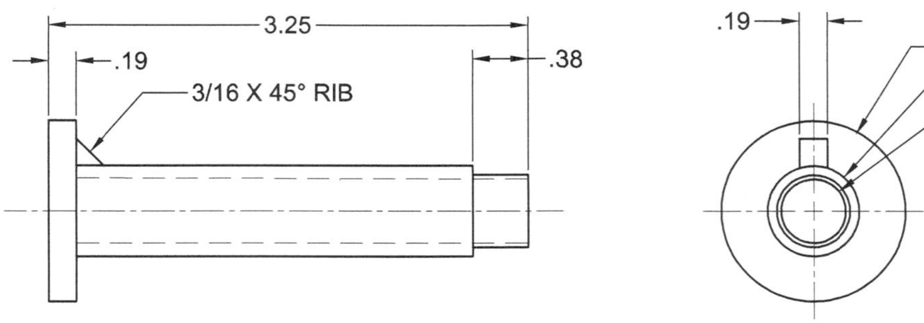

Figure 12-58 *The drawing views to be created*

Figure 12-59 *Model for Tutorial 3*

Importing the Drawing Views into Solid Edge

You will create the drawing views, as shown in Figure 12-58, in AutoCAD.

1. Create the drawing views in AutoCAD. Make sure the unit used in this drawing is in inch. Next, save the file with the name *shaft_bolt.dwg*. Alternatively, download the drawing file from the link specified in the tutorial description.

2. Invoke a new part document by selecting the **ANSI Inch** option from the **Standard Templates** drop-down list and then double-clicking on the **ansi inch part.par** template from the **New** dialog box. This template is used for creating models with inch as unit.

3. Choose the **Open** button from the **Quick Access** toolbar; the **Open File** dialog box is displayed. Select **All documents (*.*)** from the **Files of type** drop-down list. Next, browse to the *shaft_bolt.dwg* file and select it. Choose the **Options** button from the **Open File** dialog box; the **AutoCAD to Solid Edge Translation Wizard - Step 1 of 8** is displayed.

Note

*If the **Open** button is not available in the **Quick Access** toolbar, you can customize the **Quick Access** toolbar to add it.*

4. Choose the **Preview** button in this wizard; a preview of the drawing is displayed. You can use the display tools like **Zoom**, **Pan**, and **Fit** to view the drawing.

5. Switch off the unwanted layers such as Border, vports, text, if any, and choose the **Next** button.

6. Make sure the **Use template file unit** radio button is selected, so that the selected standard template unit is set as the unit for the translated *.dwg* file.

7. In the front of **Solid Edge Draft Template** of the wizard, choose the **Browse** button; the **New** dialog box is displayed. Choose **ansi inch draft. dft,** from the **ANSI Inch** option and choose **OK** to exit the dialog box. Next, choose the **Next** button; the **Step 3** of the wizard is displayed.

8. Select the **Show background** check box and then select **A4-Sheet** from the drop-down list as the background of the sheet and choose the **Next** button in the wizard; the **Step 4** page of the wizard is displayed with the **Line Type Mapping** area.

9. Accept the default values and choose the **Next** button; the **Step 5** of the wizard is displayed with the **Color to Line Width Mapping** area.

10. Accept the default settings in the **Step 5** of the wizard and then choose the **Next** button. Similarly, accept the default settings in the **Step 6** and **Step 7** of the wizard and then choose the **Next** button; the **Step 8** of the wizard is displayed.

11. Select the **Create a new configuration file** radio button from the **Step 8** of the wizard and then choose the **Copy To** button; the **Save As** dialog box is displayed.

12. Enter a name for the configuration file and then choose the **Save** button to save the file at the location *C:\Solid Edge\c12* and exit the wizard.

13. After specifying all the settings, choose the **Finish** button from the wizard; the **Open File** dialog box is displayed again.

14. Choose the **Open** button to open the AutoCAD file in Solid Edge; the *shaft-bolt.dwg* is opened in Solid Edge. Choose the **Fit** button to fit the contents into the screen, if required.

15. Choose the **2D Model** tab from the bottom of the window, if it is not chosen by default, to change the sheet from the Layout view to the Model view.

Note

1. If you are using the Draft document of Solid Edge then you can skip the 'Importing the Drawing Views into Solid Edge' section and directly move to the next heading, 'Defining Settings for Placing the Views'.

2. You can show or hide the layers of the AutoCAD file in Solid Edge. To do so, choose the ***Layers*** *tab of the docking window. Next, select the required layer from the* ***Layers*** *area or from the drawing window. Then, choose the* ***Show Layer*** *or* ***Hide Layer*** *button at the top of the* ***Layers*** *area.*

Defining Settings for Placing the Views

In this section, you need to define the settings required for aligning the views.

1. Choose the **Create 3D** tool from the **Assistants** group of the **Tools** tab; the **Create 3D** dialog box is displayed.

2. Make sure the **ansi inch part.par** template is selected in the **File** drop-down list. If not selected, then browse and select it.

3. Choose the **Options** button; the **Create 3D Options** dialog box is displayed.

4. In the **Create 3D Options** dialog box, select the **Third** radio button in the **Projection Angle** area. Next, choose **OK** and then the **Next** button.

5. In the drawing area, select the view on the right by drawing a selection box around it or by using shift and click.

6. Choose the **Next** button from the **Create 3D** dialog box and select the left side view by drawing a selection box around it.

7. Choose the **Set Fold Line** button to draw a line at a point from where you need to fold the primary view. Next, create a fold line, as shown in Figure 12-60.

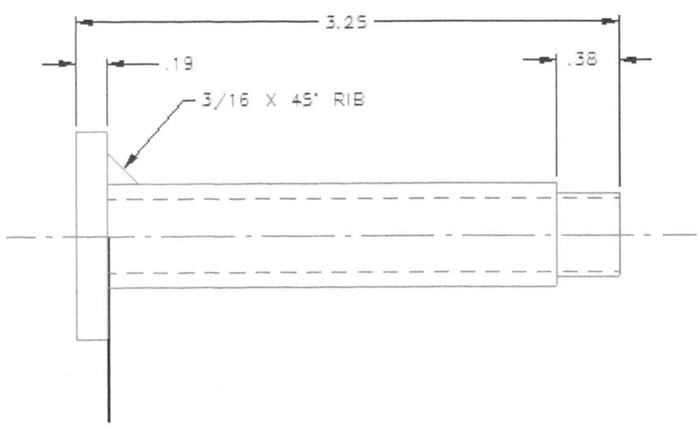

Figure 12-60 *Drawing the fold line*

8. Choose the **Finish** button; the views are oriented perpendicular to each other, as shown in Figure 12-61.

Creating the First, Second, and Third Features

Next, you need to create solid parts using the dimensions of the drawing views.

1. Choose the **Extrude** tool; the **Extrude** Command bar will be displayed. Then, select the outer circle and right click; a preview of the extrusion is displayed.

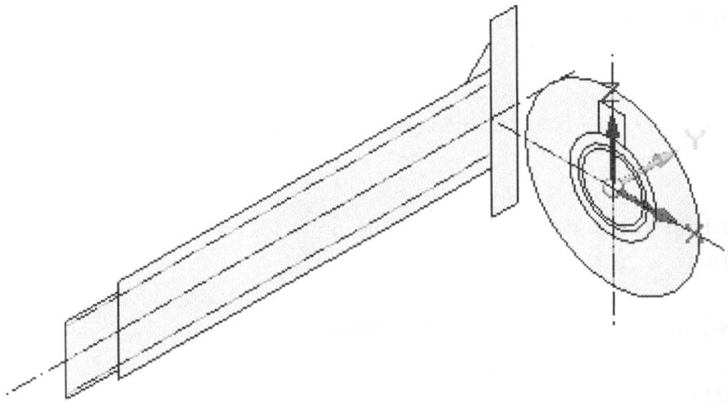

Figure 12-61 *Aligning the views perpendicularly*

2. Move the cursor toward the back view and snap to the endpoint of the first line segment to define the height of the cylinder, as shown in Figure 12-62. Click when the extrusion height snaps to the endpoint; the first feature is created.

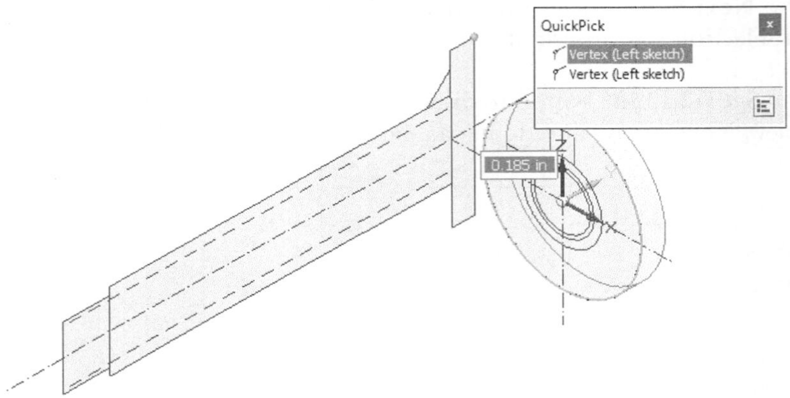

Figure 12-62 *Preview of the first feature*

Note

*If you are unable to snap to endpoints, choose the **Keypoints** button from the Command bar; a flyout is displayed. Choose the **All** option from the flyout.*

3. Choose the **Extrude** tool; the **Extrude** Command bar will be displayed. Then, select the second outer circle and right-click; a preview of the extrusion is displayed. Now, snap the extrusion height with the endpoint of the second rectangle, as shown in Figure 12-63; the second feature is created.

4. Similarly, create the third feature by snapping the extrusion height of the third outer circle with the outermost endpoint, refer to Figure 12-64.

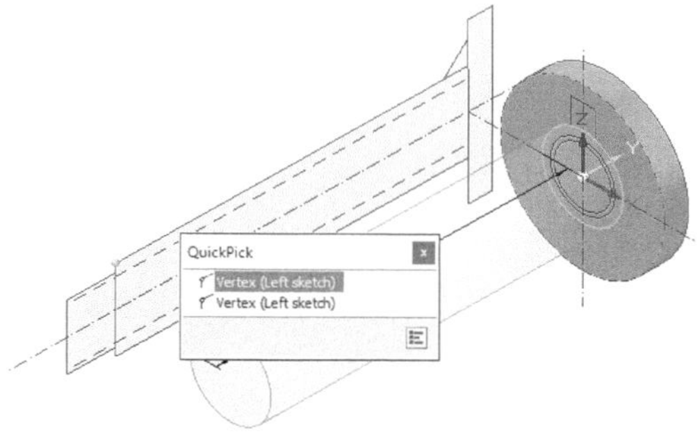

Figure 12-63 Preview of the second feature

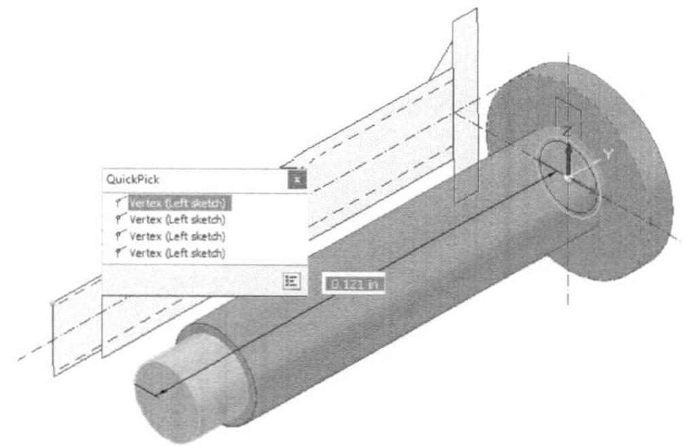

Figure 12-64 Preview of the third feature

Creating the Extrude Cut Feature

Next, you need to create a hole or a circular cutout in the third feature.

1. Invoke the **Extrude** tool; the **Extrude** Command bar is displayed. Select the innermost circle.

2. Choose the **Add/Cut** button; a flyout is displayed. Choose the **Cut** option from it.

3. Choose the **From-To** option from the **Extent type** drop-down list in the **Extrude** Command bar; you are prompted to select the **To** surface. Right-click and select the end face of the third feature as the **To** surface; the hole is created.

Creating the Rib Feature

Next, you need to create the rib feature by using the drawing views and then rotate the face to create a taper.

1. Select the rectangular section on the front view; an extrude handle is displayed. Next, click on the handle to invoke the **Extrude** tool.

2. Choose the **Finite** option from the **Extent type** drop-down list; a preview of the extruded section is displayed.

3. Snap the extrusion height to the rib on the side view, as shown in Figure 12-65; the extrusion feature is created.

4. Now to create taper, select the front face of the rib; an Extrude handle is displayed. Move the Extrude handle to the bottom edge of the face, so that the Extrude handle is modified into a steering wheel, see Figure 12-66.

5. Click on the torus of the steering wheel and rotate the front face by 45 degrees. Next, select the taper face; steering wheel is displayed on the tapered face.

6. Click on the Z-axis of the steering handle and move the cursor backward. Next, snap to midpoint of the back face of the rib, as shown in Figure 12-67.

The final model, after creating all the features in the top and front views, is shown in Figure 12-68. In this figure, the drawings are hidden because the **Sketches** check box in the **PathFinder** is cleared.

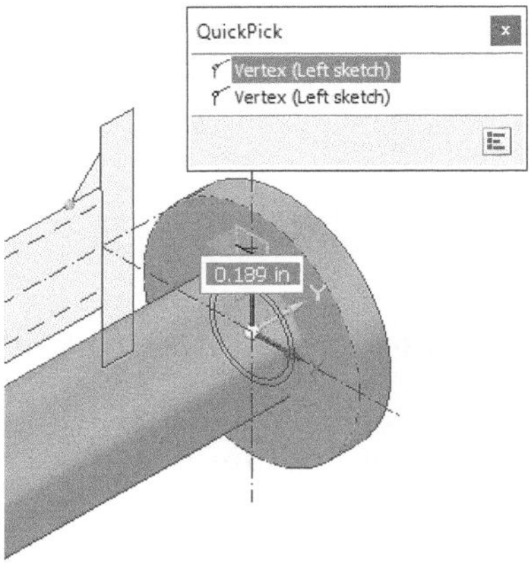

Figure 12-65 *Extrusion height of the rib*

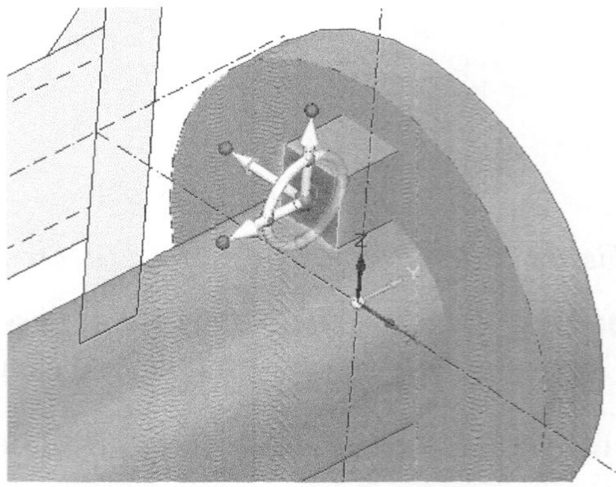

Figure 12-66 *Placing the Extrude handle*

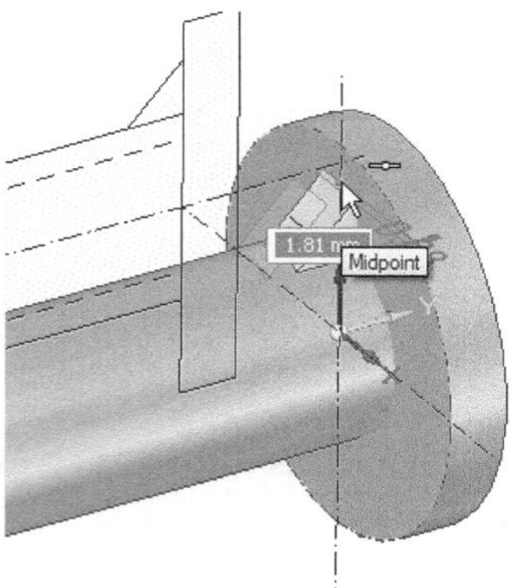

Figure 12-67 *Rotating the face for creating rib*

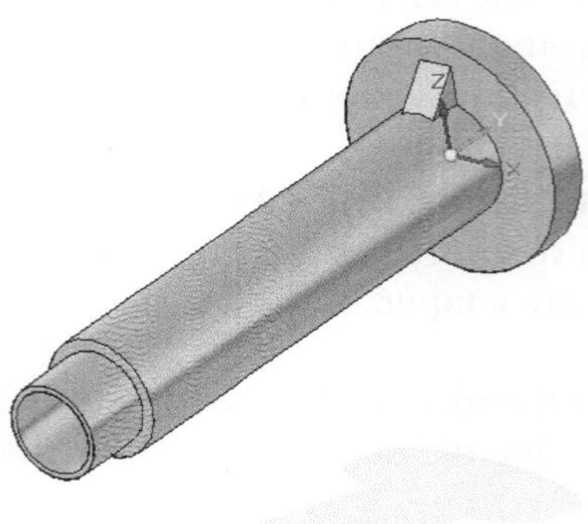

Figure 12-68 *The final model*

Saving the File

1. Save the file with the name *c12tut3.par* at the following location:
   C:\Solid Edge/c12.

Tutorial 4

In this tutorial, you will generate the exploded drawing view of the assembly created in Chapter 11. You will also add the parts list and balloons to the assembly, as shown in Figure 12-69.

(Expected time: 30 min)

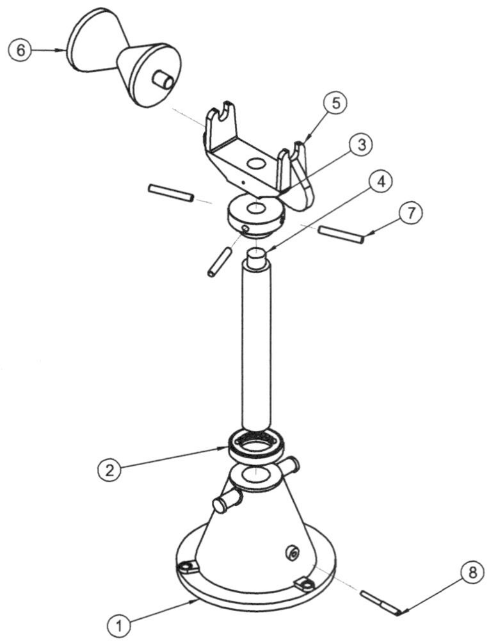

ITEM NUMBER	TITLE	MATERIAL	QUANTITY
1	STOCK SUPPORT BASE	ALUMINIUM	1
2	THRUST BEARING	ALUMINIUM	1
3	ADJUSTING SCREW	ALUMINIUM	1
4	SUPPORT ADJUSTING SCREW	ALUMINIUM	1
5	SUPPORT ROLLER BRACKET	ALUMINIUM	1
6	STOCK SUPPORT ROLLER	ALUMINIUM	1
7	ADJUSTING NUT HANDLE	ALUMINIUM	4
8	ADJUSTING SCREW GUIDE	ALUMINIUM	1

Figure 12-69 *Parts list and balloons in the exploded drawing view*

The following steps are required to complete this tutorial:

a. Start a new draft file.
b. Generate the exploded drawing view.
c. Generate the parts list and balloons.
d. Edit balloons and the text in the column, refer to Figure 12-70.
e. Save the drawing file and close the window.

Starting a New File in the Draft Environment

1. Choose the **New** button from the **Quick Access** toolbar to display the **New** dialog box.

2. Select the **Templates** option from the **Standard Templates** drop-down list. Next, select the **Template.dft** from the area adjacent to the **Standard Templates** drop-down list and choose the **OK** button to exit the dialog box and enter the **Draft** environment.

Generating the Exploded Drawing View

1. Choose the **View Wizard** tool from the **Drawing Views** group of the **Home** tab; the **Select Model** dialog box is displayed.

2. Select **Assembly Document (*.asm)** from the **Files of type** drop-down list.

3. Select the Stock Bracket assembly from the selection area and select **Stock Bracket** from the **Configuration** drop-down list located at the bottom right corner of the **Select Model** dialog box.

4. Choose the **Open** button and click in the drawing area to place the drawing view.

5. Select the drawing view and then modify the scale of the drawing view to **0.18**.

Generating the Parts List and Balloons

The parts list and balloons can be generated directly from the assembly drawing view.

1. Choose the **Parts List** tool from the **Tables** group; the **Parts List** command bar is displayed and you are prompted to select a view.

2. Select the exploded drawing view.

3. Choose the **Properties** button from the command bar to display the **Parts List Properties** dialog box.

4. Choose the **Columns** tab from the **Parts List Properties** dialog box. In the **Columns** list box, select the **Author** option and then choose the **Delete Column** button to remove this column from the table.

5. Select the **Material** option from the **Properties** list box and choose the **Add Column** button to add this column to the table.

6. Select the **Material** option from the **Columns** display box and choose the **Move Up** button.

7. Next, in the **Column Format** area, change the width value in the **Column width** edit box to **42**. Similarly, change the width value of the **Quantity** column to **42**.

   By default, the balloons display the item number and the item count. However in this case, you do not need to display the item count. Therefore, you need to modify the balloon properties accordingly by using the **Balloon** tab.

8. Choose the **Balloon** tab to display the options related to balloons.

9. Modify the value in the **Text size** edit box to **7**.

10. Next, clear the **Use Item Count for lower text** check box to make sure that the item counts are not displayed.

11. Choose the **OK** button to exit the dialog box. Make sure that the **Auto-Balloon** button is active in the command bar.

12. Click at the desired location on the drawing sheet to place the parts list table.
    You will notice that the balloons are connected by a dotted line. You can use this dotted line to adjust the position of the balloons.

Editing the Text Properties

Note that the text in the parts list is too small. Therefore, you need to increase the size of the text in the table. But before doing that, you need to confirm the table style used for the table.

1. Choose the **Styles** button from the **Style** group of the **View** tab to display the **Style** dialog box.

2. Select **Table** from the **Style type** list and then select **Normal** from the **Styles** list; the parameters of the current table style are displayed in the **Description** box.

3. To modify the parameters of the table style, choose the **Modify** button from the **Style** dialog box; the **Modify Table Style** dialog box is displayed.

4. Choose the **Text** tab in the **Modify Table Style** dialog box and then select **Normal** from the **Text styles** list; the **Modify** button gets activated.

5. Choose the **Modify** button; the **Modify Text Box Style** dialog box is invoked. In this dialog box, choose the **Paragraph** tab; the text settings are displayed in this tab.

6. Enter **7** in the **Font size** edit box and choose **OK** to close the **Modify Text Box Style** dialog box.

7. Choose **OK** from the **Modify Table Style** dialog box and then **Apply** from the **Style** dialog box to accept and exit from the dialog box.

The drawing sheet after placing the parts list and balloons is shown in Figure 12-70.

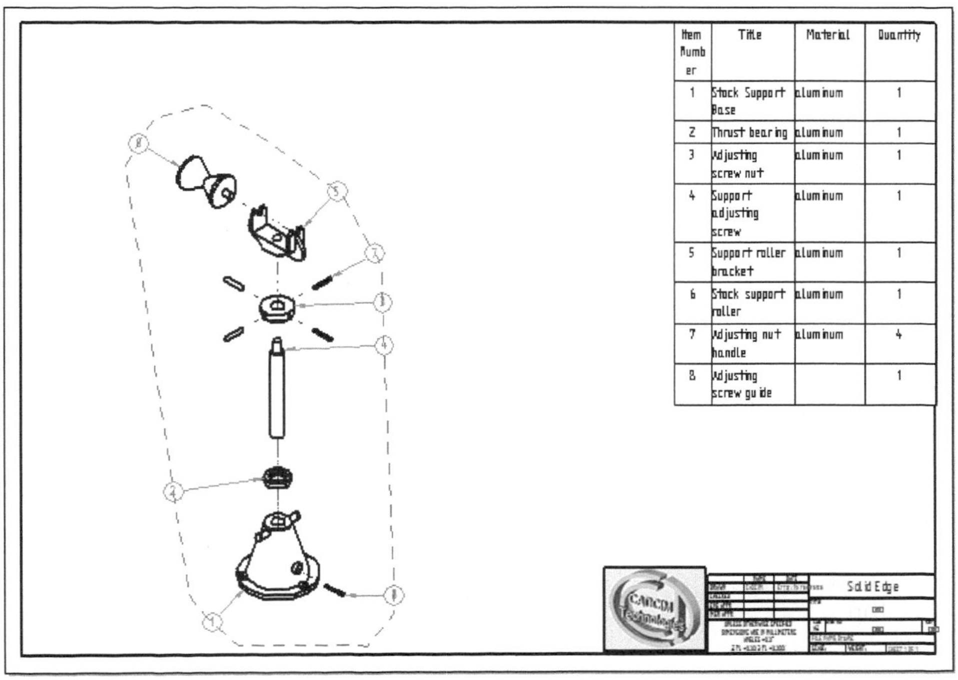

Figure 12-70 Exploded drawing view with parts list and balloons

Saving the File

1. Choose **Save** from the **Quick Access** toolbar to display the **Save As** dialog box.
2. Save the file with the name *c12tut4.dft* at the following location:
   C:\Solid Edge\c12.
3. Choose **Application Button > Close** to close the file.

Self-Evaluation Test

Answer the following questions and then compare them to those given at the end of this chapter:

1. The __________ tool is used to retrieve the dimensions that are applied to a model.
2. ____________ is the file extension of the files created in the **Draft** environment of Solid Edge.
3. The _____________ view is used for the parts that have a high length to width ratio.
4. A cutting plane can be edited by _____________ or by choosing the ___________ button from the command bar.
5. To generate a section drawing view of a part, you need a _____________.
6. When you enter the **Draft** environment of Solid Edge, only the drawing sheet is displayed. (T/F)
7. You cannot use an empty sheet for drawing. (T/F)
8. The base view is the first view that is generated on the drawing sheet. (T/F)
9. A section view is generated by cutting the part of an existing view using a plane or a line and then viewing the parent view from a direction normal to the section plane. (T/F)
10. The **View Wizard** tool is used to generate the base view. (T/F)

Review Questions

Answer the following questions:

1. In which of the following views of a part, dimensions cannot be generated?

   (a) Front (b) Right side
   (c) Top (d) None of these

2. Which of the following buttons is used to generate the BOM?

   (a) **Smart Dimension** (b) **Parts List**
   (c) **Draft View** (d) None of these

3. Which dialog box is displayed when you choose the **View Wizard** tool from the **Drawing Views** group of the **Home** tab?

   (a) **Properties** (b) **Select**
   (c) **Drawing View Properties** (d) None of these

4. The __________ tab contains the options that are used to set the dimension style, color of text, font type, font style, and size.

5. Before placing the BOM on the drawing sheet, if you choose the **Properties** button from the command bar, the **Parts List Properties** dialog box is displayed. (T/F)

6. When you enter the **Draft** environment, there are two sheets available by default. (T/F)

7. The technique of generating drawing views from a solid model is called generative drafting. (T/F)

8. A detail view is used to display the details of a portion of an existing view. (T/F)

9. The need for an auxiliary view arises when it becomes impossible to dimension a geometry in the orthographic view. (T/F)

10. In a revolved section view, the section portion revolves about an axis normal to the viewing plane such that it is straightened. (T/F)

EXERCISES

Exercise 1

Create the exploded view of the assembly that was created in Chapter 11, see Figure 12-71. Generate the BOM and balloons. **(Expected time: 30 min)**

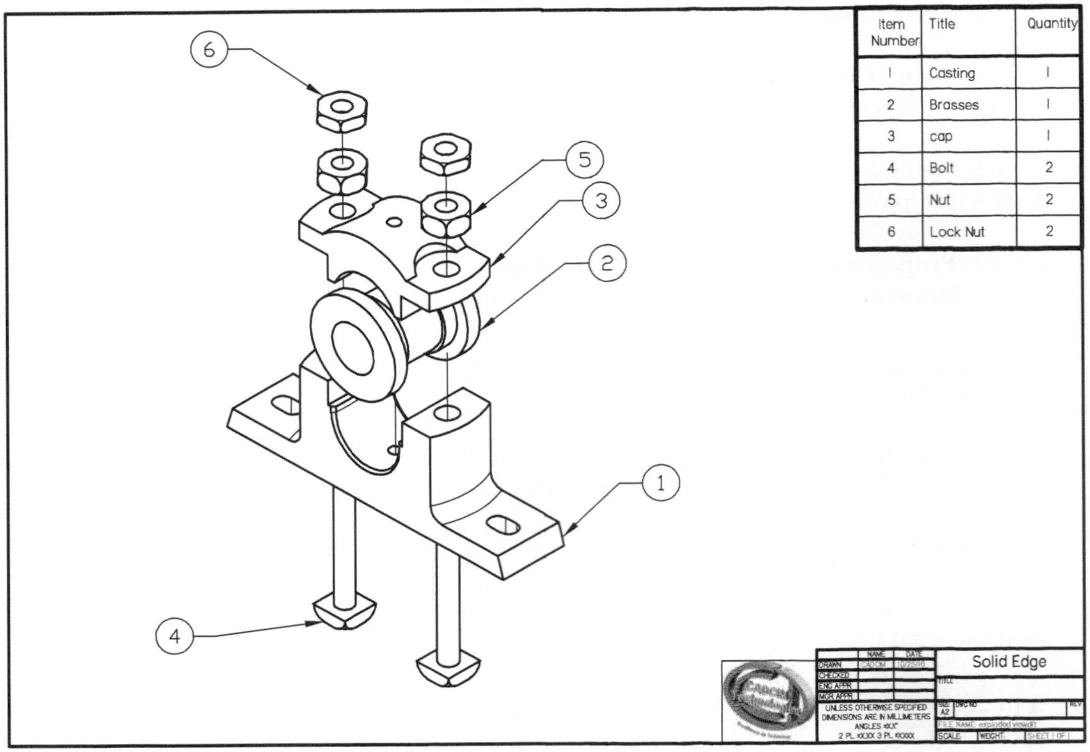

Figure 12-71 Exploded drawing view with the BOM and balloons

Exercise 2

Create the model whose drawing views are shown in Figure 12-72 and then generate the drawing views of the model. Dimension the drawing views, refer to Figure 12-72.

(Expected time: 45 min)

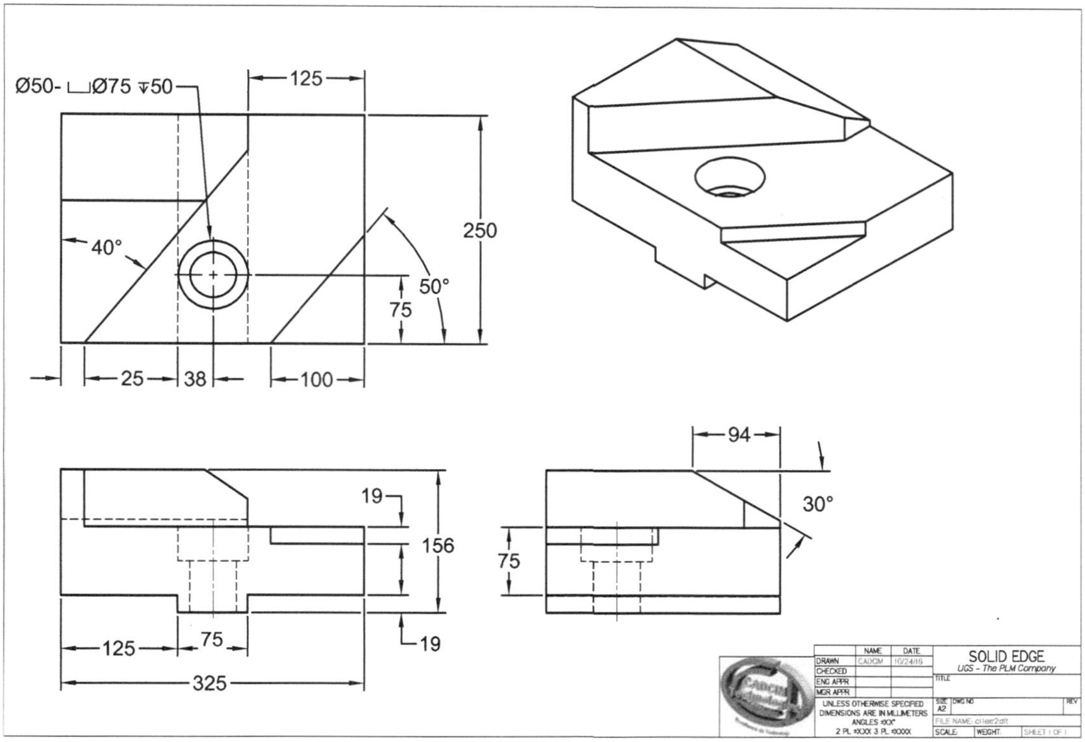

Figure 12-72 *Top, front, right side, and isometric views of the model*

Answers to Self-Evaluation Test

1. **Retrieve Dimensions**, 2. *.dft*, 3. broken, 4. double-clicking, **Edit**, 5. cutting plane, 6. F, 7. F, 8. T, 9. T, 10. T

Chapter 13

Surface Modeling

Learning Objectives

After completing this chapter, you will be able to:

- *Create extruded, revolved, and swept surfaces*
- *Create surfaces using the BlueSurf tool*
- *Create a bounded surface*
- *Stitch surfaces*
- *Use the Offset Surface and Copy Surface tools*
- *Use the BlueDot tool to join curves*
- *Create a curve at the intersection of two surfaces*
- *Trim and extend surfaces*
- *Split or replace the faces of a part*
- *Create and project curves*
- *Derive and split curves*
- *Add thickness and rounds to a surface*
- *Create a parting line and a parting surface*

SURFACE MODELING

Surface modeling is a technique of creating planar or non-planar geometries of zero thickness. Surface models are the three-dimensional (3D) models with zero thickness.

Most real world models are created using solid modeling tools. However, some models are complex. Therefore, you need to create them by surface modeling. After creating the required shape of a model using surfaces, you can convert it into a solid model. The techniques of creating surface models and solid models with the help of the surfaces are explained in this chapter. Remember that unlike solid models, surface models do not have mass properties. It becomes easier for readers to learn surface modeling if they are familiar with the solid modeling feature creation tools.

In Solid Edge, surface models are created in the **Synchronous Part** or **Ordered Part** environment using the **Surfacing** tab in the ribbon.

Note

*In the **Synchronous** environment, the **Extruded**, **Swept**, and **Revolved** tools of surface modeling are activated only when you draw a sketch. In case of the **Ordered** environment, these tools are active by default.*

CREATING SURFACES IN Solid Edge

In Solid Edge, you can create surface models using the tools from the **Surfacing** tab of the **Ribbon**. There are three tools that can be used to create three different surfaces namely, extruded surface, revolved surface, and swept surface. The tools are discussed next.

Creating an Extruded Surface

Ribbon: Surfacing > Surfaces > Extruded

To create an extruded surface, first you need to draw a profile on the required reference plane. After drawing the profile, choose the **Extruded** tool from the **Surfaces** group of the **Surfacing** tab; the **Extruded** command bar will be displayed and you will be prompted to select a profile. Select the profile and choose the **Accept** button; the **Extent Step** button in the command bar will be activated and you will be prompted to define the depth and direction of the extrusion. After specifying the depth and direction, specify whether you want to create the surface extrusion with open ends or closed ends by choosing the **Open Ends** or **Close Ends** button in the command bar. Note that these buttons will be activated only when you draw a closed profile. Choose the **Finish** button to create the extruded surface.

Similarly, you can create an extruded surface in the **Ordered Part** environment. To do so, choose the **Extruded** tool from the **Surfaces** group of the **Surfacing** tab; the **Extruded** command bar will be displayed and you will be prompted to select a planar face or a reference plane. The sketch will be drawn on this planar face or reference plane. As soon as you select a planar face or a reference plane, the sketching environment will be invoked. The remaining steps for creating an extruded surface are same as above.

Figure 13-1 shows the surface model with open ends and Figure 13-2 shows the surface model with closed ends. Remember that to create a surface model with closed ends, its profile should be closed. To provide a draft to the surfacing feature, choose the **Draft** button in the **Extruded** command bar after choosing the **Treatment Step** button. The rest of the options are same as discussed in Chapter 5.

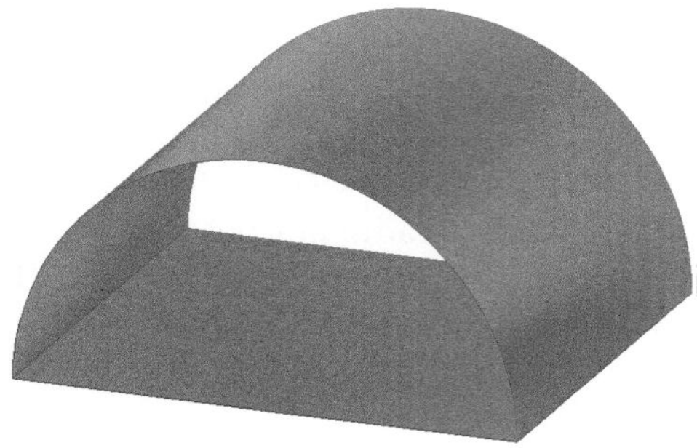

Figure 13-1 Extruded surface with open ends

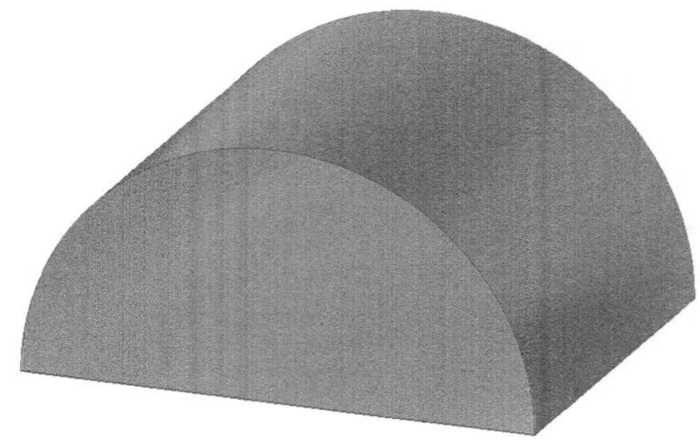

Figure 13-2 Extruded surface with closed ends

Creating a Revolved Surface

Ribbon: Surfacing > Surfaces > Revolved

To create a revolved surface, you first need to create the required profile on the desired plane and then choose the **Revolved** tool from the **Surfaces** group of the **Surfacing** tab; the **Revolved** command bar will be displayed. If you are invoking this tool in the **Ordered Part** environment, you will be prompted to select a planar face or a reference plane. Select the planar face; the **Sketching** environment will be invoked, and you will be prompted to create the required profile.

The steps required for creating a revolved surface are similar to those required for creating an extruded surface. You can also choose to close the ends of the revolved surface or keep them open. Remember that the closed or open ends option is available only when the angle of revolution is less than 360 degrees. But make sure the profile is closed. Figure 13-3 shows an open end surface model and Figure 13-4 shows a closed end surface model.

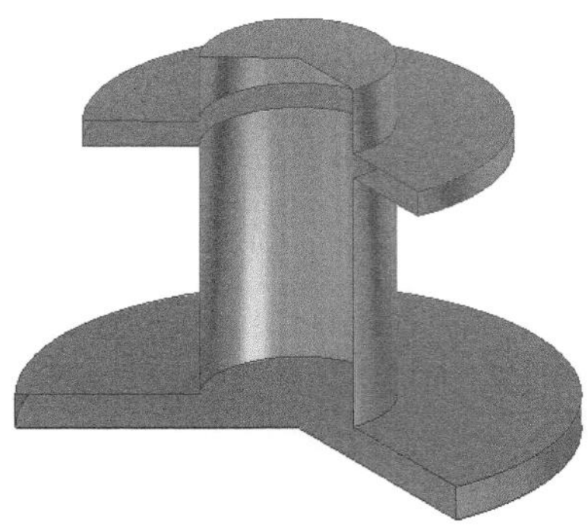

Figure 13-3 Revolved surface with open ends

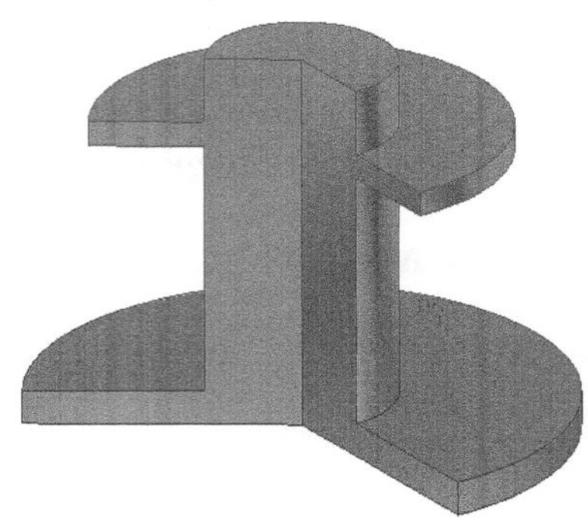

Figure 13-4 Revolved surface with closed ends

Creating a Swept Surface

Ribbon: Surfacing > Surfaces > Swept

You can create a swept surface by using the **Swept** tool from the **Ordered Part** environment. To create the surface, choose the **Swept** tool; the **Sweep Options** dialog box will be displayed, as shown in Figure 13-5. Note that if you are working in the **Synchronous Part** environment, then the **Swept** tool will be available only after creating a profile. Therefore, select the required plane and then create the sketches for the path and cross-section. In the **Default Sweep Type** area of the **Sweep Options** dialog box, there are two radio buttons that are used to specify the method of creating the swept surface. These two methods are discussed next. The rest of the options in the dialog box are the same as those discussed in solid sweeps.

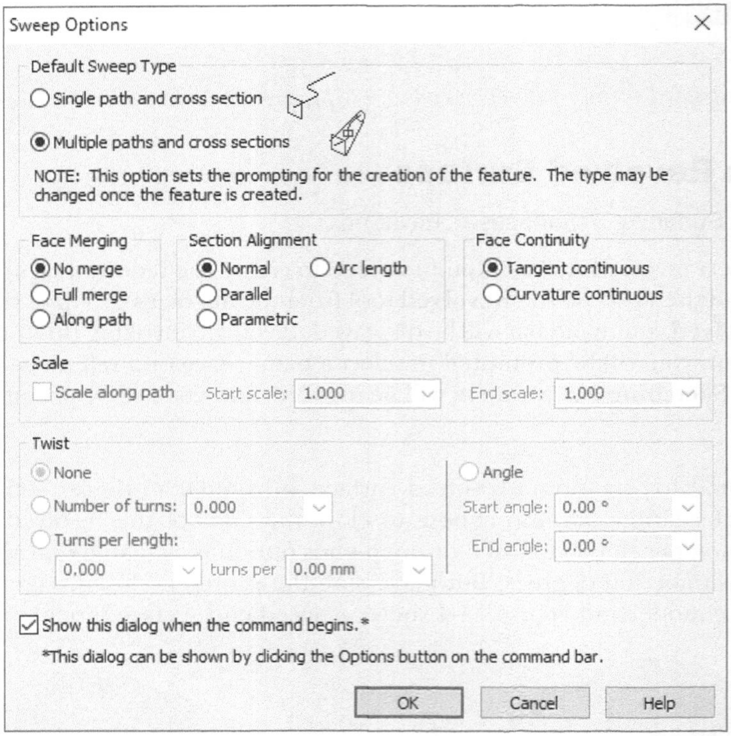

*Figure 13-5 The **Sweep Options** dialog box*

Single path and cross section Option

As the name of the radio button suggests, this method uses a single path along which the section is swept. Select this radio button in the **Sweep Options** dialog box and choose **OK**. The steps for creating a swept surface using this method are listed next.

1. After exiting the **Sweep Options** dialog box, select the type of plane from the **Create-From Options** drop-down list. Select a face or a reference plane for drawing the sketch, if you are working in the **Ordered Part** environment. Note that if you are working in the **Synchronous Part** environment, you need to select an existing path after exiting the **Sweep Options** dialog box.

2. Draw the sketch for the path of a sweep feature and exit the sketching environment. Next, choose the **Finish** button from the command bar.
3. Specify the location of the cross-section plane normal to the profile.
4. Draw the cross-section. Note that if you are working in the **Synchronous Part** environment, you need to select an existing cross-section.
5. Choose the **Finish** button; a preview of the sweep surface will be displayed. If the preview seems fine, choose the **Finish** button.

Figure 13-6 shows the cross-section and the path to create the sweep surface, and the resulting swept surface. Figure 13-7 shows the partial view of the edge of a model and the open sketch used to create the sweep surface. The swept surface created on top edge of the base is shown in Figure 13-8.

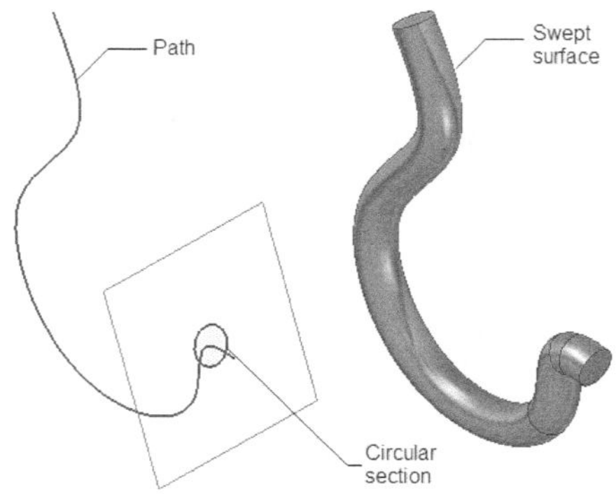

Figure 13-6 *Sweep feature*

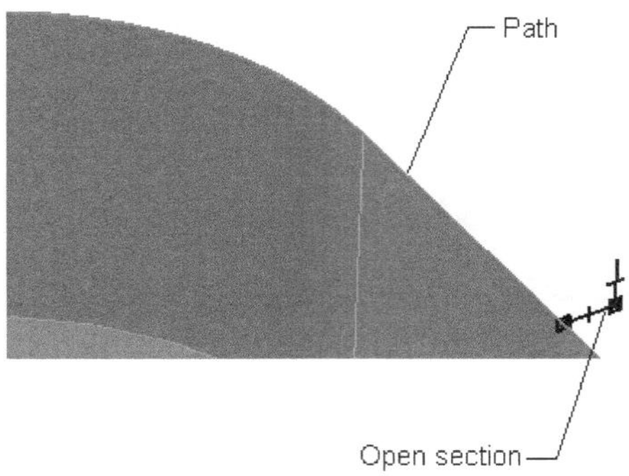

Figure 13-7 *Edge of the model and the cross-section used to create the sweep feature*

Figure 13-8 *Sweep surface created on the top edge of the base*

Multiple paths and cross sections Option

As the name suggests, when you select this method, you can use multiple paths and cross-sections to create the sweep feature. Select the **Multiple paths and cross sections** radio button and choose **OK** to exit the **Sweep Options** dialog box.

The steps for creating a swept surface using this option are listed below.

1. Select a reference plane or a planar face to draw the sketch of the path if you are working in the **Ordered Part** environment. Note that if you are working in the **Synchronous Part** environment, you need to select an existing path.
2. Draw the sketch of the first path and exit the sketching environment. Choose the **Finish** button from the command bar; the **Next** button will be displayed in the command bar. If you need to draw another path, select a reference plane or face. If you need to draw a cross-section, choose the **Next** button.
3. Specify the location on the profile where the cross-section plane will be placed. Draw the profile of the cross-section.

4. After exiting the sketching environment, choose the **Finish** button. Now, if you need to draw another cross-section, select a reference plane again and then draw the cross-section.
5. Choose the **Preview** button. If the preview seems fine, choose the **Finish** button.

Figure 13-9 shows the cross-section and the two paths needed to create a sweep feature and Figure 13-10 shows the resulting sweep surface.

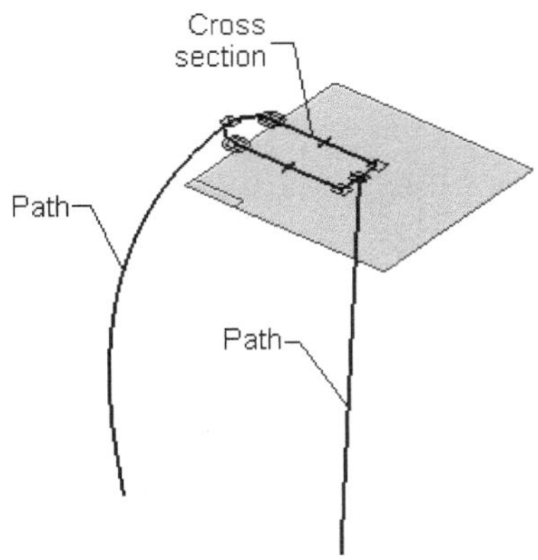

Figure 13-9 The paths and the cross-section

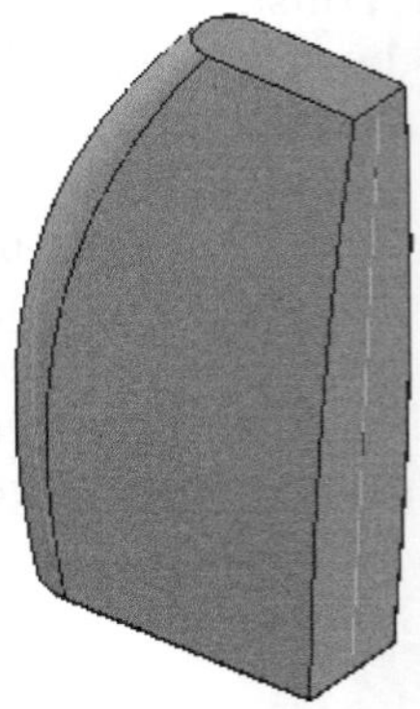

Figure 13-10 Resulting sweep surface

CREATING SURFACES USING THE BLUESURF TOOL (SYNCHRONOUS AND ORDERED)

Ribbon: Surfacing > Surfaces > BlueSurf

The **BlueSurf** tool is a multipurpose tool used for creating surfaces such as complex loft surfaces with guide curves, surface patch, and so on. This tool can be invoked from the **Surfacing** tab. Note that this button is available only after the base feature or the sketch is created. When you choose this tool, the **BlueSurf** command bar will be displayed and you will be prompted to select a point, edge chain, or curve chain. The methods used for creating surfaces are discussed next.

Creating Surfaces by Joining Two Curves

Create two curves, as shown in Figure 13-11. These curves are drawn using the sketching tools. Invoke the **BlueSurf** tool and select any one of the two curves. Now, select the other curve; a surface will be created between the two curves, as shown in Figure 13-12.

In the above case, two curves are used to create a surface. Now, you will use the **Connect** relationship to create a surface with these two curves. One of the curves will be selected as the cross-section and the other as the path or the guide curve, see Figure 13-13. To create a surface, refer to Figure 13-14, invoke the **BlueSurf** tool and select the cross-section curve. Confirm the selection by right-clicking. Choose the **Guide Curve Step** button in the command bar and select the path or the guide curve. Confirm the selection by right-clicking in the screen. Now, choose the **Next** button and then the **Finish** button from the command bar; the surface will be created, as shown in Figure 13-14.

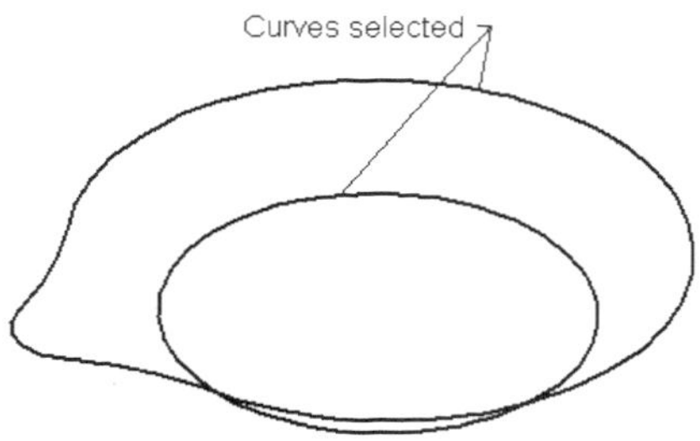

Figure 13-11 Two curves

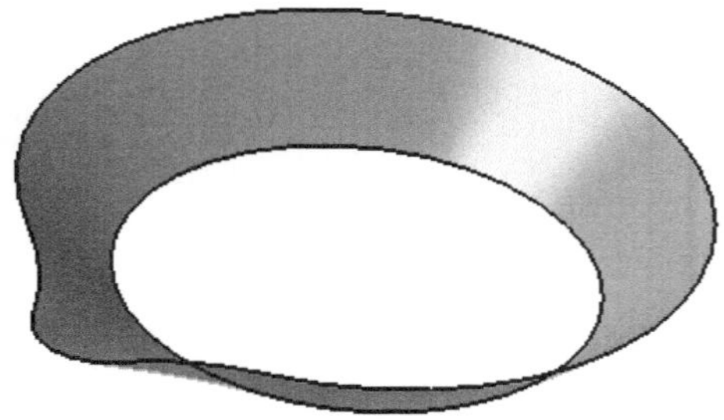

Figure 13-12 Resulting surface

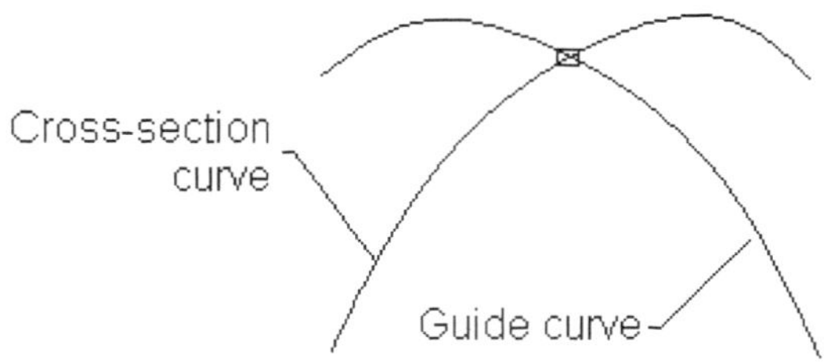

Figure 13-13 Curves that are used as the cross-section and the guide curves

Figure 13-14 Resulting surface

Note

*1. You can deselect the selected entities by using the **Deselect All** button from the **BlueSurf** command bar. If you select this button when you are in **Cross Section Step**, all the selected cross section curves will be deselected. Similarly, if you are in **Guide Curve Step**, all the selected guide curves will be deselected.*

2. You can create a plane normal to the guide curve so that the cross-section curve coincides with the guide curve.

*3. If both the curves are drawn as semicircles, you may not be able to create a surface using the **BlueSurf** tool.*

You can also use three curves to create a surface. In this case, two curves will act as cross-sections and the third curve will act as the path or the guide curve, see Figure 13-15. To create this type of surface, invoke the **BlueSurf** tool. Select the first curve and then right-click to accept the selection. Now, select the second curve and make sure that the dashed line indicating the connection points does not connect the diagonal points. Next, right-click to accept it. Then, choose the **Guide Curve Step** button from the command bar and select the path or the guide curve. Confirm the selection by right-clicking. Now, choose the **Next** button and then the **Finish** and then **Cancel** button from the command bar; the surface will be created, as shown in Figure 13-16. Make sure that the cross-sections are connected to the guide curve.

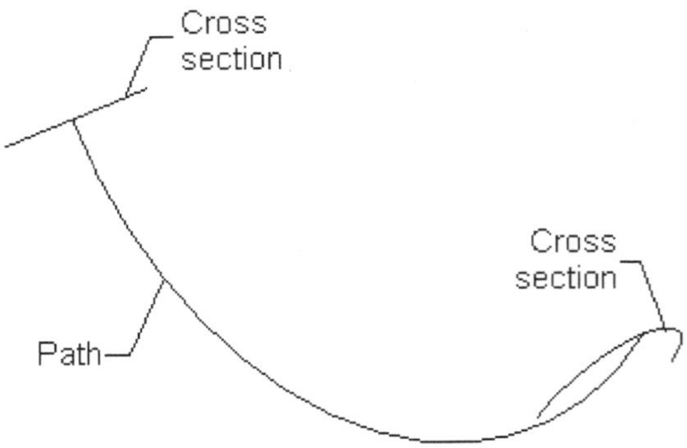

Figure 13-15 *Single path and two cross-sections*

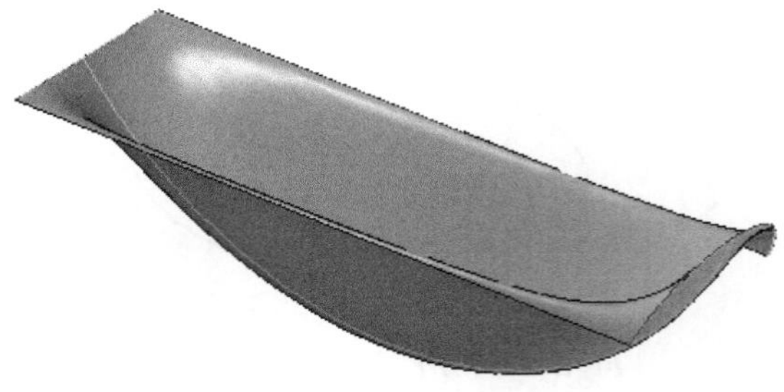

Figure 13-16 *Resulting surface*

Controlling the Shape of a Surface by Inserting a Sketch

You can modify the shape of a surface using the **BlueSurf** tool by inserting a sketch at the desired location.

Invoke the **BlueSurf** tool and select the first curve. Right-click to accept the selection. Similarly, select the other cross-section and accept it, see Figure 13-17. Choose the **Next** button from the command bar; you will notice that a surface is created between the selected cross-sections. Now, choose the **Insert Sketch Step** button from the command bar. In this step, you need to select an existing plane or create a new reference plane. You can create a new reference plane intersecting the surface. The most widely used option in the **Ordered Part** and **Synchronous Part** environments for creating a reference plane is the **Parallel Plane** option. Using this reference plane, the geometry of the curve is created. Create a parallel plane; a curve defined by the intersection of the surface and the parallel plane will be created. In this way, you can define a number of sketches by defining parallel planes. Next, exit the **BlueSurf** tool; the curve will be created on the surface, see Figure 13-18. After exiting the **BlueSurf** tool, you can select a sketch and dynamically edit it to modify the shape of the surface, see Figure 13-19. These curves appear as a separate sketch above the **BlueSurf** feature in the docking window of the **Part** environment.

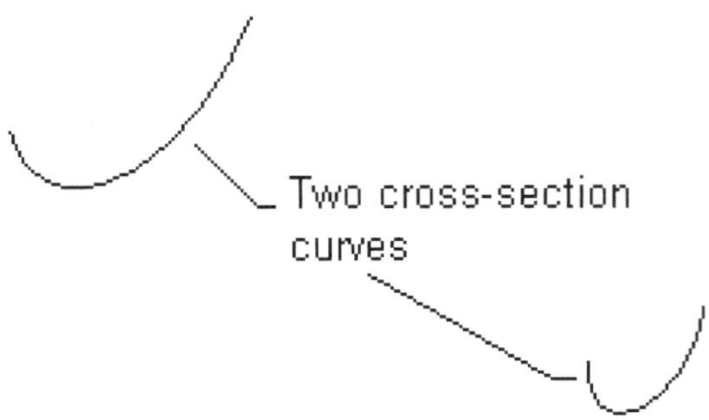

Figure 13-17 *Two cross-sections*

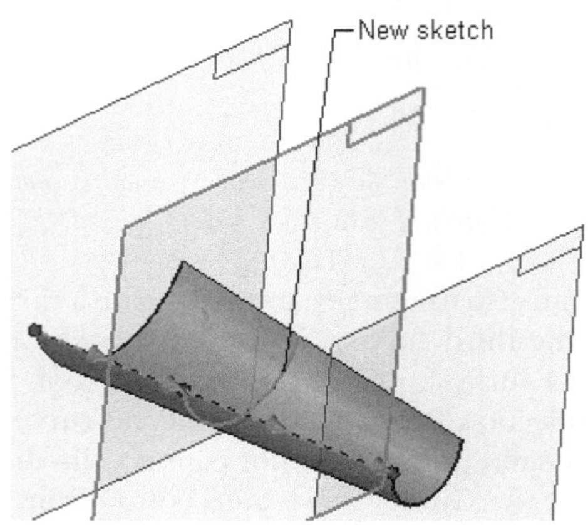

Figure 13-18 *Curve created using a plane*

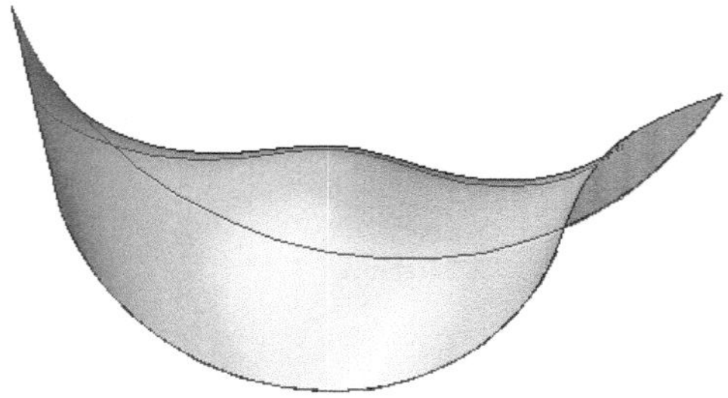

Figure 13-19 Modified surface

In the **Synchronous Part** environment, you need to create a parallel plane first and then invoke the **BlueSurf** tool. To create a parallel plane, first create a coincident plane and then move the plane to the required position by using the steering wheel. Also, the sketch will be added to the **Sketches** node in the **PathFinder**.

Closing Ends

The **BlueSurf** tool is also used to close the ends of a surface. To do so, invoke the **BlueSurf** tool and select one of the edges of the surface. Accept the edge and then select the other edge to close it, see Figures 13-20 and 13-21. Note that the surface can be created by selecting an open loop or a closed loop.

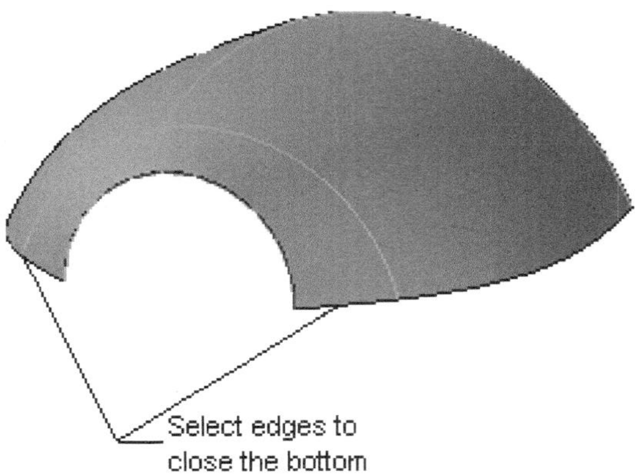

Figure 13-20 Edges of the surface

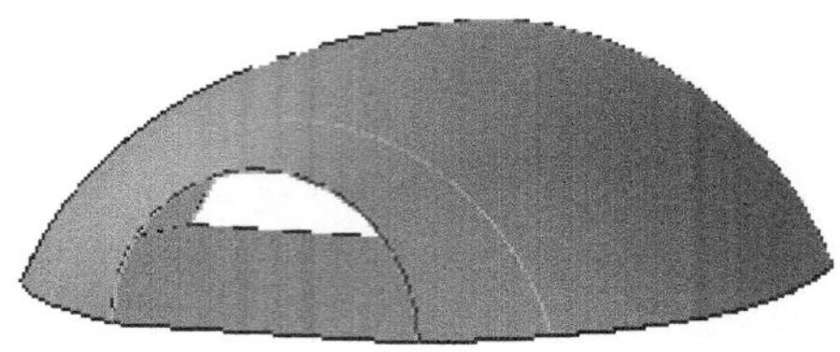

Figure 13-21 Surface created by joining edges

Controlling the Connection between Two Surfaces

The **BlueSurf** tool is used to connect or join two sets of edges formed between solid or surface features, as shown in Figure 13-22. The surface after manipulating the end conditions is shown in Figure 13-23.

There are several end conditions that are provided in the **BlueSurf Options** dialog box, see Figure 13-24. This dialog box is invoked by choosing the **BlueSurf Options** button from the command bar. The options in this dialog box can be used before or after creating the BlueSurface. You can also specify the boundary condition to the start and end surfaces by using the floating Tangency Control handle available at the two edges of the surface in the drawing area, refer to Figure 13-22. The Tangency Control handle contains a drop-down. The options in this drop-down are the same as those in the **Start section** and **End section** drop-downs of the **Standard** tab. The options in the **Standard** tab of this dialog box are discussed next.

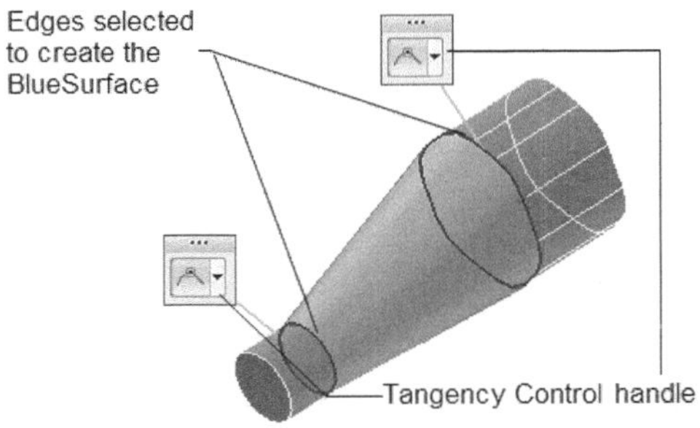

Figure 13-22 BlueSurface

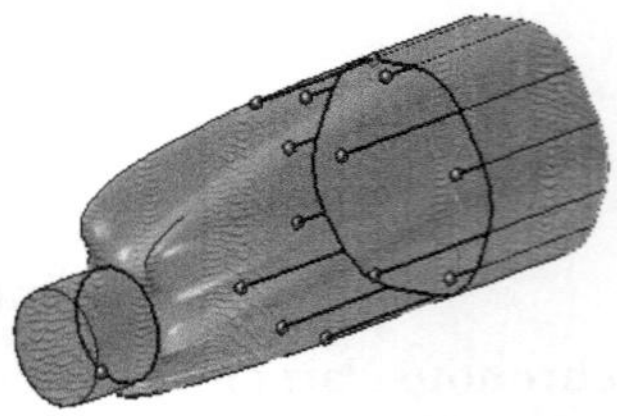

Figure 13-23 Surface after manipulation

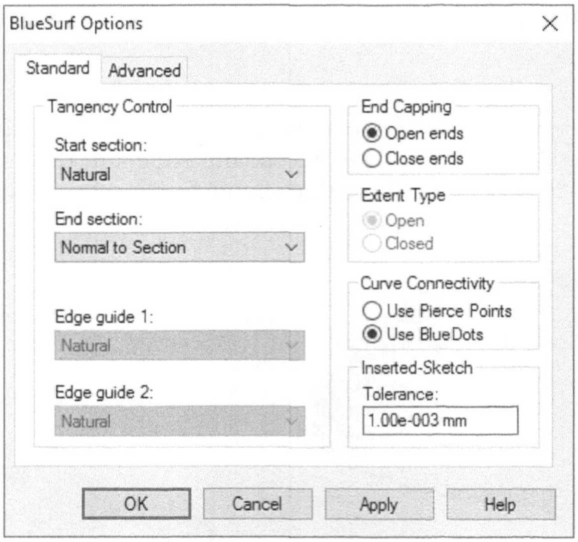

*Figure 13-24 The **Standard** tab chosen in the **BlueSurf Options** dialog box*

Note

*These Tangency Control handles are displayed with edges only when the **Show/Hide Tangency Control Handle** button is chosen in the **BlueSurf** command bar.*

Tangency Control Area

This area consists of the options that are used to specify the boundary conditions for the two end sections. The boundary condition refers to the type of joint that is required with the adjacent surface. This area has four drop-down lists, which are discussed next.

Start section

The options in this drop-down list are as follows:

Natural: This option is selected by default. It does not force any tangency conditions on the surface at the start and end sections.

Normal to Section: This option enables the boundary conditions to be modified normal to the sketched section using the drag handles (vector).

Parallel to Section: This option enables you to modify the end cross-section parallel to the sketch plane. This option is generally available when a loft surface is created by joining a point. In this case, the point acts as a cross-section. The modification can be made by dragging the handles that are displayed on the boundary of the cross-sections.

Tangent Continuous: This option is used to create a surface by lofting the edges and the cross-sections such that they are tangentially continuous. The drag handles (vector) available can be used to modify the surface.

Alternate Tangent Continuous: This option forces a surface to become alternate tangentially continuous.

Curvature Continuous: This option makes the curvature of the resulting surface continuous with the adjacent surfaces.

Alternate Curvature Continuous: This option makes the curvature of the resulting surface continuous with the alternate adjacent surfaces.

End section

The options in this list are used to determine the end conditions of the surface with respect to the adjacent surface. All the options in this list are the same as those available in the **Start section** drop-down list. Also, their availability depends on the sections to be joined.

Edge guide 1

The options in this drop-down list are used to control the tangency for the first guide curve. These options will be available only when you select the edges of existing surface as the start and end sections and the adjacent edges of same surface as the guide curve, refer to Figure 13-25. These options are the same as those available in the **Start section** drop-down list.

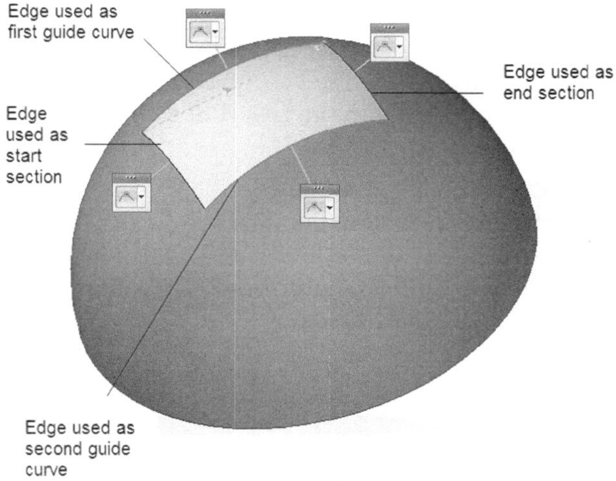

***Figure 13-25** Different edges used to create BlueSurface*

Edge guide 2

The options in this drop-down list are used to control the tangency for the second guide curve. These options will be available only when you select the edges of existing surface as the start and end sections and the adjacent edges of same surface as the guide curve refer to Figure 13-25. These options are the same as those available in the **Start section** drop-down list.

End Capping Area

The options in this area are available only when the sections are closed. The **Open ends** radio button, when selected, creates a surface that has open ends. When you select the **Close ends** radio button, a surface will be created with capped ends.

Extent Type Area

This area is available when there are at least three cross-sections. You can create a BlueSurface by closing the surface using the start section as the end section. When you select the **Open** radio button, the surface will be created by starting from the start section and ending at the end section. When you select the **Closed** radio button, a closed surface will be created between the start, end, and start sections.

Curve Connectivity Area

The options in this area are used to specify the type of connection required between the guide curve and the cross-section. These options are discussed next.

Use Pierce Points

This radio button uses the pierce point to connect the guide curve and the cross-section. It is used when you need to use dimensions for modifying the shape of a surface.

Use BlueDots

This radio button is used to connect the guide curve and the cross-section using the BlueDot. It is also used when you need to design a surface aesthetically. This is because the BlueDot enables you to modify the surface by holding it. This option will not be available in the **Synchronous Part** environment. The BlueDot is discussed later in this chapter.

Inserted-Sketch Area

The **Tolerance** edit box in this area is used to specify the tolerance value that controls the complexity of the sketch to be inserted in the **Insert Sketch Step**.

Surface Visualization Options

When you choose the **Surface Visualization Options** button; the **BlueSurf- Surface Visualization Options** dialog box is displayed, as shown in Figure 13-26. The options in this dialog box are used to display the surface mesh and curvature combs. The surface mesh is the isoparametric lines displayed along direction 1 and direction 2 of the surface, refer to Figure 13-27. They show the shape of the surface. The curvature combs show the smoothness of the surface along direction 1 and 2, refer to Figure 13-28. These are used to inspect the curvature of the surface.

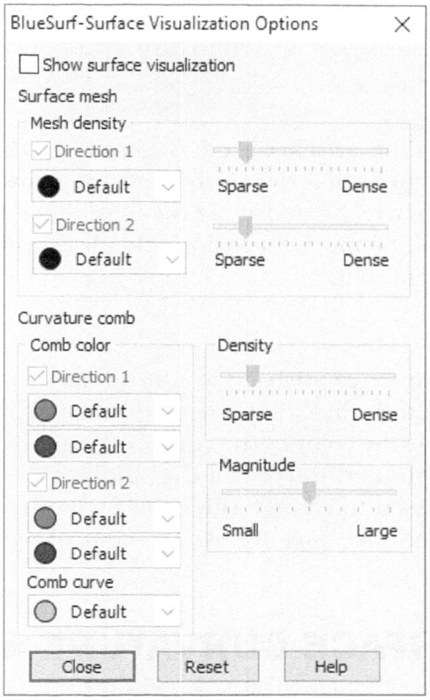

Figure 13-26 *The* ***BlueSurf-Surface Visualization Options*** *dialog box*

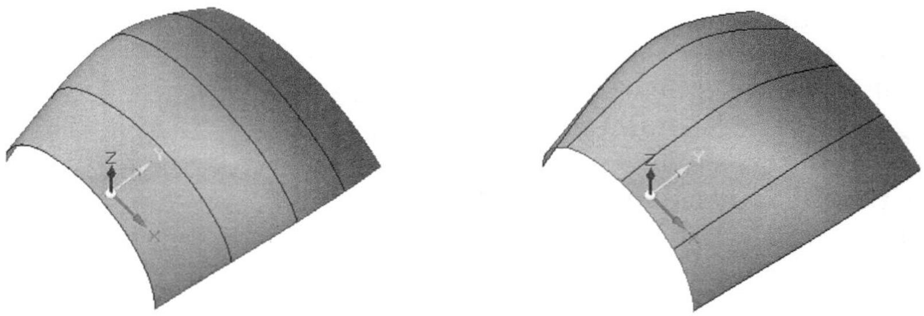

Figure 13-27 *The isoparametric lines displayed along direction 1 and 2*

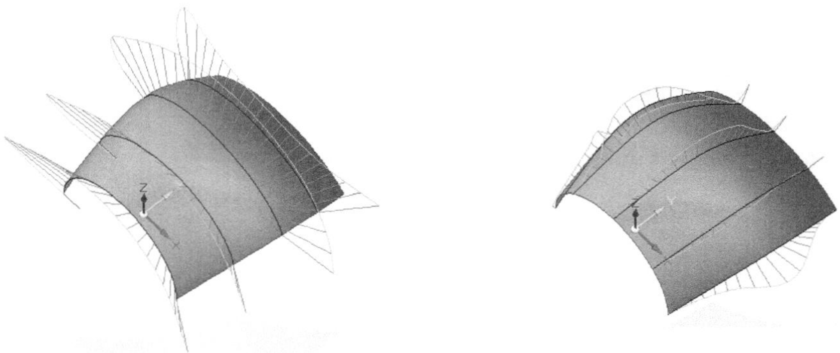

Figure 13-28 *The curvature combs displayed along direction 1 and 2*

The options in the **BlueSurf - Surface Visualization Options** dialog box are discussed next. The **Show surface visualization** check box is used to display the surface mesh and curvature comb.

Surface mesh Area

The **Mesh density** options in this area are used to control the display of the surface mesh. The **Direction 1** check box is used to display the mesh lines along direction 1. The slider bar adjacent to this check box is used to specify the density of the mesh lines along the direction 1. Similarly, you can control the display of the mesh lines along the direction 2 using the **Direction 2** check box and the slider bar adjacent to it.

Curvature comb Area

The **Comb color** options in this area are used to control the display of the curvature comb. The **Direction 1** check box is used to display the curvature comb along direction 1 and the color settings are used to the change the color of the curvature comb. Similarly, the **Direction 2** check box and the color settings are used to control the display of the curvature along direction 2. The **Comb curve** option is used to change the color of the curve connecting the comb lines. The **Density** and **Magnitude** slider bars are used to control the density and magnitude of the curvature comb.

INSPECTING SURFACE CURVATURE AT A SECTION

Ribbon: Surfacing > Inspect > Section Curvature

You can inspect the curvature of a surface at a section using the **Section Curvature** options in the **Inspect** group of the **Surfacing** tab. To do so, choose the **Settings** button from the **Section Curvature** area in the **Inspect** tab; the **Section Curvature Settings** command bar will be displayed along with the **Section Curvature Settings** dialog box. In the **Section Curvature Settings** dialog box, you can specify the density and magnitude of the curvature comb using the **Density** and **Magnitude** slider bars, respectively. Choose the **Close** button after specifying the settings in this dialog box. Next, select the surface to be inspected and right-click to accept the selection; you will be prompted to define the section plane. You can also use the **Create-From Options** drop-down list to define the plane on which the curvature comb will be displayed. By default, the **Parallel Plane** option is selected in the **Create-From Options** drop-down list. As a result, you can define a section plane parallel to an existing plane or face. The curvature comb will be displayed on the section plane, as shown in Figure 13-29. Choose the **Finish** button to close the command bar.

Figure 13-29 *A curvature comb displayed on the section plane*

CREATING SURFACES USING THE BOUNDED TOOL

Ribbon: Surfacing > Surfaces > Bounded

The **Bounded** tool is used to create a surface by using one or more edges that form a closed loop. When you choose this tool, you will be prompted to select the edges that form a closed loop. Select the curves, as shown in Figure 13-30, and then right-click to accept the selection. Next, choose the **Finish** and then **Cancel** button; the surface will be created, as shown in Figure 13-31.

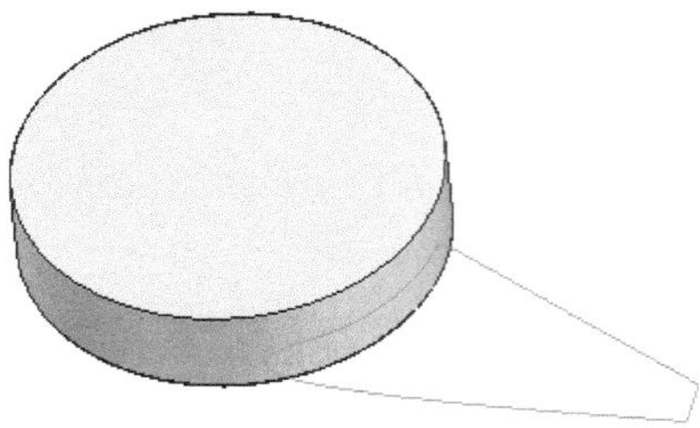

Figure 13-30 *Closed curve*

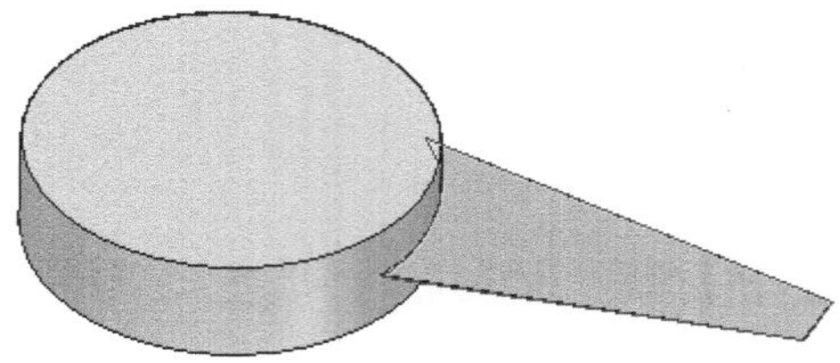

Figure 13-31 *Surface created using the curves*

To make a closed loop tangent to an existing surface, select the edges; the Tangency Control handle will be attached to the edges, as shown in Figure 13-32. Accept the selection and then choose the **Tangent Continuous** option from the Tangency Control handle; the resulting face will become tangent to an existing feature. Choose the **Finish** button to confirm and exit the command bar; the surface will be created, as shown in Figure 13-33. It is evident from this figure that when the bounded surface is created, it maintains a tangency with the selected edge. The surface created on choosing the **Natural** option from the **Tangency Control** handle is shown in Figure 13-34.

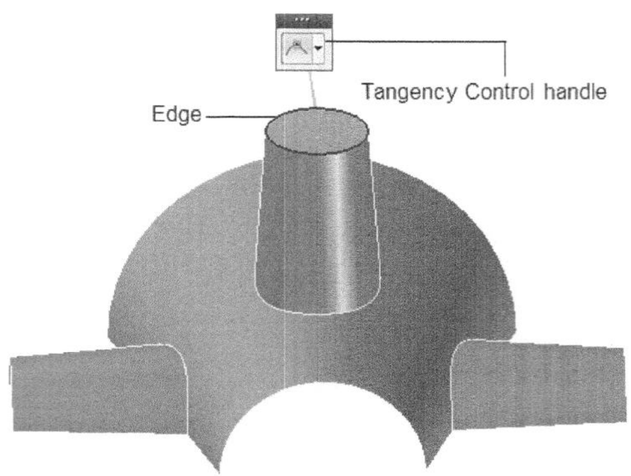

Figure 13-32 *Edge selected as a closed loop*

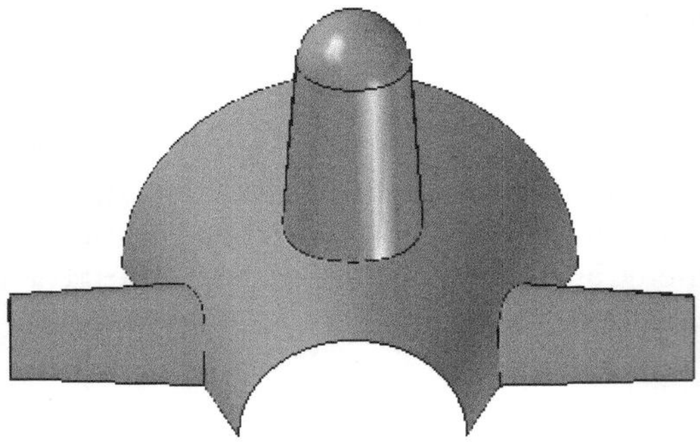

Figure 13-33 *Bounded surface created using the* ***Tangent Continuous*** *option*

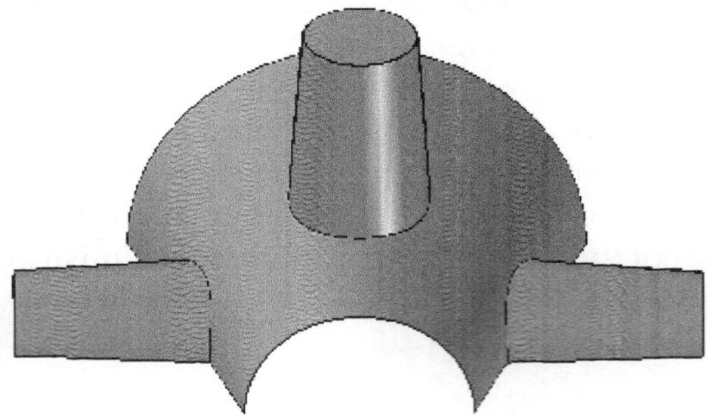

Figure 13-34 *Bounded surface created using the* ***Natural*** *option*

STITCHING MULTIPLE SURFACES TO CREATE A SINGLE SURFACE

Ribbon: Surfacing > Modify Surfaces > Stitched

The **Stitched** tool is used to join multiple individual surfaces to create a single surface. When the surface model is created, you need to join all individual surfaces and convert them into one single surface. This is because the thickness can be added to a single surface only. Remember that you cannot stitch the surfaces that do not touch each other.

To stitch surfaces, choose the **Stitched** tool from the **Modify Surfaces** group of the **Surfacing** tab; the **Stitched Surface Options** dialog box will be displayed, as shown in Figure 13-35. Change the default tolerance value to **1.00e-001** mm. This tolerance value determines the gap that is provided between the two surfaces. Choose the **OK** button to specify a value and to exit the dialog box. After exiting the **Stitched Surface Options** dialog box, you will be prompted to select two or more surfaces. Select all the surfaces that need stitching with the other surfaces and then choose the **Accept** button on the command bar. The multiple surfaces are joined to form a single surface. Next, choose the **Finish** button to complete the task and then the **Cancel** button exit the command bar. You can check whether they are joined by selecting the model. If the surfaces are joined, the entire surface model will be selected by selecting a single surface.

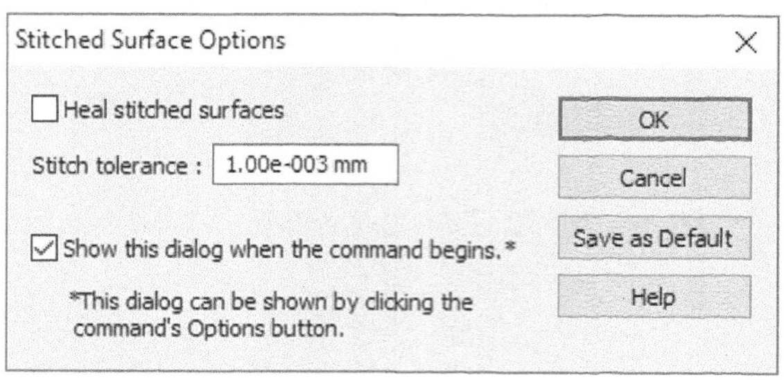

Figure 13-35 *The* ***Stitched Surface Options*** *dialog box*

You can use the **Show Non-Stitched Edges** tool from the **Stitched** drop-down in the **Modify Surfaces** group of the **Surfacing** tab to temporarily highlight the edges that are not stitched to the adjacent edges.

REPLACING THE EXISTING SURFACES

Ribbon: Surfacing > Surfaces > Redefine

The **Redefine** tool is used to create a new surface by replacing the existing surfaces. To redefine a surface, choose the **Redefine** tool from the **Surfaces** group of the **Surfacing** tab; the **Redefine** command bar will be displayed and you will be prompted to select the faces which are to be replaced by a new surface. Make sure that the surfaces to be redefined are connected to each other. You can connect the surfaces using the **Stitch** tool. Select the existing surfaces connected to each other and choose the **Accept** button from the command bar; the tangency control handles will be displayed on the surface. You can specify the connectivity between the existing surfaces using these handles. Next, choose the **Finish** button to close the command bar. Figure 13-36 shows the individual surfaces which are connected and Figure 13-37 shows a new surface created by replacing them.

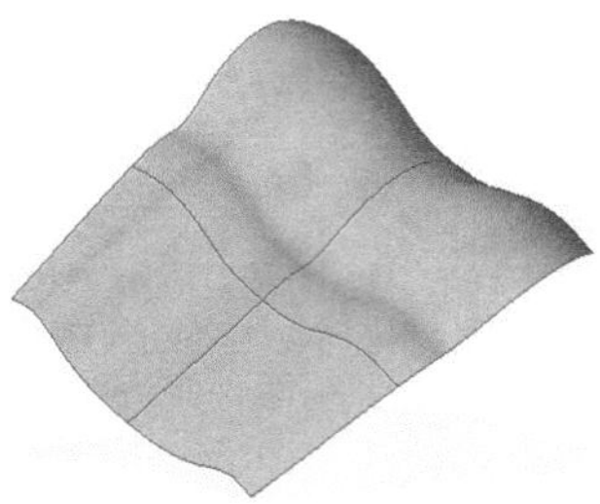

Figure 13-36 *Individual surfaces connected together*

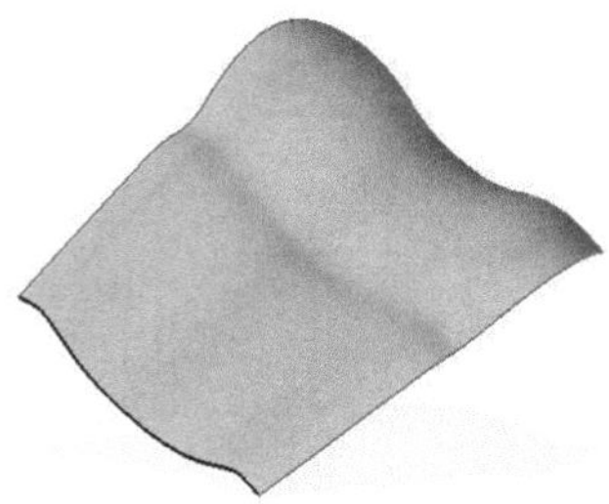

Figure 13-37 *A new surface created replacing the existing surfaces*

CREATING OFFSET SURFACES

Ribbon: Surfacing > Surfaces > Offset

The **Offset** tool enables you to offset a selected surface by a specified distance. When you choose this tool from the **Surfacing** tab, you will be prompted to select a face, chain, feature, or body depending on the options selected from the **Select** drop-down list. After selecting a surface, choose the **Accept** button; you will be prompted to specify the direction in which the offset surface will be created. This direction is pointed by a red arrow. Click in the direction of the arrow to specify the direction of the feature creation. You can specify the offset distance in the **Distance** edit box. The offset surface created is shown in Figure 13-38.

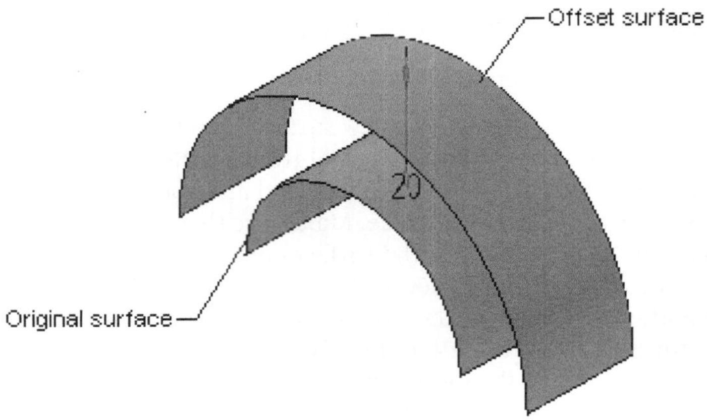

Figure 13-38 Offset surface

COPYING A SURFACE

Ribbon:	Surfacing > Surfaces > Copy

The **Copy** tool is used to copy a face of a solid or a surface feature. This tool can be used in many ways. For example, you can extract the face of a solid surface that can be further used to perform surface operations. Another application of the **Copy** tool is that if the file size of a solid model is too large, then you can extract the faces of the solid model and create a surface model out of it. The file size of this surface model will be comparatively smaller than that of the solid model.

To extract a face of the solid model or to copy the surface model, choose the **Copy** tool from the **Surfaces** group of the **Surfacing** tab; you will be prompted to select a face. After selecting the face, choose the **Accept** button; the surface will be copied. Choose the **Finish** button to exit the tool.

When you choose the **Copy** tool, the command bar will be displayed. The buttons in this command bar are discussed next.

Remove Internal Boundaries

This button enables you to remove internal boundaries from the surface and create a surface by ignoring them. For example, a face with holes on it can be selected to extract the surface. This surface, when extracted using the **Remove Internal Boundaries** button, ignores the holes and creates a plane surface. In other words, the face with holes is extracted by ignoring the holes and forming a plane surface.

Remove External Boundaries

This button enables you to remove external boundaries from a surface and create a surface by ignoring them. The resulting surface will be a surface with length and width equal to the maximum length and width of the original surface. For example, a surface with a cut at the corner, when selected to copy, results in a plane surface with four corners. Figure 13-39 shows a surface that is irregular at its boundary and Figure 13-40 shows the surface created by removing the boundary.

Figure 13-39 Irregular boundary surface

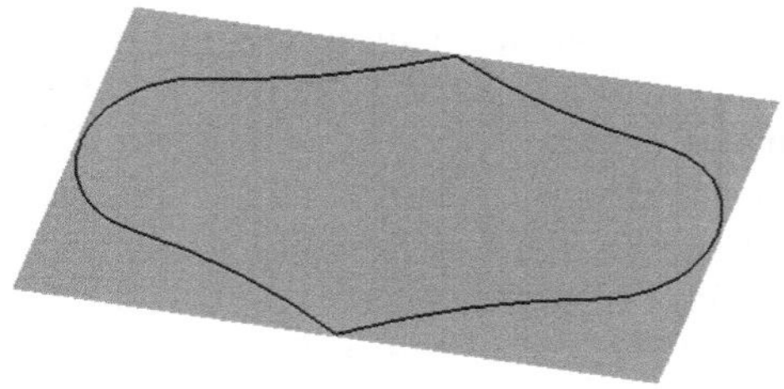

Figure 13-40 Surface created after removing the boundary

CREATING A RULED SURFACE

Ribbon: Surfacing > Surfaces > Ruled

A ruled surface is a surface which extends from an edge of a model. You can create a ruled surface using the **Ruled** tool. When you choose this tool from the **Surfaces** group in the **Surfacing** tab; the **Ruled** command bar will be displayed, as shown in Figure 13-41 and you will be prompted to select an edge or a chain of edges. As you select an edge or edge chain from the model; the preview of the ruled surface will be displayed, as shown in Figure 13-42. You can flip the direction of surface, as shown in Figure 13-43, by choosing the **Alternate Face/Side** button from the command bar.

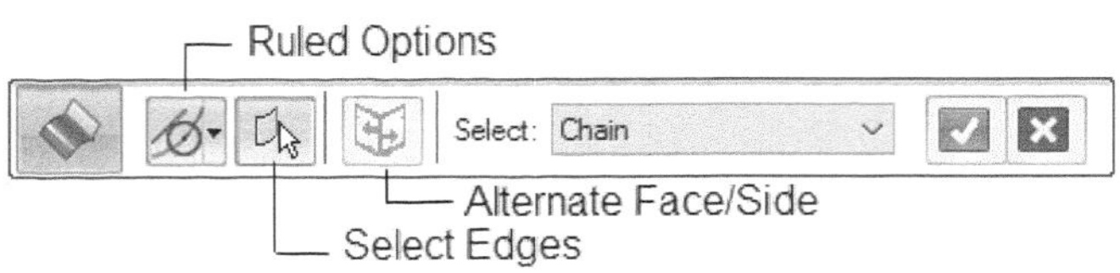

*Figure 13-41 The **Ruled** command bar*

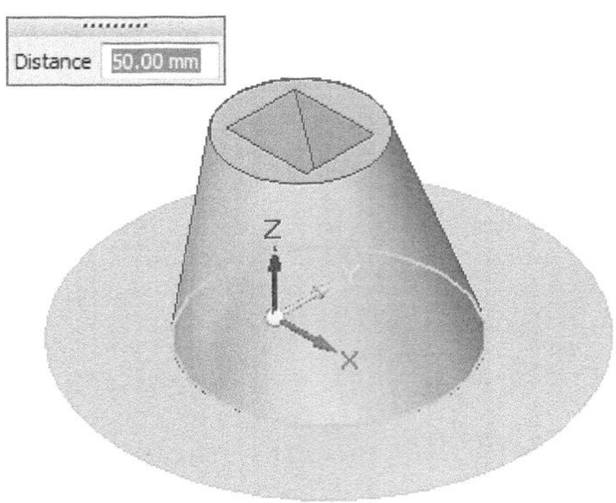

Figure 13-42 The preview of the ruled surface

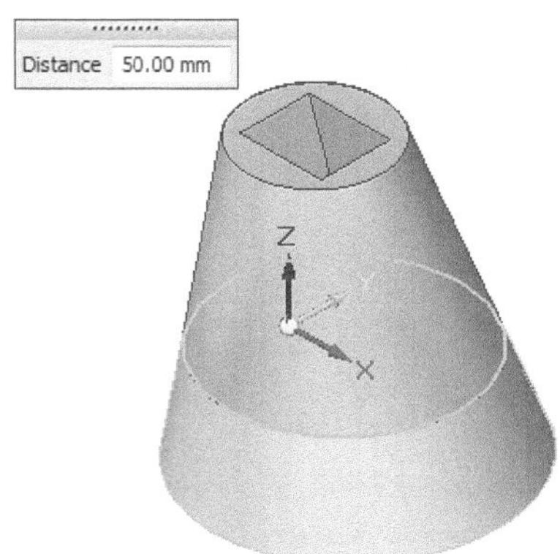

Figure 13-43 The ruled surface created in the alternate direction

By default, the **Tangent Continuous** option is selected in the **Ruled Options** drop-down. As a result, the surface will be tangent to the adjacent face of the selected edge. Also, the surface will be created as if the adjacent face of the edge is extended beyond the edge. If you select the **Normal to Face** option, the surface will be created normal to the face adjacent to the selected edge, as shown in Figure 13-44. The **Tapered to Plane** option is used to create the surface inclined to a plane or face. To create this type of surface, you need to select a plane or a surface to which the ruled surface will be inclined, and then specify the angle of inclination, refer to Figure 13-45. The **Natural** option is used to create the surface which is naturally extended without any constraining conditions, as shown in Figure 13-46. The **Along an Axis** option is used to create the ruled surface parallel to an edge or axis. To create this type of surface, you need to select an edge from the model or an axis from the Base Coordinate System, as shown in Figure 13-47. After selecting the required options from the command bar, right-click or choose the **Accept** button to create the ruled surface.

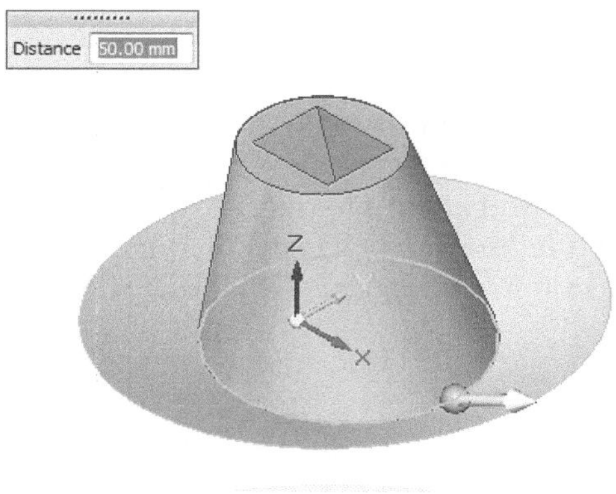

***Figure 13-44** The ruled surface created using the **Normal to Face** option*

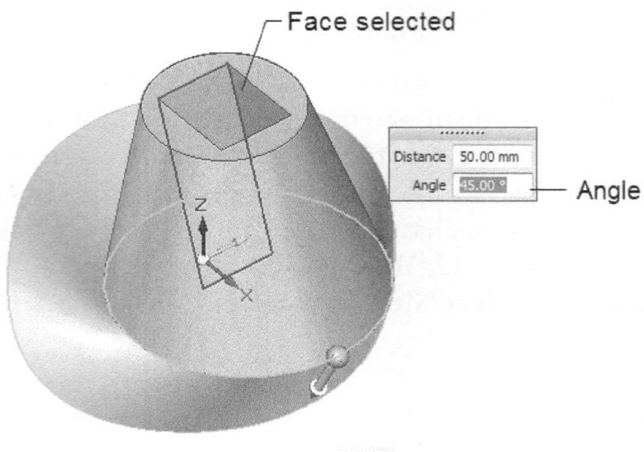

***Figure 13-45** The ruled surface created using the **Taper to Plane** option*

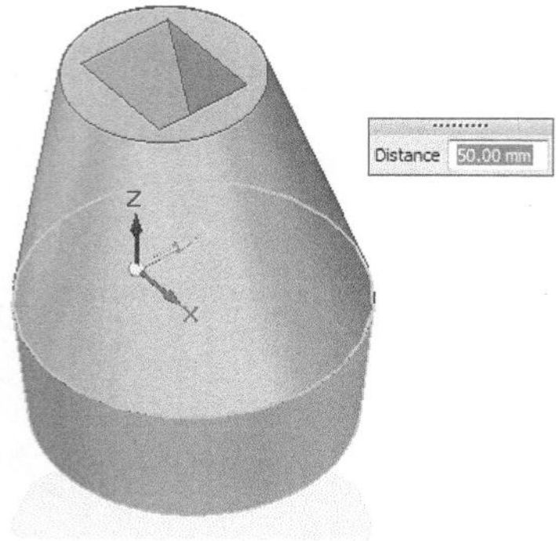

***Figure 13-46** The ruled surface created using the **Natural** option*

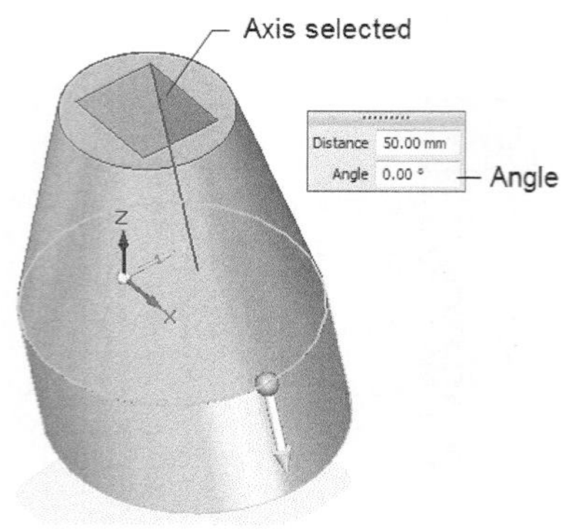

***Figure 13-47** The ruled surface created using the **Along an Axis** option*

CREATING A BLUEDOT (ORDERED ENVIRONMENT)

Ribbon: Surfacing > Modify Surfaces > BlueDot

The **BlueDot** tool is provided in the **Ordered Part** environment of Solid Edge to help you connect two curves. These curves can only be joined by selecting their keypoints. Figure 13-48 shows a table that lists the entities and their keypoints that are used to create BlueDot. Figure 13-49 shows two splines connected using the keypoints.

When you choose the **BlueDot** tool from the **Modify Surfaces** group in the **Surfacing** tab, you will be prompted to select a curve, end of sketch, or keypoint curve. Select the two curves that do not intersect in the drawing area.

Entity	Keypoints to Create BlueDot
Line	Endpoints
Arc	Endpoints
Spline	Control points
Circle	None
Ellipses	None

Figure 13-48 *Table specifying the keypoints of the entities that are used to create the BlueDot*

After the two curves are joined, you can create a surface using them, as shown in Figure 13-50. One curve acts as a cross-section and the other as a guide curve.

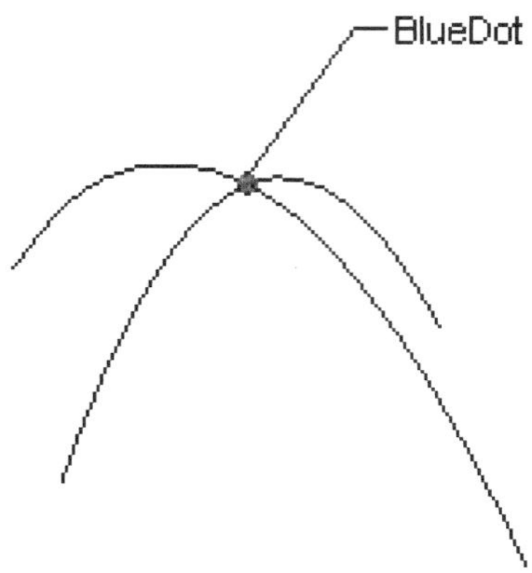

Figure 13-49 *BlueDot on splines*

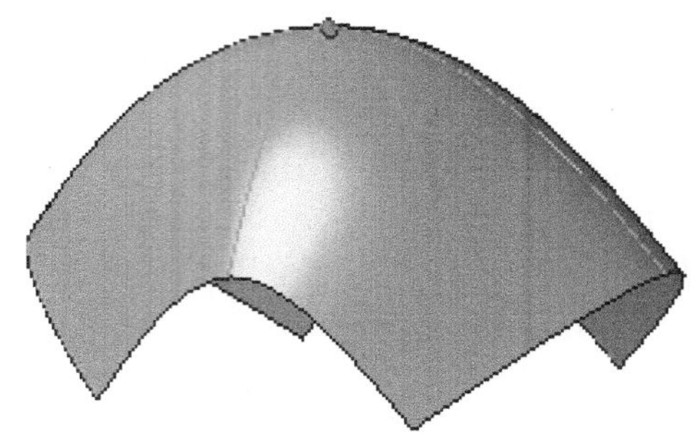

Figure 13-50 *Surface created after joining the two curves*

Note

1. The curves shown in Figure 13-49 are splines. Therefore, they are connected using control points.

2. The BlueDot does not appear in the ***PathFinder****. It cannot be added to a fully constrained sketch.*

CREATING A CURVE AT THE INTERSECTION OF TWO SURFACES

Ribbon:	Surfacing > Curves > Intersection

The **Intersection** tool is used to create a curve at the intersection of two surfaces. When you choose this tool, you will be prompted to click on a body to define set 1 and then click on the other body to define set 2. After specifying the two sets, the curve is created at the intersection of the two surfaces. Figure 13-51 shows the two surfaces that are used to create the intersection.

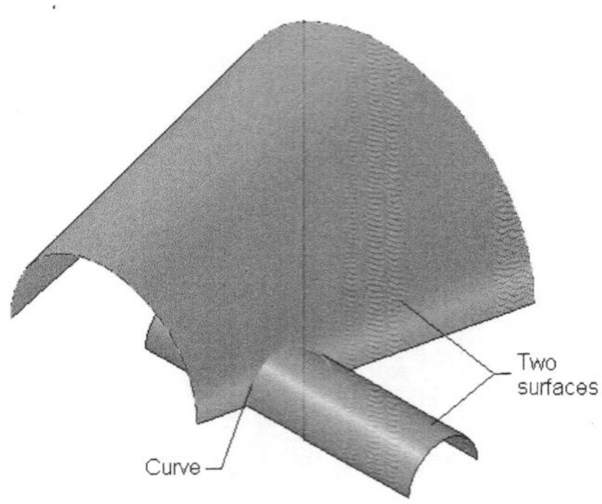

Figure 13-51 *Two surfaces and intersection curve*

TRIMMING THE SURFACES

Ribbon:	Surfacing > Modify Surfaces > Trim

The **Trim** tool is used to trim surfaces by using surfaces, sketches, or reference planes. To do so, choose the **Trim** tool; you will be prompted to select the surface to trim. Select the surface and right-click, you will be prompted to select the curve to be used to trim the surface. Remember that this curve should lie on the surface selected to be trimmed.

Figure 13-52 shows the surface selected to be trimmed. After selecting the surface, you will be prompted to specify the region of the surface you need to trim. Select the region that you need to trim. Figure 13-53 shows the trimmed surface.

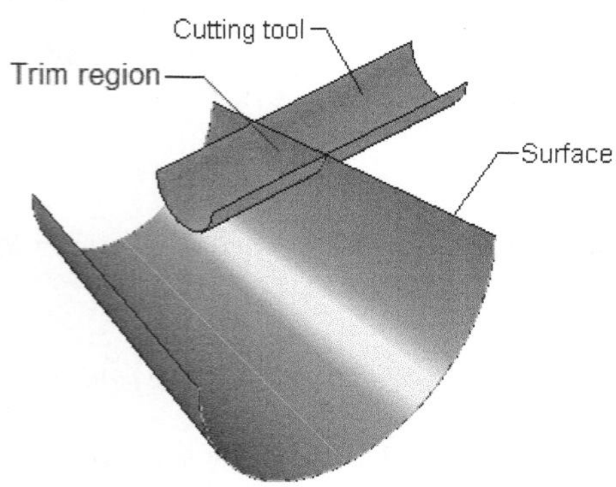

Figure 13-52 *Surface selected to be trimmed*

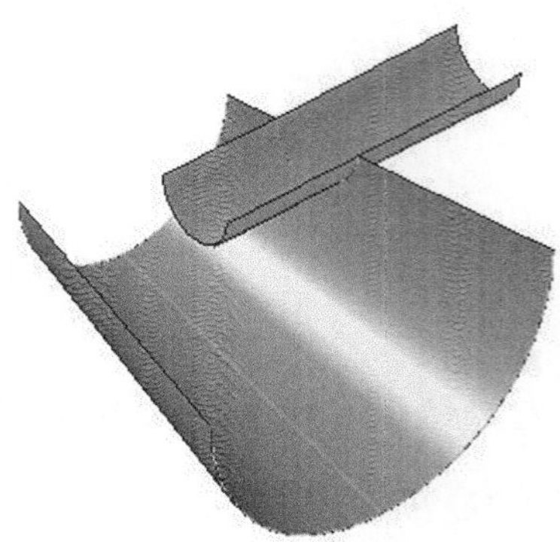

Figure 13-53 *Trimmed surface*

EXTENDING THE SURFACES

Ribbon: Surfacing > Modify Surfaces > Extend

The **Extend** tool is used to extend the selected surface. When you choose this button, you will be prompted to select a sketch or edge chain. Also the **Select Edges Step** button is chosen. Select the edge from where the surface needs to be extended. Accept the selection; the **Extent Step** button will be chosen. Next, you need specify the distance in the **Distance** edit box if the **Finite Extent** button is chosen from the command bar to extend the surface. If the **Extend To** button is chosen from the command bar then you need to select the face or plane up to which you need to extend the surface. Also note that the selected face or the plane should intersect the surface edge to be extended.

In the **Extent Step**, you are provided with three options that can be used to extend the surface. These options are discussed next.

Linear Extent

The surface extension also depends on whether the surface selected to be extended is created using the analytic element or the spline curve. The analytic element is an arc which has only two points and cannot be modified to obtain different shapes, whereas the spline has control points which can be used to modify the shape of the surface.

The **Linear Extent** button is chosen by default to extend the selected surface linearly, as shown in Figures 13-54 and 13-55.

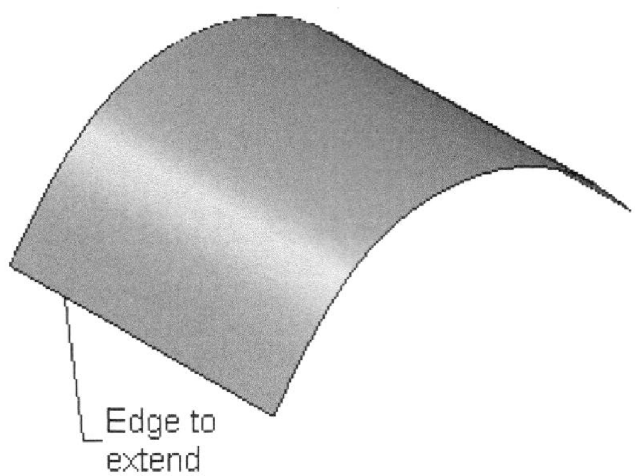

Figure 13-54 Extending the surface using the edge

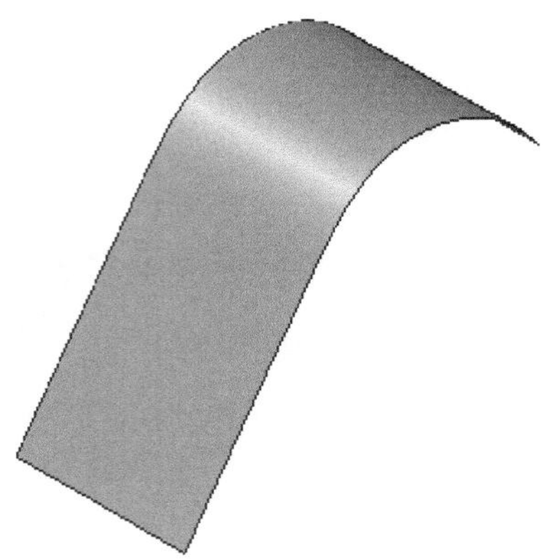

Figure 13-55 Surface extended by choosing

Curvature Continuous

This button is chosen to extend the selected surface maintaining its curvature, as shown in Figures 13-56 and 13-57.

Reflective Extent

This button is chosen to extend the selected surface as its own reflection, as shown in Figures 13-58 and 13-59.

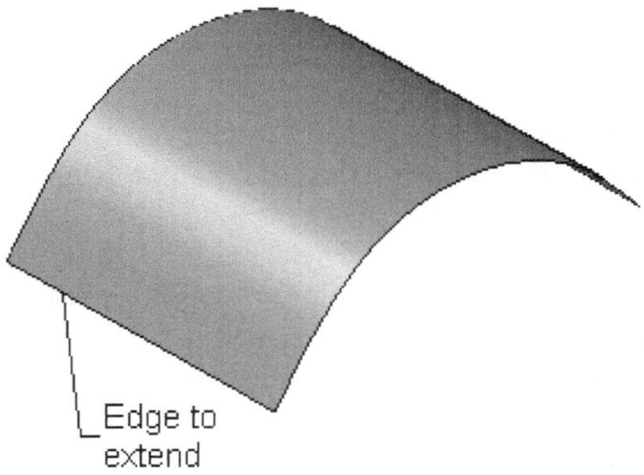

Figure 13-56 *Extending a surface using the edge*

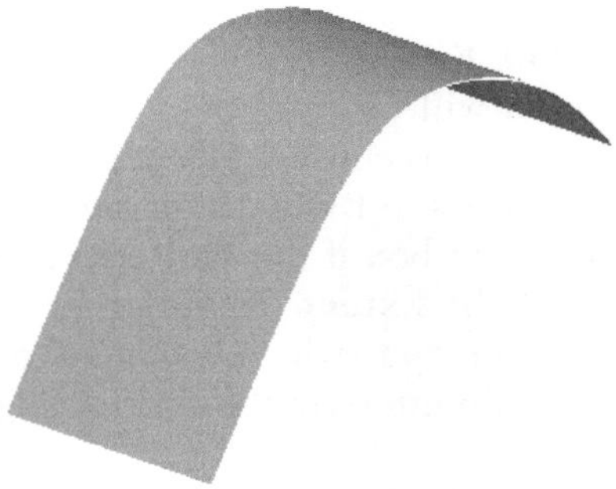

Figure 13-57 *Curvature continuous extended surface*

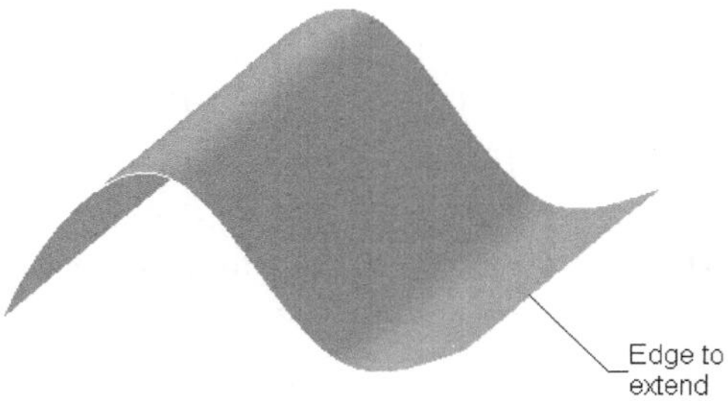

Figure 13-58 *Edge of the surface selected to extend*

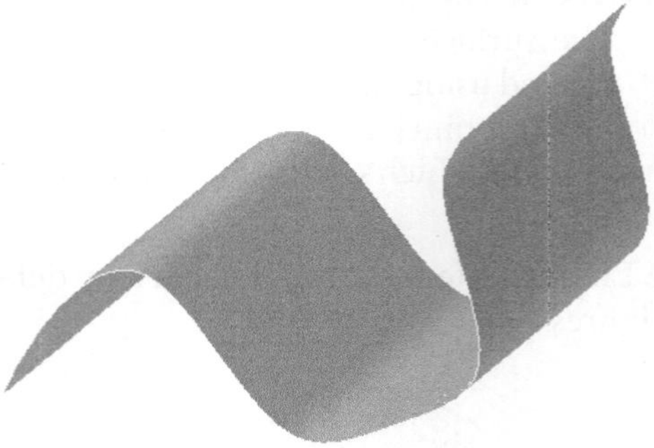

Figure 13-59 *Reflective Extent extended surface*

REPLACING THE FACES OF A PART WITH A SURFACE

Ribbon: Surfacing > Modify Surfaces > Replace Face

In Solid Edge, you can replace one or more faces of a solid model with a surface, provided that the surface selected to replace the face intersects it. To replace the faces of a solid model, first you need to create a surface for replacement. Next, choose the **Replace Face** tool from the **Modify Surfaces** group; the **Replace Face** command bar will be displayed and you will be prompted to select the faces you need to replace. Select the face to replace and right-click; you will be prompted to select the replacement surface. Next, select the replacement surface; the surface will be replaced. Remember that after the faces are replaced, the replacement surfaces will be hidden automatically.

Figure 13-60 shows the faces of the part that are selected to be replaced with the surface. The model after replacing its faces with a surface is shown in Figure 13-61.

Note

*The **Replace Face** tool will be available only if you have a surface for replacement and a solid model in the drawing area.*

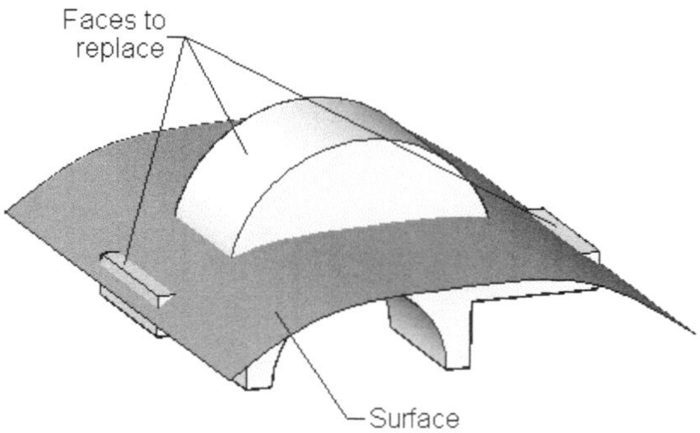

Figure 13-60 Faces to be replaced

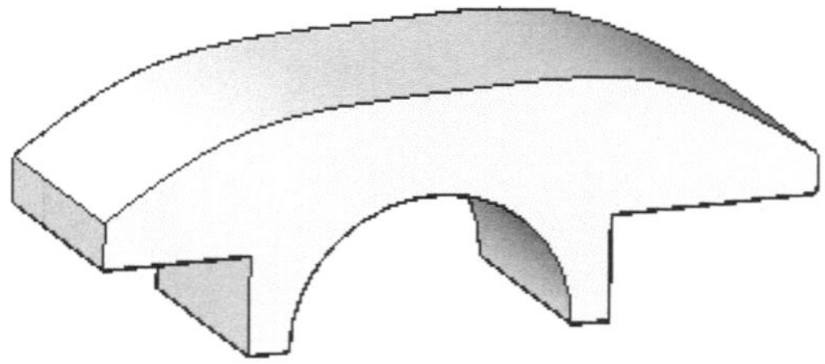

Figure 13-61 Model after replacing the faces

SPLITTING FACES

Ribbon: Surfacing > Modify Surfaces > Split

The **Split** tool is used to split a surface by using surfaces, edges, or curves. On invoking this tool, the **Select Surface Step** button will be activated and you will be prompted to select a single face. Select the surface to be split from the drawing area and right-click to accept the surface; the **Select Splitting Geometry Step** button will be activated. Next, select one or more geometries that intersect the surface you want to split and then right-click to accept the selection. Figure 13-62 shows the surfaces selected to split and Figure 13-63 shows the split surface.

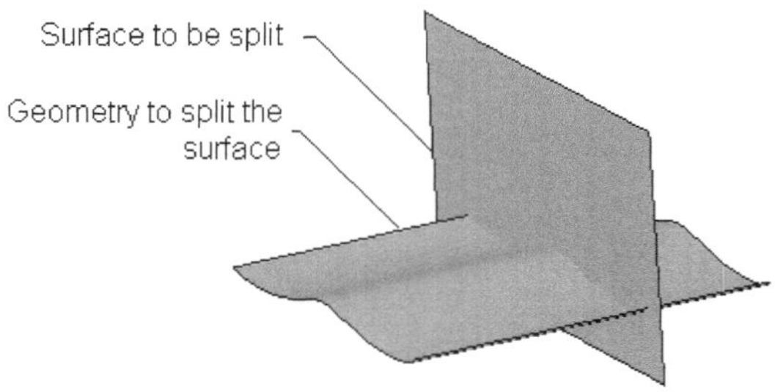

Figure 13-62 Surfaces selected to split

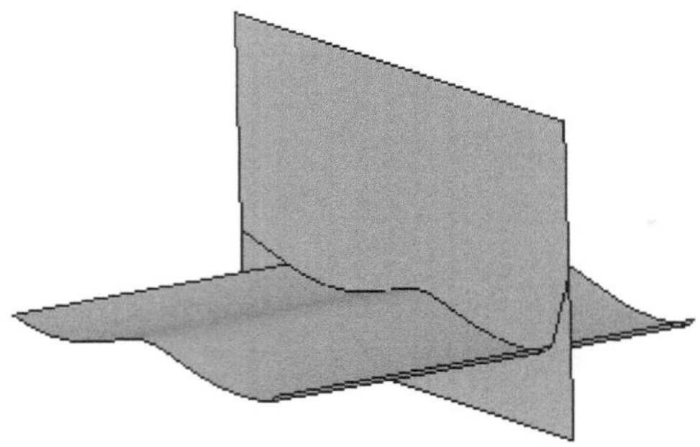

Figure 13-63 Split surface

USING THE INTERSECT TOOL

Ribbon: Surfacing > Modify Surfaces > Intersect

The **Intersect** tool is used to extend a surface up to another surface or trim a surface using an intersecting surface. On choosing this tool, you will be prompted to select two surface bodies. If you want to extend a surface, select the surface to be extended and the surface upto which you want to extend, refer to Figure 13-64. Next, right-click to accept the selection; you will be prompted to selected the edge to be extended or region to be removed. Select the edge of the surface to be extended and then right-click to accept; the surface will be extended upto the intersecting surface, as shown in Figure 13-65. If you choose the **Stitched** button on the **Intersect** command bar; the extended surface will be stitched with the intersecting surface.

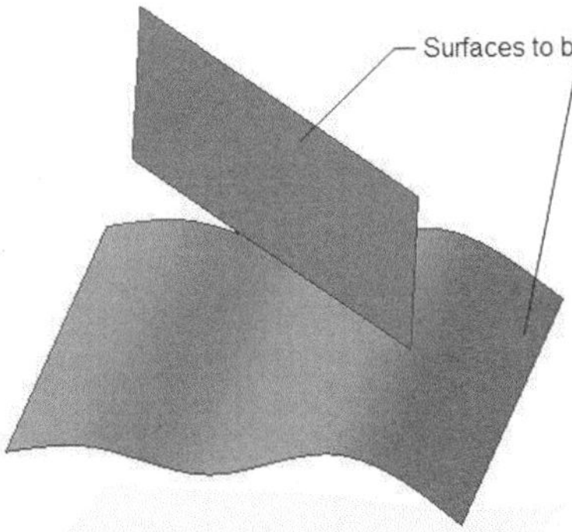

Figure 13-64 Surfaces selected to extend

Figure 13-65 Surface extended upto the intersecting surface

Note

For stitching the surfaces, the edges of the two surfaces must be connected with each other.

If you want to trim a surface, select two intersecting surfaces. Next, right-click to accept the selection; you will be prompted to select an edge to be extended or region to be removed. Select the region to be removed, as shown in Figure 13-66 and right-click to accept; the selected region will be removed, as shown in Figure 13-67.

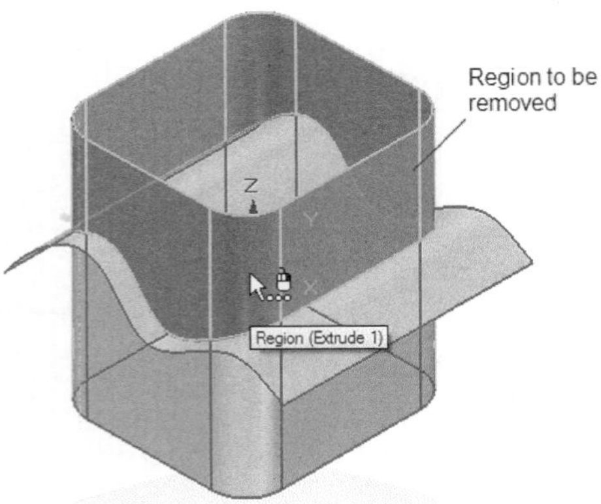

Figure 13-66 Region to be removed

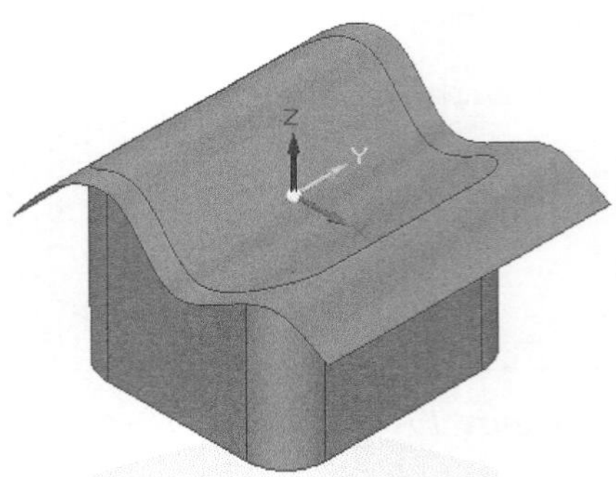

Figure 13-67 Surface after removing the region

CREATING CURVES IN 3D BY SELECTING KEYPOINTS

Ribbon: Surfacing > Curves > Keypoint Curve drop-down > Keypoint Curve

The **Keypoint Curve** tool is used to create 3D curves by joining keypoints on an existing geometry. You can also use this tool to create a curve by selecting the existing points. On choosing this tool, you will be prompted to click on a keypoint. Select the required keypoints. After you accept the keypoints, you can choose the **End Conditions Step** button to set the end conditions for the curve. The options available in various steps required to create this type of curve are discussed next.

Select Points Step

This button is chosen by default when you invoke the **Keypoint Curve** tool. The options in this step are discussed next.

Redefine Point

When you choose this button, you will be prompted to click on the point to redefine the location of an existing point. Click on the point and then click on a keypoint or in space.

Keypoints

If you choose this button, a flyout will be displayed that you can use to specify the type of keypoints to be selected.

End Conditions Step

This button can be chosen after you accept the selected points to create a curve. The options in this step are discussed next.

Open

The **Open** button is chosen by default. As a result, an open curve will be created.

Closed

The **Closed** button is chosen to create a closed curve. When you choose this button, the first keypoint will be joined with the last keypoint.

Show/Hide Tangency Control Handles

This button is chosen by default. As a result, the **Tangency Control** handles will be displayed at the end points of curve. These handles provide the options to set the end conditions of a curve. You can set the end conditions as **Natural**, **Tangent Continuous**, or **Curvature Continuous**. Figure 13-68 shows a keypoint curve created with the start and end conditions set to **Tangent Continuous**. Figure 13-69 shows the keypoint curve created with the start and end conditions set to **Natural**.

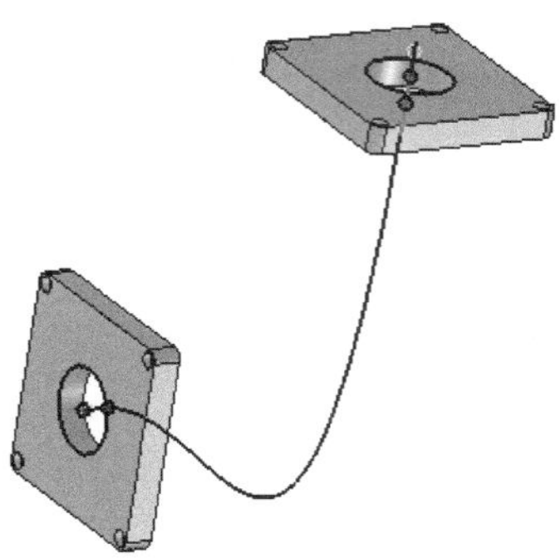

*Figure 13-68 Keypoint curve with the **Tangent Continuous** end condition*

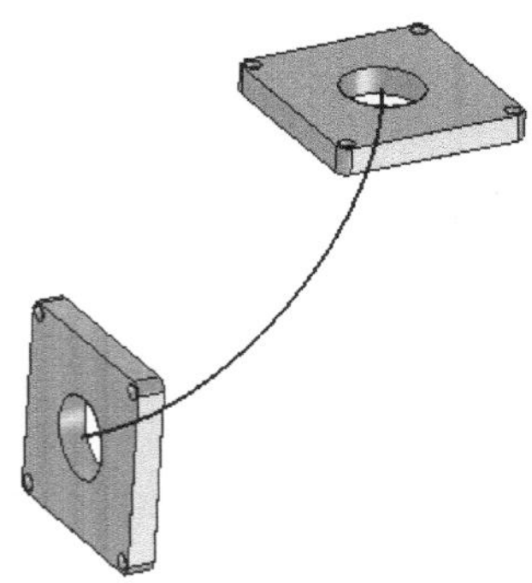

*Figure 13-69 Keypoint curve with the **Natural** end condition*

Curve Length Step

This button is chosen to give the keypoint curve a definition. The options in this step are discussed next.

Fixed Length

Choose this button to give the curve a fixed length. When you choose this button, the **Length** edit box will get activated. You can enter the length of the curve in this edit box.

Constrain Direction

Choose this button to specify the direction of control point movement when you increase or decrease the curve length. You can fix the movement of the control point along the X, Y and Z axes, any linear edge/curve, or an axis.

CREATING CURVES BY TABLE

Ribbon: Surfacing > Curves > Keypoint Curve drop-down > Curve by Table

In Solid Edge, you can enter the X, Y, and Z coordinates in an MS Excel sheet and create a curve. When you choose the **Curve by Table** tool from the **Keypoint Curve** drop-down in the **Curves** group, the **Insert Object** dialog box will be displayed, as shown in Figure 13-70, also the **Curve by Table** command bar will be displayed. You can select an existing Excel spreadsheet for an input to draw the curve or create a new spreadsheet.

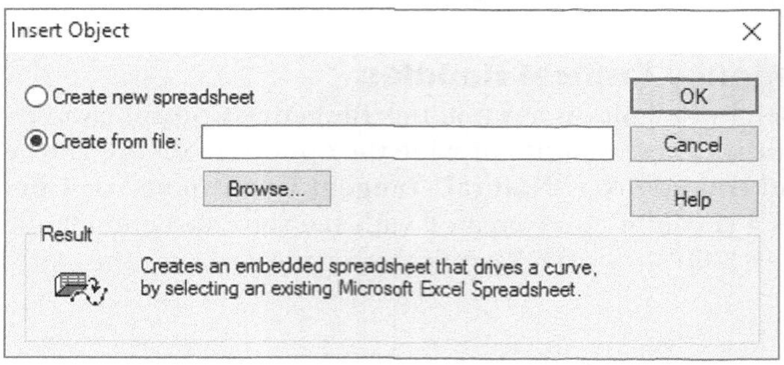

Figure 13-70 *The* ***Insert Object*** *dialog box*

When you select the **Create new spreadsheet** radio button and choose **OK**, a new excel file will open. Enter the coordinate values in this file. Some important points related to entering the coordinates in this file are listed next.

1. The X, Y, and Z values should lie under the columns A, B, and C. Any data entered outside these columns cannot be read by Solid Edge.
2. Any cell that is blank or contains a non-numeric data will not be read by Solid Edge.

After entering the coordinate values, choose the **Close** option from the **File** menu in MS Excel. You can also save the Excel file to open it later, if needed. On closing the excel file, the curve will be created in the part document with the coordinates specified in the file.

PROJECTING THE CURVES ON SURFACES

Ribbon: Surfacing > Curves > Project drop-down > Project

The **Project** tool is used to project curves on planar or non-planar surfaces. When you choose this tool, the command bar will be displayed. Choose the **Project Curve Options** button from the command bar to display the **Project Curve Options** dialog box. There are two options available in this dialog box to project the curves: **Along vector** and **Normal to selected surface**. These options are discussed next.

Along vector Option

This option projects the curve in the direction of a vector that defines the normal of the plane on which the curve is sketched. If the receiving surface is inclined or non planar, the size of the projected curve will be different from the original curve. But when you view the projected curve from the plane on which it was originally lying, the original and the projected curves will appear to be overlapping, see Figure 13-71. Figure 13-72 shows the sketched curve after projecting it on the receiving surface. Note that the original curve is drawn on the plane that is parallel to the bottom face of the model.

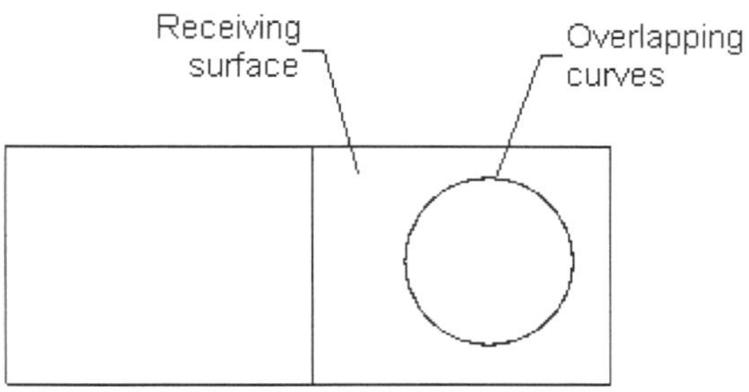

Figure 13-71 *Top view of the projected curve*

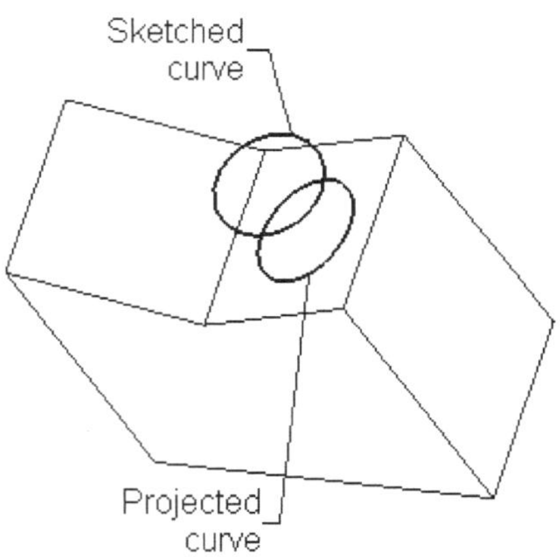

Figure 13-72 *Projecting a curve*

Normal to selected surface Option

This option projects the curve normal to the receiving surface. Figure 13-73 shows the curve selected to be projected on the receiving surface and the curve after projecting it. Notice that the geometry changes when viewed from the top. Figure 13-74 shows an alternate view of the sketched curve after projecting it on the receiving surface.

After you exit the **Project Curve Options** dialog box or when you choose the **Project** tool, you will be prompted to select the curve to be projected. Select the curve and then accept their selection. Next, select a surface or face on which you need to project the curve and right-click; an arrow will be attached to the curve and you will be prompted to select the side of the projection. Select the side when arrow points toward the model; the curve will be projected onto the selected surface. Note that when **Normal to selected surface** option is selected, the curve will be projected on the selected surface without displaying the direction arrow.

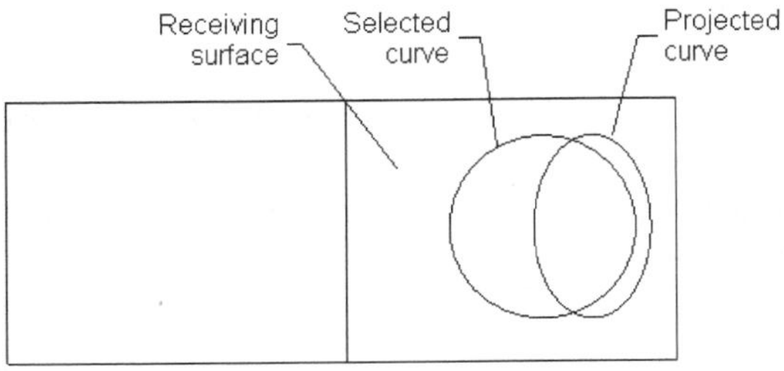

Figure 13-73 *Top view of the curve to be projected*

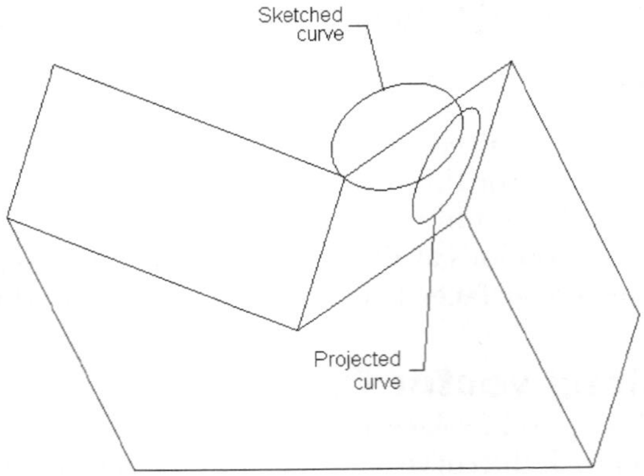

Figure 13-74 *Projecting a curve*

CREATING A CURVE AT THE PROJECTION OF TWO CURVES

Ribbon: Surfacing > Curves > Cross

The **Cross** tool is used to create a 3D curve by projecting two 2D curves on each other. This tool projects imaginary lines from both 2D curves in the direction normal to the sketching planes of the 2D curves. Then all imaginary intersecting points are joined to get the resulting 3D curve. When you choose this tool, you will be prompted to select a curve. You can select an existing curve or draw a new curve. After selecting or drawing the first curve right-click, you will be prompted to select the second curve. Select or draw the second curve and right-click; the resulting 3D curve will be created, as shown in Figure 13-75.

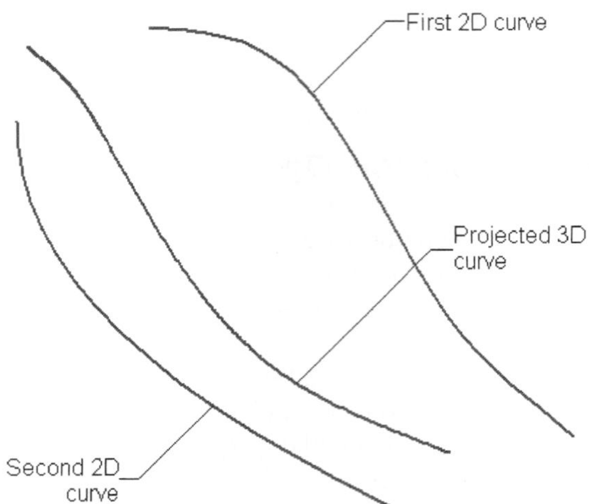

Figure 13-75 *A 3D curve projected at the intersection of two 2D curves*

DRAWING A CURVE ON A SURFACE

Ribbon: Surfacing > Curves > Contour

The **Contour** tool is used to draw a curve on the selected face. The curve is drawn by creating points on the surface. These points can be existing points such as edges, vertices, or imaginary points. The face on which the points will be drawn can be planar or non planar. When you choose this tool, you will be prompted to select a face on which the points will be drawn. Select the face and right-click,then select the points on it. You can use the **Open** and **Close** buttons on the command bar to specify the type of curve. The **Insert Point** button is used to specify the point between two points on the curve. The curve thus created can be used to trim the surface.

Figure 13-76 shows the curve that was created on the surface and Figure 13-77 shows the spherical surface that was trimmed using the curve.

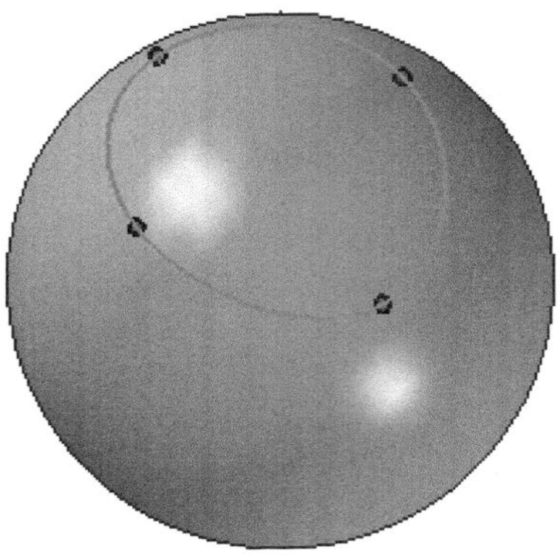

Figure 13-76 *Curve created on the surface*

Figure 13-77 *Surface trimmed using the curve*

DERIVING CURVES

Ribbon: Surfacing > Curves > Derived

The **Derived** tool is used to derive a curve from existing edges of a surface, a solid, or an existing sketch. When you choose this tool, you will be prompted to select one or more curves or edges. After selecting the curves or edges, choose the **Accept** button; the curve will be derived from the edges or curves you have chosen.

An application of the derived curve is shown in Figures 13-78 and 13-79. The outer edge of a rectangular box is used to create a derived curve.

SPLITTING A CURVE

Ribbon: Surfacing > Curves > Split

The **Split** tool is used to split a keypoint curve using an intersecting entity, such as a reference plane, keypoint, curve, and so on. When you choose this tool, you will be prompted to select a curve that you need to split. You can select more than one curve to split. After selecting and accepting the curve to split, you will be prompted to select an axis, plane, keypoint, curve, face chain, or body. This entity will be used to split the curve. You can also use the options available in the **Select** drop-down list to select the elements for splitting the curve.

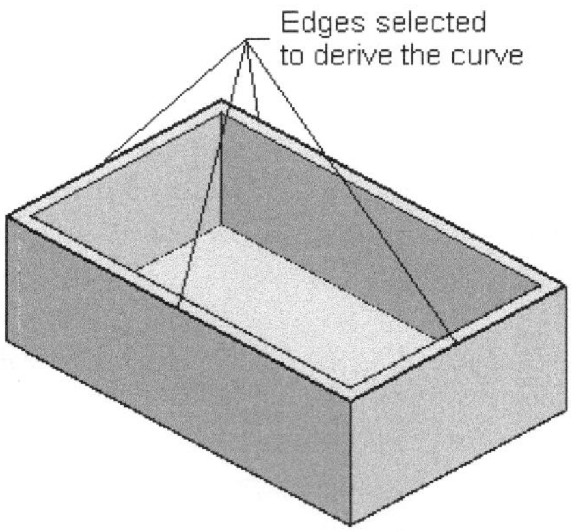

Figure 13-78 Edges selected to derive the curve

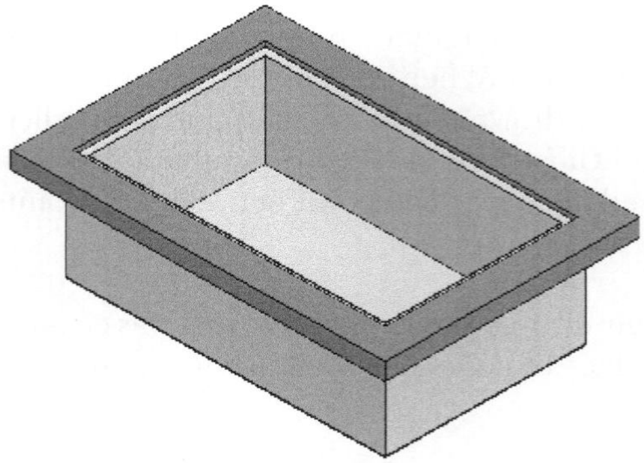

Figure 13-79 Sweep created using the derived curve

SPLITTING A BODY

Ribbon: Divide Part (Customize to add)

In the **Part** environment of Solid Edge, you can split a body using a surface or a plane and save the split files as separate part files. This tool can be used to create sections, a model of punch and die for sheet metal components, molds, and so on. This tool is available only when a solid feature exists on the screen and can be used only if the current file is saved.

Note

*You can add the **Divide Part** tool by customizing either in the new tab or in the existing tab of the ribbon.*

To split a body, choose the **Divide Part** tool from the **Select** group of the **Surfacing** tab; you will be prompted to select a surface or a plane to divide the part. After you select a surface or a plane, a red arrow will be displayed and you will be prompted to click on the side to be divided into the new file. After you select the direction, choose the **Finish** button to display the **Divide Part** dialog box, as shown in Figure 13-80. The body that you divide is saved in two separate files. Click in one of the cells under the **Filename** column of the dialog box to enter the name of the new file with one of the split portions. After naming the two files, choose the **Save Selected Files** button to save the files.

Figure 13-81 shows the part that is divided into two parts by using the surface. The resulting parts are the punch and die, refer to Figure 13-82.

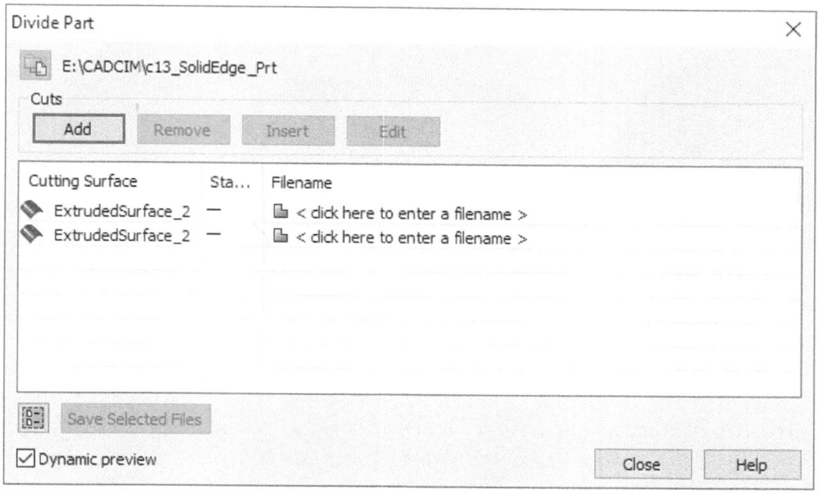

Figure 13-80 *The* ***Divide Part*** *dialog box*

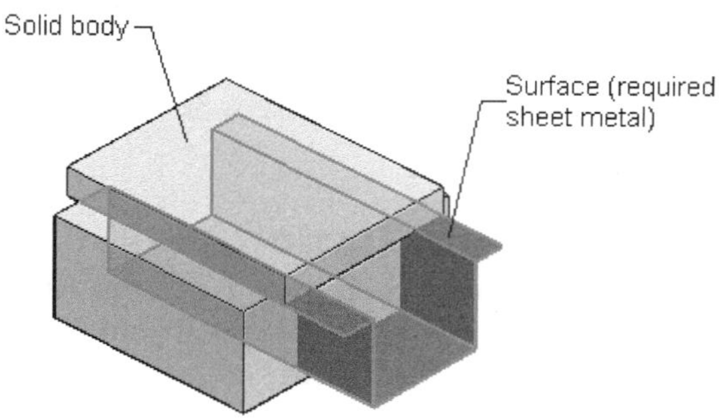

Figure 13-81 *Solid body and the surface*

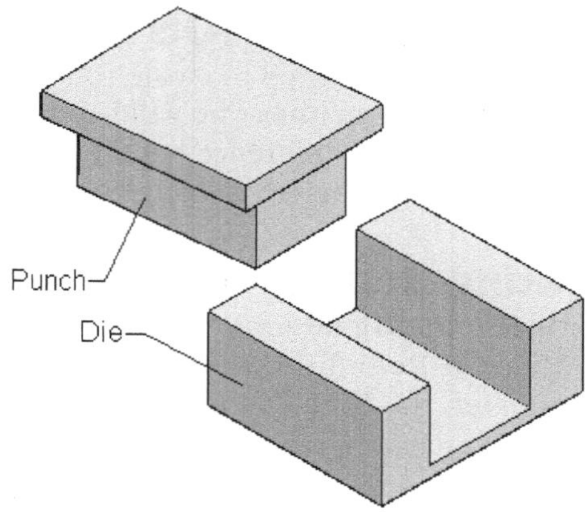

igure 13-82 *Punch and die obtained after splitting the body*

ADDING THICKNESS TO A SURFACE

Ribbon: Home > Solids > Add drop-down > Thicken

After a surface is created, you can add thickness to it to make it a solid body. Generally, the surfaces that constitute a surface model are stitched together to form a single surface, which is then thickened using the **Thicken** tool.

On choosing the **Thicken** tool from the **Add** drop-down in **Solids** group of the **Home** tab, you will be prompted to select a body. Select the body and right-click, you will be prompted to select the side to which the thickness will be added. The direction in which the thickness will be added is shown by a red arrow. Specify the side of the surface where the thickness will be added by clicking in that direction. You can also specify the thickness in the command bar. Figure 13-83 shows a stitched surface and the side to add thickness and Figure 13-84 shows the surface after adding thickness to it.

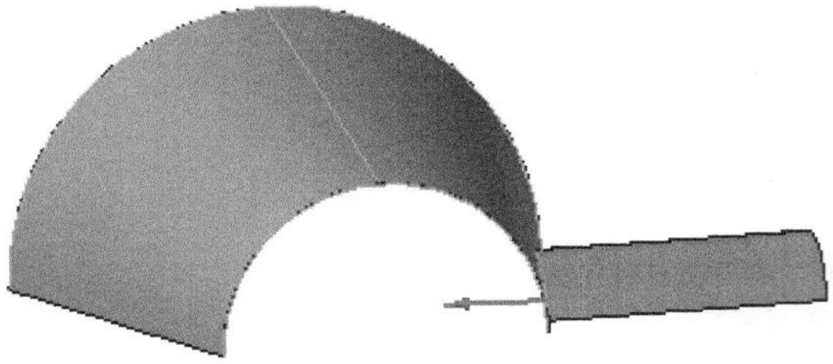

Figure 13-83 A stitched surface and the side to add thickness

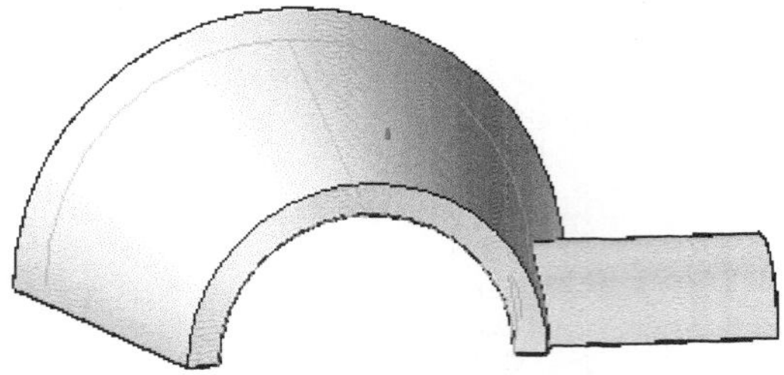

Figure 13-84 Surface after adding the thickness

Tip

An easy way of finding out whether a set of surfaces are stitched is to select any one of the surfaces. If all the surfaces are highlighted in orange, it implies that they are stitched together and represent a single surface.

CREATING ROUNDS USING BLENDING

In Chapter 6, you learned to create rounds by using the **Round** tool in the **Solids** group of the **Home** tab. In this chapter, you will learn to create rounds by blending two faces of a solid or a surface model. The difference between these methods is that in rounding, you select an edge to create a round, whereas in blending, you need to select two faces.

Creating Rounds on Solids Using the Blend Option

You can use the **Blend** tool to create rounds on solid faces only. When you invoke the **Blend** tool from the **Round** drop-down of the **Solids** group of the **Home** tab in **Synchronous Part** environment, the **Blend** command bar will be displayed. Select the **Blend** radio button from this command bar. In case you are working in the **Ordered Part** environment, choose the **Round** tool from the **Solids** group of the **Home** tab, the **Round** command bar will be displayed. Choose the **Round Options** button from the command bar to display the **Round Options** dialog box. Select the **Blend** radio button from this dialog box and choose the **OK** button to exit it; you will be prompted to select the faces to blend. Select the two faces and specify the value of radius in the **Radius** dimension box. Right-click to confirm the selection; the **Overflow Step** will be automatically invoked. The **Roll Along/Across** button will be chosen by default in the command bar and you will be prompted to select an edge. The **Tangent Hold Line** button is also available on the command bar. These two buttons are discussed next.

Roll Along/Across

The **Roll Along/Across** button creates a rounded blend on any edge it encounters. Choose this button to create a round; you will be prompted to select an edge. Select the edge, as shown in Figure 13-85; the blend round of the specified radius will be created, as shown in Figure 13-86. Remember that while creating a round blend by using this option, you need to specify the radius value.

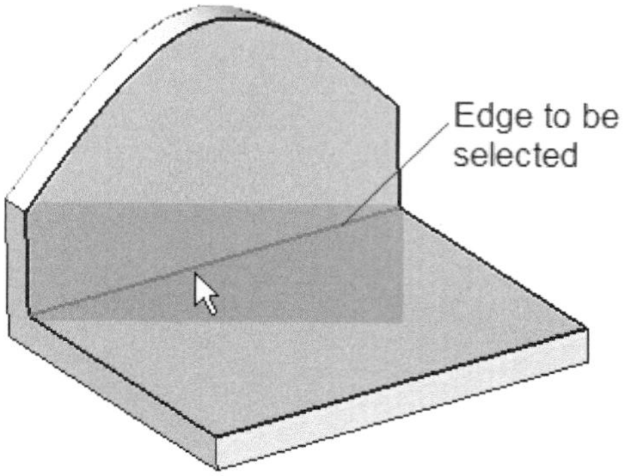

Figure 13-85 Edge to be selected

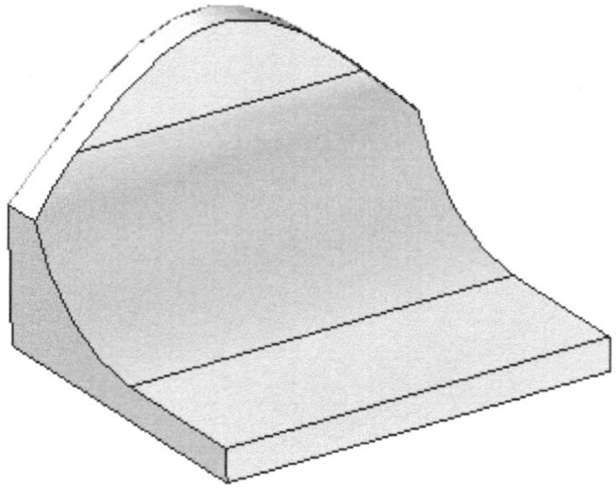

Figure 13-86 Blend round rolled across the edges

Tangent Hold Line

This option enables you to select the edges that will act as a hold line to control the blending. On choosing this button, you will be provided with two more options for defining the blending of the round. The function of these options is explained next.

Default Radius

This option enables you to create a blend between the tangent hold lines by maintaining the radius value. When you choose this option, you will be prompted to select an edge chain. Select the edge, as shown in Figure 13-87, and right-click to accept the selection; the blend round will be created, as shown in Figure 13-88.

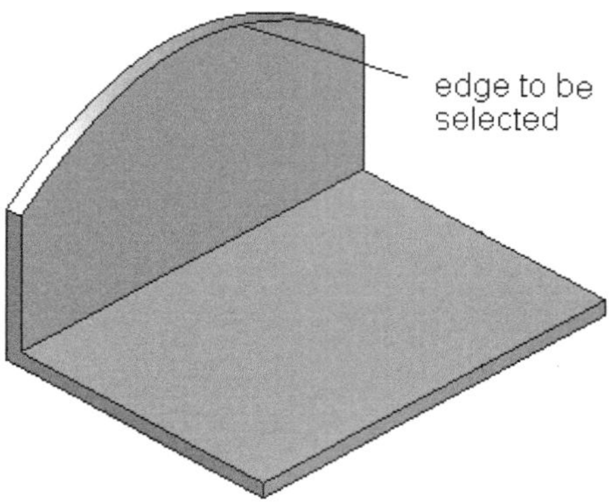

Figure 13-87 Edges to be selected

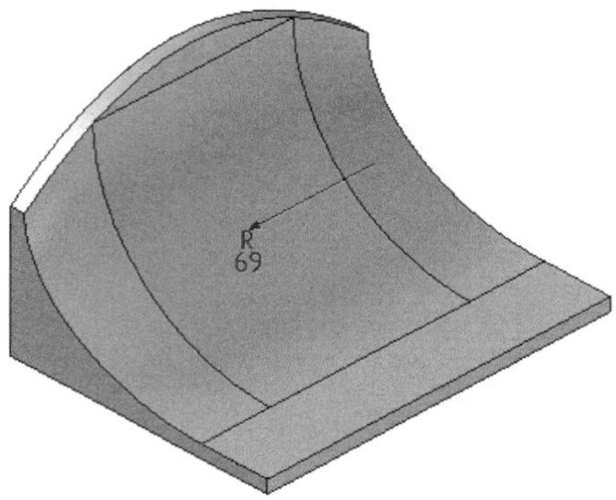

Figure 13-88 Blend round between tangent hold line with the default radius

Full Radius

This option creates a full blend between the tangent hold lines. This means that the round is created using the tangent hold lines and the tangency between the faces is maintained. Figure 13-89 shows the edges to be selected as the tangent hold line and Figure 13-90 shows the round created with full radius.

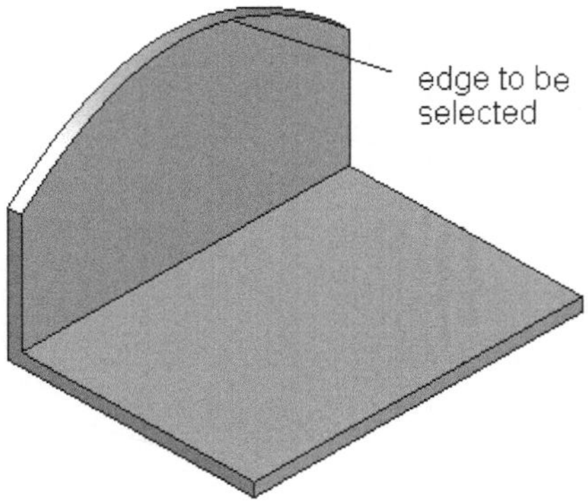

Figure 13-89 Edges to be selected

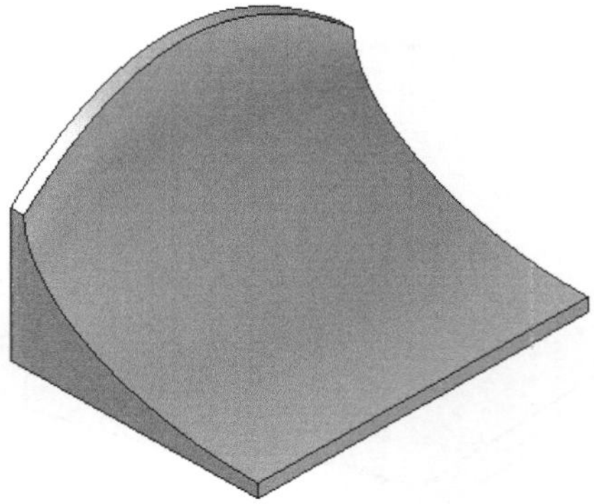

Figure 13-90 Blend round between tangent hold line with full radius

Creating Rounds by Using the Surface blend Option

You can use the **Surface blend** option to create rounds on the surfaces only. This option uses certain blend parameters that will be displayed when you choose the **Surface Blend Parameters** button from the command bar. On doing so, the **Surface Blend Parameters** dialog box will be displayed, as shown in Figure 13-91. The options in this dialog box are discussed next.

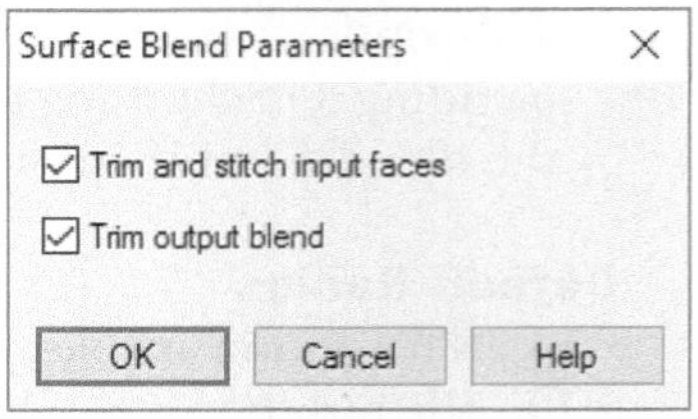

*Figure 13-91 The **Surface Blend Parameters** dialog box*

The **Trim and stitch input faces** check box, when selected, stitches the blend surface with the existing faces. Figure 13-92 shows the blend surface round created after clearing this check box and Figure 13-93 shows the blend surface round created with this check box selected.

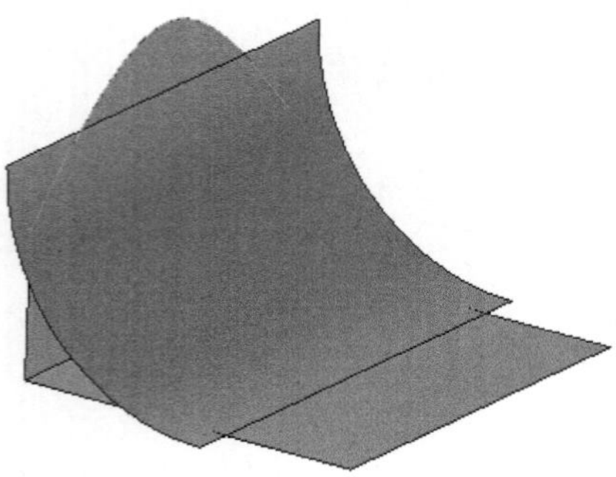

*Figure 13-92 Blend surface with the **Trim and stitch input faces** check box cleared*

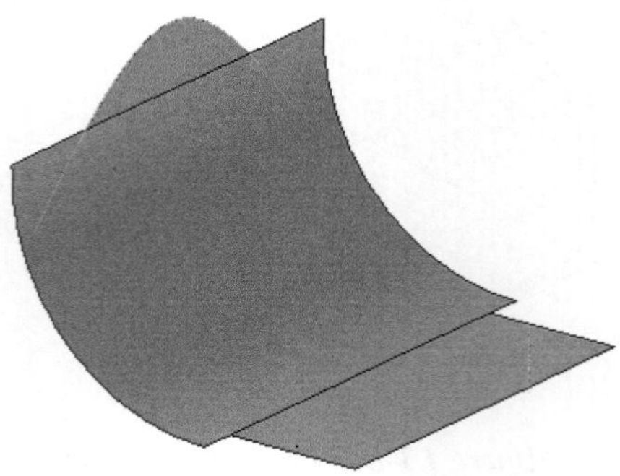

*Figure 13-93 Blend surface with the **Trim and stitch input faces** check box selected*

The **Trim output blend** check box, when selected, trims the surface blend with the faces. Figure 13-94 shows the surface blend created when the **Trim output blend** check box is selected. Figure 13-95 shows the surface blend round created when the check box is cleared.

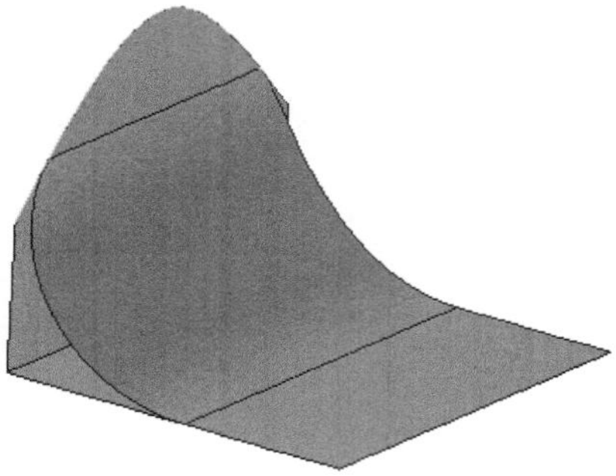

Figure 13-94 *Blend surface with the* ***Trim output blend*** *check box selected*

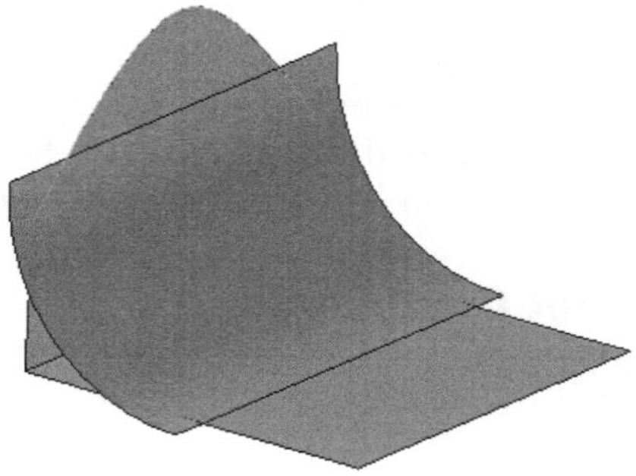

Figure 13-95 *Blend surface with the* ***Trim output blend*** *check box cleared*

Figure 13-96 shows the blend surface round when both the check boxes in the **Surface Blend Parameters** dialog box are selected.

After selecting the faces to round right-click, you will be prompted to specify the side of the face where the round will be created. Note that the buttons discussed next are available in the **Ordered Part** environment only.

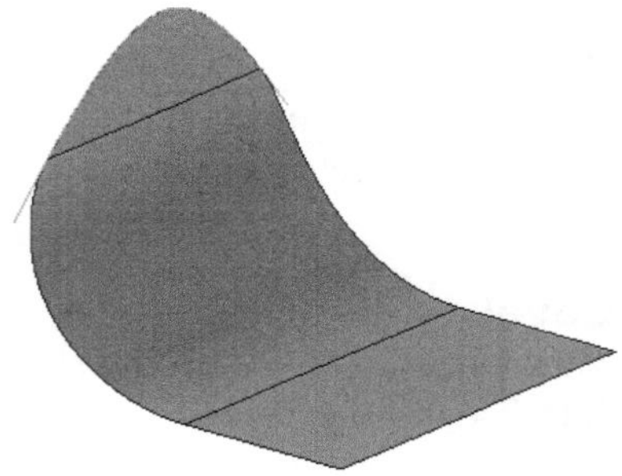

Figure 13-96 *A rounded surface*

Tangent Hold Line

This option for creating the surface blend rounds works in the same way as discussed in the **Blend** option for creating rounds. Figure 13-97 shows the surface blend round created by using the **Default Radius** option and Figure 13-98 shows the surface blend round created by using the **Full Radius** option. In both these cases, the tangent hold lines are the same as those selected in Figures 13-87 and 13-89.

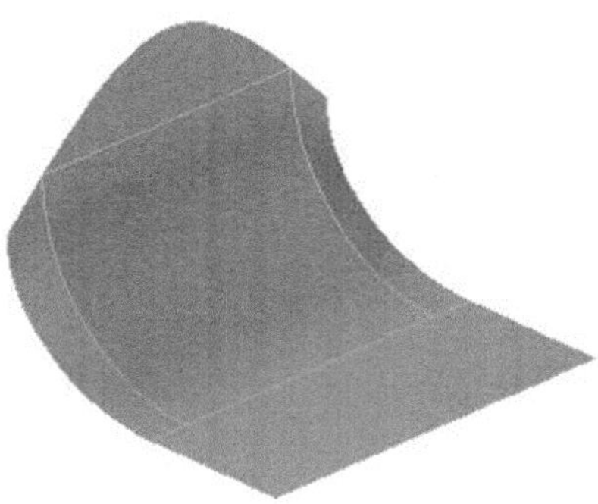

Figure 13-97 *Surface blend round created using the* ***Default Radius*** *option*

Figure 13-98 *Surface blend round created using the* ***Full Radius*** *option*

Roll Along/Across

The **Roll Along/Across** button is chosen by default. The function of this button is same as discussed in the **Blend** option for creating rounds.

Specifying the Blend Shape

You can also specify the shape of the blended rounds before creating them by using the options available in the **Shape** drop-down list in the **Select Step**, see Figure 13-99. These options are discussed next.

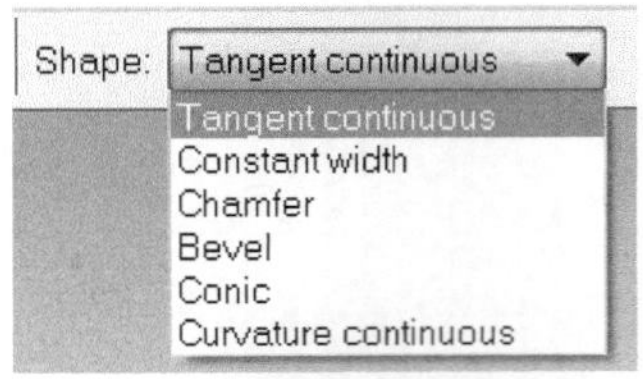

Figure 13-99 *Selecting the blend shape from the **Shape** drop-down list*

Tangent Continuous

This option uses a constant radius to create a round and is similar to creating simple rounds.

Constant width

This option creates a blend of circular cross-section with a constant chord width between two selected faces.

Chamfer

The **Chamfer** option enables you to create a chamfer on two surfaces. Figure 13-100 shows the chamfer on the surfaces.

Bevel

This option creates a bevel surface between the two selected faces. When you select this option, the **Setback** and the **Value** dimension boxes will be displayed. By default, the **Value** dimension box contains the value 1. This means that a bevel of 45-degree will be created. If you enter the value 2 in this dimension box, the resulting bevel will remove an area equal to half of the dimension value you specify in the **Setback** dimension box from the face you select first. Figure 13-101 shows a bevel surface created with a dimension 2 entered in the **Value** dimension box.

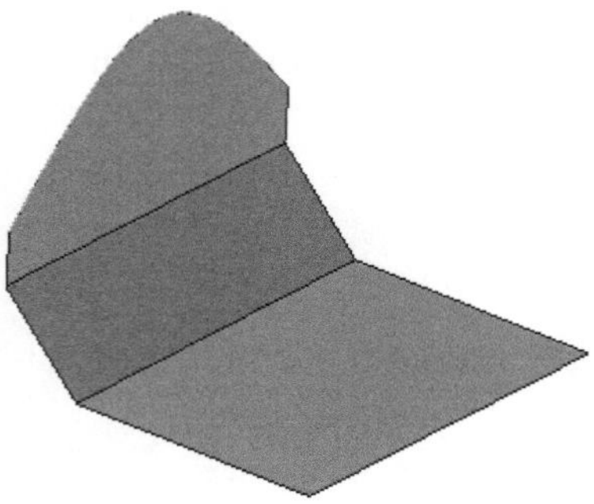

Figure 13-100 *Surface blend created using the **Chamfer** option*

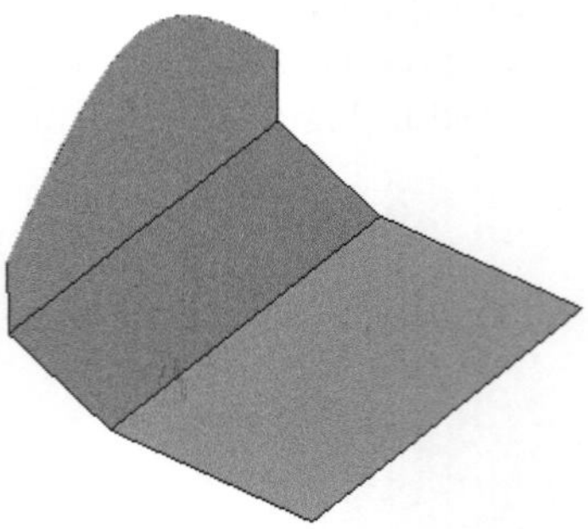

Figure 13-101 *Surface blend created using the **Bevel** option*

Conic

This option uses a conic cross-section to create a surface blend. When you select this option, the **Radius** and **Value** dimension boxes will be displayed in the command bar. The value in the **Radius** dimension box determines the width of the cross-section and the value in the **Value** dimension box changes the cross-section shape.

Curvature continuous

When you select this option, the **Radius** and **Value** dimension boxes will be displayed. This option enables you to vary the softness of the surface blend along the radius of the blend.

ADDING A DRAFT

Ribbon: Home > Solids > Draft

In earlier chapters, you learned to add a draft angle using some of the options. In this section, you will learn to add a split draft and step draft angles using the **From parting surface** and **From parting line** options.

To add a draft, choose the **Draft** tool from the **Solids** group of the **Home** tab. Next, choose the **Draft Options** button from the command bar, if you are working in the **Ordered Part** environment; otherwise, choose **Draft Options** from command bar; the **Draft Options** dialog box will be displayed. The remaining options in this dialog box are discussed next.

From parting surface Option

This option enables you to select a parting geometry that acts as a pivot point about which the draft is added to the faces. To add a draft by using this option, select the **From parting surface** option from the **Draft Options** dialog box. Then, select the plane that is perpendicular to the faces to be drafted; you will be prompted to select the parting surface. Select the construction surface, as shown in Figure 13-102. Right-click to accept the selection and choose the **Next** button from the command bar; you will be prompted to select the faces to be added to the draft. Select the faces. You need to enter the draft angle value in the **Draft angle** edit box. After specifying the draft angle, right-click to accept if you are working in the **Ordered Part** environment. Choose the **Next** button and specify the direction where the draft is needed; the draft will be added to the faces, as shown in Figure 13-103.

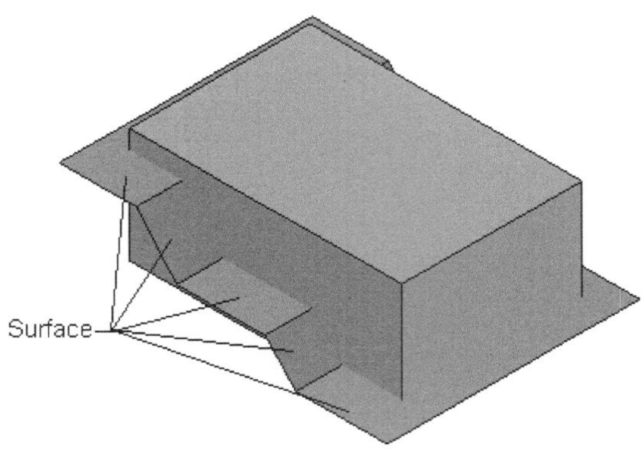

Figure 13-102 *Construction surface*

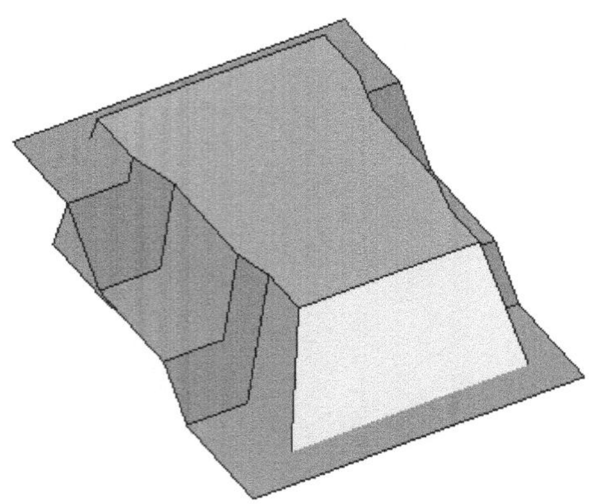

Figure 13-103 *Draft added to the faces*

If you are in the **Synchronous Part** environment, specify the draft angle value in the edit box that will be displayed after specifying the direction of draft; the draft will be created.

Note

The first plane or the face that you select to add draft is also called as neutral plane.

After the draft is added to the selected faces, refer to Figure 13-103, the single face is divided into five faces. This is because of the geometry of the construction surface that was used as the parting surface.

Split draft

To create two different drafts such that the face of a model is split using a surface, select the **From parting surface** radio button and the **Split draft** check box in the **Draft Options** dialog box. The parting surface acts as a hinge about which the draft angles will be added. Figure 13-104 shows the construction surface that is used as the parting surface. The parting surface splits the selected faces. As a result, two different draft angles are added to them, as shown in Figure 13-105.

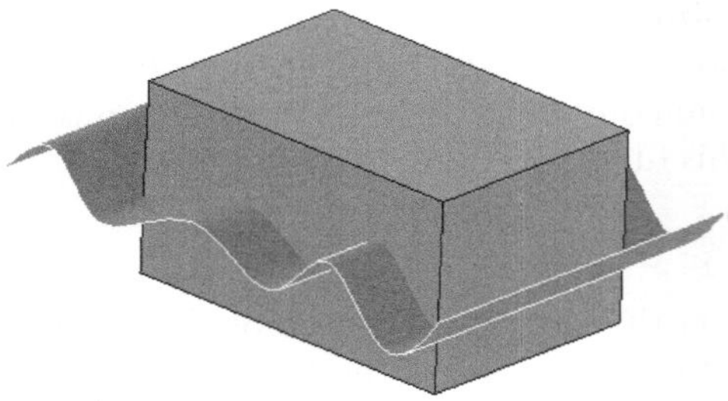

Figure 13-104 Construction surface

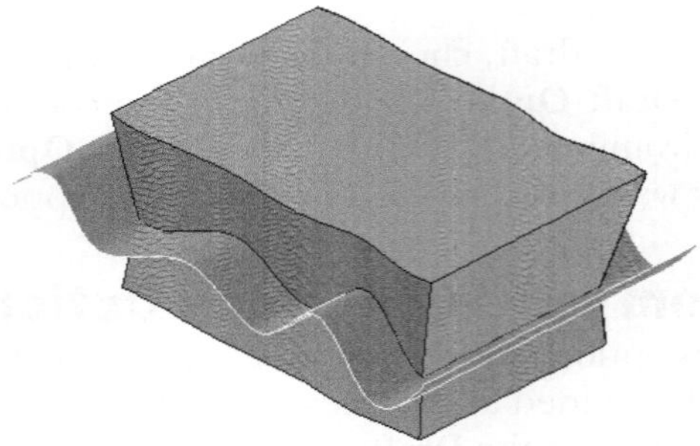

Figure 13-105 Draft added to the faces

From parting line Option

This option enables you to select a construction curve that acts as a pivot location about which the draft is added to the faces.

To add a draft by using a parting line, select the **From parting line** radio button from the **Draft Options** dialog box. The method of adding the draft angle is the same as followed earlier while using the **From parting surface** option. Figure 13-106 shows the curve and the face selected to add the draft and Figure 13-107 shows the draft added to the faces.

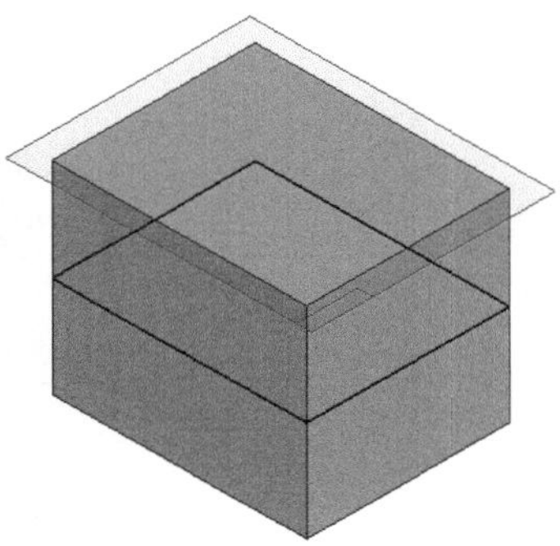

Figure 13-106 Curve and face selected to add the draft

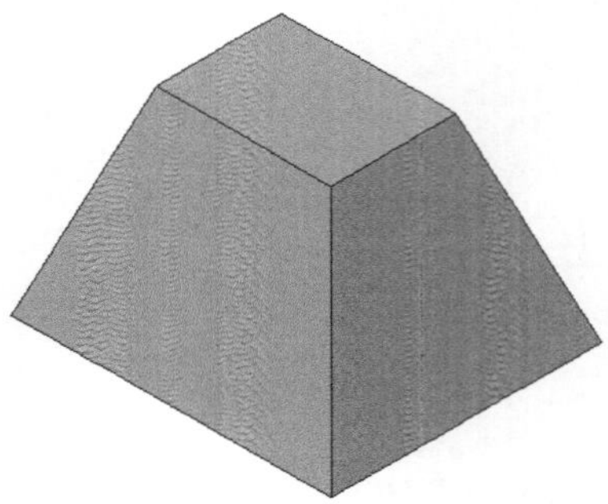

Figure 13-107 Draft added to the faces

Split draft

As discussed earlier, the **Split draft** option enables you to specify two different draft angles on the selected faces. The parting line acts as a pivot about which the draft is added. The parting line can be created by projecting a curve on the faces or by creating an intersection curve on the faces.

Step draft

The **Step draft** option will be available in the **Draft Options** dialog box when you select the **From parting line** radio button. This option is used to add a step to the draft created. The step faces can be added perpendicular to the face selected to be drafted or tapered along the draft. This can be done by selecting the **Perpendicular step faces** radio button or the **Taper step faces** radio button from the **Draft Options** dialog box.

Figure 13-108 shows the neutral plane, the curve that is projected on the face, and the face selected to be drafted. Figure 13-109 shows the step draft added perpendicular to the face selected to be drafted. The front view is also shown in this figure to show the difference between the two options of the step draft.

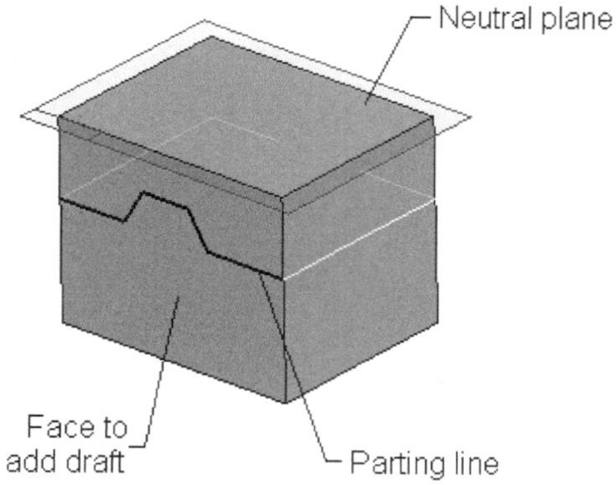

Figure 13-108 Parting line, neutral plane, and the face selected to add a draft

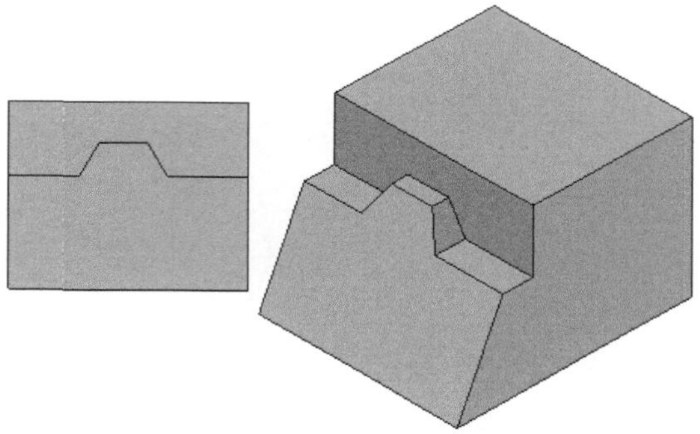

Figure 13-109 Draft added to the faces by selecting the Perpendicular step faces radio button

Figure 13-110 shows the tapered step draft added. In this figure, the front view shows the difference between the two options of the step draft. Figure 13-111 shows a split line draft created on the cylindrical face.

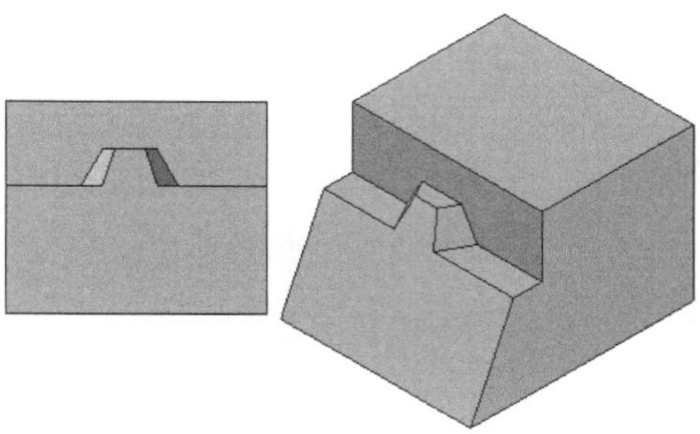

*Figure 13-110 Draft added to the faces by using the **Taper step faces** option*

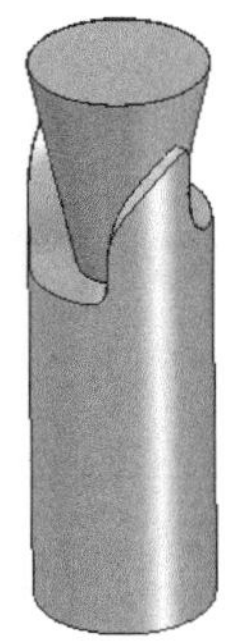

Figure 13-111 Draft added using the split line

USING THE PARTING SPLIT TOOL

Ribbon: Surfacing > Modify Surfaces > Parting Split drop-down > Parting Split

The **Parting Split** tool enables you to split the selected faces along a silhouette edge. Note that parting edges cannot be created on planar faces. To create a parting edge, choose the **Parting Split** tool; you will be prompted to select a reference plane or a face. Select a reference plane or a face to split the faces, as shown in Figure 13-112; you will be prompted to select a face. Select all faces of the part, except the two end faces, and right-click; the parting edge will be created, as shown in Figure 13-113. Choose the **Finish** and then **Cancel** button from the command bar to exit. You can check that the selected faces are divided by the parting edge.

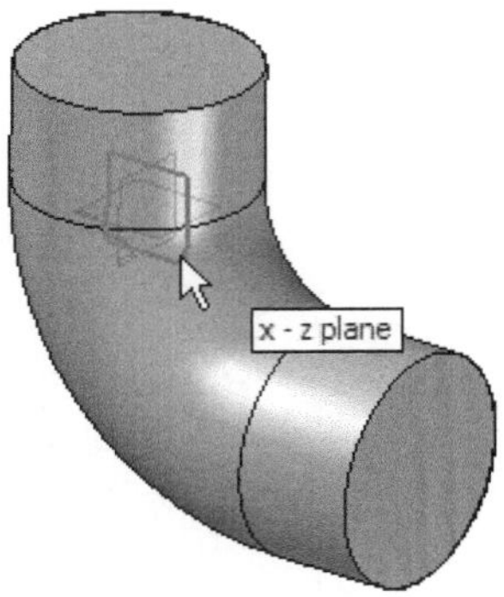

Figure 13-112 *Reference plane selected*

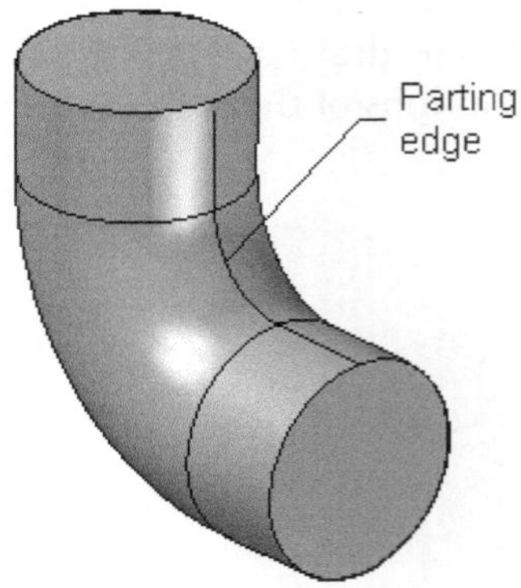

Figure 13-113 *Parting edge created*

USING THE PARTING SURFACE TOOL

Ribbon: Surfacing > Modify Surfaces > Parting Split drop-down > Parting Surface

The parting surface is used for creating molds, core, and cavity. The **Parting Surface** tool enables you to create a parting surface from a parting edge or from an edge chain. When you choose this tool, you will be prompted to select a face or a reference plane to which the parting surface will be parallel. Select a face or a reference plane; you will be prompted to select an edge, sketch, or a curve chain. Select the curve chain; you will be prompted to specify the extent and direction of the parting surface. Figure 13-114 shows the parting surface created after selecting the parting edge shown in Figure 13-113. Figure 13-115 shows the parting surface created by selecting the edge chain.

USING THE OFFSET EDGE TOOL

Ribbon: Surfacing > Modify Surfaces > Parting Split drop-down > Offset Edge

The **Offset Edge** tool is used to create the offset edges of the selected edge chain. On choosing this tool, you will be prompted to select an edge chain. Select the edge chain; you will be prompted to specify the offset distance and the direction of the offset edge. Specify the offset distance in the dynamic input box and then the direction of offset using the handle displayed on the selected edge. You can specify the offset to be formed in single direction as well as in two directions. Press 'T' to specify the offset in two directions. Figure 13-116 shows the offset edge created in single direction. Figure 13-117 shows the offset edge created in two directions.

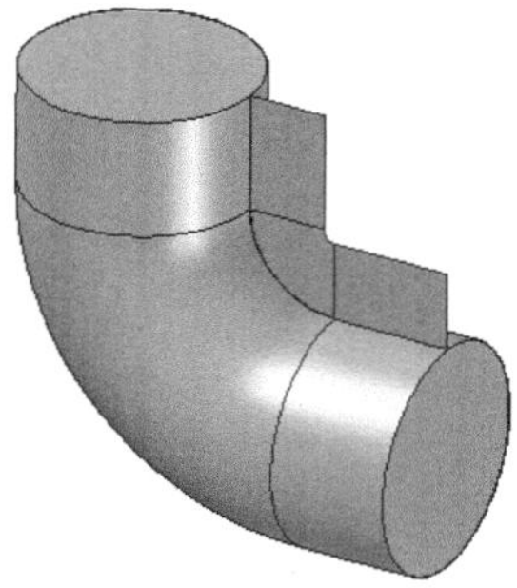

Figure 13-114 Parting surface created using the parting edge

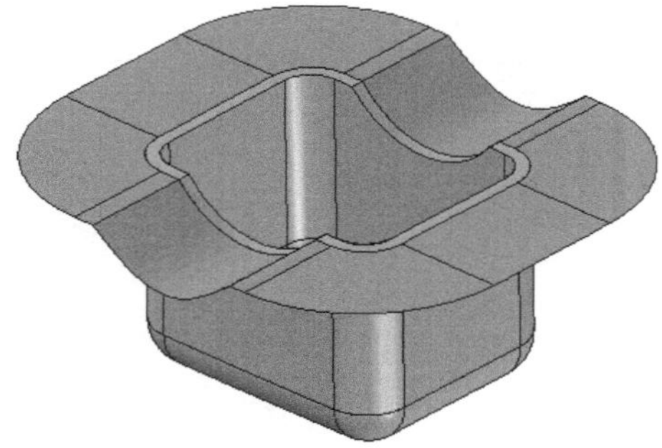

Figure 13-115 Parting surface created using the edge chain

Figure 13-116 Offset edge created in single direction

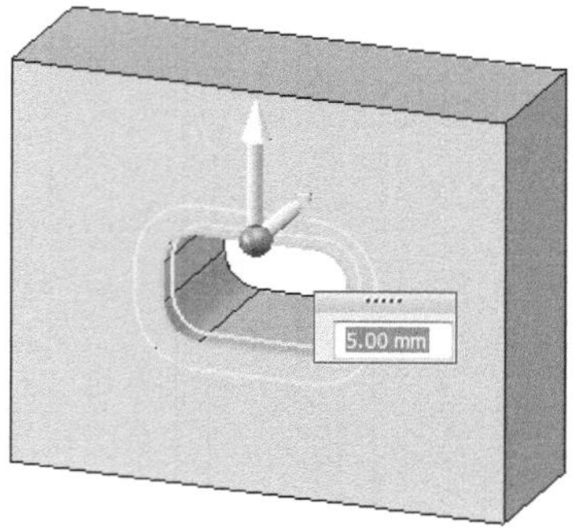

Figure 13-117 Offset edge created in two directions

TUTORIALS

Tutorial 1 Synchronous

In this tutorial, you will create the surface model shown in Figure 13-118. Its orthographic views are shown in Figure 13-119. After creating the model, save it with the name *c13tut1.par* at the location given next:

C:\Solid Edge\c13 **(Expected time: 30 min)**

The following steps are required to complete this tutorial:

a. Create the base feature by using the revolved surface tool, refer to Figures 13-120 and 13-121.
b. Create the second feature by using extruded surface tool. It will be created on a plane parallel to the top plane and at a distance of 65 mm. A draft angle will also be applied to this surface, refer to Figures 13-122 and 13-123.
c. Create the third and fourth feature by using the **Trim** tool which will trim the bottom part of the extruded surface and bottom surface of the revolved surface, refer to Figures 13-124 and 13-125.
d. Create the fifth feature by using a bounded surface, refer to Figure 13-127.
e. Create the sixth feature by using the **Stitch** tool that will stitch the revolved surface and the extruded surface.

f. Create the seventh feature by using the **Round** tool that will be created on the edges of the extruded surface, refer to Figure 13-129.

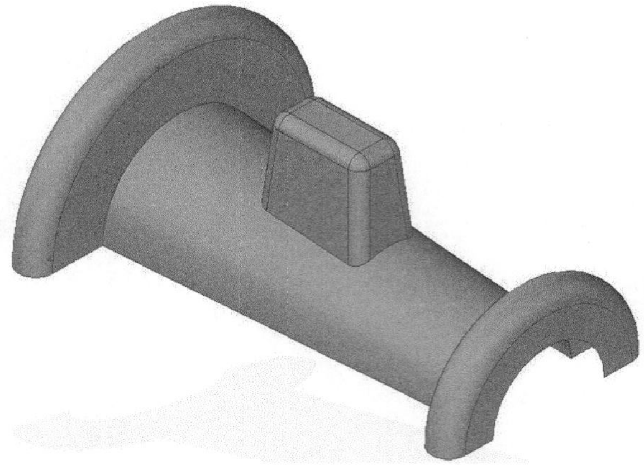

Figure 13-118 Isometric view of the surface model

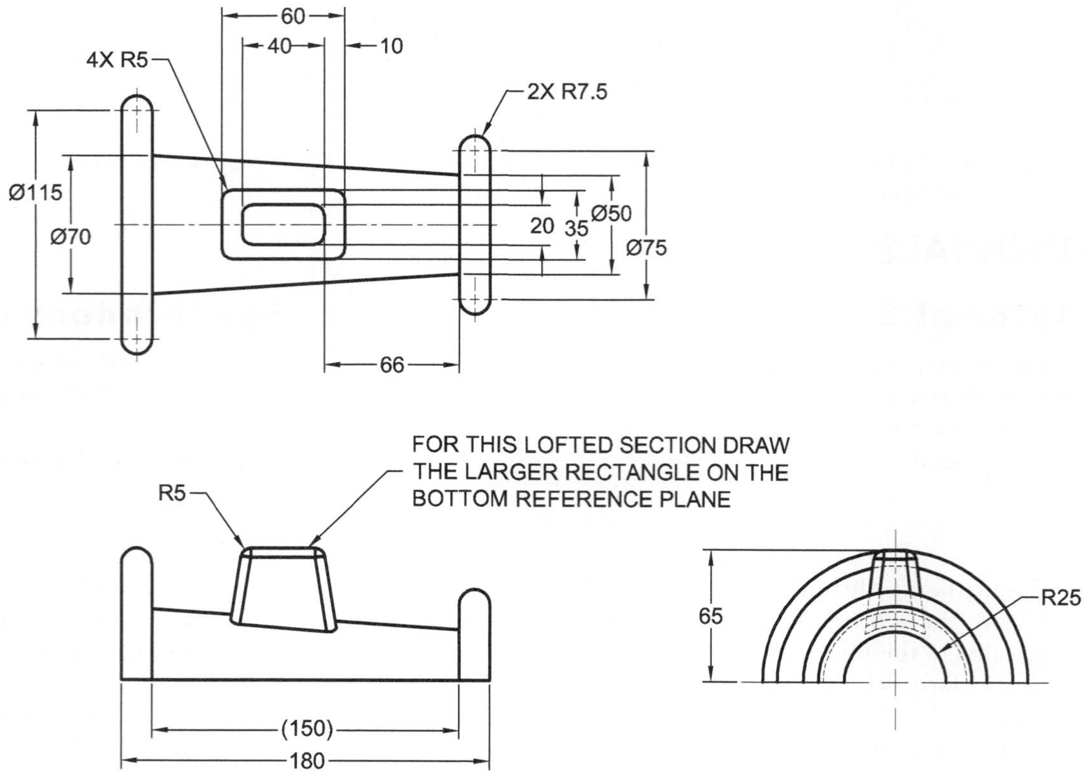

Figure 13-119 Top, front, right-side, and the detailed views of the surface model

Creating the Base Feature

The base feature is a revolved surface whose profile will be drawn on the top plane.

1. Open a new file in the part environment by choosing **ISO Metric Part** from the **Create** area. Next, draw a profile on the XZ plane and apply relations and dimensions to it, as shown in Figure 13-120.

2. Choose the **Revolved** tool from the **Surfaces** group of the **Surfacing** tab; the **Revolved** command bar is displayed and you are prompted to select the profile. Select the profile and choose the **Accept** button; the **Axis of Revolution** button is activated and you are prompted to select the axis.

3. Select the axis and revolve the sketch symmetrically through 180 degrees to create a revolved surface, as shown in Figure 13-121.

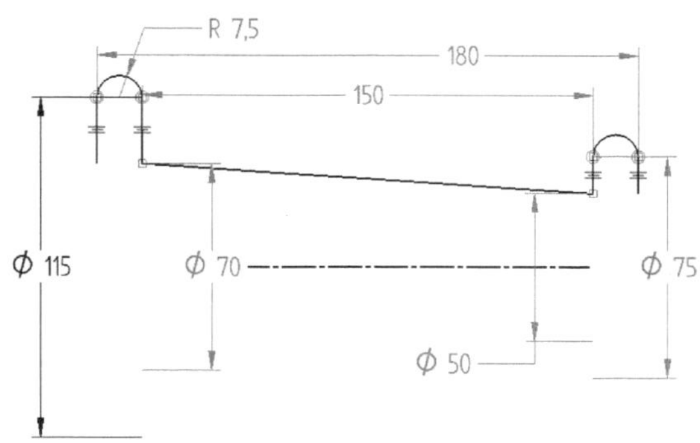

Figure 13-120 *Sketch of the base feature*

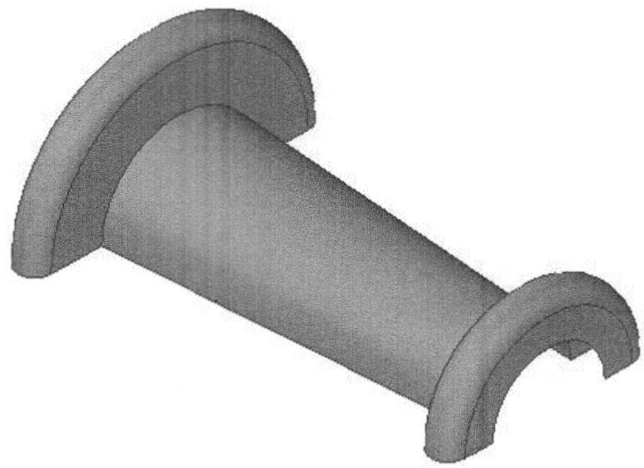

Figure 13-121 *Revolved surface*

4. Choose the **Finish** button and then exit the **Revolved** tool.

Creating the Second Feature

The second feature is an extruded surface whose sketch will be drawn on a plane created at an offset from the top plane.

1. Create a coincident plane on the XY plane and move it to an offset of 65 units from it.

2. Draw the sketch on the newly created plane, as shown in Figure 13-122.

3. Choose the **Extruded** tool from the **Surfaces** group of the **Surfacing** tab; the **Extruded** command bar is displayed and you are prompted to select a profile. Select the sketch and choose the **Accept** button; the **Extent Step** is activated and a preview of the extrusion is displayed. Also, you are prompted to specify the depth of extrusion.

4. Deactivate the **Symmetric Extent** button from the command bar.

5. Specify the depth of extrusion such that the surface is extruded up to the bottom edge of

the base feature. Also, choose the **Open Ends** button in the command bar, if it is not already chosen.

6. Choose the **Treatment Step** button from the command bar and then choose the **Draft** button.

7. Enter the value **5** in the **Angle** edit box and choose the **Flip 1** button.

8. Choose the **Preview** button from the command bar; the extruded surface with the draft is created, as shown in Figure 13-123.

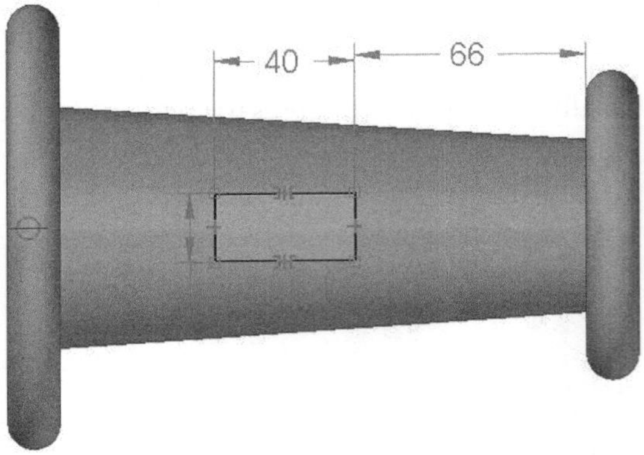

Figure 13-122 *Sketch with dimensions*

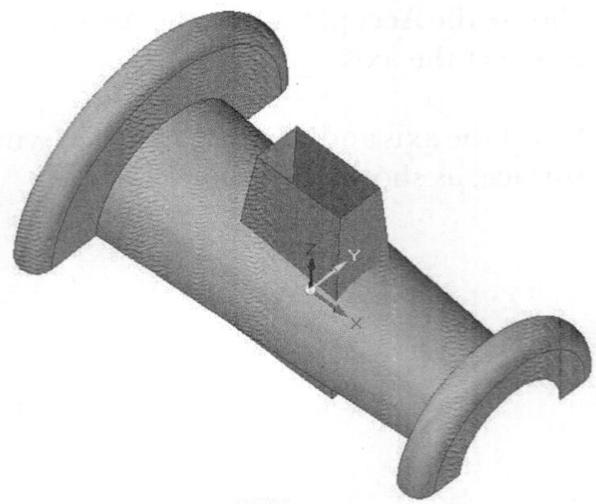

Figure 13-123 *Extruded surface with the draft*

9. Choose the **Finish** button and then the **Cancel** button to exit the **Extruded** tool.

Trimming the Extruded Surface

1. Choose the **Trim** tool from the **Modify Surfaces** group of the **Surfacing** tab; you are prompted to select a body.

   Make sure the **Single** option is selected in the **Select** drop-down list in the command bar so that a single entity can be selected.

2. Select the four vertical faces of the extruded surface. Right-click to accept the selection; you are prompted to select a curve, a face on the surface, or a plane to trim along.

3. Select the middle portion of the revolved surface and right-click to accept.

4. After selecting the surface, you are prompted to click on the region to remove. Select the lower portion of the extruded surface. Next, choose the **Accept** button or right-click.

   The extruded surface is trimmed, as shown in Figure 13-124. You will notice that the extruded surface is closed from the bottom. Therefore, you need to remove the bottom end surface of the revolved surface.

5. Choose the **Trim** tool, if it is not already chosen. Then, select the revolved surface and right-click to accept the selection.

6. Select the four faces of the extruded surface and right-click to accept the selection.

7. After selecting the faces of the extruded surface you are prompted to click on the region to remove. Specify the region to be removed and choose the **Accept** button; the specified surface is trimmed, as shown in Figure 13-125. Next exit the **Trim** tool.

Figure 13-124 *Extruded surface after trimming*

Figure 13-125 *The trimmed bottom surface*

Creating a Bounded Surface

1. Choose the **Bounded** tool from the **Surfaces** group in the **Surfacing** tab; you are prompted to select an edge or curve chain that forms a closed loop.

2. Select the edge chain on the extruded surface, as shown in Figure 13-126.

3. Right-click and choose the **Finish** button to create bounded surface, as shown in Figure 13-127.

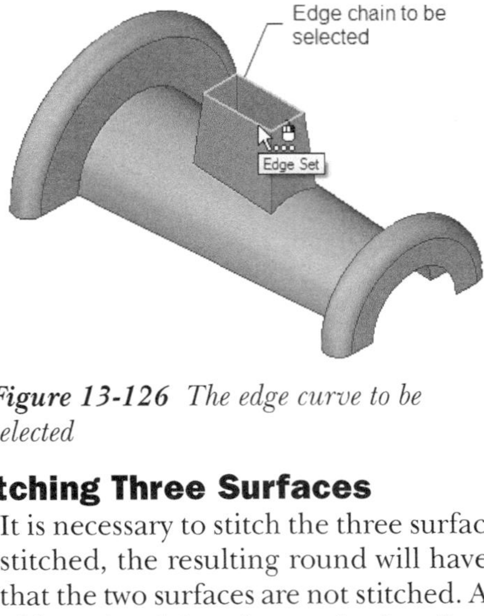

Figure 13-126 *The edge curve to be selected*

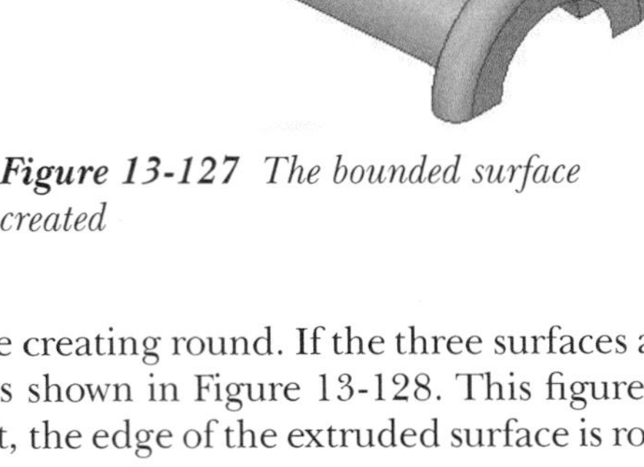

Figure 13-127 *The bounded surface created*

Stitching Three Surfaces

It is necessary to stitch the three surfaces before creating round. If the three surfaces are not stitched, the resulting round will have gaps, as shown in Figure 13-128. This figure shows that the two surfaces are not stitched. As a result, the edge of the extruded surface is rounded without involving the revolved surface.

1. Choose the **Stitched** tool from the **Modify Surfaces** group of the **Surfacing** tab; the **Stitched Surface Options** dialog box is displayed. Enter **1.00e+000 mm** in the **Stitch tolerance** edit box.

2. Choose **OK** and exit the dialog box; you are prompted to select the surfaces.

3. Select the revolved surface, bounded surface, and the drafted extruded surface. Choose the **Accept** button from the command bar; the two surfaces are stitched. Choose the **Finish** button.

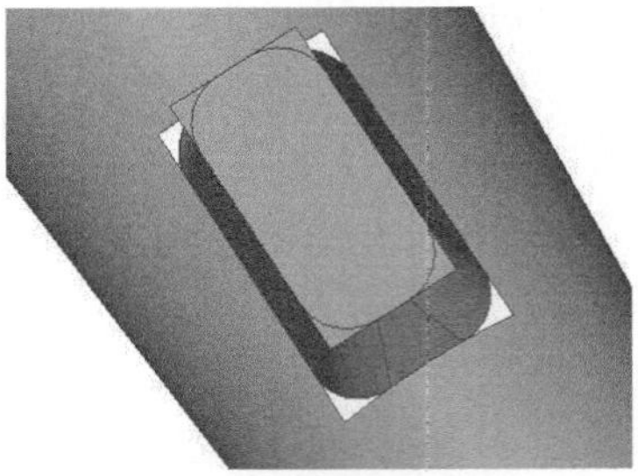

Figure 13-128 *Gaps formed in unstitched surfaces*

Creating the Round

1. Choose the **Round** tool from the **Solids** group of the **Home** tab; you are prompted to select the edges to round.

2. Select the four vertical edges and the four edges on the top face of the extruded surface. Enter **5** in the edit box displayed on the model.

3. Right-click to accept the selection; the round is created, as shown in Figure 13-129.

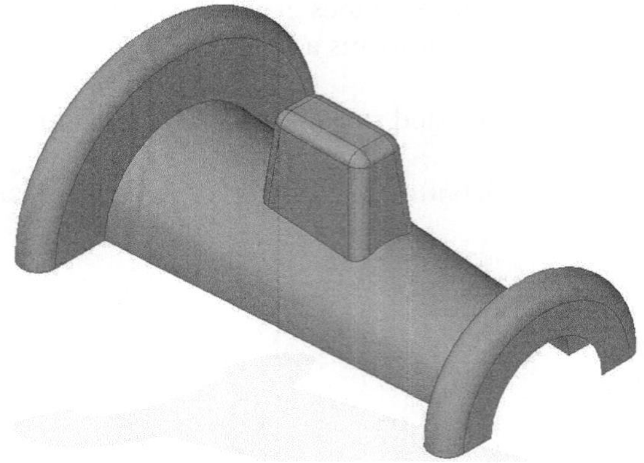

Figure 13-129 *Final surface model*

4. Save the model with the name *c13tut1.par.*

Tutorial 2 — Ordered

In this tutorial, you will create the surface model shown in Figure 13-130 in the **Ordered Part** environment. Its orthographic views are shown in Figure 13-131. After creating the model, save it with the name *c13tut2.par* at the location given next:

C:*Solid Edge**c13* **(Expected time: 45 min)**

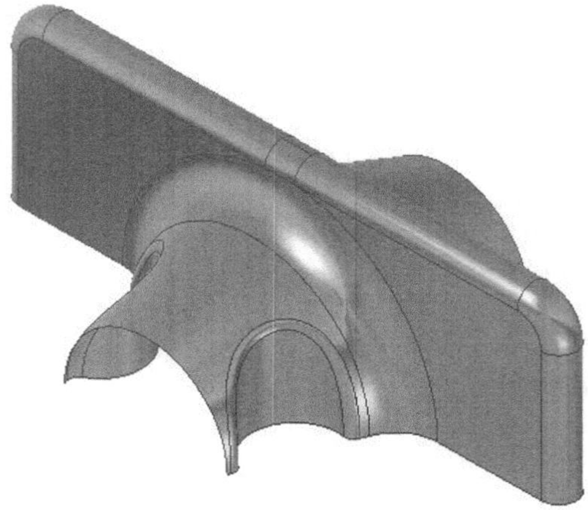

Figure 13-130 Surface model

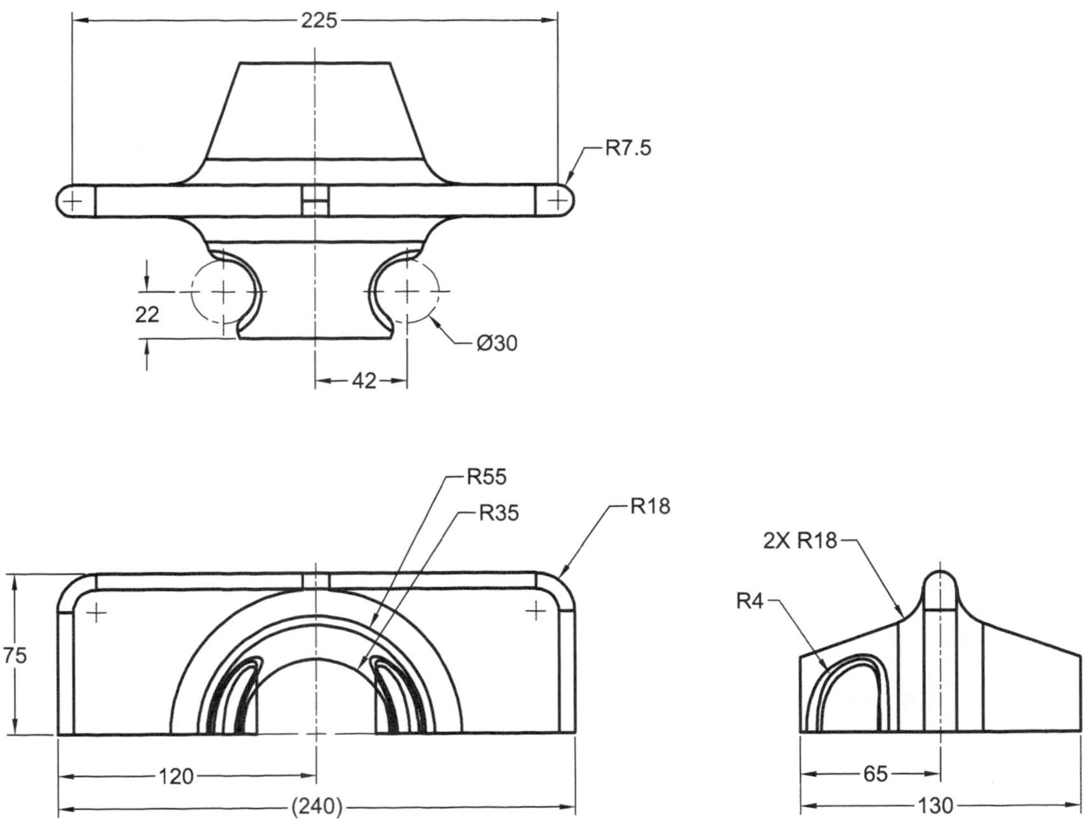

Figure 13-131 Top, front, and right side views of the surface model

The following steps are required to complete this tutorial:

a. Create the base feature on the right plane by using the extruded surface tool, refer to Figures 13-132 and 13-133.

b. Create the second feature by joining the sketches using the **BlueSurf** tool and mirror it about the front plane, refer to Figures 13-134 through 13-136.
c. Create third feature at the end of the extruded feature by using the **BlueSurf** tool, refer to Figure 13-137.
d. Create a cut feature on the second BlueSurface feature and trim it.
e. Create another cut feature by using the mirroring tool on the second feature and trim it.
f. Trim the base feature, refer to Figure 13-143.
g. Stitching all the surfaces of the model.
h. Add the round feature to the surface edges, refer to Figures 13-144 through 13-146.

Creating the Base Feature

The base feature is an extruded surface whose profile will be drawn on the right plane.

1. Open a new file in the part environment. Switch to the **Ordered Part** environment.

2. Choose the **Extruded** tool from the **Surfaces** group of the **Surfacing** tab; you are prompted to select a plane. Select the right plane.

3. Draw the profile for the extruded surface on the right plane and apply the relationships and dimensions to it, as shown in Figure 13-132.

4. Extrude the sketch symmetrically upto a depth of 240 mm; the extruded surface is created, as shown in Figure 13-133.

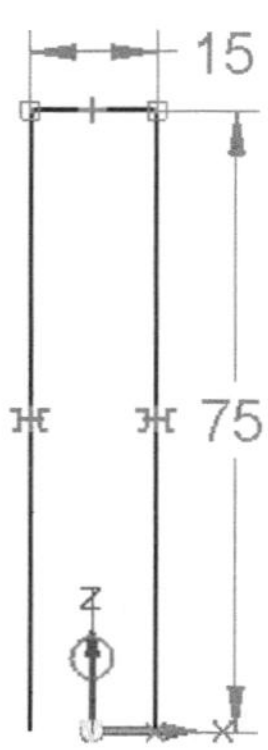

Figure 13-132 Sketch with dimensions

Figure 13-133 Extruded surface

Creating the BlueSurface by Joining Two Sketches

The second feature is the sketch that will be created on the front face of the extruded surface. The third feature is also a sketch that will be created on a parallel plane which is at an offset distance of 65 mm from the front plane. Refer to Figure 13-131 for dimensions.

Now you need to create the BlueSurface.

1. After drawing the two sketches, as shown in Figure 13-134, choose the **BlueSurf** tool from the **Surfaces** group of the **Surfacing** tab; you are prompted to select a sketch, an edge chain, or a curve chain.

2. Select a sketch, refer to Figure 13-134, and right-click. Select the other sketch and right-click to accept the selection. While selecting the sketches, remember that the keypoints should not overlap.

3. After selecting the sketches, choose the **Next** button; the BlueSurface is created with open ends, as shown in Figure 13-135. Choose the **Finish** button and then the **Cancel** button to exit the command bar.

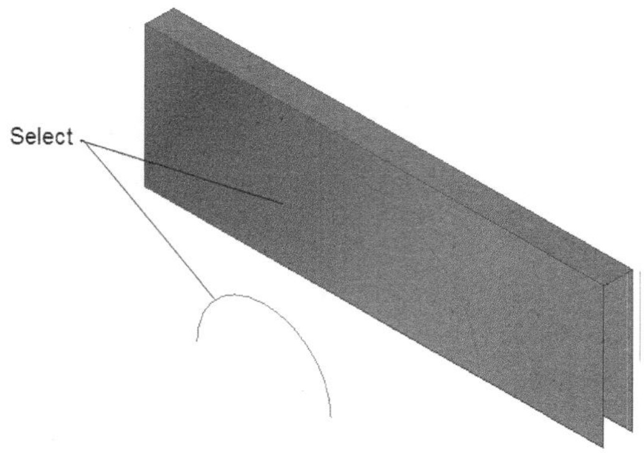

Figure 13-134 *Two sketches*

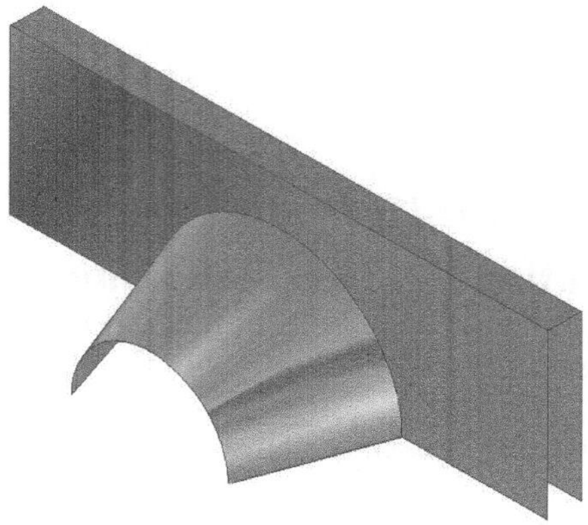

Figure 13-135 *BlueSurface with open ends*

4. Choose the **Mirror Copy Part** tool from the **Mirror Copy Feature** drop-down in the **Pattern** group of the **Surfacing** tab; you are prompted to select a surface or a curve.

5. Select the BlueSurface and right-click; you are prompted to select a planar face or a reference plane about which the mirroring will take place.

6. Select the front plane; a mirror copy of the BlueSurface is created, as shown in Figure 13-136. Choose the **Finish** button and then the **Cancel** button.

Creating the BlueSurface at the End of the Extruded Surface

Next, you need to create the BlueSurface to close the ends of the extruded surface.

1. Choose the **BlueSurf** tool from the **Surfaces** group of the **Surfacing** tab; you are prompted to select a sketch, an edge chain, or a curve chain.

2. Select the edge of the base surface, refer to Figure 13-137, as the cross-section and then choose the **Accept** button.

3. Choose the **Guide Curve Step** button from the command bar and then select the other edge of the base surface, refer to Figure 13-137. Choose the **Accept** button, the **Next** button and then the **Finish** button. Next, exit the tool; the BlueSurface is created, as shown in Figure 13-137.

4. After creating the BlueSurface, create a mirror copy of it so that the other end of the extruded surface is also closed.

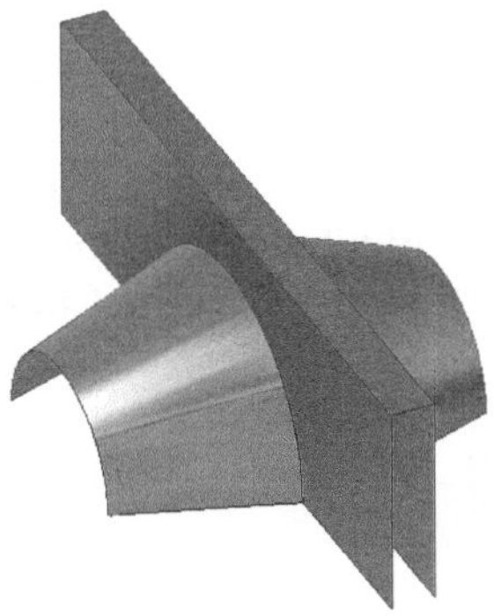

Figure 13-136 Mirror copy created

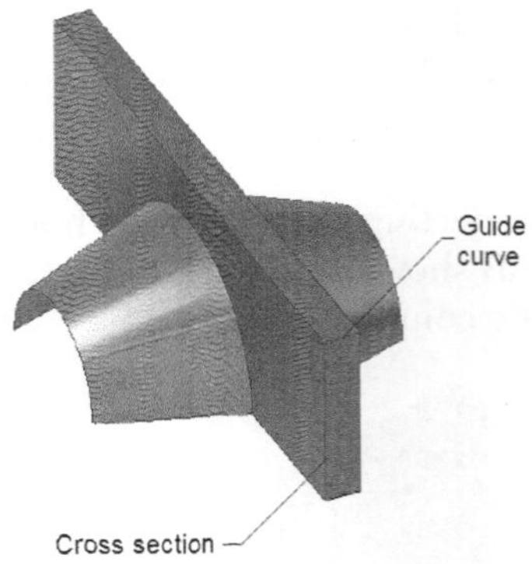

Figure 13-137 BlueSurface created

Creating the Cut on the BlueSurface

To create a cut on the BlueSurface, you first need to create a cylindrical surface. Then this surface will be used to trim the BlueSurface, thus creating the cut.

1. Create a parallel plane in the downward direction at a distance of 35 mm from the top face of the base feature and then draw the sketch. For the sketch and its dimensions, refer to Figure 13-131. Next, choose the **Extruded** tool from the **Surfaces** group of the **Surfacing** tab.

2. Extrude the sketch up to the vertex of the bottom edge of the BlueSurface, see Figure 13-138.

Note

If the sketch that is drawn to create the cylindrical surface is not extruded up to the vertex of the BlueSurface, then you will not be able to trim the surfaces later.

3. After creating the cylindrical surface, choose the **Intersect** tool from the **Modify Surfaces** group of the **Surfacing** tab; you are prompted to select the intersecting surfaces.

4. Select the BlueSurface and cylindrical surface, as shown in Figure 13-139 and right-click to accept the selection; you are prompted to select the edges to extend or regions to remove.

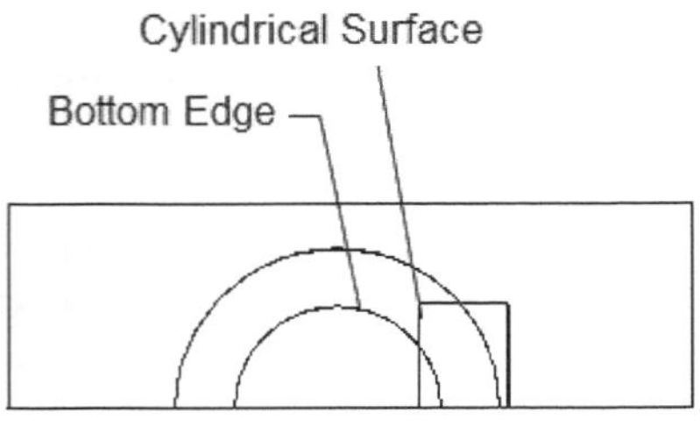

Figure 13-138 Cylindrical surface

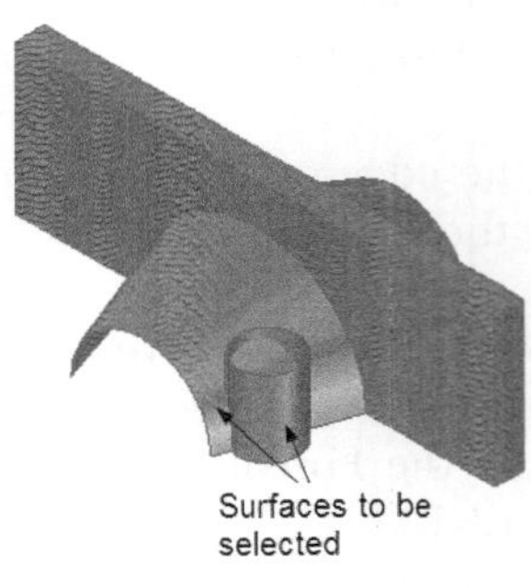

Figure 13-139 Surfaces used for trimming

5. Select the outer portion of the cylinder and intersected portion of the BlueSurface; the selected portions will be removed, as shown in Figure 13-140.

6. Right-click to accept. Next, choose **Finish** and then **Cancel** to exit the **Intersect** tool.

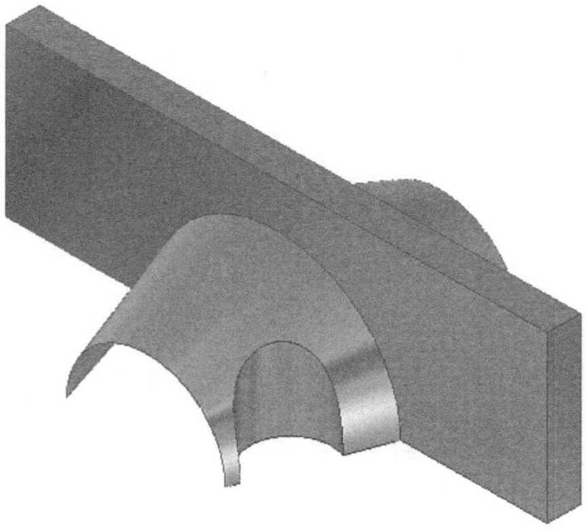

Figure 13-140 Trimmed BlueSurface

Creating a Cut on the Left of the BlueSurface

The cut on the left will be created by mirroring the trimmed surface created on the right. The mirrored surface will be used to trim the other side of the BlueSurface.

1. Mirror the cut feature to the left side, see Figure 13-141. Choose the **Intersect** tool; you are prompted to select a body.

2. Select the BlueSurface and mirrored surface, and then right-click to accept; you are prompted to select an edge to extend or region to remove.

3. Select the intersected portion of the BlueSurface to trim it, as shown in Figure 13-142.

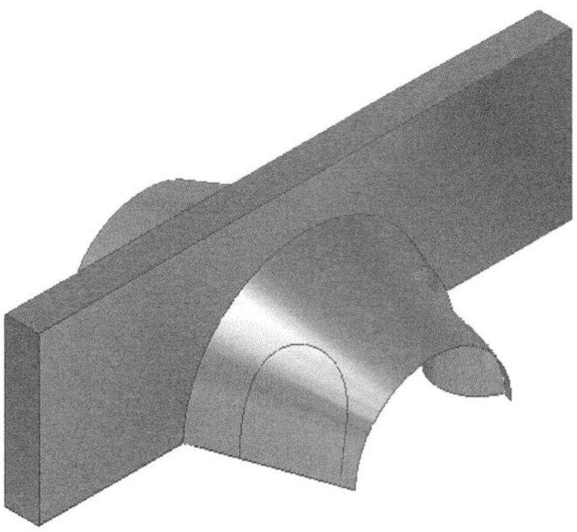

Figure 13-141 Surface after mirroring

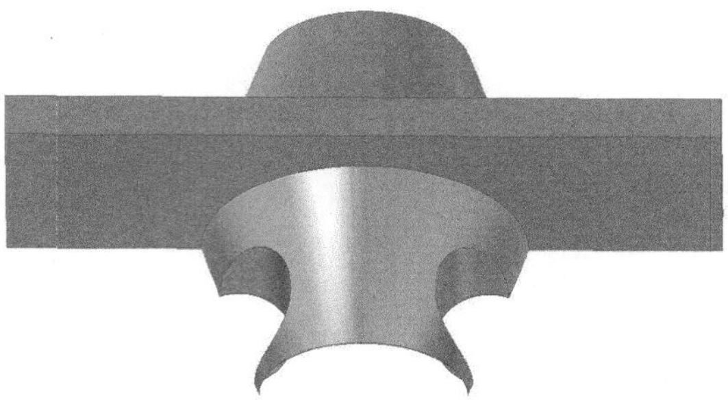

Figure 13-142 Trimmed mirror surface

Trimming the Extruded Surface

To trim the extruded surface, you need to use the semi-circular edge of the BlueSurface that intersects the extruded surface.

1. If the **Intersect** tool is not already invoked, choose it from the **Modify Surfaces** group of the **Surfacing** tab; you are prompted to select two or more surfaces.

2. Select the base feature and the two BlueSurfaces, and then right-click; you are prompted to select the regions that are to be removed.

3. Select the regions of the base feature lying at inner side of the BlueSurface; the regions are removed.

4. Choose the **Accept** button. Next, choose **Finish** and **Cancel** to exit the tool. The model after trimming the extruded surfaces is shown in Figure 13-143.

Figure 13-143 *Extruded surfaces after trimming*

Stitching the Surfaces

It is necessary to stitch all surfaces before creating the round. The steps required to stitch the surfaces are as follows:

1. Choose the **Stitched** tool from the **Modify Surfaces** group of the **Surfacing** tab; the **Stitched Surface Options** dialog box is displayed. Make sure the value 1.00e+000 mm is displayed in the **Stitch tolerance** edit box.

2. Choose **OK** to exit the dialog box; you are prompted to select the surfaces.

3. Select all surfaces one by one and then choose the **Accept** button from the command bar; the surfaces are stitched. Choose **Finish** and then **Cancel** to exit the tool.

Adding the Round Feature

After stitching the surfaces, create the rounds of radii 4 and 18.

1. Choose the **Round** tool from the **Round** drop-down of the **Solids** group in the **Home** tab; you are prompted to select the edges to round.

2. Select one of the edges of the trim feature on the BlueSurface designated as 1, see Figure 13-144. Then, enter **4** in the **Radius** edit box; a round of radius equal to **4** units is created.

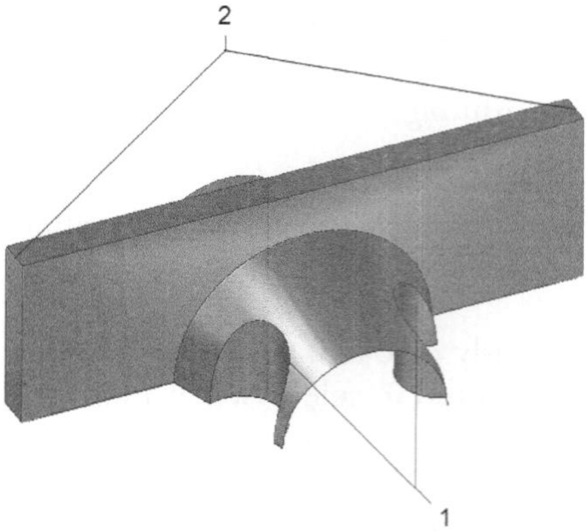

Figure 13-144 *Edges to be selected*

3. Choose the **Accept** button from the command bar and then choose the **Preview** button; the round is created, as shown in Figure 13-145.

4. Choose the **Finish** button. Select the two edges designated by 2, refer to Figure 13-144 and the edges at the front and back of the extruded surface.

5. Enter **18** in the **Radius** edit box and choose the **Accept** button.

6. Choose **Preview** and then the **Finish** button.

7. Similarly, create the remaining rounds. For dimensions, refer to Figure 13-131. The surface model after creating all rounds is shown in Figure 13-146.

8. Choose the **Save** button to save the model with the name *c13tut2.par*.

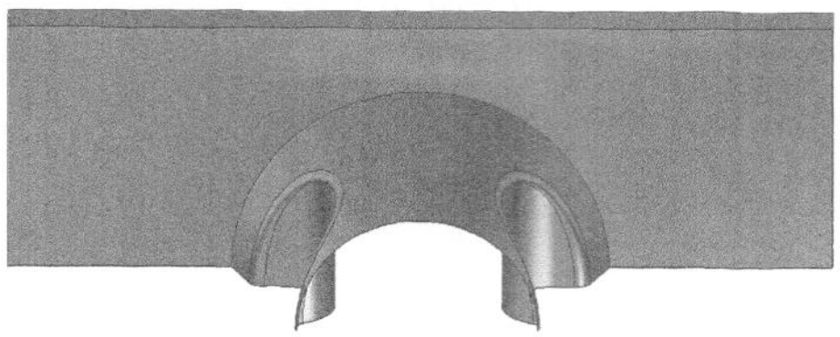

Figure 13-145 *Round of radius value 4*

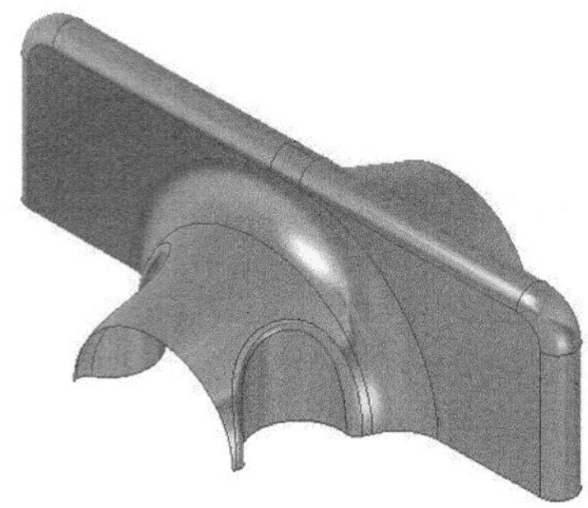

Figure 13-146 *Model after creating all rounds*

Self-Evaluation Test

Answer the following questions and then compare them to those given at the end of this chapter:

1. The _______ tool is used to connect two sketched curves in the part environment.

2. The ________ tool is used to create a curve at the intersection of two surfaces.

3. In Solid Edge, you can extend a surface using the _______ ,_______,and ______ methods.

4. Remember that after the faces are replaced by using the ________ tool, the replacement surface is automatically hidden.

5. The _________ tool is used to project curves on the surfaces.

6. The _________ tool is used to create 3D curves by joining keypoints on an existing geometry.

7. You can create a surface with closed ends by drawing an open sketch. (T/F)

8. Surface models do not have any thickness. (T/F)

9. The **BlueSurf** tool is used to create surfaces only. (T/F)

10. You can trim two surfaces by selecting them individually. (T/F)

Review Questions

Answer the following questions:

1. Which of the following is the range of the stitch tolerance for the **Stitched** tool?

   (a) **1.00e-005 to 1.00e+003** (b) **1.00e+005 to 1.00e-000**
   (c) **1.00e-005 to 1.00e+000** (d) **1.00e-000 to 1.00e+005**

2. Which of the following tabs in the **Ribbon** is used to create surface models?

   (a) **Surfacing** (b) **Solids**
   (c) **Home** (d) None of these

3. Which of the following dialog boxes is used to set the stitch tolerance?

   (a) **Sweep Options** (b) **Stitched Surface Options**
   (c) **Stitched** (d) None of these

4. Before adding thickness to a set of surfaces, they should be ________.

   (a) trimmed (b) merged
   (c) stitched (d) None of these

5. The _________ surface is used for creating molds, core, and cavity.

6. The ends of a surface can be closed by using the **BlueSurf** tool. (T/F)

7. Surface models do not have mass properties. (T/F)

8. You can select an open sketch to create a bounded surface by using the **Bounded** tool. (T/F)

9. You can add thickness to a surface. (T/F)

10. A curve that is used for trimming must lie on the surface to be trimmed. (T/F)

EXERCISES

Exercise 1

Create the surface model shown in Figure 13-147. Its orthographic views and dimensions are shown in Figure 13-148. After creating the model, save it with the name *c13exr1.par* at the location given next.

C:*Solid Edge\c13*

(Expected time: 30 min)

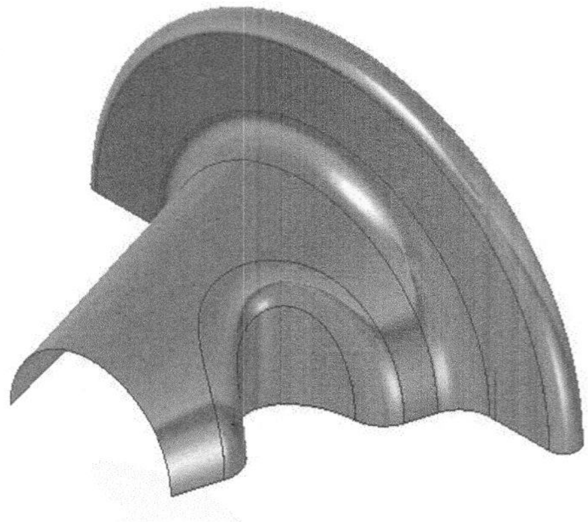

Figure 13-147 Surface model

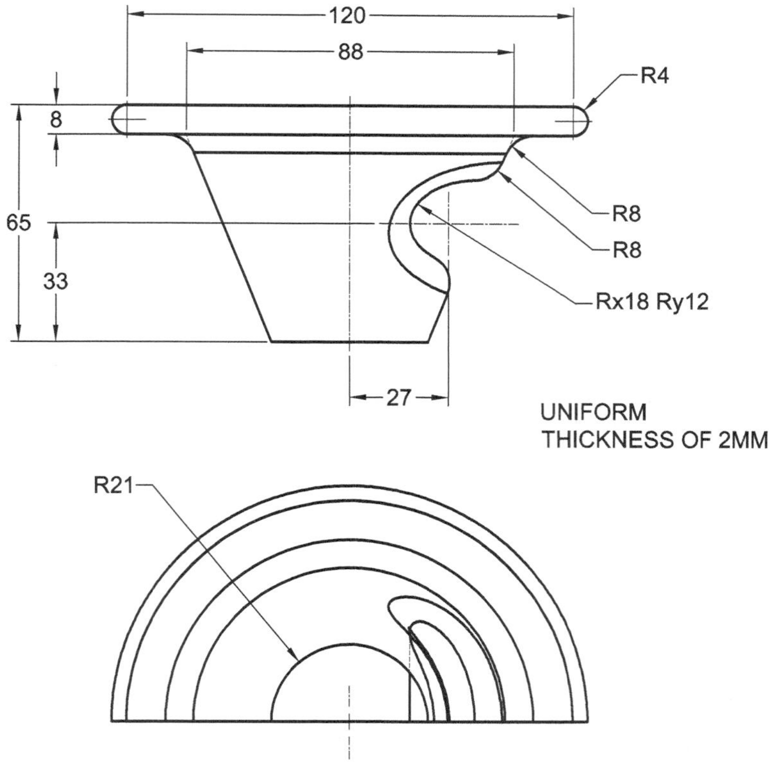

Figure 13-148 Top and front views

Exercise 2

Create the surface model shown in Figure 13-149. The orthographic views of the model with the dimensions are shown in the Figure 13-150. After creating the model, save it with the name *c13exr2.par* at the location given next.

C:*Solid Edge\c13* **(Expected time: 30 min)**

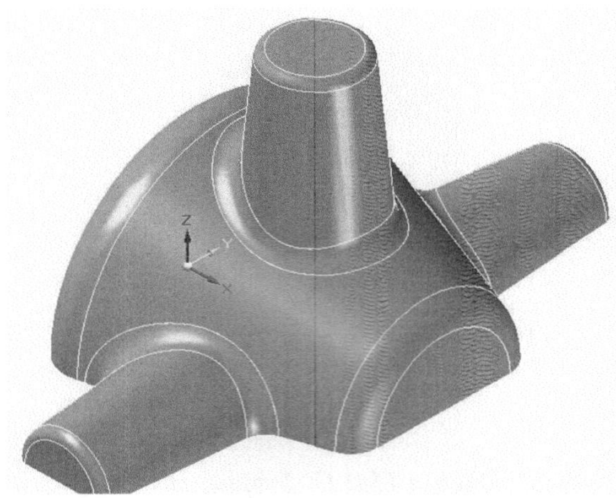

Figure 13-149 Isometric view of the surface model

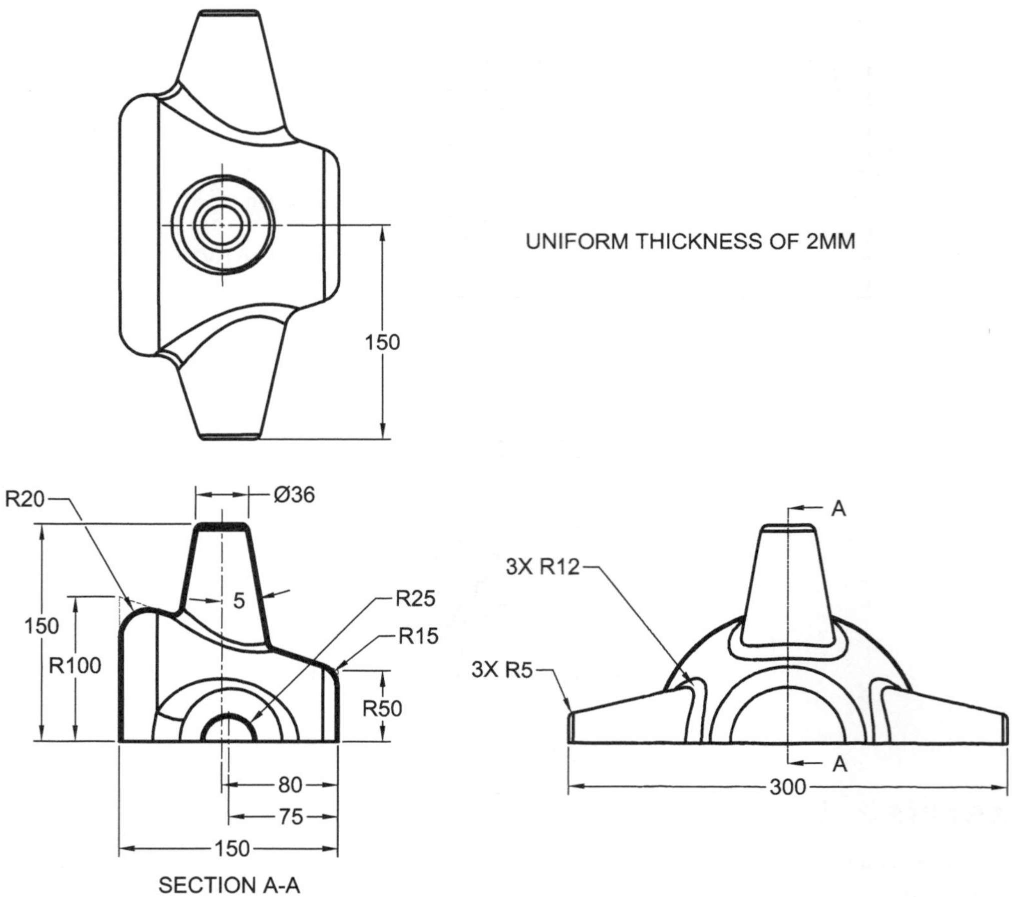

Figure 13-150 Orthographic views of the surface model

Exercise 3

In this exercise, you will create the surface model shown in Figure 13-151. The orthographic views of the surface model are shown in Figure 13-152. After creating the model, save it with the name *c13exr3.par* at the location given next.

C:*Solid Edge\c13* **(Expected time: 55 min)**

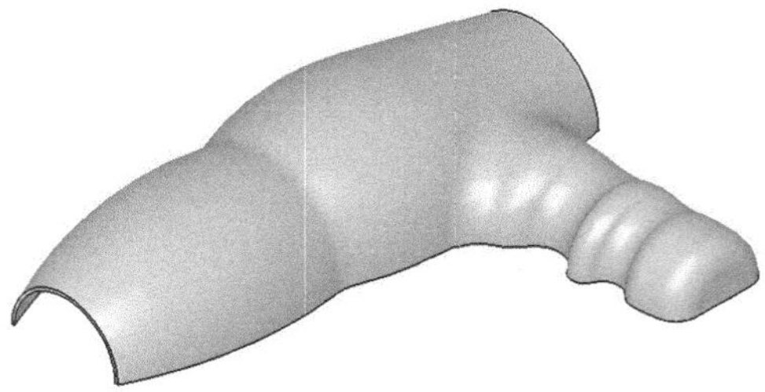

Figure 13-151 *Model of the Hair Dryer Cover*

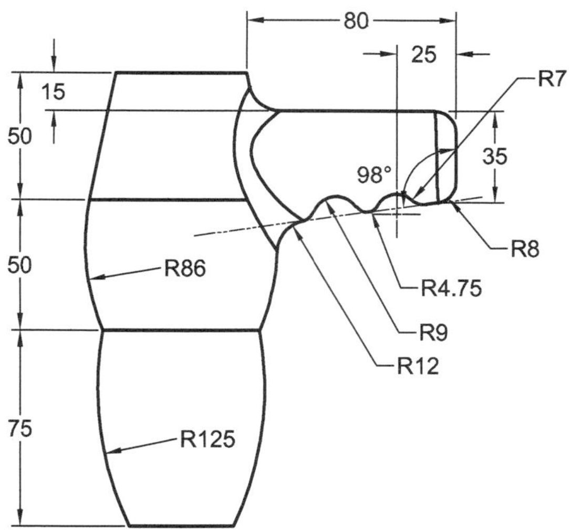

S.No.	RADIUS OF THE SECTION
1	20
2	30
3	35
4	25

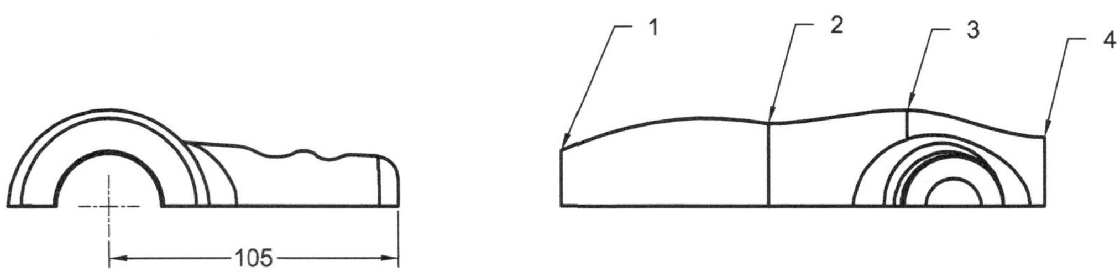

Figure 13-152 *Orthographic views and dimensions for the model*

Answers to Self-Evaluation Test

1. **BlueDot**, 2. **Intersection**, 3. **Reflective** extent, **Curvature Continuous**, **Linear** extent, 4. **Replace Face**, 5. **Project**, 6. **Keypoint Curve**, 7. F, 8. T, 9. T, 10. T

Chapter 14

Sheet Metal Design

Learning Objectives

After completing this chapter, you will be able to:
- *Set the parameters for creating the sheet metal parts*
- *Create the base of the sheet metal part*
- *Add various types of flanges to the sheet metal part*
- *Add a jog to the sheet metal part*
- *Bend or unbend a part of the sheet metal part*
- *Add corner bends to the sheet metal parts*
- *Create dimples, louvers, drawn cutouts, and beads in the sheet metal component*
- *Convert solid parts into sheet metal parts*
- *Create the flat pattern of the sheet metal parts*

THE SHEET METAL MODULE

The component with a thickness greater than 0 and less than 12 mm is called a sheet metal component. Sheet metal fabrication is a chipless process and is an easy way to create components by using the manufacturing processes such as bending, stamping, and so on.

A sheet metal component of uniform thickness is shown in Figure 14-1. It is not possible to machine such a thin component. Therefore, after creating the sheet metal component, you need to flatten it in order to find the strip layout. Based on this layout detail, you can design the punch and die. Figure 14-2 shows the flattened view of the sheet metal component.

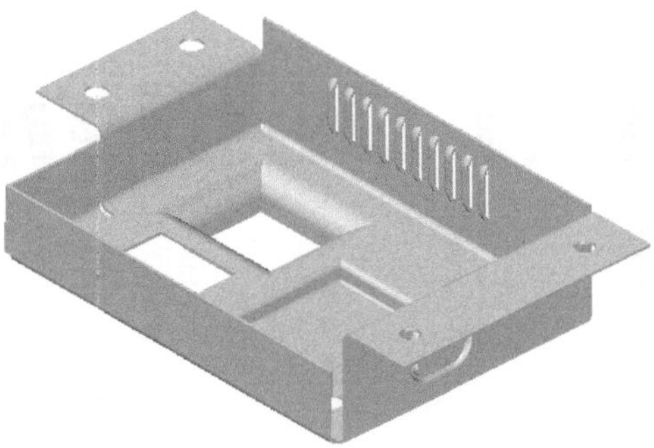

Figure 14-1 *Sheet metal component*

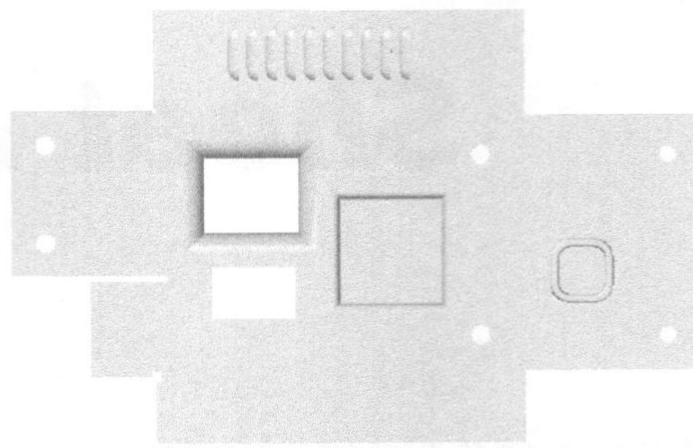

Figure 14-2 *Flattened view of the sheet metal component*

Note

All the features of a sheet metal component cannot be flattened. For example, features such as louvers, dimples, and so on cannot be flattened because they are created using a punch and a die.

Solid Edge allows you to create the sheet metal components in a special environment called the **Sheet Metal** environment. This environment provides all the tools that are required for creating the sheet metal components.

To start a new sheetmetal document in the **Synchronous Sheet Metal** environment, click on the **Application Button** and choose **New > ISO Metric Sheet Metal** from the Application menu, as shown in Figure 14-3. Alternatively, you can double-click on **iso metric sheet metal.psm** in the **New** dialog box to start a new document in the **Synchronous Sheet Metal** environment, refer to Figure 14-4. In the **Sheet Metal** environment, the **Sheet Metal** group in the **Ribbon** provides the tools that are required to create the sheet metal components. The default screen of **Synchronous Sheet Metal** environment is shown in Figure 14-5. In this environment, the sheet metal tools will not be activated until you draw a sketch to create the base for the sheet metal. After drawing the sketch, most of the sheet metal tools will become active automatically.

The Synchronous tools in this environment allow you to combine the flexibility of direct modeling and the ability to control its editing with respect to the constraints. This will enable you to dynamically add material, remove material, create flanges, and much more.

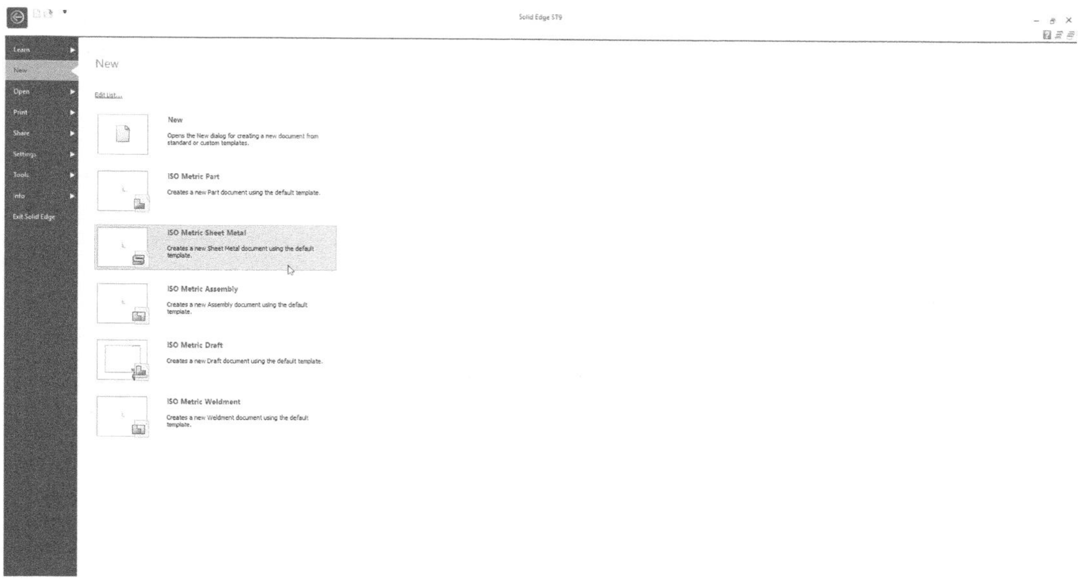

*Figure 14-3 Starting the **Sheet Metal** environment using the **New** tab of the welcome screen*

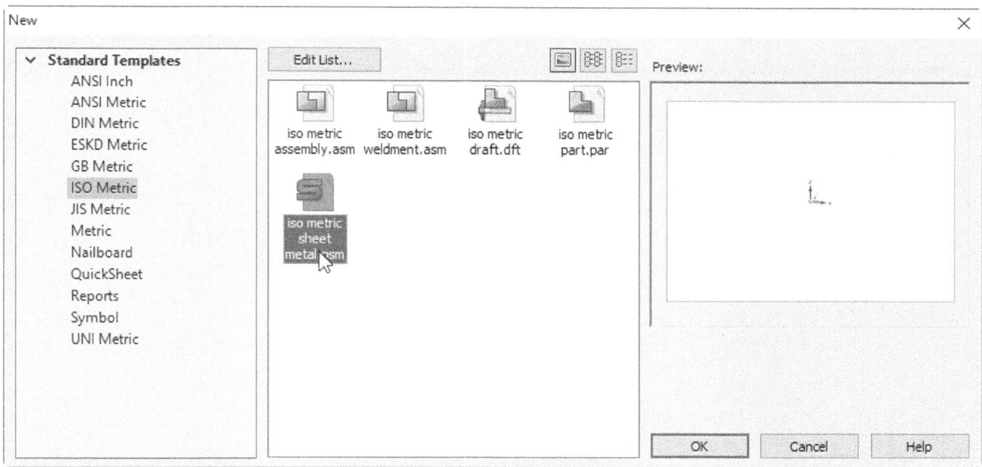

Figure 14-4 Starting a new sheet metal document

Note

*Sheet metal parts are saved in the *.psm format.*

SETTING THE SHEET METAL PART PROPERTIES

Application Button: Info > Material Table

Before you start creating the base of the sheet metal part, it is recommended that you set the options related to it. These options control the default values of the sheet thickness, bend radius, relief depth, and relief width that will be displayed in various tools.

To set these options, choose **Application Button > Info > Material Table**; the **Material Table** dialog box will be displayed with the **Material Properties** tab chosen. Choose the **Gage Properties** tab from this dialog box to display the parameters related to the sheet metal part, refer to Figure 14-6. The options available in the **Gage Properties** tab are discussed next.

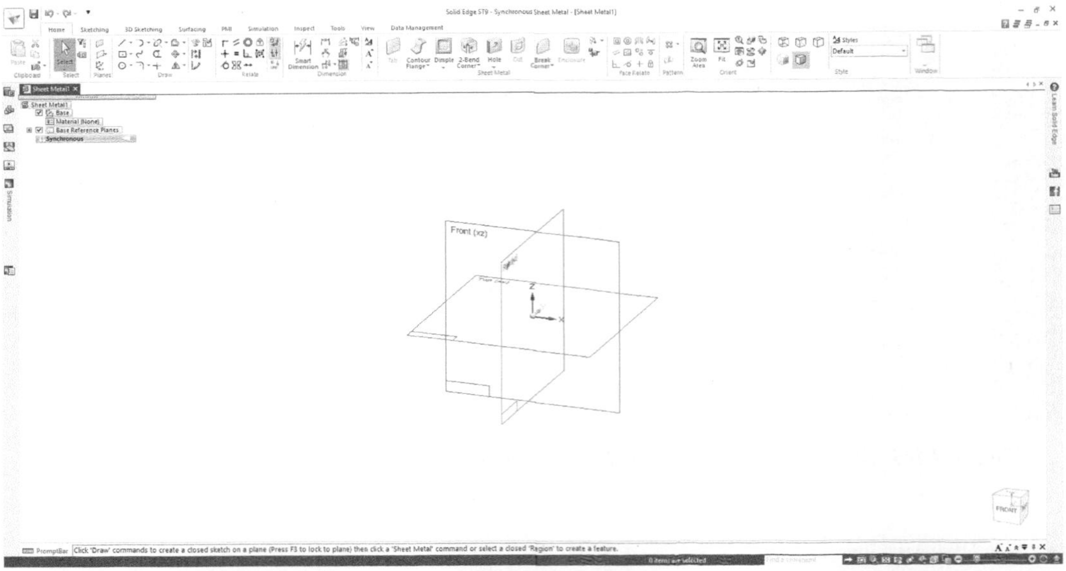

***Figure 14-5** Default screen of the **Synchronous Sheet Metal** environment*

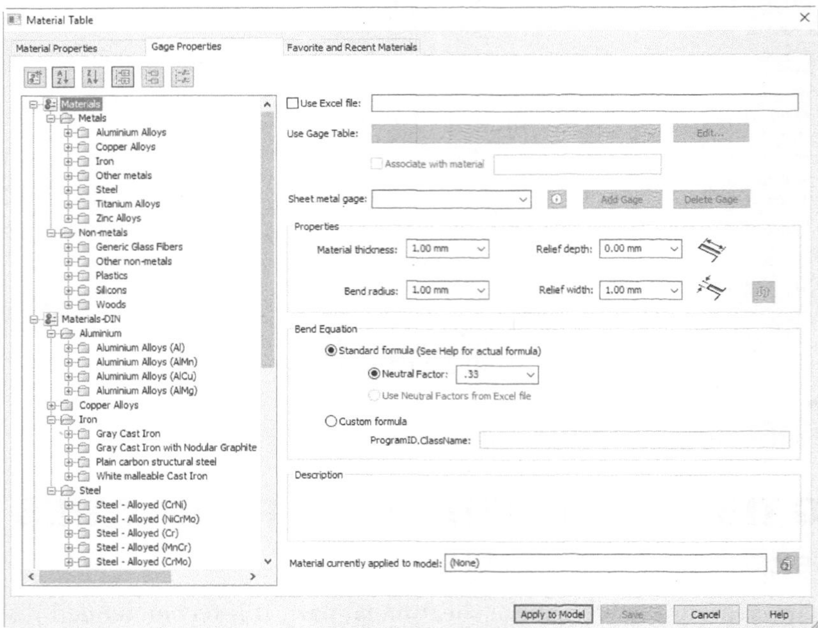

***Figure 14-6** The **Gage Properties** tab of the **Solid Edge Material Table** dialog box*

Use Excel file

In Solid Edge, you can save the sheet metal gage information in an Excel sheet. To do so, select the check box on the left of the **Use Excel file** option; the browser, the **Edit** button, and the **Use Gage Table** drop-down list will be activated. You can select the desired gage type from this drop-down list.

Use Gage Table

This drop-down list is used to select the gage type from the default gage type list present in Solid Edge. You can create a new gage file by choosing the **Edit** button next to the **Use Gage Table** drop-down list. To do so, choose the **Edit** button; a Microsoft Excel sheet will be displayed. Enter the new gage values in the excel sheet and save them with their respective names.

Sheet metal gage

This drop-down list is used to set the default gage size for the sheet metal part. The other parameters are automatically defined once you set the default sheet gage from this drop-down list. By default, no gage size is selected. As a result, you can set the custom parameters for the sheet metal part. You can add the new gage by entering the gage value in the Sheet metal gage edit box and then choose the **Add Gage** button next to the **Sheet Metal Gage** drop-down.

You can also delete the gages from this drop-down by using the **Delete Gage** button. Note that you will not be able to select the gage size from this drop-down list until you select the **Use Excel file** check box.

Properties Area

The options in this area are discussed next.

Material thickness

This edit box is used to set the default thickness for the sheet metal part. The thickness specified in this edit box will be displayed as the default thickness whenever you invoke a tool to create the sheet metal part.

Note

While creating a sheet metal part, it is not necessary to accept the default sheet thickness. You can modify the default thickness as per your requirement.

Bend radius

This edit box is used to set the default value for the bend radius. This value is used while adding flanges to the model or while bending it. Figure 14-7 shows a sheet folded with a radius of 1 mm and Figure 14-8 shows a sheet folded with a radius of 5 mm.

Relief depth

Whenever you bend a sheet metal component or create a flange such that the bend does not extend throughout the length of the edge, a groove is added at the end of the bend so that the walls of the sheet metal part do not intersect when folded or unfolded. This groove is known as relief. You can set a predefined depth for the relief using the **Relief depth** edit box. Figure 14-9 shows a sheet metal part with relief depth of 2 mm and Figure 14-10 shows a sheet metal part with relief depth of 5 mm.

Figure 14-7 Sheet with 1 mm bend radius

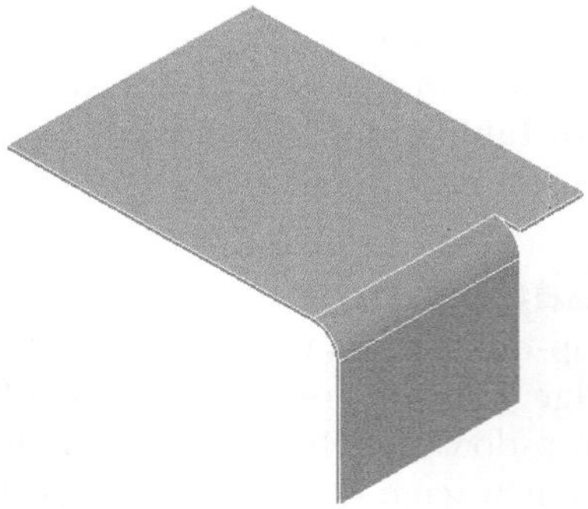

Figure 14-8 Sheet with 5 mm bend radius

Figure 14-9 Relief depth = 2 mm

Figure 14-10 Relief depth = 5 mm

Relief width

The **Relief width** edit box is used to specify the value of the width of the relief. The **default** value of the relief width is equal to the thickness of the sheet. Figure 14-11 shows a sheet metal component with a relief width of 1 mm and Figure 14-12 shows a sheet metal component with a relief width of 5 mm.

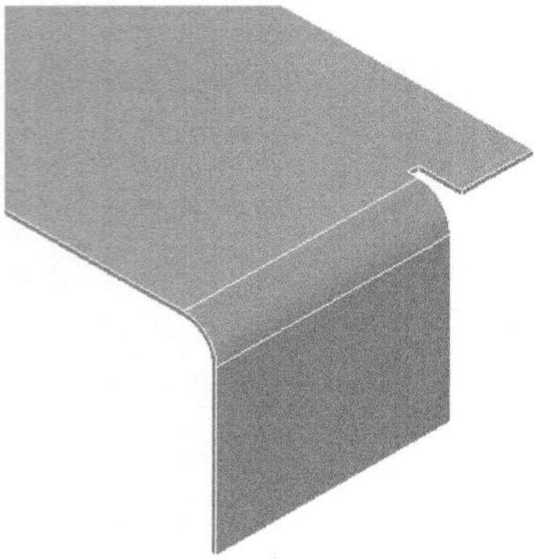

Figure 14-11 Relief width = 1mm

Figure 14-12 Relief width = 5 mm

After performing the required settings, choose the **Apply to Model** button to apply the settings to the model.

CREATING THE BASE FEATURE OF THE SHEET METAL PART

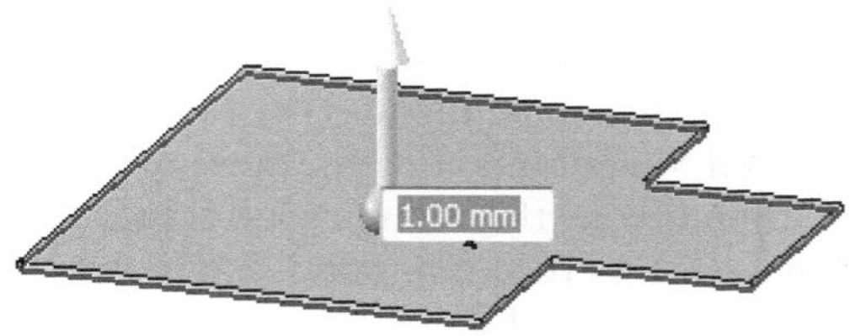

Figure 14-13 Creating the base of the sheet metal component

The tools used for creating the base feature in the **Synchronous Sheet Metal** environment are not active by default. To activate these tools, draw the sketch of the base feature and select it; an extrude handle will be displayed, as shown in Figure 14-13. Also, the **Tab** Command bar will be displayed. Note that you can also choose the **Tab** tool from the **Sheet Metal** group and then select the sketch. Click on the desired direction of the handle. Note that no matter how long you drag the handle, the tab will be created based on the thickness specified in the **Solid Edge Material Table** dialog box. You can invoke this dialog box from the Application menu and the Command bar. You can also specify the thickness of the tab feature by entering the desired value in the edit box displayed on the handle.

In the **Ordered Sheet Metal** environment, the **Tab** tool in the **Sheet Metal** group of the **Home** tab is used to create the base of the sheet metal component. You can also use this tool to add additional faces on the sheet metal component. To create the base of the sheet metal part, invoke this tool; the **Tab** Command bar will be displayed and the **Sketch Step** will be activated. You can draw the sketch for the base or select an existing sketch.

After drawing or selecting the sketch, the **Thickness Step** will be activated and the **Thickness** edit box will be displayed. You can enter the thickness value of the sheet in this edit box. Next, specify the side of feature creation; the base of the sheet metal will be created. Figure 14-14 shows the sketch for the base and Figure 14-15 shows the base of the sheet metal component.

Note

*In the **Ordered Part** environment, you can use the **Contour Flange** and **Lofted Flange** options to create the base feature.*

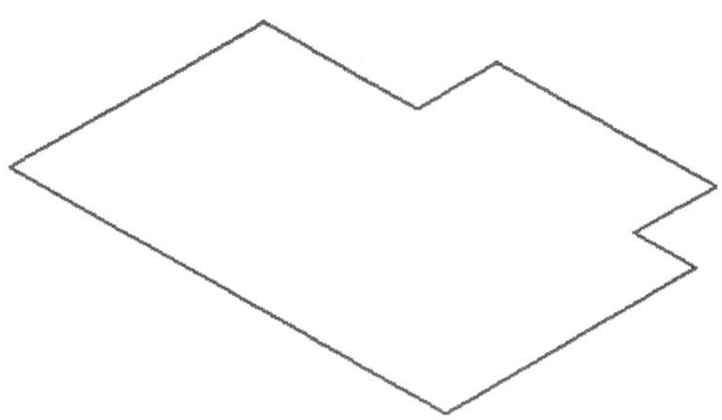

Figure 14-14 Sketch of the base of the sheet metal component

Figure 14-15 Base of the sheet metal component

ADDING FLANGES TO A SHEET METAL PART

Ribbon: Home > Sheet Metal > Flange

Flange is the bend section of the sheet metal. Solid Edge allows you to directly add a folded face to the existing sheet metal part. This is done using the **Flange** tool. This tool is available in the **Ordered Sheet Metal** environment only. First, switch to the **Ordered Sheet Metal** environment and then invoke the **Flange** tool. When you invoke this tool, the **Flange** Command bar will be displayed. It is recommended that before you create the flange, you should set its options. To do so, choose the **Flange Options** button from the Command bar; the **Flange Options** dialog box will be displayed, as shown in Figure 14-16.

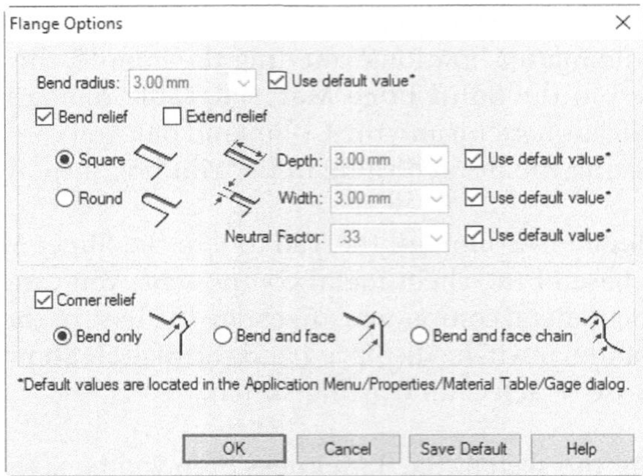

*Figure 14-16 The **Flange Options** dialog box*

Flange Options Dialog Box

The options in the **Flange Options** dialog box are discussed next.

Bend radius

This edit box is used to specify the bend radius. By default, the **Use default value*** check box is selected. As a result, the default value that was set using the **Gage Properties** tab of the **Solid Edge Material Table** dialog box will be used as the bend radius. If you want to modify the value, clear the **Use default value*** check box and then enter the required value in the **Bend radius** edit box.

Bend relief

This check box is used to specify whether or not the bend relief will be added. If this check box is selected, the other options to add the relief will be activated. You can add a square shape relief or a round shape relief. You can use the default value of the relief depth, width, and neutral factor or enter a new value in the corresponding edit boxes. Figure 14-17 shows a sheet metal part with a square relief and Figure 14-18 shows a sheet metal part with a round relief.

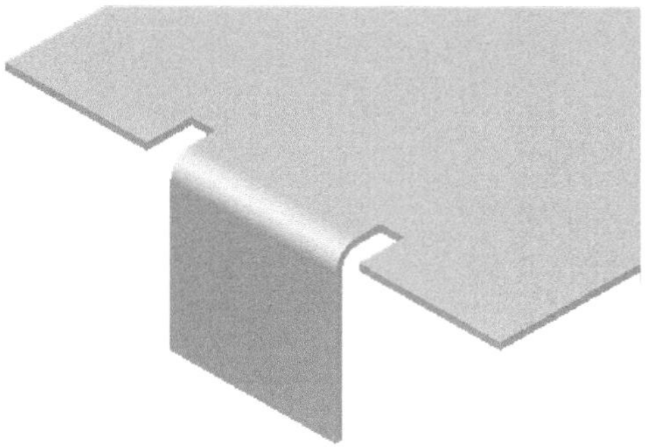

Figure 14-17 Part with square relief

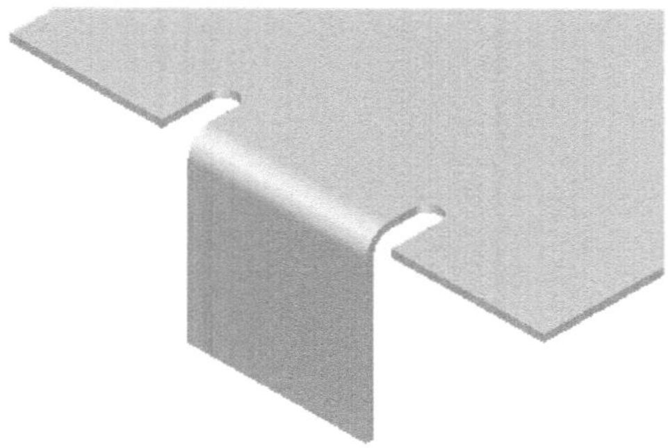

Figure 14-18 Part with round relief

Extend relief

Select this check box to extend the relief to the entire face of the sheet metal part. By default, this check box is cleared. As a result, the relief is applied only to the portion that is adjacent to the flange that you are creating.

Corner relief

This check box is selected by default and is used to add a corner relief to the flange. A corner relief is added when the flange termination forms a corner with another flange. Figure 14-19 shows flanges with no corner relief. You can add three different types of corner reliefs by selecting their corresponding radio buttons. Figure 14-20 shows the **Bend only** corner relief. Note that in this figure the corner relief is added to the existing flange and not to the one that you are creating. Figure 14-21 shows the **Bend and face** corner relief.

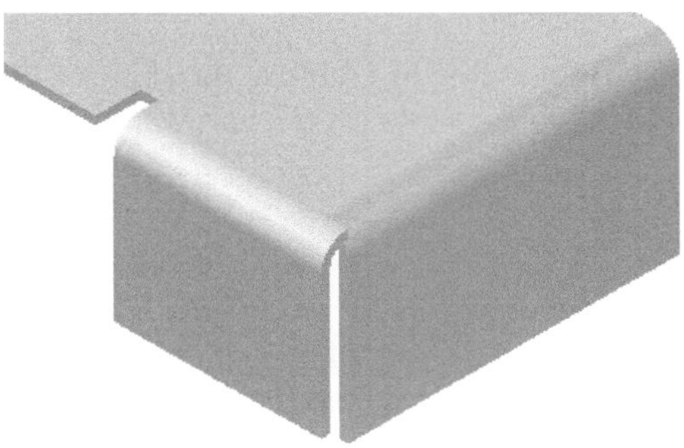

Figure 14-19 Flanges with no corner relief

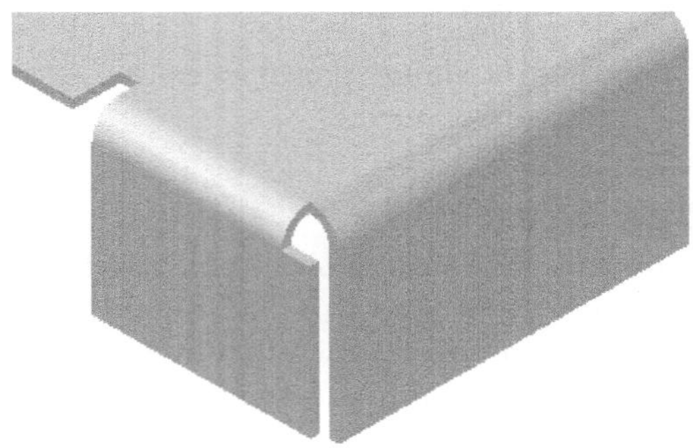

*Figure 14-20 Flanges with the **Bend only** corner relief*

The third type of corner relief, **Bend and face chain**, is used when the first flange has a chain of faces. In this case, the corner relief is applied to the face chain. Figure 14-22 shows a sheet metal part in which the first flange forms a chain with another flange. In this figure, the **Bend and face** corner relief has been added. Figure 14-23 shows the same model after adding the **Bend and face chain** corner relief.

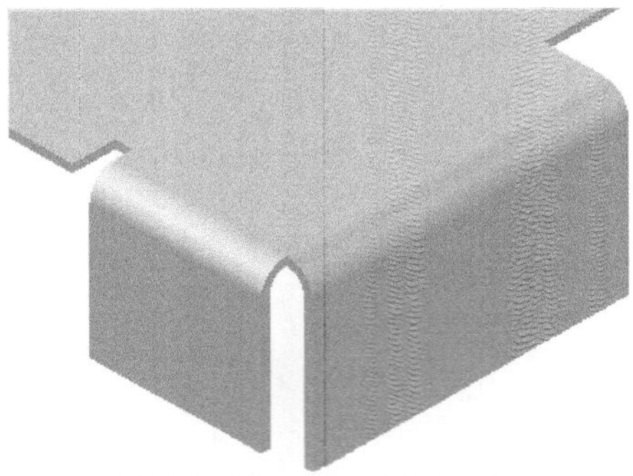

Figure 14-21 *Flanges with the* ***Bend and face*** *corner relief*

Figure 14-22 *Flanges with the* ***Bend and face*** *corner relief*

Figure 14-23 *Flanges with the* ***Bend and face chain*** *corner relief*

After setting the flange parameters, you can follow various steps for creating the flange. These steps are discussed next.

Edge Step

On invoking the **Flange** tool, the **Edge Step** in the Command bar will be activated by default. In this step, you need to select the edge to which the flange will be added. As soon as you select the edge, a preview of the flange will be displayed. The size of the flange is changed dynamically as you move the cursor. Also, note that when you select the edge, additional options are displayed in the Command bar. Before clicking in the drawing area to place the flange, you can use these options to modify the shape and size of the flange. These options are discussed next.

Material Inside

This button is chosen by default and creates a flange such that the material is added inside the profile of the flange. The profile is automatically displayed when you place the flange.

Material Outside

Choose this button to add material outside the profile of the flange. You can also choose this button after placing the flange.

Bend Outside

If this button is chosen, the bend of the flange will be placed outside the profile of the flange.

Full Width

This button is chosen by default and is used to create a flange whose width is equal to the width of the edge selected to create the flange.

Centered

Choose this button to create a flange at an equal distance from the center of the flange. After choosing this button, modify the distance of the flange in the **Distance** edit box in the Command bar and then click in the drawing area to place it. After you place the flange, its width will be displayed on the screen. To modify this value, click on it and specify the required value in the **Dimension Value** edit box.

At End

Choose this button to create the flange at one of the ends of the selected edge. When you choose this button, you will be prompted to select the desired end of the edge. Select one of the endpoints of the edge; a preview of the flange will be displayed. Click on the screen to place the flange; the width of the flange will be displayed. Click on this value to modify the width of the flange.

From Both Ends

Choose this button to create a flange at a certain offset from both ends of the selected edge. After you place the flange, its dimensions from both the ends are displayed. You can click on these dimensions to modify their values.

From End

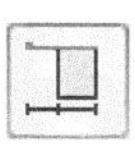

Choose this button to create a flange at a certain offset from one of the endpoints of the selected edge. When you choose this button, you will be prompted to select the desired end. Select the end and place the flange. After you place the flange, its distance from the selected end and its width will be displayed. You can click on these dimensions to modify their values.

Distance

This edit box is used to specify the distance of the flange. This value is modified dynamically as you move the cursor in the drawing window. This value is also displayed when you place the flange.

Inside Dimension

This button is chosen by default and is used to dimension the distance of the flange from inside the base sheet.

Outside Dimension

This button is chosen to dimension the flange from outside the base sheet.

Angle

This edit box is used to specify the angle of the flange. The default value is **90-degree.**

Profile Step

After you place the flange, this step will be activated. You can choose this step to modify the profile of the flange. As soon as you choose this button, the sketching environment will be invoked. The default profile in the environment is rectangular. If needed, you can remove some of the entities of the profile and add additional sketched entities to create the profile.

Offset Step

This step is used to add an offset distance between the flange and the edge selected to create the flange. To do so, choose this button; the **Distance** edit box will be displayed. When you move the cursor in the graphics window, the value in this edit box will be modified. Alternatively, you can enter an offset value in this edit box and press ENTER; the flange will be created at an offset.

ADDING FLANGES IN SYNCHRONOUS SHEET METAL

You do not need any tools to create flanges in the **Synchronous Sheet Metal** environment. You can directly create flanges using the flange start handle displayed on selecting the face of a sheet metal.

Select the face of the sheet metal where you want to add a flange; the flange start handle and a Command bar will be displayed, refer to Figure 14-24. The selection handle has two direction axes: the primary axis (longer handle) and the secondary axis (shorter handle). If you click and drag the primary axis, the length of the selected face changes dynamically. Click on the screen to define its length, refer to Figure 14-25.

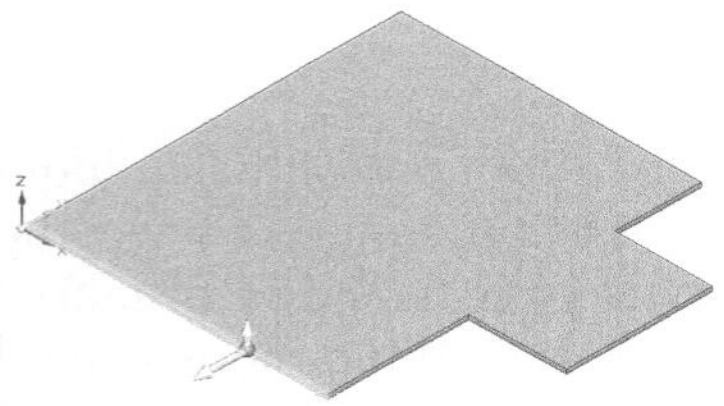

Figure 14-24 *Handle displayed on selecting the face of the sheet metal*

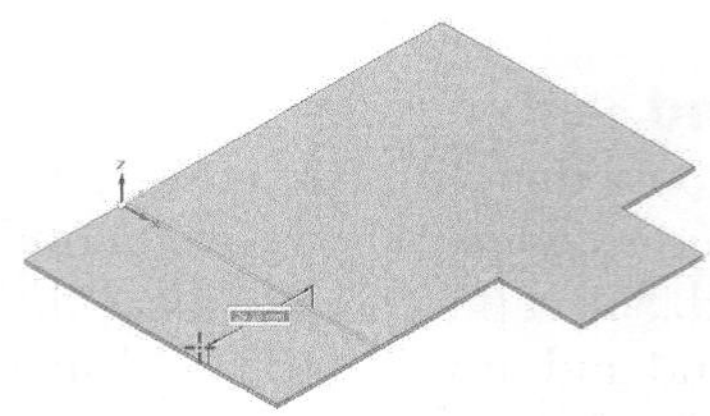

Figure 14-25 *Changing the length dynamically*

You can create the flange using the secondary axis. Alternatively, select a face and choose the down arrow on the **Move** button in the Command bar; a flyout is displayed. Choose **Flange** from the flyout; the handle on the selected face gets changed to the flange start handle. Also, the options in the Command bar get modified to the options required for creating a flange. Choose the **Flange Options** button from the Command bar; the **Flange Options** dialog box will be displayed, set the options for creating the flange, and choose the **OK** button from the dialog box. Next, click on the handle; the preview of the flange will be displayed, as shown in Figure 14-26. Next, enter the desired distance value or click at a point in the drawing area; the flange will be created. By default, the full-width flange is created. To create angular flanges, enter the desired angular value in the dynamic angle edit box which is displayed while creating the flanges. You can define the location of material creation and the measurement side of the flange in the Command bar.

To create a flange that does not extend to the full width, choose the **Partial Flange** button from the Command bar. Note that the partial flange will start from the point where you clicked to select the face. However you can change this position by moving the selection handle to the desired location before invoking the **Flange** tool. Also note that, by default, the width of the partial flange will be one-third of the width of the selected edge. However, you can modify the width or position of the flange using the dimensioning tools.

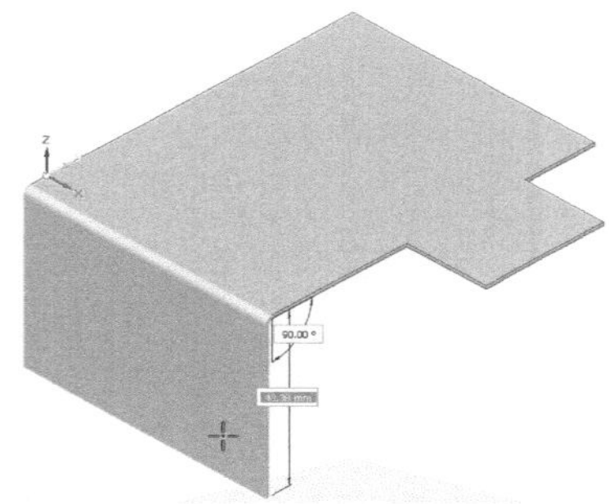

Figure 14-26 *Preview of the flange*

CREATING CONTOUR FLANGES

Ribbon:	Home > Sheet Metal > Contour Flange drop-down > Contour Flange (Ordered and Synchronous)

The flanges that are created by using an open sketched shape are called contour flanges. To create a contour flange in the **Ordered Sheet Metal** environment, invoke the **Contour Flange** tool; the **Contour Flange** Command bar will be displayed and you will be prompted to select the end of the edge at which the normal plane will be placed to create the profile of the contour flange. Select an edge to place the plane; you will be prompted to select a keypoint or enter the offset distance. Specify the location of the plane; the sketching environment will be invoked. Now, in this environment, you can draw the profile of the contour flange using lines and arcs. Note that you cannot use splines in the sketch.

After drawing the open sketch for the contour flange, exit the sketching environment; the **Extent Step** will be invoked and the preview of the contour flange will be displayed. The **Extent Step** is discussed next.

Extent Step

This step is automatically invoked when you exit the sketching environment. The options in this step are discussed next.

Finite Extent

This button is used to specify the extent of the contour flange using a distance value and is chosen by default. As a result, the **Distance** edit box is displayed in the Command bar. If this button is chosen, the **Symmetric Extent** button will also be available in the Command bar. You can use this button to create a contour flange with the symmetric extent. Figure 14-27 shows the preview of a contour flange being created. This figure also shows the open profile for the contour flange. Figure 14-28 shows the resulting contour flange with the bend relief.

To End

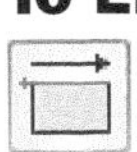

You can choose this button to terminate the contour flange at the end of the selected edge. When you choose this button, you will be prompted to specify the side for the feature creation.

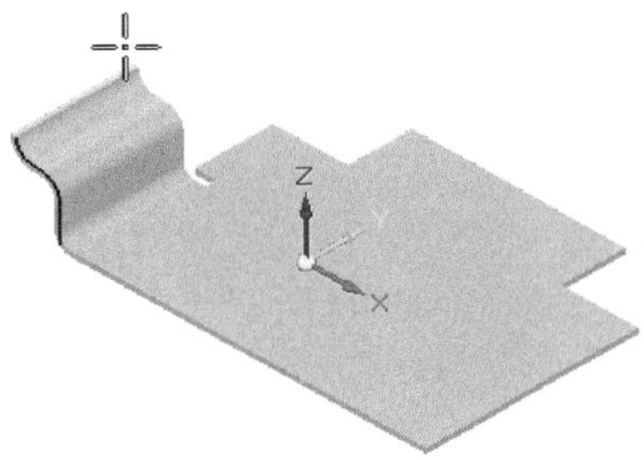

Figure 14-27 *Preview of a contour flange being created*

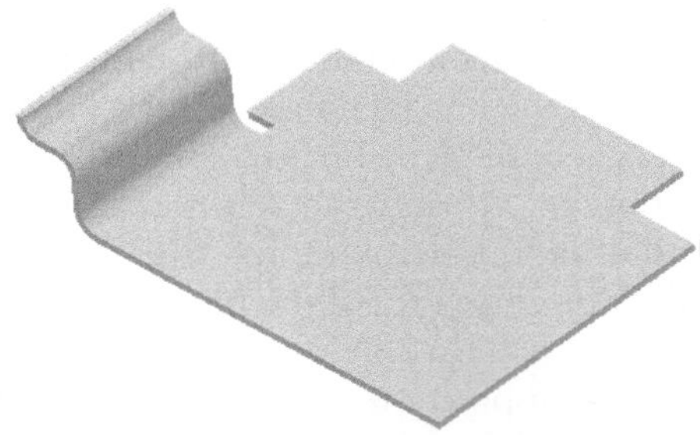

Figure 14-28 *The resulting contour flange with the bend relief*

Chain

Choose this button to select a chain of edges on which the contour flange will be created. Figure 14-29 shows the base of the sheet metal component and the sketch to be used to create the contour flange. Figure 14-30 shows the contour flange created by selecting all four edges on the top face of the base.

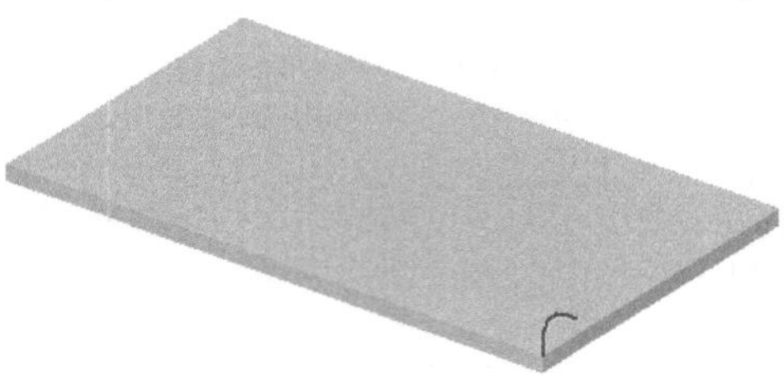

Figure 14-29 *Sketch for the contour flange*

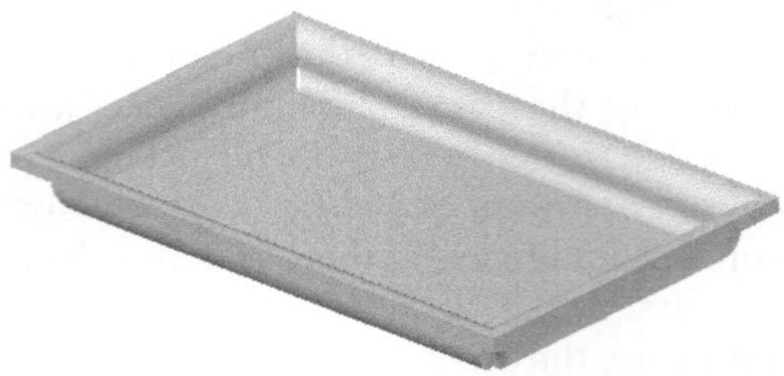

Figure 14-30 *The resulting contour flange created by selecting all four edges on the top face*

Modifying the Contour Flange Options

You can choose the **Contour Flange Options** button from the Command bar to modify the contour flange options. When you choose this button, the **Contour Flange Options** dialog box will be displayed. This dialog box has two tabs, **General** and **Miters and Corners**, refer to Figure 14-31. The options in the **General** tab are the same as those discussed while creating flanges. The options in the **Miters and Corners** tab are discussed next.

Start End/Finish End Areas

The options in these areas are used to create a miter corner at the start end and the finish end of the contour flange. By default, the **Miter** check boxes in both the areas are cleared. As a result, the options in these areas will not be available. Once you select these check boxes, the options in these area will become available. These options are discussed next.

Angle

The **Angle** edit boxes in both the areas are used to specify the miter angle at the start and finish ends. The default value is -45 degrees. Figure 14-32 shows the preview of the contour flange with miters of -45 degree at both the ends.

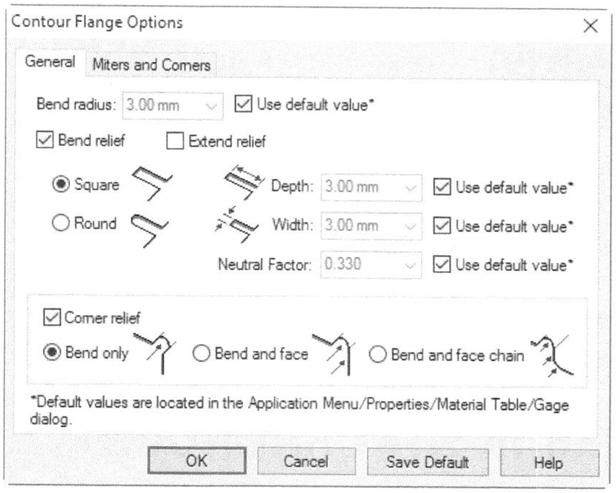

*Figure 14-31 The **Miters and Corners** tab of the **Contour Flange Options** dialog box*

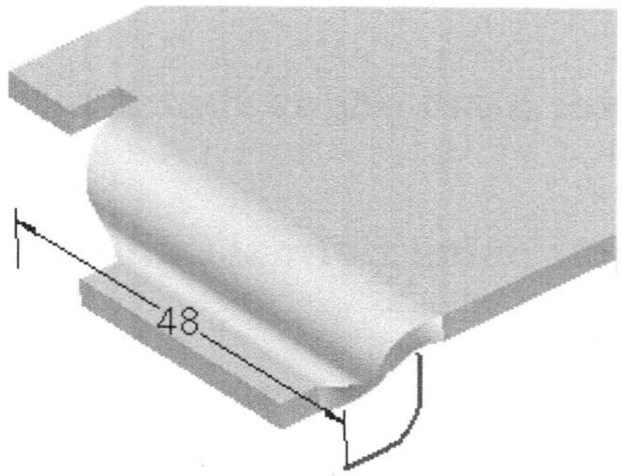

Figure 14-32 Preview of the flanges with -45 degree miter at both ends

Normal to thickness face

This radio button is used to create the miter normal to the thickness face, as shown in Figure 14-33.

Normal to source face

This radio button is used to create the miter normal to the source face, as shown in Figure 14-34.

Figure 14-33 Top view of the miter normal to the thickness face

Figure 14-34 Top view of the miter normal to the source face

Interior Corners Area

The options in this area are used to specify the corner treatment while creating the contour flange at multiple edges. You need to select the **Close Corner** check box to enable the **Treatment** drop-down list. The options available in this drop-down list are discussed next.

Open

This option is used to create an open corner.

Close

This option is used to create a close corner.

Circular Cutout

This option is used to create a circular cutout at the corner. You can specify the diameter of the circle in the **Diameter** edit box that is displayed when you select the **Circular Cutout** option.

Miter bend edges that are larger than default bend radius

This check box is selected to add a miter to the rounds that did not exist earlier.

Miter using Normal Cutout method

This check box is selected to add a miter by creating a normal cutout.

ADDING CONTOUR FLANGES IN SYNCHRONOUS SHEET METAL

To create a contour flange in the **Synchronous Sheet Metal** environment, you need to draw the sketch of the contour at a plane normal to the edge where the flange will be created. Therefore, first specify the plane and then draw the profile of the contour. Next, select the contour profile; the Command bar will be displayed. Choose the **Modify** button in the Command bar; a flyout will be displayed. Choose the **Contour Flange** tool from the flyout; the **Contour Flange** Command bar and an Extrude handle will be displayed. Click on the Extrude handle, define the direction to place the flange, and then define the extent of extrusion, refer to Figure 14-35. On doing so, the contour flange will be created along the edge perpendicular to the selected plane and you will be prompted to accept the flange created or select additional edges where the contour will sweep. Select the edges, if required, and click on the screen to accept the flange. You can also create a flange symmetrical to both sides of the contour profile by choosing the **Symmetric Extent** button from the Command bar.

To create a contour flange that does not sweep along the entire length of the selected edge, choose the **Partial Flange** button; a preview of the contour flange will be displayed along with a dynamic edit box. Enter the desired length of the flange and press ENTER; the partial flange will be created.

It is not necessary to have an existing feature to create a contour flange. The contour flange can also be the first feature of a model. To create such a flange, draw the profile of the contour in the desired plane and invoke the **Contour Flange** tool from the Command bar or from the **Ribbon**. Next, click on the Extrude handle and specify the distance of the flange, refer to Figure 14-35; the flange will be created.

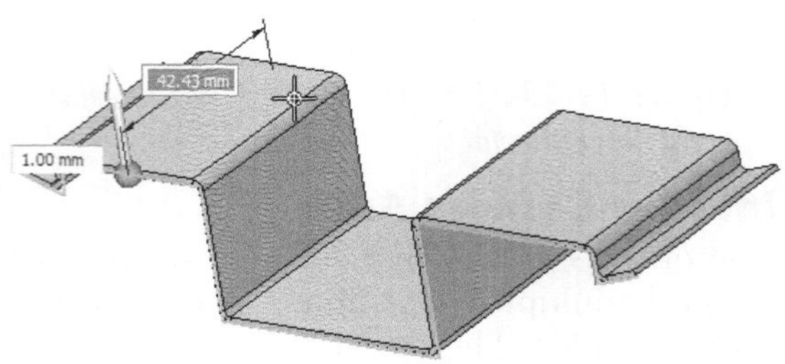

Figure 14-35 *Creating the contour flange*

In Solid Edge, you can create contour flanges along the edges of another contour flange.

CREATING LOFTED FLANGES

Ribbon:	Home > Sheet Metal > Contour Flange drop-down > Lofted Flange (Ordered)

You can create a sheet metal part between two selected profiles using the **Lofted Flange** tool. Note that the profiles being used should be open and they may or may not have the same number of elements. Figure 14-36 shows the sketches for creating the lofted flange and the parallel planes on which the two sketches are drawn. Figure 14-37 shows the preview of the resulting lofted flange.

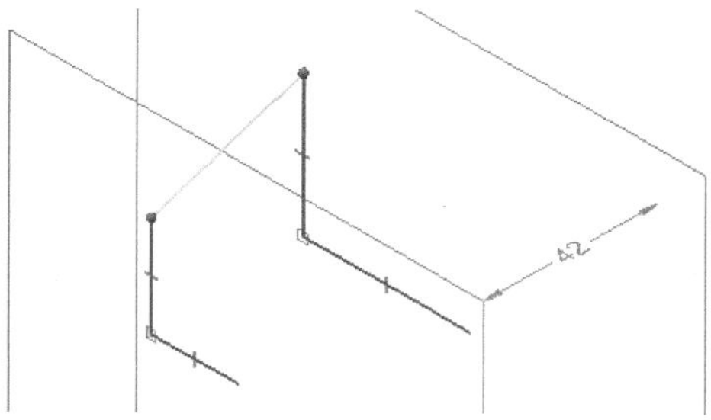

Figure 14-36 Sketches to be used to create the lofted flange

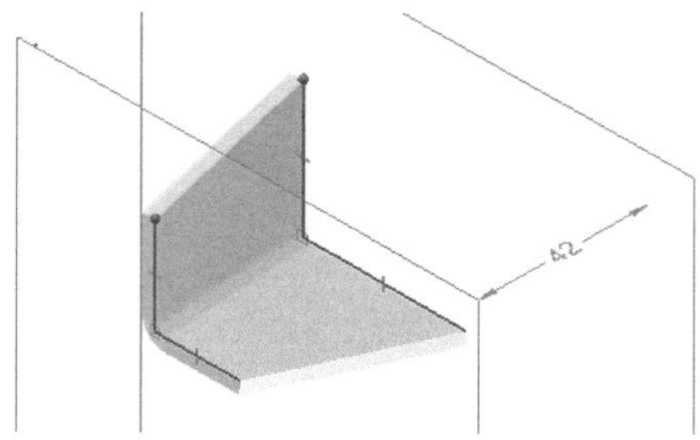

Figure 14-37 Preview of the resulting lofted flange

When you invoke this tool, the **Lofted Flange** Command bar will be displayed. Various steps required to create a lofted flange are discussed next.

Cross Section Step

This step is activated when you invoke the **Lofted Flange** tool. This step is used to create or select the profiles for the lofted flange. To draw the profile, select the sketching plane and then draw the first profile. Exit the sketching environment and then define the start point at the first profile. Choose the **Finish** button from the Command bar. Next, create a parallel plane and draw the second profile. Exit the sketching environment and specify the start point at this profile too. Next, choose the **Finish** button; the **Side Step** will be activated.

Side Step

This step is used to specify the side of the material addition. The side is indicated by a red arrow. You can move the cursor on either side of the profiles to specify the side. Once you specify the side, the preview of the contour flange will be displayed. Choose the **Finish** button to complete the feature.

Note

*You can also modify the lofted flange options by choosing the **Flange Options** button from the Command bar.*

ADDING THE JOG TO THE SHEET

Ribbon: Home >Sheet Metal > Bend drop-down > Jog (Ordered and Synchronous)

The **Jog** tool is used to add a jog to an existing sheet metal part using a sketched line segment. Figure 14-38 shows the base of a sheet metal part and the line to be used to add the jog. Figure 14-39 shows the sheet after adding the jog.

Figure 14-38 *Base sheet and the line to add the jog*

Figure 14-39 *Sheet after adding the jog*

To add a jog in the **Ordered Sheet Metal** environment, invoke the **Jog** tool; the **Jog** Command bar will be displayed. Various steps required to add the jog are discussed next.

Sketch Step

This step is used to select the plane or the face of the base feature to draw the line segment for adding the jog. Select a plane to be used for drawing the sketch.

Draw Profile Step

This step is automatically invoked when you select a planar face or a plane. In this step, you need to draw the sketch. Draw a single line that will define the jog line at the base sheet and then exit the sketching environment.

Side Step

This step is automatically activated when you exit the sketching environment. In this step, you need to define the side of the sheet on which the jog will be added.

Extent Step

This step is automatically activated after you define the side of the jog. Also, a preview of the extent of jog will be displayed in this step and you will be prompted to set the distance value for the flange. You can move the cursor on the screen to specify the distance of the jog dynamically. Alternatively, you can enter the value in the **Distance** edit box. Click on the screen to specify the distance value; a preview of the jog will be displayed with the dimension of the extent value. To edit this dimension, click on it; the **Dimension Value** edit box will be displayed on the screen with the existing dimension value. Enter the new value and press ENTER; the jog will be modified.

Note

The buttons available in the Command bar in the ***Extent*** *step are the same as those discussed in the* ***Flange*** *Command bar.*

In the **Synchronous Sheet Metal** environment, invoke the **Line** tool, select the face or plane to draw the jog line, and then draw the jog line. Next, choose the **Jog** tool from the **Bend** drop-down and then select the jog line; a handle will be displayed on the selected line. Click on the handle and specify the side of the sheet on which the jog will be added; the preview of the jog and a dynamic edit box will be displayed. Enter the distance value of the jog and press ENTER; the jog will be created.

BENDING THE SHEET METAL PART

Ribbon: Home > Sheet Metal > Bend drop-down > Bend (Ordered and Synchronous)

The **Bend** tool is used to bend an existing sheet metal part using a sketched line segment. Figure 14-40 shows a sheet metal part and the line to be used to bend it. Figure 14-41 shows the sheet after bending.

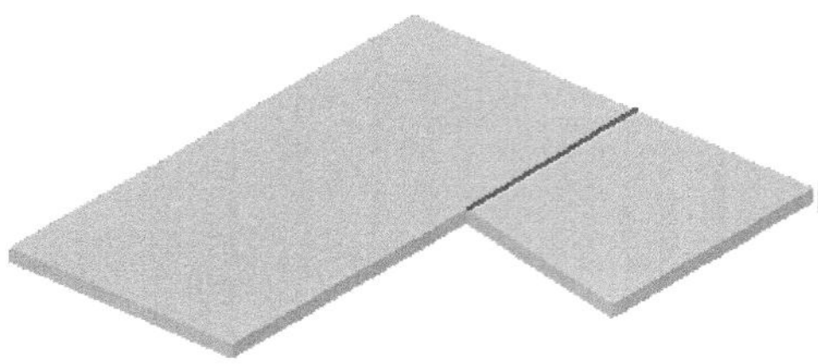

Figure 14-40 *Base sheet and the line to be bent about*

Figure 14-41 *Sheet after bending*

To bend the sheet in the **Ordered Sheet Metal** environment, invoke the **Bend** tool; the **Bend** Command bar will be displayed. Various steps required to bend the sheet are discussed next.

Sketch Step

This step is used to draw the line segment or to select an existing entity to be used for bending. Select a face of the sheet to be used for drawing the sketch or select an existing sketch.

Draw Profile Step

This step is automatically invoked when you select a planar face or a plane. Also, the sketching environment is invoked with this step and you will be prompted to draw the sketch. Draw a single line segment to define the bend line at the base sheet and then exit the sketching environment.

Bend Location

In this step, you need to define the side of the sheet that will be bent. This step is automatically activated when you exit the sketching environment. Also, a red arrow will be displayed on the bend line pointing toward the side to be bent. Click when the desired side is displayed.

Moving Side

This step is automatically activated when you define the side of the bend. In this step, you need to define the side of the sheet that will be moved after bending.

Bend Direction

This step is automatically activated when you define the side to be moved. You can bend the selected side on either side of the line segment. Also, a red arrow is displayed pointing toward the bend direction. Click when the desired direction is achieved and then choose the **Finish** button from the Command bar.

In the **Synchronous Sheet Metal** environment, you first need to draw a bend line on the desired face or plane, else the **Bend** tool will not become active. Draw the bend line and select it. Next, invoke the **Bend** tool; a handle will be displayed on the selected line. Click on the handle to define the side of bend. Next, specify the bend direction and the angle of bend; the bend will be created.

UNBENDING THE SHEET METAL PART

Ribbon: Home > Sheet Metal > Bend drop-down > Unbend (In Ordered Only)

The **Unbend** tool is used to unbend the portion of the sheet which has been bent using the **Bend** or **Flange** tools. This tool is highly useful when you want to create a feature on the bent portion of the sheet. This tool works in the following two steps:

Fixed Face Step

This step is used to specify the portion of the sheet that will be fixed while unbending. Generally, the base of the sheet metal part is selected in this step.

Select Bends

This step is automatically invoked when you select the face to fix. In this step, you need to select the rounds of the bends or flanges. Note that moving the cursor over the linear portion of the bend or flange will not select them. Select the **All Bends** option from the **Select** drop-down list to unbend all the bends in the sheet metal part.

After selecting the rounds, accept the selection. Next, choose the **Finish** button to complete the unbending of sheets.

REBENDING THE SHEET METAL PART

Ribbon: Home > Sheet Metal > Bend drop-down > Rebend (In Ordered Only)

The **Rebend** tool is used to rebend the portion of the sheet that was unbent using the **Unbend** tool. When you invoke this tool, you will be prompted to select the bends to be modified. Move the cursor over the location where the bend was placed originally; the bend will be highlighted. Next, select the bend. You can also select the **All Bends** option from the **Select** drop-down list in the Command bar to rebend all the bends. Choose the **Accept** button to accept the selection. Next, choose the **Finish** button to exit the **Rebend** tool.

Figure 14-42 shows an unbent sheet with the cut features created at the bends and Figure 14-43 shows the sheet after rebending.

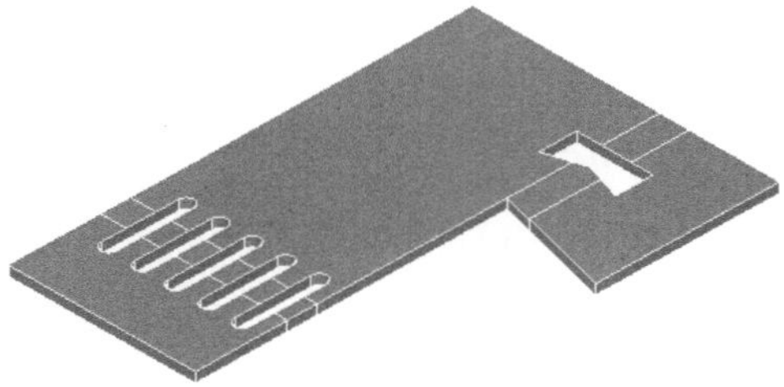

Figure 14-42 Cut features created on the unbent sheet metal part

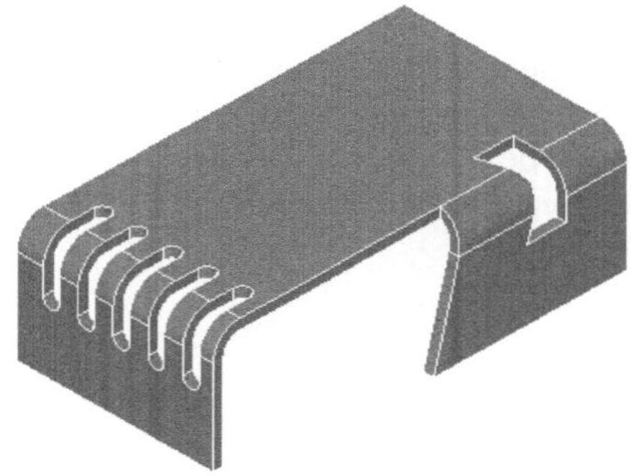

Figure 14-43 Model after rebending

FILLETING OR CHAMFERING CORNERS OF A SHEET METAL PART

Ribbon:	Home > Sheet Metal > Break Corners drop-down > Break Corner (Ordered and Synchronous)

The **Break Corner** tool is used to add fillets or chamfers to the selected corners of the sheet metal part. When you invoke this tool in the **Ordered Sheet Metal** environment, the **Break Corner** Command bar will be displayed and you will be prompted to select the edges to treat. Select the edges that you want to fillet or chamfer. By default, the **Radius Corner** button is chosen from the Command bar. As a result, a fillet is added to the model. If you want to add a chamfer, choose the **Chamfer Corner** button from the Command bar. It creates a 45-degree chamfer. You can enter the fillet or chamfer value in the **Break** edit box. This edit box will be enabled after you select the corners.

You can select the **Face** option from the **Select** drop-down list to select all corners of the selected face. Note that when you invoke this tool in the **Synchronous Sheet Metal** environment, the Command bar is displayed instead of the Command bar. You can set the required parameters in the Command bar.

CLOSING THE 2 BEND CORNERS OF A SHEET METAL PART

Ribbon:	Home > Sheet Metal > 2-Bend Corner > Close 2-Bend Corner (Ordered and Synchronous)

The **Close 2-Bend Corner** tool is used to close the corner created by two bends. When you invoke this tool, you will be prompted to click on the bends to be modified. Select the curved portion of the two bends to treat. On invoking this tool, the **Treatment** drop-down list will be displayed in the Command bar which can be used to perform seven types of treatments on the selected bends. These treatments are discussed next.

Open

This type of treatment is performed using the **Open** option from the **Treatment** drop-down list. In this type of treatment, the walls are closed but the corner is kept open. Figure 14-44 shows the two bends of a sheet metal part selected for treatment and Figure 14-45 shows the corner after treatment.

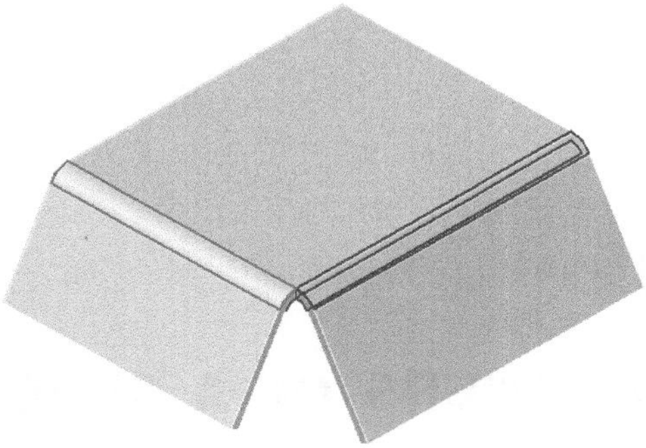

Figure 14-44 *Two bends selected for the open corner treatment*

Figure 14-45 *Model after performing the open corner treatment of the two bends*

You can also add a gap to the corner treatment by entering a value in the **Gap** edit box. Figure 14-46 shows the model after performing the open corner treatment with a gap of 2 mm.

Figure 14-46 *Model after performing the open corner treatment with a gap of 2 mm*

Note

The gap value should be less than the sheet thickness.

Closed

This type of treatment is performed using the **Closed** option from the **Treatment** drop-down list. In this type of treatment, the corners are also closed along with the walls, as shown in Figure 14-47.

Circular Cutout

This type of treatment is performed using the **Circular Cutout** option from the **Treatment** drop-down list. In this type of treatment, a circular cutout is created at the corner, as shown in Figure 14-48. You can enter the diameter of the circle in the **Diameter** edit box.

Figure 14-47 Model after performing the close corner treatment

Figure 14-48 Model after performing the circular cutout corner treatment of the two bends

U-Shaped Cutout

In this type of treatment, a U-shaped cutout is created at the corners, as shown in Figure 14-49.

V-Shaped Cutout

In this type of treatment, a V-shaped cutout is created at the corners, as shown in Figure 14-50. You can specify the angle of the V-shape in the **Angle** edit box.

Square Cutout

In this type of treatment, a square cutout is created at the corners, as shown in Figure 14-51. You can enter the width of the square in the **Width** edit box.

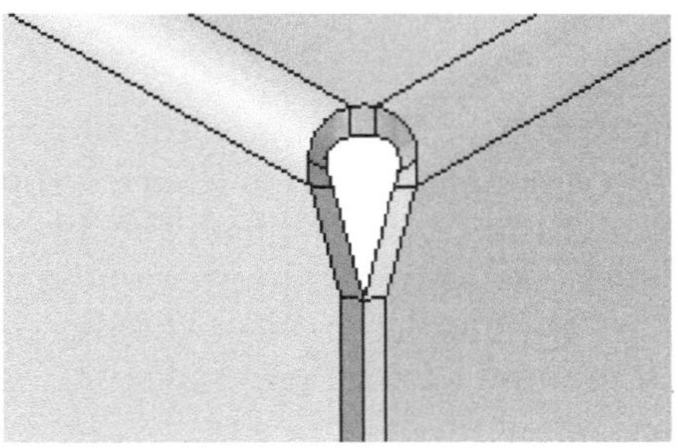

Figure 14-49 Model after performing the U-shaped cutout corner treatment of the two bends

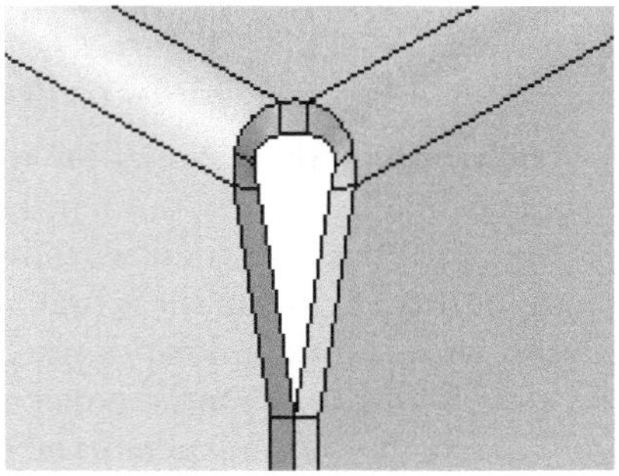

Figure 14-50 Model after performing the V-shaped cutout corner treatment of the two bends

Miter

In this type of treatment, a miter is created at the corners, as shown in Figure 14-52.

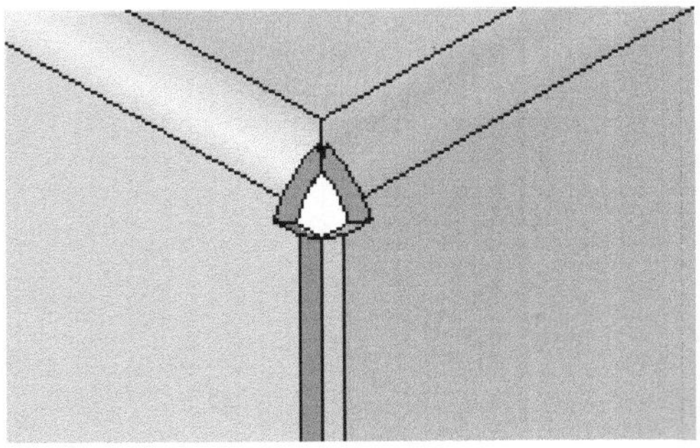

Figure 14-51 Model after performing the square cutout corner treatment of the two bends

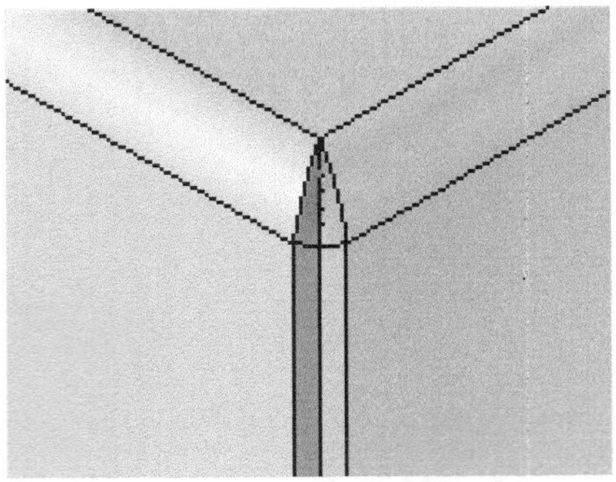

Figure 14-52 Model after performing the miter corner treatment of the two bends

You can also overlap one wall on the other by choosing the **Overlap** button from the Command bar. Figure 14-53 shows the model with an overlap.

Figure 14-53 Overlapping of walls in the corner treatment

In the **Synchronous Sheet Metal** environment, all the options for filleting or chamfering the corners are available in the Command bar instead of the Command bar. However, the options in the Command bar and their working is same as that of the Command bar. The advantage of working in this environment is that as soon as you select the corners, a preview of the model is displayed with the default options. If you modify any option, the preview will also change dynamically. Also, the dynamic edit control box corresponding to the option chosen will be displayed in which you can specify the desired values.

CREATING DIMPLES IN A SHEET METAL PART

Ribbon: Home > Sheet Metal > Dimple drop-down > Dimple (Ordered and Synchronous)

Solid Edge allows you to sketch a user-defined shape and then use it to create a dimple in the sheet metal component. To create the dimple in the **Ordered Sheet Metal** environment, invoke the **Dimple** tool. It is recommended that before starting the sketching of the dimple, you should set the dimple options. To do so, choose the **Dimple Options** button from the Command bar; the **Dimple Options** dialog box will be displayed, as shown in Figure 14-54.

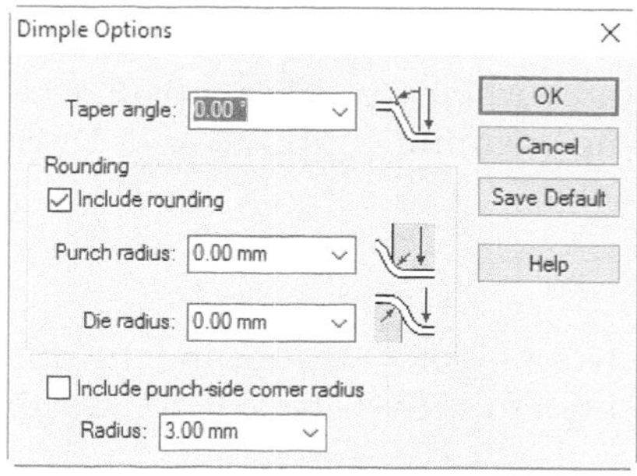

*Figure 14-54 The **Dimple Options** dialog box*

Dimple Options Dialog Box

The options available in this dialog box are discussed next.

Taper angle

This edit box is used to specify the taper angle for the dimple. Figure 14-55 shows a dimple with no taper angle and Figure 14-56 shows a dimple with a taper angle of 25 degree.

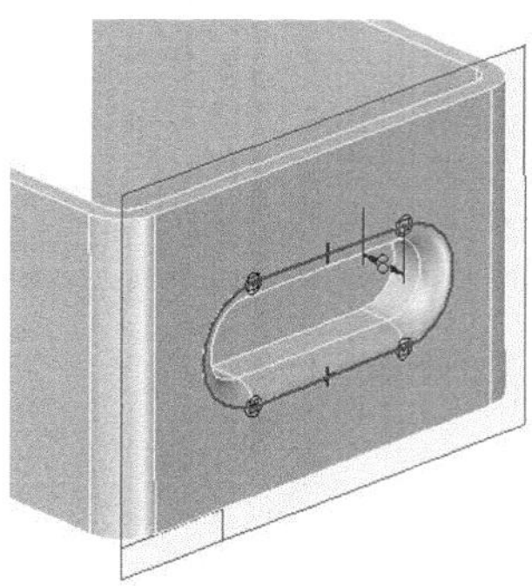

Figure 14-55 Dimple with no taper

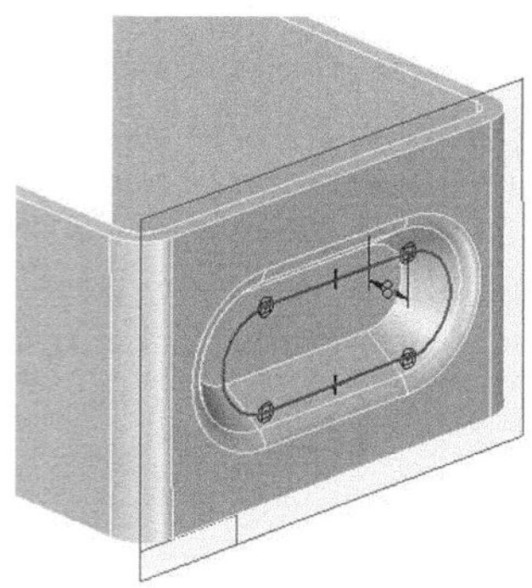

Figure 14-56 Dimple with a 25-degree taper

Rounding Area

The options in this area are used to specify the punch and die radius for creating the dimple. By default, these values are set to zero. You can set any desired value for the punch and die radius.

Include punch-side corner radius

If the profile that you have drawn for the dimple has sharp corners, you can select this check box to automatically round those corners. The radius of the round can be specified in the **Radius** edit box below this check box.

After specifying the dimple options, you can proceed with creating the dimple. Various steps to create the dimple are discussed next.

Sketch Step

This step is activated by default when you invoke the **Dimple** tool. Also, you are prompted to select a planar face. Select a face on which you want to sketch the profile of the dimple.

Draw Profile Step

This step is automatically activated when you select a planar face to draw the sketch. Also, on activating this step, the sketching environment is invoked. Draw the profile of the dimple and then exit the sketching environment.

Side Step

When you exit the sketching environment after drawing the open profile, the **Side** step will be activated and you will be prompted to specify the side for creating the feature.

Extent Step

If you draw a closed profile for the dimple and exit the sketching environment, this step is automatically activated. In this step, you can specify the distance of the depression of the dimple and the direction in which the feature will be depressed. You can specify the distance of the dimple dynamically on the screen or by entering the value in the **Distance** edit box. Figure 14-57 shows a 25-degree taper dimple created in the forward direction.

After you place the dimple, its preview will be displayed, and the **Profile Represents Die** and **Profile Represents Punch** buttons will be enabled in the Command bar. These buttons are used to specify whether the dimple walls will be placed inside or outside the profile.

Solid Edge also allows you to create open profiles for the dimple. Note that the open profile should be created such that when extended, the open entities intersect the edges of the model. Figure 14-58 shows the preview of a dimple created using an open profile. The open profile is also shown in the same figure. Note that in this profile, when the two inclined lines are extended, they intersect with the top edge of the sheet metal part.

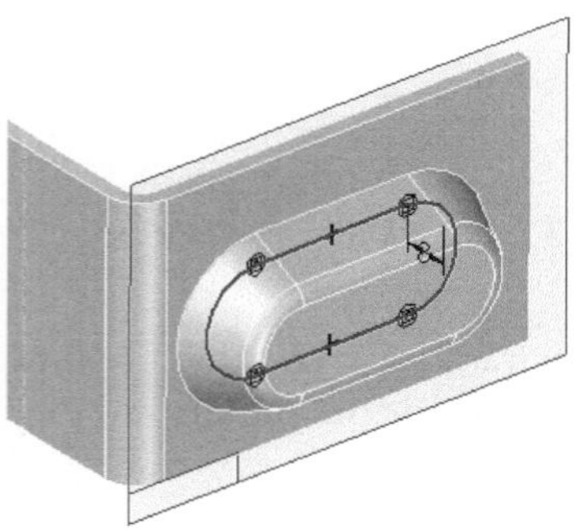

Figure 14-57 *25-degree taper dimple created in the forward direction*

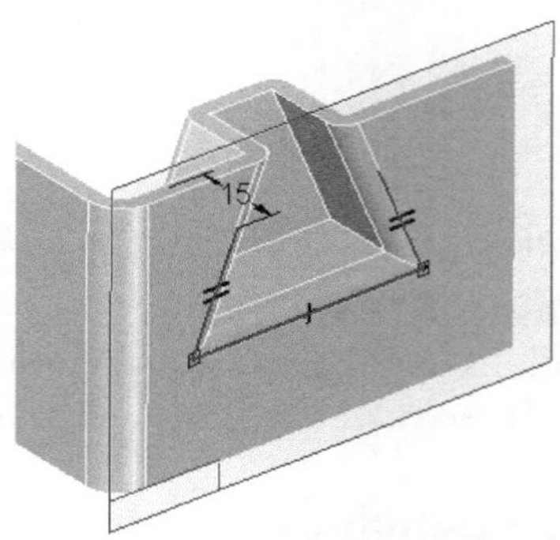

Figure 14-58 *Dimple created using an open profile*

In **Synchronous Sheet Metal** environment, you first need to draw the profile for the dimple. Next, invoke the **Dimple** tool and select the profile; the dimple will be created with default settings. You can change the direction and dimension of the dimple in the drawing area. You can also set various other parameters of the dimple using the Command bar.

Tip

In Solid Edge, you can select multiple profiles to create dimples and drawn cutouts.

CREATING LOUVERS IN A SHEET METAL PART

Ribbon:	Home > Sheet Metal > Dimple drop-down > Louver (Ordered and Synchronous)

Louvers are created in a sheet metal part to provide openings in it. Figure 14-59 shows a sheet metal part with a rectangular pattern of louvers on its top face.

In the **Ordered Sheet Metal** environment, louvers are created by sketching a single line segment defining the length of the louver. To create the louver, invoke the **Louver** tool; the **Louver** Command bar will be displayed. It is recommended that before you start creating the louver, you should set the louver options. To do so, choose the **Louver Options** button from the Command bar; the **Louver Options** dialog box will be displayed, as shown in Figure 14-60.

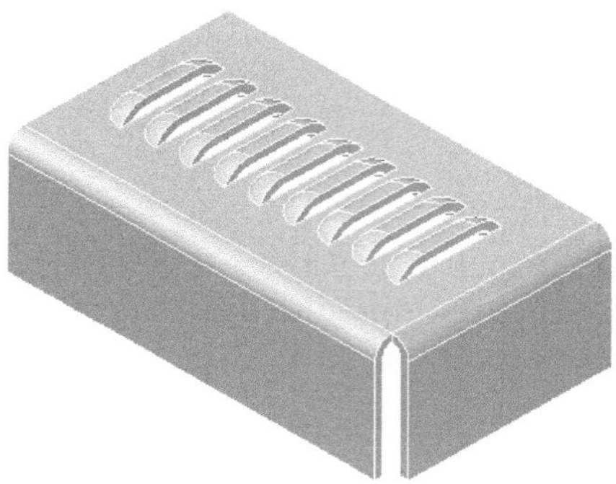

Figure 14-59 Sheet metal part with a pattern of louvers on the top face

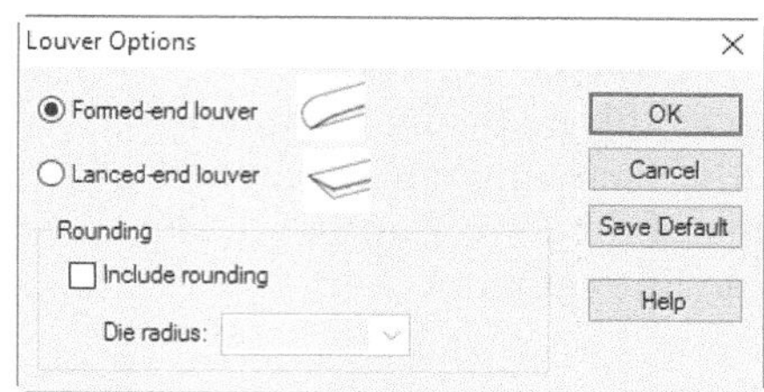

*Figure 14-60 The **Louver Options** dialog box*

Louver Options Dialog Box

The options available in the **Louver Options** dialog box are discussed next.

Formed-end louver

This radio button is selected to create a formed-end type of louver. Figure 14-61 shows a pattern of the formed-end louvers.

Lanced-end louver

This radio button is selected to create a lanced-end type of louver. Figure 14-62 shows a pattern of the lanced-end louvers.

Rounding Area

The options available in this area are used to set the die rounding. The radius for the round can be specified in the **Die radius** edit box.

After specifying the louver options, you can proceed with creating the louver. Various steps to create the louver are discussed next.

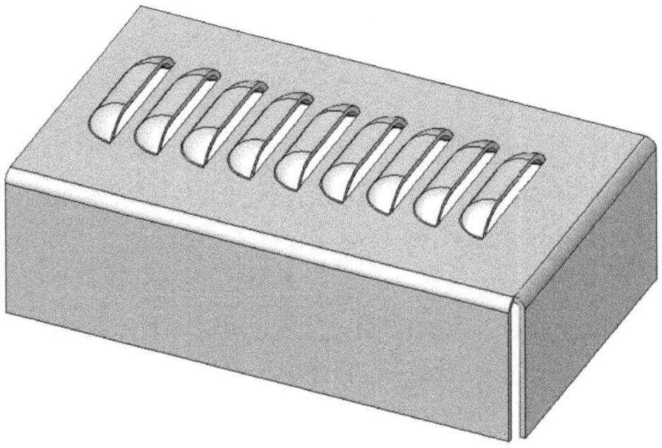

Figure 14-61 Formed-end louvers

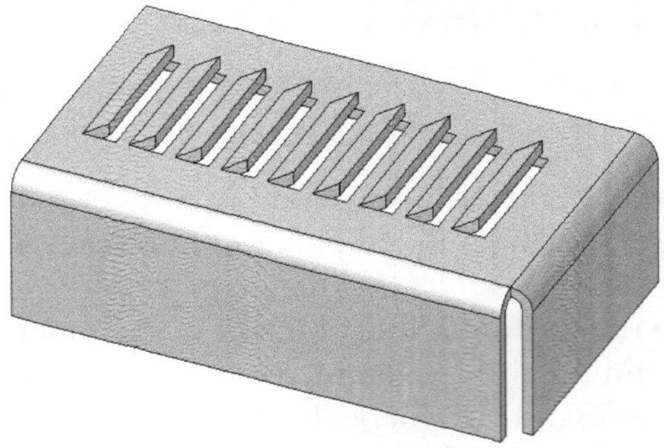

Figure 14-62 Lanced-end louvers

Sketch Step

This step is activated by default when you invoke the **Louver** tool. Also, you will be prompted to select a planar face. Select a face on which you want to sketch the profile of the louver.

Draw Profile Step

This step is automatically activated after you select a planar face. Also, with the activation of this tab, the sketching environment is invoked and you are prompted to draw the sketch. Draw the profile of the louver and then exit the sketching environment. Note that the profile has to be a single line segment.

Depth Step

This step is automatically activated when you exit the sketching environment. In this step, you need to specify the depth of the louver. You can enter the depth in the **Distance** edit box or specify it dynamically in the drawing window. Note that the distance value is specified along the face on which the sketch is drawn. You need to dynamically specify the side of the line on which the depth of the louver will be added.

Height Step

This step is automatically activated when you specify the depth of the louver. In this step, you need to specify the height of the louver. The height is specified normal to the face on which the sketch is drawn. You can enter the height in the **Distance** edit box or specify it dynamically in the drawing window. You need to specify the side of the sheet on which the louver will be added. Note that the height should be less than or equal to the difference of the depth of the louver and the sheet thickness. Also, the height should be more than the sheet thickness. For example, if the depth of the louver is 6 mm and the sheet thickness is 2 mm, the height of the louver should be more than 2 and less than or equal to 4. Figure 14-63 shows the preview of a formed-end louver. The depth of the louver is 6 mm and its height is 3.85 mm.

When you invoke the **Louver** tool in the **Synchronous Sheet Metal** environment, the louver shape with the default dimensions gets attached to the cursor. The **Louver Options** dialog box in the **Synchronous Sheet Metal** environment has some additional options in comparison to the one in the **Ordered** environment. You can specify the dimensions of the louver as per your requirement as well as the feature origin by invoking the **Louver Options** dialog box. After setting the dimensions and exiting the dialog box, move the cursor toward the face where you want to place the louver, refer to Figure 14-64. You can change the orientation of the louver by pressing the N or B key. Click at the required position. You can change the location of the louver by dimensioning its position values and editing them.

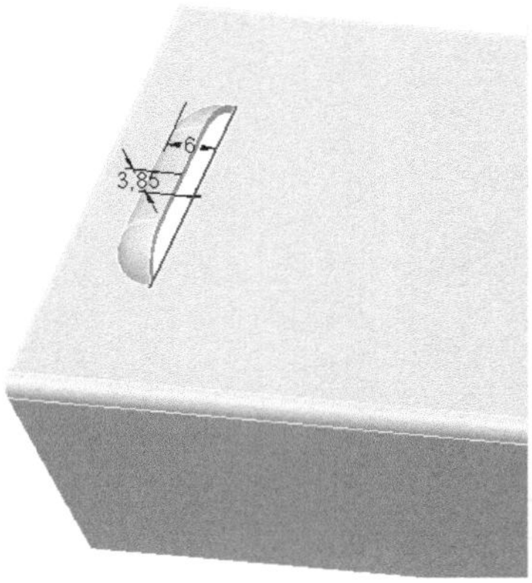

Figure 14-63 *Preview of the formed-end louver*

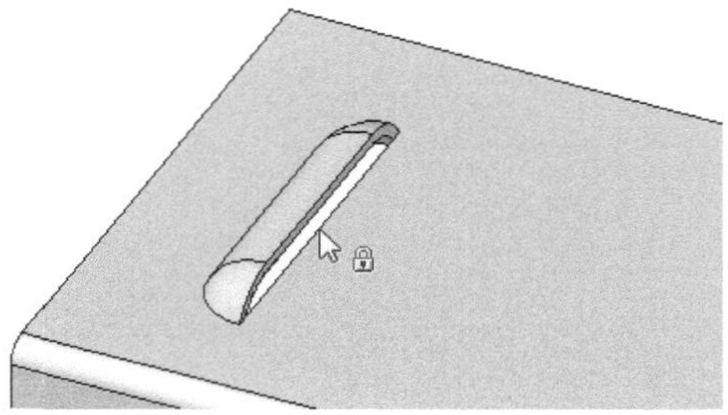

Figure 14-64 *Placing a louver in the* ***Synchronous Sheet Metal*** *environment*

After creating the louver, you can modify the louver dimensions. To do so, select the louver; a handle will be displayed with the name of the louver. Click on the louver name; the louver dimensions will be displayed with edit boxes. Enter new values in the edit boxes to modify the louver. Alternatively, you can invoke the **Louver Options** dialog box and then enter new values to modify the louver. You can change the position and orientation of the louver created using the steering wheel, which is displayed on selecting the louver.

Note

To change the alignment of the louver, you need to select it after placing; a rotate handle will be displayed. Next, you can use the rotate handle to place the louver to the correct alignment and then dimension it.

Tip

In Solid Edge, you can create a louver that lies completely on a bend.

CREATING DRAWN CUTOUTS IN A SHEET METAL PART

Ribbon: Home > Sheet Metal > Dimple drop-down > Drawn Cutout

The drawn cutouts are exactly the same as the dimples with the only difference that in drawn cutouts, the end face is open. Figure 14-65 shows a sheet metal part with two drawn cutouts of different shapes. In this figure, the rectangular cutout is created in the upward direction and the oblong cutout is created in the downward direction.

If you are working in the **Synchronous Sheet Metal** environment, you need to draw the profile of the drawn cutout. To do so, invoke the **Drawn Cutout** tool and select the profile. On doing so, a direction handle and an edit box showing the default height of the cutout will be displayed.

Specify the direction and value of the cutout; the drawn cutout will be created. You can also modify the drawn cutout after creating it. To do so, select the drawn cutout; a handle will be displayed with the name of the cutout. Click on the cutout name; an edit box with the depth value of the handle and an **Edit Profile** handle will be displayed. Enter a new depth value in the edit box if required. Else, click on the **Edit Profile** handle to edit the profile of the drawn cutout. You can change the position and orientation of the louver created using the steering wheel which is displayed on selecting the louver.

Figure 14-65 *Drawn cutouts of various shapes*

Note

The working of this tool is exactly the same as that of the ***Dimple*** *tool.*

CREATING BEADS IN A SHEET METAL PART

Ribbon: Home > Sheet Metal > Dimple drop-down > Bead

The **Bead** tool is used to create an embossed or an engraved bead on a sheet metal part using a single entity or a set of tangentially connected entities. Figure 14-66 shows an embossed bead and Figure 14-67 shows an engraved bead.

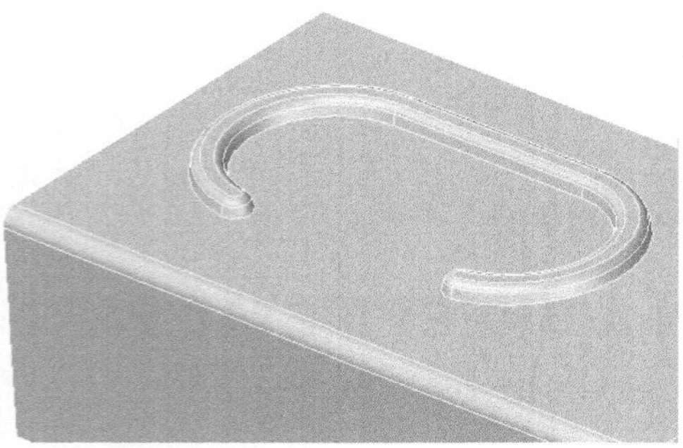

Figure 14-66 *Bead created in the upward direction, resulting in the embossed feature*

Figure 14-67 *Bead created in the downward direction, resulting in the engraved feature*

When you invoke this tool in the **Ordered Sheet Metal** environment, the **Bead** Command bar is displayed. It is recommended that before you proceed with creating the bead, you should set its options. To set the bead options, choose the **Bead Options** button from the Command bar; the **Bead Options** dialog box will be displayed, as shown in Figure 14-68.

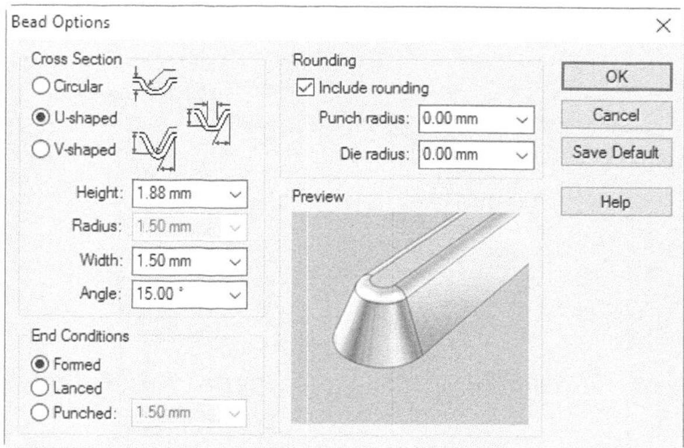

*Figure 14-68 The **Bead Options** dialog box*

Bead Options Dialog Box

The options available in this dialog box are discussed next.

Cross Section Area

The options available in this area are used to specify the cross-section of the bead. You can specify the height, radius, width, and the angle of the bead using the edit boxes available in this area. Figures 14-69 through 14-71 show beads with different cross-sections.

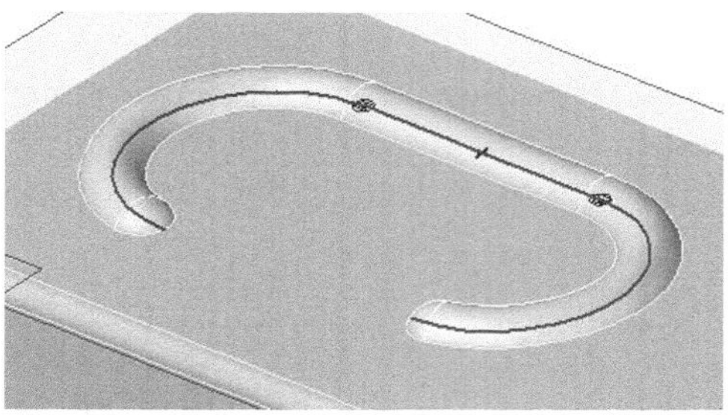

Figure 14-69 Circular cross-section bead

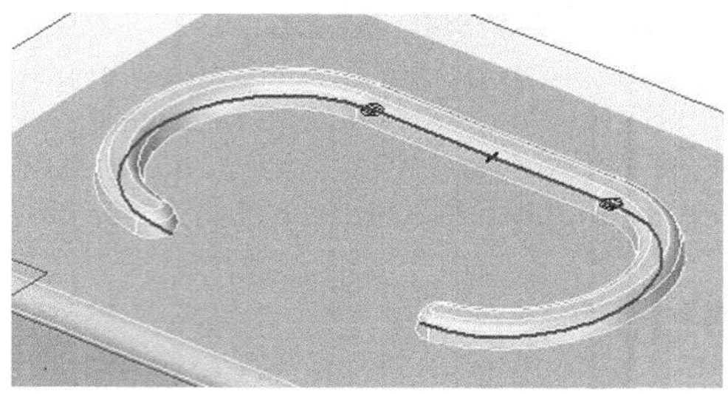

Figure 14-70 U-shaped bead

End Conditions Area

The options available in this area are used to specify the end conditions of the bead. You can specify the end condition as formed, lanced, or punched. The punch gap can be specified in the edit box that will be available on the right of the **Punched** radio button when you select it. Figures 14-72 through 14-74 show beads with different end conditions.

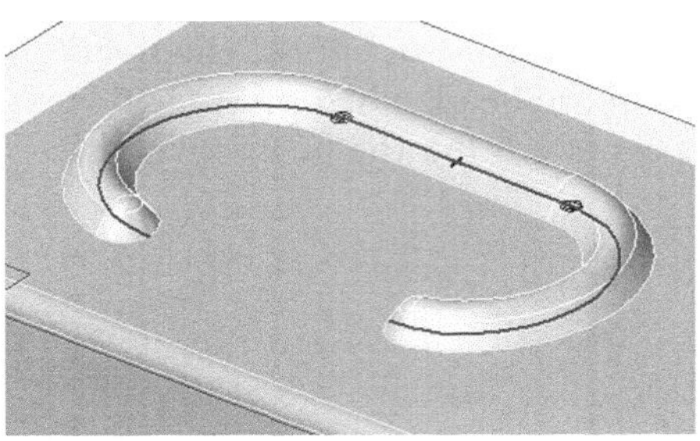

Figure 14-71 V-shaped bead

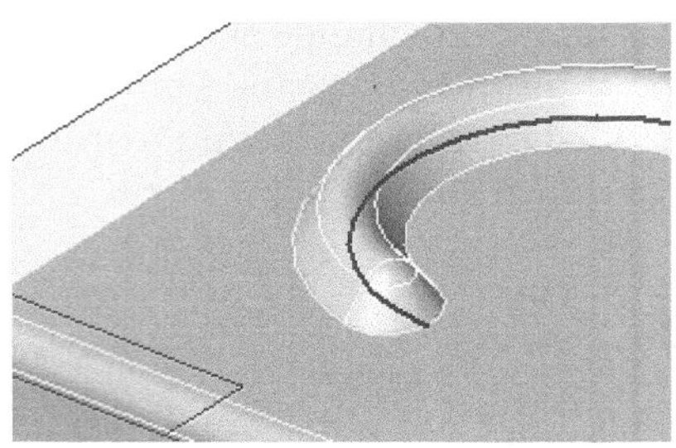

Figure 14-72 Formed end condition

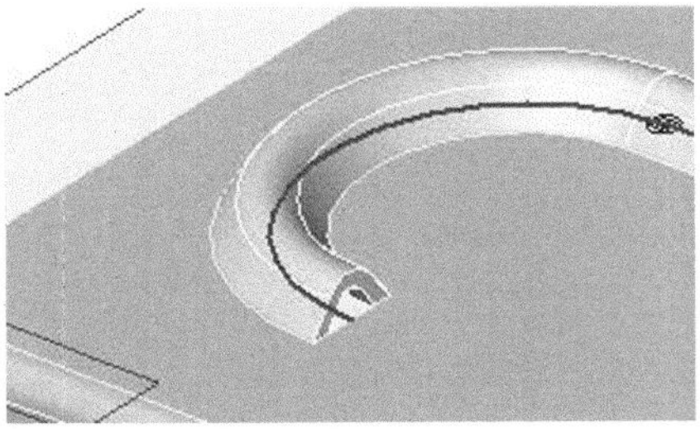

Figure 14-73 Lanced end condition

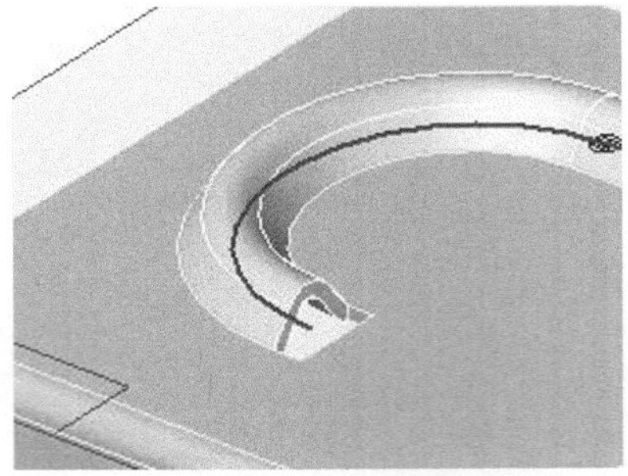

Figure 14-74 Punched end condition with a gap of 2 mm

Note

*The remaining options in the **Bead Options** dialog box are similar to those discussed earlier.*

After specifying the bead options, you can proceed with creating the bead. Various steps to create the bead are discussed next.

Sketch Step

This step is activated by default when you invoke the **Bead** tool. As a result, you are prompted to select a planar face. Select a face on which you want to sketch the profile of the bead.

Draw Profile Step

This step is automatically activated when you select a planar face. Also, the sketching environment will be invoked and you will be prompted to draw the sketch. Draw the profile of the bead and then exit the sketching environment. Note that the profile has to be a single line segment or a set of tangentially connected open or closed entities.

Side Step

This step is automatically activated when you exit the sketching environment. In this step, you need to specify the side of the feature creation. The side is displayed by a red arrow on the screen. You can specify the required side by clicking on either side of the sketch.

If you are working in the **Synchronous Sheet Metal** environment, draw the bead profile on the required plane. Next, invoke the **Bead** tool and select the bead profile. Note that this tool will be activated only when the profile for bead is already drawn on the sheet metal. Next, invoke the **Bead** tool and select the profile; the preview of the bead with default settings will be displayed. Also, a handle will be displayed on the preview showing the side of feature creation. You can click on this handle to change the direction of the feature creation. Next, choose the **Bead Options** button from the Command bar to set the parameters of the bead. The options will be same as in the **Ordered Sheet Metal** environment. The process of editing the bead created is same as that of drawn cutouts.

Tip

In Solid Edge, you can create beads, dimples, and drawn cutouts across bends.

EMBOSSING SOLIDS ONTO A SHEET METAL

Ribbon: Home > Sheet Metal > Dimple drop-down > Emboss

In Solid Edge, you can emboss solids on a sheet metal using the **Emboss** tool. This tool can be used to emboss artistic shapes, texts, company logos, and so on. The working of this tool is same in the **Ordered** and **Synchronous Sheet Metal** environments. To emboss a solid, first you need to create a solid body using the **Add body** tool. Next, switch back to the sheet metal part by double-clicking on **Design Body_1** in the **PathFinder**. Choose the **Emboss** tool from the **Dimple** drop-down in the **Sheet Metal** group; the **Emboss** Command bar will be displayed and you will be prompted to select the target body to be embossed. Select a sheet metal part; you will be prompted to select one or more tool bodies. Select one or more solid bodies and specify the clearance value in the **Clearance** edit box. If you want to subtract the solid body from the sheet metal, you need to deactivate the **Thicken** button on the Command bar and specify the emboss direction by using the **Direction** button available in the Command bar. Next, right-click to create an embossed feature. Figure 14-75 shows a sheet metal and a solid body selected and the embossed feature created.

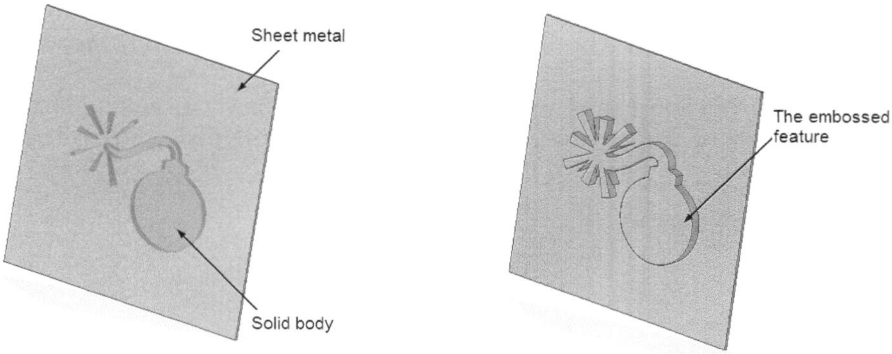

Figure 14-75 *The embossed feature created*

ADDING GUSSETS TO A SHEET METAL PART

Ribbon: Home > Sheet Metal > Dimple drop-down > Gusset (Ordered and Synchronous)

Gussets are rib like stiffeners that are added to the sheet metal part to increase its strength. In Solid Edge, you can create an automatic gusset of round or square shape or a gusset with a user-defined profile. Figures 14-76 through 14-79 show various types of gussets that can be created in Solid Edge.

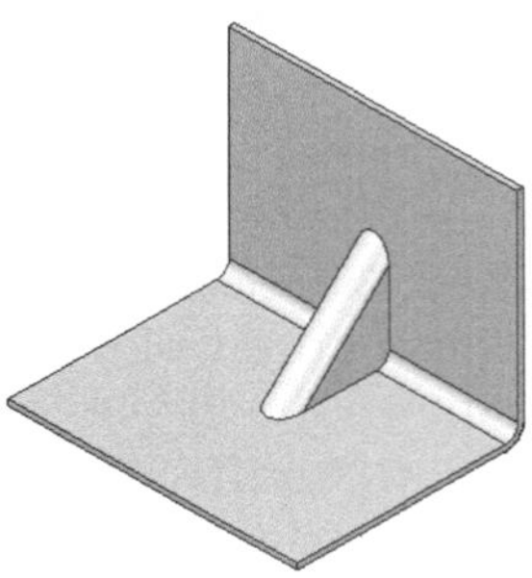

Figure 14-76 *Front view of a round gusset*

Figure 14-77 *Back view of the round gusset*

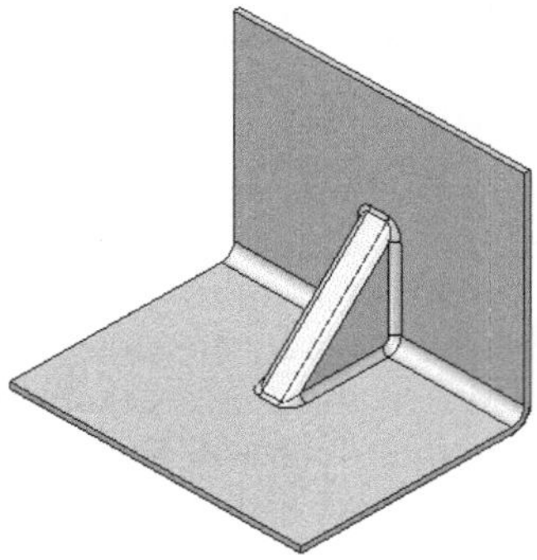

Figure 14-78 *A square gusset*

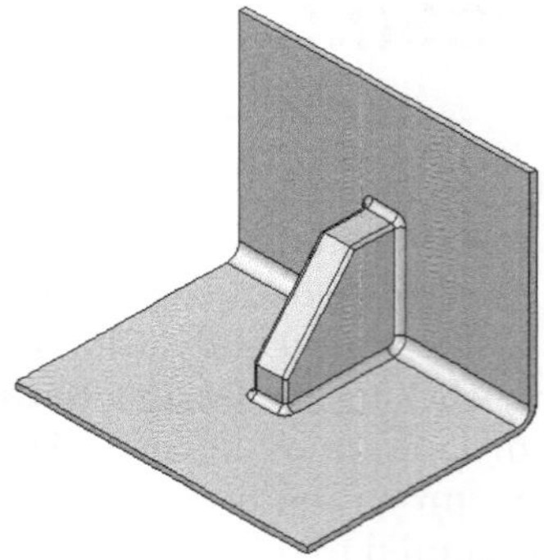

Figure 14-79 *A user-defined gusset*

To add a gusset to a sheet metal part, invoke the **Gusset** tool from the **Dimple** drop-down in the **Sheet Metal** group of the **Home** tab in the **Ordered Sheet Metal** environment; the **Gusset** Command bar will be displayed and the **Select Bend Step** will be activated. Also, you will be prompted to select a bend along which the gusset will be placed. Select the rounded portion of a bend or a flange; the **Gusset Placement Step** will be invoked and the preview of the gusset created using the current values will be displayed as you move the mouse along the selected bend.

Place the gusset and then choose the **Gusset Options** button from the Command bar to modify the gusset options. When you choose this button, the **Gusset Options** dialog box will be displayed, as shown in Figure 14-80.

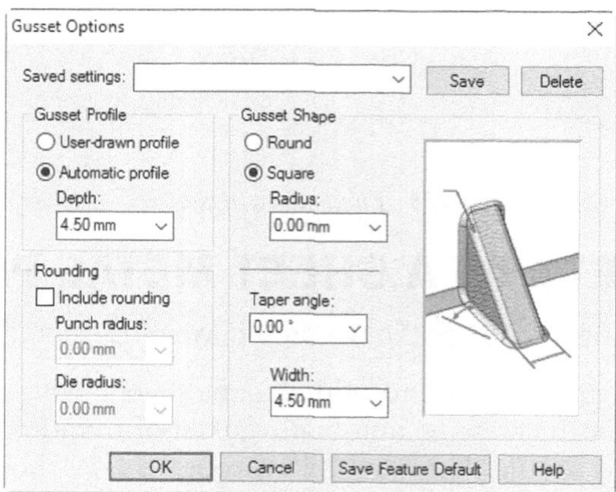

Figure 14-80 *The* ***Gusset Options*** *dialog box (Ordered)*

The options available in this dialog box are discussed next.

Saved settings

This drop-down list displays the list of settings that you have saved. By default, this drop-down list is blank. To save the settings, specify the required parameters in this dialog box, enter a name for the parameters set in the **Saved settings** edit box, and then choose the **Save** button; the settings will be saved. Now if you want to view the parameters set, select the required name from the **Saved settings** drop-down list. You can delete the unwanted settings by selecting them from this drop-down list and then choosing the **Delete** button.

Gusset Profile Area

The options in this area are used to define the profile of the gusset and depth of the gusset. These options are discussed next.

User-drawn profile (Ordered)

This is the first radio button available in the **Gusset Profile** area. You can select this radio button to create a user-drawn profile. When you exit the **Gusset Options** dialog box after selecting this option, the **Sketch Step** will be invoked. The working of this tool will then become similar to that of the **Rib** tool discussed in the earlier chapters.

Automatic profile (Ordered)

By default, the **Automatic profile** radio button is selected in this area. As a result, the automatic profile of a single inclined line is drawn as the profile of the gusset. The depth of the automatic profile can be specified in the **Depth** edit box provided below this radio button.

Depth

You can specify the depth of the gusset in this edit box.

Rounding Area

The options in this area are used to specify the punch and die radius to create the gusset. Select the **Include rounding** check box to enable the **Punch radius** and **Die radius** edit boxes. You can enter the desired values in these edit boxes.

Gusset Shape Area

The options in this area are used to define the shape of the gusset. These options are discussed next.

Round

This radio button is used to create a gusset with a round shape, as shown in Figure 14-81.

Square

This radio button is used to create a gusset with a square shape. You can also apply fillets to the sharp edges of a square gusset by entering the radius value in the **Radius** edit box. Figure 14-82 shows a square gusset without filleting the edges.

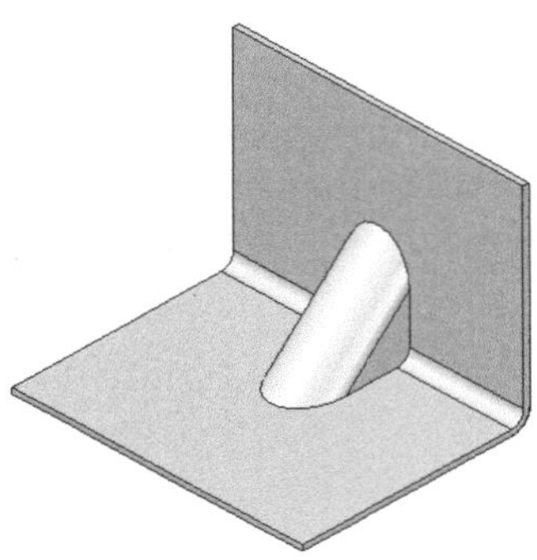

Figure 14-81 *A round gusset*

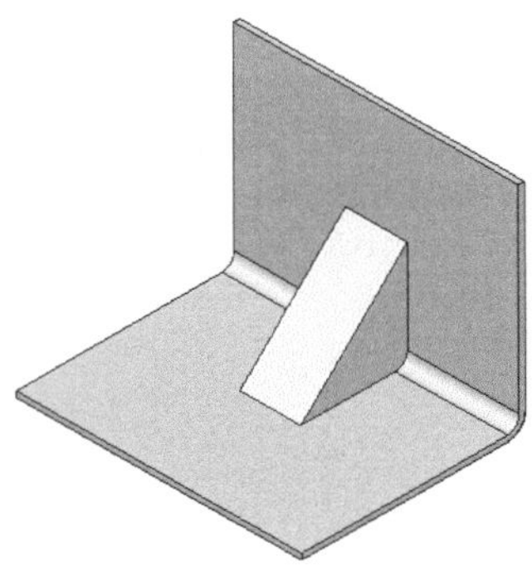

Figure 14-82 *A square gusset*

Taper angle

This edit box is used to enter the taper angle for the gusset. Figure 14-83 shows a gusset with a taper angle of 25 degrees.

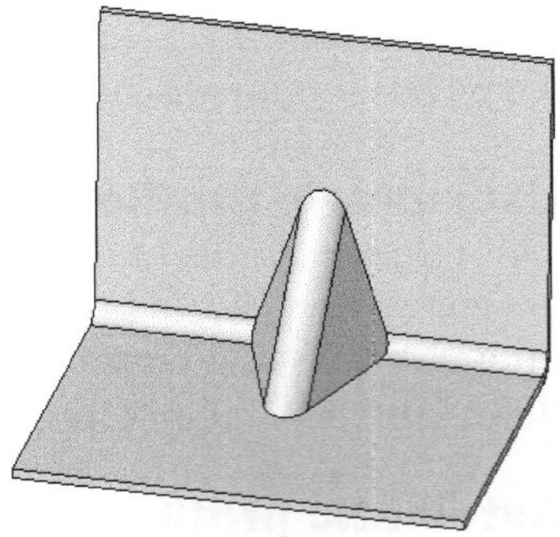

Figure 14-83 *A gusset with a taper angle of 25 degrees*

Width

This edit box is used to specify the width of the gusset. Figure 14-84 shows a gusset with a width of 10 mm and Figure 14-85 shows a gusset with a width of 20 mm.

On invoking the **Gusset** tool in the **Synchronous Sheet Metal** environment, you will be prompted to select the bend. Select the bend; a preview of the gusset will be displayed. Now as you move the mouse, the gusset preview will also move along the bend. By default, you can place a single gusset on the bend because the **Single** option is selected in the **Patterning** drop-down list of the **Gusset** Command bar. However, you can set the gusset pattern to **Fit**, **Fill**, or **Fixed**. As you set the required pattern type, the corresponding edit boxes will be displayed on the gusset. You can specify the number of gussets or spacing or both and click to place gussets on the bend.

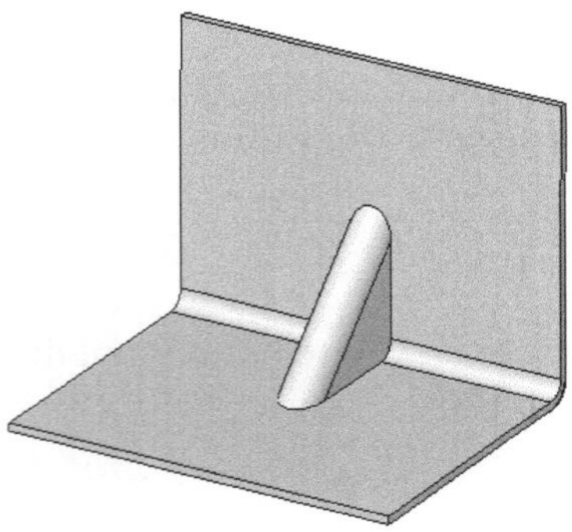

Figure 14-84 *A gusset of 10 mm width*

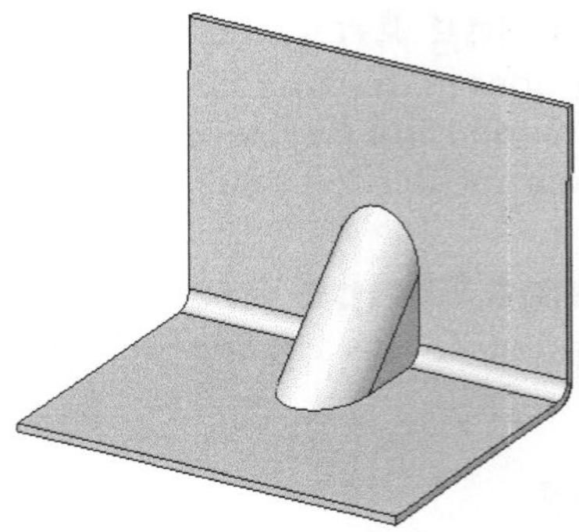

Figure 14-85 *A gusset of 20 mm width*

ADDING HEMS

Ribbon:	Sheet Metal > Contour Flange drop-down > Hem (Ordered and Synchronous)

Hems are defined as the rounded faces created on the sharp edges of a sheet metal component to reduce the area of the sharpness on the edges. This makes the sheet metal component easy to handle and assemble. To create a hem, invoke the **Hem** tool; the **Hem** Command bar will be displayed and you will be prompted to select an edge for the hem. Before you select the edge, it is recommended that you choose the **Hem Options** button to set the hem options. When you choose this button, the **Hem Options** dialog box will be displayed, as shown in Figure 14-86.

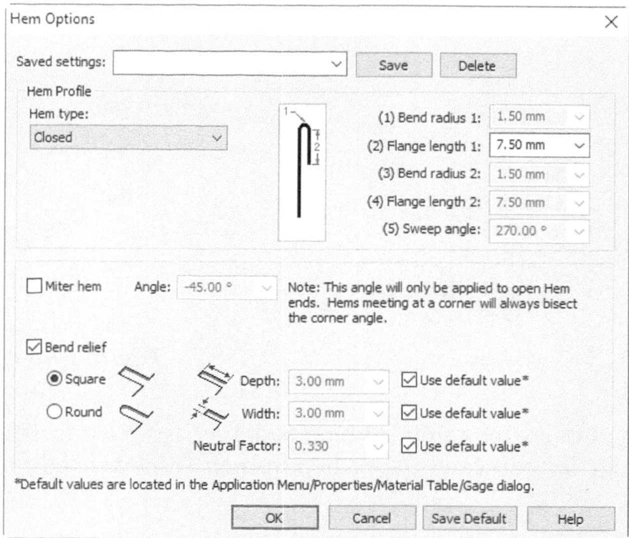

*Figure 14-86 The **Hem Options** dialog box (Ordered)*

The options in this dialog box are discussed next.

Saved settings

The options in this drop-down list are same as discussed earlier.

Hem Profile Area

The options available in this area are used to specify the profile of the hem. These options are discussed next.

Hem type

This drop-down list is used to specify the hem type. There are different types of hems available in this drop-down list. These are discussed next.

Closed

This option is used to create a closed hem, as shown in Figure 14-87. The flange length can be specified in the **Flange length 1** edit box available on the right of the preview window.

Open

This option is used to create an open hem, as shown in Figure 14-88. The bend radius and the flange length can be specified in the **Bend radius 1** and **Flange length 1** edit boxes, respectively.

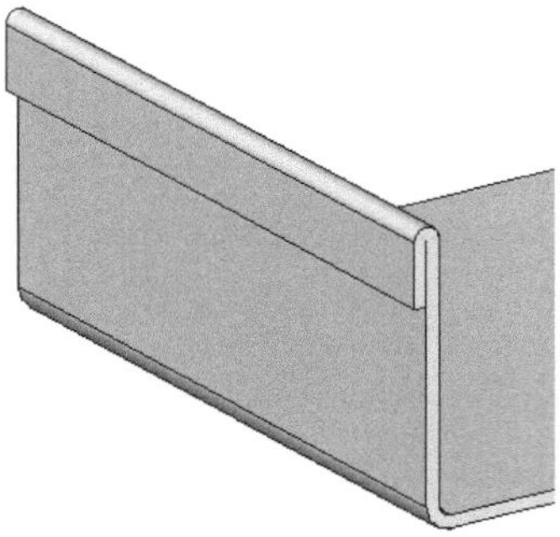

Figure 14-87 A closed hem

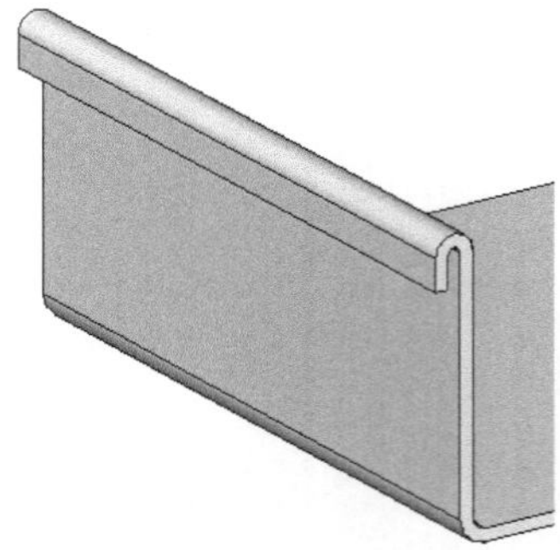

Figure 14-88 An open hem

S-Flange

This option is used to create a hem with an S shape, as shown in Figure 14-89. The bend radii and the flange lengths can be specified in their respective edit boxes.

Curl

This option is used to create a curled hem, as shown in Figure 14-90. The bend radii and the flange lengths can be specified in their respective edit boxes.

Open Loop (In Ordered only)

This option is used to create a hem that has an open loop, as shown in Figure 14-91. The bend radius and the included angle of the open loop can be specified in the **Bend radius 1** and **Sweep angle** edit boxes, respectively.

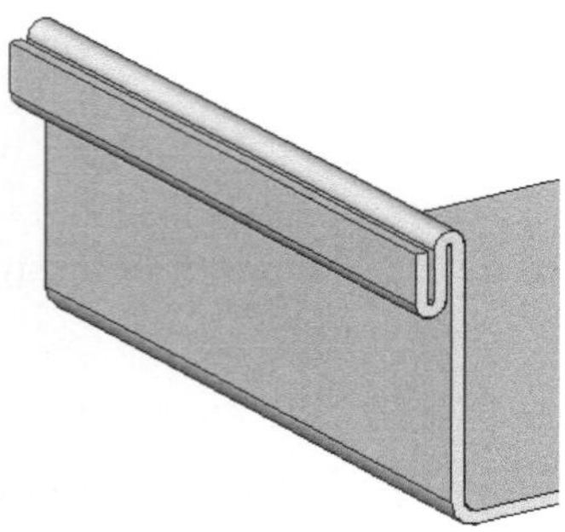

Figure 14-89 An S-shaped hem

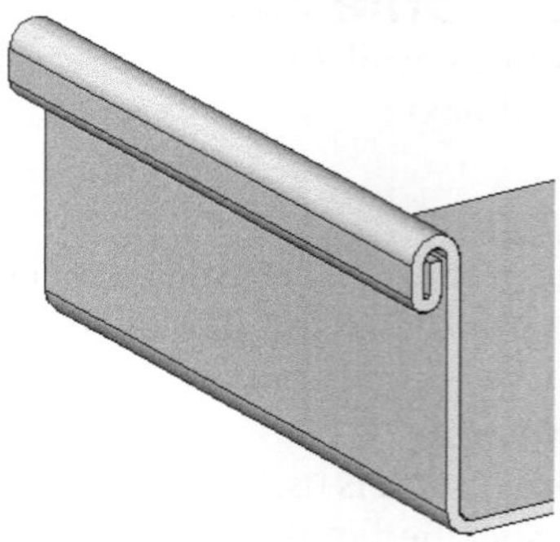

Figure 14-90 A curled hem

Closed Loop

This option is used to create a hem that has a closed loop, as shown in Figure 14-92. The bend radius and the flange length can be specified in their respective edit boxes.

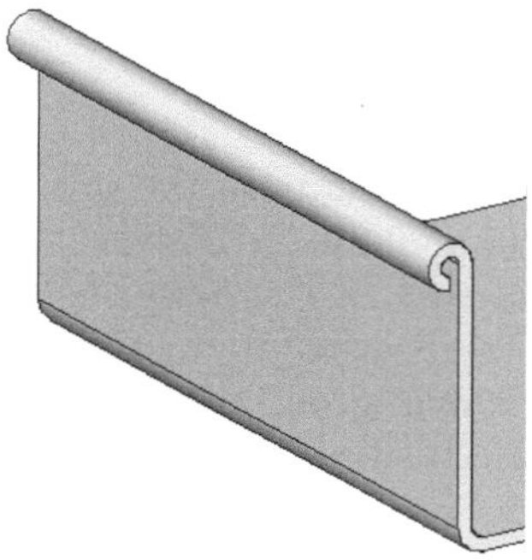

Figure 14-91 An open loop hem

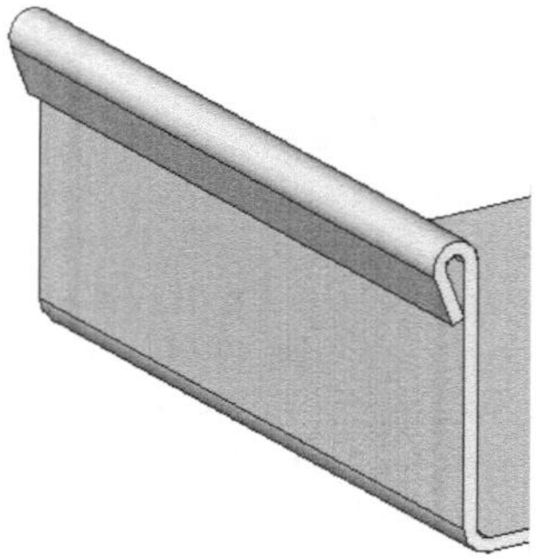

Figure 14-92 A closed loop hem

Centered Loop (In Ordered only)

This option is used to create a hem with a centered loop, as shown in Figure 14-93. The bend radii and the included angle can be specified in their respective edit boxes.

Miter hem

This check box is selected to miter a hem. You can specify a negative or a positive miter angle for the hem, as shown in Figures 14-94 and 14-95.

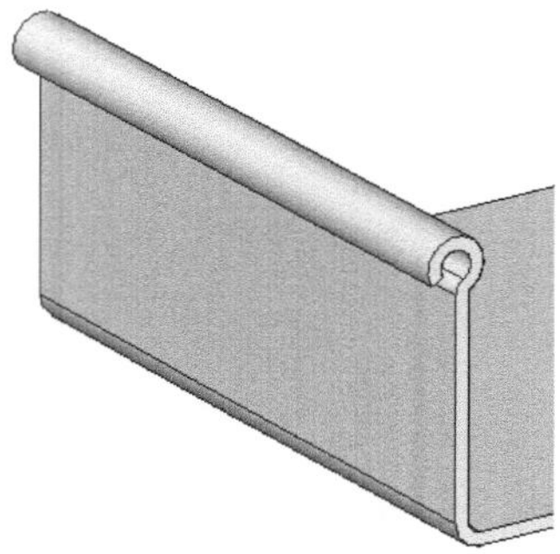

Figure 14-93 Hem with a centered loop

Note

The remaining options in this dialog box are same as those discussed earlier in this chapter.

After specifying the hem options, exit the dialog box by choosing **OK** and then select the edge on which you want to place the hem. Note that the hem will be placed on the face on which the selected edge lies. The procedure of creating hems in the **Synchronous** environment is the same as discussed in the **Ordered** environment.

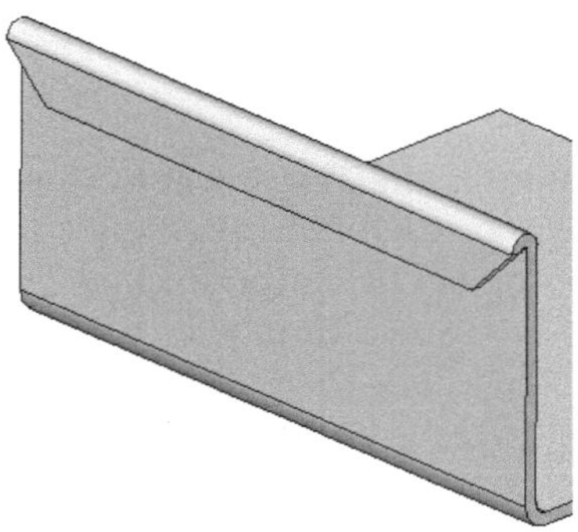

Figure 14-94 An open hem with a negative miter

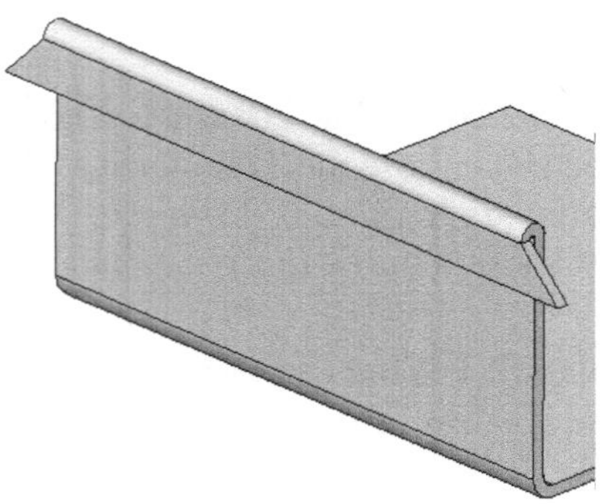

Figure 14-95 An open hem with a positive miter

CONVERTING A SOLID PART INTO A SHEET METAL PART

Solid Edge allows you to convert a solid part into a sheet metal part, the provided part is created in the solid modeling environment of a sheet metal file. To convert a solid part created in the **Ordered** environment into a sheet metal part, start a new sheet metal file and then switch to the **Ordered Sheet Metal** environment. You can switch to the **Ordered Sheet Metal** environment by using the **Switch to** tool from the **Transform** group of the **Tools** tab. On choosing this tool, the **Sheet Metal to Part** information box will be displayed. Choose **Yes** from this information box; the part modeling environment will be invoked. Now create the solid part that you want to use. For example, to create a sheet metal part, as shown in Figure 14-96, from a solid part, first you need to create a box-like solid part. Then, create a shell feature by removing one of its faces and specifying thickness. Finally, you can add the handles at the sides, as shown in Figure 14-97. After creating the required solid parts, switch back to the **Sheet Metal** environment by choosing **Switch to** tool from the **Transform** group of the **Tools** tab.

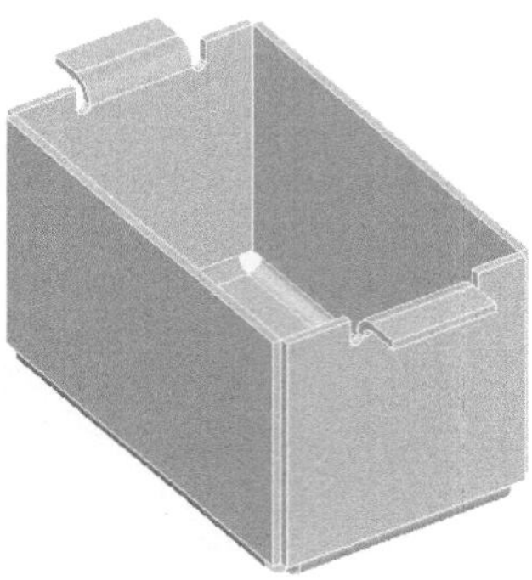

Figure 14-96 *Sheet metal component to be created*

Figure 14-97 *The part created in the **Part** environment*

After creating the solid part and switching back to the **Sheet Metal** environment, choose the **Thin Part to Sheet Metal** tool from the **Transform** group of the **Tools** tab in the **Ribbon** of the **Sheet Metal** environment; the **Thin Part to Sheet Metal** Command bar will be displayed. The options available in the Command bar are discussed next.

Transform to Sheet Metal Options

When you choose the **Transform to Sheet Metal Options** button, the **Transform to Sheet Metal Options** dialog box is displayed. The options in this dialog box have already been discussed. After specifying the desired values in the dialog box, choose the **OK** button to exit.

Select Face Step

When you invoke the **Thin Part to Sheet Metal** tool, the **Thin Part to Sheet Metal** Command bar will be displayed. Also, the **Select Face Step** button will be activated and you will be prompted to select the base face. Select the face that will act as the base of the sheet metal part. Depending on the type of model selected to be converted, the **Solid Edge** information box will be displayed, as shown in Figure 14-98. This information box will prompt you to split the edges. Choose **OK** from this box to rip the edges.

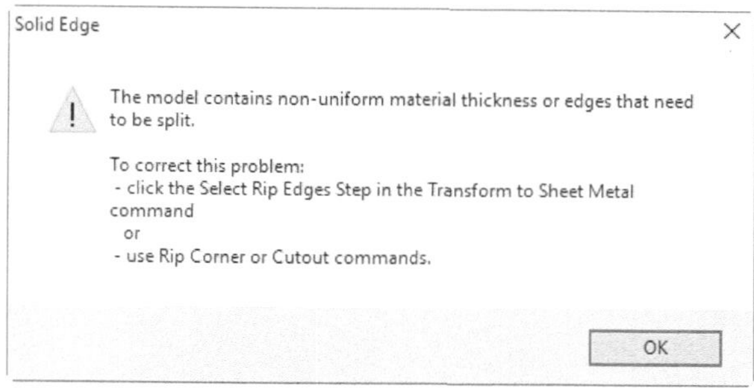

Figure 14-98 The ***Solid Edge*** *information box*

Select Rip Edges Step

You need to invoke this step manually by clicking on the **Select Rip Edges Step** button and select the edges to be ripped in the sheet metal part. Generally, the side edges of the joined faces are selected to be ripped. While the ripping takes place, the square bend relief is applied between the selected faces by default. The corner relief is also applied automatically to the corners of the edges selected to be ripped. Figure 14-99 shows the preview of the four vertical edges selected to be ripped and Figure 14-100 shows the resulting sheet metal part.

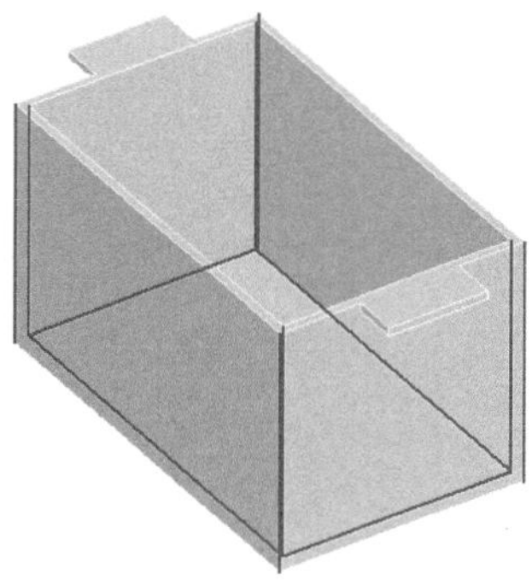

Figure 14-99 *Edges selected to be ripped*

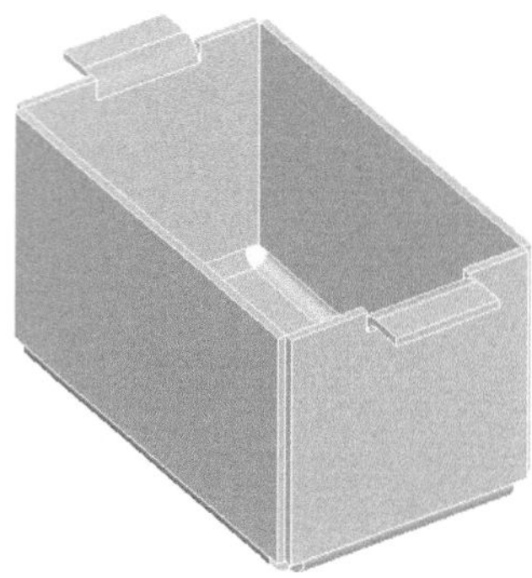

Figure 14-100 *Sheet metal part after ripping the corners*

However, if you are working in the **Synchronous Sheet Metal** environment, you need to create the required solid model in the **Synchronous Part** environment. After creating synchronous solid model, choose the **Thin Part to Synchronous Sheet Metal** tool from the **Transform** group of the **Tool** tab in the **Ribbon** of the **Synchronous Part** environment; the **Thin Part to Synchronous Sheet Metal** Command bar will be invoked in the same part environment. Select the base of the sheet metal; an information box will be displayed. Choose **OK** in the information box displayed. Choose the **Select Rip Edges Step** button from the Command bar. Then, select the edges to be ripped and accept the selection; the part will get converted into sheet metal part and can be opened in the **Synchronous Sheet Metal** environment.

RIPPING THE CORNERS OF A SOLID PART

Ribbon:	Sheet Metal > 2-Bend Corner drop-down > Rip Corner (Ordered and Synchronous)

You can rip the corners of a solid part using the **Rip Corner** tool. Note that when you use this tool, no corner relief is added to the model. To rip the corners, invoke this tool and select the edges whose corners you want to rip.

Note

You can also use the other tools such as ***Cut, Normal Cutout, Mirror****, and so on in the* ***Sheet Metal*** *environment. These tools are discussed in detail in the part modeling environment.*

ADDING SHEET METAL FEATURES TO A SOLID PART

In Solid Edge, you can add sheet metal features such as flanges, contour flanges, and dimples to a thin solid part created in the **Ordered Part** environment. To do so, create a thin walled part in the **Ordered Part** environment. Next, switch to the **Sheet Metal** environment by choosing **Switch to** tool from the **Transform** group of the **Tools** tab and create sheet metal features on the solid part, as shown in Figure 14-101.

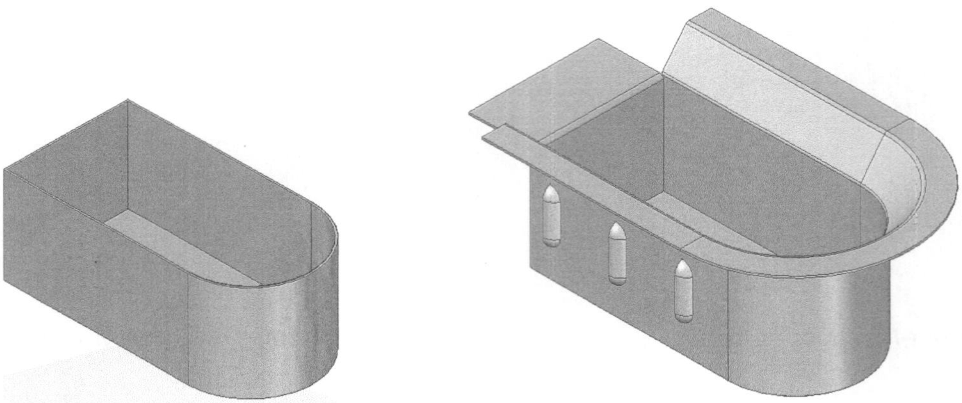

Figure 14-101 *Solid part and sheet metal features added to it*

CREATING THE FLAT PATTERN OF A SHEET METAL PART

Ribbon:	Tools > Model > Flatten (Ordered and Synchronous)

As mentioned earlier, you need to flatten a sheet metal part after creating it to generate its drawing views. Solid Edge provides a number of options to flatten a sheet metal part. Some of the options are discussed next.

Creating Flat Patterns in the Flat Pattern Environment

In Solid Edge, you need to create the flat pattern of a sheet metal component in the **Flat Pattern** environment. To invoke this environment in the **Ordered** environment, select the **Flatten** radio button from the **Model** group in the **Tools** tab. On doing so, the **Flatten** Command bar will be displayed and you will be prompted to click on the face to be oriented upward in the flat pattern. Select the base face of the sheet metal part; you will be prompted to select an edge that will define the X axis and the origin. Click on an edge close to one of its endpoints to define the orientation of the X axis. Note that after exiting the **Flatten** Command bar, you can invoke the **Flatten** tool again by choosing the **Flat Pattern** button from the **Flat** group in the **Tools** tab.

Figure 14-102 shows a sheet metal part and Figure 14-103 shows the top view of its flat pattern. Note that in the flat pattern, the lower horizontal edge close to the left endpoint was selected to define the X axis and the origin.

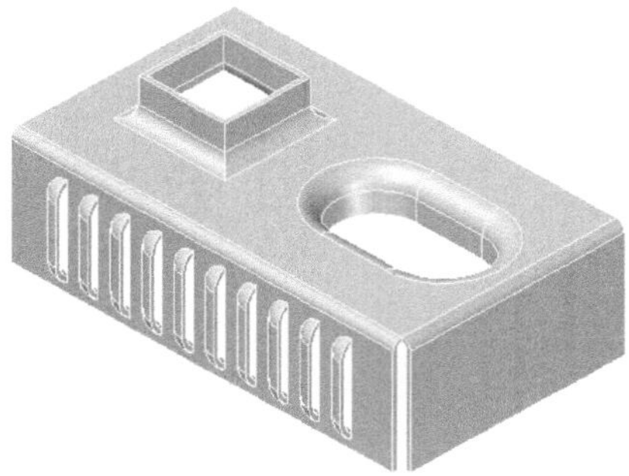

Figure 14-102 *The sheet metal part*

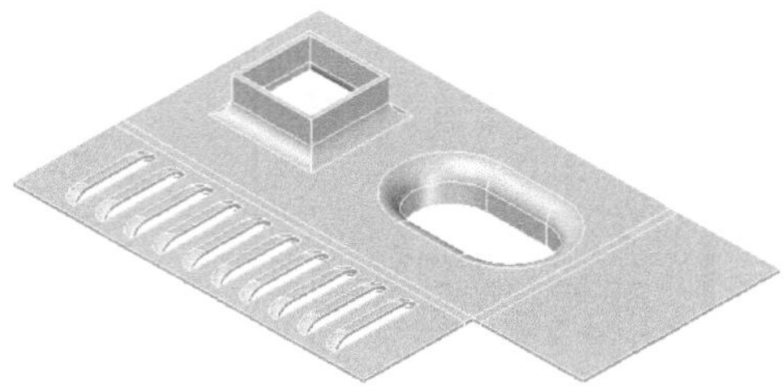

Figure 14-103 *The flat pattern*

Note

*You can create a **Tab** feature in the **Flat Pattern** environment. The **Tab** feature will be placed under the **Flat Pattern** node of the **PathFinder**. Any material added will be displayed in the **Flat Pattern** environment only.*

After creating the flat pattern, you can restore the sheet metal modeling environment by selecting the **Ordered** radio button from the **Model** group of the **Tools** tab. The flat pattern will be displayed under the **Flat Pattern** heading in the **PathFinder**. You can restore the **Flat Pattern** environment using the **Model** group in the **Tools** tab.

The working of the **Flatten** tool in the **Synchronous** environment is the same as in the **Ordered** environment. However, you can set different flat pattern treatment options using the Command bar.

In Solid Edge, you can flatten sheet metal parts with holes, deformed features, and having the bent portion.

Note

In Figure 14-102, you will observe that the features such as louvers, dimples, drawn cutouts, beads, and so on cannot be flattened, as these features are created using the punch and die.

Saving a Sheet Metal Part in the Flat Pattern Format

Application Button: Save As > Save As Flat (In both Ordered and Synchronous)

There is another method for creating a flat pattern. In this method, you need to save the sheet metal part as a flat pattern in a separate file. You can then save this file in the

AutoCAD (*.dxf), Solid Edge part, or Solid Edge sheet metal format. To save the flat pattern file, choose **Application Button > Save As > Save As Flat** in the **Sheet Metal** environment; the **Save As Flat** Command bar will be displayed. The steps in this Command bar are same as in the **Flatten** Command bar and have already been discussed. Select the face that is to be oriented upward, the edge to define the origin, and the X-axis; the **Save As Flat** dialog box will be displayed. Select the file type from the **Save as type** drop-down list and then specify the name and location of the flat pattern file to save it. Figure 14-104 shows the flattened sheet metal part. It is evident from this figure that the features such as louvers, dimples, drawn cutouts, and so on have been removed from the model.

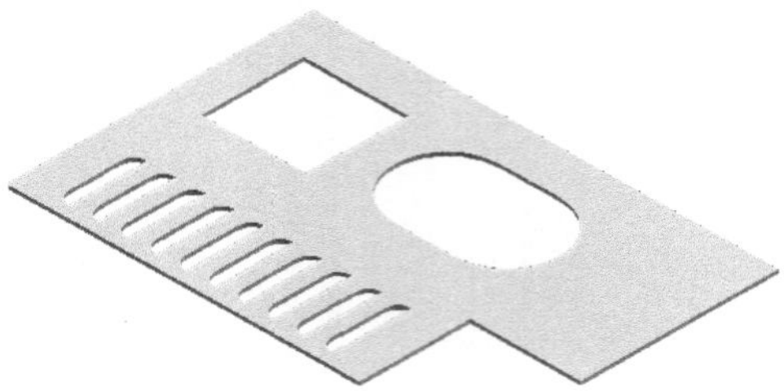

Figure 14-104 *Flat pattern saved as a separate sheet metal file*

Note

The flat pattern created in the ***Flat Pattern*** *environment will be associative to the original folded sheet metal component, whereas, the flat pattern created using the* ***Save As Flat*** *command will not be associative to the original folded sheet metal component.*

TUTORIALS

Tutorial 1 Synchronous Sheet Metal

In this tutorial, you will create the sheet metal part of the Holder Clip, shown in Figure 14-105, in the **Synchronous Sheet Metal** environment. The flat pattern of the component is shown in Figure 14-106 and its dimensions are given in Figure 14-107. Assume the missing dimensions of the part. The material thickness, bend radius, relief depth, and relief width is 1 mm each. The specifications of the louver are given next.

Type: Formed-end louver Length: 18 mm
Depth: 4 mm Height: 2.5 mm

After creating the sheet metal component, create its flat pattern. Save the component with the name *c14tut1.psm* at the location given next:

C:\Solid Edge\c14 **(Expected time: 45 min)**

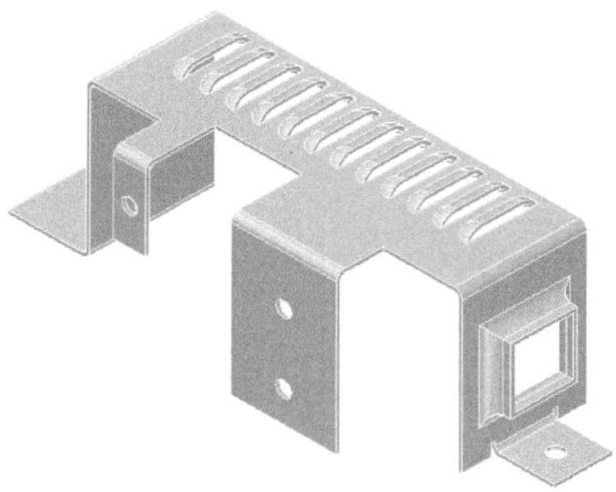

Figure 14-105 *Sheet metal part for Tutorial 1*

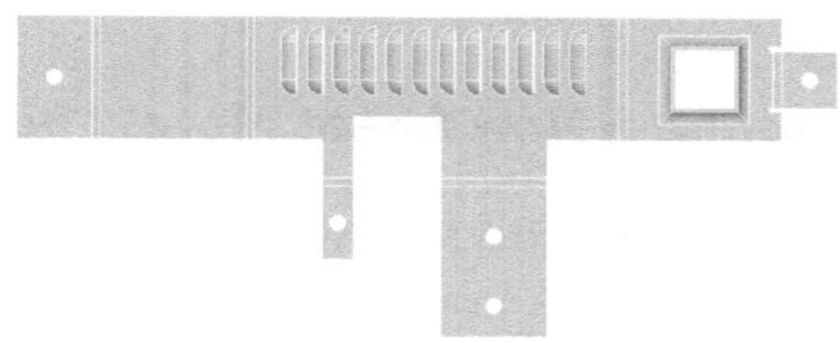

Figure 14-106 *Flat pattern of the sheet metal part for Tutorial 1*

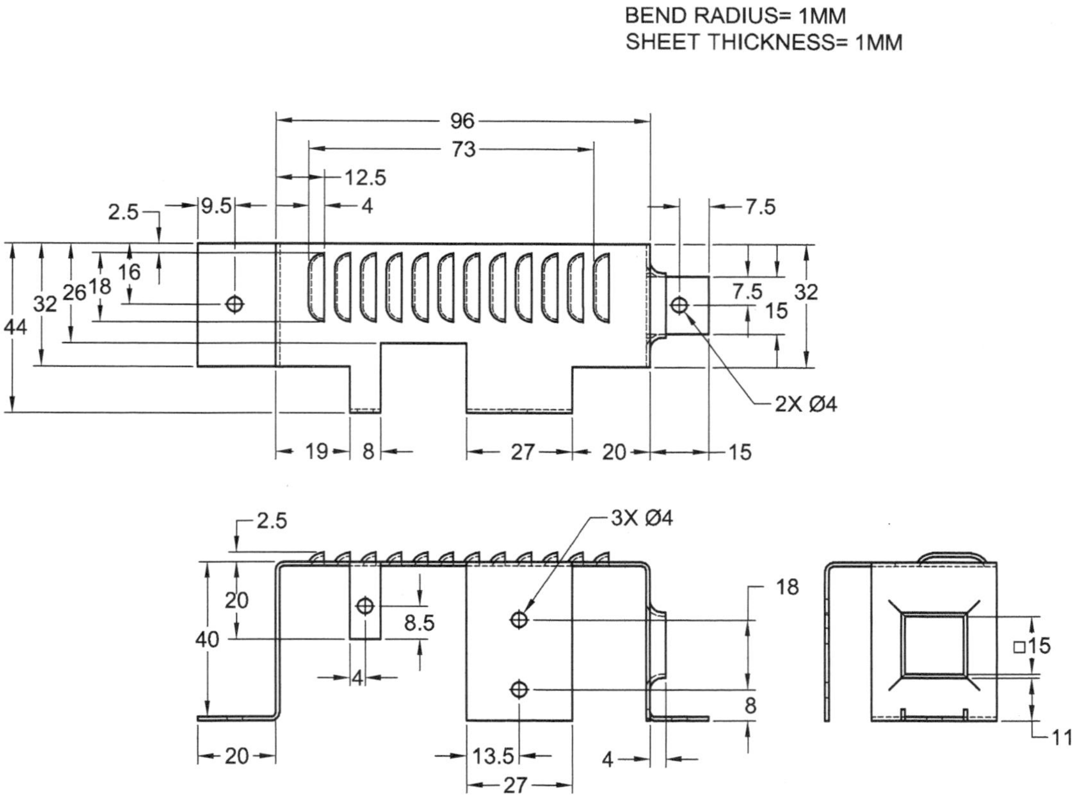

Figure 14-107 *Dimensions of the sheet metal part*

The following steps are required to complete this tutorial:

a. Start a new sheet metal file and set the sheet metal parameters.
b. Create the base feature by using the **Tab** tool, refer to Figures 14-108 and 14-109.
c. Create the flange on the front face of the base, refer to Figures 14-110 to 14-115.
d. Create a louver on the top face, refer to Figures 14-117 and 14-118.
e. Create the holes on the flanges, refer to Figure 14-119.

f. Create the drawn cutout on the right face of the model, refer to Figures 14-120 and 14-121.
g. Generate the flat pattern of the model, refer to Figure 14-122.
h. Save the model.

Starting a New Sheet Metal File

1. Choose the **ISO Metric Sheet Metal** option from the **New** tab of the welcome screen of Solid Edge; the **Synchronous Sheet Metal** screen is displayed.

2. Choose **Application Button > Info > Material Table**; the **Material Table** dialog box is displayed.

3. Choose the **Gage Properties** tab and set the value of the material thickness, bend radius, relief depth, and relief width to **1 mm** each and choose the **Apply to Model** button to apply the settings to the model.

Creating the Tab Feature

1. Invoke the **Line** tool and move the cursor toward the base coordinate system; the nearest principal plane gets highlighted.

2. Click when the XY plane gets highlighted. Use the **QuickPick** tool if the required plane does not get highlighted. You can also select the check box next to the **Base Reference Planes** node in the **PathFinder** to view the planes.

3. Choose the **Sketch View** button on the Status bar and draw the sketch for the top face of the part and apply dimensions and constraints, as shown in Figure 14-108. Make sure the **Maintain Relationships** and **Relationship Handles** buttons are activated in the **Relate** group of the **Home** tab.

4. Change the view and select the sketch region; a handle is displayed. Click on the handle; the preview of the tab feature is displayed.

5. Click when the direction of the preview is upward; the tab feature is created, as shown in Figure 14-109.

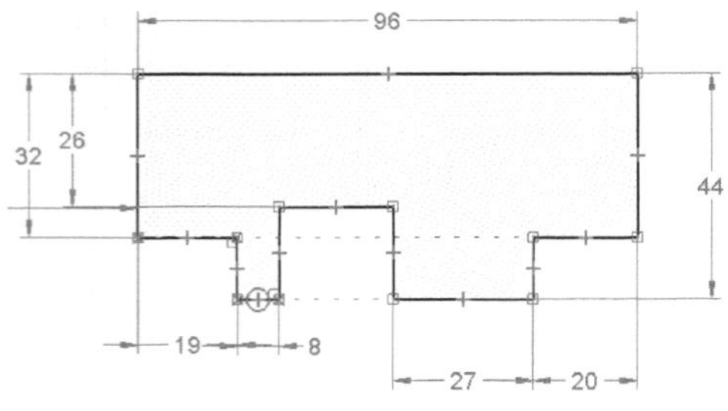

Figure 14-108 *Sketch for the top face of the part*

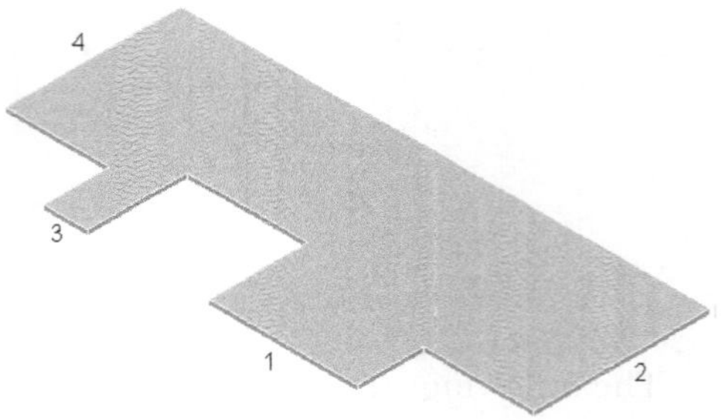

Figure 14-109 *The tab feature created*

Creating the Flanges

Next, you need to create various flanges on the top face of the sheet metal part. These flanges will be created using the Flange Start handle.

1. Select the face numbered **1** to create the flange; the Flange Start handle is displayed. Click on the Flange Start handle (the handle that is perpendicular to the selected face) and move the cursor downward; a preview of the full-width flange along with an edit box is displayed.

2. Specify **40** mm as the distance of the flange in the edit box and press ENTER. Figure 14-110 shows the preview of the flange.

   Note that the length of flange will be equal to the difference between the value entered in the edit box and the thickness of the sheet metal.

3. Similarly, create the flange of 40 mm length on the face numbered **2**, refer to Figure 14-111.

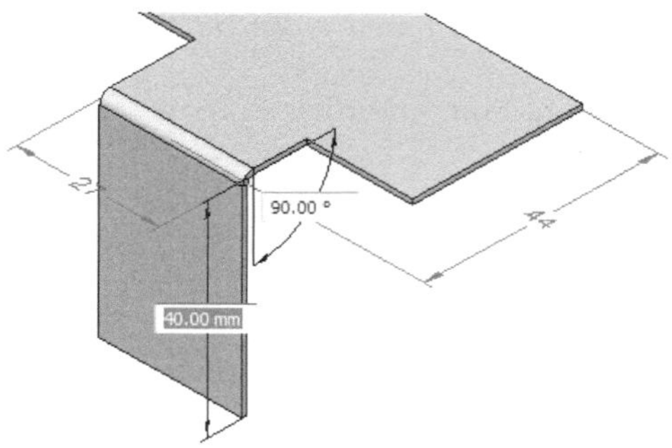

***Figure 14-110** Preview of the first flange*

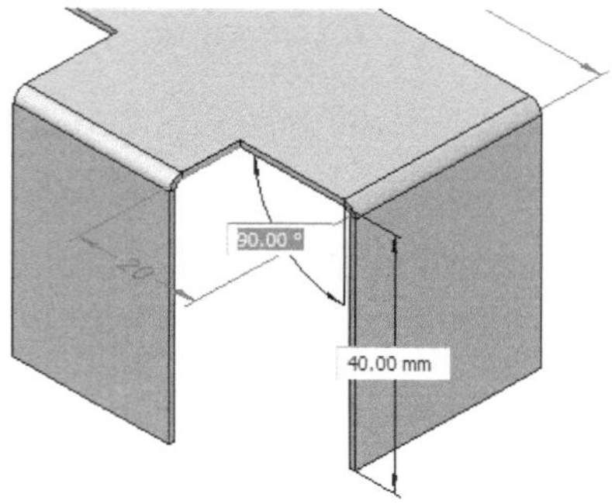

***Figure 14-111** Preview of the second flange*

Now, you need to create the centered flange.

4. Select the bottom face of the flange created last; the handles are displayed. Next, click on the Flange Start handle (shorter one); a preview of the flange is displayed. Also, the options in the Command bar change.

5. Choose the **Partial Flange** button from the Command bar to create a partial flange.

6. Specify **15** mm as the distance of the flange and then place the flange rightward.

   Now you need to position the partial flange. Refer to Figure 14-112 for dimensions.

7. Dimension the width of the flange and then dimension it again to position it at the center of the flange using the **Smart Dimension** tool. Next, modify the dimensions to the exact values and lock them.

8. Select the face numbered **3** and click on the Flange Start handle to create the fourth flange.

9. Specify **20** mm as the distance of the flange, refer to Figure 14-113, and click on the screen when the desired direction is displayed.

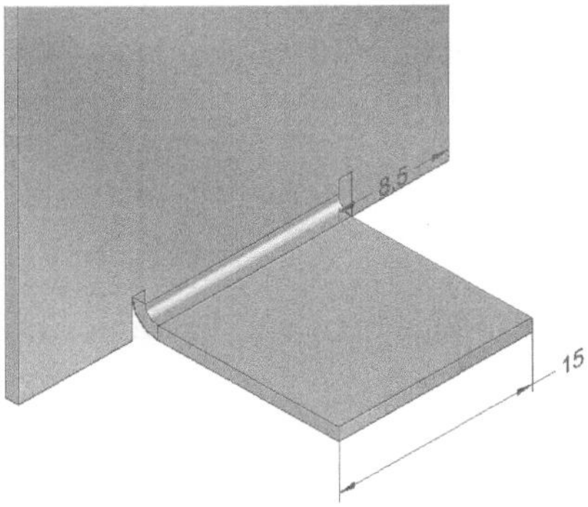

Figure 14-112 Preview of the centered flange

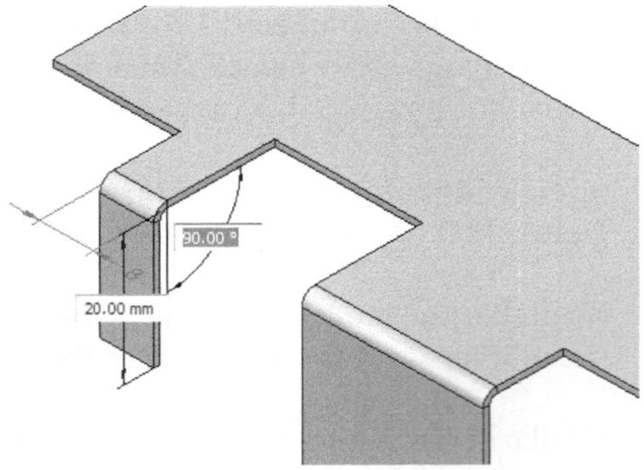

Figure 14-113 Preview of the fourth flange

10. Now, select the face numbered **4** and click on the Flange Start handle to create the fifth flange.

11. Specify **40** mm as the distance of the flange; a preview of the flange is displayed, as shown in Figure 14-114. Click when the desired direction of the flange creation is displayed.

12. Finally, create the sixth flange of **20** mm length on the bottom edge of the previous flange, refer to Figure 14-115.

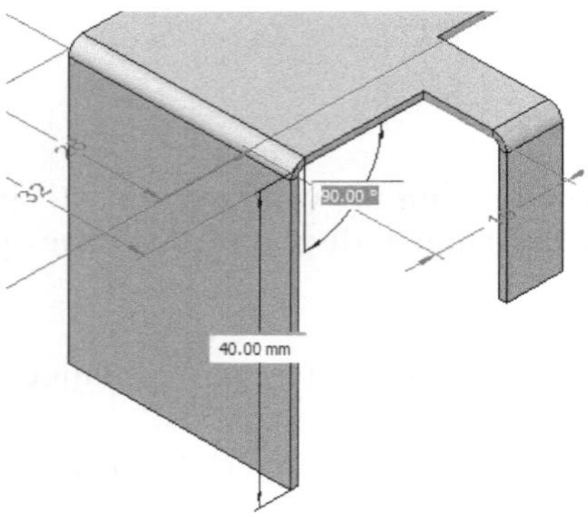

Figure 14-114 Preview of the fifth flange

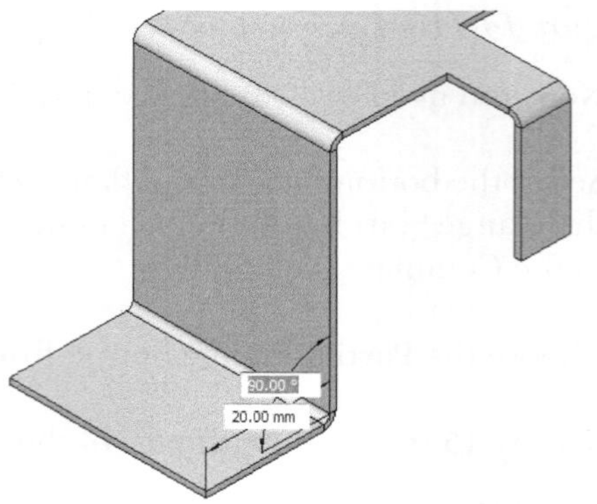

Figure 14-115 Preview of the sixth flange

Creating Louvers on the Top Face

Next, you need to create louvers on the top face. In this process, first need to create one of the louvers using the **Louver** tool and then create its rectangular pattern.

1. Choose the **Louver** tool from the **Dimple** drop-down of the **Sheet Metal** group of the **Home** tab; the **Louver** Command bar is displayed. Also, a louver is attached to the cursor and you are prompted to place it at the required plane.

2. Choose the **Louver Options** button from the Command bar; the **Louver Options** dialog box is displayed. Specify the settings, as shown in Figure 14-116, in the dialog box for the louver to be created and then exit the dialog box.

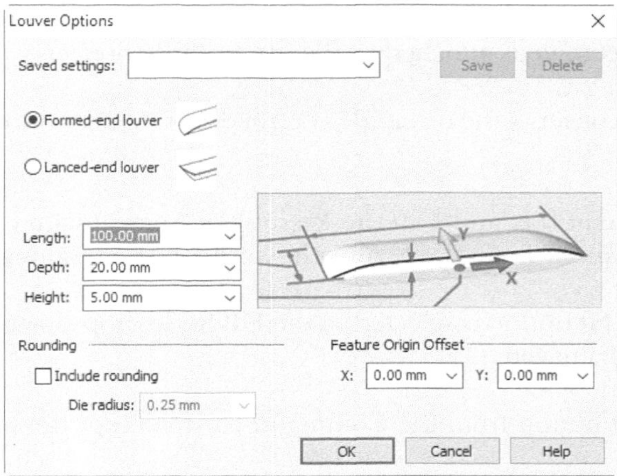

Figure 14-116 *Dialog box displaying the settings required for the louver to be created*

3. Move the cursor toward the top face of the base feature; a preview of the louver is displayed. If the orientation of the louver is incorrect, then press the N key or the B key from the keyboard to change the orientation to the possible orientations.

4. Click when the desired orientation and the approximate position is displayed.

Now you need to modify the position of the louver to an exact position.

Note

If the alignment of the louver is not appropriate after placing as shown in Figure 14-117, then you need to select it after placing; a rotate handle will be displayed. Next, you can use the rotate handle to place the louver to the correct alignment and then dimension it.

5. Create the dimensions of louver from the top and left faces and then modify them to the required values, as shown in Figure 14-117; the louver gets positioned correctly, as shown in Figure 14-118.

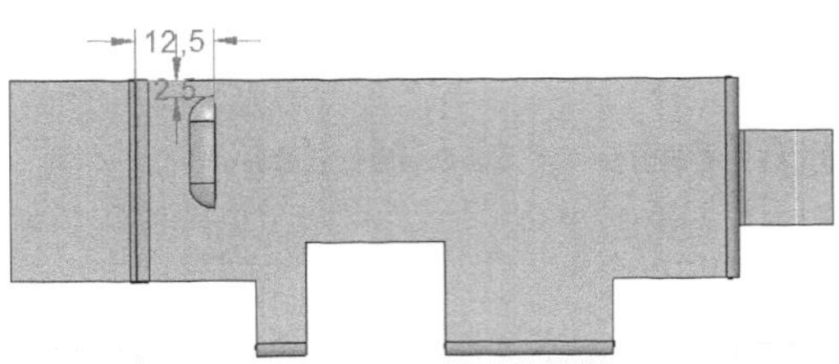

Figure 14-117 *Dimensions to position the louver*

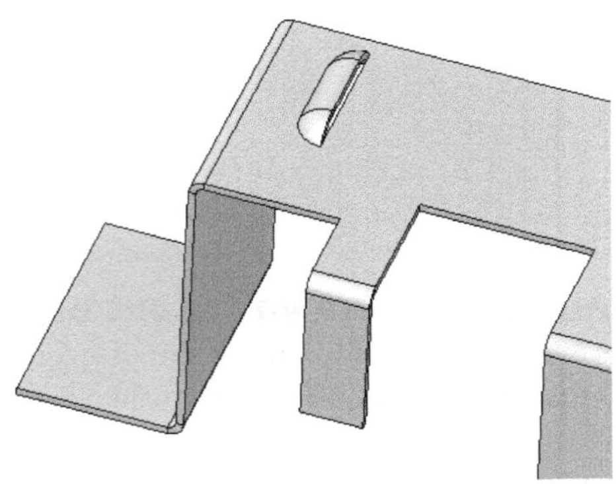

Figure 14-118 *Louver created on the top face*

Now you need to create the pattern of the louvers.

6. Select the louver and choose the **Rectangular** button from the **Pattern** group; the first corner of an imaginary rectangle is attached to the center of the louver.

7. Specify the second corner of the rectangle at right direction near the edge of the face number **2**.

8. Enter **12** in the **X** edit box and **1** in the **Y** edit box to create a rectangular pattern of the louver with 12 instances along the X direction and 1 instance along the Y direction.

9. Make sure that the **Fit** option is selected in the **Fill Style** drop-down list and enter **73** in the dynamic edit box displayed.

10. Choose the **Accept** button from the Command bar to accept the pattern created, refer to Figure 14-119.

Creating Holes

1. Invoke the **Hole** tool; a hole gets attached to the cursor. Change the dimensions of the hole by choosing the **Hole Options** button. For dimensions of the holes, refer to Figure 14-107.

2. Place the hole on the required faces of the sheet metal part. Refer to Figure 14-119 for the faces on which the hole needs to be placed.

3. Dimension the position of the holes using the **Smart Dimension** tool. Next, click on the dimension text; an edit box is displayed. Enter the required dimensions and modify the position of the holes. For dimensions of the holes, refer to Figure 14-107. The part after creating the holes is shown in Figure 14-119.

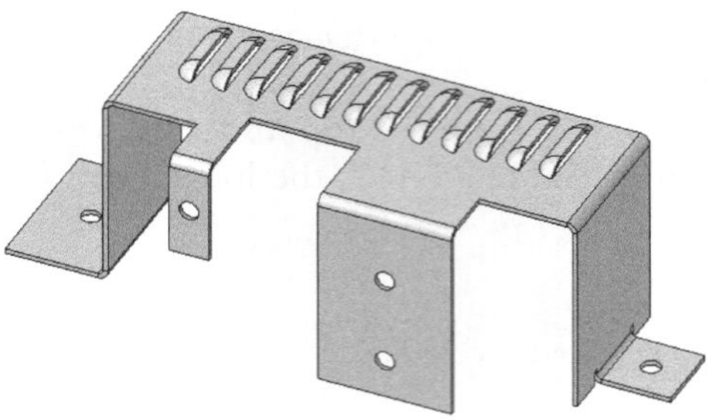

Figure 14-119 *Sheet metal part after creating five holes*

Creating the Drawn Cutout on the Right Face of the Model

Next, you need to create the drawn cutout on the right face. The sketch for this cutout is a square that will be drawn in the sketching environment.

1. Draw the profile of the drawn cutout on the right face of the model and apply dimensions and constraints to it, as shown in Figure 14-120. Make sure the **Maintain Relationships** and **Relationship Handles** buttons are activated in the **Relate** group of the **Ribbon**.

2. Choose **Drawn Cutout** from the **Dimple** drop-down of the **Sheet Metal** group of the **Home** tab and select the area of profile; a preview of the drawn cutout is displayed along with an edit box.

3. Choose the **Drawn Cutout Options** button from the Command bar; the **Drawn Cutout Options** dialog box is displayed. Next, select the **Include rounding** check box from the **Rounding** area, if it is not already selected; the **Die radius** edit box is displayed.

4. Enter **4** mm in the edit box and then clear the **Include punch-side corner radius** check box. Next, choose the **OK** button from the dialog box.

5. Next, enter **4** as the extent of the cutout in the edit box displayed on the cutout.

6. Specify the side of the cutout on the right of the face by clicking on the handle. The final sheet metal part is created, as shown in Figure 14-121.

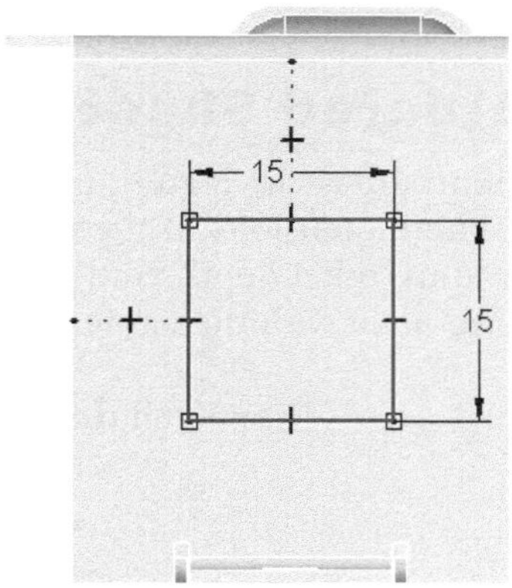

***Figure 14-120** Profile of the drawn cutout*

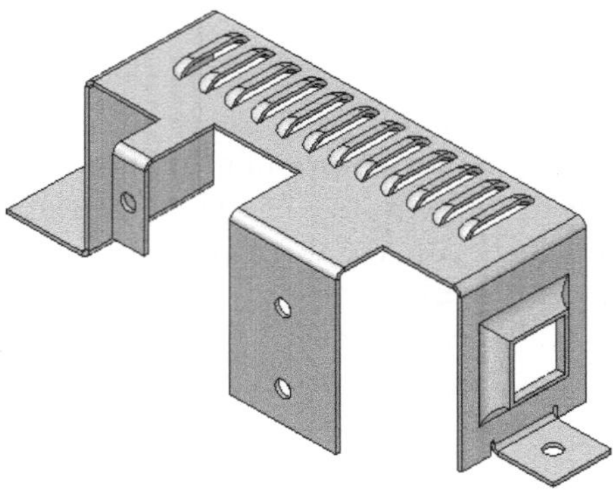

***Figure 14-121** The final sheet metal part*

Generating the Flat Pattern

Next, you need to generate the flat pattern of the sheet metal part created. The flat pattern will be generated in the **Flat Pattern** environment.

1. Select the **Flatten** radio button from the **Model** group in the **Tools** tab; the **Flatten** Command bar is displayed. Also, you are prompted to click on the face to be oriented upward.

2. Select the top face of the sheet metal part; you are prompted to click on an edge to define the X axis and the origin.

3. Select the left horizontal edge of the top face close to the left endpoint of the edge; the flat pattern of the model is created, as shown in Figure 14-122.

4. Restore the Sheet Metal modeling environment by selecting the **Synchronous** radio button from the **Model** group of the **Tools** tab.

Saving the Model

1. Save the model with the name *c14tut1.psm* at the location given next and then close the file.

    C:\Solid Edge\c14

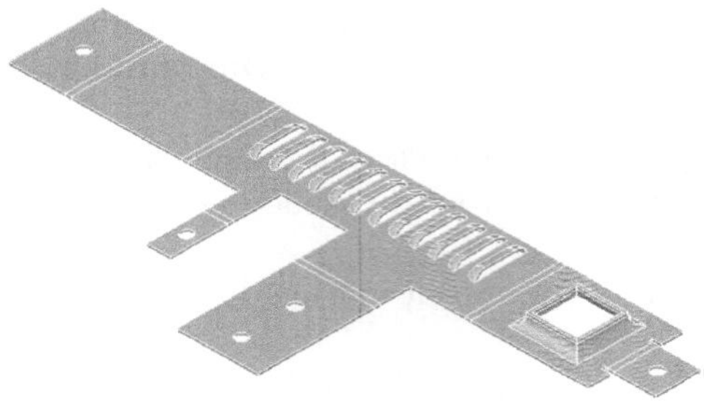

Figure 14-122 *Flat pattern of the sheet metal part*

Tutorial 2 Ordered Sheet Metal

In this tutorial, you will create the sheet metal component shown in Figure 14-123. The flat pattern of the component is shown in Figure 14-124. The dimensions of the component are shown in Figure 14-125. The material thickness, bend radius, relief depth, and relief width is 1 mm each. Assume the missing dimensions. Save the component with the name *c14tut2.psm* at the location given next:

C:\Solid Edge\c14 **(Expected time: 30 min)**

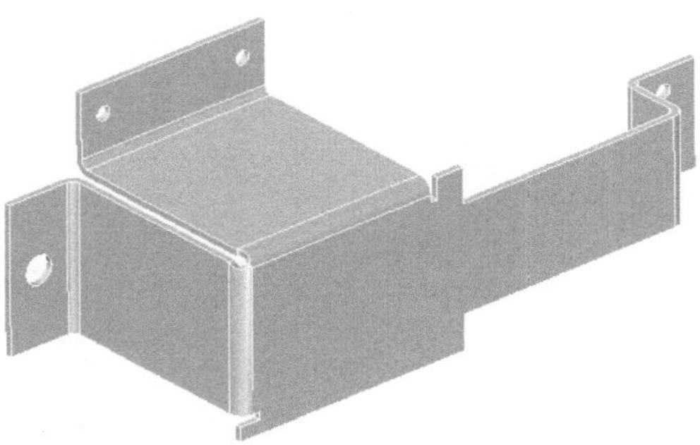

Figure 14-123 *Sheet metal part for Tutorial 2*

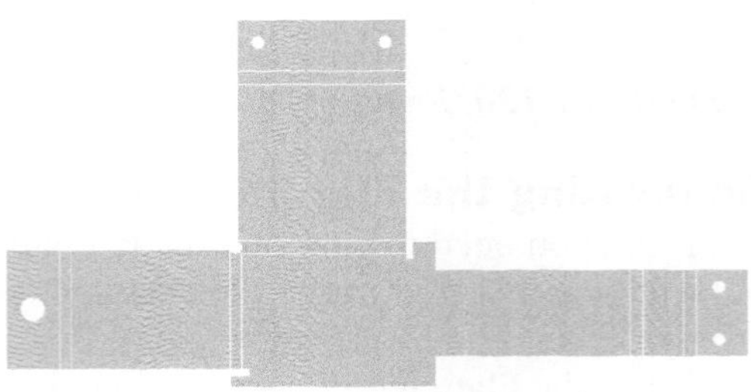

Figure 14-124 *Flat pattern of the part*

The following steps are required to complete this tutorial:

a. Start a new sheet metal file and set the sheet metal parameters.
b. Create the base feature, which is the front face, by using the tab tool, refer to Figures 14-126 and 14-127.
c. Create the flanges on the front face base feature, refer to Figures 14-128 and 14-129.
d. Close the corner of the flanges, as shown in Figure 14-131.
e. Create the holes, as shown in Figure 14-132.
f. Generate the flat pattern of the sheet metal part, as shown in Figure 14-133.

g. Save the model.

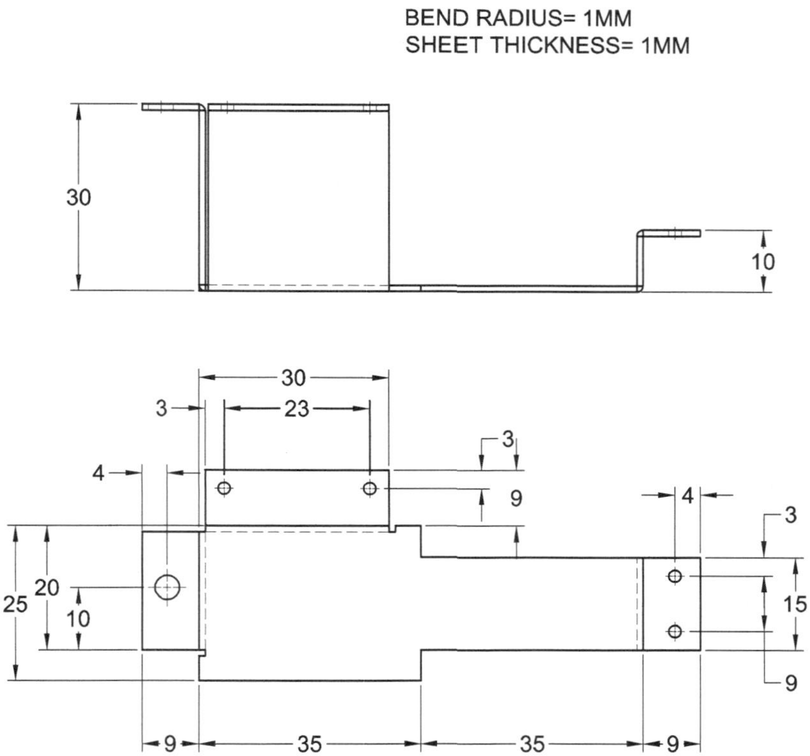

Figure 14-125 Dimensions of the sheet metal part

Starting a New Sheet Metal File

1. Start Solid Edge and then click on **ISO Metric Sheet Metal** in the **Create** area of the welcome screen to start a new sheet metal file.

2. Choose **Application Button > Info > Material Table**; the **Material Table** dialog box is invoked.

3. Choose the **Gage Properties** tab and set the value of the material thickness, bend radius, relief depth, and relief width to **1 mm**.

4. Press the ENTER key or choose the **Apply to Model** button to exit this dialog box.

5. Switch to the **Ordered Sheet Metal** environment by selecting the **Ordered** radio button from the **Model** group of the **Tools** tab.

Creating the Front Face

1. Choose the **Tab** tool from the **Sheet Metal** group of the **Home** tab; the **Tab** tool is invoked and you are prompted to click on a planar face or a reference plane.

2. Select the **Front (XZ)** plane as the sketching plane and invoke the sketching environment.

3. Draw the sketch for the front face of the part, as shown in Figure 14-126.

4. Exit the sketching environment and specify the thickness of the sheet metal part in the backward direction. Exit the **Tab** tool to create the base of the sheet metal part, as shown in Figure 14-127.

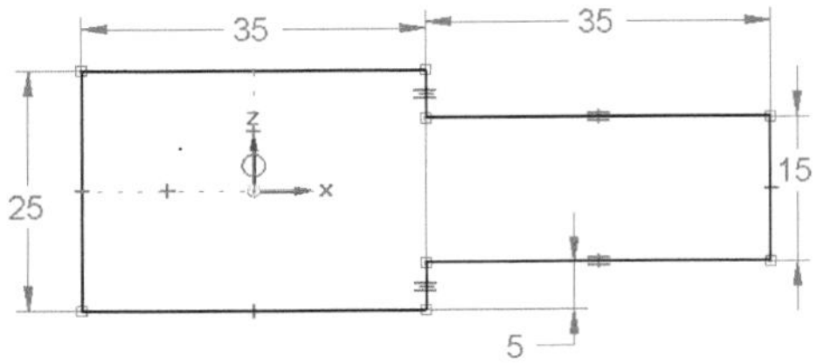

Figure 14-126 *Sketch for the front face*

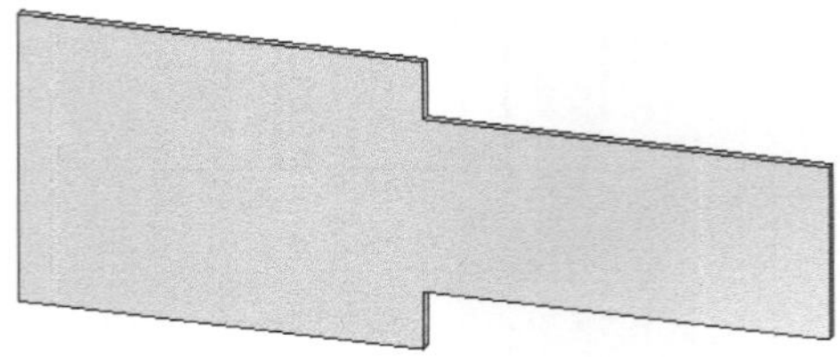

Figure 14-127 *Front face of the part*

Creating Flanges

Next, you need to create various flanges on the front face of the sheet metal part. These flanges will be created using the **Flange** tool.

1. Choose the **Flange** tool from the **Sheet Metal** group of the **Home** tab; the **Flange** tool is invoked and you are prompted to click on a thickness face edge.

2. Select the top left horizontal edge to create the flange; a preview of the flange is displayed. Now, choose the **At End** button from the Command bar. Then select the left endpoint of the top edge to locate the flange.

3. Specify the distance of the flange as **30** mm; the preview of the flange gets modified. Click on the drawing area to specify the direction of the flange. Click on the dimension of the width of the flange and modify it to **30** mm in the **Dimension Value** edit box. Figure 14-128 shows the preview of the flange after modifying the width. Choose the **Finish** button and then the **Cancel** button to create the flange.

   Now you need to create a flange on the left face of the feature.

4. Select the left vertical edge and specify the distance of the flange as **30** mm.

5. Choose the **At End** button and select the top endpoint of the edge to position the flange. Also, choose the **Material Outside** button from the Command bar. Next, click to define the side of flange and modify its width to **20** mm in the preview.

6. Choose the **Flange Options** button from the Command bar to invoke the **Flange Options** dialog box and select the **Corner relief** check box. Select the **Bend and face** radio button and choose **OK** to exit the dialog box; a preview of the second flange will be displayed, as shown in Figure 14-129. Choose the **Finish** button and then the **Cancel** button to create the flange.

7. Create the remaining flanges, as shown in Figure 14-130. For dimensions, refer to Figure 14-125.

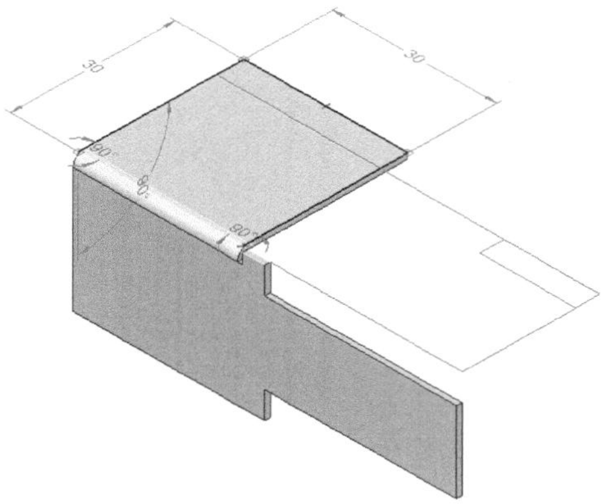

Figure 14-128 Preview of the top flange

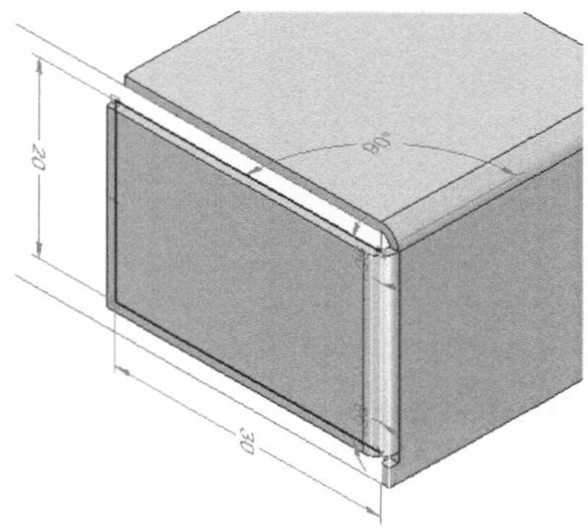

Figure 14-129 Preview of the left flange

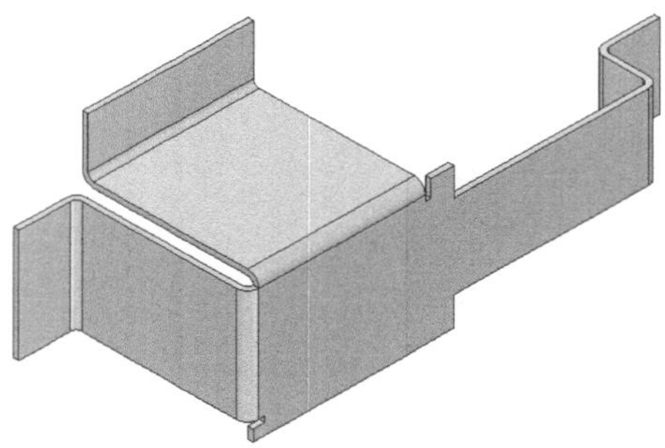

Figure 14-130 Model after creating all flanges

Closing the Corner between the First Two Flanges

The corner between the first two flanges needs to be closed. This is done by using the **Close 2-Bend Corner** tool.

1. Choose the **Close 2-Bend Corner** tool from the **2-Bend Corner** drop-down of the **Sheet Metal** group of the **Home** tab; the **Close 2-Bend Corner** tool is invoked and you are prompted to click on the bend to be modified.

2. Select the bends of the first two flanges created to define the corner to be closed.

3. Select the **Circular Cutout** option from the **Corner Treatment** drop-down list in the Command bar. Specify the gap value as **0.25** mm and the diameter as **2** mm.

4. Right-click or choose the **Accept** button and then the **Finish** button to close the corner. The part after closing the corner is shown in Figure 14-131.

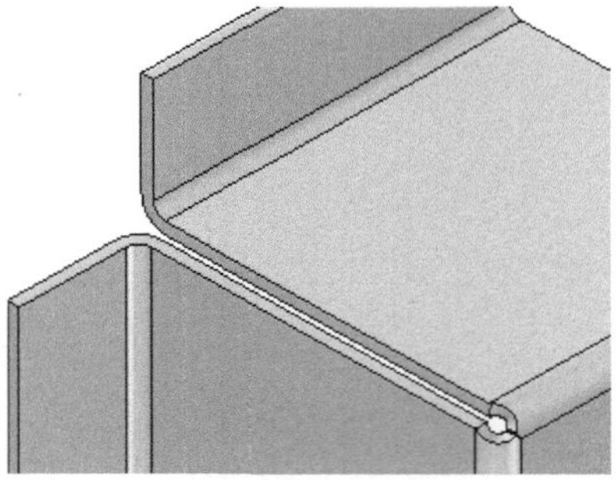

Figure 14-131 Partial view of the part after closing the corner

Creating Holes

1. Choose the **Hole** tool from the **Sheet Metal** group of the **Home** tab; the **Hole** Command bar is displayed.

2. Change the dimensions of the hole by choosing the **Hole Options** button and create the holes on the left most flange. For dimensions of the holes, refer to Figure 14-125. Similarly, create the other holes. The final sheet metal part after creating the holes is shown in Figure 14-132.

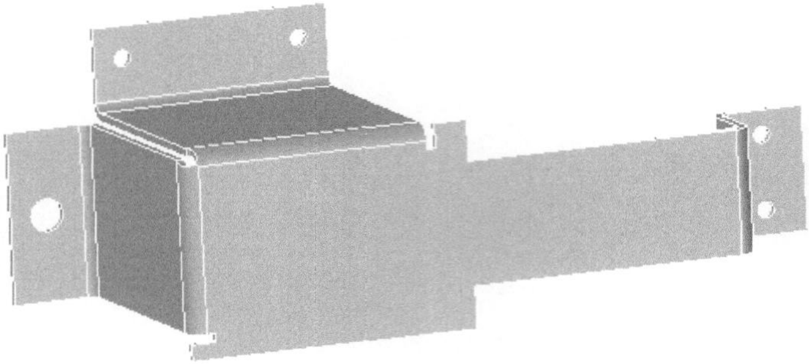

Figure 14-132 Final sheet metal part after creating the holes

Generating the Flat Pattern

Next you need to generate the flat pattern of the sheet metal part. The flat pattern will be generated in the **Flat Pattern** environment.

1. Select the **Flatten** radio button from the **Model** group in the **Tools** tab; the **Flat Pattern** environment is invoked and the **Flatten** Command bar is displayed. Also, you are prompted to click on a face to be oriented upward.

2. Select the front face of the sheet metal part; you are prompted to click on an edge to define the X-axis and the origin.

3. Select the top horizontal edge of the front face close that is to the left endpoint of the edge; the flat pattern of the model is created, as shown in Figure 14-133.

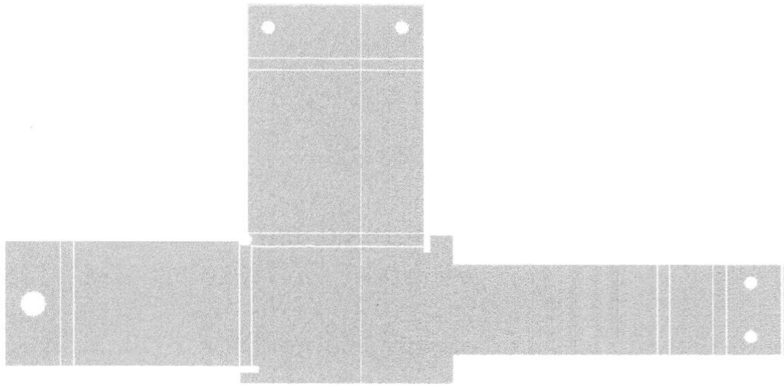

Figure 14-133 Flat pattern of the sheet metal part

Saving the Model

1. Save the model with the name *c14tut2.psm* at the location given next and then close the file.

   C:\Solid Edge\c14

Self-Evaluation Test

Answer the following questions and then compare them to those given at the end of this chapter:

1. You can unbend a sheet metal part by using the __________ tool.
2. The unbent sheet metal parts can be bent again using the __________ tool.
3. In Solid Edge, the sheet metal parts are bent using a sketched __________.
4. Solid Edge allows you to close the corner between two flanges using the __________ tool.
5. To create the flange at the center of the selected edge, you need to choose the __________ button from the **Flange** Command bar.
6. To convert a solid model into a sheet metal component, you first need to __________ it.
7. The sheet metal files are saved as the **.psm* files. (T/F)
8. When you invoke a new sheet metal file, sketching environment is invoked by default. (T/F)
9. You can use a spline to create the contour flange. (T/F)
10. You can draw a closed or an open sketch for creating the dimple feature. (T/F)

Review Questions

Answer the following questions:

1. Which of the following shapes does a louver have?

   (a) Lanced (b) Formed end
   (c) Both (a) and (b) (d) None

2. Which one of the following is not a type of treatment for a 2-bend corner?

   (a) Open (b) Close
   (c) Circular cutout (d) Square cutout

3. Which of the following tools is used to create a base of the sheet metal component?

   (a) **Flange** (b) **Contour Flange**
   (c) **Tab** (d) **Louver**

4. Which of the following tools can be used to fillet all the corners of the base feature?

   (a) **Round** (b) **Break Corner**
   (c) **Chamfer** (d) **2-Bend Corner**

5. After creating a sheet metal part, you can modify its thickness using the **Gage Properties** tab in the **Solid Edge Material Table** dialog box. (T/F)

6. The flat pattern is generated in a separate environment of sheet metal. (T/F)

7. You can set the material for the sheet metal part using the **Solid Edge Material Table** dialog box. (T/F)

8. There is no relation between the height and width of the louver. (T/F)

9. The **Drawn Cutout** tool can be invoked from the **Dimple** flyout. (T/F)

10. Beads can be created using the open or closed sketches. (T/F)

EXERCISES

Exercise 1

Create the sheet metal part shown in Figure 14-134. The flat pattern of the part is shown in Figure 14-135. Its dimensions are shown in Figure 14-136. The value of sheet thickness is 2mm and the value of bend radius, relief depth, and relief width is 1 mm.

(Expected time: 30 min)

Figure 14-134 *Sheet metal part for Exercise 1*

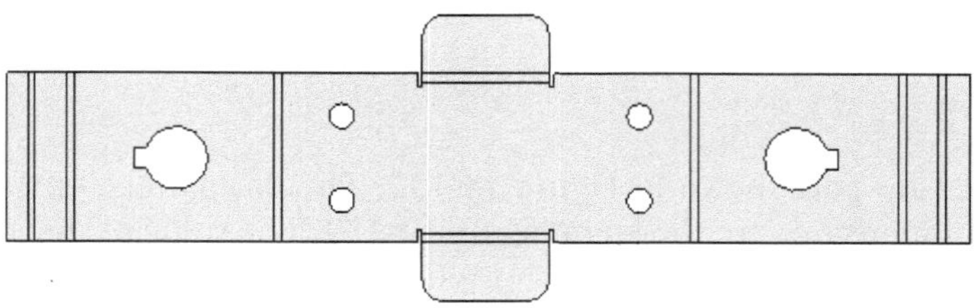

Figure 14-135 *Flat pattern of the part*

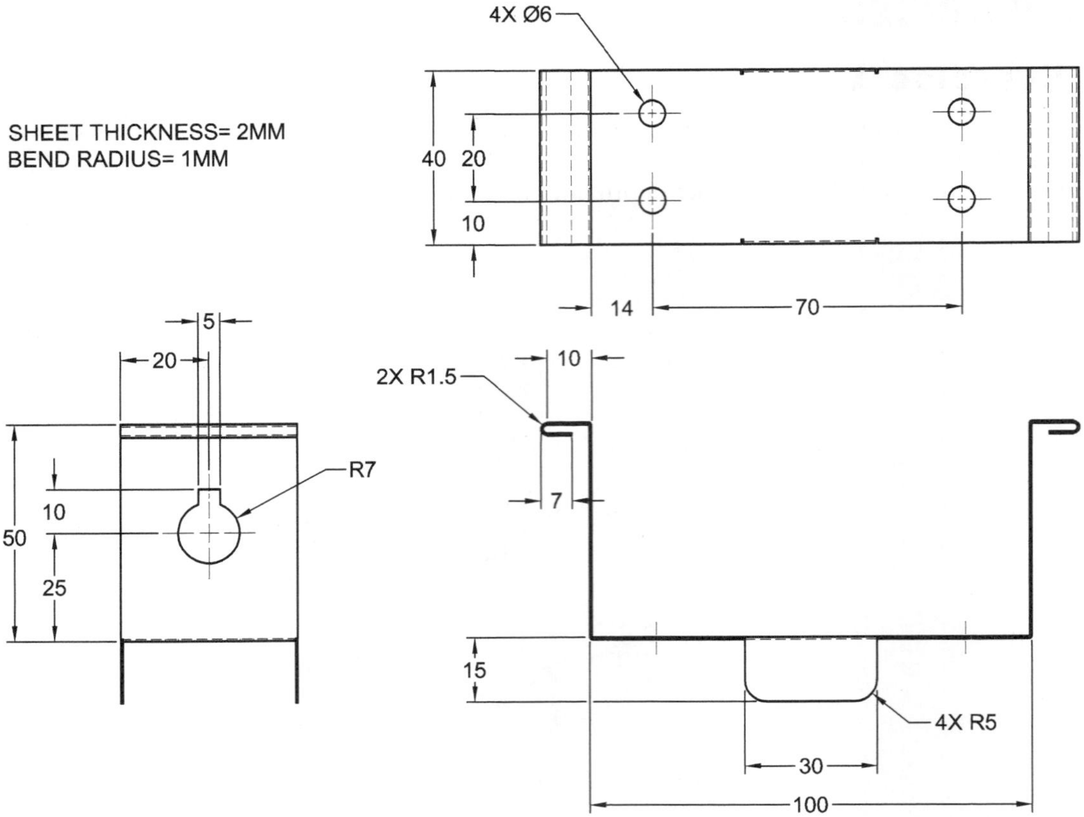

Figure 14-136 *Dimensions of the sheet metal part*

Exercise 2

Create the Holder Clip part shown in Figure 14-137. The flat pattern of the part is shown in Figure 14-138. Its dimensions are shown in Figure 14-139. The value of sheet thickness is 2 mm and the value of bend radius, relief depth, and relief width is 1 mm.

(Expected time: 30 min)

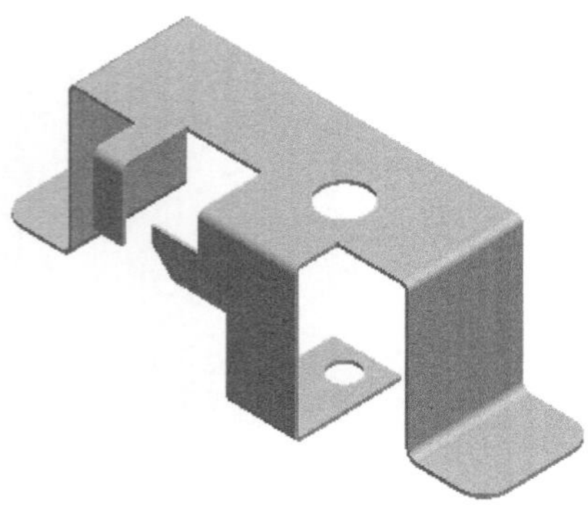

Figure 14-137 *The Holder Clip*

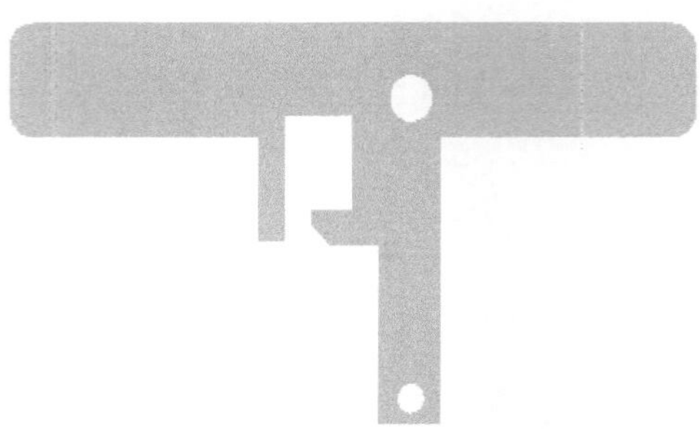

Figure 14-138 *The flat pattern of the Holder Clip*

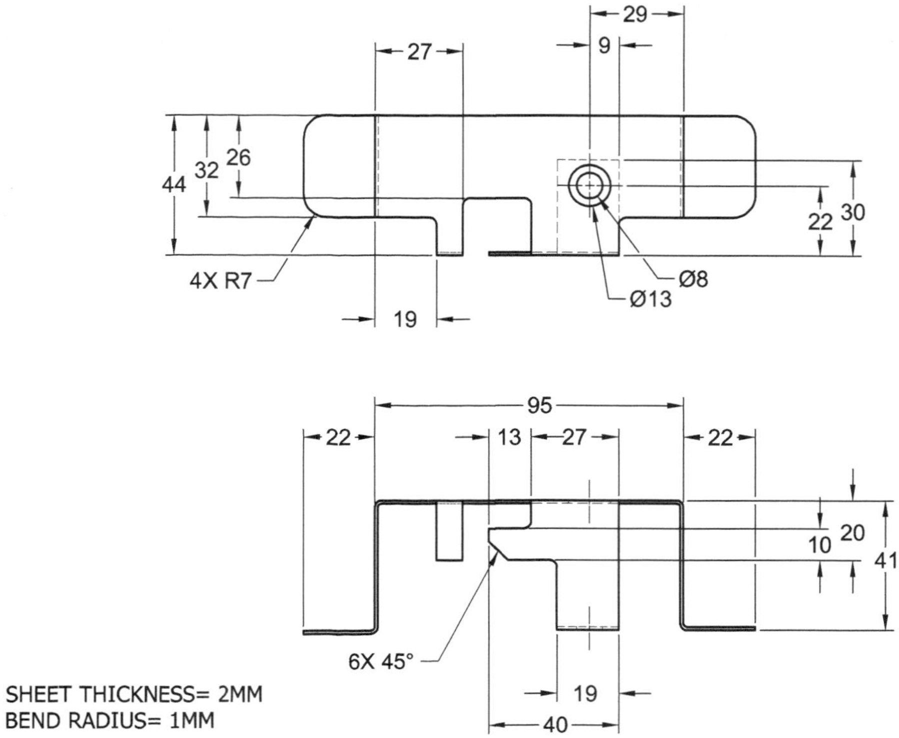

Figure 14-139 Dimensions of the sheet metal part

Answers to Self-Evaluation Test

1. **Unbend**, **2.** **Rebend**, **3.** line, **4.** **Close 2-Bend Corner**, **5.** **Centered**, **6.** shell, **7.** T, **8.** F, **9.** F, **10.** T

Chapter 15

Student Projects

Learning Objectives

After completing this chapter, you will be able to:

- *Create components of project in the Ordered Part and Synchronous Part environments*
- *Assemble components in the Assembly environment*
- *Generate drawing views of assembly in the Draft environment*

Project 1

In this project, you will create the components of a Fixture assembly in the **Synchronous Part** environment and then assemble them in the **Assembly** environment. The Fixture assembly and exploded view of the assembly are shown in Figures 15-1 and 15-2 respectively. The details of the components of the Fixture assembly are shown in Figure 15-3 through Figure 15-6. Finally, you will generate the following drawing views of the assembly, refer to Figure 15-7.

(Expected time: 3 hr)

a. Top view
b. Front view
c. Right-side view
d. Isometric view

ITEM NUMBER	PART NAME	MATERIAL	QUANTITY
1	END PLATE	STEEL	2
2	DISK	STEEL	2
3	SUPPORT PIN	STEEL	4
4	SPACER	STEEL	1
5	CENTER PIN	STEEL	1
6	BOLT	STEEL	4
7	NUT	STEEL	4

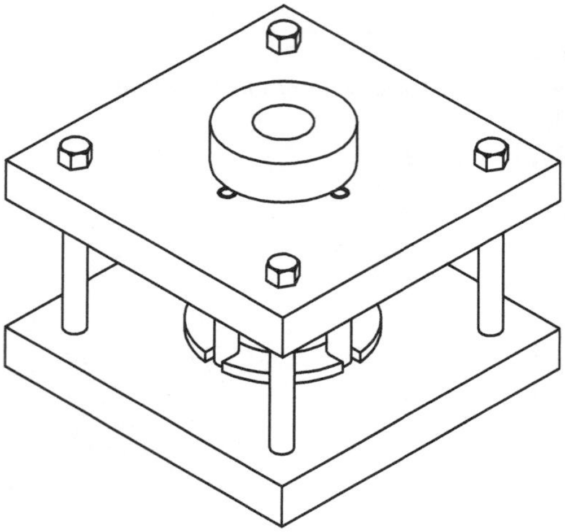

Figure 15-1 *Fixture assembly*

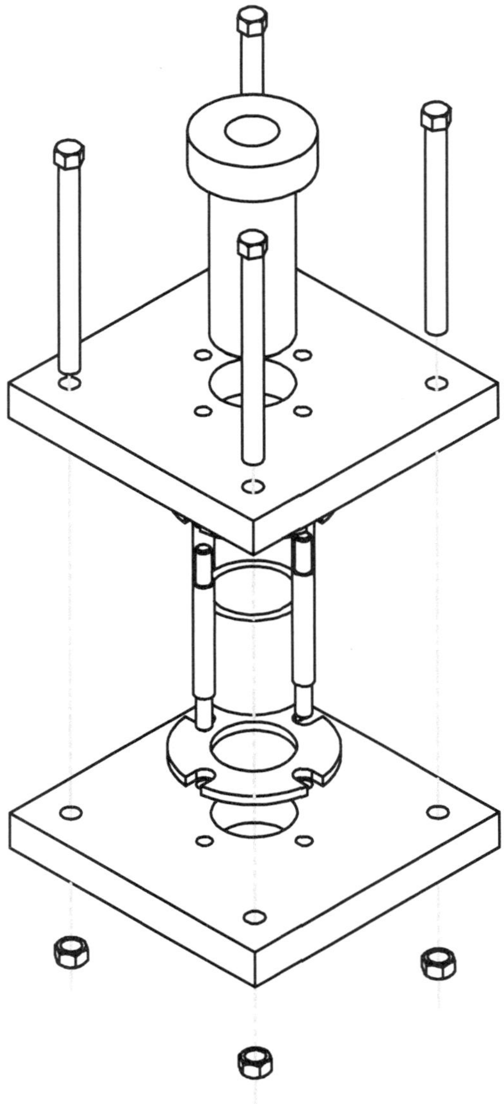

Figure 15-2 *Exploded view of the assembly*

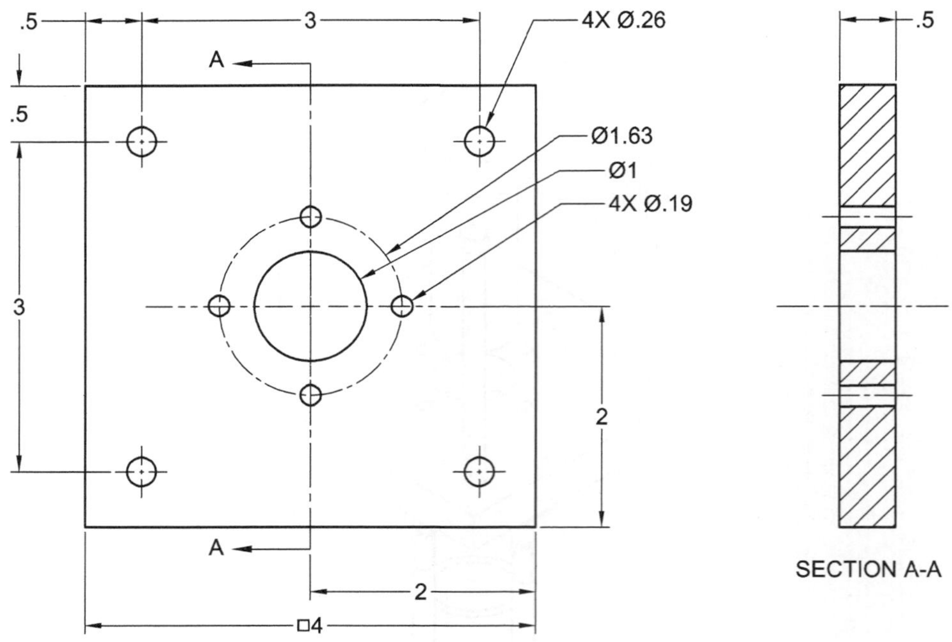

Figure 15-3 Dimensions of the End Plate

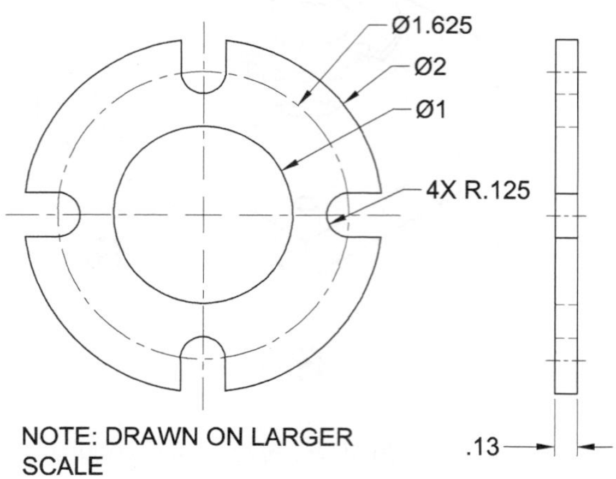

Figure 15-4 Dimensions of the Disk

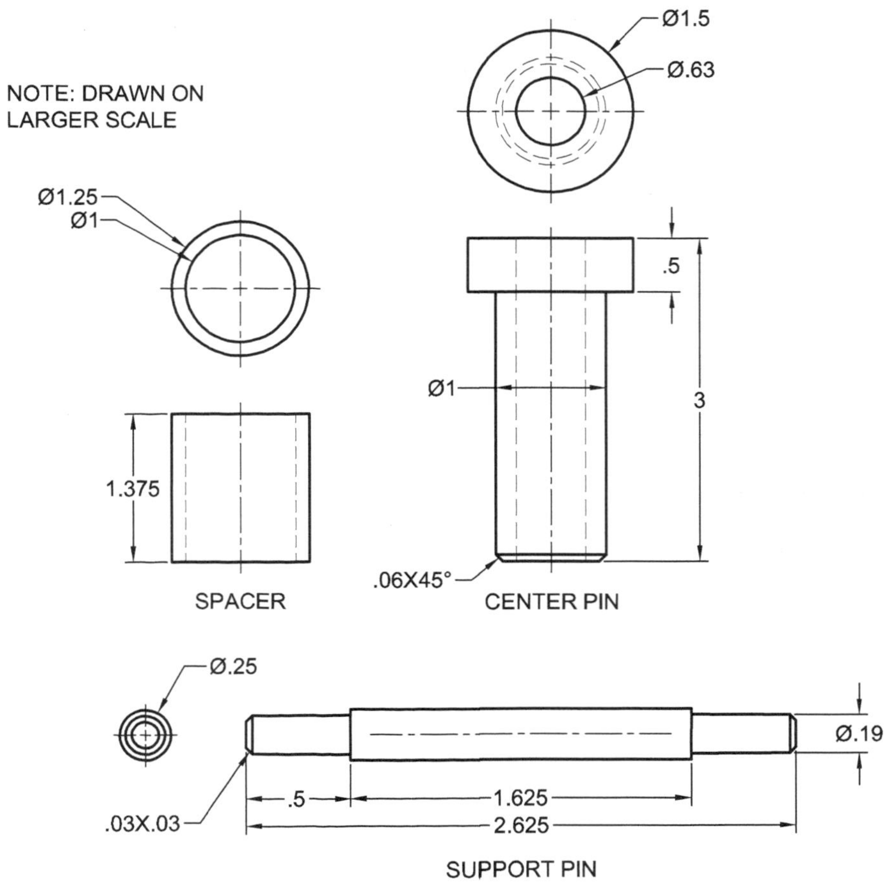

Figure 15-5 *Dimensions of the Spacer, Center Pin, and Support Pin*

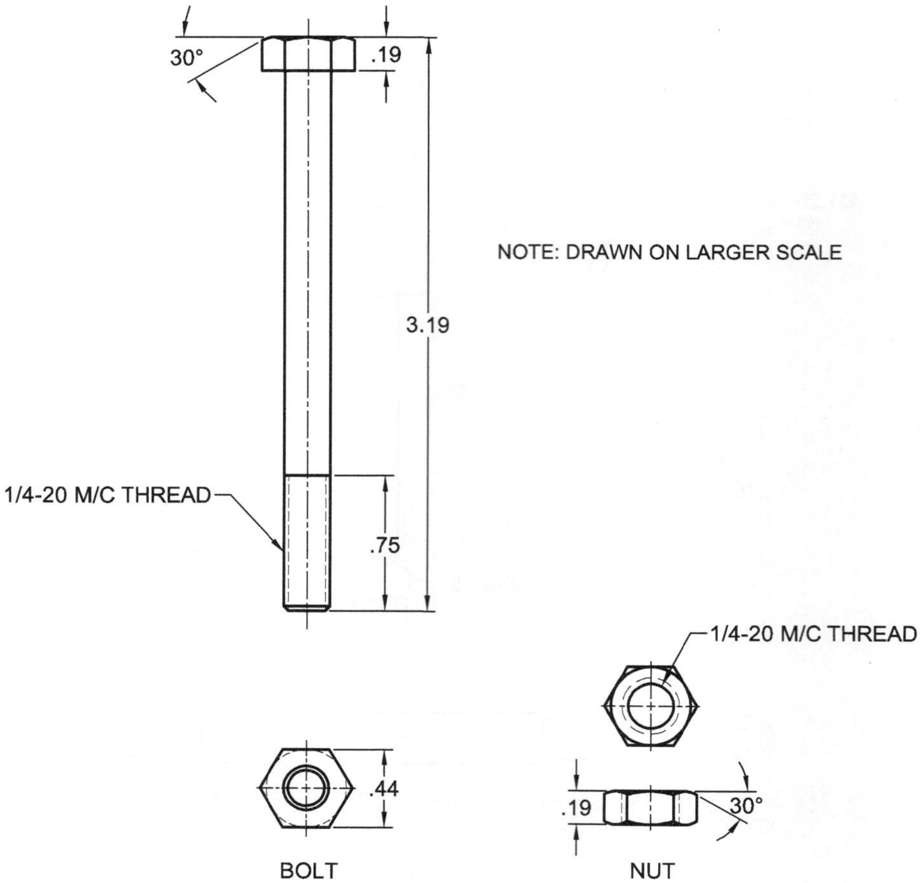

Figure 15-6 Dimensions of the Bolt and Nut

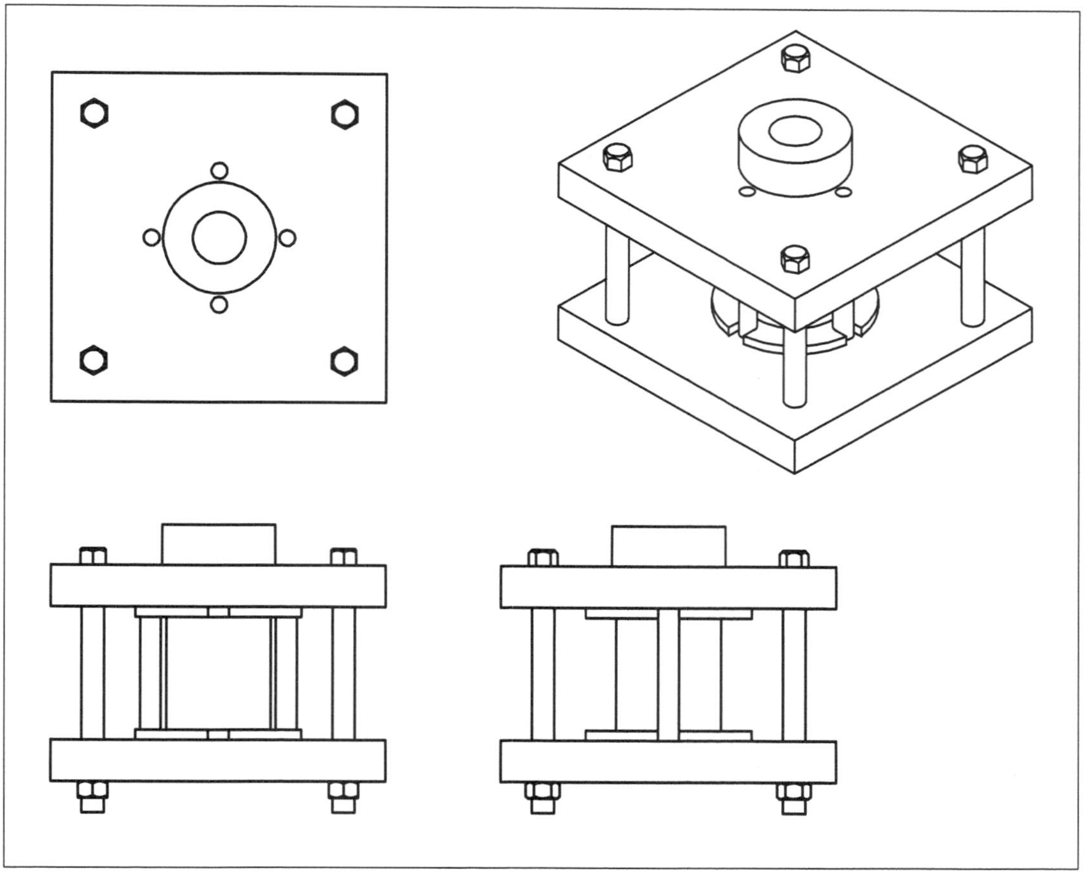

Figure 15-7 Drawing views of the Fixture assembly

The following steps are required to complete this tutorial:

a. Create components as separate part files in the **Synchronous Part** environment.
b. Open a new assembly file in the **Assembly** environment and assemble the End Plate with the assembly reference planes.
c. Assemble the Disk with the End Plate by applying assembly relationships, refer to Figure 15-19.
d. Assemble the first instance of the Support Pin with the End Plate and then create a reference pattern of the Support Pin, refer to Figures 15-21 and 15-22.
e. Assemble the Spacer with the Disk, refer to Figure 15-23.
f. Assemble the second instance of the Disk with the Spacer.
g. Assemble the second instance of the End Plate with the Spacer.
h. Assemble the Nut and Bolt with the assembly and then create their patterns to assemble their remaining instances, refer to Figure 15-24.
i. Open a new drawing file in the **Draft** environment and generate the required drawing views, refer to Figure 15-25.

CREATING COMPONENTS

To create the Fixture assembly, you first need to create its components. They are created in the **Synchronous Part** environment of Solid Edge. The unit to be followed is inch.

Creating the End Plate

As the dimensions of the End Plate are in inches, therefore you need to select a template that has units in inches.

1. Start Solid Edge and then invoke the **New** dialog box.

2. In this dialog box, choose the **ANSI Inch** from the **Standard Templates** drop-down list and double-click on **ansi inch part.par**.

3. Choose the **Rectangle by Center** tool from the **Rectangle by Center** drop-down of the **Draw** group.

4. Select the **Base Reference Planes** check box from the **PathFinder**, and then select the XY plane from the base coordinate system.

5. Change the orientation of the view normal to the sketching plane by using the **Sketch View** tool from the Status Bar. Draw a square of side measuring 4 units in the XY plane.

6. Invoke the **Select** tool and select the sketch region; an extrude handle is displayed. Click on the arrow of the handle, move the cursor upward to specify the direction of extrusion, and then specify the distance of extrusion as **.5** in the dynamic edit box; the base feature is created.

7. Invoke the **Hole** tool from the **Solids** group of **Home** tab; the **Hole Command Bar** is displayed and a hole with default settings gets attached to the cursor. Choose the **Hole Options** button in the **Command Bar** and select **inch** from the **Standard** drop-down list and then choose **OK**. Move the cursor toward the base feature and click when the preview of the hole is displayed on the top face of the base feature. Next, press the ESC key.

8. Select the hole created, if it is not selected; an Edit handle is displayed with the hole. Click on the Dimension value; an edit box is displayed. Modify the diameter value to **.26** in this edit box.

   Next, you need to specify the exact position of the hole.

9. Invoke the **Smart Dimension** tool and dimension the position of the hole with respect to the base feature, refer to Figure 15-3.

10. Select the hole and then invoke the **Rectangular** tool from the **Rectangular** drop-down of the **Pattern** group; you are prompted to click on a face or reference plane to place the pattern feature.

11. Move the cursor over top face of the End Plate and select the lock symbol displayed on it; one corner of a rectangle is attached to the center of the hole. You need to specify the second corner of the rectangle.

12. Move the cursor diagonally and specify the second corner of the rectangle; a preview of pattern is displayed with the values of the length and width as well as the number of instances in the respective directions.

13. Enter **2** as the number of instances in both the X count and Y count edit boxes displayed with the preview.

14. Enter **3** in both the length and width edit boxes of the preview rectangle. Next, choose the **Accept** button from the **Command Bar**; the pattern is created, as shown in Figure 15-8.

Note

1. To modify the rectangular pattern, double-click on the pattern node in the ***PathFinder;*** *edit boxes are displayed in the drawing area. Next, modify the parameters using these edit boxes.*

2. Dimensions, reference planes, and live section of the sketches are hidden for clarity.

15. Create a hole of diameter **1** at the center of the plate, as shown in Figure 15-9.

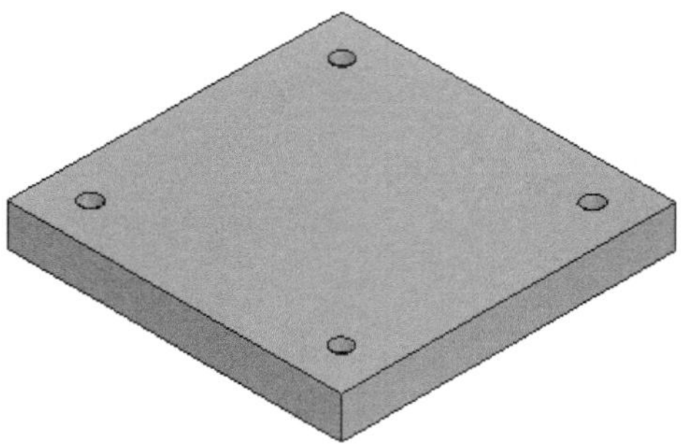

Figure 15-8 *Holes on the base feature*

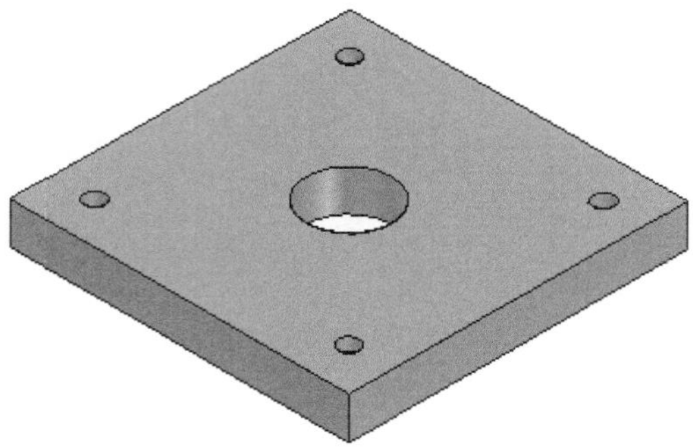

Figure 15-9 *Hole at the center*

Next, you need to create another set of holes.

16. Create a hole of diameter **.19** on the base feature. For its location, refer to Figure 15-3.

17. Select the hole created in the last step, invoke the **Circular pattern** tool, and then create the pattern of hole feature, as shown in Figure 15-10.

18. Save the component with the name *End Plate* at the location *C:\Solid Edge\c15\Fixture.*

Creating the Disk

1. Start a new part file with the **ansi inch part.par** template.

2. Draw the sketch of the base feature on the XY plane, as shown in Figure 15-11.

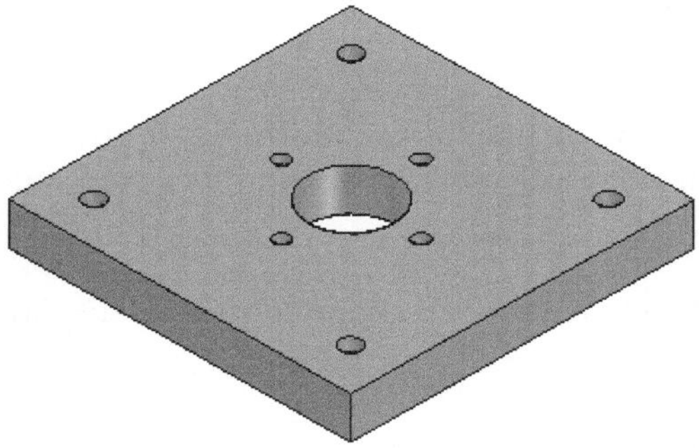

Figure 15-10 Holes created on the base feature

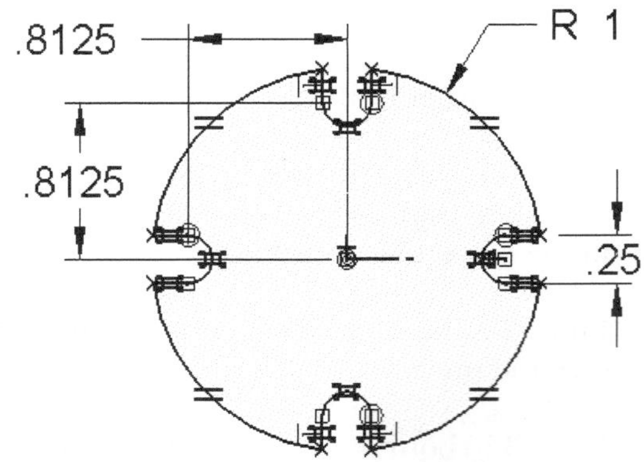

Figure 15-11 Sketch of the base feature of the Disk

Note
*To display reference planes in the graphics area, you need to select the check box beside the **Base Reference Planes** node in the **PathFinder**.*

3. Extrude the sketch to a distance of **.13**; the base feature is created, as shown in Figure 15-12.

4. Create a hole of diameter **1** at the center of the Disk, as shown in Figure 15-13.

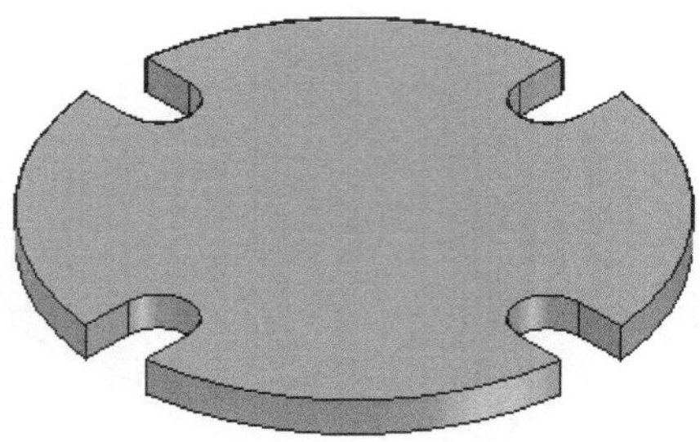

Figure 15-12 Base feature of the Disk

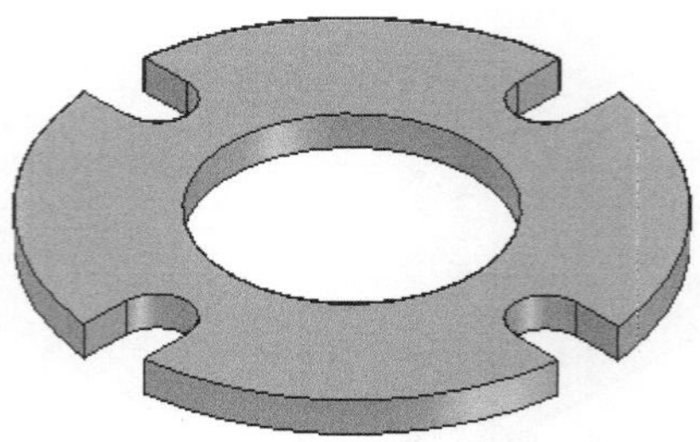

Figure 15-13 Final model of the Disk

5. Make the hole feature concentric with the Disk.

6. Save the model.

Creating the Center Pin

1. Start a new part file with the **ansi inch part.par** template.

2. Draw the sketch of the Center Pin on the XZ plane, as shown in Figure 15-14.

3. Select the sketch and then revolve it through 360 degrees using the **Revolve** handle; the base feature is created, as shown in Figure 15-15.

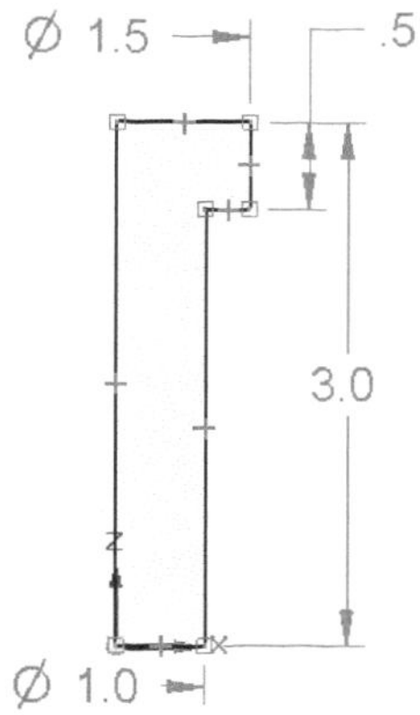

Figure 15-14 *Sketch of the base feature of the Center Pin with dimensions*

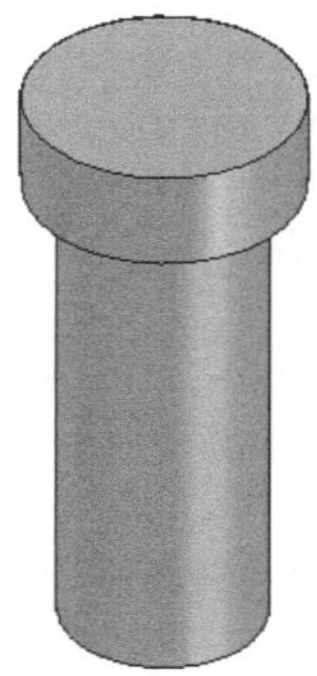

Figure 15-15 *Base feature of the Center Pin*

4. Create a through hole of diameter **.63** on the top face of the Center Pin and then make it concentric to the base feature of the Center Pin, as shown in Figure 15-16.

5. Create a chamfer at the bottom edge of the Center Pin, as shown in Figure 15-17.

6. Save the model.

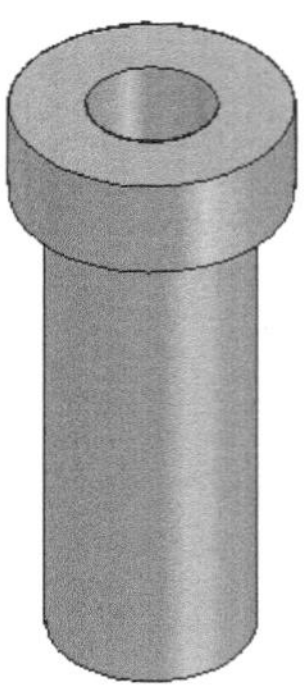

Figure 15-16 *Hole on the top face of the Center Pin*

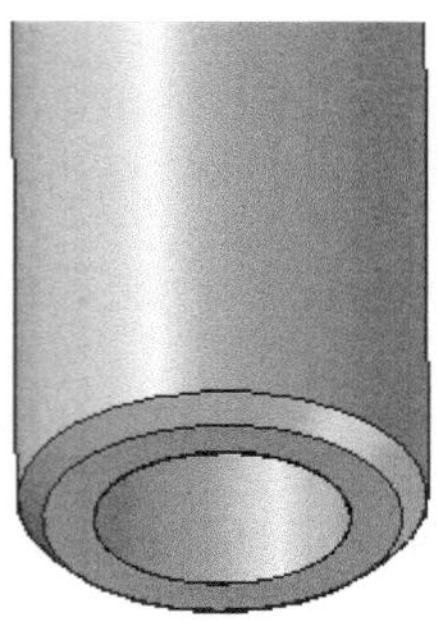

Figure 15-17 *Chamfer at the bottom edge of the Center Pin*

Create the remaining components of this assembly in the **Synchronous Part** environment.

CREATING THE ASSEMBLY

Once all parts of the Fixture assembly are created, you need to assemble them in the **Assembly** environment of Solid Edge. Remember that all parts need to be saved at the following location:

C:\Solid Edge\c15\Fixture

Note

You can also download these parts from http://www.cadcim.com. The path of the files is as follows: Textbooks>CAD/CAM>Solid Edge>SolidEdge ST9 for Designers>Tutorial Files

Starting Solid Edge Session in the Assembly Environment

As Solid Edge is already running, you can start a new file in the **Assembly** environment using the **New** dialog box.

1. Choose the **New** button from the **Quick Access** toolbar; the **New** dialog box is displayed.

2. In this dialog box, choose the **ANSI Inch** from the **Standard Templates** drop-down list and double-click on **ansi inch assembly.asm**.

Assembling the Base Component with Reference Planes

1. Choose the **Parts Library** tab from the docking window.

2. Browse and open the *Fixture* folder.

3. Double-click on the End Plate in the **Parts Library**; the End Plate is assembled with the reference planes.

Assembling the Second Component

After assembling the base component, you need to assemble the second component, which is the Disk.

1. Drag the Disk into the assembly window from the **Parts Library**.

2. Choose the Mate relationship from the **Relationship Types** flyout in the **Assemble** command bar and select the bottom face of the Disk.

3. Select the top face of the End Plate.

4. Choose the **Axial Align** button from the **Relationship Types** flyout.

5. Align the axes of the hole on the End Plate and the slot on the Disk, refer to Figure 15-18. Also, align the central axes of both components.

The two components are assembled, as shown in Figure 15-19.

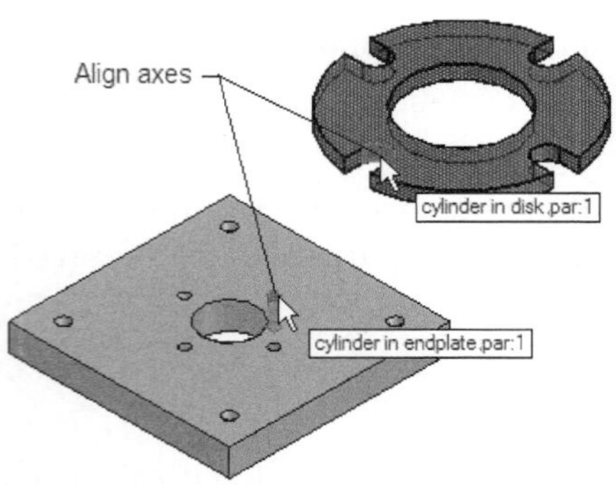

Figure 15-18 Cylindrical surfaces to be selected for aligning the axes

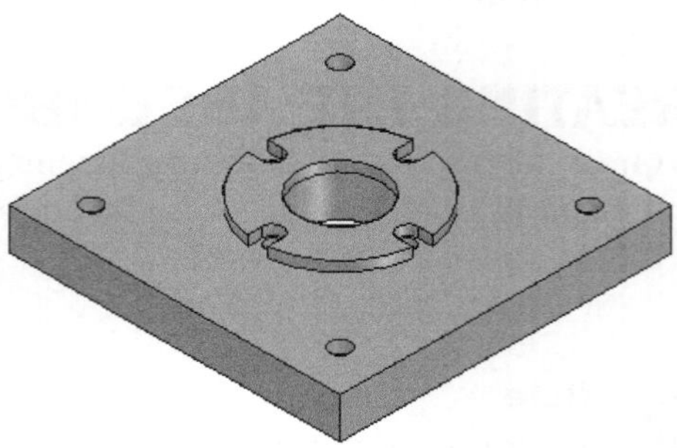

Figure 15-19 Disk assembled with the End Plate

Assembling the Third Component

Next, you need to assemble the third component. This assembly will be created by assembling the Support Pin with the End Plate.

1. Drag the Support Pin into the assembly window from the **Parts Library**.
2. Choose the **Insert** button from the **Relationship Types** flyout.
3. Select the cylindrical surface of the support pin and then any one of the holes of the End Plate. Next, select the face on the Support Pin, as shown in Figure 15-20, and then select the top face of the End Plate. The two components are assembled, as shown in Figure 15-21.

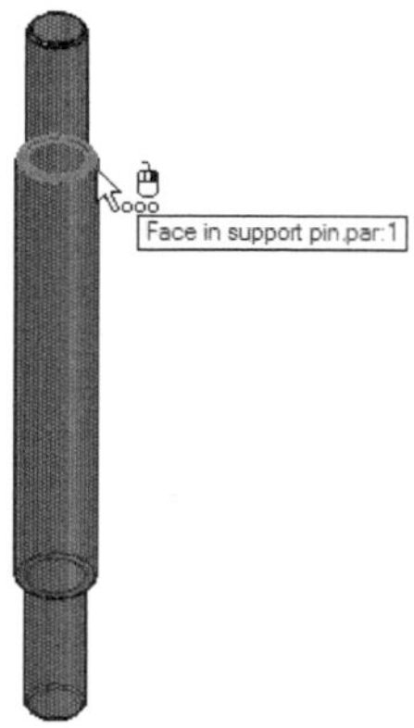

Figure 15-20 *Face to be selected to add the **Insert** relationship*

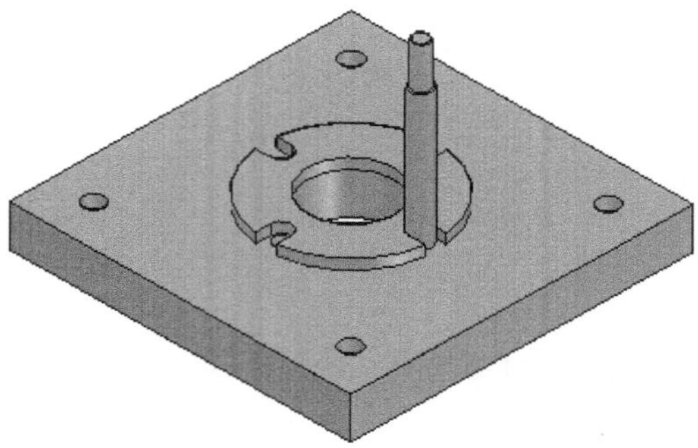

Figure 15-21 *Support Pin assembled with the End Plate*

Creating the Pattern

Now, you need to create the pattern of the Support Pin to assemble its remaining instances.

1. Choose the **Pattern** tool from the **Pattern** group; the **Pattern** command bar is displayed and you are prompted to select the part to be included in the pattern.
2. Select the Support Pin from the assembly and then choose the **Accept** button from the command bar; you are prompted to select the part or sketch that contains the pattern so that Solid Edge can refer the part to be patterned with the existing pattern.
3. Select the End Plate from the assembly; you are prompted to select an existing pattern.
4. Select the existing pattern by selecting any hole but not the parent hole; the preview of the pattern is displayed. Now, choose the **Finish** button from the command bar; the pattern is created, as shown in Figure 15-22.

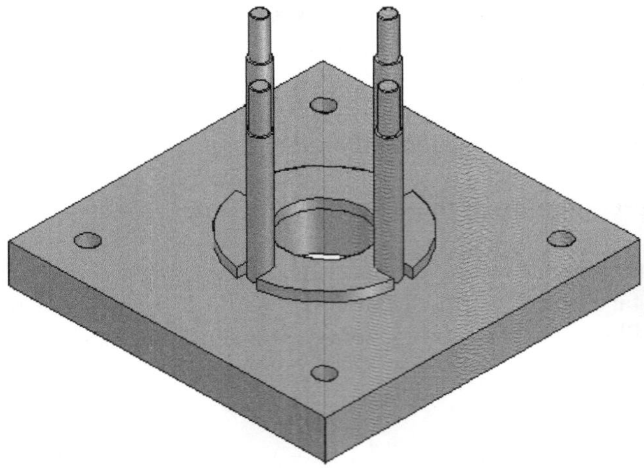

Figure 15-22 *Support Pins assembled in the assembly*

> **Tip**
> *To identify the parent hole feature, move the cursor on the holes one by one. The hole that gets highlighted alone will be the parent hole.*

Assembling the Fourth Component

After assembling the third component and creating its pattern, you need to assemble the fourth component, which is the Spacer.

1. Drag the Spacer into the assembly window from the **Parts Library**.
2. Choose the **Insert** relationship from the **Relationship Types** flyout in the command bar.
3. Align the axis of the Spacer with the axis of the hole on the Disk.
4. Select the bottom face of the Spacer and then select the top face of the Disk.

   The Spacer is assembled, as shown in Figure 15-23.

5. Similarly, using the assembly relationships in the **Assembly** environment, assemble the Disk, End Plate, Center Pin, Bolts, and Nuts in the assembly. The final Fixture assembly is shown in Figure 15-24.
6. Save the assembly with the name *Fixture* and close the file.

GENERATING DRAWING VIEWS

After creating the Fixture assembly, you can generate its drawing views in the **Draft** environment. Remember that all parts need to be saved at the following location: *C:\Solid Edge\c15\Fixture*.

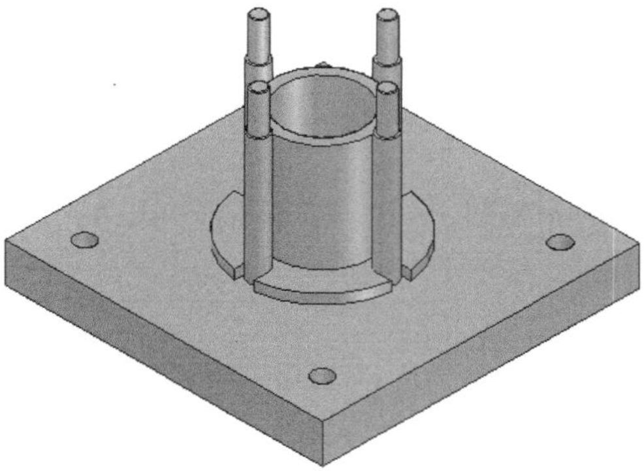

Figure 15-23 Spacer assembled in the assembly

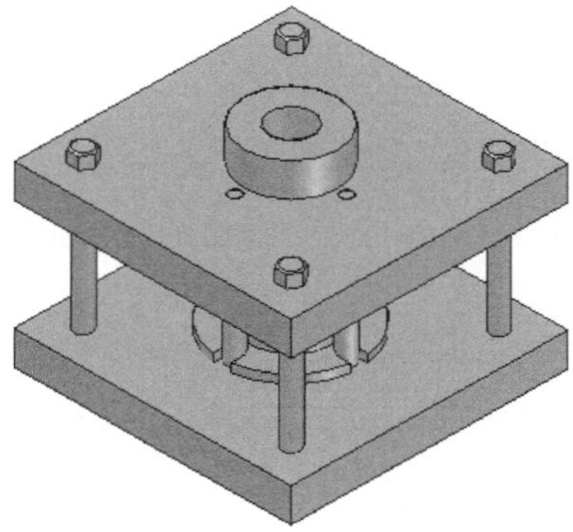

Figure 15-24 Fixture assembly

Starting a New File in the Draft Environment

You need to start a new file in which the required drawing views will be created.

1. Choose the **New** button from the **Quick Access** toolbar; the **New** dialog box is displayed.
2. Select **ansi inch draft.dft** from the dialog box, when **ANSI Inch** is chosen from the **Standard Templates** drop-down list and choose the **OK** button to exit the dialog box and start a new file. Now, you have entered into the **Draft** environment.
3. Right-click on the **Sheet 1** tab at the bottom of the drawing window; a shortcut menu is displayed. Choose the **Sheet Setup** option from it; the **Sheet Setup** dialog box is displayed.
4. Select the **D Wide(34in x 22in)** sheet from the **Standard** drop-down list of the **Size** tab in the **Sheet Setup** dialog box, if it is not already selected and then choose the **OK** button to accept the changes.

Generating the Base Drawing Views

As mentioned earlier, the drawing views are generated from their parent parts. To generate the drawing views, follow the steps discussed next.

1. Choose the **View Wizard** tool from the **Drawing Views** group; the **Select Model** dialog box is displayed.
2. Select the Fixture assembly and choose the **Open** button; the **View Wizard** command bar is displayed.
3. Choose the **Drawing View Layout** button on the command bar; the **Drawing View Creation Wizard** is displayed.
4. In the **Drawing View Creation Wizard**, select the **front** from the **Primary View** area and top, isometric, and right view buttons in the page of the wizard and then choose the **OK** button in it.

5. Place the drawing views on the sheet. After placing the views, you will notice that you need to scale them. Changing the scale of any one of the orthographic views, when modified, changes the scale of the other orthographic views also. Note that you need to scale the isometric view separately.

6. Select a view and modify the scale value to **2** in the **Scale value** edit box of the command bar. Next, press ENTER.

7. Right-click on the top view to invoke a shortcut menu. Choose the **Properties** option from the shortcut menu to invoke the **High Quality View Properties** dialog box.

8. Choose the **Display** tab and clear the **Hidden edge style** check box; the **Changing Drawing View Default Display Properties** message box is displayed.

9. Choose the **OK** button in the message box; the hidden edges become invisible in the selected drawing view.

10. Choose the **OK** button from the dialog box to close it.

11. Turn off the display of hidden edges in other views also.

12. You can move the views on the sheet by dragging them. Arrange the views as per your need, as shown in Figure 15-25.

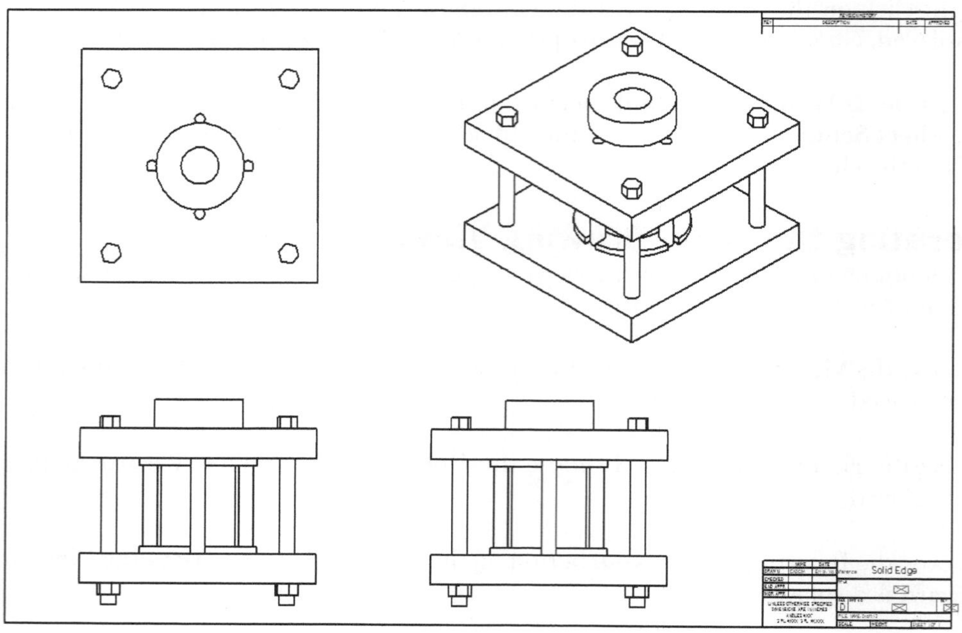

Figure 15-25 *Drawing views of the assembly*

Saving the File

1. Choose **Save** from the **Quick Access** toolbar.

2. Save the file with the name *Fixture.dft*.

3. Choose the **Close** button from the file tab bar to close the file.

Project 2

In this project, you will create the components of a Motor Blower assembly in the **Ordered Part** environment and then assemble them in the **Assembly** environment. The Motor Blower assembly and exploded view of the assembly are shown in Figures 15-26 and 15-27 respectively. The details of the components of the Motor Blower assembly are shown in Figures 15-28 through 15-33. You will also generate the following drawing views of the assembly:

(Expected time: 5 hr)

a. Top view
b. Front view
c. Left-side view
d. Isometric view

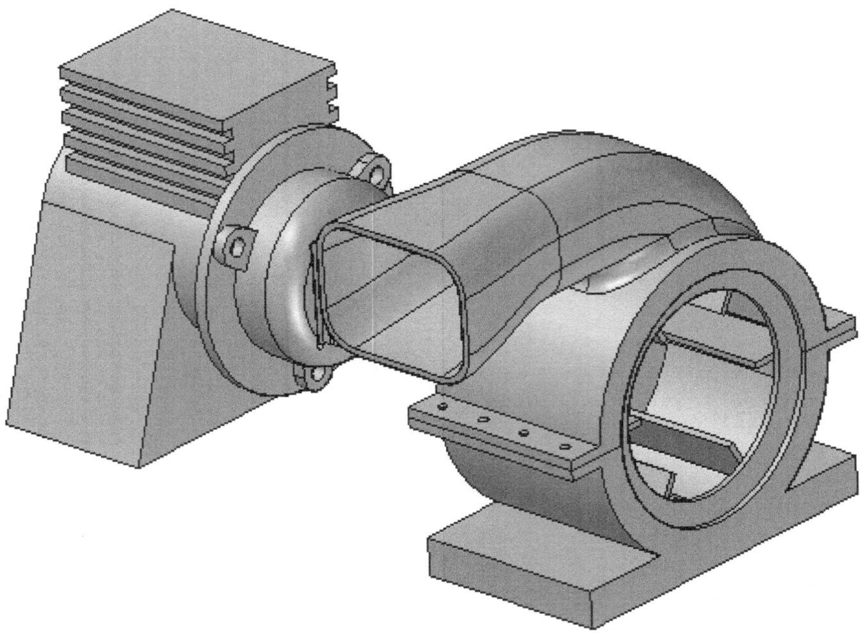

Figure 15-26 *Motor Blower assembly*

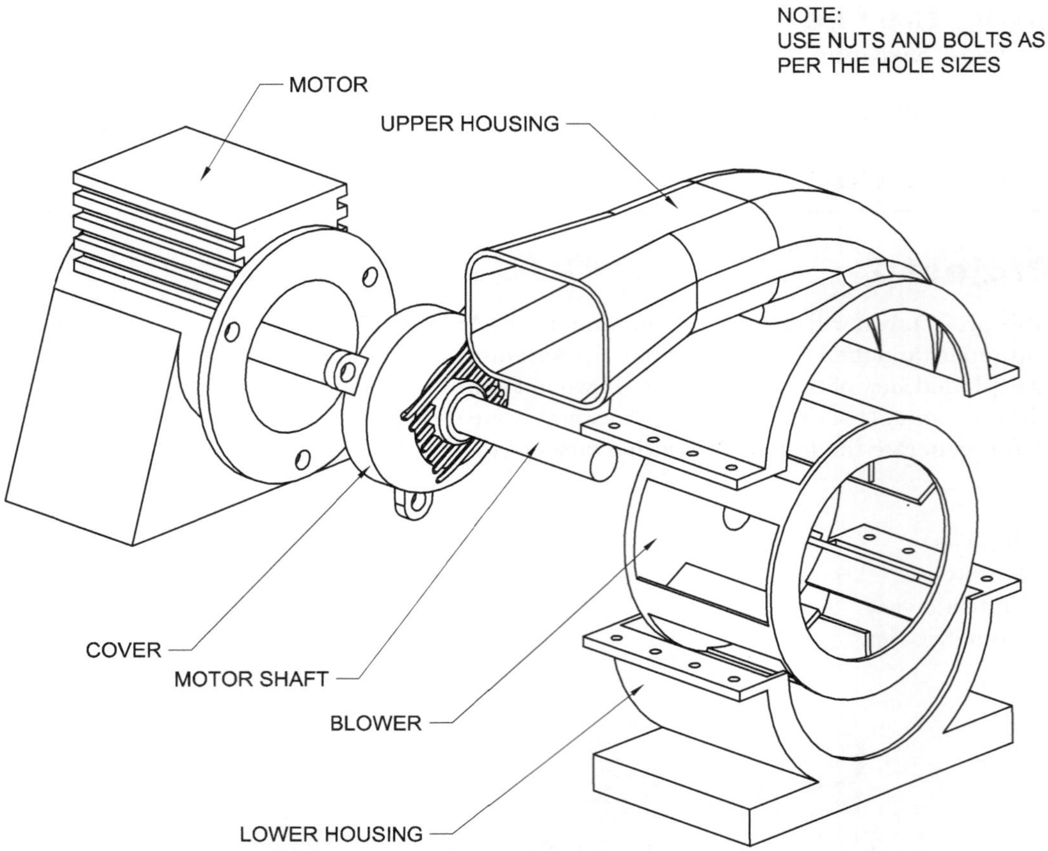

Figure 15-27 *Exploded view of the assembly*

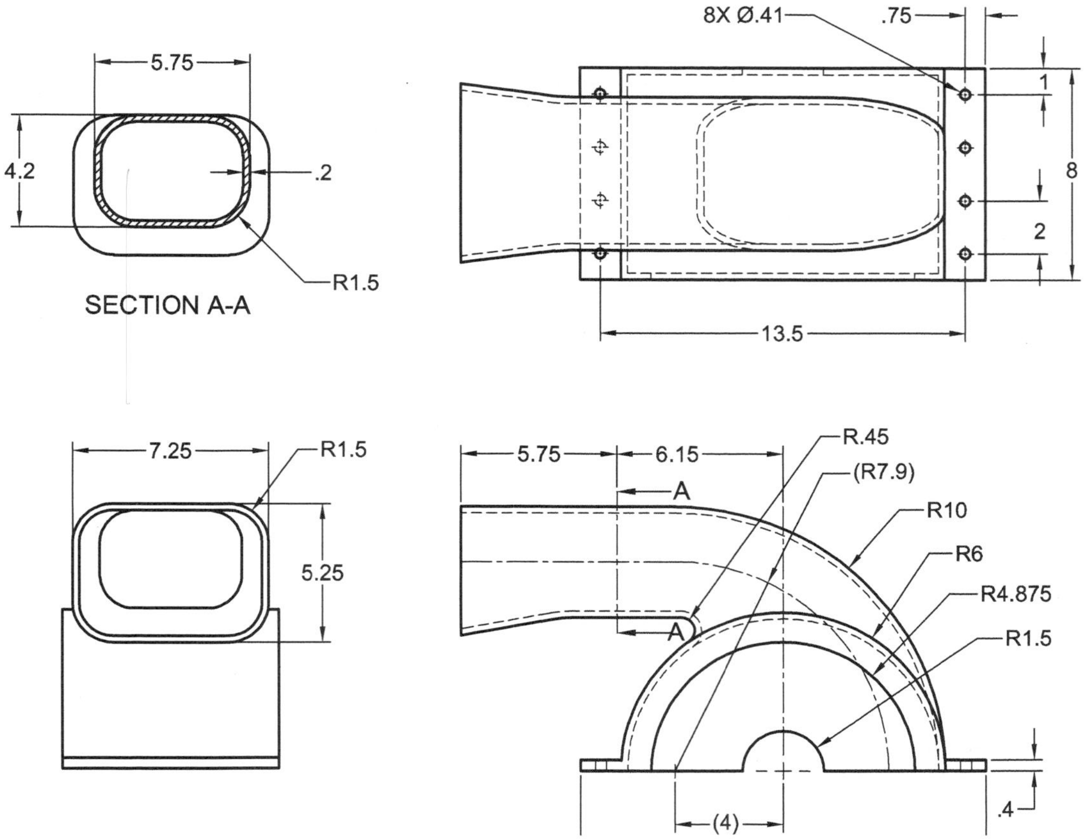

Figure 15-28 *Dimensions of the Upper Housing*

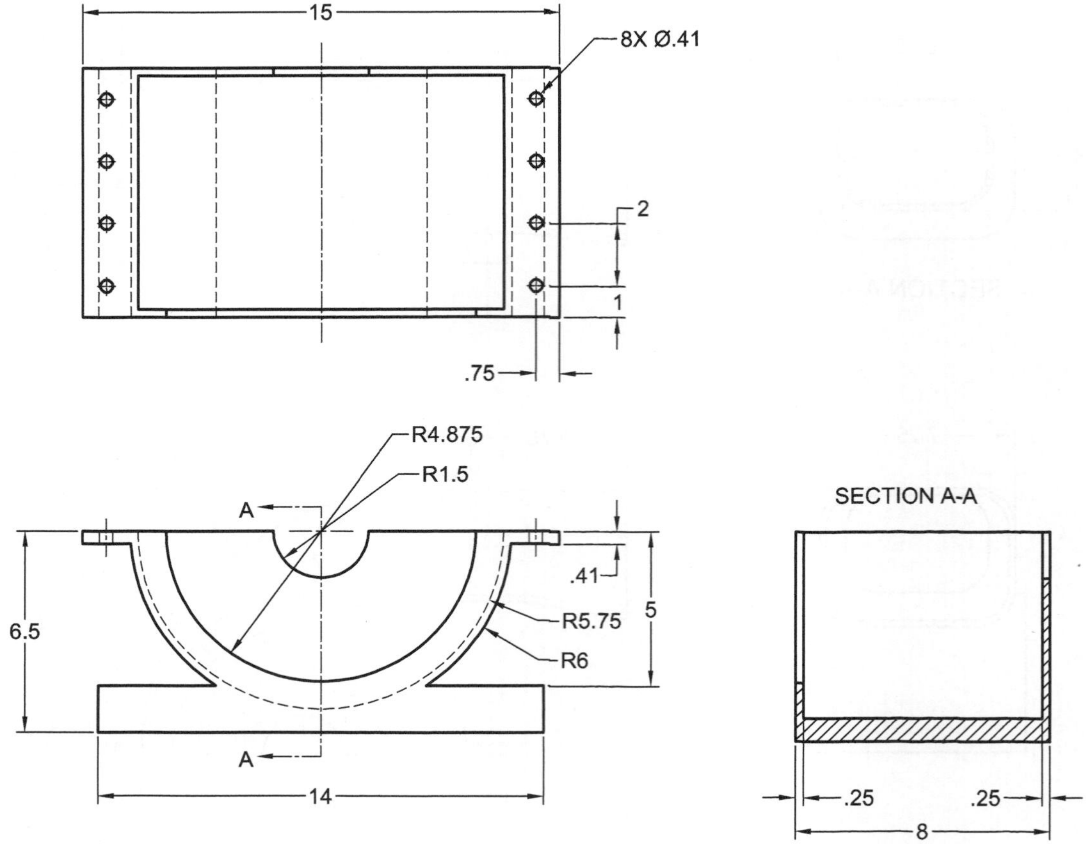

Figure 15-29 *Dimensions of the Lower Housing*

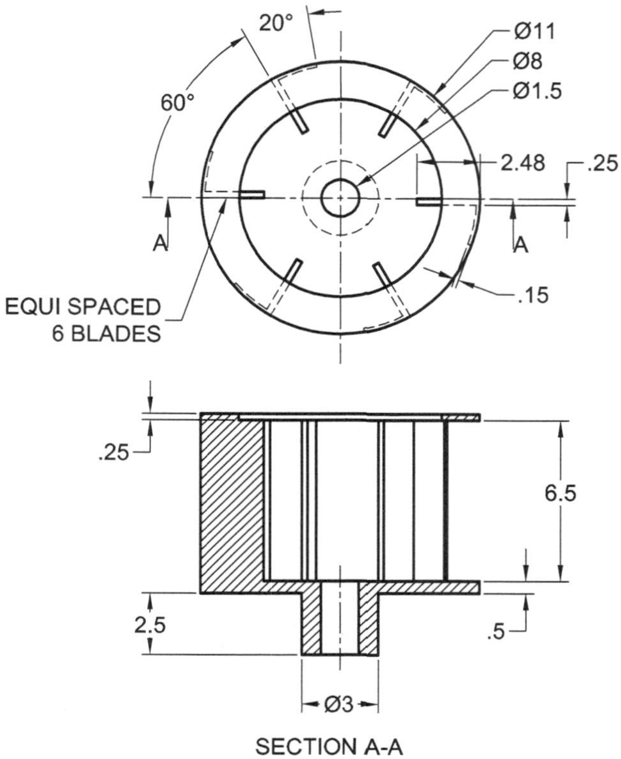

Figure 15-30 *Dimensions of the Blower*

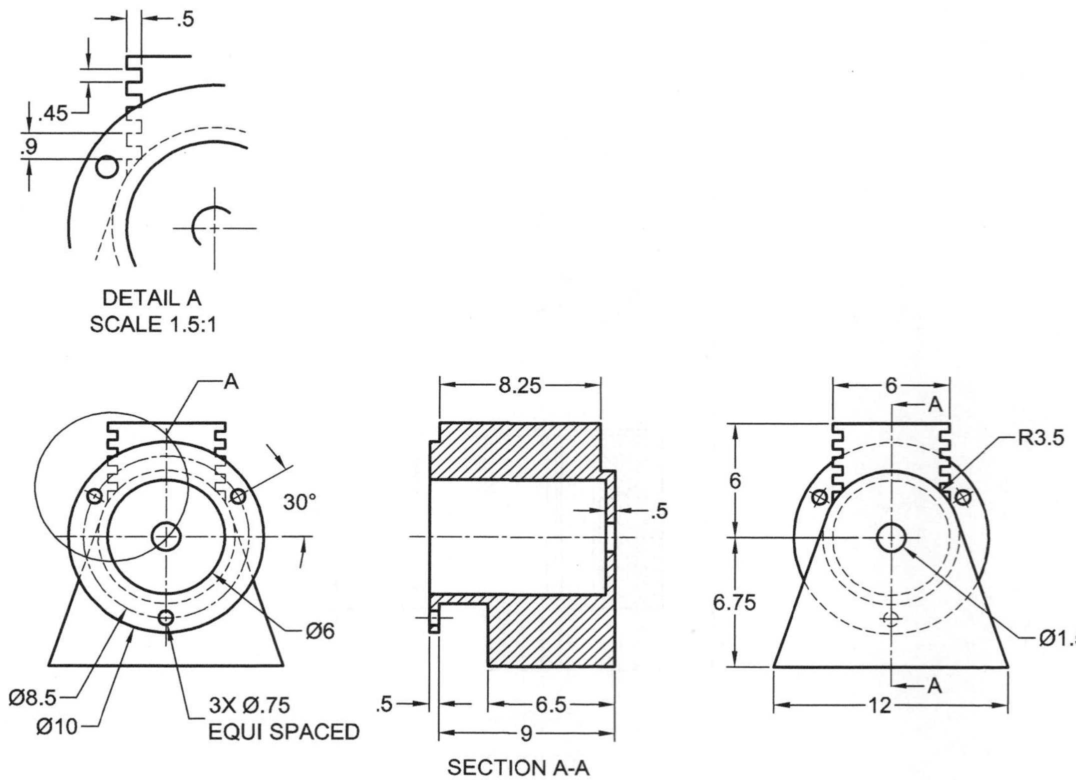

Figure 15-31 Dimensions of the Motor

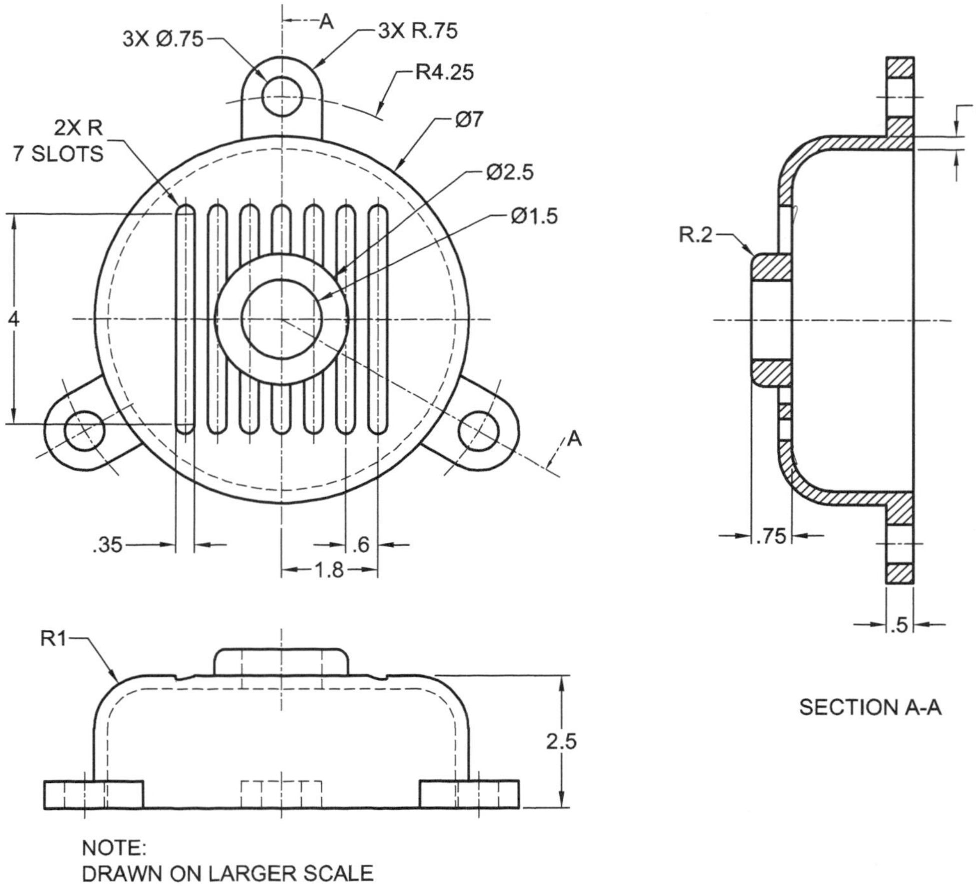

Figure 15-32 Dimensions of the Cover

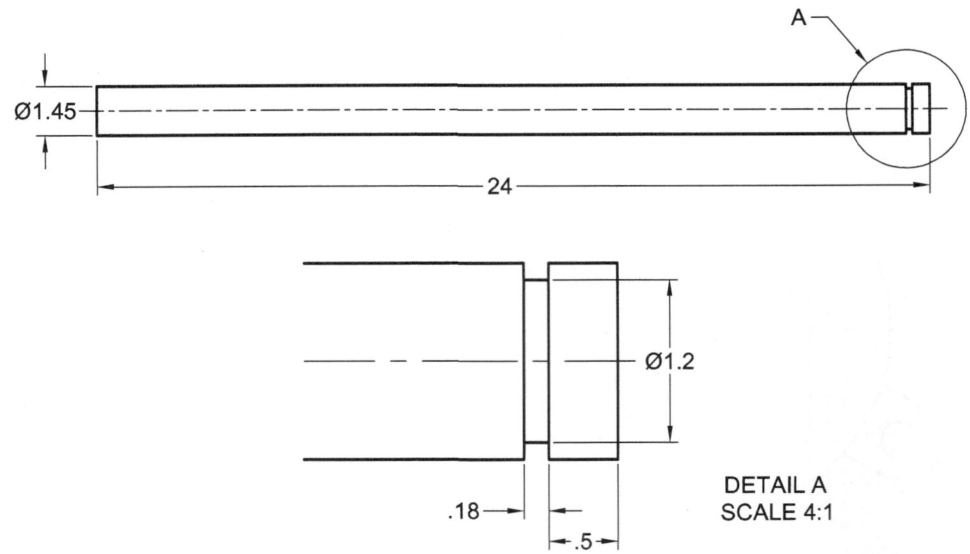

Figure 15-33 *Dimensions of the Motor Shaft*

The following steps are required to complete this project:

a. Create the components of the Motor Blower assembly in separate part files.
b. Open a new assembly file and assemble the Lower Housing with the assembly reference planes.
c. Assemble the Upper Housing with the Lower Housing by applying assembly relationships, refer to Figure 15-70.
d. Assemble the Blower with the Upper Housing, refer to Figure 15-73.
e. Assemble the Motor Shaft with the Blower, refer to Figure 15-75.
f. Assemble the Motor with the Motor Shaft and then assemble the Cap with the Motor, refer to Figures 15-77 and 15-78.
g. Open a new drawing file in the **Draft** environment and generate the required drawing views, refer to Figure 15-81.

CREATING COMPONENTS

To create the Motor Blower assembly, you first need to create its components. The components will be created in the **Part** environment of Solid Edge. The unit to be followed is inches. The Upper Housing was already created in Chapter 9. You can create it again or copy the part in the Motor Blower folder located at C:*Solid Edge\c15*.

Creating the Lower Housing

First of all, you need to create the Lower Housing.

Starting a New File

As the dimensions of the lower housing are in inches, therefore you need to select a template that has units in inches.

1. Invoke the **New** dialog box.

2. In this dialog box, choose the **ANSI Inch** from the **Standard Templates** drop-down list and then double-click on **ansi inch part.par**.

3. Switch to the **Ordered Part** environment by selecting the **Ordered** radio button from the **Model** group of the **Tools** tab.

Creating the Base Feature

The file you have opened has units set to inches. Therefore, the model created in it will have dimensions in inches.

1. Invoke the **Extrude** tool and select the front(xz) plane.

2. Draw the profile of the base feature, as shown in Figure 15-34, and exit the sketching environment. Note that the center points of the arcs are coincident with the midpoint of the top horizontal line.

3. Extrude the sketch symmetrically to both sides of the front plane up to the depth of 8. The isometric view of the base feature is shown in Figure 15-35.

Creating the Revolved Cutout

Now, you need to create the second feature, which is a revolved cutout.

1. Choose the **Revolved Cut** tool.

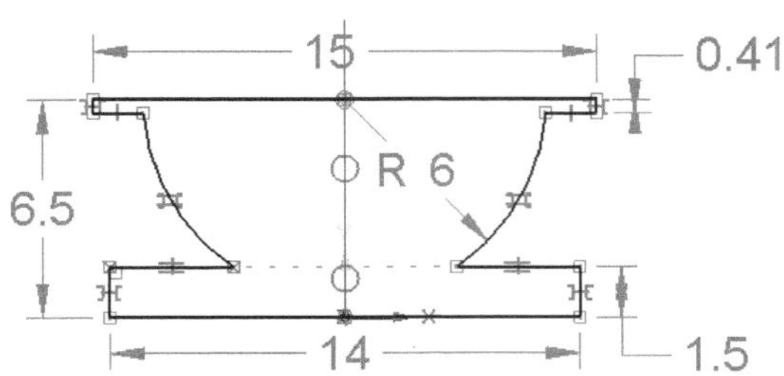

***Figure 15-34** Sketch of the base feature of the Lower Housing*

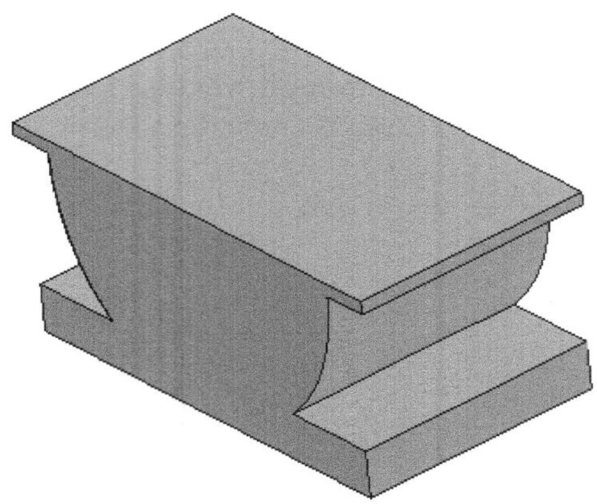

***Figure 15-35** Base feature of the Lower Housing*

2. Select the top face of the base feature and draw the sketch, as shown in Figure 15-36. Note that the sketch will be drawn on the right half of the top face. The centerline shown in the figure is the axis of revolution. After drawing the sketch, exit the sketcher environment.

3. Enter **180** as the angle of revolution in the **Angle** edit box and specify the downward direction; the cutout is created, as shown in Figure 15-37.

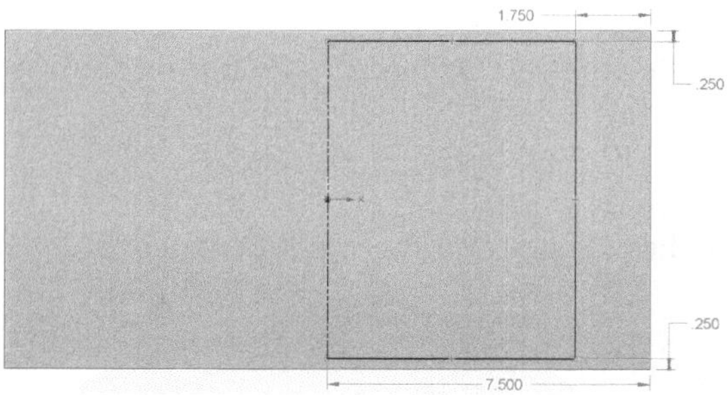

Figure 15-36 *Sketch of the revolved cutout*

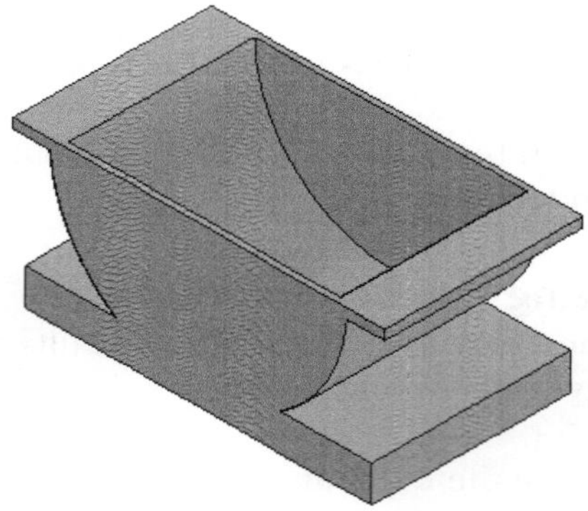

Figure 15-37 *Model after creating the revolved cutout*

Creating the Cut

You need to create a cutout on the front face of the base feature.

1. Choose the **Cut** tool and select the front face as the sketching plane.
2. Draw the sketch of the cutout feature, as shown in Figure 15-38.
3. After drawing the sketch, exit the sketching environment.
4. Specify the direction of material removal inside the sketch.
5. Choose the **Through Next** button from the command bar and specify the direction of the cut. The cutout is created, as shown in Figure 15-39.
6. Choose the **Finish** and then **Cancel** button to complete the feature creation.

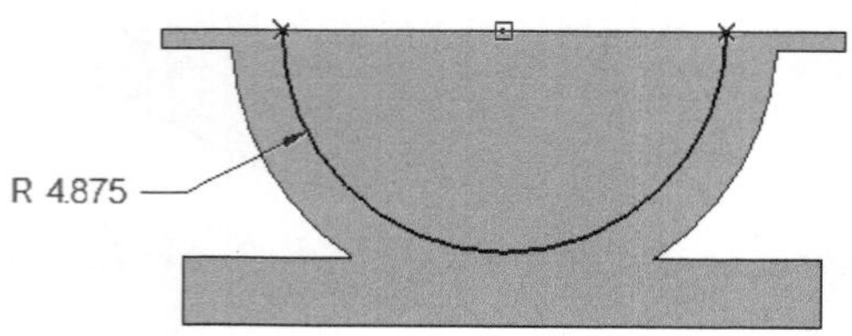

Figure 15-38 *Sketch of the cutout feature*

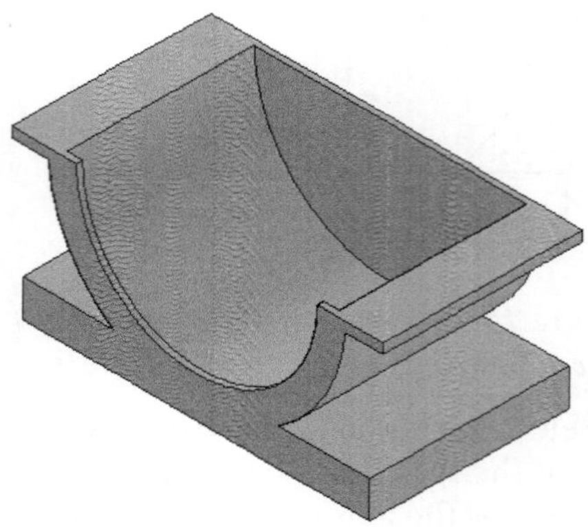

Figure 15-39 *Model after creating the cutout*

7. Similarly, create another cutout on the back face of the base feature, as shown in Figure 15-40. For dimensions, refer to Figure 15-29.

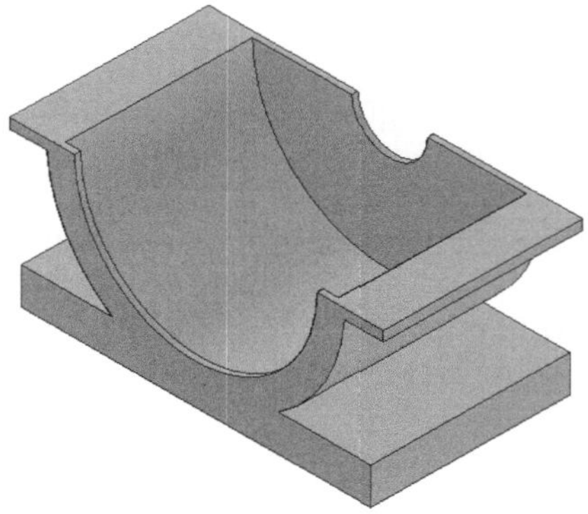

Figure 15-40 Model after creating the second cutout

Adding a Hole Feature

1. Choose the **Hole** tool from the **Solids** group to display the **Hole** command bar.
2. In the command bar, choose the **Hole Options** button to display the **Hole Options** dialog box.
3. Select **inch** from the **Standard** drop-down list and enter **.41** in the **Hole Diameter** edit box in the dialog box. Also, choose the **Through Next** button from the **Hole extents** area.
4. Accept the remaining default options and choose **OK** in the dialog box; you are prompted to click on a planar face or a reference plane.
5. Select the top face of the base feature to place the hole; the sketching environment is invoked and a circle, which is the profile of the hole feature, is attached to the cursor.
6. Place the profile of the hole on the top face of the base feature and add the required dimensions, as shown in Figure 15-41. Exit the sketching environment; the preview of the feature is displayed. Choose the **Finish** button from the command bar to complete the feature creation and then exit the **Hole** tool by choosing the **Cancel** button from the command bar. The model after creating the hole is shown in Figure 15-42.

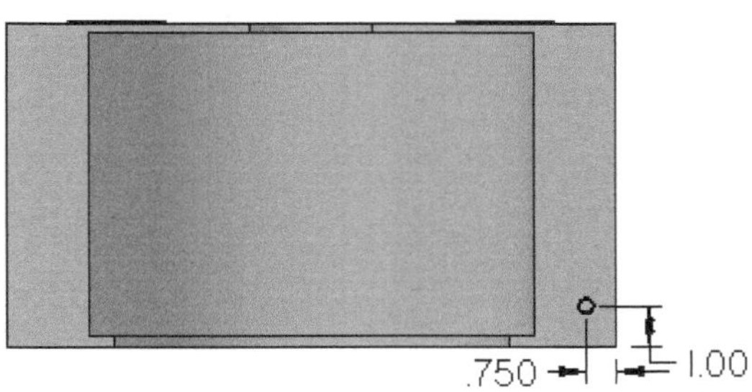

Figure 15-41 Hole profile placed on the top face

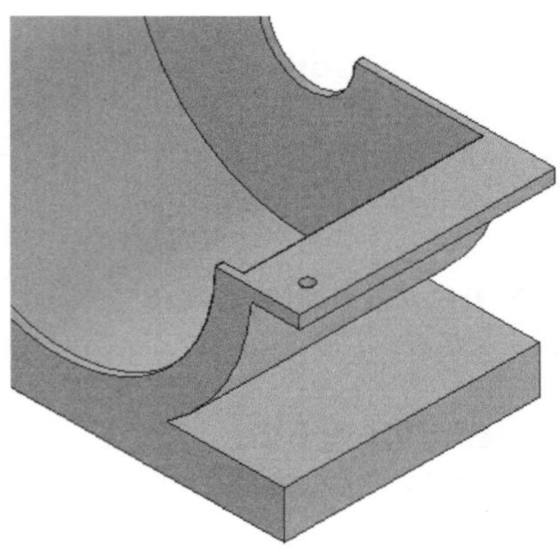

Figure 15-42 Model after creating the hole

Creating a Pattern of the Hole

Next, you need to create a rectangular pattern of the hole feature created previously. As mentioned earlier, to create a rectangular pattern, you first need to draw the profile of the pattern in the sketching environment.

1. Choose the **Pattern** tool from the **Pattern** group; the **Pattern** command bar is displayed.
2. Select **Hole 1** from the **PathFinder**; the hole is highlighted. Next, right-click to accept the feature; the **Sketch Step** is invoked and you are prompted to click on a planar face or a reference plane.
3. Select the top face of the base feature and now you need to draw the profile of the rectangular pattern.
4. In the **Features** group of the **Ribbon**, choose the **Rectangular Pattern** tool, if not chosen by default; you are prompted to click for the first point of the rectangle.
5. Select the center of the circular hole as the first point of the rectangle; you are prompted to click for the second point of the rectangle.
6. Specify the diagonally opposite corner of the rectangle. Now, select the rectangle, if it is not already selected. Next, enter **13.5** in the **Width** edit box and **6** in the **Height** edit box in the command bar.
7. Now, enter **2** and **4** in the **X** and **Y** edit boxes, respectively in the command bar to specify the number of instances to be created.
8. Choose the **Close Sketch** button from the **Ribbon** and then the **Smart** button from the command bar.
9. Choose the **Finish** button to complete the pattern. The isometric view of the final model after creating the pattern is shown in Figure 15-43.

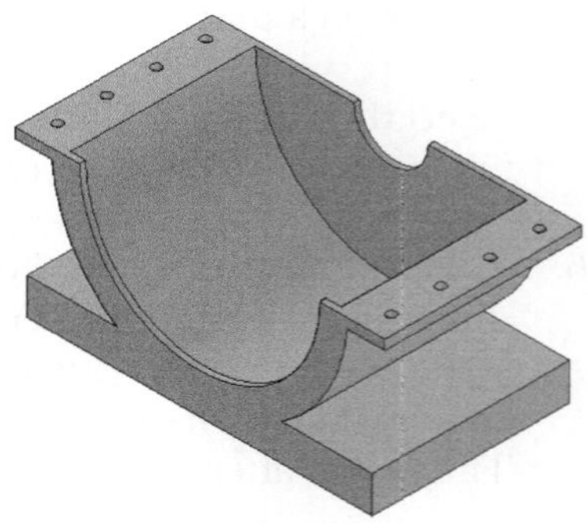

Figure 15-43 *Final model of the Lower Housing*

Saving the Model

1. Save the model with the name *Lower Housing.par* at the location given below and then close the file.
C:\Solid Edge\c15\Motor Blower

Creating the Blower

After creating the lower housing, you need to create the Blower.

Starting a New File

1. Choose the **New** button from the **Quick Access** toolbar to display the **New** dialog box.
2. In the dialog box, choose the **ANSI Inch** from the **Standard Templates** drop-down list and double-click on **ansi inch part.par**.

3. Switch to the **Ordered Part** environment.

Creating the Base Feature

1. Invoke the **Revolve** tool and then select the front plane to draw the profile of the base feature of the Blower.

2. Draw the profile of the base feature, as shown in Figure 15-44. Specify the axis of revolution and then exit the sketching environment.

3. Choose the **Revolve 360** button from the command bar to create the revolved feature, as shown in Figure 15-45. Then, choose the **Finish** and **Cancel** buttons to exit the tool.

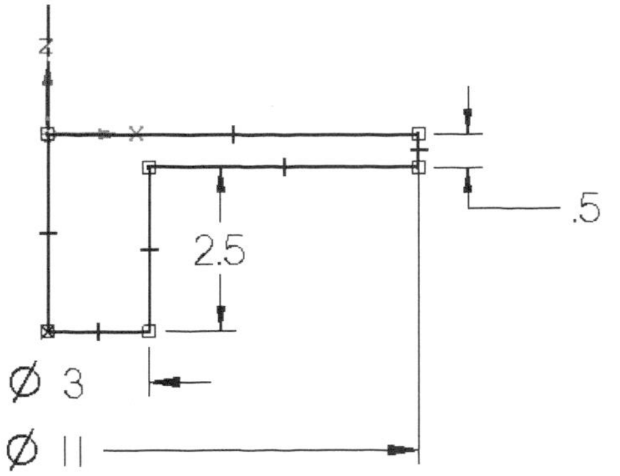

Figure 15-44 *Sketch of the base feature of the blower*

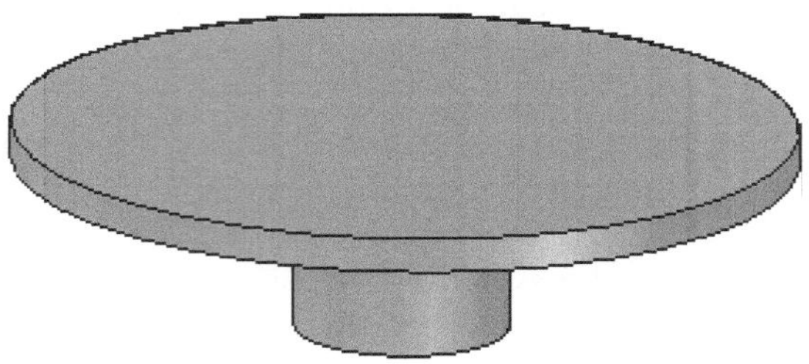

Figure 15-45 *Revolved feature*

Creating the Extruded Feature

1. Invoke the **Extrude** tool and then select the top face of the base plate to draw the profile of the extruded feature.

2. Draw the profile of the extruded feature, as shown in Figure 15-46, and then exit the sketching environment.

3. Specify the distance of extrusion as **6.5** and direction of extrusion in the upward direction. The extrude feature is created, as shown in Figure 15-47.

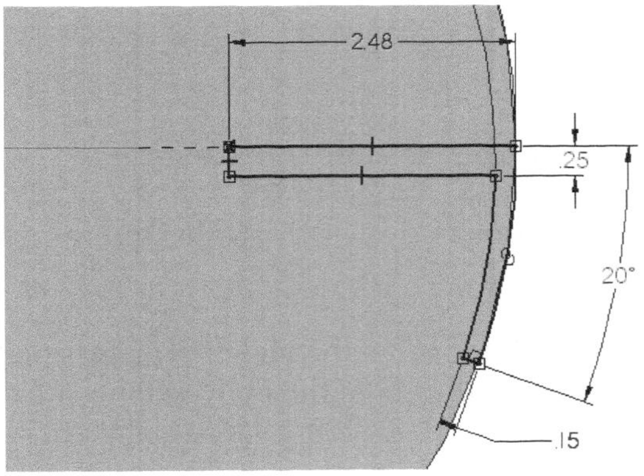

Figure 15-46 *Sketch with dimensions*

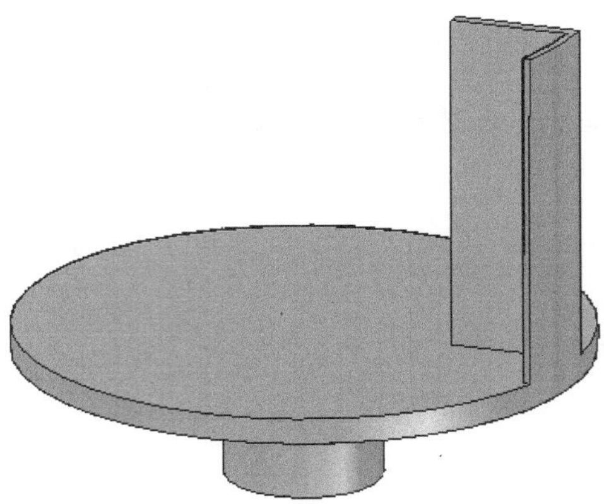

Figure 15-47 *Extrude feature*

Creating the Pattern

1. Choose the **Pattern** tool from the **Pattern** group to display the **Pattern** command bar.

2. Select the extrude feature created in the previous section from the **PathFinder**; the selected feature is highlighted. Next, right-click to accept it; the **Sketch Step** is invoked and you are prompted to click on a planar face or on a reference plane.

3. Select the top face of the bottom plate to draw the profile of the sketch.

4. As you have to create a circular pattern, choose the **Circular Pattern** tool from the **Features** group; you are prompted to click for the center of the circle.

5. Select the center of the revolved feature; you are prompted to click for the start point of the arc.

6. Move the cursor to the circumference of the base feature and click when the cursor snaps to the circumference.

7. Enter **6** in the **Count** edit box of the command bar because you have to create six instances of the extrude feature. Next, specify the direction of placement of the feature.

8. Close the sketching environment and then choose the **Smart** button from the command bar; the preview of the pattern is displayed. Choose the **Finish** button to complete the pattern creation.

Creating the Second Extruded Feature

1. Invoke the **Extrude** tool and select the top face of the pattern feature; the sketching environment is invoked.

2. Use the circular edge of the base feature by invoking the **Project to Sketch** tool and then exit the sketching environment; the preview of extrusion is displayed.

3. Move the cursor upwards and specify **.25** as the distance of extrusion.

   The isometric view of the model after creating the pattern and the second extruded feature is shown in Figure 15-48.

Adding a Hole

1. Choose the **Hole** tool from the **Solids** group to display the **Hole** command bar.

2. In the command bar, choose the **Hole Options** button to display the **Hole Options** dialog box.

3. Select **inch** from the **Standard** drop-down list and enter **1.5** in the **Hole Diameter** edit box of this dialog box. Also, choose the **Through Next** button from the **Hole extents** area.

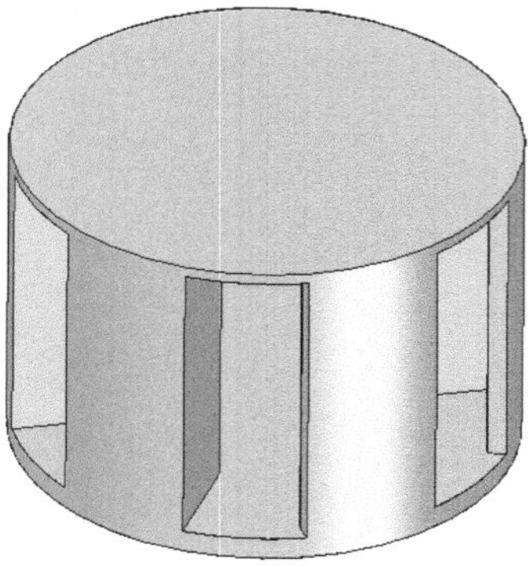

Figure 15-48 Model of the Blower after creating the pattern

4. Accept the remaining default options and choose **OK** from the dialog box; you are prompted to click on a planar face or a reference plane.

5. Select the face of the base feature, as shown in Figure 15-49, to place the hole. The sketching environment is invoked and a circle, which is the profile of the hole feature, is attached to the cursor.

6. Place the profile of the hole concentric to the profile of the circular base feature. Exit the sketching environment; the preview of the feature is displayed. Choose the **Finish** button from the command bar to complete the feature creation and then exit the **Hole** tool by choosing the **Cancel** button from the command bar. The model after creating the hole is shown in Figure 15-50.

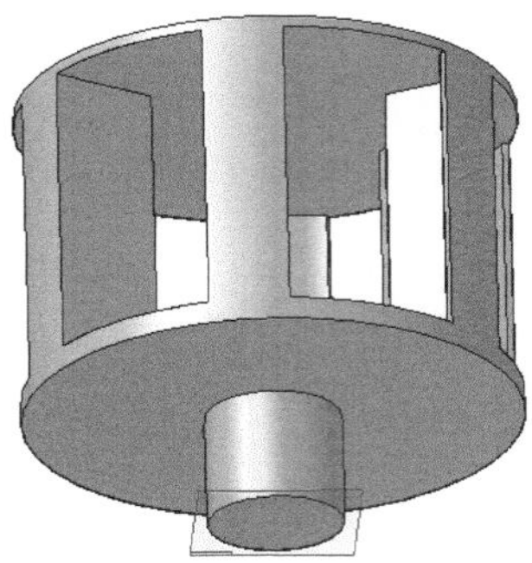

Figure 15-49 Face selected to place the hole

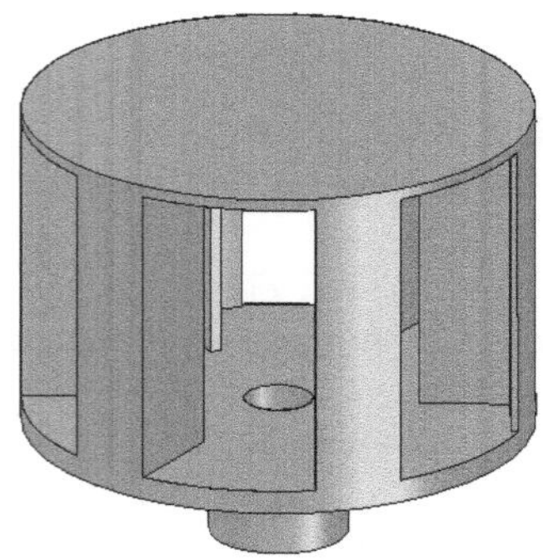

Figure 15-50 Model after creating the hole

Creating the Cutout

You need to create the cutout on the top face of the circular extruded feature.

1. Choose the **Cut** button and then select the top face of the circular extruded feature as the sketching plane.

2. Draw a circle, as shown in Figure 15-51, modify its diameter to 8, and then exit the sketching environment.

3. Choose the **Finite Extent** button from the command bar and enter **.25** in the **Distance** edit box. Next, specify the downward direction of the cut; the cutout is created, as shown in Figure 15-52.

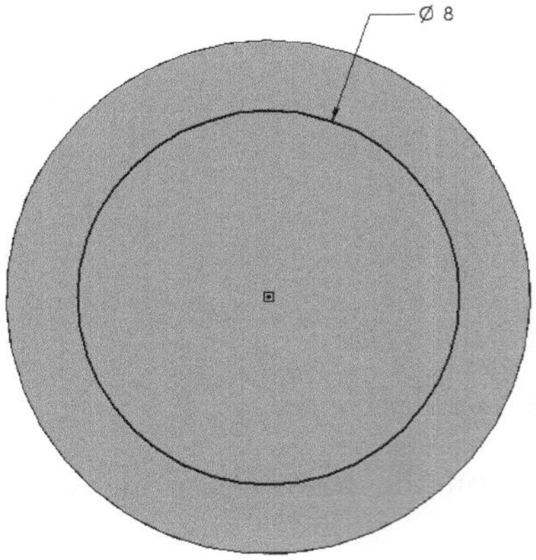

Figure 15-51 Sketch of the cutout feature

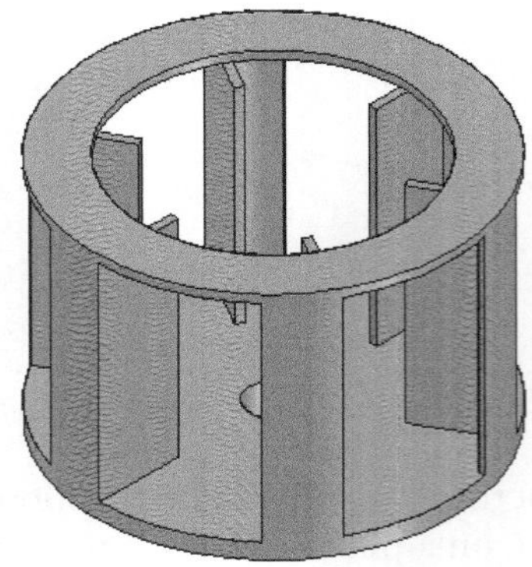

Figure 15-52 Model after creating the cutout

4. Choose **Finish** and then **Cancel** from the command bar to exit the **Cut** tool.

Saving the Model

1. Save the model with the name *Blower.par* at the location given below and then close the file.
   C:\Solid Edge\c15\Motor Blower

Creating the Motor

Next, you need to create the motor.

Starting a New File

1. Choose the **New** button from the **Quick Access** toolbar to display the **New** dialog box.

2. In the dialog box, choose **ANSI Inch** from the **Standard Templates** drop-down list and double-click on **ansi inch part.par**.

3. Switch to the **Ordered Part** environment.

Creating the First Extrude Feature

1. Invoke the **Extrude** tool and then select the front(xz) plane to draw the sketch of the base feature.

2. Draw the profile of the base feature, as shown in Figure 15-53, and then exit the sketching environment. Make sure that the center point of the arc is aligned to the origin.

3. Extrude the sketch upto the depth of **6.5**; the base feature is created, as shown in Figure 15-54. Next, choose **Finish** from the command bar.

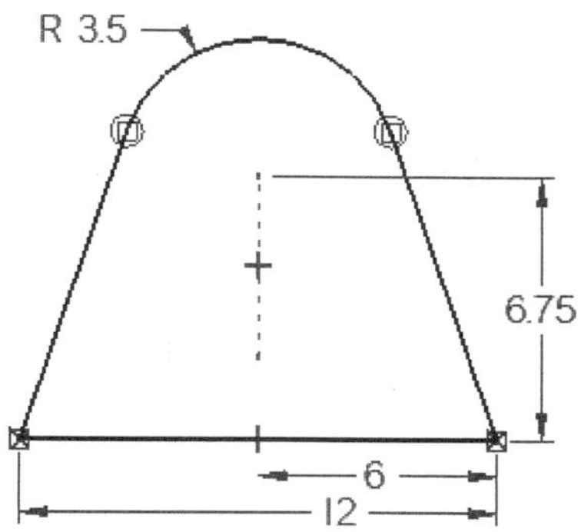

Figure 15-53 Sketch with dimensions

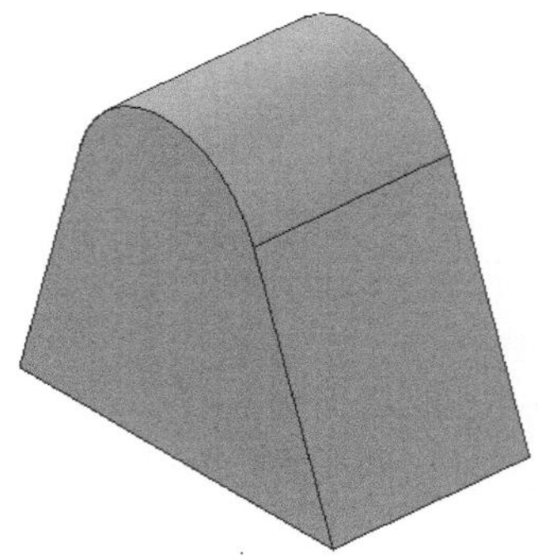

Figure 15-54 Base feature

Creating the Second Extrude Feature

1. Make sure the **Extrude** tool is active. Next, select the back face of the base feature to draw the sketch of the protrusion feature.

2. Draw the profile of the second feature concentric to the arc of the base feature, as shown in Figure 15-55, and exit the sketching environment.

3. Specify the depth of extrusion as **2.25**. Next, specify the direction of extrusion; the extruded feature is created, as shown in Figure 15-56. Next, choose **Finish** from the command bar.

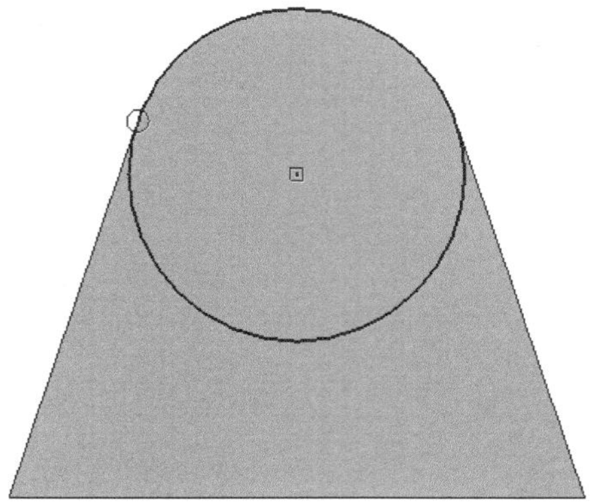

Figure 15-55 Sketch concentric to the arc of the base feature

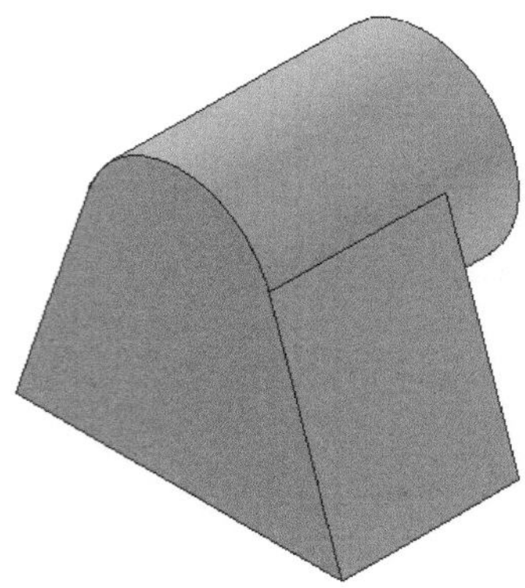

Figure 15-56 Isometric view of the model after creating the second feature

Creating the Third Extrude Feature

1. Make sure the **Extrude** tool is active. Next, select the back face of the second feature to draw the sketch of the extrude feature.

2. Draw a circle of diameter **10** unit, as shown in Figure 15-57, and then exit the sketching environment.

3. Specify the depth of extrusion as **.5** and then specify the direction of extrusion; the third feature is created, as shown in Figure 15-58. Next, choose **Finish** from the command bar.

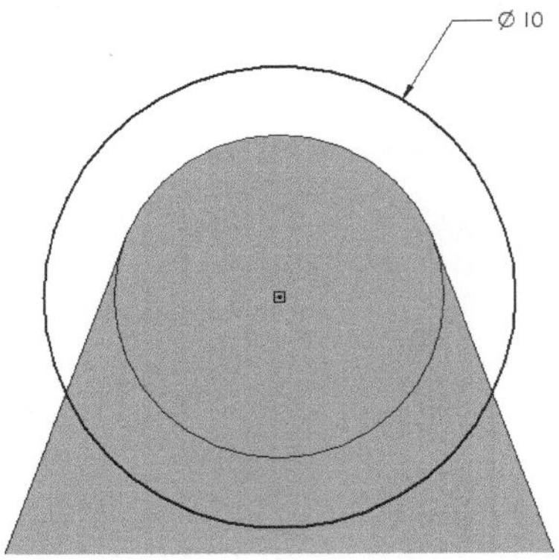

Figure 15-57 Sketch of the third feature

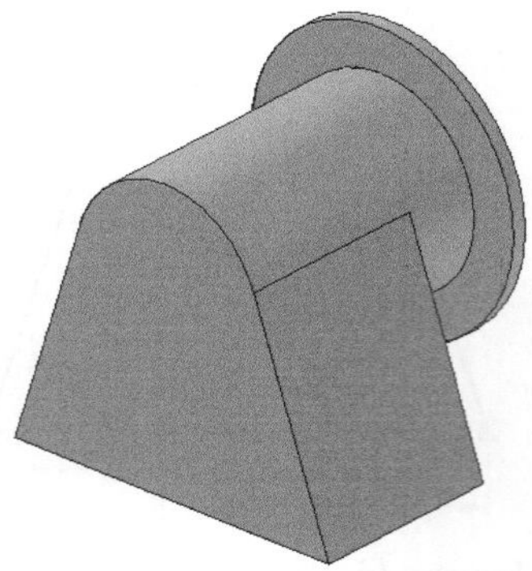

Figure 15-58 Third extrude feature created

Creating the Fourth Extrude Feature

1. Make sure the **Extrude** tool is active. Next, select the front face of the third feature to draw the sketch of the fourth feature.

2. Draw the profile of the extrude feature, as shown in Figure 15-59, and then exit the sketching environment.

3. Specify the direction of extrusion toward the first feature and then extrude the sketch to a distance of 8 unit; the fourth feature is created, as shown in Figure 15-60.

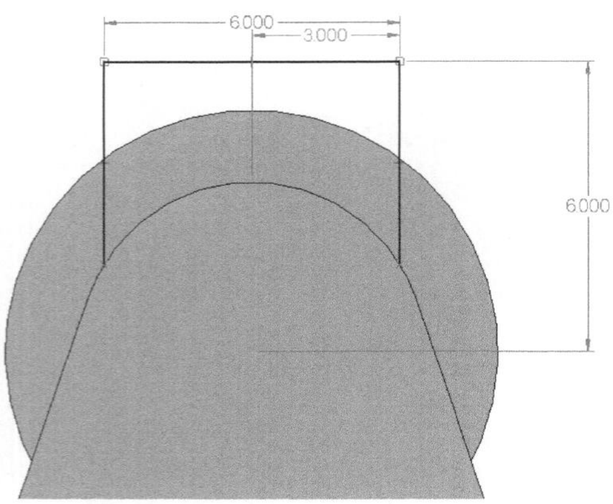

Figure 15-59 Sketch of the fourth feature with dimensions

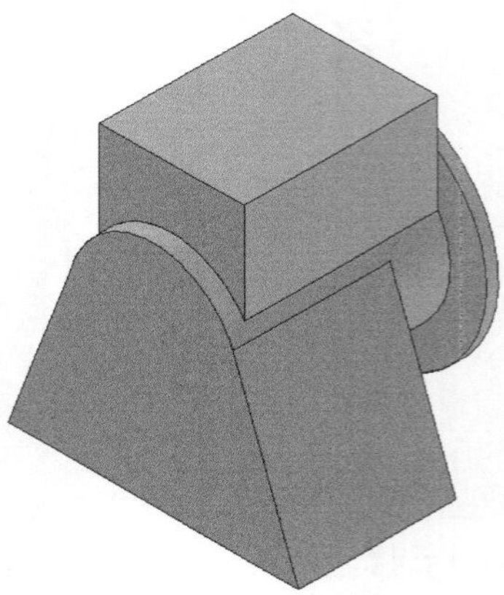

Figure 15-60 Fourth extrude feature created

4. Choose **Finish** and then **Cancel** from the command bar to exit the **Extrude** tool.

Creating the Cutout

The cutout will be created on the front face of the previous feature.

1. Choose the **Cut** tool and then select the front face of the previously created feature as the sketching plane.

2. Draw the sketch, as shown in Figure 15-61, and then exit the sketch environment.

3. Choose the **From/To Extent** button from the command bar and specify the front and back faces as the From and To faces, respectively. The cutout feature is created, as shown in Figure 15-62.

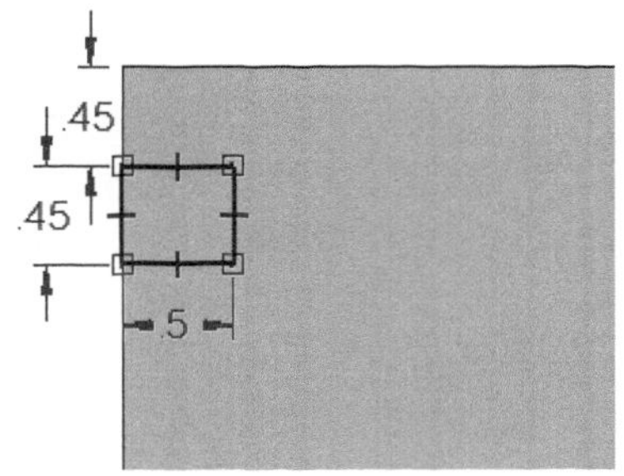

Figure 15-61 Sketch of the cutout feature

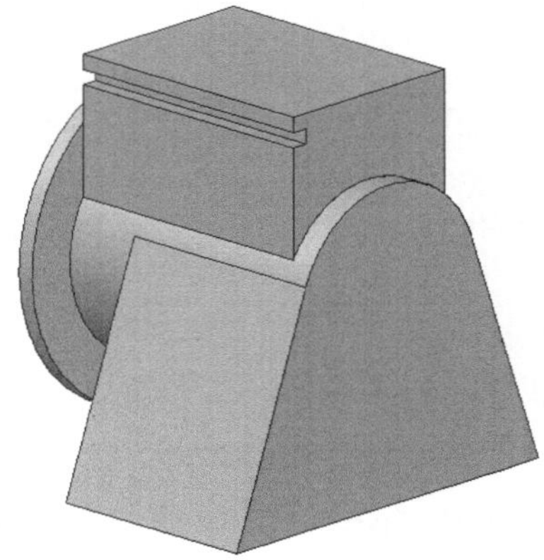

Figure 15-62 Cutout feature created

Creating a Pattern of the Cutout Feature

Next, you need to create a rectangular pattern of the cutout feature.

1. Choose the **Pattern** tool from the **Pattern** group to display the **Pattern** command bar.
2. Select **Cutout 1** from the **PathFinder**; the selected feature is highlighted in the model. Right-click to confirm the feature selection; the **Sketch Step** is invoked and you are prompted to click on a planar face or on a reference plane.
3. Select the front face of the fourth feature to draw the profile of the rectangular pattern.
4. Choose the **Rectangular Pattern** tool from the **Features** group, if it is not chosen. Next, select the top-right corner of the rectangular slot as the start point of the rectangle, see Figure 15-63; you are prompted to specify the second point of the rectangle.
5. Specify the second point; a rectangle is drawn. Next, dimension the rectangle, as shown in Figure 15-63.
6 Enter **2** and **4** in the **X** and **Y** edit boxes, respectively as you need to create four instances in the X and Y direction.
7. Exit the sketching environment.
8. Choose the **Smart** button from the command bar; the preview of the pattern is displayed. Choose the **Finish** button to complete the pattern creation.

The model after creating the pattern is shown in Figure 15-64.

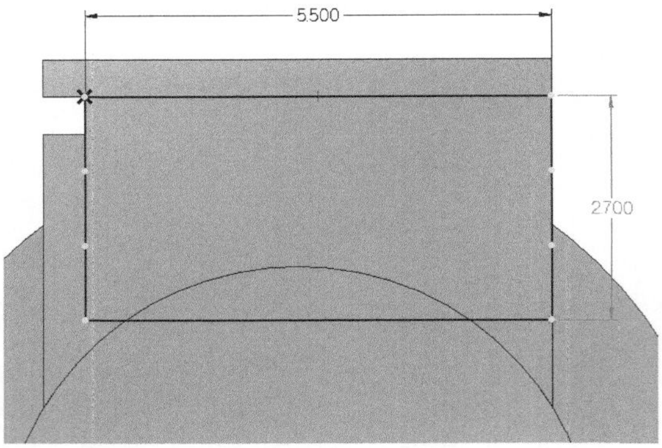

Figure 15-63 Sketch for the pattern

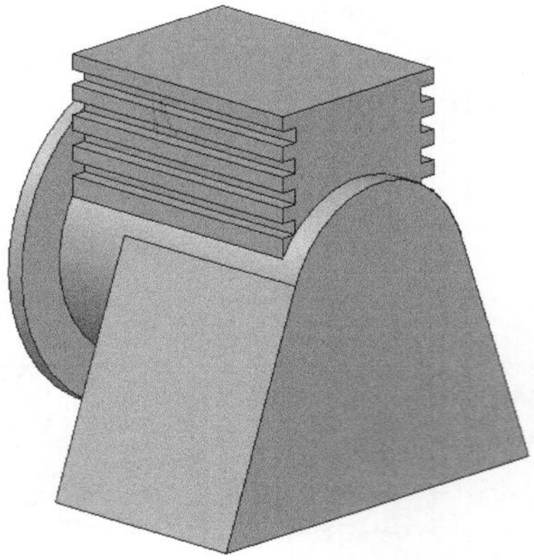

Figure 15-64 Pattern created

Adding Holes

1. Add a hole of diameter **6** on the motor, as shown in Figure 15-65. The depth of this hole is **8.25**.

2. Next, add a hole of diameter **1.5** to the motor, as shown in Figure 15-66.

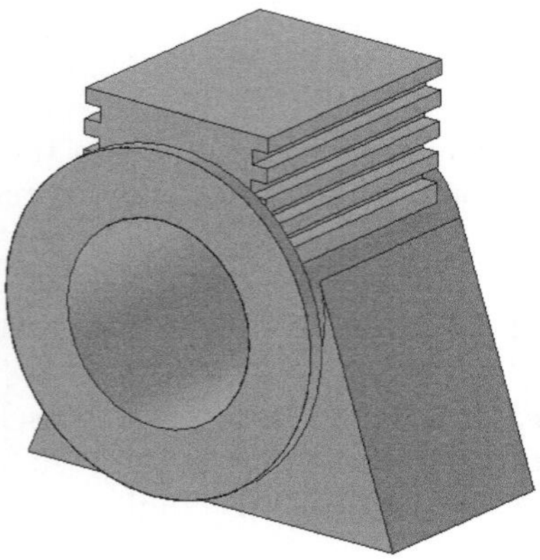

Figure 15-65 First hole created

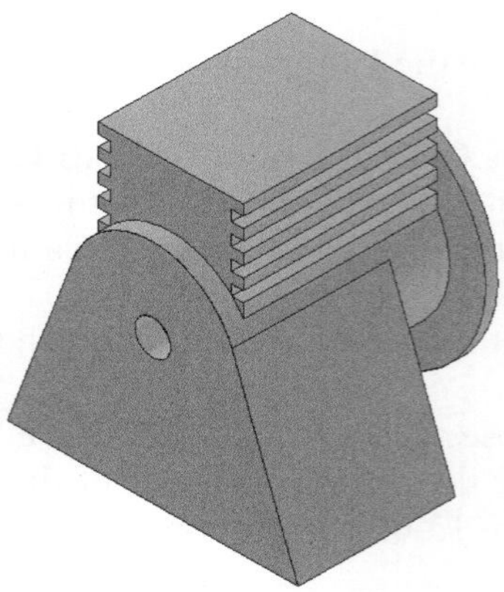

Figure 15-66 Second hole created

3. Add another hole of diameter **.75** and depth **.5** on the Pitch Circle Diameter of **8.5** units, as shown in Figure 15-67, and then create its circular pattern, as shown in Figure 15-68.

Saving the Model

1. Save the model with the name *Motor.par* at the location given below and then close the file.
   C:\Solid Edge\c15\Motor Blower

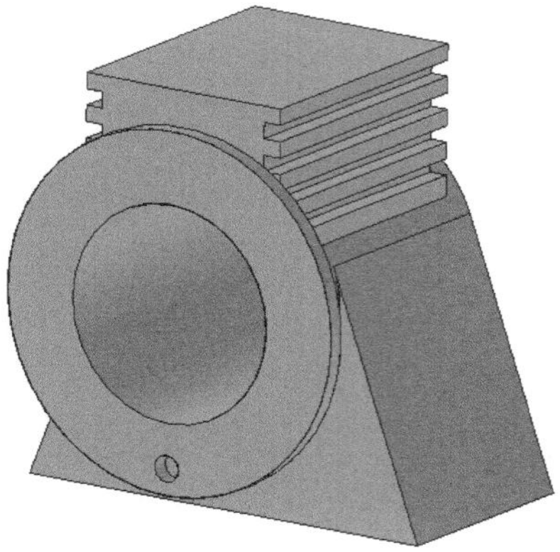

Figure 15-67 Third hole created

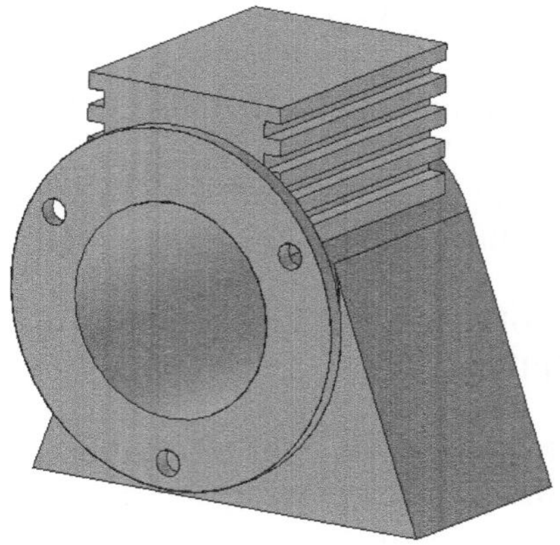

Figure 15-68 Pattern of holes created

Creating the Remaining Components

Use the **Ordered Part** environment of Solid Edge to create other components of the Motor Blower assembly. The unit to be followed is inch.

Note

You can also download components of the Motor Blower assembly from http://www.cadcim.com. The path of the files is as follows: Textbooks>CAD/CAM>Solid Edge>Solid Edge ST9 for Designers>Tutorial Files

CREATING THE ASSEMBLY

All parts of the Motor Blower assembly have now been created. Next, you need to assemble them in the **Assembly** environment of Solid Edge. Remember that all parts are saved at the following location

C:\Solid Edge\c15\Motor Blower

Starting a New Assembly File

As Solid Edge is already running, you can start a new assembly file by using the **New** dialog box.

1. Choose the **New** button from the **Quick Access** toolbar; the **New** dialog box is displayed.

2. In the dialog box, choose the **ANSI Inch** from the **Standard Templates** drop-down list and double-click on **ansi inch assembly.asm**.

3. After entering the **Assembly** environment, choose the **Parts Library** option from the **Panes** drop-down list in the **Show** group of the **View** tab to add the **Parts Library** tab to the docking window.

Assembling the Base Component with Reference Planes

As mentioned earlier, the first part that is placed in the assembly is called the base component. The base component is generally the component that does not have any motion relative to the other components in the assembly.

1. Choose the **Parts Library** button from the docking window.

2. Browse and open the folder *Motor Blower*.

3. Double-click on the *Lower Housing.par* in the docking window; the base component is assembled with the reference planes.

4. Invoke the **Solid Edge Options** dialog box by choosing **Application Button > Settings > Options**.

5. Choose the **Assembly** button from the dialog box and then select the **Do not create new window when placing component** check box, if it is not already selected. Next, choose the **OK** button to accept the changes and close the dialog box.

Assembling the Second Component

After assembling the base component, you need to assemble the second component, which is the Upper Housing.

1. Drag the Upper Housing into the assembly window from the docking window.

Note

The part that is being placed in the assembly is called the placement part. The part that is in the assembly, to which the placement part has to be constrained, is called the target part.

2. Choose the **Mate** option from the **Relationship Types** flyout in the **Assemble** command bar.

3. Choose the **Options** button to display the **Options** dialog box.

4. Select the **Use Reduced Steps when placing parts** check box in the dialog box, if it is not selected. Now, choose **OK** to exit the dialog box.

5. Select a face on the Upper Housing, as shown in Figure 15-69.

6. Select a face on the Lower Housing, as shown in Figure 15-69; the placement part is constrained to the target part.

7. Choose the **Axial Align** button from the **Relationship Types** flyout. Next, you need to align the axis of the hole in the Upper Housing with the axis of the corresponding hole in the lower housing.

8. Select the cylindrical surface of any two corresponding holes in the parts. Similarly, apply the **Axial Align** relationship to another set of holes. The Upper Housing assembled to the Lower Housing is shown in Figure 15-70.

Assembling the Third Component

Now, you need to assemble the third component, which is the Blower.

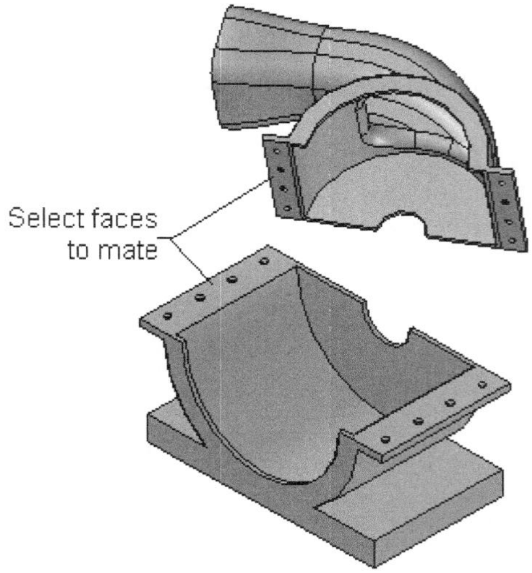

Figure 15-69 *Faces to be selected to apply the* ***Mate*** *relationship*

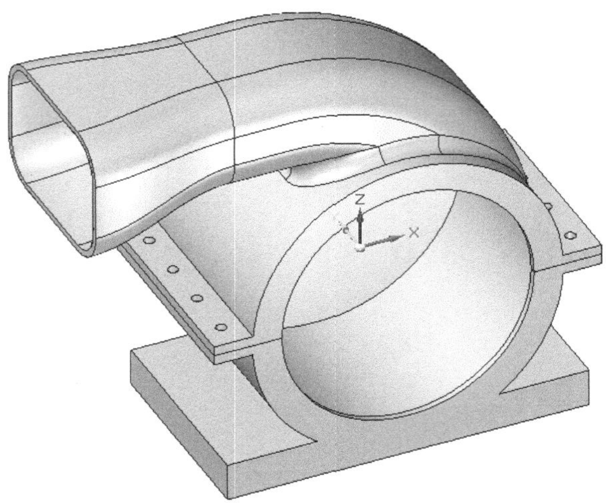

Figure 15-70 *Assembly of two components*

1. Drag the Blower into the assembly window from the docking window.

2. Choose the **Insert** button from the **Relationship Types** flyout. Remember that in the insert relationship, two constraints are used, namely **Mate** and **Axial Align**.

3. Spin the Blower in its window and select its cylindrical face, as shown in Figure 15-71. After you select the element on the placement part, you are prompted to select the corresponding element on the target part.

4. Select the cylindrical face of the Upper Housing, as shown in Figure 15-71.

Now, you need to select the faces to mate.

5. Select the face to be mated on the Blower, as shown in Figure 15-72.
6. Select the corresponding face on the Upper Housing, as shown in Figure 15-72.

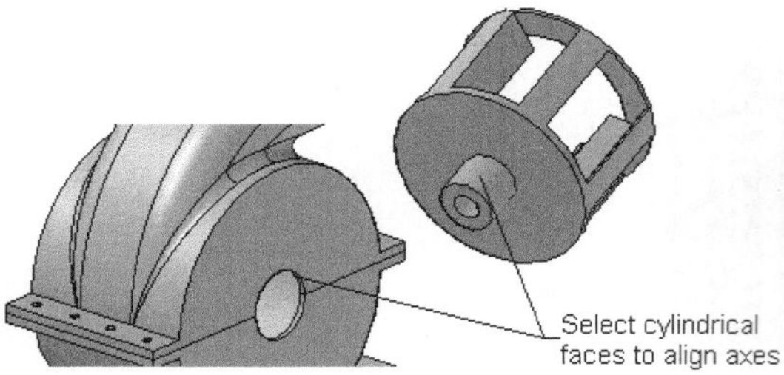

Figure 15-71 *Cylindrical faces to be selected*

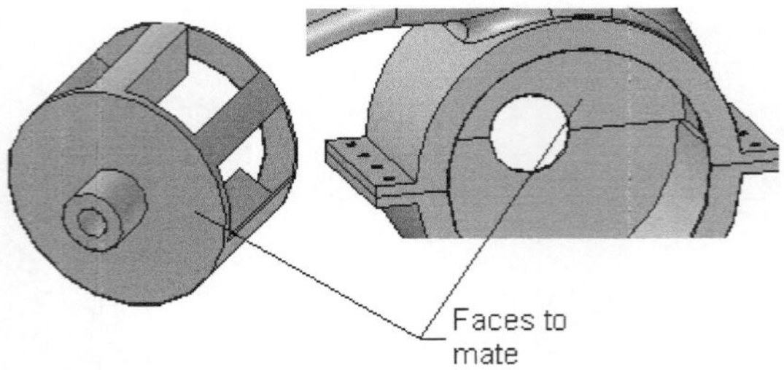

Figure 15-72 *Faces to be mated*

The Blower is assembled with the Upper Housing in the assembly, as shown in Figure 15-73.

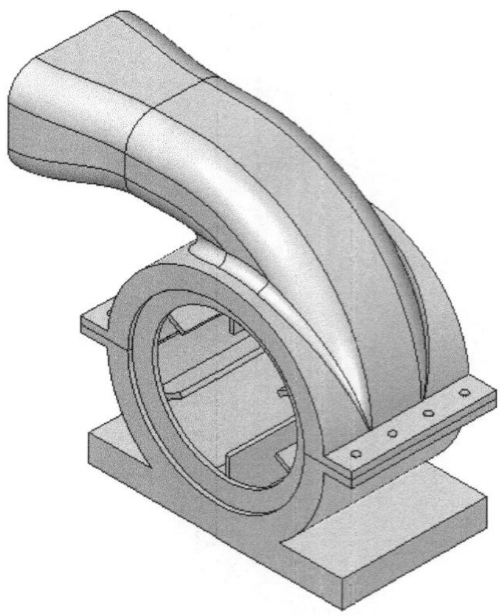

Figure 15-73 *Assembly of the Blower with the other components*

Assembling the Fourth Component

Next, you need to assemble the fourth component, which is a Shaft.

1. Drag the Motor Shaft into the assembly window from the docking window.
2. Choose the **Insert** button from the **Relationship Types** flyout.
3. Select the cylindrical face of the Motor Shaft.
4. Next, select the cylindrical face of the target part, which is the Blower.

5. Select the faces of the Motor Shaft and the Blower, as shown in Figure 15-74.

   The Shaft is assembled with the Blower, as shown in Figure 15-75. It is evident from this figure that you need to flip the Shaft.

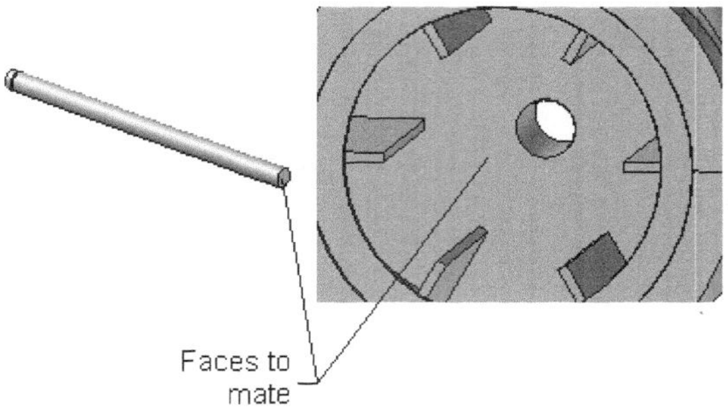

Figure 15-74 Faces to be mated

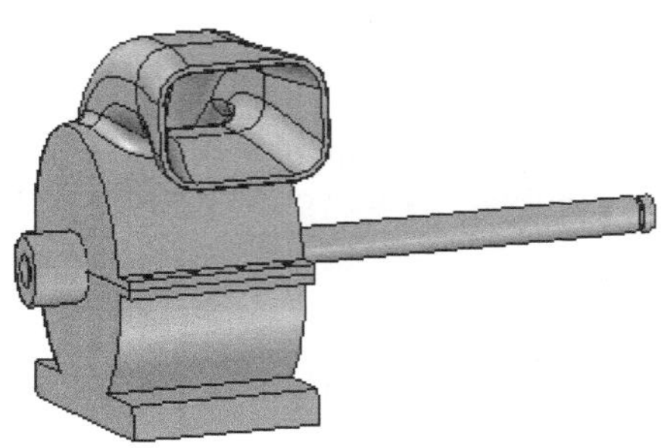

Figure 15-75 Motor Shaft partially assembled

6. Select **Motor Shaft.par:1** from the top pane of the **PathFinder**. Notice that in the bottom pane, the relationships applied to the component are displayed.

7. Select the first relationship, which is the **Mate** relationship. Right-click and choose the **Flip** option from the shortcut menu; the shaft will be flipped and the assembly will be displayed, as shown in Figure 15-76.

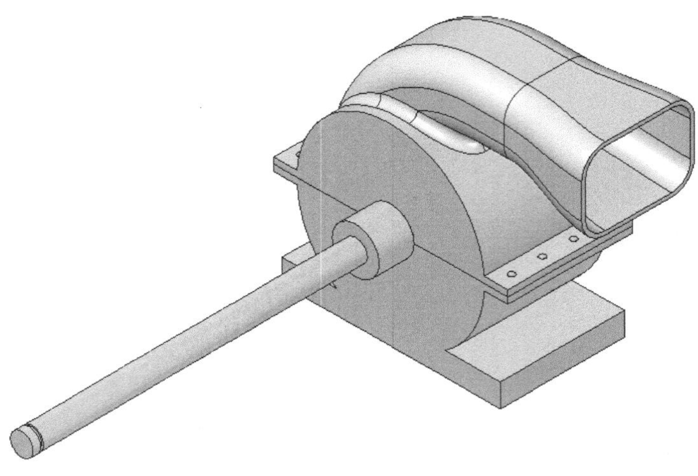

Figure 15-76 Assembly after assembling the Shaft

8. Choose the **Select** tool or click anywhere on the screen to exit.

Assembling the Fifth Component

After assembling the fourth component, you need to assemble the fifth component, which is the Motor.

1. Drag the Motor into the assembly window from the **Parts Library**.
2. Choose the **Insert** button from the **Relationship Types** flyout.
3. Select the hole (the smaller hole) on the back face of the Motor.
4. Now, select the cylindrical face of the Motor Shaft.
5. Select the back face of the Motor and then the end face of the Motor Shaft; the Motor is assembled. Now, you need to flip the orientation of the Motor.
6. Follow the steps 6, 7, and 8 given in the previous section to flip the Motor.
7. Select the Motor from the **PathFinder**.
8. Select the first relationship from the bottom of the **PathFinder**.
9. Select **Float** from the **Offset Type** flyout displayed at the bottom.
10. Next, select the second relationship from the bottom of the **PathFinder**.
11. Choose the **Unlock Rotation** button from the command bar displayed at the bottom.
12. Apply the **Planar Align** relationship between the bottom faces of the motor and Lower Housing with **Float** offset style; the Motor is assembled with the assembly, as shown in Figure 15-77.

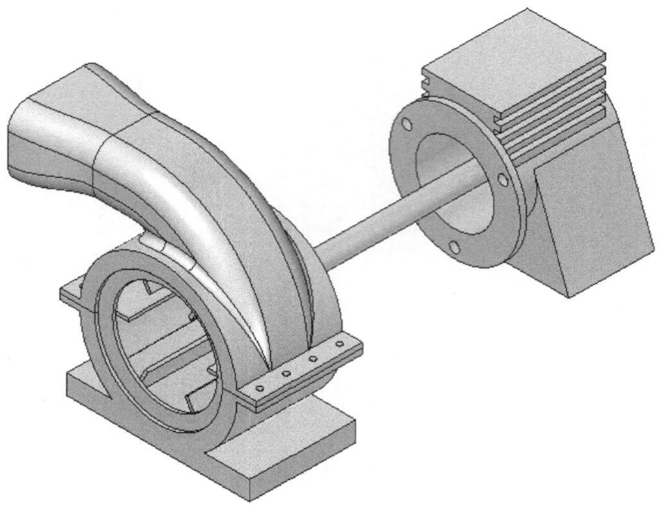

Figure 15-77 *Motor assembled with the assembly*

Assembling the Sixth Component

Next, you need to assemble the sixth component, which is the Cover.

1. Drag the Cover into the assembly window from the **Parts Library**.

2. Choose the **Axial Align** button from the **Relationship Types** flyout.

3. Select the first hole on the Cover and then the hole on the Motor, as shown in Figure 15-78; the Cover partially positions itself with the Motor.

4. Align the axis of one more hole on the Cover with the axis of another hole on the Motor.

5. Choose the **Mate** button from the **Relationship Types** flyout to align two planar faces.

6. Select the bottom planar face of the Cover and the front face of the Motor; the assembly is created, as shown in Figure 15-79.

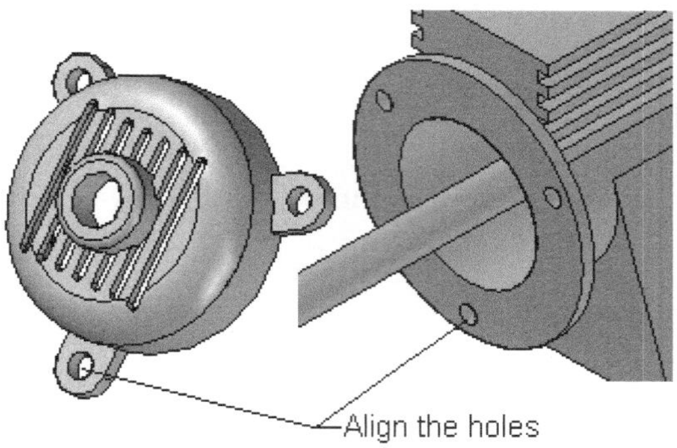

Figure 15-78 Holes to be aligned

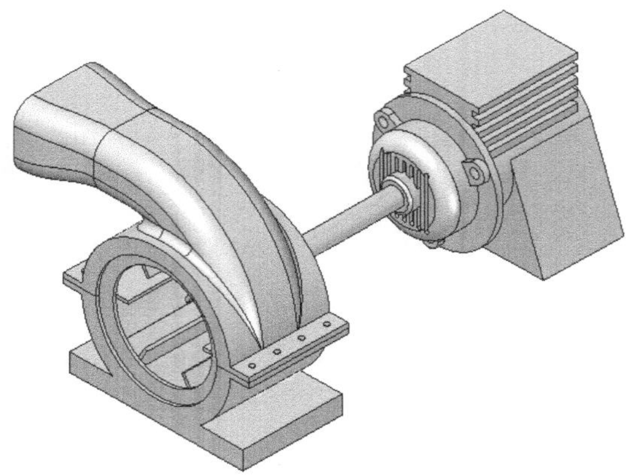

Figure 15-79 Completed assembly

Saving the File

1. Choose the **Save** button from the **Quick Access** toolbar; the **Save As** dialog box is displayed.

2. Enter **Motor Blower** as the name of the assembly and then choose the **Save** button to exit the dialog box.

3. Choose the **Close** button from the file tab bar to close the file.

GENERATING THE DRAWING VIEWS OF THE ASSEMBLY

After creating the Motor Blower assembly, you can generate its drawing views in the **Draft** environment using the third angle projection method. Remember that all parts of this assembly need to be saved at the following location :

C:\Solid Edge\c15\Motor Blower

Starting a New Draft File

As Solid Edge is already open, you can start a new file in the **Draft** environment using the **New** dialog box.

1. Choose the **New** button from the **Quick Access** toolbar; the **New** dialog box is displayed.

2. In the dialog box, choose the **ANSI Inch** from the **Standard Templates** drop-down list in the dialog box and double-click on **ansi inch draft.dft**.

Generating Drawing Views

After starting a new file in the **Draft** environment, you need to generate drawing views. To generate drawing views, follow the steps discussed next.

1. Choose **Application Button > Settings > Options** to invoke the **Solid Edge Options** dialog box. In this dialog box, choose the **Drawing Standards** button and select the **Third** radio button from the **Projection Angle** area. Next, choose the **OK** button.

2. Choose the **View Wizard** tool from the **Drawing Views** group; the **Select Model** dialog box is displayed.

3. Browse to the Motor Blower assembly and choose the **Open** button from the dialog box; the **View Wizard** command bar is displayed.

4. Choose the **Drawing View Layout** button on the command bar; the **Drawing View Creation Wizard** is displayed.

5. In the **Drawing View Creation Wizard**, select the views shown in Figure 15-80 and then choose the **OK** button.

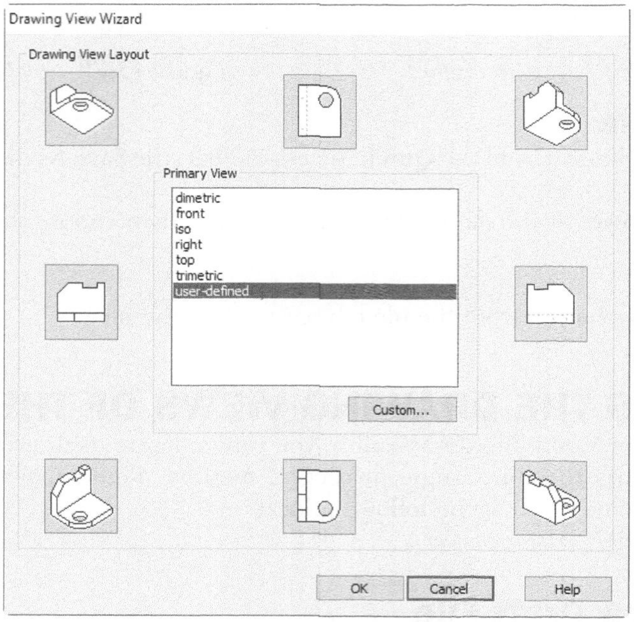

***Figure 15-80** The **Drawing View Creation Wizard** dialog box*

6. Place the drawing views on the sheet. Notice that you need to increase the scale of the views.

When you modify the scale of any one of the orthographic views, the scale of the other two orthographic views also gets modified.

7. Select an orthographic view; the command bar is displayed. Enter **0.3** in the **Scale value** edit box of the command bar; all orthographic views are scaled as specified.
8. Scale the isometric view as you did for the orthographic view.
9. Now, right-click on the top view to invoke a shortcut menu. Choose the **Properties** option from the shortcut menu to invoke the **High Quality View Properties** dialog box.
10. Choose the **Display** tab and clear the **Hidden edge style** check box; the **Changing Drawing View Default Display Properties** message box is displayed.
11. Choose the **OK** button in the message box; the hidden edges become invisible in the selected drawing view.
12. Turn off the display of hidden edges in other views also.
13. You can move the views on the sheet by dragging them. Arrange all views, as shown in Figure 15-81.

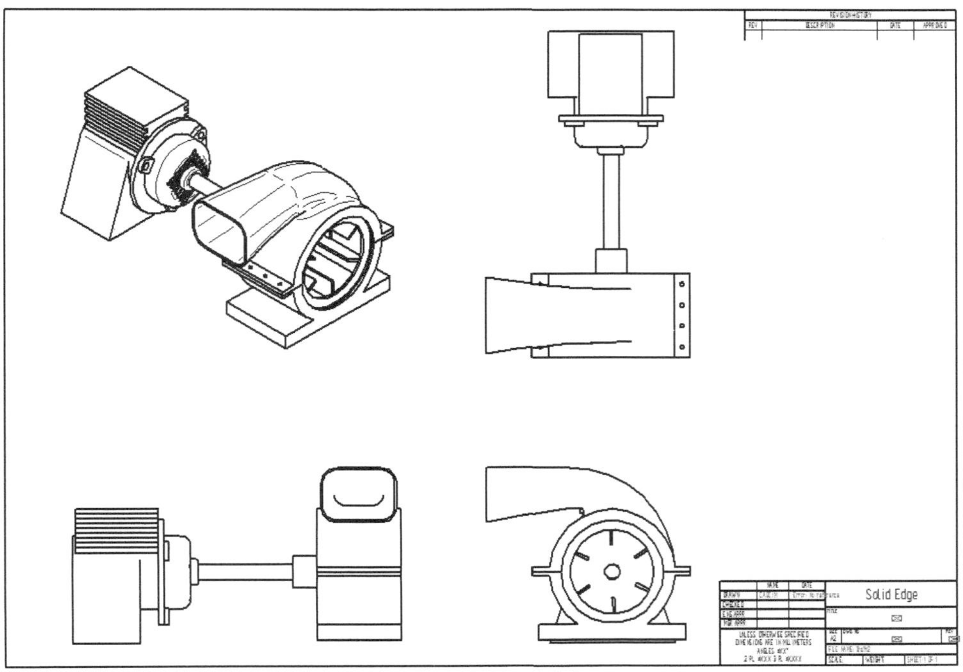

Figure 15-81 Drawing views of the assembly

Saving the File

After generating the drawing views, you need to save the file.

1. Choose **Save** from the **Quick Access** toolbar; the **Save As** dialog box is displayed.
2. Save the file with the name *motorblower.dft*.
3. Choose the **Close** button from the file tab bar to close the file.

EXERCISE

Exercise 1

In this exercise, you will create the Butterfly Valve assembly shown in Figure 15-82. The dimensions of the components are given in Figures 15-83 through 15-88.

(Expected time: 3 hr)

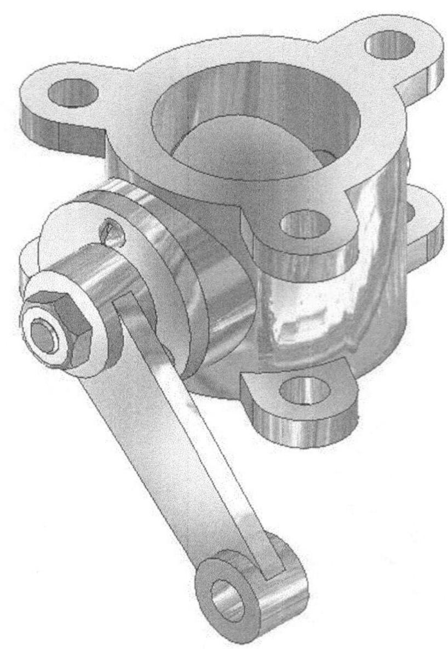

Figure 15-82 *Butterfly Valve assembly*

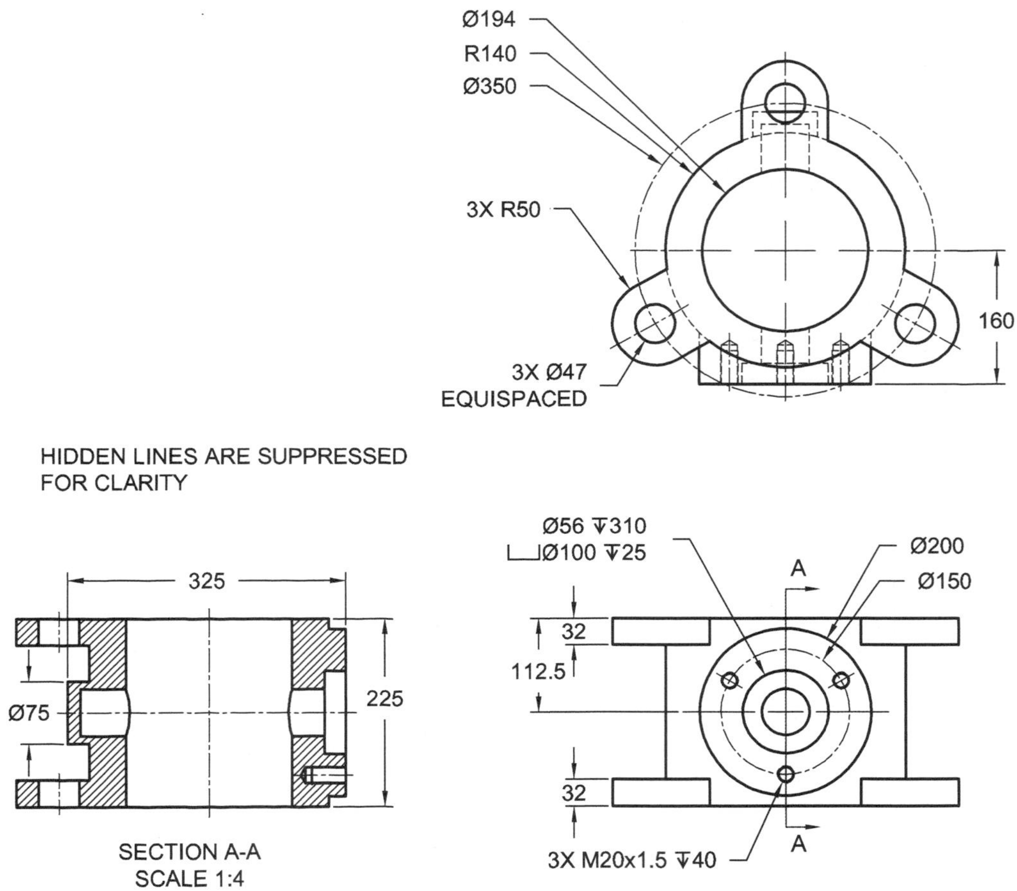

Figure 15-83 *Dimensions of the Body*

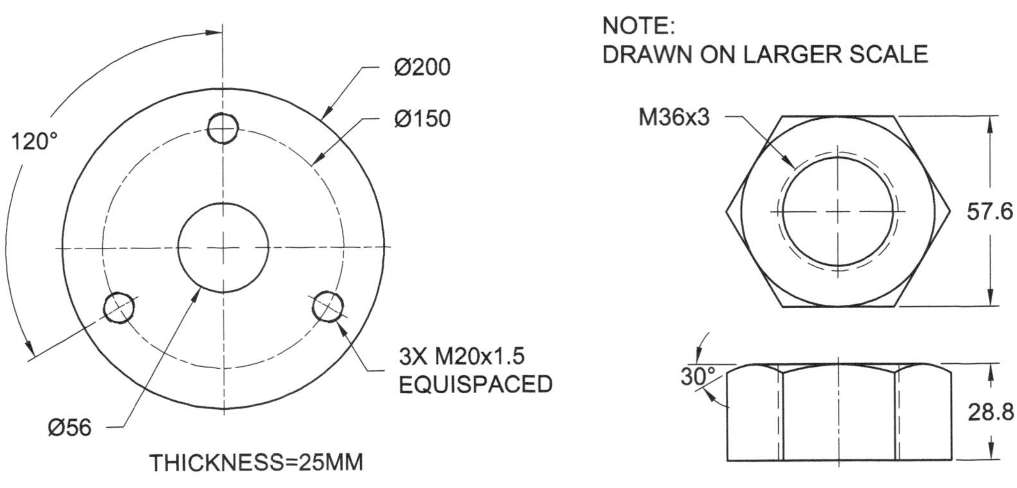

Figure 15-84 *Dimensions of the Retainer and Nut*

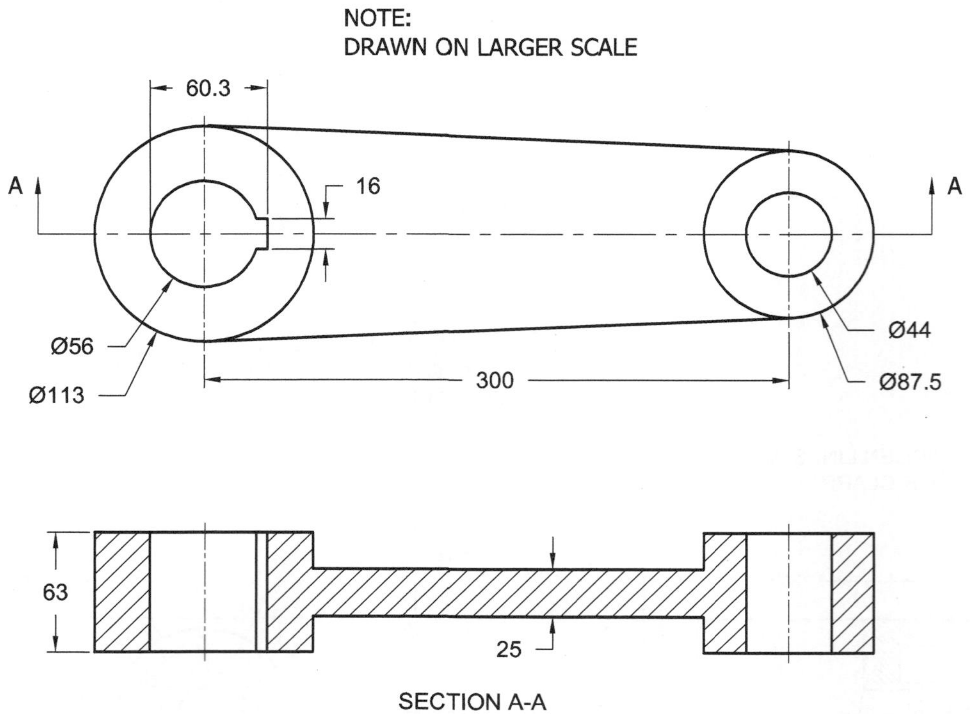

Figure 15-85 *Dimensions of the Arm*

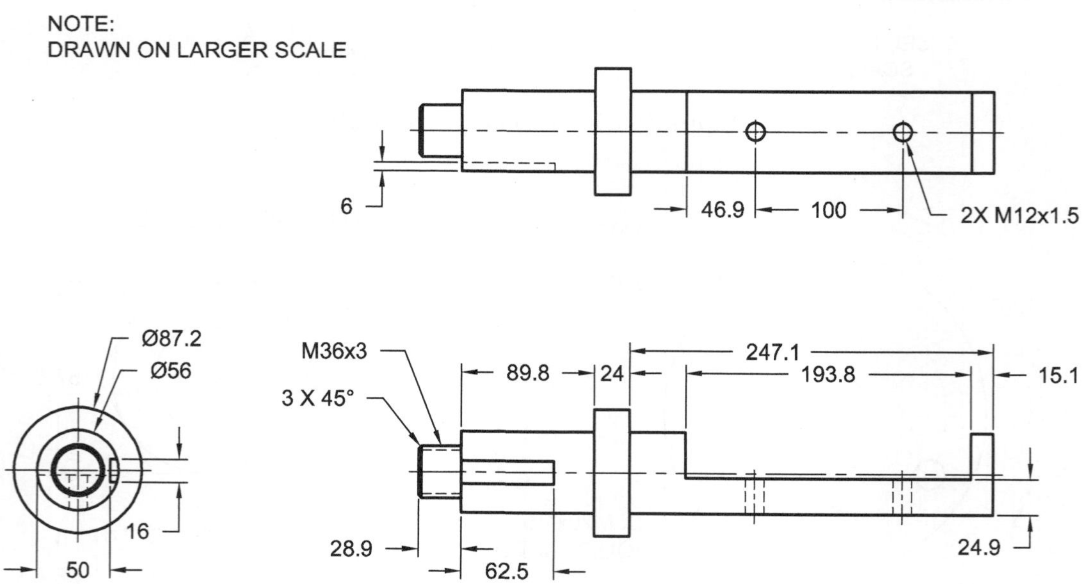

Figure 15-86 *Dimensions of the Shaft*

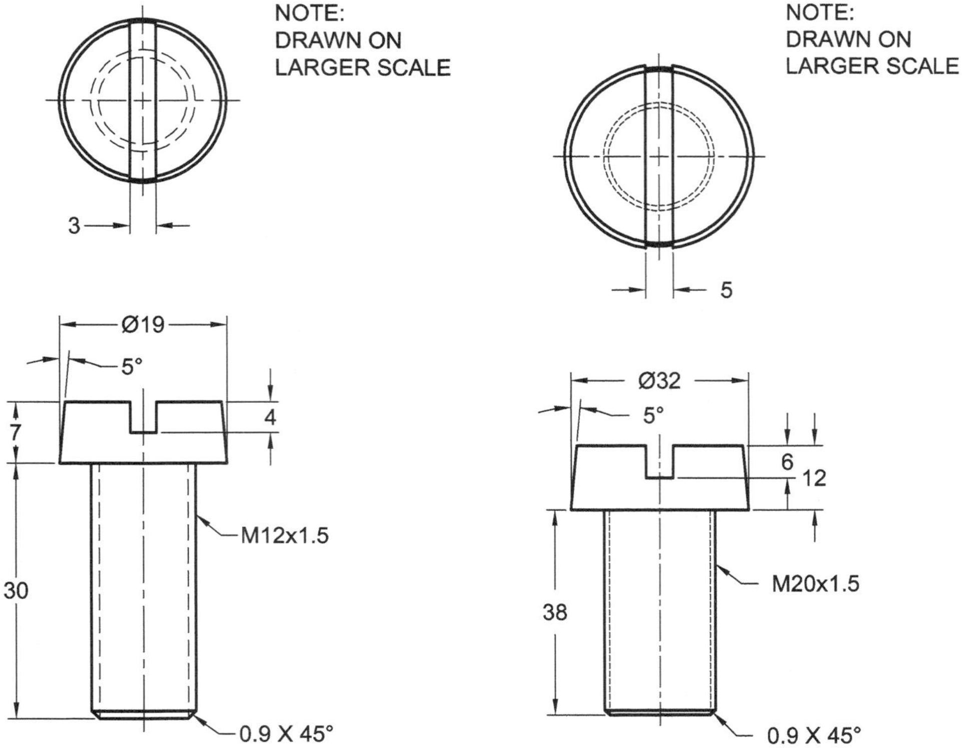

Figure 15-87 Dimensions of the Screws

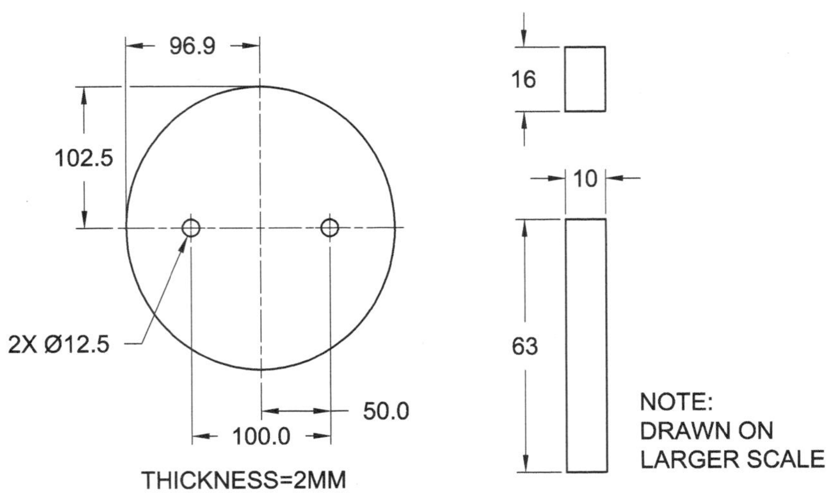

Figure 15-88 Dimensions of the Plate and Pin

This page is intentionally left blank

Index

Symbols

S

T

U

V

W

Z

Other Titles of Interest - BPB/TICKOO SERIES

Publications by BPB/TICKOO SERIES

The following is the list of some of the publications by BPB/TICKOO Series:

AutoCAD Electrical Textbook

- AutoCAD Electrical 2017 for Electrical Control Designers, 8th Edition

AutoCAD LT Textbook

- AutoCAD LT 2017 for Designers, 12th Edition

Autodesk Inventor Textbook

- Autodesk Inventor Professional 2017 for Designers, 17th Edition

NX Textbook

- NX 11.0 for Designers, 10th Edition

NX Nastran Textbook

- NX Nastran 9.0 for Designers

SolidWorks Textbook

- SOLIDWORKS 2017 for Designers, 15th Edition

CATIA Textbook

- CATIA V5-6R2016 for Designers, 14th Edition

Autodesk Revit Structure Textbook

- Exploring Autodesk Revit 2017 for Structure, 7th Edition

Autodesk Revit Architecture Textbook

- Exploring Autodesk Revit 2017 for Architecture, 13th Edition

RISA-3D Textbook

- Exploring RISA-3D 14.0

Bentley STAAD.Pro Textbook

- Exploring Bentley STAAD.Pro V8i (SELECTseries 6), 2nd Edition

AutoCAD Civil 3D Textbook

- Exploring AutoCAD Civil 3D 2017, 7th Edition

AutoCAD Map 3D Textbook
- Exploring AutoCAD Map 3D 2017, 7th Edition

Autodesk Navisworks Textbook
- Exploring Autodesk Navisworks 2017, 4th Edition

Oracle Primavera Textbook
- Exploring Oracle Primavera P6 R8.4, 2nd Edition

AutoCAD Raster Design Textbook
- Exploring AutoCAD Raster Design 2017, 2nd Edition

3ds Max Textbooks
- Autodesk 3ds Max 2017: A Comprehensive Guide, 17th Edition
- Autodesk 3ds Max 2017 for Beginners: A Tutorial Approach, 17th Edition

Autodesk Maya Textbook
- Autodesk Maya 2017: A Comprehensive Guide, 9th Edition

CINEMA 4D Textbook
- MAXON CINEMA 4D R18 Studio: A Tutorial Approach, 5th Edition

ZBrush Textbook
- Pixologic ZBrush 4R7: A Comprehensive Guide, 3rd Edition

Computer Programming Textbooks
- Introduction to C++ Programming, 2nd Edition
- Introduction to Java Programming, 2nd Edition
- Learning Oracle 12c: A PL/SQL Approach, 2nd Edition